Fifth Edition

*P*sychology Applied
to Modern Life

Adjustment in the 90s

Wayne Weiten is a graduate of Bradley University and earned his Ph.D. from the University of Illinois at Chicago in 1981. He is the author of *Psychology: Themes and Variations* (Brooks/Cole, 1995) and teaches psychology at Santa Clara University. He has received distinguished teaching awards from Division 2 of the American Psychological Association and the College of DuPage, where he taught until 1991. He will serve as President of the Society for the Teaching of Psychology (Division 2 of the American Psychological Association) in 1996–1997. He has conducted research on a wide range of topics, including cerebral specialization, educational measurement, jury behavior, attribution theory, pressure as a form of stress, and the technology of textbooks.

Margaret A. Lloyd is a graduate of the University of Denver and received her Ph.D. in psychology from the University of Arizona in 1973. She is the author of *Adolescence* (Harper & Row, 1985), is Past President of the Society for the Teaching of Psychology (Division 2 of the American Psychological Association), and currently serves as the Executive Director of the Society's Office of Teaching Resources in Psychology. She is Professor of Psychology at Georgia Southern University and a recipient of that institution's Award for Excellence for Contributions to Instruction. She has served as Chair of the psychology departments at Suffolk University (1980–1988) and Georgia Southern University (1988–1993) and is the organizer and Past Chair of the Council of Undergraduate Psychology Programs. Her scholarly interests lie in the areas of identity and gender roles.

Fifth Edition

Psychology Applied to Modern Life

Adjustment in the 90s

Wayne Weiten
Santa Clara University

Margaret A. Lloyd
Georgia Southern University

Brooks/Cole Publishing Company

I(T)P® *An International Thomson Publishing Company*

Pacific Grove • Albany • Belmont • Bonn • Boston • Cincinnati • Detroit • Johannesburg
London • Madrid • Melbourne • Mexico City • New York • Paris • Singapore
Tokyo • Toronto • Washington

To two pillars of stability in this era of turmoil—my parents
W.W.

To my father and the memory of my mother—models of integrity and courage
M.A.L.

 A CLAIREMONT BOOK

Sponsoring Editor: *Eileen Murphy*
Marketing Team: *Lauren Harp and Deborah Petit*
Editorial Assistant: *Lisa Blanton*
Production Editor: *Kirk Bomont*
Manuscript Editor: *Jackie Estrada*
Permission Editor: *May Clark*
Interior and Cover Design: *Roy R. Neuhaus*
Interior Illustration: *Lori Heckelman, Lisa Torri, and John Odam Design Associates*

Cover Illustration: *Ellen Schuster/Image Bank*
Art Coordinator: *Lisa Torri*
Photo Editor: *Kathleen Olson*
Photo Researcher: *Sue C. Howard*
Indexer: *Do Mi Stauber*
Typesetting: *GTS Graphics*
Printing and Binding: *Von Hoffman Press, Inc.*

For more information, contact:

BROOKS/COLE PUBLISHING COMPANY
511 Forest Lodge Road
Pacific Grove, CA 93950
USA

International Thomson Publishing Europe
Berkshire House 168-173
High Holborn
London WC1V 7AA
England

Thomas Nelson Australia
102 Dodds Street
South Melbourne, 3205
Victoria, Australia

Nelson Canada
1120 Birchmount Road
Scarborough, Ontario
Canada M1K 5G4

International Thomson Editores
Seneca 53
Col. Polanco
11560 México D. F. México

International Thomson Publishing GmbH
Königswinterer Strasse 418
53227 Bonn
Germany

International Thomson Publishing Asia
221 Henderson Road
#05-10 Henderson Building
Singapore 0315

International Thomson Publishing Japan
Hirakawacho Kyowa Building, 3F
2-2-1 Hirakawacho
Chiyoda-ku, Tokyo 102
Japan

Printed in the United States of America

10 9 8 7 6 5 4 3 2

Library of Congress Cataloging-in-Publication Data
Weiten, Wayne, [date]
  Psychology applied to modern life : adjustment in the 90s / Wayne
Weiten, Margaret A. Lloyd. — 5th ed.
      p.   cm.
  Includes bibliographical references and index.
  ISBN 0-534-33938-7
  1. Adjustment (Psychology). 2. Interpersonal relations. 3. Adulthood—
Psychological aspects. 4. Self-help techniques.
I. Lloyd, Margaret A. (Margaret Ann), [date]. II. Title.
BF335.W423 1997
158—dc20   96-34649
                                               CIP

Many students enter adjustment courses with great expectations. They've ambled through their local bookstores, and in the "Psychology" section they've seen numerous self-help books that offer highly touted recipes for achieving happiness for a mere $5.95. After paying far more money to enroll in a collegiate course that deals with the same issues as the self-help books, many students expect a revelatory experience. However, the majority of us with professional training in psychology or counseling take a rather dim view of self-help books and the pop psychology they represent. We tend to see this literature as oversimplified, intellectually dishonest, and opportunistic. Often we summarily dismiss the pop psychology that so many of our students have embraced. We then try to supplant it with our more sophisticated academic psychology, which is more complex and less accessible.

In this textbook, we have tried to come to grips with this problem of differing expectations between student and teacher. Our goal has been to produce a comprehensive, serious, research-oriented treatment of the topic of adjustment that also acknowledges the existence of popular psychology and looks critically at its contributions. Our approach involves the following:

- In Chapter 1 we confront the phenomenon of popular self-help books. We try to take the student beneath the seductive surface of such books and analyze some of their typical flaws. Our goal is to make the student a more critical consumer of this type of literature.
- While encouraging a more critical attitude toward self-help books, we do not suggest that they should all be dismissed. Instead, we acknowledge that some of them offer authentic insights. With this in mind, we highlight some of the better books in Recommended Reading boxes sprinkled throughout the text. These recommended readings tie in with the adjacent topical coverage and show the student the interface between academic and popular psychology.
- We try to provide the student with a better appreciation of the merit of the empirical approach. This effort to clarify the role of research, which is rare for an adjustment text, appears in the first chapter.
- Recognizing that adjustment students want to leave the course with concrete, personally useful information, we end each chapter with an application section. The Applications are "how to" discussions that address everyday problems. While they focus on issues that are relevant to the content of the particular chapter, they contain more explicit advice than the text proper.

In summary, we have tried to make this book both rigorous and applied. We hope that our approach will help students to better appreciate the value of scientific psychology.

Philosophy

A certain philosophy is inherent in any systematic treatment of the topic of adjustment. Our philosophy can be summarized as follows:

- We believe that an adjustment text should be a resource book for students. We have tried to design this book so that it encourages and facilitates the pursuit of additional information on adjustment-related topics. It should serve as a point of departure for more learning.
- We believe in theoretical eclecticism. This book will not indoctrinate your students along the lines of any single theoretical orientation. The psychodynamic, behavioral, and humanistic schools of thought are all treated with respect, as are cognitive, biological, and other perspectives.
- We believe that effective adjustment requires "taking charge" of one's own life. Throughout the book we try to promote the notion that active coping efforts are generally superior to passivity and complacency.

Changes in the Fifth Edition

One of the exciting things about psychology is that it is not a stagnant discipline. It continues to progress at what seems a faster and faster pace. A good textbook must evolve with the discipline. Although the professors and students who used the first four editions of this book did not clamor for change, there are some significant alterations.

Content Changes

To improve the book and keep up with new developments in psychology, we have made a variety of content changes—adding and deleting some topics, condensing and reorganizing others. The major alterations from the previous edition include the following.

Chapter 1: Adjusting to Modern Life. We have streamlined our discussion of the paradox of progress and compressed our coverage of the codependency movement. We have also added an excellent list of self-help books recommended by therapists and two new Recommended Reading boxes.

Chapter 2: Theories of Personality. This chapter tends to stay relatively stable, but we have managed to fit in coverage of Carl Jung, who was omitted from the previous editon. We have also expanded our discussion of self-efficacy and updated our coverage of the five-factor model.

Chapter 3: Stress and Its Effects. Besides the usual updating, we have compressed two major sections, on the nature of stress and on factors that moderate the relationship between stress and adaptational outcomes.

Chapter 4: Coping Processes. This chapter features a new overview of how to classify coping responses and new research on the benefits of meditation. The coverage of defense mechanisms and time management has been compressed.

Chapter 5: The Self. We now have an entire chapter devoted to the self, a topic that shared a chapter with material on the perception of others in the previous edition. The chapter features new discussions of self-complexity, coping with self-discrepancies, self-verification theory, and cultural influences on self-concept.

Chapter 6: Person Perception and Social Influence. Chapter 6 combines material from Chapters 5 and 7 in the previous edition. You will find new sections on culture and attribution, snap judgments versus systematic judgments, resisting social influence, and culture and social influence.

Chapter 7: Interpersonal Communication. The material found in Chapter 6 in the previous edition is now in Chapter 7. The chapter features new coverage of communication apprehension and a new discussion of the polygraph as a tool in detecting deception.

Chapter 8: Friendship and Love. Among the additions you'll find new material on culture and relationships, social skills training, and self-fulfilling prophecies in interpersonal interaction. We have also added a discussion of how evolutionary theory explains gender differences in mating preferences.

Chapter 9: Marriage and Intimate Relationships. The major change in this chapter is the new Application on violence in intimate relationships. Other changes include a streamlined discussion of the family life cycle and new coverage of stepfamilies. We have also expanded the discussion of gay relationships.

Chapter 10: Gender and Behavior. This chapter features new material on race and ethnicity as they relate to gender stereotypes, a new section on sociobiology's view of the origins of gender differences, and a new discussion of women's need to juggle multiple roles.

Chapter 11: Development in Adolescence and Adulthood. The coverage of adult development has been thoroughly revised and you will find new sections on the intensification of gender roles during adolescence and the day care–attachment controversy. A section on bereavement has been added, along with new cross-cultural material on death and dying.

Chapter 12: Work and Career Development. This chapter features a new section on diversity in the workplace, new material on repetitive strain injuries, and a new discussion of homicide under occupational hazards.

Chapter 13: Development and Expression of Sexuality. Our coverage includes new material on ethnicity as it relates to patterns of sexual behavior and a new section on sex in the age of AIDS. The coverage of sexual orientation has been reorganized. It highlights new findings on the determinants of sexual orientation.

Chapter 14: Psychology and Physical Health. The greatly expanded coverage of drinking as a health risk represents the major change in this chapter. The discussion of Type A behavior has been updated significantly, and we have added seven new figures.

Chapter 15: Psychological Disorders. In this chapter, you will find a streamlined discussion of the medical model and a new discussion of cognitive factors in anxiety disorders. Of course, all the terminology has been updated to reflect the publication of DSM-IV.

Chapter 16: Psychotherapy. The highlight of this chapter is a new discussion of the repressed memories controversy as it relates to psychotherapy. We have also compressed our descriptions of psychoanalysis and cognitive therapy and updated our coverage of research on the efficacy of insight therapy.

Other Changes

As you look through this edition, you will see many other changes besides those in content. One of the more subtle changes is that we made a conscious effort to streamline the book. Judicious efforts to compress our writing allowed us to shorten the manuscript from 277,000 words to 236,000 words, a reduction of almost 15 percent. This streamlining allowed us to shift to a more open, inviting, one-column design. You may also notice that the learning objectives that were found at the end of each chapter in the previous edition have been moved into the interiors of the chapters, where they appear in the margin adjacent to the relevant material. We hope that this arrangement will make the learning objectives more salient and more useful to your students. The chapter summaries that used to appear at the end of the main body of the chapters, but before the Applications, have been incorporated into the reviews found at the ends of the chapters. This alteration shortens the chapters while making the summaries more thorough, as they include the material in the Applications.

Writing Style

This book has been written with the student reader in mind. We have tried to integrate the technical jargon of our discipline into a relatively informal and down-to-earth writing style. We use concrete examples extensively to clarify complex concepts and to help maintain student interest.

Features

This text contains a number of features intended to stimulate interest and enhance students' learning. These special features include Applications, Recommended Reading boxes, a didactic illustration program, and cartoons.

Applications

The Applications should be of special interest to most students. They are tied to chapter content in a way that should show students how practical applications emerge out of theory and research. Although some of the material covered in these sections shows up frequently in adjustment texts, much of it is unique. Some of the Applications include the following:

- Understanding Intimate Violence
- Monitoring Your Stress
- Seeing Through Social Influence Tactics
- Getting Ahead in the Job Game
- Building Self-Esteem
- Enhancing Sexual Relationships
- Becoming an Effective Parent

Recommended Reading Boxes

Recognizing students' interest in self-help books, we have sifted through hundreds of them to identify some that may be especially useful. These are highlighted in boxes that briefly review the book and include a provocative excerpt or two. These Recommended Reading boxes are placed where they are germane to the material being covered in the text. Some of the recommended books are very well known, whereas others are obscure. Although we make it clear that we don't endorse every idea in every book, we think they all have something worthwhile to offer. This feature replaces the conventional suggested readings lists that usually appear at the ends of chapters, where they are almost universally ignored by students.

Didactic Illustration Program

The illustration program is once again in full color and we have added many new photographs and figures. Although the illustrations are intended to make the book attractive and to help maintain student interest, they are not merely decorative. They have been carefully selected for their didactic value to enhance the educational goals of the text.

Cartoons

Because a little comic relief usually helps keep a student interested, numerous cartoons are sprinkled throughout the book. Like the figures, most of these have been chosen to reinforce ideas in the text.

Learning Aids

Because this book is rigorous, substantive, and sizable, a number of learning aids have been incorporated into the text to help the reader digest the wealth of material:

- The *outline* at the beginning of each chapter provides the student with a preview and overview of what will be covered.
- *Headings* are employed very frequently to keep material well organized.
- To help alert your students to key points, *learning objectives* are sprinkled throughout the chapters, in the margins, near the relevant topical coverage.
- *Key terms* are identified with ***italicized boldface*** type to indicate that these are important vocabulary items that are part of psychology's technical language.
- An *integrated running glossary* provides an on-the-spot definition of each key term as it is introduced in the text. These formal definitions are printed in **boldface** type.
- An *alphabetical glossary* is found in the back of the book, since key terms are usually defined in the integrated running glossary only when they are first introduced.
- *Italics* are used liberally throughout to emphasize important points.
- A *chapter review* is found at the end of each chapter. Each review includes a concise but thorough summary of the chapter's key ideas, a list of the key terms that were introduced in the chapter, and a list of important theorists and researchers who were discussed in the chapter.

Supplementary Materials

A complete teaching/learning package has been developed to supplement *Psychology Applied to Modern Life*. These supplementary materials have been carefully coordinated to provide effective support for the text.

Instructor's Manual

An instructor's manual is available as a convenient aid for your educational endeavors. Written by William Addison, it provides a thorough overview of each chapter, along with a list of relevant films. It also includes a wealth of suggestions for lecture topics, class demonstrations, exercises, and discussion questions, organized around the content of each chapter in the text.

Test Bank

Pat Slocum has taken on the task of revising the test bank. It contains an extensive collection of multiple-choice questions for objective tests. The questions are closely tied to the learning objectives found in the text chapters. We're confident that you will find this to be a dependable and usable test bank.

Study Guide

The study guide has been revised by William Addison, who has built on the outstanding work of Michael Sosulski, a dear friend and colleague who passed away. The study guide is designed to help students master the information contained in the text. For each chapter, it contains a brief overview, learning objectives, a programmed review, several other types of review exercises, and a self-test. We're confident that your students will find it very helpful in their study efforts.

Culture and Modern Life

Culture and Modern Life is a small paperback that is intended to help your students appreciate how cultural factors moderate psychological processes and how the viewpoint of one's own culture can distort one's interpretation of the behavior of people from other cultures. Written by David Matsumoto, a leading authority on cross-cultural psychology, this supplementary book should greatly enhance your students' understanding of how culture can influence adjustment. *Culture and Modern Life* can be ordered shrinkwrapped with the text.

Personal Explorations Workbook

The *Personal Explorations Workbook* is a small booklet assembled by Wayne Weiten. It contains experiential exercises for each text chapter, designed to help your students achieve personal insights. The Questionnaires are psychological tests or scales that your students can administer and score for themselves. The Personal Probes consist of questions intended to help students think about themselves in relation to issues raised in the text. Most students find these exercises interesting. They can also be fruitful in stimulating class discussion. The *Personal Explorations Workbook* can be ordered shrinkwrapped with the text.

Acknowledgments

This book has been an enormous undertaking, and we want to express our gratitude to the innumerable people who have influenced its evolution. To begin with, we must cite the contribution of our students who have taken the adjustment course. It is trite to say that they have been a continuing inspiration—but they have.

We also want to express our appreciation for the time and effort invested by the authors of our ancillary books: Bill Addison (Eastern Illinois University), David Matsumoto (San Francisco State University), and Pat Slocum (College of DuPage). In spite of tight schedules, they all did commendable work.

The quality of a textbook depends greatly on the quality of the prepublication reviews by psychology professors around the country. The reviewers listed on page x have contributed to the development of this book by providing constructive reviews of various portions of the manuscript in this or earlier editions. We are very grateful to all of them.

We would also like to thank Eileen Murphy, who has served as editor of this edition. She has done an outstanding job following in the footsteps of Claire Verduin, a legend in textbook publishing circles, who we remain indebted to. We are also grateful to Jackie Estrada, for an excellent job of copy editing, Kirk Bomont, who performed capably as our production editor, Michele Mangelli, who did valiant work on the page layouts, and Fiorella Ljunggren, who shepherded previous editions into existence. Others who have made significant contributions to this book include: May Clark (permissions), Lisa Blanton (editorial assistant), Sue C. Howard (photo research), Roy Neuhaus (interior and cover design), Lisa Torri (art program), Do Mi Stauber (indexing), and Deborah Petit (marketing).

In addition, Wayne Weiten would like to thank his wife, Beth Traylor, who has been a steady source of emotional support while enduring the grueling demands of her medical career. He is also grateful to his former colleagues at the College of DuPage and his current colleagues at Santa Clara University, for their counsel and assistance. Marky Lloyd would like to thank her graduate assistants—Julie Biskner, Merry Jennifer George, Denise R. Scott, Debra Seperson, and Elisa Sullivan—and reference librarian Barbara Strickland for their help with library research. She is also grateful to her colleague, Edward W. L. Smith, and undergraduate Thea Garnes Lawton for their assistance. Finally, she wishes to thank Judith A. Holleman for her support, encouragement, and wise counsel.

Wayne Weiten
Margaret A. Lloyd

Marsha K. Beauchamp
Mt. San Antonio College

John R. Blakemore
Monterey Peninsula College

Paul Bowers
Grayson County College

George Bryant
East Texas State University

Robert Cameron
Fairmont State College

M. K. Clampit
Bentley College

Meg Clark
California State Polytechnic University–Pomona

Stephen S. Coccia
Orange County Community College

Dennis Coon
Santa Barbara City College

Salvatore Cullari
Lebanon Valley College

Kenneth S. Davidson
Wayne State University

Richard Fuhrer
University of Wisconsin–Eau Claire

Lee Gillis
Georgia College

Lawrence Grebstein
University of Rhode Island

Robert Helm
Oklahoma State University

Robert Higgins
Central Missouri State University

Clara E. Hill
University of Maryland

Michael Hirt
Kent State University

Fred J. Hitti
Monroe Community College

Joseph Horvat
Weber State University

Kathy Howard
Harding University

Walter Jones
College of DuPage

Wayne Joose
Calvin College

Margaret Karolyi
University of Akron

Susan Kupisch
Austin Peay State University

Barbara Hansen Lemme
College of DuPage

Harold List
Massachusetts Bay Community College

Louis A. Martone
Miami–Dade Community College

Richard Maslow
San Joaquin Delta College

William T. McReynolds
University of Tampa

Fred Medway
University of South Carolina–Columbia

Frederick Meeker
California State Polytechnic University–Pomona

John Moritsugu
Pacific Lutheran University

Gary Oliver
College of DuPage

Joseph Philbrick
California State Polytechnic University–Pomona

William Penrod
Middle Tennessee State University (Retired)

Barbara M. Powell
Eastern Illinois University

James Prochaska
University of Rhode Island

Joan Royce
Riverside Community College

Joan Rykiel
Ocean County College

John Sample
Slippery Rock University

Thomas K. Saville
Metropolitan State College of Denver

Norman R. Schultz
Clemson University

Dale Simmons
Oregon State University

Karl Swain
Community College of South Nevada

Kenneth L. Thompson
Central Missouri State University

David L. Watson
University of Hawaii

Deborah S. Weber
University of Akron

Clair Wiederholt
Madison Area Tech College

J. Oscar Williams
Diablo Valley College

Raymond Wolf
Moraine Park Technical College

Raymond Wolfe
State University of New York at Geneseo

Michael Wolff
Southwestern Oklahoma State University

Norbert Yager
Henry Ford Community College

Brief Contents

Contents

Part One   The Dynamics of Adjustment

1   Adjusting to Modern Life   1

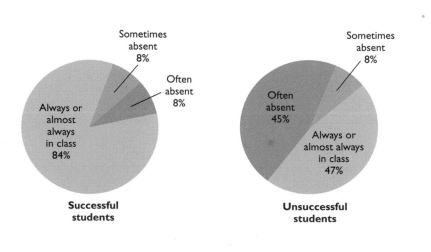

2 Theories of Personality 34

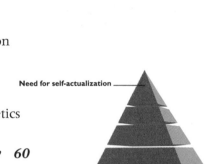

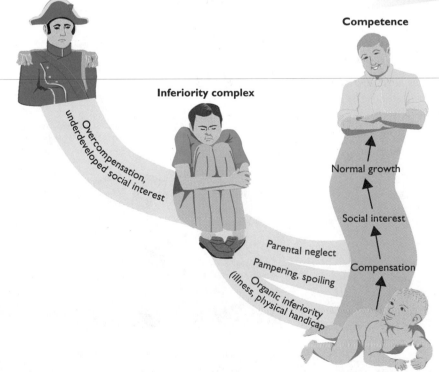

3   *Stress and Its Effects*   68

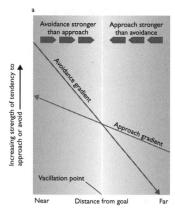

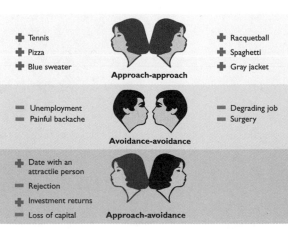

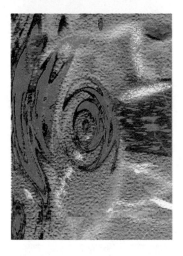

4

Coping Processes   102

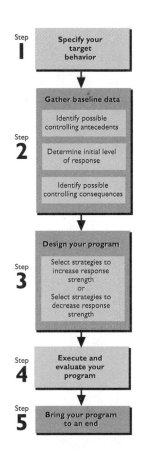

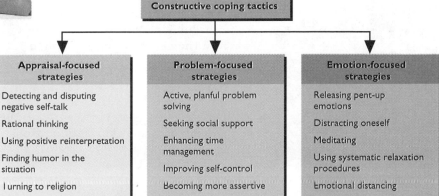

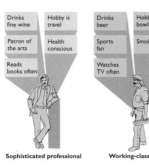

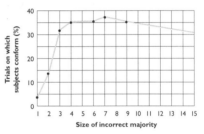

7 *Interpersonal Communication* 196

8 *Friendship and Love* 230

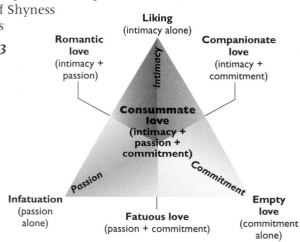

9 Marriage and Intimate Relationships 264

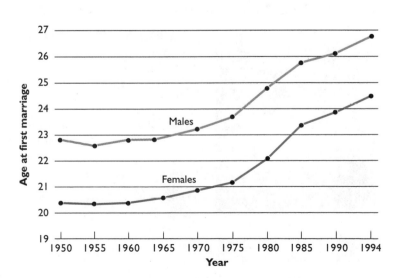

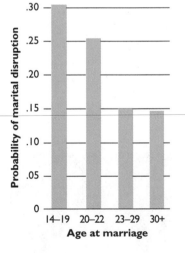

12 *Work and Career Development* 364

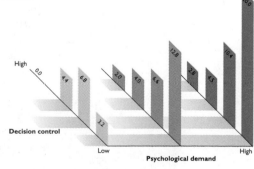

13 *Development and Expression of Sexuality* 398

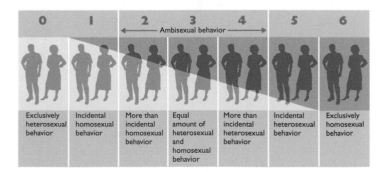

Part Four   **Mental and Physical Health**

14   *Psychology and*
       Physical Health   434

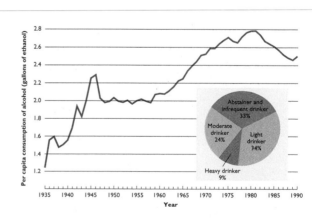

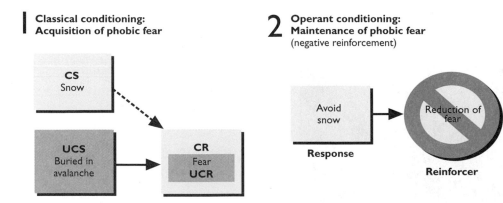

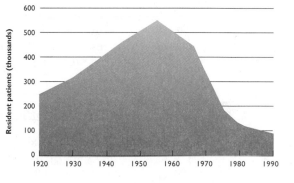

In most college courses students spend more time with their textbooks than with their professors. Given this reality, it helps if you like your textbook. Making textbooks likable, however, is a tricky proposition. By its very nature, a textbook must introduce a great many new concepts, ideas, and theories. If it doesn't, it isn't much of a textbook, and instructors won't choose to use it—so you'll never see it anyway. Consequently, we have tried to make this book as likable as possible without compromising the academic content that your instructor demands. Thus, we have tried to make the book lively, informal, engaging, well organized, easy to read, practical, and occasionally humorous. Before you plunge into Chapter 1, let us explain some of the key features that can help you get the most out of the book.

Learning Aids

Mastering the content of this text involves digesting a great deal of information. To facilitate this learning process, we've incorporated a number of instructional aids into the book.

- *Outlines* at the beginning of each chapter provide you with both a preview and an overview of what will be covered.
- *Headings* are employed very frequently to keep material well organized.
- To help alert you to key points, *learning objectives* are sprinkled throughout the chapters, in the margins near the relevant topical coverage.
- *Key terms* are identified with ***italicized boldface*** type to indicate that these are important vocabulary items that are part of psychology's technical language.
- An *integrated running glossary* provides an on-the-spot definition of each key term as it's introduced in the text. These formal definitions are printed in **boldface** type. It is often difficult for students to adapt to the jargon used by scientific disciplines. However, learning this terminology is an essential part of your educational experience. The integrated running glossary is meant to make this learning process as painless as possible.
- An *alphabetical glossary* is provided in the back of the book, since key terms are usually defined in the running glossary only when they are first introduced. If you run into a technical term that was introduced in an earlier chapter and you can't remember its meaning, you can look it up in the alphabetical glossary instead of backtracking to find the place where it first appeared.
- *Italics* are used liberally throughout the book to emphasize important points.
- A *chapter review* is found at the end of each chapter. Each review includes a thorough summary of the chapter, a list of key terms, and a list of important theorists and researchers. Reading over these review materials can help you ensure that you've digested the key points in the chapter.

Recommended Reading Boxes

This text should function as a resource book. To facilitate this goal, particularly interesting self-help books on various topics are highlighted in boxes within the chapters. Each box provides a brief description of the book and a provocative excerpt. We do not agree with everything in these recommended books, but all of them are potentially useful or intriguing. The main purpose of this feature is to introduce you to some of the better self-help books that are available.

Study Guide

The study guide that accompanies this text is an excellent resource designed to assist you in mastering the information contained in the book. It includes a wealth of review exercises to help you organize information and a self-test for assessing your mastery. You should be able to purchase it at your college bookstore. If it is not available there, you can obtain a copy by contacting the publisher (phone: 1-800-354-9706).

A Concluding Note

We sincerely hope that you find this book enjoyable. If you have any comments or advice that might help us improve the next edition, please write to us in care of the publisher, Brooks/Cole Publishing Company, Pacific Grove, California 93950. There is a form in the back of the book that you can use to provide us with feedback. Finally, let us wish you good luck. We hope you enjoy your course and learn a great deal.

Wayne Weiten
Margaret A. Lloyd

1   Adjusting to Modern Life

*T*he immense Boeing 747 lumbers into position to accept its human cargo. The eager passengers-to-be scurry on board. In a tower a few hundred yards away, air traffic controllers diligently monitor radar screens, radio transmissions, and digital readouts of weather information. At the reservation desks in the airport terminal, clerks punch up the appropriate ticket information on their computer terminals and quickly process the steady stream of passengers. Mounted on the wall are video terminals displaying up-to-the-minute information on flight arrivals, departures, and delays. Back in the cockpit of the plane, the flight crew calmly scans the complex array of dials, meters, and lights to assess the aircraft's readiness for flight. In a few minutes, the airplane will slice into the cloudy, snow-laden skies above Chicago. In a mere three hours its passengers will be transported from the piercing cold of a Chicago winter to the balmy beaches of the Bahamas. Another everyday triumph for technology will have taken place.

The Paradox of Progress

Learning Objective

Explain what is meant by the paradox of progress.

We are the children of technology. We take for granted such impressive feats as transporting 300 people over 1500 miles in a matter of hours. After all, we live in the space age—a time of unparalleled progress. Our modern Western society has made extraordinary strides in transportation, energy, communication, agriculture, and medicine. Yet in spite of our technological progress, social problems and personal difficulties seem more prevalent and more prominent than ever before. This paradox is evident in many aspects of contemporary life, as the following examples show.

Point Modern technology has provided us with countless time-saving devices—automobiles, vacuum cleaners, dishwashers, photocopiers, fax machines. Cellular phones allow people to talk to friends or colleagues while battling rush hour traffic. Personal computers can perform calculations in a few seconds that would take months if done by hand. Microwave ovens deliver full-cooked meals in a matter of minutes.

Counterpoint Nonetheless, most of us complain about not having enough time. Our schedules are overflowing with appointments, commitments, and plans. Surveys indicate that most of us spend more and more time working and have less and less time for ourselves (Gilbert, 1988). As social critic Jeremy Rifkin (1987) notes, "It is ironic in a culture so committed to saving time we feel increasingly deprived of the very thing we value. The modern world of streamlined transportation, instantaneous communication, and time-saving technologies was supposed to free us from the dictates of the clock and provide us with increased leisure. Instead there seems never to be enough time. . . . Despite our alleged efficiency, as compared to almost every other period in history, we seem to have less time for ourselves and far less time for each other" (p. 19).

Point Thanks in large part to technological advances, we live in extraordinary affluence. Undeniably, there are pockets of genuine poverty, but Paul Wachtel (1989) argues convincingly that the middle and upper classes are larger and wealthier than ever before. Most of us take for granted things that were once considered luxuries, such as color television and air-conditioning. People spend vast amounts of money on expensive automobiles, stereo systems, video equipment, clothing, and travel. Wachtel quotes a New York museum director who asserts that "shopping is the chief cultural activity in the United States" (p. 23).

Counterpoint In spite of this economic abundance, Wachtel notes that a "sense of economic decline is widespread nowadays. . . . [We feel] that declining productivity has pinched our pocketbooks, that inflation has eaten up our buying power, that we can't catch up, much less get ahead" (p. 9). According to Wachtel, our economic system's commitment to growth, coupled with the effects of mass media advertising, has created an insatiable thirst for consumption. Although our standard of living has improved, most of us feel as though we still need more goods and services.

Technology has enhanced our lives in uncountable ways; one of them is by making available to us a host of time-saving devices, from vacuum cleaners to cellular phones. But this same technology has also complicated our lives; consider for example, the hassles involved in dealing with large shopping malls or in deciding which computer or fax machine to buy.

Rich by any previous standard, we are nevertheless subjectively distressed about our economic plight.

Point   In recent years, our ability to process, store, and communicate information has improved dramatically. Using satellites, we can beam live telecasts around the globe almost instantaneously. We can access on-line computerized databases to track the stock market or to check airline schedules. Even more impressive, we can store the entire *Encyclopaedia Britannica* on a couple of compact discs.

Counterpoint   Yet Richard Saul Wurman (1989) asserts that nearly everyone suffers from *information anxiety*—concern about the ever-widening gap between what we understand and what we think we *should* understand. The crux of the problem is the explosive growth of available information, which now doubles in amount about every five years. Wurman points out that a single weekday edition of the *New York Times* "contains more information than the average person was likely to come across in a lifetime in seventeenth-century England" (p. 32). According to Wurman, people exhibit symptoms of information anxiety when they complain about stacks of unread periodicals, when they bemoan their inability to keep up with what's going on, when they pretend that they are familiar with a book or artist that they've never heard of, when they feel overwhelmed by the 50 or 60 channels available on cable TV, and when they feel bewildered by the intricacies of their computers, VCRs, and digital watches.

Point   In the medical arena, we have made stunning advances. Doctors can re-attach severed limbs, use lasers to correct microscopic defects in the eye, and even replace the human heart. Once-devastating contagious diseases such as tuberculosis, typhoid fever, smallpox, and cholera are largely under control. Since the turn of the century, life expectancy in the United States has increased from 47 to 75 years.

Counterpoint   Nonetheless, as noted in a *Time* magazine article, "Never have doctors been able to do so much for their patients, and rarely have patients seemed so ungrateful" (Gibbs, 1989, p. 49). The cost of medical care has skyrocketed and malpractice lawsuits have increased dramatically, while patients' access to quality care and their trust in the medical profession have declined noticeably (Kassler, 1994). Moreover, as we'll discuss in Chapter 14, the void left by contagious diseases has been filled all too quickly by chronic diseases that develop gradually, such as cancer, heart disease, hypertension, and ulcers. The increase in chronic diseases is partly attributable to stress and certain features of our modern lifestyle, such as our penchant for smoking and overeating, and our tendency to get little physical exercise.

The apparent contradictions just discussed all reflect the same theme: *The technological advances of the 20th century, impressive though they may be, have not led to perceptible improvement in our collective health and happiness.* Indeed, many social critics argue that the quality of our lives and our sense of personal fulfillment have declined rather than increased. This is the paradox of progress.

What is the cause of this paradox? There are many potential explanations. Erich Fromm (1963, 1981) has argued that the progress we value so much has scrambled our value systems and undermined our traditional sources of emotional security, such as family, community, and religion. Alvin Toffler (1970, 1980) attributes our collective alienation and distress to our being overwhelmed by rapidly accelerating cultural change. Robert Kegan (1994) maintains that the mental demands of modern life have become so complex, confusing, and contradictory that most of us are "in over our heads." Whatever the explanation, many theorists agree that *the basic challenge of modern life has become the search for meaning or a sense of direction* (Naylor, Willimon, & Naylor, 1994). This search involves struggling with the challenges of developing a solid sense of identity, a coherent philosophy of life, and a clear vision of a future that realistically promises fulfillment. Centuries ago, problems of this kind were probably much simpler. As we'll see in the next section, today it appears that many of us are floundering in a sea of confusion.

The Search for Direction

Our search for a sense of direction has many manifestations. Let's look at three striking expressions of this quest: the emergence of "self-realization" programs, the recent popularity of the codependency movement, and the spectacular success of best-selling "self-help" books. An examination of these phenomena can help us to better understand the modern struggle for a sense of direction and some of the ways in which it can go awry.

Self-Realization Programs

Learning Objective

Describe the key ideas of est, Scientology, and Silva Mind Control.

Since the 1960s, many Americans have shown a willingness to invest large sums of money to enroll in "self-realization" programs that are supposed to provide enlightenment and turn one's life around, usually in a short time. They vary greatly in orientation, format, and themes, but most tend to promise participants spectacular benefits. Some of these training regimens have enjoyed enormous success, earning glowing testimonials from thousands of converts. We'll look at three programs (*est*, Scientology, and Silva Mind Control) that have attained a fair amount of popularity and evaluate their worth.

est

est stands for Erhard Seminars Training, an approach to personal growth developed by Werner Erhard. Although *est* has been discontinued, similar programs based on it remain available (Pressman, 1994). The training consisted of four intensive, day-long seminars conducted on two weekends plus one weeknight seminar, with 250–300 participants who paid hundreds of dollars for their shot at enlightenment (Kaminer, 1992). The goal of *est* was "getting it." The "it" was rather mysterious, and most *est* graduates had difficulty describing or explaining it. "It" allegedly involved some profound insight that revolutionized the graduate's life.

It is hard to describe *est* without making it sound terribly bland. Proponents argued that this difficulty occurred because "The *est* experience cannot be described. It can only be experienced," but others have asserted that the seminars were simply devoid of content (Efran, Lukens, & Lukens, 1986; Kaminer, 1992). In any case, the seminars were led by a trainer who was usually extremely articulate, with a commanding presence. The trainer lectured and led discussions. The basic strategy was to break down the trainees' self-esteem and then gradually rebuild it. The trainees were told that they were bungling their way through life. They were often intimidated and made to feel foolish. After they had their self-esteem lowered, they were offered a variety of insights borrowed primarily from mainstream psychology. For example, much was made of Fritz Perls's (1969) idea that one should take

responsibility for one's own life. The training emphasized that it is useless to blame your problems on others; you can solve problems only if you accept responsibility for them.

Although many *est* graduates complained that they didn't feel any different, many others raved about the experience. Several prominent people claimed that the training significantly changed their lives (Burg, 1974). The changes most commonly reported included improvements in self-image and self-confidence, accompanied by reductions in anxiety.

Scientology/Dianetics

Scientology is a quasi-religious organization founded in the 1950s by L. Ron Hubbard. The goal in Scientology is to become "clear." Getting "clear" involves reaching a point where you are free of all programming in your mind that is not under your control. What exactly does that mean? Well, according to Hubbard (1989), people acquire automatic behavior patterns, called "engrams," which can be problematic. These engrams often involve nonadaptive emotional responses to situations. Hubbard asserts that you can rid yourself of a troublesome engram by consciously and completely reliving the original experience that created it, under the guidance of an "auditor." Scientology training may take a couple of years and can cost thousands of dollars. Some wealthy converts have spent as much as $130,000 on their training (Behar, 1991).

Like *est*, Scientology borrows liberally from the mainstream of psychological theory. An engram is very similar to the conditioned response described by Russian physiologist Ivan Pavlov some 90 years ago. The idea of reliving emotional experiences and thereby discharging the troublesome emotion was proposed by Sigmund Freud, the developer of psychoanalysis, over 100 years ago.

Silva Mind Control

Silva Mind Control courses have been available to the public since the mid-1960s. Developed by José Silva, the courses are supposed to train participants to control their brain activity (Silva & Miele, 1977). Silva maintains that it is optimal to operate at the lower rather than the higher brain-wave frequencies. Trainees are taught to use relaxation exercises and visual imagery to gain conscious control over brain activity.

As trainees acquire better mind control, behavioral self-control supposedly follows. Silva graduates purportedly can use their power of visualization to achieve great self-control. They can eat less, sleep less, work harder, or do whatever is necessary to achieve their goals in life. The mind-control training is also supposed to provide graduates with at least some extrasensory perception (ESP) capabilities. The Silva Mind Control courses resemble *est* in cost and time commitment. The sequence of courses costs a few hundred dollars and requires about a week's time. Generally, the courses are conducted in small groups.

Critique

Although their teachings are very different, *est,* Scientology, and Silva Mind Control have much in common. First, they are, above all else, money-making propositions for their developers. None of them offers self-realization free; it costs, and the fees aren't cheap. One book on Werner Erhard estimates that he has sold over $430 million worth of self-realization to people all over the world (Pressman, 1994). All three organizations seem to be more interested in making money than in spreading enlightenment.

Second, the inventors of all three systems have little or no formal training in psychology. They all appear to have emerged from the ranks of hucksterism rather than science. Werner Erhard, for instance, was previously a door-to-door salesman whose real name was Jack Rosenberg. He has had a long history of involvement with questionable sales schemes (Brewer, 1975). The Church of Scientology has a sinister reputation for coaxing large sums of money out of naive members and for subjecting its critics to vicious harassment. In a *Time* magazine exposé, Scientology was characterized as a multi-million-dollar racket and as "the most ruthless, the most classically terroristic, the most litigious and the most lucrative cult the country has ever seen" (Behar, 1991, p. 51).

Third, to be blunt, all three systems are intellectual mush. Each system offers a few worthwhile insights, but these either are borrowed from mainstream psychology or are simple common sense. Most of their principles, however, are hopelessly vague or easily refuted by available scientific data.

Scientology, *est,* and Silva Mind Control have one other perplexing thing in common. All three have many disciples, including some high-profile celebrities, who claim that the training they received revolutionized their lives. If the systems have little real merit, how do we account for this puzzling reality? In all probability, it is primarily a matter of placebo effects.

***Placebo effects* occur when people experience some change as the result of an empty, fake, or ineffectual treatment because of their positive expectations about the treatment.** Numerous studies show that if people believe a treatment or program will affect them in certain ways, they are likely to see the expected effects. For instance, many a patient has been "cured" of a physical illness by the administration of "drugs" that were really sugar pills. Placebo effects can occur even when people are likely to observe themselves very objectively—and such objectivity generally is *not* present when people are seeking self-realization. People who take self-realization training are clearly searching for something. They want, sometimes desperately, to see improvement in themselves. After investing time, money, and hope in some pathway to growth, they want to believe that it has paid off. Thus, they are exceedingly biased observers who are predisposed to see the effects that they have been led to expect. With this strong bias, it is not surprising that many participants in self-realization programs offer glowing endorsements. Unfortunately, most of their gains appear to be illusory and short-lived.

The Codependency Movement

Another manifestation of our collective malaise and never-ending search for fulfillment is the codependency movement, which has grown like a firestorm on a dry, windy prairie. The fire was ignited in 1987 with the publication of *Codependent No More* by Melody Beattie. Beattie's description of the codependency syndrome clearly struck a chord, as codependency has become "the chic neurosis of our time" (Lyon & Greenberg, 1991, p. 435). The movement spawned a host of books, workshops, seminars, support groups, and treatment programs designed to help people overcome their codependency. By 1991, there were over 500 bookstores in the United States devoted entirely to codependency literature (Jones, 1993).

Description

What is codependency? It was an obscure concept in the field of alcoholism counseling before Beattie (1987, 1989, 1993) and others (Bradshaw, 1988; Schaef, 1986,

1992; Whitfield, 1987, 1993) borrowed, broadened, and popularized it. The term originally referred to the tendency of alcoholics' spouses—typically wives of alcoholic men—to get entangled in their partner's addictions in ways that inadvertently supported the addictive behavior (Cocores, 1987). For example, the wife of an alcoholic might protect him from the consequences of his addiction by not confronting him about his problem, by lying to people to cover up his drinking, and by taking on many of his parental, household, and financial responsibilities.

Beattie (1987) greatly expanded the codependency concept. Arguing that people can be addicted to love, sex, work, food, gambling, or shopping as well as drugs and alcohol, she described the codependent person as anyone who has let another person's addictive behavior affect him or her and is obsessed with controlling that behavior. By equating any kind of self-control problem with addiction, Beattie made the notion of codependency applicable to an enormous range of people. Indeed, she estimated that as many as 80 million Americans suffer from codependency. Other theorists have offered a variety of somewhat different definitions of codependency and some are even broader than Beattie's (Whitfield, 1991).

According to most theorists, codependency is not a matter of happenstance. They maintain that many people—especially women—unwittingly *seek out* relationships with troubled individuals to satisfy an excessive need to be needed (O'Brien & Gaborit, 1992; Wright & Wright, 1991). In these relationships, codependents become obsessed with trying to protect, control, and change their partners. Pouring their energy into these largely unsuccessful efforts, codependent people consistently subordinate their own needs to those of their partner. Hence, they end up leading anguished, unfulfilling lives. The codependency literature provides a litany of personal problems that may be attributable to codependency (Loughead, 1991). These symptoms of codependency range from minor, common problems, such as boredom, indecision, and lack of spontaneity, to profound, debilitating problems, such as anorexia, depression, and suicide.

What's the solution to the widespread affliction of codependency? Most codependency experts advocate recovery programs, such as Codependents Anony-

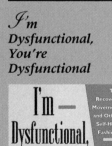
This book takes a penetrating look at self-help books, self-realization programs, the codependency movement, New Age spiritualism, and the curious tendency of people to go on TV talk shows to share their innermost secrets and their most embarrassing frailties with millions of strangers. Kaminer, a social critic who writes about politics, culture, and law, maintains that most self-help books are riddled with psychobabble and sloppy thinking, which undermine our intellectual standards. She also argues that the self-help tradition discourages independent thinking by touting the idea that there are universally applicable solutions for everyone's problems. Kaminer explains how people who jump on the self-help bandwagon give up their freedom to think for themselves by passively submitting to "expert" authority figures who provide simplistic prescriptions for attaining happiness and contentment.

In her analysis of the codependency movement, Kaminer questions the value of encouraging people to view themselves as helpless victims of their families and the wisdom of characterizing traditional feminine traits as pathological. She also questions the assertion that women remain in relationships with troubled, abusive men because they have a masochistic streak. Kaminer's book is a wide-ranging, easy-to-read, thought-provoking analysis of contemporary pop psychology.

> The self-help tradition has always been covertly authoritarian and conformist, relying as it does on a mystique of expertise, encouraging people to look outside themselves for standardized instructions on how to be, teaching us that different people with different problems can easily be saved by the same techniques. It is anathema to independent thought. [p. 6]

mous, which follow the Alcoholics Anonymous model developed in 1935 as a treatment for drinking problems. According to this model, codependency is an addictive disease and recovery can begin only when people admit that they have lost control over their disease. Victims must then commit to the Twelve-Step path to recovery. The Twelve-Step Program requires a spiritual conversion in which addicts turn their lives over to a "Higher Power." Recovery programs also depend heavily on peer self-help groups in which codependent people meet to discuss their problems, vent their emotions, exchange insights, and provide encouragement for each other.

Evaluation

Learning Objective

Summarize the text's critique of codependency theory.

Is the codependency movement just another pop psych fad? Or does it contribute genuine insights about human suffering and effective methods for alleviating this suffering? The answer appears to lie somewhere between these two extremes.

On the one hand, there is much to be said for the family systems perspective adopted by the codependency movement. Clinical work provides evidence that addicts and their family members are often enmeshed in dysfunctional relationships that contribute to the addict's problems and undermine the morale and mental health of the family members (Cermak, 1986; Mendenhall, 1989). Spouses and family members clearly have complex, reciprocal influences on each other (Robins, 1990), and the codependency movement has increased the public's appreciation of this reality. Furthermore, the popularity of the codependency movement suggests that it has uncovered a genuine malady that meshes with the subjective experience of many people in our society. As Haaken (1990) puts it, "The codependence literature expresses the pain, anguish and helplessness, combined with an overwhelming, wearisome responsibility for others, that dominates the lives of many women" (p. 397).

What about the recovery programs advocated by codependency theorists? Their efficacy hasn't been evaluated adequately (Harper & Capdevila, 1990), but they include elements that appear to have some legitimate value. For example, recovery groups seek to provide participants with social support, which can be valuable in helping people cope with stress (Hobfoll & Vaux, 1993), as we'll see in Chapter 3. Recovery groups also encourage participants to talk about their problems and vent their emotions. Research suggests that these are healthy coping strategies (Pennebaker, Colder, & Sharp, 1990), as we will learn in Chapter 4. Thus, it is plausible that many people benefit from their participation in the recovery programs promoted by the codependency movement.

On the other hand, critics argue that codependency theory is riddled with holes and that the amount of attention given to codependency has far outstripped the substance of what is known (Collins, 1993; Gomberg, 1989). Specific concerns include the following:

1. Definitions of codependency vary considerably. Whitfield (1991) reviews 23 widely disparate definitions. Thus, different theorists are often discussing different problems, and the concept of codependency remains vaguely defined, at best (Prest & Protinsky, 1993; Uhle, 1994). People who label themselves as codependent are making highly subjective self-diagnoses of dubious validity based on simplistic stereotypes.

2. Controlled, scientific research on codependency is in its infancy, and there is little or no evidence to support many of the basic tenets of codependency theory (Wright & Wright, 1991). For example, researchers have only just begun to test the idea that codependency occurs because people seek out relationships with troubled individuals (Lyon & Greenberg, 1991) or to study the applicability of the codependency concept to problems such as compulsive eating, gambling, and shopping (O'Brien & Gaborit, 1992).

3. As Kaminer (1992) notes, in codependency theory "every conceivable form of arguably compulsive behavior is classified as an addiction. We are a nation of sexaholics, rageaholics, shopaholics, and rushaholics" (p. 10). Critics assert that this view trivializes the concept of addiction, making it virtually meaningless.

4. Codependency theorists tend to blame addiction and codependence for virtually every conceivable type of psychological problem. Beattie's (1987) first book listed 234 symptoms of codependency! This tendency to explain everything in terms of addiction and codependency clearly represents a vast oversimplification of the complex causes of psychological maladies (Haaken, 1990, 1993).

5. The codependency movement speaks primarily to women, with an apparently sincere intent to help them grapple with certain problems associated with the traditional female role in our society. However, some critics argue that "codependent" has become a derogatory label that is applied to women in a discriminatory fashion (Van Wormer, 1989). There's also concern that codependency theory implicitly blames women for their own suffering, their dysfunctional relations with men, and their husbands' problems (Tavris, 1992).

In sum, codependency started out as a specific, researchable, and potentially insightful idea about how family dynamics may sometimes contribute to addictive behavior. Unfortunately, in the rush to popularize codependency, the concept has become a catchall scapegoat blamed for nearly every form of human misery. Nonetheless, the codependency movement has tapped a fountain of discontent that provides another demonstration that many people are desperately searching for simple answers to complex questions about adjustment in contemporary society.

Self-Help Books

A third example of our search for a sense of direction is the popularity of self-help books that offer do-it-yourself treatments for common personal problems. A glance at the best-seller lists of recent years reveals that our nation has displayed a voracious appetite for self-help books such as *I'm OK—You're OK* (Harris, 1967), *Your Erroneous Zones* (Dyer, 1976), *How to Be Awake and Alive* (Newman & Berkowitz, 1976), *Winning Through Intimidation* (Ringer, 1978), *Living, Loving and Learning* (Buscaglia, 1982), *The Art of Self-Fulfillment* (Litwack & Resnick, 1984), *Willpower's Not Enough* (Watson & Boundy, 1989), *Positive Solitude* (Andre, 1991), *Awakening the Giant Within* (Robbins, 1991), *Ageless Body, Timeless Mind* (Chopra, 1993), and *Liberating the Adult Within* (Kramer, 1994). With their simple recipes for achieving happiness, these books have generally not been timid about promising to change the quality of the reader's life. Consider the following excerpt from the back cover of a self-help book titled *Self Creation* (Weinberg, 1979):

> More than any book ever written, *Self Creation* shows you who you are and reveals the secret to controlling your own life. It contains an action blueprint built around a clear-cut principle as basic and revolutionary as the law of gravity. With it you will discover how to conquer bad habits, solve sexual problems, overcome depression and shyness, deal with infuriating people, be decisive, enhance your career, increase creativity. And it will show you how to love and be loved. You created you.

A glance at bookstore shelves verifies that the boom in self-help books continues unabated, fueled by people's ongoing need for guidance and direction in their personal lives.

Now you can start to reap the boundless benefits of self-confidence, self-reliance, self-determination with *Self Creation.*

If only it were that easy! If only someone could hand you a book that would solve all your problems! Unfortunately, it is not that simple. Merely reading a book is not likely to turn your life around. If the consumption of these literary narcotics were even remotely as helpful as their publishers claim, we would be a nation of serene, happy, well-adjusted people. It is clear, however, that serenity is not the dominant national mood. The multitude of self-help books that crowd bookstore shelves represent just one more symptom of our collective distress and our search for the elusive secret of happiness.

The Value of Self-Help Books

It is somewhat unfair to lump all self-help books together for a critique, because they vary widely in quality (Santrock, Minnett, & Campbell, 1994). Surveys exploring psychotherapists' opinions of self-help books suggest that there are some excellent books that offer authentic insights and sound advice (Starker, 1990, 1992). Surveys also reveal that many therapists encourage their patients to read selected self-help books (Pardeck, 1991; Warner, 1991). Thus, it would be foolish to dismiss all these books as shallow drivel. In fact, some of the better self-help books are highlighted in the Recommended Reading boxes that appear throughout this text. Unfortunately, however, the gems are easily lost in the mountains of rubbish. A great many self-help books offer little of real value to the reader. Generally, they have three fundamental shortcomings.

First, they are dominated by "psychobabble." The term *psychobabble,* coined by R. D. Rosen (1977), seems appropriate to describe the "hip" but hopelessly vague language used in many of these books. Statements such as "It's beautiful if you're unhappy," "You've got to get in touch with yourself," "You have to be up front," "You gotta be you 'cause you're you," and "You need a real high-energy experience" are typical examples of this language. At best, such terminology is ill-defined; at worst, it is meaningless. Consider the following example, taken from a question/answer booklet promoting The Forum (then called *est* training).

> The EST training doesn't change the content of anyone's life, nor does it change what anyone knows. It deals with the context or the way we hold the content. . . . Transformation occurs as a recontextualization . . . "Getting it" means being able to discover when you have been maintaining (or are stuck with) a position which costs you more in aliveness than it is worth, realizing that you are the source of that position, and being able to choose to give up that position or hold it in a way that expands the quality of your life.

What exactly does this paragraph say? Who knows? The statements are so ambiguous and enigmatic that you can read virtually any meaning into them. Therein lies the problem with psychobabble; it is often so obscure that it is unintelligible. Clarity is sacrificed in favor of a hip jargon that prevents, rather than enhances, effective communication.

A second problem is that self-help books tend to place more emphasis on sales than on scientific soundness. The advice offered in these books is far too rarely based on solid, scientific research (Ellis, 1993; Rosen, 1987). Instead, the ideas tend to come from the authors' intuitive analyses, which may be highly speculative. Moreover, even when responsible authors provide scientifically valid advice and are careful not to mislead their readers, sales-hungry publishers often slap outrageous, irresponsible promises on the books' covers (much to the dismay of some authors).

The third shortcoming is that self-help books usually don't provide explicit directions about how to change your behavior. These books tend to be smoothly and warmly written. They often strike responsive chords in the reader by aptly describing a common problem that many of us experience. The reader says, "Yes, that's me!" Unfortunately, when the book focuses on how to deal with the problem, it usually provides only a vague distillation of simple common sense, which often could be covered in two rather than two hundred pages. These books often fall back on inspirational cheerleading in the absence of sound, explicit advice.

What to Look for in Self-Help Books

Learning Objective

Summarize advice about what to look for in quality self-help books.

Because self-help books vary so widely in quality, here are some guidelines to help you find genuinely useful books.

1. Clarity in communication is essential. Advice won't do you much good if you can't understand it. Try to avoid drowning in the murky depths of psychobabble.
2. This may sound backward, but look for books that do not promise too much in the way of immediate change. The truly useful books tend to be appropriately cautious in their promises and realistic about the challenge of altering one's behavior.
3. Try to select books that mention, at least briefly, the theoretical or research basis for the program they advocate. It is understandable that you may not be interested in a detailed summary of research that supports a particular piece of advice. However, you should be interested in whether the advice is based on published research, widely accepted theory, anecdotal evidence, clinical interactions with patients, or pure speculation by the author. Books that are based on more than personal anecdotes and speculation should have a list of references in the back (or at the end of each chapter).
4. Intellectually honest authors don't just talk about what we know—they also discuss what we do *not* know. There is much to be said for books that are candid about the limits of what the so-called experts really know.

Recommended Reading

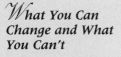

*W*hat You Can Change and What You Can't

by Martin E. P. Seligman (Knopf, 1994)

Martin Seligman is a prominent psychologist who has conducted influential research on learned helplessness, attributional style, optimism, depression, and phobias. In this book he synthesizes research on a host of issues to help people understand what they can change about themselves and what they cannot change. Seligman points out that self-improvement programs of all types—from meditation, to self-help books, to professional therapy—are predicated on the assumption that people can permanently change themselves for the better. He notes, however, that recent, highly publicized research in biological psychiatry is at odds with this assumption. This research suggests that our personality, intelligence, physique, and vulnerability to psychological disorders are predominantly determined by our genetic inheritance and hence largely immutable.

Seligman asserts that both viewpoints are too extreme, that the architects of self-improvement programs are too optimistic and the authorities on biological psychiatry too pessimistic about people's capacity for change. Thus, he sets out to review the empirical evidence on what can be modified with reliable success, and what can't be. Seligman covers a wide range of topics—treatments for sexual difficulties, alcoholism, weight problems, anxiety, depression, obsessions, and posttraumatic stress syndrome, among other things. His discussions are lively, readable, objective, sophisticated, and thoroughly grounded in research.

As the ideologies of biological psychiatry and self-improvement collide, a resolution is apparent. There are some things about ourselves that can be changed, others that cannot, and some that can be changed only with extreme difficulty. [p. 4]

5. Look for books that provide detailed, explicit directions about how to alter your behavior. Generally, these directions represent the crucial core of the book. If they are inadequate in detail, you have been shortchanged.

6. More often than not, books that focus on a particular kind of problem, such as overeating, loneliness, or marital difficulties, deliver more than those that promise to cure all of life's problems with a few simple ideas. Books that cover everything are usually superficial and disappointing. Books that devote a great deal of thought to a particular topic tend to be written by authors with genuine expertise on that topic. Such books are more likely to pay off for you. Figure 1.1 lists 15 self-help books that were among the most highly recommended in a national survey of clinical and counseling psychologists (Santrock et al., 1994). As you can see, they largely focus on specific topics.

The Approach of This Textbook

Learning Objective

Summarize the philosophy underlying the writing of this textbook.

Clearly, in spite of our impressive technological progress, we are a people beset by a great variety of personal problems. Living in our complex, modern society is a formidable challenge. This book is about that challenge. It is about you. It is about life. Specifically, it summarizes for you the scientific research on human behavior that appears relevant to the challenge of living effectively in the 1990s. It draws primarily, but not exclusively, from the science we call psychology.

This text deals with the same kinds of problems addressed by self-help books and self-realization programs: anxiety, stress, interpersonal relationships, frustration, loneliness, depression, self-control. However, it makes no boldly seductive promises about solving your personal problems, turning your life around, or helping you achieve tranquillity. Such promises simply aren't realistic. Psychologists have long recognized that changing one's behavior is a difficult challenge, fraught with frustration and failure (Seligman, 1994). Psychologists sometimes do intensive therapy with a person for years without solving the client's problem.

All this does not mean that you should be pessimistic about your potential for personal growth. You most certainly can change your behavior. Moreover, you can often change it on your own without consulting a professional psychologist. We would not be writing this text if we did not believe that some of our readers might

Figure 1.1
Top-rated self-help books
Based on a national survey of over 500 clinical and counseling psychologists, Santrock, Minnet, and Campbell (1994) compiled a list of the 25 most highly recommended self-help books. Ten of the books on their list dealt with parenting or children. These books are listed in Chapter 11, where we discuss parent-child relations. The remaining 15 titles from their top-rated list are shown here.

Top-Rated Self-Help Books

The Courage to Heal
by Ellen Bass and Laura Davis

Feeling Good
by David Burns

How to Survive the Loss of a Love
by Melba Cosgrove, Harold Bloomfield,
& Peter McWilliams

The Dance of Anger
by Harriet Lerner

The Feeling Good Handbook
by David Burns

Your Perfect Right
by Robert Alberti and Michael Emmons

What Color Is Your Parachute?
by Robert Bolles

The Relaxation Response
by Herbert Benson

The New Aerobics
by Kenneth Cooper

Learned Optimism
by Martin Seligman

Man's Search for Meaning
by Victor Frankl

You Just Don't Understand
by Deborah Tannen

The Dance of Intimacy
by Harriet Lerner

Beyond the Relaxation Response
by Herbert Benson

The Battered Woman
by Lenore Walker

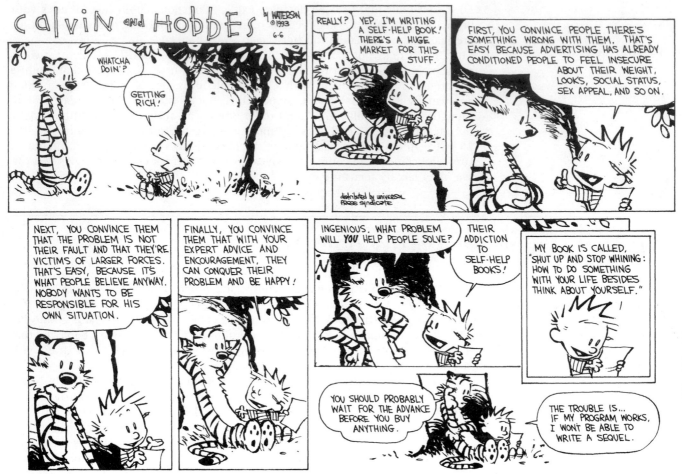

experience some personal benefit from this literary encounter. But it is important that you have realistic expectations. Reading this book will not be a revelatory experience. There are no mysterious secrets about to be unveiled before you. All this book can do is give you some potentially useful information and point you in some potentially beneficial directions. The rest is up to you.

In view of our criticisms of many self-realization programs and self-help books, it seems essential that we lay out explicitly the philosophy that underlies the writing of this text. Here, then, are the basic assumptions and goals of this book.

1. *This text is based on the premise that accurate knowledge about the principles of psychology is of value to you in everyday life.* It has been said that knowledge is power. Greater awareness of why people behave as they do should help you in interacting with others as well as in trying to understand yourself.

2. *This text attempts to foster a critical attitude about psychological issues and to enhance your critical thinking skills.* Information is important, but people also need to develop effective strategies for evaluating information. Critical thinking involves subjecting ideas to systematic, skeptical scrutiny. Critical thinkers ask tough questions, such as: What exactly is the assertion? What assumptions underlie this assertion? What evidence or reasoning supports this assertion? Are there alternative explanations? Some general guidelines for thinking critically are outlined in Figure 1.2. We have already attempted to illustrate the importance of a critical attitude in our evaluation of self-realization programs, the codependency movement, and self-help books, and we'll continue to model critical thinking strategies throughout the text.

3. *This text should open doors.* The coverage in this book is broad; we tackle many topics. Therefore, there may be places where it lacks the depth or detail that you would like. However, you should think of it as a resource book that can introduce you to other books or techniques or therapies, which you can then pursue on your own.

Figure 1.2
Guidelines for thinking critically

Critical thinking should not be equated with negative thinking; it's not a matter of learning how to tear down others' ideas. Rather, critical thinkers carefully subject others' ideas—and their own—to careful, systematic, objective evaluation. The guidelines shown here, taken from Wade and Tavris (1990), provide a succinct overview of what it means to think critically.

Guidelines for Thinking Critically

1 **Ask questions; be willing to wonder.** To think critically you must be willing to think creatively—that is, to be curious about the puzzles of human behavior, to wonder why people act the way they do, and to question received explanations and examine new ones.

2 **Define the problem.** Identify the issues involved in clear and concrete terms, rather than vague generalities such as "happiness," "potential," or "meaningfulness." What does meaningfulness mean, exactly?

3 **Examine the evidence.** Consider the nature of the evidence that supports all aspects of the problem under examination. Is it reliable? Valid? Is it someone's personal assertion or speculation? Does the evidence come from one or two narrow studies, or from repeated research?

4 **Analyze biases and assumptions**—your own and those of others. What prejudices, deeply held values, and other personal biases do you bring to your evaluation of a problem? Are you willing to consider evidence that contradicts your beliefs? Be sure you can identify the biases of others, in order to evaluate their arguments as well.

5 **Avoid emotional reasoning** ("If I feel this way, it must be true"). Remember that everyone holds convictions and ideas about how the world should operate—and that your opponents are as serious about their convictions as you are about yours. Feelings are important, but they should not substitute for careful appraisal of arguments and evidence.

6 **Don't oversimplify.** Look beyond the obvious. Reject simplistic, either-or thinking. Look for logical contradictions in arguments. Be wary of "arguments by anecdote."

7 **Consider other interpretations.** Before you leap to conclusions, think about other explanations. Be especially careful about assertions of cause and effect.

8 **Tolerate uncertainty.** This may be the hardest step in becoming a critical thinker, for it requires the ability to accept some guiding ideas and beliefs—yet the willingness to give them up when evidence and experience contradict them.

4. *This text assumes that the key to effective adjustment is to take charge of your own life.* If you are dissatisfied with some aspect of your life, it does no good to sit around and mope about it. You have to take an active role in attempting to improve the quality of your life. This action may involve learning a new skill or pursuing a particular kind of help. In any case, it is generally best to meet problems head-on rather than trying to avoid them.

The Psychology of Adjustment

Now that we have spelled out our approach in writing this text, it is time to turn to the task of introducing you to some basic concepts. In this section, we'll discuss the nature of psychology and the concept of adjustment.

What Is Psychology?

Learning Objective

Describe the two key facets of psychology.

Psychology is the science that studies behavior and the physiological and mental processes that underlie it, and the profession that applies the accumulated knowledge of this science to practical problems. Psychology leads a complex dual existence as both a *science* and a *profession.* Let's examine the science first. Psychology is an area of scientific study, much like biology or physics. Whereas biology focuses on life processes, and physics on matter and energy, psychology focuses on *behavior and related processes.*

Behavior is any overt (observable) response or activity by an organism. Psychology does not confine itself to the study of human behavior. Many psychologists believe that the principles of behavior are much the same for animals and humans. These psychologists often prefer to study animals—mainly because they can exert more control over the factors influencing the animals' behavior.

Psychology is also interested in the mental processes—the thoughts, feelings, and wishes—that accompany behavior. Mental processes are more difficult to study than behavior because they are private and not directly observable. However, they exert critical influence over human behavior, so psychologists have strived to improve their ability to "look inside the mind."

Finally, psychology includes the study of the physiological processes that underlie behavior. Thus, some psychologists try to figure out how bodily processes such as neural impulses, hormonal secretions, and genetic coding regulate behavior. Practically speaking, all this means is that psychologists study a great variety of phenomena. Psychologists are interested in maze running in rats, salivation in dogs, and brain functioning in cats, as well as visual perception in humans, play in children, and social interaction in adults.

As you probably know, psychology is not all pure science. It has a highly practical side, represented by the many psychologists who provide a variety of professional services to the public. Although the profession of psychology is prominent today, this applied aspect of psychology was actually slow to develop. Psychology emerged as an independent science back in the 19th century, but until the 1950s psychologists were found almost exclusively in the halls of academia, teaching and doing research. However, the demands of America's involvement in World War II (1942–1945) stimulated rapid growth in psychology's first professional specialty—clinical psychology. *Clinical psychology* **is the branch of psychology concerned with the diagnosis and treatment of psychological problems and disorders.** During World War II, a multitude of academic psychologists were pressed into service as clinicians to screen military recruits and treat soldiers suffering from trauma. Frequently they found their clinical work interesting, and many of them returned from the war to set up training programs to meet the continued high demand for clinical services. Soon, about half of the new Ph.D.'s in psychology were specializing in clinical work. Psychology had come of age as a profession.

What Is Adjustment?

Learning Objective

Explain the concept of adjustment.

We have referred to the term *adjustment* several times without clarifying its exact meaning. The concept of adjustment was originally borrowed from biology. It was modeled after the biological term *adaptation,* which refers to efforts by a species to adjust to changes in its environment. Just as a field mouse has to adapt to an unusually brutal winter, a person has to adjust to changes in circumstances such as a new job, a financial setback, or the loss of a loved one. Thus, *adjustment* **refers to the psychological processes through which people manage or cope with the demands and challenges of everyday life.**

The demands of everyday life are diverse, so in studying the process of adjustment we will examine a broad variety of topics. In the first section of this book, The Dynamics of Adjustment, we discuss general issues, such as how personality affects our patterns of adjustment, how we are affected by stress, and how we use coping strategies to deal with stress. In the second section, The Interpersonal Realm, we'll examine the adjustments that we make in our social relationships, exploring topics such as person perception, communication, behavior in groups, friendship, and intimate relationships. In the third section, Developmental Transitions, we'll look at how we adjust to changing demands as we grow older. We'll discuss such topics as the development of gender roles, the emergence of sexuality, phases of adult development, and transitions in the world of work. Finally, in the fourth section, Mental and Physical Health, we'll discuss how the process of adjustment influences our psychological and physical wellness.

As you can see, the study of adjustment delves into nearly every corner of our lives, and we'll be discussing a diverse array of issues and topics. Before we begin considering these topics in earnest, however, we need to take a closer look at psychology's approach to investigating behavior—the scientific method.

The Scientific Approach to Behavior

We all expend a great deal of effort in trying to understand both our own behavior and the behavior of others. We wonder about any number of behavioral questions: Why am I so anxious when I interact with new people? Why is Sam always trying to be the center of attention at the office? Why does Joanna cheat on her wonderful husband? Are extraverts happier than introverts? Is depression more common during the Christmas holidays? Given that psychologists' principal goal is to explain behavior, how are their efforts different from everyone else's? The key difference is that psychology is a *science*, committed to *empiricism*.

The Commitment to Empiricism

Learning Objective

Explain the nature of empiricism.

Empiricism is the premise that knowledge should be acquired through observation. When we say that scientific psychology is empirical, we mean that its conclusions are based on systematic observation rather than on reasoning, speculation, traditional beliefs, or common sense. Scientists are not content with having ideas that sound plausible; they conduct research to *test* their ideas. Whereas our everyday speculations are informal, unsystematic, and highly subjective, scientists' investigations are formal, systematic, and objective.

In these investigations, scientists formulate testable hypotheses, gather data (make observations) relevant to their hypotheses, use statistics to analyze these data, and report their results to the public and other scientists, typically by publishing their findings in a technical journal. The process of publishing scientific studies allows other experts to evaluate and critique new research findings.

Advantages of the Scientific Approach

Learning Objective

Explain two advantages of the scientific approach to understanding behavior.

Science is certainly not the only method we can use to draw conclusions about behavior. We all use logic, casual observation, and good old-fashioned common sense. Since the scientific method often requires painstaking effort, why should we use it?

The scientific approach offers two major advantages. The first is its clarity and precision. Commonsense notions about behavior tend to be vague and ambiguous. Consider the old truism "Spare the rod and spoil the child." What exactly does this generalization about child-rearing amount to? How severely should children be punished if we are not to "spare the rod"? How do we assess whether a child qualifies as "spoiled"? When people disagree about this assertion, it may be because they are talking about entirely different things. In contrast, the scientific approach requires that we specify *exactly* what we are talking about when we formulate hypotheses. This clarity and precision enhance communication about important ideas.

The second advantage offered by the scientific approach is its relative intolerance of error. Scientists subject their ideas to empirical tests. They also scrutinize one another's findings with a critical eye. They demand objective data and thorough documentation before they accept ideas. When the findings of two studies conflict, they try to figure out why the studies reached different conclusions, usually by conducting additional research. In contrast, common sense and casual observation often tolerate contradictory generalizations, such as "Opposites attract" and "Birds of a feather flock together." Furthermore, commonsense analyses involve little effort to verify ideas or detect errors, so that many myths about behavior come to be widely believed.

All this is not to say that science has a copyright on truth. However, the scientific approach does tend to yield more accurate and dependable information than casual analyses and armchair speculation. Knowledge of empirical data can thus provide a useful benchmark against which to judge claims and information from other kinds of sources.

Now that we have an overview of how the scientific enterprise works, we can look at some of the specific research methods that psychologists depend on most. The two main types of research methods in psychology are *experimental research methods* and *correlational research methods*. We will discuss them separately because there is an important distinction between them.

Experimental Research: Looking for Causes

Learning Objective

Describe the experimental method, distinguishing between independent and dependent variables and between experimental and control groups.

Does misery love company? This question intrigued social psychologist Stanley Schachter. When people feel anxious, do they want to be left alone, or do they prefer to have others around? Schachter's hypothesis was that increases in anxiety would cause increases in the desire to be with others, which psychologists call the *need for affiliation*. To test this hypothesis, Schachter (1959) designed a clever experiment. **The *experiment* is a research method in which the investigator manipulates an (independent) variable under carefully controlled conditions and observes whether there are changes in a second (dependent) variable as a result.** Psychologists depend on this method more than any other.

Independent and Dependent Variables

An experiment is designed to find out whether changes in one variable (let's call it *x*) cause changes in another variable (let's call it *y*). To put it more concisely, we want to know *how x affects y*. In this formulation, we refer to *x* as the independent variable, and we call *y* the dependent variable. **An *independent variable* is a condition or event that an experimenter varies in order to see its impact on another variable.** The independent variable is the variable that the experimenter controls or manipulates. It is hypothesized to have some effect on the dependent variable. The experiment is conducted to verify this effect. **The *dependent variable* is the variable that is thought to be affected by the manipulations of the independent variable.** In psychology studies, the dependent variable usually is a measurement of some aspect of the subjects' behavior.

In Schachter's experiment, *the independent variable was the subjects' anxiety level,* which he manipulated in the following way. Subjects assembled in his laboratory were told by a Dr. Zilstein that they would be participating in a study on the physiological effects of electric shock and that they would receive a series of electric shocks. Half of the subjects were warned that the shocks would be very painful. They made up the *high-anxiety* group. The other half of the subjects, assigned to the *low-anxiety* group, were told that the shocks would be mild and painless. These procedures were simply intended to evoke different levels of anxiety. In reality, no one was actually shocked at any time. Instead, the experimenter indicated that there would be a delay while he prepared the shock apparatus for use. The subjects were asked whether they would prefer to wait alone or in the company of others. *This measure of the subjects' desire to affiliate with others was the dependent variable.*

Experimental and Control Groups

To conduct an experiment, an investigator typically assembles two groups of subjects who are treated differently in regard to the independent variable. **The *experimental group* consists of the subjects who receive some special treatment in regard to the independent variable. The *control group* consists of similar subjects who do *not* receive the special treatment given to the experimental group.**

Let's return to the Schachter study to illustrate. In this study, the subjects in the high-anxiety condition were the experimental group. They received a special treatment designed to create an unusually high level of anxiety. The subjects in the low-anxiety condition were the control group.

It is crucial that the experimental and control groups be very similar, except for the different treatment they receive in regard to the independent variable. This stipulation brings us to the logic that underlies the experimental method. If the two

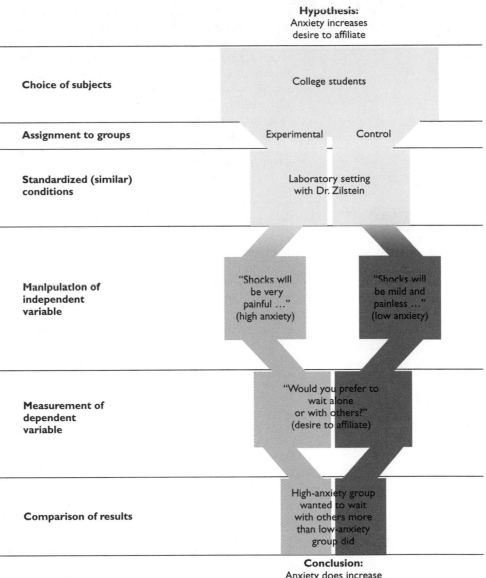

Figure 1.3
The basic elements of an experiment
This diagram provides an overview of the key features of the experimental method, as illustrated by Schachter's (1959) study of anxiety and affiliation. The logic of the experiment rests on treating the experimental and control groups alike except for the manipulation of the independent variable.

Hypothesis:
Anxiety increases desire to affiliate

Choice of subjects — College students

Assignment to groups — Experimental / Control

Standardized (similar) conditions — Laboratory setting with Dr. Zilstein

Manipulation of independent variable — "Shocks will be very painful ..." (high anxiety) / "Shocks will be mild and painless ..." (low anxiety)

Measurement of dependent variable — "Would you prefer to wait alone or with others?" (desire to affiliate)

Comparison of results — High-anxiety group wanted to wait with others more than low-anxiety group did

Conclusion:
Anxiety does increase desire to affiliate

groups are alike in all respects *except for the variation created by the manipulation of the independent variable,* then any differences between the two groups on the dependent variable ~~must be due to this manipulation of the independent variable.~~ In this way researchers isolate the effect of the independent variable on the dependent variable. Thus, Schachter isolated the impact of anxiety on need for affiliation. What did he find? As predicted, he found that increased anxiety led to increased affiliation. The percentage of subjects who wanted to wait with others was nearly twice as high in the high-anxiety group as in the low-anxiety group.

The logic of the experimental method rests heavily on the assumption that the experimental and control groups are alike—except for their different treatment in regard to the independent variable. Any other differences between the two groups cloud the situation and make it difficult to draw solid conclusions about the relationship between the independent variable and the dependent variable. Figure 1.3 summarizes the various elements in an experiment, using Schachter's study as an example.

Advantages and Disadvantages

The experiment is a powerful research method. Its principal advantage is that it allows us to draw conclusions about cause-and-effect relationships between variables. We can draw these conclusions about causation because the precise control available in the experiment permits us to isolate the relationship between the independent variable and the dependent variable. No other research method can duplicate this advantage.

For all its power, however, the experimental method has its limitations. One disadvantage is that we frequently are interested in the effects of variables that cannot be manipulated (as independent variables) because of ethical concerns or practical realities. For example, you might want to know whether being brought up in an urban area as opposed to a rural area affects people's values. A true experiment would require you to assign similar families to live in urban and rural areas, which obviously is impossible to do. To explore this question, you would have to use correlational research methods, which we turn to next.

Correlational Research: Looking for Links

In situations where psychologists cannot exert experimental control over the variables they want to study, all they can do is make systematic observations to see whether a link or association exists between the variables of interest. Such an association is called a correlation. **A *correlation* exists when two variables are related to each other.** The definitive aspect of correlational studies is that the researchers cannot control the variables under study.

Measuring Correlation

Learning Objective

Distinguish between positive and negative correlation and explain what the size of a correlation coefficient means.

The results of correlational research are often summarized with a statistic called the *correlation coefficient*. This widely used statistic will be mentioned often as we discuss studies throughout the remainder of this text. **A *correlation coefficient* is a numerical index of the degree of relationship that exists between two variables.** A correlation coefficient tells us (1) how strongly related two variables are and (2) the direction (positive or negative) of the relationship.

Two *kinds* of relationships can be described by a correlation. A *positive* correlation indicates there is a *direct* relationship between two variables. This means that high scores on variable *x* are associated with high scores on variable *y* and that low scores on variable *x* are associated with low scores on variable *y*. For example, there is a positive correlation between high school grade point average (GPA) and subsequent college GPA. That is, people who do well in high school tend to do well in college, and those who perform poorly in high school tend to perform poorly in college (see Figure 1.4).

In contrast, a *negative* correlation indicates an *inverse* relationship between two variables. This means that people who score high on variable *x* tend to score low on variable *y*, whereas those who score low on *x* tend to score high on *y*. For example, in most college courses, there is a negative correlation between how often a student is absent and how well the student performs on exams. Students who have a high number of absences tend to earn low exam scores, while students who have a low number of absences tend to get higher exam scores (see Figure 1.4).

While the positive or negative sign indicates whether an association is direct or inverse, the *size* of the coefficient indicates the *strength* of the association between two variables. This coefficient can vary between 0 and +1.00 (if positive) or between 0 and −1.00 (if negative). A coefficient near zero tells us there is no relationship between the variables. The closer the correlation is to either −1.00 or +1.00, the stronger the relationship is (see Figure 1.5). Thus, a correlation of +.90 represents a stronger tendency for variables to be associated than does a correlation of +.40. Likewise, a correlation of −.75 represents a stronger relationship than does a correlation of −.45. Keep in mind that the *strength* of a correlation depends only on the size of the coefficient. The positive or negative sign simply shows whether the correlation is direct or inverse. Therefore, a correlation of −.60 reflects a stronger relationship than a correlation of +.30.

Psychologists use a variety of correlational research methods, including naturalistic observation, case studies, and surveys. Let's examine each of these methods to see how researchers use them to detect associations between variables.

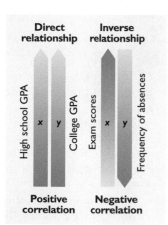

Figure 1.4
Positive and negative correlations
Variables are positively correlated if they tend to increase and decrease together and are negatively correlated if one variable tends to increase when the other decreases. Hence, the terms *positive correlation* and *negative correlation* refer to the *direction* of the relationship between two variables.

Figure 1.5
Interpreting correlation coefficients

The magnitude of a correlation coefficient indicates the strength of the relationship between two variables. The closer a correlation is to either +1.00 or −1.00, the stronger the relationship between the variables. The square of a correlation (called the coefficient of determination) is an index of the correlation's predictive power. The coefficient of determination tells us the percentage of variation in one variable that can be predicted based on the other variable. For example, the correlation between SAT scores and college grade point is roughly .50, which means that the abilities measured by SAT scores can account for about 25% of the variation among students in grade point (.50 × .50).

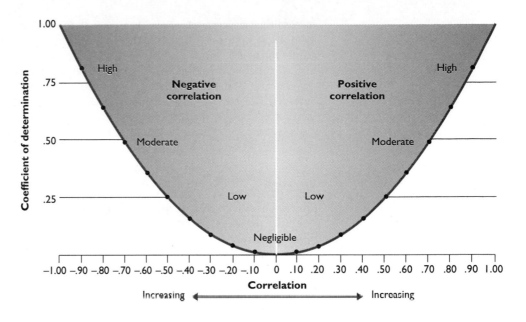

Learning Objective

Describe three correlational research methods.

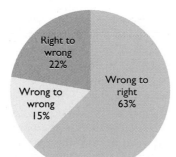

Figure 1.6
The effects of answer changing on multiple-choice exams

In a study of answer changes, Stoffer and colleagues (1977) found that wrong-to-right changes outnumbered right-to-wrong changes by a sizable margin. These results are similar to those of other studies.

Naturalistic Observation

In *naturalistic observation* a researcher engages in careful observation of behavior without intervening directly with the subjects. This type of research is called *naturalistic* because behavior is allowed to unfold naturally (without interference) in its natural environment—that is, the setting in which it would normally occur.

As an example, consider a study by Stoffer, Davis, and Brown (1977), which sought to determine whether it is a good idea for students to reconsider and change answers on multiple-choice tests. The conventional wisdom is that "your first hunch is your best hunch," and it is widely believed that students should not go back and change their answers. To put this idea to an empirical test, Stoffer and his colleagues studied the answer changes made by college students on their regular exams in a psychology course. They simply examined students' answer sheets for evidence of response changes, such as erasures or crossing out of responses. As Figure 1.6 shows, they found that changes that went from a wrong answer to a right answer outnumbered changes that went from a right answer to a wrong answer by a margin of nearly 3 to 1! The correlation between the number of changes students made and their net gain from answer changing was +.49, indicating that the more answer changing students engaged in, the more they improved their scores. These results, which have been replicated in a number of other studies (Benjamin, Cavell, & Shallenberger, 1984), show that popular beliefs about the harmful effects of answer changing are inaccurate.

Case Studies

A *case study* is an in-depth investigation of an individual subject. Psychologists typically assemble case studies in clinical settings where an effort is being made to diagnose and treat some psychological problem. To learn about an individual, a clinician may use a variety of procedures, including interviewing the subject, interviewing others who know the subject, direct observation, examination of records, and psychological testing. Usually, a single case study does not provide much basis for deriving general laws of behavior. If researchers have a number of case studies available, however, they can look for threads of consistency among them, and they may be able to draw some general conclusions.

This was the strategy employed by a research team (Farina et al., 1986) that studied psychiatric patients' readjustment to their community after their release from a mental hospital. The researchers wanted to know whether the patients' physical attractiveness was related to their success in readjustment. As we'll discuss in upcoming chapters, good-looking people tend to be treated better by others than homely people are, suggesting that attractive patients may have an easier time adjusting to life outside the hospital. To find out, the research team compiled case history data (and ratings of physical attractiveness) for patients just before their discharge and six months later. A modest positive correlation (+.38) was found between patients' attractiveness and their post-discharge social adjustment. Thus, the better-looking patients were better off, suggesting that physical attractiveness plays a role in psychiatric patients' readjustment to community living.

Surveys

Surveys are structured questionnaires designed to solicit information about specific aspects of subjects' behavior. They are sometimes used to measure dependent variables in experiments, but they are mainly used in correlational research. Surveys are frequently used to gather data on subjects' attitudes and on aspects of behavior that are difficult to observe directly (marital interactions, for instance).

As an example, consider an influential study by Thomas Holmes and his colleagues (Wyler, Masuda, & Holmes, 1971) that explored the possible relationship between life stress and physical illness. They hypothesized that high stress would be associated with a relatively high frequency of physical illness. To test this hypothesis, they gave 232 subjects a questionnaire that assessed the amount of stress the subjects had experienced in the past year and another questionnaire that assessed the amount of illness they had recently experienced. As predicted, the researchers found a positive correlation (+.32) between subjects' level of stress and their amount of illness. This groundbreaking investigation inspired hundreds of follow-up studies that have enhanced our understanding of how stress is related to physical health (see Chapter 3).

Advantages and Disadvantages

Learning Objective

Compare the advantages and disadvantages of experimental versus correlational research.

Correlational research methods give us a way to explore questions that we could not examine with experimental procedures. Consider the study we just discussed on the association between life stress and health. Obviously, Holmes could not manipulate the life stress experienced by his subjects. Their divorces, retirements, pregnancies, and mortgages were far beyond his control. But correlational methods allowed him to gather useful information on whether there is a link between life stress and illness. Thus, *correlational research broadens the scope of phenomena that psychologists can study.*

Unfortunately, correlational methods have one major disadvantage. The investigator does not have the opportunity to control events so as to isolate cause and effect. *Consequently, correlational research cannot demonstrate conclusively that two variables are causally related.* The crux of the problem is that correlation is no assurance of causation.

When we find that variables *x* and *y* are correlated, we can safely conclude only that *x* and *y* are related. We do not know *how x* and *y* are related. We do not know whether *x* causes *y, y* causes *x,* or both are caused by a third variable. For example, survey studies show that there is a positive correlation between marital satisfaction and sexual satisfaction (Hunt, 1974; Tavris & Sadd, 1977). Although it's clear that good sex and a healthy marriage go hand in hand, it's hard to tell what's causing what. We don't know whether healthy marriages promote good sex, or whether good sex promotes healthy marriages. Moreover, we can't rule out the possibility that both are caused by a third variable. Perhaps sexual satisfaction and marital satisfaction are both caused by compatibility in values. The plausible causal relationships in this case are diagrammed in Figure 1.7, which illustrates the "third-variable problem" in interpreting correlations. This is a common problem in correlational research. Indeed, it will surface in the next section, where we review the empirical research on the determinants of happiness.

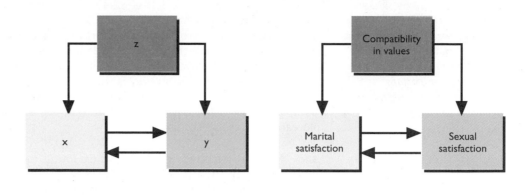

Figure 1.7
Possible causal relations between correlated variables
When two variables are correlated, there are several possible explanations. It could be that *x* causes *y*, that *y* causes *x*, or that a third variable, *z*, causes changes in both *x* and *y*. As the correlation between marital satisfaction and sexual satisfaction illustrates, the correlation itself does not provide the answer.

The Roots of Happiness: An Empirical Analysis

What exactly makes a person happy? This question has been the subject of much speculation. Commonsense hypotheses about the roots of happiness abound. For example, we have all heard that money cannot buy happiness. But do you believe it? A television commercial tells us, "If you've got your health, you've got just about everything." Is health indeed the key? What if you're healthy but poor, unemployed, and lonely? We often hear about the joys of parenthood, the joys of youth, and the joys of the simple, rural life. Are these the factors that promote happiness?

In recent years, social scientists have begun putting these and other hypotheses to empirical test. Quite a number of survey studies have been conducted to explore the determinants of happiness, or *subjective well-being,* as social scientists like to call it. The findings of these studies, which have been summarized effectively by Freedman (1978), Diener (1984), Argyle (1987), and Myers (1992), are quite interesting. We review this research because it illustrates the value of collecting data and putting ideas to an empirical test. As you will see, many commonsense notions about happiness appear to be inaccurate.

What Isn't Very Important?

Let's begin by discussing those things that are relatively unimportant in bringing happiness. A number of factors widely believed to influence one's sense of well-being turn out to be not so significant.

If wealth, fame, and success bring happiness, then rock star Bruce Springsteen should be as happy as they come. In recent interviews, however, Springsteen has revealed that his wealth and fame have not made him immune to personal doubts or depression. His story illustrates that the ingredients of happiness are more complex and subjective than many of us imagine.

Learning Objective

List the various factors that appear to be unimportant or somewhat important ingredients of happiness, based on empirical research.

Money There is a positive correlation between income and subjective feelings of happiness, but the association is surprisingly weak (Argyle, 1987). Once people ascend above the poverty level, there is little relation between income and happiness. On the average, wealthy people are only marginally happier than the middle classes. The problem with money is that in this era of voracious consumption, most of us find a way to spend all of it and come out short, no matter what our income. Complaints about not having enough money are routine even among affluent people earning six-figure incomes.

Age Age and happiness are consistently found to be unrelated. Age accounts for less than 1% of the variation in people's happiness (Myers, 1992). The key factors influencing subjective well-being may shift some as people grow older—work becomes less important, health more so—but people's average level of happiness tends to remain remarkably stable over the life span.

Gender Women are treated for depressive disorders about twice as often as men, so one might expect that women are less happy on the average. However, like age, gender accounts for less than 1% of the variation in people's subjective well-being (Myers, 1992).

Parenthood Children can be a tremendous source of joy and fulfillment, but they can also be a tremendous source of headaches and hassles. Compared to childless couples, parents worry more and experience more marital problems (Argyle, 1987). Apparently, the good and bad aspects of parenthood balance each other out, because

---

Recommended Reading

The Pursuit of Happiness: Who Is Happy—And Why

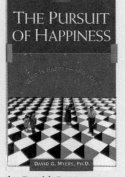

by David G. Myers
(Morrow, 1992)

The Pursuit of Happiness provides a thorough, accurate, up-to-date review of the empirical research on the determinants of happiness, seasoned nicely with illustrative personal anecdotes and low-key, practical advice. David Myers is a respected social psychologist and hard-nosed scientist who acknowledges that his reflections on happiness are "colored by Christian values and spirituality." Emphasizing the finding that objective circumstances have limited impact on happiness, Myers discusses how people might alter their subjective assessments of their lives to foster greater happiness. Working from the insight that happiness is relative, he offers suggestions for managing our comparisons to others and restraining our expectations to enhance our well-being.

Myers's book is a superb example of what self-help books could be and should be, but rarely are. It is clearly written and appropriately cautious about the limits of our knowledge. It is carefully documented, and assertions are closely tied to research and theory. The author's conjectures—which are often fascinating—are accurately presented as learned speculation rather than scientific fact, and readers are encouraged to think for themselves. Complicated issues are not reduced to sound bites and bumper sticker slogans. Myers does not encourage a self-centered approach to life (quite the opposite!), and he does not offer simple prescriptions about how to live. Given these realities, *The Pursuit of Happiness* probably won't make any best-seller lists, but it is well worth reading.

> Happiness is relative not only to our personal past experience, but also to our social experience. We are always comparing ourselves to others. And we feel good or bad depending on whom we compare ourselves to. . . . Today's middle class has double the spending power of three decades ago, yet, because the rising tide lifts all boats, feels relatively deprived compared to their better-off neighbors. Even the rich seldom *feel* rich. . . . To those earning $10,000 a year, it takes a $50,000 income to be rich. To those making $500,000, rich may be a $1 million income. . . . Advertisers exploit our eagerness to compare upward by bombarding us with images of people whose elegant possessions awaken our envy. Many television programs similarly enlarge our circle of comparisons, whetting our appetites for what some others have. [pp. 56–58]

the evidence indicates that people who have children are neither more nor less happy than people without children.

Intelligence   Intelligence is a highly valued trait in modern society, but researchers have not found an association between IQ scores and happiness. Educational attainment also appears to be unrelated to subjective well-being (Diener, 1984).

Community   According to Freedman (1978), when asked where they would most like to live, people show a clear preference for the stereotype of the tranquil, pastoral life believed to exist in rural areas. However, when actual reported happiness is related to community type, people living in urban, suburban, and rural areas are found to be equally happy.

What Is Somewhat Important?

Research has identified three facets of life that appear to have a moderate impact on subjective well-being: health, social activity, and religious belief.

Health   Good physical health would seem to be an essential requirement for happiness, but people adapt to health problems. Research reveals that individuals who develop serious, disabling health conditions aren't as unhappy as one might guess (Myers, 1992). Furthermore, Freedman (1978) argues that good health does not, by itself, produce happiness, because people tend to take good health for granted. Considerations such as these may help to explain why researchers find only a moderate positive correlation (average = .32) between health status and subjective well-being (Diener, 1984).

Social activity   Humans are social animals, and our interpersonal relations do appear to contribute to our happiness. People who are satisfied with their friendship networks and people who are socially active report above-average levels of happiness (Cooper, Okamura, & Gurka, 1992; Diener, 1984). At the other end of the spectrum, people troubled by loneliness tend to be very unhappy (Argyle, 1987).

Religion   The link between religiosity and subjective well-being is modest, but a number of large-scale surveys suggest that people with heartfelt religious convictions are more likely to be happy than people who characterize themselves as nonreligious (Argyle, 1987; Myers, 1992). Researchers aren't sure how religious faith fosters happiness (Diener, 1984), but Myers (1992) offers some interesting conjectures. Among other things, he discusses how religion can give people a sense of purpose and meaning in their lives, help them to accept their setbacks gracefully, connect them to a caring, supportive community, and comfort them by putting their ultimate mortality in perspective.

What Is Very Important?

Learning Objective

Discuss the three factors that do appear to be crucial ingredients of happiness.

The list of factors that turn out to be very important is surprisingly short. Only a few variables are strongly related to overall happiness.

Love and marriage   Romantic relationships can be stressful, but people consistently rate being in love as a critical ingredient of happiness (Diener, 1984). Furthermore, although people complain a lot about their marriages, the evidence indicates that marital status is a key correlate of happiness. Among both men and women, married people are happier than people who are single or divorced. However, the causal relations underlying this correlation are unclear. It may be that people who are happy tend to have better intimate relationships and more stable marriages, while people who are unhappy have more difficulty finding and keeping mates.

Work Given the way people often complain about their jobs, one might not expect work to be a key source of happiness, but it is. Although less critical than love and marriage, job satisfaction is strongly related to general happiness (Argyle, 1987). Studies also show that unemployment has devastating effects on subjective well-being (Diener, 1984). It is difficult to sort out whether job satisfaction causes happiness or vice versa, but evidence suggests that causation flows both ways (Argyle, 1987).

Personality The best predictor of individuals' future happiness is their past happiness (Myers, 1992). Some people seem destined to be happy and others unhappy, regardless of their triumphs or setbacks. The limited influence of life events was apparent in a study that found only marginal differences between lottery winners and quadriplegics in overall happiness (Argyle, 1987). Several lines of evidence suggest that happiness does not depend on external circumstances—having a nice house, good friends, and an enjoyable job—as much as on internal factors, such as one's outlook on life. With this reality in mind, researchers have begun to look for links between personality and subjective well-being, and they have found some relatively strong correlations. For example, self-esteem is one of the best predictors of happiness. Not surprisingly, people who like themselves tend to be happier than those who do not. Other personality correlates of happiness include extraversion, optimism, and a sense of personal control over one's life.

Conclusions

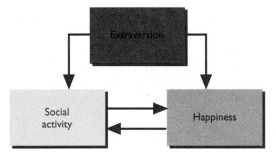

**Figure 1.8
Possible causal relations among the correlates of happiness**
Although we have considerable data on the correlates of happiness, it is difficult to untangle the possible causal relationships. For example, we know that a moderate positive correlation exists between social activity and happiness, but we can't say for sure whether high social activity causes happiness or whether happiness causes people to be more socially active. Moreover, in light of the finding that a third variable—extraversion—correlates with both variables, we have to consider the possibility that extraversion causes both greater social activity and greater happiness.

We must be cautious in drawing inferences about the causes of happiness, as most of the available data are correlational (see Figure 1.8). Nonetheless, the empirical evidence suggests that many popular beliefs about the sources of happiness are unfounded. The data also demonstrate that happiness is shaped by a complex constellation of variables. In spite of this complexity, however, a number of worthwhile insights about human adjustment can be gleaned from research on the correlates of subjective well-being.

First, research on happiness demonstrates that the determinants of subjective well-being are precisely that: subjective. Objective realities are not as important as subjective feelings. In other words, your health, your wealth, your job, and your age are not as influential as how you feel about your health, wealth, job, and age (Argyle, 1987).

Second, in making the subjective assessments that shape our happiness, everything is relative (Myers, 1992). In other words, you evaluate what you have relative to what the people around you have and relative to what you expected to have. Generally, we compare ourselves with others who are similar to us. Thus, people who are wealthy assess what they have by comparing themselves with their wealthy friends and neighbors. This is one reason why there is little correlation between wealth and happiness. You might have a lovely home, but if it sits next to a neighbor's palatial mansion, it might be a source of more dissatisfaction than happiness. In addition to comparing ourselves with other people, we compare what we have with what our expectations were. When we exceed our expectations, we are more likely to be happy. Thus, people living in a lovely home next door to a much lovelier mansion could still be quite happy—if they never expected to live in such an affluent neighborhood. To a large degree, then, happiness is measured on a relative rather than an absolute scale.

Third, although there is no simple recipe for happiness, research shows that the quest for happiness is never hopeless (Freedman, 1978). The evidence indicates that some people find happiness in spite of seemingly insurmountable problems. There is nothing, short of terminal illness—no setback, shortcoming, difficulty, or inadequacy—that makes happiness impossible.

Improving Academic Performance

Answer the following "true" or "false."

1. It's a good idea to study in as many different locations (your bedroom or kitchen, the library, lounges around school, and so forth) as possible.

2. If you have a professor who delivers chaotic, hard-to-follow lectures, there is little point in attending class.

3. Cramming the night before an exam is an efficient way to study.

4. In taking lecture notes, you should try to be a "human tape recorder" (that is, take down everything exactly as said by your professor).

5. Outlining reading assignments is a waste of time.

As you will soon learn, all of the above statements are false. If you answered them all correctly, you may already have acquired the kinds of skills and habits that lead to academic success. If so, however, you are not typical. Today, a huge number of students enter college with remarkably poor study skills and habits—and it's not entirely their fault. Our educational system generally does not provide much in the way of formal instruction on good study techniques. In this first Application, we will try to remedy this oversight to some extent by sharing with you some insights that psychology can provide on how to improve your academic performance. We will discuss how to promote better study habits, how to enhance reading efforts, how to get more out of lectures, and how to make your memory more effective.

Developing Sound Study Habits

Learning Objective

List three steps for developing sound study habits.

Effective study is crucial to success in college. You may run into a few classmates who boast about getting good grades without studying. But you can be sure that if they perform well on exams, they study. Students who claim otherwise simply want to be viewed as extremely bright rather than studious.

Learning can be immensely gratifying, but studying usually involves hard work. The first step toward effective study habits is to face this reality. You don't have to feel guilty if you don't look forward to studying. Most students don't. Once you accept the premise that studying doesn't come naturally, it should be clear that you need to set up an organized program to promote adequate study. According to Walter and Siebert (1990), such a program should include the following considerations.

1. *Set up a schedule for studying.* If you wait until the urge to study hits you, you may still be waiting when the exam rolls around. Thus, it is important to allocate definite times to studying. Review your time obligations (work, housekeeping, and so on) and figure out in advance when you can study. In allotting certain times to studying, keep in mind that you need to be wide awake and alert. Be realistic, too, about how long you can study at one time before you wear down from fatigue. Allow time for study breaks; they can revive sagging concentration.

It's important to write down your study schedule. Writing it down serves as a reminder and increases your commitment to the schedule. As shown in Figure 1.9, you should begin by setting up a general schedule for the quarter or semester. Then, at the beginning of each week, plan the specific assignments that you intend to work on during each study session. This approach should help you avoid cramming for exams at the last minute.

Figure 1.9
Example of an activity schedule
One student's general activity schedule for a semester is shown here. Each week the student fills in the specific assignments to work on during the upcoming study sessions.

	Mon	Tues	Wed	Thurs	Fri	Sat	Sun
8 A.M.						Work	
9 A.M.	History	Study	History	Study	History	Work	
10 A.M.	Psych	French	Psych	French	Psych	Work	
11 A.M.	Study		Study		Study	Work	
Noon	Math	Study	Math	Study	Math	Work	Study
1 P.M.							Study
2 P.M.	Study	English	Study	English	Study		Study
3 P.M.	Study		Study		Study		Study
4 P.M.							
5 P.M.							
6 P.M.	Work	Study	Study	Work			Study
7 P.M.	Work	Study	Study	Work			Study
8 P.M.	Work	Study	Study	Work			Study
9 P.M.	Work	Study	Study	Work			Study
10 P.M.	Work			Work			

Although some students downplay the significance of effective study, some study habits are crucial to academic success.

In planning your weekly schedule, try to avoid the tendency to put off working on major tasks such as term papers and reports. Time management experts, such as Alan Lakein (1973), point out that many of us tend to tackle simple, routine tasks first, saving larger tasks for later, when we supposedly will have more time. This common tendency leads many of us to delay working on major assignments until it's too late to do a good job. You can avoid this trap by breaking major assignments into smaller component tasks that you schedule individually.

2. *Find a place to study where you can concentrate.* Where you study is also important. The key is to find a place where distractions are likely to be minimal. Most people cannot study effectively while watching TV, listening to the stereo, or overhearing conversations. Don't depend on willpower to carry you through these distractions. It's much easier to plan ahead and avoid the distractions altogether.

There is evidence that it helps to set up one or two specific places for study. If possible, use these places for nothing else. They may become strongly associated with studying, so that they serve as cues that evoke good study behavior (Hettich, 1992). In contrast, places associated with other activities may serve as cues for these other activities. For example, studying in your kitchen may evoke more eating than reading.

3. *Reward your studying.* One of the reasons it is so difficult to motivate oneself to study regularly is that the payoffs for studying often lie in the distant future. The ultimate reward, a degree, may be years away. Even more short-term rewards, such as an A in the course, may be weeks or months away. To combat this problem, it helps to give yourself immediate rewards for studying. It is easier to motivate yourself to study if you reward yourself with a tangible payoff, such as a snack, TV show,

or phone call to a friend, when you finish. Thus, you should set realistic study goals for yourself and then reward yourself when you meet them. This systematic manipulation of rewards involves harnessing the principles of *behavior modification*, which are described in some detail in the Chapter 4 Application.

Improving Your Reading

Much of your study time is spent reading and absorbing information. *These efforts must be active.* If your reading is passive, the information will pass right through you. Many students deceive themselves into thinking that they are studying by running a marker through a few sentences here and there in their book. If this highlighting isn't done with thoughtful selectivity, the student is simply turning a textbook into a coloring book. Marking up your text can be useful, but you have to distinguish between important ideas and mere supportive material.

Learning Objective

Describe the SQ3R method and what makes it effective.

There are a number of ways of actively attacking your reading assignments. One of the more worthwhile strategies is Robinson's (1970) SQ3R method. **SQ3R is a study system designed to promote effective reading that includes five steps: survey, question, read, recite, and review.** Its name is an abbreviation for the five steps in the procedure:

Step 1: Survey. Before you plunge into the actual reading, glance over the topic headings in the chapter and try to get an overview of the material. Try to understand how the various chapter segments are related. If the chapter has an outline or summary, consult it to get a feel for the chapter. If you know where the chapter is going, you can better appreciate and organize the information you are about to read.

Step 2: Question. Once you have an overview of your reading assignment, proceed through it one section at a time. Take a look at the heading of the first section and convert it into a question. This is usually quite simple. If the heading is "Prenatal Risk Factors," your question should be "What are sources of risk during prenatal development?" If the heading is "Stereotyping," your question should be "What is stereotyping?" Asking these questions gets you actively involved in your reading and helps you identify the main ideas.

Step 3: Read. Only now, in the third step, are you ready to sink your teeth into the reading. Read only the specific section that you have decided to tackle, keeping an eye toward answering the question that you just formulated. If necessary, reread the section until you can answer that question. Decide whether the segment addresses any other important questions and answer those as well.

Step 4: Recite. Now that you can answer the key question for the section, recite it out loud to yourself in your own words. Using your own words requires understanding instead of simple memorization. Don't move on to the next section until you understand the main idea(s) of the present section. You may want to write down these ideas for review later. When you have fully digested the first section, go on to the next. Repeat steps 2 through 4 with the next section. Once you have mastered the crucial points there, you can go on again. Keep repeating steps 2 through 4, section by section, until you finish the chapter.

Step 5: Review. When you have read the chapter, test and refresh your memory by going back over the key points. Repeat your questions and try to answer them without consulting your book or notes. This review should fortify your retention of the main ideas and should alert you to any key ideas that you haven't mastered. It should also help you to see the relationships between the main ideas.

The SQ3R method does not have to be applied rigidly. For example, it is often wise to break your reading assignment down into smaller segments than those separated by section headings. In fact, you should probably apply SQ3R to many texts on a paragraph by paragraph basis. Obviously, this will require you to formulate some questions without the benefit of topic headings. However, the headings are not absolutely necessary in order to use this technique. If you don't have enough headings, you can simply reverse the order of steps 2 and 3. Read the paragraph first and then formulate a question that addresses the basic idea of the paragraph. The point is that you can be flexible in your use of the SQ3R technique. *What makes SQ3R effective is that it breaks a reading assignment down into manageable segments and requires understanding before you move on.* Any method that accomplishes these goals should enhance your reading.

It is easier to use the SQ3R method when your textbook has plenty of topic headings. This brings up another worthwhile point about improving your reading. It pays to take advantage of the various learning aids incorporated into many textbooks. Don't ignore chapter outlines or chapter summaries. They can help you recognize the important points in the chapter and understand how the various parts of the chapter are interrelated. If your book supplies learning objectives, use them. They tell you what you should get out of your reading.

Getting More out of Lectures

Learning Objective

Summarize advice on how to get more out of lectures.

Although lectures are sometimes boring and tedious, it is a simple fact that poor class attendance is associated with poor grades. For example, in one study, Lindgren (1969) found that absences from class were much more common among "unsuccessful" students (grade average of C− or below) than among "successful" students (grade average of B or above), as is shown in Figure 1.10. Even when you have an instructor who delivers hard-to-follow lectures from which you learn virtually nothing, it is still important to go to class. If nothing else, you'll get a feel for how the instructor thinks. This can help you to anticipate the content of exams and to respond in the manner your professor expects. Fortunately, most lectures are reasonably coherent.

Research indicates that accurate note taking is related to better test performance (Palkovitz & Lore, 1980). Good note taking requires you to actively process lecture information in ways that should enhance both memory and understanding. Books on study skills (Longman & Atkinson, 1991; Sotiriou, 1993) offer a number of suggestions on how to take good lecture notes, including the following:

- Extracting information from lectures requires *active listening procedures*, which are described in more detail in Chapter 6. Focus full attention on the speaker. Try to anticipate what's coming and search for deeper meanings. Pay attention to nonverbal signals that may serve to further clarify the lecturer's intent or meaning.
- When course material is especially complex and difficult, it is a good idea to prepare for the lecture by reading ahead on the scheduled subject in your text. Then you have less information to digest that is brand-new.

Figure 1.10
Successful and unsuccessful students' class attendance
Lindgren (1969) found that attendance was much better among successful students than unsuccessful students.

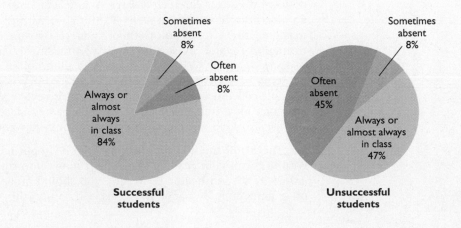

- Don't try to be a human tape recorder. Instead, try to write down the lecturer's thoughts in your own words. This practice forces you to organize the ideas in a way that makes sense to you. In taking notes, pay attention to hints about what is most important. Many instructors give subtle and not-so-subtle clues about what is important, ranging from simply repeating main points to saying things like "You'll run into this again."
- Asking questions during lectures can be very helpful. Doing so keeps you actively involved in the lecture. It also allows you to clarify points you may have misunderstood. Many students are more bashful about asking questions than they should be. They don't realize that most professors welcome questions.

Applying the Principles of Memory

Learning Objective

Summarize how memory is influenced by practice, interference, and organization.

Scientific investigation of memory processes dates back to 1885, when Hermann Ebbinghaus published a series of insightful studies. Thus, memory has been an important topic in psychology for over a century. As a result, researchers have devised a number of principles that are relevant to effective study.

Engage in Adequate Practice

Practice makes perfect, or so you've heard. In reality, practice is not likely to guarantee perfection, but repeatedly reviewing information usually leads to improved retention. Studies show that retention improves with increased rehearsal (Greene, 1992). Continued rehearsal may also pay off by improving your *understanding* of assigned material (Bromage & Mayer, 1986). As you go over information again and again, your increased familiarity with the material may permit you to focus selectively on the most important points, thus enhancing your understanding.

Recommended Reading

Learning Skills for College and Career

by Paul I. Hettich
(Brooks/Cole, 1992)

There are 20 or 30 books available on how to survive the trials and tribulations of college life. Most of them are sound books, but this new entry stands out as one of the best. The book covers the full range of topics relevant to succeeding in college, including time management, organizational skills, study techniques, memory improvement, testwiseness, reading approaches, and note-taking in class. There are unusual chapters on the covert curriculum, study groups, and interpersonal skills, and Jane Halonen has contributed a wonderful chapter on critical thinking. It is easy to read and includes an extensive collection of self-analysis exercises.

One of the most burdensome beliefs often held by the beginning student is the tendency to see the academic challenge of college as a relatively simple matter of information storage. Students with this belief see their texts as so many pages of material to be memorized and regurgitated at test time. . . . In fact, most academic disciplines are quite dynamic. Truths in one decade may be cast aside for new truths in the next. While new students may be tempted to see a discipline as finite and unchanging, most disciplines grow relentlessly. Looking at a set of introductory texts from any discipline over a span of about 30 years illustrates this principle. For one thing, the size and weight of introductory texts expand over time. Ten years from now, texts may have to be wheeled around in a cart! [pp. 244–245]

There is evidence that it even pays to overlearn material (Driskell, Wilis, & Copper, 1992). *Overlearning* **refers to continued rehearsal of material after you first appear to master it.** In one study, after subjects mastered a list of nouns (they recited the list without error), Krueger (1929) required them to continue rehearsing for 50% or 100% more trials. Measuring retention at intervals of up to 28 days, Krueger found that overlearning led to better recall of the list. The implication of this finding is simple: you should not quit rehearsing material as soon as you appear to have mastered it.

Use Distributed Practice

Let's assume that you are going to study 9 hours for an exam. Is it better to "cram" all of your study into one 9-hour period (massed practice) or distribute it among, say, three 3-hour periods on successive days (distributed practice)? The evidence indicates that retention tends to be greater after distributed practice than massed practice (Glenberg, 1992). This advantage is especially apparent if the intervals between practice periods are fairly long, such as 24 hours (Zechmeister & Nyberg, 1982). The inefficiency of massed practice means that cramming is an ill-advised study strategy for most students. Cramming will strain your memorization capabilities and tax your energy level. It may also stoke the fires of test anxiety.

Minimize Interference

Interference **occurs when people forget information because of competition from other learned material.** Research suggests that interference is a major cause of forgetting, so you'll probably want to think about how you can minimize interference. This is especially important for students because memorizing information for one course can interfere with retaining information in another course. It may help to allocate study for specific courses to specific days. Thorndyke and Hayes-Roth (1979) found that similar material produced less interference when it was learned on different days. Thus, the day before an exam in a course, it is probably best to study for that course only. If demands in other courses make that impossible, study the test material last.

Of course, studying for other classes is not the only source of interference in a student's life. Other normal waking activities also produce interference. Therefore, it is a good idea to conduct one last, thorough review of material as close to exam time as possible (Anderson, 1980). This last-minute review helps you to avoid memory loss because of interference from intervening activities.

Organize Information

Retention tends to be greater when information is well organized. Gordon Bower (1970) has shown that hierarchical organization is particularly helpful. Hence, one of the most potent weapons in your arsenal of study techniques is to *outline* reading assignments. Outlining is probably too time-consuming to do for every class. However, it is worth the effort in particularly important or particularly difficult classes, where it can greatly improve retention.

Use Verbal Mnemonics

Learning Objective

Describe several verbal and visual mnemonic devices.

People retain information better when the information is more meaningful (Raugh & Atkinson, 1975). A useful strategy is to make material *personally* relevant. When you read your textbooks, try to relate information to your own life and experience. For example, if you're reading in your psychology text about the personality trait of assertiveness, you can think of someone you know who is very assertive.

Of course, it's not always easy to make something personally meaningful. When you study chemistry, you may have a hard time relating to polymers at a personal level. This problem has led to the development of many **mnemonic devices, or strategies for enhancing memory,** that are designed to make abstract material more meaningful.

Acrostics and acronyms   Acrostics are phrases (or poems) in which the first letter of each word (or line) functions as a cue to help you recall the abstract words that begin with the same letter. For instance, you may remember the order of musical notes with the saying "**E**very **g**ood **b**oy **d**oes **f**ine" (or "**d**eserves **f**avor"). A variation on acrostics is the *acronym*—a word formed out of the first letters of a series of words. Students memorizing the order of colors in the light spectrum often store the name "Roy G. Biv" to remember **r**ed, **o**range, **y**ellow, **g**reen, **b**lue, **i**ndigo, and **v**iolet.

Narrative methods   Another useful way to remember a list of words is to create a story that includes each of the words in the right order. The narrative increases the meaningfulness of the words and links them in a specific order. Examples of this technique can be seen in Figure 1.11. Bower and Clark (1969) found that this procedure enhanced subjects' recall of lists of unrelated words.

Why—and how—would you use the narrative method? Let's assume that you always manage to forget to put one item in your gym bag on your way to the pool.

Figure 1.11
The narrative method
Two examples of the narrative method for memorizing lists are shown here (Bower & Clark, 1969). The words to be memorized are listed on the left, while the stories constructed to remember them are shown on the right.

Word Lists to Be Memorized and Stories Constructed from Them

Word lists		Stories
Bird	Nurse	A man dressed in a *Bird Costume* and wearing a *Mailbox* on his *Head* was seen leaping into the *River*. A *Nurse* ran out of a nearby *Theater* and applied *Wax* to his *Eyelids*, but her efforts were in vain. He died and was tossed into the *Furnace*.
Costume	Theater	
Mailbox	Wax	
Head	Eyelid	
River	Furnace	
Rustler	Fuzz	A *Rustler* lived in a *Penthouse* on top of a *Mountain*. His specialty was the three-toed *Sloth*. He would take his captive animals to a *Tavern* where he would remove *Fuzz* from their *Glands*. Unfortunately, all this exposure to sloth fuzz caused him to grow *Antlers*. So he gave up his profession and went to work in a *Pencil* factory. As a precaution he also took a lot of *Vitamin* E.
Penthouse	Gland	
Mountain	Antler	
Sloth	Pencil	
Tavern	Vitamin	

Figure 1.12
The method of loci
In this example from Bower (1970), a person about to go shopping pairs items to be remembered with familiar places (loci) arranged in a natural sequence: (1) hot dogs/driveway; (2) cat food/garage; (3) tomatoes/front door; (4) bananas/coat closet; (5) whiskey/kitchen sink. As the last panel shows, the shopper recalls the items by mentally touring the loci associated with them.

Short of pasting a list on the inside of the bag, how can you remember everything you need? You could make up a story that includes all the items:

> The wind and rain in COMBINATION LOCKED out the rescue efforts—nearly. CAP, the flying ace, TOWELED the SOAP from his eyes, pulled his GOGGLES from his SUIT pocket, and COMBED the BRUSH for survivors.

Rhymes Another verbal mnemonic that we often rely on is rhyming. You've probably repeated "I before E except after C" thousands of times. Perhaps you also remember the number of days in each month with the old standby, "Thirty days hath September . . ." Rhyming something to remember it is an old and useful trick.

Use Visual Imagery

Memory can be improved through the use of visual imagery. One influential theory (Paivio, 1986) proposes that visual images create a second memory code and that two codes are better than one. Many popular mnemonic devices depend on visual imagery, including the following examples.

Link method The *link method* involves forming a mental image of items to be remembered in a way that links them together. For instance, suppose that you are going to stop at the drugstore on the way home and you need to remember to pick up a news magazine, shaving cream, film, and pens. To remember these items, you might visualize a public figure likely to be in the magazine shaving with a pen while being photographed. There is evidence that the more bizarre you make your image, the more helpful it will be (McDaniel & Einstein, 1986).

Method of loci The *method of loci* involves taking an imaginary walk along a familiar path where you have placed mental images of items you want to remember at certain locations. The first step is to commit to memory a series of loci, or places along a path. Usually these loci are specific locations in your home or neighborhood. Then envision each thing you want to remember in one of these locations. Try to form distinctive, vivid images. Then, when you need to remember the items, imagine yourself walking along the path. The various loci on your path should serve as retrieval cues for the images that you formed (see Figure 1.12). The method of loci ensures that items are remembered in their correct order because the order is determined by the sequence of locations along the pathway. This method has demonstrated value for memorizing lists (Crovitz, 1971).

Key Ideas

The Paradox of Progress

• In spite of the great technological progress in our modern era, personal problems have not declined. In fact, many theorists argue that our progress has brought new, and possibly more difficult, adjustment problems.

The Search for Direction

• Self-help books, self-realization programs, and the codependency movement represent three interesting manifestations of people's struggle to find a sense of direction in our confusing world. Unfortunately, self-realization programs have little real value, and their alleged benefits are probably due to placebo effects.

• The codependency movement is motivated by good intentions, but it vastly oversimplifies the roots of human distress and has little empirical basis. Some self-help books offer worthwhile advice, but most are dominated by psychobabble and are not based on scientific research. Many also lack explicit advice on how to change behavior.

The Approach of This Textbook

• Although this text deals with many of the same issues as self-realization programs, the codependency movement, and self-help books, its philosophy and approach are quite different. Among other things, it is based on the assumption that accurate knowledge of psychology has value in everyday life and that the key to effective adjustment is to take charge of your own life.

The Psychology of Adjustment

• Psychology is both a science and a profession that focuses on behavior and related mental and physiological processes. Adjustment is a broad area of study in psychology concerned with how people adapt effectively or ineffectively to the demands and pressures of everyday life.

The Scientific Approach to Behavior

• The scientific approach to understanding behavior is empirical. Psychologists base their conclusions on formal, systematic, objective tests of their hypotheses, rather than reasoning, speculation, or common sense. The scientific approach is advantageous in that it puts a premium on clarity and has little tolerance for error.

• Experimental research involves manipulating an independent variable to discover its effects on a dependent variable. The experimenter usually does this by comparing experimental and control groups, which must be alike except for the variation created by the manipulation of the independent variable. Experiments allow us to draw conclusions about cause-effect relationships between variables, but this method isn't usable for the study of many problems.

• Psychologists conduct correlational research when they are unable to exert control over the variables they want to study. The correlation coefficient is a numerical index of the degree of relationship between two variables. Correlational research methods include naturalistic observation, case studies, and surveys. Correlational research allows us to investigate issues that may not be open to experimental study, but it cannot demonstrate that two variables are causally related.

The Roots of Happiness: An Empirical Analysis

• A scientific analysis of happiness reveals that many commonsense notions about the roots of happiness appear to be incorrect. The only factors that are clearly and strongly related to happiness are love and marriage, work satisfaction, and personality. There are no simple recipes for achieving happiness, but it helps to understand that happiness is a relative concept mediated by our highly subjective assessments of our lives.

Application: Improving Academic Performance

• To foster sound study habits, you should devise a written study schedule and reward yourself for following it. You should also try to find one or two specific places for studying that are relatively free of distractions. You should use active reading techniques, such as SQ3R, to select the most important ideas from the material you read.

• Good note-taking can help you get more out of lectures. It's important to use active listening techniques and to record lecturers' ideas in your own words. Reading ahead can also help you to prepare for lectures and ask questions as needed.

• Rehearsal, even when it involves overlearning, facilitates retention. Distributed practice tends to be more efficient than massed practice. It is wise to plan study sessions so as to minimize interference. Evidence also suggests that organization enhances retention, so outlining texts may be valuable.

• Meaningfulness can be enhanced through the use of verbal mnemonics like acrostics, acronyms, and narrative methods. The link method and the method of loci are mnemonic devices that depend on the value of visual imagery.

Key Terms

Adjustment
Behavior
Case study
Clinical psychology
Control group
Correlation
Correlation coefficient
Dependent variable
Empiricism
Experiment
Experimental group
Independent variable
Interference
Mnemonic devices
Naturalistic observation
Overlearning
Placebo effects
Psychology
SQ3R
Surveys

Key People

David Myers

2 *Theories of Personality*

Imagine that you are hurtling upward in an elevator with three other persons when suddenly a power outage causes the elevator to grind to a halt 45 stories above the ground. Your three companions might adjust to this predicament differently. One might crack jokes to relieve tension. Another might make ominous predictions that "we'll never get out of here." The third person might calmly think about how to escape from the elevator. These varied ways of coping with the same stressful situation occur because each person has a different personality. Personality differences significantly influence people's patterns of adjustment. Thus, theories intended to explain personality can contribute to our effort to understand adjustment processes.

In this chapter, we will introduce you to various theories that attempt to explain the structure and development of personality. Our review of personality theory will also serve to acquaint you with four major theoretical perspectives in psychology: the psychodynamic, behavioral, humanistic, and biological perspectives. These theoretical approaches are conceptual models that help explain behavior. Familiarity with them will help you understand many of the ideas you will encounter in this book, as well as in other books about psychology.

The Nature of Personality

To discuss theories of personality effectively, we need to digress momentarily to examine a definition of personality and to discuss the concept of personality traits.

What Is Personality?

Learning Objective

Explain the concepts of personality and personality traits, and describe the five-factor model of personality.

What does it mean if you say that a friend has an optimistic personality? Your assertion indicates that the person has a fairly *consistent tendency* to behave in a cheerful, hopeful, enthusiastic way, looking at the bright side of things, across a wide variety of situations. In a similar vein, if you note that a friend has an "outgoing" personality, you mean that she or he consistently behaves in a friendly, open, and extraverted manner in a variety of circumstances. Although none of us are entirely consistent in our behavior, this quality of *consistency across situations* lies at the core of the concept of personality.

Distinctiveness is also central to the concept of personality. We all have traits seen in other people, but we each have our own, distinctive set of personality traits. Each of us is unique. Thus, as illustrated by the elevator scenario, we use the concept of personality to explain why we don't all act alike in the same situation.

In summary, personality is used to explain (1) the stability in a person's behavior over time and across situations (consistency) and (2) the behavioral differences among people reacting to the same situation (distinctiveness). These ideas can be combined into the following definition: **personality refers to an individual's unique constellation of consistent behavioral traits.** Let's look more closely at the concept of traits.

What Are Personality Traits?

We all make remarks like "Melanie is very *shrewd*" or "Doug is too *timid* to succeed in that job" or "I wish I could be as *self-assured* as Marlene." When we attempt to describe an individual's personality, we usually do so in terms of specific aspects of personality, called *traits*. **A personality trait is a durable disposition to behave in a particular way in a variety of situations.** Adjectives such as *honest, dependable, moody, impulsive, suspicious, anxious, excitable, domineering*, and *friendly* describe dispositions that represent personality traits.

Most trait theories of personality, such as those of Gordon Allport (1937, 1961) and Raymond Cattell (1950, 1966), assume that some traits are more basic than others. According to this notion, a small number of fundamental traits determine

Figure 2.1
The five-factor model of
personality
According to McCrae and Costa
(1987), all personality traits are
derived from the five basic traits
listed in the column on the left.
These traits are viewed as
"higher-order" dimensions of
personality that determine the
"lower-order" traits listed in the
right column.

McCrae and Costa's Five-Factor Model of Personality

Basic factor	Subsidiary traits
Neuroticism	Anxious, insecure, guilt-prone, self-conscious
Extraversion	Talkative, sociable, fun-loving, affectionate
Openness to experience	Daring, nonconforming, showing unusually broad interests, imaginative
Agreeableness	Sympathetic, warm, trusting, cooperative
Conscientiousness	Ethical, dependable, productive, purposeful

other, more superficial traits. For example, a person's tendency to be impulsive, restless, irritable, boisterous, and impatient might all derive from a more basic tendency to be excitable.

In recent years, Robert McCrae and Paul Costa (1985, 1987) have stimulated a lively debate among psychologists by arguing that the vast majority of personality traits derive from just five critical traits: (1) neuroticism, (2) extraversion, (3) openness to experience, (4) agreeableness, and (5) conscientiousness. Widely dubbed the "big five," these dimensions of personality are described in Figure 2.1. McCrae and Costa maintain that personality can be described adequately by measuring the basic traits they have identified. Their bold claim that the complexity of personality can be reduced to just five fundamental dimensions has been supported in many studies by other researchers, and their *five-factor model of personality* has become the dominant conception of personality structure in contemporary psychology (Goldberg, 1993; John, 1990; Ozer & Reise, 1994). However, many theorists still maintain that more than five traits are needed to account for the variation in human personality (Briggs, 1989; Cattell, 1990; Wiggins, 1992). Ironically, other theorists have argued for even simpler three-factor or four-factor models of personality (Church & Burke, 1994; Eysenck, 1992).

The debate about how many dimensions are necessary to describe personality is likely to continue for many years to come. As you'll see throughout this chapter, the study of personality is an area in psychology that has a long history of "dueling theories." We'll begin our tour of these theories by examining the influential work of Sigmund Freud and his followers.

Psychodynamic Perspectives

Learning Objective

Discuss the nature of psychodynamic theories and Freud's background.

Psychodynamic theories include all the diverse theories descended from the work of Sigmund Freud, which focus on unconscious mental forces. Freud inspired many brilliant scholars who followed in his intellectual footsteps. Some of these followers simply refined and updated Freud's theory. Others veered off in new directions and established independent, albeit related, schools of thought. Today, the psychodynamic umbrella covers a large collection of related theories. In this section, we'll examine the ideas of Sigmund Freud in some detail and then take a brief look at the work of two of his most significant followers, Carl Jung and Alfred Adler. Another psychodynamic theorist, Erik Erikson, is covered in a later chapter on adolescent and adult development (see Chapter 11).

Freud's Psychoanalytic Theory

Born in 1856, Sigmund Freud grew up in a middle-class Jewish home in Vienna, Austria. He showed an early interest in intellectual pursuits and became an intense, hard-working young man. He dreamed of achieving fame by making an important discovery. His determination was such that in medical school he dissected 400 male eels to prove for the first time that they had testes. His work with eels did not make

Sigmund Freud

him famous. However, his later work with people made him one of the most influential and controversial figures of modern times.

Freud was a physician specializing in neurology when he began his medical practice in Vienna toward the end of the 19th century. Like other neurologists in his era, he often treated people troubled by nervous problems such as irrational fears, obsessions, and anxieties. Eventually he devoted himself to the treatment of mental disorders using an innovative procedure he developed, called *psychoanalysis*.

Psychoanalysis required lengthy verbal interactions with patients in which Freud probed deeply into their lives. Decades of experience with his patients provided much of the inspiration for Freud's theory of personality. He also gathered material by looking inward and examining his own anxieties and conflicts. For over 40 years, Freud devoted the last half-hour of each workday to self-analysis.

Freud's theory gradually gained prominence, but most of Freud's contemporaries were uncomfortable with his theory for at least three reasons. First, he argued that unconscious forces govern our behavior. This idea was disturbing because it suggested that we are not masters of our own minds. Second, he claimed that childhood experiences strongly determine adult personality. This notion distressed people because it suggested that we are not masters of our own destinies. Third, he said that our personalities are shaped by how we cope with our sexual urges. This assertion offended the conservative, Victorian values of his time. Thus, Freud endured a great deal of criticism, condemnation, and outright ridicule, even after his work began to attract more favorable attention. Let's examine the ideas that generated so much controversy.

Structure of Personality

Learning Objective

Describe Freud's three components of personality and how they are distributed across levels of awareness.

Freud (1901/1960, 1920/1924) divided personality structure into three components: the id, the ego, and the superego. He saw a person's behavior as the outcome of interactions among these three components.

The *id* is the primitive, instinctive component of personality that operates according to the pleasure principle. Freud referred to the id as the reservoir of psychic energy. By this he meant that the id houses the raw biological urges (to eat, sleep, defecate, copulate, and so on) that energize our behavior. The id operates according to the *pleasure principle*, **which demands immediate gratification of its urges.** The id engages in *primary process thinking*, which is primitive, illogical, irrational, and fantasy-oriented.

The *ego* is the decision-making component of personality that operates according to the reality principle. The ego mediates between the id, with its forceful desires for immediate satisfaction, and the external social world, with its expectations and norms regarding suitable behavior. The ego considers social realities—society's norms, etiquette, rules, and customs—in deciding how to behave. The ego is guided by the *reality principle*, **which seeks to delay gratification of the id's urges until appropriate outlets and situations can be found.** In short, to stay out of trouble, the ego often works to tame the unbridled desires of the id. As Freud put it, the ego is "like a man on horseback, who has to hold in check the superior strength of the horse" (Freud, 1923, p. 15).

In the long run, the ego wants to maximize gratification, just like the id. However, the ego engages in *secondary process thinking*, which is relatively rational, realistic, and oriented toward problem solving. Thus, the ego strives to avoid negative consequences from society and its representatives (for example, punishment by parents or teachers) by behaving "properly." It also attempts to achieve long-range goals that sometimes require putting off gratification.

While the ego concerns itself with practical realities, the *superego* **is the moral component of personality that incorporates social standards about what represents right and wrong.** Throughout our lives, but especially during childhood, we receive training about what is good and bad behavior. Eventually we internalize many of these social norms. This means that we truly *accept* certain moral principles, and then *we* put pressure on *ourselves* to live up to these standards. The superego emerges out of the ego at around 3 to 5 years of age. In some people, the superego can become irrationally demanding in its striving for moral perfection. Such people are plagued by excessive guilt.

Freud's famous psychoanalytic couch, in his office in Vienna.

Figure 2.2
Freud's model of personality structure

Freud theorized that people have three levels of awareness: the conscious, preconscious, and unconscious. To dramatize the size of the unconscious, he compared it to the portion of an iceberg that lies beneath the water's surface. Freud also divided personality structure into three components—id, ego, and superego—which operate according to different principles and exhibit different modes of thinking. In Freud's model, the id is entirely unconscious, but the ego and superego operate at all three levels of awareness.

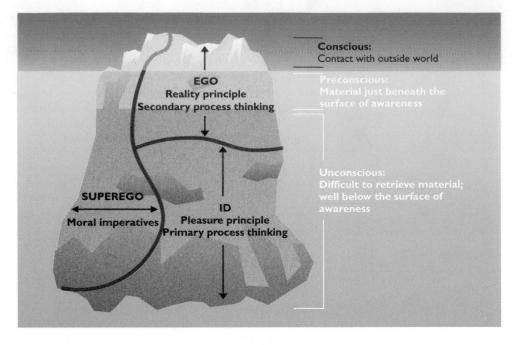

According to Freud, the id, ego, and superego are distributed across three levels of awareness. He contrasted the unconscious with the conscious and preconscious (see Figure 2.2). **The *conscious* consists of whatever you are aware of at a particular point in time.** For example, at this moment your conscious may include your train of thought in reading this text and a dim awareness in the back of your mind that your eyes are getting tired and you're beginning to get hungry. **The *preconscious* contains material just beneath the surface of awareness that can be easily retrieved.** Examples might include your middle name, what you had for supper last night, or an argument you had with a friend yesterday. **The *unconscious* contains thoughts, memories, and desires that are well below the surface of conscious awareness, but that nonetheless exert great influence on behavior.** Examples of material that might be found in your unconscious would include a forgotten trauma from childhood or hidden feelings of hostility toward a parent.

Conflict and Defense Mechanisms

Freud assumed that our behavior is the outcome of an ongoing series of internal battles between the id, ego, and superego. Why the conflict? Because the id wants to gratify its urges immediately, but the norms of civilized society frequently dictate otherwise. For example, your id might feel an urge to clobber a co-worker who constantly irritates you. However, society frowns on such behavior, so your ego would try to hold this urge in check, and you would find yourself in a conflict. You may be experiencing conflict at this very moment. In Freudian terms, your id may be secretly urging you to abandon reading this chapter so you can watch television. Your ego may be weighing this appealing option against your society-induced need to excel in school.

Freud believed that conflicts dominate our lives. He asserted that we career from one conflict to another. The following scenario provides a fanciful illustration of how the three components of personality interact to create constant conflicts.

Imagine your alarm clock ringing obnoxiously as you lurch across the bed to shut it off. It's 7 A.M. and time to get up for your history course. However, your id (operating according to the pleasure principle) urges you to return to the immediate gratification of additional sleep. Your ego (operating according to the reality principle) points out that you really must go to class since you haven't been able to decipher the stupid textbook on your own. Your id (in its typical unrealistic fashion) smugly assures you that you will get the A that you need. It suggests lying back to dream about how impressed your roommates will be. Just as you're relaxing, your superego jumps into the fray. It tries to make you feel guilty about the tuition your parents paid for the class that you're about to skip. You haven't even gotten out of bed yet—and there is already a pitched battle in your psyche.

Let's say your ego wins the battle. You pull yourself out of bed and head for class. On the way, you pass a donut shop and your id clamors for cinnamon rolls. Your ego reminds you that you're supposed to be on a diet. Your id wins this time. After you've attended your history lecture, your ego reminds you that you need to do some library research for a paper in philosophy. However, your id insists on returning to your apartment to watch some sitcom reruns. As you reenter your apartment, you notice how messy it is. It's your roommates' mess and your id suggests that you tell them off. As you're about to lash out, however, your ego convinces you that diplomacy will be more effective. Three sitcoms later you find yourself in a debate about whether to go to the gym to work out or to the student union to watch MTV. It's only midafternoon—and already you've been through a series of internal conflicts.

Freud believed that conflicts centering on sexual and aggressive impulses are especially likely to have far-reaching consequences. Why did he emphasize sex and aggression? Two reasons were prominent in his thinking. First, Freud thought that sex and aggression are subject to more complex and ambiguous social controls than other basic motives. The norms governing sexual and aggressive behavior are subtle, and we often get mixed messages about what is appropriate. Thus, he believed that these two drives are the source of much confusion.

Second, Freud noted that the sexual and aggressive drives are thwarted more regularly than other basic biological urges. Think about it: If you get hungry or thirsty, you can simply head for a nearby vending machine or a drinking fountain. But if a department store clerk infuriates you, you aren't likely to slug the clerk, because this is socially unacceptable. Likewise, when you see an attractive person who inspires lustful urges, you don't normally walk up and propose a tryst in a nearby broom closet. There is nothing comparable to vending machines or drinking fountains for the satisfaction of our sexual and aggressive urges. Thus, Freud ascribed great importance to these needs because social norms dictate that they be routinely frustrated.

Most conflicts are trivial and quickly resolved one way or the other. Occasionally, however, a conflict will linger for days, months, and even years, creating internal tension. Indeed, Freud believed that lingering conflicts rooted in childhood experiences cause most personality disturbances. More often than not, these prolonged and troublesome conflicts involve sexual and aggressive impulses that society wants to tame. These conflicts are often played out entirely in the unconscious. Although you may not be aware of these unconscious battles, they can produce *anxiety* that slips to the surface of conscious awareness. This anxiety is attributable to your ego worrying about the id getting out of control and doing something terrible.

Learning Objective

Describe seven defense mechanisms identified by Freud.

The arousal of anxiety is a crucial event in Freud's theory of personality functioning. Anxiety is distressing, so people try to rid themselves of this unpleasant emotion any way they can. This effort to ward off anxiety often involves the use of defense mechanisms. *Defense mechanisms* **are largely unconscious reactions that protect a person from painful emotions such as anxiety and guilt.** Typically, they are mental maneuvers that work through self-deception. Consider *rationalization,* **which involves creating false but plausible excuses to justify unacceptable behavior.** For example, after cheating someone in a business transaction you might reduce your guilt by rationalizing that "everyone does it."

According to Freud, the most basic and widely used defense mechanism is repression. *Repression* **involves keeping distressing thoughts and feelings buried in the unconscious.** People tend to repress desires that make them feel guilty, conflicts that make them anxious, and memories that are painful. Repression is "motivated forgetting." If you forget a dental appointment or the name of someone you don't like, repression may be at work.

Self-deception can also be seen in projection and displacement. *Projection* **involves attributing one's own thoughts, feelings, or motives to another person.** Usually, people use projection to defend against thoughts that would make them feel guilty. For example, if your lust for a co-worker makes you feel guilty, you might attribute any latent sexual tension between the two of you to the *other person's* desire to seduce you. *Displacement* **involves diverting emotional feelings (usually anger) from their original source to a substitute target.** If your boss gives you a hard time at work and you come home and slam the door, kick the dog, and scream at your spouse, you are displacing your anger onto irrelevant tar-

Defense Mechanisms, with Examples

Definition	Example
Repression involves keeping distressing thoughts and feelings buried in the unconscious.	A traumatized soldier has no recollection of the details of a close brush with death.
Projection involves attributing one's own thoughts, feelings, or motives to another person.	A woman who dislikes her boss thinks she likes her boss but feels that the boss doesn't like her.
Displacement involves diverting emotional feelings (usually anger) from their original source to a substitute target.	After a parental scolding, a young girl takes her anger out on her little brother.
Reaction formation involves behaving in a way that is exactly the opposite of one's true feelings.	A parent who unconsciously resents a child spoils the child with outlandish gifts.
Regression involves a reversion to immature patterns of behavior.	An adult has a temper tantrum when he doesn't get his way.
Rationalization involves the creation of false but plausible excuses to justify unacceptable behavior.	A student watches TV instead of studying, saying that "additional study wouldn't do any good anyway."
Identification involves bolstering self-esteem by forming an imaginary or real alliance with some person or group.	An insecure young man joins a fraternity to boost his self-esteem.

Figure 2.3
Defense mechanisms
According to Freud, we use a variety of defense mechanisms to protect ourselves from painful emotions. Definitions of seven commonly used defense mechanisms are shown on the left, along with examples of each on the right. This list is not exhaustive; additional defense mechanisms are discussed in Chapter 4.

gets. Unfortunately, social constraints often force us to hold back our anger until we end up lashing out at the people we love the most.

Other prominent defense mechanisms include reaction formation, regression, and identification. *Reaction formation* **involves behaving in a way that is exactly the opposite of one's true feelings.** Guilt about sexual desires often leads to reaction formation. Freud theorized that many males who ridicule homosexuals are defending against their own latent homosexual impulses. The telltale sign of reaction formation is the exaggerated quality of the opposite behavior. *Regression* **involves a reversion to immature patterns of behavior.** When anxious about their self-worth, some adults respond with childish boasting and bragging (as opposed to subtle efforts to impress others). For example, a fired executive having difficulty finding a new job might start making ridiculous statements about his incomparable talents and achievements. Such bragging is regressive when it is marked by massive exaggerations that anyone can see through. *Identification* **involves bolstering self-esteem by forming an imaginary or real alliance with some person or group.** For example, youngsters often shore up precarious feelings of self-worth by identifying with rock-star heroes, movie stars, or famous athletes. Adults may join exclusive country clubs or civic organizations.

Additional examples of the defense mechanisms we've described can be found in Figure 2.3. If you see defensive maneuvers that you have used, you shouldn't be surprised. According to Freud, everyone uses defense mechanisms to some extent. They become problematic only when one depends on them excessively. The seeds for psychological disorders are sown when defenses lead to wholesale distortion of reality.

Various theorists have added to Freud's original list of defenses (Vaillant, 1994). We'll examine some of these additional defense mechanisms in Chapter 4 when we discuss the role of defenses in coping with stress. For now, however, let's turn our attention to Freud's ideas about the development of personality.

Development: Psychosexual Stages

Learning Objective

Outline Freud's stages of psychosexual development and their theorized relations to adult personality.

Freud made the startling assertion that the foundation of an individual's personality is laid down by the tender age of 5! To shed light on these crucial early years, Freud formulated a stage theory of development. He emphasized how young children deal with their immature, but powerful, sexual urges (he used the term "sexual" in a general way to refer to many urges for physical pleasure, not just the urge to copulate). According to Freud, these sexual urges shift in focus as children progress from one stage to another. Indeed, the names for the stages (oral, anal, genital, and so on) are based on where children are focusing their erotic energy at the time. Thus, *psychosexual stages* **are developmental periods with a characteristic sexual focus that leave their mark on adult personality.**

Freud's Stages of Psychosexual Development

Stage	Approximate ages	Erotic focus	Key tasks and experiences
Oral	0–1	Mouth (sucking, biting)	Weaning (from breast or bottle)
Anal	2–3	Anus (expelling or retaining feces)	Toilet training
Phallic	4–5	Genitals (masturbating)	Identifying with adult role models; coping with oedipal crisis
Latency	6–12	None (sexually repressed)	Expanding social contacts
Genital	Puberty onward	Genitals (being sexually intimate)	Establishing intimate relationships; contributing to society through working

Figure 2.4
Freud's stages of psychosexual development
Freud theorized that people evolve through the series of psychosexual stages summarized here. The manner in which certain key tasks and experiences are handled during each stage is thought to leave a lasting imprint on adult personality.

Freud theorized that each psychosexual stage has its own unique developmental challenges or tasks, as outlined in Figure 2.4. The way these challenges are handled supposedly shapes personality. The notion of *fixation* plays an important role in this process. ***Fixation* involves a failure to move forward from one stage to another as expected.** Essentially, the child's development stalls for a while. Fixation is caused by *excessive gratification* or *frustration* of needs at a particular stage. Either way, fixations left over from childhood affect adult personality. Generally, fixation leads to an overemphasis on the psychosexual needs that were prominent during the fixated stage. Freud described a series of five psychosexual stages through which children progress.

Oral stage   The oral stage usually encompasses the first year of life. During this stage the main source of erotic stimulation is the mouth (in biting, sucking, chewing, and so on). How caretakers handle the child's feeding experiences is supposed to be crucial to subsequent development. Freud attributed considerable importance to the manner in which the child is weaned from the breast or the bottle. According to Freud, fixation at the oral stage could form the basis for obsessive eating or smoking later in life (among many other things).

Anal stage   In their second year, children supposedly get their erotic pleasure from their bowel movements, through either the expulsion or retention of feces. The crucial event at this time involves toilet training, which represents society's first systematic effort to regulate the child's biological urges. Severely punitive toilet training is thought to lead to a variety of possible outcomes. For example, excessive punishment might produce a latent feeling of hostility toward the "trainer," who usually is the mother. This hostility might generalize to women in general. Another possibility is that heavy reliance on punitive measures might lead to an association between genital concerns and the anxiety that the punishment arouses. This genital anxiety derived from severe toilet training could evolve into anxiety about sexual activities later in life.

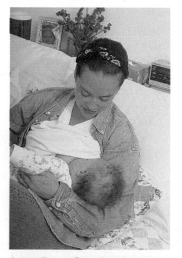

According to Freudian theory, a child's feeding experiences are crucial to later development. Fixation at the oral stage could lead to an overemphasis on, for example, smoking or eating in adulthood.

Phallic stage   Around age 4, the genitals become the focus for the child's erotic energy, largely through self-stimulation. During this pivotal stage, the *Oedipus complex* emerges. Little boys develop an erotically tinged preference for their mother. They also feel hostility toward their father, whom they view as a competitor for mom's affection. Little girls develop a special attachment to their father. Around the same time, they learn that their genitals are very different from those of little boys, and they supposedly develop *penis envy*. According to Freud, girls feel hostile toward their mother because they blame her for their anatomical "deficiency."

To summarize, **in the *Oedipus complex* children manifest erotically tinged desires for their other-sex parent, accompanied by feelings of hostility toward their same-sex parent.** The name for this syndrome was taken from a tragic myth from ancient Greece. In this myth, Oedipus is separated from his parents at birth. Not knowing the identity of his real parents, he inadvertently kills his father and marries his mother. (For many years, the term *Oedipus complex* referred to boys only, and the comparable syndrome in girls was called the *Electra complex*. However, use of a separate term for the female form of this syndrome has diminished in recent years.)

According to Freud, the way parents and children deal with the sexual and aggressive conflicts inherent in the Oedipus complex is of paramount importance. The child has to resolve the oedipal dilemma by giving up the sexual longings for the other-sex parent and the hostility felt toward the same-sex parent. Healthy psychosexual development is supposed to hinge on the resolution of the oedipal conflict. Why? Because continued hostile relations with the same-sex parent may prevent the child from identifying adequately with that parent. Without such identification, Freudian theory predicts that many aspects of the child's development won't progress as they should.

Latency and genital stages   Freud believed that from age 6 through puberty, the child's sexuality is suppressed—it becomes "latent." Important events during this *latency stage* center on expanding social contacts beyond the family. With the advent of puberty, the child evolves into the *genital stage*. Sexual urges reappear and focus on the genitals once again. At this point the sexual energy is normally channeled toward peers of the other sex, rather than toward oneself, as in the phallic stage.

In arguing that the early years shape personality, Freud did not mean that personality development comes to an abrupt halt in middle childhood. However, he did believe that the foundation for one's adult personality is solidly entrenched by this time. He maintained that future personality development is rooted in early, formative experiences and that significant conflicts in later years are replays of crises from childhood.

In fact, Freud believed that unconscious sexual conflicts rooted in childhood experiences cause most personality disturbances. His steadfast belief in the psychosexual origins of psychological disorders eventually led to bitter theoretical disputes with two of his most brilliant colleagues: Carl Jung and Alfred Adler. Jung and Adler both argued that Freud overemphasized sexuality. Freud summarily rejected their ideas, and the other two theorists felt compelled to go their own way, developing their own psychodynamic theories of personality.

Jung's Analytical Psychology

Learning Objective

Summarize Jung's views on key issues relating to personality.

Swiss psychiatrist Carl Jung called his new approach *analytical psychology* to differentiate it from Freud's psychoanalytic theory. Like Freud, Jung (1921, 1933) emphasized the unconscious determinants of personality. However, he proposed that the unconscious consists of two layers. The first layer, called the *personal unconscious,* is essentially the same as Freud's version of the unconscious. The personal unconscious houses material that is not within one's conscious awareness because it has been repressed or forgotten. In addition, Jung theorized the existence of a deeper layer he called the collective unconscious. **The *collective unconscious* is a storehouse of latent memory traces inherited from people's ancestral past that is shared with the entire human race.** Jung called these ancestral memories *archetypes*. They are not memories of actual, personal experiences. Instead, *archetypes* **are emotionally charged images and thought forms that have universal meaning.** These archetypal images and ideas show up in dreams and are often manifested in a culture's use of symbols in art, literature, and religion. Jung felt that an understanding of archetypal symbols helped him make sense of his patients' dreams. This was of great concern to him because he depended extensively on dream analysis in his treatment of patients.

Jung's unusual ideas about the collective unconscious had little impact on the mainstream of thinking in psychology. Their influence was felt more in other fields, such as anthropology, philosophy, art, and religious studies. However, many of Jung's other ideas *have* been incorporated into the mainstream of psychology. For instance, Jung was the first to describe the introverted (inner-directed) and extraverted (outer-directed) personality types. *Introverts* **tend to be preoccupied with the internal world of their own thoughts, feelings, and experiences.** They generally are contemplative and aloof. In contrast, *extraverts* **tend to be interested in the external world of people and things.** They're more likely to be outgoing, talkative, and friendly, instead of reclusive.

Adler's Individual Psychology

Alfred Adler was a charter member of Freud's inner circle—the Vienna Psychoanalytic Society. However, he soon began to develop his own theory of personality, which he christened *individual psychology*. Adler's (1917, 1927) theory stressed the social context of personality development. For instance, it was Adler who first focused attention on the possible importance of *birth order* as a factor shaping personality. Adler argued that the foremost human drive is not sexuality, but a *striving for superiority*. Adler viewed striving for superiority as a universal drive to adapt, improve oneself, and master life's challenges. He noted that young children understandably feel weak and helpless in comparison to more competent older children and adults. These early inferiority feelings supposedly motivate individuals to acquire new skills and develop new talents.

Adler asserted that everyone has to work to overcome some feelings of inferiority. *Compensation* **involves efforts to overcome imagined or real inferiorities by developing one's abilities.** Adler believed that compensation is entirely normal. However, in some people inferiority feelings can become excessive, resulting in what is widely known today as an *inferiority complex*—exaggerated feelings of weakness and inadequacy. Adler thought that either parental pampering or parental neglect (or actual physical handicaps) could cause an inferiority problem. Thus, he agreed with Freud on the importance of early childhood, although he focused on different aspects of parent-child relations.

Adler explained personality disturbances by noting that an inferiority complex can distort the normal process of striving for superiority (see Figure 2.5). He maintained that some people engage in *overcompensation* in order to conceal, even from themselves, their feelings of inferiority. Instead of working to master life's challenges, people with an inferiority complex work to achieve status, gain power over others, and acquire the trappings of success (fancy clothes, impressive cars, or whatever looks important to them). They tend to flaunt their success in an effort to cover up their underlying inferiority complex. The problem is that such people engage in unconscious self-deception, worrying more about *appearances* than *reality*.

Figure 2.5
Adler's view of personality development
Like Freud, Adler believed that early childhood experiences exert momentous influence over adult personality. However, he focused on children's social interactions rather than on their grappling with their sexuality. According to Adler, the roots of personality disturbances typically lie in excessive parental neglect or pampering. (Adapted from LeFrancois, 1983)

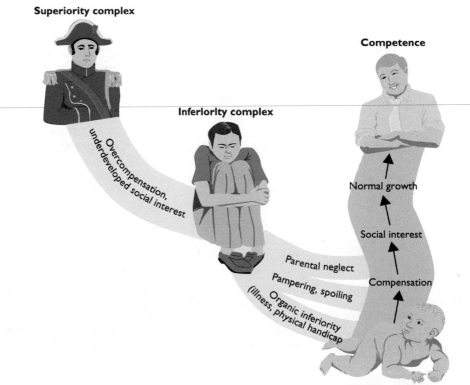

Evaluating Psychodynamic Perspectives

Learning Objective

Summarize the strengths and weaknesses of psychodynamic theories of personality.

The psychodynamic approach has given us a number of far-reaching theories of personality. These theories yielded some bold new insights (Kihlstrom, 1990; Westen, 1990). Psychodynamic theory and research have demonstrated (1) that unconscious forces can influence behavior, (2) that internal conflict often plays a key role in generating psychological distress, and (3) that early childhood experiences can exert considerable influence over adult personality. Psychodynamic models have also been praised because they probe beneath the surface of personality and because they focus attention on how personality develops over time. Many widely used concepts in psychology emerged out of psychodynamic theories, including the unconscious, defense mechanisms, introversion-extraversion, and the inferiority complex.

In a more negative vein, psychodynamic formulations have been criticized on several grounds, including the following (Fine, 1990; Fisher & Greenberg, 1985; Torrey, 1992).

1. *Poor testability.* Scientific investigations require testable hypotheses. Psychodynamic ideas have often been too vague to permit a clear scientific test. Concepts such as the superego, the preconscious, and collective unconscious are difficult to measure.

2. *Inadequate evidence.* The empirical evidence on psychodynamic theories has often been characterized as inadequate. These theories depend too much on case studies, in which it is easy for clinicians to see what they expect to see based on their theory. Recent reexaminations of Freud's own clinical work suggest that he sometimes distorted his patients' case histories to mesh with his theory (Sulloway, 1991). Furthermore, the subjects observed in clinical situations are not particularly representative of the population at large. Insofar as researchers have accumulated evidence on psychodynamic theories, it has provided only modest support for the central hypotheses.

3. *Sexism.* Many critics have argued that psychodynamic theories are biased against women. Freud believed that females' penis envy makes them feel inferior to males. He also thought that females tend to develop weaker superegos and to be more prone to neurosis than males. He dismissed female patients' reports of sexual molestation during childhood as mere fantasies. Admittedly, sexism isn't unique to Freudian theories, and the sex bias in modern psychodynamic theories has been reduced to some degree. But the psychodynamic approach has generally provided a rather male-centered viewpoint.

It's easy to ridicule Freud for concepts such as penis envy and to point to ideas that have turned out to be wrong. Remember, though, that Freud, Jung, and Adler began to fashion their theories about a century ago. It is not entirely fair to compare these theories to other models that are only a decade old. That's like asking the Wright brothers to race the Concorde. Freud and his psychodynamic colleagues deserve great credit for breaking new ground. Standing at a distance a century later, we have to be impressed by the extraordinary impact that psychodynamic theory has had on modern thought. No other theoretical perspective in psychology has been as influential, except for the one we turn to next—behaviorism.

Behavioral Perspectives

Learning Objective

Discuss behaviorism as a school of thought in psychology.

Behaviorism is a theoretical orientation based on the premise that scientific psychology should study observable behavior. Behaviorism has been a major school of thought in psychology since 1913, when John B. Watson published an influential article. Watson argued that psychology should abandon its earlier focus on the mind and mental processes and focus exclusively on overt behavior. He contended that psychology cannot study mental processes in a scientific manner because they are private and not accessible to public observation.

In completely rejecting mental processes as a suitable subject for scientific study, Watson took an extreme position that is no longer dominant among modern behaviorists. Nonetheless, his influence was enormous, as psychology did shift its primary focus from the study of the mind to the study of behavior.

The behaviorists have shown little interest in internal personality structures similar to Freud's id, ego, and superego, because such structures can't be observed. They prefer to think in terms of "response tendencies," which *can* be observed. Thus, most behaviorists view an individual's personality as a *collection of response tendencies that are tied to various stimulus situations*. A specific situation may be associated with a number of response tendencies that vary in strength, depending on an individual's past experience (see Figure 2.6).

Although behaviorists have shown relatively little interest in personality structure, they have focused extensively on personality *development*. They explain development the same way they explain everything else—through learning. Specifically, they focus on how our response tendencies are shaped through classical conditioning, operant conditioning, and observational learning. Let's look at these processes.

Pavlov's Classical Conditioning

Learning Objective

Describe Pavlov's classical conditioning and its contribution to personality.

Do you go weak in the knees when you get a note saying your boss wants to see you? Do you get anxious when you're around important people? When you're driving, does your heart skip a beat at the sight of a police car—even when you're driving under the speed limit? If so, you probably acquired these common responses through classical conditioning. **Classical conditioning is a type of learning in which a neutral stimulus acquires the capacity to evoke a response that was originally evoked by another stimulus.** This process, which is also called *respondent conditioning*, was first described back in 1903 by Ivan Pavlov.

Pavlov was a prominent Russian physiologist who did Nobel Prize–winning research on digestion. He was a dedicated scientist obsessed with his research. Legend has it that Pavlov severely reprimanded an assistant who was late for an experiment because he was trying to avoid street fighting in the midst of the Russian Revolution. The assistant defended his tardiness, saying, "But Professor, there's a revolution going on, with shooting in the streets!" Pavlov supposedly replied, "Next time there's a revolution, get up earlier!" (Fancher, 1979; Gantt, 1975).

The Conditioned Reflex

Pavlov (1906) was studying digestive processes in dogs when he discovered that the dogs could be trained to salivate in response to the sound of a bell. What was so significant about a dog salivating when a bell was rung? The key was that the bell started out as a *neutral* stimulus; that is, originally it did not produce the response

Figure 2.6
A behavioral view of personality
Behaviorists devote little attention to the structure of personality because it is unobservable, but they implicitly view personality as an individual's collection of response tendencies. A possible hierarchy of response tendencies for a specific stimulus situation is shown here.

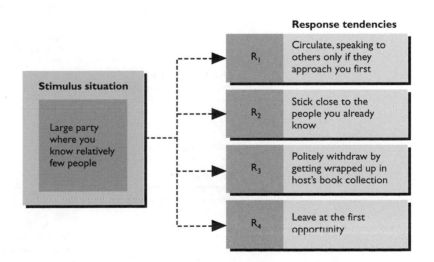

Ivan Pavlov

of salivation (after all, why should it?). However, Pavlov managed to change that by pairing the bell with a stimulus (meat powder) that *did* produce the salivation response. Through this process, the bell acquired the capacity to trigger the salivation. What Pavlov had demonstrated was *how learned reflexes are acquired.*

There is a special vocabulary associated with classical conditioning. In Pavlov's experiment the bond between the meat powder and salivation was a natural association that had not been created through conditioning. In unconditioned bonds, **the *unconditioned stimulus (UCS)* is a stimulus that evokes an unconditioned response without previous conditioning. The *unconditioned response (UCR)* is an unlearned reaction to an unconditioned stimulus that occurs without previous conditioning.**

In contrast, the link between the bell and salivation was established through conditioning. In conditioned bonds, **the *conditioned stimulus (CS)* is a previously neutral stimulus that has, through conditioning, acquired the capacity to evoke a conditioned response. The *conditioned response (CR)* is a learned reaction to a conditioned stimulus that occurs because of previous conditioning.** Note that the unconditioned response and conditioned response often involve the same behavior (although there may be subtle differences). In Pavlov's initial demonstration, salivation was an unconditioned response when evoked by the UCS (meat powder) and a conditioned response when evoked by the CS (the bell). The procedures involved in classical conditioning are outlined in Figure 2.7.

Pavlov's discovery came to be called the *conditioned reflex.* Classically conditioned responses are viewed as reflexes because most of them are relatively involuntary. Responses that are a product of classical conditioning are said to be *elicited.* This word is meant to convey that these responses are triggered automatically.

Classical Conditioning in Everyday Life

What role does classical conditioning play in shaping personality in everyday life? Classical conditioning contributes to the acquisition of emotional responses, such as anxieties, fears, and phobias (Merckelbach et al., 1989). This is a relatively small but important class of responses, as maladaptive emotional reactions underlie many

Figure 2.7
The process of classical conditioning
The sequence of events in classical conditioning is outlined here. As we encounter new examples of classical conditioning throughout the book, we will see diagrams such as in the fourth panel, which summarizes the process.

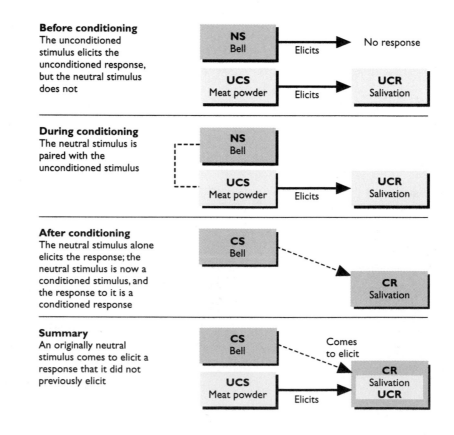

FRANK & ERNEST reprinted by permission of Newspaper Enterprise Association, Inc.

adjustment problems. For example, one middle-aged woman reported being troubled by a bridge phobia so severe that she couldn't drive on interstate highways because of all the viaducts she would have to cross. She was able to pinpoint the source of her phobia. Many years before, when her family would drive to visit her grandmother, they had to cross a little-used, rickety, dilapidated bridge out in the countryside. Her father, in a misguided attempt at humor, made a major production out of these crossings. He would stop short of the bridge and carry on about the enormous danger of the crossing. Obviously, he thought the bridge was safe, or he wouldn't have driven across it. However, the naive young girl was terrified by her father's scare tactics, and the bridge became a conditioned stimulus eliciting great fear (see Figure 2.8). Unfortunately, the fear spilled over to *all* bridges, and 40 years later she was still carrying the burden of this phobia. Although a number of processes can cause phobias (Marks, 1987), it is clear that classical conditioning is responsible for many of our irrational fears.

Classical conditioning also appears to account for more realistic and moderate anxiety. For example, imagine a news reporter in a high-pressure job who consistently gets negative feedback about his work from his bosses. The negative comments function as a UCS eliciting anxiety. These reprimands are paired with the noise and sight of the newsroom, so that it becomes a CS triggering anxiety, even when his supervisors are absent (see Figure 2.9). Our poor reporter might even reach a point at which the mere *thought* of the newsroom elicits anxiety even when he is elsewhere.

Fortunately, not every frightening experience leaves a conditioned fear in its wake. A variety of factors influence whether a conditioned response will be acquired in a particular situation. Furthermore, a newly formed stimulus-response bond does not necessarily last indefinitely. The right circumstances can lead to *extinction*—**the gradual weakening and disappearance of a conditioned response tendency.** What leads to extinction in classical conditioning? It occurs with the consistent presentation of the CS *alone,* without the UCS. For example, when Pavlov consistently presented *only* the bell to a previously conditioned dog, the bell gradually stopped eliciting the response of salivation. How long it takes to extinguish a conditioned response depends on many factors. Foremost among them is the strength of the conditioned bond when extinction begins. Some conditioned responses extinguish very quickly, while others are difficult to weaken.

Figure 2.8
Classical conditioning of a phobia
Many emotional responses that would otherwise be puzzling can be explained as a result of classical conditioning. In the case of the woman's bridge phobia, the fear originally elicited by her father's scare tactics became a conditioned response to the stimulus of bridges.

Figure 2.9
Classical conditioning of anxiety
A stimulus (in this case, a newsroom) that is frequently paired with anxiety-arousing events (reprimands and criticism) may come to elicit anxiety by itself, through classical conditioning.

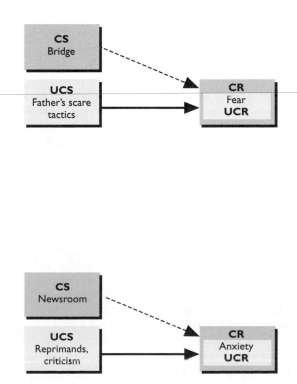

Skinner's Operant Conditioning

Discuss how Skinner's principles of operant conditioning can be applied to personality development.

B. F. Skinner

Even Pavlov recognized that classical conditioning was not the only form of conditioning. Classical conditioning best explains reflexive responding controlled by stimuli that *precede* the response. However, both animals and humans make many responses that don't fit this description. Consider the response that you are engaging in right now—studying. It is definitely not a reflex (life might be easier if it were). The stimuli that govern it (exams and grades) do not precede it. Instead, your studying response is mainly influenced by events that follow it—specifically, its *consequences*.

This kind of learning is called *operant conditioning*. **Operant conditioning is a form of learning in which voluntary responses come to be controlled by their consequences.** Operant conditioning probably governs a larger share of human behavior than classical conditioning, since most of our responses are voluntary rather than reflexive. Because they are voluntary, operant responses are said to be *emitted* rather than *elicited*.

The study of operant conditioning was led by B. F. Skinner (1953, 1974, 1990), a Harvard University psychologist who spent most of his career studying simple responses made by laboratory rats and pigeons. The fundamental principle of operant conditioning is uncommonly simple. Skinner demonstrated that *organisms tend to repeat those responses that are followed by favorable consequences, and they tend not to repeat those responses that are followed by neutral or unfavorable consequences*. In Skinner's scheme, favorable, neutral, and unfavorable consequences involve reinforcement, extinction, and punishment, respectively. We'll look at each of these in turn.

The Power of Reinforcement

According to Skinner, reinforcement can occur in two different ways, which he called *positive reinforcement* and *negative reinforcement*. **Positive reinforcement occurs when a response is strengthened (increases in frequency) because it is followed by the arrival of a (presumably) pleasant stimulus.** Positive reinforcement is roughly synonymous with the concept of reward. Notice, however, that reinforcement is defined *after the fact*, in terms of its effect on behavior. Why? Because reinforcement is subjective. Something that serves as a reinforcer for one person may not function as a reinforcer for another person. For example, peer approval is a potent reinforcer for most people, but not all.

Positive reinforcement motivates much of our everyday behavior. You study hard because good grades are likely to follow as a result. You go to work because this behavior produces paychecks. Perhaps you work extra hard in the hopes of winning a promotion or a pay raise. In each of these examples, certain responses occur because they have led to positive outcomes in the past.

Positive reinforcement influences personality development in a straightforward way. Responses followed by pleasant outcomes are strengthened and tend to become habitual patterns of behavior. For example, a youngster who clowns around in class might gain appreciative comments and smiles from his schoolmates. This social approval will probably reinforce clowning-around behavior, which, if reinforced with some regularity, will gradually become an integral element of his personality (see Figure 2.10). Similarly, whether or not a child develops traits such as independence, assertiveness, or selfishness depends on whether he or she is reinforced for such behaviors by parents and by other influential persons.

Negative reinforcement occurs when a response is strengthened (increases in frequency) because it is followed by the removal of a (presumably) unpleasant stimulus. Don't let the word *negative* here confuse you. Negative reinforcement *is* reinforcement. Like positive reinforcement, it strengthens a response. However, this strengthening occurs because the response gets rid of an aversive stimulus. Consider a few examples. You rush home in the winter to get out of the cold. You may clean your bedroom to get rid of a mess. Parents often give in to their children's begging, simply to halt the whining.

Negative reinforcement plays a major role in the development of avoidance tendencies. As you may have noticed, many people tend to avoid facing up to awk-

Skinner placed rats and other animal subjects in controlled environments where reinforcement could be regulated and responses accurately measured.

ward situations and sticky personal problems. This personality trait typically develops because avoidance behavior gets rid of anxiety and is therefore negatively reinforced. Recall our imaginary newspaper reporter whose work environment (the newsroom) elicits anxiety (due to classical conditioning). He might notice that on days when he calls in sick, his anxiety evaporates; this response is thus gradually strengthened—through negative reinforcement (see Figure 2.10). If his avoidance behavior continues to be successful in reducing his anxiety, it might carry over into other areas of his life and become a central aspect of his personality.

Extinction and Punishment

Like the effects of classical conditioning, the effects of operant conditioning may not last forever. In both types of conditioning, *extinction* refers to the gradual weakening and disappearance of a response. In operant conditioning, extinction begins when a previously reinforced response stops producing positive consequences. As extinction progresses, the response typically becomes less and less frequent and eventually disappears.

Thus, the response tendencies that make up one's personality are not necessarily permanent. For example, the youngster who found that his classmates reinforced clowning around in grade school might find that his attempts at comedy earn nothing but indifferent stares in high school. This termination of reinforcement would probably lead to the gradual extinction of the clowning-around behavior. How quickly an operant response extinguishes depends on many factors in the person's earlier reinforcement history.

Some responses may be weakened by punishment. In Skinner's scheme, **punishment occurs when a response is weakened (decreases in frequency) because it is followed by the arrival of a (presumably) unpleasant stimulus.** The concept of punishment in operant conditioning confuses many students on two counts. First, it is often mixed up with negative reinforcement because both involve aversive stimuli. Please note, however, that they are altogether different events with opposite outcomes. In negative reinforcement, a response leads to the *removal* of something aversive, thereby *strengthening* the response. In punishment, a response leads to the *arrival* of something aversive, thereby *weakening* the response.

The second source of confusion involves viewing punishment as only a disciplinary procedure used by parents, teachers, and other authority figures. In the operant model, punishment occurs whenever a response leads to negative consequences. Defined in this way, the concept goes far beyond actions like parents spanking children or teachers handing out detentions. For example, if you wear a new outfit and your friends make fun of it and hurt your feelings, your behavior has been punished, and you are less likely to wear it again. Similarly, if you go to a restaurant and have a horrible meal, in Skinner's terminology your response has led to punishment.

The impact of punishment on personality development is just the opposite of reinforcement. Generally speaking, those patterns of behavior that lead to punishing (that is, negative) consequences tend to be weakened. For instance, if your impulsive decisions always backfire, your tendency to be impulsive should decline.

Figure 2.10
Positive and negative reinforcement in operant conditioning
Positive reinforcement occurs when a response is followed by a favorable outcome, so that the response is strengthened. In negative reinforcement, the removal (symbolized here by the "No" sign) of an aversive stimulus serves as a reinforcer. Negative reinforcement produces the same result as positive reinforcement: the person's tendency to emit the reinforced response is strengthened (the response becomes more frequent).

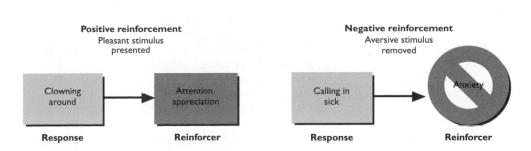

According to Skinner (1987), conditioning in humans operates much as it does in the rats and pigeons that he studied in his laboratory. Hence, he assumed that conditioning strengthens and weakens response tendencies "mechanically"—that is, without conscious participation. Like John Watson (1913) before him, Skinner asserted that we can explain behavior without being concerned about individuals' mental processes.

Skinner's ideas continue to be influential, but his mechanical view of conditioning has not gone unchallenged by other behaviorists. Theorists such as Albert Bandura have developed somewhat different behavioral models in which *cognition* plays a role. **Cognition refers to the thought processes involved in acquiring knowledge.** In other words, cognition is another name for the mental processes that behaviorists have traditionally shown little interest in.

Bandura and Social Learning Theory

Learning Objective

Describe Bandura's social learning theory and its relation to personality.

Albert Bandura is one of several behaviorists who have added a cognitive flavor to behaviorism since the 1960s. Bandura (1977), Walter Mischel (1973), and Julian Rotter (1982) take issue with Skinner's view. They point out that humans obviously are conscious, thinking, feeling beings. Moreover, they argue that in neglecting cognitive processes, Skinner ignored the most distinctive and important feature of human behavior. Bandura and like-minded theorists call their modified brand of behaviorism *social learning theory.*

Bandura (1977, 1986) agrees with the basic thrust of behaviorism in that he believes that personality is largely shaped through learning. However, he contends that conditioning is not a mechanical process in which people are passive participants. Instead, he maintains that people actively seek out and process information about their environment in order to maximize favorable outcomes.

Observational Learning

Bandura's foremost theoretical contribution has been his description of observational learning. **Observational learning occurs when an organism's responding is influenced by observing others, who are called models.** Bandura does not view observational learning as entirely separate from classical and operant conditioning. Instead, he asserts that both classical and operant conditioning can take place indirectly when one person observes another's conditioning (see Figure 2.11).

To illustrate, suppose you observe a friend behaving assertively with a car salesman. Let's say that her assertiveness is reinforced by the exceptionally good buy she gets on the car. Your own tendency to behave assertively with salespeople might well be strengthened as a result. Notice that the favorable consequence is experienced by your friend, not you. While your friend's tendency to bargain assertively should be reinforced directly, your tendency to bargain assertively may also be reinforced indirectly.

The theories of Skinner and Pavlov make no allowance for this type of indirect learning. After all, observational learning requires that you pay *attention* to your friend's behavior, that you *understand* its consequences, and that you store this *information* in *memory.* Obviously, attention, understanding, information, and memory involve cognition, which behaviorists used to ignore.

As social learning theory has been refined, it has become apparent that some models are more influential than others (Bandura, 1986). Both children and adults tend to imitate people they like or respect more than people they don't. Individuals are also likely to imitate the behavior of those they consider attractive or powerful (such as rock stars). In addition, imitation is more likely when people see similarity between the model and themselves. Thus, children imitate same-sex role models somewhat more than other-sex models. Finally, as noted before, people are more likely to copy a model if they see the model's behavior leading to positive outcomes.

According to social learning theory, models have a great impact on personality development. Children learn to be assertive, conscientious, self-sufficient, dependable, easygoing, and so forth by observing others behaving in these ways. Parents,

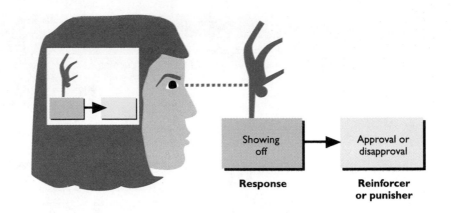

Figure 2.11
Observational learning
In observational learning, an observer attends to and stores a mental representation of a model's behavior (for example, showing off by doing handstands) and its consequences (such as approval or disapproval from others). According to social learning theory, many of one's characteristic responses are acquired through observation of others' behavior.

Showing
off

Approval or
disapproval

Response

**Reinforcer
or punisher**

teachers, relatives, siblings, and peers serve as models for young children. Bandura and his colleagues have done extensive research showing how models influence the development of aggressiveness, sex roles, and moral standards in children (Bandura, 1973; Bussey & Bandura, 1984; Mischel & Mischel, 1976). Their research on the modeling of aggressive behavior has been particularly influential.

Self-Efficacy

Bandura (1990a, 1993) believes that *self-efficacy* is a crucial element of personality. **Self-efficacy is the belief about one's ability to perform behaviors that should lead to expected outcomes.** A person high in self-efficacy feels confident that he or she can execute the responses necessary to earn reinforcers. A person low in self-efficacy worries that the necessary responses may be beyond his or her abilities. Perceptions of self-efficacy are subjective and specific to different kinds of tasks. For instance, you might feel extremely confident about your ability to handle difficult social situations but doubtful about your ability to handle academic challenges. Although specific perceptions of self-efficacy predict behavior best, these perceptions are influenced by general feelings of self-efficacy, which can be measured with the scale shown in Figure 2.12 (Sherer et al., 1982). Perceptions of self-efficacy can influence which challenges you tackle and how well you perform. Studies have found that feelings of greater self-efficacy are associated with greater success in giving up smoking (Garcia, Schmitz, & Doerfler, 1990), higher levels of academic performance (Multon, Brown, & Lent, 1991), enhanced performance in athletic competition (Bandura, 1990a), and consideration of a broader range of occupations in making career choices (Bores-Rangel et al., 1990), among many other things.

Evaluating Behavioral Perspectives

Learning Objective

Summarize the strengths and weaknesses of behavioral theories of personality.

Behavioral theories are firmly rooted in empirical research rather than clinical intuition. Pavlov's model has shed light on how conditioning can account for our sometimes troublesome emotional responses. Skinner's work has demonstrated how our personalities are shaped by the consequences of our behavior. Bandura's social learning theory has shown how our observations mold our characteristic behavior.

Behaviorists, in particular Walter Mischel (1973, 1990), have also provided the most thorough account of why people are only moderately consistent in their behavior. For example, a person who is shy in one context might be quite outgoing in another. Other models of personality largely ignore this inconsistency. The behaviorists have shown that this inconsistency occurs because people behave in ways they think will lead to reinforcement in the situation at hand. In other words, situational factors play a significant role in controlling a person's behavior.

Of course, each theoretical approach has its shortcomings, and the behavioral approach is no exception. Major lines of criticism include the following (Liebert & Spiegler, 1990; Maddi, 1989).

1. *Overdependence on animal research.* Many principles in behavioral theories were discovered through research on animals. Some critics, especially humanistic theo-

Figure 2.12
Sample items from the Self-Efficacy Scale
The eight items shown here are taken from the Self-Efficacy Scale, developed by Sherer et al. (1982). The 23-item scale measures general expectations of self-efficacy that are not tied to specific situations. The more items you agree with, the stronger your self-efficacy. High scores on the complete scale are predictive of vocational and educational success.

The Self-Efficacy Scale

Instructions: This questionnaire is a series of statements about your personal attitudes and traits. Each statement represents a commonly held belief. Read each statement and decide to what extent it describes you. There are no right or wrong answers. You will probably agree with some of the statements and disagree with others. Please indicate your own personal feelings about each statement below by marking the letter that best describes your attitude or feeling. Please be very truthful and describe yourself as you really are, not as you would like to be.

A = Disagree strongly
B = Disagree moderately
C = Neither agree nor disagree
D = Agree moderately
E = Agree strongly

1. ____ When I make plans, I am certain I can make them work.

2. ____ If I can't do a job the first time, I keep trying until I can.

3. ____ If I see someone I would like to meet, I go to that person instead of waiting for him or her to come to me.

4. ____ When I have something unpleasant to do, I stick to it until I finish it.

5. ____ When I decide to do something, I go right to work on it.

6. ____ When I'm trying to become friends with someone who seems uninterested at first, I don't give up very easily.

7. ____ Failure just makes me try harder.

8. ____ I am a self-reliant person.

rists, argue that behaviorists depend too much on animal research and that they indiscriminately generalize from the behavior of animals to the behavior of humans.

2. *Dilution of the behavioral approach.* The behaviorists used to be criticized because they neglected cognitive processes, which clearly are important factors in human behavior. The rise of social learning theory, which focuses heavily on cognitive factors, blunted this criticism. However, social learning theory undermines the foundation on which behaviorism was built—the idea that psychologists should study only observable behavior. Thus, some critics complain that behavioral theories aren't very behavioral anymore.

Humanistic Perspectives

Learning Objective

Discuss humanism as a school of thought in psychology.

Humanistic theory emerged in the 1950s as something of a backlash against the behavioral and psychodynamic theories. The principal charge hurled at these two models was that they were dehumanizing. Freudian theory was criticized for its belief that primitive, animalistic drives dominate behavior. Behaviorism was criticized for its preoccupation with animal research. Critics argued that both schools viewed people as helpless pawns controlled by their environment and their past, with little capacity for self-direction. Many of these critics blended into a loose alliance that was christened the "third force" in psychology because it surfaced as an alternative to the two dominant "forces" at the time (the psychodynamic and behavioral).

This third force came to be known as humanism because of its exclusive interest in human behavior. **Humanism is a theoretical orientation that emphasizes the unique qualities of humans, especially their free will and their potential for personal growth.** Humanistic psychologists are interested only in issues important to human existence, such as love, creativity, loneliness, and personal growth. They do not believe that we can learn anything of any significance about the human condition from animal research.

Humanistic theorists take an optimistic view of human nature. In contrast to most psychodynamic and behavioral theorists, humanistic theorists believe (1) that human nature includes an innate drive toward personal growth, (2) that individuals have the freedom to chart their own courses of action and are not pawns of their environment, and (3) that people are largely conscious and rational beings who are not dominated by unconscious, irrational needs and conflicts. Humanistic theorists also maintain that a person's subjective view of the world is more important than objective reality. According to this notion, if you *think* you are homely, or bright, or sociable, then these beliefs will influence your behavior more than the actual realities of how homely, bright, or sociable you actually are.

The humanistic approach clearly provides a different perspective on personality than either the psychodynamic or behavioral approaches. In this section we'll review the ideas of the two most influential humanistic theorists, Carl Rogers and Abraham Maslow.

Rogers's Person-Centered Theory

Learning Objective

Explain Rogers's views on self-concept, development, and defensive behavior.

Carl Rogers (1951, 1961, 1980) was one of the founders of the human potential movement, which emphasizes personal growth through sensitivity training, encounter groups, and other exercises intended to help people get in touch with their true selves. Working at the University of Chicago in the 1940s, Rogers devised a major new approach to psychotherapy. Like Freud, Rogers based his personality theory on his extensive therapeutic interactions with many clients. Because of his emphasis on a person's subjective point of view, Rogers called his approach a *person-centered theory.*

The Self and Its Development

Rogers saw personality structure in terms of just one construct. He called this construct the *self*, although it is more widely known today as the *self-concept*. **A self-concept is a collection of beliefs about one's personal qualities and typical**

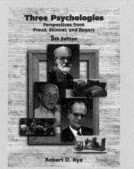

Recommended Reading

Three Psychologies: Perspectives from Freud, Skinner, and Rogers

by Robert D. Nye (Brooks/Cole, 1992)

One would be hard pressed to identify anyone who has had more influence on the evolution of psychology in the 20th century than Sigmund Freud, B. F. Skinner, and Carl Rogers. In this concise (160-page), highly readable book, Robert Nye gives readers a simple—but not oversimplified—introduction to the theories of these three giants. After providing a brief overview of all three theories in the first chapter, Nye devotes a chapter to each theorist, attempting to present that psychologist's ideas "as convincingly as possible, holding back judgments and criticisms until later" (p. vii). These chapters include short biographical sketches and discuss practical examples and real-world implications of each theorist's provocative ideas. In the fifth and final chapter, Nye systematically compares the three theories, reviews criticism of each, and adds his own personal comments.

> *Freud* makes me ask myself "Do I really know why I'm doing what I'm doing?" He causes me to question my motives and to try to reduce my possible blindness to characteristics, prejudices, and biases I might have. . . .
>
> With regard to *Skinner,* he made an extremely important contribution by pointing repeatedly to the environment's effects on behavior. . . . Skinner drew attention to an obviously important aspect of human life: reinforcement. It is significant for controlling our own behaviors, raising children, improving education, getting along with others, and most other activities. Reinforcement seems so simple that we often ignore it. . . .
>
> What about *Rogers*? Well, after I read his works, I generally come away feeling good. However, this is sometimes tempered by my impression that he was overly optimistic about the force toward growth and fulfillment that supposedly resides within us. [pp. 148–150]

Figure 2.13
Rogers's view of personality structure
In Rogers's model, the self-concept is the only important structural construct. However, Rogers acknowledges that one's self-concept may not jibe with the realities of one's actual experience—a condition called incongruence. People have varied amounts of incongruence between their self-concept and reality.

Self-concept   Actual experience

Congruence
Self-concept meshes well with actual experience (some incongruence is probably unavoidable)

Self-concept   Actual experience

Incongruence
Self-concept does not mesh well with actual experience

Carl Rogers

behavior. Your self-concept is your mental picture of yourself. It is a collection of self-perceptions. For example, a self-concept might include beliefs such as "I am easygoing" or "I am pretty" or "I am hard-working."

Rogers stressed the subjective nature of the self-concept, suggesting that it may not be entirely consistent with the person's actual experiences. To put it more bluntly, one's self-concept may be inaccurate. Most people tend to distort their experiences to some extent to promote a relatively favorable self-concept. For example, you may believe that you are quite bright academically, but your grades might suggest otherwise. Rogers used the term ***incongruence*** **to refer to the disparity between one's self-concept and one's actual experience.** In contrast, if a person's self-concept is reasonably accurate, it is *congruent* with reality. Everyone experiences *some* incongruence; the crucial issue is how much (see Figure 2.13). Rogers maintained that a great deal of incongruence undermines a person's psychological well-being.

In terms of personality development, Rogers was concerned with how childhood experiences promote congruence or incongruence. He believed that people have a strong need for affection, love, and acceptance from others. Early in life, parents provide most of this affection. Rogers held that when parents make their affection *conditional*—that is, make it depend on the child's behaving well and living up to expectations—children may distort or block out of their self-concept any experiences that make them feel unworthy of love. At the other end of the spectrum, Rogers asserted that when parents make their affection *unconditional*, children have less need to block out unworthy experiences because they have been assured that they are worthy of affection, no matter what they do.

Rogers believed that unconditional love from parents fosters congruence and that conditional love fosters incongruence. He further theorized that if individuals grow up believing that affection from others (besides their parents) is conditional, they go on to distort more and more of their experiences to feel worthy of acceptance from a wider and wider array of people, so that incongruence continues to grow.

Anxiety and Defense

According to Rogers, experiences that threaten one's self-concept are the principal cause of troublesome anxiety. The more inaccurate your self-concept is, the more likely you are to have experiences that clash with your self-perceptions. Thus, people with highly incongruent self-concepts are especially likely to be plagued by recurrent anxiety.

To ward off this anxiety, people often behave defensively; they ignore, deny, and twist reality to protect their self-concept. Consider a young woman who, like most of us, considers herself a "nice person." But suppose that in reality she is rather conceited and selfish, and she gets feedback from friends that she is a "self-centered, snotty brat." How might she react in order to protect her self-concept? She might ignore or block out those occasions when she behaves selfishly and then deny the accusations that she is self-centered. She might attribute her girlfriends' negative comments to their jealousy of her good looks and blame her boyfriends' negative remarks on their disappointment that she won't get more serious with them. Meanwhile, she might start doing some kind of charity work to show everyone (including herself) that she really is a nice person. As you can see, people can go to great lengths to defend their self-concept.

Rogers's theory can explain defensive behavior and personality disturbances, but he also emphasized psychological health. He suggested that psychological health is rooted in a congruent self-concept. In turn, congruence is rooted in a sense of personal worth, which stems from a childhood saturated with unconditional affection from parents and others. These themes are similar to those emphasized by the other major humanistic theorist, Abraham Maslow.

Maslow's Theory of Self-Actualization

Learning Objective

Describe Maslow's hierarchy of needs and summarize his findings on self-actualizing persons.

Abraham Maslow grew up in Brooklyn and spent much of his career at Brandeis University, where he provided crucial leadership for the fledgling humanistic movement. Like Rogers, Maslow (1968, 1970) argued that psychology should take a greater interest in the nature of the healthy personality, instead of dwelling on the causes of disorders. "To oversimplify the matter somewhat," he said, "it is as if Freud supplied to us the sick half of psychology and we must now fill it out with the healthy half" (Maslow, 1968, p. 5). Maslow's key contributions were his analysis of how motives are organized hierarchically and his description of the healthy personality.

Hierarchy of Needs

Maslow proposed that human motives are organized into a *hierarchy of needs*—a **systematic arrangement of needs, according to priority, in which basic needs must be met before less basic needs are aroused.** This hierarchical arrangement is usually portrayed as a pyramid (see Figure 2.14). The needs toward the bottom of the pyramid, such as physiological or security needs, are the most basic. Higher levels in the pyramid consist of progressively less basic needs. When a person manages to satisfy a level of needs reasonably well (complete satisfaction is not necessary), *this satisfaction activates needs at the next level.*

Like Rogers, Maslow argued that humans have an innate drive toward personal growth—that is, evolution toward a higher state of being. Thus, he described the needs in the uppermost reaches of his hierarchy as *growth needs*. These include the needs for knowledge, understanding, order, and aesthetic beauty. Heading the list is **the *need for self-actualization*, which is the need to fulfill one's potential; it is the highest need in Maslow's motivational hierarchy.** Maslow summarized this concept with a simple statement: "What a man *can* be, he *must* be." According to Maslow, people will be frustrated if they are unable to fully utilize their talents or pursue their true interests. For example, if you have great musical talent but must work as an accountant, or if you have scholarly interests but must work as a salesclerk, your need for self-actualization will be thwarted.

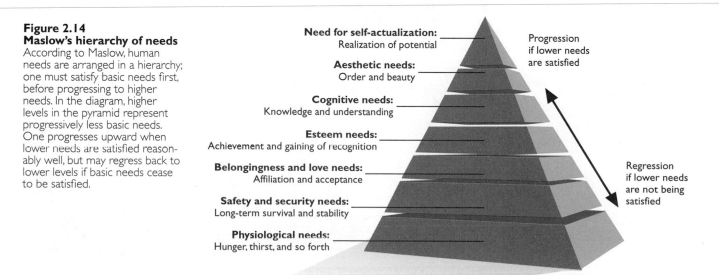

Figure 2.14
Maslow's hierarchy of needs
According to Maslow, human needs are arranged in a hierarchy; one must satisfy basic needs first, before progressing to higher needs. In the diagram, higher levels in the pyramid represent progressively less basic needs. One progresses upward when lower needs are satisfied reasonably well, but may regress back to lower levels if basic needs cease to be satisfied.

Need for self-actualization:
Realization of potential

Aesthetic needs:
Order and beauty

Cognitive needs:
Knowledge and understanding

Esteem needs:
Achievement and gaining of recognition

Belongingness and love needs:
Affiliation and acceptance

Safety and security needs:
Long-term survival and stability

Physiological needs:
Hunger, thirst, and so forth

Progression if lower needs are satisfied

Regression if lower needs are not being satisfied

PEANUTS reprinted by permission of United Feature Syndicate, Inc.

The Healthy Personality

Because of his interest in self-actualization, Maslow set out to discover the nature of the healthy personality. He tried to identify people of exceptional mental health so that he could investigate their characteristics. In one case, he used psychological tests and interviews to sort out the healthiest 1% of a sizable population of college students. He also studied admired historical figures (such as Thomas Jefferson and psychologist/philosopher William James) and personal acquaintances characterized by superior adjustment. Over a period of years, he accumulated his case histories and gradually sketched, in broad strokes, a picture of ideal psychological health.

Maslow called people with exceptionally healthy personalities *self-actualizing persons* because of their commitment to continued personal growth. He identified various traits characteristic of self-actualizing people, which are listed in Figure 2.15. In brief, Maslow found that self-actualizers are accurately tuned in to reality and that they are at peace with themselves. He found that they are open and spontaneous and that they retain a fresh appreciation of the world around them. Socially, they are sensitive to others' needs and enjoy rewarding interpersonal relations. However, they are not dependent on others for approval. Nor are they uncomfortable with solitude. They thrive on their work, and they enjoy their sense of humor. Maslow also noted that they have "peak experiences" (profound emotional highs) more often than others. Finally, he found that they strike a nice balance between many polarities in personality, so that they can be both childlike and mature, rational and intuitive, conforming and rebellious.

Evaluating Humanistic Perspectives

Learning Objective

Summarize the strengths and weaknesses of humanistic theories of personality.

The humanists added a refreshing perspective to the study of personality. Their argument that a person's subjective views may be more important than objective reality has proven compelling. Today, even behavioral theorists have begun to consider subjective personal factors such as beliefs and expectancies. The humanistic approach also deserves credit for making the self-concept an important construct in

**Figure 2.15
Characteristics of self-actualizing people**
Humanistic theorists emphasize psychological health instead of maladjustment. Maslow's sketch of the self-actualizing person provides a provocative picture of the healthy personality. (Adapted from Potkay & Allen, 1986)

Characteristics of Self-Actualizing People

- Clear, efficient perception of reality and comfortable relations with it.
- Spontaneity, simplicity, and naturalness
- Problem centering (having something outside themselves they "must" do as a mission)
- Detachment and need for privacy
- Autonomy, independence of culture and environment
- Continued freshness of appreciation
- Mystical and peak experiences

- Feelings of kinship and identification with the human race
- Strong friendships, but limited in number
- Democratic character structure
- Ethical discrimination between means and ends, between good and evil
- Philosophical, unhostile sense of humor
- Balance between polarities in personality

psychology. Finally, the humanists have often been applauded for focusing attention on the issue of what constitutes a healthy personality.

Of course, there is a negative side to the balance sheet as well. Critics have identified some weaknesses in the humanistic approach to personality, including the following (Burger, 1993).

1. *Poor testability.* Like psychodynamic theorists, the humanists have been criticized for proposing hypotheses that are difficult to put to a scientific test. Humanistic concepts such as personal growth and self-actualization are difficult to define and measure.

2. *Unrealistic view of human nature.* Critics also charge that the humanists have been overly optimistic in their assumptions about human nature and unrealistic in their descriptions of the healthy personality. For instance, Maslow's self-actualizing people sound *perfect.* In reality, Maslow had a hard time finding self-actualizing persons. When he searched among the living, the results were so disappointing that he turned to the study of historical figures. Thus, humanistic portraits of psychological health are perhaps a bit unrealistic.

3. *Inadequate evidence.* Humanistic theories are based primarily on discerning but uncontrolled observations in clinical settings. Case studies can be valuable in generating ideas, but they are ill-suited for building a solid database. More experimental research is needed to catch up with the theorizing in the humanistic camp. This is precisely the opposite of the situation that we'll encounter in the next section, on biological perspectives, where more theorizing is needed to catch up with the research.

Biological Perspectives

The striking parallels in the lives of Jim Lewis and Jim Springer, identical twins separated soon after birth and reunited as adults, suggest that heredity may have a powerful impact on personality.

Like many identical twins reared apart, Jim Lewis and Jim Springer found they had been leading eerily similar lives. Separated four weeks after birth in 1940, the Jim twins grew up 45 miles apart in Ohio and were reunited in 1979. Eventually, they discovered that both drove the same model blue Chevrolet, chain-smoked Salems, chewed their fingernails, and owned dogs named Toy. Each had spent a good deal of time vacationing at the same three-block strip of beach in Florida. More important, when tested for such personality traits as flexibility, self-control and sociability, the twins responded almost exactly alike. [Leo, 1987, p. 63]

So began a *Time* magazine summary of a major twin study conducted at the University of Minnesota, where investigators have been exploring the hereditary roots of personality. The research team has managed to locate and complete testing on 44 rare pairs of identical twins separated early in life. Not all the twin pairs have been as similar as Jim Lewis and Jim Springer, but many of the parallels have been uncanny. Identical twins Oskar Stohr and Jack Yufe were separated soon after birth. Oskar was sent to a Nazi-run school in Czechoslovakia, while Jack was raised in a Jewish home on a Caribbean island. When they were reunited for the first time during middle age, they both showed up wearing similar mustaches, haircuts, shirts, and wire-rimmed glasses. A pair of previously separated female twins both arrived at the Minneapo-

lis airport wearing seven rings on their fingers. One had a son named Richard Andrew, and the other had a son named Andrew Richard! Still another pair of separated twin sisters shared the same phobia of water. They even dealt with it in the same peculiar way—by backing into the ocean.

Could personality be largely inherited? These anecdotal reports of striking resemblances between identical twins reared apart certainly raise this possibility. In this section we'll discuss Hans Eysenck's theory, which emphasizes the influence of heredity, and look at recent research on the biological bases of personality.

Eysenck's Theory

Learning Objective

Describe Eysenck's biological theory of personality.

Hans Eysenck

Hans Eysenck was born in Germany but fled to London during the era of Nazi rule. He went on to become one of Britain's most prominent psychologists. According to Eysenck (1967), "Personality is determined to a large extent by a person's genes" (p. 20). How is heredity linked to personality in his model? In part, through conditioning concepts borrowed from behavioral theory. Eysenck (1967, 1982, 1991) theorizes that some people can be conditioned more readily than others because of inherited differences in their physiological functioning (specifically, their level of arousal). These variations in "conditionability" are assumed to influence the personality traits that people acquire through conditioning.

Eysenck views personality structure as a hierarchy of traits. Numerous superficial traits are derived from a smaller number of more basic traits, which are derived from a handful of fundamental higher-order traits, as shown in Figure 2.16. Eysenck has shown a special interest in explaining variations in *extraversion-introversion*, the trait dimension first described years earlier by Carl Jung. He has proposed that introverts tend to have higher levels of physiological arousal than extraverts. This higher arousal supposedly motivates them to avoid social situations that will further elevate their arousal and makes them more easily conditioned than extraverts. According to Eysenck, people who condition easily acquire more conditioned inhibitions than others. These inhibitions, coupled with their relatively high arousal, make them more bashful, tentative, and uneasy in social situations. This social discomfort leads them to turn inward. Hence, they become introverted.

Is there any research to support Eysenck's explanation of the origins of introversion? Yes, but the evidence is inconsistent. Many studies *have* found that introverts tend to exhibit higher levels of arousal than extraverts (Bullock & Gilliland, 1993; Wilson, 1990), but many studies have also failed to find the predicted differences (Gale, 1983). Even Eysenck (1990) acknowledges that the evidence on his theory is mixed and that the concept of physiological arousal has turned out to be much more multifaceted and difficult to measure than he originally anticipated. It will be interesting to see whether more consistent results are obtained in the future, as investigators improve and refine their methods for measuring physiological arousal.

Recent Research in Behavioral Genetics

Learning Objective

Summarize recent twin studies that support the idea that personality is largely inherited.

Recent twin studies have provided impressive support for Eysenck's hypothesis that personality is largely inherited. **In *twin studies* researchers assess hereditary influence by comparing the resemblance of identical twins and fraternal twins on a trait.** The logic underlying this comparison is as follows. *Identical twins* emerge from one egg that splits, so that their genetic makeup is exactly the same (100% overlap). *Fraternal twins* result when two eggs are fertilized simultaneously; their genetic overlap is only 50%. Both types of twins *usually* grow up in the same home, at the same time, exposed to the same relatives, neighbors, peers, teachers, events, and so forth. Thus, both kinds of twins normally develop under similar environmental conditions, but identical twins share more genetic kinship. Hence, if sets of identical twins exhibit more personality resemblance than sets of fraternal twins, this greater similarity is probably due to heredity rather than environment.

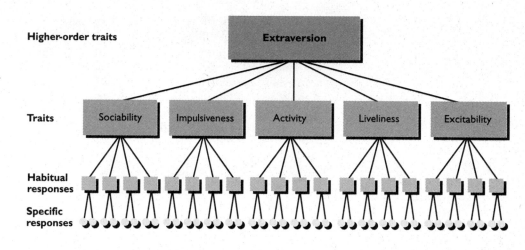

Figure 2.16
Eysenck's model of personality structure
Eysenck describes personality structure as a hierarchy of traits. In this scheme, a few higher-order traits (such as extraversion) determine a host of lower-order traits (such as sociability), which determine a person's habitual responses (such as going to lots of parties). In turn, these determine the person's specific responses to situations. (From Eysenck, 1967)

In one large study, 573 pairs of twins responded to five personality scales that measured altruism, empathy, nurturance, aggressiveness, and assertiveness (Rushton et al., 1986). Figure 2.17 shows the mean correlations observed on three of these traits. Higher correlations are indicative of greater similarity on a trait. On all five traits, identical twins were found to be much more similar to each other than fraternal twins were. The investigators attribute the identical twins' greater personality resemblance to their greater genetic similarity. Based on the observed correlations, they *estimate* that genetic factors account for about 56% to 72% of the variation in the five traits studied.

Some skeptics still wonder whether identical twins might exhibit more personality resemblance than fraternal twins because they are raised more similarly. In other words, they wonder whether environmental factors (rather than heredity) could be responsible for identical twins' greater similarity. This nagging question can be answered only by studying identical twins who have been reared apart. This is why the twin study at the University of Minnesota is so important.

The Minnesota study (Tellegen et al., 1988) is the first to administer the same personality test to identical and fraternal twins reared together as well as apart. Most of the twins reared apart were separated quite early in life (median age of 2.5 months) and remained separated for a long time (median period of almost 34 years). Nonetheless, on all three of the higher-order traits examined, the identical twins reared apart displayed more personality resemblance than fraternal twins reared together. Based on the pattern of correlations observed, the researchers estimate that genetic inheritance accounts for at least 50% of the variation among people in personality.

Figure 2.17
Heredity and personality
Selected results from the twin study of personality conducted by Rushton et al. (1986) are shown here. Identical twins showed stronger correlations in personality than fraternal twins, suggesting that personality is partly inherited. The correlational data yielded rather high estimates of hereditary influence for the personality traits examined in the study.

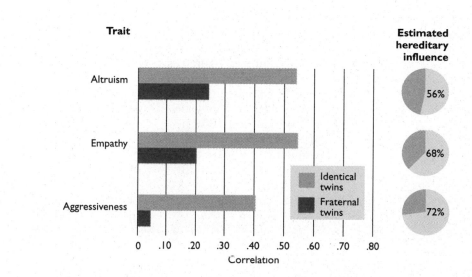

Research on the genetic bases of personality has inadvertently turned up another interesting finding. A number of recent studies have found that shared family environment has surprisingly little impact on personality (Hoffman, 1991; Plomin & Daniels, 1987). For many years, social scientists have assumed that the environment shared by children growing up together leads to some personality resemblance among them. However, recent findings seriously undermine this widespread belief.

These findings have led Robert Plomin (1990) to ask, "Why are children in the same family so different from one another?" Researchers have only just begun to explore this perplexing question. Plomin speculates that children in the same family experience home environments that are not nearly as homogeneous as previously assumed. He notes that children in the same home may be treated quite differently, because gender and birth order can influence parents' approaches to child-rearing. Temperamental differences between children may also evoke differences in styles of parenting. Focusing on how environmental factors vary *within* families represents a promising new way to explore the determinants of personality (Baker & Daniels, 1990).

Evaluating Biological Perspectives

Learning Objective

Summarize the strengths and weaknesses of biological theories of personality.

Recent studies have provided convincing evidence that biological factors help shape personality. Nonetheless, we must take note of some weaknesses in biological approaches to personality.

1. *Problems with estimates of hereditary influence.* Efforts to carve personality into genetic and environmental components with statistics are ultimately artificial. The effects of heredity and environment are bound together in complicated interactions that can't be separated cleanly. Although estimates of the genetic component in personality sound very precise, they are estimates based on a complicated chain of inferences that are subject to debate. Some theorists argue that twin studies inflate the apparent influence of heredity and that the genetic component of personality is closer to 20% than 50% (Plomin, Chipuer, & Loehlin, 1990).

2. *Lack of adequate theory.* At present there is no comprehensive biological theory of personality. Eysenck's model does not provide a systematic overview of how biological factors govern personality development (and was never intended to). Additional theoretical work is needed to catch up with recent empirical findings on the biological basis for personality.

An Epilogue on Theoretical Diversity

Learning Objective

Discuss why the subject of personality has generated so much theoretical diversity.

Figure 2.18 provides a comparative overview of the ideas of Freud, Skinner, Rogers, and Eysenck, as representatives of the pyschodynamic, behavioral, humanistic, and biological approaches to personality. Most of this information was covered in the chapter, but the figure organizes it so that the similarities and differences between the theories become more apparent. As you can see, there are many fundamental points of disagreement. Our review of perspectives on personality should have made one thing abundantly clear: Psychology is marked by theoretical diversity.

Why are there so many competing points of view? One reason is that no single theory can adequately explain everything that we know about personality. Sometimes different theories focus on different aspects of behavior. Sometimes there is simply more than one way of looking at something. Is the glass half empty or half full? Obviously, it is both. To take an example from another science, physicists wrestled for years with the nature of light. Is it a wave or is it a particle? In the end, it proved useful to think of light sometimes as a wave and sometimes as a particle. Similarly, if a business executive lashes out at her employees with stinging criticism, is she releasing pent-up aggressive urges (a psychoanalytic view)? Is she making a habitual response to the stimulus of incompetent work (a behavioral view)?

Overview of Four Approaches to Personality

	Sigmund Freud: A psychodynamic view	B. F. Skinner: A behavioral view	Carl Rogers: A humanistic view	Hans Eysenck: A biological view
Source of data and observations	Case studies from clinical practice of psychoanalysis	Laboratory experiments, primarily with animals	Case studies from clinical practice of client-centered therapy	Twin, family, and adoption studies of hereditary influence; factor analysis studies of personality structure
Key motivational forces	Sex and aggression; need to reduce tension produced by internal conflicts	Pursuit of primary (unlearned) and secondary (learned) reinforcers; priorities depend on personal history	Actualizing tendency (need for personal growth) and self-actualizing tendency (need to maintain self-concept)	No specific motivational forces singled out
Model of personality structure	Three interacting components (id, ego, superego) operating at three levels of consciousness	Collection of response tendencies tied to specific stimulus situations	Self-concept, which may or may not be congruent with actual experience	Hierarchy of traits, with specific traits derived from more fundamental, general traits
View of personality development	Emphasis on fixation or progress through psychosexual stages; experiences in early childhood leave lasting mark on adult personality	Personality evolves gradually over the life span (not in stages); responses followed by reinforcement become more frequent	Children who receive unconditional love have less need to be defensive; they develop more accurate, congruent self-concepts; conditional love fosters incongruence	Emphasis on unfolding of genetic blueprint with maturation; inherited predispositions interact with learning experiences
Roots of disorders	Unconscious fixations and unresolved conflicts from childhood, usually centered on sex and aggression	Maladaptive behavior due to faulty learning; the "symptom" is the problem, not a sign of underlying disease	Incongruence between self-concept and actual experience; overdependence on others for approval and sense of worth	Genetic vulnerability activated in part by environmental factors
Importance of nature (biology, heredity) vs. nurture (environment, experience)	Nature: emphasis on biological basis of instinctual drives	Nurture: strong emphasis on learning, conditioning, role of experience	Nurture: interested in innate potentials, but humanists believe we can rise above our biological heritage	Nature: strong emphasis on how hereditary predispositions shape our personalities
Importance of person factors vs. situation factors	Person: main interest is in internal factors (id, ego, conflicts, defenses, etc.)	Situation: strong emphasis on how we respond to specific stimulus situations	Person: focus on self-concept, which is stable	Person: interested in stable traits molded by heredity

Figure 2.18
Comparison of four theoretical perspectives on personality
This chart compares the theories of Freud, Skinner, Rogers, and Eysenck to highlight the similarities and differences among the psychodynamic, behavioral, humanistic, and biological approaches to personality.

Is she trying to act like a tough boss because that's a key aspect of her self-concept (a humanistic view)? Or is she exhibiting an inherited tendency to be aggressive (a biological view)? In some cases, all four of these explanations might have some validity.

In short, it is an oversimplification to expect that one view has to be right while all others are wrong. Life is rarely that simple. In view of the complexity of personality, it would be surprising if there were *not* a number of different theories. It's probably best to think of the various theoretical orientations in psychology as complementary viewpoints, each with its own advantages and limitations. Indeed, modern psychologists increasingly recognize that theoretical diversity is a strength rather than a weakness (Hilgard, 1987; Kleinginna & Kleinginna, 1988). As we proceed through this text, you will see how differing theoretical perspectives often inspire fruitful research and how they sometimes converge on a more complete understanding of behavior than could be achieved by any one perspective alone.

Assessing Your Personality

Answer the following "true" or "false."

1. Responses to personality tests are subject to unconscious distortion.

2. The results of personality tests are often misunderstood.

3. Personality test scores should be interpreted with caution.

4. Personality tests may be quite useful in helping people to learn more about themselves.

If you answered "true" to all four questions, you earned a perfect score. Yes, personality tests are subject to distortion. Admittedly, test results are often misunderstood, and they should be interpreted cautiously. In spite of these problems, however, psychological tests can be useful.

All people engage in efforts to size up their own personality as well as that of others. When you think to yourself that "this salesman is untrustworthy," or when you remark to a friend that "Howard is too timid and submissive," you are making personality assessments. In a sense, then, personality assessment is part of daily life. However, psychological tests provide much more systematic assessments than do casual observations.

The value of psychological tests lies in their ability to help people form a realistic picture of their personal qualities. In light of this value, we have included a variety of personality tests in the *Personal Explorations Workbook* that is available to accompany this text and we have sprinkled a number of short tests throughout the text itself. Most of these questionnaires are widely used personality tests. We hope that you may gain some insights by responding to these scales. But it's important to understand the logic and limitations of such tests. To facilitate your use of these and other tests, this Application discusses some of the basics of psychological testing.

Key Concepts in Psychological Testing

Learning Objective

Explain the concepts of standardization, test norms, reliability, and validity.

A *psychological test* is a standardized measure of a sample of a person's behavior. Psychological tests are measurement instruments. They are used to measure abilities, aptitudes, and personality traits.

Keep in mind that your responses to a psychological test represent a *sample* of your behavior. This reality should alert you to one of the key limitations of psychological tests. It's always possible that a particular behavior sample is not representative of your characteristic behavior. We all have our bad days. A stomachache, a fight with a friend, a problem with your car—all might affect your responses to a particular test on a particular day. Because of the limitations of the sampling process, test scores should always be interpreted *cautiously*. Most psychological tests are sound measurement devices, but test results should *not* be viewed as the "final word" on one's personality and abilities, because of the ever-present sampling problem.

Most psychological tests can be placed in one of two broad categories: (1) mental ability tests and (2) personality tests. *Mental ability tests*, such as intelligence tests, aptitude tests, and achievement tests, often serve as gateways to schooling, training programs, and jobs. *Personality tests* measure various aspects of personality, including motives, interests, values, and attitudes. Many psychologists prefer to call these tests personality *scales*, since the questions do not have right and wrong answers as do those on tests of mental abilities.

Figure 2.19
Test reliability
Subjects' scores on the first administration of an assertiveness test are represented on the left, while their scores on a second administration (a few weeks later) are represented on the right. If subjects obtain similar scores on both administrations, the test measures assertiveness consistently and is said to have high reliability. If subjects get very different scores when they take the test a second time, the test is said to have low reliability.

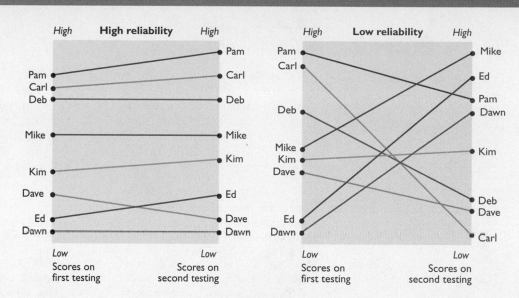

Standardization and Norms

Both personality scales and tests of mental abilities are *standardized* measures of behavior. **Standardization refers to the uniform procedures used to administer and score a test.** All subjects get the same instructions, the same questions, the same time limits, and so on, so that their scores can be compared meaningfully.

The standardization of a test's scoring system includes the development of test norms. ***Test norms* provide information about where a score on a psychological test ranks in relation to other scores on that test.** Why do we need test norms? Because in psychological testing, everything is relative. Psychological tests tell you how you score *relative to other people*. They tell you, for instance, that you are average in impulsiveness, or slightly above average in assertiveness, or far below average in anxiety. These interpretations are derived from the test norms.

Reliability and Validity

Any kind of measuring device, whether a tire gauge, a stopwatch, or a psychological test, should be reasonably consistent. That is, repeated measurements should yield reasonably similar results. To appreciate the importance of reliability, think about how you would react if a tire pressure gauge gave you several very different readings for the same tire. You would probably conclude that the gauge was broken and toss it into the trash because you know that consistency in measurement is essential to accuracy.

***Reliability* refers to the measurement consistency of a test.** A reliable test is one that yields similar results for people upon repetition of the test (see Figure 2.19). Like most other types of measuring devices, psychological tests are not perfectly reliable. They usually do not yield the exact same score when repeated. A certain amount of inconsistency is unavoidable because human behavior is variable. Personality tests tend to have lower reliability than mental ability tests because daily fluctuations in mood influence how people respond to such tests.

Even if a test is quite reliable, we still need to be concerned about its validity. ***Validity* refers to the ability of a test to measure what it was designed to measure.** If we develop a new test of assertiveness, we have to provide some evidence that it really measures assertiveness. Validity can be demonstrated in a variety of ways, most of them involving correlating scores on a test with other measures of the same trait, or with related traits.

Self-Report Inventories

Learning Objective

Discuss the value and
limitations of self-report
inventories.

The vast majority of personality tests are self-report inventories. *Self-report inventories* **are personality scales that ask individuals to answer a series of questions about their characteristic behavior.** When you take a self-report personality scale, you endorse statements as true or false as applied to you, or indicate how often you behave in a particular way, or rate yourself with respect to certain qualities. For example, on the Minnesota Multiphasic Personality Inventory, people respond "true," "false," or "cannot say" to 550 statements such as the following:

I get a fair deal from most people.
I have the time of my life at parties.
I am glad that I am alive.
Several people are following me everywhere.

The logic underlying this approach is simple. Who knows you better than you do? Who has known you longer? Who has more access to your private feelings?

The entire range of personality traits can be measured with self-report inventories. Some scales measure just one trait dimension, such as the Self-Efficacy Scale (see Figure 2.12) or the measure of introversion-extraversion shown in Figure 2.20. Others simultaneously assess a multitude of traits. The Sixteen Personality Factor Questionnaire (16PF), developed by Raymond Cattell and his colleagues (Cattell, Eber, & Tatsuoka, 1970), is a representative example of a multitrait inventory. The 16PF is a 187-item scale that measures 16 basic dimensions of personality, called *source traits*, which are shown in Figure 2.21.

To appreciate the strengths of self-report inventories, consider how else you might assess your personality. For instance, how assertive are you? You probably have some vague idea, but can you accurately estimate how your assertiveness compares to others'? To do that, you need a great deal of comparative information about others' usual behavior—information that all of us lack. In contrast, a self-report inventory inquires about your typical behavior in a wide variety of circumstances requiring assertiveness and generates an exact comparison with the typical behav-

Figure 2.20
The Maudsley Personality Inventory, Short Form
The items shown here, taken from the Maudsley Personality Inventory, provide a brief measure of extraversion-introversion. The items are worded so that a "yes" response is indicative of extraverted tendencies. If you answered "yes" to all six questions, you are probably more extraverted than introverted, although you should be cautious about drawing conclusions based on such a short scale. (Adapted from Eysenck & Eysenck, 1969)

The Maudsley Personality Inventory, Short Form

Instructions: The following questions pertain to the way people behave, feel, and act. Decide whether the items represent your *usual* way of acting or feeling, and circle either a "yes" or "no" for each. If you find it absolutely impossible to decide, circle the "?" answer, but use this answer sparingly.

1. Do you prefer action to planning for action?
   YES　　　?　　　　NO

2. Are you happiest when you get involved in some project that calls for rapid action?
   YES　　　?　　　　NO

3. Do you usually take the initiative in making new friends?
   YES　　　?　　　　NO

4. Are you inclined to be quick and sure in your actions?
   YES　　　?　　　　NO

5. Would you rate yourself as a lively individual?
   YES　　　?　　　　NO

6. Would you be very unhappy if you were prevented from making numerous social contacts?
   YES　　　?　　　　NO

Figure 2.21
The Sixteen Personality
Factor Questionnaire
(16PF)

Cattell's 16PF is designed to
assess 16 basic dimensions of
personality. The pairs of traits
listed across from each other in
the figure define the 16 factors
measured by this self-report
inventory. The profile shown is
the average profile seen among a
group of airline pilots who took
the test. (From Cattell, 1973)

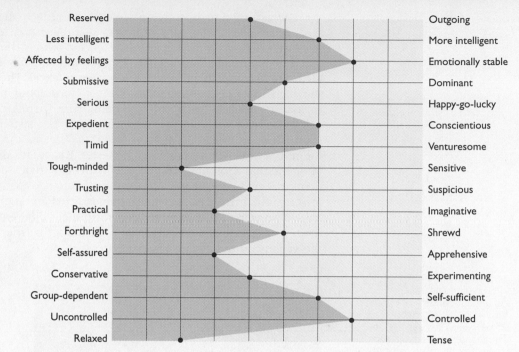

Reserved	Outgoing
Less intelligent	More intelligent
Affected by feelings	Emotionally stable
Submissive	Dominant
Serious	Happy-go-lucky
Expedient	Conscientious
Timid	Venturesome
Tough-minded	Sensitive
Trusting	Suspicious
Practical	Imaginative
Forthright	Shrewd
Self-assured	Apprehensive
Conservative	Experimenting
Group-dependent	Self-sufficient
Uncontrolled	Controlled
Relaxed	Tense

ior reported by many other respondents for the same circumstances. Thus, self-report inventories are much more thorough and precise than our casual observations.

However, these tests are only as accurate as the information that we give them. Deliberate deception can be a problem. For example, some people are unconsciously influenced by the social desirability or acccptability of specific statements (Paulhus, 1991). Without realizing it, they endorse only those statements that make them look good. This problem provides another reason why personality test results should always be regarded as suggestive rather than definitive.

Projective Tests

Learning Objective

Discuss the value and limitations of projective tests.

Projective tests, which take an indirect approach to the assessment of personality, are used extensively in clinical work. ***Projective tests* ask subjects to respond to vague, ambiguous stimuli in ways that may reveal the subjects' needs, feelings, and personality traits.** The

In projective tests, such as the Rorschach, stimuli are deliberately vague and ambiguous to serve as a blank screen onto which subjects can project their concerns, conflicts, and desires.

Rorschach test, for instance, consists of a series of ten inkblots. Respondents are asked to describe what they see in the blots (see the adjacent photo). In the Thematic Apperception Test (TAT), a series of pictures of simple scenes is presented to subjects who are asked to tell stories about what is happening in the scenes and what the characters are feeling. For instance, one TAT card shows a young boy contemplating a violin resting on a table in front of him.

The assumption underlying projective testing is that ambiguous materials can serve as a blank screen onto which people project their characteristic concerns, conflicts, and desires. Thus, a competitive person who is shown the TAT card of the boy and the violin might concoct a story about how the boy is contemplating an upcoming musical competition at which he hopes to excel. The same card shown to a person high in impulsiveness might elicit a story about how the boy is planning to sneak out the door to go dirt-bike riding with friends.

Proponents of projective tests assert that the tests have two unique strengths. First, they are not transparent to subjects. That is, the subject doesn't know how the test provides information to the tester. Hence, it's difficult for people to engage in intentional deception. Second, the indirect approach used in these tests may make them especially sensitive to unconscious features of personality. Critics of projective tests maintain that they are poorly standardized and highly subjective, such that different clinicians will administer and score them differently, making the reliability of the tests distressingly low. Critics also maintain that there is inadequate evidence on the validity of most projective measures.

In taking the Thematic Apperception Test (TAT), a respondent is asked to tell stories about scenes such as this one. The themes apparent in each story can be scored to provide insight about the respondent's personality.

Key Ideas

The Nature of Personality

• The concept of personality explains the consistency in a person's behavior over time and across situations as well as each person's distinctiveness. Personality traits are dispositions to behave in certain ways. Recent research suggests that the complexity of personality can be reduced to just five basic traits.

Psychodynamic Perspectives

• Freud's psychoanalytic theory emphasizes the importance of the unconscious. Freud saw personality structure in terms of three components (the id, ego, and superego) that are involved in internal conflicts, which generate anxiety. According to Freud, we ward off anxiety and other unpleasant emotions with defense mechanisms, which work through self-deception. Freud believed the first five years of life are extremely influential in shaping adult personality. He described five psychosexual stages that children undergo through adolescence.

• Jung's analytical psychology stresses the importance of the collective unconscious and archetypes. Adler's individual psychology emphasizes how people strive for superiority in order to compensate for their feelings of inferiority.

• Psychodynamic theories have produced many groundbreaking insights about the unconscious, the role of conflict, and the importance of early, formative childhood experiences. However, they have been criticized for their poor testability, their inadequate base of empirical evidence, and their male-centered views of the human condition.

Behavioral Perspectives

• Behavioral theories view personality as a collection of response tendencies shaped through learning. Pavlov's classical conditioning can explain how people acquire emotional responses. Skinner's model of operant conditioning shows how consequences such as reinforcement, extinction, and punishment shape habitual patterns of behavior. Bandura's social learning theory adds a cognitive flavor to behaviorism. It shows how people can be conditioned indirectly through observation.

• Behavioral approaches to personality are based on rigorous research. They have provided ample insights about how situational factors and learning mold people's personalities. However, the behaviorists have been criticized for their overdependence on animal research, and behavioral theories aren't all that behavioral anymore.

Humanistic Perspectives

• Humanistic theories take an optimistic view of people's conscious, rational ability to chart their own courses of action. Rogers focused on the self-concept as the critical aspect of personality. He maintained that incongruence between one's self-concept and reality creates anxiety and leads to defensive behavior. Maslow theorized that human needs are arranged hierarchically. He asserted that psychological health depends on fulfilling the need for self-actualization.

• Humanistic theories deserve credit for highlighting the importance of subjective views of oneself and for confronting the question of what makes for a healthy personality. However, they lack a firm base of research, are difficult to put to an empirical test, and may be overly optimistic about human nature.

Biological Perspectives

• Eysenck believes that individual differences in physiological functioning affect conditioning and thus influence personality. Recent twin studies have provided impressive evidence that genetic factors shape personality. The biological approach has been criticized because of problems with estimates of hereditary influence and because it offers no comprehensive model of personality.

An Epilogue on Theoretical Diversity

• The study of personality illustrates the great theoretical diversity in psychology. This diversity is a strength in that it fuels research that moves us toward a more complete understanding of behavior.

Application: Assessing Your Personality

• Psychological tests are standardized measures of behavior—usually mental abilities or aspects of personality. Test scores are interpreted by consulting test norms to find out what represents a high or low score. As measuring devices, psychological tests should produce consistent results, a quality called reliability. Validity refers to the degree to which a test measures what it was designed to measure.

• Self-report measures, such as the MMPI and 16PF, ask subjects to describe themselves. Self-report inventories can provide a better snapshot of personality than can casual observations, but they are vulnerable to certain sources of error, including deception and social desirability bias.

• Projective tests, such as the Rorschach and TAT, assume that subjects' responses to ambiguous stimuli reveal something about their personality. Projective tests may discourage deception by subjects and facilitate the exploration of unconscious dimensions of personality. While the projective hypothesis seems plausible, projective tests' reliability and validity are disturbingly low.

Key Terms

Archetypes
Behaviorism
Classical conditioning
Cognition
Collective unconscious
Compensation
Conditioned response (CR)
Conditioned stimulus (CS)
Conscious
Defense mechanisms
Displacement
Ego
Extinction
Extraverts
Fixation
Hierarchy of needs
Humanism
Id
Identification
Incongruence
Introverts
Need for self-actualization
Negative reinforcement
Observational learning
Oedipus complex
Operant conditioning
Personality
Personality trait
Pleasure principle
Positive reinforcement
Preconscious
Projection
Projective tests
Psychodynamic theories
Psychological tests
Psychosexual stages
Punishment
Rationalization
Reaction formation
Reality principle
Regression
Reliability
Repression
Self-concept
Self-efficacy
Self-report inventories
Standardization
Superego
Test norms
Twin studies
Unconditioned response (UCR)
Unconditioned stimulus (UCS)
Unconscious
Validity

Key People

Alfred Adler
Albert Bandura
Hans Eysenck
Sigmund Freud
Carl Jung
Abraham Maslow
Ivan Pavlov
Carl Rogers
B. F. Skinner

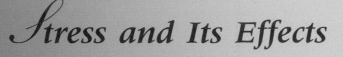

3 *Stress and Its Effects*

$\mathcal{Y}$ou're in your car headed home from school with a classmate. Traffic is barely moving. A radio report indicates that the traffic jam is only going to get worse. You groan audibly as you fiddle impatiently with the radio dial. Another motorist nearly takes your fender off trying to cut into your lane. Your pulse quickens as you shout insults at the unknown driver, who cannot even hear you. You think about the term paper that you have to work on tonight. Your stomach knots up as you recall all the crumpled drafts you tossed into the wastebasket last night. If you don't finish the paper soon, you won't be able to find any time to study for your math test, not to mention your biology quiz. Suddenly you remember that you promised the person you're dating that the two of you would get together tonight. There's no way. Another fight looms on the horizon. Your classmate asks how you feel about the tuition increase the college announced yesterday. You've been trying not to think about it. You're already in debt up to your ears. Your parents are bugging you about changing schools, but you don't want to leave your friends. Your heartbeat quickens as you contemplate the debate you'll have to wage with your parents. You feel wired with tension as you realize that the stress in your life never seems to let up.

Many different circumstances can create stress. It comes in all sorts of packages: large and small, pretty and ugly, simple and complex. All too often, the package is a surprise. In this chapter, we'll try to sort out these packages. We'll analyze the nature of stress, outline the major types of stress, and discuss how people respond to stressful events at several levels.

In a sense, stress is what a course on adjustment is all about. Recall from Chapter 1 that adjustment essentially deals with how people manage to cope with various demands and pressures. These demands or pressures that require adjustment represent the core of stressful experience. Thus, the central theme in a course such as this is: How do people adjust to stress, and how might they adjust more effectively?

The Nature of Stress

Learning Objective

Summarize four general points about the nature of stress.

Over the years, the term *stress* has been used in different ways by different theorists. Some have viewed stress as a *stimulus* event that presents difficult demands (a divorce, for instance), while others have viewed stress as the *response* of physiological arousal elicited by troublesome events (Whitehead, 1994). However, the emerging consensus among contemporary researchers is that stress is neither a stimulus nor a response but a special stimulus-response transaction in which one feels threatened. Hence, we will define **stress as any circumstances that threaten or are perceived to threaten one's well-being and thereby tax one's coping abilities.** The threat may be to immediate physical safety, to long-range security, to self-esteem, to reputation, or to peace of mind. This is a complex concept—so let's dig a little deeper.

Stress Is an Everyday Event

The term *stress* tends to spark images of overwhelming, traumatic crises. People think of hijackings, hurricanes, military combat, and nuclear accidents. Undeniably, these are extremely stressful events. Studies conducted in the aftermath of tornadoes, floods, earthquakes, and the like typically find elevated rates of anxiety, depression, and drug abuse in the communities affected by these disasters (Rubonis & Bickman, 1991; Weisaeth, 1993). However, these unusual and infrequent events represent the tip of the iceberg. Many everyday events—from waiting in line or having car trouble to shopping for Christmas presents, misplacing your checkbook, and staring at bills you can't pay—are also stressful.

You might guess that minor stresses would produce minor effects, but that isn't necessarily true. Research shows that routine hassles may have significant negative effects on one's mental and physical health (Delongis, Folkman, & Lazarus, 1988).

Richard Lazarus and his colleagues have devised a scale to measure stress in the form of daily hassles. Their scale lists 117 everyday problems, such as misplacing things, struggling with rising prices, dealing with delays, and so forth. When they compared their hassles scale against another scale that assessed stress in the form of major life events (Kanner et al., 1981), they found that scores on their scale were more strongly related to subjects' mental health than scores on the stressful events scale. Other investigators, working with different types of samples and different measures of hassles, have also found that everyday hassles are predictive of mental and physical health (Kohn, Lafreniere, & Gurevich, 1991; Rowlison & Felner, 1988).

Why would minor hassles be more strongly related to mental health than major stressful events? The answer isn't entirely clear yet, but most theories of stress assume that stressful events have a *cumulative* impact (Seta, Seta, & Wang, 1991). In other words, stress adds up. Routine stresses at home, at school, and at work might be fairly benign individually, but collectively they could create great strain.

Stress Lies in the Eye of the Beholder

Richard Lazarus

The experience of feeling threatened depends on what events one notices and how one chooses to appraise or interpret them. Events that are stressful for one person may be "ho-hum" routine for another. For example, many people find flying in an airplane somewhat stressful, but frequent fliers may not even raise an eyebrow. Some people enjoy the excitement of going out on a date with someone new; others find the uncertainty terrifying.

In discussing appraisals of stress, Lazarus and Folkman (1984) distinguish between primary and secondary appraisal. *Primary appraisal* **is an initial evaluation of whether an event is (1) irrelevant to you, (2) relevant, but not threatening, or (3) stressful.** When you view an event as stressful, you are likely to make a *secondary appraisal,* **which is an evaluation of your coping resources and options for dealing with the stress.** Thus, your primary appraisal would determine whether you see an upcoming job interview as stressful. Your secondary appraisal would determine how stressful the interview seems in light of your assessment of your ability to deal with it.

Often, people are not very objective in their appraisals of potentially stressful events. A study of hospitalized patients awaiting surgery showed only a slight correlation between the objective seriousness of a person's upcoming surgery and the amount of fear the person experienced (Janis, 1958). Clearly, some people are more prone to feel threatened by life's difficulties than are others. A number of studies have shown that anxious, neurotic people report more stress than others (Brett et al., 1990), as do people who are relatively unhappy (Seidlitz & Diener, 1993). Thus, stress lies in the eye (actually, the mind) of the beholder, and people's appraisals of stressful events are highly subjective.

Stress May Be Embedded in the Environment

Although the perception of stress is a highly personal matter, many kinds of stress emanate from environmental circumstances. *Ambient stress* **consists of chronic environmental conditions that, although not urgent, are negatively valued and place adaptive demands on people** (Holahan, 1986). Such features of the environment as excessive noise, heat, and pollution can threaten people's well-being and leave their mark on individuals' mental and physical health. For example, investigators have found an association between exposure to high levels of noise and elevated blood pressure among children attending school near Los Angeles International Airport (Cohen, et al., 1980). Research has also revealed that people exposed to excessive noise at work experience more headaches, nausea, and moodiness than others (Cohen, Glass, & Phillips, 1977). Evidence suggests that excessive heat may impair task performance and increase the likelihood of aggressive behavior (Fisher, Bell, & Baum, 1984). In a study conducted in Dayton, Ohio, Rotton and Frey (1984) found that psychiatric emergencies increased when air pollution was high.

Stress can be caused by environmental circumstances such as excessive noise, crowding, and risk of disaster.

Crowding is another source of environmental stress. Temporary experiences of crowding, such as when you're packed into a rock concert with thousands of other fans, can be stressful, but most of the research on crowding has been concerned with the effects of residential density. Generally, studies find an association between high density and aggression, poor task performance, and social withdrawal (Sundstrom, 1978). One does not have to live in an urban skyscraper or tenement to experience crowding. Even an overcrowded dormitory, with three students in rooms built for two, can be stressful (Mullen & Felleman, 1990). Psychologists have also explored the repercussions of living in areas that are at risk for disaster. For instance, studies suggest that people who live near a nuclear power plant or in an area subject to earthquakes may experience increased stress (Baum, 1990; Nolen-Hoeksema & Morrow, 1991).

Reprinted by permission: Tribune Media Services.

As with other types of stress, the experience of environmental stress is subjective. A level of noise, heat, or crowding that is aversive for one person may not be bothersome to another. Even in the aftermath of a major disaster, only some people will feel stressed out. For example, in a study of Stanford students' adjustment to the 1989 Loma Prieta earthquake that crippled the San Francisco Bay Area, Nolen-Hoeksema and Morrow (1991) found negative emotional effects primarily among students who tended to ruminate about their problems and those who were depressed before the earthquake.

Stress May Be Self-Imposed

We tend to think of stress as something imposed from without by others and their demands. However, a recent study of college students' stress found that stress is self-imposed surprisingly often (Epstein & Katz, 1992). For example, you might sign up for extra classes to get through school quickly. Or you might actively seek additional responsibilities at work to impress your boss. People frequently put pressure on themselves to get good grades or to climb the corporate ladder rapidly. Many people create stress by embracing unrealistic expectations for themselves. Because stress is often self-imposed, individuals have more control over their stress than many people realize. However, to exert this control, we need to be able to recognize the sources of stress in our lives. Hence, in the next section we'll discuss the major types of stress.

Major Types of Stress

Learning Objective

List and describe four principal types of stress.

An enormous variety of events can be stressful for one person or another. To achieve a better understanding of stress, theorists have tried to organize it into principal types. None of their organizational schemes has turned out to be altogether satisfactory. It's virtually impossible to classify stressful events into nonintersecting categories. Although this problem presents conceptual headaches for researchers, it need not prevent us from describing four major types of stress: frustration, conflict, change, and pressure. As you read about each of these, you'll surely recognize familiar adversaries.

Frustration

Learning Objective

Describe frustration as a form of stress.

"It has been very frustrating to watch the rapid deterioration of my parents' relationship. Over the last year or two they have argued constantly and have refused to seek any professional help. I have tried to talk to them, but they kind of shut me and my brother out of their problem. I feel very helpless and sometimes even very angry, not at them, but at the whole situation."

This scenario illustrates frustration. As psychologists use the term, **frustration occurs in any situation in which the pursuit of some goal is thwarted.** In essence, you experience frustration when you want something and you can't have it. We all have to deal with frustration virtually every day. Traffic jams, for instance, are a routine source of frustration that can affect mood and blood pressure (Schaeffer et al., 1988). Fortunately, most frustrations are brief and insignificant. You may be quite upset when you go to a repair shop to pick up your ailing computer and find that it hasn't been fixed as promised. However, a week later you'll probably have your precious computer, and all will be forgotten.

Of course, some frustrations can be sources of significant stress. *Failures* and *losses* are two common kinds of frustration that can be highly stressful. Everyone fails in at least some of his or her endeavors. Some people make failure almost inevitable by setting unrealistic goals for themselves. They tend to forget that for every newly appointed vice-president in the business world, there are dozens of middle-level executives who don't get promoted. Losses may be especially frustrating because one is deprived of something one is accustomed to having. For example, few things are more frustrating than losing a dearly loved boyfriend, girlfriend, or spouse.

More often than not, frustration appears to be the culprit at work when people are troubled by environmental stress (Graig, 1993). To the extent that excessive noise, heat, pollution, and crowding are stressful, it's probably because they frustrate the individual's desire for quiet, a comfortable body temperature, clean air, and adequate privacy.

Conflict

Learning Objective

Describe three types of conflict and discuss our reactions to conflicts.

Neal Miller

"Should I or shouldn't I? I became engaged at Christmas. My fiancé surprised me with a ring. I knew if I refused the ring he would be terribly hurt and our relationship would suffer. However, I don't really know whether or not I want to marry him. On the other hand, I don't want to lose him either."

Like frustration, conflict is an unavoidable feature of everyday life. That perplexing question "Should I or shouldn't I?" comes up countless times in our lives. **Conflict occurs when two or more incompatible motivations or behavioral impulses compete for expression.** As we discussed in Chapter 2, Sigmund Freud proposed nearly a century ago that internal conflicts generate considerable psychological distress. This link between conflict and distress was measured with new precision in recent studies by Laura King and Robert Emmons (1990). Using an elaborate questionnaire to assess the overall amount of internal conflict experienced by subjects, they found in several studies that higher levels of conflict were associated with higher levels of psychological distress.

Conflicts come in three types, which were originally described by Kurt Lewin (1935) and investigated extensively by Neal Miller (1944, 1959). These three types—approach-approach, avoidance-avoidance, and approach-avoidance—are diagrammed in Figure 3.1.

In an *approach-approach conflict* a choice must be made between two attractive goals. The problem, of course, is that you can choose just one of the two goals. For example, you have a free afternoon; should you play tennis or racquetball? You're out for a meal; do you want the pizza or the spaghetti? You can't afford both; should you buy the blue sweater or the gray jacket?

Among the three kinds of conflict, the approach-approach type tends to be the least stressful. People usually don't stagger out of restaurants exhausted by the stress of choosing which of several appealing entrees to eat. In approach-approach

Figure 3.1
Types of conflict
Psychologists have identified three basic types of conflict. In approach-approach or avoidance-avoidance conflicts, the person is torn between two goals. In an approach-avoidance conflict there is only one goal under consideration, but it has both positive and negative aspects.

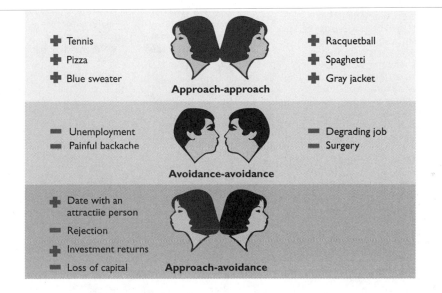

+ Tennis
+ Pizza
+ Blue sweater
Approach-approach
+ Racquetball
+ Spaghetti
+ Gray jacket

− Unemployment
− Painful backache
Avoidance-avoidance
− Degrading job
− Surgery

+ Date with an attractiie person
− Rejection
+ Investment returns
− Loss of capital
Approach-avoidance

conflicts you typically have a reasonably happy ending, whichever way you decide to go. Nonetheless, approach-approach conflicts centering on important issues may sometimes be troublesome. If you are torn between two appealing college majors or two attractive boyfriends, you may find the decision-making process quite stressful.

In an *avoidance-avoidance conflict* **a choice must be made between two unattractive goals.** Forced to choose between two repelling alternatives, you are, as they say, "caught between the devil and the deep blue sea." For example, let's say you have painful backaches. Should you submit to surgery that you dread, or should you continue to live with the pain?

Obviously, avoidance-avoidance conflicts are most unpleasant and very stressful. Typically, people keep delaying their decision as long as possible, hoping they will somehow be able to escape the conflict situation. For example, you might delay surgery in the hope that your backaches will disappear on their own.

In an *approach-avoidance conflict* **a choice must be made about whether to pursue a single goal that has both attractive and unattractive aspects.** For instance, imagine that you're offered a career promotion that will mean a large increase in pay. The catch is that you will have to move to a city that you hate. Approach-avoidance conflicts are very common, and they can be quite stressful. Any time you have to take a risk to pursue some desirable outcome, you are likely to find yourself in an approach-avoidance conflict. Should you risk rejection by asking out that attractive person in class? Should you risk your savings by investing in a new business that could fail?

Approach-avoidance conflicts often produce *vacillation*. That is, we go back and forth, beset by indecision. We decide to go ahead, then we decide not to, then we decide to go ahead again. Humans are not unique in this respect. Many years ago, Neal Miller (1944) observed the same vacillation in his groundbreaking research with rats. Miller created approach-avoidance conflicts in hungry rats by alternately feeding and shocking them at one end of a runway apparatus. Eventually, these rats tended to hover near the center of the runway. They would alternately approach and retreat from the goal box at the end of the alley.

In a series of studies, Miller (1959) plotted out how an organism's tendency to approach a goal (the approach gradient in Figure 3.2a) and to retreat from a goal (the avoidance gradient in Figure 3.2a) increase as the organism nears the goal. He found that avoidance motivation increases more rapidly than approach motivation (as reflected by the avoidance gradient's steeper slope in Figure 3.2a). Based on this principle, Miller concluded that *in trying to resolve an approach-avoidance conflict, we should focus more on decreasing avoidance motivation than on increasing approach motivation.*

Figure 3.2
Approach-avoidance conflict
(a) According to Neal Miller (1959), as you near a goal that has positive and negative features, avoidance motivation tends to rise faster than approach motivation (that's why the avoidance gradient has a steeper slope than the approach gradient), sending you into retreat. However, if you retreat far enough, you'll eventually reach a point where approach motivation is stronger than avoidance motivation, and you may decide to go ahead once again. The ebb and flow of this process leads to vacillation around the point where the two gradients intersect. (b) As the avoidance gradient is lowered, the person comes closer and closer to the goal. If the avoidance gradient can be lowered far enough, the person should be able to resolve the conflict and reach the goal.

How would this insight apply to complex human dilemmas? Imagine you are counseling a friend who is vacillating over whether to ask someone out on a date. Miller would assert that you should attempt to downplay the negative aspects of possible rejection (thus lowering the avoidance gradient) rather than emphasize how much fun the date could be (thus raising the approach gradient). Figure 3.2b shows the effects of lowering the avoidance gradient. If it is lowered far enough, the person should reach the goal (make a decision and take action).

Change

Learning Objective

Summarize evidence on life change as a form of stress.

"After my divorce, I lived alone for four years. Six months ago, I married a wonderful woman who has two children from her previous marriage. My biggest stress is suddenly having to adapt to living with three people instead of by myself. I was pretty set in my ways. I had certain routines. Now everything is chaos. I love my wife and I'm fond of the kids, and they're not really doing anything wrong, but my house and my life just aren't the same and I am having trouble dealing with it all."

There is evidence that life changes may represent a key type of stress. *Life changes are any noticeable alterations in one's living circumstances that require readjustment.* Research on life change began when Thomas Holmes, Richard Rahe, and their colleagues set out to explore the relation between stressful life events and physical illness (Holmes & Rahe, 1967; Rahe & Arthur, 1978). They interviewed thousands of tuberculosis patients to find out what kinds of events preceded the onset of their disease. Surprisingly, the frequently cited events were not uniformly negative. The patients listed plenty of aversive events, as expected, but they also mentioned many seemingly positive events, such as getting married, having a baby, or getting promoted.

Why would positive events, such as moving to a nicer home, produce stress? According to Holmes and Rahe, it is because they produce *change*. Their thesis is that disruptions of our daily routines are stressful. According to their theory, changes in personal relationships, changes at work, changes in finances, and so forth can be stressful even when the changes are welcomed.

Based on this analysis, Holmes and Rahe (1967) developed the Social Readjustment Rating Scale (SRRS) to measure life change as a form of stress. The scale assigns numerical values to 43 major life events that are supposed to reflect the magnitude of the readjustment required by each change (see Figure 3.3). In taking the scale, respondents are asked to indicate how often they experienced any of these 43 events during a certain time period (typically, the past year). The person then adds up the numbers associated with each event checked. This sum is an index of the amount of change-related stress the person has recently experienced.

The SRRS and similar scales have been used in thousands of studies by researchers all over the world. Overall, these studies have shown that people with higher scores on the SRRS tend to be more vulnerable to many kinds of physical illness and many types of psychological problems as well (Creed, 1993; Derogatis & Coons, 1993; Gruen, 1993). These results have attracted a great deal of attention, and the SRRS has been reprinted in many newspapers and popular magazines. The attendant publicity has led to the widespread conclusion that life change is inherently stressful.

More recently, however, experts have criticized this research, citing problems with the methods used (Johnson & Bornstein, 1991; Monroe & McQuaid, 1994; Raphael,

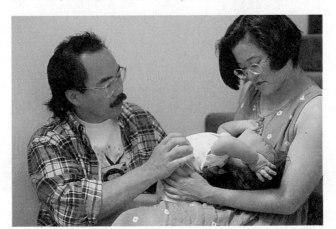

Are major life changes inherently stressful? Empirical evidence suggests that they are not. Although many life changes can be very difficult, stress lies in the eye of the beholder. The transition to parenthood, for example, is stressful for some people but not for others.

Cloitre, & Dohrenwend, 1991) and in interpreting the findings (Brett et al., 1990; Watson & Pennebaker, 1989). At this point, it is a key interpretive issue that concerns us. Many critics have argued that the SRRS does not measure *change* exclusively. The main problem is that the list of life changes on the SRRS is dominated by events that are clearly negative or undesirable (death of a spouse, fired at work, and so on). These negative events probably generate great frustration. Although there are some positive events on the scale, it could be that frustration (generated by negative events), rather than change, creates most of the stress assessed by the scale.

To investigate this possibility, researchers have begun to take into account the desirability and undesirability of subjects' life changes. Subjects are asked to indicate the desirability of the events that they check off on the SRRS and similar scales. The findings in these studies clearly indicate that life change is *not* the crucial dimension measured by the SRRS. Rather, undesirable or negative life events cause most of the stress tapped by the SRRS (Smith, 1993; Turner & Wheaton, 1995).

Should we discard the notion that change is stressful? Not entirely. Other lines of research, independent of work with the SRRS, support the hypothesis that change is an important form of stress. For instance, researchers have found associations between geographic mobility and impaired mental and physical health that presumably reflect the impact of change (Brett, 1980; Shuval, 1993). And research on becoming a parent, which is a highly positive life change for the vast majority of people, shows that the transition to parenthood can be extremely stressful (Miller & Sollie, 1986). A study by Brown and McGill (1989) suggests that desirable life changes may be stressful for some people but not for others. They found a link between positive life changes and increased illness only among subjects low in self-esteem. In contrast, positive events were correlated with improved health among their high self-esteem subjects. Based on these results, Brown and McGill suggest that positive events are stressful to the extent that they disrupt one's sense of identity.

More research is needed, but it is quite plausible that change constitutes a major type of stress in people's lives. However, right now we have little reason to believe that change is *inherently* or *inevitably* stressful. Some life changes may be quite challenging, while others may be quite benign.

Figure 3.3
Social Readjustment Rating Scale (SRRS)
Devised by Holmes and Rahe (1967), this scale measures the change-related stress in one's life. The numbers on the right are supposed to reflect the average amount of stress (readjustment) produced by each event. Respondents check off the events that have occurred to them recently and add up the associated numbers to arrive at their stress scores. See the Application for a detailed critique of the SRRS.

Social Readjustment Rating Scale

Life event	Mean value	Life event	Mean value
Death of a spouse	100	Son or daughter leaving home	29
Divorce	73	Trouble with in-laws	29
Marital separation	65	Outstanding personal achievement	28
Jail term	63	Wife begins or stops work	26
Death of close family member	63	Begin or end school	26
Personal injury or illness	53	Change in living conditions	25
Marriage	50	Revision of personal habits	24
Fired at work	47	Trouble with boss	23
Marital reconciliation	45	Change in work hours or conditions	20
Retirement	45	Change in residence	20
Change in health of family member	44	Change in school	20
Pregnancy	40	Change in recreation	19
Sex difficulties	39	Change in church activities	19
Gain of a new family member	39	Change in social activities	18
Business readjustment	39	Mortgage or loan for lesser purchase (car, TV, etc.)	17
Change in financial state	38	Change in sleeping habits	16
Death of a close friend	37	Change in number of family get-togethers	15
Change to a different line of work	36	Change in eating habits	15
Change in number of arguments with spouse	35	Vacation	13
Mortgage or loan for major purchase (home, etc.)	31	Christmas	12
Foreclosure of mortgage or loan	30	Minor violations of the law	11
Change in responsibilities at work	29		

Pressure

"My father questioned me at dinner about some things I did not want to talk about. I know he doesn't want to hear my answers, at least not the truth. My father told me when I was little that I was his favorite because I was 'pretty near perfect' and I've spent my life trying to keep that up, even though it's obviously not true. Recently, he has begun to realize this and it's made our relationship very strained and painful."

At one time or another, most of us have probably remarked that we were "under pressure." What does this mean? **Pressure involves expectations or demands that one behave in a certain way.** Pressure can be divided into two subtypes: the pressure to *perform* and the pressure to *conform*. You are under pressure to perform when you are expected to execute tasks and responsibilities quickly, efficiently, and successfully. For example, salespeople usually are under pressure to move lots of merchandise. Professors at research institutions are often under pressure to publish in prestigious journals. Comedians are under pressure to be amusing. Secretaries are often under pressure to complete lots of clerical work in very little time. Pressures to conform to others' expectations are also common. Businessmen are expected to wear suits and ties. Suburban homeowners are expected to keep their lawns manicured. Teenagers are expected to adhere to their parents' values and rules. Young adults are expected to be married by the time they're 30.

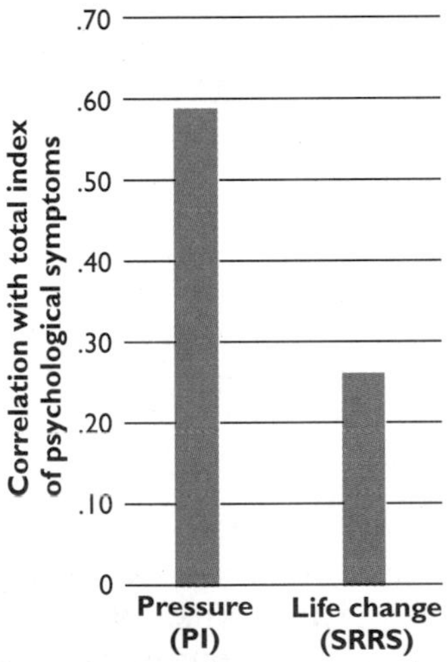

Although widely discussed by the general public, the concept of pressure has received scant attention from researchers. However, Weiten (1988) has devised a scale to measure pressure as a form of life stress. The result is a 48-item self-report measure, called the Pressure Inventory, which is still undergoing development. In the first two studies with this scale, a strong relationship has been found between pressure and a variety of psychological symptoms and problems. In fact, pressure has turned out to be more strongly related to measures of mental health than the SRRS and other established measures of stress (see Figure 3.4). These findings suggest that pressure may be an important form of stress that merits more attention from researchers.

Figure 3.4
Pressure and psychological symptoms
A comparison of pressure and life change as sources of stress suggests that pressure may be more strongly related to mental health than change is. In one study, Weiten (1988) found a correlation of .59 between scores on the Pressure Inventory (PI) and symptoms of psychological distress. In the same sample, the correlation between SRRS scores and psychological symptoms was only .28.

Key Factors in the Appraisal of Stress

We noted earlier that stress lies in the eye of the beholder. Quite a variety of factors influence our subjective appraisals of potentially stressful events. Four that stand out are (1) familiarity with the challenge, (2) the controllability of the events, (3) the predictability of the events, and (4) the imminence of the threat.

Familiarity

Learning Objective

Explain how familiarity and controllability influence one's appraisal of stress.

An important consideration in your appraisal of stress is your familiarity with the stressful demands. Generally, the more unfamiliar you are with a potentially stressful event, the more threatened you are likely to feel (McGrath, 1977). The importance of familiarity was apparent in a study that compared the arousal of novice and experienced parachute jumpers as they prepared for a jump (Fenz & Epstein, 1967). As one might expect, and as Figure 3.5 shows, the novices experienced considerably more arousal during the jump than the experienced parachutists. Given the influence of familiarity, a person's first major job interview, first appearance in

Figure 3.5
Familiarity and physiological arousal

Using heart rate as an index of stress-induced physiological arousal, Fenz and Epstein (1967) compared a group of experienced parachute jumpers against a group of novices as both groups went through a jump. As the graph shows, the two groups started out with similar levels of arousal, but as the time for the jump approached, the novices experienced greater arousal. The lower arousal seen in the experienced jumpers shows how familiarity with a stressful event can sometimes make it less stressful.

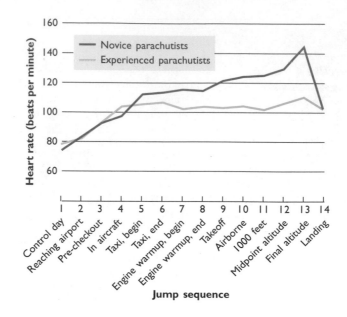

a courtroom, or first purchase of a home tends to be more stressful than subsequent similar events. Familiarity with a challenge can make yesterday's crisis today's routine.

Controllability

Another factor that influences your appraisal of stress is your perception of how much control you can exert over the event in question. For example, if you are facing surgery and a lengthy rehabilitation period, your feelings might range from a sense of powerlessness to a firm belief that you will be able to speed up the recovery process. Stern, McCants, and Pettine (1982) found that when events are viewed as controllable, they tend to be less stressful.

The finding that controllability reduces stress is fairly typical for this line of research, although it is not universal (Thompson & Spacapan, 1991). Jerry Burger (1989) has identified some situations in which greater control is associated with *increased* stress. He points out that when events are controllable, people have to accept greater responsibility for their outcomes. *Hence, people who are particularly concerned about how others will evaluate them often find being in control quite stressful.* Nonetheless, the general trend is for people to view events over which they have more control as less stressful.

Predictability

If you experience a stressful event—for instance, being fired at work—is it more traumatic when it comes out of nowhere (unpredictable stress) or when you can see it coming for some time (predictable stress)? In general, it appears that people prefer predictable stress over surprise packages. When researchers expose subjects to the stress of predictable and unpredictable noise, they usually find that subjects are bothered more by the unpredictable noise (Matthews et al., 1989). Major stressors, such as a serious illness or a job loss, seem to be less devastating when they can be anticipated over a period of time. We may prefer predictability because it allows us to engage in anticipatory coping to prepare for the stress.

However, the effects of predictability are complex. There are situations in which people prefer *not* to know about stress in advance (Burger, 1989). For instance, when understudy actors or rookie athletes are pressed into service as last-minute substitutes for more experienced performers, many comment, "It was better that way. I didn't have time to dwell on it and get nervous." The value of predictability probably depends on whether there's anything you can do to prepare for the stress. If preparation won't help (or if you already feel prepared), knowing about stress in advance may only allow you to dwell on the threatening event, which will usually make it all the more threatening.

Imminence

If you *do* know about a threatening event in advance, your stress usually increases as the event becomes more imminent (closer in time). When a threat lies in the distant future, its stressfulness may be minimal. However, as the challenge looms near, concern and distress typically escalate (Lazarus & Folkman, 1984). Thus, as you approach the day on which you have to take a critical exam, or submit to serious surgery, or speak at a convention, you generally will find the stress increasing (Bolger, 1990). In fact, your stress may peak during the period of anticipation, rather than with the event itself (see Figure 3.6). For example, after a big exam, students often remark, "Taking it wasn't nearly as bad as anticipating it and worrying about it."

In summary, the appraisal of stress is a complicated process. Factors such as controllability and predictability have varied effects on a person's appraisal of stress, depending on the exact circumstances. However, research on this process is important because stress appraisals make all the difference in the world to how people respond to stress, which is our next topic.

Responding to Stress

The human response to stress is complex and multidimensional. Stress affects people at several levels. Consider again the chapter's opening scenario, in which you're driving home in heavy traffic, thinking about overdue papers, tuition increases, and parental pressures. Let's look at some of the reactions we mentioned. When you groan audibly in reaction to the traffic report, you're experiencing an *emotional response* to stress—in this case, annoyance and anger. When your pulse quickens and your stomach knots up, you're exhibiting *physiological responses* to stress. When you shout insults at another driver, your verbal aggression is a *behavioral response* to the stress. Thus, we can analyze reactions to stress at three levels: (1) emotional responses, (2) physiological responses, and (3) behavioral responses. Figure 3.7 depicts these three levels of response.

Figure 3.6
Imminence as a factor in appraisals of stress
In a study of personality and coping styles, Bolger (1990) tracked daily levels of anxiety in 50 premedical students for 35 days surrounding the administration of the highly stressful Medical College Admissions Test (MCAT). As you can see, anxiety increased steadily as the stressful event became more imminent, and it peaked just prior to the event rather than during the event itself. (Based on Bolger, 1990)

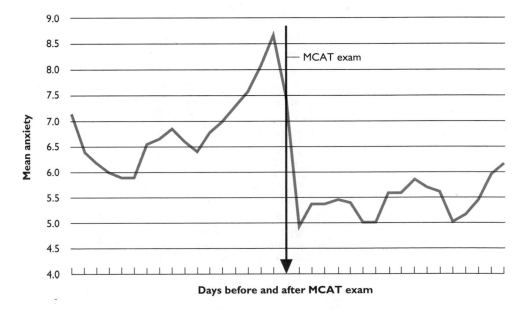

Days before and after MCAT exam

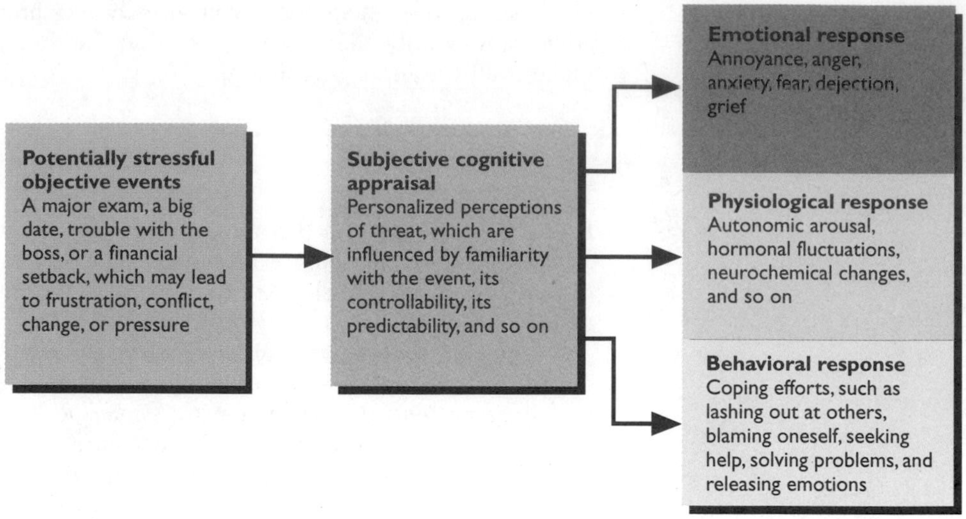

Figure 3.7
The multidimensional response to stress
A potentially stressful event, such as a major exam, will elicit a subjective, cognitive appraisal of how threatening the event is. If the event is viewed with alarm, the stress may trigger emotional, physiological, and behavioral reactions.

Potentially stressful objective events
A major exam, a big date, trouble with the boss, or a financial setback, which may lead to frustration, conflict, change, or pressure

Subjective cognitive appraisal
Personalized perceptions of threat, which are influenced by familiarity with the event, its controllability, its predictability, and so on

Emotional response
Annoyance, anger, anxiety, fear, dejection, grief

Physiological response
Autonomic arousal, hormonal fluctuations, neurochemical changes, and so on

Behavioral response
Coping efforts, such as lashing out at others, blaming oneself, seeking help, solving problems, and releasing emotions

Emotional Responses

Emotion is an elusive concept. Psychologists debate about how to define emotion, and they offer many conflicting theories that purport to explain emotion. However, everybody has extensive personal experience with and knowledge of emotions. Everyone has a good idea of what it means to be anxious, elated, gloomy, jealous, disgusted, excited, guilty, or nervous. Rather than pursue the technical debates about emotion, we'll rely on your familiarity with the concept and simply note that *emotions* **are powerful, largely uncontrollable feelings, accompanied by physiological changes.** When people are under stress, they often react emotionally. More often than not, stress tends to elicit unpleasant emotions rather than pleasurable feelings (Lazarus, 1993).

The link between stress and emotion was apparent in a study of 96 women who filled out diaries about the stresses and moods they experienced over a 28-day period (Caspi, Bolger, & Eckenrode, 1987). The investigators found that daily fluctuations in stress correlated with daily fluctuations in mood. As stress increased, mood tended to become more negative. As the researchers put it, "Some days everything seems to go wrong, and by day's end, minor difficulties find their outlet in rotten moods" (p. 184). Other studies that have tracked daily stress and mood fluctuations have also found strong relations between the two (Affleck et al., 1994; Repetti, 1993).

Emotions Commonly Elicited

Learning Objective

List three dimensions of emotion commonly elicited by stress.

Although there are no simple one-to-one connections between certain types of stressful events and particular emotions, researchers *have* begun to uncover some strong links between specific *cognitive reactions to stress (appraisals)* and specific emotions (Smith & Lazarus, 1993). For example, self-blame tends to lead to guilt, helplessness to sadness, and so forth. Although many emotions can be evoked by stressful events, some are certainly more likely than others. Common emotional responses to stress include the following (Lazarus, 1993; Woolfolk & Richardson, 1978):

- *Annoyance, anger, and rage.* Stress can produce feelings of anger ranging in intensity from mild annoyance to uncontrollable rage. Frustration is particularly likely to generate anger.
- *Apprehension, anxiety, and fear.* Stress probably evokes anxiety and fear more frequently than any other emotions. As we saw in Chapter 2, Freudian theory has long recognized the link between conflict and anxiety. However, anxiety can also be created by the pressure to perform, the threat of impending frustration, or the uncertainty associated with change.
- *Dejection, sadness, and grief.* Sometimes stress—especially frustration—simply brings you down. Routine setbacks, such as traffic tickets and poor grades, often pro-

duce feelings of dejection. More profound setbacks, such as deaths and divorces, typically leave one grief-stricken.

Of course, this list is not exhaustive. In his insightful analyses of stress-emotion relations, Richard Lazarus (1991, 1993) mentions five other emotions that often figure prominently in reactions to stress: guilt, shame, envy, jealousy, and disgust.

Effects of Emotional Arousal

Learning Objective

Discuss the effects of emotional arousal on coping efforts, and describe the inverted-U hypothesis.

Emotional responses are a natural and normal part of life. Even unpleasant emotions fill important functions. Like physical pain, painful emotions can serve as warnings that one needs to take action. However, strong emotional arousal *can* sometimes interfere with efforts to cope with stress. For example, there's evidence that high emotional arousal can interfere with attention and memory retrieval and can impair judgment and decision making (Janis, 1993; Mandler, 1993).

The well-known problem of *test anxiety* illustrates how emotional arousal can hurt performance. Often students who score poorly on an exam will nonetheless insist that they know the material. Many of them are probably telling the truth. A number of researchers have found a negative correlation between test-related anxiety and exam performance. That is, students who display high test anxiety tend to score low on exams (Hembre, 1988). Test anxiety can interfere with test taking in several ways, but the critical consideration appears to be the disruption of attention to the test (Sarason, 1984). Many test-anxious students waste too much time worrying about how they're doing and wondering whether others are having similar problems. In other words, their minds wander too much from the task of taking the test.

Although emotional arousal may hurt coping efforts, this isn't *necessarily* the case. The *inverted-U hypothesis* predicts that task performance should improve with increased emotional arousal—up to a point, after which further increases in arousal become disruptive and performance deteriorates (Anderson, 1990; Mandler, 1993). This idea is referred to as the inverted-U hypothesis because when performance is plotted as a function of arousal, the resulting graphs approximate an upside-down U (see Figure 3.8). In these graphs, the level of arousal at which performance peaks is characterized as the *optimal level of arousal* for a task.

This optimal level of arousal appears to depend in part on the complexity of the task at hand. The conventional wisdom is that *as a task becomes more complex, the optimal level of arousal (for peak performance) tends to decrease.* This relationship is depicted in Figure 3.8. As you can see, a fairly high level of arousal should be optimal on simple tasks (such as driving eight hours to help a friend in a crisis). However, performance should peak at a lower level of arousal on complex tasks (such as making a major decision in which you have to weigh many factors).

The research evidence on the inverted-U hypothesis is inconsistent and subject to varied interpretations (Neiss, 1988, 1990). Hence, it may be risky to generalize this principle to the complexities of everyday coping efforts. Nonetheless, the

Figure 3.8
Arousal and performance
Graphs of the relationship between emotional arousal and task performance tend to resemble an inverted U, as increased arousal is associated with improved performance up to a point, after which higher arousal leads to poorer performance. The optimal level of arousal for a task depends on the complexity of the task. On complex tasks, a relatively low level of arousal tends to be optimal. On simple tasks, however, performance may peak at a much higher level of arousal.

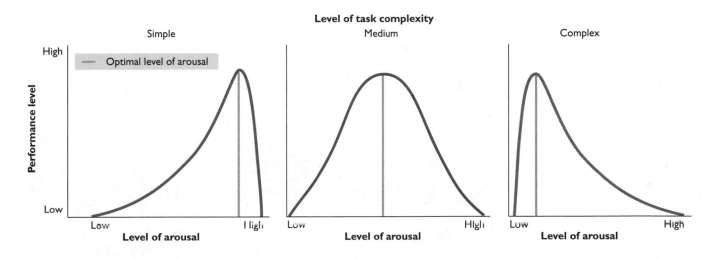

inverted-U hypothesis provides a plausible model of how emotional arousal could have either beneficial or disruptive effects on coping, depending on the nature of the stressful demands.

Physiological Responses

As we have seen, stress frequently elicits strong emotional responses. These emotional responses bring about important physiological changes. Even in cases of moderate stress, you may notice that your heart has started beating faster, you have begun to breathe harder, and you are perspiring more than usual. How does all this (and much more) happen? Let's see.

The "Fight-or-Flight" Response

The *fight-or-flight response* is a physiological reaction to threat that mobilizes an organism for attacking (fight) or fleeing (flight) an enemy. First described by Walter Cannon (1932), the fight-or-flight response occurs in the body's autonomic nervous system. **The *autonomic nervous system (ANS)* is made up of the nerves that connect to the heart, blood vessels, smooth muscles, and glands.** As its name hints, the autonomic nervous system is somewhat *autonomous*. That is, it controls involuntary, visceral functions that we don't normally think about, such as heart rate, digestion, and perspiration.

The autonomic nervous system can be broken into two divisions (see Figure 3.9). The *parasympathetic division* of the ANS generally conserves bodily resources. For instance, it slows heart rate and promotes digestion to help the body save and store energy. The fight-or-flight response is mediated by the *sympathetic division* of the ANS, which mobilizes bodily resources for emergencies. In one experiment, Cannon studied the fight-or-flight response in cats by confronting them with dogs. Among other things, he noticed an immediate acceleration in breathing and heart rate and a reduction in digestive processes.

Elements of the fight-or-flight response are also seen in humans. Imagine your reaction if your car were to nearly spin out of control on the highway. Your heart would race, and your blood pressure would surge. You might get "goose bumps" and experience a "knot in your stomach." These reflex responses are part of the fight-or-flight response.

In a sense, this automatic reaction is a leftover from our evolutionary past. It is clearly an adaptive response in the animal kingdom, where the threat of predators often requires a swift response of fighting or fleeing. But among humans, the fight-or-flight response appears less adaptive. Most of our stresses cannot be han-

Figure 3.9
The autonomic nervous system (ANS)
The ANS is composed of the nerves that connect to the heart, blood vessels, smooth muscles, and glands. The ANS is subdivided into the *sympathetic division*, which mobilizes bodily resources in times of need, and the *parasympathetic division*, which conserves bodily resources. Some of the key functions controlled by each division of the ANS are summarized in the center of the diagram.

Sympathetic		Parasympathetic
Pupils dilated; dry; far vision	**Eyes**	Pupils constricted; moist; near vision
Goose bumps	**Skin**	No goose bumps
Dry	**Mouth**	Salivating
Sweaty	**Palms**	Dry
Passages dilated	**Lungs**	Passages constrictee
Increased rate	**Heart**	Decreased rate
Supply maximum to muscles	**Blood**	Supply maximum to internal organs
Increased activity	**Adrenal glands**	Decreased activity
Inhibited	**Digestion**	Stimulated
Climax	**Sexual functions**	Arousal

dled simply through fight or flight. Work pressures, marital problems, and financial difficulties require far more complex responses. Moreover, our stresses often continue for lengthy periods of time, so that our fight-or-flight response leaves us in a state of enduring physiological arousal. Concern about the effects of prolonged physical arousal was first voiced by Hans Selye, a Canadian scientist who conducted extensive research on stress.

The General Adaptation Syndrome

Learning Objective

Describe the three stages of the general adaptation syndrome.

Hans Selye

The concept of stress was added to our language by Hans Selye (1936, 1956, 1982). Selye was born in Vienna but spent his entire professional career at McGill University in Montreal. Beginning in the 1930s, Selye exposed laboratory animals to a diverse array of both physical and psychological stressors (heat, cold, pain, mild shock, restraint, and so on). The patterns of physiological arousal seen in the animals were largely the same, regardless of the type of stress. Thus, Selye concluded that stress reactions are *nonspecific*. In other words, he maintained that they do not vary according to the specific type of stress encountered. Initially, Selye wasn't sure what to call this nonspecific response to a variety of noxious agents. In the 1940s, he decided to call it *stress,* and the word has been part of our vocabulary ever since.

Selye (1956, 1974) formulated an influential theory of stress reactions called the general adaptation syndrome. **The *general adaptation syndrome* is a model of the body's stress response, consisting of three stages: alarm, resistance, and exhaustion.** In the first stage of the general adaptation syndrome, an *alarm reaction* occurs when an organism recognizes the existence of a threat. Physiological arousal increases as the body musters its resources to combat the challenge. Selye's alarm reaction is essentially the fight-or-flight response originally described by Cannon.

However, Selye took his investigation of stress a couple of steps further by exposing laboratory animals to *prolonged* stress, similar to the chronic stress often endured by humans. If stress continues, the organism may progress to the second phase of the general adaptation syndrome, called the *stage of resistance.* During this phase, physiological changes stabilize as coping efforts get under way. Typically, physiological arousal continues to be higher than normal, although it may level off somewhat as the organism becomes accustomed to the threat.

If the stress continues over a substantial period of time, the organism may enter the third stage, called the *stage of exhaustion.* According to Selye, the body's resources for fighting stress are limited. If the stress cannot be overcome, the body's resources may be depleted, and physiological arousal will decrease. Eventually, the organism may collapse from exhaustion. During this phase, resistance declines, potentially leading to what Selye called "diseases of adaptation," such as ulcers or high blood pressure.

Selye's theory and research forged a link between stress and physical illness. He showed how prolonged physiological arousal that is meant to be adaptive could lead to diseases. His theory has been criticized because it ignores individual differences in the appraisal of stress (Lazarus & Folkman, 1984), and his belief that stress reactions are nonspecific remains controversial (Baum, 1990; Hobfoll, 1989), but his model provided guidance for a generation of researchers who worked out the details of how stress reverberates throughout the body. Let's look at some of those details.

Brain-Body Pathways

Learning Objective

Describe the two major pathways along which the brain sends signals to the endocrine system in response to stress.

When a person experiences stress, the brain sends signals to the endocrine system along two major pathways (Asterita, 1985; Koranyi, 1989). **The *endocrine system* consists of glands that secrete chemicals called hormones into the bloodstream.** The major endocrine glands, such as the pituitary, pineal, thyroid, and adrenal glands, are shown in Figure 3.10.

The hypothalamus, a small structure near the base of the brain, appears to initiate action along both of the pathways. The first pathway (shown on the right in Figure 3.11) is routed through the autonomic nervous system. The hypothalamus activates the sympathetic division of the ANS. A key part of this activation involves stimulating the central part of each adrenal gland (the adrenal medulla) to

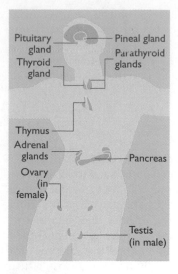

Figure 3.10
The endocrine system
The endocrine glands secrete hormones into the bloodstream. The locations of the principal endocrine glands are shown here. The hormones released by these glands regulate a variety of physical functions and play a key role in people's response to stress.

release large amounts of *catecholamines* into the bloodstream. These hormones radiate throughout the body, producing many important physiological changes. The net result of catecholamine elevation is that the body is mobilized for action. Heart rate and blood flow increase, pumping more blood to the brain and muscles. Respiration and oxygen consumption speed up, facilitating alertness. Digestive processes are inhibited to conserve energy. The pupils of the eyes dilate, increasing visual sensitivity.

The second pathway (shown on the left in Figure 3.11) involves more direct communication between the brain and the endocrine system. The hypothalamus sends signals to the so-called master gland of the endocrine system, the pituitary gland. The pituitary in turn secretes a hormone (ACTH) that stimulates the outer part of each adrenal gland (the adrenal cortex) to release another important set of hormones—*corticosteroids*. These hormones stimulate the release of more fats and proteins into circulation, thus helping to increase the body's energy. They also mobilize chemicals that help inhibit tissue inflammation in case of injury.

Stress can also produce other physiological changes that we are just beginning to understand. The most critical changes occur in the immune system. The immune system provides the body with resistance to infections. However, mounting evidence indicates that stress can suppress the functioning of the immune system, making it less effective in repelling invasions by infectious agents (Stein & Miller, 1993; Stone et al., 1994). The exact mechanism underlying immunal suppression remains a mystery for the moment, although it may be mediated by the release of *endorphins*, internally produced chemicals that resemble opiate drugs (such as morphine) in structure and effects (Meyerhoff, Oleshansky, & Mougey, 1988). In any case, it is becoming clear that physiological responses to stress extend into every corner of the body. Moreover, some of these responses may persist long after a stressful event has ended (Esterling et al., 1994). As you will see, these physiological reactions can have an impact on both mental and physical health.

Behavioral Responses

Learning Objective

Describe the nature of behavioral responses to stress.

Although people respond to stress at several levels, behavior is the crucial dimension of these reactions. Emotional and physiological responses to stress—which are often undesirable—tend to be largely automatic. However, dealing effectively with

Figure 3.11
Brain-body pathways in stress
In times of stress, the brain sends signals along two pathways. The pathway through the autonomic nervous system (shown in blue boxes on the right) controls the release of catecholamine hormones that help mobilize the body for action. The pathway through the pituitary gland and the endocrine system (yellow boxes on the left) controls the release of corticosteroid hormones that increase energy and ward off tissue inflammation.

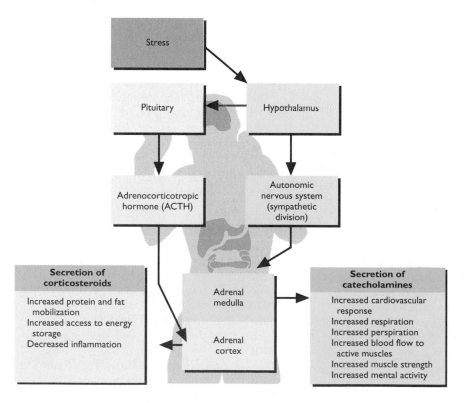

stress at the behavioral level can shut down these potentially harmful emotional and physiological responses.

Most behavioral responses to stress involve coping. *Coping* **refers to active efforts to master, reduce, or tolerate the demands created by stress.** Notice that this definition is neutral as to whether coping efforts are healthful or maladaptive. The popular use of the term often implies that coping is inherently positive. When we say that someone "coped with her problems," we imply that she handled them effectively.

In reality, coping responses may be either healthful or unhealthful (Moos & Schaefer, 1993). For example, if you were flunking a history course at midterm, you might cope with this stress by (1) increasing your study efforts, (2) seeking special help from a tutor, (3) blaming your professor for your poor grade, or (4) giving up on the class without really trying. Clearly, the first two coping responses would be more healthful than the second two.

People cope with stress in an endless variety of ways. Because of the complexity and importance of coping processes, we'll devote all of the next chapter to ways of coping. At this point, it is sufficient to note that our coping strategies help determine whether stress has any positive or negative effects on us. In the next section, we'll see what some of those effects can be as we discuss the possible outcomes of people's struggles with stress.

The Potential Effects of Stress

Individuals struggle with many stresses every day, most of which come and go without leaving any enduring imprint. However, when stress is severe or when demands pile up, stress may have lasting effects. These effects are often called "adaptational outcomes." They are relatively durable (though not necessarily permanent) consequences of exposure to stress. Although stress can have beneficial effects, research has focused mainly on possible negative outcomes (Cohen, 1988), so you'll find our coverage slanted in that direction.

Recommended Reading

Comprehensive Stress Management

by Jerrold S. Greenberg (William C. Brown, 1990, 1992)

This practical book serves as a textbook in many of the courses on stress that are popping up in colleges and universities. Although its principal focus is on stress *management*, which we cover in the next chapter, it contains more information on the nature and causes of stress than any comparable book. Written in a highly personable manner, it is also well illustrated.

In the first part of the book, Greenberg elaborates on the concept of stress, describes how stress affects physiological functioning, and discusses the connection between stress and a host of physical diseases. The final part includes unusual chapters on stress in specific populations: occupational stress, college stress, family stress, stress linked to sex roles, and stress among the elderly. Between the first and final parts of the book, Greenberg provides ten chapters on approaches to stress management, including meditation, biofeedback, relaxation techniques, and ways to change appraisals of stress.

> Women experience stressors . . . that are based [on] sex-role stereotyping. Their work in the home is not valued, they earn less than they should earn when working outside the home, or they are expected to be "superwomen," that is, excellent lovers, wives, mothers, and employees. However, men, too, experience stress as a result of sex-role stereotyping. Do you think it's easy being ashamed to show fear? Men are supposed to be strong, and many consider fear a sign of weakness. Don't you think it stressful to have the responsibility of being the "breadwinner"? [1990, p. 321]

Impaired Task Performance

Stress often takes its toll on one's ability to perform effectively on the task at hand. For instance, Roy Baumeister's work shows how pressure can interfere with performance. Baumeister's (1984) theory assumes that pressure to perform often makes people self-conscious and that this elevated self-consciousness disrupts their attention. He theorizes that attention may be distorted in two ways. First, elevated self-consciousness may divert attention from the demands of the task, creating distractions. Second, on well-learned tasks that should be executed almost automatically, the self-conscious person may focus *too much* attention on the task. Thus, the person thinks too much about what he or she is doing.

Baumeister (1984) found support for his theory in a series of laboratory experiments in which he manipulated the pressure to do well on a simple perceptual-motor task. Even more impressive, his theory was supported in a study of the past performance of professional sports teams in championship contests (Baumeister & Steinhilber, 1984). According to Baumeister, when a championship series such as baseball's World Series goes to the final, decisive game, the home team is under greater pressure than the visiting team. Why? Because players desperately want to succeed in front of their hometown fans. As a result, they experience elevated self-consciousness. Conventional wisdom suggests that home teams have the advantage in sports. But Baumeister argues that the performance of the home team declines when pressure mounts in the final game of a championship series.

To test this hypothesis, Baumeister and Steinhilber (1984) analyzed past championships in professional baseball and basketball. These sports settle their championships with a series of games. Thus, the performance of the home teams in early games can be compared against their performance in the final game. As hypothesized, Baumeister and Steinhilber found that the winning percentage for home teams was significantly lower in final games than in early games in both sports (see Figure 3.12). Furthermore, statistics showed that the home team in baseball made more fielding errors in game 7 than in early games. In basketball, the home team's free-throw shooting percentage went down in the last game. The most obvious explanation for these findings is that the home team "chokes under pressure," as predicted by Baumeister's theory. Thus, stress can impair task performance—even in gifted professional athletes.

Olympic athletes like pole vaulter Sergei Bubka, left, are under intense pressure to succeed. High-pressure situations can produce heightened self-consciousness and impaired performance—what has been described as "choking under pressure."

Figure 3.12
Choking under pressure
In early World Series and NBA championship contests that involve less pressure, the home team enjoys an advantage. But when it comes to the last game, the home team frequently chokes under pressure, as evidenced by the decreased winning percentages shown here. (Data from Baumeister & Steinhilber, 1984)

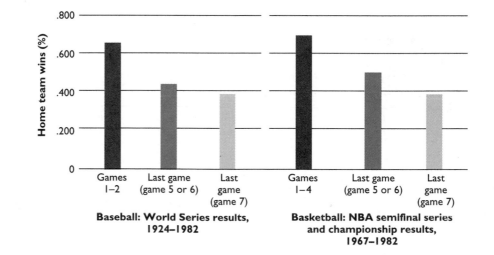

Disruption of Cognitive Functioning

An interesting experimental study suggests that Baumeister is on the right track in looking to *attention* to explain how stress impairs task performance. In a study of stress and decision making, Keinan (1987) was able to measure three specific aspects of subjects' attention under stressful and nonstressful conditions. The researcher placed subjects under stress by telling them that they might receive painful but harmless electric shocks while working on a decision-making task at a computer. No one was actually shocked, and subjects were given the option of quitting the study when they were told about the shock. Keinan found that stress disrupted two out of the three aspects of attention measured in the study. Stress increased subjects' tendency (1) to jump to a conclusion too quickly without considering all their options and (2) to do an unsystematic, poorly organized review of their available options.

Severe stress may leave people dazed and confused, in a state of shock (Weisaeth, 1993). In these states, people report feeling emotionally numb, and they respond in a flat, apathetic fashion to events around them. They often stare off into space and have difficulty maintaining a coherent train of thought. Their behavior often has an automatic, rigid, stereotyped quality. Fortunately, this disorientation usually occurs only in extreme situations involving overwhelming stress. For instance, you will sometimes see shock among people who have just been through a major disaster, such as a fire, flood, or tornado.

Burnout

Learning Objective

Describe burnout and posttraumatic stress disorders.

Burnout is an overused buzzword that means different things to different people. Nonetheless, Ayala Pines and her colleagues have described burnout in a systematic way that has facilitated scientific study of the syndrome (Pines, 1993; Pines & Aronson, 1988). **Burnout involves physical, mental, and emotional exhaustion that is attributable to work-related stress.** The physical exhaustion includes chronic fatigue, weakness, and low energy. The mental exhaustion is manifested in highly negative attitudes toward oneself, one's work, and life in general. The emotional exhaustion includes feeling hopeless, helpless, and trapped.

What causes burnout? According to Pines and her colleagues (1981), "it usually does not occur as the result of one or two traumatic events but sneaks up through a general erosion of the spirit" (p. 3). They view burnout as an emotional disturbance brought on gradually by heavy, chronic, job-related stress.

Initially, theorists thought that burnout was unique to the helping professions, such as social work, clinical psychology, and counseling. The high burnout rate in the helping professions was blamed on helpers' emotionally draining relations with their clients. However, it has gradually become clear that burnout is a potential problem in all occupations (Maslach, 1982). Indeed, work stress may not be the only cause of burnout. It's possible that chronic stress from other roles, such as parenting or being a student, may lead to burnout.

CATHY copyright Cathy Guisewite. Reprinted with permission of UNIVERSAL PRESS SYNDICATE. All rights reserved.

Delayed Effects: Posttraumatic Stress Disorders

The effects of stress are not necessarily apparent right away. A time lag may occur between the occurrence of stress and the appearance of its effects. **The *posttraumatic stress disorder* (PTSD) involves disturbed behavior that emerges sometime after a major stressful event is over.** Post-traumatic stress disorders have mostly been seen in veterans of the Vietnam War. Among Vietnam veterans, posttraumatic disorders typically began to surface anywhere from 9 to 60 months after the soldier's discharge from military service. There were, of course, immediate stress reactions among the soldiers as well—but these were expected. The delayed reactions were something of a surprise, and they continue to be a problem for many former soldiers today. Studies suggest that nearly half a million Vietnam veterans still suffer from PTSD (Schlenger et al., 1992).

Experiencing the horrors of natural disasters can sometimes lead to posttraumatic stress disorder.

Although posttraumatic stress disorders are most widely associated with Vietnam veterans, they have been seen in response to other cases of severe stress as well. A study of mental health by Helzer, Robins, and McEvoy (1987) suggests that posttraumatic stress disorders have been experienced by roughly 5 out of every 1000 men and 13 out of every 1000 women in the general population.

What types of stress besides combat are severe enough to produce PTSD? Among women, the most common cause found by Helzer and his colleagues was a physical attack, such as a rape. Other causes among women included seeing someone die (or seeing someone seriously hurt), close brushes with death, serious accidents, and discovering a spouse's affair. Among men, all the posttraumatic disorders were due to combat experiences or to seeing someone die. Studies indicate that PTSD is also somewhat common in the wake of major disasters, such as floods, hurricanes, earthquakes, fires, and so forth (Green, 1991; Koopman, Classen, & Spiegel, 1994).

What are the symptoms of PTSD? Common symptoms seen in combat veterans have included nightmares, paranoia, emotional numbing, guilt about surviving, alienation, and problems in social relations (A. Blank, 1982). In the more diverse collection of cases identified by Helzer et al. (1987), the most common symptoms were nightmares, difficulties in sleeping, and feelings of jumpiness. PTSD is also associated with an elevated risk for substance abuse, depression, and suicide attempts (Warshaw et al., 1993).

Psychological Problems and Disorders

Learning Objective

Discuss the potential impact of stress on mental and physical health.

Posttraumatic stress disorders are caused by a single episode of extreme stress. Of greater relevance to most of us are the effects of chronic, prolonged, everyday stress. On the basis of clinical impressions, psychologists have long suspected that chronic stress might contribute to many types of psychological problems and mental disorders. Since the late 1960s, advances in the measurement of stress have allowed researchers to verify these suspicions in empirical studies. When it comes to common psychological problems, studies indicate that stress may contribute to poor academic performance (Lloyd et al., 1980), insomnia (Hartmann, 1985), nightmares (Cernovsky, 1989), sexual difficulties (Malatesta & Adams, 1984), alcohol abuse (Jennison, 1992), drug abuse (Lester, Nebel, & Baum, 1994), and unhappiness (Heady & Wearing, 1989). Above and beyond these everyday problems, research reveals that stress often contributes to the onset of full-fledged psychological disorders, including depression (Gruen, 1993), schizophrenia (Spring, 1989), anxiety disorders (Lester et al., 1994; McKeon, Roa, & Mann, 1989), and eating disorders (Strober, 1989).

We'll discuss these relations between stress and mental disorders in detail in Chapter 15. Of course, stress is only one of many factors that may contribute to psychological disorders. Nonetheless, it is sobering to realize that stress can have a dramatic impact on people's mental health.

Physical Illness

It is just as sobering to realize that stress can have a dramatic impact on physical health. The idea that stress can contribute to physical diseases is not entirely new. Evidence that stress can cause physical illness began to accumulate back in the 1930s. By the 1950s, the concept of psychosomatic disease was widely accepted. *Psychosomatic diseases* **are genuine physical ailments caused in part by psychological factors, especially emotional distress.** The underlying assumption is that stress-induced autonomic arousal contributes to most psychosomatic diseases. Please note that these diseases are not *imagined* physical ailments. The term *psychosomatic* is often misused to refer to ailments that are "all in the head." This is an entirely different syndrome, which we'll discuss in Chapter 15.

Common psychosomatic diseases include high blood pressure, ulcers, asthma, skin disorders such as eczema and hives, and migraine and tension headaches (Kaplan, 1989). These diseases do not *necessarily* have a strong psychological component in every affected individual. There is a genetic predisposition to most psychosomatic diseases, and in some people these diseases are largely physiological in origin (Weiner & Fawzy, 1989). More often than not, however, psychological factors contribute to psychosomatic diseases. When they do, stress is one of the chief culprits at work (Creed, 1993).

Prior to the 1970s, it was thought that stress contributed to the development of only a few physical diseases (the psychosomatic diseases). In the 1970s, however, researchers began to uncover new links between stress and a great variety of diseases previously believed to be purely physiological in origin. Although there is room for debate on some specific diseases, stress may influence the onset and course of heart disease, stroke, tuberculosis, multiple sclerosis, arthritis, diabetes, leukemia, cancer, various types of infectious diseases, and the common cold (Elliott, 1989; Elliott & Eisdorfer, 1982; Miller, 1983). We'll take a more detailed look at the evidence linking stress to some of these diseases in Chapter 14.

Beneficial Effects

Learning Objective

Discuss three ways in which stress might have beneficial effects.

The beneficial effects of stress are more difficult to pinpoint than the harmful effects because they tend to be more subtle. Although research data are sparse, there are at least three ways in which stress can have positive effects.

First, stressful events help to satisfy our need for stimulation and challenge. Studies suggest that most people prefer an intermediate level of stimulation and challenge in their lives (Suedfeld, 1979). Although we think of stress in terms of stimulus overload, underload can be extremely unpleasant as well (Goldberger, 1993). Thus, most people would experience a suffocating level of boredom if they lived a stress-free existence. In a sense, then, stress fulfills a basic need of the human organism.

Second, stress can promote personal growth or self-improvement (Holahan & Moos, 1990). Stressful events sometimes force people to develop new skills, learn new insights, and acquire new strengths. In other words, the adaptation process initiated by stress may lead to personal changes that are for the better. Confronting and conquering a stressful challenge may lead to improvements in specific coping abilities and to an enhanced self-concept (Schaefer & Moos, 1992). For example, a breakup with a boyfriend or a girlfriend often leads individuals to change aspects of their behavior that they find unsatisfactory. Moreover, even if people do not conquer stressors, they may be able to learn from their mistakes. Recognizing these opportunities, Crystal Park and colleagues (1994) have recently developed a systematic measure of *stress-related growth* and begun to explore its determinants.

Third, today's stress can inoculate people so that they are less affected by tomorrow's stress. Some studies suggest that exposure to stress can increase stress tolerance—as long as the stress isn't overwhelming (Meichenbaum, 1993). Thus, a woman who has previously endured business setbacks may be much better prepared than most people to deal with a bank foreclosure on her home. In light of the negative effects that stress can have, improved stress tolerance is a desirable goal. We'll look next at the factors that influence people's ability to tolerate stress.

Factors Influencing Stress Tolerance

Some people seem to be able to better withstand the ravages of stress than others can (Holahan & Moos, 1990, 1994). Why? Because a number of *moderator variables* can reduce the impact of stress on physical and mental health. To shed light on differences in how well people tolerate stress, we'll look at five key moderator variables: social support, hardiness, optimism, sensation seeking, and autonomic reactivity. As you'll see, these factors influence people's appraisals of potentially stressful events and their emotional, physical, and behavioral responses to stress. These complexities are diagrammed in Figure 3.13, which builds on Figure 3.7 to provide a more complete overview of all the factors involved in people's reactions to stress.

Social Support

Learning Objective

Discuss how social support and hardiness influence stress tolerance.

Friends may be good for your health! This startling conclusion emerges from studies on social support as a moderator of stress. **Social support refers to various types of aid and succor provided by members of one's social networks.** In one study, Jemmott and Magloire (1988) examined the effect of social support on immunal functioning in a group of students going through the stress of final exams. They found that students who reported stronger social support had higher levels of an antibody that plays a key role in warding off respiratory infections. Positive correlations between high social support and greater immunal functioning were also seen in a study that focused on spouses of cancer patients (Baron et al., 1990).

Many studies have found evidence that social support is favorably related to physical health (Cohen, 1988; Vogt et al., 1992). Indeed, in a major review of the relevant research, House, Landis, and Umberson (1988) argue that the evidence linking social support to health is roughly as strong as the evidence linking smoking to cancer. Social support seems to be good medicine for the mind as well as the body, as most studies find an association between social support and mental health (Leavy, 1983; Sarason, Pierce, & Sarason, 1994). The mechanisms underlying the connection between social support and wellness are the subject of considerable debate (Hobfoll & Vaux, 1993). It appears that social support serves as a protective buffer for individuals during times of high stress, reducing the negative impact of stressful events. Furthermore, social support has its own positive effects on health, which may be apparent even when one isn't under great stress (Cohen & Syme, 1985).

The power of social support is such that even pets may provide social bonds that buffer the effects of stress. For instance, Siegel (1990) found that elderly pet owners required less medical care than comparable subjects who did not own pets. In another study, women exposed to brief stress showed less physiological reaction when in the company of their pets (Allen et al., 1991).

Of course, social *bonds* are not equivalent to social *support* (Rook, 1990). Indeed, some people in one's social circles may be a source of more *stress* than *support* (Lepore, 1992; Vinokur & van Ryn, 1993). Friends and family can put one under pressure, make one feel guilty, break promises, and so forth. Pagel, Erdly, and Becker (1987) looked at both the good and the bad sides of social relations in measuring subjects' satisfaction with their social networks. They found that the helpfulness of friends and family wasn't as important as whether friends and family caused emotional distress. Adapting a line from an old Beatles song, the investigators concluded

Figure 3.13
Overview of the stress process
This diagram builds on Figure 3.7 (the multidimensional response to stress) to provide a more complete overview of the factors involved in stress. This diagram adds the potential effects of stress (seen on the far right) by listing some of the positive and negative adaptational outcomes. It also completes the picture by showing that moderating variables (seen at the top) can intervene to influence the effects of stress.

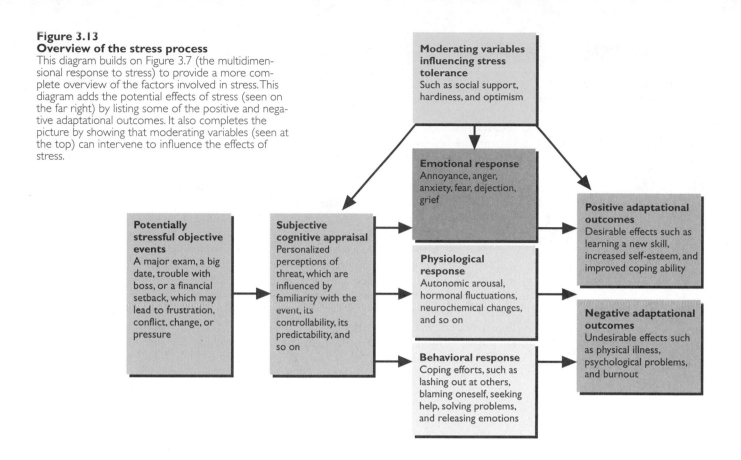

that "We get by with (*and in spite of*) a little help from our friends." To some extent, then, people who report good social support may really mean that their friends and family aren't driving them crazy.

Hardiness

Suzanne Ouellette
(formerly Kobasa)

Another line of research indicates that certain personality traits may moderate the impact of stressful events. Suzanne Ouellette (formerly Kobasa) reasoned that if stress affects some people less than others, then some people must be *hardier* than others. She set out to determine whether personality factors might be the key to these differences in hardiness.

Kobasa (1979) used a modified version of the Holmes and Rahe (1967) stress scale (SRRS) to measure the amount of stress experienced by a group of executives. As in most other studies, she found a modest correlation between stress and the incidence of physical illness. However, she carried her investigation one step further than previous studies. She compared the high-stress executives who exhibited the expected high incidence of illness against the high-stress executives who stayed healthy. She administered a battery of psychological tests, comparing the executives along 18 dimensions of personality. She found that the hardier executives "were more committed, felt more in control, and had bigger appetites for challenge" (Kobasa, 1984, p. 70). These traits have also shown up in many other studies of hardiness (Ouellette, 1993).

Thus, **hardiness is a personality syndrome marked by commitment, challenge, and control that is purportedly associated with strong stress resistance.** Hardiness may reduce the effects of stress by altering stress appraisals. Hardy subjects tend to appraise potentially stressful events as less threatening and less undesirable than others do (Rhodewalt & Zone, 1989). However, some doubts have been expressed about the relevance of the hardiness syndrome to women (Wiebe, 1991), and active debate continues about the key elements of hardiness (Funk, 1992). Nonetheless, Ouellette's work has stimulated research on how personality affects one's health and tolerance of stress. Of particular interest is new work on optimism, a trait that researchers have paid little attention to until recently.

Optimism

Learning Objective

Discuss how optimism, sensation seeking, and autonomic reactivity influence stress tolerance.

Defining *optimism* **as a general tendency to expect good outcomes,** Michael Scheier and Charles Carver (1985) found a correlation between optimism and relatively good physical health in a sample of college students. In another study that focused on surgical patients, optimism was found to be associated with a faster recovery and a quicker return to normal activities after coronary artery bypass surgery (Scheier et al., 1989). Research suggests that optimists cope with stress in more adaptive ways than pessimists (Aspinwall & Taylor, 1992; Scheier & Carver, 1992). Optimists are more likely to engage in action-oriented, problem-focused coping, are more willing than pessimists to seek social support, and are more likely to emphasize the positive in their appraisals of stressful events. In comparison, pessimists are more likely to deal with stress by giving up or by engaging in denial.

In a related line of research, Christopher Peterson and Martin Seligman have studied how people explain bad events (personal setbacks, mishaps, disappointments, and such). They identified a *pessimistic explanatory style* in which some people tend to blame setbacks on their personal shortcomings. In a retrospective study of men who had graduated from Harvard back in the 1940s, they found an association between this pessimistic explanatory style and relatively poor health (Peterson, Seligman, & Vaillant, 1988). In their attempt to explain this association, they speculate that pessimism leads to passive coping efforts and poor health care practices. A subsequent study also found an association between pessimism and suppressed immune function (Kamen-Siegel et al., 1991).

Sensation Seeking

Sensation seeking is yet another personality trait that affects how people respond to stress. First described by Marvin Zuckerman (1971, 1979, 1990), *sensation seeking* **is a generalized preference for high or low levels of sensory stimulation** (see Figure 3.14). People who are high in sensation seeking prefer, and perhaps even need, a high level of stimulation. They are easily bored, and they enjoy challenges. They like activities that may involve some physical risk, such as mountain climbing, whitewater rafting, and surfing. They may satisfy their appetite for stimulation by experimenting with drugs, numerous sexual partners, and novel experiences (such as travel to unusual places). They tend to relish gambling, spicy foods, provocative art, wild parties, and unusual friends.

High sensation seekers actively pursue stimulation and risk. They enjoy experiences, such as snowboarding, that most of us would find stressful and unpleasant.

Obviously, high sensation seekers actively pursue experiences that many people would find stressful. However, now that you know how subjective stress is, it should come as no surprise that sensation seekers see these experiences as less threatening, risky, and anxiety-provoking than other people would (Franken, Gibson, & Rowland, 1992). Zuckerman (1991) believes that there is a biological predisposition toward high sensation seeking.

Although sensation seeking may be associated with stress resistance, we hasten to point out that high sensation seeking may often be more maladaptive than adaptive. In comparison to others, high sensation seekers are more likely to indulge in drug abuse, have difficulty in school, exhibit unhealthy habits (such as smoking or driving too fast), and engage in impulsive behavior, including fighting

Reprinted with special permission of King Features Syndicate.

with others (Zuckerman, 1979, 1990). Some studies have even found an association between high sensation seeking and criminal behavior (Stacy, Newcomb, & Bentler, 1993; Young, 1990). Thus, the disadvantages of high sensation seeking may well outweigh the advantages.

Autonomic Reactivity

In light of the physiological response that people often make to stress, it makes sense that physical makeup might influence stress tolerance. According to this line of thinking, those individuals who have a relatively placid autonomic nervous system should be less affected by stress than those who are equipped with a highly reactive ANS. Thus far, most of the research on autonomic reactivity has focused on autonomically regulated cardiovascular (heart rate and blood pressure) reactivity in response to stress.

Figure 3.14
A brief scale to assess sensation seeking as a trait
As the text explains, people high in sensation seeking tend to appraise potentially stressful events as less threatening than others do. Follow the instructions for this scale to obtain a rough estimate of your own sensation-seeking tendencies. (From Grasha & Kirschenbaum, 1986)

Measuring Sensation Seeking

Answer "true" or "false" to each of the items listed below by circling "T" or "F." A "true" means that the item expresses your preference most of the time. A "false" means that you do not agree that the item is generally true for you. After completing the test, score your responses according to the instructions that follow the test items.

T F   1. I would really enjoy skydiving.
T F   2. I can imagine myself driving a sports car in a race and loving it.
T F   3. My life is very secure and comfortable—the way I like it.
T F   4. I usually like emotionally expressive or artistic people, even if they are sort of wild.
T F   5. I like the idea of seeing many of the same warm, supportive faces in my everyday life.
T F   6. I like doing adventurous things and would have enjoyed being a pioneer in the early days of this country.
T F   7. A good photograph should express peacefulness creatively.
T F   8. The most important thing in living is fully experiencing all emotions.
T F   9. I like creature comforts when I go on a trip or vacation.
T F 10. Doing the same things each day really gets to me.
T F 11. I love snuggling in front of a fire on a wintry day.
T F 12. I would like to try several types of drugs as long as they didn't harm me permanently.
T F 13. Drinking and being rowdy really appeals to me on the weekend.
T F 14. Rational people try to avoid dangerous situations.
T F 15. I prefer Figure A to Figure B.

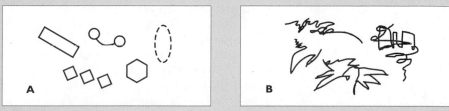

Give yourself 1 point for answering "true" to the following items: 1, 2, 4, 6, 8, 10, 12, and 13. Also give yourself 1 point for answering "false" to the following items: 3, 5, 7, 9, 11, 14, and 15. Add up your points, and compare your total to the following norms: 11–15, high sensation seeker; 6–10, moderate sensation seeker; 0–5, low sensation seeker. Bear in mind that this is a shortened version of the Sensation Seeking Scale and that it provides only a rough approximation of your status on this personality trait.

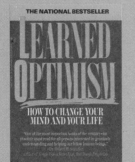
Martin Seligman is an outstanding researcher who has done pioneering work in a number of areas. *Learned Optimism* is a highly personal book in which Seligman describes how his research on optimism grew out of his earlier work on learned helplessness and depression. It offers some interesting insights into how a scientist's thinking evolves as research progresses and new evidence emerges.

According to Seligman, people have characteristic ways of explaining and thinking about their successes, their failures, and their challenges in life. Pessimists expect the worst possible scenario from every setback and they blame themselves for their failures. Optimists are much the opposite. They see life's difficulties in the least threatening light and tend to attribute setbacks to circumstances rather than their personal flaws and inadequacies. Seligman reviews research on how these differences in explanatory style affect mental and physical health, as well as performance in school, in sports, and at work.

Seligman also offers extensive advice about how people can change their characteristic way of thinking, borrowing liberally from the ideas of such other influential theorists as Albert Ellis and Aaron Beck. *Learned Optimism* is a well-written, readable, practical book, loaded with fascinating anecdotes and firmly grounded in empirical research.

> There was a lot of hype in the press about Berkeley swimming star Matt Biondi's chances in the 1988 Seoul Olympics . . .
>
> The first event Biondi swam was the two-hundred-meter freestyle. He finished a disappointing third. The second event was the one-hundred-meter butterfly, not his premier event. Overpowering the field, he led all the way. But in the last two meters, rather than taking one extra stroke and crashing into the finish wall, he appeared to relax and coast the final meter. You could hear the groan in Seoul, and imagine it across America, as he was inched (centimetered?) out by Anthony Nesty of Surinam, who took the extra stroke to win Surinam's first medal ever. The "agony of defeat" interviewers hammered Biondi on the disappointment of a bronze and a silver medal and speculated that he might not be able to rebound. Would Biondi carry home gold in his five remaining events after this embarrassing start?
>
> I sat in my living room confident that he would. I had reason to believe this, because we had tested Matt Biondi in Berkeley four months before to determine his capacity to do just what he had to do now—come back from defeat.
>
> Along with his teammates, he had taken the Attributional Style Questionnaire, and he had come out in the top quarter of optimism of an optimistic bunch. We had then simulated defeat under controlled conditions in the pool. Nort Thornton, Biondi's coach, had him swim the one-hundred-yard butterfly all out. Biondi swam it in 50.2 seconds, a very respectable time. But Thornton told him he had swum 51.7, a very slow time for Biondi. Biondi looked disappointed and surprised. Thornton told him to rest up for a few minutes and then swim it again—all out. Biondi did. His actual time got even faster, 50.0. Because his explanatory style was highly optimistic and he had shown us that he got faster—not slower—after defeat, I felt he would bring back gold from Seoul.
>
> In his last five events in Seoul, Biondi won five gold medals. [pp. 163–164]

Subjects who are exposed to stressful tasks in laboratory settings show fairly consistent personal differences in cardiovascular reactivity over time and across a variety of tasks (Manuck et al., 1993; Sherwood, 1993). There may be a genetic basis for these differences in cardiovascular reactivity (Smith et al., 1987), which can be seen even in children (Matthews, Woodall, & Stoney, 1990). However, the research thus far has largely focused on reactions to simple, short-term stressors in the laboratory (challenging mental tasks) that are relatively pale imitations of real-life stress. Hence, more research is needed on reactions to chronic, ongoing stress and stress emanating from social interactions (Kelsey, 1993; Lassner, Matthews, & Stoney, 1994). Nonetheless, the preponderance of evidence suggests that certain patterns of cardiovascular reactivity *probably* make some people more vulnerable than others to stress-related heart disease (Blascovich & Katkin, 1993).

Application Monitoring Your Stress

Rank the following five events in terms of how stressful they would be for you (1 = most stressful, 5 = least stressful).

_____ **1.** *Change in residence.*

_____ **2.** *Fired at work.*

_____ **3.** *Death of a close family member.*

_____ **4.** *Pregnancy.*

_____ **5.** *Personal injury or illness.*

All five events appear on the Social Readjustment Rating Scale (SRRS), developed by Holmes and Rahe (1967), which we described earlier in this chapter (see Figure 3.3). If you ranked them in the same order as Holmes and Rahe's subjects, the rankings would be 5, 3, 1, 4, and 2. If you didn't rank them in that order, don't worry about it. That merely shows that the perception of stress is personal and subjective. Unfortunately, the SRRS fails to take this subjectivity into account. That is just one of a number of basic problems with the SRRS.

The SRRS and the research associated with it have received a great deal of publicity. The scale has been reprinted in many popular newspapers and magazines. In these articles, readers have been encouraged to attribute great significance to their scores. They have sometimes been told that they should reduce or minimize change in their lives if their scores are high (Cohen, 1979). Such bold advice could be counterproductive and needs to be qualified carefully. Therefore, in this Application we'll elaborate on some of the problems with the SRRS as a measurement scale, introduce you to an improved scale for measuring stress, and explain why your scores on any stress scale should be interpreted with caution.

Problems with the SRRS

Learning Objective

List five problems with the Social Readjustment Rating Scale.

Thomas Holmes

As you learned earlier in this chapter, the SRRS was developed in the early 1960s by Thomas Holmes and Richard Rahe (1967). They designed the scale to measure the amount of change-related stress that people experience. The scale assigns normative values to 43 life events that supposedly indicate how stressful those events are. You respond to the scale by checking off those events that have happened to you in a recent time period. Then you add up the values of the checked events to arrive at your score. In a host of studies, these scores have been found to be related to the likelihood of developing an intimidating array of physical illnesses and psychological problems (Creed, 1993; Derogatis & Coons, 1993; Elliott, 1989; T. W. Miller, 1989).

Before we discuss the shortcomings of the SRRS, we should emphasize that Holmes and Rahe deserve enormous credit for having the imagination to tackle the difficult task of measuring life stress. They had the insight to recognize the potential importance of stress and the ingenuity to develop a scale that would permit its measurement. They pioneered a new area of research that has turned out to be extremely productive. However, their groundbreaking foray into the assessment of stress was not without its flaws, and their scale has been improved on. So, borrowing from the analyses of a number of critics (notably, Cleary, 1980; Derogatis, 1982; Monroe & McQuaid, 1994; Rabkin, 1993; Schroeder & Costa, 1984), let's look at some of the major problems with the SRRS. Although our list is not exhaustive, there are five key problems.

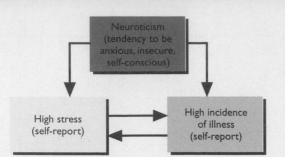

**Figure 3.15
Neuroticism as a possible factor underlying the stress-illness correlation**
Many studies have found a correlation between subjects' scores on self-report stress scales, such as the SRRS, and their reports of how much illness they have experienced. However, neurotic subjects, who are anxious, insecure, and self-conscious, tend to recall more stress and more illness than others. Although a great deal of evidence suggests that stress contributes to the causation of illness, some of the stress-illness correlation may be due to neuroticism causing both high stress and high illness.

First, as mentioned earlier, the assumption that the SRRS measures change exclusively has been shown to be inaccurate. We now have ample evidence that the desirability of events affects adaptational outcomes more than the amount of change that the events require (Brown & McGill, 1989; Smith, 1993). Thus, it seems prudent to view the SRRS as a measure of diverse forms of stress, rather than as a measure of change-related stress.

Second, the SRRS fails to take into account differences among people in their subjective perception of how stressful an event is. For instance, while divorce may deserve a stress value of 73 for *most* people, a particular person's divorce might generate much less stress and merit a value of only 25. Thus, the normative weights assigned to events on the SRRS may not capture the true impact of an event on a particular person. Cohen, Kamarck, and Mermelstein (1983) have suggested that it might be better to have respondents rate how personally stressful events are, rather than use the standardized, average weights.

Third, many of the events listed on the SRRS and similar scales are highly ambiguous, leading people to be inconsistent as to which events they report experiencing (Raphael, Cloitre, & Dohrenwend, 1991). For instance, what qualifies as "trouble with boss"? Should you check that because you're sick and tired of your supervisor? What constitutes a "change in living conditions"? Does your purchase of a great new stereo qualify? How should the "pregnancy" item be interpreted? Should a man who has a pregnant wife check that item? As you can see, the SRRS includes many "events" that are described inadequately, producing considerable ambiguity about the meaning of one's response. Problems in recalling events over a period of a year also lead to inconsistent responding on stress scales, thus lowering their reliability (Klein & Rubovits, 1987).

Fourth, the SRRS does not sample from the domain of stressful events very thoroughly. Could the 43 events listed on the SRRS exhaust all the major stresses that people typically experience? Studies designed to explore that question have found many significant omissions (Dohrenwend et al., 1993; Kanner et al., 1981; Turner & Wheaton, 1995).

Fifth, the correlation between SRRS scores and health outcomes may be inflated because subjects' neuroticism (anxiety-proneness) affects both their responses to stress scales and their self-reports of health problems. Neurotic individuals have a tendency to recall more stress than others and to recall more symptoms of illness than others (Brett et al., 1990; Watson & Pennebaker, 1989). These tendencies mean that some of the correlation between high stress and high illness may simply reflect the effects of subjects' neuroticism. This is another case of the third-variable problem in correlation that we introduced in Chapter 1 (see Figure 3.15). The possible contaminating effects of neuroticism obscure the meaning of scores on the SRRS and similar measures of stress.

The Life Experiences Survey

In light of the problems we have outlined, a number of researchers have attempted to develop improved versions of the SRRS (for instance, Dohrenwend et al., 1978; Paykel, 1974). The scale that seems to be gaining the greatest use is the Life Experiences Survey (LES), assembled by Irwin Sarason and colleagues (Sarason, Johnson, & Siegel, 1978). The LES (see Figure 3.16) has become a widely used measure of stress in contemporary research (for examples see Gillis, 1993; Lightsey, 1994; Mullis et al., 1993). The LES revises and builds on the SRRS in a variety of ways that correct, at least in part, most of the problems we've discussed.

Specifically, the LES recognizes that stress involves more than mere change and asks respondents to indicate whether events had a positive or negative impact on them. This strategy permits the computation of positive change, negative change, and total change scores, which helps researchers to gain much more insight into which facets of stress are most crucial. The LES also takes into consideration differences among people in their appraisal of stress. It does so by dropping the normative weights and replacing them with personally assigned weightings of the impact of relevant events. Ambiguity in items is decreased by providing more elaborate descriptions of many items to clarify their meaning. The scale still contains some ambiguity, but there is no complete solution for this problem.

The failure of the SRRS to sample the full domain of stressful events is dealt with in several ways. First, some significant omissions from the SRRS were added to the LES. Second, the LES allows the respondent to write in personally important events that are not included on the scale. Third, the LES, reprinted here (Figure 3.16), has an extra section just for students. Sarason et al. (1978) suggest that

Figure 3.16
The Life Experiences Survey (LES)
Like the SRRS, the LES is designed to measure change-related stress. However, Sarason, Johnson, and Siegel (1978) corrected many of the problems apparent in the SRRS. Follow the instructions in the text to determine your positive, negative, and total change scores.

INSTRUCTIONS. Listed below are a number of events that sometimes bring about change in the lives of those who experience them and that necessitate social readjustment. Please check those events you have experienced in the recent past and indicate the time period during which you have experienced each event. Be sure that all checkmarks are directly across from the items that they correspond to. Also, for each item checked below, please indicate the extent to which you viewed the event as having either a positive or a negative impact on your life at the time the event occurred. That is, indicate the type and extent of impact that the event had. A rating of −3 would indicate an extremely negative impact. A rating of 0 suggests no impact, either positive or negative. A rating of +3 would indicate an extremely positive impact.

The Life Experiences Survey (LES)

	0 to 6 mo	7 mo to 1 yr	Extremely negative	Moderately negative	Somewhat negative	No impact	Slightly positive	Moderately positive	Extremely positive
Section I									
1. Marriage			−3	−2	−1	0	+1	+2	+3
2. Detention in jail or comparable institution			−3	−2	−1	0	+1	+2	+3
3. Death of spouse			−3	−2	−1	0	+1	+2	+3
4. Major change in sleeping habits (much more or much less sleep)			−3	−2	−1	0	+1	+2	+3
5. Death of a close family member:			−3	−2	−1	0	+1	+2	+3
a. Mother			−3	−2	−1	0	+1	+2	+3
b. Father			−3	−2	−1	0	+1	+2	+3
c. Brother			−3	−2	−1	0	+1	+2	+3
d. Sister			−3	−2	−1	0	+1	+2	+3
e. Grandmother			−3	−2	−1	0	+1	+2	+3
f. Grandfather			−3	−2	−1	0	+1	+2	+3
g. Other (specify)			−3	−2	−1	0	+1	+2	+3
6. Major change in eating habits (much more or much less food intake)			−3	−2	−1	0	+1	+2	+3
7. Foreclosure on mortgage or loan			−3	−2	−1	0	+1	+2	+3
8. Death of close friend			−3	−2	−1	0	+1	+2	+3
9. Outstanding personal achievement			−3	−2	−1	0	+1	+2	+3
10. Minor law violations (traffic tickets, disturbing the peace, etc.)			−3	−2	−1	0	+1	+2	+3

(continued)

The Life Experiences Survey (LES) *(continued)*

	0 to 6 mo	7 mo to 1 yr	Extremely negative	Moderately negative	Somewhat negative	No impact	Slightly positive	Moderately positive	Extremely positive
11. *Male:* Wife/girlfriend's pregnancy			−3	−2	−1	0	+1	+2	+3
12. *Female:* Pregnancy			−3	−2	−1	0	+1	+2	+3
13. Changed work situation (different work responsibility, major change in working conditions, working hours, etc.)			−3	−2	−1	0	+1	+2	+3
14. New job			−3	−2	−1	0	+1	+2	+3
15. Serious illness or injury of close family member:									
a. Father			−3	−2	−1	0	+1	+2	+3
b. Mother			−3	−2	−1	0	+1	+2	+3
c. Sister			−3	−2	−1	0	+1	+2	+3
d. Brother			−3	−2	−1	0	+1	+2	+3
e. Grandfather			−3	−2	−1	0	+1	+2	+3
f. Grandmother			−3	−2	−1	0	+1	+2	+3
g. Spouse			−3	−2	−1	0	+1	+2	+3
h. Other (specify)			−3	−2	−1	0	+1	+2	+3
16. Sexual difficulties			−3	−2	−1	0	+1	+2	+3
17. Trouble with employer (in danger of losing job, being suspended, being demoted, etc.)			−3	−2	−1	0	+1	+2	+3
18. Trouble with in-laws			−3	−2	−1	0	+1	+2	+3
19. Major change in financial status (a lot better off or a lot worse off)			−3	−2	−1	0	+1	+2	+3
20. Major change in closeness of family members (increased or decreased closeness)			−3	−2	−1	0	+1	+2	+3
21. Gaining a new family member (through birth, adoption, family member moving in, etc.)			−3	−2	−1	0	+1	+2	+3
22. Change of residence			−3	−2	−1	0	+1	+2	+3
23. Marital separation from mate (due to conflict)			−3	−2	−1	0	+1	+2	+3
24. Major change in church activities (increased or decreased attendance)			−3	−2	−1	0	+1	+2	+3
25. Marital reconciliation with mate			−3	−2	−1	0	+1	+2	+3
26. Major change in number of arguments with spouse (a lot more or a lot fewer)			−3	−2	−1	0	+1	+2	+3
27. *Married male:* Change in wife's work outside the home (beginning work, ceasing work, changing to a new job, etc.)			−3	−2	−1	0	+1	+2	+3
28. *Married female:* Change in husband's work (loss of job, beginning new job, retirement, etc.)			−3	−2	−1	0	+1	+2	+3
29. Major change in usual type and/or amount of recreation			−3	−2	−1	0	+1	+2	+3
30. Borrowing for a major purchase (buying a home, business, etc.)			−3	−2	−1	0	+1	+2	+3
31. Borrowing for smaller purchase (buying a car or TV, getting school loan, etc.)			−3	−2	−1	0	+1	+2	+3

(continued)

The Life Experiences Survey (LES) *(continued)*

	0 to 6 mo	7 mo to 1 yr	Extremely negative	Moderately negative	Somewhat negative	No impact	Slightly positive	Moderately positive	Extremely positive
32. Being fired from job			−3	−2	−1	0	+1	+2	+3
33. *Male:* Wife/girlfriend having abortion			−3	−2	−1	0	+1	+2	+3
34. *Female:* Having abortion			−3	−2	−1	0	+1	+2	+3
35. Major personal illness or injury			−3	−2	−1	0	+1	+2	+3
36. Major change in social activities, e.g., parties, movies, visiting (increased or decreased participation)			−3	−2	−1	0	+1	+2	+3
37. Major change in living conditions of family (building new home, remodeling, deterioration of home or neighborhood, etc.)			−3	−2	−1	0	+1	+2	+3
38. Divorce			−3	−2	−1	0	+1	+2	+3
39. Serious injury or illness of close friend			−3	−2	−1	0	+1	+2	+3
40. Retirement from work			−3	−2	−1	0	+1	+2	+3
41. Son or daughter leaving home (due to marriage, college, etc.)			−3	−2	−1	0	+1	+2	+3
42. End of formal schooling			−3	−2	−1	0	+1	+2	+3
43. Separation from spouse (due to work, travel, etc.)			−3	−2	−1	0	+1	+2	+3
44. Engagement			−3	−2	−1	0	+1	+2	+3
45. Breaking up with boyfriend/girlfriend			−3	−2	−1	0	+1	+2	+3
46. Leaving home for the first time			−3	−2	−1	0	+1	+2	+3
47. Reconciliation with boyfriend/girlfriend			−3	−2	−1	0	+1	+2	+3
Other recent experiences that have had an impact on your life. List and rate.									
48. _____			−3	−2	−1	0	+1	+2	+3
49. _____			−3	−2	−1	0	+1	+2	+3
50. _____			−3	−2	−1	0	+1	+2	+3

Section 2. Students only

	0 to 6 mo	7 mo to 1 yr	Extremely negative	Moderately negative	Somewhat negative	No impact	Slightly positive	Moderately positive	Extremely positive
51. Beginning a new school experience at a higher academic level (college, graduate school, professional school)			−3	−2	−1	0	+1	+2	+3
52. Changing to a new school at same academic level (undergraduate, graduate, etc.)			−3	−2	−1	0	+1	+2	+3
53. Academic probation			−3	−2	−1	0	+1	+2	+3
54. Being dismissed from dormitory or other residence			−3	−2	−1	0	+1	+2	+3
55. Failing an important exam			−3	−2	−1	0	+1	+2	+3
56. Changing a major			−3	−2	−1	0	+1	+2	+3
57. Failing a course			−3	−2	−1	0	+1	+2	+3
58. Dropping a course			−3	−2	−1	0	+1	+2	+3
59. Joining a fraternity/sorority			−3	−2	−1	0	+1	+2	+3
60. Financial problems concerning school (in danger of not having sufficient money to continue)			−3	−2	−1	0	+1	+2	+3

special, tailored sections of this sort be added for specific populations whenever it is useful.

We suggest that you respond to the LES in Figure 3.16. Although we have been critical of people overinterpreting SRRS scores, there is much to be said for making an estimate of how much stress you've been under recently. If you score high, you may want to think about ways to reduce some of the stress in your life.

Arriving at your scores is very simple. Just add up all the positive impact ratings on the right side. That sum is your positive change score. Then add up your negative impact ratings to arrive at your negative change score. Adding these two values yields your total change score. Approximate norms for all three of these scores are listed in Figure 3.17, so that you can get some idea of what your score means.

Research to date suggests that your negative change score is the crucial one. Positive change has not been found to be a very good predictor of adaptational outcomes. In direct comparisons with the SRRS, the negative change score has turned out to be a better predictor of mental and physical health than SRRS scores (Sarason et al., 1978). Thus far, research has shown that negative change scores are related to a variety of negative adaptational outcomes.

A Cautionary Note

Learning Objective

Explain why one should be cautious in interpreting scores on stress scales.

There is merit in getting an estimate of how much stress you have experienced lately, but scores on the LES or any measure of stress should be interpreted with caution. You need not panic if you add up your negative change score and find that it falls in the "high" category. Although a connection clearly exists between stress and a variety of undesirable adaptational outcomes, there are a couple of reasons why a high score shouldn't cause undue concern.

First, the strength of the association between stress and adaptational problems is modest. Most of the correlations observed between stress scores and illness have been relatively low, often less than .30 (Dohrenwend & Dohrenwend, 1981; Kobasa, 1979). For researchers and theorists, it is very interesting to find any relationship at all. However, the link between stress and adaptational problems is too weak to permit us to make confident predictions about individuals. Many people endure high levels of stress without developing significant problems.

Second, stress is only one of a multitude of variables that affect your susceptibility to various maladies. Stress interacts with such other factors as your lifestyle, coping skills, social support, hardiness, and genetic inheritance in influencing your mental and physical health. It's important to remember that stress is only one actor on a crowded stage. In light of these considerations, you should evaluate the potential meaning of SRRS or LES scores with caution. A high score should be food for thought, but not reason for alarm.

Figure 3.17
Norms for the Life Experiences Survey (LES)
Approximate norms for college students taking the LES are shown for negative, positive, and total change scores. These norms are based on 345 undergraduates studied by Sarason, Johnson, and Siegel (1978). Data for males and females were combined, as gender differences were negligible. Negative change scores prove to be the best predictor of adaptational outcomes.

Norms for LES			
Score category	Negative change	Positive change	Total change
High	14 and above	16 and above	28 and above
Medium	4–13	7–15	12–27
Low	0–3	0–6	0–11

Key Ideas

The Nature of Stress

• Stress involves transactions with the environment that are perceived to be threatening. Stress is a common, everyday event, and even routine hassles can be problematic. To a large degree, stress lies in the eye of the beholder. Whether one feels threatened by events depends on how one appraises them.

• Some of the stress that people experience emanates from their environment. Examples of environmental stimuli that can be stressful include excessive noise, heat, pollution, and crowding. Much everyday stress is self-imposed.

Major Types of Stress

• Major types of stress include frustration, conflict, change, and pressure. Frustration occurs when an obstacle prevents one from attaining some goal. There are three principal types of conflict: approach-approach, avoidance-avoidance, and approach-avoidance. The latter is especially stressful. Vacillation is a common response to approach-avoidance conflict.

• A large number of studies with the SRRS suggest that change is stressful. Although this may be true, it is now clear that the SRRS is a measure of general stress rather than just change-related stress. Two kinds of pressure (to perform and to conform) also appear to be stressful.

Key Factors in the Appraisal of Stress

• Appraisals of potentially threatening events are highly subjective. Stressful events are usually viewed as less threatening when they are familiar, controllable, and predictable, and when they lie in the distant future. However, controllability and predictability have varied effects on the appraisal of stress.

Responding to Stress

• Emotional reactions to stress typically involve anger, fear, or sadness. Emotional arousal may interfere with coping. The optimal level of arousal on tasks varies, depending on the complexity of the task. Physiological arousal in response to stress was originally called the fight-or-flight response by Cannon. Selye's general adaptation syndrome describes three stages in the physiological reaction to stress: alarm, resistance, and exhaustion. Diseases of adaptation may appear during the stage of exhaustion.

• There are two major pathways along which the brain sends signals to the endocrine system in response to stress. Actions along these paths release two sets of hormones into the bloodstream, catecholamines and corticosteroids. Stress can also affect the immune system. Behavioral responses to stress involve coping. Coping efforts may be healthy or maladaptive. If people cope effectively with stress, they can short-circuit potentially harmful emotional and physical responses.

The Potential Effects of Stress

• Although stress can have positive effects, research on the effects of stress has concentrated on negative outcomes. Common negative effects include impaired task performance, disruption of attention and other cognitive processes, pervasive exhaustion known as burnout, posttraumatic stress disorders, a host of everyday psychological problems, full-fledged psychological disorders, and varied types of damage to physical health. However, stress fulfills a basic human need for challenge and can lead to personal growth and self-improvement.

Factors Influencing Stress Tolerance

• People differ in how much stress they can tolerate without experiencing ill effects. A person's social support is a key consideration. The personality factors associated with hardiness—commitment, challenge, and control—may increase stress tolerance. People high in optimism and sensation seeking also have advantages in coping with stress. A relatively placid autonomic nervous system may also shield people from some of the detrimental health effects associated with stress.

Application: Monitoring Your Stress

• It can be useful to attempt to measure the amount of stress in one's life, but the much-used SRRS is marred by a variety of shortcomings. It does not really measure change exclusively and it fails to account for the subjective nature of stress. Some of the items on the SRRS are ambiguous, and the scale does not sample the domain of stress thoroughly.

• In contrast, the LES is an improved measure of stress that recognizes the subjectivity of stress and the importance of the desirability of many life events. The LES also samples the domain of stressful events a little more thoroughly and is characterized by less ambiguity than the SRRS. Negative change scores on the LES have been found to be predictive of a variety of adaptational outcomes.

Key Terms

Ambient stress
Approach-approach conflict
Approach-avoidance conflict
Autonomic nervous system (ANS)
Avoidance-avoidance conflict
Burnout
Conflict
Coping
Emotions
Endocrine system
Fight-or-flight response
Frustration
General adaptation syndrome
Hardiness
Life changes
Optimism
Posttraumatic stress disorder (PTSD)
Pressure
Primary appraisal
Psychosomatic diseases
Secondary appraisal
Sensation seeking
Social support
Stress

Key People

Thomas Holmes and Richard Rahe
Richard Lazarus
Neal Miller
Suzanne Ouellette (Kobasa)
Hans Selye
Marvin Zuckerman

4 Coping Processes

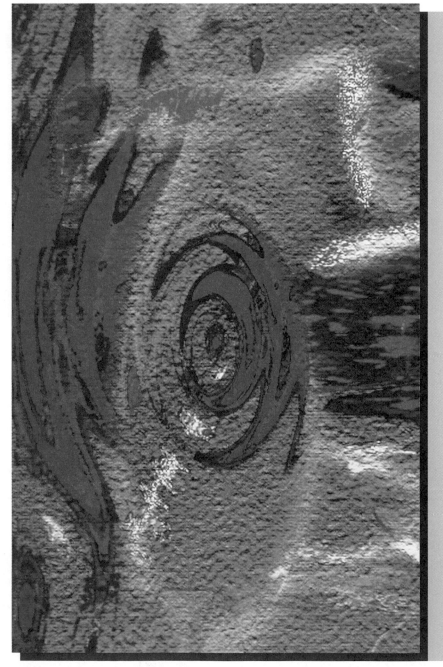

"I have begun to believe that I have intellectually and emotionally outgrown my husband. However, I'm not really sure what this means or what I should do. Maybe this feeling is normal and I should ignore it and continue my present relationship. This seems to be the safest route. Maybe I should seek a lover while continuing with my husband. Then again, maybe I should start anew and hope for a beautiful ending with or without a better mate."

*T*he woman quoted here is in the throes of a thorny conflict. Although it is hard to tell just how much emotional turmoil she is experiencing, it's clear that she is under substantial stress. What should she do? Is it psychologically healthy to remain in an emotionally hollow marriage? Is seeking a secret lover a reasonable way to cope with this unfortunate situation? Should she just strike out on her own and let the chips fall where they may? There are no simple answers to these questions. As you'll soon see, decisions about how to cope with life's difficulties can be terribly complex.

This chapter focuses on how people cope with stress. In the previous chapter we discussed the nature of stress and its potential effects. We learned that stress can be a challenging, exciting stimulus to personal growth. However, we also saw that stress can prove damaging to psychological and physical health because it often triggers emotional and physiological responses that may be harmful. These emotional and physiological responses tend to be largely automatic. Controlling them depends on the coping responses people make to stressful situations. Thus, a person's mental and physical health depend, in part, on his or her ability to cope effectively with stress.

In this chapter we begin with a general discussion of the concept of coping. Then we review some common coping patterns that tend to have relatively little value in reducing stress. We then go on to discuss what it means to engage in healthier, "constructive" coping. The remainder of the chapter expands on the specifics of constructive coping.

The Concept of Coping

Learning Objective

Discuss three general points about coping.

In Chapter 3, we saw that *coping* **refers to efforts to master, reduce, or tolerate the demands created by stress.** Let's take a closer look at this concept and discuss some general points about coping.

People cope with stress in many different ways. In recent years, a number of researchers have attempted to identify and classify the various coping techniques used to deal with stress. Their work reveals that people use quite a variety of coping strategies. For instance, in a study of how 255 adult subjects dealt with stress, McCrae (1984) identified 28 different coping techniques. In another study, Carver, Scheier, and Weintraub (1989) found that they could sort their subjects' coping tactics into 14 categories, which are listed in Figure 4.1. Thus, in grappling with stress, people select their coping tactics from a large and varied menu of options.

Individuals exhibit styles of coping. Most people come to rely on some coping strategies more than others (Folkman, Lazarus, Gruen, & DeLongis, 1986). Of course, situational demands can influence which strategies are used. For instance, in situations involving severe stress, emotion-focused coping may be especially likely (Terry, 1994). Nonetheless, coping strategies show moderate stability across situations (Carver & Scheier, 1994). To some extent, each person has a personal style of coping with life's difficulties. As we progress through this chapter, it may be fruitful for you to analyze your style of coping.

Coping strategies vary in their adaptive value. In everyday terms, when we say that someone "coped with his problems," we imply that he handled them effectively. In reality, however, coping processes range from the helpful to the destructive (Carver et al., 1989). For example, coping with the disappointment of not getting a promotion by plotting to sabotage your company's computer system would be a negative way of coping. Hence, we will distinguish between coping patterns that tend to be helpful and those that tend to be maladaptive. Bear in mind, however, that our generalizations about the adaptive value of various coping strategies are based on trends or tendencies. No coping strategy can ensure a successful outcome. Further-

Figure 4.1
Classifying coping strategies
Carver, Scheier, and Weintraub
(1989) sorted their subjects'
coping responses into 14 categories. The categories are listed
here (column 1) with a representative example from each category (column 2). As you can see,
people use quite a variety of
coping strategies.

Types of Coping Strategies

Coping strategy	Example
Active coping	I take additional action to try to get rid of the problem.
Planning	I come up with a strategy about what to do.
Suppression of competing activities	I put aside other activities in order to concentrate on this.
Restraint coping	I force myself to wait for the right time to do something.
Seeking social support for instrumental reasons	I ask people who have had similar experiences what they did.
Seeking social support for emotional reasons	I talk to someone about how I feel.
Positive reinterpretation and growth	I look for the good in what is happening.
Acceptance	I learn to live with it.
Turning to religion	I seek God's help.
Focus on and venting of emotions	I get upset and let my emotions out.
Denial	I refuse to believe that it has happened.
Behavioral disengagement	I give up the attempt to get what I want.
Mental disengagement	I turn to work or other substitute activities to take my mind off things.
Alcohol-drug disengagement	I drink alcohol or take drugs in order to think about it less.

more, the adaptive value of a coping technique depends on the exact nature of the situation. As you'll see in the next section, even ill-advised coping strategies may have adaptive value in some instances.

Common Coping Patterns of Limited Value

"Recently, after an engagement of 22 months, my fiancée told me that she was in love with someone else, and that we were through. I've been a wreck ever since. I can't study because I keep thinking about her. I think constantly about what I did wrong in the relationship and why I wasn't good enough for her. Getting drunk is the only way I can get her off my mind. Lately, I've been getting plastered about five or six nights a week. My grades are really hurting, but I'm not sure that I care."

This young man is going through a difficult time and does not appear to be han-
dling it well. He's blaming himself for the breakup with his fiancée. He's turning to alcohol to dull the pain that he feels, and it sounds like he may be giving up on school. Given his situation, these coping responses aren't particularly unusual, but they're only going to make his problems worse.

In this section, we'll examine some relatively common coping patterns that tend to be less than optimal. Specifically, we'll discuss giving up, aggression, indulging yourself, blaming yourself, and defense mechanisms. Some of these coping tactics may be helpful in certain circumstances, but more often than not, they are counterproductive.

Giving Up

When confronted with stress, people sometimes simply give up and withdraw from the battle. This response of apathy and inaction tends to be associated with the emotional reactions of sadness and dejection. Bruno Bettelheim (1943) observed this reaction among prisoners in the Nazi concentration camps of World War II. Some

Martin Seligman

prisoners aggressed against their captors through acts of sabotage and worked valiantly to maintain their will to live. However, many others sank into apathy and made no effort to adapt and survive.

Martin Seligman (1974, 1992) has developed a model of this giving-up syndrome that sheds some light on its causes. In Seligman's original research, animals were subjected to electric shocks they could not escape. The animals were then given an opportunity to learn a response that would allow them to escape the shock. However, many of the animals became so apathetic and listless they didn't even try to learn the escape response. When researchers made similar manipulations with *human* subjects using inescapable noise (rather than shock) as the stressor, they observed parallel results (Hiroto & Seligman, 1975). This syndrome is referred to as learned helplessness. ***Learned helplessness* involves passive behavior produced by exposure to unavoidable aversive events.** Unfortunately, this tendency to give up may be transferred to situations in which one is not really helpless. Hence, some people routinely respond to stress with fatalism and resignation, passively accepting setbacks that might be dealt with effectively.

Seligman originally viewed learned helplessness as a product of conditioning. However, research with human subjects has led Seligman and his colleagues to revise their theory. The current model proposes that one's *cognitive interpretation* of aversive events determines whether one develops learned helplessness. Specifically, helplessness seems to occur when individuals come to believe that events are beyond their control. This belief is particularly likely to emerge in people who exhibit a pessimistic explanatory style. Among other things, these people tend to attribute setbacks to personal inadequacies instead of situational factors (Abramson, Seligman, & Teasdale, 1978; Seligman, 1990).

As you might guess, giving up is not a highly regarded method of coping. Carver and his colleagues (1989, 1993) have studied this coping strategy, which they refer to as *behavioral disengagement*, and found that it is associated with increased rather than decreased distress. Furthermore, many studies suggest that learned helplessness can contribute to depression (Peterson & Seligman, 1984). A related coping tactic that may have more adaptive value is *social withdrawal*. In response to stress, many people pull back from their interactions with others, becoming socially distant and preoccupied. This coping strategy has not yet been the focus of much research. Repetti (1992) speculates that social withdrawal may be adaptive in the short run, perhaps allowing people to reduce stress-induced arousal and replenish their energy, but that it is probably maladaptive as a long-term coping response.

However, giving up could be adaptive in some instances. For example, if you were thrown into a job that you were not equipped to handle, it might be better to quit rather than face constant pressure and diminishing self-esteem. There is something to be said for recognizing one's limitations. In other cases, individuals need to recognize that their goals are unrealistic. The highly competitive nature of American society leads many to push themselves toward heights that are very difficult to achieve. Goals such as gaining admission to medical school, becoming a professional actress, or buying an expensive home may be better abandoned if they are unrealistic. The value of any coping response thus depends on the situation. As you will see again and again, there are no simple rules regarding the best ways to cope with life's challenges.

Striking Out at Others

"A young man, aged 17, cautiously edged his car into traffic on the Corona Expressway in Los Angeles. His slow speed apparently aggravated the men in a pickup truck behind him. Unfortunately, he angered the wrong men—they shot him to death. During that same weekend in 1987 there were six other roadside shootings in the Los Angeles area. All of them were triggered by minor incidents or "fender benders." Frustrated motorists are attacking each other more and more frequently, especially on the overburdened highways of Los Angeles."

Such tragic incidents of highway violence vividly illustrate that people often respond to stressful events by striking out at others with aggressive behavior. ***Aggression* involves any behavior intended to hurt someone, either physically or verbally.** Snarls, curses, and insults are much more common than shootings or fist-

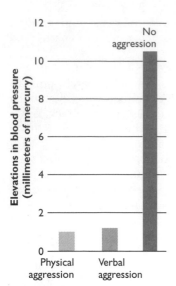

12 ┤ ─────────────────── ┌────┐ No
                          │   │ aggression
10 ┤ ─────────────────── │   │

8 ┤

6 ┤

4 ┤

2 ┤
     ┌───┐ ┌───┐
0 ┴───┴───┴─┴───┴──┴────┴──
   Physical Verbal
  aggression aggression

Elevations in blood pressure (millimeters of mercury)

Figure 4.2
Aggression and blood pressure
After frustrating subjects, Hokanson and Burgess (1962) found that those who were allowed to engage in either physical or verbal aggression showed smaller increases in blood pressure than subjects who had no opportunity for aggression. These findings support the idea that aggressive behavior permits people to cathart (drain off) emotional tension. As the text notes, however, many other studies have failed to support the cathartic value of aggression.

fights, but aggression of any kind can be problematic. Many years ago, a team of psychologists (Dollard et al., 1939) proposed the *frustration-aggression hypothesis,* which held that aggression is always due to frustration. Decades of research have verified their suggested causal link between frustration and aggression.

However, this research has also shown that there isn't an inevitable, one-to-one correspondence between frustration and aggression. In discussing qualifications to the frustration-aggression hypothesis, Leonard Berkowitz (1969, 1989) concludes (1) that frustration does not *necessarily* lead to aggression, (2) that many factors in addition to frustration (such as one's personality) influence the likelihood of aggression, and (3) that frustration may produce responses other than aggression (for example, apathy). Although these are important qualifications, it is clear that frustration often leads to aggression.

People often lash out at others who had nothing to do with their frustration, usually because they cannot vent their anger at the real source of the frustration. Thus, you'll probably suppress your anger rather than verbally attack a police officer who gives you a speeding ticket. Twenty minutes later, however, you might be downright brutal in rebuking a gas station attendant who is slow in servicing your car. As we discussed in Chapter 2, this diversion of anger to a substitute target was noticed long ago by Sigmund Freud, who called it *displacement.*

Freud theorized that behaving aggressively can free pent-up emotion and thus be adaptive. He coined the term **catharsis to refer to this release of emotional tension.** There is some experimental evidence to support Freud's theory of catharsis. In a widely cited study, Hokanson and Burgess (1962) found that the opportunity to aggress physically or verbally after frustration led to a smaller increase in subjects' blood pressure (see Figure 4.2). Given the potential negative effects of emotional arousal, this study suggests that expressing aggression may have some adaptive value.

However, after reviewing additional research by Hokanson and others, Carol Tavris (1982, 1989) concludes that aggressive behavior does not reliably lead to catharsis. She asserts, "Aggressive catharses are almost impossible to find in continuing relationships because parents, children, spouses, and bosses usually feel obliged to aggress back at you; and indirect, 'displaced' aggression does nothing but make you angrier and more upset" (1982, p. 131). Thus, the adaptive value of aggressive behavior tends to be minimal. Hurting someone, especially an irrelevant someone,

Recommended Reading

Anger: The Misunderstood Emotion

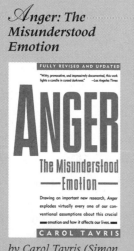

by Carol Tavris (Simon & Schuster, 1989)

With the possible exception of anxiety, anger is the emotion elicited by stress more than any other. Anger is a powerful emotion that can be harnessed to achieve admirable goals. The work of some of the world's great reformers and leaders has been fueled by moral outrage. However, anger also lies at the center of many human woes—wrecked friendships, destroyed marriages, murders, and wars. Thus, anger is a profoundly important emotion. Carol Tavris analyzes virtually every facet of anger in her book. She carefully scrutinizes common beliefs about anger and concludes that many of them are inaccurate. For instance, she argues convincingly against the idea that aggression can drain off anger through catharsis and the idea that anger and aggression are overpowering, instinctual responses. Tavris's book is a delight to read. It's witty, lively, practical, thought provoking, and frequently eloquent.

Our contemporary ideas about anger have been fed by the anger industry, psychotherapy, which too often is based on the belief that inside every tranquil soul a furious one is screaming to get out. Psychiatric theory refers to anger as if it were a fixed amount of energy that bounces through the system: if you pinch it in here, it is bound to pop out there—in bad dreams, neurosis, hysterical paralysis, hostile jokes, or stomachaches. Therapists are continually "uprooting" anger or "unearthing" it, as if it were a turnip. [p. 23]

Some people cope with stress by indulging themselves—with a shopping spree or eating, for instance, or with some other type of enjoyable activity. There's nothing inherently wrong with a little self-indulgence, but this coping strategy sometimes leads to injudicious spending, eating, drinking, or drug use.

is not likely to alleviate frustration. Moreover, the interpersonal conflicts that often emerge from aggressive behavior may produce additional stress. If you pick a fight with your spouse after a terrible day at work, you may create new stress and lose valuable empathy and social support from him or her.

Indulging Yourself

Stress sometimes leads to self-indulgence. When troubled by stress, many people engage in excessive consummatory behavior: injudicious patterns of eating, drinking, smoking, using drugs, spending money, and so forth. For instance, after an exceptionally stressful day, some people head for their refrigerator, a grocery store, or a restaurant in pursuit of something chocolate. In a similar vein, others cope with stress by making a beeline for the nearest shopping mall for a spending spree.

In their classification of coping responses, Moos and Billings (1982) list *developing alternative rewards* as a common response to stress. It makes sense that when things are going poorly in one area of their lives, people may try to compensate by pursuing substitute forms of satisfaction. When this happens, consummatory responses probably rank high. They are relatively easy to execute, and they tend to be very pleasurable. Thus, it is not surprising that there is evidence relating stress to increases in eating (Grunberg & Straub, 1992), smoking (Cohen & Lichtenstein, 1990), and the consumption of alcohol and drugs (Peyser, 1993).

There is nothing inherently maladaptive about indulging oneself as a way of coping with life's stresses. The pursuit of alternative rewards is a readily available coping strategy that may have merit if kept under control. If a hot fudge sundae or

CATHY copyright Cathy Guisewite. Reprinted with permission of UNIVERSAL PRESS SYNDICATE. All rights reserved.

some new clothes calm your nerves after a major setback, who can argue? However, if a person consistently responds to stress with chronic and excessive consummatory behavior, obvious problems are likely to develop. Excesses in eating may produce obesity. Excesses in drinking can lead to alcoholism, drunk driving, and a host of other problems. Excesses in drug use may endanger one's health and result in drug dependence. Excesses in spending may create havoc in one's personal finances. Given the risks associated with self-indulgence, it has rather marginal adaptive value.

Blaming Yourself

Learning Objective

Discuss the adaptive value of negative self-talk.

In a postgame interview after a tough defeat, a prominent football coach was brutally critical of himself. He said that he was outcoached, that he had made poor decisions, and that his game plan was faulty. He almost eagerly assumed all the blame for the loss himself. In reality, he had taken some reasonable chances that didn't go his way and had suffered the effects of poor execution by his players. Looking at it objectively, the loss was attributable to the collective failures of 50 or so players and coaches. However, the coach's unrealistically negative self-evaluation was a fairly typical response to frustration. When confronted by stress (especially frustration and pressure), many people become highly self-critical.

The tendency to engage in "negative self-talk" in response to stress has been noted by a number of influential theorists. Albert Ellis (1973, 1987) calls this phenomenon *catastrophic thinking* and focuses on how it is rooted in irrational assumptions. Amplifying on Ellis's approach, Aaron Beck (1976, 1987) asserts that people often (1) unreasonably attribute their failures to personal shortcomings, (2) focus on negative feedback from others while ignoring favorable feedback, and (3) make unduly pessimistic projections about the future. Thus, if you performed poorly on an exam, you might blame it on your woeful stupidity, dismiss a classmate's comment that the test was unfair, and hysterically predict that you will flunk out of school.

Although recognizing one's weaknesses does have some value, Ellis and Beck agree that negative self-talk tends to be counterproductive. According to Ellis, catastrophic thinking causes, aggravates, and perpetuates emotional reactions to stress that are often problematic. Along even more serious lines, Beck marshals evidence that negative self-talk can contribute to the development of depressive disorders. The upshot is that people who blame themselves for their difficulties tend to be less happy and less well adjusted than those who do not display this coping style (Revenson & Felton, 1989; Vitaliano et al., 1989). In general, then, it appears that self-blame and self-criticism are not very useful ways to cope with stress.

Defensive Coping

Defensive coping is a common response to stress. As we noted in Chapter 2, the concept of defense mechanisms was originally developed by Sigmund Freud. Building on Freud's initial insights, modern psychologists have broadened the scope of the concept and added to Freud's list of defense mechanisms.

The Nature of Defense Mechanisms

Learning Objective

Explain how defense mechanisms work.

Defense mechanisms are largely unconscious reactions that protect a person from unpleasant emotions such as anxiety and guilt. A number of strategies fit this definition. For example, Laughlin (1979) lists 49 different defenses. In our discussion of Freud's theory in Chapter 2, we described seven common defense mechanisms. Figure 4.3 introduces another five defenses that people use with some regularity. Although widely discussed in the popular press, defense mechanisms are often misunderstood. We will use a question-answer format to elaborate on the nature of defense mechanisms in the hopes of clearing up any misconceptions.

Common Defense Mechanisms

Mechanism	Example
Denial of reality. Protecting oneself from unpleasant reality by refusing to perceive or face it.	A smoker concludes that the evidence linking cigarette use to health problems is scientifically worthless.
Fantasy. Gratifying frustrated desires by imaginary achievements.	A socially inept and inhibited young man imagines himself chosen by a group of women to provide them with sexual satisfaction.
Intellectualization (isolation). Cutting off emotion from hurtful situations or separating incompatible attitudes in logic-tight compartments.	A prisoner on death row awaiting execution resists appeal on his behalf and coldly insists that the letter of the law be followed.
Undoing. Atoning for or trying to magically dispel unacceptable desires or acts.	A teenager who feels guilty about masturbation ritually touches door knobs a prescribed number of times after each occurrence of the act.
Overcompensation. Covering up felt weaknesses by emphasizing some desirable characteristic, or making up for frustration in one area by overgratification in another.	A dangerously overweight woman goes on eating binges when she feels neglected by her husband.

Figure 4.3
Additional defense mechanisms
Like the seven defense mechanisms described in our discussion of Freudian theory in Chapter 2 (see Figure 2.3), these five defenses are frequently used in efforts to cope with stress. (Adapted from Carson, Butcher, & Coleman, 1988)

What do defense mechanisms defend against? Above all else, defense mechanisms shield one from the *emotional discomfort* elicited by stress. Their main purpose is to ward off unwelcome emotions or to reduce their intensity. The chief emotion guarded against is anxiety. The psyche is especially protective when the anxiety is caused by some threat to self-esteem. People also use defenses to suppress dangerous feelings of anger so that they do not explode into acts of aggression. Guilt and dejection are two other emotions that people often try to evade through defensive maneuvers.

How do they work? Defense mechanisms work through *self-deception*. They accomplish their goals by distorting reality so it does not appear so threatening. For example, suppose you're doing poorly in school and are in danger of flunking out. Initially, you might use *denial* to block awareness of the possibility that you could flunk out. This might temporarily fend off feelings of anxiety. If it becomes difficult to deny the obvious, you might resort to *fantasy*, daydreaming about how you will salvage adequate grades by getting spectacular scores on the upcoming final exams, when the objective fact is that you are hopelessly behind in your studies. Thus, defense mechanisms work their magic by bending reality in self-serving ways.

Are they conscious or unconscious? Freud originally assumed that defenses operate entirely at an unconscious level. However, the concept of defense mechanisms has been broadened by other theorists to include maneuvers that people may be aware of. Thus, defense mechanisms operate at varying levels of awareness, although they are largely unconscious.

Are they normal? Definitely. Everyone uses defense mechanisms on a fairly regular basis. They are entirely normal patterns of coping. The notion that only neurotic people use defense mechanisms is inaccurate.

Can Illusions Be Healthy?

Learning Objective

Discuss the adaptive value of defense mechanisms, including recent work on healthy illusions.

The most critical question concerning defense mechanisms is, *Are they healthy?* This is a complicated question. More often than not, the answer is no. Generally, defense mechanisms are poor ways of coping for a number of reasons. First, defensive coping is an avoidance strategy, and avoidance rarely provides a genuine solution to one's problems. Holahan and Moos (1985, 1990) have found that people who exhibit relatively high resistance to stress use avoidance strategies less than people who are frequently troubled by stress. Second, defenses such as denial, fantasy, and projection represent "wishful thinking," which is likely to accomplish little. In fact, in a study of how students coped with the stress of taking the Medical College Admissions Test (MCAT), Bolger (1990) found that students who engaged in a lot of wishful thinking experienced greater increases in anxiety than other students as the exam approached. Third, a repressive coping style has been found to relate to poor health, in part because repression often leads people to delay facing up to their problems (Weinberger, 1990). For example, if you were to block out obvious warning signs of cancer or diabetes and fail to obtain needed medical care, your defensive behavior could be fatal. Fourth, defensive tactics use up energy that could be spent more wisely by tackling the problem. In other words, defensive pseudosolutions may prevent people from employing more constructive coping strategies.

The shortcomings of defensive coping were highlighted in a long-term study of men who had graduated from Harvard. Periodic interviews and tests allowed George Vaillant (1977) to distinguish between men who depended on "immature" defense mechanisms that involved radical distortions of reality and those who depended on "mature" defenses that involved much less distortion of reality. He found that the men who used immature defenses experienced much poorer outcomes than those who relied on the more mature defenses. They exhibited less happiness, poorer adjustment, fewer harmonious marriages, more barren friendship networks, and a higher incidence of mental illness. Thus, when defenses lead to wholesale distortions of reality, they clearly are not healthy.

Although defensive behavior tends to be relatively unhealthful, Vaillant (1994) emphasizes that some defenses are healthier than others and that defense mechanisms can sometimes be adaptive. For example, *overcompensation* for athletic failures could lead you to work extra hard in the classroom. Creative use of *fantasy* is sometimes the key to dealing effectively with a temporary period of frustration, such as a stint in the military service or a period of recovery in the hospital.

Most theorists used to regard accurate contact with reality as the hallmark of sound mental health (Jahoda, 1958; Jourard & Landsman, 1980). However, after studying *denial* and other defenses, Richard Lazarus acknowledges that sometimes "illusion and self-deception can have positive value in a person's psychological economy" (Goleman, 1979, p. 47). Consistent with this notion, Ward, Leventhal, and Love (1988) found that cancer patients who relied on repression experienced fewer treatment side effects than did patients who carefully monitored the course of their disease.

Shelley Taylor (1989) has reviewed several lines of evidence suggesting that "certain illusions may be adaptive for mental health and well-being" (p. 193). First, she notes that "normal" people tend to have overly favorable self-images. In contrast, depressed subjects exhibit less favorable—but more realistic—self-concepts. Second, normal subjects overestimate the degree to which they control chance events. In comparison, depressed subjects are less prone to this illusion of control. Third, normal individuals are more likely than depressed subjects to display unrealistic optimism in making projections about the future.

Thus, it is hard to make sweeping generalizations about the adaptive value of self-deception. Some of the personal illusions that people create through defensive coping may help them to deal with life's difficulties. Roy Baumeister (1989) theorizes that it's all a matter of degree and that there is an "optimal margin of illusion." According to Baumeister, extreme distortions of reality are maladaptive, but small illusions are often beneficial.

In summary, defensive coping and self-deception can be healthful or harmful, depending on the circumstances. As a rule, the more your defenses prevent you from engaging in constructive coping, the more harmful they probably are. To fully appreciate this point, we need to consider what it is that makes coping "constructive."

Shelley Taylor

The Nature of Constructive Coping

Learning Objective

Describe the nature of constructive coping.

Our discussion thus far has focused on coping strategies that tend to be less than ideal. Of course, people also exhibit many healthful strategies for dealing with stress. We use the term **constructive coping to refer to efforts to deal with stressful events that are judged to be relatively healthful.** No strategy of coping can *guarantee* a successful outcome. Even the best coping responses may turn out to be

ineffective in some cases. Thus, the concept of constructive coping is simply meant to have a healthful, positive connotation, without promising success.

Constructive coping does *not* appear to depend particularly on one's intelligence—at least not the abstract, "academic" intelligence measured by conventional IQ tests. Seymour Epstein (1990), a professor at the University of Massachusetts, has shown an interest in "why smart people think dumb." His interest was stimulated in part by a course that he teaches in which students keep daily records of their most positive and negative emotional experiences for class discussion. Commenting on these discussions, Epstein says, "One cannot help but be impressed, when observing students in such a situation, with the degree to which some otherwise bright people lead their lives in a manifestly unintelligent and self-defeating manner" (Epstein & Meier, 1989, p. 333).

To investigate this matter more systematically, Epstein and Petra Meier (1989) devised an elaborate scale to assess the degree to which people engage in constructive coping and thinking. They found that constructive thinking was favorably

---

Recommended Reading

You're Smarter Than You Think

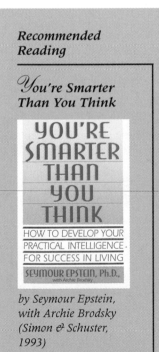

by Seymour Epstein, with Archie Brodsky (Simon & Schuster, 1993)

In an ongoing effort to understand "why smart people think dumb," Seymour Epstein has conducted pioneering research on what he calls *constructive thinking*. In this book, he summarizes his research for the layperson and offers sage advice on how people can make their thinking more constructive. He begins with a self-administered scale intended to measure the reader's tendency to engage in constructive thinking. This brief (30 items) version of the scale that he has used extensively in his research assesses the reader's emotional coping, behavioral coping, categorical thinking, superstitious thinking, esoteric thinking, and naive optimism. He provides test norms so readers can understand how they stack up on each dimension.

After this intriguing venture in self-assessment, Epstein tackles the paradox of how bright people can be remarkably foolhardy. He argues that people operate with two minds—a rational mind and an experiential mind. Although a person's rational mind may rack up high scores on IQ and academic tests, the experiential mind has more influence over everyday coping behavior. The metaphor of two minds may be more confusing than helpful to many readers, but Epstein goes on to provide a great deal of worthwhile advice on how to cope more effectively with emotional distress, relationship problems, work stress, and the challenge of parenting, among other things.

> Why do "smart" people think "dumb" and vice versa? The answer, I have found, is that there is a second kind of intelligence that is unrelated to IQ tests, but is related, instead, to common sense, social skills, and coping with emotions. . . . Your experiential mind is much more closely connected with your emotions than is your rational mind. Operating outside of rational awareness, it comes up with automatic, gut-level, reactions based on memories of past experiences. Your experiential mind is vital to your well-being because it automatically interprets what is going on around you, how you feel about it, and what you should do about it. [pp. 11–12]

related to mental and physical health and to measures of "success" in work, love, and social relationships. However, subjects' IQ scores were only weakly related to their constructive coping scores and largely unrelated to the measures of success in work, love, and social relationships.

In a subsequent study, Katz and Epstein (1991) compared good versus poor constructive thinkers as they worked on laboratory tasks that subjected them to modest stress. Under stress, the good constructive thinkers reported fewer negative thoughts and less negative emotion. They also exhibited lower physiological arousal as indexed by heart rate. In another follow-up study, Epstein and Katz (1992) uncovered a negative correlation between constructive thinking and a measure of self-produced stress, thus supporting the notion that "some people, because of their disorganized, provocative, or otherwise maladaptive behavior, instigate more stressors in their lives than do others" (p. 814). In other words, they found that good constructive thinkers not only cope more effectively with stress, they also create less stress for themselves than poor constructive thinkers.

What makes certain coping strategies constructive? Frankly, it's a gray area in which psychologists' opinions vary to some extent. Nonetheless, some consensus among the experts emerges from the burgeoning research on coping and stress management. Key themes in this literature include the following:

1. Constructive coping involves confronting problems directly. It is task relevant and action oriented. It involves a conscious effort to rationally evaluate one's options in an effort to solve one's problems.
2. Constructive coping is based on reasonably realistic appraisals of one's stress and coping resources. A little self-deception may sometimes be adaptive, but excessive self-deception and highly unrealistic negative thinking are not.
3. Constructive coping involves learning to recognize, and in some cases inhibit, potentially disruptive emotional reactions to stress.
4. Constructive coping involves learning to exert some control over potentially harmful or destructive habitual behaviors. It requires the acquisition of some behavioral self-control.

Learning Objective

List the three categories of constructive coping tactics.

These points should give you a general idea of what we mean by constructive coping. They will also guide our discussion on how to cope more effectively with stress. In the remainder of this chapter we will use a classification scheme proposed by Rudolph Moos and Andrew Billings (1982) to divide constructive coping techniques into three broad categories, grouped according to their focus or goals (see Figure 4.4):

- *Appraisal-focused coping* involves efforts to reevaluate the apparent demands or redefine the apparent meaning of stressful events. Its goal is to alter one's appraisal of the threat in the situation.
- *Problem-focused coping* involves efforts to circumvent, modify, remedy, or conquer the problem and its consequences. Its goal is to directly master the threat or problem itself.

Figure 4.4
Overview of constructive coping tactics
Coping tactics can be organized in several ways, but we will use the classification scheme shown here, which has three categories: appraisal-focused, problem-focused, and emotion-focused. The list of coping tactics in each category is not exhaustive.

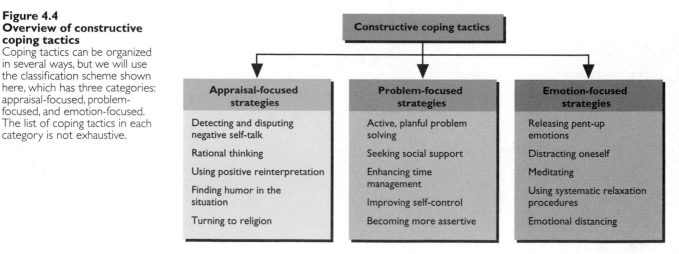

Constructive coping tactics		
Appraisal-focused strategies	**Problem-focused strategies**	**Emotion-focused strategies**
Detecting and disputing negative self-talk	Active, planful problem solving	Releasing pent-up emotions
Rational thinking	Seeking social support	Distracting oneself
Using positive reinterpretation	Enhancing time management	Meditating
Finding humor in the situation	Improving self-control	Using systematic relaxation procedures
Turning to religion	Becoming more assertive	Emotional distancing

- *Emotion-focused coping* involves efforts to control and usually reduce the emotional reactions aroused by stress. Its goal is to reestablish a healthy emotional equilibrium.

Of course, like most efforts to classify complex behavior, this scheme is not entirely satisfactory. Some coping tactics are difficult to categorize because they have more than one goal. Nonetheless, this scheme gives us a framework for analyzing healthful approaches to coping.

Appraisal-Focused Constructive Coping

People often underestimate the importance of the appraisal phase in the stress process. They fail to appreciate the highly subjective feelings that color the perception of threat to one's well-being. A useful way to deal with stress is to alter your appraisal of threatening events. In this section, we'll examine Albert Ellis's ideas about reappraisal and discuss the value of using humor and positive reinterpretation to cope with stress.

Ellis's Rational Thinking

Learning Objective

Describe Ellis's analysis of how catastrophic thinking causes maladaptive emotions.

Albert Ellis (1977, 1985) is a prominent theorist who believes that we can short-circuit our emotional reactions to stress by altering our appraisals of stressful events. Ellis's insights about stress appraisal are the foundation for a widely used system of therapy that he devised. **Rational-emotive therapy is an approach to therapy that focuses on altering clients' patterns of irrational thinking to reduce maladaptive emotions and behavior.**

Ellis maintains that *you feel the way you think*. He argues that problematic emotional reactions are caused by negative self-talk, which he calls catastrophic thinking. **Catastrophic thinking refers to unrealistic appraisals of stress that exaggerate the magnitude of one's problems.** Ellis uses a simple A-B-C sequence to explain his ideas (see Figure 4.5).

A. *Activating event.* The A in Ellis's system stands for the activating event that produces the stress. The activating event may be any potentially stressful transac-

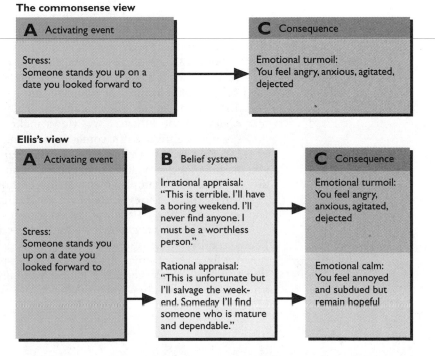

Figure 4.5
Albert Ellis's A-B-C model of emotional reactions
Most people are prone to attribute their negative emotional reactions (C) directly to stressful events (A). However, Ellis argues that emotional reactions are really caused by the way people think about these events (B).

Albert Ellis

tion. Examples might include an automobile accident, the cancellation of a date, a delay while waiting in line at the bank, or a failure to get a promotion you were expecting.

B. *Belief system.* B stands for your belief about the event. This represents your appraisal of the stress. According to Ellis, people often view minor setbacks as disasters. Thus, they engage in catastrophic thinking: "How awful this is. I can't stand it!" "Things never turn out right for me." "I'll be in this line forever." "I'll never get promoted."

C. *Consequence.* C stands for the consequence of people's negative thinking. When appraisals of stressful events are terribly negative, the consequence tends to be emotional distress. Thus, one feels angry, outraged, anxious, panic-stricken, disgusted, or dejected.

Ellis asserts that most people don't understand the importance of phase B in this three-stage sequence. They unwittingly believe that the activating event (A) *causes* the consequent emotional turmoil (C). However, Ellis maintains that A does not cause C. It only appears to do so. Instead, Ellis asserts that B causes C. Emotional distress is actually caused by one's catastrophic thinking in appraising stressful events.

According to Ellis, it is commonplace for people to turn inconvenience into disaster and make "mountains out of molehills." For instance, imagine that someone stands you up on a date that you were eagerly looking forward to. You might think "Oh, this is terrible. I'm going to have another rotten, boring weekend. People always mistreat me. I'll never find anyone to fall in love with. I must be a crummy, worthless person." Ellis would argue that such thoughts are irrational. He would point out that it does not follow logically from being stood up that you (1) must have a lousy weekend, (2) will never fall in love, or (3) are a worthless person.

The Roots of Catastrophic Thinking

Ellis theorizes that unrealistic appraisals of stress are derived from irrational assumptions that people hold. He maintains that if you scrutinize your catastrophic thinking, you will find that your reasoning is based on an indefensibly unreasonable premise, such as "I must have approval from everyone" or "I must perform well in all endeavors." These faulty assumptions, which people often hold unconsciously, generate catastrophic thinking and emotional turmoil. To facilitate emotional self-control, it is important to learn to spot irrational assumptions and the unhealthful patterns of thought they generate. Let's look at four particularly common irrational assumptions. A lengthier list can be found in Figure 4.6.

1. *I must have love and affection from certain people.* Everyone wants to be liked and loved. There is nothing wrong with that. However, many people foolishly believe that they should be liked by everyone they come in contact with. If you stop to think about it, that's clearly unrealistic. Once individuals fall in love, they tend to believe that their future happiness depends absolutely on the continuation of that one, special relationship. They believe that if their current love relationship were to end, they would never again be able to achieve a comparable one. This is an unrealistic view of the future. Such views make people anxious during a relationship and severely depressed if it comes to an end.

2. *I must perform well in all endeavors.* Ours is a highly competitive society. We are taught that victory brings happiness. Consequently, people feel that they must always win. For example, many sports enthusiasts are never satisfied unless they perform at their best level. However, by definition, their best level is not their typical level, and they set themselves up for inevitable frustration.

3. *Other people should always behave competently and be considerate of me.* Everyone is angered by others' stupidity and selfishness. For example, you may become outraged when a mechanic fails to fix your car properly or when a salesperson treats you rudely. It would be nice if people were always competent and considerate, but you know better—they are not! Yet many people go through life unrealistically expecting others' efficiency and kindness.

Irrational Assumptions in Everyday Thinking

Irrational assumption	Rational alternative
1 I must be loved or approved of by everyone for everything I do.	It's best to concentrate on my own self-respect, on winning approval for practical purposes, and on loving rather than being loved.
2 I must be thoroughly competent, adequate, and achieving in order to be worthwhile.	I'm an imperfect creature who has limitations and fallibilities like anyone else—and that's okay.
3 It's horrible when things aren't the way I'd like them to be.	I can try to change or control the things that disturb me—or temporarily accept conditions I can't change.
4 There isn't much I can do about my sorrows and disturbances, because unhappiness comes from what happens to you.	I feel how I think. Unhappiness comes mostly from how I look at things.
5 If something is dangerous or fearsome, I'm right to be terribly upset about it and to dwell on the possibility of its occurring.	I can frankly face what I fear and either render it nondangerous or accept the inevitable.
6 It's easier to avoid facing difficulties and responsibilities than to face them.	The "easy way out" is invariably the much harder alternative in the long run.
7 I'm dependent on others and need someone stronger than I am to rely on.	It's better to take the risk of relying on myself and thinking and acting independently.
8 There's always a precise and perfect solution to human problems, and it's catastrophic not to find it.	The world is full of probability and chance, and I can enjoy life even though there isn't always an ideal solution to a problem.
9 The world—especially other people—should be fair, and justice (mercy) must triumph.	I can work toward seeking fair behavior, realizing that there are few absolutes in life.
10 I must not question the beliefs held by society or respected authorities.	It's better to evaluate beliefs for myself—on their own merits, not on who happens to hold them.

Figure 4.6
Irrational assumptions that can cause emotional disturbance
Irrational assumptions like those listed here are often held unconsciously. According to Ellis, constructive coping depends on detecting these assumptions and replacing them with more rational views, like these examples. (Adapted by Basil Najjar from Ellis, 1977)

4. *Events should always go the way I like.* Some people simply won't tolerate any kind of setback. They assume that things should always go their way. For example, some commuters become tense and angry each time they get stuck in a rush-hour traffic jam. They seem to believe that they are entitled to coast home easily every day, even though they know that rush hour rarely is a breeze. Such expectations are clearly unrealistic and doomed to be violated. Yet few people recognize the obvious irrationality of the assumption that underlies their anger unless it is pointed out to them.

Reducing Catastrophic Thinking

How can you reduce your unrealistic appraisals of stress? Ellis asserts that you must learn (1) how to detect catastrophic thinking and (2) how to dispute the irrational assumptions that cause it. Detection involves acquiring the ability to spot unrealistic pessimism and wild exaggeration in your thinking. Examine your self-talk closely.

Ask yourself why you're getting upset. Force yourself to verbalize your concerns, covertly or out loud. Look for key words that often show up in catastrophic thinking, such as *should, ought, never,* and *must.*

Disputing your irrational assumptions requires subjecting your entire reasoning process to scrutiny. Try to root out the assumptions from which your conclusions are derived. Once they are unearthed, their irrationality may be quite obvious. If your assumptions seem reasonable, ask yourself whether your conclusions follow logically. Try to replace your catastrophic thinking with more low-key, rational analyses. These strategies should help you redefine stressful situations in ways that are less threatening. Strangely enough, another way to defuse such situations is to turn to humor.

Humor as a Stress Reducer

Learning Objective

Discuss the merits of humor and positive reinterpretation as coping strategies.

A few years ago, the Chicago area experienced its worst flooding in about a century. Thousands of people saw their homes wrecked when two rivers spilled over their banks. As the waters receded, the flood victims returning to their homes were subjected to the inevitable TV interviews. A remarkable number of victims, surrounded by the ruins of their homes, *joked* about their misfortune. When the going gets tough, it may pay to laugh about it. In a study of coping styles, McCrae (1984) found that 40% of his subjects reported using humor to deal with stress.

In analyzing the stress-reducing effects of humor, Dixon (1980) emphasizes its impact on the appraisal of stress. Finding a humorous aspect in a stressful situation redefines the situation in a less threatening way. Dixon notes that laughter can also discharge pent-up emotions. These dual functions of humor may make joking about life's difficulties a particularly useful coping strategy.

Some psychologists have long suspected that humor might be a worthwhile coping response. But empirical evidence to that effect has emerged only in recent years (Martin & Lefcourt, 1983; Nezu, Nezu, & Blissett, 1988). For instance, Martin and Lefcourt (1983) found that a good sense of humor functioned as a buffer to lessen the negative impact of stress on mood. Some of their results are shown in Figure

Recommended Reading

How to Stubbornly Refuse to Make Yourself Miserable About Anything—Yes, Anything!

by Albert Ellis (Carol Communications, 1988)

This is one of the most recent "popular" books by Albert Ellis, the world-renowned architect of rational-emotive therapy. At last count, Ellis had written around 50 books, about evenly divided between popular books intended for a general audience and technical books intended for mental health professionals. This book doesn't break any new ground for Ellis, but it does bring his ideas together in one succinct, readable summary, complete with exercises. Ellis is a bit prone to overstatement, asserting that his book "will help you achieve a profound philosophic change and a radically new outlook on life." Whether it does so or not, his ideas clearly can help people cope with stress more effectively. If you're a victim of catastrophic thinking, this book is worth reading. The writing is casual and down-to-earth. For instance, the following passage comes from a chapter titled "Forget Your 'Godawful' Past."

> For several years I was a highly successful psychoanalyst and thought that I was greatly helping my clients by exploring the gory details of their early life and showing them how these experiences made them disturbed—and how they could now understand and remove these early influences.
>   How wrong I was!
>   After I honestly admitted that my psychoanalytic "cures" were hardly as good as I would have liked them to be, I began to see that helping people to understand their past was not only doing them little good but was actually blocking their dealing with their present problems. [p. 69]

Figure 4.7
Humor and coping
Martin and Lefcourt (1983) related stress to mood disturbance in subjects who were either high or low in their use of humor. Increased stress led to smaller increases in mood disturbance in the high humor group, suggesting that humor has some value in efforts to cope with stress.

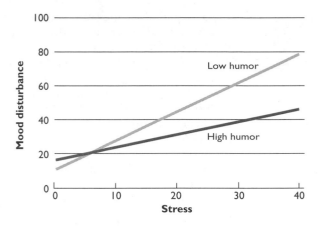

4.7. It plots how mood disturbance increased as stress went up in two groups of subjects—those who were high or low in their use of humor. Notice how higher stress led to a smaller increase in mood disturbance in the high humor group.

Positive Reinterpretation

When you are feeling overwhelmed by life's difficulties, you might try the commonsense strategy of recognizing that "things could be worse." No matter how terrible your problems seem, you probably know people who have even bigger troubles. That is not to say that you should derive satisfaction from others' misfortune. However, comparing your own plight with others' even tougher struggles can help you put your problems in perspective. Research by McCrae (1984) suggests that this strategy of making positive comparisons with others is a widely used coping mechanism. It seems to be a relatively healthful one, in that it can facilitate calming reappraisals of stress without the necessity of distorting reality.

Another way to engage in positive reinterpretation is to search for something good in a bad experience. Distressing though they may be, many setbacks have positive elements. After experiencing divorces, illnesses, firings, financial losses, and such, many people remark that "I came out of the experience better than I went in," or "I grew as a person." The positive aspects of a personal setback may be easy to see after the stressful event is behind you. The challenge is to recognize these positive aspects while you are still struggling with the setback, so that it becomes less stressful. Research suggests that positive reinterpretation is an effective coping method (Folkman, Lazarus, Gruen, & DeLongis, 1986).

Problem-Focused Constructive Coping

Problem-focused coping includes efforts to remedy or conquer the stress-producing problem itself. In this category, we'll discuss systematic problem solving, the importance of seeking help, effective time management, and improving self-control.

Using Systematic Problem Solving

Learning Objective

List and describe four steps in systematic problem solving.

In dealing with life's problems, the most obvious course of action is to tackle the problems head-on. In the study of coping by Carver, Scheier, and Weintraub (1989), the two coping tactics that reflect this approach (active coping and planning) were favorably related to higher self-esteem and lower anxiety. In another study, D'Zurilla and Sheedy (1991) took a more focused look at the link between problem solving and stress. They used two scales to evaluate key aspects of subjects' social problem-solving ability. One scale gauged subjects' *problem orientation*—that is, whether they approached problems with a positive attitude, viewing them as challenges and opportunities. The other scale assessed a set of four *problem-solving skills:* (1) defining and formulating the problem, (2) generating alternative solutions, (3) making decisions, and (4) implementing and verifying solutions. Three months after the assessment of their problem-solving ability, subjects completed the Derogatis Stress Profile (Derogatis, 1987), which measures various symptoms of stress. D'Zurilla and Sheedy found that subjects' level of stress symptoms correlated $-.53$ with their problem orientation and $-.23$ with their problem-solving skills. In other words, the better subjects' problem-solving abilities were, the fewer stress-related difficulties they experienced. Consistent with this finding, research reveals that the acquisition of systematic problem-solving skills can help depressed patients reduce their feelings of depression (Nezu, 1986).

Because there are an infinite number of personal problems that may arise, we can only sketch a general outline of how to engage in systematic problem solving. The problem-solving plan described here is a synthesis of observations by various experts, especially Mahoney (1979) and Miller (1978). The four steps, which closely parallel the four problem-solving skills measured by D'Zurilla and Sheedy (1991), include the following: (1) clarify the problem, (2) generate alternative courses of action, (3) evaluate your alternatives and select a course of action, and (4) take action while maintaining flexibility.

Clarify the Problem

You can't tackle a problem head-on if you're not sure what the problem is. Therefore, the first step in any systematic problem-solving effort is to clarify the nature of the problem. Sometimes the problem will be all too obvious. At other times the source of trouble may be quite difficult to pin down. In any case, you need to arrive at a specific and concrete definition of your problem.

Two common tendencies typically hinder efforts to get a clear picture of one's problems. First, people often describe their problems in vague generalities (for example, "My life isn't going anywhere" or "I never have enough time"). Second, people tend to focus too much on negative feelings. This tendency confuses the consequences of problems ("I'm so depressed all the time" or "I'm so nervous I can't concentrate") with the problems themselves.

Generate Alternative Courses of Action

The second step in systematic problem solving is to generate alternative courses of action. Notice that we did not call these alternative *solutions*. Many problems do not have a readily available solution that will completely resolve the problem. If you think in terms of searching for complete solutions, you may prevent yourself from considering many worthwhile courses of action. Instead, it is more realistic to search for alternatives that may produce some kind of improvement in your situation.

Besides avoiding the tendency to insist on solutions, you need to avoid the temptation to go with the first alternative that comes to mind. Many people are a little trigger-happy. They thoughtlessly try to follow through on the first response that occurs to them. Various lines of evidence suggest that it is wiser to engage in brainstorming about a problem. **Brainstorming involves generating as many ideas as possible while withholding criticism and evaluation.** In other words, you generate alternatives without paying any attention to their apparent practicality. This approach facilitates creative expression of ideas.

Evaluate Your Alternatives and Select a Course of Action

Once you generate as many alternatives as you can, you need to start evaluating them. There are no simple criteria for judging the relative merits of your alternatives. However, you will probably want to address three general issues. First, ask yourself whether each alternative is a *realistic plan*. In other words, what is the probability that you can successfully execute the intended course of action? Try to think of any obstacles you may have failed to anticipate. In making this assessment, it is important to try to avoid both foolish optimism and unnecessary pessimism. Second, consider any *costs* or *risks* associated with each alternative. The "solution" to a problem can sometimes be worse than the problem itself. Assuming you can successfully implement your intended course of action, what are the possible negative consequences? Finally, compare the *desirability* of the probable outcomes of each alternative. After eliminating the unrealistic possibilities, list the probable consequences (both good and bad) associated with each alternative. Then review and compare the desirability of these potential outcomes. In making your decision, you have to ask yourself "What is important to me? Which outcomes do I value the most?"

Take Action While Maintaining Flexibility

Once you have chosen your course of action, you should try to implement your plan. In doing so, try to maintain flexibility. Don't get locked into a particular course of action. Few choices are truly irreversible. You need to monitor results closely and be willing to revise your strategy.

In evaluating your course of action, try to avoid the simplistic success/failure dichotomy. You should look for improvement of any kind. If your plan doesn't work out too well, consider whether it was undermined by any circumstances that you could not have anticipated. Finally, remember that you can learn from your failures. Even if things didn't work out, you may now have new information that will facilitate a new attack on the problem.

Seeking Help

In Chapter 3, we learned that social support can be a powerful force that helps buffer the deleterious effects of stress. We discussed social support as if it were a stable, external resource available to different people in varying degrees. In reality, people's social supports fluctuate over time and evolve out of their interactions with others (Newcomb, 1990). For example, some people have more support than others because they have personal characteristics that attract more support or because they make more effort to seek support.

In trying to tackle problems directly, it pays to keep in mind the value of seeking aid from friends, family, co-workers, and neighbors. Because of potential embarrassment, many people are reluctant to acknowledge their problems and to seek help from others. What makes this situation so lamentable is that others can provide a great deal of help in many ways.

Using Time More Effectively

Learning Objective

Discuss five common causes of wasted time.

Do you constantly feel as though you have too much to do and too little time to do it in? Do you feel overwhelmed by your responsibilities at work, at school, and at home? Do you feel like you're always rushing around, trying to meet an impossible schedule? If so, you're struggling with time pressure. You can estimate how well you manage time by responding to the brief questionnaire in Figure 4.8. If the results suggest that your time is out of your control, you may be able to make your life less stressful by learning sound time-management strategies.

R. Alec Mackenzie (1972), a prominent time-management researcher, points out that time is a nonrenewable resource. It can't be stockpiled like money, food, or other precious resources. You can't turn back the clock. Furthermore, everyone, whether rich or poor, gets an equal share of time—24 hours per day, seven days a week. Although time is our most equitably distributed resource, some people spend it much more wisely than others. Let's look at some of the ways in which people let time slip through their fingers without accomplishing much.

The Causes of Wasted Time

When people complain about "wasted time," they're usually upset because they haven't accomplished what they really wanted to with their time. Wasted time is

**Figure 4.8
Assessing your time management**
This brief questionnaire is designed to evaluate the quality of one's time management. Although it is geared more for working adults than college students, it should allow you to get a rough handle on how well you manage your time. (From LeBoeuf, 1980)

How Well Do You Manage Your Time?

Listed below are ten statements that reflect generally accepted principles of good time management. Answer these items by circling the response most characteristic of how you perform your job. Please be honest. No one will know your answers except you.

1 Each day I set aside a small amount of time for planning and thinking about my job.
   0. Almost never 1. Sometimes 2. Often 3. Almost always

2 I set specific, written goals and put deadlines on them.
   0. Almost never 1. Sometimes 2. Often 3. Almost always

3 I make a daily "to do list," arrange items in order of importance, and try to get the important items done as soon as possible.
   0. Almost never 1. Sometimes 2. Often 3. Almost always

4 I am aware of the 80/20 rule and use it in doing my job. (The 80/20 rule states that 80 percent of your effectiveness will generally come from achieving only 20 percent of your goals.)
   0. Almost never 1. Sometimes 2. Often 3. Almost always

5 I keep a loose schedule to allow for crises and the unexpected.
   0. Almost never 1. Sometimes 2. Often 3. Almost always

6 I delegate everything I can to others.
   0. Almost never 1. Sometimes 2. Often 3. Almost always

7 I try to handle each piece of paper only once.
   0. Almost never 1. Sometimes 2. Often 3. Almost always

8 I eat a light lunch so I don't get sleepy in the afternoon.
   0. Almost never 1. Sometimes 2. Often 3. Almost always

9 I make an active effort to keep common interruptions (visitors, meetings, telephone calls) from continually disrupting my work day.
   0. Almost never 1. Sometimes 2. Often 3. Almost always

10 I am able to say no to others' requests for my time that would prevent my completing important tasks.
   0. Almost never 1. Sometimes 2. Often 3. Almost always

To get your score, give yourself
   3 points for each "almost always"
   2 points for each "often"
   1 point for each "sometimes"
   0 points for each "almost never"
Add up your points to get your total score.

If you scored
   0–15   Better give some thought to managing your time.
   15–20   You're doing OK, but there's room for improvement.
   20–25   Very good.
   28–30   You cheated!

time devoted to unnecessary, unimportant, or unenjoyable activities. Why waste time on such activities? There are many reasons.

Inability to set or stick to priorities   Time consultant Alan Lakein (1973) notes that it's often tempting to deal with routine, trivial tasks ahead of larger and more difficult tasks. Thus, students working on a major term paper often read their mail, do the dishes, fold the laundry, reorganize their desk, or dust the furniture instead of concentrating on the paper. Routine tasks are easy, and working on them allows one to rationalize the avoidance of more important tasks. Unfortunately, so much time is spent on trivial pursuits that more important tasks are left undone.

Inability to say no   Other people are constantly making demands on our time. They want us to exchange gossip in the hallway, go out to dinner on Friday night, cover their hours at work, help with a project, listen to their sales pitch on the phone, join a committee, or coach Little League. Clearly, we can't do everything that everyone wants us to. However, some people just can't say no to others' requests for their time. Such people end up fulfilling others' priorities instead of their own. Thus, McDougle (1987) concludes, "Perhaps the most successful way to prevent yourself from wasting time is by saying *no*" (p. 112).

Inability to delegate responsibility   Some tasks should be delegated to others—secretaries, subordinates, fellow committee members, other coaches, spouses, children, and so on. However, many people have difficulty delegating work to others. Barriers to delegation include unwillingness to give up any control, lack of confidence in subordinates, fear of being disliked, the need to feel needed, and the attitude that "I can do it better myself" (Mitchell, 1987). The problem, of course, is that people who can't delegate waste a lot of time on trivial work or others' work.

Inability to throw things away   Some people are "pack rats" who can't throw anything into the wastebasket. Their desks are cluttered with piles of mail, newspapers, magazines, reports, and books. Their filing cabinets overflow with old class notes or ancient memos. At home, their kitchen drawers bulge with rarely used utensils, their closets bulge with old clothes that are never worn, and their attics bulge with discarded junk. Pack rats waste time in at least two ways. First, they lose time looking for things that are lost amid all the chaos. Second, they end up reshuffling the same paper, rereading the same mail, re-sorting the same reports, and so on. They would be better off if they made more use of their wastebaskets. Indeed, Mackenzie (1972) notes that "the art of wastebasketry has been designated by at least one management consultant as the most critical skill in managing one's work" (p. 69).

Inability to accept anything less than perfection   High standards are admirable, but some people have difficulty finishing projects because they expect them to be flawless. They can't let go. They dwell on minor problems and keep making microscopic changes in their papers, projects, and proposals. They are caught in what Emanuel (1987) calls the "paralysis of perfection." They end up spinning their wheels, redoing the same work over and over.

Time-Management Techniques

Learning Objective

Summarize advice on managing time effectively.

What's the key to better time management? Most people assume that it's increased *efficiency*—that is, learning to perform tasks more quickly. Improved efficiency may help a little, but time-management experts maintain that efficiency is overrated. They emphasize that the key to better time management is increased *effectiveness*—that is, learning to allocate time to your most important tasks. This distinction is captured by a widely quoted slogan in the time-management literature: "Efficiency is doing the job right, while effectiveness is doing the right job." Let's look at the experts' suggestions for using time more effectively (based on Lakein, 1973; Lebov, 1980; Mackenzie, 1972).

1. *Monitor your use of time.* The first step toward better time management is to monitor your use of time to see where it all goes. This requires keeping a written record of your activities, similar to that shown in Figure 4.9. At the end of each week, you should analyze how your time was allocated. Based on your personal roles and responsibilities, create categories of time use such as studying, child care, housework, commuting, work at the office, work at home, eating, and sleeping. For each day, add up the hours consumed by each category. Record this information on a summary sheet like that in Figure 4.10. Two weeks of record keeping should allow you to draw some conclusions about where your time goes. Your records will help you make informed decisions about reallocating your time. When you begin your time-management program, these records will also give you a baseline for comparison, so that you can see whether your program is working.

2. *Clarify your goals.* You can't wisely allocate your time unless you decide what you want to accomplish with your time. Lakein (1973) suggests that you ask yourself "What are my lifetime goals?" Write down all the goals that you can think of, even relatively frivolous things like going deep-sea fishing or becoming a wine expert. Some of your goals will be in conflict. For instance, you can't become a vice-president at your company in Wichita and move to the West Coast. Thus, the tough part comes next. You have to wrestle with your goal conflicts. Figure out which

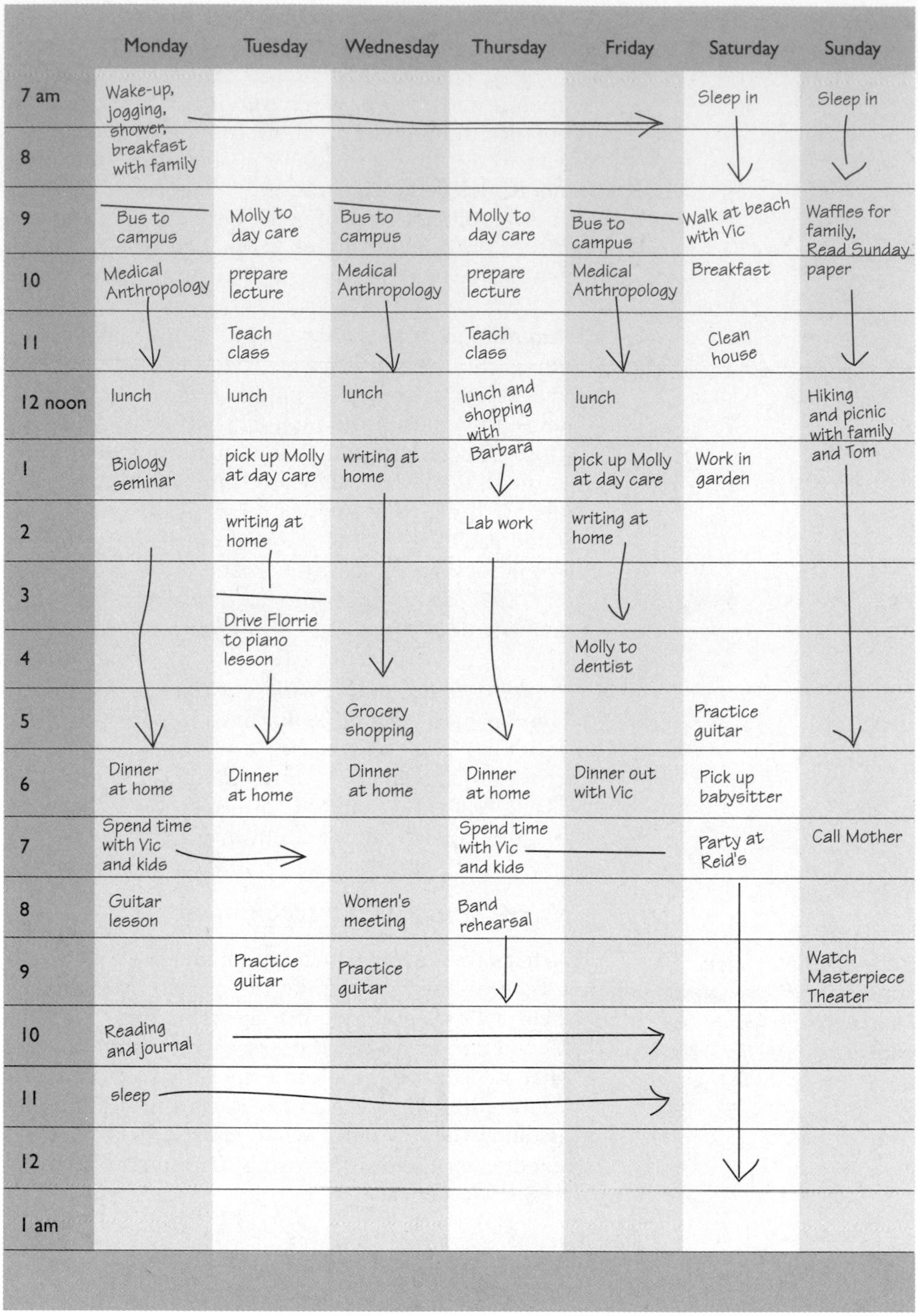

Figure 4.9
Example of a time log
To improve your time management, experts recommend keeping a detailed record of how you use your time. This example shows the kind of record keeping that should be done.

	Monday	Tuesday	Wednesday	Thursday	Friday	Saturday	Sunday
7 am	Wake-up, jogging, shower, breakfast with family					Sleep in	Sleep in
8							
9	Bus to campus	Molly to day care	Bus to campus	Molly to day care	Bus to campus	Walk at beach with Vic	Waffles for family, Read Sunday paper
10	Medical Anthropology	prepare lecture	Medical Anthropology	prepare lecture	Medical Anthropology	Breakfast	
11		Teach class		Teach class		Clean house	
12 noon	lunch	lunch	lunch	lunch and shopping with Barbara	lunch		Hiking and picnic with family and Tom
1	Biology seminar	pick up Molly at day care	writing at home		pick up Molly at day care	Work in garden	
2		writing at home		Lab work	writing at home		
3							
4		Drive Florrie to piano lesson			Molly to dentist		
5			Grocery shopping			Practice guitar	
6	Dinner at home	Dinner at home	Dinner at home	Dinner at home	Dinner out with Vic	Pick up babysitter	
7	Spend time with Vic and kids			Spend time with Vic and kids		Party at Reid's	Call Mother
8	Guitar lesson		Women's meeting	Band rehearsal			
9		Practice guitar	Practice guitar				Watch Masterpiece Theater
10	Reading and journal						
11	sleep						
12							
1 am							

goals are most important to you, and order them in terms of priority. These priorities should guide you as you plan your activities on a daily, weekly, and monthly basis.

3. *Plan your activities using a schedule.* People resist planning because it takes time, but in the long run it saves time. Thorough planning is essential to effective time management. At the beginning of each week, you should make up a list of short-term goals. This list should be translated into daily "to do" lists of planned activities. To avoid the tendency to put off larger projects, break them into smaller, manageable components, and set deadlines for completing the components. Your planned activities should be allocated to various time slots on a written schedule. Schedule your most important activities into the time periods when you tend to be most energetic and productive.

4. *Protect your prime time.* The best-laid plans can quickly go awry because of interruptions. There's no foolproof way to eliminate interruptions, but you may be

Figure 4.10
Time use summary
To analyze where your time goes, you need to review your time log and create a weekly time use summary, like the one shown here. The exact categories to be listed on the left depend on your circumstances and responsibilities.

Time Use Summary Form

Activity	Mon.	Tues.	Wed.	Thurs.	Fri.	Sat.	Sun.	Total	%
1 Sleeping	8	6	8	6	8	7	9	52	31
2 Eating	2	2	3	2	3	2	3	17	10
3 Commuting	2	2	2	2	2	0	0	10	6
4 Housework	0	1	0	3	0	0	2	6	4
5 In class	4	2	4	2	4	0	0	16	9
6 Part-time job	0	5	0	5	0	3	0	13	8
7 Studying	3	2	4	2	0	4	5	20	12
8 Relaxing	5	4	3	2	7	8	5	34	20
9									
10									

able to shift most of them into certain time slots while protecting your most productive time. The trick is to announce to your family, friends, and co-workers that you're blocking off certain periods of "quiet time" when visitors and phone calls will be turned away. Of course, you also have to block off periods of "available time" when you're ready to deal with everyone's problems.

5. *Increase your efficiency.* Although efficiency is not the key to better time management, it's not irrelevant. Time-management experts do offer some suggestions for improving efficiency, including the following (Klassen, 1987; Schilit, 1987).

- *Handle paper once.* When memos, letters, reports, and such arrive on your desk, they should not be stashed away to be read again and again before you deal with them. Most paperwork can and should be dealt with immediately.

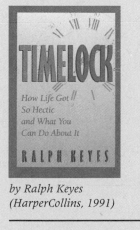
If you're locked in a perennial struggle with time—and if you're losing the battle—this book may be worth your time. In *Timelock*, Ralph Keyes offers insightful analyses, peppered with interesting case studies, of why most people never have enough time. He discusses how the pressure to produce and the wealth of choices in everyday life lead people to try to do too much, turning them into "rushaholics." He also explains how modern conveniences, such as computers and videotape recorders, often create new demands on our time that far exceed the time they save. Most important, Keyes discusses how cultural norms program people to constantly try to squeeze more and more activities into less and less time. What's the solution? Keyes argues convincingly that most people should reevaluate what they want out of life and try to do less instead of more. He offers a host of practical suggestions for achieving this end in this fascinating and thought-provoking book.

There are two basic approaches to coming to terms with time. The more prevalent one—the don't waste a minute school—emphasizes squeezing maximum productivity out of each second with better planning, list making, and high-tech tools. The less conventional, but more pertinent approach proposes just the opposite: reducing the volume of one's activities and becoming less concerned about time as such in an effort to better see the big picture, reflect regularly, and stay focused on what really matters . . .

The ongoing theme of this book has been that the harder we try to control time, the more time controls us. By the same token, once we stop trying to wrestle time to the ground, its grip on our throat eases. We may not "manage" our schedules better by getting on friendlier terms with time, but we no longer mind as much. Best of all we lose the feeling that time is our enemy. [pp. 162–164]

- *Tackle one task at a time.* Jumping from one problem to another is inefficient. Insofar as possible, stick with a task until it's done. In scheduling your activities, try to allow enough time to complete tasks.
- *Group similar tasks together.* It's a good idea to bunch up small tasks that are similar. This strategy is useful when you're paying bills, replying to letters, returning phone calls, and so forth.
- *Make use of your downtime.* Most of us endure a lot of "downtime," waiting in doctors' offices, sitting in needless meetings, riding on buses and trains. In many of these situations, you may be able to get some of your easier work done—if you think ahead and bring it along.

Improving Self-Control

Self-discipline and self-control are the key to handling many of life's problems effectively. All four forms of stress described in Chapter 3 can create challenges to your self-control. Whether you're struggling with the *frustration* of poor grades in school, constant *conflicts* about your overeating, *pressure* to do well in sports, or *changes* in finances that require readjustment, you will need reasonable self-control if you expect to make much progress.

For many people, however, satisfactory self-control is difficult to achieve. Fortunately, the last several decades have produced major insights into the mechanisms of self-control. These insights have emerged from research on *behavior modification,* an approach to controlling behavior based on the principles of learning and conditioning. Because of its importance, we'll devote the entire Application at the end of this chapter to improving self-control through behavior modification.

Emotion-Focused Constructive Coping

Let's be realistic: There are going to be occasions when appraisal-focused coping and problem-focused coping are not successful in warding off emotional turmoil. Some problems are too serious to be whittled down much by reappraisal, and others simply can't be "solved." Moreover, even well-executed coping strategies may take time to work before emotional tensions begin to subside. Hence, it is helpful to have some coping mechanisms that are useful in reducing emotional arousal. Here we'll discuss the merits of four such coping strategies: releasing pent-up emotions, distracting yourself, meditating, and using relaxation exercises.

Releasing Pent-Up Emotions

Learning Objective

Discuss the adaptive value of releasing pent-up emotions and of distracting yourself.

Because of the potential negative physiological effects of emotional arousal, it's not a good idea to let strong emotions seethe within you for a long time. One study of high school students found that those who tended to hold their anger in were more likely to have higher blood pressure (Spielberger et al., 1985). In short, it probably pays to try to release pent-up emotions.

For example, when you're dejected, it may be worthwhile to go ahead and cry your heart out. Humans have a natural inclination to use this simple response. Unfortunately, many people—especially men—are taught that crying is inappropriate. Admittedly, the evidence for beneficial effects from crying is rather weak, coming mostly from clinical reports and anecdotal accounts (Kraemer & Hastrup, 1988). Nonetheless, crying may be a reasonable, albeit unproven, coping strategy.

Recent studies suggest that verbalization may have considerable value in releasing anxiety and calming other stress-related emotions (Clark, 1993). In other words, it could help to "talk it out." James Pennebaker and his colleagues have shown that talking or writing about traumatic events can have beneficial effects. According to Pennebaker (1990), a large proportion of people do not discuss their personal problems—even major trauma—with others. This situation is unfortunate in light of the

In times of stress, seeking support from one's friends and releasing pent-up emotions are very useful coping strategies.

finding that people who do not talk about traumatic events suffer more health problems than those who confide in others (Pennebaker & O'Heeron, 1984; Pennebaker & Susman, 1988). To test the value of talking it out, Pennebaker, Kiecolt-Glaser, and Glaser (1988) asked college students to write four brief essays about their difficulties in adjusting to college. The subjects who wrote about their personal problems and traumas showed better immune function than control subjects who wrote essays about superficial topics. In a subsequent, similar study, the students who wrote about their personal problems enjoyed better health in the following months than the other subjects (Pennebaker, Colder, & Sharp, 1990). Thus, if you can find a good listener, it may be wise to try to discharge problematic emotions by letting your secret fears, misgivings, and suspicions spill out in a candid conversation. Admittedly, talking about one's problems can be awkward and difficult. Pennebaker's research suggests that confiding in others does have short-term costs in that it may elicit anxiety and other negative emotions. However, in the long run, those who open up to others enjoy better mental and physical health than those who hold back.

Distracting Yourself

Distraction involves diverting your attention from a problem by thinking about other things or engaging in other activities. Substantial reliance on this strategy was observed in the coping efforts of 60 married couples (Stone & Neale, 1984). If your stomach is churning over a snafu at work, it may be a good idea to go out to a movie, read a good thriller, or head for the bowling alley. Activities that require focused attention are probably best when using this strategy.

The adaptive merits of distraction are open to debate. On the one hand, distracting yourself is probably inferior to problem-focused coping that might yield a longer-lasting solution. On the other hand, distracting yourself clearly is a better idea than self-indulgence, lashing out at others, or getting bogged down in negative self-talk. Thus, it appears to be a strategy that has modest, short-term value when more direct tactics have failed to produce progress.

Meditating

Learning Objective

Summarize the evidence on the effects of meditation.

Recent years have seen an explosion of interest in meditation as a method for relieving stress. *Meditation* **refers to a family of mental exercises in which a conscious attempt is made to focus attention in a nonanalytical way.** There are many approaches to meditation. In the United States, the most widely practiced approaches are those associated with yoga, Zen, and transcendental meditation

(TM). Although all three are rooted in Eastern religions (Hinduism, Buddhism, and Taoism), most Americans who practice meditation have only vague ideas regarding its religious significance. Of interest to us is the idea that meditation can calm inner emotional turmoil.

Most meditative techniques look deceptively simple. For example, in TM a person is supposed to sit in a comfortable position with eyes closed and silently focus attention on a *mantra*, a specially assigned Sanskrit word that creates a resonant sound. This exercise in mental self-discipline is to be practiced twice daily for 20 minutes. The technique has been described as "diving from the active surface of the mind to its quiet depths" (Bloomfield & Kory, 1976, p. 49).

Advocates of TM claim that it can improve learning, energy level, work productivity, physical health, mental health, and general happiness while reducing tension and anxiety caused by stress (Alexander et al., 1990; Bloomfield & Kory, 1976). These are not exactly humble claims. Moreover, TM advocates assert that they can back up their claims with scientific evidence. Let's examine that evidence.

What are the *physical effects* of going into the meditative state? Some studies suggest that it produces changes in the electrochemical activity of the brain. Most studies also find decreases in subjects' heart rate, respiration rate, oxygen consumption, and carbon dioxide elimination (see Figure 4.11). Many researchers have also observed increases in skin resistance and decreases in blood lactate—physiological indicators associated with relaxation. Taken together, these bodily changes suggest that meditation can lead to a potentially beneficial physiological state characterized by relaxation and suppression of arousal (Carrington, 1993; Fenwick, 1987).

These findings generated quite a bit of excitement in the 1970s. However, additional research using better experimental controls soon dampened some of this enthusiasm. It turns out that these physical changes may not be unique to meditation. A variety of systematic relaxation training procedures may be able to produce similar results (Holmes, 1987; Shapiro, 1984).

The findings on the *psychological effects* of meditation are also promising but controversial. Some studies have found that meditation can improve mood, lessen fatigue, and reduce anxiety and drug abuse (Carrington, 1987; Eppley, Abrams, & Shear, 1989; Gelderloos et al., 1991). Studies also suggest that meditation is associated with improved physical health (Orme-Johnson, 1987), superior mental health (Alexander, Rainforth, & Gelderloos, 1991), and even increased longevity among the elderly (Alexander et al., 1989). However, some psychologists argue that at least some of these effects may be just as attainable through systematic relaxation or other mental focusing procedures (Holmes, 1984; Shapiro, 1987). At present, the evidence on this issue is too inconsistent and fragmentary to permit any solid conclusions (Lehrer & Woolfolk, 1993).

What's the bottom line? If you are troubled by chronic emotional tension, learning to meditate may be an effective way to reduce your troublesome arousal. Bear in mind, however, that the benefits of meditation may not be as spectacular as some proponents have claimed. Furthermore, you may be able to attain some of the same benefits through less exotic techniques, such as the relaxation procedures that we discuss next.

Figure 4.11
Transcendental meditation (TM) and physiological arousal
The physiological changes shown on this graph (based on Wallace & Benson, 1972) indicate that meditation suppresses arousal, thus leading to a physical state that may have beneficial effects.

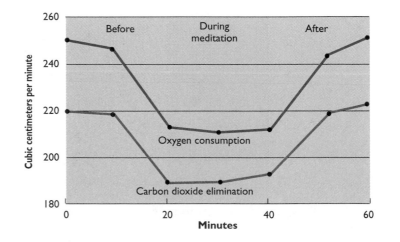

Using Relaxation Procedures

Learning Objective

Describe the requirements and procedure for Benson's relaxation response.

Herbert Benson

Ample evidence suggests that systematic relaxation procedures can soothe emotional turmoil and reduce problematic physiological arousal (Lehrer & Woolfolk, 1984, 1993). One study even proposes that relaxation training may improve the effectiveness of one's immune response (Kiecolt-Glaser et al., 1985). There are a number of worthwhile approaches to achieving beneficial relaxation. The most prominent systems are Jacobson's (1938) *progressive relaxation* (see McGuigan, 1993), Schultz and Luthe's (1969) *autogenic training* (see Linden, 1993), and Benson's (1975; Benson & Klipper, 1988) *relaxation response.* We'll discuss Benson's approach because it is a simple one that virtually anyone can learn to use.

After studying various approaches to meditation, Herbert Benson, a Harvard Medical School cardiologist, concluded that elaborate religious rituals and beliefs are not necessary to profit from meditation. He also concluded that what makes meditation beneficial is the relaxation it induces. After "demystifying" meditation, Benson (1975) set out to devise a simple, nonreligious procedure that could provide similar benefits. He calls his procedure the "relaxation response." According to Benson, the following four factors are critical to effective practice of the relaxation response:

1. *A quiet environment.* It is easiest to induce the relaxation response in a distraction-free environment. After you become skilled at the relaxation response, you may be able to accomplish it in a crowded subway. Initially, however, you should practice it in a quiet, calm place.
2. *A mental device.* To shift attention inward and keep it there, you need to focus it on a constant stimulus, such as a sound or word that you recite over and over. You may also choose to gaze fixedly at a bland object, such as a vase. Whatever the case, you need to focus your attention on something.
3. *A passive attitude.* It is important not to get upset when your attention strays to distracting thoughts. You must realize that such distractions are inevitable. Whenever your mind wanders from your attentional focus, calmly redirect attention to your mental device.
4. *A comfortable position.* Reasonable body comfort is essential to avoid a major source of potential distraction. Simply sitting up straight works well for most people. Some people can practice the relaxation response lying down, but for most people such a position is too conducive to sleep.

Benson's (1975, pp. 114–115) actual procedure for inducing the relaxation response is described in Figure 4.12. For full benefit, it should be practiced daily.

Figure 4.12
Benson's relaxation response
The relaxation procedure advocated by Herbert Benson is a simple one that should be practiced daily. (From Benson, 1975)

1 Sit quietly in a comfortable position.

2 Close your eyes

3 Deeply relax all your muscles, beginning at your feet and progressing up to your face. Keep them relaxed.

4 Breathe through your nose. Become aware of your breathing. As you breathe out, say the word "one" silently to yourself. For example, breathe in . . . out, "one"; in . . . out, "one"; and so forth. Breathe easily and naturally.

5 Continue for 10 to 20 minutes. You may open your eyes to check the time, but do not use an alarm. When you finish, sit quietly for several minutes, at first with your eyes closed and later with your eyes opened. Do not stand up for a few minutes.

6 Do not worry about whether you are successful in achieving a deep level of relaxation. Maintain a passive attitude and permit relaxation to occur at its own pace. When distracting thoughts occur, try to ignore them by not dwelling on them, and return to repeating "one." With practice, the response should come with little effort. Practice the technique once or twice daily but not within two hours after any meal, since digestive processes seem to interfere with the elicitation of the relaxation response.

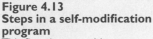

Answer the following "yes" or "no."

1. Do you have a hard time passing up food, even when you're not hungry?

2. Do you wish you studied more often?

3. Would you like to cut down on your smoking or drinking?

4. Do you experience difficulty in getting yourself to exercise regularly?

5. Do you wish you had more willpower?

Figure 4.13
Steps in a self-modification program
This flowchart provides an overview of the steps necessary to execute a self-modification program.

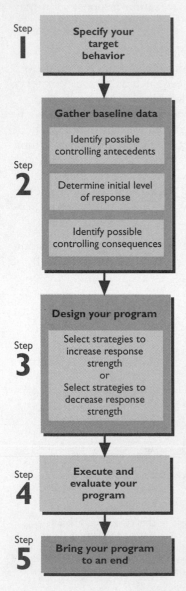

If you answered "yes" to any of these questions, you have struggled with the challenge of self-control. This Application discusses how you can use the techniques of behavior modification to improve your self-control. If you stop to think about it, self-control—or rather a lack of it—underlies many of the personal problems that people struggle with every day.

***Behavior modification* is a systematic approach to changing behavior through the application of the principles of conditioning.** Advocates of behavior modification assume that behavior is a product of learning, conditioning, and environmental control. They further assume that *what is learned can be unlearned.* Thus, they set out to "recondition" people to produce more desirable patterns of behavior.

The technology of behavior modification has been applied with great success in schools, businesses, hospitals, factories, child care facilities, prisons, and mental health centers (Goodall, 1972; Kazdin, 1982; Rachman, 1992). Moreover, behavior modification techniques have proven particularly valuable in efforts to improve self-

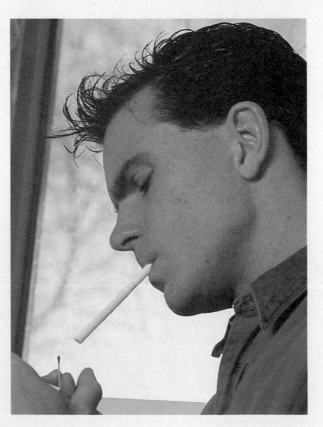

Self-control problems, such as cigarette smoking, can often be improved through the use of self-modification techniques.

control. Our discussion borrows liberally from an excellent book on self-modification by David Watson and Roland Tharp (1993). We will discuss five steps in the process of self-modification, which are outlined in Figure 4.13.

Specifying Your Target Behavior

Learning Objective

Explain why traits cannot be target behaviors in self-modification programs.

The first step in a self-modification program is to specify the target behavior(s) that you want to change. Behavior modification can only be applied to a clearly defined, overt response, yet many people have difficulty pinpointing the behavior they hope to alter. They tend to describe their problems in terms of unobservable personality *traits* rather than overt *behaviors*. For example, when asked what behavior he would like to change, a man might say, "I'm too irritable." That may be true, but it is of little help in designing a self-modification program. To use a behavioral approach, you need to translate vague statements about traits into precise descriptions of specific target behaviors.

To identify target responses, you need to ponder past behavior or closely observe future behavior and list specific *examples* of responses that lead to the trait description. For instance, the man who regards himself as "too irritable" might identify two overly frequent responses, such as arguing with his wife and snapping at his children. These are specific behaviors for which he could design a self-modification program.

Gathering Baseline Data

Learning Objective

Discuss the three kinds of information you should pursue in gathering your baseline data for a self-modification program.

The second step in behavior modification is to gather baseline data. You need to systematically observe your target behavior for a period of time (usually a week or two) before you work out the details of your program. In gathering your baseline data, you need to monitor three things.

First, you need to determine the initial response level of your target behavior. After all, you can't tell whether your program is working effectively unless you have a baseline for comparison. In most cases, you would simply keep track of how often the target response occurs in a certain time interval. Thus, you might count the daily frequency of snapping at your children, smoking cigarettes, or biting your fingernails. If studying is your target behavior, you will probably monitor hours of study. If you want to modify your eating, you will probably keep track of how many calories you consume. Whatever the unit of measurement, *it is crucial to gather accurate data*. You should keep permanent written records, preferably in some type of chart (see Figure 4.14).

Second, you need to monitor the antecedents of your target behavior. **Antecedents are events that typically precede the target response.** Often these events play a major role in evoking your target behavior. For example, if your target is overeating, you might discover that the bulk of your overeating occurs late in the evening while you watch TV. If you can pinpoint this kind of antecedent-response connection, you may be able to design your program to circumvent or break the link.

Third, you need to monitor the typical consequences of your target behavior. Try to identify the reinforcers that are maintaining an undesirable target behavior or the unfavorable outcomes that are suppressing a desirable target behavior. In trying to identify reinforcers, remember that avoidance behavior is usually maintained by negative reinforcement (see Chapter 2). That is, the payoff for avoidance is usually the removal of something aversive, such as anxiety or a threat to self-esteem. You should also take into account the fact that a response may not be reinforced every time, as most behavior is maintained by intermittent reinforcement.

Figure 4.14
Example of record keeping in a self-modification program for losing weight
Graphic records are ideal for tracking progress in behavior modification efforts.

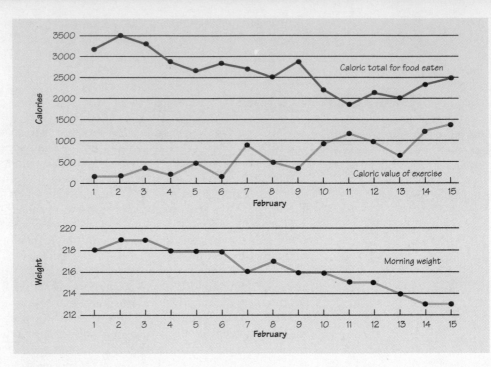

Designing Your Program

Once you have selected a target behavior and gathered adequate baseline data, it is time to plan your intervention program. Generally speaking, your program will be designed either to increase or to decrease the frequency of a target response.

Increasing Response Strength

Efforts to increase the frequency of a target response depend largely on the use of positive reinforcement. In other words, you reward yourself for behaving properly. Although the basic strategy is quite simple, doing it skillfully involves a number of considerations.

Selecting a reinforcer   To use positive reinforcement, you need to find a reward that will be effective for you. Reinforcement is subjective. What is reinforcing for one person may not be reinforcing for another. Figure 4.15 lists questions you can ask yourself to help determine your personal reinforcers. Be sure to be realistic and choose a reinforcer that is really available to you.

You don't have to come up with spectacular new reinforcers that you've never experienced before. *You can use reinforcers that you are already getting.* However, you have to restructure the contingencies so that you get them only if you behave appropriately. For example, if you normally buy two compact discs per week, you might make these purchases contingent on studying a certain number of hours during the week. Making yourself earn rewards that you used to take for granted is often a useful strategy in a self-modification program.

Arranging the contingencies   Once you have chosen your reinforcer, you have to set up reinforcement contingencies. These contingencies describe the exact behavioral goals that must be met and the reinforcement that may then be awarded. For

Figure 4.15
Selecting a reinforcer
These questions may help you identify your personal reinforcers. (From Watson & Tharp, 1993)

What Are Your Reinforcers?

1 What will be the rewards of achieving your goal?

2 What kind of praise do you like to receive, from yourself and others?

3 What kinds of things do you like to have?

4 What are your major interests?

5 What are your hobbies?

6 What people do you like to be with?

7 What do you like to do with those people?

8 What do you do for fun?

9 What do you do to relax?

10 What do you do to get away from it all?

11 What makes you feel good?

12 What would be a nice present to receive?

13 What kinds of things are important to you?

14 What would you buy if you had an extra $20? $50? $100?

15 On what do you spend your money each week?

16 What behaviors do you perform every day? (Don't overlook the obvious or commonplace.)

17 Are there any behaviors you usually perform instead of the target behavior?

18 What would you hate to lose?

19 Of the things you do every day, which would you hate to give up?

20 What are your favorite daydreams and fantasies?

21 What are the most relaxing scenes you can imagine?

example, in a program to increase exercise, you might make spending $40 on clothes (the reinforcer) contingent on having jogged 15 miles during the week (the target behavior).

Try to set behavioral goals that are both challenging and realistic. You want your goals to be challenging so that they lead to improvement in your behavior. However, setting unrealistically high goals—a common mistake in self-modification—often leads to unnecessary discouragement.

You also need to be concerned about doling out too much reinforcement. If reinforcement is too easy to get, you may become *satiated*, and the reinforcer may lose its motivational power. For example, if you were to reward yourself with virtually all the compact discs you wanted, this reinforcer would lose its incentive value.

One way to avoid the satiation problem is to put yourself on a token economy. **A *token economy* is a system for doling out symbolic reinforcers that are exchanged later for a variety of genuine reinforcers.** Thus, you might develop a point system for exercise behavior, accumulating points that can be spent on compact discs, movies, restaurant meals, and so forth. You can also use a token economy to reinforce a variety of related target behaviors, as opposed to a single, specific response. The token economy in Figure 4.16, for instance, is set up to strengthen three different, though related, responses (jogging, tennis, and sit-ups).

Shaping In some cases, you may want to reinforce a target response that you are not currently capable of making, such as speaking in front of a large group or jog-

Figure 4.16
**Example of a token
economy to reinforce
exercise**
This token economy was set up
to strengthen three types of
exercise behavior. The person
can exchange tokens for four
different types of reinforcers.

Responses Earning Tokens

Response	Amount	Number of tokens
Jogging	1/2 mile	4
Jogging	1 mile	8
Jogging	2 miles	16
Tennis	1 hour	4
Tennis	2 hours	8
Sit-ups	25	1
Sit-ups	50	2

Redemption Value of Tokens

Reinforcer	Tokens required
Purchase one compact disc of your choice	30
Go to movie	50
Go to nice restaurant	100
Take special weekend trip	500

ging ten miles a day. This situation calls for *shaping,* **which is accomplished by
reinforcing closer and closer approximations of the desired response.** Thus,
you might start jogging two miles a day and add a half-mile each week until you
reach your goal. In shaping your behavior, you should set up a schedule spelling
out how and when your target behaviors and reinforcement contingencies should
change. Generally, it is a good idea to move forward gradually.

Decreasing Response Strength

Learning Objective

*Discuss how to use
reinforcement, control of
antecedents, and punishment to
decrease the strength of a
response in self-modification
efforts.*

Let's turn now to the challenge of reducing the frequency of an undesirable
response. You can go about this task in a number of ways. Your principal options
include reinforcement, control of antecedents, and punishment.

Reinforcement Reinforcers can be used in an indirect way to decrease the frequency of a response. This may sound paradoxical, since you have learned that reinforcement strengthens a response. The trick lies in how you define the target
behavior. For example, in the case of overeating you might define your target behavior as eating more than 1600 calories a day (an excess response that you want to
decrease) or eating less than 1600 calories a day (a deficit response that you want
to increase). You can choose the latter definition and reinforce yourself whenever
you eat less than 1600 calories in a day. Thus, you can reinforce yourself for *not*
emitting a response, or for emitting it less, and thereby decrease the response
through reinforcement.

Control of antecedents A worthwhile strategy for decreasing the occurrence of an
undesirable response may be to identify its antecedents and avoid exposure to them.
This strategy is especially useful when you are trying to decrease the frequency of
a consummatory response, such as smoking or eating. In the case of overeating, for
instance, the easiest way to resist temptation is to avoid having to face it. Thus, you
might stay away from enticing restaurants, minimize time spent in your kitchen,
shop for groceries just after eating (when willpower is higher), and avoid purchas-

ing favorite foods. Figure 4.17 lists a variety of suggestions for controlling antecedents to reduce overeating. Control of antecedents can also be helpful in a program to increase studying. The key often lies in *where* you study. You can reduce excessive socializing by studying somewhere devoid of people. Similarly, you can reduce loafing by studying someplace where there is no TV, stereo, or phone to distract you.

Punishment   The strategy of decreasing unwanted behavior by punishing yourself for that behavior is an obvious option that people tend to overuse. The biggest problem with punishment in a self-modification effort is that it is difficult to follow through and punish yourself. Nonetheless, there may be situations in which your manipulations of reinforcers need to be bolstered by the threat of punishment. If

Figure 4.17
Control of antecedents
Controlling antecedents that trigger overeating is often a crucial part of behavioral programs for weight loss. The tips listed here have proven useful to many people.

Controlling the Antecedents of Overeating

A. Shopping for food

1. Do not purchase problematic foods. These include
   a. very fattening, high-calorie foods
   b. your favorite foods, unless they have very low caloric values (you will be tempted to overconsume favorite foods)
   c. foods requiring little preparation (they make it too easy to eat)

2. To facilitate the above, you should
   a. use a shopping list from which you do not deviate
   b. shop just after eating (your willpower is reduced to jelly when you're hungry)
   c. carry only enough money to pay for items on your list

B. In your kitchen

1. Don't use your kitchen for anything other than food preparation and consumption. If you study or socialize there, you'll be tempted to eat.
2. Keep food stock stored out of sight.
3. If you have problematic foods in your kitchen (for other household members, of course), arrange cupboards and the refrigerator so that these foods are out of reach or in the rear.
4. Don't hover over cooking food. It will cook itself.
5. Prepare only enough food for immediate consumption.

C. While eating

1. Don't do anything besides eating. Watching TV or reading promotes mindless consumption.
2. Leave serving dishes on the kitchen counter or stove. Don't set them right in front of you.
3. Eat from a smaller dish. It will make a quantity of food appear greater.
4. Slow the pace of eating. Relax and enjoy your food.

D. After eating

1. Quickly put away or dispose of leftover foods.
2. Leave the kitchen as soon as you are through.

E. In regard to restaurants

1. Insofar as possible, do not patronize restaurants. Menus are written in a much too seductive style.
2. If social obligations require that you eat out, go to a restaurant that you don't particularly like.
3. When in restaurants, don't linger over the menu, and don't gawk at the food on other tables.
4. Avoid driving down streets and going to shopping centers that are loaded with alluring fast-food enterprises.

F. In general

1. Try to avoid boredom. Keep yourself busy.
2. Try to avoid excessive sleep loss and fatigue. Your self-control diminishes when you are tired.
3. Avoid excessive fasting. Skipping meals often leads to overeating later.

you're going to use punishment, keep two guidelines in mind. First, do not use punishment alone. Use it in conjunction with positive reinforcement. If you set up a program in which you can earn only negative consequences, you probably won't stick to it. Second, use a relatively mild punishment so that you will actually be able to administer it to yourself. Nurnberger and Zimmerman (1970) developed a creative method of self-punishment. They had subjects write out a check to an organization they hated (for instance, the campaign of a political candidate whom they despised). The check was held by a third party who mailed it if subjects failed to meet their behavioral goals. Such a punishment is relatively harmless, but it can serve as a strong source of motivation.

Executing and Evaluating Your Program

Learning Objective

Discuss issues related to fine-tuning and ending a self-modification program.

Once you have designed your program, the next step is to put it to work by enforcing the contingencies that you have carefully planned. During this period, you need to continue to accurately record the frequency of your target behavior so you can evaluate your progress. The success of your program depends on your not "cheating." The most common form of cheating is to reward yourself when you have not actually earned it.

You can do two things to increase the likelihood that you will comply with your program. One is to make up a *behavioral contract*—**a written agreement outlining a promise to adhere to the contingencies of a behavior modification program.** The formality of signing such a contract in front of friends or family seems to make many people take their program more seriously. You can further reduce the likelihood of cheating by having someone other than yourself dole out the reinforcers and punishments.

Behavior modification programs often require some fine-tuning. So don't be surprised if you need to make a few adjustments. Several flaws are especially common in designing self-modification programs. Among those that you should look out for are (1) depending on a weak reinforcer, (2) permitting lengthy delays between appropriate behavior and delivery of reinforcers, and (3) trying to do too much too quickly by setting unrealistic goals. Often, a small revision or two can turn a failing program around and make it a success.

Ending Your Program

Generally, when you design your program you should spell out the conditions under which you will bring it to an end. This involves setting terminal goals such as reaching a certain weight, studying with a certain regularity, or going without cigarettes for a certain length of time. Often, it is a good idea to phase out your program by planning a gradual reduction in the frequency or potency of your reinforcement for appropriate behavior.

If your program is successful, it may fade away without a conscious decision on your part. Often, new, improved patterns of behavior become self-maintaining. Responses such as eating right, exercising regularly, and studying diligently may become habitual. Whether you end your program intentionally or not, you should always be prepared to reinstitute the program if you find yourself slipping back to your old patterns of behavior.

Key Ideas

The Concept of Coping

• Coping involves behavioral efforts to master, reduce, or tolerate the demands created by stress. People cope with stress in many different ways, but most have certain styles of coping. Coping strategies vary in their adaptive value.

Common Coping Patterns of Limited Value

• Giving up, possibly best understood in terms of learned helplessness, is a common coping pattern that tends to be of limited value. Another is striking out at others with acts of aggression. Frequently caused by frustration, aggression tends to be counterproductive because it often creates new sources of stress. Blaming yourself with negative self-talk and indulging yourself are other relatively nonadaptive coping patterns.

• Particularly common is defensive coping, which may involve any of a number of defense mechanisms. Although the adaptive value of defensive coping tends to be less than optimal, it depends on the situation. Some of one's illusions may be healthful.

The Nature of Constructive Coping

• Constructive coping, which includes efforts to deal with stress that are judged as relatively healthful, does not appear to depend on one's intelligence. Constructive coping is rational, realistic, and action oriented. It also involves inhibiting troublesome emotions and learning self-control.

Appraisal-Focused Constructive Coping

• Appraisal-focused constructive coping is facilitated by Ellis's suggestions on how to reduce catastrophic thinking by digging out the irrational assumptions that cause it. Other valuable strategies in-clude using humor to deal with stress and looking for the positive aspects of setbacks and problems.

Problem-Focused Constructive Coping

• Systematic problem solving can be facilitated by following a four-step process: (1) clarify the problem, (2) generate alternative courses of action, (3) evaluate your alternatives and select a course of action, and (4) take action while maintaining flexibility.

• Other problem-focused coping tactics with potential value include seeking social support and acquiring strategies to improve self-control. Better time management can also aid problem-focused coping. Effective time management doesn't depend on increased efficiency as much as on setting priorities and allocating time wisely.

Emotion-Focused Constructive Coping

• Our discussion of emotion-focused coping noted the possible value of releasing pent-up emotions and the occasional efficacy of distracting yourself. Research suggests that meditation can be helpful in reducing emotional turmoil. Although less exotic, systematic relaxation procedures, such as Benson's relaxation response, can also be effective in coping with troublesome emotional arousal.

Application: Achieving Self-Control

• In behavior modification, the principles of learning are used to change behavior directly. Behavior modification techniques can be used to increase one's self-control. The first step in self-modification is to specify the overt target behavior to be increased or decreased. The second step is to gather baseline data about the initial rate of the target response and identify any typical ante-cedents and consequences associated with the behavior.

• The third step is to design a program. If you are trying to increase the strength of a response, you'll depend on positive reinforcement. The reinforcement contingencies should spell out exactly what you have to do to earn your reinforcer. A number of strategies can be used to decrease the strength of a response, including reinforcement, control of antecedents, and punishment. The fourth step is to execute and evaluate the program. Self-modification programs often require some fine-tuning. The final step is to determine how and when you will phase out your program.

Key Terms

Aggression
Antecedents
Behavioral contract
Behavior modification
Brainstorming
Catastrophic thinking
Catharsis
Constructive coping
Coping
Defense mechanisms
Learned helplessness
Meditation
Rational-emotive therapy
Shaping
Token economy

Key People

Herbert Benson
Albert Ellis
Seymour Epstein
Sigmund Freud
James Pennebaker
Martin Seligman
Shelley Taylor

5 *The Self*

You've just taken your first exam in your first psychology course. Expecting a B, you're looking forward to getting your test back. Your instructor hands you your exam and you look at your grade: a C−. You're shocked! How could this be? You thought that you knew the material really well. As you sit there taking in this disappointing and disturbing turn of events, you search for possible explanations for your performance. "Did I study long enough? Do I need to revamp my study methods? Is this course a lot harder than I had thought? Am I really 'college material'?" As you leave the class, your mood has shifted from up to down. You're feeling dejected and are already worrying about how you'll do on the next exam. This scenario illustrates the process of self-perception and the effect self-perception can have on emotions, self-esteem, and goal setting. People engage in this process constantly to understand the causes of their own behavior.

In this chapter, we focus on the self and its role in adjustment. We'll start off by looking at three major components of the self: self-concept, self-esteem, and identity. Then, we'll review some basic principles of the self-perception process. Next, we'll turn to the topic of self-regulation. Finally, we'll focus on how people present themselves to others. In the Application, we offer some suggestions for building self-esteem.

Self-Concept

Learning Objective

Define self-concept and explain how it guides current and future behavior.

The *self-concept* **is a collection of beliefs about one's basic nature, unique qualities, and typical behavior.** A person's self-concept might include beliefs such as "I'm tall," "I'm blond," "I play the clarinet," "I'm a good student," and "I'm friendly." As you can see from these examples, the self-concept includes many separate but interrelated dimensions. Although we usually talk about the self-concept as a single entity, it is probably more accurate to say that individuals have a number of specific self-concepts that operate in different situations (Harter, 1990). Don Hamachek (1992) has suggested that people have separate concepts of their physical, social, emotional, and intellectual selves.

These various self-concepts are characterized by relatively distinct thoughts and feelings. That is, you might have considerable information about your social skills and feel quite capable about them but have limited information about your physical skills and feel less confident about this aspect of your self. Current thinking is that only a portion of the total self-concept operates at any one time (Markus & Nurius, 1986; Markus & Wurf, 1987). The self-concept that is currently accessible is termed the *working self-concept*. When a particular self-concept is operating, its attendant thoughts and feelings strongly influence the way one processes information about that aspect of one's self. When you're in class, for example, the beliefs and emotions associated with your intellectual self-concept usually dominate how you process information you receive in that setting. Similarly, when you're at a party (or thinking about a party when you're in class!), you tap into your social self-concept and the thoughts and feelings related to it.

Not only do self-concepts affect current behavior, they also influence future behavior. The term *possible selves* **refers to one's conceptions about the kind of person one might become in the future** (Markus & Nurius, 1986). If you have narrowed your career choices to personnel manager and psychologist, these represent two possible selves in the career realm. Possible selves are developed from past experiences, current behavior, and future expectations. They make people more attentive to goal-related information and role models and more mindful of the need to practice goal-related skills. As such, they help individuals not only to envision desired future goals but also to achieve them (Markus & Ruvolo, 1989). Sometimes, possible selves are negative and represent what the person fears he or she might become—an alcoholic like Uncle George or an adult without an intimate relationship. In this case, possible selves function as images to be avoided.

Self-concepts are not set in concrete, but they are not easily changed, either. As you will see, people are strongly motivated to maintain a consistent view of the self. Thus, once the self-concept is established, one has a tendency to preserve and defend it. In the context of this stability, however, self-concepts do have a certain dynamic quality (Markus & Wurf, 1987). Although they rarely change overnight, self-concepts may very well undergo gradual change over time.

Self-concepts are not merely an abstract idea of interest to psychologists. Because they guide the processing of self-relevant information, self-concepts obviously play a powerful role in how people see themselves and others, how they feel, and how they behave. For instance, if you have been eyeing an attractive classmate recently, your social self-concept may be the critical factor that determines whether you actually approach that person.

Self-Complexity

Learning Objective

Define self-complexity and explain how it operates to protect against stress.

Individuals' self-concepts vary in complexity. *Self-complexity* **refers to how simple or elaborate one's self-concept is.** People with greater self-complexity have a number of different aspects to their self-concept, so each single component makes up a small part of the whole self-concept (see Figure 5.1a). In contrast, those who are low in self-complexity have relatively few self-components, so each one makes up a large part of the self-concept (see Figure 5.1b). According to Patricia Linville (1985, 1987), a positive or negative event (winning a tennis match or having a fight with one's partner) directly affects only that self-component that is related to the event. When one of only a few components is affected, the impact will be greater than when one of many components is involved. Thus, if you have many different selves and have a fight with your partner, you may feel bad, but not as bad as a person who has only a few self-components. Conversely, if you have many differ-

Recommended Reading

Encounters with the Self

by Don Hamachek (Harcourt Brace Jovanovich, 1992)

This book is about the many aspects of the self-concept. It describes how the contours of the self-concept are molded by one's interactions with others, how the self-concept continues to undergo metamorphosis throughout life, and how the self-concept is expressed in everyday behavior. Though reasonably compact in size, the book is quite broad in scope, and Hamachek manages to cover a number of intriguing topics, including defense mechanisms, how people perceive others, the role of physical appearance in shaping self-concept, how child-rearing styles influence self-concept, how self-perceptions affect academic adjustment, and how to pursue a more positive self-image.

This is one of those rare books that can provide satisfactory reading for both the layperson and the sophisticated professional. Academicians will appreciate the well-documented and thorough review of relevant research. Nonprofessional readers will find the book highly readable and brimming with practical insights and advice. Although the author disavows any intention of writing a "self-help" book, this volume is likely to be about as helpful to readers as any mere book can be.

Some individuals avoid finding out more about themselves for fear of having to give up a self with which they have grown comfortable or "satisfied." Most people have an initial inclination to resist personal change anyway, but this resistance is even stronger for those who refuse to insert new or changed behavior into their current concept of self. For example, a shy, timid, submissive person may not want to know his strengths and assets for fear that he might have to be more assertive and socially aggressive. If shyness has become a way of life designed to protect him from the risks of social disapproval (in this case, nothing ventured, nothing lost—in terms of self-esteem), then it may be difficult indeed for him to give up being timid. Other individuals are reluctant to find out more about themselves because of the threat of having to become more personally mature. Maturity implies many things, among which are a certain degree of independence and autonomy, capacity for self-discipline, certainty about goals and values, and motivation toward some level of personal achievement. Most of all, greater maturity means greater responsibility, and for some this may be a frightening possibility. [p. 53]

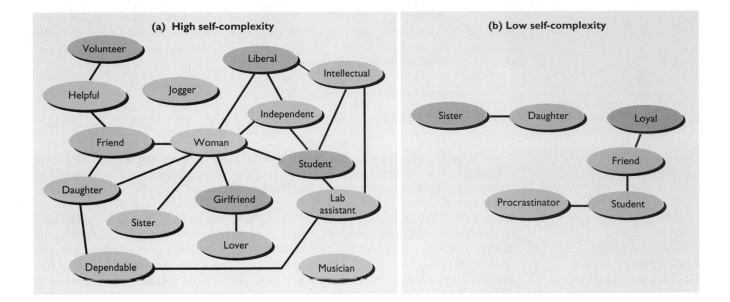

(a) High self-complexity

Volunteer · Liberal · Intellectual · Helpful · Jogger · Independent · Friend · Woman · Student · Daughter · Girlfriend · Lab assistant · Sister · Lover · Dependable · Musician

(b) Low self-complexity

Sister · Daughter · Loyal · Friend · Procrastinator · Student

Figure 5.1
Self-complexity
(a) This woman perceives herself to have many different self-components, so she rates high in self-complexity. (b) This woman sees herself as having relatively few self-components and thus has low self-complexity.

ent selves and win a tennis match, your elation will be less intense than that experienced by a person with fewer selves. In other words, according to Linville, people who are low in self-complexity should experience greater swings in emotion and self-esteem than those who are high in self-complexity.

Are there any data to support this idea? In one study, college students who differed in self-complexity were told either that they had done well or had failed on an aptitude test (Linville, 1985). Those who were low in self-complexity reported more positive moods if they experienced success and more negative moods if they experienced failure compared to those who were high in self-complexity. In other words, those with low self-complexity experienced greater mood fluctuations than did those with high self-complexity (see Figure 5.2). Linville also found that college students who were low in self-complexity had more emotional ups and downs over a two-week period than did those who were high in self-complexity.

Because self-complexity contributes to stable emotions and self-esteem, it seems to be a desirable quality. Is it something people can develop? According to Linville (1987), it helps to be involved in a variety of roles, relationships, and situations (student, worker, friend, sibling, son or daughter, musician, tennis player, community volunteer, romantic partner). She also believes that having a broad range of experiences in these different roles and relationships can foster self-complexity. Once people have developed self-complexity, there is more good news. Research has shown that people with high self-complexity can offset the impact of negative events by setting up positive events that affect other self-components (Linville & Fischer,

Figure 5.2
Self-complexity as a buffer against depression
The moods of high self-complexity subjects fluctuated less in response to failure and success experiences than did the moods of low self-complexity subjects. (Based on Linville, 1985)

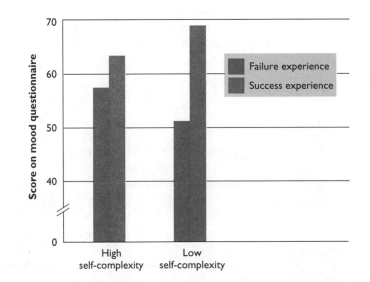

1991). For instance, if you have a disagreement with a co-worker (negative experience for the "work self"), you can arrange to socialize with a friend (positive experience for the "friend self"), thereby diminishing to a degree the negative experience affecting the "work self."

Self-Discrepancies

Some people perceive themselves pretty much the way they'd like to see themselves. Others experience a gap between what they actually see and what they'd like to see. For example, Jack describes his actual self as "shy," but his ideal self as "outgoing." **This mismatching of self-perceptions is termed** *self-discrepancy.* According to E. Tory Higgins (1989), individuals have three types of self-perceptions: the *actual self* (qualities that you or others believe you *actually* possess), the *ideal self* (characteristics that you or others would *like* you to have), and the *ought self* (traits that you or others believe that you *should* possess). Although self-discrepancy theory is concerned both with personal self-perceptions and perceptions of how a significant other (parent, good friend, or lover) sees one, we'll limit our discussion to the self-discrepancies associated with one's own self-perceptions.

Self-Discrepancies and Their Effects

Learning Objective

Describe two types of self-discrepancies and their specific effects.

According to Higgins, when people live up to their personal standards (ideal or ought selves), they experience high self-esteem; when they don't meet their own expectations, self-esteem suffers (Moretti & Higgins, 1990). In addition, he says, certain types of self-discrepancies are associated with specific emotions (see Figure 5.3). One type of self-discrepancy occurs when the *actual* self is at odds with the *ideal* self. *Dejection-related* emotions (sadness, disappointment) are triggered in these instances. Consider Mary's situation: She knows that she's attractive, but she is also overweight and would like to be thinner. Self-discrepancy theory would predict that she would feel dissatisfied and dejected. Interestingly, research has shown an association between discrepant actual/ideal views of body shape and eating disorders (Strauman et al., 1991).

A second type of discrepancy involves a mismatch between *actual* and *ought* selves. Think of an instance in which your self-concept doesn't match your sense of responsibility. Perhaps you don't stay in touch with your grandparents as often as you feel you should. As a result of this actual/ought self-discrepancy, Higgins predicts that you would experience *agitation-related* emotions (irritability, anxiety, and guilt). Extreme discrepancies of this type can result in anxiety-related psychological disorders.

Everyone experiences self-discrepancies, yet most people manage to feel reasonably good about themselves. How is this possible? Two factors seem to be important: (1) the amount of discrepancy experienced and (2) awareness of the discrepancy. Thus, those with self-discrepancies feel more emotional discomfort than those who are self-congruent. Similarly, those who are more aware of self-discrepancies are more vulnerable to negative feelings than those who are less aware of them (Higgins et al., 1986).

Figure 5.3
Types of self-discrepancies, their effects on emotional states, and possible consequences
According to E. Tory Higgins (1989), discrepancies between actual and ideal selves produce disappointment and sadness, whereas discrepancies between actual and ought selves result in irritability and guilt. Such self-discrepancies can make individuals vulnerable to more serious psychological problems, such as depression and anxiety-related disorders.

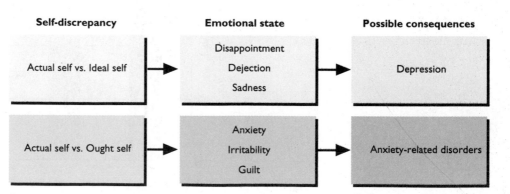

Can people do anything to blunt the negative emotions and blows to self-esteem associated with self-discrepancies? Well, for one thing, people can *change their behavior* to bring it more in line with personal standards (ideal or ought selves). For instance, if your ideal self is a person who gets above-average grades and your actual self just got a D on a test, you can study more effectively for the next test to improve your grade. But what about the times you can't match your ideal standards? Perhaps you had your heart set on making the varsity tennis team but didn't make the cut. Or maybe you had planned to go to medical school but barely eked out C's in your science courses. One way to ease the discomfort associated with such discrepancies is to bring your actual self a bit more in line with your actual abilities. You may also look for ways to *blunt self-awareness*. Sometimes you do this by avoiding situations that increase your self-awareness—you don't go to a party if you expect to spend a miserable evening talking to yourself.

Some people use alcohol to blunt self-awareness. In one study, college students were first put into either a high or a low self-awareness group based on test scores (Hull & Young, 1983). Then both groups were given a brief version of an intelligence test as well as false feedback on their test performance. Half of the high self aware group were told that they had done quite well on the test, while the other half were told that they had done quite poorly. Then, supposedly as part of a separate study, these participants were asked to taste and evaluate different wines for 15 minutes. The experimenters predicted that the high self-aware participants who had been told that they had done poorly on the IQ test would drink more than the other groups, and this is what the study found (see Figure 5.4). In other words, those who couldn't escape negative information about themselves drank more alcohol to reduce their self-awareness.

Heightened self-awareness doesn't *always* make people focus on self-discrepancies and negative aspects of the self. If that were true, most people would feel a lot worse about themselves than they actually do! As you recall, self-concepts are made up of many self-beliefs, many of them positive, some negative. Because people have a need to feel good about themselves, they tend to focus on their positive features rather than their "warts" (Showers, 1992).

Factors Shaping Your Self-Concept

A variety of sources influence your self-concept. Chief among them are your own observations, feedback from others, and cultural values.

Figure 5.4
Self-awareness and alcohol consumption
Individuals who were high in self-awareness drank significantly more wine in a 15-minute period if they believed that they had performed poorly on an IQ test than did any other group. (From Hull & Young, 1983)

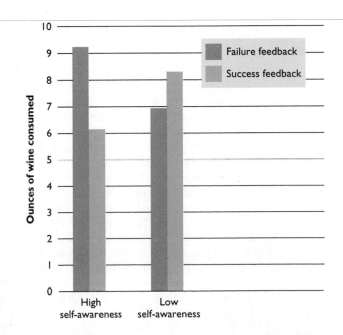

When people don't live up to their personal standards, self-esteem suffers, and some turn to alcohol to blunt their awareness of the discrepancy.

Your Own Observations

Learning Objective

Describe how social comparisons influence the self-concept.

Leon Festinger

Your observations of your own behavior are obviously a major source of information about what you are like. Early in childhood, individuals start observing their own behavior and drawing conclusions about themselves. Young children will make statements about who is the tallest, who can run the fastest, or who can swing the highest. Leon Festinger's (1954) *social comparison theory* **proposes that individuals compare themselves with others in order to assess their own behavior.** People compare themselves to others to determine how attractive they are, how they did on the history exam, how their social skills stack up, and so forth.

Although Festinger's original theory claimed that people engage in social comparison for the purpose of accurately assessing their abilities, recent research suggests that they also use social comparison to maintain their self-image and to improve their skills (Goethals, 1986; Wood, 1989). Furthermore, the reasons people engage in social comparison determine whom they choose for a point of comparison. **A *reference group* is a set of people against whom people compare themselves.** For example, if you want to know how you did on your first test in social psychology (ability appraisal), your reference group will be the entire class. On the other hand, if you want to improve your tennis game (skill development), your reference group will probably be limited to those of superior ability, because their skills give you something to strive for. And, if your self-esteem needs bolstering, you will probably compare yourself to those whom you perceive to be worse off than you so you can feel better about yourself.

The potential impact of such social comparisons was dramatically demonstrated in the classic "Mr. Clean/Mr. Dirty" study (Morse & Gergen, 1970). Subjects thought they were being interviewed for a job. Half the subjects met another applicant who was neatly dressed and who appeared to be very competent. The other half were exposed to a competitor who was unkempt and disorganized. All subjects filled out measures of self-esteem both before and after the bogus job interviews. The results indicated that subjects who encountered the impressive competitor showed a decrease in self-esteem after the interview, while those who met the unimpressive competitor showed increases in self-esteem. Thus, comparisons with others can have immediate effects on one's self-concept.

People's observations of their own behavior are not entirely objective. The general tendency is to distort reality in a positive direction (see Figure 5.5). Research findings support the idea that most people tend to evaluate themselves in a more positive light than they really merit (Markus & Wurf, 1987; Taylor & Brown, 1988, 1994). The strength of this tendency was highlighted in a large survey conducted, as part of the Scholastic Aptitude Test (SAT), of some 829,000 high school seniors (Myers, 1980). In this survey, 70% of the students rated themselves above average

Figure 5.5
Distortions in self-images
How people see themselves may be very different from how others see them. These pictures and text illustrate the subjective quality of self-concept and perception of others. Generally, self-images tend to be distorted in a positive direction.

As she sees herself: Unchanged since age 22. Sociable, scintillating, sexy.

As the husband sees her: Older than her years. Someone more suited to suburban domesticity and PTA.

As he sees himself: Stylish haircut, rakish moustache; benevolent, generous, powerful. A smooth operator.

As the wife sees him: Somewhat of a slob, moody, not very decisive or strong.

in "leadership ability." Only 2% rated themselves below average. Obviously, by definition, 50% must be "above average" and 50% below. Nonetheless, in regard to "ability to get along with others," 100% of the subjects saw themselves as above average! Furthermore, 25% of the respondents thought that they belonged in the top 1%. These findings call to mind Garrison Keillor's description of the inhabitants of Lake Woebegone, the mythical Minnesota town where "all the women are strong, all the men are good-looking, and all the children are above average."

Although the general tendency is to distort reality in a positive direction, most people tend to make both negative and positive distortions. For example, you might overrate your social skill, emotional stability, and intellectual ability while underrating your physical attractiveness. Also, a minority of people constantly evaluate themselves in an unrealistically negative way. Thus, the tendency to see oneself in an overly favorable light is strong but not universal.

Feedback from Others

Learning Objective

Describe how feedback from others shapes one's self-concept.

Your self-concept is obviously shaped by the feedback that you get about your behavior from other people. Of course, it is obvious that not everyone has equal influence in your life. Early on, your parents and other family members played a dominant role in providing you with feedback. As you grew older, the number of significant others who gave you feedback increased (Harter, 1990).

Parents give their children a great deal of direct feedback. They constantly express approval or disapproval, making statements such as "I'm so proud of you" or "You're a lazy bum just like your Uncle Patrick." Most people, especially when young, take this sort of feedback to heart. Thus, it comes as no surprise that studies find an association between parents' views of a child and the child's self-concept (Wylie, 1979). There is even stronger evidence for a relationship between children's perceptions of their parents' attitudes toward them and their own self-perceptions (Felson, 1989; Wylie, 1979).

Interestingly, people are not particularly accurate perceivers of how specific individuals evaluate them; they are better at judging how other people, in general, view

them (DePaulo et al., 1987; Kenny & DePaulo, 1993). Also, when people have access to "objective" information (course grades), their perceptions of others' judgments don't seem to carry as much weight as when they are evaluating themselves in areas for which they must rely solely on socially defined standards, such as physical attractiveness (Felson, 1989).

Parents and family are not the only source of feedback during childhood. Teachers, Little League coaches, Scout leaders, and others also provide significant feedback. In adolescence, as one's peer group becomes more influential, friends play an important role in the development of self-concept (Harter, 1990; Smollar & Youniss, 1985). Of course, feedback from others is filtered through one's social perception systems. As a consequence, it may be as distorted as one's own self-observations.

Cultural Guidelines

Your self-concept is also shaped by cultural values. The society in which you are brought up defines what is desirable and undesirable in personality and behavior. For example, American culture tends to put a premium on individuality, competitive success, strength, and skill. When people meet cultural expectations, they feel good about themselves and experience increases in self-esteem, and vice versa (Matsumoto, 1994).

Recent cross-cultural studies suggest that different cultures shape different conceptions of the self (Markus & Kitayama, 1991). One important way cultures differ is on the dimension of individualism versus collectivism (Hofstede, 1983; Triandis, 1989, 1994). *Individualism* **involves putting personal goals ahead of group goals and defining one's identity in terms of personal attributes rather than group memberships.** In contrast, *collectivism* **involves putting group goals ahead of personal goals and defining one's identity in terms of the groups to which one belongs** (such as one's family, tribe, work group, social class, caste, and so on). In comparison to individualistic cultures, collectivist cultures place a higher priority on shared values and resources, cooperation, mutual interdependence, and concern for how one's actions will affect other group members. Childrearing patterns in collectivist cultures emphasize the importance of obedience, reliability, and proper behavior, whereas individualistic cultures emphasize the development of independence, self-esteem, and self-reliance.

A variety of factors influence whether societies cherish individualism as opposed to collectivism. Among other things, increases in a culture's affluence, education, urbanization, and social mobility tend to foster more individualism (Triandis, 1994). Many contemporary societies are in transition, but generally speaking, North American and Western European cultures tend to be individualistic, whereas Asian, African, and Latin American cultures tend to be higher in collectivism (Hofstede, 1980, 1983).

Define individualism and collectivism, and summarize recent findings about the effect of culture on self-concept.

Figure 5.6
Independent and inter-dependent views of the self
(a) Individuals in cultures that support an independent view of the self perceive the self as clearly separated from significant others. (b) Individuals in cultures that support an interdependent view of the self perceive the self as inextricably connected to others. (Adapted from Markus & Kitayama, 1991)

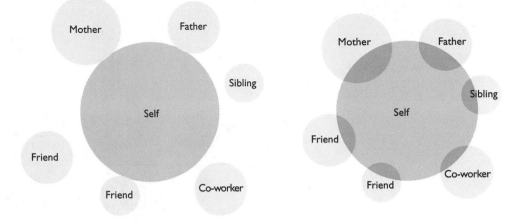

Individuals reared in individualistic cultures usually have an *independent* view of the self, perceiving themselves as unique, self-contained, and distinct from others. In contrast, individuals reared in collectivist cultures typically have an *interdependent* view of the self. They see themselves as inextricably connected to others and believe that harmonious relationships with others are of utmost importance. Figure 5.6 depicts the self-conceptions of individuals from these contrasting cultures.

Individuals with an independent view of the self are socialized to maintain their sense of self as a separate person—to "look out for number one," claim more than their share of credit for group successes, and disavow responsibility for group failure. Those with an interdependent view of the self are socialized to adjust themselves to the needs of the groups to which they belong and to maintain the interdependence among individuals. Thus, social duties and obligations assume great importance and individuals are likely to see themselves as responsible for group failures (Matsumoto, 1994).

A number of researchers have noted parallels between the self-views promoted by individualistic and collectivist cultures and the self-views of many Northern American men and women, respectively (Dion & Dion, 1993; Lykes, 1985). That is, many American men seem to have an independent view of the self and many American women tend to have an interdependent view of the self. These hypothesized gender differences in self-conceptions are provocative and warrant further investigation. For instance, this research might be able to shed light on gender differences related to the experience of romantic love and the capacity for intimacy (see Chapter 8).

Cultural values are also responsible for various stereotypes that may mold self-perceptions. For instance, gender stereotypes influence males' and females' self-perceptions and behavior. One study found that college students' gender stereotypes predicted which activities they tried and how much they enjoyed them (Carter & Myerowitz, 1984). In a similar manner, stereotypes about race, class, sexual orientation, and religion can influence self-conceptions.

Self-Esteem

Learning Objective

Define self-esteem and describe some correlates of self-esteem.

Self-esteem refers to one's overall assessment of one's worth as a person; it is the evaluative component of one's self-concept. Self-esteem is a global evaluation that blends many specific evaluations about one's adequacy as a student, an athlete, a worker, a spouse, a parent, or other relevant role. Figure 5.7 shows how specific elements of self-concept may contribute to self-esteem. If you feel basically good about yourself, you would be said to have high self-esteem. Sometimes, the term "positive self-concept" is used as a synonym for self-esteem.

Figure 5.7
The structure of self-esteem
Self-esteem is a global evaluation that combines assessments of different aspects of one's self-concept, each of which is built up from many specific behaviors and experiences. (Adapted from Shavelson, Hubner, & Stanton, 1976)

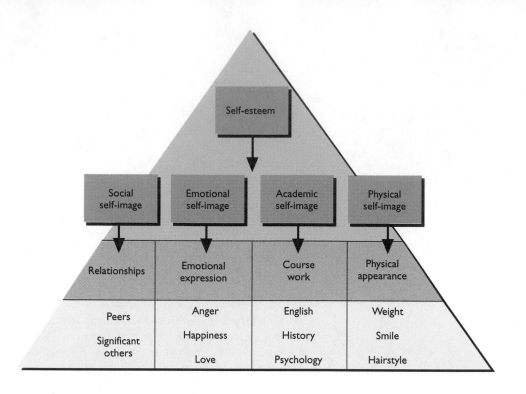

Self-esteem is a difficult concept to investigate, for two reasons. First, there is some doubt about the validity of many measures of self-esteem. The problem is that researchers tend to rely on self-reports from subjects, which obviously may be biased. For many people, the self-esteem they really feel and the level of self-esteem that they report on a questionnaire may be quite different (Wells & Marwell, 1976). Second, in probing self-esteem it is often quite difficult to separate cause from effect. A large volume of correlational data indicates that certain behavioral characteristics are associated with positive or negative self-esteem. For instance, we saw in Chapter 1 that self-esteem is a good predictor of happiness. However, it is hard to tell whether these behavioral tendencies are the cause or the effect of a particular level of self-esteem. This problem in pinpointing causation should be kept in mind as we look at the determinants and effects of self-esteem.

The Importance of Self-Esteem

The importance of adequate self-esteem can hardly be overestimated. To illustrate the potential influence of self-esteem, we will review some of the many problematic characteristics that often accompany low self-esteem. Before we do so, we should point out that individuals characterized as having low self-esteem really have moderate or average self-esteem. It is only because they score lower on tests of self-esteem than individuals who rate themselves very positively that they are classified as having low self-esteem. Very few individuals actually score "low" on tests of self-esteem.

People with low self-esteem tend to develop more emotional problems than people with high self-esteem (Pillow, West, & Reich, 1991; Rosenberg, 1985; Wylie, 1979). Among other things, they are more likely to report that they are troubled by anxiety, depression, irritability, aggressiveness, feelings of resentment and alienation, unhappiness, insomnia, and psychosomatic symptoms. There also is an association between low self-esteem and shyness (Cheek & Buss, 1981). People low in self-esteem often feel socially awkward, self-conscious, and especially vulnerable to rejection (Rosenberg, 1985). They have a particularly great need for acceptance from others, but they are often unable to take the initiative in seeking it out. Thus, they rarely join formal groups and do not participate very actively in social encounters. As a result, they are also often lonely (Jones, Freemon, & Goswick, 1981; Olmstead et al., 1991).

Figure 5.8
The vicious circle of low-self-esteem and poor performance

Low self-esteem is associated with low or negative expectations about performance. These often result in inadequate preparation and high anxiety, which heighten the likelihood of poor performance. Unsuccessful performance triggers self-blame, which feeds back to low self-esteem. (From Brehm & Kassin, 1993)

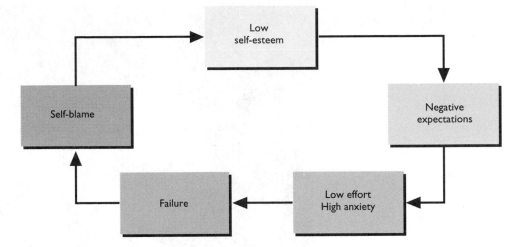

Because self-esteem affects expectations, it operates in a self-perpetuating fashion. As can be seen in Figure 5.8, individuals with low self-esteem may have negative expectations about their performance (on a test, in a social situation, at a job interview). As a result, they feel anxious and may not prepare for the challenge. Then, when they fail, they often blame themselves—delivering one more blow to their already battered self-esteem (Brockner, 1983). This repeating loop also works for those with high self-esteem: Positive expectations usually produce high effort, low anxiety, successful outcomes, and self-praise. Thus, positive feelings about the self are perpetuated.

Determinants of Self-Esteem

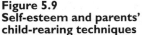

Learning Objective

Discuss the determinants of self-esteem.

The foundations for high or low self-esteem appear to be laid very early in life. Thus, psychologists have focused much of their attention on the role of parenting in self-esteem development. Indeed, there is ample evidence that parental involvement, acceptance, support, and provision of clearly defined limits have marked influence on children's self-esteem (Buri et al., 1988; Felson, 1989; Grolnick & Ryan, 1989). Let's review the findings of a classic study of self-esteem in young boys conducted by Stanley Coopersmith (1967, 1975). When he compared the child-rearing styles of mothers of boys with high self-esteem and low self-esteem, he found that mothers whose sons had high self-esteem (1) expressed more affection to their children, (2) were more interested in their children's activities, (3) were more accepting of their children, (4) used sound, consistent disciplinary procedures, and (5) had relatively high self-esteem themselves (see Figure 5.9). In particular, it was mothers' sincere interest in their children that seemed most strongly related to the development of a positive self-concept.

Figure 5.9
Self-esteem and parents' child-rearing techniques

Parents strongly influence youngsters' self-esteem. Coopersmith (1975) found interesting differences in child-rearing practices among the mothers of boys with high, medium, and low self-esteem.

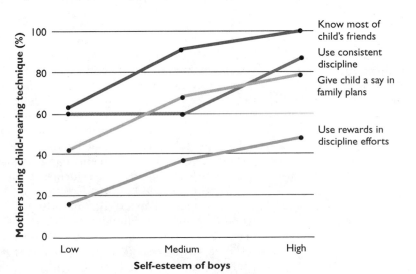

While parental feedback may be the crucial childhood determinant of self-esteem, it is clear that children (and adults) make their own judgments about themselves as well. An important basis for self-judgments is how well one "stacks up" against others one chooses as a reference group. For example, one study found that preadolescents' self-esteem was affected by the quality of competition they faced in school (Marsh & Parker, 1984). This study compared children from schools in higher socioeconomic areas with "high quality" competition (high-ability reference group) to children of similar ability from schools in lower socioeconomic areas with "low quality" competition (low-ability reference group). Surprisingly, the children in the low-quality schools tended to display greater self-esteem than children of similar academic ability who were enrolled in the high-quality schools. The reason for this finding appears to be that students compare themselves to others in their own schools, not to a hypothetical reference group of, say, all bright students in the country (Rosenberg, 1979). Thus, it has been suggested that it may be beneficial to one's self-esteem to be "a large fish in a small pond" (Davis, 1966; Marsh & Parker, 1984). This finding that kids with similar talents vary in self-esteem depending on their reference group demonstrates the immense importance of social comparison in the development of self-esteem.

Minority Group Membership and Self-Esteem

Learning Objective

Explain why members of minority groups do not have lower self-esteem than those in the dominant majority.

We have seen that perceptions of the self develop in a social context. Thus, minority group membership is a factor in the development of self-esteem. Morris Rosenberg (1979), a well-known researcher in this area, has asserted that a key factor in self-esteem development is the extent to which people perceive themselves to be similar to others in their social environment. If individuals live in an environment that makes them feel different and deficient, they can suffer from lowered self-esteem.

Because of the existence of prejudice and discrimination in the United States, it has generally been assumed (and sometimes found) that members of minority groups have lower self-esteem than members of the dominant majority group. In fact, there is a good deal of evidence to the contrary (Crocker & Major, 1989; Garnets & Kimmel, 1991; Rosenberg, 1979).

How does it happen that minority group members often have high self-esteem when it seems they shouldn't? A review of studies in this area suggested a number of strategies minority group members use to protect their self-esteem from the effects of being stigmatized (Crocker & Major, 1989). These include attributing negative appraisals to prejudice against their group instead of to themselves, and devaluing those qualities on which their group fares poorly and valuing those attributes on which their group excels. In addition, minority group members use their own group as their dominant reference group, not the relatively advantaged majority group. This in-group comparison ensures that minority group individuals are similar to others and, therefore, that they compare positively to them. This experience leads them to feel good about themselves.

An important implication here is that minority group role models play a critical part in the development of self-esteem. Because of recognizable markers (skin color, sex, body weight, physical handicaps), many minority groups are visible. This enables minority group members to easily identify in-group role models. Of course, this isn't true in the case of homosexuals, because sexual orientation isn't obvious unless individuals choose to make it so. Because of the social stigma still attached to homosexuality, many homosexual individuals prefer not to declare their sexual orientation openly. Although this is understandable, it means that gay and lesbian role models are more difficult to identify. Obviously, role models are important for self-esteem development for anyone. However, members of the dominant majority typically have lots of role models to choose from, whereas minority group members do not. Hence, it's the relative availability of role models that distinguishes minority and majority group members, not the need for them.

Identity

Learning Objective

Define identity and discuss its development.

A widely discussed concept related to self-perception is "ego identity." According to Erik Erikson (1968), a highly influential psychoanalytic theorist (see Chapter 11), **identity refers to having a relatively clear and stable sense of who one is and what one stands for.** This means that although you have a multiplicity of thoughts and feelings and engage in many diverse activities, you remain "familiar" to yourself in a fundamental way. In addition, your own sense of who you are must match pretty well with other people's views of you. This latter idea reflects Erikson's assertion that identity is rooted in both self and society.

James Marcia (1976), another authority on this subject, suggests that identity may be viewed from three perspectives. First, a sense of identity depends on the ability to integrate one's own and one's parents' expectations into a relatively congruent sense of self. Again, we see the emphasis on self and society (the latter, mediated through parental expectations). Although much of the process of identity formation is unconscious, the key point is that individuals create their own identity. They do not just unquestioningly assume the roles and beliefs designated for them by parents and society. Second, developing a sense of identity gives people the ability to perceive themselves as ongoing entities—as beings who have a past, present, and future, all of which feel connected. Finally, Marcia says that a person's unique identity will be reflected in his or her choices of career, personal values, and beliefs.

Development of Identity

Obviously, your identity has its roots in childhood. Ideally, it continues to develop throughout adulthood (Marcia, 1991). However, Erikson views adolescence as the most significant period for identity development, and research has supported his view. Studies show that identity concerns are particularly prominent among those in late adolescence (college-age individuals) (Archer, 1982; Marcia, 1980; Meilman, 1979). The fact that identity achievement is a concern during late adolescence probably reflects the conjunction of several developmental milestones during this time (Lloyd, 1985). That is, the achievement of a stable and familiar sense of self depends on physical and sexual maturity, competence in abstract thought, and a degree of emotional stability. In addition, identity achievement requires a certain amount of freedom from the constraining influences of parents and peers. As it happens, late adolescence is the period during which such conditions are first likely to exist.

Identity Statuses

According to Erikson, identity emerges out of crisis. For Erikson, the term "identity crisis" refers to a period of personal questioning during which individuals reflect on and experiment with various occupational possibilities and value choices (political, religious, and so forth). For most people, an identity crisis is not a sudden or personally agonizing experience but rather the gradual evolution of a sense of who one is. This search for identity is part of the normal developmental process.

The experience of an identity crisis usually results in a commitment to a specific career and personal ideology. According to Marcia, these two factors of crisis and commitment combine in various ways to produce four different identity statuses (see Figure 5.10). These are not stages that people pass through, but rather statuses that characterize a person's identity orientation at any particular time. In other words, it is possible that a person may never experience some of the statuses, including that of identity achievement. Let's examine these four identity statuses.

Identity foreclosure Not everyone develops a unique, personal identity. Rather than going through the process of developing their own beliefs and career choices (identity crisis), individuals in the foreclosure status unquestioningly adopt the values and expectations of their parents. For example, adolescents (or adults) who select careers because this is what their parents want for them would be classified as "foreclosures." These individuals have made commitments—or, rather, adopted the commitments of others—but because they haven't gone through an identity crisis, they don't qualify as having achieved an independent identity.

Moratorium Individuals in the midst of struggling with a sense of identity are classified as being in the moratorium status. As part of the process of evolving a personally satisfying identity, adolescents are likely to engage in a variety of identity experiments, trying on different roles, beliefs, and behaviors. Most move on to the identity achievement status, but some drift into the status of identity diffusion.

Identity diffusion Identity diffusion is characterized by a failure to achieve a stable and integrated sense of self. Individuals in this category experience considerable self-doubt, but they don't appear to be concerned about doing anything to change their circumstances. Hence, they are different from those in the moratorium status, who are still struggling to resolve identity conflicts. People in the diffusion status are not currently experiencing an identity crisis, nor are they able to make career or value commitments. Identity diffusion is a serious problem for only a small number of adolescents, usually in cases where it is prolonged.

Identity achievement The preferred identity status, of course, is that of identity achievement. In this case, a person has successfully passed through an identity crisis and is now able to make a commitment to a career objective and a set of personally meaningful beliefs.

Both identity achievement and identity foreclosure can be seen as resolutions of the identity crisis, because a sense of commitment characterizes both. Of course, in foreclosure, the commitment is not an independently developed one, as is desir-

**Figure 5.10
Marcia's four identity statuses**
According to Marcia, the occurrence of an identity crisis and the development of personal commitments can combine into four possible identity statuses, as shown in this diagram.

Marcia's Four Identity Statuses		
	Crisis present	**Crisis absent**
Commitment present	Identity achievement (successful achievement of a sense of identity)	Identity foreclosure (unquestioning adoption of parental or societal values)
Commitment absent	Identity moratorium (active struggling for a sense of identity)	Identity diffusion (absence of struggle for identity, with no obvious concern about this)

able. Individuals in both the moratorium and diffusion statuses have only vague, or sometimes no, commitments. While those in identity diffusion have given up the search for identity, those in moratorium are still pursuing it.

Considerable research has been done on identity statuses and their characteristics (Marcia, 1980, 1991). Compared to those in other statuses, *identity achievers* are more cognitively flexible, function at higher levels of moral reasoning, and have the capacity for more emotionally intimate relationships (Marcia, 1991). Those in the *moratorium* status are conflicted between conforming and rebelling, have ambivalent feelings toward their parents, and are perceived by others to be very intense. *Foreclosures* are strongly connected to their families, are cognitively rigid, conventional, and hold conservative values. Those in the *identity diffusion* status feel alienated from their parents, are at the lower levels of moral reasoning, and are less capable of emotional intimacy than those in the other statuses.

Basic Principles of Self-Perception

Now that you're familiar with some of the major aspects of the self, let's explore some of the processes people use to construct and maintain a coherent view of the self. We'll look at self-attributions, attributional style, two important motives that influence self-perception, and some interesting strategies people use to maintain positive feelings about the self.

Self-Attributions

Learning Objective

Define self-attributions and describe the key dimensions of attributions.

Let's say that you do well on a statistics test. To what do you attribute your performance? Did your new study routine pay off? Could you relate easily to the material? Perhaps math is one of your favorite subjects. This example from everyday life illustrates the nature of the self-attribution process. *Self-attributions* **are inferences that people draw about the causes of their own behavior.** People routinely make attributions to make sense out of their experiences. These attributions involve inferences that ultimately represent guesswork on the individual's part.

Fritz Heider (1958) was the first to assert that people tend to locate the cause of a behavior either within a person, attributing it to personal factors, or outside of a person, attributing it to environmental factors. He thus established one of the crucial dimensions along which attributions are made. (His theory is a general one which pertains not only to self-attributions but also to the attributions people make to explain the causes of events and the behavior of other people. In this chapter, we'll review Heider's theory only as it applies to self-attributions; we'll take up the other applications of his theory in the next chapter.)

"I think you'll find my test results are a pretty good indication of your abilities as a teacher."

Internal or External

Elaborating on Heider's insight, various theorists have agreed that explanations of behavior and events can be categorized as internal or external attributions (Jones & Davis, 1965; Kelley, 1967; Weiner, 1974). *Internal attributions* **ascribe the causes of behavior to personal dispositions, traits, abilities, and feelings.** *External attributions* **ascribe the causes of behavior to situational demands and environmental constraints.** For example, if you attribute your poor statistics grade to your failure to prepare adequately for the test or to getting overly anxious during the test, you are making an internal attribution.

Whether one's attributions are internal or external can have a tremendous impact on one's personal adjustment. As we'll see in Chapter 8, lonely people tend to attribute the cause of their loneliness to stable, internal causes ("I'm unlovable"). Similarly, studies suggest that people who attribute their setbacks to internal, personal causes while

Unstable cause
(temporary)

Stable cause
(permanent)

Internal-external dimension

Internal cause

| Effort Mood Fatigue | Ability Intelligence |

External cause

| Luck Chance Opportunity | Task difficulty |

Figure 5.11
Key dimensions of attributional thinking
Weiner's model of attributions assumes that people's explanations for success and failure emphasize internal versus external causes and stable versus unstable causes. For example, if you attribute an outcome to great effort or to lack of effort, you are citing causes that lie within the person. Since effort can vary over time, the causal factors at work are unstable. Other examples of causal factors that fit into each of the four cells in Weiner's model are shown in the diagram. (From Weiner et al., 1972)

discounting external, situational explanations may be more prone to depression than people who display opposite tendencies (Alloy, Clements, & Kolden, 1985; Huesmann & Morikawa, 1985).

Stable or Unstable

A second dimension people use in making causal attributions is the stability of the causes underlying behavior (Weiner, 1974; Weiner et al., 1972). A stable cause is one that is more or less permanent and unlikely to change over time. For example, a sense of humor and intelligence are *stable internal* causes of behavior. *Stable external* causes of behavior include such things as laws and rules (speed limits, no smoking areas). An unstable cause of behavior is one that is variable or subject to change. *Unstable internal* causes of behavior include such things as mood (good or bad) and motivation (strong or weak). *Unstable external* causes could be the weather and the presence or absence of other people. According to Bernard Weiner (1974), the stable-unstable dimension in attribution cuts across the internal-external dimension, creating four types of attributions for success and failure, as shown in Figure 5.11.

Let's apply Weiner's model to a concrete event. Imagine that you are contemplating why you just landed the job you wanted. You might attribute your success to internal factors that are stable (excellent ability) or unstable (hard work on your eye-catching résumé). Or you might attribute the outcome to external factors that are stable (lack of top-flight competition) or unstable (good luck). If you failed to get the job, the explanations you might offer for the outcome would fall in the same four categories: internal-stable (lack of ability), internal-unstable (inadequate effort on your résumé), external-stable (too much competition in your field), and external-unstable (bad luck).

Controllable or Uncontrollable

A third dimension in the attribution process is the *controllability* of the causes underlying one's actions (Weiner, 1986). For example, the amount of effort you expend on a task is typically perceived as something under your control, whereas an aptitude for music, say, is viewed as something you are born with (beyond your control). This dimension acknowledges the fact that sometimes behavior is under one's control and sometimes it isn't. Controllability can vary with each of the other two factors.

These three dimensions appear to be the central ones in the attribution process. Research has documented that self-attributions can influence future expectations (success or failure) and emotions (pride, hopelessness, guilt), and that these combine to influence subsequent performance (Fiske & Taylor, 1991; Weiner, 1986).

Attributional Style

Imagine that you and a friend are reasonably bright college freshmen who have just received the results of your first psychology exam, for which you both studied moderately hard. Both of you are disappointed to get C's on the exam. After class, you talk to each other about the situation. You attribute your grade to not studying hard enough and vow to really be prepared for the next exam. Your friend, though, mumbles, "I guess I'm just not that smart. I'm probably going to flunk out of school." On the basis of these comments, who do you think is likely to do better on the next exam? If you guessed that you will, you are probably correct. Let's see why.

Attributional style **refers to the tendency to use similar causal explanations for a wide variety of events in one's life.** According to Martin Seligman (1990), people tend to exhibit, to varying degrees, one of two attributional styles: an *optimistic explanatory style* or a *pessimistic explanatory style* (see Figure 5.12). The person with an optimistic explanatory style has a tendency to attribute setbacks to external, unstable, and specific factors. A person who failed to get a desired job, for example, might attribute this misfortune to bad luck in the interview rather than

Learning Objective

Describe Seligman's two attributional styles and their relationship to psychological adjustment.

to personal shortcomings. This style can help people discount their setbacks and thus maintain positive expectations for the future and a favorable self-image. Not surprisingly, an optimistic attributional style is associated with students' academic success and salespersons' job success (Fiske & Taylor, 1991).

In contrast, people with a pessimistic explanatory style tend to attribute their setbacks to internal, stable, and global (or pervasive) factors. These attributions make them feel bad about themselves and pessimistic about their ability to handle challenges in the future. Research shows that such a style appears to foster passive behavior and to make one more vulnerable to learned helplessness and depression (Peterson & Seligman, 1987; Sweeney, Anderson, & Bailey, 1986). This attributional style has also been tied to shyness and loneliness. In other words, lonely people may tell themselves that they're lonely because they're basically unlovable. Not only is that a devastating belief, but it provides no way to change the situation. Of course, people can make alternative attributions to explain their loneliness that can lead to more positive outcomes, as we'll see in Chapter 8.

The Premium on Consistency

The desire to maintain a consistent self-image is a powerful motive. This tendency to strive for a consistent self-image is the major reason that people's self-concepts are relatively stable, as we discussed earlier. People maintain consistent self-perceptions in a number of subtle ways and are often unaware of doing so. For example, individuals tend to reconstruct their personal history to match new information about themselves. Thus, they are able to maintain consistency between past and present behavior by erasing past memories that conflict with current behaviors. To illustrate, people who were once shy and who later became outgoing have been shown to recall memories about themselves that indicate they now perceive themselves as having always been outgoing (Ross & Conway, 1986). This inclination to revise the past in favor of the present may lie behind the oft-heard parental reproof, "When I was your age . . ." (Ross, McFarland, & Fletcher, 1981). What may be going on here, says Michael Ross, is that parents have conveniently erased memories of their childhood behavior—which was probably similar to that of their children— and, instead, compare their children's behavior to their own *current* behavior.

Another way people maintain self-consistency is by seeking out feedback and situations that will confirm their existing self-perceptions and avoiding situations or feedback that might disconfirm their self-image. According to William Swann's *self-verification theory*, **people prefer to receive feedback from others that is con-**

Figure 5.12
The effects of attributional style on expectations, emotions, and behavior
The pessimistic explanatory style is seen in the top set of boxes. This attributional style, which attributes setbacks to internal, stable, and global causes, tends to result in an expectation of lack of control over future events, depressed feelings, and passive behavior. A more adaptive, optimistic attributional style is shown in the bottom set of boxes.

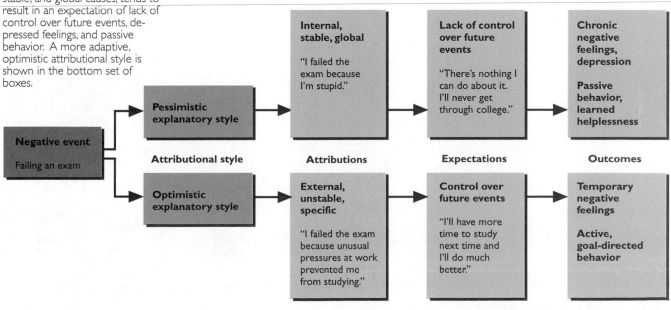

sistent with their own self-views. Thus, those with positive self-concepts should prefer positive feedback from others and those with negative self-concepts should prefer negative feedback. And research has found this is usually the case (Swann, Stein-Seroussi, & Giesler, 1992; Swann et al., 1990). In one study, college men were divided into either a positive self-concept group or a negative self-concept group based on test scores. Then, they were asked to choose a partner for a subsequent 2- to 3-hour interaction. Participants were led to believe that one of the prospective partners held views of him that were consistent with his self-views and that the other held views of him that were inconsistent with his self-views. As predicted, subjects with positive self-views preferred partners who viewed them positively, whereas those with negative self-views chose partners who viewed them negatively (Swann et al., 1992).

The Need for Self-Enhancement

Typically, self-perceptions are biased in a positive direction. **This tendency to maintain positive feelings about the self is termed** *self-enhancement.* Evidence of self-enhancement is widespread. For example, individuals exaggerate their control over life events (Wright, Zautra, & Braver, 1985), predict they will have a brighter future than others (Weinstein, 1980), view themselves as better than others (Allison, Messick, & Goethals, 1989), seek more information about their strengths than their weaknesses (J. D. Brown, 1990), and perceive that skills at which they excel are more important than those at which they don't (Campbell, 1986). While self-enhancement is quite common, it is not universal. As we noted in Chapter 4, high self-esteem and nondepressed individuals have more positive self-views than do those individuals who have low self-esteem or who are moderately depressed (Taylor & Brown, 1988, 1994). Thus, self-enhancement seems to operate less in the latter group. Let's explore some cognitive strategies individuals frequently use to maintain positive feelings about the self.

Downward Comparisons

Learning Objective

Discuss how downward comparisons and the self-serving bias contribute to self-enhancement.

Earlier in the chapter, we mentioned that people compare themselves to others as a means of learning more about themselves (social comparison). Individuals engage in social comparison whether or not they expect to feel threatened by the information they receive. Once threat enters the picture, however, it seems to change the type of person one chooses to compare oneself with. That is, when people feel threatened, they frequently choose to compare themselves with someone who is worse off than they are (Wills, 1981). **This defensive tendency to compare oneself with someone whose troubles are more serious than one's own is termed** *downward social comparison.* Studies show positive increases in both mood and self-esteem when downward social comparisons are made (Reis, Gerrard, & Gibbons, 1993).

If you have ever been in a serious car accident in which your car was "totaled," you probably reassured yourself by reflecting on the fact that at least no one was seriously injured. Similarly, people with chronic illnesses may compare themselves with those who have life-threatening diseases. Talk shows that feature people with assorted life tragedies provide numerous opportunities for downward social comparison. No doubt, this contributes to their popularity.

PEANUTS reprinted by permission of United Feature Syndicate, Inc.

The Self-Serving Bias

Suppose that you and three other individuals apply for a part-time job in the psychology department and you are selected for the position. Chances are, you believe that you were hired because you had the most outstanding qualifications for the job. But how do the other three people who weren't hired interpret the negative outcome? Do they tell themselves that you got the job because you were the most able? Unlikely! Instead, they probably attribute their loss to "bad luck" or to not having had time to prepare for the interview. These different explanations for success and failure reflect **the *self-serving bias*, or the tendency to attribute one's successes to personal factors and one's failures to situational factors** (Miller & Ross, 1975).

Research indicates that the self-serving bias is quite a potent one, although it seems that people are more likely to take credit for their successes than they are to disavow their failures (Fiske & Taylor, 1991). And, there are some occasions when people don't rush to take credit for their successes. For instance, if your role in a success is quite obvious to others, you may opt for modesty—at least to others (Schlenker, Weigold, & Hallam, 1990). Ironically, this strategy also turns out to be self-serving, because you may fear that "blowing your horn" too loudly could cause others to dislike you.

Interestingly, studies have shown that subjects who publicly take credit for their successes and disavow responsibility for their failures actually perceive themselves this way (Greenberg, Pyszczynski, & Solomon, 1982; Reiss et al., 1981). Hence, it is likely that people portray themselves favorably not only for the purpose of impression management but also to maintain self-esteem.

The Self-Centered Bias

Learning Objective

Discuss how the self-centered bias contributes to self-enhancement.

Reflect for a minute on who does the most cleaning in your apartment, you or your roommate. You were probably quick to name yourself. However, if we asked your roommate the same question, she would probably tell us that she did most of the cleaning! Since both of you can't be right, what's going on here? This is an example of **the *self-centered bias*, or the tendency for individuals to take more than their share of credit for a joint venture** (Ross & Sicoly, 1979). There are some noteworthy differences between this bias and the self-serving bias. For one thing, the self-centered bias involves a joint outcome, whereas the self-serving bias concerns only one individual's performance. For another, the success or failure of the outcome is irrelevant in the self-centered bias, but it is central to the self-serving bias.

Studies of the self-centered bias have asked married couples and college roommates to review a list of household chores and indicate the degree of responsibility they or the other person had for these tasks (Ross & Sicoly, 1979; Thompson & Kelley, 1981). Then the researchers have computed a "responsibility score" for each person and added the two scores together. Surprisingly, the two scores usually add up to more than 100%—that is, each person thinks that he or she does more chores than the other believes to be true. In addition, individuals in these studies have been asked to list examples of the chores that they and the other person have completed. Again, each gives more examples of his or her own chores than of the other person's.

What seems to be behind the self-centered bias? An intuitively obvious explanation is that claiming more than one's share of responsibility for joint ventures can raise one's self-esteem. However, the fact that a person will take more credit for outcomes whether or not they result in success seems to refute such an interpretation (Ross & Sicoly, 1979). Two other explanations do seem to be supported by research: (1) individuals are better at recalling instances of their own behaviors than those of others, and (2) when people perceive that they are the kind of person who would typically perform such a task, they are likely to believe that they have contributed more to it (Fiske & Taylor, 1991).

If we had to make a summary statement to pull together this wide-ranging discussion of the basic principles of self-perception, we would say that the process of self-perception is highly subjective. People's attributions are ultimately guesses about the causes of their thoughts, feelings, and behavior. Moreover, self-perceptions are influenced by self-protecting motives, and people use a number of strategies to maintain positive feelings about the self.

Self-Regulation

Learning Objective

Define self-regulation and self-efficacy.

People are constantly making decisions about goals to pursue and developing strategies by which to reach those goals. If they fall short of a goal, they take stock and often devise a different way to get where they want to go. **This work of directing and controlling one's behavior is termed** *self-regulation.* We'll review self-regulation from the perspective of Albert Bandura's theory of self-efficacy. As you may recall from our brief discussion of this topic in Chapter 2, *self-efficacy* **refers to people's conviction that they can achieve specific goals.** Simply having a skill doesn't guarantee that one will be able to put it into practice; one must also *believe* that one is capable of doing so. Obviously, efficacy beliefs vary according to one's skills. A person may have high self-efficacy when it comes to making friends but low self-efficacy when it comes time to speak in front of a group.

Correlates of Self-Efficacy

A number of studies show that self-efficacy affects individuals' commitments to goals, their performance on tasks, and their persistence toward goals in the face of obstacles (Bandura, 1990b). In addition, people with high self-efficacy anticipate success in future outcomes and can "tune out" negative thoughts that can lead to failure (Bandura, 1989). Research has also demonstrated that self-efficacy is related to career choice (Betz & Hackett, 1986), health habits, and responses to stress (Bandura, 1992).

Because of its importance in psychological adjustment, it is worth noting that self-efficacy is learned and can be changed. Studies have demonstrated that increasing a person's self-efficacy is an effective way to treat psychological problems such as test anxiety (Smith, 1989), fear of sexual assault (Ozer & Bandura, 1990), posttraumatic stress disorder (Solomon et al., 1988), and drug addiction (DiClemente, 1986).

Developing Self-Efficacy

Learning Objective

Describe four means for developing self-efficacy.

Self-efficacy plays a key role in the ability to make commitments to goals and to meet the goals one sets. How do people acquire this valuable characteristic? Bandura (1986) suggests there are four sources of self-efficacy:

• *Mastery experiences.* The most important path to self-efficacy is through a history of mastering new skills. Sometimes new skills come easily—learning how to use the copy machine in the library, for instance. Some skills are harder to master—learning how to use a new word-processing program or how to play the piano. In acquiring more difficult skills, people usually make mistakes. How one handles these failure experiences is the key to learning self-efficacy. If you give up when you make mistakes, your failure instills self-doubts or low self-efficacy. On the other hand, if you persist through failure experiences to eventual success, you learn the lesson of self-efficacy: I *can* do it! A practical implication for parents, teachers, and coaches is that they should set high, but attainable, goals for children, encourage them to learn from their mistakes, and inspire them to persevere until they succeed. This approach provides the mastery experiences children need to build self-efficacy and will enable them to approach future challenges with confidence. Well-intentioned parents, teachers, and supervisors who sometimes do their children's or employees' work or who regularly allow others to opt out of obligations with no consequences are unwittingly depriving individuals of opportunities to develop self-efficacy.

In overcoming obstacles to master new skills, children build self-efficacy, enabling them to approach new challenges with confidence.

• *Vicarious experiences.* Another way to improve self-efficacy is by watching others perform a skill you want to learn. It's important that the model you choose be competent at the task, and it helps if the model is similar to you (in age, gender, and race). For example, if you're afraid of speaking up for yourself, observing someone who is skilled at doing so can help you develop the necessary confidence. In addition, it's important that the person you use as a model not experience negative consequences; watching someone engage in behavior that results in adverse effects can undermine self-efficacy.

• *Persuasion and encouragement.* Although it is less effective than the first two approaches, a third way to develop self-efficacy is through others' telling you that you are "up" to a particular task. For example, if you're having a hard time asking someone for a date, a friend's encouragement might give you just the push you need. Of course, persuasion doesn't always work. And, unless encouragement is accompanied by specific and concrete suggestions, this tactic is unlikely to be successful. Too, if people attempt a skill they're doubtful about and perform poorly, they can experience a blow to self-efficacy.

• *Interpretation of emotional arousal.* The physiological responses that accompany feelings and one's interpretations of these responses are another source of self-efficacy. Let's say you're sitting in class waiting for the instructor to distribute an exam. You notice that your palms are moist and your heart is pounding. If you attribute these behaviors to fear, you can temporarily lower your self-efficacy, thus increasing the chances that you will do poorly on the test. Alternatively, if you interpret your sweaty palms and racing heart to the arousal everyone needs to perform well, you may be able to boost your self-efficacy and increase your chances of doing well.

To summarize, the ability to set goals, to design strategies by which to actually accomplish these goals, and to persist through failure to eventual success plays a key role in psychological adjustment.

Albert Bandura

Self-Presentation

Learning Objective

Explain why we may have many public selves.

Whereas your self-concept involves how you see yourself, your public self involves how you want *others* to see you. **A *public self* is an image or facade presented to others in social interactions.** People rarely behave totally spontaneously. Let's face it: Most people see only an edited version of your behavior, which is usually calculated to present a certain image. This presentation of a public self may sound deceitful, but it is perfectly normal, and everyone does it (Alexander & Knight, 1971; Goffman, 1959, 1971). Actually, most people are not limited to a single public self.

Typically, individuals have a number of public selves that are tied to certain situations and to certain people with whom they interact. For instance, you may have one public self for your parents and another for your siblings. You may have still others for your teachers, your same-sex friends, your other-sex friends, your spouse, your boss, your colleagues, your customers, and your neighbors.

Impression Management

Learning Objective

Explain why people engage in impression management.

Impression management **refers to usually conscious efforts by people to influence how others think of them.** Why do people engage in impression management? Basically, it's a matter of necessity. Social norms virtually require everyone to engage in careful self-presentation (Goffman, 1959). In other words, people are expected to portray themselves in certain ways when interacting with their parents, peers, co-workers, and so forth. Furthermore, social norms also support others' acceptance of these efforts at impression management (Goffman, 1959). Although others may be skeptical, they rarely challenge a person's self-presentations. Unless one's self-presentation is clearly and extremely out of line with reality, people will keep their suspicions to themselves.

Normally, people try to make a positive impression on others (Baumeister, Tice, & Hutton, 1989). This is obviously important if they want to be liked, respected, hired, and so forth. Let's take a look at the operation of impression management by reviewing a study of behavior in job interviews (von Baeyer, Sherk, & Zanna, 1981). In this study, female job applicants were led to believe that the man who would interview them held either very traditional, "chauvinistic" views of women or more egalitarian views. Applicants who expected a chauvinist presented themselves in a more "traditionally feminine" manner than subjects in the other condition. Their self-presentation efforts affected both their appearance (they wore more makeup) and their communication style (they talked less and gave more traditional answers to a question about marriage and children). The bottom line is this: Impression management is a normal feature of everyday social interactions. Although people certainly don't do it all the time, they probably do it a lot more than many realize. Individuals use a number of strategies to make favorable impressions on others (Jones, 1964; Jones & Pittman, 1982). We'll briefly describe three that are commonly used: ingratiation, basking in reflected glory, and self-handicapping.

Using Ingratiation

Learning Objective

Describe the impression management strategies of ingratiation and basking in reflected glory.

As we noted, people want others to like them and actively engage in behavior they hope will result in favorable evaluations from others. **These efforts to make oneself likable to others are termed** *ingratiation.* One of the most common ingratiation tactics is *giving compliments.* Good old-fashioned flattery is far from obsolete. Still, sincerity is important because people can often detect insincerity by mismatches between verbal and nonverbal messages. Another way people try to get others to like them is by *doing favors* for them. Generally, people like these little attentions. However, the favors shouldn't be too spectacular, or they may leave the target person with the uncomfortable feeling of social indebtedness. A third strategy is *going along with others.* To get others to like you, it helps to do the things that they want to do. Finally, *presenting a favorable self-image* by playing up your strong points can be a way to get others to like you. Depending on the situation, some display of false modesty can also be useful.

Basking in Reflected Glory

When your favorite sports team won the national championship last year, did you make a point of wearing the team cap? And, when your best friend won that special award, do you recall looking for opportunities to tell others the good news about *your* friend? Of course, if you played a role in someone's success, it's understandable that you would want to share in the recognition. However, people often bask in reflected glory even when they've had nothing to do with an outstanding

Robert Cialdini

achievement. Robert Cialdini and his colleagues (1976) describe **the tendency to enhance one's image by publicly announcing one's association with those who are successful as** *basking in reflected glory.*

Cialdini and his colleagues (1976) studied this phenomenon on college campuses with nationally ranked football teams. They predicted that, when asked how their team had fared in a recent football game, students would be more likely to say "*we* won" (in other words, to bask in reflected glory, or to "BIRG") when the home team had been successful than to identify with the team when it lost. In addition, they reasoned that students who had just experienced a personal failure would be more likely to BIRG than would students who had just experienced a personal success. They tested their hypotheses by having college students take a test on their knowledge of various campus issues. Afterward, half the students were told that they had done very well on the test and the other half were told that they had done rather poorly. Then participants were asked to describe the outcome of a recent school football game. As predicted, students were more likely to BIRG when their team won than when it lost. Also, subjects who believed that they had just failed the test were more likely to use the words "*we* won" than those who believed they had performed well.

There is evidence not only for basking in reflected glory but also for the opposite tendency: cutting off reflected failure. That is, when people find themselves associated with those who are *un*successful, they often distance themselves from the "failures" to protect their public image (Cialdini et al., 1976; Snyder, Lassegard, & Ford, 1986).

Self-Handicapping

Learning Objective

Explain how self-handicapping can contribute to impression management.

Another impression management strategy comes into play when people need to "save face" because they have failed at an important task. Maybe they got cut from the soccer team, failed to get a job they wanted, or did poorly on an algebra test. When this happens, they can usually come up with a face-saving excuse, and such excuses are even more convincing if used *before* an outcome is known: "I'm having a hard time studying for my biology exam because I'm not feeling very well." However, some people use a different, but related, strategy to avoid the disapproval that follows poor performance. They actually behave in a way that sets them up to fail, so that they have a ready-made excuse for failure, should it occur. For example, when a big exam is coming up, these individuals might put off studying until the last minute or go out drinking the night before the test. When exam day arrives, chances are they don't do very well. How do these individuals explain their poor performance to others? Obviously, they didn't do well because they didn't prepare for the test. (After all, wouldn't you rather have others believe that your poor performance is due to inadequate preparation rather than lack of ability?) **This tendency to sabotage one's performance to provide an excuse for possible failure is termed** *self-handicapping* (Berglas & Jones, 1978). A number of studies have revealed that people use a variety of tactics by which to handicap their performance, including use of alcohol or drugs, procrastination, a bad mood, a distracting stimulus, anxiety, depression, and being overcommitted (Fiske & Taylor, 1991).

Some people engage in self-handicapping more than others. Men use this strategy more often than women, as do those who are more conscious of how others view them (Shepperd & Arkin, 1989). Moreover, individuals vary in the *means* they use for self-handicapping. For example, men are more likely to use the strategies of not practicing or taking drugs, whereas women more often report physical symptoms or stress (Hirt, Deppe, & Gordon, 1991). Finally, there are individual differences in the *reasons* for self-handicapping. People with low self-esteem more often engage in self-handicapping to maintain a positive impression (or to avoid failing), while those with high self-esteem are more likely to handicap themselves to enhance their image (Rhodewalt et al., 1991; Tice, 1991). That is, if they happen to do well, they can claim that they are especially capable, given their excellent performance with minimal preparation. In one study, college students were categorized as high or low in self-esteem based on test scores (Tice, 1991). They were then told that they would soon be completing either a test of nonverbal intelligence (a task important to their self-esteem) or a test of eye-hand coordination (a task unimpor-

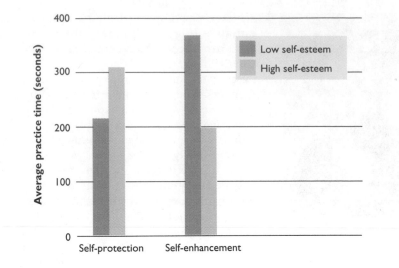

Figure 5.13
Motives for self-handicapping vary depending on self-esteem
When subjects were told that they would be taking a test that identified only people who were intellectually deficient (self-esteem protection condition), low self-esteem subjects practiced less (self-handicapped) than high self-esteem subjects. In contrast, when subjects were told that the test identified only people who were highly gifted (self-esteem enhancement condition), high self-esteem subjects practiced less (self-handicapped) than low self-esteem subjects. Thus, both high and low self-esteem individuals self-handicap, but they have different motives for doing so. (Based on Tice, 1991)

tant to their self-esteem). Finally, half the subjects taking each test were told that it identified only individuals who were intellectually deficient (motivating them to want to protect their self-esteem by avoiding failure), and half were told that the test identified only those who were highly gifted (motivating them to want to enhance their image). After hearing this information, all subjects were allowed to practice as long as they wished. As predicted, when the task was important to their self-esteem, those who practiced less (self-handicapped) were the low self-esteem subjects in the self-protection condition and the high self-esteem subjects in the self-enhancement condition (see Figure 5.13).

Thus, self-handicapping seems like a "win-win" strategy: If you fail, you have a face-saving excuse at the ready, and if you happen to succeed, you can claim that you are unusually gifted! However, it probably has not escaped your attention that there is a big risk associated with self-handicapping. That is, in the process of giving yourself an attributional "out" to use in case of failure, your self-defeating behavior is likely to result in poor performance (Baumgardner & Brownlee, 1987). Moreover, although self-handicapping may prevent others from attributing your poor performance to low ability, it does not prevent them from making negative attributions about you. For example, people tend to believe that individuals are less competent when they self-handicap than when they don't (Arkin & Baumgardner, 1985). Also, if you self-handicap, others may perceive you as lazy, inclined to drink too much, or highly anxious, depending on the means you use to self-handicap. Consequently, this impression management tactic has serious drawbacks.

Self-Monitoring

Learning Objective

Describe how high and low self-monitors tend to behave.

According to Mark Snyder (1979, 1986), people vary in their awareness of how they are perceived by others. *Self-monitoring* **refers to the degree to which people attend to and control the impressions they make on others.** People who are high self-monitors are sensitive to their impact on others. Those who are low self-monitors are less concerned about impression management and behave more spontaneously.

Compared to low self-monitors, high self-monitors actively seek information about how they are expected to behave and try to tailor their actions accordingly (Snyder & Campbell, 1982); they are sensitive to situational cues and relatively skilled at deciphering what others want to see; and they tend to act more in accordance with situational expectations than with their true feelings or attitudes (Zanna & Olson, 1982). Because high self-monitors control their emotions well and deliberately regulate nonverbal signals that are more spontaneous in others, they are relatively talented at self-presentation (Friedman & Miller-Herringer, 1991). In addition, they have been shown to be more accurate in judging other people's feelings

(Geiser, Rarick, & Soldow, 1977). In contrast, low self-monitors are more likely to express their true beliefs, since they are more motivated to behave consistently with their internal feelings (McCann & Hancock, 1983).

Self-Presentation and Authenticity

Although people may be aware of the dubious accuracy of their self-presentations, research indicates that individuals sometimes come to believe their fabrications (Jones et al., 1981; Rhodewalt & Agustsdottir, 1986). In other words, if you present yourself in a certain way often enough, you may begin to actually see yourself in that way. For example, if you are really quite conceited but you incorporate false humility into many of your public selves, you might begin to view yourself as a humble person.

Although everyone engages in some impression management, people vary greatly in how much they edit their behavior. As we have seen, some people are more concerned than others about portraying themselves appropriately for various audiences. Moreover, people differ in the degree of congruence or overlap among their various public selves (see Figure 5.14). Recall Erikson's emphasis on the congruence between people's own sense of self and others' perceptions of them. In a similar fashion, Sidney Jourard (1971) maintained that constant misrepresentation for purposes of impression management may lead people to lose touch with their "authentic" selves. Jourard argued that this kind of confusion is dangerous and may cause much psychological distress.

It is this identity-related confusion that leads many people to be concerned about "finding" themselves. This search for the real self became something of a fad in the 1970s, and many people used the concept to rationalize their "rudderless" lives. It has since become common to ridicule people who say they are "looking for the real me." However, this search for the authentic self may often be a genuine effort to come to grips with a self-concept and an identity that are in disarray.

To conclude, it is probably a good idea to avoid going overboard on self-presentation efforts. Taken to an excess, impression management may be harmful to accurate self-perception. Also, most people are sensitive to sincerity in others; when they doubt the sincerity of flattering statements, they may like the flatterer less (Kauffman & Steiner, 1968; Lowe & Goldstein, 1970).

In the upcoming Application, we'll redirect our attention to the critical issue of self-esteem and outline seven steps for building self-esteem.

Figure 5.14
Public selves and identity confusion
Person 1 has very divergent public selves with relatively little overlap among them. Person 1 is more likely to develop identity confusion than Person 2, whose public selves are more congruent with each other.

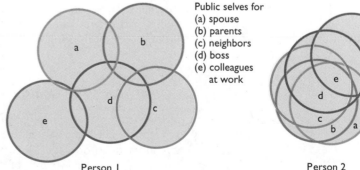

Public selves for
(a) spouse
(b) parents
(c) neighbors
(d) boss
(e) colleagues
  at work

Person 1

Person 2

Application

Building Self-Esteem

Answer the following "yes" or "no."

1. *I am very sensitive to criticism.*

2. *I tend to have a hard time accepting praise or flattery.*

3. *I have very little confidence in my abilities.*

4. *I often feel awkward in social situations and just don't know how to take charge.*

5. *I tend to be highly critical of other people.*

If you answered "yes" to most of these questions, you may be suffering from what Alfred Adler called an *inferiority complex* (see Chapter 2). This syndrome, which is dominated by low self-esteem, is fairly common. It is also quite unfortunate. People with very low self-esteem tend to develop more emotional problems than others, set low goals for themselves, become socially invisible, conform against their better judgment, and court rejection by putting down others.

Self-esteem is obviously an important component of the self-concept. An overly negative self-image can contribute to many kinds of behavioral problems. An overly positive image can also cause problems, but people characterized by excessive conceit do not suffer in the same way that self-critical people do.

In this Application, we describe seven guidelines for building self-esteem. These guidelines are based on our own distillation of the advice of many theorists, including Rogers (1977), Ellis (1984), Jourard (Jourard & Landsman, 1980), Hamachek (1992), Mahoney (1979), and Zimbardo (1977).

1. Recognize That You Control Your Self-Image

The first thing you must do is recognize that *you* ultimately control how you see yourself. You *do* have the power to change your self-image. True, we have discussed at length how feedback from others influences your self-concept. Yes, social comparison theory suggests that you need such feedback and that it would be unwise to ignore it completely. However, the final choice about whether to accept or reject such feedback rests with you. Your self-image resides in your mind and is a product of your thinking. Although others may influence your self-concept, you are the final authority.

2. Don't Let Others Set Your Goals

A common trap that many people fall into is letting others set the standards by which they evaluate themselves. Others are constantly telling you that you *should* do this or that you *ought* to do that. Thus, you hear that you "should study computer science" or "ought to lose weight" or "must move to a better neighborhood." Most of these people are well-intentioned, and many of them may have good ideas. Still, it is important that you make your *own* decisions about what you will do and what you will believe in. For example, consider a business executive in his early 40s who sees himself in a negative light because he has not climbed very high in the corporate hierarchy. The crucial question is: Did he ever *really* want to make that arduous climb? It could be that he has misgivings about the value of such an effort. Perhaps he has gone through life thinking he should pursue that kind of success only because that standard was imposed on him by society. You should think about the source of and basis for your personal goals and standards. Do they really

Learning Objective

List seven suggestions to build self-esteem.

"I don't suppose it's much compared with other inferiority complexes"

© Punch/Rothco

represent ideals that *you* value? Or are they beliefs that you have passively accepted from others without thinking?

3. Recognize Unrealistic Goals

Even if you truly value certain ideals and sincerely want to achieve certain goals, another question remains. Are your goals realistic? Many people get in the habit of demanding too much of themselves. They always want to perform at their best, which is obviously impossible. For instance, you may have a burning desire to achieve international acclaim as an actor. However, the odds against such an achievement are enormous. It is important to recognize this reality so that you do not condemn yourself for failure. Some overly demanding people pervert the social comparison process by always comparing themselves against the *best* rather than against similar others. They assess their looks by comparing themselves with famous models, and they judge their finances by comparing themselves with the wealthiest people they know. Such comparisons are unrealistic and almost inevitably undermine self-esteem.

4. Modify Negative Self-Talk

The way you analyze your life influences how you see yourself (and vice versa). People who are low in self-esteem tend to engage in various counterproductive modes of thinking. For example, when they succeed, they may attribute their success to good luck, and when they fail, they may blame themselves. Quite to the contrary, you should take credit for your successes and consider the possibility that your failures may not be your fault. As discussed in Chapter 4, Albert Ellis has

Recommended Reading

Self-Esteem

by Matthew McKay and Patrick Fanning (New Harbinger Publications, 1992)

If you want to assess, raise, and maintain your self-esteem, this book can help you. The authors work from the premise that everyone has a "pathological critic," an inner voice that is judgmental and faultfinding. Some people have an overly active and harsh pathological critic that, over time, erodes self-esteem. Through the use of cognitive restructuring, the reader is shown how to deal with these destructive self-statements.

This book is easily understood, is written in an interesting style, and packs a lot of information in a few pages. It is most useful for those whose self-esteem problems are limited to a specific area (such as work, parenting, or sex). While also helpful to those whose esteem problems are more serious, the authors suggest that the book will be most effective for this group when used along with psychotherapy.

In the following excerpt, the authors discuss how parents' reactions to children can contribute to low self-esteem.

Many parents label poor judgment as moral error. For example, a child who puts off a school project until the very end and is then forced to stay up late doing a rather slipshod job is guilty of poor judgment or poor impulse control (or both). But a parent who labels this behavior as lazy or stupid or "screwed up" is communicating to the child that he is morally bad. . . . The more your parents confused matters of taste, preference, judgment, and convenience with moral issues, the more likely you are to have fragile self-esteem. [p. 112]

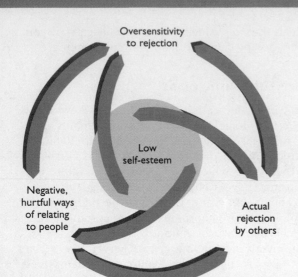

Figure 5.15
The vicious circle of low self-esteem and rejection
A negative self-image can make expectations of rejection a self-fulfilling prophecy, because people with low self-esteem tend to approach others in negative, hurtful ways. Real or imagined rejections lower self-esteem still further, creating a vicious circle.

pointed out that people often think irrationally and draw unwarranted negative conclusions about themselves. For example, if you apply for a job and are rejected, you might think, "They didn't hire me. I must be a worthless, inept person." The conclusion that you are a "worthless person" does *not* follow logically from the fact that you were not hired. Such irrational thinking and negative self-talk breed poor self-esteem. It is important to recognize the destructive potential of negative self-talk and bring it to a halt.

5. Emphasize Your Strengths

The advice to emphasize your strengths may seem trite, but it has genuine merit. People with low self-esteem often derive little satisfaction from their accomplishments and virtues. They dismiss compliments as foolish, unwarranted, or insincere. They pay little heed to their good qualities while talking constantly about their defeats and frailties. The fact is that everyone has strengths and weaknesses. You should accept those personal shortcomings that you are powerless to change and work on those that are changeable, without becoming obsessed about it. At the same time, you should take stock of your strengths and learn to appreciate them.

6. Work to Improve Yourself

As just mentioned, some personal shortcomings *can* be overcome. Although it is important to reassess your goals and discard those that are unrealistic, this advice is not intended to provide a convenient rationalization for complacency. There is much to be said for setting out to conquer personal problems. In a sense, this entire text is based on a firm belief in the value of self-control and self-improvement. As we saw in our discussion of self-efficacy, there is ample evidence that efforts at self-improvement can pay off by boosting self-esteem.

7. Approach Others with a Positive Outlook

People who are low in self-esteem often try to cut others down to their (subjective) size through constant criticism. As you can readily imagine, this faultfinding and generally negative approach to interpersonal transactions does not go over well with other people. Instead, it leads to tension, antagonism, and rejection. This rejection lowers self-esteem still further (see Figure 5.15). Efforts to build self-esteem can be facilitated by recognizing and reversing this self-defeating tendency. Approaching people with a positive, supportive outlook will promote rewarding interactions and help you earn their acceptance. There is probably nothing that enhances self-esteem more than acceptance and genuine affection from others.

5 Review

Key Ideas

Self-Concept
• The self-concept, self-esteem, and identity are three major components of the self. The self-concept is composed of a number of beliefs about what one is like, and it is not easily changed. It governs both present and future behavior. Individuals' self-concepts vary in complexity. People with complex self-concepts are likely to have stable emotions and high self-esteem. When there are discrepancies between one's ideal self and actual or ought self, negative emotions and lowered self-esteem may result. To cope with these negative states, individuals may bring their behavior in line with their ideal selves or blunt their awareness of self-discrepancies.

Self-Esteem
• The self-concept is shaped by several factors. These include individuals' observations of their own behavior, which often involve social comparisons with others—usually similar others who make up a reference group. Self-observations tend to be biased in a positive direction. In addition, feedback from others shapes the self-concept; this information is also filtered to some extent. Cultural guidelines also affect the way people see themselves. Those who are reared in individualistic cultures usually have an independent view of the self, whereas those in collectivist cultures tend to have an interdependent view of the self.

Identity
• Self-esteem is a person's global evaluation of his or her worth. Low self-esteem is associated with emotional problems and difficulties in social interactions. Because self-esteem affects expectations, it operates in a self-perpetuating fashion. Parents are especially important in determining self-esteem. Members of minority groups use a number of strategies to protect their self-image from the effects of being stigmatized.
• Identity is a relatively clear and stable sense of who one is and what one stands for. According to Erik Erikson, developing a sense of identity is a key challenge of adolescence. James Marcia has proposed that identity outcomes include foreclosure, moratorium, diffusion, and achievement. A number of theorists emphasize the importance of congruence between one's public selves and one's self-concept and sense of identity.

Basic Principles of Self-Perception
• Individuals make use of a number of processes to construct and maintain a coherent view of the self. To explain the causes of their behavior, individuals make self-attributions. Generally, people attribute their behavior to internal or external factors and to stable or unstable factors. Controllability-uncontrollability is another key dimension of self-attributions. People tend to use either an optimistic explanatory style or a pessimistic explanatory style to explain various events that occur in their lives, and these attributional styles are related to psychological adjustment.
• Individuals strive to maintain a consistent self-view, even though this means that self-perceptions are not necessarily accurate. Individuals actively strive to maintain a positive view of themselves. Common self-enhancement strategies include downward comparisons, the self-serving bias, and the self-centered bias.

Self-Regulation
• Self-regulation involves setting goals and directing behavior to meet those goals. A key aspect of self-regulation is self-efficacy—an individual's belief that he or she can achieve specific goals. Self-efficacy plays a key role in adjustment and can be learned through mastery experiences, vicarious experiences, persuasion, and positive interpretations of emotional arousal.

Self-Presentation
• Public selves are the various images that individuals project to others. Generally, people try to create positive impressions for others by employing impression management strategies such as ingratiation, basking in reflected glory, and self-handicapping. People who are high in self-monitoring are especially sensitive to the impressions they make on others.
• In striving to make positive impressions on others, it is unwise to stray too far from the truth. This misguided tactic may interfere with accurate self-perception and cause others to distrust and dislike us.

Application: Building Self-Esteem
• The seven building blocks to higher self-esteem include (1) recognize that you control your self-image, (2) don't let others set your goals, (3) recognize unrealistic goals, (4) modify negative self-talk, (5) emphasize your strengths, (6) work to improve yourself, and (7) approach others with a positive outlook.

Key Terms

Attributional style
Basking in reflected glory
Collectivism
Downward social comparison
External attributions
Identity
Impression management
Individualism
Ingratiation
Internal attributions
Possible selves
Public self
Reference group
Self-attributions
Self-centered bias
Self-complexity
Self-concept
Self-discrepancy
Self-efficacy
Self-enhancement
Self-esteem
Self-handicapping
Self-monitoring
Self-regulation
Self-serving bias
Self-verification theory
Social comparison theory

Key People

Albert Bandura
Robert Cialdini
Erik Erikson
James Marcia
Mark Snyder

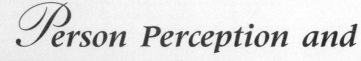

6 Person Perception and
Social Influence

You've had your eye on that attractive brunette in the first row of your algebra class since the term began. Should you ask her out? As you ponder about the wisdom of this action, you watch her, hoping to pick up some clues to help you make your decision. You notice a sorority decal on her notebook. You don't belong to a fraternity and you've never dated a sorority woman. You've heard that some of them can be snobbish, although she seems to be friendly and approachable. Still, you're only a sophomore; what if she's a senior? That could be awkward. As you continue to contemplate what to do, similar thoughts flit through your mind.

In this scenario, we see the process of person perception at work. People are constantly constructing impressions of others to try to understand them and predict their behavior. In this chapter, we'll explore what's involved in forming these impressions. We'll also pay special attention to inaccuracies in person perception and the problem of prejudice. Then we'll change perspectives and look at how other people influence one's own beliefs and behavior. Among other issues, we'll examine persuasion, conformity, and obedience to authority figures. As you'll see, both person perception and social influence play significant roles in social interactions and personal adjustment.

The Process of Person Perception

Can you remember the first time you met your freshman roommate? She seemed pleasant enough but came across as a little reserved. In fact, you were worried whether you would become friends. To your relief, within a week it seemed as though you had known each other for years. As people interact with others, they constantly engage in *person perception,* **the process of forming impressions of others.** Impression formation is usually such an easy and automatic process that people are unaware it is taking place. Nonetheless, the process is a complex one. Let's review some of its essential aspects.

Key Sources of Information

Learning Objective

Describe five key sources of information used to form impressions of others.

Because you can't read other people's minds, you are dependent on *observations* of them to determine what they are like. In forming impressions of others, people rely on four key sources of observational information: appearance, verbal statements, actions, and nonverbal messages. In addition, the *situation* in which behavior occurs provides useful information about others.

• *Appearance.* Despite the admonition "You can't judge a book by its cover," people frequently do just that. Physical features such as height, weight, skin color, and hair color are some of the cues used to "read" other people. Regardless of their accuracy, beliefs about physical features are used to form impressions of others (Bull & Rumsey, 1988). For example, Americans learn to associate red hair with "hot" tempers and the wearing of eyeglasses with studiousness.

• *Verbal statements.* Another obvious source of information about others is what they say. If Ethan tells you that he goes out drinking every weekend and Jack says that he never drinks, you form quite different impressions of these two individuals. If Mary speaks negatively about most people she knows, you will probably conclude that she is a critical person.

• *Actions.* Because people don't always tell the truth, one must rely heavily on people's behavior to provide insights about them (Newtson, 1974). In impression formation, people follow the adage "Actions speak louder than words." If you know that Linda volunteers 5 hours a week at the local homeless shelter, you are likely to infer that she is a caring person.

• *Nonverbal messages.* Another key source of information about others is nonverbal communication: facial expressions, eye contact, body language, and gestures (Ambady & Rosenthal, 1992; Ekman, 1992). These nonverbal cues provide information about people's emotional states and dispositions. For example, a bright smile and good eye contact signal friendliness and openness. Also, because people know that verbal behavior is more easily manipulated than nonverbal behavior, they often rely on nonverbal cues to determine the truth of what others say (DePaulo, LeMay, & Epstein, 1991).

• *Situations.* The setting in which behavior occurs provides critical information about how to interpret a person's behavior. For example, if Doug guffaws at a joke at a local student hangout, no one bats an eye. But if he bursts out laughing in the middle of a serious lecture, it raises eyebrows and generates speculations about why he is behaving this way. As this example illustrates, people pay particular attention to behavior that is negative or unexpected (B. Weiner, 1985).

Social Schemas

Learning Objective

Define social schemas and explain their role in person perception.

Although every individual is unique, people tend to categorize each other. For example, in our opening scenario, the prospective dating partner is described as an "attractive brunette" and as a sorority woman. Once you knew these facts, certain associations probably came to mind. Labels such as "sorority woman," "art major," "professor," "airhead," and "jock" reflect the role of social schemas in person perception. **Social schemas are organized clusters of ideas about categories of people.** When a social schema is activated, it usually influences your perception of a person (see Figure 6.1). For example, being told that Jack is a "nice guy" will probably increase your tendency to notice behaviors that fit your schema for "nice guy." In addition, you may overlook behaviors that contradict this schema. People depend on social schemas because they help to efficiently process and store the countless bits and pieces of information about others that come to people in their interactions (Fiske & Taylor, 1991).

Snap Judgments Versus Systematic Judgments

Learning Objective

Explain the difference between snap judgments and systematic judgments.

Snap judgments about others are those made on the basis of only a few bits of information and preconceived notions. Thus, they may not be particularly accurate. Nevertheless, people get by with superficial assessments of others quite often. As Susan Fiske (1993) puts it: "People are good enough perceivers" (p. 156). Often, interactions with others are so fleeting or inconsequential that it makes little difference that such judgments are imprecise. Does it really matter that you mistakenly infer that the blond postal clerk is a fun-loving person, or that your bespectacled restaurant server is an intellectual? You may never interact with the person again, and even if you do, your interactions are not likely to be significant to either of you.

On the other hand, when it comes to selecting an employee, a boss, or a mate, it's critical that impressions be as accurate as possible. Hence, it's not surprising that people are motivated to take more care in these assessments. In forming impressions of those who can affect their welfare and happiness, people make *systematic judgments* rather than snap decisions (see Figure 6.2). That is, they take the time to observe the person in a variety of situations and to compare the person's behavior with that of others in similar situations. In assessing what a significant individual is like, people are particularly interested in learning *why* the person behaves in a certain way. This deeper level of understanding is vital if one is to make accurate predictions

Figure 6.1
Examples of social schemas
Everyone has social schemas for various "types" of people, such as sophisticated professionals or working-class stiffs. Social schemas are clusters of beliefs that guide information processing.

Sophisticated professional   **Working-class stiff**

about their future behavior. After all, when you're looking for a roommate, you don't want to end up with an inconsiderate slob. To determine the causes of others' behavior, people engage in the process of causal attribution.

Attributions

Learning Objective

Define attributions and explain when people are likely to make them.

As we have seen in earlier chapters, ***attributions* are inferences that people draw about the causes of their own behavior, others' behavior, and events.** In the previous chapter, we focused on *self*-attributions. Here, we'll apply attributions to the behavior of *other people*. For example, suppose that your boss bawls you out for doing a sloppy job on an insignificant project. To what do you attribute this tongue-lashing? Was your work really that sloppy? Was your boss just in a grouchy mood? Is your boss under too much pressure? Or let's say that you overhear Amy compliment Tracy on her clothing. To what do you attribute the compliment? Does Amy really like Tracy's outfit? Or was the compliment merely part of everyday social routine? Is it possible that the compliment was an attempt to butter Tracy up?

In Chapter 5, we noted that there are three key dimensions of attributions: internal/external, stable/unstable, and controllability/uncontrollability. For the purposes of this discussion, we'll focus only on the internal/external dimension. When people ascribe the causes of someone's behavior to personal dispositions, traits, abilities, or feelings, they are making *internal* attributions. When people impute the causes of the person's behavior to situational demands and environmental constraints, they are making *external* attributions. For example, if a friend's business fails, you might attribute the failure to her lack of business acumen (an internal factor) or to negative trends in the economy (an external explanation). Parents who discover that their teenage son just banged up the family car may blame it on his carelessness (an internal attribution) or on slippery road conditions (an external attribution).

The types of attributions people make about others can have a tremendous impact on everyday social interactions. For example, blaming a friend's business failure on poor business "smarts" rather than on a poor economy will obviously affect how you view your friend—not to mention whether you'll lend her money! Likewise, if parents attribute their son's automobile accident to slippery road conditions, they are likely to deal with him very differently than if they attribute it to his carelessness. In addition, there is evidence that the attributions spouses make to explain each other's behavior can affect their marital satisfaction (Bradbury & Fincham, 1988).

Obviously, people don't make attributions about everyone they meet. Research suggests that people are relatively selective about this (Hilton, Fein, & Miller, 1993; E. Jones, 1990; B. Weiner, 1985). It seems that people are most likely to make attributions (1) when unusual events grab their attention, (2) when events have personal consequences, (3) when others behave in unexpected ways, and (4) when they are suspicious about the motives underlying someone's behavior.

Some aspects of the attribution process are relatively logical (Brewer, 1988). Nonetheless, research also shows that the process of person perception is sometimes unsystematic, illogical, and subject to biases (Fiske & Taylor, 1991). Snap judgments are one example of unsystematic and illogical judgments. Biases also creep into the person perception process. We'll consider some of these biases next.

Figure 6.2
The process of person perception
In forming impressions of others, perceivers rely on four different sources of observational information. When it's important to form accurate impressions of others, we are motivated to make systematic judgments about them, including attributions. When accuracy isn't a priority, we make snap judgments about others. (Adapted from Brehm & Kassin, 1993)

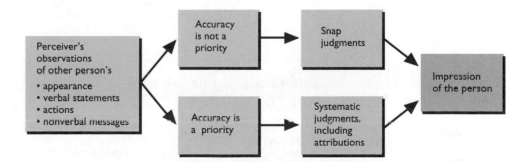

Confirmatory Biases

Soon after you begin interacting with someone, you start forming hypotheses about what the person is like. In turn, these hypotheses can influence your behavior toward that person in such a way as to confirm your expectations. Thus, if when you first meet Jack he has a camera slung around his neck, you will probably hypothesize that he has an interest in photography and question him selectively about his interests in this area. You might also neglect to ask more wide-ranging questions that would give you a more accurate picture of him. **This tendency to behave toward others in ways that confirm your hypotheses about them is termed** *confirmatory hypothesis testing.* Let's look at a study that shows confirmatory hypothesis testing at work. In this experiment, male students were asked to have a brief telephone conversation with a female student (Snyder, Tanke, & Berscheid, 1977). Before their conversations, the men were given a folder with a photo of and background information on their telephone partners. Half the men saw a photo of an attractive woman and half saw a photo of an unattractive woman. (In reality, the women in the photos did not participate in the study, and there was no difference in the attractiveness of the actual female telephone partners. The background information was provided by the real phone partners.) Prior to the telephone conversations, the men were asked to rate their partners-to-be on a variety of dimensions. Those men who believed their partners to be attractive judged that they would be poised, humorous, outgoing, and socially adept. Men who believed their partners to be unattractive judged them to be awkward, serious, unsociable, and socially inept. Generalizing from this example, we can surmise that confirmatory hypothesis testing occurs not only in casual social interactions but also in job interviews and in courtrooms, in which the interviewer or attorney may ask leading questions (Fiske & Taylor, 1991).

Although there is research support for confirmatory hypothesis testing, there is some question about how pervasive it is. For example, Susan Fiske (1993) notes that when people have a high need for accuracy in their impression of someone, they are less likely to engage in selective questioning. Instead, they ask *diagnostic* questions, such as, "Would you rather have a few, close relationships or many less intimate ones?" Diagnostic questions provide people with information about the accuracy of their initial hypotheses, in contrast to biased questions that seek mainly to confirm their expectations.

Memory processes can also contribute to confirmatory biases in person perception. Often, individuals selectively recall facts that fit with the schemas they apply to others. Evidence for such a tendency was found in a study by Cohen (1981). In this experiment, participants watched a videotape of a woman who engaged in a variety of activities, including listening to classical music, drinking beer, and watching TV. Half the participants were told that the woman was a waitress and half were led to believe that she was a librarian. When asked to recall what the woman did during the filmed sequence, participants tended to remember activities consistent with their stereotypes of waitresses and librarians. For instance, participants who thought that the woman was a waitress recalled her drinking beer, while participants who thought she was a librarian recalled her listening to classical music.

Normally, people remain unaware of the biases in their perceptions. They go blithely along, assuming that their version of reality is accurate. And most of the time this works (Fiske, 1993). It's only when someone else disagrees with a perception that a person is brought up short. When this happens, the individual may alter his or her views, conclude that the other person's perception is "off," or look for another, satisfactory explanation for the difference in perceptions.

Susan Fiske

Self-Fulfilling Prophecies

Sometimes confirmatory hypothesis testing can actually alter another person's behavior in the direction of one's hypotheses about them. For instance, in the study by Snyder and colleagues, after the men had completed their ratings of their part-

Figure 6.3
The three steps in a self-fulfilling prophecy
Through a three-step process, your expectations about a person can cause the person to behave in ways that confirm those expectations. First, you form an impression of someone. Second, you behave toward that person in a way that is consistent with your impression. Third, the person exhibits the behavior you encourage, thereby confirming your initial impression. (Adapted from Smith & Mackie, 1995)

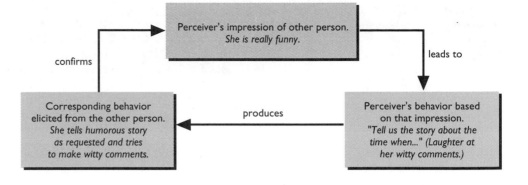

Learning Objective

Define the self-fulfilling prophecy and describe the three steps involved in the process.

ners, they spoke with their partners for 10 minutes on the telephone. Later, audiotapes of these conversations were analyzed by judges who were blind to the nature of the study. The judges rated the comments of the men with "attractive" partners as more sociable and outgoing than those of the men with "unattractive" partners. How did independent judges rate the women's comments? The "attractive" women were rated as more confident and animated than the "unattractive" women; they were also judged to have enjoyed their conversations and liked the men they spoke with more than the "unattractive" women did.

This process whereby expectations about a person cause the person to behave in ways that confirm the expectations is termed the *self-fulfilling prophecy.* This term was coined by sociologist Robert Merton (1948) as an explanation for such phenomena as the runs on banks that occurred during the Depression. That is, when unfounded rumors would circulate that a bank couldn't cover its deposits, people would rush to the bank and withdraw their funds, thereby draining the deposits from the bank and making real what was initially untrue.

In Figure 6.3, you can see the three steps in a self-fulfilling prophecy. First, the perceiver has an initial impression of someone (the target person). Then the perceiver behaves toward the target person in line with his or her expectations. The third step in the process occurs when the target person adjusts his or her behavior to the perceiver's actions, which confirms the perceiver's hypothesis about the target person. Note that both individuals are unaware that this process is operating. Also note that because perceivers are unaware of their expectations and of the effect they can have on others, they mistakenly attribute the target person's behavior to an internal cause (personal disposition) rather than an external one (the perceiver's behavior/expectations).

The best-known experiments on self-fulfilling prophecy have been conducted in the classroom setting, examining the effect of teachers' expectations on students' academic performance (Rosenthal, 1985). In a review of 400 studies on this question over a period of 30 years, it was reported that teacher expectations significantly influenced student performance in 36% of the experiments. Of course, the self-fulfilling prophecy can also work in other settings.

Thankfully, research also indicates that there are limits on self-fulfilling prophecy. Two conditions seem to minimize the effects of the perceiver's expectations on a target person's behavior. First, if a target person is aware of another's beliefs and these beliefs contradict his or her self-view, the target person works hard to change the perceiver's perceptions and is usually successful in doing so (Hilton & Darley, 1985). Second, target persons who are confident about their self-views are less likely to be influenced by a perceiver with different perceptions (Swann & Ely, 1984). But when perceivers are confident about their beliefs and target persons are uncertain about their self-views, the self-fulfilling prophecy comes into play.

Key Themes in Person Perception

As you have seen, the process of person perception is complex. Nonetheless, we can detect three recurrent themes in this process: efficiency, selectivity, and stability.

Efficiency

In forming impressions of others, people prefer to exert no more effort or time than is necessary. According to Susan Fiske (1993), like government bureaucrats, people "only bother to gather information on a 'need to know' basis" (p. 175). After all, you're a busy person with lots of important things to attend to. It boggles the mind to consider what life would be like if you had to take the time to make careful observations and judgments of everyone you meet. Obviously, the human penchant for efficiency has advantages: People can make judgments quickly and keep things simple. Of course, there is a big disadvantage: Errors occur in these judgments. Still, on balance, efficiency works pretty well as an operating principle.

Selectivity

There is an old saying that "people see what they expect to see." As we noted earlier, this commonsense notion that expectations influence perceptions has been confirmed repeatedly by social scientists. For example, in a classic study, Harold Kelley (1950) showed how a person is preceded by his or her reputation. Students in a class at the Massachusetts Institute of Technology (MIT) were told that a new lecturer would be speaking to them that day. Before the instructor arrived, the students were given a short description of him, with one important variation. Half the students were led to expect a "warm" person, while the other half were led to expect a "cold" one (see Figure 6.4). All the participants were exposed to the same 20 minutes of lecture and interaction with the new instructor. However, those who were led to expect a warm person rated the instructor as significantly more considerate, sociable, humorous, good-natured, informal, and humane than those who were led to expect a cold person.

Especially if there's any ambiguity in someone's behavior, people are likely to interpret what they see in a way that fits their expectations (E. Jones, 1990). Thus, after dealing with an assertive female customer, a salesman who holds traditional gender stereotypes might characterize her as "pushy." In contrast, he might fail to notice the same behavior in a man, because he would have unthinkingly interpreted the assertiveness as appropriate male behavior.

Stability

Although the evidence is not overwhelming, some studies suggest that first impressions have a powerful influence on perceptions of others (Asch, 1946; Friedman, 1983; Hodges, 1974). **A *primacy effect* occurs when initial information carries more weight than subsequent information.** There are a couple of reasons that first impressions tend to be particularly potent. In part, this tendency is caused by the fact that people see what they expect to see. Moreover, as we have already noted, confirmatory biases may lead people to discount later information that contradicts their initial impression. Interestingly, one study suggests that it may be easier to override positive first impressions than negative ones (Rothbart & Park, 1986). When the initial impression is negative, it may be especially difficult to change. Thus, getting off on the wrong foot may be particularly damaging to a person.

Of course, it is possible to override a primacy effect. If you're *actively* looking for change in a person or receive compelling evidence that contradicts your initial impression, you can change your opinion. Still, since people usually expect others to stay the same, their initial impressions don't change very often.

In summary, the process of person perception is highly subjective. In forming impressions of others, people are efficient and selective perceivers. Their impressions also tend to be stable. And, although perceptions of others can be erroneous, they are usually "good enough" for everyday purposes (Fiske, 1993).

Figure 6.4
Descriptions of the guest lecturer in Kelley's (1950) study
These two descriptions, provided to two groups of students before the lecturer spoke, differ by only two words, but that small difference caused the two groups to form altogether different perceptions of the lecturer.

Mr. Blank is a graduate student in the Department of Economics and Social Science here at M.I.T. He has had three semesters of teaching experience in psychology at another college. This is his first semester teaching Ec. 70. He is 26 years old, a veteran, and married. People who know him consider him to be a rather cold person, industrious, critical, practical, and determined.

Mr. Blank is a graduate student in the Department of Economics and Social Science here at M.I.T. He has had three semesters of teaching experience in psychology at another college. This is his first semester teaching Ec. 70. He is 26 years old, a veteran, and married. People who know him consider him to be a very warm person, industrious, critical, practical, and determined.

Perceiving Others: Sources of Error

Mistakes in person perception are quite common (Buckhout, 1980). And, as you have no doubt learned from experience, faulty judgments of others can cause serious problems in people's lives and relationships. Of course, an obvious source of error in person perception is the pervasive tendency of people to create false impressions for each other. In this section, however, we want to focus on some of an individual's *own* perceptual tendencies that contribute to perceptual inaccuracies. Perhaps by being more knowledgeable about these tendencies, you can minimize their negative influences in your life.

Categorizing

Learning Objective

Describe three consequences of categorizing.

People commonly categorize others on the basis of race, gender, age, sexual orientation, and so forth. People perceive those like themselves as being members of their *in-group* ("us") and those who are dissimilar as being in the *out-group* ("them"). Such categorizing has three important results. First, people usually have more favorable attitudes toward in-group members than out-group members (Tajfel et al., 1971). Second, people usually see out-group members as being much more similar to each other than they really are, whereas they see members of their in-group as unique individuals. In other words, people frequently explain the behavior of out-group members on the basis of the characteristic that sets them apart ("Those Nerdians are all drunks"), while attributing the same behavior by an in-group member to unique personality traits ("Jack's a heavy drinker"). This phenomenon is termed the *out-group homogeneity effect*. This tendency to see out-group members as similar is heightened if the behavior in question is perceived as negative.

A third result of categorizing is that it heightens the visibility of out-group members when there are only a few of them within a larger group. In other words, minority group status in a group makes the quality that distinguishes the person more salient—race, gender, whatever. When people are perceived as unique or distinctive, they are seen as having more influence in a group, and extra weight is given to their good and bad qualities (Crocker & McGraw, 1984). Distinctiveness also makes it more likely that stereotypes will be invoked. This explains why many people notice nagging women (but not men), noisy blacks (but not whites), and Jewish names among cheating stockbrokers (but not white, Anglo-Saxon Protestant names).

Another phenomenon related to distinctiveness occurs when minority group members voice opinions—especially if the opinions vary from those of the domi-

The extremely hostile reactions of some of the white male senators on the Judiciary Committee to Anita Hill's allegations of sexual harassment were due in part to her distinctiveness.

nant majority. When minority group members disagree with majority opinion, they are often derided as loud, offensive, and "pushy" and as trying to "take over." One example of this is the strong negative reaction of some individuals to the idea of allowing homosexuals to serve in the military. What accounts for these intense reactions? In large part, they're a response to the violation of an unarticulated belief held by the majority group. That belief is that minorities should remain silent and invisible, so as to keep things the way they are (Patai, 1991). But, because members of minority groups have less than their fair share of political and economic resources in a society, it's understandable that they want things to change. This state of affairs places minority group members who are struggling for increased power in a "double bind." If they remain silent and invisible, they're ignored by the dominant majority; if they speak up, they often generate hostility.

Stereotypes

Learning Objective

Define stereotypes and give three reasons why they persist.

Stereotypes **are widely held beliefs that people have certain characteristics simply because of their membership in a particular group.** For example, many people assume that Jews are shrewd and ambitious, that African Americans have special athletic and musical abilities, that women are dependent and concerned about their appearance, and that men are unemotional and domineering. Although a kernel of truth may underlie some stereotypes, it should be readily apparent that not all Jews, African Americans, women, and so forth behave alike. There is enormous diversity in behavior within any group. Stereotyping is a process of overgeneralizing that leads to a great deal of inaccuracy in social perception.

The most prevalent kinds of stereotypes are those based on gender, race, and age (Fiske, 1993). Gender stereotypes, although in transition, remain pervasive. For example, in a study of gender stereotypes in 30 countries, males were typically characterized as adventurous, powerful, and independent, whereas females were characterized as sentimental, submissive, and superstitious (Williams & Best, 1982). Ethnic and racial stereotypes have also undergone some changes but remain quite common (Dovidio & Gaertner, 1991; T. Smith, 1991). Because of their wide-ranging significance, we'll explore gender stereotypes in detail in Chapter 10.

Why do stereotypes persist? One reason is that they are functional. Because people are deluged with much more information than they can process, their tendency is to reduce complexity to simplicity. As we noted earlier, the tradeoff for such simplification is inaccuracy, much of which people are unaware of. Stereotypes also endure because of the selectivity in social perception and confirmatory biases that we discussed earlier. Thus, when people encounter members of groups they view with prejudice, they are likely to see what they expect to see (Stephan, 1989). The self-fulfilling prophecy is a third reason stereotypes persist. That is, beliefs about another person may actually elicit the anticipated behavior and confirm biased expectations.

People confirm and perpetuate their stereotypes in several ways. The unfortunate result of this process is that stereotypes often lead to unfair treatment of others. In particular, women, African Americans, members of certain ethnic groups, homosexuals, and the elderly are often victims of discrimination.

Excessive Focus on Physical Appearance

Learning Objective

Discuss how aspects of physical appearance influence our perceptions of others.

People often draw inferences about others' personality on the basis of physical appearance. In particular, there is plenty of evidence that physically attractive people are believed to possess many desirable personality traits. In fact, this perception is so widespread that social psychologists have developed a term for it: the *"what-is-beautiful-is-good"* stereotype (Dion, Berscheid, & Walster, 1972). That is, compared to those who are less attractive, beautiful people are usually viewed as more socially competent, more assertive, better adjusted, and more intellectually competent (Eagly et al., 1991). Yet research has found little basis in fact for most of these perceptions. Attractive people *do* have an advantage in the social arena. For example, they have better social skills, are more popular, are less socially anxious (especially about interactions with the other gender), are less lonely, and are more sexually experienced. However, they are not any different from others when it comes to intelligence, personality traits, mental health, or self-esteem (Feingold, 1992b).

It does seem that attractive people are perceived in a more favorable light than is actually justified (Dion, 1986; Eagly et al., 1991; Feingold, 1992b). As you may have inferred, all of these biases can also be reversed. Thus, unattractive people are unjustifiably seen as less well adjusted and less intellectually competent than others. This prejudice against the plain and homely is clearly unfair.

Social perceptions are also affected by other aspects of physical appearance. Tall people have been perceived, at various times, to be delicate, introverted, and intelligent, whereas short people have been viewed as passionate, petty, and negative (Roberts & Herman, 1986). In both the United States and Korea, adults with baby-faced features are judged as more warm, kind, naive, and submissive, while adults with more mature facial features are judged as strong, worldly, and dominant (McArthur & Berry, 1987). People who are neat dressers are thought to be conscientious (Albright, Kenny, & Malloy, 1988). Those who wear glasses are perceived as being relatively intelligent, industrious, and reliable. On the other hand, they are not judged to be as attractive, outgoing, or athletic as those who don't wear glasses (Harris, Harris, & Bochner, 1982).

Television, movies, and magazines constantly brainwash us into placing great emphasis on physical beauty. Our culture emphasizes physical appearance to such an extent that it is a central factor in our perception and judgment of others.

The Fundamental Attribution Error

Learning Objective

Describe the fundamental attribution error and how cultural values can influence its operation.

In trying to explain the causes of others' behavior, people invoke personality-based attributions and discount the importance of situational factors. Although this tendency is not universal (Harvey, Town, & Yarkin, 1981), it is strong enough that Lee Ross (1977) called it the *"fundamental* attribution error." **The *fundamental attribution error* is the tendency to explain other people's behavior as the result of personal, rather than situational, factors.** This bias leads people to leap to conclusions about others' personal qualities.

The fundamental attribution error is different from stereotyping or focusing on physical appearance in that the inferences are based on actual behavior. Nonetheless, those inferences may still be inaccurate. Because the importance of situational factors is underestimated, one may attribute to people motives and traits that they don't actually have. For instance, imagine that you're at your bank and the person

Lee Ross

in line ahead of you flies into a rage over an error made in his account. You will probably infer that this person is temperamental or quarrelsome—and you may be right. However, this person may normally be an easygoing individual who is late for an appointment, has waited in line for 30 minutes, and already straightened out a similar error by the same bank just last week. Thus, a person's behavior at a given time may or may not be reflective of his or her personality—but others tend to assume that it is.

As you might expect, cultural values seem to promote different attributional errors. You'll recall from our discussion in Chapter 5 that Western societies tend to be *individualistic,* viewing people as autonomous individuals who are responsible for their actions (Matsumoto, 1994). Endorsing beliefs such as "You can do anything you put your mind to" and "You have no one to blame but yourself," Westerners typically explain behavior in terms of people's personality traits and unique abilities. In contrast, members of *collectivist* societies value interdependence and obedience; hence, they are more likely to assume that an individual's behavior reflects adherence to group norms. Consistent with this analysis, researchers have found that American subjects explain others' behavior in terms of internal attributions more than Hindu (Miller, 1984) or Japanese subjects do (Weisz, Rothbaum, & Blackburn, 1984). A recent study found that English-language newspapers used more dispositional explanations and Chinese-language newspapers used more situational explanations for the same crimes (Morris & Peng, 1994).

Defensive Attribution

In attempting to explain the calamities and setbacks that befall other people, an observer's tendency to make internal attributions becomes even stronger than normal. Let's say that a friend is mugged and severely beaten. You may attribute the mugging to your friend's carelessness or stupidity ("He should have known better than to be in that neighborhood at that time") rather than to bad luck. Why? Because if you attribute your friend's misfortune to bad luck, you have to face the ugly reality that it could just as easily happen to you. To avoid disturbing thoughts such as these, people often attribute mishaps to victims' negligence (Salminen, 1992; Thornton, 1984, 1992).

Defensive attribution is the tendency to blame victims for their misfortune, so that one feels less likely to be victimized in a similar way. Blaming victims for their calamities also helps people to maintain their belief that they live in a "just world" where people get what they deserve and deserve what they get

Defensive attribution is one aspect of social perception that contributes to prejudice. For example, some people blame the homeless for their plight in an attempt to avoid the unpleasant thought that they themselves could one day suffer the same misfortune.

(Lerner & Miller, 1978). Acknowledging to oneself that the world is not just—that unfortunate events can happen as a result of chance factors—would mean having to admit the frightening possibility that the catastrophes that happen to others could also happen to oneself. By using defensive attribution, people can avoid such disturbing thoughts. Unfortunately, when victims are blamed for their setbacks, people unfairly attribute undesirable traits to them, such as incompetence, foolishness, laziness, and greed. Thus, defensive attribution often leads people to derogate victims of misfortune.

A common example of "blaming the victim" is reflected in comments that rape victims "asked for it." Similarly, when a woman is abused by a boyfriend or husband, people frequently blame the victim by remarking how stupid she is to stay with the man, rather than condemning the aggressor for his behavior (Kristiansen & Giulietti, 1990).

As we have seen, people's perceptions of others are quite subjective. Many of the tendencies exhibited in person perception contribute to inaccurate views of others. Much of the time these inaccurate perceptions are harmless. However, there clearly are occasions when these inaccuracies interfere with rewarding social interactions. This is certainly true in the case of prejudice, which we consider next.

Person Perception Errors and Prejudice

Learning Objective

Distinguish between prejudice and discrimination, and between traditional and modern forms of prejudice.

In this section, we'll consider how distortions in the process of person perception contribute to prejudice. To illustrate these ideas, we'll draw on examples of prejudice based on race, gender, ethnicity, and sexual orientation. But before we address these topics, we need to clarify a couple of terms that are often confused. ***Prejudice* is a negative attitude toward members of a group; *discrimination* is behaving differently, usually unfairly, toward the members of a group.** Prejudice and discrimination do tend to go together, but there is no necessary correspondence between the two (see Figure 6.5). For example, a restaurant owner might be prejudiced against Chicanos and yet treat them like anyone else because he needs their business. This is an example of prejudice without discrimination. Although it is probably less common, discrimination without prejudice may also occur. For example, an executive who has favorable attitudes toward African Americans may not hire them because his boss would be upset.

Overt racism has declined in the past 50 years (Crosby, Bromley, & Saxe, 1980; Pettigrew, 1979). Yet many people are opposed to programs designed to reduce the social and economic inequalities between ethnic groups, such as school busing and affirmative action. To explain this seeming paradox, researchers suggest that a new, more subtle form of racial prejudice has emerged (Gaertner & Dovidio, 1986; Ponterotto & Pedersen, 1993). *Modern racism* is prejudice combined with the perception that members of minority groups are benefiting unfairly from social and legislative changes. It manifests itself in the beliefs that discrimination no longer exists, that African Americans are pushing too hard and too fast for advancement, and that black Americans are undeserving of recent economic and social gains (McConahay, 1986; Sears, 1987). Evidence exists for similar beliefs about women—termed *modern sexism* (Swim et al., 1995; Tougas et al., 1995). Hence, although many people carefully avoid overt expressions of prejudiced attitudes, they may privately harbor negative views of minority groups. Still, if they believe that prejudiced views are socially acceptable or that it is safe to do so, they may express these views and engage in discriminatory acts.

Inaccuracy in person perception is both a cause and an effect of prejudice. Following is a rundown of how the four sources of inaccuracy that we discussed earlier contribute to prejudice.

• *Categorizing.* When people categorize others on the basis of race, gender, age, or sexual orientation, the out-group homogeneity effect kicks in. That means that members of that category will be perceived as much more homogeneous than they really are and that people will probably try to explain their behavior on the basis of stereotypes associated with the characteristic that distinguishes them. Thus, they

Figure 6.5
Prejudice and discrimination
Prejudice and discrimination are highly correlated, but they don't necessarily go hand in hand. As the examples in the yellow cells show, there can be prejudice without discrimination and discrimination without prejudice.

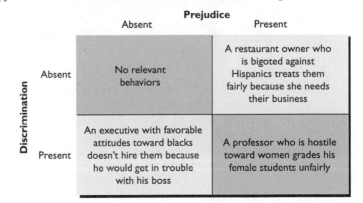

	Prejudice	
Discrimination	Absent	Present
Absent	No relevant behaviors	A restaurant owner who is bigoted against Hispanics treats them fairly because she needs their business
Present	An executive with favorable attitudes toward blacks doesn't hire them because he would get in trouble with his boss	A professor who is hostile toward women grades his female students unfairly

Learning Objective

Discuss four sources of error in person perception that contribute to prejudice.

will probably be viewed as tokens of their group rather than as individuals in their own right. Thus, the only woman in an all-male organization is more likely to be stereotyped than a woman in an organization that is more gender-balanced (Kanter, 1977; Pettigrew & Martin, 1987).

• *Stereotypes.* Perhaps no factor plays a larger role in prejudice than stereotyping. Many people subscribe to derogatory stereotypes of various ethnic groups. As we noted earlier, racial stereotypes have declined over the past 50 years, but they're not a thing of the past (Dovidio & Gaertner, 1991). Unfortunately, the selectivity of person perception makes it likely that people will see what they expect to see when they actually come into contact with minorities they view with prejudice. For example, Duncan (1976) had white participants watch and evaluate an interaction on a TV monitor that was supposedly live (it was actually a videotape). Participants saw two people get into an argument, during which one of them gave the other a slight shove. The race of the person giving the shove was varied across groups of participants. The shove was coded as "violent behavior" by 73% of the white participants when the actor was black, but by only 13% when the actor was white. Moreover, recent research shows that stereotypes are insidious in that they can operate unconsciously (Banaji, Hardin, & Rothman, 1993; Devine, 1989) and can even infiltrate the thinking of people who are genuinely low in prejudice (Monteith, 1993). According to Patricia Devine (1989), prejudiced stereotypes come readily to mind and are often activated automatically, even in people who truly renounce prejudice. Thus, a man who rejects prejudice against homosexuals may still feel uncomfortable sitting next to a gay man on a bus, even though he regards his reaction as inappropriate.

• *Fundamental attribution error.* Recall that the fundamental attribution error is the tendency to explain the causes of events by pointing to the personal characteristics of the actors (internal attributions). Pettigrew (1979) maintains that people are particularly prone to this error when evaluating targets of prejudice. Thus, when people take note of ethnic neighborhoods dominated by crime and poverty, they tend to blame these problems on the personal qualities of the residents. Other explanations emphasizing situational factors are downplayed or ignored (job discrimination, poor police service, and so on). The old saying "They should be able to pull themselves up by their bootstraps" is a blanket dismissal of how situational factors may make it especially difficult for minorities to achieve upward mobility.

• *Defensive attribution.* We have already seen that people sometimes unfairly blame victims of adversity to reassure themselves that they are unlikely to experience a similar fate. There is evidence that many people engage in such defensive attribution when they encounter people who have been victimized by prejudice and discrimination. For example, it has been suggested that many Germans who lived through the Nazi persecutions of Jews somehow convinced themselves that those sent to concentration camps deserved their fate (Hallie, 1971). Individuals who say that those who contract AIDS deserve it may be "blaming the victim" to reassure themselves that they won't get the disease.

In the first part of this chapter, we have explored the process of person perception and the effects of *one's beliefs on others.* In the second half of the chapter, we want to turn the tables and consider how *others influence one's beliefs and behavior.* In our discussion of social influence, we'll address such questions as the following:

• Why do so many commercials feature physically attractive actors and upbeat music?
• What role did social influence play in the tragedies of Jonestown and Waco?
• What tactics do advertisers, salespeople, charlatans, and other influence artists use to gain their ends?

We'll begin our coverage by discussing the principles of persuasion—attempts to change attitudes and beliefs. Then we'll move to the subject of social influence—attempts to change behavior—and look at the principles of conformity, compliance, and obedience to authority. Next, we'll consider some contemporary examples of yielding to and resisting social influence. Last, we'll examine the relation of culture to social influence.

Persuasion: The Power of Rhetoric

Every day you are bombarded by efforts to alter your attitudes through persuasion. To illustrate, let's trace the events of an imaginary morning. You may not even be out of bed before you start hearing radio advertisements meant to persuade you to buy specific mouthwashes, computers, and athletic shoes. When you open your newspaper, you find statements from numerous government officials, all of which have been carefully crafted to shape your opinions. On your way to school, you see billboards showing attractive models draped over automobiles and bottles of scotch in an effort to affect your feelings about these products. Arriving on campus, you find a group passing out leaflets urging you to recant your sins and join the group in worship. In class, your economics professor champions the wisdom of the free market in international trade. At lunch, the person you've been dating argues about the merits of an "open relationship." Your discussion is interrupted by someone who wants both of you to sign a petition for nuclear disarmament. "Does it ever let up?" you wonder.

When it comes to persuasion, the answer is "no." As Anthony Pratkanis and Elliot Aronson (1992) put it, we live in "the age of propaganda." In light of this reality, let's examine some of the factors that determine whether persuasion works.

***Persuasion* is the communication of arguments and information intended to change another person's attitudes.** What are attitudes? For the purposes of our discussion, we'll define ***attitudes* as beliefs and feelings about people, objects, and ideas.** Let's look more closely at two of the terms in this definition. We use the term *beliefs* to mean thoughts and judgments about people, objects, and ideas. For example, you may *believe* that equal pay for equal work is a fair policy or that capital punishment is not an effective deterrent to crime. The "feeling" component of attitudes refers to how positively or negatively one feels about an issue, as well as how strongly one feels about it. For example, you may *strongly favor* equal pay for equal work, but only *mildly disagree* with the idea that capital punishment reduces the crime rate.

The process of persuasion includes four basic elements (see Figure 6.6). **The *source* is the person who sends a communication, and the *receiver* is the person to whom the message is sent.** Thus, if you watched a presidential address on TV, the president would be the source, and you and millions of other listeners would be the receivers in this persuasive effort. **The *message* is the information transmitted by the source. The *channel* is the medium through which the message is sent.** In examining communication channels, investigators have often compared face-to-face interaction against appeals sent via mass media (for example, television and radio). Although the research on communication channels is interesting, we'll confine our discussion to source, message, and receiver variables. Let's examine some of the factors that determine whether persuasion works.

Learning Objective

Define persuasion and attitudes and list the four elements in the persuasion process.

Figure 6.6
Overview of the persuasion process
The process of persuasion essentially boils down to *who* (the source) communicates *what* (the message) *by what means* (the channel) *to whom* (the receiver). Thus, there are four sets of variables that influence the process of persuasion: source, message, channel, and receiver factors. The diagram lists some of the more important factors in each category (including some that are not discussed in the text due to space limitations). (Based on Lippa, 1994)

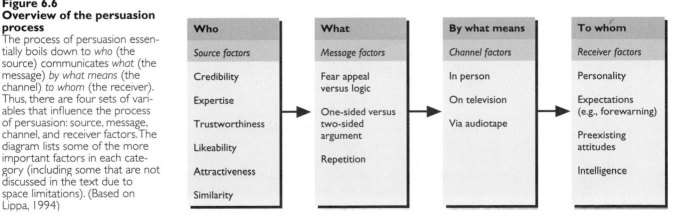

Who	What	By what means	To whom
Source factors	*Message factors*	*Channel factors*	*Receiver factors*
Credibility	Fear appeal versus logic	In person	Personality
Expertise	One-sided versus two-sided argument	On television	Expectations (e.g., forewarning)
Trustworthiness		Via audiotape	Preexisting attitudes
Likeability	Repetition		Intelligence
Attractiveness			
Similarity			

Source Factors

Learning Objective

Discuss credibility and likability and give some examples of these source factors.

Persuasion tends to be more successful when the source has high *credibility* (O'Keefe, 1990). What gives a person credibility? Either expertise or trustworthiness. People try to convey their *expertise* by mentioning their degrees, their training, and their experience, or by showing an impressive grasp of the issue at hand (Hass, 1981; Wood & Kallgren, 1988).

Expertise is a plus, but *trustworthiness* is even more important (McGinnies & Ward, 1980). Whom would you believe if you were told that your state needs to reduce corporate taxes to stimulate its economy—the president of a huge corporation in your state or an economics professor from out of state? Probably the latter. Trustworthiness is undermined when a source, such as the corporation president, appears to have something to gain. In contrast, trustworthiness is enhanced when people appear to argue against their own interests (Hunt, Smith, & Kernan, 1985). This effect explains why salespeople often make remarks like "Frankly, my snowblower isn't the best and they have a better brand down the street if you're willing to spend a bit more . . ."

Likability also increases the effectiveness of a persuasive source (Roskos-Ewoldsen & Fazio, 1992). Likability depends on a host of factors (see Chapter 8). A key consideration is a person's physical attractiveness. The favorable effect of physical attractiveness on persuasion was apparent in a study by Chaiken (1979), in which students were asked to obtain signatures for a petition. Chaiken found that the more attractive students were more successful. Other studies have also shown the effect of physical attractiveness on persuasion (Kahle & Homer, 1985; Pallak, 1983). People also respond better to sources who are *similar* to them in ways that are relevant to the issue at hand (Mackie, Worth, & Asuncion, 1990).

The importance of source variables is obvious in advertising. Many companies spend a fortune to obtain an ideal spokesperson, such as Bill Cosby, who combines trustworthiness, expertise (a doctorate in education), likability, and a knack for connecting with the average person. Companies quickly abandon spokespersons whose likability declines. For example, Pepsi immediately canceled an advertising campaign centered on the rock star Madonna when one of her videos offended many people's religious values. And Hertz dropped O. J. Simpson as their spokesperson when he became a controversial figure.

Message Factors

Learning Objective

Discuss three message factors and give some examples.

Imagine that you are going to give a speech to a local community group advocating a reduction in state taxes on corporations. In preparing your speech, you will probably wrestle with questions about how to structure your message. Should you look at both sides of the issue, or just present your own side? Should you deliver a low-key, logical speech, or should you try to strike fear in the hearts of your listeners? Should you spell out your conclusions for your listeners, or use rhetorical questions to stimulate their thinking? Let's look at these message factors.

We'll assume that you're aware that there are two sides to the taxation issue. On the one hand, you are convinced that lower corporate taxes will bring new companies and factories to your state, stimulate economic growth, and create jobs. On the other hand, you realize that the reduced tax revenues may gradually hurt the quality of education and roads in your state. Nevertheless, you believe that the benefits of a lower tax rate will outweigh the costs. Should you present a *one-sided argument* that ignores the possible effects on education and road quality? Or should you present a *two-sided argument* that acknowledges concern about education and road quality and then downplays the magnitude of these problems?

In general, two-sided arguments seem to be more effective. Just mentioning that there are two sides to an issue can increase your credibility with an audience (Jones & Brehm, 1970). One-sided messages work only when your audience is uneducated about the issue or when they are already very favorably disposed to your point of view (Lumsdaine & Janis, 1953).

Persuasive messages commonly attempt to arouse fear. Opponents of nuclear power scare us with visions of meltdowns. Antismoking campaigns emphasize the threat of cancer. Deodorant ads highlight the risk of embarrassment. Does *fear arousal* work? Yes, in many cases. Studies involving a wide range of issues (nuclear policy, auto safety, and dental hygiene, among others) have shown that the arousal of fear often increases persuasion (Boster & Mongeau, 1985; Perloff, 1993). However, there are limiting conditions (Johnson, 1991).

For fear arousal to work, listeners must view the dire consequences as exceedingly unpleasant, as fairly probable if they don't take the suggested advice, and as avoidable if they do. People will surely agree that lung cancer is a disease no one wants. But you may have trouble convincing smokers that their pack-a-day habit puts them at risk for lung cancer, because they may rationalize that they smoke too few cigarettes to be at risk. Should you press your point with graphic descriptions of what smokers' lungs look like and stories about the awful last days of your Uncle Jack who died from lung cancer? Probably not, unless you can offer them a sure-fire stop-smoking program. Research shows that if you induce a high level of fear in your audience without providing a manageable solution to the problem, you may make your audience defensive, causing them to tune you out (Jepson & Chaiken, 1986).

Generating *positive feelings* is also an effective way to persuade people. Familiar examples of such tactics include the use of music in TV commercials, the practice of wining and dining prospective customers, and the ploy of offering small gifts (key chains, pencils, etc.). Research has shown that producing positive feelings in order to win people over *can* be effective—provided they don't care too much about the issue. If they do care about the topic, it takes more than good feelings to move them. For example, one study showed that the use of music in TV commercials was effective in persuading viewers, but only when the message concerned a trivial topic (Park & Young, 1986).

Receiver Factors

Learning Objective

Discuss two receiver factors and give some examples.

What about the receiver of the persuasive message? Are some people easier to persuade than others? Undoubtedly, but the personality traits that account for these differences interact with other considerations in complicated ways. Transient factors, such as forewarning the receiver about a persuasive effort and the receiver's initial position on an issue, seem to be more influential than the receiver's personality. When you shop for a new TV, you expect salespeople to work at persuading you. To some extent this *forewarning* reduces the impact of their arguments (Petty & Cacioppo, 1979; Pfau et al., 1990). Thus, there is some truth to the old saying, "To be forewarned is to be forearmed."

The effect of a persuasion attempt also depends on the discrepancy between a *receiver's initial position* on an issue and the position advocated by the source. Persuasion tends to work best when a moderate discrepancy exists between the two. Why? According to *social judgment theory,* people are usually willing to consider alternative views on an issue if the views aren't too different from their own (Sherif & Hovland, 1961; Upshaw, 1969). This range of potentially acceptable positions on an issue is referred to as the *latitude of acceptance.* Persuasive messages that fall outside a receiver's latitude of acceptance usually fall on deaf ears. When a message falls within a receiver's latitude of acceptance, successful persuasion is much more likely (Atkins, Deaux, & Bieri, 1967).

Within the latitude of acceptance, however, a *larger* discrepancy between the receiver's initial position and the position advocated should produce greater attitude change than a smaller discrepancy. The reason is that people often "meet partway" to resolve disagreement. Figure 6.7 shows how this theory could apply to an audience member who hears your presentation advocating reduced corporate taxation.

We hope that this review of source, message, and receiver variables will make you a more thoughtful consumer of the countless persuasive efforts made by other individuals and the media. Of course, persuasion is not the *only* method through

Figure 6.7
Latitude of acceptance and attitude change
A, B, and C are positions on the tax rate that one might advocate. A and B both fall within the receiver's latitude of acceptance, but position B should produce a larger attitude shift. Position C is outside the receiver's latitude of acceptance and should fall on deaf ears.

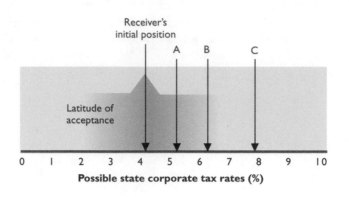

which people influence you. There are many other techniques that don't depend on the communication of arguments and information. We'll examine some of these fascinating tactics in the Application.

Conformity and Compliance: The Power of Social Pressure

Learning Objective

Define conformity and summarize Asch's findings on conformity.

If you keep a well-manicured lawn, or extol the talents of popular rock star Bruce Springsteen, are you exhibiting conformity? According to social psychologists, it depends on whether your behavior is the result of group pressure. **Conformity occurs when people yield to real or imagined social pressure.** For example, if you maintain a well-groomed lawn only to avoid complaints from your neighbors, you are yielding to social pressure. If you like Springsteen because you genuinely enjoy his records, that's not conformity. However, if you like Springsteen because it's "fashionable" and your friends would question your taste if you didn't, then you're conforming.

Asch's Studies

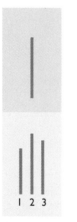

Figure 6.8
Stimuli used in Asch's conformity studies
Subjects were asked to match a standard line (top) with one of three other lines displayed on another card (bottom). The task was easy—until experimenter accomplices started responding with obviously incorrect answers, creating a situation in which Asch evaluated subjects' conformity. (Adapted from Asch, 1955)

In the 1950s, Solomon Asch (1951, 1955, 1956) devised a clever procedure that minimized ambiguity about whether participants were conforming, allowing him to investigate the variables that govern conformity. Let's re-create one of Asch's (1955) classic experiments. The participants are male undergraduates recruited for a study of visual perception. A group of seven participants are shown a large card with a vertical line on it. Then they are asked to indicate which of three lines on a second card matches the original "standard line" in length (see Figure 6.8). All seven participants are given a turn at the task, and each announces his choice to the group. The subject in the sixth chair doesn't know it, but everyone else in the group is an accomplice of the experimenter. They're about to make him wonder whether he has taken leave of his senses.

The accomplices give accurate responses on the first two trials. On the third trial, line 2 clearly is the correct response, but the first five participants all say that line 3 matches the standard line. The genuine subject can't believe his ears. Over the course of the experiment, the accomplices all give the same incorrect response on 12 out of 18 trials. Asch wanted to see how the subject would respond in these situations. The line judgments are easy and unambiguous. Working alone, people achieve better than 95% accuracy in matching the lines. So, if the subject consistently agrees with the accomplices, he isn't making honest mistakes—he is conforming. Will the subject stick to his guns and defy the group? Or will he go along with the group?

Averaging across 50 participants, Asch (1955) found that the young men conformed on 37% of the trials. The participants varied considerably in their tendency to conform, however. Out of the 50 participants, 26% never caved in to the group, while 28% conformed on more than half the trials.

Figure 6.9
Conformity and group size
This graph shows the percentage of trials on which subjects conformed as a function of group size in Asch's research. Asch found that conformity became more frequent as group size increased, up to about seven persons, and then leveled off. (Adapted from Asch, 1955)

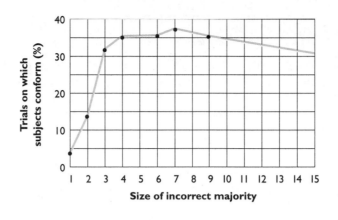

In subsequent studies, group size and group unanimity turned out to be key determinants of conformity (Asch, 1956). To examine the effects of group size, Asch repeated his procedure with groups that included 1 to 15 accomplices. Little conformity was seen when a subject was pitted against just one accomplice, but conformity increased rapidly as group size went from 2 to 4, peaked at a group size of 7, and then leveled off (see Figure 6.9). Thus, Asch concluded that as groups grow larger, conformity increases—up to a point.

Interestingly, group size made little difference if just one accomplice "broke" with the others, wrecking their unanimous agreement. The presence of another dissenter lowered conformity to about one-quarter of its peak, even when the dissenter made inaccurate judgments that happened to conflict with the majority view. Apparently, the participants just needed to hear someone else question the accuracy of the group's perplexing responses.

Conformity Versus Compliance

At first, Asch wasn't sure whether conforming participants were really changing their beliefs in response to social pressure or just pretending to change them. A study that included a condition in which participants made their responses anonymously, instead of publicly, settled the question. Conformity declined dramatically when participants recorded their responses privately. This finding suggested that participants in the Asch studies were not really changing their beliefs (Deutsch & Gerard, 1955). Based on this evidence, theorists concluded that Asch's experiments evoked a particular type of conformity, called compliance. **Compliance occurs when people yield to social pressure in their public behavior, even though their private beliefs have not changed.** In the Asch studies, compliance resulted from subtle, implied pressure. However, compliance usually occurs in response to explicit rules, requests, and commands. For example, if you agree to wear formal clothes to a fancy restaurant that requires formal attire, even though you scorn such rules, you're displaying compliance. Similarly, if you reluctantly follow a supervisor's suggestions at work, even when you think that they're lousy ideas, you're complying with a superior's wishes. Compliance with an authority figure's directions is commonplace, as you'll see in the next section.

Obedience: The Power of Authority

Obedience is a form of compliance that occurs when people follow direct commands, usually from someone in a position of authority. In itself, obedience isn't good or bad. To get at that important issue, we need to consider what one is being asked to do. For example, if the fire alarm goes off in your classroom and your instructor "orders" you to leave, obedience is a good idea. On the other hand, if you're asked to engage in an illegal act by your boss or to do something that goes against your conscience, *disobedience* is probably in order. Because the consequences of obedience can be so serious, it's important to know how it operates.

Milgram's Studies

Stanley Milgram

Stanley Milgram was a brilliantly creative social psychologist who set out to study the tendency to obey authority figures. Like many other people after World War II, he was troubled by how readily the citizens of Germany had followed the orders of dictator Adolf Hitler, even when the orders required morally repugnant actions, such as the slaughter of millions of Jews. Milgram, who had worked with Solomon Asch, set out to design a standard laboratory procedure for the study of obedience, much like Asch's procedure for studying conformity.

Milgram's (1963) participants were a diverse collection of 40 men from the local community. They were told that the study was concerned with the effects of punishment on learning. When they arrived at the lab, they drew slips of paper from a hat to get their assignments. The drawing was rigged so that the subject always became the "teacher" and an experimenter accomplice (a likable 47-year-old accountant) became the "learner."

The teacher watched while the learner was strapped into a chair and as electrodes were attached to his arms (to be used to deliver shocks whenever he made a mistake on the task). The subject was then taken to an adjoining room that housed the "shock generator" that he would control in his role as the teacher. Although the apparatus looked and sounded realistic, it was a fake, and the learner was never shocked. The experimenter played the role of the authority figure who told the teacher what to do and who answered any questions that arose.

The experiment was designed so that the learner would make many mistakes, and the teacher was instructed to increase the shock level after each wrong answer. At 300 volts, the learner began to pound on the wall between the two rooms in protest; soon he stopped responding to the teacher's questions altogether. From this point forward, participants frequently turned to the experimenter for guidance. Whenever they did so, the experimenter (authority figure) firmly stated that the teacher should continue to give stronger and stronger shocks to the now-silent learner. The dependent variable was the maximum shock the subject was willing to administer before refusing to cooperate.

As Figure 6.10 shows, 26 of the 40 participants (65%) administered all 30 levels of shock. Although they tended to obey the experimenter, many participants voiced and displayed considerable distress about harming the learner. They groaned, bit their lips, stuttered, trembled, and broke into a sweat—but they continued administering the shocks. Based on these findings, Milgram concluded that obedience to authority was even more common than he or others had anticipated.

Milgram found that obedience increased (1) when the authority figure was physically near the participants rather than distant, (2) when the victim was less visible and less audible to the participants, and (3) when the experiment was conducted at a prestigious university rather than at an unimpressive-looking office building. These findings suggest that actions are determined not so much by the *kind of person* one is as by the *kind of situation* one is in. According to Milgram, situational factors (the appropriate trappings of authority) combine to produce a shift in perspective that leads to obedience to the authority figure. That is, people begin focusing on how well they're living up to the expectations of the authority figure instead of evaluating their actions in terms of harmful effects on the victim. Applying this insight to Nazi war crimes and other atrocities, Milgram made a chilling assertion: Inhuman and evil visions may originate in the disturbed mind of an authority figure like Hitler, but it is only through the obedient actions of normal people that such ideas can be turned into frightening reality.

After his initial demonstration, Milgram (1974) tried about 20 variations on his experimental procedure, looking for factors that influenced participants' obedience. As a whole, Milgram was surprised at how stable participants' obedience remained as he changed various aspects of his experiment. In one of these later experiments, Milgram studied female participants to see whether there were gender differences in obedience to authority. He found no significant differences between men and women in obedience behavior. (Women *did* report higher levels of tension than men

Figure 6.10
Milgram's (1963) experiment on obedience
The photos show the fake shock generator and the "learner" being connected to the shock generator during an experimental session. The results of the study are summarized in the bar graph. The vast majority of subjects (65%) delivered the entire series of shocks to the learner.

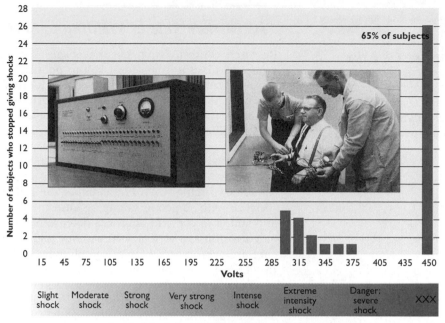

65% of subjects

Number of subjects who stopped giving shocks

Volts: 15 45 75 105 135 165 195 225 255 285 315 345 375 405 435 450

Slight shock | Moderate shock | Strong shock | Very strong shock | Intense shock | Extreme intensity shock | Danger: severe shock | XXX

Level of shock (as labeled on Milgram's shock machine)

did, but this difference may have been because women felt freer to report high tension levels rather than actually having experienced more tension.)

If you're like most people, you're confident that you wouldn't follow an experimenter's demands to inflict harm on a helpless victim. But research findings suggest that you're probably wrong. After many replications, the data are clear, and their implications are frightening and deplorable. Most people can be coerced into engaging in actions that violate their morals and values.

The Ensuing Controversy

The clever experiment that Milgram devised became one of the most famous and controversial studies in the annals of psychology. It has been hailed by some as a "monumental contribution" to science and condemned by others as "dangerous, dehumanizing, and unethical research" (Ross, 1988). Some critics argued that Milgram's results wouldn't generalize to the real world (Baumrind, 1964; Orne & Holland, 1968). Yet the results were consistently replicated for many years, in diverse settings, with a variety of participants and procedural variations (Miller, 1986). Overall, the weight of evidence supports the generalizability of Milgram's results.

Critics also questioned the ethics of Milgram's procedure (Baumrind, 1964). His defenders argued that the brief distress experienced by his participants was a small price to pay for the insights that emerged from his obedience studies. However, by contemporary standards of research ethics, his procedure is questionable. At most universities it would be difficult to obtain permission to replicate Milgram's study today—a bizarre epitaph for what may be psychology's best-known experiment.

Perspectives on Social Influence

In this section, we'll explore how social influence operates in real-life situations. We'll start with a brief discussion of peer pressure and how it can result in tragedy. Next, we'll examine the role of persuasion and social influence in the "Jonestown massacre" and the "Waco conflagration." Then, we'll take a look at "whistleblowers" to show how individuals are able to resist social influence. Finally, we'll discuss how culture affects individuals' responses to social influence.

The Darker Side of Yielding to Social Pressure

Research confirms what every teenager knows—namely, that conformity to peer group norms is an important key to popularity (Sebald, 1981). When people yield to social influence, it is often on relatively trivial matters, such as dressing up to go to a nice restaurant. In these cases, conformity and compliance to social norms help minimize the confusion and anxiety people experience when they find themselves in unfamiliar situations. However, when individuals feel pressured to conform to antisocial norms, tragic consequences can sometimes result. Familiar examples of the negative effects of "going along with the crowd" include drinking more than one knows one should because others say, "C'mon, have just one more"; driving at someone's urging when one is under the influence of alcohol or drugs; refusing to socialize with someone simply because the person isn't liked by one's social group; and failing to come to another's defense when it might make one unpopular. Compared to those who feel secure about their status in a group, those who feel insecure are even more likely to comply when peers put down members of out-groups (Noel, Wann, & Branscombe, 1995).

Peer pressure also plays a role in campus gang rape. One factor that distinguishes gang rape from other forms of rape is peer pressure. That is, one man might initiate the rape, but others go along with it for fear of being seen as sexually inadequate. Because male peers play an important role in confirming each other's sexual competence (Gagnon & Simon, 1973; Miller & Simon, 1974), sex can be a vehicle by which men confirm their social status with other males—sometimes with tragic consequences for females.

A Case of Fatal Social Influence: The Jonestown Massacre

The power of social influence was made vividly apparent in the infamous "Jonestown massacre" that took place in Guyana, South America, in 1978. As you may know, Jim Jones was the charismatic leader of an American religious cult called the People's Temple, which had set up a large encampment ("Jonestown") in the isolated wilderness of Guyana. Feeling pressured by a U.S. congressional investigation, Jones persuaded all his followers to commit mass suicide by drinking cyanide-laced Kool-Aid. Although a small minority of Jones's followers refused to cooperate (a few escaped, a few were shot), most went along with him and took their own lives. In all, 913 Americans died at Jonestown, including more than 200 children who were poisoned by their parents. How can we explain such extraordinary behavior?

Social psychologists who have studied this event tell us that this unusual behavior was due to Jim Jones's highly skilled use of persuasion and social influence tactics (Galanter, 1989; Zimbardo & Leippe, 1991). To begin with, Jonestown members were already heavily dependent on and trusting of Jones, as evidenced by their joining his movement and leaving the United States. These individuals were persuaded to join Jonestown in the first place because they felt alienated from American society and, therefore, were particularly vulnerable to Jones's promise of a better life in a better place (*receiver* factors). But the fact that Jones could persuade individuals to move to an isolated location in a foreign country gives us an idea of his impressive rhetorical skills. As a *source*, Jones was perceived by his followers as an expert who was credible and trustworthy (Zimbardo & Leippe, 1991).

Jones also had an unusual amount of control over the content of the information his followers received and how it was presented to them (*message* factors). Specifically, he could prevent his people from coming into contact with ideas or values that differed from those he espoused and permit them to receive only the information he wanted them to have. Of course, to have this degree of control over people is quite unusual, and it is one of the key factors that explains how Jones was able to persuade hundreds of individuals to kill themselves.

What happened was this: Because of charges of abuse by some concerned relatives back home, a congressman and some reporters had come to Jonestown to investigate. Jonestown passed the inspection, but Jones panicked when some cult members asked Jones if they could return to the United States on the plane with the congressman. Under the influence of drugs and suffering from paranoid delusions, Jones believed word would get out and that the U.S. military would invade Jonestown and kill his people—and that he would lose control of the Temple (Galanter, 1989; Zimbardo & Leippe, 1991).

Panic-stricken, Jones ordered the murder of the congressman and the small group from the People's Temple as they were getting ready to board the plane. Realizing that this turn of events made it even more likely that the U.S. military would invade Jonestown, he gathered the faithful together and told them that the visiting congressman was going to be killed by an angered cult member acting on his own, and that this would prompt intervention by the U.S. military. He also told them it was likely that they would all be killed and that the only way to prevent this was to commit mass "revolutionary suicide." Jones's ability to invoke, intuitively, the tactics of persuasion is vividly portrayed in the following description based on the videotape that Jones made of the last hour of Jonestown:

> Masterfully, Jones destroyed dissent by first inviting it. When a vocal young woman made reasonable arguments for alternative solutions short of suicide, Jones conveyed an air of support and fair-mindedness. "I like you Christina: I've always liked you," he told her. But he refuted her arguments with platitudes that stirred the crowd and ultimately compelled his most committed followers to come forth and publicly question her faith and allegiance. In the end, she was shouted down—and with her defeat, Jones won and the people lost.
>
> As the universal approval for this prophet's visionary "final solution" began carrying people up to the Kool-Aid crucible, Jones began to express displeasure with those who still hesitated. He alternated between a soothing tone ("Go with your child—I think it's humane . . . it is painless") and the impatient tone of a disappointed parent ("Lay down your life with dignity . . . stop these hysterics"). [Zimbardo & Leippe, 1991, p. 20]

Social influence tactics were also at work here: the power of social pressure (going along with others), the power of authority (doing what you are told), the power of group dynamics (violating personal standards in order to be liked by other members of a cohesive group), modeling, and playing on guilt. The persuasion and social influence tactics used by Jim Jones are normal and familiar to everyone. What was unusual was the degree of control he had over his members' psychological environment; this situation allowed him to use a large number of techniques that combined to produce uncommonly powerful—and tragic—results.

There are obvious parallels between the dynamics of the Jonestown massacre and the 1993 tragedy at the Branch Davidian compound in Waco, Texas. After 51

Like Jim Jones, David Koresh, the leader of the Branch Davidians at Waco, Texas, held an unusual amount of control over the members of his group. This intensified his persuasiveness and influence within his group and contributed to the tragic Waco conflagration.

days of an armed standoff, a catastrophic fire of unknown origin swept through the compound on April 20, killing over 80 adults and children (Gibbs, 1993). (David Koresh, the leader of the Branch Davidians, and several others died of gunshot wounds to the head and not from the fire or smoke inhalation.) Although we will probably never know all the facts about Waco, we do know that there were remarkable similarities between Jim Jones and David Koresh and in the tactics of persuasion and social influence that they both so skillfully used to such tragic ends.

Resisting Social Influence: Whistleblowing

Learning Objective

Give some examples of whistleblowing and describe four factors that determine whether people will resist social influence and take principled action.

Despite the fact that three employees of Rockwell International informed NASA that the space shuttle *Challenger* was not safe, NASA officials refused to postpone the fateful launch on January 20, 1986. Because decision-making authority for the launch was transferred from engineers to administrators and because administrators were unwilling to assume responsibility for the costly decision to postpone the launch, seven lives and a multimillion-dollar spacecraft were lost (Romzek & Dubnick, 1987). The behavior of the NASA authorities serves as another example of yielding to social influence. The actions of the Rockwell "whistleblowers," on the other hand, demonstrate the phenomenon of *resisting* social influence.

Some experts on "whistleblowing" use the term to refer to situations in which employees take concerns about organizational practices *outside* the organization (Graham, 1986). These cases are relatively rare because of the high risk involved: Karen Silkwood probably died for trying to report unsafe practices at the nuclear power plant where she worked. Other writers use *whistleblowing* to apply to a wide variety of actions taken by employees to protest or change ethically questionable organizational practices (Glazer & Glazer, 1990). Although their actions may be less dramatic and less dangerous, these "ethical resisters" also risk the loss of credibility, friends, and jobs for the sake of important principles (Glazer & Glazer, 1990). We'll use *whistleblowing* in this broader sense.

Is it common for employees to report wrongdoings they observe on the job to their superiors? In a large-scale survey, 8500 civilian employees of the federal government were asked if they had observed any wrongdoing at work during a 12-month period (Graham, 1986). Nearly half the participants reported that they had personally observed a serious case of wrongdoing, such as tolerating a situation that was dangerous to public safety, accepting bribes, or stealing federal funds. Of those who had witnessed such transgressions, almost 30% said that they had told their bosses about the problem (72% reported that they had done nothing about the situation).

Because the risks of whistleblowing can be quite high, it's understandable that relatively few people are willing to engage in such actions. Still, some do. What prompts them to blow the whistle? Generalizing from research on social influence and helping behavior, the following factors stand out (Graham, 1986; Latané & Darley, 1970).

1. *Individuals must be aware of a problem.* Obviously, those who don't know that a wrongdoing has taken place or who don't view an activity as unethical have no reason to report a problem. Merely noticing that wrongdoing has occurred, however, does not ensure that a person will do anything about it. For that to happen, additional factors must come into play.

2. *People must perceive the problem as serious and believe that they are capable of taking effective action.* Ethical dissenters typically take the view that they are demonstrating company loyalty by helping the organization correct its mistakes rather than ignoring them (Graham, 1986). Moreover, they place loyalty to the public or principles over loyalty to the company. Nonetheless, even if people view an issue as serious, they also must feel that

Three courageous "whistleblowers" from Rockwell International—Ria Solomon, Sylvia Robins, and Al Bray—warned NASA about the faulty O-ring seals in the *Challenger.*

there is a feasible solution to the problem before they take action. In other words, they need to believe that something can be done and that they possess the necessary skills and resources to do so. Self-esteem is an issue here, as is the person's position in the organization (Graham, 1986). People also weigh the perceived costs of acting (and not acting). In some organizations, being demoted or fired is a realistic possibility. In others, whistleblowing may be dealt with constructively.

3. *Social support is important.* The presence of co-dissenters increases the likelihood that individuals will take action. Recall that in Asch's study, the presence of just one agreeing partner decreased conformity to incorrect responses. Also, because whistleblowing usually involves some degree of risk, aligning oneself with others can decrease anxiety and increase safety. Discussing the problem with others who are sympathetic can provide helpful perspectives on the issue. In some organizations, individuals are designated to handle such problems to protect employees from reprisals. If not, there are usually resources outside the organization.

4. *People must take responsibility for acting and follow through.* In a large organization, individuals who are aware of a problem may persuade themselves that someone else will take responsibility for reporting the issue. **This phenomenon is termed** *diffusion of responsibility,* **or the expectation that others who are present will take responsibility for action.** If individuals decide to act, then they must decide precisely what to do and how. Should they keep the information inside the organization or should they go outside the organization? Should they take indirect action (reporting the problem to someone else or reporting it anonymously), or should they act directly (quitting, for example)? In deciding how to respond, individuals obviously consider how the organization is likely to respond to their possible actions.

In summary, we see that resisting social influence involves the interplay of both personality and situational factors, as does yielding to social pressure. We hope our contemporary examples of resisting and conforming to social influence will motivate you to examine how these factors operate in your own life.

Culture and Social Influence

A number of studies have explored cultural differences in conformity, compliance, and obedience. This research shows that people in Asian countries view conformity and obedience more positively than do either Americans or citizens of some other Western countries (Matsumoto, 1994). For example, on a values survey, Asian participants endorsed items related to conformity and obedience, whereas British participants endorsed items related to individualism (independence and freedom) (Punetha, Giles, & Young, 1987). In addition, it appears that Japanese and Hong Kong Chinese value obedience more than the British and Italians do (Argyle et al., 1986).

Individuals in countries where conformity is valued also show higher levels of conformity *behavior* than those where such behavior is viewed negatively. Hence, it has been shown that Japanese are more conforming than Americans (Buck, Newton, & Muramatsu, 1984) and that Italians are more conforming than Anglo-Australians (Cashmore & Goodnow, 1986). Such findings are consistent with the individualistic orientation of Western cultures and the collectivist orientation of other cultures.

In the upcoming Application, we'll alert you to some social influence strategies at work in everyday situations.

Seeing Through Social Influence Tactics

Which of the following statements is true?

1. *It's a good idea to ask for a small favor before soliciting the larger favor that you really want.*

2. *It's a good idea to ask for a large favor before soliciting the smaller favor that you really want.*

Would you believe that *both* of these statements are true? Although the two approaches involve opposite strategies, both can be very effective ways to get people to do what you want. This paradox illustrates the complexity of social influence processes, which we'll examine from a practical standpoint in this Application. It pays to understand these strategies, because advertisers, salespeople, and fundraisers (not to mention friends and neighbors) use them frequently to influence your behavior. We'll begin by looking at the contradictory strategies described in our opening questions.

The Foot-in-the-Door Technique

Learning Objective

Describe the foot-in-the-door and door-in-the-face compliance strategies.

Door-to-door salespeople have long recognized the importance of gaining a *little* cooperation from sales targets (getting a "foot in the door") before hitting them with the real sales pitch. **The *foot-in-the-door technique* involves getting people to agree to a small request to increase the chances that they will agree to a larger request later** (see Figure 6.11). This technique is widely used in all walks of life. For example, groups seeking donations often ask people to simply sign a petition first. Salespeople routinely ask individuals to try a product with "no obligations" before they launch their hard sell. In a similar vein, a wife might ask her husband to get her a cup of coffee, and when he gets up to fetch it say, "While you're up, would you make me a grilled cheese?"

The foot-in-the-door technique was first investigated by Jonathon Freedman and his colleagues. In one study (Freedman & Fraser, 1966), the large request involved telephoning homemakers to ask whether a team of six men doing consumer research could come into their home to classify all their household products. Imagine six strangers tramping through your home, pulling everything out of your closets, cupboards, and drawers, and you can understand why only 22% of the subjects in the control group agreed to this outlandish request. Subjects in the experimental group were contacted three days before the unreasonable request was made and asked to answer a few questions about the soaps used in their home. When the large request was made three days later, 53% of the experimental group complied with that request.

Many other studies have also shown that the foot-in-the-door technique is an effective strategy. Researchers aren't entirely sure *why* the technique is effective. One explanation is that granting the initial favor makes people feel more favorable about whatever is being requested (DeJong, 1979; Dillard, 1991). This change in attitude makes them more willing to go along with a subsequent request. Of course, no strategy works all the time. The foot-in-the-door technique may be ineffective if the initial request is too small to create a sense of commitment or if the second request is so large it's unreasonable (Foss & Dempsey, 1979; Zuckerman, Lazzaro, & Waldgeir, 1979).

The Door-in-the-Face Technique

The door-in-the-face technique reverses the sequence of requests employed with the foot-in-the-door technique. **The *door-in-the-face technique* involves making a very large request that is likely to be turned down to increase the chances that people will agree to a smaller request later** (see Figure 6.11). The name for this strategy is derived from the expectation that the initial request will be quickly rejected. For example, a husband who wants to coax his frugal wife into agreeing to buy a $20,000 sports car might begin by proposing that they purchase a $30,000 sports car. By the time she has talked her husband out of the $30,000 car, the $20,000 price tag may look quite reasonable to her.

The door-in-the-face technique works for two reasons (Cialdini, 1993). First, everything is relative, and people are easily swayed by *contrast effects*. A 6'3" basketball player, who is really quite tall, can look downright small when surrounded by teammates who all are over 6'8". Similarly, a $20,000 car may seem cheap relative to a $30,000 car. Second, when people make concessions by reducing the size of their requests, most targets feel obliged to reciprocate by making concessions of their own. Hence, they agree to the smaller request.

The belief that people should reciprocate others' kindness is a powerful norm. Let's examine some of the other ways in which it is used in social influence efforts.

Figure 6.11
The foot-in-the-door and the door-in-the-face techniques
These two influence techniques are essentially the reverse of each other, but both can work. In the foot-in-the-door technique, you begin with a small request and work up to a larger one. In the door-in-the-face technique, you begin with a large request and work down to a smaller one.

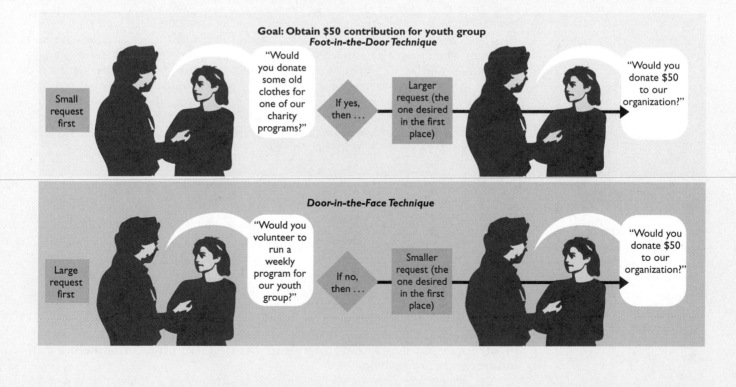

Using the Reciprocity Norm

Learning Objective

Explain how the reciprocity norm is used in social influence.

Most people have been socialized to believe in the *reciprocity norm*—**the rule that one should pay back in kind what one receives from others.** Robert Cialdini (1993) has written extensively about how the reciprocity norm is used in social influence efforts. Charities frequently make use of the reciprocity principle. Groups seeking donations for the disabled, the homeless, and so forth routinely send address labels, key rings, and other small gifts with their pleas for donations.

Salespeople using the reciprocity principle distribute free samples to prospective customers. Cialdini (1993) describes the procedures used by the Amway Corporation, which sells such household products as detergent, floor wax, and insect spray. Amway's door-to-door salespeople give homemakers many bottles of their products for a "free trial." When the salesperson returns a few days later, the homemaker feels obligated to buy some of the products.

The reciprocity rule is meant to promote fair exchanges in social interactions. However, when people manipulate the reciprocity rule, they usually give something of minimal value in the hopes of getting far more in return. For example, a person selling large computer systems may wine and dine a potential customer at a nice restaurant in an effort to close a deal worth hundreds of thousands of dollars. According to Cialdini, the reciprocity norm is so powerful that it often works even when (1) the gift is uninvited, (2) the gift comes from someone you dislike, or (3) the gift results in an uneven exchange.

The Lowball Technique

Learning Objective

Explain how lowballing is used in social influence.

Manipulations of the reciprocity rule can involve some trickery, but the *lowball technique* is even more deceptive. The name for this technique derives from a common practice in automobile sales, in which a customer is offered a terrific bargain on a car. The bargain price gets the customer to commit to buying the car. Soon after this commitment is made, the dealer starts revealing that there are some hidden costs. Typically, the customer learns that options apparently included in the original price are actually going to cost extra. Once they have committed to buying a car, most customers are unlikely to cancel the deal. **Thus, the *lowball technique* involves getting someone to commit to an attractive proposition before its hidden costs are revealed.**

Car dealers aren't the only ones who use this technique. For instance, a friend might ask if you want to spend a week with him at his charming backwoods cabin. After you accept this seemingly generous proposition, he may add, "Of course there's some work for us to do. We need to repair the pier, paint the exterior, and . . . " Lowballing is very dishonest. You might guess that people would become angry and back out of a deal once its hidden costs are revealed. Although this certainly happens on occasion, lowballing is a surprisingly effective strategy (Burger & Petty, 1981).

Reactance and Feigned Scarcity

A number of years ago, Jack Brehm demonstrated that telling people they can't have something only makes them want it more. This finding emerged in his research on reactance. *Reactance* **occurs when a person's freedom to behave in a certain way is impeded, thus leading to efforts to restore the threatened freedom.**

In one study of reactance (Brehm, 1966), subjects listened to four records and then were asked to rate how much they liked each one. As a reward for participating in the study, some subjects were told that they could have the record of their choice when they returned to make additional ratings on a second occasion. When subjects returned for the second session, they were told that one of the four records would not be available as their reward. The excluded record varied from subject to subject. It was always the record ranked third best by that individual in the first set of ratings. The subjects listened to the four records again and made their second set of ratings. Brehm found that the ratings of the excluded records increased significantly. In other words, the record that a subject could not have became all the more desirable!

Learning Objective

Discuss how reactance and feigned scarcity can increase someone's attraction to something.

Recommended Reading

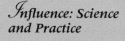

by Robert B. Cialdini (HarperCollins, 1993)

This brilliant book examines the dynamics of social influence. Cialdini, a social psychologist, draws on his extensive empirical research on influence tactics such as the door-in-the-face technique and lowballing. However, what makes his book unique is that he has gone far beyond laboratory research in his effort to better understand the ins and outs of social influence. For three years, he immersed himself in the real world of influence artists, becoming a "spy of sorts." As he puts it, "When I wanted to learn about the compliance tactics of encyclopedia (or vacuum cleaner, or portrait photography, or dance lessons) sales organizations, I would answer a newspaper ad for sales trainees and have them teach me their methods. Using similar but not identical approaches, I was able to penetrate advertising, public relations, and fund-raising agencies to examine their techniques" (from the preface). The result is an insightful book that bolsters scientific data with anecdotal accounts of how influence artists ply their trade. Familiarity with their strategies can help you to avoid being an easy mark or a "patsy."

A few years ago, a university professor tried a little experiment. He sent Christmas cards to a sample of perfect strangers. Although he expected some reaction, the response he received was amazing—holiday cards addressed to him came pouring back from people who had never met nor heard of him. The great majority of those who returned cards never inquired into the identity of the unknown professor. . . . While small in scope, this study nicely shows the action of one of the most potent of the weapons of influence around us—the rule of reciprocation. The rule says that we should try to repay, in kind, what another person has provided us. [p. 19]

This reactance effect helps explain why companies often try to create the impression that their products are in scarce supply. Scarcity threatens your freedom to choose a product, thus creating reactance and an increased desire for the scarce product. Advertisers frequently feign scarcity to drive up the demand for products. Thus, we constantly see ads that scream "limited supply available," "for a limited time only," "while they last," and "time is running out."

The Power of Modeling

Learning Objective

Explain how modeling effects can be used in social influence.

As we noted in Chapter 2, *observational learning* occurs when people's behavior is swayed by their observations of others, who, in this context, are called *models*. According to Albert Bandura (1986), a great deal of behavior is the product of imitation or modeling effects. These modeling effects are sometimes used in social influence efforts.

The power of modeling was demonstrated in an experiment designed to increase the contributions dropped into a Salvation Army kettle during the Christmas holiday (Bryan & Test, 1967). In this study, experimental accomplices posing as shoppers tossed money into a Salvation Army kettle as they walked by. Thus, they modeled generous behavior for real shoppers who witnessed their contributions. As predicted, the shoppers exposed to these generous models made more contributions than the shoppers in a control condition, where the models were absent.

Advertisers are well aware of people's tendency to be influenced by what others do. That's why they run television ads in which both celebrities and "ordinary people" testify about how they use a particular detergent, deodorant, or gasoline. Modeling effects also explain why television producers use laugh tracks in their comedy shows. Research reveals that canned laughter leads audiences to laugh at jokes more frequently and longer (Fuller & Sheehy-Skeffington, 1974; Smyth & Fuller, 1972). People try to take advantage of modeling effects in many different situations. For instance, bartenders often slip a few dollar bills into their tip jars to fraudulently "model" healthy tipping from previous customers.

In summary, people use a host of methods to coax compliance from one another. Despite the fact that many of these influence techniques are more or less dishonest, they're still widely used. There is no way to completely avoid being hoodwinked by influence strategies. However, understanding these various tactics can reduce the likelihood that you'll be a victim of influence artists. As we noted in our discussion of persuasion, "to be forewarned is to be forearmed."

6 Review

Key Ideas

The Process of Person Perception
• In forming impressions of other people, individuals rely on appearance, verbal statements, actions, nonverbal messages, and situational cues. Individuals usually make snap judgments about others unless accurate impressions are important. To explain the causes of other people's behavior, individuals make attributions (either internal or external).
• People often try to confirm their hypotheses about what others are like, and this can result in biased impressions. Self-fulfilling prophecies can actually change a target person's behavior in the direction of a perceiver's expectations. The process of person perception is characterized by the themes of efficiency, selectivity, and stability.

Perceiving Others: Sources of Error
• Many aspects of person perception lead us to see others inaccurately. We may be swayed by categorizing, stereotypes, or excessive attention to physical attractiveness or other features of appearance. Misperceptions are also fostered by the fundamental attribution error and defensive attribution.
• Prejudice is a particularly unfortunate outcome of our tendency to view others inaccurately. Most of the usual sources of error in person perception contribute to prejudicial beliefs about minority groups.

Persuasion: The Power of Rhetoric
• The success of persuasive efforts depends on several factors. A source of persuasion who is expert, trustworthy, likable, physically attractive, and similar to the receiver tends to be relatively effective. Although there are some limitations, two-sided arguments, arousal of fear, and generation of positive feelings

are effective elements in persuasive messages. Persuasion is undermined when receivers are forewarned or have beliefs that are extremely discrepant from the position being advocated.

Conformity and Compliance: The Power of Social Pressure
• Asch found that subjects often conform to the group, even when the group reports inaccurate judgments. Asch's experiments may have produced public compliance while subjects' private beliefs remained unchanged.

Obedience: The Power of Authority
• In Milgram's landmark study of obedience to authority, subjects showed a remarkable tendency to follow orders to shock an innocent stranger. Milgram concluded that situational pressure can make decent people do indecent things.

Perspectives on Social Influence
• When antisocial norms are dominant, yielding to peer pressure can result in unfortunate outcomes. Extremely effective communicators with almost complete control over groups are able to produce powerful, and sometimes tragic, results. Although people often yield to social pressure, they sometimes resist, as exemplified by whistleblowing. The value that cultures place on conformity influences the extent to which individuals are likely to conform.

Application: Seeing Through Social Influence Tactics
• A variety of tactics have been shown to be effective in influencing the behavior of others. These include the foot-in-the-door technique, the door-in-the-face technique, the reciprocity norm, the lowball technique, reactance, feigned scarcity, and modeling.

Key Terms

Attitudes
Attributions
Channel
Compliance
Confirmatory hypothesis testing
Conformity
Defensive attribution
Diffusion of responsibility
Discrimination
Door-in-the-face technique
Foot-in-the-door technique
Fundamental attribution error
Lowball technique
Message
Obedience
Person perception
Persuasion
Prejudice
Primacy effect
Reactance
Receiver
Reciprocity norm
Self-fulfilling prophecy
Social schemas
Source
Stereotypes

Key People

Solomon Asch
Robert Cialdini
Susan Fiske
Robert Merton
Stanley Milgram
Philip Zimbardo

Interpersonal Communication

*H*ave you ever hurried home, eager to tell someone about something that happened that day, only to find no one there to listen to your story? It may not have been a spectacular or earthshaking tale; maybe you simply picked up an intriguing bit of gossip or met someone who was a little unusual. Still, it was something you wanted to share with others. Chances are you rehearsed your fascinating account all the way home. On finding no receptive ears for your story, do you remember how frustrated you felt? As this common experience illustrates, people have a powerful need to share information about interesting or important events with others and to hear their reactions.

Interpersonal communication is an integral part of human experience. Moreover, interpersonal skills are highly relevant to adjustment, because they can be critical to one's happiness and success in life. In this chapter, we'll look at the process of interpersonal communication, covering both nonverbal and verbal communication. Then, we'll turn our attention to communication problems and interpersonal conflict, including some suggestions for dealing constructively with conflict. In the Application, we'll consider ways to develop an assertive communication style.

The Process of Interpersonal Communication

Learning Objective

Define interpersonal communication and describe the four components of the communication process.

Communication can be defined as the process of sending and receiving messages that have meaning. Our personal thoughts have meaning, of course, but when we "talk to ourselves," we are engaging in *intra*personal communication. This chapter focuses on *inter*personal communication—the face-to-face transmission of meaning between two or more people. For the most part, we'll concentrate on two-person interactions. We will define **interpersonal communication as an interactional process whereby one person sends a message to another.**

It is important to note several points about this definition. First, for communication to qualify as *interpersonal,* at least two people must be involved. Second, interpersonal communication is a *process*. By this, we simply mean that it is usually composed of a series of actions: Mary talks/John listens, John responds/Mary listens, and so on. Third, this process is *interactional*. Communication is generally not a one-way street: Both participants send as well as receive information when they're interacting. An important implication of this fact is that you need to pay attention to both your *speaking* and *listening* skills if you want to improve the effectiveness of your communication.

Components of the Communication Process

Let's take a look at the essential components of the interpersonal communication process. The four elements are the same as those in persuasion, the form of interpersonal communication discussed in Chapter 6: (1) the source of the message, (2) the message itself, (3) the channel in which the message is sent, and (4) the receiver of the message (Berlo, 1960). We'll briefly review these four components as they relate to our current discussion (see Figure 7.1).

The *source* is the person who initiates, or sends, the message. In a typical two-way conversation, both people serve as sources (as well as receivers) of messages. Keep in mind that each source person brings a unique set of expectations and under-

Figure 7.1
A model of interpersonal communication
According to David Berlo (1960), interpersonal communication involves four elements: the source, the receiver, the message, and the channel through which the message is transmitted. In conversations, both participants function as source and receiver.

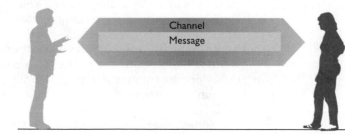

Source   Receiver standings to each communication situation. We will return to this important point shortly.

The *message* is the information or meaning that is transmitted from one person to another. The message is the content of the communication—that is, the ideas and feelings conveyed to another person. Language is the primary means of sending messages, but people also communicate to others nonverbally. Nonverbal communication includes the facial expressions, gestures, and vocal inflections used to supplement (and sometimes entirely change) the meaning of verbal messages. For example, when you say, "Thanks a lot," your nonverbal communication can convey either sincere gratitude or heavy sarcasm.

The *channel* refers to the medium through which the message reaches the receiver. People receive verbal messages, of course, by hearing them. They hear both the literal content of messages and the vocal inflections others use to communicate. Sometimes sound is the only channel available for receiving information—when you talk on the telephone, for instance. More often, however, people receive information from multiple channels simultaneously. They not only hear what the other person says, they also see the facial expressions, observe the gestures, experience eye contact, and sometimes feel the physical touch of the speaker. Note that the messages in the various channels may be consistent or inconsistent with each other, making interpretation of them more or less difficult.

The *receiver* is the person to whom the message is targeted. As we have noted, in a two-person interaction, each participant serves as both a source and a receiver. Each source/receiver has a unique history and set of beliefs and expectations that influence the communication process (Chelune, 1987). Communication is more effective (and less problematic) when people have similar frames of reference (Clark, 1985).

The Importance of Communication

Before we get into the details of interpersonal communication, let's take a moment to emphasize its significance. Communication with others—friends, lovers, parents, spouses, children, employers, employees—is such an essential and commonplace aspect of everyday life that it's hard to overstate the importance of communicating effectively. Many of life's satisfactions (and frustrations and heartaches, as well) hinge on one's ability to communicate effectively with others. Research has shown that good communication can enhance satisfaction in marriage and that poor communication can be a factor in marital dissatisfaction (Cleek & Pearson, 1985; Fitzpatrick, 1987). Most of our coverage in this chapter will be organized around two basic categories of communication: verbal (linguistic) and nonverbal. We'll tackle nonverbal communication first.

Nonverbal Communication

Learning Objective

Define nonverbal communication and list five general principles of nonverbal communication.

You're standing at the bar in your favorite lounge, gazing across a dark, smoky room filled with people drinking, dancing, and talking. You motion to the bartender that you'd like another drink. Your companion comments on the loudness of the music, and you nod your head in agreement. You spot an attractive stranger across the bar; your eyes meet for a moment and you smile. In a matter of seconds, you have sent three messages without uttering a syllable. To put it another way, you have just sent three nonverbal messages. **Nonverbal communication is the transmission of meaning from one person to another through means or symbols other than words.** Communication at the nonverbal level takes place through a variety of behaviors: interpersonal distance, facial expression, eye contact, body posture and movement, gestures, physical touch, and tone of voice. We will discuss each of these in this section.

Some experts maintain that most of the message transmissions in face-to-face interactions actually occur at the nonverbal level (Mehrabian, 1971; Philpott, 1983).

Clearly, a great deal of information is exchanged through nonverbal channels—probably more than most people realize. Thus, to enhance your effectiveness in communication, it's helpful to become more knowledgeable about the nature of nonverbal cues.

General Principles

Let's begin by examining some general principles of nonverbal communication.

1. *Nonverbal communication is multichanneled.* Nonverbal communication typically involves simultaneous messages sent through a number of channels. For instance, information may be transmitted through gestures, facial expressions, eye contact, and vocal tone at the same time. In contrast, verbal communication is limited to a single channel: speech. If you have ever tried to follow two people speaking at once, you are aware of how difficult it is to process multiple inputs of information. The multichanneled nature of nonverbal communication is one of the reasons that many nonverbal transmissions sail by the receiver unnoticed.

2. *Nonverbal communication frequently conveys emotions.* Sometimes you can communicate your feelings without saying a word—for example, "a look that 'kills.'" Nonverbal demonstrations of positive feelings include sitting or standing close to those you care for, touching them often, and looking at them frequently (Fletcher & Fitness, 1990; Patterson, 1988).

3. *Nonverbal communication is relatively ambiguous.* Nonverbal messages tend to be less clear than spoken words. A shrug or a raised eyebrow can mean different things to different people. Moreover, it is always difficult to know whether nonverbal messages are being sent intentionally. Although some popular books on body language imply otherwise, very few nonverbal signals carry universally accepted meanings (Swenson, 1973). Hence, they should be interpreted with caution.

4. *Nonverbal communication may contradict verbal messages.* We have all seen people who proclaim "I'm not angry" while their bodies clearly convey that they are positively furious. It is well known that verbal and nonverbal messages may be quite inconsistent. When confronted with such inconsistency, which message should you believe? Because of their greater spontaneity, you're probably better off heeding the nonverbal signs. Research shows that when someone is instructed to tell a lie, deception is most readily detected in the nonverbal channel of communication (DePaulo, Lanier, & Davis, 1983; DePaulo, LeMay, & Epstein, 1991).

5. *Nonverbal communication is culture-bound.* As with verbal language, nonverbal signals are different in different cultures (Matsumoto, 1996). For instance, people of Northern European heritage tend to engage in less physical contact and keep a greater distance between themselves than do people of Latin or Middle Eastern heritage. Thus, an Englishman might be quite upset when a well-meaning Brazilian "trespasses" on his personal space. Sometimes cultural differences can be quite pronounced. For example, in Tibet people greet their friends by sticking out their tongues (Ekman, 1975)!

Nonverbal signals can provide information about many things in interpersonal interactions. As we discuss specific nonverbal behaviors, we will focus on the information they provide regarding social affiliation (or liking for another person) and social status.

Personal Space

Learning Objective

Define proxemics and personal space.

Proxemics is the study of people's use of interpersonal space. *Personal space* is a zone of space surrounding a person that is felt to "belong" to that person. The personal space that you consider "yours" is like an invisible bubble you carry around with you in your social interactions. As we will see, although the boundaries of personal space are imaginary, this space may be marked off in tangible ways under some conditions. The size of this mobile zone is related to cultural background, social status, personality, age, and gender. Interestingly, animals show a similar tendency, called *territoriality*—the marking off and defending of certain areas as their own.

As you might guess, the amount of social distance people feel comfortable with depends on the nature of the relationship and the situation (Darley & Gilbert, 1985; J. A. Hall, 1990). The appropriate distance between people is regulated by social norms and varies by culture. Anthropologist Edward Hall (1990) has described four interpersonal distance zones that are appropriate for particular kinds of encounters in American culture (see Figure 7.2). The general rule is that the more you like someone, the more comfortable you feel being physically close to him or her. Of course, there are obvious exceptions, such as in crowded subways and elevators, but these situations are often experienced as stressful. Women seem to have smaller personal-space zones than men do. When talking, women sit or stand closer together than men (Sussman & Rosenfeld, 1982). There seem to be two reasons for this: women approach others more closely than men do, and others approach women more closely than they approach men (Hall, 1990).

As with other aspects of nonverbal communication, personal distance can convey information about status. People of similar status tend to stand closer together than do people whose status is unequal (J. A. Hall, 1990). Moreover, it is the prerogative of the more powerful person in an interaction to set the "proper" interpersonal distance (Henley, 1977).

What happens when someone approaches you more closely than you feel is appropriate? Such invasions of personal space invariably result in feelings of discomfort as well as attempts to bring the interpersonal distance more in line with your expectations. To illustrate, let's say that you have staked out some territory for yourself at a table in the library. When a stranger sits down at "your" table and forces you to share it, how might you react? One option is to move to another table to reestablish a distance that feels comfortable to you. If moving away is not practical, you will probably reorient your body away from the intruder or place some barrier (for example, a stack of books) between you and the invader. Whatever response you choose, the point is that invasions of personal space rarely go unnoticed, and they usually elicit a variety of reactions.

Figure 7.2
Interpersonal distance zones
According to Edward Hall (1990), people like to keep a certain amount of distance between themselves and others. The distance that makes one feel comfortable depends on whom one is interacting with and the nature of the situation. Generally, the zones depicted on the left are appropriate for the people and situations listed on the right.

Zone and distance

Zone 1: Intimate distance zone

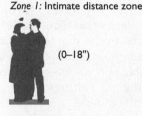

(0–18")

Zone 2: Personal distance zone

(18"– 4')

Zone 3: Social distance zone

(4'–12')

Zone 4: Public distance zone

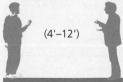

(12'+)

Appropriate people and situations

Parents and children, lovers, husband and wife

Close friends

Co-workers, social gatherings, friends, work situations

Actors, total strangers, important officials

Facial Expression

Define display rules and discuss what can be discerned from facial cues.

Facial expressions convey emotions more than they convey anything else. In an extensive research program, Paul Ekman and his colleagues have identified six primary emotions that have distinctive facial expressions: anger, disgust, fear, happiness, sadness, and surprise (Ekman, 1992; Ekman & Friesen, 1984). The facial expressions conveying these six emotions appear to be universal. That is, individuals from a variety of cultures are able to identify them correctly (Ekman & Friesen, 1984, 1986; Ekman et al., 1987). Typically, in such studies, subjects from a variety of Western and non-Western cultures are shown photographs depicting various emotions and are asked to match the photographs with the appropriate emotions. Some representative results from this research are shown in Figure 7.3.

Although a small number of basic facial expressions are universally recognizable, other expressions of emotions can vary from culture to culture—as we saw in the earlier example of Tibetans sticking out their tongues to greet their friends. In addition, social rules govern when (and whether) it is appropriate to express one's feelings. The facial expression of emotion is regulated by a given society's norms. **Display rules are norms that govern the appropriate display of emotions.**

Sometimes we may not want to communicate all that we feel to someone else, or they to us. It is considered bad form, for instance, to gloat over one's victories or to show envy or anger in defeat. This regulation of facial expression is an aspect of impression management that we discussed in Chapter 5. Is it possible to deliberately deceive others through facial expression? Yes, indeed. In fact, it appears that people are better at sending deceptive messages with their faces than with other areas of their bodies (Ekman, Friesen, & Ellsworth, 1982). Recall the term "poker face," an allusion to poker players who are skilled at controlling their excitement about a good hand of cards (or their dismay about a bad one). As you might predict, high self-monitors are better than low self-monitors at managing their facial expressions when it is inappropriate to show them (Friedman & Miller-Herringer, 1991). At this point, we don't know whether high-self-monitors are really more skilled at regulating their behavior or whether they are just more motivated to do so.

Figure 7.3
Facial expressions and emotions
Ekman and Friesen (1984) found that people in highly disparate cultures showed fair agreement on the emotions portrayed in these photos. This consensus across cultures suggests that the facial expressions associated with certain emotions may have a biological basis.

Facial Expressions and Emotions

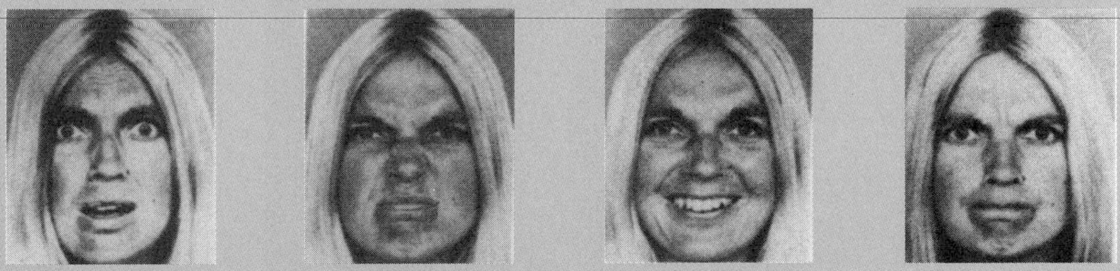

	Emotion displayed			
	Fear	*Disgust*	*Happiness*	*Anger*
Country	*Agreement in judging photos (%)*			
United States	85	92	97	67
Brazil	67	97	95	90
Chile	68	92	95	94
Argentina	54	92	98	90
Japan	66	90	100	90
New Guinea	54	44	82	50

Eye Contact

Learning Objective

Discuss the characteristics associated with high levels of eye contact.

Eye contact (also called mutual gaze) is another major channel of nonverbal communication. Above all, the *duration* of eye contact between people is what is most meaningful. A great deal of research has been done on communication through the eyes; we will briefly summarize some of the more interesting findings (Kleinke, 1986).

People who engage in high levels of eye contact are usually judged as more attentive than those who maintain less eye contact. Speakers, interviewers, and experimenters receive higher ratings of competence when they maintain high rather than low eye contact with their audience. Similarly, those who engage in high levels of mutual gaze are likely to be perceived as having effective social skills and credibility. Gaze is also a means of communicating the *intensity* (but not the positivity or negativity) of feelings.

The *positivity and negativity* of feelings are communicated by the context of the communication, timing, and accompanying nonverbal behaviors (position of the mouth, for example) (J. A. Hall, 1990). On the positive side, eye contact is strongly related to feelings of interpersonal attraction (Kleinke, 1986). For example, couples who say they are in love spend more time gazing at each other than do other couples (Patterson, 1988). Also, people who engage in high mutual gaze are judged by observers as liking each other more than those who engage in relatively little eye contact. Finally, maintaining eye contact with others generally causes them to like

Strong eye contact often conveys intense positive feelings; reduced eye contact usually signals negative feelings.

Figure 7.4
Visual dominance, status, and gender

Women typically show low visual dominance (see control condition) because they are usually accorded lower status than men (Dovidio et al., 1988). However, when researchers placed women in a high-power position and measured their visual behavior, women showed the high visual dominance pattern, and men, the low visual dominance pattern. When men were placed in the high-power position, the visual dominance patterns reversed. Thus, visual dominance seems to be more a function of status than of gender.

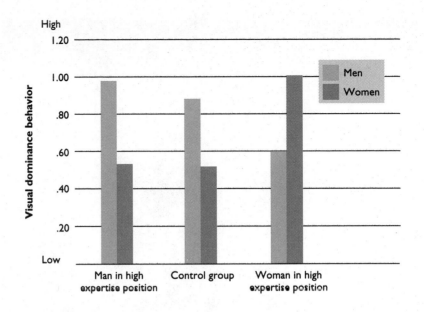

us, although people prefer a moderate amount of eye contact rather than constant (or no) mutual gaze.

In a negative interpersonal context, a steady gaze becomes a stare. A stare causes most people to feel uncomfortable and to flee the situation (Kleinke, 1986). Moreover, like threat displays among nonhuman primates such as baboons and rhesus monkeys, a stare can convey aggressive intent (Henley, 1986). People can also communicate by *reducing* their eye contact with others. For example, mutual gaze usually is reduced when an interaction is unpleasant or embarrassing (Edelman & Hampson, 1981) or when people feel that their personal space is being invaded (Kleinke, 1986).

Culture affects patterns of eye contact. For example, Americans get annoyed with people from Asian cultures because they look less directly at others during interactions. On the other hand, people from Arab countries get frustrated with Americans because we gaze less than they are used to (Matsumoto, 1996).

In the United States, gender and racial differences have been found in eye contact. Women tend to gaze more at others in interactions than men do (Giles & Street, 1985). However, the patterning of eye contact also reflects status, and gender and status are often confounded, as we have noted. Higher-status individuals look at the other person more when speaking than when listening, while lower-status people behave just the opposite. Women usually show the lower-status visual pattern because they are typically accorded lower status than men. As you can see in Figure 7.4, when women are in high-power positions, they show the high-status visual pattern to the same extent that men do (Dovidio et al., 1988). Several studies have found that this pattern is reversed among African Americans: Black listeners tend to gaze less than white listeners (Fehr & Exline, 1987; LaFrance & Mayo, 1976). Obviously, such differences in nonverbal communication can lead to misunderstandings if gazing behaviors intended to convey interest and respect are interpreted as being disrespectful or dishonest.

Body Language

Learning Objective

Define kinesics and discuss the characteristics associated with body movement and posture.

Body movements—those of the head, trunk, hands, legs, and feet—also provide nonverbal avenues of communication. **Kinesics is the study of communication through body movements.** What does body movement convey? For one thing, it provides information about the level of tension or relaxation that a person is experiencing. For example, frequent touching or scratching suggests nervousness (Harrigan, 1985). A person's *gait* (way of walking) can provide cues about age: Younger people walk with more bounce, hip sway, and loose-jointedness than older individuals (Montepare & Zebrowitz-McArthur, 1987).

Body posture also conveys information. For instance, leaning back with arms or legs arranged in an asymmetrical position (an "open" position) conveys a feeling of

People in higher-status positions tend to adopt an "open" body posture, and those in lower-status roles usually adopt a "closed" position.

relaxation. Posture can also indicate a person's attitude toward you (McKay, Davis, & Fanning, 1995). Someone's leaning toward you typically indicates interest and a positive attitude. When people angle their bodies away from you or cross their arms, their posture may indicate a negative attitude or defensiveness.

In addition, body posture can convey status differences. Generally, a higher-status person will look more relaxed. In contrast, a lower-status person will tend to exhibit a more rigid body posture, often sitting up straight with feet together, flat on the floor, and arms close to the body (a "closed" position) (Mehrabian, 1972). Again, as we saw with eye contact, status and gender differences are frequently parallel. That is, men are more likely to exhibit the high-status "open" posture and women the lower-status "closed" posture (J. A. Hall, 1990).

Hand gestures are used primarily to regulate conversations and to supplement speech (McKay et al., 1995). The *referencing gesture* is used to refer to an object or person who is the subject of conversation. For example, you might point at a car that you're commenting on. The *gesture of emphasis* is used to stress a point that is being made verbally. Thus, you might slam your fist onto a desk to emphasize the importance of your statement. *Demonstrative gestures* mimic what is being said: In discussing a cutoff of someone's financial support, you might make chopping motions with your hand.

Touch

Learning Objective

Discuss some of the research findings on touching.

Touch takes many forms and can express a variety of meanings, including support, consolation, and sexual intimacy (DeVito, 1992). Touch can also convey messages of status and power; those who initiate a touch are generally assumed to have higher status than those who receive a touch. It's more common, for example, to see teachers touch students than vice versa. How people interpret the possible messages communicated by touch depends on their age and gender, the setting in which the touching takes place, and the relationship between the toucher and recipient, among other things (Major, Schmidlin, & Williams, 1990). Also, there are strong norms about *where* people are allowed to touch friends. These norms are quite different for same-gender as opposed to cross-gender interactions, as can be seen in Figure 7.5.

The results of a large-scale observational study conducted in the Boston area provide several generalizations about touching behavior (Hall & Veccia, 1990, 1991). In this study, researchers observed 4500 pairs of people interacting in a variety of public places (shopping malls, hotel lobbies, subway stations). Observers recorded instances of touching with the hand as well as other parts of the body and esti-

Figure 7.5
Where friends touch each other
Social norms govern where friends tend to touch each other. As these figures show, the patterns of touching are different in same-gender as opposed to cross-gender interactions. (Adapted from Marsh, 1988)

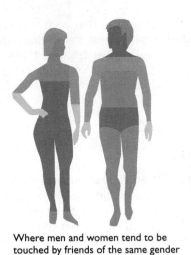

■ Seldom (0–25%)

■ Quite often (26–50%)

■ Often (51–75%)

■ Very often (76–100%)

Where men and women tend to be touched by friends of the same gender

Where men and women tend to be touched by friends of the other gender

mated (based on training) the age of the pairs. First, it was found that female-female pairs touch each other significantly more than male-male pairs do. Second, although there were no overall differences between the number of men who touched women and vice versa, if we look at these pairs by age, a different pattern emerges. That is, as they age, men tend to touch women less and women tend to touch men more. Comparable age changes were not found for same-gender pairs.

Regarding people's *responses* to touching, it has been found that women generally respond more favorably to touching than men do (Henley & Freeman, 1981). This gender difference may depend on status differences. Support for this interpretation comes from the finding that both women and men react favorably to touching when the person initiating the touch is higher in status than the recipient (Major, 1981). Of course, in cases where touching is unwelcome (for example, sexual harassment), these findings do not hold.

Paralanguage

Learning Objective

Define paralanguage and describe its role in communication.

The term *paralanguage* refers to *how* something is said rather than *what* is said. Thus, **paralanguage includes all vocal cues other than the content of the verbal message itself.** These cues may include how loudly or softly people speak, how fast they talk, and the rhythm and quality of their speech (Burgoon, 1990). Each of these aspects of vocalization can affect the message being transmitted.

Variations in vocal emphasis can give the same set of words very different meanings. Consider the sentence "I really enjoyed myself!" If you vary the word that is accented, you can speak this sentence in three different ways, each resulting in a different meaning:

- *I* really enjoyed myself!
  (Even though others may not have had a good time, I did.)
- I *really* enjoyed myself!
  (My enjoyment was exceptional or greater than expected.)
- I really *enjoyed* myself!
  (Much to my surprise, I had a great time.)

As you can see from these examples, the way something is said can make a considerable difference in the meaning conveyed. In fact, you can actually reverse the literal meaning of a verbal message by how you say it (such as by using sarcasm).

Aspects of vocalization can also communicate emotions. For example, rapid speech may mean that a person is happy, frightened, or nervous. Slower speech might be used when the person is uncertain or when he or she wants to emphasize a point. Loud vocalization often indicates anger. A relatively high pitch may indicate anxiety (Verderber & Verderber, 1995). Slow speech, low volume, and low pitch are often associated with sadness. Thus, vocal quality is another clue that you can use to discern someone's true feelings. Keep in mind, however, that it is easy to assign meanings to voice quality that aren't valid. For example, it is quite common for people to stereotype certain vocal characteristics as indicative of specific personality traits even though research doesn't support such associations (Heun & Heun, 1978). Examples of common vocal stereotypes include associating a deep voice with masculinity and maturity, and a high, breathy voice with femininity and youth.

Detecting Deception

Learning Objective

Summarize the evidence on detecting deception from nonverbal cues.

The spontaneous nature of nonverbal communication often makes it a better index of a person's true feelings than what the person actually says. This reality raises an obvious question. Is it possible to detect deceit by monitoring nonverbal signals? Yes, but it isn't easy. Interestingly, the clues that suggest dishonesty don't necessarily correspond to popular stereotypes about how liars give themselves away.

Evidence on the nonverbal behaviors associated with deception is summarized in Figure 7.6 (based on DePaulo, Stone, & Lassiter, 1985). The vocal and visual cues that have been studied are listed in the first column. The second column indicates whether these cues are really associated with deception. The third column indicates whether the same cues are widely believed to be associated with deception. As you can see, research does not support many stereotypical notions about lying. Contrary to popular belief, lying is *not* associated with slow talking, long pauses before speaking, excessive shifting of posture, reduced smiling, or lack of eye contact.

Nonetheless, there are some cues that do seem to be associated with dishonesty. Vocal cues include excessive hesitations and stammering, speaking with a

Figure 7.6
Detecting deception from nonverbal behaviors
This chart summarizes evidence on which nonverbal cues are *actually* associated with deception and which are *believed* to be a sign of deception, based on a research review by DePaulo, Stone, and Lassiter (1985).

Nonverbal Cues and Deception

Kind of cue	***Are cues associated with actual deception?***	***Are cues believed to be a sign of deception?***
Vocal cues		
Speech hesitations	YES: Liars hesitate more.	YES
Voice pitch	YES: Liars speak with higher pitch.	YES
Speech errors (stutters, stammers)	YES: Liars make more errors.	YES
Speech latency (pause before starting to speak or answer)	NO	YES: People think liars pause more.
Speech rate	NO	YES: People think liars talk slower.
Response length	YES: Liars give shorter answers.	NO
Visual cues		
Pupil dilation	YES: Liars show more dilation.	(No research data)
Adaptors (self-directed gestures)	YES: Liars touch themselves more.	NO
Blinking	YES: Liars blink more.	(No research data)
Postural shifts	NO	YES: People think liars shift more.
Smiling	NO	YES: People think liars smile less.
Gaze (eye contact)	NO	YES: People think liars engage in less eye contact.

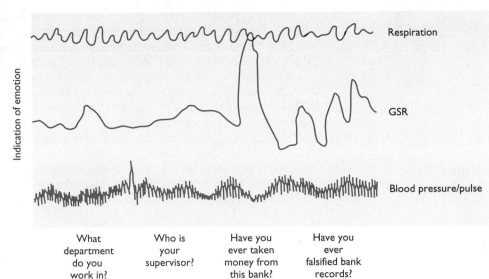

Figure 7.7
The polygraph and emotional reactions
A lie detector measures the physiological arousal that most people experience when they tell a lie. After using nonthreatening questions to establish a baseline, a polygraph examiner looks for signs of arousal (such as the sharp change in galvanic skin response, or GSR, shown here) on incriminating questions.

Learning Objective

Describe what polygraphs do, how accurate they are, and some problems with their use.

higher pitch, and giving relatively short answers. Visual cues include excessive blinking and dilation of the pupils. Also, liars nervously touch themselves more than normal. Too, it's helpful to look for inconsistencies between messages expressed through the face and those from the lower part of the body. For example, a friendly smile accompanied by a nervous shuffling of feet may be cause for concern. Another clue is whether there is any lack of spontaneity in the facial message compared to the verbal message. People tend to take more time to muster and send deceptive nonverbal signals than authentic ones. Because of this tendency, liars' verbal and facial expressions may be out of sync.

If people have trouble detecting deception, might a *machine* be more accurate? **The *polygraph* is a device that records fluctuations in physiological arousal as a person answers questions.** Although called a "lie detector," it's really an emotion detector. The polygraph monitors key indicators of autonomic arousal, such as heart rate, blood pressure, respiration rate, and perspiration (or GSR). The assumption is that when subjects lie, they experience emotion that produces noticeable changes in these physiological indicators (see Figure 7.7). Research indicates that polygraphs are inaccurate about one-fourth to one-third of the time (Kleinmuntz & Szucko, 1984; Lykken, 1981). One problem is that people who are telling the truth may experience emotional arousal when they respond to incriminating questions. Thus people who are actually innocent may "fail" a polygraph test. Another problem is that some people can lie without experiencing physiological arousal. Because of the high error rates, polygraph results cannot be submitted as evidence in most types of courtrooms. In spite of the courts' conservatism, many companies have required prospective and current employees to take lie detector tests to weed out thieves. In 1988, the U.S. Congress passed a law curtailing this practice.

In conclusion, deception is potentially detectable, but detecting it is not a simple matter. The nonverbal behaviors that tend to accompany lying are subtle and can be difficult to spot.

The Significance of Nonverbal Communication

Learning Objective

Discuss the significance of nonverbal messages in interpersonal relationships.

Although people often are unaware of nonverbal communication, it clearly plays an important role in everyone's life. You constantly use nonverbal cues to convey your own feelings to others and to "read" theirs (DePaulo, 1992). Let's consider some ways that nonverbal communication can affect adjustment.

In our society, if you dislike someone, you don't usually say so (Tesser & Rosen, 1975). Instead, your negative feelings will "leak" through nonverbal channels (DePaulo, 1992). Individuals with negative self-concepts seem to have difficulty detecting these nonverbal messages of aversion, which puts them at a social disadvantage (Rosenthal et al., 1979). To study this issue, researchers tape-recorded 10-minute interactions between two-person, same-gender pairs (Swann, Stein-Seroussi,

& McNulty, 1992). Replicating the findings of previous studies, the study found that participants with negative self-views were perceived less favorably than those with positive self-concepts. However, those with negative self-concepts failed to perceive this fact. In another phase of the study, judges evaluated the verbal and nonverbal (voice quality) messages received by the positive- and negative-self-concept individuals. While there were no significant differences in the nature of the verbal messages received by these two groups, there were significant differences in the nonverbal messages. Apparently, those with negative self-views attended to the positive verbal cues and disregarded the negative nonverbal cues. Deprived of this important information, these individuals may fail to learn that (or why) they alienate others, making it difficult for them to correct their behavior.

Research has also been done on other aspects of nonverbal communication, such as its importance in marital relationships. For example, it has been shown that husbands and wives in unhappy marriages send more negative nonverbal messages and fewer positive nonverbal messages than do couples who are happily married (Noller, 1982, 1985). Of course, relationships also depend heavily on verbal communication, which we'll explore in the next section.

Verbal Communication

Verbal communication is sending and receiving messages through written or spoken words. In this section, we'll explore effective speaking and listening as well as the important topic of self-disclosure. Because effective communication rests on the foundation of a positive interpersonal climate, we'll start with this topic.

Creating a Positive Interpersonal Climate

A positive interpersonal climate exists when people feel that they can be open rather than guarded or defensive in their communication. You can go a long way toward creating such a climate by putting the following suggestions into practice.

1. *Learn to feel and communicate empathy.* **Empathy is adopting another's frame of reference to understand his or her point of view.** Empathy includes being sensitive to others' needs and accepting of their feelings. To clarify the meaning of empathy, it may be helpful to make a distinction between a person and his or her behavior. Being accepting and understanding toward a person does *not* necessarily mean that you must also condone or endorse the individual's behavior. For example, what if your roommate confides in you that he is worried about his drinking? In discussing the issue with him, you can come to understand the reasons for his excessive drinking without condoning this behavior. You can communicate your support for him, as a person, by continuing to be his friend—without encouraging him to continue drinking.

2. *Practice withholding judgment.* You can promote an open climate for communication by trying to be nonjudgmental. This doesn't mean that you give up your right to have opinions and make judgments. It merely means that you should strive to interact with people in ways that don't put them on the spot (forced to offer an opinion when they would rather not) or make them feel "put down" or inadequate.

3. *Strive for honesty.* Mutual trust and respect thrive on authenticity and honesty. So-called hidden agendas don't stay hidden very long. Even if others don't know exactly what your underlying motives are, they often can sense that you're not being entirely honest. Of course, striving for honesty does not mean that you are bound to communicate everything that you feel at any time to any person. While it is true that some interactions necessarily involve pain—for example, breaking up with a girlfriend or boyfriend—you can avoid many unpleasant interactions by being truthful without being needlessly hurtful.

4. *Approach others as equals.* You may know from personal experience that most people don't like to be reminded of another's higher status or greater ability. You

can go a long way toward effective communication by disregarding status differences in your conversations. Especially when you have the higher status, it is better to approach people on equal terms.

5. *Express your opinions tentatively.* Rather than giving the impression that you know all the answers, strive to communicate that your beliefs and attitudes are flexible and subject to revision. You can do this by using qualifying words or phrases. For instance, instead of saying, "This is how we should do it," you might say, "There seem to be several possible approaches; the one that seems the best to me is . . . What do you think?"

Effective Speaking and Listening

Communication is effective when the message you intend to convey is the message that is actually received. To be an effective communicator, you must be able to accurately transmit a message as well as accurately receive it.

Too often, people are careless in their speech, which can result in misunderstanding. For example, you can probably recall an instance in which you hurt someone's feelings unintentionally because you said the first thing that came to mind. At other times, miscommunication occurs because people aren't clear about what they are trying to express. It's important to take the time to think carefully about what you want to say and how you can best express it when you are talking about serious issues.

Speaking effectively requires skills that are developed over a lifetime. Thus, we realize that a few paragraphs of advice won't produce dramatic changes in your speaking skills. Nonetheless, observing a few general guidelines can enhance the effectiveness of your communication. These suggestions appear in Figure 7.8. If you want more detailed information on this topic, we suggest that you consult Verderber and Verderber (1995), an excellent communications text.

Effective *listening* is a vastly underappreciated skill. To paraphrase an old saying, "We have two ears and only one mouth, so we should listen twice as much as we speak." Because listeners process speech much more rapidly than people speak (600 words per minute versus 100–140 words per minute), it is understandable that receivers can become bored, distracted, and inattentive (Adler & Towne, 1987). This is likely to be true when the listener knows the speaker well (and, therefore, expects that he or she knows what the speaker will say). Fatigue and preoccupation with one's own thoughts are other factors that interfere with effective listening.

**Figure 7.8
Guidelines for effective speaking**
You can enhance your communication skills by following these suggestions for effective speaking.

Hints for Effective Speaking

1. *Consider the frame of reference of your listener or listeners.* When talking with others, consider their background, intelligence, attitudes, and so forth, and speak in terms that they can understand. Avoid talking over the heads of your audience and using terms that are foreign to them. Illustrate your ideas with examples your listeners can relate to from their own experience.

2. *Use an assertive communication style.* Express your thoughts and feelings directly and honestly. Assertiveness means standing up for your rights when someone else infringes on them. For a more detailed discussion of assertive communication, see the Application at the end of this chapter.

3. *Be specific and concrete.* Effective communication is hampered when you speak in vague generalities. This can leave your listeners confused and frustrated. And don't confuse lengthy talk with clear communication. You can speak for a long time without saying anything.

4. *Avoid "loaded" words.* Certain words are "loaded" in the sense that they tend to trigger negative emotional reactions in listeners. You can communicate more effectively if you avoid such words. For example, you can discuss politics without using terms such as "right-winger" and "knee-jerk liberal."

5. *Make your verbal and nonverbal messages congruent.* Inconsistency between the verbal and nonverbal channels can generate confusion and mistrust in your listeners. Work at becoming more aware of your nonverbal signals. If you strive for honesty in your verbal communications, you will lessen the likelihood of incongruence in the nonverbal channel.

Figure 7.9
Guidelines for effective listening
These suggestions for improving listening skills are based on the recommendations of a number of experts.

Hints for Effective Listening

1. *Position yourself so that you can see and hear the speaker.* Face the person squarely and maintain good eye contact to signal your attentiveness to the speaker. Also, adopting an "open" posture and leaning forward will send a clear nonverbal message that you are interested in what the other person has to say (Egan, 1990).

2. *Actively attend to and process the verbal message.* Because listeners process speech faster than speakers talk, your attention can wander. Try to devote this extra time to the incoming information rather than to irrelevant thoughts. You can review points already made, anticipate what the speaker will say next, and search for deeper meanings that may underlie the surface message (Huseman, Lahiff, & Hatfield, 1976).

3. *Pay attention to nonverbal signals.* While people use verbal cues to get the "objective" meaning of a message, they depend on nonverbal cues for information about the emotional and interpersonal meanings of the message (Burgoon, 1990). When verbal and nonverbal messages conflict with each other, people are more likely to rely on nonverbal cues.

4. *Check your understanding of the message.* Check with the speaker from time to time to be sure that you have understood the message properly. Translate the ideas (including the underlying ones) into your own words to see whether the speaker agrees with your interpretation.

To be an effective listener, you must be able to receive the message that the sender intends. The key to effective listening is to devote active effort to the task. As you can see in Figure 7.9, successful listening requires that you actively attend to and process incoming information. Although you are not likely to experience a dramatic change in your speaking skills overnight, you *may* be able to substantially improve your listening fairly quickly. For one thing, most people probably are ineffective listeners because they are unaware of the elements of effective listening. Also, effective listening hinges largely on your attitude. If you're willing to work at it, you can become a good listener.

In this short book, readers will find a wealth of information to help improve their communication skills in a wide variety of situations. *Messages* is organized according to six types of communication skills: basic, advanced, conflict, social, family, and public. Within each of these sections, chapters address important issues. For example, the section on family skills includes chapters on sexual communication, parent effectiveness, and family communications; the section on public skills addresses communication in small groups and public speaking; and "advanced skills" deals with hidden agendas, transactional analysis, and the role of culture and gender in communication. The authors have a breezy writing style and use lots of examples to illustrate their points. They have also included numerous exercises to help readers assess their communication skills and practice more effective ways of interacting with others. The following excerpt addresses one of several common "hidden agendas" individuals use in talking with others.

I'm Helpless, I Suffer
This is the agenda of the victim. The stories focus on misfortune, injustice, abuse. The stories are about someone who's stuck, who tries but can't escape, who endures without hope of remedy. The person is implicitly saying, "Don't ask me to do anything about all this pain, I'm not responsible."

A classic I'm Helpless, I Suffer game is Why Does This Always Happen To Me? One man, who'd gotten a little break from his ulcer symptoms, complained of a reoccurrence after he got stuck in traffic without his antacids. "This always happens. I feel a little better and then some crazy thing comes up to set me back. Somebody puts pepper on my salad or sales take a plunge at work. It never fails." The I'm Helpless, I Suffer agenda is ideal for avoiding scary new solutions, or for accepting pain that otherwise suggests the need for a major life decision. "I'm ugly, ill, too nervous" will often help put off the change indefinitely. [pp. 75–76]

Self-Disclosure: The Key to Intimacy

Learning Objective

Define self-disclosure and explain why it is important to adjustment.

Self-disclosure is the voluntary act of verbally communicating information about oneself to another person. This information doesn't have to be a deeply hidden secret, but it may be. In general terms, self-disclosure involves opening up about yourself to others. Conversations that include self-disclosure are experienced as deeper and more personally meaningful than more routine, superficial interactions.

Self-disclosure has both breadth and depth (Altman & Haythorn, 1965). *Breadth* refers to the number of different topics discussed with another person. *Depth* refers to the degree to which personal information is disclosed to another. For example, you would probably feel quite comfortable chatting about your feelings about the weather and today's sports scores with strangers (not much breadth or depth). In contrast, your best friend probably knows a wide variety of information about you (greater breadth) as well as how you feel about more private concerns, such as your jealousy toward your sister or your self-consciousness about your weight (greater depth). Figure 7.10 is a visual representation of breadth and depth in self-disclosure.

Self-disclosure is of critical importance to adjustment for several reasons. First, it is the key to emotional intimacy (McKay et al., 1995; Taylor & Altman, 1987). And intimacy is the element that distinguishes those relationships experienced as meaningful and sustaining from those experienced as superficial and unsupportive. Intimate relationships in this sense may be platonic or sexual. Indeed, as you may have discovered, a sexually intimate relationship is not necessarily an emotionally intimate relationship. In emotional intimacy, the important factor is the degree to which people are open and honest with each other.

A second important function of self-disclosure is aiding self-understanding. As we discussed in Chapter 5, people need to compare themselves with others to gain a better understanding of themselves. To obtain the information they seek, they often need to engage in self-disclosure. For instance, if you want to know whether your anxiety about your history class is realistic, you will probably have to divulge your concerns to your fellow students to get the feedback you need. Third, sharing fears and problems with others who are trustworthy and supportive plays a key role in mental health. As we saw in Chapter 4, expressing your feelings to someone else can reduce stress.

Who Reveals What to Whom, When, and Under What Circumstances?

Self-disclosure can be risky. When you reveal important and private things about yourself to others, you become more vulnerable to them. What if they reject you, or share your confidences with someone else? How can you know whether it's safe

Figure 7.10
Breadth and depth of self-disclosure
Breadth of self-disclosure refers to how many things one opens up about; depth refers to how far one goes in revealing private information. Both the breadth and depth of disclosures are greater with best friends as opposed to casual acquaintances or strangers. (Based on Altman & Taylor, 1983)

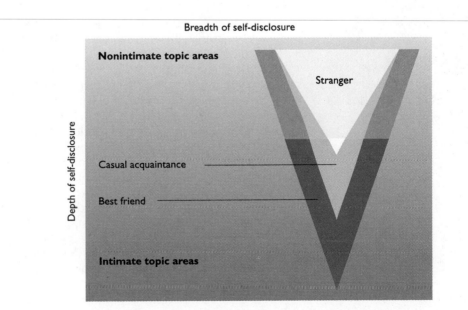

Learning Objective

Summarize the evidence on
who tends to disclose what to
whom and under what
circumstances.

to share personal information with another? In the discussion that follows, we'll try to respond to these and related questions about self-disclosure.

Who? In general, it has been found that females tend to be more openly self-disclosing than males, although the disparity seems smaller than once believed (Dindia & Allen, 1992). This disparity is typically attributed to differences in gender-role socialization. In our culture, most men are taught to be inexpressive, particularly about tender emotions and feelings of vulnerability. Thus, it isn't surprising that females disclose more personal information and feelings, whereas males disclose more nonpersonal information (Rubin, Peplau, & Hill, 1981). When disclosing emotions, females talk more often about negative feelings, while males more often disclose feelings that are positive or neutral. Here, we might point out that there is an inverse relationship between disclosure and power. To the extent that men have more power in a relationship, they need not disclose as much personal information (Henley & Freeman, 1981).

In *some* situations, however, men may be more prone to self-disclosure than women. For example, in dealing with strangers (as opposed to friends), males tend to be more self-disclosing than females (Rosenfeld, Civikly, & Herron, 1979; Rubin, 1974). Also, in the beginning stages of an other-gender relationship, men may disclose more than women (Derlega et al., 1985). This finding is consistent with the traditional gender-role expectation that males should initiate relationships and females should encourage males to talk. Thus, it is an oversimplification to say that women are more open than men.

What? Obviously, it is easier to be open about some topics than others. Individuals quickly give biographical information (for example, where they live, their age, or their education) but are understandably reluctant to divulge inner fears, such as insecurities about their work. Also, people are generally willing to reveal socially desirable things about themselves, such as their membership in the Jaycees. In contrast, they tend to be reticent about socially undesirable things, such as a conviction for tax evasion (Altman & Taylor, 1983).

When? *Social penetration theory* **focuses on how relationships develop and, sometimes, dissolve** (Taylor & Altman, 1987). This theory, developed by Irwin Altman and Dalmas Taylor, has contributed significantly to our understanding of the role of self-disclosure in relationship development. Among other things, it predicts that gradual changes occur in the breadth and depth of self-disclosure as relationships develop. Thus, early in a relationship, disclosures are restricted to a narrow range of impersonal topics; however, as the relationship grows, the number of topics increases, as does the willingness to discuss more personal concerns. Research generally supports these predictions, and it also shows that individuals expand the range of topics they discuss with others before they increase the depth of their personal revelations (Altman, Vinsel, & Brown, 1981). Once people begin sharing personal information with another, the depth of their disclosures increases without much change in their breadth.

Not all relationships develop according to the principle of gradual self-disclosure. Many individuals seem to be capable, early on, of distinguishing between those relationships they wish to remain relatively superficial and those they would like to become more intimate (Berg & Clark, 1986). At least one study on friendship development has reported that the progression of relationships to more intimate levels is not as gradual as social penetration theory would predict (Hays, 1985). Obviously, then, there is variability in the timing of self-disclosure in relationship development. Still, saying too much too soon can nip a relationship in the bud. Moreover, those who disclose in this way may be viewed as maladjusted and less likable (Collins & Miller, 1994). Because it entails less risk and stress, we suggest that gradual self-disclosure may be the optimal route to close relationships.

To whom? A critical factor in self-disclosure is the target person who will receive the information. Usually, people are more likely to disclose personal information to females than to males. However, this trend is moderated by situational variables,

Irwin Altman

such as the exact nature of the topic (Hill & Stull, 1987). As you might expect, people tend to disclose more to those they like and to those they know relatively well (Derlega et al., 1987).

As individuals move from adolescence toward adulthood, they tend to disclose less to their parents and same-gender friends and more to their other-gender friends. Usually, they disclose more to a spouse or partner than to anyone else. Consistent with the predictions of social penetration theory, partners who engage in a good deal of self-disclosure report relatively high levels of satisfaction in relationships (Hansen & Schuldt, 1984; Rubin et al., 1980). On the other hand, it has also been suggested that *equity* in self-disclosure, rather than high self-disclosure, may be the critical factor that helps couples avoid stress (Bowers, Metts, & Duncanson, 1985).

Under what circumstances? A situational variable that figures prominently in self-disclosure is *reciprocity*. Typically, a person returns a disclosure of approximately the same intimacy as that revealed by the other person (Cunningham, Strassberg, & Haan, 1986). A number of studies have shown that *people disclose more when another reciprocates by making disclosures to them.* Thus, in a cyclical manner, self-disclosure breeds more self-disclosure. The reciprocity norm governing self-disclosure appears to be most influential in the early stages of a relationship (Cunningham et al., 1986; Taylor & Altman, 1987). Hence, unless there are special circumstances operating, you can usually assume that if you engage in appropriate self-disclosure with a person to whom you'd like to feel closer, your listener will reciprocate. Being aware of this may alleviate some of your anxiety about opening up to others you do not know well.

Once relationships are well-established, reciprocity in self-disclosure seems to taper off (Taylor & Altman, 1987). Instead of reciprocating to a personal revelation by a close friend or lover, people frequently respond with statements of sympathy and understanding. This movement away from equal exchanges of self-disclosure appears to be based on needs that emerge as intimate relationships develop: (1) the need for support from those one feels close to and (2) the need to maintain privacy in close relationships (Altman et al., 1981). Reciprocating support with friends and lovers, then, enables people to strengthen their relationships while allowing them to maintain a sense of privacy. In fact, the ability to balance the needs for self-disclosure and privacy seems to be an important factor in maintaining satisfying close relationships (Baxter, 1988).

Altman and Taylor use the term *depenetration* to describe the dynamics of relationships that are moving toward dissolution. Although there is not much research on the topic, self-disclosure seems to change when relationships are in distress. For example, one or both individuals may decrease the breadth and depth of their self-disclosures, indicating that they are emotionally withdrawing (Baxter, 1988). Also, another study of troubled relationships found that the breadth of self-disclosure decreased, but the depth increased due to the rise in the number of *negative* personal statements expressed (Tolstedt & Stokes, 1984).

When Is Self-Disclosure Appropriate?

To disclose or not to disclose—that is the question. By now, you should be able to appreciate the complexity of this question. The crucial issue concerning self-disclosure is: When is it appropriate?

The answer is both simple and complex. We'll give you the simple part first. *Self-disclosure is appropriate when your listener is sincerely interested and willing to hear what you have to say.* But how do you know whether your target person is interested? This is where the answer gets complex. It helps to go slowly and pay close attention to the other person's reaction. It's something like testing the water to see whether it's warm enough instead of jumping in all at once.

In assessing the other person's reaction, you need to pay close attention to both verbal and nonverbal cues. Verbally, the positive signs to listen for are empathy and reciprocity. In particular, the other person's reciprocating with self-disclosure generally indicates a willingness on his or her part to proceed to a more intimate level of communication. Of course, some people who aren't very comfortable engaging

in self-disclosure themselves are sincerely willing to listen to you anyway. Thus, you cannot depend on reciprocity alone as an indicator of the other person's interest.

This is why tuning in to nonverbal signals is of crucial importance. Commonly, when people are uncomfortable with your self-disclosure, they will try to send you a nonverbal message to that effect, to avoid embarrassing you with a more obvious verbal warning. They will most likely deliver this "stop" message by reducing eye contact and by displaying a puzzled, apprehensive, or pained facial expression. If seated, the other person may angle his or her body away from you; if the person is standing, he or she may increase the distance between you or shuffle his or her feet impatiently. In contrast, if your target person faces you squarely, leans forward, appears relaxed, and maintains good eye contact, you can be fairly certain that he or she is willing to listen to your self-disclosure.

Communication Problems and Interpersonal Conflict

Up to now, we've considered verbal and nonverbal communication separately. From now on, we'll use the term "communication" to mean both types of messages. In this section, we'll discuss communication apprehension and barriers to effective communication. We'll also consider how miscommunication can contribute to date rape. We'll close on a positive note and offer some suggestions for dealing constructively with conflict when it arises.

Communication Apprehension

Learning Objective

Define communication apprehension and four responses to it.

It's the first day of child psychology class and you have just learned that 30-minute oral reports are a course requirement. Do you welcome this as an opportunity to polish your public speaking skills, or, panic-stricken, do you race to the Registrar's office to drop the class? If you opted for the latter, you may suffer from ***communication apprehension,* or the anxiety caused by having to talk with others.** Some people experience communication apprehension in all speaking situations (including one-on-one encounters), but most people who have the problem notice it when they have to speak before groups.

Bodily experiences associated with communication apprehension can range from small increases in heart rate to "butterflies" in the stomach, cold hands, dry mouth, and a racing heart rate (McKay, Davis, & Fanning, 1983). These physiological effects are stress-induced "fight or flight" responses of the autonomic nervous system (see Chapter 3). Interestingly, it isn't the physiological responses themselves that are the root of communication apprehension, but rather it is one's *interpretation* of these bodily responses (McCroskey & Beatty, 1986). That is, individuals who score high on measures of communication apprehension frequently interpret the bodily changes they experience in public speaking situations as indications of fear. In contrast, those who score low on these measures are likely to interpret such physiological reactions as excitement and as normal in such a situation (McCroskey & Beatty, 1986).

Four responses to communication apprehension have been identified. The most common is *communication avoidance,* a reaction that occurs when people are confronted with a communication situation and can choose whether they want to participate in it. If they believe that speaking will make them uncomfortable, these individuals will typically avoid participating. *Communication withdrawal* occurs when people unexpectedly find themselves in a communication situation that they can't get out of. In this case, people may clam up entirely or say as little as possible. *Communication disruption* involves the inability to make fluent oral presentations or the use of inappropriate verbal or nonverbal behavior. Of course, inadequate communication skills can produce this same behavioral effect, and it isn't always possible for the average person to identify the actual cause of the problem. *Excessive communication* is a relatively unusual response to high communication apprehension, but it does occur. An example would be the person who attempts to dominate social situations. Although individuals who exhibit this response are perceived as poor communicators, they are not usually identified by the average person as having communication apprehension. This is because we expect to see it only in people who don't talk very much. Of course, excessive communication may be caused by factors other than communication apprehension.

James McCroskey, an expert who has written extensively on this topic, suggests that avoidance and withdrawal tactics are only effective *short-term* strategies for coping with communication apprehension (McCroskey & Beatty, 1986). Because it is unlikely that one can go through life without having to speak in front of a group, it is important to learn to cope with this stressful event rather than avoid it time and again (McKay, Davis, & Fanning, 1995). Allowing the problem to get out of hand can result in self-limiting behavior, such as refusing a job promotion that would entail public speaking. (The Recommended Reading on page 210, *Messages,* offers some helpful suggestions for dealing with "stage fright.") Not unexpectedly, research indicates that people with high levels of communication apprehension are likely to have difficulties in interpersonal relationships and in work and educational settings (McCroskey & Beatty, 1986). Both cognitive restructuring (Chapter 4) and systematic desensitization (Chapter 16) have proved to be effective methods for dealing with this problem (McCroskey & Beatty, 1986).

Barriers to Effective Communication

Learning Objective

Describe five communication barriers.

A *communication barrier* is anything in the communication process that inhibits or blocks the accurate transmission and reception of messages. Barriers to effective communication can reside in the source, in the receiver, or sometimes in both. Common barriers to effective communication include defensiveness, motivational distortion, self-preoccupation, game playing, and collusion.

Defensiveness

Perhaps the most basic barrier to effective communication is *defensiveness*—an excessive concern with protecting oneself from being hurt. People are prone to react defensively when they feel threatened, such as when they feel that others are going to evaluate them or when they believe that others are trying to control or manipulate them. Defensiveness is also easily elicited when others act in a superior manner. Thus, those who overemphasize their status, wealth, brilliance, or power often put receivers on the defensive. Dogmatic people who convey "I'm always right" also tend to breed defensiveness. Although you should try to cultivate a communication style that reduces the likelihood of arousing defensiveness in others, you need to remember that you don't have complete control over others' perceptions and reactions.

A threat need not be real to elicit defensive behavior. If you expect that another person won't like you, for example, your interactions with that person will probably not be very positive. And, if the self-fulfilling prophecy kicks in, you may produce the negative reaction you fear.

Motivational Distortion

In Chapter 6, we discussed biases and distortions in person perception. The same processes commonly take place in communication. That is, people can hear what they want to hear instead of what is actually being said.

Each person has a unique frame of reference—certain attitudes, values, and expectations—that can influence what he or she hears. Information that contradicts one's views often produces emotional discomfort. One way of avoiding these unpleasant feelings is to engage in *selective attention*, or actively choosing to attend to information that supports one's beliefs and to ignore information that contradicts them. Similarly, an individual may read meanings into statements that are not intended or jump to erroneous conclusions. This tendency to distort information occurs most often in discussions of issues that people feel strongly about. Certain issues (politics, racism, sexism, abortion) are often highly charged for both the source and receiver. Misperceptions are especially likely to occur in these situations and to interfere with effective communication.

Self-Preoccupation

Everyone has had the experience of trying to communicate with someone who is so self-focused as to make enjoyable two-way conversation impossible. Such people seem to talk to hear themselves talk. When someone else tries to slip in a word about his or her problems, the self-preoccupied speaker may cut the person off by saying, "That's nothing. Listen what happened to me!" Further, self-preoccupied people rarely listen attentively. When another person is talking, they're wrapped up in rehearsing what they're going to say when they get a chance. These people show little awareness of the negative effects they have on their listeners.

People who are self-preoccupied can cause negative reactions in others for several reasons. First, the content of their remarks is usually so self-serving (seeking to impress, to gain unwarranted sympathy, and so on) that others find it offensive. Another problem is that these people consistently take up more than their fair share of conversation time. Some individuals do both—that is, they talk only about themselves *and* they do so at great length. After a "conversation" with someone like this, listeners feel that their need to communicate has been ignored. Usually they try to avoid such individuals if they can. If they can't, they tend to respond only minimally to try to end the conversation as quickly as possible. Needless to say, people who fail to respect the social norm that conversations entail a mutual sharing of information risk alienating others.

Game Playing

"Game playing" is another barrier to effective communication. Game playing was first described by Eric Berne (1964), who originated transactional analysis. **Transactional analysis is a broad theory of personality and interpersonal relations that emphasizes patterns of communication.** In Berne's scheme, **games are manipulative interactions progressing toward a predictable outcome, in which people conceal their real motivations.** In the broadest sense, game playing can include the deliberate (or sometimes unintentional) use of ambiguous, indirect, or deceptive statements. Some game playing involves "verbal fencing" to avoid having to make clear one's meaning or intent. Particularly problematic are repetitive games that result in bad feelings and erode the trust and respect that are essential to good relationships. Games interfere with effective communication and are a destructive element in relationships.

Collusion

In contrast to the other barriers to effective communication, collusion requires at least two willing partners. These partners are usually involved in an intimate relationship. **In *collusion*, two people have an unspoken agreement to deny some problematic aspect of reality in order to sustain their relationship.** To accomplish this mutual denial, both suppress all discussion of the problem area. The classic example of collusion is the alcoholic partnership. In this case, the alcoholic person requires the partner to join him or her in denying the existence of a drinking problem. To maintain the relationship, the partner goes along with the tacit agreement. The two people go to great lengths to avoid any comment about alcohol-related difficulties. Over time, the drinking usually gets worse and the relationship often deteriorates, thereby making it more difficult for the partner to continue the collusion. Because it is based on a mutual agreement to deny a specific aspect of reality, collusion obviously prevents effective communication.

Miscommunication and Date Rape

Learning Objective

Distinguish between date rape and acquaintance rape.

Although date rape involves more than just communication gone awry, poor communication is a key factor surprisingly often. We have chosen to discuss this subject here, rather than in our chapter on sexuality, because the evidence indicates that rape is *not* really an expression of sexuality but rather an act of aggression. Sex is the means by which the rapist expresses power and hostility, not attraction and passion (Browne & Williams, 1993; Knight, Rosenberg, & Schneider, 1985). Although the vast majority of rape survivors are women, about 5% of rape survivors are men. Male rape usually occurs in prison settings, where sex is used to establish dominance. While rare, there are instances of women raping men (men don't have total voluntary control over erections) (Sarrel & Masters, 1982). Obviously, the experience of rape is traumatic, regardless of one's gender. Because the vast majority of rapes are committed by men, our discussion will center on women as the victims of rape. Although sexual aggression is typically discussed in a heterosexual context, it also occurs among homosexual couples; however, little if any research exists on this topic (Lobel, 1986; Rozee, Bateman, & Gilmore, 1991).

Acquaintance rape **occurs when a woman is forced to have unwanted intercourse with someone she knows.** Acquaintance rape includes not only rapes committed on dates but also those committed by nonromantic acquaintances ("friends," co-workers, neighbors, relatives). *Date rape* **is a more restrictive term that refers to forced and unwanted intercourse with someone in the context of dating.** Date rape can occur on a first date, with someone one has dated for a while, or with someone to whom one is engaged. Many people confuse date rape with seduction. The latter occurs when a woman is persuaded *and agrees* to have sex. Date rape often occurs when seduction fails and the man has sex with the woman without her consent.

The force involved in date rape typically can be verbal or physical coercion, but it may sometimes involve the use of a weapon. One study of 190 male undergraduates at a Southern university found that the following tactics were used: verbal persuasion (70%), ignoring a woman's protests (35%), physical restraint (11%), threats of physical aggression (3%), and physical aggression (3%) (Rapaport & Burkhart, 1984).

Incidence of Rape

Learning Objective

Discuss the incidence and consequences of rape.

It is difficult to obtain accurate information about the prevalence of any form of rape (it is estimated that 90% of all rapes are never reported). Experts estimate that the chances of a woman being raped sometime in her lifetime range between 14% and 25% (Koss, 1993). Contrary to popular belief, only a minority of reported rapes are committed by strangers: 1 out of 5. The majority of rape victims are between the ages of 15 and 25.

How common is rape among *college students*? In a widely cited study, Mary Koss and her colleagues surveyed approximately 7000 students at 32 colleges about their sexual experiences since age 14 (Koss, Gidycz, & Wisniewski, 1987). They found that 15% of the women had been victims of actual rape and that another 12% had experienced attempted rape. Moreover, 8% of the men admitted to either having forced a woman to have intercourse or having tried to do so. However, *none* of these men identified himself as a rapist. Similarly, among the women who reported experiencing sexual aggression that met the legal definition of rape, only 27% actually labeled their own experience "rape."

Mary Koss

These results suggest that there is a lot of confusion and self-deception about what constitutes rape. Many people seem to believe that if a stranger leaps out of the bushes and sexually attacks you, it is rape. On the other hand, if someone you know forces you to have sex, then it isn't rape. In fact, of the women in the college survey who reported experiences that met the legal definition of rape, only 11% had been raped by strangers. The vast majority had been raped by someone they knew: 30% by steady dates, 25% by nonromantic acquaintances, and 9% by husbands or other family members. Because of the widespread reluctance to see acquaintance rape for what it is, Koss (1985) has labeled it "a hidden crime." Its hidden nature causes women who have been raped to question and doubt themselves and allows men to deny responsibility for their behavior. These patterns of thinking also encourage "blaming the victim."

Consequences of Rape

All rape is traumatic, but it is particularly shattering when a woman is raped by someone she has cared for and trusted. In addition, because most women are not used to the idea that rape can occur with someone they know, it is particularly difficult for a victim of date or acquaintance rape to deal with her feelings of betrayal, rage, and shame (Katz, 1991). (A helpful book for survivors of date and acquaintance rape, *Recovering from Rape*, is described in the Recommended Reading.) Rape survivors typically experience the same symptoms as others coping with posttraumatic stress disorder, as we noted in Chapter 4 (Koss, 1993). Although not all women are affected by rape in the same way, most rape survivors go through three stages: trauma, denial, and resolution.

1. *Trauma.* Women experience a variety of emotional reactions to rape. Chief among them are fear of being alone, fear of men, fear of retaliation (especially if charges are filed), and fear of trusting subsequent dating partners. Feelings of depression, anger, helplessness, guilt, pain, shame, and anxiety are also common. Many

---

Recommended Reading

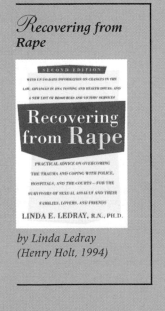

Recovering from Rape

by Linda Ledray
(Henry Holt, 1994)

This comprehensive handbook offers rape survivors and their loved ones both emotional support and practical guidance in overcoming the trauma of rape. Each chapter contains a section addressed to the survivor and to the significant other. The author, both a nurse and clinical psychologist who has worked with rape survivors for 20 years, guides the reader through the painful and complex initial emotional reactions toward recovery. The book also offers expert advice for the many practical issues that must be confronted: coping with the police, getting medical attention, getting tested for sexually transmitted diseases and pregnancy, telling other people (who, when, and how), and whether to prosecute the rapist. Other chapters address such topics as childhood sexual assault, rapists and their motives, and the prevention of rape. At the end of the book, the author provides suggested readings as well as a list of resources and victims' services, by state. The following excerpt addresses the importance of social support in the recovery process.

Numerous reports, books, and articles resulting from years of study and research in all types of crises, including rape, show that next to your own resilience, the key factor in your recovery is support from family and friends. Their support and understanding are important in helping you better deal with the emotional trauma and resolve the fear, anxiety, and depression. It's much easier to take risks and face what you see as potentially dangerous, uncomfortable, frightening situations with someone beside you. Although social support cannot make up for feeling that you lack control over your life and surroundings, it certainly can give you the extra confidence necessary to take calculated risks, face your fears, and overcome the immobilizing effects of anxiety and depression. [p. 105] rape victims show signs of stress-related physical problems. Emotional reactions can be exacerbated if the woman's family and friends are not supportive—particularly if family or friends blame the victim for the attack. As we saw in Chapter 6, it is common for people to blame victims of calamities (defensive attribution).

2. *Denial.* In this stage—which may last for months or years—rape victims try to put the trauma behind them and get on with their lives. During this period, women avoid talking about their rape as they try to deny that it took place. This strategy generally fails as a long-term solution because the powerful and painful emotions don't just go away.

3. *Resolution.* In order to move beyond the experience, a woman needs to deal with her feelings by talking with someone who is supportive and understanding: a friend, a counselor, or a member of the clergy. Once she has worked through her feelings and fears, she may be able to put the trauma in the past and begin to feel in control of her life again. Still, it is likely that she will always be haunted by the experience.

There are other consequences of rape, some affecting both the man and the woman. It is not uncommon for women to drop out of school because of the trauma and lack of social support. Also, the grades of the man and woman may suffer because of emotional distress and inability to concentrate on their studies. Moreover, if the rape survivor prosecutes her attacker, the man faces criminal proceedings. If he is a student, he may be suspended from school whether or not the woman takes the case to court. And both may have to deal with negative publicity and social stigma.

Factors Contributing to Date Rape

Learning Objective

Discuss three noncommunication factors that contribute to rape.

The phenomenon of date rape can be traced to a variety of underlying factors. Communication problems are often critical, but before we focus on those, let's briefly examine some other contributing factors.

- *Gender roles.* Traditional norms of courtship suggest that males should initiate dates and sex, while females either consent or decline these advances. Society still encourages a double standard for males and females when it comes to sexual behavior. Men are encouraged to have sexual feelings, to act on them, and to "score," whereas women are discouraged from being sexual unless they are "carried away" by passion. This double standard promotes hidden norms that condone sexual aggression by men in dating relationships. These values are also reflected in men's and women's beliefs about when sexual intercourse is appropriate in a relationship. In one survey, half of the men felt sexual intercourse was appropriate by the fifth date; however, only 23% of the women felt this way (Knox & Wilson, 1981).

- *Alcohol and drugs.* Drinking heavily or taking drugs on dates makes it likely that a person's judgment will be impaired. In these circumstances, both men and women are likely to be less inhibited. Unfortunately, alcohol and drugs make some men more willing to use force and women more vulnerable to the use of force (Shotland & Hunter, 1995). If a woman passes out, she is easy prey for anyone who is willing to take advantage of her.

- *Sexual violence in the media.* Laboratory research on the effects of aggressive pornography (depicting rape and other sexual violence against women) suggests that such material elevates some men's tendency to behave aggressively toward women (Malamuth & Donnerstein, 1982). Related research has shown that exposure to such material can increase male viewers' willingness to say that they would commit a rape, while decreasing their sensitivity to rape and the plight of rape victims (Donnerstein & Linz, 1984). Furthermore, men who have viewed sexually violent films report greater acceptance of rape myths as well as greater acceptance of interpersonal violence against women (Malamuth & Check, 1981). Figure 7.11 presents selected items from two scales often used to measure sexual aggression. Because aggressive pornography is being displayed more frequently in films and on television, it is reasonable to speculate that media depictions are contributing to an increase in rape.

Figure 7.11
Assessing attitudes about sexual aggression
Researchers use carefully constructed scales to assess individuals' attitudes about sexual aggression. Sample items from two such scales are shown here. (Adapted from Burt, 1980)

Measuring Attitudes Toward Sexual Aggression

Rape Myth Acceptance Scale	Acceptance of Interpersonal Violence Scale
1 When women go around braless or wearing short skirts and tight tops, they are just asking for trouble.	1 Being roughed up sexually is stimulating to many women.
2 If a girl engages in necking or petting and she lets things get out of hand, it is her own fault if her partner forces sex on her.	2 Sometimes the only way a man can get a cold woman turned on is to use force.
3 Many women have an unconscious wish to be raped, and may then unconsciously set up a situation in which they are likely to be attacked.	3 A man is never justified in hitting his wife.
SCORING: People who score high on this scale agree with all of the above items.	SCORING: People who score high on this scale agree with items 1 and 2 and disagree with item 3.

The Role of Miscommunication in Date Rape

Learning Objective

Discuss the role of miscommunication in date rape.

Miscommunication between dating partners often is a key factor contributing to date rape. Among dating couples, frank conversations about whether to engage in sexual activities, which behaviors are permissible, and what to do about birth control are, regrettably, the exception rather than the rule (Abbey, 1991; Knox & Wilson, 1981). For one thing, most people (young people, especially) are embarrassed to talk about sex. For another, many feel that talking about sex takes the mystery out of it. Also, because there aren't any hard and fast rules about when sexual activities should occur in dating, sexual decision making is highly dependent on situational forces.

Another problem is that dating partners often misunderstand what the other means. For instance, research shows that males are more likely than females to perceive friendly behavior as having sexual intent (Kowalski, 1993; Muehlenhard, 1988; Shotland, 1989). This is particularly true for men who endorse traditional attitudes toward women and who score high on scales of rape myth acceptance and adversarial sexual beliefs, such as that women are manipulative in sexual relationships (Kowalski, 1993). Such men can think a woman has communicated sexual interest (and act accordingly) when, in fact, she has not. If a man doesn't make an effort to clarify a woman's intentions, he can easily let himself feel that he has been "led on." He may then use his anger as an excuse to force the woman to have sex. Also, some men still believe that if they spend money on a woman, she owes them sex (Shotland, 1989).

Misunderstandings also occur in dating relationships because social norms encourage game playing. Thus, dating partners may not always say what they mean or mean what they say. Some women may say "no" (in words or in nonverbal behavior) to sexual activity when they actually mean "maybe" or "yes." Studies surveying the extent of "token resistance" among college women report that approximately 38% of them have engaged in this behavior (Muehlenhard & Hollabaugh, 1988; Shotland & Hunter, 1995).

The researchers were also interested in why the women engaged in token resistance (Muehlenhard & Hollabaugh, 1988). Participants' responses were grouped into three categories: (1) *practical reasons* (fear of pregnancy), (2) *inhibition-related reasons* (emotional, religious, and moral worries), and (3) *manipulative reasons* (getting the man more aroused, being in control). Looking more carefully at these reasons, other researchers reasoned that practical and inhibition-related concerns seemed to explain sexual refusal but not token resistance (Shotland & Hunter, 1995). And, although manipulative reasons could explain token resistance, the number of women who engage in token resistant behavior for these reasons is relatively small (23%).

As a more viable explanation, these researchers hypothesized that token resistance reflects women's changing sexual intentions as relationships develop over time. In other words, as dating proceeds, both pressure to have sex and sexual

The trials of Mike Tyson and William Kennedy Smith focused public attention on the problem of date rape. The different perceptions of defendants and victims in both trials attested to the key role of miscommunication, among other factors, in date rape.

arousal usually increase. Too, some of women's concerns may diminish. Thus, women may change their intentions to have sex. Several findings seem to support this view. First, sexual refusals occurred before the 11th date, while token resistant behavior occurred after this time. Second, on a given date, refusals occurred earlier and token resistance, later. Third, 83% of women who used token resistance reported having more than one sexual intention during a date, while only 34% of women who said "no" and meant it reported having multiple sexual intentions. Note that neither the patterning of token resistant behavior nor a change in sexual intentions would be predicted by a "manipulation" explanation.

Of course, some women *do* engage in token resistance for manipulative purposes. This behavior occurs more often among women who are already involved in a sexual relationship than among those who are not, and it is often related to the woman's dissatisfaction with sexual practices in the relationship. The most frequently given "manipulative" reason for token resistance was "I wanted to be in control—the one to say when"—probably a reflection of women's role as regulators of sexual activity and its timing (Shotland & Hunter, 1995). Relatively few women gave patently manipulative reasons such as "I was angry with him and wanted to get back" or "I wanted him to beg." These findings are important because research has shown that men who believe that women are sexually manipulative are likely to be sexually aggressive and may rape their partners (Koss et al., 1985; Muehlenhard & Linton, 1987). It is important that men recognize that most women do not engage in token resistance for hostile and manipulative reasons.

The double standard presents women with an avoidance-avoidance conflict. If they openly acknowledge their interest in sex (don't use token resistance), they risk being perceived as "easy" by men who believe in the double standard. But, if women use token resistance as a tactic for coping with their dates' standards, they also put themselves at risk because using token resistance sets the stage for miscommunication—and sometimes for tragedy (Kowalski, 1993; Muehlenhard & McCoy, 1991).

Reducing the Incidence of Date Rape

Learning Objective

List some suggestions for reducing the incidence of date rape.

What can be done to reduce the incidence of date rape? We offer the following suggestions to people in dating relationships: (1) Recognize date rape for what it is: an act of sexual aggression. (2) Think through your feelings, values, and intentions about sexual relations *before* the question of having sex arises. (3) Communicate your feelings and expectations about sex by engaging in appropriate self-disclosure. (4) Listen carefully to each other and respect each other's wishes. (5) Beware of excessive alcohol and drug use, which may deprive you of control. (6) Exercise control over your environment: Agree to go only to *public* places (not apartments) until you know someone very well, and always carry enough money for transportation back home. (7) Know the warning signs associated with pre-rape behavior (see Figure 7.12), and be cautious in dating those who exhibit more than one of them. (8) Be prepared to act *aggressively* if assertive refusals don't stop unwanted advances.

Many of these suggestions involve efforts to improve interpersonal communication. Obviously, improved communication will not eliminate date rape, but it can go a long way toward reducing the problem.

Dealing Constructively with Conflict

Learning Objective

Define interpersonal conflict and discuss how constructive confrontation can be helpful.

Conflict is an unavoidable feature of interpersonal interaction. Therefore, learning to deal with it constructively is an important aspect of effective communication. People do not have to be enemies to be in conflict, and being in conflict does not make people enemies. **Interpersonal conflict exists whenever two or more people disagree.** By this definition, conflict will occur between friends and lovers, as well as

Typical Characteristics of Date Rapists

Sexual entitlement	Power and control	Hostility and anger	Acceptance of interpersonal violence
Touching women with no regard for their wishes	Interrupting people, especially women	Showing a quick temper	Using threats in displays of anger
Sexualizing relationships that are appropriately not sexual	Being a bad loser	Blaming others when things go wrong	Using violence in borderline situations
Engaging in conversation that is inappropriately intimate	Exhibiting inappropriate competitiveness	Tending to transform other emotions into anger	Approving observed violence
Telling sexual jokes at inappropriate times or places	Using intimidating body language		Justifying violence
Making inappropriate comments about women's bodies, sexuality, and so on	Game playing		

Figure 7.12
Date rapists: Warning signs
According to Rozee, Bateman, and Gilmore (1991), four factors appear to distinguish date rapists: feelings of sexual entitlement, a penchant for exerting power and control, high hostility and anger, and acceptance of interpersonal violence. The presence of more than one of these characteristics is an important warning sign (Malamuth, 1986). When sexual entitlement is coupled with any other factor, special heed should be taken.

Learning Objective

Describe five personal styles of dealing with interpersonal conflict.

between competitors and enemies. The discord may be caused by a simple misunderstanding or be a product of incompatible goals, values, attitudes, or beliefs.

Many people have the impression that conflict is inherently bad and that it should be suppressed if at all possible. In reality, conflict is neither inherently bad nor inherently good. Conflict is a natural phenomenon that may lead to either good or bad outcomes, depending on how people deal with it. Avoidance tends to be one of the worst ways of coping with conflict. Interpersonal discord that is suppressed usually affects a relationship in spite of efforts to conceal it, and the effects of suppressing it tend to be negative (Baxter & Wilmot, 1985). When dealt with openly and constructively, interpersonal conflict can lead to a variety of valuable outcomes (Johnson & Johnson, 1994). Among other things, constructive confrontation may (1) bring problems out into the open where they can be solved, (2) put an end to chronic sources of discontent in a relationship, and (3) lead to new insights through the clashing of divergent views.

Personal Styles of Dealing with Conflict

How do you react to conflict? Most people have a certain personal style in dealing with conflict (Sternberg & Soriano, 1984). We will describe five common styles in this section, so that you can see where you fit in (see Figure 7.13). These five modes of dealing with conflict—avoidance, accommodation, domination, compromise, and integration—are based on theoretical models pioneered by Blake and Mouton (1964) and Thomas (1976).

Avoidance Some people simply don't like to face up to the existence of conflict. They operate under the unrealistic hope that if they ignore the problem, it will go away. When a conflict emerges, the avoider will change the subject, make a hasty exit, or pretend to be preoccupied with something else. This person finds conflict extremely unpleasant and distasteful and will go to great lengths to avoid being drawn into a confrontation. Of course, most problems will not go away while one pretends they don't exist. This style generally just delays the inevitable clash. Avoidance is not an adequate means of dealing with conflict.

Accommodation Like the avoider, the accommodating person feels uncomfortable with conflict. However, instead of ignoring the disagreement, this person brings the conflict to a quick end by giving in easily. This style grows out of basic feelings of insecurity. People who are overly worried about acceptance and approval from others are likely to use this strategy of surrender. Accommodation is a poor way of dealing with conflict because it does not generate creative thinking and genuine solutions. Moreover, feelings of resentment (on both sides) may develop because the accommodating person often likes to play the role of a martyr.

Domination   The dominator turns every conflict into a black-and-white, win-or-lose situation. This person will do virtually anything to emerge victorious from the confrontation. The dominator tends to be aggressive and deceitful. This person rigidly adheres to one position and will use threats and coercion to force the other party to submit. Giving no quarter, the dominator will often get personal and "hit below the belt." This style is undesirable because, like accommodation, it does not generate creative thinking aimed at mutual problem solving. Moreover, this approach is particularly likely to lead to postconflict tension, resentment, and hostility.

Compromise   Compromise is a pragmatic approach to conflict that acknowledges the divergent needs of both parties. A compromise approach involves negotiation and a willingness to meet the other person halfway. While trying to be reasonable, the compromiser nonetheless works hard to maximize the satisfaction of his or her own needs. Thus, the compromise approach may involve some manipulation and misrepresentation. Compromise is a fairly constructive approach to conflict, but its manipulative aspects make it somewhat inferior to the final approach, that of integration.

Integration   While compromise simply entails "splitting the difference" between positions, integration involves a sincere effort to find a solution that will maximize the satisfaction of both parties. When this approach is used, the conflict is viewed as a mutual problem to be solved as effectively as possible. Integration thus encourages openness and honesty. Also, integration stresses the importance of criticizing the other person's *ideas* in a disagreement rather than the other *person*. Integration requires putting a lot of effort into clarifying differences and similarities in positions, so that both can build on the similarities. Generally, this is the most productive approach for dealing with conflict. Instead of resulting in a postconflict residue of tension and resentment, integration tends to produce a climate of trust.

Figure 7.13
Johnson's (1981) characterization of the five styles of dealing with interpersonal conflict
David Johnson has playfully used the stereotypic characteristics of five animals to capture the essence of the five basic styles of dealing with conflict.

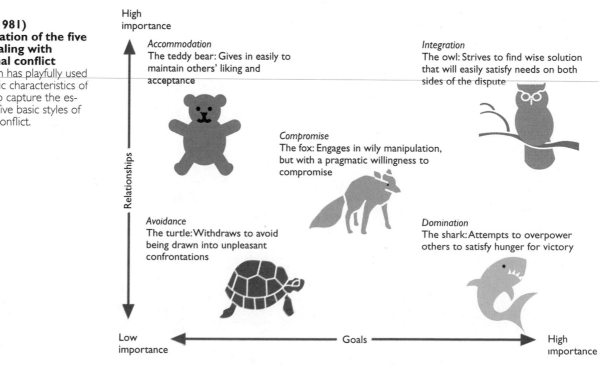

High importance

Accommodation
The teddy bear: Gives in easily to maintain others' liking and acceptance

Integration
The owl: Strives to find wise solution that will easily satisfy needs on both sides of the dispute

Compromise
The fox: Engages in wily manipulation, but with a pragmatic willingness to compromise

Avoidance
The turtle: Withdraws to avoid being drawn into unpleasant confrontations

Domination
The shark: Attempts to overpower others to satisfy hunger for victory

Relationships

Low importance   Goals   High importance

Guidelines for Constructive Conflict Resolution

In the preceding section, we emphasized the desirability of integration as an approach to conflict resolution. In this section, we offer some specific suggestions to help you implement such an approach. Before you actually get down to talking, though, there are some things you need to keep in mind (Alberti & Emmons, 1990; Johnson & Johnson, 1994). First, it's important to acknowledge the existence of a conflict. Second, you should approach the conflict as equals, with a balance of power between the two of you. If you have a higher status or more power (parent, supervisor), try to set this difference aside. Third, define the conflict as a mutual problem to be solved cooperatively, rather than as a win-lose proposition. Fourth, choose a mutually acceptable time to sit down and work on resolving the conflict. It is not always best to tackle the conflict when and where it first arises. Finally, remember to show respect for the other person's position. Try to empathize with, and fully understand, his or her frame of reference.

Here now are some explicit guidelines to help you achieve an integrative style of dealing with interpersonal conflict (Alberti & Emmons, 1990; Johnson & Johnson, 1994):

- Make communication honest and open. Don't withhold information or misrepresent your position. Avoid deceit and manipulation.
- Phrase your statements about another person's annoying habits in terms of specific behaviors rather than global personality traits. (Remarks of the latter sort are more likely to be taken personally.) Similarly, avoid saying things like "You always . . ."
- Assume responsibility for your own feelings and preferences. Instead of "*You* make me mad," say "*I* am angry." Or, try "I'd appreciate it if you'd water the garden" rather than "Don't you think the garden needs watering?"
- Put a great deal of effort into clarifying your respective positions. It is imperative that each of you understands the exact nature of your disagreements.
- Communicate your flexibility and willingness to modify your position.
- Emphasize the similarities in your positions rather than the differences. Try to use those similarities to build toward a mutually satisfactory solution.

In our upcoming Application, we will discuss assertive communication, a communication style that has proved extremely effective across a wide variety of interpersonal communication situations, including making acquaintances, developing relationships, and resolving interpersonal conflicts.

Application

Learning to Be Assertive

Answer the following questions "yes" or "no."

1. When someone asks you for an unreasonable favor, do you have difficulty saying "no"?

2. Do you feel timid about returning flawed merchandise?

3. Do you have a hard time requesting even small favors from others?

4. When you're in a group that is hotly debating an issue, are you shy about speaking up?

5. When a salesperson pressures you to buy something you don't want, do you have a hard time expressing your lack of interest?

If you answered "yes" to several of these questions, you may have difficulty being assertive. Many people have a hard time being assertive; however, this problem is more common among females, because they are socialized to be more submissive than males—for example, to "be nice" and not to "make waves." Consequently, assertiveness training has become especially popular among women. Men, too, find assertiveness training helpful, both because some males have been socialized to be passive and because some men want to learn to be less aggressive and more assertive. In this Application, we'll elaborate on the differences between assertive, submissive, and aggressive behavior and discuss some procedures for increasing assertiveness.

The Nature of Assertiveness

Learning Objective

Differentiate assertive communication from submissive and aggressive communication and discuss the adaptiveness of each style.

Assertiveness involves acting in one's own best interests by expressing one's thoughts and feelings directly and honestly (Alberti & Emmons, 1990; Bower & Bower, 1991). Essentially, assertiveness involves standing up for your rights when someone else is about to infringe on them. To be assertive is to speak out openly rather than pull your punches.

The nature of assertive communication can best be clarified by contrasting it with submissive communication and aggressive communication. *Submissive communication* is consistently giving in to others on points of possible contention. Submissive people tend to let others take advantage of them. Typically, their biggest problem is that they cannot say "no" to unreasonable requests. A common example is the college student who can't tell her roommate not to borrow her clothes. They also have difficulty voicing disagreement with others and making requests themselves. In traditional trait terminology, they are timid. Although the roots of submissiveness have not been investigated fully, they appear to lie in excessive concern about gaining the social approval of others. However, the strategy of not making waves is more likely to garner others' contempt than their approval. Moreover, individuals who use this style often feel bad about themselves (for being "pushovers") and resentful of those whom they allow to take advantage of them. These feelings often lead the submissive individual to try to punish the other person by withdrawing, sulking, or crying (Bower & Bower, 1991). These manipulative attempts to get one's own way are sometimes referred to as "passive aggression" or "indirect aggression."

It is sometimes difficult to differentiate between assertive communication and aggressive communication. In principle, the distinction is fairly simple. *Aggressive communication* involves an intention to hurt or harm another. Assertive behavior includes no such intention to inflict harm, but it does involve defending your rights. The problem in real life is that assertive and aggressive behavior *may* overlap. When someone is about to infringe on their rights, people often lash out at the other party (aggression) while defending their rights (assertion). The challenge, then, is to learn to be firm and assertive without going a step too far and becoming aggressive.

Advocates of assertive communication argue that it is much more adaptive than either submissive or aggressive communication (Alberti & Emmons, 1990; Bower & Bower, 1991). They maintain that submissive behavior leads to poor self-esteem, self-denial, emotional suppression, and strained interpersonal relationships. They assert that aggressive communication tends to promote guilt, alienation, and disharmony. In contrast, assertive behavior is said to foster high self-esteem and satisfactory interpersonal relationships.

Of course, behaving assertively does *not ensure* that you will always get what you want. The essential point with assertiveness is that you are able to state what you want clearly and directly. Being able to do so makes you feel good about yourself and will usually make others feel good about you, too. And, although being assertive doesn't guarantee your chances of getting what you want, it certainly enhances them.

Steps in Assertiveness Training

Numerous assertiveness training programs are available in book form or through seminars. Some recommendations about books appear in the Recommended Reading box in this section. Most of the programs are behavioral and emphasize gradual improvement and reinforcement of appropriate behavior. Here we will summarize the key steps in assertiveness training.

1. Clarify the Nature of Assertive Communication

Most programs begin, as we have, by clarifying the nature of assertive communication. In order to produce assertive behavior, you need to understand what it looks and sounds like. One way to accomplish this is to imagine situations calling for assertiveness and compare hypothetical submissive (or passive), assertive, and aggressive responses. Let's consider one such comparison. In this example, a woman in assertiveness training is asking her roommate to cooperate in cleaning the apartment once a week. The roommate, who is uninterested in the problem, is listening to music when the conversation begins. In this example, the roommate is playing the role of the antagonist—called "Downer" in the following scripts (excerpted from Bower & Bower, 1991, pp. 8, 9, 11).

> *The Passive Scene*
> SHE: Uh, I was wondering if you would be willing to take time to decide about the housecleaning.
> DOWNER: *(listening to the music)* Not now, I'm busy.
> SHE: Oh, okay.
>
> *The Aggressive Scene*
> SHE: Listen, I've had it with you not even talking about cleaning this damn apartment. Are you going to help me?
> DOWNER: *(listening to the music)* Not now, I'm busy.
> SHE: Why can't you look at me when you turn me down? You don't give a damn about the housework or me! You only care about yourself!
> DOWNER: That's not true.
> SHE: You never pay any attention to the apartment or to me. I have to do everything around here!

DOWNER: Oh, shut up! You're just neurotic about cleaning all the time. Who are you, my mother? Can't I relax with my stereo for a few minutes without you pestering me? This was my apartment first, you know!

The Assertive Scene
SHE: I know housework isn't the most fascinating subject, but it needs to be done. Let's plan when we'll do it.
DOWNER: *(listening to the music)* Oh, c'mon—not now! I'm busy.
SHE: This won't take long. I feel that if we have a schedule, it will be easier to keep up with the chores.
DOWNER: I'm not sure I'll have time for all of them.
SHE: I've already drawn up a couple of rotating schedules for housework, so that each week we have an equal division of task. Will you look at them? I'd like to hear your decisions about them, say, tonight after supper?
DOWNER: *(indignantly)* I have to look at these now?
SHE: Is there some other time that's better for you?
DOWNER: Oh, I don't know.
SHE: Well, then let's discuss plans after supper for fifteen minutes. Is that agreed?
DOWNER: I guess so.
SHE: Good! It won't take long, and I'll feel relieved when we have a schedule in place.

For people to whom assertive communication is unfamiliar, the process of clarifying the nature of assertiveness can be critical. In such cases, it may be a good idea to read two or three books on assertiveness to get a good picture of assertive behavior. The differences between the three types of behavior may best be conceptualized in terms of how people deal with their own rights and the rights of others. Submissive people sacrifice their own rights. Aggressive people tend to ignore

There are more than 20 books on assertiveness training, and many of them are fairly good. However, the Bowers' book is especially strong because it is specific, detailed, and concrete. Bower and Bower put the problem of nonassertiveness into perspective, relating it to self-esteem and anxiety. They then lay out a systematic program for increasing assertive behavior. They make extensive use of probing questions to help you work out a plan of action that is personally relevant. They also provide sample verbal scripts for numerous common situations that typically call for assertive behavior. Among other topics they cover are requesting a raise, saying "no" to unreasonable demands, protesting unjust criticism, dealing with a substance abuser, protesting annoying habits, and dealing with the silent treatment. Also, they devote a whole chapter to the role of assertive behavior in developing friendships—initiating and ending conversations, keeping conversations going, making dates, using self-disclosure, listening, and coping with social anxieties. The book is smoothly written in a nonpatronizing tone. (An excerpt is included in this Application.)

Other books on assertiveness can also be recommended highly. Especially noteworthy is one of the very first entries in this area, *Your Perfect Right*, by Robert E. Alberti and Michael L. Emmons (1990), which is now in its sixth edition. Many books have been written with women in mind and focus on the unique problems women encounter. Of these, *The Assertive Woman*, by Stanlee Phelps and Nancy Austin (1987) appears particularly useful.

the rights of others. Assertive people consider both their own rights and the rights of others.

As we learned earlier in this chapter, the nonverbal aspect of communication is extremely important. To ensure that your assertive words have impact, it is important that you back them up with congruent nonverbal messages. That is, you'll come across as more assertive if you face the person you're talking with, look directly at him or her, and maintain eye contact, rather than looking away, fidgeting, slouching, and shuffling your feet (Bower & Bower, 1991).

2. Monitor Your Assertive Communication

Most people vary in assertiveness from one situation to another. In other words, they may be assertive in some social contexts and timid in others. Consequently, once you understand the nature of assertive communication, you should monitor yourself and identify when you are nonassertive. In particular, you should figure out *who* intimidates you, on *what topics*, and in *which situations*.

3. Observe a Model's Assertive Communication

Once you have identified the situations in which you are nonassertive, think of someone who communicates assertively in those situations and observe that person's behavior closely. In other words, find someone to model yourself after. This person should help you to learn how to behave assertively in situations crucial to you. Your observations should also allow you to see how rewarding assertive communication can be, which should strengthen your assertive tendencies.

4. Practice Assertive Communication

Ultimately, the key to achieving assertive communication is to practice it and work toward gradual improvement. Your practice can take several forms. In *covert rehearsal*, you can imagine a situation requiring assertion and the dialogue that you would engage in. In *role playing*, you might get a therapist or friend to play the role of an antagonist, then practice communicating assertively in this artificial situation.

Eventually, of course, you want to transfer your assertiveness skills to real-life situations. Most experts recommend that you use *shaping* to increase your assertive communication gradually. As we discussed in the Chapter 4 Application, shaping involves rewarding yourself for making closer and closer approximations of a desired behavior. For example, in the early stages of your behavior-change program, your goal might be to make at least one assertive comment every day, while toward the end you might be striving to make at least eight such comments every day. Obviously, in designing a shaping program, it is important to set realistic goals for yourself.

5. Adopt an Assertive Attitude

Most assertiveness training programs use a behavioral orientation and focus on specific responses for specific situations. However, it's obvious that real-life situations are only rarely just like those portrayed in books. Hence, some experts maintain that acquiring a repertoire of verbal responses for certain situations is not as important as developing a new attitude that you're not going to let people push you around (or let yourself push others around, if you're the aggressive type) (Alberti & Emmons, 1990). Although most programs don't talk explicitly about attitudes, they do appear to instill a new attitude indirectly. A change in attitude is probably crucial to achieving flexible, assertive behavior.

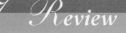

Key Ideas

The Process of Interpersonal Communication

• Interpersonal communication is the interactional process that occurs when one person sends a message to another. Communication takes place when a source sends a message to a receiver either verbally or nonverbally. Although people often take it for granted, effective communication contributes to their satisfaction and success in relationships and on the job.

Nonverbal Communication

• Nonverbal communication tends to be more spontaneous than verbal communication, and it is also more ambiguous. Sometimes it contradicts what is communicated verbally. It is often multichanneled, and, like language, it is culturally bound. Nonverbal communication frequently conveys emotions. Elements of nonverbal communication include personal space, facial expression, eye contact, body language, touch, and paralanguage.

• Proxemics deals with the use of personal space. Edward Hall has described how specific distances are maintained in certain kinds of social relationships. When these norms are violated and personal space is invaded, people tend to react negatively.

• Facial expressions often convey emotional states. However, it is relatively easy to send deceptive signals with the face. The duration of eye contact is an important cue and may communicate either highly positive or strongly negative feelings. Cultural, gender, racial, and status differences have been found in patterns of eye contact.

• Body movements and posture may indicate a person's relaxation and attitude toward others. Hand gestures are used primarily to regulate and supplement speech. Touching can convey a variety of meanings. Paralanguage is concerned with the use of vocal emphasis in speaking. Slight variations in vocal emphasis can reverse the literal meaning of a message.

• Certain nonverbal cues are associated with deception, but many of these cues do not correspond to popular beliefs about how liars give themselves away. Discrepancies between facial expressions and other nonverbal signals may suggest dishonesty. The vocal and visual cues associated with lying are so subtle, however, that the detection of deception is difficult. Machines that are used for detecting deception (polygraphs) are not particularly accurate.

• Nonverbal communication plays an important role in adjustment, especially in the quality of interpersonal relationships.

Verbal Communication

• Verbal communication consists of both speaking and listening. Effective communication rests on a foundation of a positive interpersonal climate. To promote a positive interpersonal climate, it helps to show empathy, treat people as equals, withhold judgment, strive for honesty, and express opinions tentatively. To be an effective communicator, it's essential to have good speaking and listening skills. We are often careless and sloppy speakers as well as inattentive and preoccupied listeners.

• Self-disclosure, or opening up to others, is the key to developing emotional intimacy in relationships. Inappropriate self-disclosure, however, can cause interpersonal difficulties. Women tend to engage in more self-disclosure than men, but this disparity is not so consistent as it was once believed to be. The reciprocity norm is an important situational factor that influences self-disclosure.

Communication Problems and Interpersonal Conflict

• A number of problems can arise that interfere with effective communication. Individuals who become overly anxious when they talk with others suffer from communication apprehension. This difficulty can cause problems in relationships and in work and educational settings. Barriers to effective communication include defensiveness, motivational distortion, self-preoccupation, game playing, and collusion.

• Occasionally, miscommunication figures in tragic situations such as date rape (forced intercourse in the context of dating). Date rape appears to be increasingly common, especially on college campuses, where most victims are raped by someone they know. Misunderstandings about sexual intentions are common in dating relationships because partners often fail to engage in adequate self-disclosure, misinterpret ambiguous nonverbal signals, and engage in game playing.

• Dealing constructively with interpersonal conflict is an important aspect of effective communication. Five common styles of dealing with conflict, ranging from least to most effective, are avoidance, accommodation, domination, compromise, and integration.

Application: Learning to Be Assertive

• An assertive style enables individuals to stand up for themselves and to respect the rights of others. To become more assertive, individuals need to understand what assertive communication is, monitor assertive communication, observe a model's assertive communication, practice being assertive, and adopt an assertive attitude.

Key Terms

Acquaintance rape
Assertiveness
Collusion
Communication apprehension
Communication barrier
Date rape
Display rules
Empathy
Games
Interpersonal communication
Interpersonal conflict
Kinesics
Nonverbal communication
Paralanguage
Personal space
Polygraph
Proxemics
Self-disclosure
Social penetration theory
Transactional analysis
Verbal communication

Key People

Irwin Altman and Dalmas Taylor
Sharon Anthony Bower and Gordon
    Bower
Paul Ekman and Wallace Friesen
Edward T. Hall
Mary Koss

8 Friendship and Love

Ellen Berscheid

$\mathscr{B}$ill was so keyed up, he tossed and turned all night. When morning finally arrived, he was elated. In less than 2 hours, he would be meeting Susan for coffee! When he got to his first class, he found it practically impossible to keep his mind on the lecture. He was constantly distracted by thoughts and images of Susan. When class was finally over, he had to force himself not to walk too fast to the Student Union, where they had agreed to meet. Sound familiar? Chances are that you recognize Bill's behavior as that of someone falling in love.

Love and friendship play vital roles in people's lives. They also play a large role in psychological adjustment. Given their importance, it's ironic that psychologists didn't start studying these phenomena scientifically until the 1970s (Rubin, 1973). Why did research on romantic love get off to such a late start? In part, it was because many people don't believe that love is an appropriate topic for scientific study. For example, in 1975 then-Senator William Proxmire bestowed his infamous Golden Fleece Award (for waste of taxpayers' money) on two social psychologists who had had the audacity to study love. Ellen Berscheid and Elaine Hatfield (then Walster) had conducted pioneering research on love that was funded, in part, by a grant from the National Science Foundation. Despite the fact that their research was widely lauded in scientific circles, Senator Proxmire was not impressed. "Americans want to leave some things in life a mystery," he asserted, "and right at the top of things we don't want to know is why a man falls in love with a woman and vice versa." Because many people shared Proxmire's view, psychological research on love and friendship was slow in getting off the ground.

Currently, however, interpersonal relationships are an active area of research, and we have a wealth of interesting findings to explore. First, we will look at some general theories about how close relationships develop and explore how culture affects people's views of relationships. Next, we'll review some of the factors that are important in determining who is initially attracted to whom. Following that, we'll discuss what psychologists are discovering about friendships and romantic relationships, and we'll consider the problem of loneliness. In the Application section, we'll focus on shyness.

Perspectives on Close Relationships

Learning Objective

Define close relationships and give some examples.

Social psychologists define *close relationships* **as relatively long-lasting relationships in which frequent interactions occur in a variety of settings and in which the impact of these interactions is strong.** In other words, people spend a lot of time and energy maintaining close relationships, and what the other person says or does matters a lot. It matters so much that close relationships have the capacity to arouse intense feelings—both positive (passion, concern, caring) and negative (rage, jealousy, despair).

Close relationships come in many forms: friendships, relationships with family members and co-workers, romantic relationships, marriage. Although many close relationships are based on mutual, intimate self-disclosure, many are not. When college students were asked to identify that person to whom they felt closest, 47% named a romantic partner, 36% listed a friend, 14% mentioned a family member, and 3% listed another individual such as a co-worker (Berscheid, Snyder, & Omoto, 1989). Hence, not all close relationships are characterized by emotional intimacy, as we'll see next.

Identity and Intimate Relationships

Learning Objective

Distinguish among Orlofsky's five intimacy statuses.

As you'll recall from Chapter 5, Erik Erikson posited that identity is a central issue in personality that typically develops during late adolescence (ages 17–22). In addition, he theorized that individuals need to be in the status of identity achievement in order to establish committed, intimate relationships that typically develop in early adulthood (see Chapter 11). Elaborating on Erikson's concept of intimacy, Jacob Orlofsky and his colleagues (1973) constructed interview questions to measure inti-

Drawing by Weber; © 1989 The New Yorker Magazine, Inc.

"My preference is for someone who's afraid of closeness, like me."

macy development based on the criteria of depth and mutuality of interpersonal relationships with same- and other-gender peers. As a result, they established five statuses of intimacy: intimate, preintimate, stereotyped, pseudointimate, and isolate.

Individuals in the *intimate* status form close, open relationships with male and female friends and are involved in a committed relationship. *Preintimate* individuals are also capable of mature, reciprocal relationships, but because of ambivalence about commitment, they have not yet had a relationship to which they are strongly committed. Individuals in the *stereotyped* status have relationships that are superficial. That is, there isn't much openness or closeness, and others are often seen as objects to manipulate rather than persons to share with. Those in the *pseudointimate* status are typically involved in a relatively permanent relationship, but it is one that resembles the stereotyped relationship in quality. *Isolates* avoid social situations and appear to be loners whose social interactions consist of casual conversations after class with a few acquaintances. Note that with the exception of the isolate status, a person's intimacy status isn't determined by whether he or she is *in* a relationship but rather by the *quality* of the relationship he or she has. That is, the distinctions among the statuses hinge on the person's ability to engage in self-disclosure, to feel emotionally close to another person, and to make a commitment to a relationship.

In line with Erikson's theory, research provides some evidence that emotional and sexual intimacy and identity are related. Several studies have found that college men and women in the more advanced identity statuses (achievement and moratorium) are most likely to be in the more advanced intimacy statuses (intimate and preintimate) (Fitch & Adams, 1983; Kacerguis & Adams, 1980). Likewise, foreclosures and diffusions are predominant in the less advanced intimacy statuses (stereotyped, pseudointimate, and isolate). A similar pattern has been found in adults up to 35 years of age (Raskin, 1986; Tesch & Whitbourne, 1982).

Research supports the notion that intimacy and identity are related. What we still need to know is whether identity precedes intimacy or vice versa. Although one study has demonstrated that identity precedes intimacy (Dyk & Adams, 1990), we need more research on this question. In addition, we need to know more about the roles that gender and gender-role orientation play in this process (Adams, 1992). Some theorists (and some research) suggest that intimacy precedes identity development in females (Chodorow, 1978; Gilligan, 1982; Josselson, 1987). Nonetheless, even without answers to these questions, Erikson offers a thought-provoking explanation for why some people are motivated to develop and are capable of developing committed, intimate relationships while others are not.

Social Exchange in Relationships

Let's look at some important principles by which relationships operate. *Social exchange theory* **postulates that interpersonal relationships are governed by perceptions of the rewards and costs exchanged in interactions.** Basically, this model predicts that interactions between acquaintances, friends, and lovers are likely to continue as long as the participants feel that the benefits they derive from the relationship are reasonable in comparison to the costs of being in the relation-

Figure 8.1
Figure 8.1
The key elements of social exchange theory and their effects on a relationship
According to social exchange theory, relationship outcome is determined by the rewards minus the costs of a relationship. Relationship satisfaction is based on the outcome matched against comparison level (expectations). Commitment to a relationship is determined by one's satisfaction minus one's comparison level for alternatives plus one's investments in the relationship. (Adapted from Brehm & Kassin, 1993)

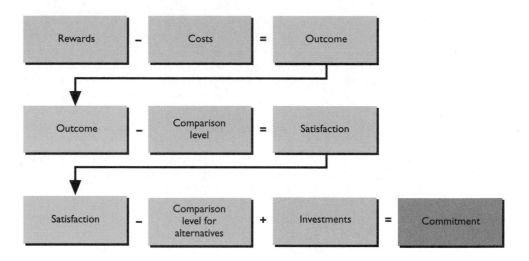

Learning Objective

Define the elements of social exchange theory and explain how they work in relationships.

ship (Kelley & Thibaut, 1978; Thibaut & Kelley, 1959). Harold Kelley and John Thibaut based their theory on B. F. Skinner's principle of reinforcement, which assumes that individuals try to maximize their rewards in life and minimize their costs (see Chapter 2). Of course, it is important to note that what is considered a reward or a cost in a relationship is highly subjective.

According to social exchange theory, people assess a relationship according to its *outcome*—their subjective perception of the rewards of the relationship minus its costs (see Figure 8.1). Rewards include such things as emotional support, status, and sexual gratification (in romantic relationships); costs are things like the time and energy that a relationship requires, emotional conflicts, and the inability to engage in other rewarding activities because of relationship obligations.

Individuals gauge their *satisfaction* with a relationship by comparing the outcomes (rewards minus costs) to their subjective expectations (see Figure 8.1). **This standard of what constitutes an acceptable balance of rewards and costs in a relationship is called the *comparison level*.** It is based on the outcomes one has experienced in previous relationships and the outcomes one has seen others experience in their relationships. A person's comparison level may also be influenced by exposure to fictional relationships, such as those in books or on television. Consistent with the predictions of social exchange theory, research indicates that there is higher relationship satisfaction when rewards are perceived to be high and costs are perceived to be low.

To understand the role of *commitment* in relationships, we need to look at two additional factors (see Figure 8.1). The first is the *comparison level for alternatives,* **or one's estimation of the available outcomes from alternative relationships.** In using this standard, individuals assess their current relationship outcomes in comparison to the potential outcomes of other similar relationships that are actually available to them. This principle helps explain why many unsatisfying relationships are not terminated until another love interest actually appears.

The second factor that figures in relationship commitment is ***investments,* or things that people contribute to a relationship that they can't get back if the relationship ends.** Investments include past costs (time, money) that they can never recover if the relationship fails. Understandably, putting investments into a relationship strengthens one's commitment to it.

But what happens if individuals feel they have invested a lot in a relationship that starts to feel bad? Because they're unwilling to forfeit their investments, some people put even more into such a relationship. Others decide that they will probably have to forfeit their investment sooner or later, so they choose not to wait—especially if an attractive alternative comes into the picture.

We'll use a hypothetical example to illustrate how social exchange theory works. If both people in a romantic relationship feel that they are getting a lot out of the relationship (lots of strokes, high status) compared to its costs (a few arguments, occasionally giving up preferred activities), the relationship will probably be perceived as satisfactory and will be maintained. However, if either person begins to feel that the ratio of rewards to costs is falling below his or her comparison level, then dissatisfaction is likely to occur. The dissatisfied person may attempt to alter the balance of costs and rewards or try to ease out of the relationship. The likelihood of ending the relationship depends on the number of important investments a person has made in the relationship and whether the person believes that an alternative relationship is available that could yield greater satisfaction.

Exchange theory principles seem to operate in a similar fashion regardless of a couple's sexual orientation (Peplau, 1991). Moreover, heterosexual and homosexual couples seem quite similar with regard to important aspects of relationships. For example, studies of heterosexual males and females, gay males, and lesbians found that all groups report high satisfaction with their relationships (Duffy & Rusbult, 1986; Kurdek & Schmitt, 1986b), as well as moderately high investments in their relationships, moderately poor alternatives, and strong commitment (Duffy & Rusbult, 1986).

This theory of an "interpersonal marketplace" provides a useful model for analyzing many types of relationships. Nonetheless, many people resist the idea that close relationships operate according to an economic model. Much of this resistance probably stems from discomfort with the idea that self-interest plays such an important role in the maintenance of relationships. Some of this resistance may also be due to a feeling that the principles of social exchange theory don't apply well to close relationships. In fact, there is some empirical support for this position. Margaret Clark and her colleagues (Clark & Bennett, 1992) distinguish between *exchange relationships* (with strangers, acquaintances, co-workers) and *communal relationships* (with close friends, lovers, family members). Research suggests that in exchange relationships, the usual principles of social exchange dominate. Social exchange principles also operate in communal relationships, but people seem to apply the principles differently. For example, in communal relationships, rewards are usually given freely, without any expectation of prompt reciprocation (Clark, 1984). Also, individuals pay more attention to the needs of a partner in a communal relationship than in an exchange relationship (Clark, Mills, & Powell, 1986). In other words, when people close to us need us, we help them without stopping to calculate whether and when they will reward us in kind.

Culture and Relationships

Learning Objective

Describe how members from individualistic cultures and collectivist cultures view love and marriage.

Most cross-cultural research on close relationships focuses on romantic relationships rather than on friendships or family relationships. Cultures vary in their emphasis on love—especially romantic love—as a prerequisite for marriage. Love as the basis for marriage is an 18th-century invention of Western culture (Stone, 1977). As Elaine Hatfield and Richard Rapson (1993) note, "Marriage-for-love represents an ultimate expression of individualism" (p. 2). In contrast, marriages arranged by families and other go-betweens remain common in cultures high in collectivism, including India (Gupta, 1992); Japan (Iwao, 1993); and China (Xiaohe & Whyte, 1990). This practice is declining in some societies as a result of Westernization, but in collectivist societies, people contemplating marriage still tend to think in terms of "What will my parents and other people say?" rather than "What does my heart say?" (Triandis, 1994). Studies show that attitudes about love in collectivist societies reflect these cultural priorities (Moghaddam, Taylor, & Wright, 1993). For example, in comparison to Western respondents, Japanese respondents report that they value romantic love less (Simmons, von Kolke, & Shimizu, 1986) and rate their relationships as being lower in love commitment (Ting-Toomey, 1991). When compared to Europeans, respondents from India and South Africa also indicated that they valued romantic love less (Furnham, 1984). And a cross-cultural investigation of the meaning of various emotions found that Italian and American participants equated love with happiness, whereas Chinese participants associated it with sadness and tended to envision unrequited love (Shaver, Wu, & Schwartz, 1991).

People from Western societies are often dumbfounded by collectivist cultures' deemphasis on love and their penchant for arranged marriages. Most of us assume that our modern conception of love as the basis for marriage must result in better marital relationships than collectivist cultures' "antiquated" beliefs and practices. However, a variety of researchers have noted that there is little empirical support

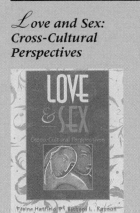
The authors examine romantic relationships and sex from a cross-cultural perspective. Hatfield, a social psychologist, is a distinguished pioneer in research on passionate and companionate love. Rapson, a historian, has long had an interest in the psychological side of American life, past and present.

Hatfield and Rapson, who are husband and wife, have done a fine job of melding research and thinking not only from psychology and history but also from anthropology, sociology, biology, literature, and art. Moreover, they have pulled together all this fascinating information with an interesting and involving writing style. They make ample use of first-person accounts and easily readable graphs to illustrate their points. They have also included a number of exercises and tests so readers can assess their own feelings and attitudes.

The book is organized into seven chapters that address key aspects of relationships or, in their words, "how people meet, mate, fall in love, make love, and fall out of love, usually only to risk it all over again" (p. viii). As they explore these topics, they attempt to sort out what is biological and universal and what is culturally specific. The reader will come away with much broader perspectives on love and sex and a greater appreciation for the role culture plays in shaping people's lives.

Today in many parts of the world, parents and matchmakers still arrange their children's marriages. Arranged marriages are common in India, in the Muslim countries, in sub-Saharan Africa, and in cultural enclaves throughout the remainder of the world. . . .

Some problems are serious enough to rule out any thought of marriage. Sometimes, religious advisors would chart the couples' horoscope. Couples born under the wrong sign may be forbidden to marry. . . . Generally, young people are forbidden to marry anyone who is too closely related (say, a brother or a sister or a certain kind of cousin). Sometimes, they are forbidden to marry foreigners. . . . If things look promising, parents and go-betweens begin to talk about the exchange of property, dowries, and the young couple's future obligations and their living arrangements. [p. 46]

for this ethnocentric view (Dion & Dion, 1993; Triandis, 1994). They cite, for example, a study of couples in India, which found that love tended to grow over the years in arranged marriages, whereas it tended to decline among couples who married for love (Gupta & Singh, 1982). Also, the expectation that marriage will fill diverse psychological needs places greater pressure on marital relationships in individualistic societies than on those in collectivist cultures. These high expectations for personal fulfillment in marriage might be linked to the rapidly escalating divorce rates in these societies (Dion & Dion, 1993). The dearth of cross-cultural research on love means that we can only speculate on these matters. But smug assumptions about the superiority of Western ways look very shaky given our extremely high divorce rates. The Recommended Reading on this page provides a fascinating look at cultural variability in love and sex.

Factors Influencing Interpersonal Attraction

"I just don't know what she sees in him. She could do so much better for herself." "Sure, she's an okay person, but he's too good for her." How many times have you heard remarks like these? Such comments illustrate the great interest people have in analyzing the dynamics of attraction. **Interpersonal attraction refers to positive feelings toward another person.** Who is attracted to whom is an exceedingly complex topic. A multitude of factors influence your assessment of another person's attractiveness. Furthermore, attraction is a two-way street, so there are intricate interactions between factors.

Our review of research in this area pertains to initial attraction in friendships as well as in heterosexual and homosexual romantic relationships. Although liking and loving represent two different types of relationships, we believe that the dynamics of *initial attraction* in each case are sufficiently similar to justify a unified discussion. In some cases, a particular factor, such as physical attractiveness, may play a more influential role in love than in friendship, or vice versa. However, all the factors to be discussed in this section appear to enter into both types of attraction.

To simplify this complex issue, we'll divide our coverage into three segments. In the first part, we'll review the *characteristics of other people* that tend to make them attractive. In the second, we'll discuss how *one's own characteristics* influence one's assessment of others' attractiveness. Finally, we'll look at *interaction factors*—those that don't reside in either person alone but rather emerge out of a pair's relationship to each other.

Characteristics of the Other Person

Have you ever had a friend attempt to set you up for a blind date? If so, what kinds of questions did you ask about your prospective date? Did you inquire about the person's manners, attitudes, and moral character? Probably not. Chances are, you wanted to know about his or her looks, personality, and intelligence. Research suggests that these are the main characteristics of individuals that influence others' attraction to them. Let's examine the evidence.

Physical Attractiveness

Statements such as "Beauty is only skin deep" and "You can't judge a book by its cover" imply that people should be cautious about being seduced by physical beauty. However, research suggests that most people pay little attention to this advice!

Learning Objective

Summarize the findings on the importance of physical attractiveness in relationships.

Emphasis on physical attractiveness Studies of physical beauty have been conducted in a variety of settings, from college dances to commercial dating services (Walster et al., 1966; Woll, 1986). All show that attractiveness is an important factor in dating. Good looks also play a role in friendships. People, especially males, prefer attractiveness in their same- and other-gender friends (Berscheid et al., 1971; Feingold, 1988, 1990). Although women are more likely to report that physical attractiveness is less important to them than males do, some recent research suggests that these differences have been exaggerated (Sprecher, 1989a; Stevens, Owens, & Schaefer, 1990). It seems that women are as influenced by physical attractiveness as men, but downplay this in their self-reports. And because most of this research is based on self-reports, the gender difference is artificially heightened.

Do heterosexuals and homosexuals differ on the importance of physical attractiveness in prospective dating partners? One study looked at similarities and differences in how gay and straight individuals worded personal advertisements in newspapers (Deaux & Hanna, 1984). Some 800 ads were analyzed—200 each from heterosexual males, heterosexual females, homosexual males, and homosexual females. Interestingly, gender (male or female) turned out to be a more important factor than sexual orientation (heterosexual or homosexual). That is, both heterosexual and homosexual men placed more emphasis on physical attractiveness when describing themselves and their preferences in partners than did either heterosexual or homosexual women. Regardless of sexual orientation, women placed more importance on psychological characteristics when describing themselves and their preferences in partners. A later study found that gay men emphasized physical characteristics most and lesbians, least (Gonzales & Meyers, 1993).

The emphasis on beauty may not be quite as great as the evidence reviewed thus far suggests. Figure 8.2 summarizes the results of a cross-cultural study conducted in 37 different countries on the characteristics commonly sought in a mate (Buss, 1985). As you can see, personal qualities, such as kindness/understanding and intelligence, are ranked higher than physical attractiveness by both genders. These results are somewhat reassuring. Still, as we saw in earlier chapters, verbal reports are not necessarily an accurate reflection of how people actually behave.

Figure 8.2
Characteristics sought in a mate
Buss (1989) surveyed individuals in 37 countries on the characteristics they sought in a mate. Both kindness/understanding and intelligence were ranked higher than physical attractiveness by both genders. Statistically significant gender differences in rankings were found for a variety of characteristics, which are shown in italics. For example, males ranked physical attractiveness higher than females did.

Characteristics Commonly Sought in a Mate

Rank	Characteristics preferred by men	Characteristics preferred by women
1	Kindness and understanding	Kindness and understanding
2	Intelligence	Intelligence
3	*Physical attractiveness*	Exciting personality
4	Exciting personality	Good health
5	Good health	Adaptability
6	Adaptability	*Physical attractiveness*
7	Creativity	Creativity
8	Desire for children	*Good earning capacity*
9	College graduate	College graduate
10	Good heredity	Desire for children
11	*Good earning capacity*	Good heredity
12	Good housekeeper	Good housekeeper
13	Religious orientation	Religious orientation

What makes someone attractive?   The advertising industry has fostered a rather narrow conception of physical attractiveness. The truth is, people differ in regard to what they actually find attractive. In one study, subjects were asked, "When you first meet someone, which one or two things about physical appearance do you tend to notice first?" As can be seen in Figure 8.3, responses varied widely. Also from Figure 8.3, you can see that what a person notices in others often depends on whether they are a member of the same or the other gender. Other research suggests that both facial and bodily appearance are important factors in perceived attractiveness, but an unattractive body is perceived as being a greater liability than an unattractive face (Alicke, Smith, & Klotz, 1986). Males, especially, place more emphasis on body build.

Males are rated as highly attractive if they have broad shoulders, slim waists and legs, and small buttocks (Lavrakas, 1975). Tall men are viewed as attractive (Eisenberg et al., 1984; Lynn & Shurgot, 1984), as are men who are not obese (Harris, Harris, & Bochner, 1982). Women who are rated high in attractiveness are not overweight (Franzoi & Herzog, 1987) and have medium-sized breasts (Kleinke & Staneski, 1980). A study of preferences for body types among white college students found that men exaggerated the extent to which same- and other-gender peers perceived large physiques as most desirable for males. Similarly, women believed that their male and female peers preferred a much thinner female silhouette than was actually the case (Cohn & Adler, 1992). Incidentally, the modern emphasis on thinness as the ideal female body shape has been suggested as a major cause of the high incidence of eating disorders among adolescent, Caucasian girls (Boskind-Lodahl, 1976; Garner et al., 1980). We'll discuss this issue in more detail in Chapter 10 ("Gender and Behavior").

Because our culture values attractiveness in females, being physically attractive appears to be more important for females than for males (Feingold, 1990). This gender gap was apparent in a recent study of the tactics heterosexual individuals use in pursuing romantic relationships. David Buss (1988) asked 208 newlywed individuals to describe the things they did when they first met their spouse, and during the remainder of their courtship, to make themselves more appealing to their partner. Buss found that men were more likely than women to emphasize their material resources by doing such things as flashing lots of money, buying nice gifts, showing off expensive possessions, and bragging about their importance at work (see Figure 8.4). In contrast, women were more likely than men to work at enhancing their appearance by dieting, wearing stylish clothes, trying new hairstyles, and getting a tan. Although there were relative differences between the genders in emphasis on physical attractiveness, the data in Figure 8.4 show that *both* genders relied on tactics intended to enhance or maintain good looks.

Figure 8.3
What men and women first notice about physical appearance

In a Roper Poll, people were asked, "When you first meet someone, which one or two things about physical appearance do you tend to notice first?" The subjects' responses depended to some extent on their gender and on whether they were meeting someone of the same gender or the other gender. Overall, the subjects' responses were highly varied.

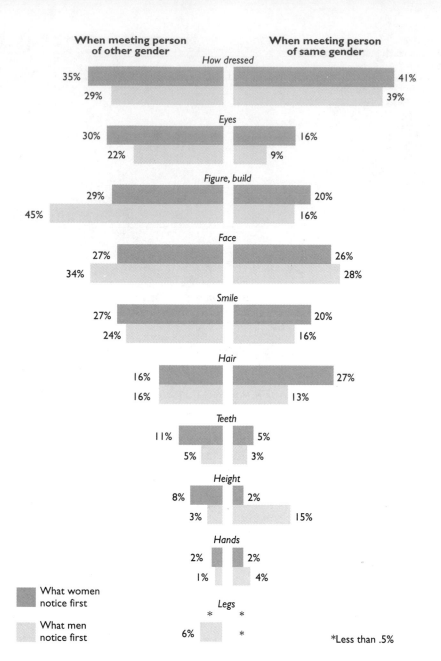

When meeting person of other gender | When meeting person of same gender

How dressed
35% / 29% — 41% / 39%

Eyes
30% / 22% — 16% / 9%

Figure, build
29% / 45% — 20% / 16%

Face
27% / 34% — 26% / 28%

Smile
27% / 24% — 20% / 16%

Hair
16% / 16% — 27% / 13%

Teeth
11% / 5% — 5% / 3%

Height
8% / 3% — 2% / 15%

Hands
2% / 1% — 2% / 4%

Legs
* / 6% — * / *

What women notice first

What men notice first

*Less than .5%

Learning Objective

Define the matching hypothesis and summarize the evidence for it.

Thankfully, a person does not have to be spectacularly good-looking in order to enjoy a rewarding social life. People apparently take into consideration their own level of attractiveness in the process of dating and mating. **The *matching hypothesis* proposes that people of similar levels of physical attractiveness gravitate toward each other.** The matching hypothesis is supported by evidence that both heterosexual dating couples and those who are married tend to be similar in physical attractiveness (Feingold, 1988, 1990). (We are unaware of research on this question regarding homosexual couples.) There is some debate, however, about whether people match up by their own choice (Aron, 1988; Kalick & Hamilton, 1986). Some theorists believe that individuals mostly pursue high attractiveness in partners and that their matching is the result of social forces beyond their control, such as rejection by more attractive others.

Researchers have also found evidence for matching effects in same-gender friendships (McKillip & Riedel, 1983). As we mentioned earlier, matching effects appear stronger among males than females, regardless of sexual orientation (Berscheid et al., 1971; Feingold, 1988, 1990). The reasons for this gender difference are not readily apparent. Overall, additional research is needed on the matching hypothesis as it relates to friendship formation.

Figure 8.4
Similarities and differences
between the genders in the
tactics of attraction

Buss (1988) asked newlywed
subjects to rate how often they
had used 23 tactics of attraction
to make themselves more appealing to their partner. The tactics
used by one gender significantly
more often than the other are
listed in the first two sections of
the figure. Although there were
significant differences between
the genders, there were also
many similarities. The 11 tactics
used most frequently by each
gender (those above the median)
are highlighted, showing considerable overlap between males and
females in the tactics they used
most. (Note: Higher means in the
data reflect higher frequency of
use, but the numbers do not
indicate frequency per day or
week.)

Tactics of Attraction

	Mean frequency	
Tactics used significantly more by males	Men (N = 102)	Women (N = 106)
Display resources	0.67	0.44
Brag about resources	0.73	0.60
Display sophistication	**1.18**	0.88
Display strength	0.96	0.44
Display athleticism	**1.18**	0.94
Show off	0.70	0.47
Tactics used significantly more by females		
Wear makeup	0.02	**1.63**
Keep clean and groomed	**2.27**	**2.44**
Alter appearance—general	0.39	**1.27**
Wear stylish clothes	**1.22**	**2.00**
Act coy	0.54	0.73
Wear jewelry	0.25	**2.21**
Wear sexy clothes	0.68	0.91
Tactics for which no significant gender differences were found		
Act provocative	0.77	0.90
Flirt	**2.13**	**2.09**
Keep hair groomed	**2.20**	**2.31**
Increase social pressure	0.89	0.90
Act nice	**1.77**	**1.86**
Display humor	**2.42**	**2.28**
Act promiscuous	0.30	0.21
Act submissive	**1.24**	**1.11**
Dissemble (feign agreement)	**1.26**	1.09
Touch	**2.26**	**2.16**

Desirable Personality Characteristics

Learning Objective

Describe the personality traits that people find desirable.

Personality characteristics are another obvious factor influencing interpersonal attraction. Subjects rate a hypothetical person's likability much higher when the person is described as sincere, honest, and dependable rather than loudmouthed, deceitful, and obnoxious. A large-scale survey on people's perceptions of the ideal man and woman revealed that the most sought after qualities are confidence, integrity, warmth, gentleness, and the ability to love (Tavris, 1977). Similar results were reported in a more recent study of British college students and dating agency members regarding the personality characteristics they preferred in romantic partners (Goodwin, 1990). That is, the most preferred qualities were kindness/consideration, honesty, and humor. In another study on dating criteria, American college students gave the highest ratings to qualities such as emotionally stable, easygoing, friendly, exciting, and good sense of humor (Kenrick et al., 1993).

In another study, heterosexual college students were asked to rate the physical and psychological characteristics they deemed desirable for both sexual relationships and meaningful, long-term relationships (Nevid, 1984). As you might expect, personal qualities were rated as more important than physical characteristics for meaningful romantic relationships. Also, men placed greater emphasis than women on the physical characteristics of prospective romantic partners, whereas women stressed personal qualities. However, since this research was based on self-reports, these gender differences are probably exaggerated.

According to the matching hypothesis, we tend to wind up with someone similar to ourselves in attractiveness. However, other factors such as personality, intelligence, and social status also influence attraction.

Intelligence and Competence

Learning Objective

Summarize the findings regarding competence and likability.

Generally, people prefer others who are bright and competent over those who are not. The data in Figure 8.2 support this idea. The characteristics of intelligence, "college graduate," and "good earning capacity" were ranked as important ones in an ideal mate.

Sometimes, however, extremely competent people may be threatening, and others may occasionally dislike them. Interestingly, highly competent people may be able to enhance their attractiveness by showing themselves to be fallible and thus more "human." In a study that tested this idea, male students listened to a tape recording of another male student who was supposedly being interviewed for an important position on campus. The interviewee was portrayed differently in four conditions: (1) unusually competent, (2) unusually competent and makes an embarrassing blunder (he spills coffee on himself), (3) somewhat inept, and (4) somewhat inept and makes the same embarrassing blunder (Aronson, Willerman, & Floyd, 1966). Which interviewee did the subjects like best? They preferred the highly competent student who committed the blunder. But, before you start making frequent blunders to enhance your likability, please note that the person the subjects liked least was the inept student who committed the blunder.

This preference for competent people who make humanizing mistakes may be limited to individuals of the same gender. Kay Deaux (1972) conducted an experiment that was basically the same as the one conducted by Aronson and associates except that she added female participants and had both males and females play the role of the stimulus person. As before, men liked the competent male more when he made a blunder. However, women preferred the competent male who did *not* blunder. Similarly, men rated the competent female who did not commit a blunder higher than the one who did. In explaining these perplexing findings, Deaux suggests that people may empathize more with those of their own gender and hence be more tolerant of their blunders. She also suggests that idealized images of the other gender may make it more difficult to accept their mistakes.

Age and Social Status

Learning Objective

Summarize the findings regarding the effects of age and social status on likability.

A number of studies indicate that American women usually marry men who are somewhat older than they are and that American men prefer women who are somewhat younger than they (Kenrick & Keefe, 1992). These findings have been found in other cultures as well (Kenrick & Keefe, 1992).

Regarding social status, several studies have shown that, in heterosexual dating, males "trade" occupational status for physical attractiveness in females, and vice versa (Deaux & Hanna, 1984; Feingold, 1992a). This finding also appears to hold true in many other cultures. As we already saw in the cross-cultural study summarized in Figure 8.2, men in most countries rate physical attractiveness in a prospective mate as more important than women do, whereas women rate "good earning capacity" as a more important characteristic than do men (Buss, 1989). Moreover, several studies have shown that more attractive women are more likely to demand high status in their prospective dates than less attractive women are (Harrison & Saeed, 1977).

Evolutionary social psychologists such as Arnold Buss (1988) believe that these findings on age, status, and physical attractiveness reflect gender differences in our inherited reproductive strategies (Kenrick & Keefe, 1992). According to this view, men are attracted to women of childbearing age because women are limited in the number of years they can reproduce (and men are not). Hence, men display more interest in characteristics that denote a woman's *reproductive capacity* (youth, attractiveness, health). Women, on the other hand, invest more resources in their offspring than do men and are especially desirous of mates who can help feed and protect her and her children. So women focus on a man's capacity for *resource acquisition* (maturity, earning capacity, status). Of course, there are other explanations for gender differences in attraction and mate selection. Chief among these are traditional gender-role socialization and poorer economic opportunities for women (Sprecher, Sullivan, & Hatfield, 1994).

One's Own Characteristics

Thus far, we have discussed how others' characteristics influence your attraction to them. Now we are ready to turn the spotlight on you, examining the role that such internal factors as social motives, self-esteem, and self-perception processes play in attraction.

Social Motives

Learning Objective

Describe how social motives, self-esteem, and misattributions of emotional arousal can influence one's attraction to others.

Social motives are what impel people to engage in social interaction and relationships. Obviously, there are individual differences in the strength of these motives. As a result, some people thrive on many acquaintances and friends, while others are perfectly content with only a few close relationships. Dan McAdams (1982) has found some interesting differences between two important social motives. If you have a strong *need for affiliation,* you probably enjoy establishing and maintaining many rewarding interpersonal relationships as well as joining and participating in groups. Individuals who are low on this need feel less drawn to interact with others. If you prefer a few, intimate relationships, you probably have a strong *need for intimacy.* Research has shown that individuals with high intimacy needs engage in deeper self-disclosure and experience a greater sense of well-being than do those with low intimacy needs (McAdams & Bryant, 1987; McAdams, Healy, & Krause, 1984).

Self-Esteem

As we noted in Chapter 5, your self-esteem influences how you relate to others. For example, subjects with low self-esteem select less attractive dates than those with high self-esteem do (Kiesler & Baral, 1970). Thus, people with a favorable self-concept may see themselves as having a wider range of dating choices than those with an unfavorable self-concept do.

Self-esteem also affects your reactions to others' evaluations of you (Berscheid, 1985; Jones, 1973). Individuals with low self-esteem tend to react more positively to favorable evaluators and more negatively to unfavorable evaluators than people with high self-esteem do (Dion & Dion, 1988). Thus, people may be more vulnerable to others' views of them—for better and for worse—if their self-esteem is low.

Misattributions and Emotions

Stanley Schachter's (1964) theory of emotion proposes that when people experience the physiological arousal usually associated with emotion, they try to explain the reasons for the arousal by looking at the situation they are in. Researchers used a naturalistic setting to examine this theory (Dutton & Aron, 1974). Participants were young men crossing a footbridge who encountered a good-looking young woman (actually a confederate of the experimenters). The woman stopped the men on the bridge, asking them to complete a questionnaire for a class project she was doing. When the men returned the questionnaire, she offered to explain the research at some future time and gave them her phone number. The key to the experiment was that this procedure was enacted on two very different bridges. One was a long suspension bridge that swayed precariously over a 230-foot drop. The other was a solid, safe structure a mere 10 feet above a small stream.

The experimenters reasoned that men crossing the high suspension bridge would experience emotional arousal and that some of them might misinterpret their arousal as being caused by the woman rather than the bridge. If these men attributed their arousal to the woman, they would probably infer that they found her very attractive. The dependent variable in the study was the percentage of men who later called the woman to pursue a date. As predicted, those men who met the woman in an aroused state (on the precarious bridge) were more likely to ask her out than were those who met her in a normal emotional state (on the safe bridge).

It has been suggested that misattributing the causes of emotional arousal may be the basis for the tendency to mistake lust for love. Although sexual arousal is an important aspect of romantic love, love is more than mere lust. Nonetheless, research on self-perception shows just how easy it may be for people to mix up sexual arousal and more profound feelings of love.

Interaction Factors

Some factors in the dynamics of attraction lie neither in you nor in the other person. Instead, they emerge out of your unique relationship with each other. Hence, they are called *interaction factors*. These factors include proximity, similarity, and reciprocity.

Proximity

It would be difficult for you to develop a friendship with someone you never met. Although it happens occasionally (between pen pals and on computer bulletin boards, for instance), attraction usually depends on proximity: People have to be in the same place at the same time. **Proximity refers to geographic, residential, and other forms of spatial closeness.** Generally, people become acquainted with, and attracted to, those who live, work, shop, or play nearby.

The importance of proximity was apparent in a classic study of friendship patterns among married graduate students living in a university housing project (Festinger, Schachter, & Back, 1950). People whose doors were close together were most likely to become friends. Moreover, those whose homes faced the central court area had more than twice as many friends in the complex as those whose homes faced outward. Using the centralized court area apparently increased the likelihood that people would meet and befriend others.

Proximity effects were also found in a study of Maryland state police trainees (Segal, 1974). At the training academy, both dormitory rooms and classroom seats were assigned on the basis of alphabetical order. Six months after their arrival, participants were asked to name their closest three friends among the group of trainees. Trainees whose last names were closer together in the alphabet were much more likely to be friends than were trainees whose names were widely separated in the alphabet.

Proximity effects may seem self-evident, but it is sobering to realize that your friendships and love interests are shaped by seating charts, desk arrangements in offices, and floor assignments in residence halls. In spite of the increasing geographic mobility in modern society, people still tend to marry someone who grew up nearby (Ineichen, 1979).

Similarity

Is it true that "birds of a feather flock together," or do "opposites attract"? Research provides far more support for the first adage than for the second (Cappella & Palmer, 1990). Heterosexual married and dating couples tend to be similar in age, race, religion, social class, education, intelligence, physical attractiveness, and attitudes (Brehm, 1992; Hendrick & Hendrick, 1992). We are unaware of research on similarity effects among homosexual couples; however, in one study that compared heterosexual, homosexual, and bisexual individuals, members of all three groups agreed that it was important for lovers to have similar interests, share the same religious beliefs, and have similar values (Engel & Saracino, 1986). The factor on which the groups differed was similarity in ethnic background. That is, heterosexuals were significantly more likely than homosexuals or bisexuals to say that having a partner from the same ethnic background was important.

Also, people with similar *personalities* are more likely to be attracted to each other than to those with dissimilar personalities. For example, it has been found that males and females who identify strongly with traditional gender-role characteristics are more likely to be attracted to each other than to others who identify less strongly with stereotypic gender roles (Pursell & Banikiotes, 1978). Similarly, "Type A" individuals are attracted to each other (Morell, Twillman, & Sullaway, 1989).

In married couples, personality similarity appears to be associated with greater marital happiness (Caspi & Herbener, 1990). Similarity is also important among friends (Newcomb, 1961). For instance, among adolescents, best friends are similar in age, gender, race, educational goals and performance, political and religious activities, and illicit drug use (Deutsch et al., 1991; Kandel, 1978). Adult friends also tend to be relatively similar in terms of education, occupational status, ethnicity, and religion (Blieszner & Adams, 1992).

The most obvious explanation for these correlations is that similarity causes attraction. Laboratory experiments on *attitude similarity* conducted by Donn Byrne and his colleagues suggest that similarity does cause liking (Byrne, 1971; Byrne, Clore, & Smeaton, 1986). In these studies, subjects who have previously provided information on their own attitudes are led to believe that they will be meeting a stranger. They are given information about the stranger's views that has been manipulated to show various degrees of similarity to their own views. As attitude similarity increases, subjects' ratings of the likability of the stranger increase (see Figure 8.5). This evidence supports the notion that similarity promotes attraction. However, it's also consistent with a somewhat different explanation proposed by Rosenbaum (1986).

Rosenbaum has marshaled evidence suggesting that similarity effects occur in attraction not because similarity fosters liking, but because *dis*similarity leads people to *dis*like others (he termed this phenomenon the *repulsion hypothesis*). In one study of this hypothesis, Rosenbaum (1986) found that Democrats did not rate other Democrats (similar others) higher than controls as much as they rated Republicans (dissimilar others) lower than controls. Thus, Rosenbaum downplays the importance of attitude similarity, arguing instead that *dissimilarity causes disdain*. More recent evidence suggests that liking is influenced by *both* similarity and dissimilarity in attitudes (Singh & Tan, 1992; Smeaton, Byrne, & Murnen, 1989).

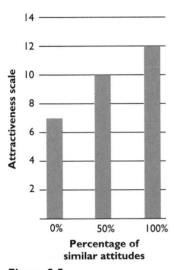

Figure 8.5
Attitude similarity and attraction
When asked to rate the likability of a hypothetical stranger, subjects give progressively higher ratings to people who share more attitudes with them. (Adapted from Gonzales et al., 1983)

Learning Objective

Explain how reciprocity affects attraction.

Reciprocity

A critical factor that determines your liking for others is the extent to which you believe that they like you (Berscheid & Walster, 1978; Hays, 1984). If you believe that others are sincere, you like it when they flatter you, do favors for you, and use nonverbal behavior to signal their interest in you (eye contact, leaning forward). Moreover, you usually reciprocate. In interpersonal attraction, **reciprocity involves liking those who show that they like you.** In general, it appears that liking breeds liking and loving promotes loving (Byrne & Murnen, 1988).

You can see the self-fulfilling prophecy at work here. If you believe that someone likes you, you behave in a friendly manner toward him or her. Your behavior

Figure 8.6
Reciprocity and liking
Research participants were led to believe that their research partner either did or did not like them. The participants who believed that their partners liked them liked their partners more than did the participants who believed that their partners did not like them. These results illustrate how reciprocity and the self-fulfilling prophecy can influence attraction to others. (Based on Curtis & Miller, 1986)

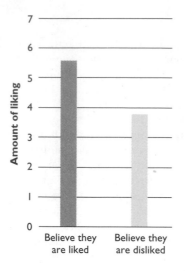

encourages the other person to respond positively, and this confirms your initial expectation. A study by Rebecca Curtis and Kim Miller (1986) shows this self-fulfilling prophecy in action. College students who were strangers were divided into pairs and had a 5-minute "get acquainted" conversation. Afterward, one member of each pair was led to believe that the other student either did or did not like them. Then, the pairs met again and talked about current events for 10 minutes. Raters, blind to the experimental condition of the participants, listened to tape recordings of the 10-minute interactions and rated the participants on a number of behaviors. As predicted, the individuals who believed that they were liked were rated as disclosing more about themselves, behaving more warmly, disagreeing less, and having a more positive tone of voice and general attitude than those who believed that they were disliked (see Figure 8.6).

A qualification to the reciprocity principle involves the widely discussed strategy of playing "hard to get." According to this strategy, showing relatively little interest in the social overtures of a person of the other sex (nonreciprocity) may make the other person even more eager to pursue the relationship. However, the empirical evidence suggests that playing hard to get may not be advisable. Research indicates that people prefer members of the other gender who appear hard for *others* to get but who eagerly accept them (Walster et al., 1973).

Our review of the dynamics of attraction has shown that many factors influence the emergence of close relationships. In the next two sections we'll probe more deeply into the nature of friendship and romantic love.

Friendship

Friends play a significant role in everyone's lives. They may provide help in times of need, advice in times of confusion, consolation in times of failure, and praise in times of achievement. The importance of friends was underscored in a survey of 40,000 readers of *Psychology Today* magazine. In that survey, 51% of the respondents indicated that in a crisis they were more likely to turn to friends than to family for help (Parlee et al., 1979).

Several studies have compared same-gender friendships with heterosexual romantic relationships. Qualities such as acceptance, trust, respect, confidence,

Friends play a very important role in our lives. Research suggests that loyalty is the heart and soul of friendship.

understanding, spontaneity, mutual assistance, and happiness are valued in both kinds of relationships (K. E. Davis, 1985). Romantic relationships also involve fascination and exclusiveness. Friendships were perceived to be more stable than romantic relationships among those who were unmarried. Another study found that friends report higher levels of contentment and commitment than do dating partners (Winn, Crawford, & Fischer, 1991). In this section, we'll explore what makes a good friend and how gender and marital status affect patterns of friendship.

What Makes a Good Friend?

Learning Objective

Summarize the research on what makes a good friend.

The most intriguing aspect of the *Psychology Today* survey was its investigation of what makes a "good friend." Figure 8.7 lists the most frequently endorsed qualities. The results suggest that loyalty is the heart and soul of friendship. As you can see, the top two qualities in Figure 8.7 are keeping confidences (an aspect of loyalty) and loyalty itself. As one might guess, the next most important ingredients of friendship are warmth/affection and supportiveness. The high ratings for candor (frankness) and a sense of humor are interesting and well worth keeping in mind.

These results generally coincide with those of another survey on friendship, although one other important factor emerged in this second survey (Block, 1980). That additional factor was a willingness to let friends be themselves. Block points out that people often put others under pressure to behave in ways that are consistent with their own expectations. Such "conditional" expectations would appear to resemble those held by many parents for their children. As we discussed in Chapter 2, Carl Rogers believes that conditional affection contributes to distortions in people's self-concepts, and for this reason he advocates unconditional acceptance in child-rearing. Consistent with Rogers's theory, Block's respondents emphasized the importance of relatively unconditional acceptance from their friends.

A slightly different way of looking at what is important in friendship comes from a cross-cultural study of students in England, Italy, Japan, and Hong Kong (Argyle & Henderson, 1984). The investigators wanted to see whether they could find enough agreement on how friends should conduct themselves to permit the formulation of some informal rules governing friendships. For a behavior to qualify as a rule, subjects had to agree that the behavior was important in a friendship, that failure to behave this way could destroy the friendship, and that the behavior could differentiate between current and former friends and between intimate and nonintimate friends. On the basis of the students' responses, the authors identified

Figure 8.7
Important qualities in a friend
The traits listed here are those that subjects cited most often when asked what makes a good friend. (Adapted from Parlee et al., 1979)

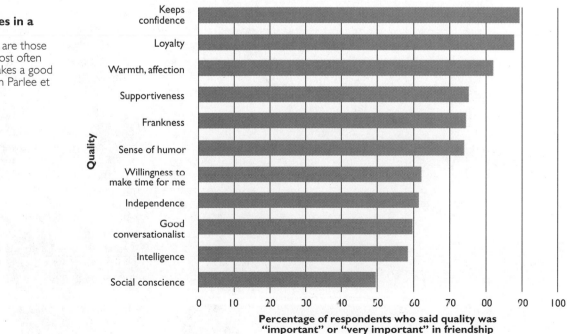

Percentage of respondents who said quality was "important" or "very important" in friendship

Figure 8.8
Vital behaviors in friendship
A cross-cultural inquiry into the behaviors that are vital to friendship identified the six rules of friendship listed here. (Adapted from Argyle & Henderson, 1984)

The Rules of Friendship

Share news of success with a friend

Show emotional support

Volunteer help in time of need

Strive to make a friend happy when in each other's company

Trust and confide in each other

Stand up for a friend in his or her absence

six informal rules. As Figure 8.8 shows, the common thread running through these rules seems to be providing emotional and social support. Hence we can conclude that loyalty, emotional support, and letting friends be themselves are the most important expectations for friendship.

Gender Differences in Friendship

Learning Objective

Describe gender differences in friendships.

Men's and women's same-gender friendships have a lot in common, but there are some interesting differences that appear to be rooted in traditional gender roles and socialization. For one thing, men's friendships tend to be based on shared interests and doing things together (Hays, 1985; Sherrod, 1989). In contrast, women's friendships are more likely to focus on talking and emotional intimacy. Men seem to view their friends as serving specific functions (one may be a fishing partner; another, a traveling companion). Women seem to react to their friends in a more "global" way (Wright, 1982). Also, many men seem willing to tolerate and work around sources of tension in friendships, whereas women are more likely to confront friends about conflicts to resolve them (Wright, 1982).

Men's and women's friendships can also be differentiated in terms of their topics of conversation. Women are far more likely than men to discuss personal problems, feelings, and people (Caldwell & Peplau, 1982; Davidson & Duberman, 1982). Men who don't adhere to traditional gender roles are an exception to this rule. That is, these men appear to divulge as much to their best male friend as most women do to their best female friend (Lavine & Lombardo, 1984).

Friendships between men tend to be regulated by social roles. That is, men usually relate to each other as business partners, as tennis rivals, or as baseball fans.

Recommended Reading

Just Friends:
The Role of Friendship in Our Lives

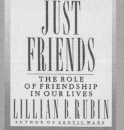

by Lillian Rubin
(Harper & Row, 1985)

Based on in-depth interviews with 300 men and women ages 25–55, from a variety of walks of life, Lillian Rubin examines the complex phenomenon of friendship. She has also conducted 100 interviews with gay males and lesbians, focusing on their love relationships, their friendships, and the interactions between the two. She draws on this information to make comparisons between homosexual and heterosexual experiences of friendship. The topics she addresses include differences between family relationships and friendships, the role of friendship in psychological development, men's and women's friendships, the effect of marriage on friendship, and friendships between women and men. In addition, there is a chapter on "best friends," from which the following excerpt is taken:

> Unlike other friendships, where expectations are more modest, we usually expect our best friends to meet us at many different levels. We want best friends to respond to the many selves inside us, to understand our feelings, and, if not to share them, at least to know their value. A thirty-eight-year-old artist, married fourteen years, said of her best friend:
>> The fundamental thing about my friendship with Nancy, and what I prize so, is that I feel free to be all the different things I am with her—including a depressed drag sometimes. I don't have to be on stage or be clever and amusing for her to want to be with me. It's like there's a sign on our friendship for both of us that says, "No cute person wanted here; only the real stuff."
>> She's not an artist, but she has such a deep appreciation of my artistic side that it thrills me. Except for Stuart, she's the only person in years who I've felt understands me in my core self. [pp. 184–185]

Moreover, men generally rate their same-gender friendships as less intimate than women rate theirs. Men also perceive less emotional support to be available from their friends than most women do (Sherrod, 1989).

There are several likely reasons for these gender differences in friendships (Reis, Senchak, & Solomon, 1985). First, men and women appear to have different pathways to intimacy (shared activities versus self-disclosure, respectively). Second, men may have less need for intimacy than women do. Third, traditional gender-role expectations encourage men to be "strong and silent." As we saw in Chapter 7, when self-disclosure is socially acceptable for men, they sometimes engage in more self-disclosure than women.

We noted in Chapter 3 that social support from friends (and others) reduces the impact of stress and is associated with better mental health. This finding raises an interesting question: Do women's same-gender friendships yield greater mental health benefits than men's because of women's greater intimacy? There is evidence on both sides of this question. On one hand, evidence suggests that same-gender friendships buffer stress and reduce depression in both males and females (Cohen, Sherrod, & Clark, 1986; Cohen & Wills, 1985). On the other, the relative lack of emotional support from same-gender male friends often means that men are heavily dependent on their wives for such support. Should this be the case, a man whose marriage ends in divorce will have less emotional support from friends than will his former wife (Gerstel, 1988). This may be one of the reasons that men typically have a harder time adjusting to divorce than women do (Price & McKenry, 1988).

Romantic Love

Wander through a bookstore and you'll see an overwhelming array of titles such as *Love Can Be Found, Men Who Can't Love, Women Who Love Too Much*, and *How to Survive the Loss of a Love*. Turn up your radio and you'll hear the refrains of "I Will Always Love You," "Love Will Find a Way," "Prove Your Love," and "Endless Love." Although there are other forms of love, such as parental love and platonic love, these books and songs are all about *romantic love*, a subject of consuming interest for almost everyone.

People have always been interested in love and romance. However, the scientific study of love has a short history that dates back only to the 1970s. Love has proven to be an elusive subject of study. It is difficult to define, difficult to measure, and frequently difficult to understand. Nonetheless, psychologists have begun to make some progress in their study of love. Given all the confusion about love, we'll first attempt to debunk some myths about it.

Myths About Love

Learning Objective

Discuss four myths about romantic love.

Romantic love is a highly idealized concept in our culture. Some interesting as well as troublesome myths have been nurtured by this idealism—as well as by American television and movies. Accordingly, our first task is to take a realistic look at love and dispel some of these problematic notions. Most of our discussion will be based on the writings of Elaine Hatfield (formerly Walster) and Ellen Berscheid (Berscheid, 1988; Berscheid & Walster, 1978; Hatfield, 1988; Walster & Berscheid, 1974), who probably have conducted more research on love than anyone else. Although they're rigorous researchers who have made major contributions to the scientific study of love, Berscheid and Hatfield have also been willing to offer down-to-earth, practical insights about the nature of love. Following are some myths they have identified.

Myth 1: When you fall in love, you'll know it. People often spend a great deal of time agonizing over whether they are experiencing true love or mere infatuation. When individuals consult others about their doubts, they're often told, "If it's true love, you'd know it." This assertion, which amounts to replying, "You must not really be in love," simply isn't accurate. As we noted, it's often difficult to distin-

Elaine Hatfield

guish lust from love. Studies also show that dating couples engage in increased attributional guesswork at transition points in their relationships—to figure out their feelings (Fletcher et al., 1987). Thus, confusion about a romantic relationship is not the least bit unusual, and it does not mean that you aren't really in love.

Myth 2: When love strikes, you have no control over it. This myth suggests that love is so powerful that people are incapable of behaving wisely once they are under its spell. While it may be comforting to tell yourself that you have no control in matters of the heart, this rationalization encourages people to act irresponsibly when they are "in love." But irresponsible behavior can result in tragic outcomes—sexually transmitted diseases (including AIDS), unwanted pregnancy, and unhappy marriages, to name a few. In the early stages of romantic relationships, it's especially hard to sort out the many, intense feelings. However, because of this, individuals need to proceed cautiously in making important decisions about sexual involvements and long-term commitments.

Myth 3: True love lasts forever. Love *may* last forever, but unfortunately, you can't count on it. People perpetuate this myth in an interesting way. If their love relationship disintegrates, they conclude that it was never genuine love, only infatuation or comfortable compatibility. This rationalization allows them to continue their search for the one, great, idealized lover who will supposedly bring complete happiness. It's more realistic to view love as a sometimes wonderful, sometimes frustrating experience that might be encountered a number of times in one's life.

Myth 4: Love can conquer all problems. This myth is the basis for many unsuccessful marriages. Numerous couples, fully aware of problems in their relationship (for example, poor communication, disagreement about gender roles), forge ahead into marriage anyway. Well-intentioned but naive, they say to themselves, "As long as we love each other, we'll be able to work it out." While authentic love certainly helps in tackling marital problems, it is no guarantee of success. In fact, there is some provocative evidence that how much you *like* your lover may be more important than how much you *love* your lover. When researchers correlated a host of variables with a measure of the "successfulness" of romantic relationships, liking for one's partner was more highly correlated (.62) with relationship success than was love (.50) of one's partner (Sternberg & Grajek, 1984). A small difference such as this in just one study is hardly definitive. However, it raises the possibility that liking may conquer problems more effectively than love.

Sexual Orientation and Love

Learning Objective

Define sexual orientation, and summarize the research findings on the experience of love in heterosexual and homosexual relationships.

Sexual orientation **refers to a person's preference for emotional and sexual relationships with individuals of the same gender, the other gender, or either gender.** *Heterosexuals* **seek emotional-sexual relationships with members of the other gender.** *Homosexuals* **seek emotional-sexual relationships with members of the same gender.** *Bisexuals* **seek emotional-sexual relationships with members of both genders.** In recent years, the terms *gay* and *straight* have become widely used to refer to homosexuals and heterosexuals, respectively. *Gay* can refer to homosexuals of either gender, but most homosexual women prefer to call themselves *lesbians*.

Most studies of romantic love and relationships suffer from *heterosexism,* **or the assumption that** *all* **individuals and relationships are heterosexual.** Most questionnaires on romantic love and romantic relationships fail to ask subjects about their sexual orientation. When data are analyzed, there is no way to know whether subjects are referring to same- or other-gender romantic partners. Assuming that their subjects are all heterosexuals, researchers proceed to describe their findings without any mention of homosexuality. Of course, because many more people identify themselves as heterosexual, heterosexism in research probably doesn't distort the conclusions about heterosexuals very much. A more important problem of heterosexism is that it renders homosexual relationships invisible. Consequently, psychologists don't know as much about the role of sexual orientation as they would like to. Currently, more research attention is being devoted to the experience of being homosexual. Where evidence is available, we'll mention it.

The experience of romantic love seems to be the same regardless of a person's sexual orientation.

Strandtman - Umminger

Ms. Sara Dee Strandtman and Ms. Karen Marie Umminger were married Sunday, July 12, 1992, at the First Unitarian Church of Austin. The Reverend Linda R. Pendergrass officiated. A reception followed at the Hancock Recreation Center.

In the experience of love relationships, gender and identification with traditional or nontraditional gender roles seem to be more critical factors than sexual orientation (Garnets & Kimmel, 1991; Peplau, 1981). According to Linda Garnets and Doug Kimmel (1991), two psychologists well known for their research and writing on gay and lesbian issues, "Many similarities are found between heterosexual and homosexual couples, indicating commonality in dynamics within the relationship and a similar range of diversity among relationships" (p. 170). Both heterosexual and homosexual couples say they want their partners to have characteristics similar to theirs, hold similar values about relationships, report similar levels of relationship satisfaction, and perceive their relationships to be loving and satisfying.

For these reasons, our discussion of love will presume that the *experience of love* is similar regardless of a person's sexual orientation. Research has shown some differences between homosexual and heterosexual *relationships*—for example, in the division of labor and the balance of power—but we will hold our discussion of these issues for the next chapter, which is concerned with marriage and other intimate relationships.

Gender Differences Regarding Love

Learning Objective

Summarize the findings on gender differences and romanticism.

The differences in how males and females are socialized in our society appear to affect their attitudes toward love. The traditional stereotype suggests that women are more romantic than men. Nonetheless, much of the research evidence suggests just the opposite—men are the more romantic gender. For example, several studies have found that men hold more romantic beliefs than women do (Frazier & Esterly, 1990; Peplau, Hill, & Rubin, 1993; Sprecher & Metts, 1989). Other researchers report that men tend to fall in love more easily than women, whereas women fall out of love more easily than men (Hill, Rubin, & Peplau, 1976; Rubin, Peplau, & Hill, 1981). Furthermore, these researchers found that women seem to experience less emotional turmoil than men when romantic relationships break up.

Thus, as a whole, the evidence suggests that men are more romantic than women. However, we should note that women do seem more romantic with regard to *expressions* of love. That is, women are more willing to verbalize and display their affection (Balswick & Avertt, 1977). There is also evidence that women may be more sensitive than men to problems that occur in relationships (Hill et al., 1976). These gender differences seem in line with the observation in Chapter 5 that many men seem to have independent self-views whereas many women hold interdependent self-views (Dion & Dion, 1993; Lykes, 1985). Of course, without empirical data, this possible connection is only a thought-provoking speculation.

Another possible explanation for the finding that men appear to be more romantic than women is one based on economics. Heterosexual women are still more economically dependent on their partners than vice versa. According to this view, being romantic in the choice of a potential partner may be a luxury that men can afford more readily than women can. (We are unaware of research on this question with homosexual subjects. Hence, we don't know if this principle holds for all couples and, if it does, whether the reasons for it are similar.)

Theories of Love

Can the experience of love be broken down into certain key components? Are some of these elements more important than others? How are romantic love relationships different from other types of close relationships? These are the kinds of questions addressed by new theories of love that have emerged from the recent explosion of research on romantic relationships. In this section we'll look at two prominent theories of love.

Triangular Theory of Love

Learning Objective

Define passion, intimacy, and commitment, and describe Sternberg's eight types of love.

Robert Sternberg's (1986, 1988) *triangular theory of love* posits that all love experiences have three components: intimacy, passion, and commitment. Each of these components is represented as a point of a triangle, from which the theory derives its name (see Figure 8.9).

Passion **refers to the intense feelings (both positive and negative) experienced in love relationships, including sexual desire.** Sternberg suggests that while sexual needs may be dominant in many close relationships, other needs also figure in the experience of passion. Among them are the needs for affiliation, self-esteem, dominance, submission, and self-actualization. For example, self-esteem is threatened when one experiences jealousy.

Intimacy **refers to warmth, closeness, and sharing in a relationship.** Signs of intimacy include giving and receiving emotional support, wanting to promote the welfare of the loved one, and sharing one's self and one's possessions with another. As we've already discussed, self-disclosure is necessary to achieve and maintain feelings of intimacy in a relationship.

Commitment **involves the decision and intent to maintain a relationship in spite of the difficulties and costs that may arise.** According to Sternberg, commitment has a short-term and a long-term aspect. The short-term aspect concerns the conscious decision to love someone. The long-term aspect reflects the determination to make a relationship endure. Although the decision to love someone usually comes before commitment, some people make a commitment without consciously deciding that they love the other person.

Sternberg has described eight different types of relationships that can result from the presence or absence of each of the three components of love (see Figure 8.9). One of these relationship types, *nonlove,* is not pictured in the diagram because it is defined as the absence of any of the three components. Most interpersonal relationships—casual interactions—fall into this category. When all three components are present, *consummate love* is said to exist.

Sternberg's model is relatively new and hasn't generated much research to date. One study found little support for the notion that the various types of love can be accounted for by different weightings of intimacy, passion, and commitment (Hendrick & Hendrick, 1989). However, another study of dating couples found that measures of their commitment and intimacy were among the best predictors of whether their relationships continued (Hendrick, Hendrick, & Adler, 1988).

Figure 8.9
Sternberg's triangular theory of love
According to Robert Sternberg (1986), love includes three components: intimacy, passion, and commitment. These components are portrayed here as points on a triangle. The absence of all three components is called nonlove, which is not shown in the diagram. The other possible combinations of these three components yield the seven types of relationships mapped out here.

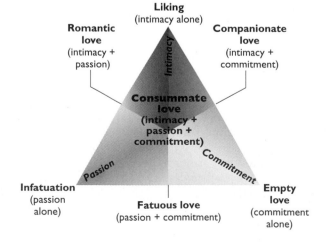

Romantic Love as Attachment

In another groundbreaking theory of love, Cindy Hazan and Phillip Shaver (1987) have looked at similarities between adult romantic love and attachment relationships in infancy. *Infant attachment* **refers to the strong emotional bond that infants usually develop with their caregivers during the first year of their lives.** Hazan and Shaver suggest that infant attachments and romantic attachments share a number of features: intense fascination with the other person, distress at separation, and efforts to stay close and spend time together. They also make the provocative suggestion that romantic relationships in adulthood follow the same form as attachments in infancy (see Figure 8.10).

What forms do attachments in infancy take? Research indicates that these early attachments vary in quality and that infants tend to fall into three groups (Ainsworth et al., 1978). Most infants develop a *secure attachment*. However, some are very anxious when separated from their caretaker, a syndrome called *anxious-ambivalent attachment*. A third group of infants, characterized by *avoidant attachment*, never connect very well with their caretaker.

How do attachments in infancy develop? The evidence indicates that these early attachments are related to parent-child interactions. (While earlier research focused mainly on mother-child interactions, more recent research looks at father-child interactions as well.) In the domain of attachment research, three parenting styles have been identified as possible determinants of attachment quality. A *warm/responsive* approach in caregiving is thought to promote secure attachments. A *cold/rejecting* style of caregiving is thought to be associated with avoidant attachments, and an *ambivalent/inconsistent* style with anxious-ambivalent attachments.

According to Hazan and Shaver, early bonding experiences produce relatively enduring relationship styles, including adult romantic partnerships. They theorize, for example, that an adult who had an anxious-ambivalent attachment in infancy will tend to have romantic relations marked by anxiety and ambivalence. Hazan and Shaver's (1987) initial survey study provided some support for their theory. They found that adults' love relationships could be sorted into groups that paralleled the patterns of attachment seen in infants. Specifically, they found that their subjects fell into the following three categories:

Figure 8.10
Infant attachment and romantic relationships
According to Hazan and Shaver (1987), romantic relationships in adulthood are similar in form to attachment patterns in infancy, which are determined in part by parental caregiving styles. The theorized relations between parental styles, attachment patterns, and intimate relations are outlined here. Hazan and Shaver's (1987) study sparked a flurry of follow-up research, which has largely supported the basic premises of their groundbreaking theory, although the linkages between infant experiences and close relationships in adulthood appear to be somewhat more complex than those portrayed here (Shaver & Hazan, 1992). (Parental caregiving styles and adult attachment styles based on Hazan and Shaver, 1986, 1987; infant attachment patterns adapted from Shaffer, 1989)

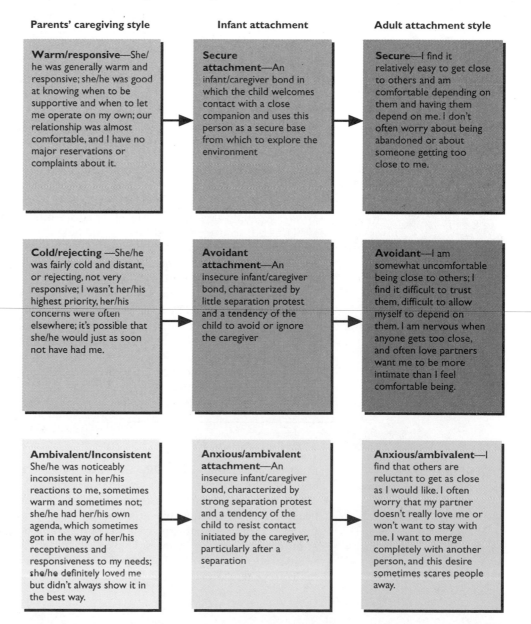

Parents' caregiving style	Infant attachment	Adult attachment style
Warm/responsive—She/he was generally warm and responsive; she/he was good at knowing when to be supportive and when to let me operate on my own; our relationship was almost comfortable, and I have no major reservations or complaints about it.	**Secure attachment**—An infant/caregiver bond in which the child welcomes contact with a close companion and uses this person as a secure base from which to explore the environment	**Secure**—I find it relatively easy to get close to others and am comfortable depending on them and having them depend on me. I don't often worry about being abandoned or about someone getting too close to me.
Cold/rejecting—She/he was fairly cold and distant, or rejecting, not very responsive; I wasn't her/his highest priority, her/his concerns were often elsewhere; it's possible that she/he would just as soon not have had me.	**Avoidant attachment**—An insecure infant/caregiver bond, characterized by little separation protest and a tendency of the child to avoid or ignore the caregiver	**Avoidant**—I am somewhat uncomfortable being close to others; I find it difficult to trust them, difficult to allow myself to depend on them. I am nervous when anyone gets too close, and often love partners want me to be more intimate than I feel comfortable being.
Ambivalent/Inconsistent—She/he was noticeably inconsistent in her/his reactions to me, sometimes warm and sometimes not; she/he had her/his own agenda, which sometimes got in the way of her/his receptiveness and responsiveness to my needs; she/he definitely loved me but didn't always show it in the best way.	**Anxious/ambivalent attachment**—An insecure infant/caregiver bond, characterized by strong separation protest and a tendency of the child to resist contact initiated by the caregiver, particularly after a separation	**Anxious/ambivalent**—I find that others are reluctant to get as close as I would like. I often worry that my partner doesn't really love me or won't want to stay with me. I want to merge completely with another person, and this desire sometimes scares people away.

Cindy Hazan

Phillip Shaver

- *Secure adults* (56% of subjects). People in this category found it easy to get close to others, trusted other people, and were comfortable with mutual dependence. Further, they rarely worried about being abandoned by their partner. Of the three groups of adults, these subjects were found to have the longest lasting relationships and the fewest divorces. They described their parents as behaving warmly to them and to each other.
- *Avoidant adults* (24% of subjects). These individuals felt somewhat uncomfortable getting close to others and had difficulty trusting their partners completely. They reported experiencing jealousy, emotional highs and lows, and a fear of intimacy in their relationships. They described their parents as less warm than secure adults did, and saw their mothers as cold and rejecting.
- *Anxious-ambivalent adults* (20% of subjects). Subjects in this category found their partners unwilling to get as close as they would like and they worried about their lovers leaving them. They also reported feelings of extreme sexual attraction and jealousy in their relationships. They described their relationship with their parents as less warm than secure adults did, and felt that their parents had unhappy marriages.

Hazan and Shaver found that the percentage of adults falling into each category was roughly the same as the percentage of infants in each comparable category. Also, subjects' recollections of their childhood relations with their parents were consistent with the idea that people relive their infant attachment experiences in adulthood. Of course, longitudinal studies are needed to demonstrate conclusively a causal link between infant and adult attachment styles. One longitudinal study has found evidence for consistency on some dimensions up to 10 years of age (Sroufe, Egeland, & Kreutzer, 1990).

Understandably, Hazan and Shaver's theory has attracted considerable interest among psychologists. Research has shown that securely attached individuals have more committed, satisfying, interdependent, and well-adjusted relationships compared to people with either anxious-ambivalent or avoidant attachment styles (Collins & Read, 1990; Hendrick & Hendrick, 1989). Studies have also found that an anxious-ambivalent style is associated with not being in a relationship and with being in relationships of shorter duration, and that an avoidant style is associated with shorter relationships (Collins & Read, 1990; Shaver & Brennan, 1992).

Research on adult *attachment styles and self-disclosure* with Israeli undergraduates indicates that both secure and anxious-ambivalent individuals disclose more than avoidant people in the early stages of social interaction (Mikulincer & Nachshon, 1991). Also, secure people showed more flexibility in self-disclosure and were more responsive to their conversation partners than those who were ambivalent and anxious-avoidant. These findings generally support Hazan and Shaver's theory of adult attachment styles and romantic love.

Attachment patterns may also have far-reaching repercussions that extend into many aspects of people's lives besides their romantic relationships. For instance, researchers have found correlations between attachment styles and job satisfaction, gender roles, religious beliefs, vulnerability to drinking problems, and attitudes about work (Shaver & Hazan, 1993, 1994). Thus, Hazan and Shaver's innovative ideas about the long-term effects of infant attachment experiences have triggered an avalanche of thought-provoking research.

The Course of Romantic Love

Learning Objective

Discuss the course of romantic love over time, why love relationships fail, and what couples can do to help relationships last.

Must passion fade? Regrettably, the answer to this question appears to be yes. Several theorists suggest that the intense attraction and arousal one feels for a lover seems destined to subside. Sternberg (1986) hypothesizes that passion reaches its peak early in a relationship and then declines in intensity. In contrast, both intimacy and commitment appear to increase as time progresses, although they develop at different rates (see Figure 8.11).

Berscheid and Hatfield's research also led them to conclude that passionate love tends to peak early and then fights a difficult battle against the erosion of time. At

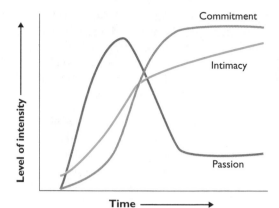

Figure 8.11
The course of love over time
According to Sternberg (1986), the three components of love typically progress differently over time. He theorizes that passion peaks early in a relationship and then declines. In contrast, intimacy and commitment are thought to build gradually.

first, love is "blind," so individuals usually develop a highly idealized picture of their lover (often a projection of their own needs). However, as time passes, the intrusion of reality often undermines this idealized view.

Must the decline of passion lead to the demise of a relationship? Not necessarily. Some relationships do dissolve when passion fades. However, many others evolve into different, but still satisfying, phases such as companionate love. Let's examine the research on why some romantic relationships endure while others end.

Why Relationships Fail

Most people find being in love exhilarating and wish it could last forever. Indeed, when consumed by passionate love, it's hard to believe these feelings for the other person won't last forever. Unfortunately, while many relationships do withstand the test of time, many others do not.

A longitudinal study of undergraduate dating couples revealed that 42% of couples who had designated their relationship as their closest interpersonal relationship had split up within nine months (Berscheid, Snyder, & Omoto, 1989). Similarly, the Boston Couples Study, a longitudinal study of dating couples in the Boston area, reported that almost half (45%) of the relationships had dissolved at the end of two years (Hill et al., 1976). A 15-year follow-up to the Boston Couples Study reported that 32% of the initial dating couples had married and that 64% of them had not (Peplau, Hill, & Rubin, 1993). Among the couples who had married at some time during the study, 68% were still together at the time of the follow-up.

The results from the initial Boston Couples Study provide some interesting insights about what causes couples to break up. In this study, 200 couples (predominantly college students) were followed over a period of two years. To participate in the study, couples had to be "going steady" and believe that they were in love. The reasons that couples gave for going their separate ways are shown in Figure 8.12. The results of this and other studies (Brehm, 1992) suggest that three prominent factors contribute to romantic breakups:

1. *Premature commitment.* Virtually all of the reasons for breakups involved things that could be known only after some sharing of personal information over time. Hence it seems that many couples make romantic commitments without taking the time to really get to know each other. These individuals may find out later that they

Figure 8.12
Factors contributing to breakups
Couples who broke up after dating steadily were asked why by Hill, Rubin, and Peplau (1976). The factors commonly cited are listed here. The researchers distinguished between *interactive factors*, which consisted of problems that emerged out of the partners' ways of relating to each other, and *noninteractive factors*.

What Causes Couples to Break Up?

Factors	Women's reports (%)	Men's reports (%)
Interactive factors		
Becoming bored with relationship	77	77
Differences in interests	73	61
Differences in backgrounds	44	47
Differences in intelligence	20	10
Conflicting sexual attitudes	48	43
Conflicting marriage ideas	43	29
Noninteractive factors		
Woman's desire to be independent	74	50
Man's desire to be independent	47	61
Woman's interest in someone else	40	31
Man's interest in someone else	18	29
Living too far apart	28	41
Pressure from woman's parents	18	13
Pressure from man's parents	10	9

Couples who focus on one another's positive qualities and the benefits of their relationship reduce relationship distress.

don't really like each other or that they have very little in common. For these reasons, "whirlwind courtships" are risky. Intimacy needs to be combined with commitment if relationships are to survive (Hendrick et al., 1988).

2. *Ineffective conflict resolution skills.* The vast majority of couples reported having disagreements. Research indicates that the likelihood of disagreements increases as couples learn more about each other and become more interdependent. One study reported that disagreements among casually dating couples were significantly lower than among couples who were dating seriously (Braiker & Kelley, 1979). Unfortunately, as we discussed in Chapter 7, many people do not know how to deal with conflict constructively. This inability to resolve conflicts effectively appears to be a key factor in romantic breakups (Brehm, 1992).

3. *Availability of a more attractive relationship.* Whether a deteriorating relationship actually ends depends, in great part, on the availability of a more attractive alternative (Felmlee, Sprecher, & Bassin, 1990). We all know of individuals who bided their time in unsatisfying relationships only until they met someone new.

Helping Relationships Last

Are there things people can do to increase the chances that their love relationships will last? Amazingly, it has been only recently that researchers have addressed this critical question. Fortunately, enough research has been done to date to permit us to offer some tentative advice.

1. *Engage in extensive self-disclosure and take plenty of time to get to know the other person before you make a long-term commitment.* Recent research based on Sternberg's theory found that the best predictors of whether dating couples' relationships would continue were their levels of commitment and intimacy (Hendrick et al., 1988). Hence, it appears that early attention to the intimacy foundations of a relationship and ongoing, mutual efforts to build a commitment can help foster more enduring love. These factors are evident in the responses of long-married couples to the question of why they thought that their relationship had lasted (Lauer & Lauer, 1985). The most frequently given responses of 351 couples, who had been married for 15 years or more, were (1) friendship ("I like my spouse as a person"); (2) commitment to the relationship ("I want the relationship to succeed"); (3) similarity in values and relationship issues ("We agree on how and how often to show affection"); and (4) positive feelings about each other ("My spouse has grown more interesting").

2. *Emphasize the positive qualities in your partner and in your relationship.* It is crucial to communicate more positive feelings than negative ones to your partner (Byrne & Murnen, 1988). People find this easy to do early in a relationship, but harder as the relationship continues. For one thing, once the initial "glow" of the relationship wears off, a common attributional error comes into play. **The *actor-observer effect* is the tendency to attribute one's own behavior to situational factors and others' behavior to personal factors.** This tendency can set up the destructive habit of chronically blaming the other person for problems and not taking responsibility when one should. Ironically, married couples generally make more negative and fewer positive statements to their spouse than to strangers (we presume this holds true for those in other types of committed relationships as well) (Koren, Carlton, & Shaw, 1980; Miller, 1991). This tendency is more prevalent among distressed than among nondistressed couples (Bradbury & Fincham, 1990; Halford & Sanders, 1990). Unfortunately, when one partner engages in this behavior, the other often responds in kind. This can set in motion a pattern of reciprocal negativity that makes things worse. Hence, there's a lot of good sense in the old song that advises people to "accentuate the positive and eliminate the negative."

3. *Develop effective conflict resolution skills.* Because conflicts arise in all relationships, it's important to be able to deal successfully with them. For one thing, it's

useful to distinguish between minor annoyances and important relationship issues. You need to learn to see minor irritations in perspective and recognize how little they matter. When problems are really important, however, it's usually best to avoid the temptation to sweep them under the rug in the hope that they'll disappear. Important issues rarely disappear on their own, and if you postpone the inevitable discussion, the "sweepings" will have accumulated, making it more difficult to sort out the various issues and feelings. For more specific suggestions, refer to our discussion of this issue in Chapter 7.

Loneliness

Although individuals vary in their need for affiliation, friendship and love play important roles in people's lives. Let's see what happens when this fundamental need for these social relations is thwarted. **Loneliness occurs when a person has fewer interpersonal relationships than desired or when these relationships are not as satisfying as desired.** *Loneliness is not the same as spending time alone.* People can feel lonely even when surrounded by others (at a party or concert, for instance). Conversely, some people cherish solitude and are content with less social interaction than most others prefer. Thus, loneliness is a highly subjective and personal feeling.

Learning Objective

Describe the three kinds of loneliness identified by Young.

Jeffrey Young (1982) has identified three kinds of loneliness. *Chronic loneliness* is a condition that affects people who have been unable to develop a satisfactory interpersonal network over a period of years. *Transitional loneliness* occurs when people who have had satisfying social relationships in the past become lonely because of a specific disruption of their social network (the death of a loved one, say, or divorce, or moving to a new locale). One study reported that 75% of new college students reported experiencing loneliness in their first few weeks on campus (Cutrona, 1982). *Transient loneliness* involves brief and sporadic feelings of loneliness, which many people may experience even when their social lives are reasonably adequate.

Loneliness may not occur in all areas of a person's life. For instance, you might be highly satisfied with your friendship network but feel dissatisfied about not having a suitable romantic relationship. Research suggests that loneliness can be attributed to perceived deficits in four types of relationships: (1) romantic/sexual relationships, (2) friendship relationships, (3) family relationships, and (4) community relationships (Schmidt & Sermat, 1983). Because it is likely that each problem can have different solutions, it's important to pinpoint the exact nature of your social deficits to better understand how to cope with loneliness.

Prevalence and Consequences of Loneliness

Learning Objective

Summarize the evidence on the prevalence and consequences of loneliness.

How many people are chronically tormented by severe loneliness? Although we don't have sound data for a precise answer to this question, anecdotal evidence suggests that the number of people plagued by severe loneliness is substantial. Telephone hotlines for troubled people report that complaints of loneliness dominate their calls.

Research on the prevalence of loneliness in specific age groups reveals some statistics that many will find surprising because they contradict stereotypes: (1) adolescents and young adults are the loneliest age group, and (2) loneliness decreases with age, at least until the much later years of adulthood when one's friends begin to die (Peplau et al., 1982; Rubenstein & Shaver, 1982).

The *personal* consequences of loneliness can be overwhelming. Painful thoughts of one's plight may come to dominate one's consciousness. As might be expected, studies have found a strong correlation between feelings of loneliness and feelings of depression (Anderson & Harvey, 1988; Young, 1982). Similarly, researchers have reported a relationship between loneliness and poor physical and psychological health (Rubenstein & Shaver, 1982).

Unfortunately, loneliness seems to have some *social* consequences, too. Several studies have found that when a hypothetical target person was characterized as socially isolated and lonely, participants rated that person as less well adjusted, less achieving and intellectually competent, and less socially competent than a nonlonely target person (Lau & Gruen, 1992; Rotenberg & Kmill, 1992). In addition, the lonely person was less preferred as a friend by others and was rated as weaker, more passive, less attractive, and less sincere compared to a nonlonely target person. Lonely men were evaluated more negatively than lonely women. Of course, we need to be careful about generalizing too much from a single study, but it does seem that poor social skills are evaluated negatively by others. The good news is that effective social skills can be learned—recall our discussion of assertive communication in the Application for Chapter 7.

The Roots of Loneliness

A number of factors can contribute to feelings of loneliness. Since any event that ruptures the social fabric of a person's life may lead to loneliness, no one is immune. Social trends and personal qualities are among the more prominent causes of loneliness.

Contributing Social Trends

Learning Objective

Explain how social trends and low self-esteem contribute to loneliness.

A major reason people have difficulty overcoming loneliness is that many tend to withdraw socially, even when surrounded by others.

A number of theorists have commented on various social trends that have undermined the sharing of intimacy in our culture (Flanders, 1982; Keyes, 1980). Because of people's busy schedules, social interactions at home are reduced as family members eat on the run, on their own, or in front of the TV. And the fact that people watch television so much tends to diminish meaningful family conversation. While technology makes life easier in some respects, it can also have negative effects on personal lives. For example, superficial social interactions become prevalent as people order their meals at drive-up windows, do their banking at ATMs or over the phone, and so forth. Finally, with the advent of personal computers, more and more people will spend time at terminals in their offices and homes, alone.

As you might expect, individuals whose parents have been divorced report feeling more lonely than those from intact families (Rubenstein & Shaver, 1982; Shaver & Rubenstein, 1980). Moreover, the earlier in their lives the divorce occurred, the stronger the feelings of loneliness experienced in adulthood. In contrast, no differences in loneliness are seen between individuals who have lost a parent through death and those from intact families. Interestingly, research does not support two intuitive expectations regarding loneliness. That is, loneliness doesn't correlate with the nature of residential setting (urban or rural) or with the frequency of changes in location (Rubenstein & Shaver, 1982).

Low Self-Esteem

A key personal factor that seems to promote loneliness is low self-esteem and related negative attitudes about

PEANUTS reprinted by permission of United Feature Syndicate, Inc.

oneself (Hanson, Jones, & Carpenter, 1984; Rubenstein & Shaver, 1982). Lonely people often have cynical and pessimistic attitudes and believe that life is uncontrollable (Anderson & Riger, 1991; Davis et al., 1992). They seem to selectively attend to negative information about themselves, thereby reinforcing an already negative self-concept (Frankel & Prentice-Dunn, 1990). Individuals who have unfavorable opinions of themselves often do not feel worthy of others' affection. They may make little effort to pursue close relationships. This lack of confidence probably has a spiraling effect, as low self-esteem begets loneliness and loneliness begets still lower self-esteem.

Negative Attitudes About Others

Lonely individuals seem to hold negative attitudes toward others when compared to those who aren't lonely. That is, research has found that those who describe themselves as lonely don't like others very much (Rubenstein & Shaver, 1980), don't trust others very much (Vaux, 1988), often evaluate others negatively (Jones, Sansome, & Helm, 1983; Wittenberg & Reis, 1986), and have hostile attitudes toward others (Check, Perlman, & Malamuth, 1985). As with self-esteem and loneliness, negative attitudes about others and loneliness probably interact.

Poor Social Skills

Poor social skills prevent many people from experiencing rewarding social interactions. One study found that lonely people tend to pay inadequate attention to their conversational partners (Jones, Hobbs, & Hockenbury, 1982). Other research has found that lonely people are relatively inhibited, speaking less than nonlonely people (Sloan & Solano, 1984) and disclosing less about themselves than those who are not lonely (Davis & Franzoi, 1986; Sloan & Solano, 1984; Solano, Batten, & Parish, 1982; Williams & Solano, 1983). This (often unconscious) tendency has the effect of keeping people at an emotional distance and limits interactions to a relatively superficial level. Anxiety about social skills is also correlated with loneliness (Anderson & Harvey, 1988; Solano & Koester, 1989) and shyness (Anderson & Harvey, 1988), a topic we'll consider in the upcoming Application.

Negative Self-Talk

Ultimately, what underlies many of the factors just discussed is negative self-talk. Lonely people are prone to irrational thinking about their social skills, the probability of achieving intimacy, the likelihood of rejection, and so forth. For example, there is evidence that lonely people blame themselves for their painful state and tend to attribute their loneliness to *stable, internal causes* (Anderson, Horowitz, & French, 1983; Anderson et al., 1994; Michela, Peplau, & Weeks, 1982). That is, lonely people might tell themselves that they're lonely because they're basically unlovable individuals. Not only is this a devastating belief, it also provides no way to change the situation. From our discussion on attribution in Chapter 5, recall that there are *other* attributions a lonely person could make *and* that these explanations point to solutions. If a person says, "My conversational skills are weak" (unstable,

Clusters of Cognitions Typical of Lonely Clients

Clusters	Cognitions	Behaviors
A	1. I'm undesirable. 2. I'm dull and boring.	Avoidance of friendship
B	1. I can't communicate with other people. 2. My thoughts and feelings are bottled up inside.	Low self-disclosure
C	1. I'm not a good lover in bed. 2. I can't relax, be spontaneous, and enjoy sex.	Avoidance of sexual relationships
D	1. I can't seem to get what I want from this relationship. 2. I can't say how I feel, or he/she might leave me.	Lack of assertiveness in relationships
E	1. I won't risk being hurt again. 2. I'd screw up any relationship.	Avoidance of potentially intimate relationships
F	1. I don't know how to act in this situation. 2. I'll make a fool of myself.	Avoidance of other people

Figure 8.13
Patterns of thinking underlying loneliness
According to Young (1982), negative self-talk contributes to loneliness. Six clusters of irrational thoughts are shown here. Each cluster of cognitions leads to certain patterns of behavior (right) that promote loneliness.

internal cause), this leads to the solution: "I'll try to find out how to improve them." Or, if a person tells herself, "It always takes time to meet people when you move to a new location" (unstable, external cause), this leads to the solution of trying harder to develop new relationships and giving them time to work. The attribution "I've really looked hard, but there just don't seem to be very many people in the organization who share my interests and attitudes" (stable, external cause) may lead to the decision, "I guess it's time to look for a new job." As you can see, the last three attributions lead to active modes of coping.

Young (1982) points out that lonely people engage in negative self-talk that prevents them from pursuing intimacy in an active and positive manner. He has identified some clusters of ideas that foster loneliness. Figure 8.13 gives examples of typical thoughts from six of these clusters of cognitions and the overt behaviors that result.

Coping with Loneliness

Learning Objective

Give some suggestions for coping with loneliness.

For those who suffer from loneliness, there are no simple solutions, but there are some effective ones. A major reason that people have difficulty overcoming loneliness is that they tend to withdraw socially. For example, one study that asked people what they did when they felt lonely found that the top responses were "read" and "listen to music" (Rubenstein & Shaver, 1982). If used only occasionally, reading and listening to music can be constructive ways of dealing with loneliness. However, as long-term strategies, they do nothing to help a lonely person acquire new friends.

Effective self-help strategies for overcoming loneliness include engaging in positive self-talk, avoiding the temptation to withdraw from social situations, and working on one's conversational skills (Brehm, 1992). The importance of staying active socially cannot be overemphasized. As we noted earlier in this chapter, proximity is a powerful factor in the development of close relationships. You have to be around people in order to expand your network of friends.

For those who seek professional help for their loneliness, there is good news: Both the negative perceptions that often underlie loneliness and poor social skills can be changed relatively easily and quickly (Young, 1982). Most college counseling centers are staffed with professionals who are experts in *social skills training*. Over a series of sessions, they can help individuals learn to change their negative views of themselves ("I'm boring") and others ("They're cold and unfriendly"). In addition, clients watch videotapes of socially skilled models demonstrating appropriate social behavior in a variety of settings. Then they practice these behaviors in the counselor's office. Sometimes these practice sessions are taped so clients can actually see how they are coming across.

In the Application, we'll discuss a common, and related, problem: shyness.

Application

Understanding Shyness

*A*nswer the following "yes" or "no."

1. *When I am the focus of attention, I often become anxious.*

2. *In interacting with people, I tend to be very self-conscious.*

3. *I get embarrassed quite easily in social situations.*

4. *I wish that I could be more assertive about pursuing social relationships.*

5. *I am often concerned about being rejected by others.*

Learning Objective

Define shyness and list some of its common characteristics, its prevalence, and its consequences.

If you answered yes to several of these questions, you may be hampered in your social life by a common problem—shyness. Loneliness and shyness are intersecting problems. Although many lonely people are not shy, and many shy people are not lonely, it is nonetheless true that loneliness is a common consequence of shyness (Cheek & Busch, 1981). Given this, it isn't surprising that shy and lonely people share some common characteristics. Two of these are poor social skills and negative attitudes toward others (Jones & Carpenter, 1986).

Shyness refers to discomfort, inhibition, and excessive caution in interpersonal relations. Specifically, shy people tend (1) to be timid about expressing themselves, (2) to be overly self-conscious about how others are reacting to them, (3) to embarrass easily, and (4) to experience physiological symptoms of their anxiety, such as a racing pulse, blushing, or an upset stomach.

Prevalence and Consequences of Shyness

Philip Zimbardo (1977, 1990) has done pioneering research on shyness. His survey data indicate that shyness may be more common than previously realized. Over 80% of the respondents to his survey reported having been shy during some stage of

Recommended Reading

Shyness

by Philip G. Zimbardo (Addison Wesley, 1977)

Zimbardo, an outstanding social psychologist, focuses his keen insight on the frustrations of being shy. A lack of jargon and ample use of actual case histories make this book highly readable. Zimbardo explores the roots of shyness in Part I of the book and then addresses the question of "what to do about it" in Part II. The second part of the book is full of exercises and sound advice for tackling this problem head-on.

Theories are like enormous vacuum cleaners, sucking up everything in their paths. Each of the theories outlined here has vigorous backers, hawkers of the best vacuum cleaner on the market. We shall borrow freely from any and all of them when we come to design programs for coping with shyness. [1977, p. 55] their lives. Moreover, 40% indicated that they were currently troubled by shyness. The personal implications of shyness are generally quite negative. Most shy people report that they do not like being shy. This is understandable in view of the common consequences of shyness. Shy people tend to have difficulty making friends, and they tend to be sexually inhibited. They also are lonely and depressed more often than others.

Situational Nature of Shyness

Learning Objective

Discuss the situational nature of shyness and distinguish between state shyness and trait shyness.

The traditional stereotype of the shy person as one who is timid all the time appears to be somewhat inaccurate. In Zimbardo's study, 60% of the shy people reported that their shyness was *situationally specific*. That is, they experienced shyness only in certain social contexts, such as asking someone for help or interacting with a large group of people. Figure 8.14 lists the situations that most commonly elicited shyness in Zimbardo's subjects.

The situational nature of shyness has led researchers to distinguish between state shyness and trait shyness (Asendorpf, 1989). *State shyness* is a temporary elevation in anxiety in reaction to certain social situations. According to Asendorpf (1986), the crux of the problem is that people experience an approach-avoidance conflict (see Figure 8.15). They are torn between their desire to interact with someone (approach motivation) and their fear of making a social blunder (avoidance motivation). What types of situations tend to elicit state shyness? According to Asendorpf, the most common triggers appear to be the presence of strangers and the expectation of being evaluated by others.

Trait shyness is a consistent tendency to feel anxious and inhibited in a wide variety of social situations. People who are chronically tormented by discomfort in social interactions exhibit shyness as a stable personality trait (Jones, Briggs, & Smith, 1986). Some studies suggest that there is a genetic predisposition toward trait shyness (Daniels & Plomin, 1985).

Coping with Shyness

Learning Objective

Discuss Zimbardo's three steps for coping with shyness.

It would be naive to pretend that shyness can be overcome easily. However, it is important to emphasize that shyness *can* be overcome successfully! Think about it. In Zimbardo's survey, 40% of the respondents reported that they were *currently* shy, while 80% indicated that they *had been* shy at some previous time. Obviously, half of the once-shy subjects felt that they had conquered their shyness.

Much of Zimbardo's (1977) book is devoted to how to deal with the problem of shyness. Basically, the three key steps in this process are (1) analyzing one's shyness, (2) building self-esteem, and (3) improving social skills.

Analyzing One's Shyness

The first step is the easiest. Individuals should analyze their shyness and try to pinpoint exactly which social situations tend to elicit their shy behavior. They should further try to ascertain what causes their shyness in the specific situations. To help identify situations that trigger their shyness, individuals can use some of the techniques for gathering baseline data that are used with behavior modification programs (see the Chapter 4 Application).

Figure 8.14
The situational determinants of shyness
Zimbardo (1977) asked subjects about the people and circumstances that made them feel shy. The results showed that shyness depends to a large degree on situational factors.

"What Makes You Shy?"

	Percentage of shy students
Other people	
Strangers	70
Opposite sex	64
Authorities by virtue of their knowledge	55
Authorities by virtue of their role	40
Relatives	21
Elderly people	12
Friends	11
Children	10
Parents	8
Situations	
Where I am focus of attention—large group (as when giving a speech)	73
Large groups	68
Of lower status	56
Social situations in general	55
New situations in general	55
Requiring assertiveness	54
Where I am being evaluated	53
Where I am focus of attention—small group	52
Small social groups	48
One-to-one different-sex interactions	48
Of vulnerability (need help)	48
Small task-oriented groups	28
One-to-one same-sex interactions	14

A number of reasons or combinations of reasons may account for trait shyness. Zimbardo listed eight common reasons: (1) concern about negative evaluation, (2) fear of rejection, (3) lack of self-confidence, (4) lack of specific social skills, (5) fear of intimacy, (6) preference for being alone, (7) emphasis on and enjoyment of nonsocial activities, and (8) personal inadequacy or handicap.

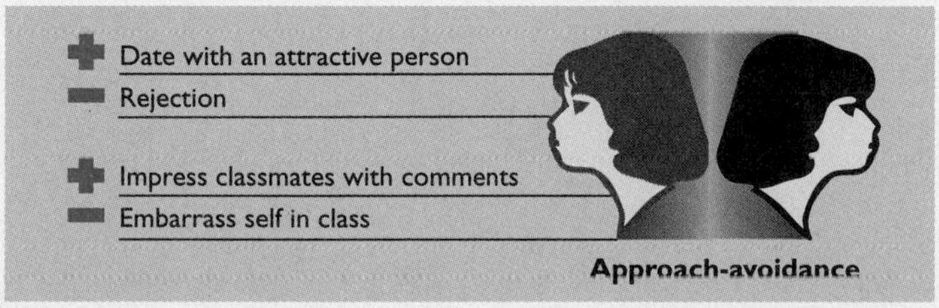

Figure 8.15
Shyness as an approach-avoidance conflict
State shyness involves an approach-avoidance conflict in which a person both desires and fears social interaction. As we noted in Chapter 3, approach-avoidance conflicts can be highly stressful.

+ Date with an attractive person
− Rejection

+ Impress classmates with comments
− Embarrass self in class

Approach-avoidance

Building Self-Esteem

Poor self-esteem appears to be a key factor underlying trait shyness (Crozier, 1981). Hence, it is important for shy people to work on improving their self-confidence. In his book, Zimbardo spells out "fifteen steps to a more confident you." Many of these steps coincide with the suggestions made in the Chapter 5 Application on building self-esteem.

Improving Social Skills

Philip Zimbardo

The third step is the most difficult. As we have discussed repeatedly, it is not easy to change deeply ingrained habits. Zimbardo suggests using many of the behavior modification techniques covered in the Chapter 4 Application. Specifically, he recommends specifying certain target social responses to be increased and then setting up a reward system for engaging in these responses. He further emphasizes that one has to be realistic and work toward *gradual* improvement. For example, he suggests that people start with relatively simple and nonthreatening social behaviors, such as anonymous conversations. These are conversations with strangers in public places, such as a theater line, a bank, or a stadium. Other simple social responses that one might start with include saying "Hello" to strangers or giving compliments to others.

Zimbardo offers other suggestions for improving social skills that are too numerous to detail here. However, we can mention a few ideas to consider if you are troubled by shyness. First, it's a good idea to select a nonshy role model to watch closely. Identify someone in your personal sphere who is extraverted. It's probably a good idea to use a same-gender model. Observe how your role model handles various kinds of social situations. In particular, pay attention to how he or she acts in the situations that trigger your shyness. Second, develop "expertise" in some area so that you have something to contribute to conversations. In other words, become a movie buff or a sports buff or an amateur political analyst. Third, listen actively and attentively. People love to talk about themselves. Encourage them to do so. After going on and on about themselves, they'll probably compliment you on what an interesting and enjoyable "conversation" the two of you just had!

As you work on developing your social skills, bear in mind that your progress will probably be gradual. Social skills are honed over a lifetime. Although they *can* be improved with practice, it normally takes a good bit of time, and your progress may seem barely perceptible. However, if you stick with it, you can conquer shyness.

Key Ideas

Perspectives on Close Relationships

• Close relationships are characterized as long-lasting ones in which two people interact frequently in a variety of settings and in which the impact of these interactions is strong. Close relationships include friendships as well as work, family, and romantic relationships. The ability to establish and maintain committed, intimate relationships appears to be related to identity development.

• Social exchange theory uses principles of reinforcement to predict relationship satisfaction and commitment. Individuals seem to apply social exchange principles depending on whether they are in an exchange or communal relationship. People in individualistic cultures believe that romantic love is a prerequisite for marriage, whereas those in collectivist cultures prefer arranged marriages.

Factors Influencing Interpersonal Attraction

• The dynamics of attraction are similar for friendship and love. People are drawn to others whom they find physically attractive, pleasant to be with, and intelligent and competent. Women tend to marry men who are somewhat older than they are, and men seem to prefer women who are somewhat younger. In heterosexual dating, men often trade status for attractiveness in women and vice versa. One's own needs for affiliation and intimacy, as well as one's self-esteem and self-perception processes, also figure importantly in one's attraction to others. The interaction factors of proximity, similarity, and reciprocity promote attraction.

Friendship

• The key ingredients of friendship are loyalty, emotional support, and letting friends be themselves. Women's same-gender friendships tend to be characterized by intimacy and self-disclosure, whereas men's same-gender friendships typically involve doing things together.

Romantic Love

• Myths about romantic love include the idea that when people fall in love they know it and the notion that people have no control over themselves when love strikes. Other myths are that love lasts forever and that it can conquer all problems. Research indicates that the experience of romantic love is the same for heterosexual and homosexual individuals. Gender differences regarding love do not support the traditional stereotype that women are more romantic than men.

• Sternberg's triangular theory of love proposes that passion, intimacy, and commitment combine into eight different types of love. Hazan and Shaver theorize that love relationships follow the form of attachments in infancy.

• Initially, romantic love is usually characterized by passion, but strong passion appears to fade over time. In relationships that continue, passionate love evolves into a less intense, more mature form of love. The chief causes of relationship failure are the tendency to make premature commitments, ineffective conflict resolution skills, and the availability of a more attractive relationship. To help relationships last, couples should engage in extensive self-disclosure, take plenty of time to get to know each other, emphasize the positive qualities in their partner and relationship, and develop effective conflict resolution skills.

Loneliness

• Loneliness involves discontent with the extent and quality of one's interpersonal network. A surprisingly large number of people in our society are troubled by loneliness, which is often associated with depression, as well as poor physical and psychological health. Although loneliness is promoted by a number of social trends, it appears to be caused mainly by personal factors such as low self-esteem, negative attitudes about others, poor social skills, and negative self-talk. The keys to coping with loneliness are engaging in positive self-talk, avoiding the temptation to withdraw from social situations, and working on one's communication skills.

Application: Understanding Shyness

• Shy people are usually uncomfortable and inhibited around others. A large number of people seem to be troubled by shyness. Although most cases of shyness seem to stem from situational causes, some individuals suffer from trait shyness. To cope with shyness, Zimbardo suggests that individuals analyze the causes of their shyness, build their self-esteem, and improve their social skills.

Key Terms

Actor-observer effect
Bisexuals
Close relationships
Commitment
Comparison level
Comparison level for alternatives
Heterosexism
Heterosexuals
Homosexuals
Infant attachment
Interpersonal attraction
Intimacy
Investments
Loneliness
Matching hypothesis
Passion
Proximity
Reciprocity
Sexual orientation
Shyness
Social exchange theory

Key People

Ellen Berscheid and Elaine Hatfield (Walster)
Cindy Hazan and Philip Shaver
Harold Kelley and John Thibaut
Robert Sternberg
Philip Zimbardo

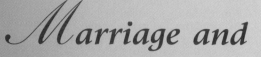

9 Marriage and
Intimate Relationships

"My hands are shaky. I want to call her again but I know it is no good. She'll only yell and scream. It makes me feel lousy. I have work to do but I can't do it. I can't concentrate. I want to call people up, go see them, but I'm afraid they'll see that I'm shaky. I just want to talk. I can't think about anything besides this trouble with Nina. I think I want to cry."

—A recently separated man quoted in *Marital Separation* (Weiss, 1975, p. 48)

*T*his man is an emotional wreck. He is describing his feelings a few days after he and his wife broke up. He is still hoping for a reconciliation. In the meantime he feels overwhelmed by anxiety, remorse, and depression. He feels alone and is scared by the prospect of remaining alone. His emotional distress is so great that he can't think straight or work effectively.

This man's reaction to the loss of an intimate relationship is not unusual. Marital breakups are devastating for most people—a reality that illustrates the enormous importance of intimate relationships in our lives.

In this chapter we will take a look at marriage and other intimate relationships. We will discuss why people marry and how they progress toward the selection of a mate. To shed light on marital adjustment, we will describe the life cycle of the family, highlighting key vulnerable spots in marital relations. We will also address issues related to divorce, cohabitation, remaining single, and being gay. Finally, in the Application, we will examine the important problem of intimate violence. Let's begin by discussing recent challenges to the traditional concept of marriage.

Challenges to the Traditional Model of Marriage

Marriage is the legally and socially sanctioned union of sexually intimate adults. Traditionally, the marital relationship has included economic interdependence, common residence, sexual fidelity, and shared responsibility for children. Although the institution of marriage remains popular, it sometimes seems to be under assault from shifting social trends. This assault has prompted many experts to ask whether the institution of marriage is in serious trouble (Rodman & Sidden, 1992). It appears that marriage will weather the storm. But it's worth looking at some of the social trends that are shaking the traditional model of marriage.

1. *Increased acceptance of singlehood.* An increasing proportion of the adult population under age 35 is remaining single (Stein, 1989). In part, this trend reflects longer postponement of marriage than before. The median age at which people marry has been increasing gradually since the mid-1960s, as Figure 9.1 shows. Thus, remaining single is becoming a more viable lifestyle. Furthermore, the negative stereotype of people who remain single, which pictures them as lonely, frustrated, and unchosen, is gradually evaporating.

Figure 9.1
Median age at first marriage
The median age at which people marry for the first time has been creeping up for both males and females since the mid-1960s. This trend indicates that more people are postponing marriage.

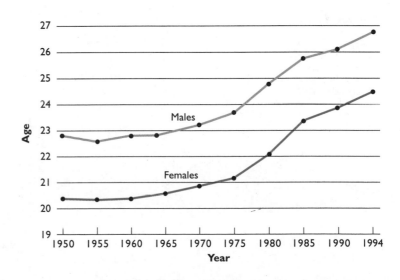

Thanks in part to television portrayals of the family, people cling to an idealized image of the traditional nuclear family, despite the fact that only 7% of American families match this stereotype.

2. *Increased acceptance of cohabitation.* **Cohabitation** **is living together in a sexually intimate relationship without the legal bonds of marriage.** Negative attitudes toward couples "living together" appear to be declining, although many people continue to disapprove of the practice. It is difficult to get accurate information on the number of couples who cohabit. However, various sources of data suggest that cohabitation has increased dramatically (Bumpass, Sweet, & Cherlin, 1991). Census data, for instance, indicate that the number of couples living together increased more than sevenfold between 1970 and 1993.

3. *Reduced premium on permanence.* Most people still view marriage as a permanent commitment, but many people are also strongly committed to their own personal growth. Marriage is often seen as just one context in which such growth can occur. Thus, an increasing number of people regard divorce as justifiable if their marriage fails to foster their interests as individuals (Popenoe, 1993). Accordingly, the social stigma associated with divorce has lessened and divorce rates have risen. Some experts estimate that roughly two of every three marriages will ultimately result in separation or divorce (Wisensale, 1992).

4. *Transitions in gender roles.* The women's movement and economic pressures have led to substantial changes in the expectations of many people entering marriage today. The traditional breadwinner and homemaker roles for the husband and wife are being discarded by many couples, as more and more married women enter the workforce (see Figure 9.2). Role expectations for husbands and wives are becoming more varied, more flexible, and more ambiguous (Fine, 1992). Many people regard this trend as a step in the right direction (see Chapter 10). However, changing gender roles create new potential for conflict between marital partners.

5. *Increased voluntary childlessness.* In the past two decades, the percentage of women without children has climbed in all age groups (see Figure 9.3) as an increasing number of married couples have chosen not to have children (Seccombe, 1991). This trend is probably due to new career opportunities for women, the tendency to marry at a later age, and changing attitudes. Since 1962, the percentage of American mothers who agree that "all couples should have children" has declined from 84% to 43% (Thornton, 1989).

Figure 9.2
Women in the workforce
The percentage of women (over age 16) who work outside the home has been rising steadily throughout this century. Even among women with children under 6 years of age, about 57% are employed. (Data from U.S. Bureau of Labor Statistics, 1991)

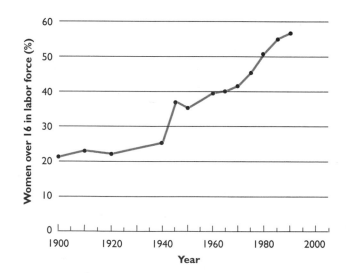

Figure 9.3
Percentage of women without children by age group
The proportion of adult women in the United States who have never had a child has been increasing gradually over the last two decades. (Data from U.S. Bureau of Labor Statistics, 1991)

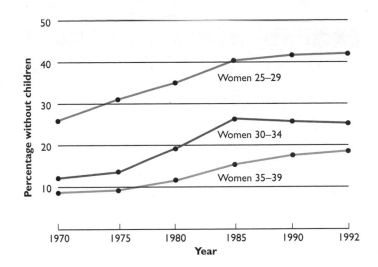

6. *The decline of the traditional nuclear family.* Thanks to televison shows like *Happy Days* and *Home Improvement*, in the eyes of most people, the normal American family should consist of a husband and wife married for the first time, rearing two or more children, with the man serving as the main breadwinner and the woman filling the homemaker role (Coontz, 1992). As Demo (1992) notes, "This ideal continues to serve as the reference point against which contemporary families are judged, despite the fact that many families did not conform to these ideals even during the nostalgic 1950s and early 1960s" (p. 105). Today, it is estimated that only 7% of American families match this idealized image of the "normal" family (Otto, 1988). The increasing prevalence of single-parent homes, stepfamilies, childless marriages, unwed parents, and working wives has conspired to make the traditional nuclear family a highly deceptive mirage that does not reflect the diversity of family structures in America.

In summary, the norms that mold marital and intimate relationships have been restructured in fundamental ways in recent decades. Traditional values have eroded as people have increasingly embraced more individualistic values (Popenoe, 1993; Thornton, 1989). Thus, the institution of marriage is in a period of transition, creating new adjustment challenges for modern couples. Support for the concept of monogamy remains strong, but changes in American society are altering the traditional model of marriage. The impact of these changes will be seen throughout this chapter as we discuss various facets of married life.

Moving Toward Marriage

"I'm ashamed of being single, I have to admit it. I have grown to hate the word. The worst thing someone can say is, 'How come you're still not married?' It's like saying, 'What's wrong with you.' I look at women who are frumpy and physically undesirable and they're monochromatic and uninteresting and they don't seem unselfish and giving and I wonder, 'How did they become such an integral part of a man's life that he wanted to marry them and spend his life with them?' I'm envious. They're married and I date."

—A woman quoted in *Tales from the Front* (Kavesh & Lavin, 1988, p. 91)

This woman desperately wants to be married. The intensity of her motivation for marriage may be a bit unusual, but otherwise she is fairly typical. Like most people, she has been socialized to believe that her life won't be complete until she finds a mate. Although alternatives to marriage are more viable than ever, experts project that over 90% of Americans will marry at least once. Some will even do it several times! But why? What motivates people to marry? And how do individuals choose their partners? We'll address these questions as we discuss the factors that influence a person's movement toward marriage.

The Motivation to Marry

A variety of motivational factors propel people into marriage. Foremost among these is the desire to participate in a socially sanctioned, mutually rewarding, intimate relationship. Another key factor is the social pressure exerted on people to marry. Getting married is still the norm in our society. Parents, relatives, and friends expect one to marry eventually, and they often make this abundantly clear with their comments and inquiries.

The popular view in American culture is that people marry because they have fallen in love. Although partially accurate, this view is terribly oversimplified. A multitude of motivational factors are involved in the decision to marry. Peter Stein (1975, 1976) interviewed single men and women aged 22 to 45 who were judged to be neither unattractive nor socially inept. As you can see in Figure 9.4, he learned that many forces push and pull people toward marriage or singlehood.

Selecting a Mate

Learning Objective

Discuss several factors influencing the selection of a mate.

Modern Western cultures are somewhat unusual in permitting free choice of one's marital partner. Most societies rely on parental arrangements and severely restrict the range of acceptable partners along religious and class lines (Bumiller, 1989). Mate selection in American culture is a gradual process that begins with dating and moves on to sometimes lengthy periods of courtship. In this section, we will look at the impact of endogamy, homogamy, and gender on marital choice. We'll also discuss Bernard Murstein's S-V-R theory, which provides a good overview of the process of mate selection.

Endogamy

***Endogamy* refers to the tendency of people to marry within their own social group.** Buss (1985) reviewed extensive evidence indicating that people tend to marry others of the same race, religion, ethnic background, and social class. This endogamy is promoted by cultural norms and by the way proximity and similarity influence interpersonal attraction (see Chapter 8). Although endogamy appears to be gradually declining, it's likely to remain influential for the foreseeable future (Surra, 1990).

Homogamy

***Homogamy* refers to the tendency of people to marry others who have similar personal characteristics.** Among other things, marital partners tend to be sim-

Figure 9.4
The decision to marry
Stein (1975) interviewed single people between 22 and 45 to ascertain the motivational factors that influence the decision to marry. *Pushes toward marriage* involve deficits supposedly felt by single persons. *Pushes toward singlehood* involve deficits felt by married people. *Pulls* are positive factors associated with marriage or being single. Not everyone weighs all these factors, but this list illustrates the complexity of the decision to marry.

The Decision to Marry

Pushes toward marriage	Pulls toward marriage	Pushes toward singlehood	Pulls toward singlehood
Economic security	Influence of parents	Restrictions	Career opportunities
Influence from mass media	Desire for family	Suffocating one-to-one	Variety of experiences
Pressure from parents	Example of peers	relationships, feeling trapped	Self-sufficiency
Need to leave home	Romanticization of marriage	Obstacles to self-development	Sexual availability
Interpersonal and personal reasons	Love	Boredom, unhappiness, anger	Exciting lifestyle
Fear of independence	Physical attraction	Role playing and conformity to	Freedom to change and
Loneliness	Emotional attachment	expectations	experiment
Alternatives did not seem feasible	Security, social status, prestige	Poor communication with mate	Mobility
Cultural expectations, socialization		Sexual frustration	Sustaining friendships
Regular sex		Lack of friends, isolation, loneliness	Supportive groups
Guilt over singlehood		Limitations on mobility and	Men's and women's groups
		available experience	Group living arrangements
		Influence of and participation in	Specialized groups
		women's movement	

People tend to marry others who are similar in race, religion, social class, education, and other personal characteristics.

ilar in age and education (Schoen & Wooldredge, 1989), physical attractiveness (Folkes, 1982), attitudes and values (Honeycutt, 1986), and even vulnerability to psychological disorders (McLeod, 1995). Deviations from homogamy in age and education tend to be one-sided, as husbands are usually older and better educated than their wives (South, 1991). Cultural norms that discourage women from dating younger men may contribute to a "marriage squeeze" for women. Without the freedom to date younger men, women are likely to find their pool of potential partners dwindling more rapidly than is the case for men of similar age (Oppenheimer, 1988).

Gender and Mate Selection Preferences

Research reveals that males and females exhibit both similarities and differences in what they look for in a marital partner. Many characteristics, such as kindness, emotional stability, dependability, and a pleasant disposition, are rated highly by both sexes (Buss, 1989; Kenrick et al., 1993). However, a few crucial differences between males' and females' priorities are found, and these differences appear to be nearly universal across cultures. As a group, women place a higher value than men on potential partners' socioeconomic status, intelligence, character, ambition, and financial prospects (Buss, 1989; Feingold, 1992a). In contrast, men consistently show more interest than women in potential partners' youthfulness, physical attractiveness, and interest in raising a family (Buss, 1994; Kenrick et al., 1993).

Most theorists explain these gender disparities in terms of evolutionary concepts (Feingold, 1992a). According to evolutionary theories, all organisms, including humans, are motivated to enhance their chances of passing on their genes to subsequent generations. Human females supposedly accomplish this end, not by seeking larger or stronger partners, as in the animal kingdom, but by seeking male partners who possess or are likely to acquire more material resources that can be invested in children. Men, on the other hand, are assumed to maximize their reproductive outlook by seeking female partners with good breeding potential. Thus, men are thought to look for youth, attractiveness, good health, and other characteristics presumed to be associated with higher fertility. Although these evolutionary analyses of gender differences in mating preferences are rather speculative, they fit with the evidence remarkably well.

Stimulus-Value-Role Theory

Learning Objective

Outline Murstein's stage theory of mate selection.

A number of theories have attempted to shed light on the process of mate selection and the development of premarital relationships (see Berg & McQuinn, 1986; Cate, Huston, & Nesselrode, 1986; Stephen, 1985). We'll focus on one particularly prominent model, Bernard Murstein's (1976, 1986) *stimulus-value-role (S-V-R) theory*. According to Murstein, couples generally proceed through three stages, which he calls the stimulus, value, and role stages, as they move toward marriage.

During the first stage, a person's attraction to members of the other gender depends mainly on their *stimulus value*. At this point, the individual focuses on relatively superficial and easily identifiable characteristics of the other person. Foremost among these are the person's physical attractiveness, social status, occupational success, and reputation. Borrowing from *social exchange theory* (see Chapter 8), Murstein argues that progress to the next stage depends on the pair's having relatively similar stimulus value, so as to produce an "even" exchange. The two persons may derive their stimulus value from different characteristics—one from wealth, say, and the other from beauty. However, progress to stage 2 is thought to depend on the couple's subjective perception that they possess similar stimulus value.

If a couple makes it to the second stage, involving *value comparison*, the significance of stimulus variables may be reduced. Further progress now depends on compatibility in values. Typically, the pair will begin to explore each other's attitudes about religion, politics, sex, gender roles, leisure activities, and so forth. If fundamental incompatibilities are uncovered, the relationship may stall at stage 2, or it may come to an end. However, if the two persons discover similarity in values as they open up to each other, they are more likely to progress to stage 3.

In the *role stage*, the couple begin to consider marriage. Hence, they start evaluating whether the other person does a satisfactory job in the role of intimate companion. At this point, individuals focus on the distribution of power in their relationship, the reliability of emotional support, and the quality of their sexual liaison (if they have formed one). Although some people may marry after progressing through only the first two stages, Murstein maintains that marriage is generally delayed until couples are comfortable with role enactments in stage 3.

Murstein's theory has been questioned on the grounds that courtship relationships do not really evolve through distinct stages. Critics argue that individuals in romantic relationships acquire information about each other's stimulus characteristics, values, and roles continuously rather than in discrete stages (Leigh, Holman, & Burr, 1984, 1987). Although there is some merit to this criticism, S-V-R theory provides a useful overview of the factors that influence whether romantic relationships progress toward marriage.

Predictors of Marital Success

Learning Objective

Summarize evidence on predictors of marital success.

Are there any factors that predict marital success? Research devoted to this question has been hampered by one obvious problem: How do you measure "marital success"? Some researchers have simply compared divorced and intact couples in regard to premarital characteristics. The problem with this strategy is that many intact couples obviously do not have happy or successful marriages. Other researchers have used elaborate questionnaires to measure couples' marital satisfaction. Unfortunately, these scales are plagued by a number of problems. Among other things, they appear to measure complacency and lack of conflict more than satisfaction (Fowers et al., 1994). Although our measures of marital quality are rather crude, some predictors of marital success have been found. These relations are all statistically weak, but they are intriguing nonetheless.

Family background   The marital adjustment of partners is correlated with the marital satisfaction of their parents. People whose parents were divorced are more likely than others to experience divorce themselves (White, 1990). For a number of reasons, marital instability appears to run in families (Teachman, Polonko, & Scanzoni, 1987).

Age   The ages of the bride and groom are also related to the likelihood of success. Couples who marry young have higher divorce rates (London & Wilson, 1988; White, 1990), as Figure 9.5 shows. Surprisingly, couples who marry late also have a higher propensity to divorce. Because they are selected from a smaller pool of potential mates, older newlyweds are more likely to differ in age, religion, social status, and education (Bitter, 1986). Such differences may make marriage more challenging regardless of age.

Figure 9.5
Age at marriage and probability of marital disruption in the first five years
Martin and Bumpass (1989) estimated the likelihood of marital disruption (either divorce or separation) within five years for various groups. The data summarized here, based on people who married between 1980 and 1985, show that the probability of marital disruption is substantially higher among those who marry young.

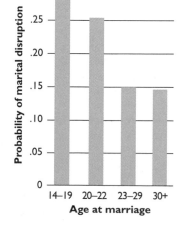

Length of courtship Longer periods of courtship are associated with a greater probability of marital success (Cate & Lloyd, 1988). Longer courtships may allow couples to evaluate their compatibility more accurately. Alternatively, the correlation between courtship length and marital success may exist because people who are cautious about marriage have attitudes and values that promote marital stability.

Socioeconomic class The frequency of divorce is higher in the working and lower classes than in the upper and middle classes. There are probably many reasons for this situation, but a key reason appears to be the greater financial stress in lower socioeconomic strata (Conger et al., 1990).

Personality Generally, studies have found that partners' specific personality traits are *not* particularly predictive of marital success. However, the presence of psychological distress and emotional disorders in one or both partners is associated with marital problems (Mastekaasa, 1994; Raschke, 1987). One recent study (Long & Andrews, 1990) found an interesting association between a trait called *perspective taking* and marital adjustment. **Perspective taking is a component of empathy that involves the tendency to put oneself in another person's place.** For both husbands and wives, high scores in perspective taking were found to be positively correlated with marital adjustment. Thus, individuals who work to understand their partner's viewpoint appear to have a better chance of marital success.

In summary, there are some thought-provoking correlations between couples' premarital characteristics and their marital adjustment. However, many of the relevant studies are getting rather dated given the shifting landscape of modern marriage (Cate & Lloyd, 1992), and most of the correlations are relatively small. Thus, there are no proven, reliable premarital predictors of marital success. However, researchers have found some stronger correlations when they have investigated the relationship between marital adjustment and the family life cycle. We'll examine this research next.

Marital Adjustment Across the Family Life Cycle

"Jennifer has taken a lot of time away from us, the time that we normally spend doing things together or talking. It seems like maybe on a weekend when we would normally like to sleep in, or just have lazy sex, Jennifer wakes up and needs to be fed. . . . But I'm sure that will pass as soon as Jennifer gets a little older. We're just going through a phase."

—A new mother quoted in *American Couples* (Blumstein & Schwartz, 1983, p. 205)

Learning Objective

Describe the relationship between the family life cycle and marital satisfaction.

"We're just going through a phase." That statement highlights an important point: There are predictable patterns of development for families, just as there are for individuals. These patterns make up the *family life cycle,* **an orderly sequence of developmental stages that families tend to progress through.** The institutions of marriage and family are inevitably intertwined. With the advent of marriage, two persons add a new member to their existing families and create an entirely new family. Typically, this new family forms the core of one's life as an adult.

Sociologists have proposed a number of models to describe family development (Mattessich & Hill, 1987). Our discussion will be organized around a six-stage model of family development outlined by Carter and McGoldrick (1988; McGoldrick & Carter, 1989). Figure 9.6 provides an overview of their model. It spells out the developmental tasks during each stage of the life cycle for families that eventually have children and remain intact. Carter and McGoldrick have described variations on this basic pattern that are associated with remaining childless or going through a divorce. However, we will mostly focus on the basic pattern in this section.

Research suggests that the family life cycle is an important determinant of marital satisfaction. Numerous studies that have measured spouses' overall satisfaction in different stages of the family life cycle have found a U-shaped relationship like

The Family Life Cycle

Family life cycle stage	Emotional process of transition: Key developmental task	Additional changes in family status required to proceed developmentally
1 Between families: The unattached young adult	Accepting parent/offspring separation	a. Differentiation of self in relation to family of origin b. Development of intimate peer relationships c. Establishment of self in work
2 The joining of families through marriage: The newly married couple	Commitment to new system	a. Formation of marital system b. Realignment of relationships with extended families and friends to include spouse
3 The family with young children	Accepting new members into the system	a. Adjusting marital system to make space for child(ren) b. Taking on parenting roles c. Realignment of relationships with extended family to include parenting and grandparenting roles
4 The family with adolescents	Increasing flexibility of family boundaries to include children's independence	a. Shifting of parent-child relationships to permit adolescent to move in and out of system b. Refocus on midlife marital and career issues c. Beginning shift toward concerns for older generation
5 Launching children and moving on	Accepting a multitude of exits from and entries into the family system	a. Renegotiation of marital system as a dyad b. Development of adult-to-adult relationships between grown children and their parents c. Realignment of relationships to include in-laws and grandchildren d. Dealing with disabilities and death of parents (grandparents)
6 The family in later life	Accepting the shifting of generational roles	a. Maintaining own and/or couple functioning and interests in face of physiological decline; exploration of new familial and social role options b. Support for a more central role for middle generation c. Making room in the system for the wisdom and experience of the elderly; supporting the older generation without overfunctioning for them d. Dealing with loss of spouse, siblings, and other peers and preparation for own death; life review and integration

Figure 9.6
Stages of the family life cycle
The family life cycle can be divided into six stages, as shown here (based on Carter & McGoldrick, 1988). The family's key developmental task during each stage is identified in the second column. The third column lists additional developmental tasks at each stage.

the one shown in Figure 9.7 (Belsky, 1990a; Glenn, 1990). This U shape reflects the fact that satisfaction tends to be greatest at the beginning and at the end of the family life cycle, with a noticeable decline occurring in the middle. The conventional explanation for this pattern is that the burdens of child-rearing undermine couples' satisfaction, which gradually begins to climb back up again as children grow up and these burdens ease. This explanation is plausible, but alternative explanations might also account for the U-shaped pattern. For example, the decline in satisfaction after the first few years of marriage could simply reflect the normal erosion of passionate love that is frequently seen in couples whether or not they are married or have children (see Chapter 8). The increase in satisfaction in the later stages of the family life cycle could be due to diminishing demands and stresses from spouses' work roles, which often have a deleterious effect on marital interactions. Although the exact reasons for the U-shaped pattern in marital satisfaction are not clear yet, virtually all of the potential explanations are based on the assumption that marital adjustment is influenced by the nature of the challenges that couples confront at various points in the family life cycle. Let's look at these challenges.

Between Families: The Unattached Young Adult

As young adults become independent of their parents, they go through a transitional period during which they are "between families" until they form a new family through marriage. What is interesting about this stage is that it is being prolonged by more and more people. The percentage of young adults who are postponing marriage until their late twenties or early thirties has risen dramatically

Figure 9.7
Marital satisfaction across the family life cycle
This graph depicts the percentage of husbands and wives studied by Rollins and Feldman (1970) who said their marriage was going well "all the time" at various stages of the family life cycle. Rollins and Feldman broke the family life cycle into eight stages instead of six. The U-shaped relationship shown here has been found in many other studies as well.

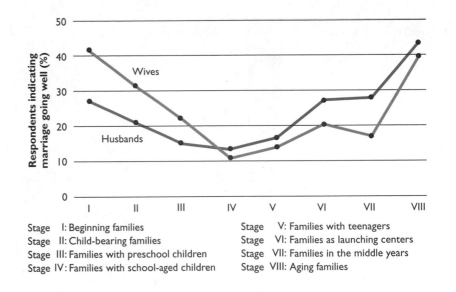

Stage I: Beginning families
Stage II: Child-bearing families
Stage III: Families with preschool children
Stage IV: Families with school-aged children
Stage V: Families with teenagers
Stage VI: Families as launching centers
Stage VII: Families in the middle years
Stage VIII: Aging families

(Sporakowski, 1988). The extension of this stage is probably due to a number of factors, among them the availability of new career options for women, increased educational requirements in the world of work, and increased emphasis on personal autonomy.

Joining Together: The Newly Married Couple

Learning Objective

Discuss changing attitudes about couples remaining childless.

In this phase, the newly married couple gradually settle into their roles as husband and wife. This phase *can* be quite troublesome, as the early years of marriage are often marred by numerous problems and disagreements (Johnson et al., 1986). *In general, however, this stage tends to be characterized by great happiness—the proverbial "marital bliss."* Spouses' satisfaction with their relationship tends to be relatively high early in marriage, before the arrival of the first child (Glenn & McLanahan, 1982).

The prechildren phase used to be rather short for most newly married couples, as they quickly went about the business of starting a family. Traditionally, couples simply *assumed* that they would proceed to have children. Remaining childless by choice used to be virtually unthinkable. Although attitudes about voluntary childlessness remain largely negative, the percentage of childless couples has doubled since 1960 (Somers, 1993). Thus, more and more couples find themselves struggling to *decide* whether to have children. Often, this decision occurs after numerous postponements, when the couple finally acknowledges that "the right time" is never going to arrive (Crane, 1985).

Couples who choose to remain childless cite the great costs incurred in rearing children. In addition to the financial burdens, they mention costs such as giving up educational or career opportunities, loss of time for leisure activities and each other, loss of privacy and autonomy, and worry about the responsibility associated with child-rearing (Bram, 1985; Seccombe, 1991). In contrast, couples who decide to have children cite many reasons, including the responsibility to procreate, the joy of watching youngsters mature, the sense of purpose that children create, and the satisfaction associated with emotional nurturance and the challenge of child-rearing (Goetting, 1986). In spite of the costs involved in raising children, most parents report no regret about their choice. The vast majority of parents rate parenthood as a very positive and satisfying experience (Demo, 1992).

Family with Young Children

Learning Objective

Discuss the dynamics of the transition to parenthood.

Although most parents are happy with their decision to have children, the arrival of the first child represents a major transition, and the disruption of old routines can be extremely stressful. The new mother, already physically exhausted by the birth process, is particularly prone to postpartum distress (Hock et al., 1995). The

Although children can be unparalleled sources of joy and satisfaction, the transition to parenthood can be extremely stressful, especially for the mother.

transition to parenthood tends to be more difficult for older women and for working wives. Women who have to shoulder the major burden of infant care and those whose babies have difficult temperaments are also especially vulnerable to distress (Kalmuss, Davidson, & Cushman, 1992).

Crisis during the transition to parenthood is far from universal, however (Ruble et al., 1988). Couples who have high levels of intimacy, closeness, and commitment prior to the first child's birth are likely to maintain a high level of satisfaction after the child's birth (Lewis, 1988). Interestingly, older males who father their first child relatively late tend to experience a smoother transition to parenthood than younger men (Cooney et al., 1993). The key to making this transition less stressful may be to have *realistic expectations* about parental responsibilities (Belsky, 1985; Kalmuss et al., 1992). Studies find that stress tends to be greatest in new parents who have overestimated the benefits and underestimated the costs of their new role. This is especially true for new moms.

Although children bring their share of trials and tribulations to a marriage, evidence suggests that they should not have to shoulder all the blame for their parents' sagging marital satisfaction. Studies that have compared young married couples with children to similar couples without children have found that the early years of marriage typically bring a decline in marital satisfaction for both groups (Glenn, 1990; Kurdek, 1993). This decline may be somewhat steeper for parents because of the stress associated with raising children (Belsky, 1990a), but it appears that some of the negative effects attributed to parenthood may be due to other processes that unfold as marriages evolve over the years.

In any case, parenting is a complex topic to which many entire books have been devoted. There are diverse styles of parenting, and they each tend to yield different results (Baumrind, 1991). We will consider this topic in earnest in the Chapter 11 Application.

Family with Adolescent Children

Learning Objective

Identify common problems that surface as a family's children reach adolescence.

Although the adolescent years have long been viewed as a period of great stress and turmoil, research from the past decade has led to the conclusion that adolescence is not as turbulent or difficult for youngsters as once believed (Offer et al., 1988; see Chapter 11). Ironically, though, studies indicate that it is an especially stressful period for adolescents' parents. Parents overwhelmingly rate adolescence as the most difficult stage of parenting (Gecas & Seff, 1990).

Couples have more time to enjoy leisure activities once their work and parental responsibilities decrease.

As adolescent children seek to establish their own identities, parental influence tends to decline while the influence of their peer groups tends to increase. Parents tend to retain more influence than peers over important matters, such as educational goals and career plans, but peers gradually tend to gain more influence over less critical matters, such as style of dress and recreational plans (Gecas & Seff, 1990). Thus, conflicts between adolescent children and their parents tend to involve everyday matters (such as chores and appearance) more than substantive issues (such as sex and drugs) (Barber, 1994). Conflict is particularly likely to surface between adolescents (of both genders) and their mothers. Moreover, when conflict does occur, mothers are more adversely affected by it than fathers (Steinberg & Silverberg, 1987). This may be because women's self-esteem has tended to be more closely tied than men's to the quality of their family relationships.

In addition to worrying about their adolescent children, middle-aged couples often must worry about the care of their parents. Thanks to increased longevity and decreased family size, today's average married couple has more parents than children (Wisensale, 1992). Females tend to assume most of the responsibility for elderly relatives, and it is estimated that in the future women can expect to spend more years caring for their aging parents than for their dependent children (Brubaker, 1990). Many theorists are concerned that these multigenerational caregiving responsibilities may prove burdensome. However, the available evidence to date suggests that this shift in family responsibilities has had relatively little impact on caregivers' well-being (Loomis & Booth, 1995).

Launching Children into the Adult World

Learning Objective

Discuss the transitions that occur in the later stages of the family life cycle.

When a couple's children begin to reach their twenties, the family has to adapt to a multitude of exits and entries, as children leave and return, sometimes with their own spouses. During this period, children have to progress from dependence to independence. Their progress is sometimes complicated when parents have difficulty letting go.

One might argue that launching children into the adult world tends to be a lengthier and more difficult process today than it once was. The percentage of 18- to 29-year-olds who live with their parents has climbed in recent years (Aquilino, 1990; Glick & Lin, 1986). The rapidly rising cost of a college education and the shrinking job market have probably led many young adults to linger in their parents' homes. Moreover, crises such as separation, divorce, job loss, and pregnancy out of wedlock are increasingly forcing children who have ventured out on their own to return to their parents. The repercussions of these new trends are sure to be the subject of future research.

When parents do manage to get all their children launched into the adult world, they find themselves faced with an "empty nest." This was formerly thought to be a difficult transition for many parents, especially mothers who were familiar only with the maternal role. Today, however, more women have experience with other roles outside the home, and most look forward to their "liberation" from child-rearing responsibilities (Reinke et al., 1985).

The Family in Later Life

Marital satisfaction tends to climb in the postparental period as couples find that they have more time to devote attention to each other (Brubaker, 1990). Whether this satisfaction is due to reduced parental responsibilities, reduced work responsibilities, or other considerations remains unclear (Lee, 1988). In any case, many couples take advantage of their newfound freedom, traveling or developing new leisure interests. For many people this can be a period of increased intimacy. Spouses do have to adapt to spending more time with each other, but most seem to make the adjustment without major problems (Treas, 1983). Of course, age-related considerations that are independent of the relationship, such as the increased likelihood of physical illness, can make the later years stressful. In general, however, the trend is for couples to report fairly high satisfaction until one of the spouses (usually the husband) dies.

Vulnerable Areas in Marital Adjustment

"When we first got married, the first six months of conflicts were all about getting him to take account of what I had planned for him at home. . . . He would come waltzing in an hour and a half late for dinner, or cancel an evening with friends, because he had to close a deal. . . . We would argue and argue . . . not because I didn't want him to make a living . . . but because I thought he had to be more considerate."

—A wife quoted in *American Couples* (Blumstein & Schwartz, 1983, p. 174)

An unavoidable reality of marriage is that couples must confront a legion of problems together. During courtship, couples mostly focus on pleasurable activities. But when people marry, they must face many problems, such as arriving at acceptable role compromises, paying bills, and raising a family. There is no such thing as a problem-free marriage. Successful marriages depend on couples' ability to handle their problems. In this section we will analyze the major kinds of difficulties that are likely to emerge. We can't offer simple solutions for these problems. However, in navigating one's way through life, it helps to know where the most perilous reefs are.

Unrealistic Expectations

Learning Objective

Discuss how unrealistic expectations may affect marital adjustment.

Sabatelli (1988) notes that many people enter marriage with unrealistic expectations about how wonderful it's going to be. When expectations are too high, disappointment is likely. Part of the problem is the degree to which media portrayals romanticize love and marriage. Films and TV shows tend to focus on the excitement of falling in love rather than the sacrifice of caring for a sick spouse. Further, people who marry quickly may not know each other very well and tend to have an idealized picture of their new mate. This idealized picture often turns out to be inaccurate when they see their new partner in a wider variety of less pleasant situations. This kind of letdown can best be avoided by trying to be realistic about a prospective mate's qualities. Such realism is more likely if lovers are open with each other during the courtship period and disclose their frailties instead of hiding them.

Gaps in Role Expectations

Learning Objective

Discuss the causes and ramifications of gaps in marital role expectations.

When a couple marries, each partner assumes new roles—those of husband and wife. With each role goes certain expectations that the partners hold about how wives and husbands should behave. These expectations may vary greatly from one person to another. Gaps between partners in their role expectations appear to have a negative impact on their marital satisfaction (Lye & Biblarz, 1993). Unfortunately, substantial differences in role expectations seem particularly likely in this era of transition in gender roles.

An individual's marital role expectations are shaped significantly by exposure to his or her parents' relationship. The traditional role expectations passed on by parents used to be fairly clear. A husband was supposed to act as the principal breadwinner, make the important decisions, and take care of certain household chores, such as car and yard maintenance. A wife was supposed to raise the children, cook, clean, and follow the leadership of her husband. Spouses had different spheres of influence. The working world was the domain of the husband, the home the domain of the wife.

In recent decades, however, the women's movement and other forces of social change have led to new expectations about marital roles. Young adults no longer blindly follow the traditions of their elders. Today, there are *options* from which to choose, so prospective mates can't assume that they share the same views on the appropriate responsibilities of spouses. Interestingly, husbands and wives with nontraditional attitudes about gender roles in marriage report somewhat lower marital satisfaction than those with more traditional views, probably because they view alternatives to married life more favorably and because they place greater emphasis on personal fulfillment (Lye & Biblarz, 1993).

Women may be especially vulnerable to ambivalence and confusion about shifting marital roles. Surveys of college women (Baber & Monaghan, 1988; Machung, 1989) show that more women than ever are aspiring to demanding professional careers. At the same time, virtually all these women plan to marry and have children. Most expect to marry a man who will assume equal responsibility for childrearing and domestic chores. Clearly, these women want to "have it all." Yet, research shows that husbands' career demands continue to take priority over their wives' vocational ambitions. It is wives who are expected to interrupt their career to raise young children, stay home when children are sick, and abandon their jobs when husbands' careers require relocation (Silberstein, 1992). Moreover, even when both spouses are employed, many husbands maintain traditional role expectations about housework, child care, decision making, and so forth (Blair, 1993).

Reflective of this reality, studies indicate that wives are still doing the bulk of the household chores in America, even when they work outside the home. For example, Blair and Johnson (1992) found that working wives devoted an average of 31 hours per week to housework (not including child care), while their husbands contributed only 15 hours on the average. The gap was even greater for nonemployed wives, who averaged 42 hours per week of housework in comparison to 12 hours per week for their husbands. Moreover, Blair and Johnson found that wives still do the vast majority of "women's work," such as cooking, cleaning, and laundry, while men continue to do mostly traditional "male chores," such as auto maintenance and outdoor tasks (see Figure 9.8).

Of course, housework patterns vary and some husbands do more than others. Gilbert (1994) estimates that about one-third of dual-career couples have reasonably equitable role-sharing arrangements. Men tend to do more housework when they have lighter work demands, when their wives earn a larger portion of the family income or work longer hours, and when they or their wives hold less traditional beliefs about gender roles (Almeida, Maggs, & Galambos, 1993; Coltrane & Ishii-Kuntz, 1992). A study by McHale and Crouter (1992) suggests that housework arrangements are most likely to be a source of discontent when spouses' expectations and preferences clash with reality. They found lower marital satisfaction when

Figure 9.8
Who does the housework?
Blair and Johnson (1992) studied the proportion of housework done by husbands and wives. These charts, based on employed wives, show that even working women continue to do a highly disproportionate share of most household tasks and that the division of labor still meshes with traditional gender roles.

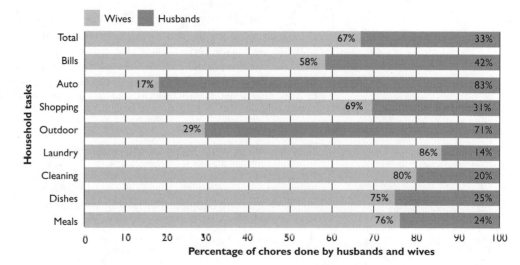

wives with nontraditional attitudes about gender roles had to live with a traditional division of household labor and when husbands with traditional attitudes had to adapt to a more equal division of labor. Obviously, women's and men's varied expectations about housework roles create considerable potential for conflict.

In light of this reality, it is imperative that couples discuss role expectations in depth before marriage. If they discover that their views are very different, they need to take the potential for problems seriously. Many people casually dismiss gender-role disagreements, thinking they can "straighten out" their partner later on. But assumptions about marital roles, whether traditional or not, may be deeply held and not easily changed.

Work and Career Issues

Learning Objective

Summarize how spouses' work affects their marital satisfaction and their children.

The possible interactions between one's occupation and one's marriage are numerous and complex. Individuals' satisfaction and involvement in their job can affect their own marital satisfaction, their partners' marital satisfaction, and their children's development.

Husbands' Work and Marital Adjustment

Work has traditionally played a central role in men's lives. Hence, a host of studies have investigated the relationship between husbands' job satisfaction and their marital adjustment. We could speculate that these two variables might be either positively *or* negatively related. On the one hand, if a husband is highly committed to a satisfying career, he may have less time and energy to devote to his marriage and family. On the other hand, the frustration and stress of an unsatisfying job might spill over to contaminate a man's marriage.

The research on this issue suggests that both scenarios are realistic possibilities. Husbands who try to balance a high commitment to work with a strong commitment to parenting report more role strain than husbands who have a low commitment to their work (O'Neil & Greenberger, 1994). Moreover, studies find that husbands' stress at work can have a substantial negative effect on their wives' emotional health and marital satisfaction (Rook, Dooley, & Catalano, 1991; Small & Riley, 1990).

Wives' Work and Marital Adjustment

Although few studies have looked at the impact of wives' work on their own marital satisfaction, many have examined the effect of wives' work on their husbands' well-being or the couple's marital adjustment. This slant arises from traditional views that regard men's *lack* of employment, but women's *employment,* as departures from the norm. Typically, these studies simply categorize women as working or nonworking and compare the husbands' (or couples') marital satisfaction.

Most of these studies find no consistent differences in the marital adjustment of male-breadwinner couples versus dual-career couples (Piotrkowski, Rapoport, & Rapoport, 1987; Spitze, 1988). Recently, some investigators have begun to study the mediating influence of spouses' *attitudes* toward married women's employment, with enlightening results. It appears that marital satisfaction tends to be highest when partners share similar gender-role expectations and when the wife's employment status matches her own (and her husband's) preference about it (Menaghan & Parcel, 1990). In summary, although dual-career couples do face special problems in negotiating career priorities, child care arrangements, and other practical matters, their marriage need not be negatively affected.

Parents' Work and Children's Development

Another issue of concern has been the potential impact of parents' employment on their children. Virtually all of the research in this area has focused on the effects of mothers' employment outside the home. This research has been guided by two implicit assumptions. The first assumption is that the more time mothers spend with their children, the better off the children are. The second assumption is that the full-time housewives of previous generations devoted more time to their children than today's employed wives. Both assumptions have been questioned (Hoffman, 1987). Extremely high levels of mother-child interaction can backfire, contributing to excessive dependency in children. Furthermore, yesterday's full-time mothers did not have modern, time-saving household conveniences, and they had more children. Thus, they may not have devoted any more time to each individual child than today's working mothers do. Furthermore, when mothers work outside the home, fathers tend to devote more time to child care so that the combined time that both parents spend with their children is about the same as in traditional male-breadwinner families (Gilbert, 1994).

What does the research on maternal employment show? Although most Americans believe that mothers' employment is detrimental to children's development (Greenberger et al., 1988), a host of empirical studies have found that maternal employment is *not* harmful to children (Demo, 1992; Etaugh, 1993; Greenstein, 1993; MacEwen & Barling, 1991). For instance, studies generally have not found a link between mothers' employment status and the quality of infant-mother emotional attachment (Easterbrooks & Goldberg, 1985; Etaugh, 1993). Clearly, a child can form a strong attachment to a working mother. Furthermore, the *attitudes* of both parents are important. Families in which both the wife and her husband are satisfied with the wife's role (whether she is employed or not) tend to have the most well-adjusted offspring (Easterbrooks & Goldberg, 1985).

Some researchers even suggest that maternal employment can have *positive* effects on children (Demo, 1992). For instance, studies have found that children of working mothers tend to be especially self-reliant and responsible. This advantage appears to be particularly pronounced for girls. Daughters of working mothers also tend to exhibit higher than average academic competence and career aspirations (Hoffman, 1987).

Financial Difficulties

Learning Objective

Discuss how financial issues are related to marital adjustment.

How do couples' financial resources affect their marital adjustment? Neither financial stability nor wealth can ensure marital satisfaction. However, poverty can produce serious problems (Conger et al., 1990; Voydanoff, 1990). Without money, families live in constant dread of financial drains such as illness, layoffs, or broken appliances. Husbands tend to view themselves as poor providers and become hostile and irritable. Their hostility can undermine the warm, supportive exchanges that help to sustain relationships. This problem is sometimes aggravated by disappointed wives who criticize their husbands. Spontaneity in communication may be impaired by an understandable reluctance to talk about financial concerns. Thus, it is clear that poverty can have negative effects on married couples and their children (Klebanov, Brooks-Gunn, & Duncan, 1994).

Even when financial resources are plentiful, money can be a source of marital strain. Quarrels about how to spend money are common and potentially damaging at all income levels. Pittman and Lloyd (1988), for instance, found that perceived financial stress (regardless of a family's actual income) was associated with decreased marital satisfaction. A study that examined how happily married couples handled their money in comparison to couples that eventually divorced found that the happy couples engaged in more joint decision making on finances (Schaninger & Buss, 1986). Thus, the best way to avoid troublesome battles over money is probably to engage in extensive planning of expenditures together.

Inadequate Communication

Effective communication is crucial to the success of a marriage. The damaging role that poor communication can play was clearly demonstrated in a study by Fowers and Olson (1989). They identified areas of marital functioning that differentiated between satisfied and dissatisfied couples. Of the three most important areas of functioning, two involved communication: spouses' comfort in sharing information with each other and their willingness to recognize and resolve conflicts between them. (The third area was the quality of their sexual relationship.) Similarly, in a study of couples getting a divorce (Cleek & Pearson, 1985), communication difficulties were the most frequently cited problem among both husbands and wives (see Figure 9.9). A couple's strategy for resolving conflicts may be particularly crucial to marital satisfaction (Kurdek, 1995).

Recommended Reading

Love Is Never Enough

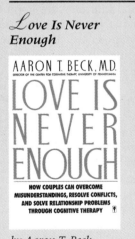

by Aaron T. Beck
(Harper & Row, 1988)

There are innumerable books that attempt to tell couples how to make it all work. Aaron Beck's entry in this market appears to be superior to most of the others. Beck, the founder of cognitive therapy (see Chapter 16), is a renowned expert on the distorted thought patterns that promote anxiety and depression. He argues that many married couples (especially those in distress) engage in the same errors of thinking as depressed and anxious people: namely, negativity, rigidity, and selectivity. If each spouse thinks about the other in such a distorted manner, then disillusionment, miscommunication, and frustration are inevitable. Most of the chapters include one or more questionnaires that readers can use to probe their own relationships. In addition, Beck provides a great deal of practical advice about how to identify and change the distorted thought patterns that undermine the marital satisfaction of so many couples. A unique feature of Beck's book is its inclusion of many actual conversations of troubled couples, along with the unspoken thoughts that lie behind each line of dialogue.

The following interchange occurred when Marjorie wanted to hang a picture but had difficulty driving the nail into the wall:

KEN: [She's having a problem. I'd better help her.] Let me do it for you.
MARJORIE: [He has no confidence in my ability.] That's all right. I can do it myself [angrily].
KEN: What's the matter with you? I was only trying to help.
MARJORIE: That's all you ever do. You don't think I can do anything.
KEN: Well, you can't even drive a nail straight [laughs].
MARJORIE: There you go again—always putting me down.
KEN: I was just trying to help.

The spouses had completely different versions of Ken's intervention. Marjorie's goal of hanging the picture was to assure herself that she could handle manual tasks; in fact, she was looking forward to Ken's praise for her demonstration of competence and independence. His intrusion, though, brought her sense of incompetence to the surface. While each was correct in the belief that Ken lacked confidence in Marjorie's manual ability, Ken perceived himself as kind and considerate, while Marjorie viewed him as intrusive and patronizing. What started as an innocent gesture of helpfulness on his part led to hurt feelings and antagonism. [p. 59]

Figure 9.9
Causes of divorce
When Cleek and Pearson (1985) asked divorcing couples about their perceptions regarding the causes of their divorce, both men and women cited communication difficulties more than any other cause.

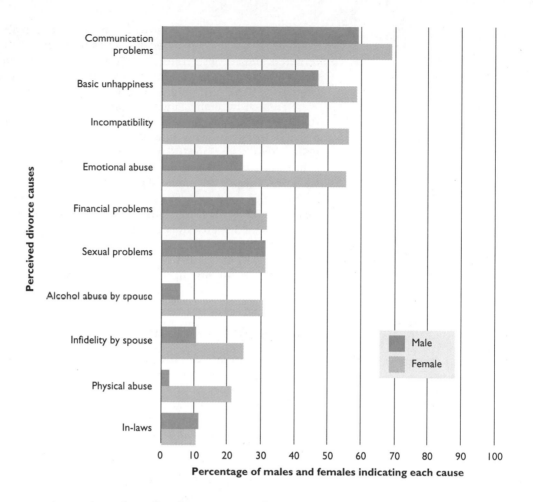

A number of studies have compared communication patterns in happy and unhappy marriages. This research indicates that unhappily married spouses (1) find it difficult to convey positive messages, (2) misunderstand each other more often, (3) are less likely to recognize that they have been misunderstood, (4) use more frequent, and more intense, negative messages, and (5) often differ in the amount of self-disclosure they prefer in the relationship (Noller & Fitzpatrick, 1990; Noller & Gallois, 1988; Sher & Baucom, 1993). Moreover, gender differences in approaches to communication (see the Chapter 10 Application) are frequently exaggerated in unhappily married couples (Gottman & Levenson, 1988).

The importance of marital communication was underscored in a widely cited study that attempted to predict the likelihood of divorce in a sample of 52 married couples (Buehlman, Gottman, & Katz, 1992). Each couple provided an oral history of their relationship and a 15-minute sample of their interaction style, during which they discussed two problem areas in their marriage. The investigators rated the spouses on a variety of factors that mostly reflected the subjects' ways of relating to each other. Based on these ratings, they were able to predict which couples would divorce within three years with 94% accuracy!

In recent years, investigators have increasingly turned to attribution theory to better understand marital miscommunication (Fincham & Bradbury, 1992). As explained in Chapters 5 and 6, *attributions* are inferences that people draw about the causes of events, others' behavior, and even their own behavior. Attributing events to internal versus external factors, or stable versus unstable factors, can make all the difference in the world in how one relates to other people.

A couple's willingness to recognize and resolve conflict is a key factor in marital satisfaction, as many movies have portrayed in a tragicomic fashion.

Married people routinely make attributions to explain each other's behavior. For example, if a wife forgets her husband's birthday, he might conclude that she's self-centered and inconsiderate (an internal, stable attribution). Or he might conclude that she's drained by work overload at the office (an external, unstable attribution). Obviously, these attributions don't have the same implications for their relationship.

Research by Frank Fincham and his colleagues indicates that distressed spouses (usually defined as those seeking marital therapy) tend to explain their partners' negative behavior with internal, stable attributions that have global implications ("She doesn't love me"). In contrast, they tend to explain their partners' positive behaviors with external, unstable attributions that have specific implications ("She was nice because she made a big sale today"). Patterns of attribution in happily married couples tend to be just the opposite (Bradbury & Fincham, 1988; Fincham, Beach, & Baucom, 1987; Karney et al., 1994). Thus, in comparison to happy couples, distressed spouses blame their problems on each other and view good behavior as a temporary aberration. Unhappy spouses' biases in attribution could be either a cause or an effect of marital distress, but their biases clearly aren't a promising foundation for marital bliss.

Problems with In-Laws

Learning Objective

Discuss how in-law problems and growing in different directions are related to marital adjustment.

Research on in-law conflict has diminished in recent years. This may indicate that in-law trouble is less of a problem in our more mobile society. When intergenerational conflict does occur, it typically involves the wife and her mother-in-law. In fact, in-law trouble has been characterized as a "female problem," perhaps because women have traditionally shouldered the responsibility for maintaining kinship ties (Marotz-Baden & Cowan, 1987). Fischer (1983) found that wives tend to turn to their own mothers for help after giving birth. Yet they may regard their mother-in-law's concern over her new grandchild as "interference." In general, in-law strife tends to be greatest for couples who have not yet attained emotional or financial independence from their parents.

Growing in Different Directions

We have already mentioned the tendency for people to marry others similar to themselves (homogamy). However, it is always possible that partners will diverge in terms of their values and activity preferences. For instance, in the early years of a marriage, both members of a couple might enjoy a moderate amount of social entertaining with their friends. As the years wear on, one partner might find such activity tedious, while the other comes to enjoy it even more. Neither partner is wrong. They are simply evolving in different directions. However, this divergence can lead to bitter disagreements about how the partners should spend their time.

Although sometimes difficult, it is important that spouses allow each other room for personal growth. They should recognize that it is unrealistic to expect one's partner to remain exactly the same forever. In this era, with recreation playing an increasingly large role in people's lives, more spouses may have to learn to engage in individual activities. At the same time, it is important to strive to maintain joint activities as well. Studies have uncovered a positive correlation between the amount of spouses' interaction and their marital satisfaction (Zuo, 1992). Joint leisure activities that involve high levels of communication may be especially valuable in fostering marital happiness (Holman & Jacquart, 1988; Smith, Snyder, et al., 1988).

Divorce

"In the ten years that we were married I went from 24 to 34 and they were a very significant ten years. I started a career, started to succeed, bought my first house, had a child, you know, very significant years. And then all of a sudden, every god-

KUDZU by Doug Marlette. By permission of Doug Marlette and Creators Syndicate.

damn thing, I'm back to zero. I have no house. I don't have a child. I don't have a wife. I don't have the same family. My economic position has been shattered. And nothing recoverable. All these goals which I had struggled for, every goddamn one of them, is gone."

—A recently divorced man quoted in *Marital Separation* (Weiss, 1975, p. 75)

The dissolution of a marriage tends to be a bone-jarring event for most people, as this bitter quote illustrates. Any of the problems discussed in the previous section might lead a couple to consider divorce. However, people appear to vary in their threshold for divorce, just as they do in their threshold for marriage. Some couples will tolerate a great deal of disappointment and bickering without seriously considering divorce. Other couples are ready to call an attorney as soon as it becomes apparent that their expectations for marital bliss were somewhat unrealistic. Typically, however, divorce is the culmination of a gradual disintegration of the relationship brought about by an accumulation of many interrelated problems.

Increasing Rate of Divorce

Learning Objective

Summarize evidence on changing divorce rates.

Although relatively accurate statistics are available on divorce rates, it is still difficult to estimate the percentage of marriages ending in divorce. The usually cited ratio of marriages in a year to divorces in the same year is highly misleading. It would be more instructive to follow people married in a particular year over a period of time, but little research of this nature has been done. In any case, it is clear that divorce rates have increased substantially in recent decades, as Figure 9.10 shows. The most widely cited recent estimates of future divorce risk are well over 50%. Martin and Bumpass (1989) project that if you include couples who separate per-

Figure 9.10
Increasing divorce rates
The percentage of marriages ending in a divorce has been going up steadily for over 100 years. Today, experts estimate that over 50% of marriages will end in divorce. (Source: Cherlin, 1981; Martin & Bumpass, 1989)

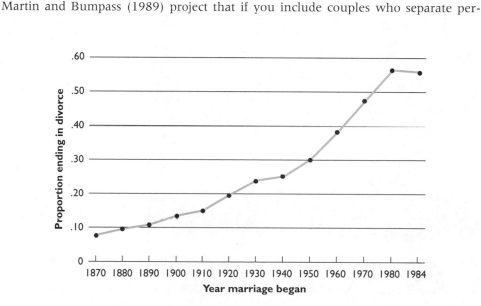

manently but never bother to file for divorce, *two-thirds* of today's marriages in the United States will result in marital dissolution. Divorce rates are higher among blacks than whites, among lower-income couples, and among people who marry at a relatively young age (White, 1991).

A wide variety of social trends have probably contributed to the increasing divorce rates (Raschke, 1987; White, 1990). The stigma attached to divorce has gradually eroded. Many religious denominations are becoming more tolerant of divorce, and marriage has thus lost some of its sacred quality. The declining fertility rate and the consequent smaller families probably make divorce a more viable possibility. The entry of more women into the workforce has made many wives less financially dependent on the continuation of their marriage. New attitudes emphasizing individual fulfillment seem to have counterbalanced older attitudes that encouraged dissatisfied spouses to suffer in silence. Reflecting all these trends, the legal barriers to divorce have also diminished.

Deciding on a Divorce

Learning Objective

Summarize evidence on the effects of divorce on spouses and their children.

Divorces are often postponed repeatedly, and they are rarely executed without a great deal of forethought. Indecision is common, as roughly two out of five divorce petitions are eventually withdrawn (Donovan & Jackson, 1990). The decision to divorce is not usually a singular event, but rather the outcome of a long series of smaller decisions that may take years to unfold.

It is difficult to generalize about the relative merit of divorce as opposed to remaining in an unsatisfactory marriage. There is evidence that people who are currently divorced suffer a higher incidence of both physical and psychological maladies and are less happy than those who are currently married (Frank, 1985; Kitson & Morgan, 1990). Furthermore, the process of getting divorced is usually very stressful for both spouses. One might guess that as divorce becomes more commonplace it should also become less stressful and traumatic, but available evidence does not support this supposition (Kitson, 1992).

As painful as marital dissolution may be, remaining in an unhappy marriage is also potentially detrimental. A longitudinal study of wives (Schaefer & Burnett, 1987) found that marital quality was an even better predictor of a woman's psychological health three years later than her psychological health at the initial measurement. In particular, poor marital adjustment at time 1 was predictive of significant depression and anxiety at time 2. Other studies have found an association between marital distress and elevated rates of anxiety, depression, and drug disorders in both men and women, although it's hard to tell what's causing what in many of these studies (Gotlib & McCabe, 1990). These findings suggest that sticking it out in an unhappy marriage may be counterproductive to one's adjustment.

The high divorce rate has led to some novel ways of dealing with its worrisome legal aspects. Attorney Robert Nordyke discovered that the drive-up window at his new office— a former savings and loan branch in Salem, Oregon—was perfect for serving legal papers on his clients' spouses.

Decisions about divorce must take into account the impact on a couple's children. Weighing this consideration is difficult, however, because divorces have highly varied effects on children, depending on a complex constellation of interacting factors (Furstenberg & Cherlin, 1991). There has been much debate about whether children benefit if parents persevere and keep an unhappy marriage intact. Children whose parents divorce may exhibit a variety of adjustment problems that can continue for years (Amato & Keith, 1991b). However, so do children from intact homes characterized by persistent marital discord (Amato, 1993; Grynch & Fincham, 1990). All in all, the weight of evidence suggests that in the long run it is less damaging to the children if unhappy parents divorce than if the children grow up in an intact but dissension-ridden home (Demo & Acock, 1988). However, this assertion is based on the assumption that the parents' divorce brings their bickering to an end.

Unfortunately, the conflicts between divorcing spouses often continue unabated for many years after they part ways. Goldberg (1985), for instance, describes a case history in which a man's ex-wife was still calling him 10 to 15 times a day to disturb and berate him three years after their divorce.

In any case, one should not underestimate the trauma that most children go through when their parents divorce. After a divorce, children may exhibit depression, anxiety, nightmares, dependency, aggression, withdrawal, distractibility, lowered academic performance, and reduced physical health (Bray & Hetherington, 1993; Guidubaldi, Perry, & Nastasi, 1987). Although these effects begin to dissipate in many children after a couple of years (Hetherington, 1991), divorce can have a lasting impact that may extend into adulthood. Amato and Keith (1991a) studied *adults* whose parents divorced when they were children and found elevated rates of maladjustment, antisocial behavior, and marital instability—as well as lower educational and occupational attainments—in comparison to adults whose parents stayed married.

Children have more adjustment problems when their parents go through a particularly bitter, acrimonious, and conflict-ridden divorce (Tschann et al., 1989, 1990). Divorce also tends to be especially tough on boys whose mothers have sole custody and who therefore are denied a stable male role model (Hetherington, 1991). The children's recovery and subsequent adjustment seem to depend primarily on the quality of their relationship with the custodial parent, the quality of the child-rearing skills exhibited by the custodial parent, and the custodial parent's level of adjustment to the divorce (Amato, 1993).

Adjusting to Divorce

Learning Objective

Discuss how men and women adjust to divorce.

It is clear that divorce is an exceedingly stressful life event (Buehler & Langenbrunner, 1987). It often combines all four major sources of stress described in Chapter 3: frustration, conflict, pressure, and change. In most respects, divorce appears to be more difficult and disruptive for women than for men (Clarke-Stewart & Bailey, 1989). Women are more likely to assume the responsibility of rearing the children, whereas fathers tend to reduce their contact with their children (Albiston, Maccoby, & Mnookin, 1990). After divorce, over one-third of children see their father only a few times a year or not at all (Seltzer, 1991). Another key consideration is that divorced women are less likely than their ex-husbands to have adequate income or a satisfying job. Paradoxically, although divorced women experience greater stress and feel more financially strapped than divorced men (Weitzman, 1989), women tend to experience serious mental health problems less often and have more positive feelings about their divorce than men (Diedrick, 1991; Kitson & Morgan, 1990). The reasons for these perplexing gender differences are not clear.

Remarriage

Learning Objective

Summarize data on the frequency and success of remarriage and its impact on children.

Roughly three-quarters of divorced women and five-sixths of divorced men eventually remarry (Glick, 1984). About half of these remarriages occur within three years of the divorce. Among women, less education and lower income are associated with more rapid remarriage. In contrast, men who are better educated and financially well-off tend to remarry more quickly. The greater one's age at the time of divorce, the lower the likelihood of remarriage, especially among women (Bumpass, Sweet, & Martin, 1990).

How successful are second marriages? The answer depends on one's standard of comparison. Divorce rates *are* higher for second than for first marriages (White & Booth, 1985). However, this may simply indicate that this group of people sees divorce as a reasonable alternative to an unsatisfactory marriage. Nonetheless, studies of marital adjustment suggest that second marriages are slightly less successful than first marriages and that marital satisfaction in remarriages is somewhat lower for women than for men (Vemer et al., 1989). Of course, if you consider that in

Figure 9.11
Children's adjustment in four types of families

Acock and Demo (1994) assessed children's adjustment in four types of family structures: first marriages, divorced single-parent homes, stepfamilies, and families in which the mother never married. The comparisons of 2457 families did turn up some statistically significant differences, as children's overall well-being was highest in intact first marriages and lowest in divorced homes. However, as you can see, the differences were rather small, and the authors conclude that "family structure has a modest effect on children's well-being" (p. 183).

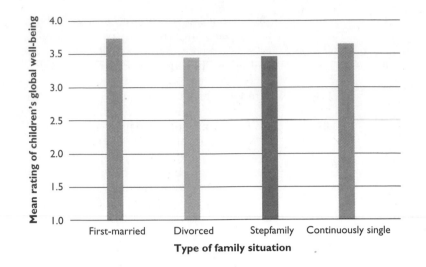

this pool of people *all* the first marriages ran into serious trouble, then the second marriages look rather good by comparison. On the up side, remarried couples report more open communication, more willingness to confront conflict, and more egalitarian housekeeping and child-rearing roles than couples in their first marriage (Furstenberg, 1990; Giles-Sims, 1987; Hetherington & Clingempeel, 1992).

Another major issue related to remarriage is its effect on children. When children from stepfamilies are compared to children from first marriages, investigators find no differences in the youngsters' self-esteem or academic achievement (Pasley, Ihinger-Tallman, & Lofquist, 1994). However, adaptation to remarriage can be difficult. On the average, interaction in stepfamilies appears to be somewhat less cohesive and warm than in first-marriage families, and stepparent-child relations tend to be more negative and distant than parent-child relations in first marriages (Bray & Hetherington, 1993). However, most studies find modest differences between stepfamilies and other types of families in the adjustment of their children. For example, Figure 9.11 highlights some representative results from one recent, large-scale study (Acock & Demo, 1994).

Alternatives to Marriage

We noted at the beginning of the chapter that the traditional model of marriage has been undermined by a variety of social trends. More and more people are choosing alternatives to marriage. We will examine some of these alternatives in this section. Specifically, we'll discuss remaining single, cohabitation, and gay relationships.

Remaining Single

Learning Objective

Describe stereotypes of single life and summarize evidence on the adjustment of single people.

The pressure to marry is substantial in our society. Americans are socialized to believe that they are not complete until they have found their "other half" and have entered into a partnership for life (Shostak, 1987). Staying unattached is often referred to as "failure" to marry. In spite of this pressure, an increasing proportion of young adults are remaining single, as Figure 9.12 shows.

Does the increased number of single adults mean that people are turning away from the institution of marriage? Perhaps a little, but for the most part, no. A variety of factors have contributed to the growth of the single population. Much of this growth is due to the increase in the median age at which people marry and the increased rate of divorce. The vast majority of single, never-married people *do* expect to marry eventually. There has been no rush among young people to embrace lifetime singlehood, as the percentage of high school seniors expecting to marry (95%

Figure 9.12
The proportion of young people who remain single
This graph shows the percentage of single men and women, aged 20–24 or 25–29, in 1993 as compared to 1960 (based on U.S. Census data). The proportion of people remaining single has increased substantially for both genders, in both age brackets. Single men continue to outnumber single women in these age brackets.

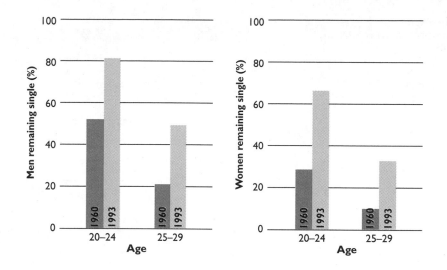

for females and 90% for males) has remained high and very stable since the 1960s (Thornton, 1989).

Singlehood has been plagued by two very disparate stereotypes of the single life (Keith, 1986). On the one hand, single people are sometimes portrayed as carefree swingers who are too busy enjoying the fruits of promiscuity to shoulder marital responsibilities. On the other hand, they are seen as losers who did not succeed in snaring a mate. They may be portrayed as socially inept, maladjusted, frustrated, lonely, and bitter. These stereotypes do a great injustice to the diversity that exists among those who are single.

The "swinging single" stereotype appears to be a media-manufactured illusion designed to lure singles' spending power into nightclubs and bars. In reality, the singles-bar circuit is frequently described as an experience in alienation and disappointment. In comparison to married people, single people do have sex with more partners. However, they have sex less frequently, and they rate their sexual relations as less satisfying than their married counterparts do (Cargan & Melko, 1982).

As for the "maladjusted, bitter" stereotype, it is true that single people have an elevated incidence of mental and physical health problems (Gotlib & McCabe, 1990; Trovato & Lauris, 1989), and they do rate themselves as less happy than married people (Lee, Seccombe, & Shehan, 1991). However, the differences are modest and the happiness gap has shrunk in recent years, especially among women (Glenn & Weaver, 1988). Although popular stereotypes suggest that being single is more difficult for women than for men, the empirical data suggest just the opposite. Most studies find that single women are healthier and more satisfied with their lives than single men are, and various lines of evidence suggest that women get along without men better than men get along without women (Cargan & Melko, 1982; Glenn & Weaver, 1988).

Although the increase in the single population does not reflect a widespread rejection of marriage, it is leading to more favorable attitudes toward singles. People used to assume that there was something wrong with an adult who remained single. Today, more people view singlehood as a reasonable option rather than a deviant lifestyle.

Cohabitation

Learning Objective

Discuss the prevalence of cohabitation and whether it improves the probability of marital success.

As we saw earlier in the chapter, *cohabitation* refers to living together in a sexually intimate relationship outside of marriage. Recent years have witnessed a tremendous increase in the number of cohabiting couples (see Figure 9.13). In 1993 there were slightly over 3.5 million unmarried couples living together in the United States. They represented about 5–6% of all couples (married and unmarried) sharing living quarters at that time. However, the percentage of couples living together at any one time does not accurately convey how widespread this phenomenon has become,

Figure 9.13
Cohabitation in the United States
The number of unmarried couples living together has been increasing rapidly since 1970 (based on U.S. Census data). This increase shows no signs of leveling off.

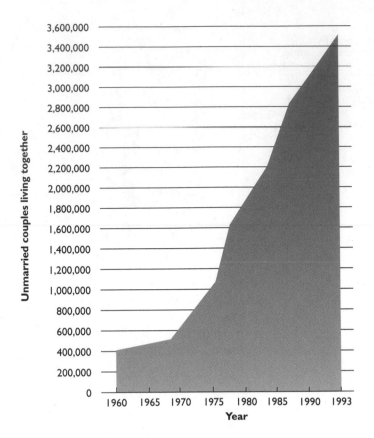

because cohabiting unions tend to be short—about half of cohabiting couples either get married or break up within 18 months (Bumpass & Sweet, 1989). It is more instructive to study people getting married for the first time and determine what percentage of them have cohabited prior to their marriage (either with their spouse-to-be or someone else). Studies indicate that this percentage has increased dramatically, from around 11% in 1970 to nearly 50% in the 1990s (Bumpass et al., 1991).

Cohabitation tends to conjure up images of college students or other well-educated young couples without children, but these images are misleading. In reality, cohabitation rates have always been higher in the less educated segments of the population. Moreover, almost half of cohabitants have been married previously, and one study found that 40% of cohabitating couples had children, mostly from previous marriages (Bumpass et al., 1991).

The principal motivations for cohabitation (as opposed to marriage) include more individualism, more freedom, no need to divorce, the advantage of sharing living expenses, and the opportunity to determine compatibility before marriage (Bumpass et al., 1991; Kotkin, 1985). Those who choose cohabitation tend to be liberal in values, nonreligious, and pragmatic about intimate relationships (Macklin, 1983; Newcomb, 1983; Tanfer, 1987).

Although many people see cohabitation as a threat to the institution of marriage, most theorists see it as a new stage in the courtship process—a sort of trial marriage. Consistent with the latter view, about three-quarters of cohabitants expect to marry their current partner (Bumpass et al., 1991). Thus, it appears that cohabitation does not represent a repudiation of marriage.

In discussing the pros and cons of cohabitation, White (1987) points out that it may provide an opportunity for young people to experiment with marital-like responsibilities. As a prelude to marriage, it should reduce the likelihood of entering marriage with unrealistic expectations. Living together may also permit people to identify incompatible mates more effectively than a traditional courtship might. These considerations suggest that couples who cohabit before they marry should go on to more successful marriages than those who do not.

Although White's analyses seem plausible, researchers have *not* found that premarital cohabitation increases the likelihood of subsequent marital success. In fact, studies have found an association between premarital cohabitation and *higher*

Figure 9.14
Cohabitation and marital instability
Comparisons of people who cohabit before marriage and those who do not have generally found higher rates of marital dissolution among the cohabiters. The data summarized here compare rates of marital disruption (either divorce or separation) in the first four years of marriage for cohorts of women born in various periods, based on research by Schoen (1992). These data suggest that the differences between cohabiters and noncohabiters in marital instability are shrinking.

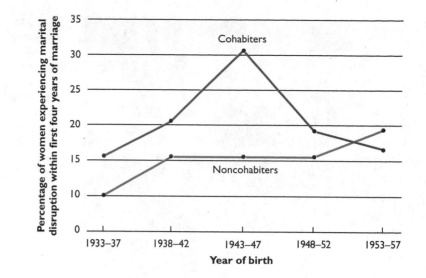

divorce rates in Canada, Sweden, and the United States (DeMaris & Rao, 1992; Schoen, 1992). Why is cohabitation associated with marital instability? Most theorists argue that it's because this nontraditional lifestyle has historically attracted a liberal and unconventional segment of the population with a weak commitment to the institution of marriage and relatively few qualms about getting divorced. There is some empirical support for this explanation (Glenn, 1990; Thomson & Colella, 1992), but the evidence is mixed (DeMaris & MacDonald, 1993). If this explanation is accurate, the elevated divorce rates among cohabitants should gradually shrink to normal as cohabitation becomes more common, because the population of cohabitants will increasingly resemble the general population. A trend in this direction is already apparent (Schoen, 1992), as you can see in Figure 9.14.

Gay Relationships

Learning Objective

Discuss the stability and dynamics of intimate relationships among homosexual couples.

Up until this point, we have, for purposes of simplicity, focused our attention on *heterosexuals,* those who seek emotional/sexual relationships with members of the other sex. However, we have been ignoring a significant minority group: *homosexual* men and women, who seek emotional/sexual relationships with members of the same sex. (In everyday language, the term *gay* is used to refer to homosexuals of both sexes, although many homosexual women prefer the term *lesbian* for themselves.) How large is this minority group? It's difficult to say because negative attitudes about homosexuality in our society continue to prevent many gays from "coming out of the closet" (Gonsiorek & Weinrich, 1991). A frequently cited estimate of the number of people who are homosexual is 10%. If homosexuals and bisexuals are lumped together, recent studies *suggest* that this figure is reasonably accurate for males, but an overestimate for females (Ellis & Ames, 1987; Janus & Janus, 1993).

Devoting a separate section to gay couples may seem to imply that the dynamics of their close relationships are different from those seen in heterosexual couples. Actually, this appears to be much less true than widely assumed, even though gays' close relationships unfold in a radically different social context than heterosexuals' marital relationships. As Garnets and Kimmel (1991) point out, gay relationships "develop within a social context of societal disapproval with an absence of social legitimization and support; families and other social institutions often stigmatize such relationships and there are no prescribed roles and behaviors to structure such relationships" (p. 170). About two-thirds of Americans still condemn homosexual relations as morally wrong, and gays continue to be victims of employment and housing discrimination, not to mention verbal and physical abuse (Herek, 1991). Gay couples cannot legally formalize their unions by getting married, and in fact, laws prohibiting same-gender sexual relations are still on the books in 24 states in the United States. Gay couples are also denied various economic benefits available to married couples (Rivera, 1991). For example, they can't file joint tax returns and

Despite the common stereotype that homosexuals rarely form long-term relationships, the fact is that they are similar to heterosexual couples in their attitudes and behaviors, and many enjoy long-term commitments in marriage-like arrangements.

Learning Objective

List five misconceptions about gay couples.

they generally can't obtain employer-provided health insurance for their partner.

Given the lack of moral, social, legal, and economic supports for gay relationships, are gay unions less stable than marital unions? Researchers have not been able to collect adequate data on this question yet, but the very limited data available suggest that gay couples' relationships *are* somewhat briefer and more prone to breakups than heterosexual marriages (Peplau, 1991). Insofar as this may be true, Letitia Anne Peplau suggests that it's probably because gay relationships face fewer barriers to dissolution—that is, fewer practical problems that make breakups difficult or costly (Peplau, 1981; Peplau & Cochran, 1990). Married couples considering divorce often face a variety of such barriers (attorneys' fees, concerns about children, wrangling over joint investments, the disapproval of their families), which may motivate them to salvage their deteriorating relationship. In contrast, gay couples do not have to wrestle with the legal formalities of divorce, and they are less likely to have children, joint investments, or family opposition to worry about.

Although gay relationships evolve in a different social context than heterosexual relationships, recent studies have documented striking commonalities between both types of couples. They report similar levels of love and commitment in their relationships, similar levels of overall satisfaction with their relationships, and similar levels of sexual satisfaction (Peplau, 1991). Resemblance is also apparent when researchers study what gays and heterosexuals want out of their relationships (Peplau, 1988; see Figure 9.15) and what they look for in a prospective partner (Laner, 1988). Homosexual and heterosexual couples are also similar in terms of the factors that predict relationship satisfaction (Kurdek & Schmitt, 1988) and the problems that contribute to breakups (Blumstein & Schwartz, 1983). Moreover, recent studies indicate that both types of couples generally wrestle with the same sources of conflict in their relationships and that their patterns of conflict resolution are largely the same (Kurdek, 1994a, 1994b).

Although research indicates a considerable continuity between homosexual and heterosexual relationships, basic misconceptions about the nature of gay relationships remain widespread. Let's look at some of these inaccurate stereotypes.

First, many people assume that most gay couples adopt traditional masculine and feminine roles in their relationships, with one partner behaving in a cross-gendered manner. This appears to be true in only a small minority of cases. In fact, on the whole, gay couples appear to be more flexible about role expectations than heterosexuals (Marecek, Finn, & Cardell, 1988; Zacks, Green, & Marrow, 1988). In comparison to married couples, gay couples display a more equitable balance of power in their relationships and are less likely to adhere to traditional gender roles.

Second, it is widely believed that gays are characterized by exceptionally high levels of sexual activity and that they engage in casual sex with many partners. In reality, high levels of sexual activity are characteristic only in certain segments of the gay male population and are virtually nonexistent among lesbians (Tripp, 1987). In fact, within the context of committed relationships, lesbians exhibit strikingly low rates of sexual activity (Blumstein & Schwartz, 1990; Nichols, 1990). Regardless of their sexual orientation (gay or straight), males tend to have somewhat different motivations than females for engaging in sex. Women are more likely to regard sexual activity as an expression of affection and commitment. Men tend to attach more importance to sexual pleasure and conquest (Leigh, 1989). Their socialization is more likely than women's to stress the desirability of varied and frequent sexual activity. The gay male, being free of the strictures of marriage and having his choice of like-minded partners, has simply been in a better position than his heterosexual counterpart to act on this masculine socialization (Blasband & Peplau, 1985).

Figure 9.15
Comparing priorities in intimate relationships
Peplau (1981) asked heterosexual men and women and homosexual men and women to rate the significance (9 = high importance) of various aspects of their intimate relationships. As you can see, all four groups returned fairly similar ratings. Peplau concludes that homosexuals and heterosexuals largely want the same things out of their relationships.

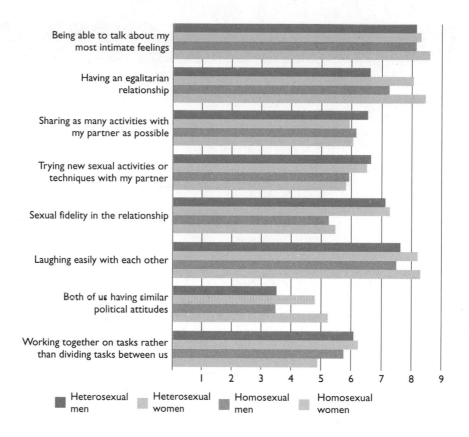

Third, popular stereotypes suggest that gays only rarely get involved in long-term intimate relationships. In reality, most homosexual men, and nearly all homosexual women, prefer stable, long-term relationships, and at any one time roughly half of gay males and three-quarters of lesbians are involved in committed relationships (Macklin, 1987; Peplau, 1991). Lesbian relationships are generally sexually exclusive. About half of committed male couples have "open" relationships, allowing for the possibility of sexual activity (but not affection) with outsiders. While intimate relationships among gays appear to be less stable than marriages among straights, they may compare favorably with heterosexual cohabitation, which would be a more appropriate baseline for comparison. Both gays and heterosexual cohabitants may face opposition to their relationship from their families and from society in general, and neither enjoys the legal and social sanctions of marriage.

Fourth, lesbians and gay men tend to be thought of as individuals rather than as members of families. This thinking reflects a society-wide bias that homosexuality and family just don't mesh (Allen & Demo, 1995). In reality, gays are very much involved in families as sons and daughters, as parents and stepparents, as aunts, uncles, and grandparents. Although exact data are not available, far more are parents than most people realize. Many of these parental responsibilities are left over from previous marriages, as about one-fifth of gay men and one-third of lesbians have been heterosexually married (Harry, 1983). But an increasing number of homosexuals are opting to have children in the context of their gay relationships (Barret & Robinson, 1994; Falk, 1994). Unfortunately, researchers have largely neglected gays' family life (Allen & Demo, 1995), so we know virtually nothing about gay fathers and only very little about lesbian mothers. The preliminary evidence on lesbian mothers suggests that they are similar to their heterosexual counterparts and that their children do not experience any unique ill effects due to being reared by a gay parent (Falk, 1994).

Finally, an inevitable fate for any stereotyped group is that its members are lumped together and simplistically assumed to be identical. In reality, there is as much diversity among gays as there is among straights, dooming to failure any attempt to classify gays into "types" (Tripp, 1987). To identify an individual as "homosexual" is to say nothing more about that person's unique lifestyle, personality, or values than to describe someone as "heterosexual."

Application

Understanding Intimate Violence

Answer the following statements "true" or "false."

1. Most women in abusive relationships are attracted to violent men.

2. Most men who have witnessed domestic violence as children will batter their intimate partners.

3. Severe child abuse is more often inflicted by strangers than by parents.

4. Incest usually develops out of an already close father-daughter relationship.

Learning Objective

Define intimate violence and give some examples of it.

All of these statements are false and are myths that many people believe. Most of us assume that we will be safe with those whom we love and trust. Unfortunately, some individuals live with the terrible irony that they fear those to whom they feel closest. **Intimate violence is aggression toward those who are in close relationship to the aggressor.** Intimate violence takes many forms: psychological, physical, and sexual abuse of intimate partners and children. Tragically, sometimes violence against partners and children ends in homicide. In this Application, we'll focus on three of these serious social problems: partner abuse, child abuse, and child sexual abuse.

Partner Abuse

Learning Objective

Give some statistics regarding partner abuse.

The O. J. Simpson trial dramatically heightened public awareness of partner violence, particularly wife-battering and homicide. People found it difficult to reconcile the image of the smiling sports hero with the fact that he was a convicted wife-batterer with a history of terrorizing his former wife. Physical abuse can include hitting, kicking, burning, using a weapon, and rape. Examples of psychological abuse are humiliation, name calling, and refusing to speak. Exercising unreasonable control over a woman's access to money is also a form of abuse (Schechter & Gary, 1988).

As with other taboo topics, obtaining accurate estimates of physical abuse is difficult. One estimate is that about 28% of all married couples experience some form of physical aggression (slapping, beating) over the life of their marriage (Straus & Gelles, 1990; Straus, Gelles, & Steinmetz, 1980). A study of relationship abuse in lesbian couples found that this problem occurs at about the same rate (27%) (Brand & Kidd, 1986). Thus, domestic violence is not limited to heterosexual couples. These figures don't include the battering that goes on among cohabiting heterosexual couples, and some estimate that violence is even more common in these relationships (Stets & Straus, 1989). Moreover, this estimate excludes the physical abuse that goes on in some dating relationships and says nothing at all about psychological abuse. We also know that domestic violence is under-reported because of the stigma attached to it. Figure 9.16 provides additional statistics on partner abuse.

Some studies of physical aggression in married couples have reported higher rates of wife-to-husband abuse than husband-to-wife abuse (Hampton, Gelles, & Harrop, 1989; Straus & Gelles, 1986). There are some important weaknesses in these studies, however; among other things, they have failed to examine the consequences of abuse. Although we don't want to discount women's aggressive behavior in relationships, we need to point out that women are much more likely than men to suffer serious injuries and death as a result of physical assaults (Browne, 1993; Koss et al., 1994).

Figure 9.16
Facts on partner abuse
These grim statistics illustrate the seriousness of the problem of intimate violence in the United States.

Partner Abuse Statistics

- Approximately 90% of reported victims of domestic violence are women (U.S. Department of Justice, 1988).

- Domestic violence is the single largest cause of injury among women aged 15–44 (Novello et al., 1992).

- In 1994, 28% of female murder victims were killed by husbands or boyfriends; whereas only 3% of male murder victims were killed by wives or girlfriends (Federal Bureau of Investigation, 1995).

Characteristics of Batterers

Learning Objective

Summarize the characteristics of batterers and battered women.

Research shows that characteristics of the batterer are much better predictors of violence than are characteristics of the battered woman (Hotaling & Sugarman, 1986). Nonetheless, men who batter women are a diverse group, so a single profile has not emerged. Batterers typically have low self-esteem (Sigler, 1989; Walker, 1984) and are overly jealous and possessive (Okun, 1985). They are also likely to have been beaten as children or to have witnessed their mothers being beaten (Hotaling & Sugarman, 1986). One well-sampled study found that men who had observed violence between their parents were nearly three times as likely to hit their wives as were men whose parents had not been violent (Strauss et al., 1980). It's important to note, however, that most men who grow up in these difficult circumstances do not become batterers—only about a third do.

Abuse is more likely among men in the military (where hyper-aggressivity is encouraged), when men are unemployed (a serious threat to masculinity), and among men who have problems with alcohol or drugs (which impairs judgment) (Okun, 1986). Batterers often deny the seriousness of their behavior and deny responsibility for it. Battering appears to be slightly more common in families of lower socioeconomic status, but no social class is immune (Okun, 1986; Schuller & Vidmar, 1992). Ethnicity doesn't appear to be related to abuse when groups are equated for socioeconomic status and employment (Coley & Beckett, 1988; Gondolf, 1988).

Characteristics of Battered Women

Although some characteristics of battered women have been identified, it isn't clear whether these traits trigger the abuse or whether they are the result of the abuse. That is, it is easy to understand why an abused woman might begin to feel that she is worthless. Battered women typically have low self-esteem, blame themselves, change their own behavior to minimize the abuse rather than trying to change that of their partner, and often deny what is really going on (Sigler, 1989; Walker, 1984). Battered women are more likely to have a feminine or undifferentiated gender-role identity, and less likely to be androgynous (Mattley & Schwartz, 1990).

Why Women Stay in Abusive Relationships

Learning Objective

Explain why some women stay in abusive relationships.

Why do some women remain in an abusive relationship? One reason is that a woman may love her husband and truly believe that his behavior will change. And even if she is convinced that he won't change, she may remain in the relationship to avoid the social stigma of being divorced (remember the "marriage mandate") or to avoid disapproval from her family and friends (who are likely to "blame the victim"). The economic factor is an extremely important roadblock to her leaving, and

293

one that is often overlooked. That is, an abused woman probably has children and will need to support both them and herself. If they are young, she may not want to leave them to go to work. Even if she does want to work, she will probably have difficulty obtaining a job that would pay for child care on top of other living expenses. A related problem is that abused women and their families often have nowhere to go (McHugh, Frieze, & Browne, 1993). Furthermore, there is ample evidence that trying to leave an abusive relationship may precipitate brutal attacks or murder. Despite the many difficulties of leaving abusive relationships, attention is still focused on why women stay rather than on why men batter and on what interventions will prevent women from being brutalized or killed when they do leave (Koss et al., 1994).

Child Abuse

As hard as it is to believe, experts estimate that over a million children a year are physically abused (National Center on Child Abuse and Neglect, 1988). Sadly, most physical abuse of children is inflicted by family members and caregivers. And younger children are at greater risk for abuse than older ones. According to a 1994 Gallup poll, one in eight Americans reported being punched, kicked, or choked by a parent or adult guardian, and one in twenty suffered even more severe physical punishment during childhood (Moore, 1994). Mothers are more likely than fathers to physically abuse their children (Strauss et al., 1980), but fathers are more likely to sexually abuse their children (Russell, 1984). Boys are more likely to suffer from physical abuse, and girls, sexual abuse. There are conflicting findings on whether mothers or fathers are more likely to murder their children.

What leads parents to engage in child abuse? A number of factors appear to play a role (Belsky, 1993). A factor that is frequently cited is acceptance of violence as a legitimate disciplinary technique. Also, parents who have substance abuse problems are more likely to abuse their children. Child abuse is also linked to families that are large and poor, but it's important to note that not all poor parents abuse their children. Parents who themselves have been abused as children are more likely to abuse their children; however, most are *not* likely to abuse their children (Emery, 1989; Malinosky-Rummell & Hansen, 1993). Brandt Steele (1980) has suggested that four conditions appear necessary for child abuse to occur:

1. A caregiver who is predisposed to child abuse because of a history of neglect or abuse in his or her own life.
2. A crisis that places extra stress on the caregiver.
3. Lack of sources of support for the caregiver, either because he or she is unable to reach out, or because facilities are unavailable.
4. A child who is perceived as being unsatisfactory in some way.

Taking this view, it is easy to understand why child abuse is more likely to occur in poorer, larger, and less-educated families. Obviously, the levels of deprivation and stress in such families are much greater than for families with higher socioeconomic status.

The short- and long-term effects of child abuse vary depending on a variety of factors, including the age of the child when abuse was experienced, whether abuse occurred rarely or repeatedly, and the severity of the abuse. Those who experience repeated, severe abuse—especially at ages younger than 3 years—are more likely to have emotional difficulties (Kinard, 1982). Childhood physical abuse has been found to be linked, in adulthood, to aggressiveness toward dating partners, spouses, and children; substance abuse; emotional problems; and self-injurious and suicidal behaviors (Malinosky-Rummell & Hansen, 1993).

Figure 9.17
Actions taken by individuals who suspect child abuse
In a 1994 Gallup poll, 13% of the respondents indicated that they personally knew children they suspected had been physically or sexually abused. These same individuals were also asked what they did about their suspicions. Their responses are given here. (Data from Moore, 1994)

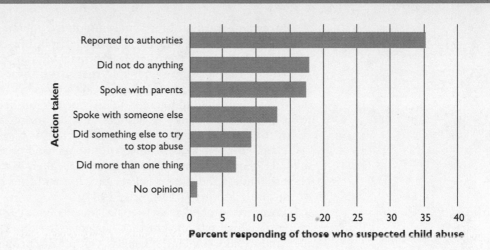

People are becoming more sensitized to the seriousness of child abuse. And when they suspect such a problem exists, many say they are willing to act to stop it (see Figure 9.17).

Child Sexual Abuse

The idea of sexual abuse of any kind is abhorrent to most people. The sexual abuse of children is viewed as particularly despicable because it involves helpless victims and is frequently perpetrated by individuals who are supposed to be the protectors of children (Densen-Gerber, 1984). Some definitions of child sexual abuse include physical contact and some do not (Haugaard & Reppucci, 1988). For the purposes of our discussion, we'll define *child sexual abuse* **as sexual experiences in which the victim is younger than 18 and the perpetrator is at least five years older than the victim.** The variability in definitions of childhood sexual abuse contributes to the difficulty of obtaining accurate estimates of the problem. Experts estimate that between 10% and 67% of children have experienced some kind of sexual abuse (Haugaard & Reppucci, 1988; Pope & Hudson, 1992). Although boys are sometimes the victims of sexual abuse, some 80% to 90% of the targets are girls (Trickett & Putnam, 1993). The most common form of sexual abuse is fondling (Haugaard & Reppucci, 1988).

Incest

Learning Objective

Define incest and discuss the nature of the problem.

Incest is a particular form of child sexual abuse. *Incest* **is sexual activity between close relatives.** Traditionally, incest referred to sexual activities between blood relatives, but the term now usually includes sexual activities between nonblood relatives as well (for instance, between stepfathers and stepdaughters). For reasons we have already mentioned, it is difficult to obtain accurate estimates of incest. Sexual activity between stepfather and stepdaughter occurs more frequently than between daughters and their biological fathers. For example, in a study of 930 sexually abused women, 1 in 6 had been molested by a stepfather compared to 1 in 40 by a biological father (Stark, 1984). Reports of incest by mothers or stepmothers are much lower (Stark, 1984). Although few incidents are reported, it is believed that the most common form of incest is between brothers and sisters while they are growing up. Since this usually takes the form of mutual experimentation and is usually not exploitive, mental health professionals worry less about its effects.

Incestuous relationships between fathers and daughters typically start when the daughter is between 6 and 11 years of age, and they continue for at least two years. Most encounters don't involve intercourse; among prepubescent girls, they consist of fondling the breasts and genitals, masturbation, and oral sex (Stark, 1984).

Incest occurs in families across all socioeconomic levels. Its causes are not entirely understood and agreed upon, but mental health professionals believe that it occurs most frequently in families (1) that are socially isolated, (2) that are controlled by strong, domineering fathers, and (3) in which the wife is either financially and emotionally dependent on the husband or sick, absent, alcoholic, or mentally ill. Frequently, the oldest daughter has taken over the household and child care responsibilities, and the sexual relationship with her father evolves as an extension of the "little mother" role (Stark, 1984).

Contrary to popular stereotype, incest doesn't usually develop out of a loving father-daughter relationship that has gone too far. The abuser's motives are complex and usually combine sexuality with power, hostility, and the need for a dependent "partner." Daughters usually cooperate with their father's sexual advances, so that physical force is seldom used. For this reason, victims of sexual abuse usually suffer considerable guilt and shame, making it difficult for them to seek help. Although some victims cooperate with their fathers because they are desperate for any kind of affection, many others do so and remain silent because they believe that they are keeping the family together, that their fathers will go to jail, or that there isn't anyone who can help them (Stark, 1984).

Effects of Incest

Learning Objective

Describe the effects of incest.

As with physical abuse, the effects of incest vary depending on how frequently it occurred, whether physical abuse was also involved, the nature of the relationship between the victim and the abuser, and the availability of nonabusing caregivers. Incest victims often suffer from depression, anxiety, guilt, anger, and helplessness (Haugaard & Reppucci, 1988; Trickett & Putnam, 1993). They typically also have difficulty trusting others. Some survivors may develop anxiety disorders, eating disorders, or behavior disorders, and some may have problems with substance abuse. Often, not knowing how else to cope with the situation, they run away from home. Suicide attempts are also common among victims; one study reported that 38% had attempted to kill themselves (Stark, 1984). (The controversial issue of psychotherapy and recovered memories among survivors of sexual abuse is discussed in Chapter 16.)

Although most of us would prefer not to think about this darker side of relationships, intimate violence is a reality we can ill-afford to ignore. It deeply touches the lives of millions of individuals. Hopefully, increased public awareness of intimate violence will help reduce its incidence and its tragic effects.

Key Ideas

Challenges to the Traditional Model of Marriage

• The traditional model of marriage is being challenged by the increasing acceptability of singlehood, the increasing popularity of cohabitation, the reduced premium on permanence, changes in gender roles, the increasing prevalence of voluntary childlessness, and the decline of the traditional nuclear family. Nonetheless, marriage remains quite popular.

Moving Toward Marriage

• A multitude of factors influence one's motivation to marry. Mate selection is influenced by endogamy, homogamy, and gender. Women place more emphasis on potential partners' character and financial prospects, whereas men are more interested in youthfulness and physical attractiveness.

• According to Murstein, the process of mate selection goes through three stages, which emphasize the stimulus value of the potential partner, value compatibility, and adequacy of role enactments. There are some premarital predictors of marital success, such as family background, age, length of courtship, social class, and personality, but the relations are weak.

Marital Adjustment Across the Family Life Cycle

• When marital satisfaction is mapped across the family life cycle, researchers find a U-shaped curve reflecting lower satisfaction in the middle stages. Newly married couples tend to be very happy before the arrival of children. Today more couples are struggling with the decision about whether to have children. The arrival of children is a major transition that is handled best by parents who have realistic expectations about the difficulties inherent in raising a family.

• As children reach adolescence, parents should expect more conflict as their influence declines. They must learn to relate to their children as adults and help launch them into the adult world. Once the children have struck out on their own, marital satisfaction tends to rise once again.

Vulnerable Areas in Marital Adjustment

• Gaps in expectations about marital roles, or unrealistic expectations in general, may create marital stress. Disparities in expectations about gender roles and the distribution of housework may be especially common and problematic. Work concerns can clearly spill over to influence marital functioning, but the links between parents' employment and marital adjustment are complex.

• Wealth does not ensure marital happiness, but a lack of money can produce marital problems. Inadequate communication is a commonly reported marital problem, which is increasingly analyzed from an attributional perspective. In-law problems appear to be declining. Sexual difficulties, jealousy, and growing in different directions are other common problems in marital relationships.

Divorce

• Divorce is becoming increasingly common for a variety of reasons. Unpleasant as divorce may be, the evidence suggests that toughing it out in an unhappy marriage is often worse. Divorce can create problems for children, but so does a strife-ridden intact home. Divorce is quite stressful and may lead to a variety of emotional and practical problems associated with the crisis of change. A substantial majority of divorced people remarry. These second marriages have a somewhat lower probability of success than first marriages.

Alternatives to Marriage

• An increasing proportion of the young population is remaining single, but this does not mean that people are turning away from marriage. Single people are often stereotyped as unhappy losers or carefree swingers. Both pictures are largely inaccurate. Although singles generally have the same adjustment problems as married couples, evidence suggests that singles tend to be slightly less happy. The prevalence of cohabitation has increased dramatically. Logically, one might expect cohabitation to facilitate marital success, but research has consistently found an association between cohabitation and marital instability.

• Gay relationships develop in a starkly different social context than marital rela-tionships. Nonetheless, studies have found that heterosexual and homosexual couples are similar in many ways. Gay relationships are characterized by great diversity. It is not true that gays usually assume traditional masculine and feminine roles. Nor is it true that they rarely get involved in long-term intimate relationships or family relations.

Application: Understanding Intimate Violence

• Intimate violence is a serious social problem that involves the emotional, physical, and sexual abuse of romantic partners and children. Men who batter their partners typically have low self-esteem, are possessive of their partners, and deny responsibility for their behavior. Battered women also have low self-esteem, but it isn't clear whether this is a cause or a result of abuse. Women stay in abusive relationships for a variety of reasons.

• One in eight Americans report having been physically abused in childhood. A history of abuse as a child combined with stress and deprivation predispose individuals to abusiveness. Childhood physical abuse can have serious short- and long-term effects.

• Estimates of childhood sexual abuse are wide-ranging. Girls are the most common targets; stepfathers and fathers are usually the perpetrators. Sexual abuse occurs most commonly in families that are socially isolated and that have domineering fathers and vulnerable mothers. The effects of incest can be quite serious for survivors.

Key Terms

Child sexual abuse
Cohabitation
Endogamy
Family life cycle
Homogamy
Incest
Intimate violence
Marriage
Perspective taking

Key People

Bernard Murstein
Letitia Anne Peplau

10   *Gender and Behavior*

"In classes, I experienced myself as a person to be taken lightly. In one seminar, I was never allowed to finish a sentence. There seemed to be a tacit understanding that I never had anything to say."

> —A woman quoted in *The Classroom Climate: A Chilly One for Women* (Hall & Sandler, 1982, p. 7)

"I get a feeling, like I want to say 'I love you' or just put my arms around my girlfriend. But then, for some reason, I just shut down and I don't do anything. It seems like I am going to give up too much by getting too close. Maybe she'll want more than I have to give. This way I can cover myself. But I wind up feeling guilty about not showing her I care."

> —A man quoted in *Man Alive: A Primer of Men's Issues* (Rabinowitz & Cochran, 1994, p. 55)

*T*his woman and man feel boxed in by gender roles. They're struggling with the limitations placed on their behavior because of their gender. They aren't unique or unusual. Think about the times *you* have changed *your* behavior to bring it in line with society's concepts of masculinity and femininity.

Before proceeding further, we need to define some terms. Some scholars prefer to use the term *gender* to refer to male-female differences that are learned, and *sex* to designate biologically based differences between males and females. However, as well-respected authority Janet Shibley Hyde (1996) points out, making this sharp distinction between *sex* and *gender* fails to recognize that biology and culture may interact. Following this reasoning, we'll use **gender to mean the state of being male or female.** (When we use the term *sex*, we're referring to sexual behavior.) It's important to note that, as *we* use the term, *gender* says nothing about the *causes* of behavior. In other words, if we say that there are gender differences in aggressive behavior, we are simply stating that males and females differ in this area; we are saying nothing about what might be the cause of these differences. Because visible physical differences exist between males and females, you might be tempted to leap to the conclusion that it is this biological difference that is responsible for gender differences in aggressive behavior. Nonetheless, this conclusion would be incorrect. Figure 10.1 lists a number of gender-related terms for easy comparison.

In this chapter, we'll examine the role of gender in people's lives. We'll address a number of complex and controversial questions. Are there genuine behavioral differences between males and females? If so, what are their origins? Are traditional gender-role expectations healthy or unhealthy? Why are gender roles in our society changing, and what does the future hold? In the Application, we'll explore gender and communication styles.

Figure 10.1
Terminology related to gender
The topic of gender involves many closely related ideas that are easy to confuse. The gender-related concepts introduced in this chapter are summarized here for easy comparison.

Gender-Related Concepts	
Gender	The state of being male or female
Gender identity	An individual's perception of himself or herself as male or female
Gender stereotypes	Widely held and often inaccurate beliefs about males' and females' abilities, personality traits, and social behavior
Gender differences	Actual disparities in behavior between males and females, based on research observations
Gender roles	Culturally defined expectations about appropriate behavior for males and females
Gender-role identity	A person's identification with the traits regarded as masculine or feminine (one's sense of being masculine or feminine)
Sexual orientation	A person's preference for sexual partners of the other gender (heterosexual), the same gender (homosexual), or both genders (bisexual)

Gender Stereotypes

Learning Objective

Define gender stereotypes and discuss three important points about them.

Obviously, women and men are biologically different, with regard to their genitals and other aspects of their anatomy and with regard to their physiological functioning. The readily apparent physical disparities between males and females lead us to expect other differences as well. Recall from Chapter 6 that *stereotypes* are widely held beliefs that people have certain characteristics simply because of their membership in a particular group. **Gender stereotypes are widely shared beliefs about males' and females' abilities, personality traits, and social behavior.** Research indicates that there is a great deal of consensus on *supposed* behavioral differences between men and women (Bergen & Williams, 1991; Martin, 1987). For example, a survey of gender stereotypes in 25 countries revealed considerable similarity of views (Williams & Best, 1990). Because of the widespread gains in educational and occupational attainment by American women since the 1970s, we might expect to find changes in gender stereotypes from then to now. But in fact, gender stereotypes in this country have largely remained stable since 1972 (Bergen & Williams, 1991; Martin, 1987; Ruble, 1983).

Gender stereotypes are too numerous to summarize here. Instead, refer to Figure 10.2, which lists a number of behavioral characteristics thought to be associated with femininity and masculinity. This list is based on a study in which subjects were asked to indicate the extent to which various traits are characteristic of each gender (Ruble, 1983). Although the list may contain a few surprises, you have probably encountered most of these stereotypes before. After all, everyone knows that women are more dependent, emotional, irrational, and talkative than men. Or are they?

Before we review the actual evidence on gender differences in behavior, we want to emphasize several additional points. First, although there is general agreement on a number of gender stereotypes, there are variations as well (Williams & Best, 1990). The characteristics in Figure 10.2 represent the prototypical American male and female: white, middle-class, heterosexual, and Christian (Basow, 1992). Obviously, however, not everyone fits this set of characteristics. For those who differ from the prototype, there are also variations in some gender stereotypes. For example, the stereotypes for African American males and females are more similar on the dimensions of competence and expressiveness than those for white Ameri-

**Figure 10.2
Traditional gender stereotypes**
This is a partial list of the characteristics that college students associate with a typical man and a typical woman. (Adapted from Ruble, 1983)

Elements of Traditional Gender Stereotypes

Masculine	Feminine
Active	Aware of others' feelings
Adventurous	Considerate
Aggressive	Creative
Ambitious	Cries easily
Competitive	Devotes self to others
Dominant	Emotional
Independent	Enjoys art and music
Leadership qualities	Excitable in a crisis
Likes math and science	Expresses tender feelings
Makes decisions easily	Feelings hurt
Mechanical aptitude	Gentle
Not easily influenced	Home oriented
Outspoken	Kind
Persistent	Likes children
Self-confident	Neat
Skilled in business	Needs approval
Stands up under pressure	Tactful
Takes a stand	Understanding

can males and females (Smith & Midlarsky, 1985). Also, African American women are viewed as less passive, dependent, emotional, intelligent, vain, and warm than white American women (Landrine, 1985; Romer & Cherry, 1980).

A second point we want to make is that the traditional male stereotype is more complimentary than the conventional female stereotype. This fact is related to **androcentrism, or the belief that the male is the norm** (Bem, 1993). In other words, our society is organized in a way that favors "masculine" characteristics and modes of behavior. Figure 10.3 gives examples of androcentrism in the workplace. Of course, male gender-role stereotypes also have some negative aspects.

A final point about gender stereotypes is that since the 1980s, the boundaries between male and female stereotypes seem to have become less rigid (Deaux & Lewis, 1983, 1984). Prior to the 1980s, the male and female stereotypes were perceived to be separate and distinct categories (for example, men are strong and women are weak). Now it seems that people see gender stereotypes as overlapping categories. That is, when participants are asked to estimate the probability that a hypothetical man or woman is strong, estimates for a hypothetical man are .66 and for a hypothetical woman, .44 (Deaux & Lewis, 1983, 1984).

Now that we've examined gender stereotypes, let's see what the research shows about the *actual* behavior of males and females. Keep in mind that we'll be looking at gender comparisons in modern Western societies. The story may be different in other cultures.

Research on Gender Comparisons

Research on *gender comparisons* seeks to discover the actual similarities and differences between males and females in their typical (average) behavior. A vast number of studies have been conducted in this area, and many report conflicting findings. Moreover, new evidence is pouring in constantly. Needless to say, it is almost an overwhelming task to keep up with trends in the field. Thankfully, a new

Figure 10.3
Male bias on the job
In the world of work, women who exhibit traditional "masculine" characteristics are often perceived negatively. Thus, a man and a woman may display essentially the same behavior but elicit very different reactions.

Androcentrism in the Workplace	
He's good on details.	She's picky.
He follows through.	She doesn't know when to quit.
He's assertive.	She's pushy.
He stands firm.	She's rigid.
He's a man of the world.	She's been around.
He's not afraid to say what he thinks.	She's outspoken.
He's close-mouthed.	She's secretive.
He exercises authority.	She's power-mad.
He climbed the ladder of success.	She slept her way to the top.
He's a stern taskmaster.	She's difficult to work for.

research technique has come to the rescue. *Meta-analysis* **is a statistical technique that evaluates the results of many studies on the same question.** Using this technique to synthesize the research on gender comparisons yields two critical pieces of information: (1) how large a gender difference exists (if there is one), and (2) which group scores higher (males or females). We've reviewed a number of studies based on meta-analysis to give you an up-to-date picture of the research evidence on gender comparisons. We'll look at three areas: cognitive abilities, personality traits and social behavior, and psychological disorders.

Cognitive Abilities

Learning Objective

Summarize the research findings on gender similarities and differences in verbal, mathematical, and spatial abilities.

Janet Shibley Hyde

Perhaps we should first point out that gender differences have *not* been found in *overall* intelligence. Of course, this shouldn't be surprising, because intelligence tests are intentionally designed to minimize differences between the scores of males and females.

What about gender differences in *specific* cognitive skills? Until very recently, it was generally agreed that females scored higher than males on measures of *verbal ability* and that this gap opened up during early adolescence (Hyde, 1981; Petersen, Crockett, & Tobin-Richards, 1982). However, Janet Shibley Hyde and Marcia Linn (1988) conducted a meta-analysis in this area that has altered the thinking on this issue. (The analysis included a variety of verbal behaviors: vocabulary, analogies, reading comprehension, and essay writing.) The meta-analysis showed no gender differences in verbal ability (or that differences are so small as to be unimportant). In addition, Hyde and Linn *did* find evidence of gender differences (favoring females) in verbal ability in those studies that had been conducted before 1974. Thus, it seems that there has been an actual change in gender differences in verbal ability, perhaps due to changes in gender-role socialization or in the testing of verbal ability.

Hyde and her colleagues performed another major meta-analysis on tests of *mathematical ability* (Hyde, Fennema, & Lamon, 1990). Again, the conclusion represents a change from earlier thinking on the question: Gender differences in mathematical ability in the general population no longer exist. (As with verbal ability, gender differences favoring males were found in the studies published before 1974.) Interestingly, when specific domains of mathematics are analyzed, some age trends emerge. On mathematical *problem solving*, males and females essentially perform the same until high school, when boys begin to outperform girls. The authors note that in high school, boys are more likely to elect math courses over girls, and that is probably one reason for the obtained gender difference in mathematical problem solving. Nonetheless, Hyde and her colleagues are concerned about this finding because problem-solving ability is essential for success in science courses and careers, arenas currently underpopulated by women.

A third important meta-analysis conducted by Hyde and her colleagues is in the area of *spatial ability*. Gender differences favoring males were found in one type of spatial ability: mental rotation (Linn & Petersen, 1986). This is the ability to mentally rotate a figure in three dimensions, a skill that is important in occupations such as engineering. Apparently, spatial ability can be improved by training (Baenninger & Newcombe, 1989).

To summarize, males and females seem to be similar regarding mental abilities. The differences that do exist are limited. We'll examine the possible causes of these differences after we have examined gender comparisons in some additional areas.

Personality Traits and Social Behavior

Investigators of gender differences have examined a variety of personality traits. We will discuss those that have attracted the most attention.

Self-Confidence

Many studies support the conclusion that, on average, males are more self-confident than females (Mednick & Thomas, 1993). Self-confidence is most likely to be low

Learning Objective

Summarize the research on
gender differences in
personality and social behavior.

among females in academic areas or tasks that are stereotyped as "masculine," such as math and science (Mednick & Thomas, 1993). This finding holds for both African American and white girls and women. Even when they receive the same grades as males in math and science courses, females perceive themselves as less competent than males consider themselves.

Women's self-confidence seems to fluctuate depending on the situation. That is, when women perform tasks that they view as gender-appropriate, when they get clear and direct feedback on their task performance, and when they work alone, their performance estimates are similar to men's (Mednick & Thomas, 1993). Women also deliberately lower their achievement predictions when they have to make them in public but do not do so in private (Heatherington et al., 1993). If women believe they are interacting with someone who is not as competent as they are, they also make lower estimates (Heatherington et al., 1993). Thus, while it is true that women often give lower estimates of their achievement than men, this does not necessarily mean that women lack self-confidence in achievement situations. Rather, this behavior may reflect conformity to a modesty norm for women or concern about others' feelings.

Aggression

Aggression is behavior that is intended to hurt someone, either physically or verbally (see Chapter 4). Research reveals that males are more aggressive than females, although the size of this difference is moderate (Hyde, 1984; Hyde & Frost, 1993). Furthermore, when distinctions are made among different types of aggression, some researchers have found that girls tend to engage in more verbal and disobedient aggressive acts, while boys engage in more physical and destructive aggressive acts (Hyde, 1984; Katz, Boggiano, & Silvern, 1993). Research also suggests that the genders may *think* differently about aggression (Eagly, 1987). For example, women report being aware of the danger of behaving aggressively and feeling more guilt and anxiety about engaging in aggressive behavior. These patterns of thinking probably inhibit women's expression of aggression.

The disparity between the genders in aggressive behavior shows up early in childhood. That it continues through adulthood is supported by the fact that men account for a grossly disproportionate share of violent crime (Kenrick, 1987). Figure 10.4 summarizes the stark gender differences in aggressive crimes such as assault, armed robbery, rape, and homicide.

Helping Behavior

Although helping others is a key aspect of the female gender role, a meta-analysis of studies in this area shows that men are more helpful than women (Eagly & Crowley, 1986; Hyde & Frost, 1993). If this surprises you, consider how helping behavior is usually operationally defined. That is, research on helping behavior typically looks at acts of chivalry and rescuing those in need. Obviously, this type of helping behavior matches better with male role expectations. Gender differences in helping

Figure 10.4
Gender differences in violent crimes
Males are arrested for violent crimes far more often than females, as these statistics show. These data support the findings of laboratory studies indicating that males tend to be more physically aggressive than females. (Data from U.S. Bureau of the Census, 1995)

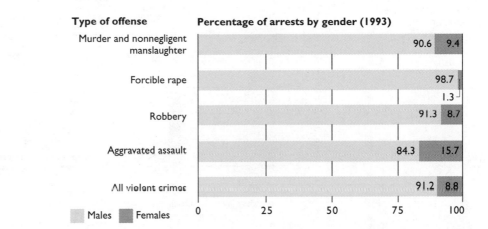

CALVIN AND HOBBES copyright Watterson. Reprinted with permission of UNIVERSAL PRESS SYNDICATE. All rights reserved.

behavior seem rooted in conformity to gender-role expectations rather than biology. For instance, men are even more likely than women to help when their behavior is observed by others than when seen by only the helper and "helpee," and they are more likely to help when the situation might involve danger (helping a stranger change a flat tire).

Conformity

Conformity **is yielding to real or imagined social pressure.** Traditional beliefs hold that females are more conforming than males, who are viewed as more independent-minded. Nonetheless, research has demonstrated that females *don't* conform to peer standards more than males *unless* there is group pressure to do so (Eagly & Carli, 1981; Hyde & Frost, 1993). As we noted earlier, race and gender often interact. For example, African American females seem to be less easily influenced and more assertive than either African American males or white females (Adams, 1980, 1983). The traditional explanation for gender differences in conformity is that women are more gullible than men, but there are alternative explanations as well: Women typically hold lower status in groups than do men, and women may be more concerned about preserving social harmony than men (Eagly, 1987).

Communication

Popular stereotypes have it that females talk a lot more than males do. In fact, the opposite is true: Men talk more than women (Aries, 1987; Swacker, 1975). In addition, men interrupt women more than women interrupt men (Natale, Entin, & Jaffe, 1979; West & Zimmerman, 1983). Nonetheless, there is evidence that women talk more than men when they have more power in a relationship (Kollock, Blumstein, & Schwartz, 1985). Thus, this gender difference seems to reflect status and power differences between men and women.

Another gender difference in verbal communication is tentativeness. Linda Carli (1990) looked for gender differences in three different types of tentative language (see Figure 10.5). She found that women are more likely than men to use *hedges* ("kind of" or "you know") or *disclaimers* ("I may be wrong" or "I'm not sure"). Also, women are twice as likely to use *tag questions* at the ends of sentences than are males (Carli, 1990; Lakoff, 1973; McMillan et al., 1977). For example, a woman might say, "Let's go to a movie, *OK?*" or "That was a terrific con-

Figure 10.5
Gender differences in the use of tentative language in mixed-gender groups
When men and women talked together for 10 minutes, it was found that women used significantly more hedges, disclaimers, and tag questions than men. (Data from Carli, 1990)

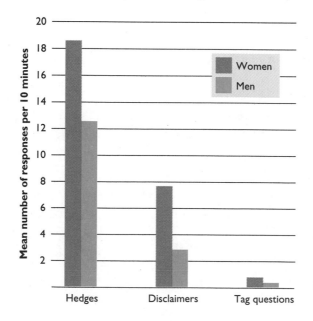

DEVELOPMENTAL TRANSITIONS   PART III

cert, *wasn't it?*" The reasons for this gender difference have been attributed both to women's greater insecurity and their greater interpersonal sensitivity (Wood, 1994).

Researchers have also studied how the genders compare in the realm of *non-verbal* communication. Regarding the *display* of nonverbal cues, the typical finding is that females display more submission and warmth cues, while males display more dominance and high-status cues (Frieze & Ramsey, 1976). It is quite likely that status differences are responsible for these findings (Henley, 1977; Mayo & Henley, 1981). A gender difference has also been found in *sensitivity* to nonverbal cues favoring women (Briton & Hall, 1995; Hall, 1984).

Psychological Disorders

Learning Objective

Summarize the research on gender and psychological disorders.

With regard to psychological disorders, the *overall* incidence of mental disorders is roughly the same for both genders. It seems that about one out of every three people will develop a psychological disorder at one time or another, and that this is true for both males and females (Robins et al., 1984).

When researchers assess the prevalence of *specific* disorders, they do find gender differences (Regier et al., 1988; Russo & Green, 1993). Antisocial behavior, alcoholism, and other drug-related disorders are more prevalent among men. Women, on the other hand, are more likely to suffer from depression and anxiety disorders (phobias, for example). They also show higher rates of eating disorders (Travis, 1988). In addition, women *attempt* suicide more often than men, but men *complete* suicides (actually kill themselves) more frequently than women (Cross & Hirschfeld, 1986; Strickland, 1988).

What accounts for these gender differences in mental illnesses? For one thing, there is a relatively obvious connection between the symptoms of "male" and "female" disorders and traditional gender roles (Katz, Boggiano, & Silvern, 1993). That is, women's disorders seem to reflect a turning *inward*—negative, hostile, and anxious feelings and conflicts are directed against the self. In men, these same feelings and conflicts are typically directed *outward*—against other individuals or society. (Suicide is one obvious exception.)

Putting Gender Differences in Perspective

Learning Objective

Summarize the findings regarding overall behavioral differences between males and females.

Although there are some genuine gender differences in behavior, remember that these are *group* differences. That is, they tell us nothing about individuals. Essentially, we are comparing the "average man" with the "average woman." Furthermore, the differences between these groups are relatively small. Figure 10.6 shows how scores on a trait might be distributed for men and women. Although the group averages are detectably different, you can see that there is great variability within each group (gender) and huge overlap between the two groups. Thus, a gender difference that shows up on the average does not by itself tell us anything about you or any other unique individual.

Figure 10.6
The nature of group differences
Gender differences are group differences that indicate little about individuals because of the great overlap between the groups. For a given trait, one gender may score higher on the average, but there is far more variation within each gender than between the genders.

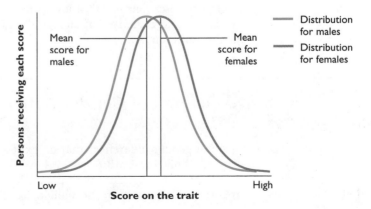

Figure 10.7
Meta-analyses of gender differences

Meta-analysis allows researchers to combine the results of many studies and estimate the amount of variation in a trait accounted for by a particular factor (in this case, gender). Some influential meta-analyses of gender differences are summarized here. They suggest that gender accounts for only a tiny portion of the variation among people in cognitive abilities and social behavior. (Adapted from Brigham, 1986)

Summary of Research on Gender Differences

Characteristic	Researcher	Number of studies analyzed	Variance accounted for by gender (%)
Verbal abilities	Hyde & Linn (1988)	165	<1
Mathematical abilities	Hyde, Fennema, & Lamon (1990)	254	<1
Visual-spatial abilities	Hyde (1981)	10	4.5
Aggression	Hyde (1984)	143	6
Decoding of nonverbal cues	Hall (1978)	75	4
Susceptibility to social influence	Eagly & Carli (1981)	148	1

Another way to gauge the influence of gender on behavior is to estimate how much of the variation among people on a trait is accounted for by a person's gender. Estimates of these proportions can be made through meta-analysis. Figure 10.7 summarizes the findings of meta-analyses on gender effects by Janet Shibley Hyde and others. These meta-analyses suggest that gender accounts for 1% or less of the variation among people in verbal ability, mathematical ability, and conformity (susceptibility to social influence). Furthermore, on the traits with the largest gender differences, gender accounts for only about 4–6% of the variation among individuals. Other factors besides gender, therefore, are far more important in accounting for the differences between individuals.

To summarize, the behavioral differences between males and females are fewer in number and smaller in size than popular stereotypes suggest. Moreover, gender-relevant behavior often seems to appear and disappear as gender-role expectations become more or less salient (Unger, 1981). *Ultimately, the similarities between women and men greatly outweigh the differences.*

If gender differences in personality and behavior are relatively modest, why does it seem otherwise? One explanation focuses on gender-based differences in social roles. Alice Eagly's (1987) *social role theory* **asserts that minor gender differences are exaggerated by the different social roles that males and females occupy.** For example, because women are assigned the role of caregiver, they learn to behave in nurturing ways. Moreover, people come to associate such role-related behaviors with individuals of a given gender, not with the actual roles they play. In other words, we come to see nurturing as a female trait rather than as a characteristic that anyone in a nurturing role would demonstrate. This is one way that stereotypes develop and persist.

Another explanation for the discrepancy between beliefs and reality is that the differences actually reside in the eye of the beholder, not the beholdee. *Social constructionism* **asserts that individuals construct their own reality based on societal expectations, conditioning, and self-socialization.** According to social constructionists, both the tendency to look for gender differences and people's specific beliefs about gender are rooted in the "gendered" messages and conditioning that permeate their socialization experiences. To better understand these issues, we need to explore the role of biological and environmental factors as likely sources of gender differences.

Alice Eagly

Biological Origins of Gender Differences

Are the gender differences that do exist acquired through learning, or are they biologically built in? Until now, we have deferred tackling this controversial question. Essentially, it represents the age-old issue of nature versus nurture. The "nature" theorists concentrate on how biological disparities between the genders contribute to differences in behavior. "Nurture" theorists, on the other hand, emphasize the role of learning and the environment. Although we will discuss biological and environmental influences separately, keep in mind that the distinctions between nature and nurture are less sharp today than they once were. As you'll see, a number of contemporary researchers and theorists in this area are interested in how biological and environmental factors interact. In this section, we'll look at the sociobiological explanation of gender differences, as well as two other biologically based lines of inquiry in this area: brain organization and hormonal influences.

Sociobiology

Learning Objective

Summarize the sociobiological explanation of gender differences.

Sociobiology **is the study of the genetic and evolutionary basis of social behavior in all organisms, including humans.** Sociobiologists assert that natural selection favors social behaviors that maximize reproductive success—that is, passing on genes to the next generation (Wilson, 1980). Thus, they explain social behaviors such as aggression and mating patterns in terms of their evolutionary value. Sociobiologists use the same reasoning to explain gender differences. Take, for example, the question of why the female of the species typically provides most of the care of the offspring. According to Trivers (1972), *parental investment* is the key. That is, each parent devotes time and energy to the care of offspring proportional to his or her investment in the offspring. By increasing the offspring's chance of survival, parents maximize the transmission of their genes to the next generation. Human females invest one of their few eggs (only one a month is produced), as well as weeks or months to carry and nourish offspring. Males, on the other hand, contribute but one of hundreds of millions of sperm and do not carry the young during the gestation period. According to sociobiologists, it is adaptive for the female to continue to care for the offspring after birth (to ensure that her genes are passed on) because she has already invested so much in the offspring. However, the male's situation is different. Because he has invested relatively little in the offspring, he doesn't have the same incentive to take care of them.

Recommended Reading

The New Our Bodies, Ourselves: A Book By and For Women

by The Boston Women's Health Book Collective (Simon & Schuster, 1992)

The New Our Bodies, Ourselves is a revised and greatly expanded version of a remarkably popular and worthwhile book. As its title suggests, it is primarily about the female body and women's health issues. This latest edition contains 27 chapters, including ones on body image; food; alcohol, mood-altering drugs, and smoking; environmental and occupational health; violence against women; sexual relationships with men and women; birth control; sexually transmitted diseases; AIDS; pregnancy; childbirth; growing older; and medical care for women.

The book grew spontaneously out of a women's discussion group that began meeting in Boston in 1969. Part of the book's charm lies in its unique mixture of information drawn from technical sources and information drawn from personal experiences. These two disparate sources of insight are interwoven nicely through the use of numerous quotations. The book is illustrated where necessary, and it provides many suggestions for additional reading.

> Every society throughout history has had standards of beauty, but at no time before has there been such an intense media blitz telling us what we should look like. Magazine covers, films, TV shows, and billboards surround us with images which fail to reflect the tremendous diversity among us. Never before have there been hundreds of profitable businesses set up to convince us we don't look good enough. [p. 23]

Sociobiological theories are post hoc explanations of gender differences that are difficult to test empirically. Moreover, efforts to apply sociobiological concepts to *human* behavior have generated a highly charged debate (Ruse, 1987). While many social psychologists might be sympathetic with the idea that genetic and biological factors play some role in human social behavior, they have serious questions about some of the basic assumptions of sociobiology (Cantor, 1990). In particular, they reject the view that behaviors or traits that are affected by genetic factors cannot be altered. To cite an example, increasing numbers of people are voluntarily cutting back on foods high in cholesterol, despite the fact that humans are genetically programmed to find such foods highly tasty.

Other critics suggest that sociobiological theory can be used to claim that the status quo in society is the inevitable outcome of evolutionary forces (Lewontin, Rose, & Kamin, 1984). For example, if males have dominant status over females, then natural selection must have favored this arrangement. These and other problems lead us to conclude that sociobiological explanations for human gender differences remain highly speculative. Let's look at two alternative biological explanations for gender differences.

Brain Organization

Some theorists assert that male and female brains are organized differently and that this might account for gender differences in some cognitive abilities. As you may know, the human brain is divided into two halves. **The *cerebral hemispheres* are the right and left halves of the cerebrum, which is the convoluted outer layer of the brain.** The largest and most complicated part of the human brain, the cerebrum is responsible for most complex mental activities.

Some evidence suggests that the right and left cerebral hemispheres are specialized to handle different cognitive tasks (Halpern, 1992; Springer & Deutsch, 1993). For example, it appears that the *left hemisphere* is more actively involved in *verbal and mathematical processing*, while the *right hemisphere* is specialized to handle *visual-spatial and other nonverbal processing*. This pattern is generally seen in both right-handed and left-handed people, although it is less consistent among those who are left-handed.

After these findings on hemispheric specialization surfaced, various theorists began to wonder whether a connection might exist between this division of labor in the brain and the then-observed gender differences in verbal and spatial skills. Consequently, researchers began looking for disparities between males and females in brain organization.

They found some evidence that males exhibit more cerebral specialization than females (Bryden, 1988; Hines, 1990). In other words, there is a trend for males to depend more heavily than females on the left hemisphere in verbal processing and on the right hemisphere in spatial processing. Gender differences have also been found in the size of the corpus callosum, the band of fibers that connects the two hemispheres (Hines, 1990). More specifically, some studies suggest that females tend to have a larger corpus callosum. This might allow for better interhemispheric transfer of information, which, in turn, might underlie the more bilateral organization of females' brains. Thus, some theorists have argued that these differences in brain organization are responsible for gender differences in verbal and spatial ability (Halpern, 1992; Kimura, 1987). As a result of the interest aroused by these findings, the popular press has often touted the idea that there are "male brains" and "female brains" which are fundamentally different (Bleier, 1984).

This idea is intriguing, but we have a long way to go before we can attribute gender differences in verbal and spatial ability to right brain/left brain specialization. For one thing, as we noted earlier, recent studies indicate that there aren't any real

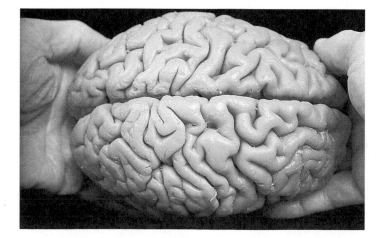

Studies have shown that the brain's cerebral hemispheres, shown here, are somewhat specialized in the kinds of cognitive tasks they handle and that such specialization is more pronounced in males than in females. Whether this difference bears any relation to gender differences in behavior is yet to be determined.

gender differences in verbal ability to be explained. Second, studies have not consistently found that males have more specialized brain organization than females (Fausto-Sterling, 1992; Halpern, 1992), and the finding of a larger corpus callosum in females does not always appear (Halpern, 1992; Hines, 1990). Third, because a significant amount of brain development occurs over the first 5 to 10 years after birth, during which time males and females are socialized differently, it is possible that different life experiences may accumulate to produce slight differences in brain organization (Hood et al., 1987). Finally, it's important to remember that male and female brains are much more similar than they are different. Thus, the notion that cerebral specialization is linked to gender differences in mental abilities is still under debate.

Hormonal Influences

Learning Objective

Review the evidence relating hormones to gender differences.

Biological explanations of gender differences have also focused on the possible role of hormones. **Hormones are chemical substances released into the bloodstream by the endocrine glands.** We'll examine the role hormones play in sexual differentiation and in sexual and aggressive behavior.

Prenatal Gender Differentiation

We know that hormones play a key role in gender differentiation during *prenatal* development. One's biological gender is determined by one's sex chromosomes. An XX pairing produces a female, and an XY pairing produces a male. However, both male and female embryos are essentially the same until about 8 to 12 weeks after conception. Around this time, male and female gonads (sex glands) begin to produce different hormonal secretions. The high level of *androgens* (male hormones) in males and the low level of androgens in females leads to the differentiation of male and female genital organs.

The influence of prenatal hormones on gender differentiation becomes apparent when something interferes with normal prenatal hormonal secretions. John Money and his colleagues have tracked the development of a small number of females who were exposed to high levels of androgens during their prenatal development. The girls were born to mothers who either had a hormonal malfunction during pregnancy or were given an androgenlike drug to prevent miscarriage. These *androgenized females* were born with genitals that appeared to be male. The degree of masculinization of their genitals varied, depending on the extent of their prenatal hormonal imbalance. In some cases, the masculinization was so subtle that it went unnoticed for months and even years. Once noticed, most cases were treated with a combination of hormone therapy and surgical correction of the genitals to match the gender they were assigned at birth.

Money and his colleagues wondered whether the prenatal dose of male hormones would affect the behavioral tendencies of these androgenized females. Sure enough, they found that the androgenized females showed "tomboyish" interests in vigorous outdoor activities. They also showed preferences for male playmates and "male" toys (Money & Ehrhardt, 1972). More recently, several other researchers have compared groups of these girls with their "normal" sisters (Berenbaum & Hines, 1992; Hines & Kaufman, 1994). Consistent with Money's findings, the later research showed that the androgenized girls preferred male-stereotyped toys for play, whereas their sisters did not. Contrary to earlier results, however, there were no differences between the groups in the amount of rough play.

The findings on androgenized females suggest to many theorists that prenatal hormones shape gender differences in humans. But there are a few problems with this evidence. First, it's always dangerous to draw conclusions about the general population based on a handful of subjects who have an abnormal condition. Second, most of the androgenized girls received drug treatments (cortisone) for their condition, and these treatments could have influenced their activity levels. Third, the girls were born with masculine-appearing genitals that often were not surgically corrected until age 2 or 3. Hence, their families may not have reared them in quite the same way as they would have reared "normal" girls. In light of these problems, research on androgenized females cannot conclusively demonstrate that prenatal hormones, alone, cause gender differences in behavior.

Sexual and Aggressive Behavior

Research on testosterone suggests that this hormone plays an important role in *sexual desire* for both men and women (Everitt & Bancroft, 1991). When testosterone is reduced or eliminated, both men and women show decrements in sexual drive. A handful of studies have also reported associations between levels of male and female hormones and specific traits. So far, however, the results of these studies are inconsistent (Fausto-Sterling, 1992; Hines, 1982). For instance, testosterone has been linked with higher levels of *aggression* in humans (Inoff-Germain et al., 1988). Still, the picture is complicated because it has also been found that aggressive behavior can produce increases in testosterone (Rose, Gordon, & Bernstein, 1972).

In summary, hormones probably do play a role in some aspects of sexual and aggressive behavior, although the nature of the connections are not well understood. Also, hormones have less influence on human behavior than they do on animal behavior because humans are more susceptible to environmental influences. We still have much to learn about the complicated ways in which hormones interact with social and psychological factors.

The overall evidence suggests that biological factors play a relatively minor role in gender differences, creating predispositions that are largely shaped by experience. In contrast, efforts to link gender differences to disparities in the way males and females are reared have proved more fruitful. We'll consider this perspective next.

Environmental Origins of Gender Differences

Learning Objective

Define socialization and gender roles, and describe Margaret Mead's findings on the variability of gender roles.

Socialization is the acquisition of the norms and roles expected of people in a particular society. This process includes all the efforts made by a society to ensure that its members learn to behave in a manner that's considered appropriate. The socialization process includes efforts to teach children about gender roles. **Gender roles are cultural expectations about what is appropriate behavior for each gender.** For example, in our culture women have widely been expected to rear children, cook meals, clean house, and do laundry. On the other hand, men have been expected to be the family breadwinner, do yardwork, and tinker with cars.

Are gender roles in other cultures similar to those seen in our society? Generally, yes—but not necessarily. Despite a fair amount of cross-cultural consistency in gender roles, some dramatic variability exists as well (Munroe & Munroe, 1975). For instance, when anthropologist Margaret Mead (1950) conducted a now-classic study of three tribes in New Guinea, she found one tribe (the Mundugumor) in which *both* genders followed our masculine role expectations and another tribe (the Arapesh) in which *both* genders approximated our feminine role. She found a third tribe (the Tchambuli) in which the male and female roles were roughly the *reverse* of our own. Such remarkable discrepancies between cultures existing within 100 miles of one another demonstrate that gender roles are not a matter of biological destiny. Instead, like other roles, gender roles are acquired through socialization.

As we noted earlier, Eagly's social role theory suggests that gender differences occur because males and females are guided by different role expectations. In the next section, we'll discuss how our society teaches individuals about gender roles.

Processes in Gender-Role Socialization

How do people acquire gender roles? Gender-role socialization takes place through several key learning processes. These include reinforcement and punishment, observational learning, and self-socialization.

Children learn behaviors appropriate to their gender roles very early in life. According to social learning theory, boys tend to follow in their father's footsteps, while girls tend to do the sorts of things their mother does.

Learning Objective

Explain how reinforcement and punishment, observational learning, and self-socialization operate in gender-role socialization.

Reinforcement and Punishment

One important way children learn gender roles is by being reinforced for "gender-appropriate" behaviors and punished for "gender-inappropriate" ones (recall our discussion of operant conditioning in Chapter 2). Parents, teachers, peers, and others often reinforce (usually with tacit approval) "gender-appropriate" behavior and respond negatively to "gender-inappropriate behavior" (Fagot & Leinbach, 1987; Fagot, Leinbach, & O'Boyle, 1992). For example, a young boy who has just hurt himself may be told by his dad that "big boys don't cry." If the child succeeds in inhibiting his crying, he may get a pat on the back or a warm smile—both potent reinforcers. Over time, a consistent pattern of such reinforcement will strengthen the boy's tendency to "act like a man" and suppress emotional displays.

Many parents probably take gender-appropriate behavior for granted and don't go out of their way to reward it. But they usually react very negatively to gender-inappropriate behavior (O'Leary, 1977). For instance, a 10-year-old boy who enjoys playing with dollhouses may elicit strong disapproval. Parents pay more attention to discouraging gender-inappropriate behavior in boys than in girls. Fathers are especially likely to punish gender-inappropriate behavior in their sons (Lytton & Romney, 1991). This punishment usually involves verbal reprimands or ridicule rather than physical punishment.

Observational Learning

As explained in Chapter 2, *observational learning* occurs when a person's behavior is influenced by observations of others, who are called *models*. Parents serve as models for children, as do siblings, teachers, relatives, and other people who are important in children's lives. Note that models are not limited to real people. For example, characters on television and in films also function as role models.

According to *social learning theory* (see Chapter 2), young children are more likely to imitate people who are nurturant, powerful, and similar to them (Mischel, 1970). Children imitate both genders, but most children tend to imitate same-gender models more than other-gender models (Bussey & Bandura, 1984; Perry & Bussey, 1979). Thus, observational learning often leads young girls to play with dolls, toy stoves, and so forth. In contrast, young boys are more likely to tinker with toy trucks, miniature gas stations, and such. Similarly, girls and boys spend more time with same-gender peers, who serve as each other's models.

Self-Socialization

Children are not merely passive recipients of gender-role socialization. Rather, they play an active role in this process (Bem, 1993; Martin & Halverson, 1987). Self-socialization entails three steps. First, children learn to classify themselves as male or female and to recognize their gender as a permanent quality (around age 5 or 6). Second, this self-categorization motivates them to value those characteristics and behaviors that are associated with their gender. Third, they strive to bring their behavior in line with what is considered gender-appropriate in their culture. In other words, children get involved in their own socialization, working diligently to discover the rules that are supposed to govern their behavior.

Sources of Gender-Role Socialization

There are four major sources of gender-role socialization: parents, peers, schools, and the media. Our discussion of gender-role socialization will primarily reflect white, middle-class experiences because researchers have focused on this group (Reid & Paludi, 1993). It's important to keep in mind, however, that individuals who have grown up in different types of households may have had different experiences. For example, traditional gender roles are relatively rigidly defined in Hispanic families (Comas-Diaz, 1987). Also, gender roles are changing, so the generalizations that follow may say more about how you were socialized than about how your children will be.

Parents

Learning Objective

Describe how parents, peers, and schools influence gender-role socialization.

A great deal of gender-role socialization takes place in the home. Nonetheless, a meta-analysis of 172 studies of parental socialization practices suggests that parents don't treat girls and boys as differently as one might expect (Lytton & Romney, 1991). Still, there are some important dissimilarities. For one thing, there is a strong and consistent tendency for both mothers and fathers to emphasize and encourage *play activities* that are "gender-appropriate." Other studies have found that boys and girls are encouraged to play with different types of toys (Etaugh & Liss, 1992). As Figure 10.8 shows, substantial gender differences are found in toy preferences. Generally, boys have less leeway to play with "feminine" toys than girls do with "masculine" toys. As children grow older, their leisure activities often vary by gender: Johnny plays in Little League and Mary gets ballet lessons.

A second finding from the meta-analysis of parenting practices was that mothers and fathers consistently assign *household chores* in line with gender stereotypes (Lytton & Romney, 1991; McHale et al., 1990). Girls usually do laundry and dishes, whereas boys mow the lawn and take out the trash.

Parents' attitudes about gender roles have been shown to influence the gender roles acquired by their children (Jackson, Ialongo, & Stollak, 1986; Weisner &

Figure 10.8
Toy preferences and gender
This graph depicts the percentage of boys and girls asking for various types of toys in letters to Santa Claus (adapted from Richardson & Simpson, 1982). As you can see, boys and girls differ substantially in their toy preferences. These differences show the effects of gender-role socialization.

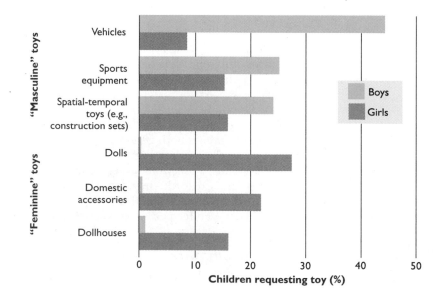

Wilson-Mitchell, 1990). For example, several studies have found that only mothers with nontraditional views of gender roles seemed to encourage their daughters to be independent (Brooks-Gunn, 1986; Carr & Mednick, 1988). In this context, we might mention that middle-class parents may allow their children to deviate more from traditional gender roles than lower-class parents do (Reid & Paludi, 1993). Also, African American families seem to place less emphasis on traditional gender roles than white American families (Smith & Midlarsky, 1985). In contrast, Asian American families typically encourage subservience in their daughters (Tsai & Uemura, 1988), and Hispanic families usually encourage traditional gender-role behavior.

Peers

Peers form an important network for learning about gender-role stereotypes, as well as gender-appropriate and gender-inappropriate behavior. Between the ages of 4 and 6, children seem to separate into same-gender groups. A longitudinal study showed that the ratio of time spent with same-gender playmates versus other-gender playmates rose from 3:1 to 11:1 between these ages (Maccoby, 1990; Maccoby & Jacklin, 1987). Therefore, it seems that, during these ages, same-gender peers are the most powerful instruments of such learning (Fagot, 1985).

Play among same-gender peers takes different forms for boys and girls. Boys play in larger groups and roam farther away from home, whereas girls prefer smaller groups and stay near the house (Feiring & Lewis, 1987). In addition, high status in boys' groups is achieved by engaging in dominant behavior (telling others what to do and enforcing orders). In contrast, girls usually express their wishes as suggestions rather than demands (Maltz & Borker, 1983). Also, boys engage in rough-and-tumble play much more frequently than do girls (Maccoby, 1988).

Peers seem to play a different and more important role for boys than for girls. For boys, male peers seem to assume more importance than adult models relatively early in life, for several reasons. First, adult males are relatively invisible to male children because they are at work and don't typically work in settings where children are present. Also, boys spend much of their time in the presence of females (mothers and female teachers). Thus, it has been suggested that males use the male peer group for information about the male role in the absence of adult male models (Hartley, 1959) and to resist female influence (Maccoby & Jacklin, 1987). Because girls have easy access to information about the female role and feel at ease with female adults, they don't need to rely on same-gender peers in the way boys do. Research seems to support such an interpretation. For example, male peers appear to play a particularly important role for African American males, who are more likely to be reared in a female-headed home than are white males (Coates, 1987; Rashid, 1989). In contrast, African American girls report that they feel close both to family members and to male and female peers.

Little boys who show an interest in dolls are likely to lose status among their male peers.

Schools

Schools also make a major contribution to the socialization of gender roles (Best, 1983; Busch-Rossnagel & Vance, 1982; Wellesley College Center for Research on Women, 1992). The *books* that children use in learning to read can influence their ideas about what is suitable behavior for males and females (Schau & Scott, 1984). Traditionally, males have been more likely to be portrayed as clever, heroic, and adventurous in these books, whereas females have been more often shown performing domestic chores. Although the depiction of stereotypical gender roles has declined considerably since the 1970s, researchers still find significant differences in how males and females are portrayed (Noddings, 1992; Purcell & Stewart, 1990). Many high school and college textbooks also contain gender bias. The most common problems are the use of

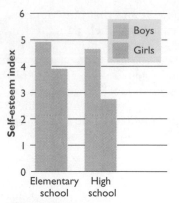

Figure 10.9
The gender gap in self-esteem between elementary school and high school
Girls experience a significant drop in self-esteem between elementary school and high school, whereas boys do not. In this study, self-esteem was measured by responses to five statements: "I like the way I look," "I like most things about myself," "I'm happy the way I am," "Sometimes I don't like myself that much," and "I wish I were somebody else." (AAUW, 1994)

Learning Objective

Describe how television influences gender-role socialization.

generic masculine language ("policeman" versus "police officer," and so forth) and portraying males and females in stereotypical roles.

Gender bias in schools also shows up in *teachers' behaviors*. Preschool and grade-school teachers frequently reward gender-appropriate behavior in their pupils (Fagot et al., 1985). Also, teachers tend to pay greater attention to males—helping them, praising them, and scolding them more than females (Sadker & Sadker, 1985; Wellesley College Center for Research on Women, 1992). In contrast, girls tend to be relatively invisible in the classroom and receive little encouragement for academic achievement from teachers. A recent national report in this area concluded that girls' self-esteem is gradually eroded through such experiences as (1) teachers paying less attention to them, (2) sexual harassment by male peers, (3) the stereotyping and invisibility of females in textbooks, and (4) test bias that restricts girls' chances of getting into college and obtaining scholarships (Wellesley College Center for Research on Women, 1992). Figure 10.9 depicts the development of this gender-gap in self-esteem.

Gender bias also shows up in *academic and career counseling*. Despite the fact that females obtain higher grades than males do in all subjects from elementary school through college (Eccles, 1989; Kimball, 1989), many counselors still encourage male students to be physicians and engineers and guide female students toward teaching, nursing, and homemaking (Read, 1991).

The Media

Television is yet another source of gender-role socialization (Morgan, 1982). Youngsters in the United States spend a lot of time watching TV (see Figure 10.10). Children between the ages of 3 and 11 watch an average of 2–4 hours of TV per day (Huston et al., 1990; Liebert & Sprafkin, 1988). African American children and youth spend more time in front of the TV than their white peers (Brown et al., 1990).

An analysis of male and female TV characters showed that males outnumber females 2 to 1, the same ratio that existed in the 1950s (D. M. Davis, 1990). Television programs have traditionally depicted men and women in highly stereotypical ways (Basow, 1992). On prime-time programs today, more women are portrayed as having jobs. Still, most female TV characters have professional jobs such as lawyers, whereas most real women work in low-paying, low-status jobs. The "up" side of this unbalanced portrayal is that professional women characters can serve as positive role models for girls and women, but the "down" side is that viewers are led to underestimate the degree of inequity in the workplace (Basow, 1992).

Television commercials are even more gender-stereotyped than programs (Bretl & Cantor, 1988; Lovdal, 1989). Women are shown worrying about how white "their" laundry is and how to use expensive cosmetics to "snare" a man, although at least one study of gender bias in television commercials reported that men are increasingly being shown in the roles of spouse and parent (Bretl & Cantor, 1988). Music videos frequently portray women as sex objects, and these portrayals appear to influence viewers' attitudes about sexual conduct (Hansen & Hansen, 1988).

There appears to be a clear link between the number and type of television programs children watch and acquiring gender-stereotyped beliefs. Children who are frequent viewers have been found to hold more stereotyped beliefs about gender than children who watch less TV (Kimball, 1986; Signorielli & Lears, 1992). Children who watch a great deal of educational TV tend to be less traditional about gender roles than other children (Repetti, 1984), no doubt because many children's shows on educational TV promote nontraditional gender roles. As we saw in Chapter 6, once stereotypes are learned, they are difficult to change.

Figure 10.10
Television viewing habits
As children grow up, they spend more and more time watching TV until viewing time begins to decline slightly at around age 12. Research shows that children's conceptions of gender roles are influenced to a considerable degree by what they watch on television. (Data from Liebert & Sprafkin, 1988)

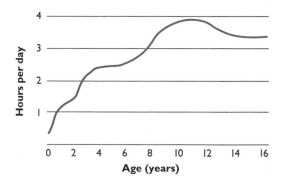

Another form of gender bias in television is its inordinate emphasis on physical attractiveness in women. Males on television may or may not be good-looking, but the vast majority of females are young, attractive, and sexy (D. M. Davis, 1990). Exposure to such role models means that females experience much more pressure to be youthful, thin, and physically attractive than males do (Feingold, 1990). These cultural expectations have been frequently cited as a cause of the disproportionately high incidence of eating disorders in females (Levenkron, 1982; Polivy & Thomsen, 1988).

Traditional Gender Roles

The social norms that characterize traditional gender roles are based on several assumptions: that all members of the same gender have basically the same traits, that the traits of one gender are different from the traits of the other gender, and that masculine traits are more highly valued. Because traditional gender roles are based on the assumption that everyone is heterosexual (heterosexism), they say nothing about homosexual individuals. This fact and the relative invisibility of gay males and lesbians mean that young homosexuals are deprived of positive role models. This state of affairs obviously makes it more difficult for them to sort through the interrelated issues of identity, gender-role identity, and sexual orientation. Let's look at traditional gender-role expectations.

Role Expectations for Males

Learning Objective

List five elements of the traditional male role.

A number of psychologists have characterized the traditional male role (Kilmartin, 1994; Pleck, 1981a). According to James Doyle and Michele Paludi (1991), it contains five key elements:

- *The anti-feminine element.* As we have seen, "real men" shouldn't act in any way that might be perceived as feminine. As Robert Brannon (1976) puts it, "No sissy stuff."
- *The success element.* To prove their masculinity, men need to beat out other men at sports and at work. Having a high-status job, driving an expensive car, and making lots of money are aspects of this element.
- *The aggressive element.* Men are expected to fight for what they believe is right and to aggressively defend themselves against threats. Aggression may take the form of verbal or physical force, even violence.
- *The sexual element.* "Real men" should be the initiators and controllers of sexual activity.
- *The self-reliant element.* Being "in control" and remaining cool and calm under pressure are aspects of this element.

Gender-role expectations for boys have remained relatively stable for years. However, it appears that the male role may be undergoing some changes. According to Joseph Pleck (1981a), who has written extensively on this issue, in the *traditional male role*, masculinity is validated by individual physical strength, aggressiveness, and emotional inexpressiveness. In the *modern male role*, masculinity is validated by economic achievement, organizational power, emotional control (even over anger), and emotional sensitivity and self-expression (but only with women).

The traditional role exists along with the new expectations, so males may experience role inconsistencies. Pleck (1976) explains: "Where childhood socialization valued physical strength and athletic ability and taught boys to shun girls, adulthood confronts males with expectations for intellectual and social skills and for the capacity to relate to females as work peers and emotional intimates" (p. 16). The recent rise in popularity of various men's groups suggests that many men are feeling uncomfortably constrained by traditional gender roles.

Problems with the Male Role

It is a common misconception that only women suffer from narrow gender roles. Although the women's movement stimulated concern about the costs of females' roles during the 1950s and 1960s, only more recently have similar concerns been raised about the costs of males' roles (Doyle, 1989; Keen, 1991; Kilmartin, 1994; Pleck, 1981a).

Pressure to Succeed

Most men are socialized to believe that job success is everything. They are encouraged to be highly competitive and are taught that a man's masculinity is measured by the size of his paycheck and job status (Doyle, 1989; Gould, 1978; Keen, 1991). As Christopher Kilmartin (1994) notes, "There is always another man who has more money, higher status, a more attractive partner, or a bigger house. The traditional man . . . must constantly work harder and faster" (p. 13). Small wonder, then, that so many men pursue success with a fervor that is sometimes dangerous to their health. The extent of this danger is illustrated by males' life expectancy, which is about seven years shorter than females' (of course, factors besides gender roles contribute to this difference).

The majority of men who have internalized this success ethic are unable to realize their dreams. How does this "failure" affect them? While many are able to adjust to it, many are not. Those in the latter group are likely to suffer from poor self-esteem and a diminished sense of virility (Doyle, 1989). Males' obsession with success also creates problems for females. For instance, many men want to "keep women in their place" because their self-esteem is threatened when a woman earns more than they do (Astrachan, 1992; Blumstein & Schwartz, 1983). Men's emphasis on success also makes it more likely that they will spend long hours on the job. This decreases the amount of time families can spend together and increases the amount of time wives spend on housework and child care.

The Emotional Realm

Most young boys are trained to believe that men should be strong, tough, cool, and detached. Also, men learn to direct their negative and anxious feelings toward others, as we noted earlier. These experiences increase the tendency for males to behave aggressively, and sometimes violently (Tavris, 1989). Intimate violence and sexual assaults are almost exclusively perpetrated by males, and almost 90% of violent crimes in the United States are committed by men (U.S. Bureau of the Census, 1995).

In contrast, males learn early to hide emotions such as love, joy, and sadness because they believe that such feelings are "feminine" and imply weakness. Unfortunately, some men inhibit emotions for so long that they become unable even to identify them. This condition is termed *alexithymia* ("no words for emotions") (Kilmartin, 1994; Sifneos, 1972). These problems with "tender" emotions have serious consequences. First, it makes it difficult for males to express feelings of affection and causes problems in their relationships with partners and children (Katz, Boggiano, & Silvern, 1993). Second, as we saw in Chapter 3, there are risks inherent in bottling up emotions. Suppressed emotions contribute to many stress-related disorders.

Sexual Problems

Men often experience sexual problems that derive partly from their gender-role socialization. The problem stems from having a "macho" sexual image to live up to. Thus, there are few things that most men fear more than a sexual encounter in which they are unable to achieve an erection (Doyle, 1989). Unfortunately, these very fears often *cause* the impotence that men dread (see Chapter 13). The upshot is that males' obsession with sexual performance often produces anxiety that may interfere with their sexual responsiveness.

Another problem is that many men learn to confuse feelings of intimacy with sex. In other words, if a man experiences strong feelings of connectedness, he is likely to understand these as sexual feelings. This confusion has a number of consequences (Kilmartin, 1994). For one thing, sex may be the only way some men can allow themselves to feel intimately connected to another. Thus, men's keen interest in sex may be driven, in part, by strong needs for emotional intimacy that don't get satisfied in other ways. The confusion of intimacy and sex also explains why some men misperceive a woman's friendly touch as a sexual invitation, as we noted in our discussion of date rape. Finally, the sexualization of intimate feelings causes inappropriate anxiety when men feel affection for another man and is related to the problem of homophobia.

Homophobia is the intense fear and intolerance of homosexuality. Because homosexuality is still largely unaccepted, fear of being labeled homosexual keeps many people, but especially males, adhering to traditional gender roles who might otherwise be more flexible. One reason that homophobia is more prevalent among males is that the male role is rooted in the fear of appearing feminine—and feminine characteristics are mistakenly associated with gayness (Herek, 1986; McCreary, 1994). Second, homophobia is much more common in men than in women because males feel more pressure to avoid any behavior characteristic of the other gender (Herek, 1988; Kite, 1984). Although they will tolerate "tomboyism" in girls, parents (especially fathers) are highly intolerant of any "sissy" behavior exhibited by their sons. This intense pressure against appearing feminine contributes not only to homophobia among heterosexual males (Herek, 1988; Kite, 1984) but also to negative attitudes toward females (Friedman, 1989).

Role Expectations for Females

Learning Objective

List two major expectations of the traditional female role.

The traditional female role consists of two major expectations (Doyle & Paludi, 1991):

- *The marriage mandate.* "Real women" attain adult status when they get married. In marriage, women are expected to be responsible for housework and cooking. That a large number of lesbians have previously been married indicates the power of the marriage mandate (Bell & Weinberg, 1978; Chapman & Brannock, 1987).
- *The motherhood mandate.* The imperative of the female role is to have children. This expectation has been termed the "motherhood mandate" by Nancy Felipe Russo (1979). Preferably, a woman should have at least two children, and at least one of them should be a son. Moreover, it is important that she be a "good mother."

Although women are increasingly opting for jobs and careers, the expectation for a career is still not widespread enough to be called a "mandate" except among African American women (Dickson, 1993). In fact, the traditional female role is incompatible with achievement in traditionally masculine areas (Hyde, 1996; Lloyd, 1985).

Both the marriage and motherhood mandates fuel women's intense focus on *heterosexual success*—learning how to attract and interest males as prospective mates. The resulting emphasis on dating and marriage causes most women to feel ambivalent about a challenging career so as not to drive away a prospective mate who might be threatened by a high-achieving woman. If gender-role expectations continue to change such that females have a wider variety of lifestyle options and career opportunities, increasing numbers of heterosexual women will be faced with the inherent conflict between family responsibilities and career (a conflict most heterosexual men don't currently face).

Problems with the Female Role

Concerns about the limitations of women's roles have received the lion's share of attention. These concerns first became prominent with the advent of the feminist movement, which generated some compelling analyses of the problems associated with the traditional female role (for example, Friedan, 1964; Millett, 1970). Since then, research has shown that many of these concerns are justified.

Diminished Aspirations

Learning Objective

Describe three common problems associated with the traditional female role.

Despite recent efforts to increase women's opportunities for achievement, young women continue to have lower aspirations than young men with comparable backgrounds and abilities (Mednick & Thomas, 1993). Higher intelligence and grades are generally associated with higher career aspirations, but this is less likely to hold true for girls than for boys (Danziger, 1983; Marini, 1978). This discrepancy between women's abilities and their level of achievement has been termed the *ability-achievement gap* (Hyde, 1996). As we noted, the roots of this gap seem to lie in the conflict between achievement and femininity that is built into the traditional female role (Earle & Harris, 1985). Some women worry that they will be seen as unfeminine if they boldly strive for success.

Juggling Multiple Roles

Another problem with the female role is that role expectations and societal institutions have not kept pace with the reality of women's lives. Traditional gender roles dictate that husbands go to work and wives and mothers stay home and take care of the house and children. Today, however, 62% of married women with children under the age of 6 work outside the home (U.S. Bureau of the Census, 1995). This gap between roles and reality means that women who want to "have it all" experience burdens and conflicts that men do not. That is, men's roles include worker, spouse, and parent with relatively little competition among these roles. This is because men typically have major day-to-day responsibilities in only *one* role (worker), which is also a high-status role. Most women, on the other hand, have day-to-day responsibilities as *both* spouse and parent. Furthermore, when women decide to work, they have major responsibilities in all *three* areas.

It's important to note that multiple roles, themselves, are not the problem. In fact, there is evidence that multiple roles can be beneficial for mental health, as we'll see in Chapter 12. Rather, the problem stems from unequal sharing of role responsibilities (women usually do more work). In addition, some women may experience psychological conflicts related to multiple roles that are fueled by the husband's negative attitudes about his wife's working outside the home or from her own attitudes about working, if she has been reared according to traditional gender roles (Basow, 1992). Subsidized child care programs and the equal participation of fathers in child-rearing and household tasks would go a long way toward alleviating women's stress in this area (Pleck, 1981b).

Ambivalence About Sexuality

Like men, women may have sexual problems that stem, in part, from their gender-role socialization. For many females, the problem is that they have difficulty enjoying sex. Why is this? For one thing, rather than being encouraged to focus directly on getting sexual experience, as boys are, girls are encouraged to focus on romance (Simon & Gagnon, 1977). Also, compared to males, more females are brought up in ways that generate guilt, shame, and fears about sex. These negative emotions stem in part from the experience of menstruation (and its association with blood and pain) and fear of pregnancy. Females' concerns about sexual exploitation, rape, and incest can also contribute to the development of negative feelings about sex. Thus, many women approach sex with "emotional baggage" that men are less likely to carry. This means that women are likely to have ambivalent feelings about sex instead of the largely positive feelings that most men have (Hyde, 1996).

Sexism: A Special Problem for Females

Intimately intertwined with the topic of gender roles is the issue of sexism. **Sexism is discrimination against people on the basis of their gender.** (Using our terminology, the term should probably be "genderism," but we'll stick with standard terminology for the sake of clarity.) Generally, sexism is used to describe discrimination by men against women. However, sometimes *women* discriminate against other women, and sometimes men are the victims of gender-based discrimination. In this section, we'll mention two specific problems for women: economic discrimination and aggression toward women.

Economic discrimination usually takes the form of differential access to jobs and differential treatment once on the job. Concerning *job access*, the problem is that women still don't have the same employment opportunities as men. For example, in 1993 only 19% of architects were women; similarly, only 22% of physicians and 11% of members of Congress were women (U.S. Bureau of the Census, 1994). Ethnic minority women were even less likely than white women to work in these occupations. On the other hand, women were overrepresented in such "pink-collar ghetto" occupations as secretary and preschool and kindergarten teacher (see Figure 10.11). The second aspect of economic discrimination involves women being *treated differently at work.* Examples of differential treatment include lower job evaluations for women whose performance is equal to men's (Dobbins, Cardy, & Truxillo, 1986, 1988) and lower salaries for women employed in the same jobs as men (see Figure 10.12). In addition, many more women than men must cope with sexual harassment at work.

Examples of *aggression toward females* include rape, intimate violence, sexual harassment, sexual abuse, incest, and violent pornography. We've discussed a number of these problems elsewhere, so we'll make only a few points here. *Sexual harassment* is being recognized as a widespread problem that occurs not only on the job but also at home (obscene telephone calls), on the street (catcalls and whistles), and in medical and psychotherapy settings. It also takes place in schools and colleges.

Figure 10.11
Women in the world of work
The percentage of women who work outside the home has been increasing steadily over the past century. Nonetheless, women remain underrepresented in many traditionally masculine occupations and overrepresented in many traditionally feminine occupations. (Data from U.S. Bureau of the Census, 1995)

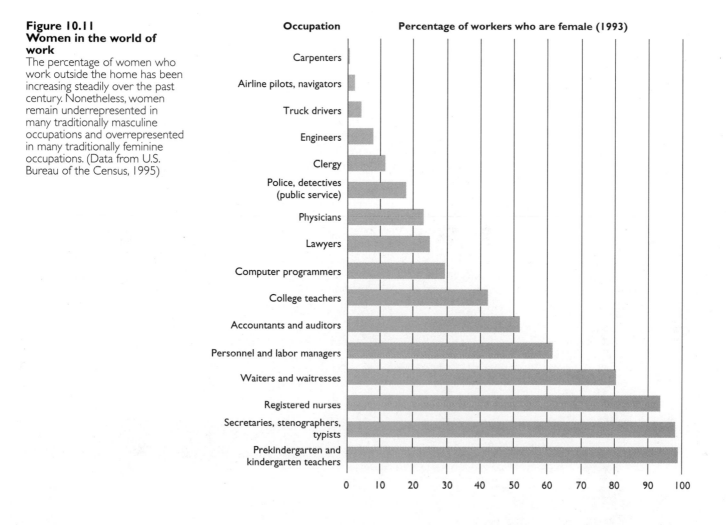

Figure 10.12
The gender gap in weekly
wages
Women continue to earn less
than men in all occupational
categories, as these 1994 data for
selected occupations make clear.
(Data from U. S. Bureau of Labor
Statistics, 1995)

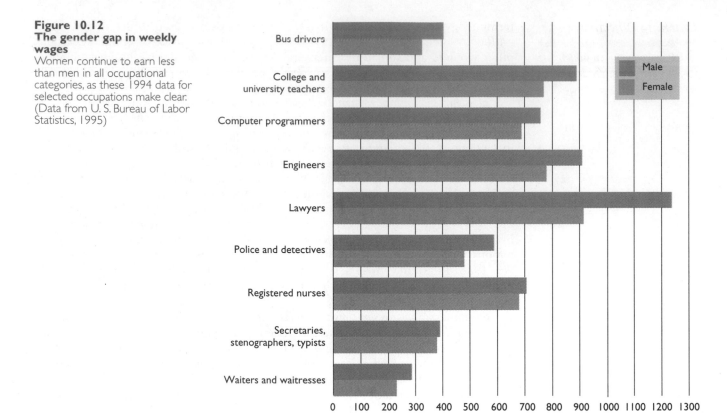

Figure 10.13 reports the results of a survey on the most common forms of sexual harassment in grades 2 through 12. Teachers and professors who pressure students for sexual favors in exchange for grades have been singled out for strong criticism (Dziech & Weiner, 1990; Quina & Carlson, 1989). Regarding *intimate violence*, four women are killed per day by men who batter (Walker, 1989). In a nationwide survey of college women on 32 campuses, 32% reported that they had experienced physical aggression from a date or other intimate partner (White & Koss, 1991).

Although there are costs associated with traditional roles for *both* genders, sexism causes serious problems in the lives of girls and women. In addition, when prejudice and discrimination prevent talented individuals from making contributions from which all could benefit, society as a whole suffers.

**Figure 10.13
Reported incidence of
sexual harassment in the
schools**
This figure depicts common forms of sexual harassment in grades 2 through 12 and the percentage of girls reporting them. (Adapted from Stein, Marshall, & Tropp, 1993)

Type of harassment	Percentage reporting
Received suggestive gestures, looks, comments, or jokes	89
Touched, pinched, or grabbed	83
Leaned over or cornered	47
Received sexual notes or pictures	28
Pressured to do something sexual	27
Forced to do something sexual	10
Other form of harassment	7

Note: Percentages do not add to 100 because readers could indicate more than one type of harassment.

The title and thesis of this book make reference to Protagoras's statement, "Man is the measure of all things." Tavris, a social psychologist who has written this book for the nonprofessional audience, uses her natural wit and humor to excellent advantage. She points out the fallacy of using a male-centered standard for evaluating "what is normal" for both men and women. Using research findings, she exposes numerous myths about males and females that are the source of misunderstanding and frustration for many.

Tavris is not interested in replacing a male-centered view with a female-dominant view, but rather in expanding people's view of what it means to be human. She urges people to move away from the tendency to think in "us–them" terms about gender issues. Rather, she suggests that men and women need to work together and rethink how they need to be in order to have the kinds of relationships and work that are life enhancing. In the following excerpt, she explains how gender-based attributions of behavior can be triggered by situational factors:

> . . . men and women do not have a set of fixed masculine or feminine traits; the qualities and behaviors expected of women and men vary, depending on the situation the person is in. A token woman in a group of men will feel highly aware of her femaleness and so will the group. Almost everything she does will be attributed to her gender, which is why she is likely to be accused of being too feminine (thus not "one of the boys") or too masculine ("trying to be something she's not")—but what's really at issue is her visible difference from the majority. A token man in a group of women will have the comparable experience. [p. 292]

Gender in the Past and in the Future

Until now, we have focused largely on *traditional* gender roles and some of the difficulties they tend to generate. In Western society, however, gender roles are in a state of transition (Dambrot, Papp, & Whitmore, 1984; Weeks & Gage, 1984). Sweeping changes have already occurred. It's hard to imagine today, but less than 100 years ago, women were not allowed to vote or manage their own finances. Only a few decades ago, it was virtually unheard of for a woman to initiate a date, manage a corporation, or run for public office. In this section, we'll discuss *why* gender roles are changing and what the future might hold.

Why Are Gender Roles Changing?

Learning Objective

Explain the basis for traditional gender roles and why they are changing.

Many people are baffled about why gender roles are changing. They can't understand why age-old traditions are being flouted and discarded. A number of theories attempt to explain why gender roles are in transition. Basically, these theories look at the past to explain the present and the future. A key consideration is that gender roles have always constituted a division of labor. In earlier societies, the division of labor according to gender was a natural outgrowth of some simple realities. In most hunting-and-gathering societies, as well as most herding societies, an economic premium was put on physical strength. Men tend to be stronger than women, so they were better equipped to handle such jobs as hunting and farming. In most societies they got those assignments, whereas the women were responsible for gathering plants for food, taking care of the home, and child rearing (Nielsen, 1990). Another consideration was that women had to assume responsibility for nursing young children. In summary, although people might have worked out other ways of doing things (and some cultures did), there were some basic reasons for dividing labor according to gender in premodern societies.

A division of labor based on gender no longer makes economic sense in our society. Relatively few jobs require great physical strength; the rest call for skills possessed by both men and women.

Today's traditional gender roles are a carryover from the past. Once traditions are established, they have a way of perpetuating themselves. Moreover, males have had a vested interest in maintaining these traditions, since the arrangements made them a privileged class. During the last century or so in Western society, these divisions of labor have become increasingly antiquated. Therein lies the prime reason for changes in gender roles. *Traditional gender roles no longer make economic sense.* In our mechanized, industrial economy, physical strength has become much less important in a job. And as we move toward a service economy, physical strength is even less relevant.

The future is likely to bring even more dramatic shifts in gender roles. We can see the beginnings of some of these changes now. For example, although women still bear children, nursing responsibilities are now optional. Moreover, as women become more economically independent, they will have less need to get married solely for economic reasons. The possibility of developing a fetus outside the uterus may seem far-fetched now, but some experts predict that it is only a matter of time. If so, both men and women could choose to be "mothers."

Traditional gender roles used to be considered a "God-given" fact of life. As we have seen, however, what appear to be obvious behavioral differences between males and females are often found to be stereotypes instead. In addition, most of the gender differences that do exist can be traced to differences in socialization. Consequently, we are now more aware of the social and political bases for gender roles (Tavris, 1992). This awareness has focused attention and public debate on the prejudices that underlie unequal treatment of females (and sometimes males). This attention seems likely to add momentum to the movement toward nontraditional gender roles. It is safe to conclude that gender roles will remain in flux for some time to come.

Alternatives to Traditional Gender Roles

Learning Objective

Define gender-role identity and discuss two main alternatives to traditional gender roles.

Gender-role identity is a person's identification with the traits regarded as masculine or feminine. Initially, gender-role identity was conceptualized as either "masculine" or "feminine." All males were expected to develop masculine gender-role identities and females, feminine gender-role identities. Individuals who did not identify with the expectations for their gender or who identified with the characteristics for the other gender were judged to be few in number and to have psychological problems.

In the 1970s, psychologists began to rethink their ideas about gender-role identity. One assumption that was called into question is that males are and should be "masculine" and females, "feminine." For one thing, it appears that the number of people who don't conform to gender-role norms is relatively high, as is the amount of strain that accompanies trying to conform to gender-role stereotypes (Pleck, 1981a). Also, research suggests that strong identification with traditional gender-role expectations may produce negative psychological and behavioral outcomes in both genders. For example, high femininity in females is associated with low self-esteem (Whitley, 1983) and increased psychological distress (Helgeson, 1994). High masculinity in males has been linked to increased Type A behavior (see Chapter 14), poor health care (Helgeson, 1994), greater likelihood of committing physical and sexual aggression in relationships (Mosher, 1991), and psychopathology (Evans & Dinning, 1982). Furthermore, heterosexual couples with traditional gender-role identities appear to have unsatisfying relationships, compared to androgynous couples (Ickes, 1993). (Problems seem to stem from the masculine gender-role's emphasis on dominance and low self-disclosure [Pleck, Sonenstein, & Ku, 1993].) Thus, the evidence does not support the assertion that "masculine" males and "feminine" females are particularly well adjusted.

As people have become aware of the costs of traditional gender roles, there has been a lot of debate about moving beyond them. A big question in these discussions has been: What should we move toward? To date, two ideas have received the most attention: (1) androgyny and (2) gender-role transcendence. Let's examine these concepts.

Androgyny

Like masculinity and femininity, androgyny is a type of gender-role identity. **Androgyny refers to the coexistence of both masculine and feminine personality traits in an individual.** In other words, an androgynous person is one who scores above average on measures of *both* masculinity and femininity.

To fully appreciate the nature of androgyny, we need to briefly review other kinds of gender identity (see Figure 10.14). Males who score high on masculinity and low on femininity and females who score high on femininity and low on masculinity are said to be *gender-typed*. Males who score high on femininity but low on masculinity and females who score high on masculinity but low on femininity are said to be *cross-gender-typed*. Finally, males and females who score low on both masculinity and femininity are characterized as *gender-role undifferentiated*.

Keep in mind that we are referring to individuals' descriptions of themselves in terms of personality traits traditionally associated with each gender (dominance, nurturance, and so on). People sometimes confuse gender-role identity with sexual orientation. These are not the same thing. One can be homosexual, heterosexual, or bisexual (sexual orientations) and be androgynous, gender-typed, cross-gender-typed, or gender-role undifferentiated (gender-role identities).

As we have mentioned, it used to be assumed that males who scored high in masculinity and females who scored high in femininity were better adjusted than "masculine" women and "feminine" men. Sandra Bem (1975) challenged this prevailing view. She argued that traditionally masculine men and feminine women feel compelled to adhere to rigid and narrow gender roles that unnecessarily restrict their behavior. In contrast, androgynous individuals ought to be able to function more flexibly. She also advanced the idea that androgynous people tend to be psychologically healthier than those who exhibit conventional gender-typing.

What about Bem's ideas? First, androgynous people do seem more flexible than others (Bem, 1975). That is, they can be nurturing ("feminine") or independent ("masculine"), depending on the situation. In contrast, gender-typed males have difficulty behaving nurturantly, and gender-typed females have difficulty with independence. Also, individuals whose partners are either androgynous or feminine (but not masculine or undifferentiated) report higher relationship satisfaction (Antill, 1983). This finding holds for both cohabiting heterosexuals and lesbian and gay couples (Kurdek & Schmitt, 1986b). Furthermore, a study of married couples revealed that the happiest couples were those in which both partners were androgynous (Zammichieli, Gilroy, & Sherman, 1988). Thus, in these areas, androgyny seems to be advantageous.

Bem's second assertion (that androgynous people are psychologically healthier than gender-typed individuals) requires a more complicated response. Since 1976 over a hundred studies have been conducted to try to answer this question. Some early studies *did* find a positive correlation between androgyny and mental health. Ultimately, however, the weight of the evidence did not support Bem's hypothesis that androgyny is especially healthful (Hyde & Frost, 1993). In fact, several comprehensive surveys of the research reported that *masculine* traits (in either gender) were more strongly associated with psychological health than androgyny was (Hyde & Frost, 1993; Taylor & Hall, 1982, Whitley, 1984). (Because most tests of self-esteem measure traits consistent with the male role, such as

Sandra Bem

Figure 10.14
Possible gender-role identities
This diagram summarizes the relations between subjects' scores on measures of masculinity and femininity and four possible gender identities.

	Femininity Score	
	High	**Low**
Masculinity Score — **High**	Androgynous males and females	Masculine gender-typed (if male) or cross-gender-typed (if female)
Masculinity Score — **Low**	Feminine gender-typed (if female) or cross-gender-typed (if male)	Undifferentiated males and females

achievement and independence, we would expect to find a positive relationship between masculinity and self-esteem [Whitley, 1988b].) These findings, as well as some problems with the concept of androgyny, have led Bem and other psychologists to take a different view of gender roles, as we shall see.

Gender-Role Transcendence

Some conceptual problems with androgyny caused theorists in this area to rethink their views. One of these problems is that androgyny requires people to develop both masculine and feminine characteristics, rather than one or the other. While it can be argued that androgyny is less restrictive than traditional gender roles, it may also lead people to feel that they have two sources of inadequacy to contend with, as opposed to only one (Bem, 1993).

Furthermore, the idea that people should have both masculine and feminine traits reinforces the assumption that gender is an integral part of human behavior (Bem, 1983; Lott, 1981). In other words, the androgyny perspective presupposes that masculine and feminine traits actually exist within everyone. Another way of saying this is that our current system is one that sets up self-fulfilling prophecies. That is, if people use gender-based labels ("masculine" and "feminine") to identify certain human characteristics and behaviors, then they'll always, but wrongly, associate these traits with one gender or the other.

Many theorists maintain that masculinity and femininity are really only arbitrary labels that people have learned to impose on certain traits through societal conditioning. This assertion is the foundation for the *gender-role transcendence* perspective (Bem, 1983, 1993; Spence, 1983). **Gender-role transcendence means that to be fully human, people need to move beyond gender roles as a way of organizing the world and of perceiving themselves and others.** This goal requires that we *not* simply divide human characteristics into masculine and feminine categories (and then combine them, as the androgyny perspective suggests). Rather, we need to dispense with the artificially constructed gender categories and labels. What might this mean? Instead of the labels "masculine" and "feminine," we would use gender-neutral terms such as "instrumental" and "expressive" to describe personality traits and behaviors. This "decoupling" of traits and gender would eliminate the self-fulfilling prophecy problem.

The advocates of gender-role transcendence argue that this practice would help people break their current habits of "projecting gender into situations irrelevant to genitalia" (Bem, 1985, p. 222) and hasten the advent of a gender-free society. They believe that if gender were eliminated (or even reduced) as a means of categorizing traits, each individual's unique capabilities and interests would assume greater importance. This would mean that individuals would be more free to develop their own unique potentials.

Although many social scientists find the concept of a gender-free society appealing, some social critics are concerned about the decline of traditional gender roles (Davidson, 1988; Gilder, 1986). For instance, George Gilder (1986) maintains that conventional gender roles provide a fundamental underpinning for our economic and social order. Furthermore, he asserts that changes in gender roles will damage intimate relationships between women and men and have a devastating impact on family life. Gilder argues that women are needed in the home in their traditional homemaker role to provide for the socialization of the next generation. Without this traditional socialization, he predicts that our moral fabric will decay, leading to an increase in crime, violence, and drug abuse. Given these starkly contrasting projections, it will prove most interesting to see what unfolds during the next few decades.

In the Application, we'll explore gender and communication styles.

Bridging the Gender Gap in Communication

Answer the following questions "true" or "false."

1. Men talk much more than women in mixed-gender groups.

2. Women are more likely to ask for help than men.

3. Women are more willing to initiate confrontations in relationships than men.

4. Men talk more about nonpersonal issues with their friends than women do.

If you answered "true" to all of the above statements, you were correct. These are just some of the observed differences in communication styles between males and females. While not descriptive of all men and women or of all mixed-gender conversations, these style differences appear to be the source of many misunderstandings between the genders.

When confronted with one of these distressing encounters in our personal or work relationships, we often attribute them to the other person's individual quirks or "failings." Instead, it seems that some of these frustrating experiences may be due to gender differences in style. That is, men and women learn to speak different "languages" in social interactions, but don't realize this. In this Application, we'll explore the nature of these gender-based style differences, how they develop, and how they can contribute to interpersonal conflicts. We'll also offer some suggestions for dealing more effectively with these style differences.

The Clash of Two "Cultures"

Learning Objective

Describe how the different socialization experiences of males and females contribute to communication problems between the genders.

According to sociolinguist Deborah Tannen (1990), males and females are typically socialized in different "cultures." That is, males are likely to learn a language of "status and independence," while females learn a language of "connection and intimacy" (p. 42). Tannen likens male-female communications to other "cross-cultural" communications—full of opportunities for misunderstandings to develop.

These differences in communication styles develop in childhood and are fostered by traditional gender stereotypes and the socializing influences of parents, teachers, media, and childhood social interactions—usually with same-gender peers. As we noted earlier, boys play in larger groups, usually outdoors, and farther away from home than girls (Feiring & Lewis, 1987). Thus, boys are less under the scrutiny of adults and are therefore more likely to engage in activities that encourage exploration and independence (Feiring & Lewis, 1987). Also, boys' groups are often hierarchically organized (structured in terms of high- and low-status roles). Boys achieve high status in their groups by engaging in dominant behavior (telling others what to do and enforcing compliance). The games that boys play often result in winners and losers, and boys frequently bid for dominance by interrupting each other, calling each other names, boasting to each other about their abilities, and refusing to cooperate with each other (Maltz & Borker, 1983).

In contrast, girls usually play in small groups or in pairs, often indoors, and gain high status through popularity, the key to which is intimacy with peers. Many of the games girls play do not have winners or losers. And, while it is true that girls vary in abilities and skills, to call attention to oneself as better than others is frowned upon. Girls are likely to express their wishes as suggestions rather than demands or orders (Maltz & Borker, 1983). Similarly, dominance is gained by verbal persuasion rather than the direct bids for power characteristic of boys' social interactions

(Charlesworth & Dzur, 1987). These two cultures shape the functions of speech in different ways. According to Eleanor Maccoby (1990), among boys, "speech serves largely egoistic functions and is used to establish and protect an individual's turf. Among girls, conversation is a more socially binding process" (p. 516).

These different styles carry over into adult social interactions. According to Tannen, because of different socialization experiences, many males learn to see the social world as hierarchical. To maintain independence and avoid failure (in their own eyes and in the eyes of other men), they have to jockey for high status. Hence, she says, men tend to approach conversations as "negotiations in which people try to achieve and maintain the upper hand if they can and protect themselves from others' attempts to put them down and push them around" (p. 25). Females, on the other hand, learn to see the social order as a community in which individuals are connected to others and one where the task is to preserve these connections. Consequently, women tend to approach conversations as "negotiations for closeness in which people try to seek and give confirmation and support, and to reach consensus. They try to protect themselves from others' attempts to push them away" (p. 25). These different views of the social order are the root of the oft-heard complaint, "You just don't understand"—the title of Tannen's book (see the Recommended Reading below).

Recommended Reading

You Just Don't Understand: Women and Men in Conversation

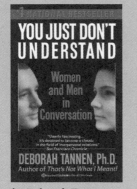

by Deborah Tannen
(Ballantine, 1990)

This bestseller addresses the "communication gap" between males and females. According to Tannen, a sociolinguist, boys and girls learn different styles of communication through same-gender social interactions in childhood. When used in other-gender interactions, these different styles can result in miscommunication and frustration, because men and women often approach social interactions from different (and sometimes conflict-producing) perspectives. Tannen describes a wide variety of problematic interactions that result from style differences and offers numerous examples. In addition, she "translates" many examples of conversations between men and women as a way of illustrating how the different styles operate, showing the reader the difference between what individuals think they are saying and how their messages may actually be interpreted. Tannen believes that many frustrations caused by gender differences in styles of communication could be alleviated if men and women learned to understand each other's perspective.

One of the many interesting issues Tannen discusses is the role and importance of *metamessages*—the attitudes, feelings, and status information behind the actual words people speak. According to her, "metamessages *frame* a conversation much as a picture frame provides a context for the images in the picture" (p. 33); they help people interpret what is going on in a conversation. To help readers understand how they operate in communication, she provides a number of helpful examples of metamessages.

> The chivalrous man who holds a door open or signals a woman to go ahead of him when he's driving is negotiating both status and connection. The status difference is implied by a metamessage of control. The woman gets to proceed not because it is her right but because he has granted her permission, so she is being framed as subordinate. Furthermore, those in a position to grant privileges are also in a position to change their minds and take them away. This is the dimension to which some women respond when they protest gallant gestures as "chauvinist." Those who appreciate such gestures as "polite" see only the connection: He's being nice. And it is also the dimension the man performing the generous gesture is likely to see, and the reason he may be understandably incensed if his polite gesture sparks protest rather than thanks. [p. 34]

Instrumental and Expressive Styles

While not true of all men and women, there is evidence that men are more likely to use an "instrumental" style of communication and women, an "expressive" style (Block, 1973; Tannen, 1990). Interestingly, this gender difference has been found across a number of cultures (D'Andrade, 1966). **An *instrumental style* focuses on reaching practical goals and finding solutions to problems; an *expressive style* is characterized by being able to express tender emotions easily and being sensitive to the feelings of others.** Obviously, many individuals use both styles, depending on the situation.

As we mentioned, men tend to use instrumental communication styles more often than women. For example, research has shown that, in conflict situations, husbands are more likely to stay calm and problem-oriented (Gottman, 1979) and make more efforts to find compromise solutions to problems (Raush et al., 1974). However, an instrumental style can have a "darker" side. When the instrumental behavior of calmness changes to coldness and unresponsiveness, it becomes negative. Research has shown that this emotional unresponsiveness is characteristic of many men and that it seems to figure importantly in marital dissatisfaction (Kilmartin, 1994).

A large number of studies indicate that women, on the average, are more skilled than men in *nonverbal* communication—a key component of the expressive style. For example, they are better at reading and sending nonverbal messages (J. A. Hall, 1990). Regarding *verbal* communication, women are better listeners (Miller, Berg, & Archer, 1983) and better at consoling individuals in emotional distress (Burleson, 1982). On the other hand, besides the already mentioned "positive" behaviors associated with the expressive style, women have been found to engage in some "negative" expressive behaviors as well (Brehm, 1992). For example, research has shown that, during relationship conflicts, women are more likely to (1) display strong negative emotions (Noller, 1985, 1987); (2) use psychologically coercive tactics (guilt, verbal attack, power plays) (Barnes & Buss, 1985); (3) reject attempts at reconciliation (Barnes & Buss, 1985); and (4) send double-messages (making a negative verbal statement while smiling) (Noller, 1985, 1987). Women's greater use of such tactics may be attributable to their greater desire to modify relationships (Christensen & Heavey, 1990).

The idea of "two cultures" and of gender-based communication styles has intuitive appeal because it confirms our stereotypes and reduces complex issues to simple explanations. But, there's an important caveat here. As we have often noted, research shows that status and power differences sometimes hide behind what seem to be gender differences. That is, because power and biological gender are often linked (males typically have more status; females, less) and because biological gender is a more visible factor than status, people often attribute differences in behavior to gender rather than power. Also, there are individual differences in preferred styles: some women will prefer the "male style" and some men, the "female style"; many will use either style, depending on the situation. Therefore, we caution you not to reduce *all* communication problems between males and females to "two cultures" and gender-based style differences.

Common Mixed-Gender Communication Problems

In this section, we'll briefly review some common mixed-gender communication problems noted by Tannen. To keep things simple, we'll refer to "she" and "he" to illustrate various scenarios, but you should interpret these labels loosely for the reasons we have mentioned.

Mismatches

Learning Objective

Describe five mixed-gender communication problems.

People expect their friends and partners to support and reassure them. When a mismatch exists between people's expectations and reality, they become confused and frustrated. Sometimes they are hurt or angry, as well. Consider a woman who describes a recurring problem she is having at work to her partner because she wants some sympathy. Thinking that she is seeking a solution to the problem, he gives her advice. Not receiving the consolation she seeks, she believes that he doesn't care. He, for his part, is frustrated about her repeated complaining, since he has offered her the same advice in the past. Instead of taking his advice, she persists in complaining about the problem. In this scenario, neither wants to frustrate the other, but that's exactly what is happening because the two are talking at cross-purposes. She wants him to commiserate with her, but he thinks she wants him to help her solve a problem. Each assumes he or she knows what the other wants, but neither does. These mismatches crop up quite frequently between couples.

Rapport Talk and Report Talk

Tannen suggests that most women engage in *rapport talk* (displaying similarities and matching experiences with others). Many men, on the other hand, seem to be more comfortable with *report talk* (exhibiting knowledge and skill to get and keep the attention of others). Also, men and women often have different ideas about what is important to talk about. She wants to talk about the personal details of her life and her feelings. He wants to talk about activities—things they do together or politics or sports. In this situation, his failure to talk about personal things confirms her worst expectations (the relationship is falling apart). He fears that if he says anything about emotions that might be fleeting—especially negative ones—they'll get blown out of proportion and create a problem where one doesn't exist. Again, these differences are rooted in childhood experiences.

Talking About People Versus Things

Women's conversations frequently involve sharing the details of their personal lives or "talking about people." It's important to understand that "talking *about* people" isn't necessarily destructive (although it can be if it turns into "talking *against* people"). As they did in childhood, women share secrets with one another as a way of being close. Men are interested in details, too, but those of a different kind: politics, news, and sports. Women fear being left out by not knowing what is going on in friends' lives; men fear being left out by not knowing what is going on in the world. Interestingly, Tannen notes that exchanging information about public events (men's style) has an advantage over sharing private information (women's style): It doesn't make men personally vulnerable.

Tannen suggests that frustrations can be reduced if men and women understand how their style differences operate here. That is, men need to understand why many women like to talk about the details of their personal lives and women need to understand that most men don't have this need. In addition, she says that both women and men need to extend their communication strategies by adding aspects of the other style to their own. Thus, some men may need to learn to be more comfortable talking about their personal lives, whereas some women could benefit by talking more about impersonal topics and talking in a more assertive manner.

Lecturing and Listening

In many mixed-gender conversations, particularly those in public settings, women often end up playing the listener to the man's "lecture." While this fact illustrates that women often don't get the same attention as men, Tannen suggests that we look more closely here. How does this situation come about? Are men self-centered big mouths? Are women meek and passive creatures? Instead of these interpretations, Tannen suggests that men and women are playing different games that are rooted in childhood experiences. Men are playing "Do you respect me?" and women, "Do you like me?"

As we noted, boys and men use words to jockey for status and to challenge the authority of others, both men and women. Women who lack experience defending themselves against these challenges can easily misinterpret an assertive man's style as an attack on her credibility. Similarly, women have been taught to "hand off" the conversational ball and expect that others will do the same. While most women reciprocate, many men don't. When this happens, some women may feel awkward drawing the focus of the conversation back to themselves because this style was frowned upon during childhood play with other girls.

To improve this kind of mixed-gender communication problem, Tannen suggests that women who tire of listening need to be more assertive and take some control of the conversation. Also, some men might be relieved to learn that they don't always have to be the one to talk. As you saw in Chapter 7, effective listening is a much-underrated communication skill.

The Woman's Double-Bind

According to Tannen, mixed-gender communication situations often place women at a disadvantage because the "male style" of communication is likely to predominate. If this were the only consideration, it wouldn't present much of a difficulty for women—they would just need to be proficient in the "male style." The problem arises because the male style is used as the norm against which both women's and men's speech is evaluated (recall androcentrism). This means that a woman will be evaluated negatively regardless of which style (male or female) she adopts. The female style is devalued, and a woman using a male style is also evaluated negatively. Women in positions of authority experience a special version of this double-bind. According to Tannen, "If they speak in ways expected of women, they are seen as inadequate leaders. If they speak in ways expected of leaders, they are seen as inadequate women" (p. 244).

Research supports this contention. When women failed to offer support for their arguments or used tag questions, subjects judged them to be less intelligent and less knowledgeable than men who behaved in an identical manner (Bradley, 1981). Similarly, students judged female professors as incompetent when they generated classroom discussion, but they did not negatively evaluate male professors who did this (Macke, Richardson, & Cook, 1980).

Toward a "Shared Language"

Tannen asserts that many frustrations in personal and work relationships could be avoided if men and women were more aware of gender-based differences in communication styles. Many people misperceive style differences as the other's personal failings. If we could see the style differences for what they are, we could eliminate

Figure 10.15
Hints for men to improve gender-based communication
Having productive personal and work relationships in today's world demands that one be knowledgeable about gender and communication styles. Men may be able to benefit from the suggestions compiled here. Among other things, many men need to learn to listen more effectively when conversing with women. (Based on insights from Tannen, 1990.)

Bridging the Communication Gap: Hints for Men

1 Notice whether or not you have a tendency to interrupt women. If you do, work on breaking this habit. When you catch yourself interrupting, say, "I'm sorry, I interrupted you. Go ahead with what you were saying."

2 Avoid responding to a woman's questions in monosyllables ("Yep," "Nope," "Uh-huh"). Give her more details about what you did and explain why.

3 Learn the art of conversational give and take. Ask women questions about themselves. And listen carefully when they respond.

4 Don't order women around. For example, don't say, "Get me the newspaper." First, notice whether it might be an inconvenience for her to do something for you. If it isn't, say, "Would you mind giving me the newspaper?" or "Would you please give me the newspaper?" If she's busy, get it yourself!

5 Don't be a space hog. Be more aware of the space you take up when you sit with others (especially women). Watch that you don't make women feel crowded out.

6 Learn to open up about personal issues. Talk about your feelings, interests, hopes, and relationships. Talking about personal things helps others know who you are (and probably helps you clarify your self-perceptions, too).

7 Learn to convey enthusiasm about things in addition to the victories of your favorite sports teams.

8 Don't be afraid to ask for help if you need it.

a lot of blaming and negative feelings. As Tannen says, "Nothing hurts more than being told your intentions are bad when you know they are good, or being told that you are doing something wrong when you know you're just doing it your way" (pp. 297–298). People need to understand that there are different ways of listening, talking, and of having conversations, not just their own way. Some advice on how to improve communication between the genders can be found in Figure 10.15, which lists specific pointers for men, and in Figure 10.16, which lists specific suggestions for women.

Figure 10.16
Hints for women to improve gender-based communication
Women can also help bridge the gender gap in communication. Suggestions for women emphasize the need to be more assertive in interacting with men. (Based on insights from Tannen, 1990.)

Bridging the Communication Gap: Hints for Women

1 When others interrupt you, politely but firmly redirect the conversation back to you. You can say, for example, "Excuse me, I haven't finished my point."

2 Look the person you're talking with directly in the eye.

3 A lower-pitched voice gets more attention and respect than a higher-pitched one, which is associated with little girls. Keeping your abdominal muscles firm as you speak will help keep your voice low.

4 Learn to be comfortable claiming more space (without becoming a space hog). If you want your presence to be noted, don't fold yourself up into an unobtrusive object.

5 Talk more about yourself and your accomplishments. This isn't offensive as long as others are doing the same and the circumstances are appropriate. If the conversation turns to photography and you know a lot about the topic, it's perfectly OK to share your expertise.

6 Make a point of being aware of current events so you'll be knowledgeable about what others are discussing and have an opinion to contribute.

7 Resist the impulse to be overly apologetic. Although many women say "I'm sorry" to convey sympathy or concern (not apology), these words are likely to be interpreted as an apology. Because apologizing puts one in a lower-power position, women who use apologetic words inappropriately put themselves at a disadvantage.

Key Ideas

Gender Stereotypes

• Many stereotypes have developed around behavioral differences between the genders, although the distinctions between the male and female stereotypes are less rigid than they used to be. Gender stereotypes may vary depending on race or ethnicity, and they typically favor males.

Research on Gender Comparisons

• Research generally does not support gender stereotypes. There are no gender differences in general intelligence, verbal ability, or mathematical ability. If males have any advantage in visual-spatial ability, it appears to be slight.

• Research shows that males typically are more self-confident and more aggressive than females. Males also appear to help more than females, but this finding is related to the way that helping behavior is typically measured. Females seem to conform to group pressure slightly more than males. They also talk less than males and display more tentativeness in their speech. Women appear to have the advantage in sensitivity to nonverbal communication. The genders are similar in overall mental health, but they differ in prevalence rates for specific psychological disorders.

• All in all, the gender differences that do exist are quite small. Moreover, they are group differences that tell us little about individuals. Nonetheless, the belief persists that dramatic psychological differences exist between males and females. Social role theory and social constructionism provide two explanations for this phenomenon.

Biological Origins of Gender Differences

• Biological explanations of gender differences have focused on sociobiology, brain organization, and hormonal influences. Sociobiologists explain gender differences on the basis of evolutionary value. Because sociobiological theories are difficult to test empirically, they remain highly speculative. Regarding brain organization, some studies suggest that males exhibit more cerebral specialization than females. However, linking this finding to gender differences in cognitive abilities is questionable, especially because cognitive differences appear to be disappearing.

• Efforts to tie hormone levels to gender differences have also been troubled by interpretive problems. Nonetheless, there probably is some hormonal basis for gender differences in aggression and in some aspects of sexual behavior. Most experts believe that socialization plays a more important role than biology in most behavioral disparities between the genders.

Environmental Origins of Gender Differences

• The socialization of gender roles appears to take place through (1) reinforcement and punishment, (2) observational learning, and (3) self-socialization. These processes operate through many social institutions, but parents, peers, schools, and the media are the four primary sources of gender-role socialization.

Traditional Gender Roles

• The five elements of the traditional male role include the anti-feminine element, the success element, the aggressive element, the sexual element, and the self-reliant element. Problems associated with the traditional male role include (1) excessive pressure to succeed, (2) difficulty dealing with emotions, and (3) sexual problems. Homophobia is a particular problem for men.

• The traditional role expectations for females include the "motherhood mandate" and "marriage mandate." Among the principal costs of the traditional female role are (1) diminished aspirations, (2) juggling of multiple roles, and (3) ambivalence about sexuality. In addition to these psychological problems, women also face sexist hurdles in the economic domain and are victims of aggression.

Gender in the Past and in the Future

• Gender roles have always represented a division of labor. They are changing today, and they seem likely to continue changing because they no longer mesh with economic reality. Consequently, an important question is how we might move beyond traditional gender roles. The perspectives of androgyny and gender-role transcendence provide two possible answers to this question.

Application: Bridging the Gender Gap in Communication

• Because of different socialization experiences, males and females usually learn different communication styles. These differences in experience and style seem to underlie a number of mixed-gender communication problems. Both men and women need to understand these style differences to reduce interpersonal conflicts and the frustrations they cause.

Key Terms

Aggression
Androcentrism
Androgyny
Cerebral hemispheres
Conformity
Expressive style
Gender
Gender-role identity
Gender roles
Gender-role transcendence
Gender stereotypes
Homophobia
Hormones
Instrumental style
Meta-analysis
Sexism
Social constructionism
Social role theory
Socialization
Sociobiology

Key People

Sandra Bem
Alice Eagly
Janet Shibley Hyde
John Money
Joseph Pleck
Deborah Tannen

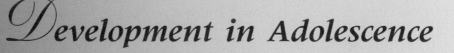

11 Development in Adolescence and Adulthood

"My mother always complains that I spend too much time on the telephone. She thinks that I'm just gossiping with my friends and feels that my time would be better spent studying. She can't seem to understand that my friends and I help each other through some pretty rough situations. She thinks that way because she doesn't believe that anything a teenager does besides homework is important. My Mom tells me to learn in school, but she doesn't realize that I'm actually trying to learn to survive school. Attending school is like a tryout for life. I know that it sounds silly to adults, but at times getting a date, being invited to a certain party, or being chosen to work on the school's newspaper can mean more than getting an A on a test."

—"Tracy," quoted in *Teenagers Talk About School* (Landau, 1988, p. 31)

*D*o Tracy's—or her mother's—complaints sound familiar? Have you ever been frustrated by your parents' or your child's inability to understand your point of view? Psychologists attribute these contrasting perspectives to differences in development. In the above scenario, Tracy and her mother are at different levels of development in a number of areas: physical, cognitive, personality, and social. This means that they have different perspectives on themselves and on the world.

Although the period of adolescence has been studied since the early 1900s, it is only since the 1970s that psychologists have given serious attention to development after adolescence. Until that time, it was widely assumed that developmental processes slowed to a crawl as people moved into adulthood. Now, however, social scientists realize that important developmental changes continue throughout adult life. As a result, they are probing into these changes to identify crucial patterns and trends. In this chapter, we'll review the major changes that take place during adolescence and adulthood. We'll also examine the topics of dying and death. In the Application, we'll offer some suggestions for effective parenting.

The Transition of Adolescence

Adolescence is a transitional period between childhood and adulthood. Its age boundaries are not exact, but in our society adolescence begins at around age 13 and ends at about age 22. In some ways, adolescents resemble the children they were, yet the many changes they undergo during this stage ensure that they will be different from children in many respects. Similarly, we see glimpses of the adults that adolescents will become, but we more often observe that they don't behave much like

As they mature, adolescents look and act increasingly like adults, although boys typically lag two years behind girls in physical development.

adults. As adolescents mature, we see fewer resemblances to children and more similarities to adults.

Although most societies have at least a brief period of adolescence, this stage is *not* universal across cultures (Schlegel & Barry, 1991; Whiting, Burbank, & Ratner, 1986). In some cultures, young people move directly from childhood to adulthood. A protracted period of adolescence is seen primarily in industrialized nations. In these societies, rapid technological progress has made lengthy education, and therefore prolonged economic dependence, the norm. Thus, in our own culture, junior high school, high school, and college students often have a "marginal" status. They are capable of reproduction and so are physiologically mature. Yet they have not achieved the emotional and economic independence from their parents that are the hallmarks of adulthood. Let's begin our discussion of adolescent development with its most visible aspect: the physical changes that transform the body of a child into that of an adult.

Physical Changes

Learning Objective

Describe the physical changes that accompany pubescence and puberty and some of their psychological effects.

Recall for a moment your junior high school days. Didn't it seem that your body grew so fast about this time that your clothes just couldn't "keep up"? This phase of rapid growth in height and weight is called the *adolescent growth spurt*—"spurt" because of the relatively sudden increases in body height and weight. Brought on by hormonal changes, it typically starts at about 11 years of age in girls and about two years later in boys (Malina, 1990). (Technically, this spurt should be called the *pre*adolescent growth spurt because it actually occurs *prior* to puberty, which is generally recognized as the beginning of adolescence.)

Psychologists use the term *pubescence* to describe **the two-year span preceding puberty during which the changes leading to physical and sexual maturity take place.** Besides growing taller and heavier during pubescence, children begin to take on the physical features that characterize adults of their respective genders. These bodily changes are termed *secondary sex characteristics*—**physical features that distinguish one gender from the other but that are not essential for reproduction.** For example, boys go through a voice change, develop facial hair, and experience greater skeletal and muscle growth in the upper torso, leading to broader shoulders and enhanced upper body strength. Females experience breast growth and a widening of the pelvic bones as well as increased fat deposits in this area, resulting in wider hips (Litt & Vaughan, 1992). Figure 11.1 details these physical changes in boys and girls.

These various physical changes are triggered by activities of the pituitary gland. This "master gland" sends signals to the adrenal glands (on top of the kidneys) and gonads (ovaries and testes). These glands in turn secrete the hormones responsible for the changes in physical characteristics that differentiate males and females.

For Better or For Worse®   by Lynn Johnston

 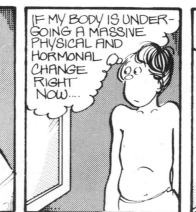 

Figure 11.1
Physical development during pubescence and puberty
During pubescence, the two years prior to puberty, a growth spurt occurs and secondary sex characteristics develop. During puberty, the primary sex characteristics mature. These various physical changes are caused by hormonal secretions.

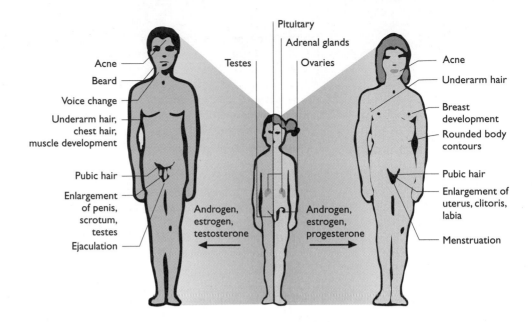

Note that the capacity to reproduce is not attained in pubescence. That comes later. *Puberty* **is the stage during which sexual functions reach maturity and that marks the beginning of adolescence.** It is during puberty that the *primary sex characteristics*—**the structures necessary for reproduction**—develop fully. In the male, these include the testes, penis, and related internal structures; in the female they include the ovaries, vagina, uterus, and other internal structures (see Figure 11.1).

Recommended Reading

The Hurried Child: Growing Up Too Fast, Too Soon

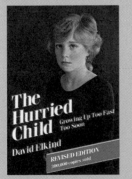

by David Elkind
(Addison-Wesley, 1988)

In this fascinating book, David Elkind shows how recent changes in the structure of family life have altered prevalent views of children and their needs. Earlier generations saw children as needing adult protection and guidance, a view consistent with the "traditional" family structure in which at least one parent was available to the children at all times. Today, in many step-, single-parent, and dual-earner families, such nurturing is impossible for parents to provide. Many of these parents have alleviated their anxiety about parenthood by adopting a new conception of children as "superkids" who can take care of themselves.

This new view of children as "miniature adults" is mirrored in every facet of children's culture: education, television, movies, and music. Thus, society as a whole conspires with the parents to "hurry" children to outgrow their need for nurturance as quickly as possible.

According to Elkind, pressuring children to grow up fast can produce negative outcomes ranging from academic failure to psychosomatic illness to teenage suicide. Nevertheless, he maintains an attitude of optimism and hope that, with awareness of the pressures today's children face, parents can and will seek to alleviate their children's stress. Reading this book can help a concerned parent do just that.

The conception of children as competent to deal with, and indeed as benefitting from, everything and anything that life has to offer was an effective rationalization for parents who continue to love their children but who have neither the time, nor the energy, for childhood. . . .

If child-rearing necessarily involves stress, then by hurrying children to grow up, or by treating them as adults, we hope to remove a portion of our burden of worry and anxiety and to enlist our children's aid in carrying life's load. We do not mean our children harm in acting thus—on the contrary, as a society we have come to imagine that it is good for young people to mature rapidly. Yet we do our children harm when we hurry them through childhood. [pp. xiii, 3]

In females, the onset of puberty is typically signaled by *menarche*—**the first occurrence of menstruation.** American girls typically reach menarche at about age 13, with further sexual maturation continuing until approximately age 16 (Malina, 1990). Most girls are sterile for 12 to 18 months following menarche. (Of course, pregnancy is a possibility for *some* girls at this age, so those who have begun to menstruate should assume that they can become pregnant.) Breast development and the presence of pubic hair serve as important social criteria of adolescence for girls in the absence of visible external genitals.

In males, there is no comparable clear-cut marker of the onset of sexual maturity. The capacity to ejaculate sperm is used as a popular index of puberty (the onset of sperm production not being a visible event). The first ejaculation usually occurs through masturbation, rather than nocturnal emissions (Hyde, 1994). (With the latter, also called "wet dreams," ejaculation occurs during sleep and is sometimes accompanied by erotic dreams.) Experts note that ejaculation may not be a valid index of actual maturity because early ejaculations may contain seminal fluid but not active sperm. American boys begin to produce sperm and ejaculate between ages 12 and 14, with complete sexual maturation occurring at about age 18 (Brooks-Gunn & Reiter, 1990; Tanner, 1978).

As we have noted, puberty arrives about two years later in boys than in girls. Indeed, the major reason that adult males are taller than adult females is that males typically experience two additional years of development before the onset of the growth spurt (Brooks-Gunn & Reiter, 1990). Interestingly, there have been *generational* changes in the timing of puberty, at least in industrialized countries (Chumlea, 1982). Today's adolescents begin puberty earlier, and complete it more rapidly, than did their counterparts in earlier generations. This trend apparently reflects improvements in nutrition and medical care. In the United States, this trend appears to have leveled off, probably a reflection of the attainment of higher standards of living for most Americans. Thus, the onset of sexual maturation may have a genetically predetermined age "floor."

Puberty also brings important changes in other body organs. For instance, the heart and lungs increase considerably in size, and the heart rate drops. These changes are more marked for boys than for girls and are responsible, in part, for the superior performance of males in certain physical activities relative to females. Before about age 12, boys and girls are similar in physical strength, speed, and endurance. After puberty, boys have a clear advantage in all three areas (Smoll & Schutz, 1990).

After attaining sexual maturation, adolescents continue to mature physically until the secondary sex characteristics are fully developed and the body has reached adult height and proportions. In girls, such growth continues until about age 17; in boys, it goes on until about age 20 (Brooks-Gunn & Reiter, 1990).

Variation in the onset of pubescence and puberty is normal. Still, the timing of these physical changes figures importantly in adjustment. More specifically, research suggests that girls who mature early and boys who mature late seem to feel particularly anxious and self-conscious about their changing bodies (Siegel, 1982). The early-maturing girl is taller and heavier than most of the girls and nearly all the boys her age. The late-maturing boy is shorter and slighter than most of the boys and nearly all the girls his age. To make matters worse, both groups have body types that are at odds with cultural ideals of extreme slenderness for females and muscular physique for males.

Research has shown that early maturation in girls is correlated with poorer school performance, earlier experience of intercourse, and more unwanted pregnancies (Stattin & Magnusson, 1990). They also have more negative body images (Petersen, 1988) and are more likely to be depressed (Rierdan & Koff, 1991). Late-maturing boys have been found to feel more inadequate and more insecure and to think less of themselves than other boys do (Siegel, 1982). Optimal adjustment for girls is associated with puberty coming "on time," whereas optimal adjustment for boys is related to puberty arriving early. Also, girls' and boys' *perceptions* of the timing of their puberty and their feelings of attractiveness follow this same pattern (see Figure 11.2).

Figure 11.2
Perceived timing of puberty and optimal adjustment
For girls, feelings of attractiveness and a positive body image are associated with the perception that puberty arrives "on time"; for boys, these feelings are associated with the perception that puberty arrives early. (Adapted from Tobin-Richards, Boxer, & Petersen, 1983)

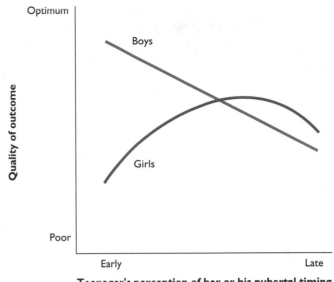

Cognitive Changes

Learning Objective

Summarize the cognitive changes that occur during adolescence.

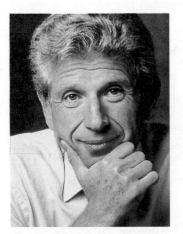

David Elkind

Around the time of early adolescence, major changes take place in thinking and problem solving (Keating, 1990). Compared to those who are younger, adolescents can think abstractly (not merely concretely) and more efficiently. They also become more self-aware and self-reflective and can view problems from several different perspectives rather than only one. Thus, the thinking of adolescents is qualitatively different from that of younger children. Whereas the latter go about solving problems on a trial-and-error basis, most adolescents are capable of solving problems by generating a number of possible hypotheses and systematically testing them.

One of the significant outcomes of these cognitive changes is that adolescents are freed from the cognitive limitations of concrete reality. This means that they can apply their logical skills to abstract concepts such as love, justice, and truth and can contemplate heady social and political issues that would never occur to a younger child. The ability to engage in abstract thinking also frees adolescents from existing solely in the present. This newly developed ability to conceive of future events is one reason they spend so much time fantasizing, planning, and worrying about their lives to be.

A particularly interesting aspect of cognitive development is egocentrism. Jean Piaget, an early theorist of cognitive development, used the term *egocentrism* **to refer to the tendency to view reality in line with one's own idiosyncratic perceptions.** According to David Elkind (1988), egocentrism in adolescence appears to account for much of the experience and behavior typical at this age. Elkind aptly labels one form of adolescent egocentrism the *imaginary audience*. Because adolescents are so focused on themselves, they wrongly assume that they are the center of others' attention as well. Hence, adolescents often act as if they are performing for an audience. Examples of the imaginary audience at work include adolescents' self-consciousness (both unwarranted self-criticism or self-admiration) and their fantasies about how others will react to the news of their death (others recall—too late, of course—what a good person they really were).

A second form of adolescent egocentrism is the *personal fable*. In this case, adolescents believe that they are unique and, therefore, that others (especially parents) can't comprehend their special experiences. Familiar examples of the personal fable come readily to mind: the ecstasy of one's first romantic love experience (no one else has ever loved as deeply) and the utter devastation of one's first "break-up" (no one else has ever suffered so much).

Elkind suggests that much of the high-risk behavior of some adolescents is attributable to the personal fable. For example, the high incidence of injury and death by accident in this group is likely based in adolescents' belief that they are immortal (even though others are not). Also, the high incidence of pregnancy due to the failure to use birth control probably reflects the personal fable that "other girls can get pregnant, but not me."

Egocentrism seems to disappear as individuals learn more about others through social interactions and through intimate relationships in which there is mutual self-disclosure. That is, when they learn that others often have views that differ from their own, they replace the imaginary audience with a more realistic sense of the beliefs of others. Likewise, the ideas of the personal fable are eventually overcome as individuals come to see that their own experiences are not so different from those of others (Enright, Shukla, & Lapsley, 1980).

Personality Changes

Adolescents are faced with a number of challenges in the realm of personality. These include grappling with identity questions, coping with changes in gender-role expectations, and dealing with the stresses of moving from childhood to adulthood.

The Search for Identity

Learning Objective

Describe Erikson's psychosocial crisis of adolescence and Marcia's four identity statuses.

Erik Erikson (1963) devised a theory of personality development that views adolescence as a period of pivotal importance. (Figure 11.3 depicts all eight of Erikson's stages, although we will focus on only the last four in this chapter.) According to Erikson (1968), the premiere challenge of adolescence is developing a clear sense of identity. This involves wrestling with such important issues as "Who am I?" "What do I stand for?" and "What kind of work do I want to do?" Sexual orientation is also an important aspect of identity development.

As we explained in Chapter 5, Marcia (1976) suggested that there are actually four possible outcomes of the psychosocial crisis of adolescence instead of just the two Erikson proposed. Each of these "identity statuses" represents a different way of dealing with the identity crisis. *Foreclosure* involves a premature commitment to visions, values, and roles prescribed by one's parents (identity crisis bypassed). *Moratorium* involves delaying commitment for a while to experiment with alternative ideologies (currently experiencing identity crisis). *Identity diffusion* involves an inability

Figure 11.3
Overview of Erikson's stages
Building on earlier work by Freud, Erik Erikson (1963) divided the life span into eight stages. Each stage involves a psychosocial crisis (column 2) that is played out in certain social relationships (column 3). If a crisis is handled effectively, a favorable outcome results (column 4).

Erikson's Stages of Psychosocial Development

Stage	Psychosocial crisis	Significant social relationships	Favorable outcome
1 First year of life	Trust vs. mistrust	Mother or mother substitute	Trust and optimism
2 Second and third years	Autonomy vs. doubt	Parents	A sense of self-control and adequacy
3 Fourth through sixth years	Initiative vs. guilt	Basic family	Purpose and direction; ability to initiate one's own activities
4 Age 6 through puberty	Industry vs. inferiority	Neighborhood; school	Competence in intellectual, social, and physical skills
5 Adolescence	Identity vs. diffusion	Peer groups and outgroups; models of leadership	An integrated image of oneself as a unique person
6 Early adulthood	Intimacy vs. isolation	Partners in friendship and sex; competition, cooperation	An ability to form close and lasting relationships, to make career commitments
7 Middle adulthood	Generativity vs. stagnation	Divided labor and shared household	Concern for family, society, and future generations
8 The aging years	Integrity vs. despair	"Humankind," "my kind"	A sense of fulfillment and satisfaction with one's life; willingness to face death

to make identity commitments (unresolved identity crisis). *Identity achievement* involves arriving at a sense of self and direction after some consideration of alternative possibilities (resolved identity crisis).

A sense of identity usually evolves gradually as a result of innumerable daily decisions: whether to date a particular person, take a particular course, use drugs, become sexually active, become politically involved, go to college, and so forth. At the end of this period of questioning (identity crisis), adolescents typically feel committed to an occupational direction and a system of values they can embrace as their own (Marcia, 1991). As they formulate their identity, adolescents gradually achieve psychological distance from their parents, becoming autonomous individuals with their own consciously chosen values and goals.

Although the struggle for a sense of identity neither begins nor ends in adolescence, it does tend to be especially intense during this period. Why should this be the case? First, the physical changes of puberty force adolescents to revise their self-image and confront their sexuality. Second, the advent of formal operations promotes self-reflection. Third, faced with the end of mandatory schooling, adolescents must contemplate occupational choices and make decisions about their future.

Erikson and many other theorists believe that identity achievement is a cornerstone of sound psychological health. Identity diffusion can interfere with important developmental transitions that should unfold during the adult years.

Intensification of Gender Roles

Learning Objective

Discuss how gender roles influence adolescent development.

Some theorists suggest that gender-role expectations intensify around the time of puberty (Brooks-Gunn & Reiter, 1990). That is, the changes in appearance that signal the onset of physical and sexual maturation are directly tied to gender-role issues. More specifically, these external changes produce alterations in self-perceptions and intensify other people's expectations that one will conform closely to gender-role expectations. Research findings support this idea (Simmons & Blyth, 1987).

If males are to function successfully in designated adult roles, they must achieve a sense of identity, become independent of their family, and decide on an occupation (Lloyd, 1985). These developmental tasks are usually achieved during adolescence and young adulthood. In their classic study of adolescence, Elizabeth Douvan and Joseph Adelson (1966) found that occupational choice was the central identity issue for adolescent boys: "For most boys the question of 'what to be' begins with work and the job, and he is likely to define himself and to be identified by occupation" (p. 17). Numerous studies support this finding (Marcia, 1980, 1991).

Adolescent girls are pressured to give up so-called masculine characteristics and behavior that were acceptable in childhood, especially those involving autonomy and achievement in "masculine" areas (Brooks-Gunn & Reiter, 1990; Morgan & Farber, 1982). They are encouraged to focus on dating and social skills instead. Much of this energy is focused on learning skills that will ensure *heterosexual success*—learning how to attract and interest boys as prospective mates. This focus on attracting a mate typically results in excessive concern about body image and ambivalence about a career (Holland & Eisenhart, 1990).

The emphasis on heterosexual success may also delay the development of an independent sense of identity. Traditional female norms dictate that a woman should build her identity around her roles as wife and mother rather than around a career, as men are expected to do. Also, a girl cannot take the initiative in realizing these roles (she must be chosen as a mate, not do the choosing). For these reasons, gender-role expectations may delay identity achievement until adult roles are assumed. As you can see, the culturally created incompatibilities between femininity and achievement cause psychological conflicts for both adolescent and adult females (Hyde, 1996; Lloyd, 1985).

Time of Turmoil?

Is adolescence a period of emotional upheaval and turmoil? G. Stanley Hall (1904), one of the first psychologists to study adolescence, thought so. In fact, he specifically characterized adolescence as a period of "storm and stress." Hall attributed this turmoil to the conflicts between the physical changes of puberty and society's demands for social and emotional maturity.

Does research support the idea that adolescence is a period especially marked by emotional turbulence? There is evidence that adolescents do seem to experience more stress and more negative emotions than younger children do (Larson & Asmussen, 1991; Larson & Ham, 1993). And, there is a modest increase in parent-adolescent conflict (Eccles et al., 1993). Still, parent-adolescent relations are not as difficult or contentious as advertised (Galambos, 1992). On the whole, the evidence indicates that a majority of teenagers make it through adolescence without any more turmoil than one is likely to encounter in other periods of life (Hauser & Bowlds, 1990; Petersen, 1988). Based on her extensive studies of adolescents, Anne Petersen (1987) has concluded, "The adolescent's journey toward adulthood is inherently marked by change and upheaval, but need not be fraught with chaos or deep pain" (p. 34).

No doubt because of popular expectations that the adolescent period will be filled with "storm and stress," many parents, teachers, and counselors view the onset of the teenage years with anxiety and dread. Young people, caught up in their own experiences and lacking a broader perspective, may perceive their conflicts and frustrations as an indication of serious psychological disturbance rather than as normal responses to adolescent transitions.

As youngsters progress through adolescence, the differences between the vast majority who can cope with the transition to adulthood and the small minority who cannot become increasingly obvious. Symptoms of those in the latter group include depression, suicidal behavior, drug and alcohol abuse, and chronic delinquency (Petersen, 1988; Takanishi, 1993). Because the incidence of such problems is relatively low, attention should be paid to such behavior when it does appear (Petersen, 1988). Well-intentioned adults make a serious mistake by passing off problems as "normal adolescent turmoil" that will be "outgrown." Early professional attention in such cases can often prevent more major problems from developing.

Although the number of adolescents with serious problems remains relatively small, in recent years alarming increases have occurred in the incidence of some of these psychological and social problems. For example, homicide accounts for 33% of the deaths among 15- to 19-year-old African American males and is the leading cause of death in this group (Millstein & Litt, 1990). Youth who live in poor, high-density metropolitan areas are most at risk. Another disturbing finding is that suicide rates increased 214% among 15- to 19-year-olds between 1960 and 1990 (Garland & Zigler, 1993). In the next section, we'll look more closely at adolescent suicidal behavior.

Adolescent Suicide

As noted, recent years have seen a surge in adolescent suicide. This is apparent in Figure 11.4a, which shows that suicide among 15- to 24-year-olds increased by more than 154% between 1960 and 1990, while it rose only slightly in the general population during this period. Despite these increases, only a small minority of adolescents attempt suicide (Meehan et al., 1992). Also, white males are more likely to commit suicide than black males (Millstein & Litt, 1990). Figure 11.4b plots suicide rates as a function of age. Here you can see that, even with this steep increase, the incidence of suicide in the 15–24 age group is lower than that for any older age group.

Actually, the suicide crisis among teenagers involves *attempted* suicide more than *completed* suicide. Experts estimate that when all age groups are lumped together, suicide attempts outnumber actual suicidal deaths by a ratio of about 8:1 (Cross & Hirschfeld, 1986). However, the ratio of attempted to completed suicides among adolescents is much higher than for any other age group. Studies suggest that the ratio among adolescents may be anywhere from 50:1 to 200:1 (Garland & Zigler, 1993). According to David Curran (1987), suicide attempts by adolescents tend to be a "communicative gesture designed to elicit caring" (p. 12). Put another way, they are desperate cries for attention, help, and support.

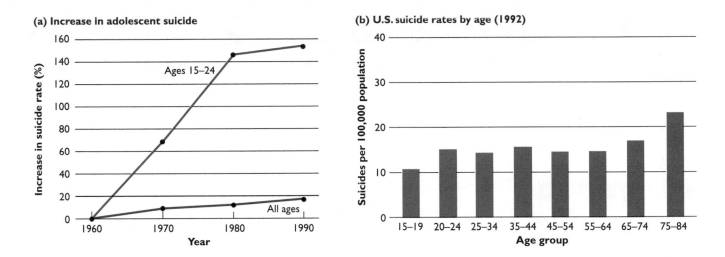

(a) Increase in adolescent suicide

Increase in suicide rate (%)

160
140 Ages 15–24
120
100
80
60
40
20
0
      1960   1970   1980   1990
              Year
                            All ages

(b) U.S. suicide rates by age (1992)

Suicides per 100,000 population

40

30

20

10

0
   15–19 20–24 25–34 35–44 45–54 55–64 65–74 75–84
                      Age group

Figure 11.4
Adolescent suicide
(a) The suicide rate for adolescents has increased in recent decades far more than the suicide rate for the population as a whole. (b) Nonetheless, the suicide rate for the 15–19 age group remains lower than the suicide rates for older adults. (Data from *Statistical Abstract of the United States*, 1995)

What drives an adolescent to such a dramatic, but dangerous, gesture? Research suggests that the "typical" suicidal adolescent has a long history of stress and personal problems extending back into childhood (de Wilde et al., 1992; Jacobs, 1971). Unfortunately, for some teenagers these problems—conflicts with parents, difficulties in school, problems with girlfriends and boyfriends—escalate during adolescence. As their efforts to cope with these problems fail, many teenagers rebel against parental authority, withdraw from social relationships, and make dramatic gestures such as running away from home. These actions often lead to progressive social isolation.

When a person feels socially isolated, a pressing problem with great emotional impact may precipitate an attempted suicide. The precipitating problem—a poor grade in school, not being allowed to go somewhere or buy something special—may appear trivial to an objective observer. But the seemingly trivial problem may serve as the final thread in a tapestry of frustration and distress.

The increase in adolescent suicide is a disturbing social tragedy that requires attention from parents, schools, and the helping professions (see the Chapter 15 Application for a discussion of suicide prevention).

The Expanse of Adulthood

Learning Objective

Explain the role of social clocks in adult development.

As people progress through adulthood, they periodically ask themselves, "How am I doing for my age?" In pondering this question, they are likely to be influenced by their social clocks. **A *social clock* is a person's notion of a developmental schedule that specifies what the person should have accomplished by certain points in life.** For example, if you feel that you should be married by the time you're 30, that belief creates a marker on your social clock. While everyone has his or her own social clock, they are very much a product of socialization.

Social clocks can exert considerable influence over decisions concerning education, career moves, marriage, parenting, and other life choices. Adhering to a social clock based on prevalent age norms brings social approval and is thus a way to evaluate one's own development. Important life events that come too early or too late according to one's social clock produce more stress than transitions that occur "on time" (Chiriboga, 1987). It is easy to imagine how an early marriage, delayed career promotion, or premature retirement might be especially stressful. In particular, it appears that lagging behind one's personal schedule in regard to certain achievements produces chronic frustration and reduced self-esteem (Helson, Mitchell, & Moane, 1984). In short, many people listen carefully to their social clocks ticking in the background as they proceed through adulthood. With this thought in mind, let's explore development in adulthood.

Erikson's View of Adult Development

Describe Erikson's psychosocial crises of young, middle, and late adulthood.

Erik Erikson

Insofar as personality changes during the adult years, Erik Erikson's (1963) theory offers some clues about the nature of changes people can expect. Recall that each of Erikson's eight stages focuses on a *psychosocial crisis* involving transitions in social relationships (see Figure 11.3). As we noted earlier, in adolescence the key crisis is identity versus identity diffusion. Let's see how Erikson viewed psychosocial development in adulthood.

Stage Six: Intimacy Versus Isolation

During young adulthood, Erikson's sixth stage, the psychosocial crisis centers on whether a person can develop the capacity to share intimacy with others. Erikson is not concerned simply with the young adult's need to find a marriage partner. Rather, he is concerned with more subtle issues, such as whether one can learn to open up to others, truly commit to others, and give of oneself unselfishly. The person who can experience genuine intimacy is thought to be more likely to develop a mature and successful long-term relationship. Failure to resolve this psychosocial crisis favorably leads to difficulties in relating to others in a genuine fashion. The resulting sense of isolation often fosters manipulative interactions with friends and troublesome committed relationships.

As we noted in Chapter 8, Jacob Orlofsky and his colleagues (1973) found support for five different intimacy statuses, based on the quality of a person's relationships with others:

- *Intimate.* Individuals in this status are capable of forming open and close relationships with both male and female friends and are involved in a committed relationship.
- *Preintimate.* Although people in this category are capable of mature, reciprocal relationships, they haven't yet experienced a committed relationship because they are ambivalent about making commitments.
- *Stereotyped.* Men and women in this status have relationships that are superficial and not very close. They often see others as objects to manipulate rather than to share with.
- *Pseudointimate.* These individuals are typically involved in a relatively permanent relationship, but it is one that resembles the stereotyped relationship in quality.
- *Isolate.* Isolates avoid social situations and appear to be loners whose social interactions consist of casual conversations with a few acquaintances.

According to Erikson, the ability to establish and maintain intimate relationships depends on having successfully weathered the identity crisis of adolescence. In line with this prediction, at least one study has found that identity precedes intimacy rather than vice versa (Dyk & Adams, 1990). Also, researchers have found that college males and females in the more advanced identity statuses (achievement and moratorium) are most likely to be in the more advanced intimacy statuses (intimate and preintimate) (Fitch & Adams, 1983; Kacerguis & Adams, 1980). Similarly, foreclosures and diffusions are predominantly in the less advanced intimacy statuses (stereotyped, pseudointimate, and isolate). A similar pattern has been found in adults up to 35 years of age (Raskin, 1986; Tesch & Whitbourne, 1982).

Additional support for Erikson's hypothesis comes from a study on identity status and marriage, with an interesting gender difference (Kahn et al., 1985). This study found that men who had achieved a stable sense of identity were more likely to be married earlier than those who had not done so. Also, those men who had not achieved a stable sense of identity tended to remain single. In contrast, women's likelihood of marrying was not affected by their identity status. This is no doubt because women experience stronger pressure to marry (recall our discussion of the "marriage mandate" in Chapter 10). However, women who lacked a strong sense of identity were more likely to experience marital breakups. Thus, this study showed that a stable sense of identity is related to men's *entering* committed relationships and to women's *remaining* in them.

Stage Seven: Generativity Versus Stagnation

In middle adulthood, the challenge is to acquire generativity, or a concern for the welfare of future generations. Adults demonstrate generativity when they provide unselfish guidance to younger people. The recipients of this guidance are often their children, but not necessarily. For example, a middle-aged college professor may gain great satisfaction from working with undergraduate and graduate students. Or a 50-year-old attorney might take on the role of "mentor" for a younger woman in her law firm. Thus, generativity and its opposite, stagnation, do not hinge on whether one has children. Stagnation is characterized by self-absorption and self-indulgent preoccupation with one's own needs.

Stage Eight: Integrity Versus Despair

In Erikson's last stage, during the retirement years, the challenge is to achieve (ego) integrity. People who achieve integrity are able to look back on their lives with a sense of satisfaction and to find meaning and purpose there. Its opposite, despair, is the tendency to dwell on the mistakes of the past, bemoan paths not chosen, and contemplate with bitterness the approach of death. Erikson suggests that it is better to face the future in a spirit of acceptance than to wallow in regret and resentment.

A recent study tested some aspects of Erikson's theory using male and female subjects over a 20-year span of adulthood (Whitbourne et al., 1992). By using a complicated research design, the authors were able to demonstrate support for several of Erikson's propositions. For example, they found that psychosocial develop-

---

Recommended Reading

Necessary Losses: The Loves, Illusions, Dependencies and Impossible Expectations That All of Us Have to Give Up in Order to Grow

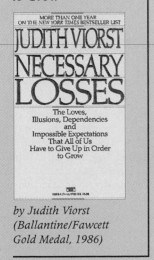

MORE THAN ONE YEAR ON THE NEW YORK TIMES BESTSELLER LIST

JUDITH VIORST
NECESSARY LOSSES

The Loves,
Illusions, Dependencies
and
Impossible Expectations
That All of Us
Have to Give Up in Order
to Grow

by Judith Viorst
(Ballantine/Fawcett
Gold Medal, 1986)

Author Judith Viorst views personal loss as an inevitable fact of life. And, although loss is painful and often depressing, she strongly believes that these unavoidable losses can help us grow. For Viorst, loss encompasses a much broader range of experiences than the traditional loss of loved ones through death. She discusses losses as a result of leaving and being left; changing, letting go, and moving on; and giving up our romantic dreams, impossible expectations, and illusions of freedom, power, and safety. She also addresses the loss of our own younger self, the self we always believed would be unwrinkled, invulnerable, and immortal.

The author is a popular writer who has had a number of years of psychoanalytic training and experience as a therapist. In keeping with this background, she emphasizes the role of past experiences and unconscious forces in shaping our lives. She, like Freud, believes that becoming aware of these forces can help us become more self-directing. In writing this book, she wants to help readers understand how losses and growth are intricately intertwined as well as understand how they have reacted to their own losses. She believes that this experience will enable readers to increase their self-awareness, which, in turn, will foster important personal growth. In the excerpt below, Viorst examines the experience of loss in marriage.

The contrast between the marriage we wanted and the marriage we got spans more than romantic and sexual disappointment. For even when we marry with an earthier vision of what a good marriage should be, the married state—and the person with whom we are sharing it—may fail to meet some, sometimes all, of our expectations: That we will always be there for each other. That we will always be faithful and loyal to each other. That we will accept each other's imperfections. That we will never consciously hurt each other. That although we expect to disagree on many minor matters, we surely will be in agreement on major matters. That we will be open and honest with each other. That we will always go to bat for each other. That our marriage will be our sanctuary, our refuge, our "haven in a heartless world."

Not necessarily. Certainly, not all the time. [p. 210]

ment proceeds in an orderly sequence of stages and that favorable resolutions of earlier stages lead to favorable resolutions of later stages.

Erikson's theory provides a useful and relatively accurate view of the key psychosocial issues confronting adults. Still, each of the three stages of adulthood pose additional developmental challenges. Next, we'll turn our attention to the major personal and social transitions that take place during early, middle, and late adulthood.

Early Adulthood (from about age 20 to 40)

Learning Objective

Summarize the key developmental transitions in early adulthood.

Between the ages of about 20 and 30, adults must learn a number of new and important roles. Take Jack, for example. He graduated from college at age 22 and then left his family and moved to Atlanta to start work as a management trainee. Shortly thereafter, he got involved in a serious relationship (which later broke up). Then, at age 25, Jack got engaged and married; at 26, he changed jobs; and at 28, he and his wife had their first child. It's easy to see why the years from 20 to 30 have been described as "demographically dense," referring to the fact that more role changes occur during this period than any other (Rindfuss, 1991). For a number of reasons (discussed in Chapter 13), gay males and lesbians take longer to recognize their sexual orientation than heterosexuals do (Garnets & Kimmel, 1991). Much of this sorting out process takes place during early adulthood and adds further stress to an already difficult period.

To cope successfully with all these developmental challenges, young adults must have developed certain psychological and social competencies. These include a set of personal values to guide their life decisions and enough self-control to reach their goals. In addition, they must have a sense of the kind of work they want to do, the competencies necessary for the job they want, and social skills by which to develop and maintain relationships at work and with friends and partners or mates. Also, most young adults are still struggling to become fully independent of their parents.

Adjusting to Family Life

Although the age of marriage seems to be getting later and later in our culture, most people still marry in their 20s. The first few years of married life tend to be very happy (Belsky, 1990a; Glenn, 1990). The early years of committed gay and lesbian relationships also follow this pattern (Kurdek & Schmitt, 1988). Although an increasing number of people are choosing not to have children, the vast majority of married couples plan to do so (Roosa, 1988). Still, the arrival of the first child represents a major transition. Postpartum depression can be a problem for new mothers, especially those who have to shoulder the major burden of infant care (Harriman, 1986; Kalmuss, Davidson, & Cushman, 1992). After the arrival of children, marital satisfaction typically declines and continues to be low until middle adulthood, when it rises (Belsky, 1990a; Glenn, 1990).

Adjusting to the World of Work

In addition to adjusting to committed relationships and parenting, young adults are also confronted with major challenges in their work lives (Super, 1957, 1985, 1988). Individuals need to complete their schooling and secure their first job. At this point in career development, many people are still only tentatively committed to their chosen occupational area. If their first experiences are not rewarding, they may shift to another area, where they continue to explore their work options. Ideally, people are able to find work that is gratifying; when this happens, they typically commit to an occupational area. Once individuals make a commitment to a particular kind of work, their future job moves usually take place within this field. During early adulthood, workers learn new skills and develop work attitudes that affect their job success.

Middle Adulthood (from about age 40 to 65)

Compared to early adulthood, which requires the learning of so many new roles, middle adulthood is an easier period. Nonetheless, middle adulthood has its share of challenges.

Confronting the Aging Process

Chief among the challenges of middle adulthood is confronting the aging process. Middle-aged adults notice a number of physical transformations: changes in vision that often require glasses or bifocals for reading, the onset of wrinkles and sagging skin, and more bodily aches and pains and general "creakiness." In addition, people are forced to acknowledge their mortality as they witness the deaths of parents, colleagues, and friends.

Transitions in the Parenting Role

As children grow up, parental influence over them tends to decline, and the early years of parenting—which once seemed so difficult—are often recalled with fondness. When youngsters reach adolescence and seek to establish their own identities, gradual realignment occurs in parent-child relationships. It is worth noting that parent-adolescent relations generally are not as bitter or contentious as widely assumed. Nonetheless, conflicts over values are common, and power struggles frequently ensue (Silverberg, Tennenbaum, & Jacob, 1992). When conflict does occur, mothers are often more adversely affected than fathers (Steinberg & Silverberg, 1987). This may be because the woman's self-esteem tends to be more closely tied to the quality of family relationships.

Ironically, although recent studies have shown that adolescence is not as turbulent or difficult for youngsters as once believed, their parents *are* stressed out. Parents overwhelmingly rate adolescence as the most difficult stage of child-rearing (Gecas & Seff, 1990). Still, on balance, most parents seem to have little regret about their decision to have children and rate parenthood as a very positive experience (Demo, 1992; Goetting, 1986). A related challenge for most middle-aged adults is learning the grandparent role. In addition, some individuals (typically women) may assume responsibility for the care of their aging parents and relatives.

Although the "emptying of the nest" is widely believed to be a traumatic event for parents, especially women, few seem to experience it as such (Birchler, 1992; Reinke et al., 1985). The postparental period often provides couples with new freedom to devote their attention to each other. Many couples take advantage of this opportunity by traveling or developing new leisure interests. And as offspring strike out on their own, couples' marital satisfaction tends to start climbing to higher levels once again (Brubaker, 1990). It tends to remain fairly high until one of the spouses (usually the husband) dies.

Transitions in the Work Role

At midlife, workers seem to follow one of two patterns (Papalia & Olds, 1994). Those in the *stable career pattern* are at the peak of their careers. They have more responsibility, earn more money, and wield more influence than their younger co-workers. Some workers in this group continue to work at a frantic pace, struggling to accomplish their goals as they hear their social clocks ticking. Others seem content with their work achievements and begin to shift some of their attention and energy to family and leisure activities.

Workers in the *changing careers pattern* are a more varied group. Whereas all are seeking to begin a different type of work, their reasons for doing so may be quite different. Some are looking for a new line of work because they have been forced out of a job by cutbacks. Others are seeking new careers because they want new work challenges at this time in their lives. A third group consists of women who are entering or reentering the workforce because family concerns now occupy less of their time and energy.

Is There a Midlife Crisis?

There has been a spirited debate about whether most people go through a *midlife crisis*. Two influential studies of adult development in the 1970s both concluded that a midlife crisis is a normal transition experienced by a majority of people. Daniel Levinson and his colleagues (1978) found that most of their subjects (all men) went through a midlife crisis around the ages of 40 to 45. This transition was marked by reappraisal of one's life and emotional turmoil. Roger Gould (1978) found that the men in his study tended to go through a midlife crisis between the ages of 35 and 45. Gould's subjects reported feeling pressed by time. They heard their social clocks ticking loudly as they struggled to achieve their life goals.

Since the landmark studies of Levinson and Gould, many other researchers have questioned whether the midlife crisis is a normal developmental transition. A host of studies have failed to detect an increase in emotional turbulence at midlife (Eisler & Ragsdale, 1992; Roberts & Newton, 1987). How can we explain this discrepancy? Levinson and Gould both depended primarily on interview and case study methods to gather their data. As we noted in Chapter 2, when knitting together impressionistic case studies, it is easy for investigators to see what they expect to see. Given that the midlife crisis has long been a part of developmental folklore, Levinson and Gould may have been prone to interpret their case study data in this light (McCrae & Costa, 1984). In any case, investigators relying on more objective measures of emotional stability have found signs of midlife crises in only a tiny minority (2–5%) of subjects (Chiriboga, 1989; McCrae & Costa, 1990). Thus, it's clear that the fabled midlife crisis is not universal, and it probably isn't even typical.

Late Adulthood (after age 65)

Late adulthood also has its share of developmental transitions. These include adjusting to retirement, adapting to changes in one's support network, coping with health problems, and confronting death.

Retirement

As retirement looms near, people prepare to leave the workplace. Although 65 is the age typically associated with retirement, today individuals are retiring earlier (Clark, 1988). More men and women retire between the ages of 60 and 65 than later. This decrease in the age of retirement is occurring both in the United States and in other industrialized countries (Inkeles & Usui, 1989).

Individuals approach retirement with highly variable attitudes (Atchley, 1982, 1991). Many are filled with apprehension, usually about how they will occupy themselves and how they will manage financially. Nonetheless, many studies have shown that retirement has no adverse effect on overall health or life satisfaction (Smith, Patterson, & Grant, 1992). However, retirement can pose a problem for those who are forced to leave work because of such things as ill health, mandatory retirement policies, or job elimination (Herzog, House, & Morgan, 1991). Retirement can also be stressful if it comes at the same time as other life changes, such as widowhood (Stull & Hatch, 1984). And, although retirement may result in decreased income, it also provides more time for travel, hobbies, household tasks, and friends (George, Fillenbaum, & Palmore, 1984).

Changes in Support Networks

As we noted earlier, couples' relationship satisfaction tends to start climbing to higher levels later in life and tends to remain fairly high until one of the spouses or partners dies. In addition, most older adults maintain their ties to their children

Friendships play an important role in older adults' life satisfaction.

and grandchildren. One large study of over 11,000 adults aged 65 and over found that 63% of the participants reported that they saw at least one of their children once a week or more often, and another 16% saw a child one to three times a month. Only 20% indicated that they saw their children once a month or less (Crimmins & Ingegneri, 1990). Surprisingly, elderly parents who see their children regularly or who report positive interactions with them don't describe themselves as happier than those who see their children less often or who have less positive relationships with their offspring (Markides & Krause, 1985; Seccombe, 1987).

Older adults report that siblings may become more important than they were earlier and may play an important role in adjustment at this age, but this finding appears to be limited to relationships involving sisters (Cicirelli, 1989). A few studies have explored this issue in ethnic minority families. This research indicates that Hispanics have extensive family relationships, with frequent visiting and exchanges not only with the immediate family but also with grandparents and cousins (Keefe, 1984). Also, there is some evidence that Italian American and African American siblings may have closer relationships than siblings from nonethnic families, although the number of these intimate relationships appears to be relatively small (Gold, 1990; Johnson, 1982).

Friends seem to play a more significant role in life satisfaction for older adults than family members do, at least for most white Americans. This is especially true for those who are unmarried, but it also holds true to some degree for those who are still married (Antonucci, 1990; Lee & Shehan, 1989). Friendships provide companionship, as well as opportunities for sharing activities and reflecting on common experiences. The gender differences in friendships we noted in Chapter 8 continue throughout adulthood. Thus, older men may have a larger network of friends than older women, but women's friendships are more intimate (Wright, 1989). Men rely heavily on their wives for emotional support, whereas women derive support from children and friends, as well as from their spouse (Antonucci & Akiyama, 1987). This differential in social support appears to place husbands at higher risk than wives for health and adjustment problems when a spouse dies.

For African American elders *fictive kin* are an important component of social support networks. In these relationships, neighbors or peers acquire the status of a close family member and render mutual aid and support (Taylor et al., 1990). Also, for many elderly African Americans, participation in church activities plays a central role in psychological adjustment (Bryant & Rakowski, 1992).

Other significant challenges for older adults include coping with health problems, dealing with the deaths of friends and partners, and confronting one's own mortality. We'll address these issues in the last two sections of the chapter.

Aging: A Gradual Process

As an alternative to the ages-and-stages approach to adult development, many psychologists have simply set out to identify changes in physical, cognitive, and personality functioning across the expanse of adulthood. While some of these age-related developments are quite obvious, others are subtle. In either case, the changes take place gradually. We'll begin with key changes in the physical realm.

Physical Changes

The physical changes that take place during adulthood affect one's appearance, nervous system, vision and hearing, hormone functioning, and health. (Unless we indicate otherwise, the following summary of trends is based on Whitbourne, 1985.)

Changes in Appearance

Height is rather stable in adulthood, although it does tend to decline by an inch or so after age 55, as the spinal column "settles." Weight is more variable and tends to increase in most adults up through the mid-50s, when a gradual decline typically begins. Although weight often goes down late in life, the percentage of body weight that is fat tends to increase throughout adulthood, much to the chagrin of many. The skin of the face and body tends to wrinkle and sag. The appearance of the face may change, as the nose and ears tend to become longer and wider, and the jaw appears to shrink. Hair tends to thin out and become gray in both genders, and many males have to confront receding hairlines and baldness.

The net impact of these changes is that many older people view themselves as less attractive. This unfortunate reality is probably aggravated by the media's obsession with youthful attractiveness. Older women suffer more than older men as a result of the decline in physical attractiveness. For example, one study showed that attractiveness ratings declined with age when the subject was a woman, but not when the subject was a man (Mathes et al., 1985). Some refer to this phenomenon as a "double standard" of aging (Sontag, 1972). That is, because much of a woman's worth is determined by her physical attractiveness to men, her social status declines along with her attractiveness (Bell, 1989). In contrast, older men don't have to rely on their looks for social status. Instead, they can use their occupational achievements and money for this purpose.

Neurological Changes

The nervous system is composed of *neurons,* **individual cells that receive, integrate, and transmit information.** The number of active neurons in the brain declines steadily during adulthood. As neurons die, the brain decreases in both weight and volume, especially after age 50. Although this progressive neuronal loss sounds alarming, it is a normal part of aging that may not have much functional significance. The brain has billions of neurons, so these losses may be mere drops in a bucket. At present, there is little reason to suspect that this normal process contributes to the onset of *senile dementia,* **or the abnormal and progressive decline in general cognitive functioning that is observed in some people over age 65.** Senile dementia occurs in about 15% of people over age 65 (Elias, Elias, & Elias, 1990).

Alzheimer's disease is a specific form of senile dementia. Although the precise causes of this disease are not yet known, it is associated with changes in brain chemistry (Coyle, Price, & DeLong, 1983) and structure (Hyman et al., 1984). Alzheimer's disease is a vicious affliction that can strike during middle age (40–65) or later in life (after 65). The disease is one of progressive deterioration, ending in death, and may take from one to ten years to run its course. Tragically, there is no cure for the disease at this time, nor can the course of the disease be slowed down or reversed (Biegel, Sales, & Schulz, 1991).

The beginnings of Alzheimer's disease are so subtle that they are difficult to detect (Biegel et al., 1991). Individuals often forget common words, may report reduced energy, and may lose their temper. Later, obvious problems begin to emerge. These include difficulties in speaking and comprehending as well as in performing complicated tasks. The person doesn't seem to have trouble with familiar activities. Sometimes, victims are insensitive to the feelings of others.

From this point, profound memory loss develops, especially for recent events. For example, patients may forget the time, date, current season of the year, and where they are. They may also fail to recognize familiar people, an occurrence that is particularly devastating to family and friends. Sometimes, they experience hallucinations, delusions, and paranoid thoughts. Later, individuals become completely disoriented and lose control of bladder and bowel functions (Biegel et al., 1991). At this point, they are unable to care for themselves at all. Finally, the disease results in death.

Changes in Vision and Hearing

The most important changes in sensory reception occur in vision and hearing. The proportion of people with 20/20 vision declines steadily as age increases. From about age 30 to the mid-60s, most people become increasingly farsighted. After the mid-60s, the trend is toward greater nearsightedness. Older people commonly have difficulty adapting to darkness, recover poorly from glare, and have reduced peripheral vision. Depth perception begins to decline in the mid-40s. These changes in vision may be responsible for accidents in and outside the home but most seriously affect the activity of driving (particularly at night). For instance, drivers over 65 have a high proportion of accidents, which are typically caused by failing to obey traffic signs, not yielding the right of way, and making improper turns, rather than speeding (Sterns, Barrett, & Alexander, 1985).

Noticeable hearing losses usually do not show up until people reach their 50s. Whereas the vast majority of the elderly require corrective treatment for visual losses, only about one-third of older adults suffer hearing losses that require corrective treatment. In addition, small sensory losses in touch, taste, and smell have been detected, usually after age 50. These losses generally have little impact on day-to-day functioning, although older people often complain that their food is somewhat tasteless. In contrast, visual and hearing losses often make interpersonal interaction more awkward and difficult, thus promoting social withdrawal in some older people.

Hormonal Changes

Age-related changes occur in hormonal functioning, but their significance is not well understood. They do *not* appear to be the chief cause of declining sexual activity during the later years. Rather, this decline seems to be more from acceptance of social norms that older people don't have sexual desires and that sexual activity in the elderly is "inappropriate." For women, decreased sexual activity may simply reflect lack of opportunity, since the proportion of widows increases dramatically with age (Turner & Adams, 1988). The vast majority of older adults remain physically capable of engaging in rewarding sexual encounters right on through their 70s, although arousal tends to be somewhat slower and less intense.

Among women, menopause is a rather dramatic transition that typically occurs in the early 50s. *Menopause* **is the time when menstruation ceases.** Not so long ago, it was thought that menopause was almost universally accompanied by severe emotional strain. However, it is now clear that women's reactions to menopause vary greatly, depending on their expectations (Matthews, 1992). Most women suffer little psychological distress (McKinlay, McKinlay, & Brambilla, 1987). Episodes of moderate physical discomfort during the transitional phase are fairly common. However, many women find this discomfort no more troublesome than that associated with menstruation itself. The loss of fertility that accompanies menopause is not necessarily traumatic, since it comes at an age when few women would realistically plan to have more children. When emotional distress does occur, it is more often a reaction to a perceived loss of physical attractiveness than to a loss of reproductive capacity.

Although there has been much discussion in recent years of "male menopause," there really is no equivalent experience among men. Significant endocrine changes do occur in males in their later years. However, these changes are very gradual and are largely unrelated to physical or psychological distress.

Changes in Health Status

Unfortunately, the quality of health does tend to diminish with increasing age (Siegler, Nowlin, & Blumenthal, 1980). There are many reasons for this trend. Vital organ systems lose some of their functional capacity. Vulnerability to some diseases (such as heart disease) increases with age. For other diseases (such as pneumonia), the vulnerability may remain unchanged, but the effects of the condition, if contracted, may be more serious. In any case, there is a clear trend in the direction of declining health. The proportion of people with a chronic health problem climbs steadily with age. As you can see in Figure 11.5, the most common chronic health problems among those over 65 are arthritis, hypertension, hearing impairment, and heart disease (U.S. Bureau of the Census, 1994). Women over 65 have a 1-in-5 chance of breaking a hip (Brody, 1992).

Factors such as lifestyle differences and access to and affordability of health care play an important role in maintaining good health. For instance, among the elderly, the affluent have better health than the poor and white people are healthier than African Americans (Markides, Coreil, & Rogers, 1989). The health of elderly Hispanics seems to fall between that of whites and African Americans.

Only a few elderly Americans live in nursing homes at any one time, although these numbers do increase with age. That is, only about 2% of individuals aged 65 to 74 live in nursing homes, whereas 22% of those over 85 do so (U.S. Bureau of the Census, 1992). However, with "the graying of America" due to the aging of the baby boom generation, the number of elderly individuals needing nursing home care is expected to soar (Kunkel & Applebaum, 1992).

Regular exercise can help protect against deterioration of health at any age.

Although it's a given that you will grow older, there are some things you can do to increase the likelihood of good health regardless of your age. For one thing, we know that those who exercise tend to be healthier and live longer than those who do not (Blair et al., 1989). Regular exercise during adulthood has been shown to protect against hypertension, heart disease, and osteoporosis (Hill, Storandt, & Malley, 1993). Because exercise increases the strength and flexibility of joints and muscles, it also reduces the chance of injuries. In addition, there is evidence that regular exercise may amelio-

**Figure 11.5
Chronic health problems in
those over age 65**
Although most people over age
65 are in good health, they suffer
from a number of chronic conditions. Note: These data refer only
to noninstitutionalized individuals.
(Data from U. S. Bureau of the
Census, 1995)

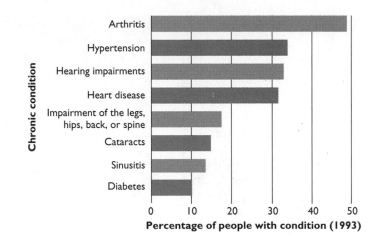

rate anxiety and mild depression (Blumenthal et al., 1991). A healthful diet is
another habit that helps maintain health. The topics of exercise and nutrition are
discussed more fully in Chapter 14.

Cognitive Changes

Learning Objective

*Describe cognitive changes that
occur with aging.*

There are many widely held notions about intellectual decline during adulthood. It
is commonly believed that intelligence drops during middle age and that memory
lapses become more frequent in the later years. Are these common conceptions correct? Let's review the evidence on cognitive functioning during adulthood.

Intelligence

Researchers have long been interested in whether general intelligence, as measured
by IQ tests, remains stable throughout the adult years. The current evidence suggests that IQ is fairly stable throughout most of adulthood. However, a small decline
often begins after age 60 (Hertzog & Schaie, 1988; Schaie, 1990). This post-60
decline appears to be associated with failing health (Field, Schaie, & Leino, 1988)
and with problems in focusing attention (Stankov, 1988). These studies also indicate that there are large individual differences among people in IQ fluctuations.
Although some people experience a modest decline during middle age, many others actually show an *increase* in IQ as late as their 50s. Overall, general intelligence
seems to be stable throughout most of adulthood.

It does appear that people's IQ scores drop precipitously within the last several
years before death (Berg, 1987). This phenomenon is referred to as "terminal drop."
It probably reflects the effects of declining health in those who are approaching their
death.

Memory

Many elderly people feel that their memory "isn't what it used to be." In support
of this perception, numerous studies report declines in the proficiency of long-term
memory in older adults (Baltes & Kleigl, 1992; Hultsch & Dixon, 1990). However,
most of these studies have been based on artificial laboratory tasks that bear little
resemblance to the memory challenges that people encounter in everyday life. Thus,
it's hard to say whether the memory losses seen in these studies have much practical significance.

Investigators have only recently begun to study age-related changes in memory
for more meaningful, realistic content. There *do* seem to be some modest declines
with age in memory for prose, television shows, conversations, past activities, and
personal plans (Kausler, 1985). Such memory impairments could conceivably interfere with older adults' daily activities. However, the memory losses associated with

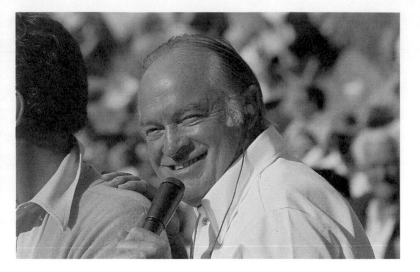

Many people, such as author Betty Friedan and comic Bob Hope, remain active and productive in their 70s, 80s, and even 90s.

aging are moderate in size and are *not* universal. According to Salt-house (1991), age-related decreases in the capacity of short-term or working memory are the crucial factor underlying older adults' poorer performance on memory tasks and other changes in their cognitive functioning. Some older people, especially those who remain mentally active, suffer little memory impairment.

A popular misconception is that older people have vivid recollections of events in the distant past while being very forgetful about recent events. In actuality, there is no evidence that the elderly have more numerous, or more vivid, early memories (Rabbitt & McGinnis, 1988). Their memories of events long ago may be loose reconstructions that are less accurate than is assumed.

Learning and Problem Solving

Although intelligence and memory during adulthood may be more stable than widely believed, there *are* some significant cognitive changes during the adult years. These changes show up most clearly when researchers look at specific aspects of learning and problem solving.

There is ample evidence that the ability to narrow one's focus of attention diminishes somewhat with increasing age, as does the ability to handle simultaneous multiple inputs (Plude & Hoyer, 1985; Stankov, 1988). These changes may be due to decreased efficiency in filtering out irrelevant stimuli. Most of the studies have simply compared extreme age groups (very young participants against very old participants). Hence, we're not sure about the age at which these changes tend to emerge.

In the cognitive domain, age seems to take its toll on *speed* first. Many studies indicate that one's speed in learning, solving problems, retrieving memories, and processing information tends to decline with age, probably commencing in middle adulthood (Drachman, 1986). The general nature of this trend (across differing tasks) suggests that it may be due to age-related changes in neurological functioning (Birren & Fisher, 1995).

Overall *success* on laboratory problem-solving tasks also appears to decrease as people grow older (Charness, 1985). This decline is not as clear or as strong as that observed for speed of processing (Reese & Rodeheaver, 1985). For the most part, problem-solving ability is unimpaired if older people are given adequate time to compensate for their reduced speed in cognitive processing. Furthermore, many of the age-related decrements in cognitive functioning can be partly compensated for by increases in older adults' knowledge.

It should be emphasized that many people remain capable of great intellectual accomplishment well into their later years (Simonton, 1990). This reality was verified in a study of scholarly, scientific, and artistic productivity that examined life-long patterns of work among 738 men who lived at least through the age of 79 (Dennis, 1966). Figure 11.6 plots the percentage of professional works completed

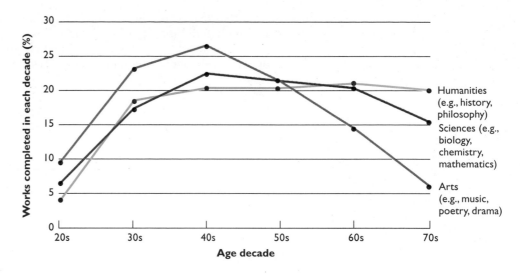

Figure 11.6
Age trends in professional productivity
Dennis (1966) compiled the percentage of professional works completed in each decade of life by 738 men who lived to at least age 79. Productivity peaked in the 40s decade, but professional output remained strong through the 60s decade, and even through the 70s decade for the humanities and sciences.

by these men in their 20s, 30s, 40s, 50s, 60s, and 70s. As you can see, in most professions the 40s decade was the most productive. However, in many areas productivity was remarkably stable through the 60s and even the 70s. Other researchers have focused on the *quality*, rather than the quantity, of output. They typically find that "masterpieces" occur at the same relative frequency among the works of creators of all ages (Simonton, 1990).

Personality Changes

Summarize the evidence on personality change and stability in adulthood.

At midlife, Jerry Rubin went from being an outraged, radical political activist to being a subdued, conventional Wall Street businessman. His transformation illustrates that major personality changes sometimes occur during adulthood. But how common are such changes? Is a grouchy 20-year-old destined to be a grouchy 40-year-old and a grouchy 65-year-old? Or can the grumpy young adult become a mellow senior citizen? How stable is personality over the life span? Let's examine these questions.

Psychologists have engaged in lively debate about whether personality remains stable in adulthood, and both sides have been able to cite supportive research. On the one hand, a number of large-scale longitudinal studies using objective assessments of personality traits provide evidence for long-term stability in personality. The general conclusion that emerges from these longitudinal studies is that personality tends to be quite stable over periods of 20 to 40 years (Caspi & Herbener, 1990; Costa & McCrae, 1994). For example, Paul Costa and Robert McCrae (1988) conducted a six-year longitudinal study of 983 men and women, aged 21 to 76 at the time of the first testing. Over this six-year period, they looked at the stability of the traits in their five-factor model of personality (see Chapter 2). The stability of the participants' self-ratings on these five traits over six years was quite high. (Correlation coefficients for men and women were essentially the same.) Costa and McCrae also asked the spouses of the participants to rate the subjects over the same six-year interval. They found that the stability of the spousal ratings closely matched that of the participants' self-ratings.

On the other hand, some studies suggest that substantial personality changes continue to occur throughout the life span (Helson & Moane, 1987; Whitbourne et al., 1992). For example, in a study of women graduates of Mills College, few personality changes were found between the ages of 21 and 27; however, between the ages of 27 and 43 the women increased in dominance (including confidence) and independence (Helson, Mitchell, & Moane, 1984; Helson & Moane, 1987). According to Susan Whitbourne and her colleagues (1992), "there is a growing body of evidence indicating the existence of adult personality changes on a variety of . . . variables" (p. 268).

In sum, researchers assessing the stability of personality in adulthood have reached very different conclusions (Kogan, 1990). How can these contradictory conclusions be reconciled? This appears to be one of those debates in which researchers are eyeing the same findings, but from different perspectives. Hence, some conclude that the glass is half full, whereas others conclude that it's half empty. In his discussion of this controversy, Lawrence Pervin (1994) concludes that personality is characterized by *both* stability and change. It appears that some personality traits (such as emotional stability, extraversion, and assertiveness) tend to remain stable, while others (such as masculinity and femininity) tend to change systematically as people grow older (Conley, 1985; Helson & Stewart, 1994).

Death and Dying

Dealing with the deaths of close friends and loved ones is an increasingly frequent adjustment problem as people move through adulthood. Moreover, the final challenge of life is to confront one's own death gracefully. In this section, we'll discuss research on death and dying.

Attitudes About Death

Learning Objective

Discuss cultural and individual attitudes about death.

Research on death was relatively scarce until recently because death is a taboo topic in modern Western society. The most common strategy for dealing with death in our culture is *avoidance*. Evidence of the inability to confront death comfortably is plentiful. It is apparent in how people talk about death, using euphemisms such as "passed away" to avoid even the word itself. People's discomfort often leads them to unnecessarily quarantine the dying in hospitals and nursing homes to minimize exposure to the specter of death. These are all manifestations of what Kastenbaum (1986) calls a **death system—the collection of rituals and procedures used by a culture to handle death.** Death systems vary from one culture to another. Ours happens to be rather negative and evasive.

Negativism and avoidance are *not* universal features of all death systems. In Mexican culture, death is discussed frequently and even celebrated on a national feast day, the Day of the Dead (DeSpelder & Strickland, 1983). Also, the Amish view death as a natural transition rather than a dreaded adversary (Bryer, 1979). Thus, some cultures and subcultures display less fear of death than our majority culture.

Within our culture, individuals differ greatly in their attitudes about death. There are conflicting findings about whether *preoccupation* with thoughts about death peaks in middle or old age. However, the evidence is fairly clear that *fear* of death tends to decline after middle age (Gesser, Wong, & Reker, 1987–1988; Kastenbaum, 1986). Elderly adults are more likely to fear the period of uncertainty that comes before death than death itself (Marshall & Levy, 1990). Thus, they are concerned about where they will live, who will take care of them, and how they will cope with the loss of control and independence they may experience before death.

Religious affiliation isn't especially influential in determining feelings about death, but a strong, deeply felt religious commitment (regardless of denomination) is associated with lower death anxiety (Kalish, 1986). There is some evidence that those who are disappointed in themselves or who haven't accomplished all that they had hoped may be more fearful of death than others (Neimeyer & Chapman, 1980–1981). Ultimately, fear of death is an individual matter, greatly influenced by personality and family background (Rosenheim & Muchnik, 1984–1985).

The Process of Dying

Pioneering research on the experience of dying was conducted by Elisabeth Kübler-Ross (1969, 1970) during the 1960s. At first, her project met with immense resistance. Fellow physicians at the hospital where she worked were not inclined to cooperate with her requests to interview dying patients. Gradually, however, it

Learning Objective

Summarize the five stages of dying identified by Kübler-Ross and what more recent research concludes about the dying process.

Elisabeth Kübler-Ross

became apparent that many such patients were enthusiastic about the discussions. They were frustrated by the "conspiracy of silence" that surrounds death and relieved to get things out in the open.

Eventually, Kübler-Ross interviewed over 200 terminally ill patients and developed a model of the process of dying. According to her model, people evolve through a series of five stages as they confront their own death. Huyck and Hoyer (1982, pp. 506–507) provide a succinct description of these reactions:

Stage 1: Denial. Denial, shock, and disbelief are the first reactions to being informed of a serious, life-terminating illness. According to Kübler-Ross, few patients maintain this stance to the end.

Stage 2: Anger. After denial, the patient often becomes nasty, demanding, difficult, and hostile. Asking and resolving the question "Why me?" can help the patient reduce resentment.

Stage 3: Bargaining. In this stage the patient wants more time and asks for favors to postpone death. The bargaining may be carried out with the physician or, more frequently, with God.

Stage 4: Depression. Depression is a signal that the acceptance process has really begun. Kübler-Ross has referred to this stage as *preparatory grief*—the sadness of anticipating an impending loss.

Stage 5: Acceptance. The person who achieves acceptance has taken care of unfinished business. The patient has relinquished the unattainable and is now ready to die. He or she will want to be with close family members, usually a wife or husband and children; dying children want to be with their parents. Although patients desire the presence of someone warm, caring, and accepting at this time, verbal communication may be totally unnecessary.

There is no question that Kübler-Ross greatly improved our understanding of the process of dying and stimulated research that continues to add to our knowledge. Nonetheless, her views have been heavily criticized (Kastenbaum, 1985). For one thing, because her findings were based almost entirely on cancer patients, critics have questioned whether individuals who die from other causes might have different death experiences. Second, because cultures vary widely in their views of death, many suggest that Kübler-Ross's patients represented only the American experience of dying rather than a universal human response. Finally, Kübler-Ross has been most strongly criticized for characterizing the dying process as stage-based. More systematic studies of dying patients have not always observed the same five emotions or the same progression of emotions she described (Baugher et al., 1989–1990). Instead of progressing though a common, five-stage process, dying people seem to show "a jumble of conflicting or alternating reactions running the gamut from denial to acceptance, with tremendous variation affected by age, sex, race, ethnic group, social setting, and personality" (Butler & Lewis, 1982, p. 370).

Bereavement and Grieving

Learning Objective

Define bereavement and mourning and describe what is known about the process of grieving.

When a friend, spouse, or relative dies, individuals must cope with **bereavement, or the painful loss of a loved one through death.** The death of an intimate typically brings forth the painful and complex emotions of grief. Cultural and religious rituals are designed to help survivors adjust to and cope with their loss. **These formal practices of an individual and a community in response to a death are termed *mourning.*** Considerable variation exists between and within cultures regarding how this major life event is acknowledged. In America, the bereaved are typically encouraged to break their emotional ties with the deceased relatively quickly and to return to their regular routines. In contrast, in Japan the bereaved are encouraged to maintain emotional ties to their dead loved ones. Almost all Japanese homes have altars dedicated to family ancestors, and family members routinely talk to the deceased and offer them food (Stroebe et al., 1992). Regardless of the particular form that mourning takes, all such rituals are designed to make death meaningful and to help the bereaved cope with the pain and disruption of death (Marshall & Levy, 1990).

There are several conceptualizations of the grieving process. According to John Bowlby (1980), a prominent theorist in this area, grieving is a four stage process:

Stage 1: Numbness. In this initial phase, survivors are typically dazed and confused. There may be accompanying physical reactions such as nausea or tightness in the chest or throat. This phase may last several days or, in cases when death is unexpected, several weeks.

Stage 2: Yearning. In this phase, survivors try to recover the lost person. Individuals may report that they see the deceased and may wander as if they are searching for the loved one. They often feel frustration, anger, and guilt. In addition, they may experience intense feelings of sadness and may cry and sob uncontrollably. Loss of appetite and insomnia may also be present.

Stage 3: Disorganization and despair. Searching for the loved one ceases as the loss is accepted as real. However, accepting the loss brings feelings of helplessness, despair, and depression. Survivors often experience extreme fatigue and a need to sleep much more than usual.

Stage 4: Reorganization. Individuals are able to resume their normal routines at home and at work. Depression lifts, regular sleeping habits return, and energy increases. Thoughts of the loved one may bring sadness, but these feelings are no longer overwhelming.

Research on the process of grieving suggests that grief does not follow such a straightforward path. Just as there is variability in people's reactions to dying, there are also variable responses to bereavement. In fact, some recent findings have challenged the traditional view of grieving, which holds that distress is an inevitable response to loss and that failure to experience distress is a sign that the individual has not grieved "properly" (Stroebe et al., 1992). As a result, the person is expected to suffer negative consequences later.

As a way of testing these views, Camille Wortman and Roxane Silver (1990) summarized the results of four studies that looked at the amount of distress experienced by widows one month after the death of their husbands and the distress experienced a year or two later. They found four distinct patterns of grieving. The *normal* pattern is characterized by high levels of immediate distress and low levels of distress at the time of the second measurement. The *chronic* pattern is typified by high levels of distress both immediately after the death and later on. In the *delayed* pattern, there is low immediate distress followed by high distress later on. Finally, the *absent* pattern is characterized by low levels of distress both shortly after the husband died as well as later.

As you can see in Figure 11.7, the least common pattern is delayed grief—only 1–5% of mourners fall into this category. Also, "absent grief" appears to be relatively common—30–78% of widows show this pattern. Thus, according to Wortman and Silver, there appears to be little support for the traditional view of grieving. Instead, it appears that many individuals are able to handle bereavement without significant distress. Still, it's important to note that bereaved persons, on the average, score higher on depression and lower in life satisfaction and are at greater risk for illness than are the nonbereaved (Wortman & Silver, 1990).

In the upcoming Application, we'll look at some of the ways parents can facilitate the development of their children by providing optimal combinations of affection and discipline.

Figure 11.7
Four patterns of grieving
Using data from four different studies, Camille Wortman and Roxane Silver (1990) divided widows according to their levels of distress a month after their husbands died (immediate distress) and one to two years later (later distress). This arrangement of data produced four patterns of grieving. Within each category, we have given the lowest and highest percentages reported among the four studies. Although the traditional view of grief holds that the "normal" pattern is the only healthy response to loss, these data show that there are other adaptive patterns of grieving.

Later distress		
	High	**Low**
Immediate distress — High	Chronic 8%–26%	Normal 9%–41%
Immediate distress — Low	Delayed 0%–5%	Absent 30%–78%

Becoming an Effective Parent

Answer the following statements "true" or "false."

1. Infant-mother emotional attachments are natural and formed readily.

2. Placing infants and children in day care negatively affects their development.

3. Extensive use of punishment is the key to effective discipline.

4. Parents shouldn't have to explain their reasons for punishing their children.

All these statements are false. All represent popular myths about child-rearing that we will encounter in our discussion of effective parenting.

Many parents are eager to learn all they can about children's development. They search to find new and better ways to ensure optimal physical, emotional, and cognitive development in their children. In this Application, we'll explore some key issues in modern parenting.

Maternal Behavior and Infant-Mother Attachment

During the first few months of life, infants rely on built-in behaviors such as crying, cooing, and smiling to initiate and maintain contact with adult caregivers. Before long, infants start to recognize their most frequent caregiver (typically, the mother) and are more easily soothed by that person. By the age of 7 months or so, most babies develop a strong emotional attachment to a single, familiar caregiver (hereafter assumed to be the mother, to simplify our discussion).

However, contrary to popular belief, infants' attachment to their mothers is *not* automatic. Indeed, as we mentioned in Chapter 8, not all infants develop a secure attachment to their mothers. Sometimes, mothers are insensitive or inconsistent in responding to their infants' needs (Isabella & Belsky, 1991). Problems with attachment may also arise with "difficult" infants. For instance, some babies are prone to distress, spit up most of their food, make bathing a major battle, refuse to go to sleep, and rarely smile. It is easy to see that such behavior could undermine a mother's responsiveness (Mangelsdorf et al., 1990).

Learning Objective

Describe Ainsworth's three attachment styles and how caregivers can promote secure attachment in their infants.

After extensive study of infant-mother attachments, Mary Ainsworth and her colleagues (1978) concluded that infants could be grouped into three attachment styles. One style is described as *avoidant*. Babies in this group tend to ignore their mothers. A second group is *anxious-ambivalent*. These infants seem to desire contact with the mother, yet they actively resist her when she comes near. Fortunately, the majority of infants are *securely attached* and welcome contact with their mothers. A secure attachment to a caregiver during infancy is important because it seems to provide a basis for successful social relationships later in life (Elicker, Englund, & Sroufe, 1992). In Erik Erikson's terms, the securely attached baby has developed a sense of trust in the caregiver and toward the world at large.

Recent research in this area suggests that there is a fourth attachment style—*disorganized/disoriented* (Main & Solomon, 1990). These infants are both drawn to their caregivers and fear them because of negative past experiences with them. Disorganized/disoriented attachment styles appear to be common among abused children (Carlson et al., 1989).

Can a mother promote a secure attachment in her baby? Ainsworth and her associates reported that the mothers of securely attached infants enjoyed physical contact with the baby, were perceptive about the baby's needs, and had a good sense of timing (for instance, they knew when the baby wanted to be picked up or put down). The implication is that these are among the key attributes of effective parenting of infants.

Day Care and Attachment

Learning Objective

Summarize the research on the effects of day care on infants and children.

The impact of day care on attachment is a hotly debated topic these days. The crucial question is whether daily infant-mother separations might disrupt the attachment process. The issue is an important one, given that 58% of mothers with an infant under the age of 1 work outside the home (U.S. Bureau of the Census, 1994). Research by Jay Belsky (1988, 1990b, 1992) suggests that babies who receive nonmaternal care for more than 20 hours per week have an increased risk of developing insecure attachments to their mothers. Belsky's findings have raised many eyebrows, but they need to be put in perspective. First, the data suggest that the proportion of day-care infants who exhibit insecure attachment is only slightly higher than the norm in American society and even lower than the norm in some other societies (Lamb, Sternberg, & Prodromidis, 1992). Second, many studies have found that maternal employment is not harmful to children (Demo, 1992), and some studies have even found that day care can have beneficial effects on youngsters' intellectual and social development (Andersson, 1992; Caldwell, 1993). Third, the effects of day care appear to depend on the quality of the care provided. Negative effects seem minimal and may even be outweighed by positive effects when children are cared for in spacious, well-equipped, adequately staffed facilities that provide lots of individual attention and carefully planned activities (Howes, Phillips, & Whitebrook, 1992; Scarr et al., 1993).

Dimensions of Child-Rearing

Learning Objective

Describe Baumrind's parenting styles and the effects of these styles on children's development.

As children move from infancy into toddlerhood, the role of parenting broadens. The manner in which parents react to a child's actions communicates their standards of appropriate and inappropriate behavior. Parents fulfill this role with varying degrees of conscious awareness.

Two major dimensions underlie parenting behavior (Maccoby & Martin, 1983). The first, and most important, is *parental acceptance*. Although most parents are at least moderately accepting of their children, some are indifferent or even hostile and rejecting. Parental acceptance and warmth appear to influence the degree to which children internalize the behavioral standards of their parents (Greenberger & Goldberg, 1989). Children whose parents hold them in high regard are likely to incorporate parental values into their own personalities. This should enable them to exercise self-control and to behave appropriately even when the parents are not present. In contrast, children whose parents show less acceptance may fail to internalize their parents' values and tend to be less self-controlled. They may comply with parents' demands in the parents' presence (perhaps out of fear of punishment), but misbehave on their own.

The second dimension of parenting behavior is *parental control*. This concerns the degree of strictness of parental standards. For example, a parent who is moderately controlling sets high performance standards and expects increasingly mature behavior. A parent who is uncontrolling expects little of the child. The absence of control is related to high levels of aggression and maladjustment. Too strict and punitive control is associated negatively with moral development and also leads to rebellion in adolescents (Lloyd, 1985).

Figure 11.8
Baumrind's parenting styles
Four parenting styles result from the interactions of parental acceptance and parental control. (Adapted from Baumrind, 1971)

		Parental acceptance	
		Low	*High*
Parental control	**High**	Authoritarian (low acceptance, high control)	Authoritative (high acceptance, high control)
	Low	Neglectful (low acceptance, low control)	Permissive (high acceptance, low control)

Diana Baumrind

Diana Baumrind (1967, 1971, 1978) looked at specific parenting styles as interactions between the two dimensions of acceptance and control. In addition, she was interested in the effects of these parenting styles on children's social and intellectual competence. In her initial study, Baumrind observed a sample of preschool children and their parents and rated both groups on a number of dimensions. Additional data were obtained through interviews with the parents. Baumrind was able to identify four distinct "parenting styles": authoritarian, permissive, authoritative, and neglectful (see Figure 11.8), although she reported results on only the first three of these styles.

Authoritarian parents (low acceptance, high control) are highly demanding and controlling and use physical punishment or the threat of it with their children. By virtue of their higher status, they issue commands that are to be obeyed without question ("Do it because I said so"). Such parents rigidly maintain tight control even as their children mature. They also tend to be somewhat emotionally distant and may also be rejecting.

Permissive parents (high acceptance, low control) make few or no demands of their children. They allow children free expression of impulses and set few limits on appropriate behavior. Permissive parents are responsive and warmly accepting and indulge their children's desires.

Authoritative parents (high acceptance, high control) set high goals for their children but are also very accepting of their children and responsive to their needs. They encourage verbal give-and-take and allow their children to question parental requests. They also provide age-appropriate explanations that emphasize the consequences of "good" and "bad" behavior. Authoritative parents maintain firm control but also take into account each child's unique and changing needs. They are willing to negotiate with their children, setting new and less restrictive limits when appropriate, particularly as children mature.

Effects of Parenting Styles

Baumrind found that these parenting styles were associated with different clusters of traits in children, as summarized in Figure 11.9. The children of authoritarian parents tended to be moody, fearful, resentful, irritable, and unfriendly. Children of permissive parents tended to be rebellious, undisciplined, impulsive, aggressive, and domineering. Authoritative parenting, in contrast, was associated with more positive outcomes. The children of authoritative parents tended to be self-reliant, self-disciplined, cooperative, friendly, and intellectually curious.

Of course, these data are correlational and they do *not* establish that parenting style was the *cause* of the children's traits. The direction of influence probably goes both ways. For instance, parents may become increasingly authoritarian *in response to* their child's increasing resentment and irritability. Even so, Baumrind's results imply that authoritative parenting is most likely to foster social and cognitive competence in children.

Parenting Styles and Children's Traits

	Parenting style		
	Authoritative	Authoritarian	Permissive
Children's behavioral profile	Energetic-friendly	Conflicted-irritable	Impulsive-aggressive
	Self-reliant	Fearful, apprehensive	Rebellious
	Self-controlled	Moody, unhappy	Low in self-reliance and self-control
	Cheerful and friendly	Easily annoyed	Impulsive
	Copes well with stress	Passively hostile	Aggressive
	Cooperative with adults	Vulnerable to stress	Domineering
	Curious	Aimless	Aimless
	Purposive	Sulky, unfriendly	Low in achievement
	Achievement-oriented		

Figure 11.9
Baumrind's findings on parenting style and children's traits
Diana Baumrind has studied three styles of parenting and their relations to children's social and intellectual competence. As you can see, authoritative parenting is associated with the most desirable outcomes. (Summary adapted from Schaffer, 1989)

What happened when these children got older? Baumrind made follow-up observations of her subjects when they were 8 to 9 years old. She found that the children of authoritative parents were still the highest in both social and cognitive competence. This was especially true for the girls.

Baumrind (1978) points out that authoritative parents make adjustments for a child's increasing age and maturity. As their children get older, authoritative parents set increasingly high standards of behavior—high enough to encourage the child to "try," but not so high that the child is doomed to fail. These parents also take into account the child's age when they explain and enforce these standards.

Issues in Rearing Adolescents

Learning Objective

Discuss issues related to the effective parenting of adolescents.

Parent-adolescent relations generally are not as bitter or contentious as widely assumed, but conflicts over values are common and power struggles frequently ensue (Silverberg, Tennenbaum, & Jacob, 1992). As noted earlier, parents overwhelmingly rate adolescence as the most difficult stage of child-rearing (Gecas & Seff, 1990). Adolescents' emerging cognitive abilities enable them to question parental values and to formulate a personal philosophy to guide their own behavior. One of the undercurrents in parent-adolescent relationships is the fact that the balance of power between parent and child is shifting. Younger children accept their parents' power as a legitimate source of authority, especially if they have a warm relationship. The increasing autonomy of adolescents, however, requires a more equal parent-child relationship. While this is a necessary step on the road to autonomous adulthood, negotiating these shifts in power can sometimes be difficult.

Authoritarian parents who are unwilling to relinquish their control promote hostility and rebellion in their adolescent children. Permissive parents, who never exercised control over their children, may find themselves faced with adolescents whose behavior is completely out of hand. Authoritative parents who are willing to respond to their teenagers' input are most likely to avoid such turmoil (Baumrind, 1978). As Baumrind continues to follow her subjects, she expects to find that effective parenting of adolescents involves increasing parental responsiveness and decreasing parental demandingness (Baumrind, 1989).

Toward Effective Parenting

Learning Objective

List five suggestions for more effective parenting.

Are there some "basic rules" for effective parenting? We offer five key principles. Of course, it's essential to tailor these suggestions to the age and developmental level of a specific child. (For additional perspectives, see Figure 11.10, which lists ten of the best books on parenting.)

1. *Set high, but reasonable standards.* Children should be expected to behave in a socially appropriate manner for their age and to do as well as they can in school and in other activities. Parents who don't expect much from their children are teaching them not to expect much from themselves.

2. *Stay alert for "good" behavior and reward it.* Most parents pay attention to children when they are misbehaving and ignore them when they're being good. This is backward! Develop the habit of praising good behavior so a child knows what you want.

3. *Explain your reasons when you ask a child to do something.* Don't assume that a child can read your mind. Explaining the purpose of a request can transform what might appear to be an arbitrary request into a reasonable one. It also encourages self-control in a child.

4. *Encourage children to take the perspective of others.* Talk to children about the effects of their behavior on others ("How would you feel if Mary did that to *you*?"). This role-playing approach fosters moral development and empathy in children.

Figure 11.10
Top-rated self-help books on parenting
Based on a national survey of over 500 clinical and counseling psychologists, Santrock, Minnet, and Campbell (1994) compiled a list of the 25 most highly recommended self-help books. The ten books listed here deal with parenting or children. The other 15 self-help books, which deal with a variety of topics, are listed in Chapter 1.

Top-Rated Self-Help Books

Infants and Mothers
by T. Barry Brazelton

What Every Baby Knows
by T. Barry Brazelton

Dr. Spock's Baby and Child Care
by Benjamin Spock and Michael Rothenberg

To Listen to a Child
by T. Barry Brazelton

The Boys and Girls Book About Divorce
by Richard Gardner

Toddlers and Parents
by T. Barry Brazelton

Between Parent and Teenager
by Haim Ginott

The First Three Years of Life
by Burton White

Between Parent and Child
by Haim Ginott

Children: The Challenge
by Rudolph Dreikurs

5. *Enforce rules consistently.* Children need to have a clear idea about what is expected of them and to know that there will be consequences when they fail to meet your standards. This practice also fosters self-control in children.

Parents often wonder how punishment can be used more effectively in disciplinary efforts. In the next section, we'll elaborate on the principles of effective punishment.

Using Punishment Effectively

Learning Objective

List five suggestions for the effective use of punishment.

To use punishment effectively, parents should use it less often. This is because punishment often has unintended, negative side effects (Newsom, Favell, & Rincover, 1983; Van Houten, 1983). One of these side effects is that punishment often triggers *strong, negative emotional responses*, including fear, anxiety, anger, and resentment. These emotional reactions can create a variety of problems, including hostility toward parents. A second side effect is that heavy punishment can result in the *general suppression of behavioral activity*. In other words, children who are strongly and frequently punished can become withdrawn, inhibited, and less active than other children. Finally, studies show that *harsh physical punishment* often leads to an *increase in aggressive behavior* (Weiss et al., 1992). Children who are subjected to a lot of physical punishment tend to become more aggressive than the average youngster. The truckload of side effects associated with punishment make it less than ideal as a disciplinary procedure.

Although parents probably overuse punishment as a means of behavioral control, it does have a role to play in disciplinary efforts. The following guidelines summarize research evidence on how to make punishment effective while minimizing its side effects (Berkowitz, 1993).

1. *Punishment should be swift.* A delay in delivering punishment undermines its impact. Saying "Wait until your father (or mother) gets home . . ." is a fundamental mistake in the use of punishment. (This also unfairly sets up the other parent as the "heavy.") Quick punishment highlights the connection between the prohibited behavior and its negative outcome.

2. *Punishment should be consistent.* If you want to eliminate an undesirable behavior, you should punish it each and every time it occurs. When parents are inconsistent about punishing a particular behavior, they only create confusion in the child.

3. *Punishment should be explained.* When children are punished, the reason for their punishment should be explained as fully as possible, given the constraints of their age. The more children understand the reason why they are punished, the more effective the punishment tends to be. These explanations, characteristic of the authoritative style, also foster the development of self-control.

4. *Punishment should not damage the child's self-esteem.* To be effective, punishment should get across the message that it is the *behavior* that is undesirable, not the child. Unduly harsh physical punishment, derogatory accusations, and other hurtful words erode the child's self-esteem.

5. *The parent should point out alternative, positive ways for the child to behave and reinforce these actions.* One shortcoming of punishment is that it only tells a child what *not* to do. A better strategy is to punish an undesirable response *and* reward a positive alternative behavior. Children usually engage in undesirable behavior for a purpose. The parent should suggest another response that serves the same purpose and reward the child for doing it. For example, many troublesome behaviors exhibited by children are primarily attention-seeking devices. Punishment of these responses will be more effective if the parent can provide a child with more acceptable ways to gain attention.

Key Ideas

The Transition of Adolescence
• During pubescence, the adolescent growth spurt takes place and secondary sex characteristics develop. During puberty, which begins several years later, the primary sex characteristics mature. The onset of puberty marks the beginning of adolescence. Girls typically mature two years earlier than boys. Boys who mature late and girls who mature early may find puberty particularly stressful. During adolescence, cognitive changes also occur. These include developing the ability to think logically about hypothetical possibilities and abstract concepts.

• In the realm of personality, adolescents must develop a clear sense of identity and cope with intensified gender-role expectations. Some theorists assert that adolescence is a period of turmoil; however, research does not support this view. For this reason, careful attention should be paid to youth who display symptoms of serious problems such as depression, suicidal behavior, drug and alcohol abuse, and chronic delinquency. Suicide among adolescents has been increasing, but fewer than 1% of young people actually take their lives. Social isolation seems to increase the emotional impact of personal problems and often precipitates suicide attempts.

The Expanse of Adulthood
• Erikson's theory of personality development focuses on psychosocial crises in each of eight successive stages, centering on transitions in social relations. In adulthood, these crises are intimacy vs. isolation, generativity vs. stagnation, and integrity vs. despair.

• During early adulthood, individuals make more major role changes than in any other developmental stage. These typically include leaving one's family, entering the workplace and developing one's career, finding a mate, having and rearing children, and adjusting to family life.

• In middle adulthood, people must come to terms with the fact that their bodies are aging. In addition, they must deal with transitions in the parental role as children mature and leave home. Coping with the "empty nest" seems to be less of a problem than popular wisdom suggests. Workers at midlife seem to fall into one of two paths: the stable career pattern or the changing careers pattern. Very few individuals seem to experience a midlife crisis. Older adults must adjust to retirement, adapt to changes in their social networks, cope with health problems, and confront death.

Aging: A Gradual Process
• Physical development during adulthood leads to many obvious changes in physical appearance and sensory acuity. After age 30 there is a steady loss of active brain cells; however, this loss has not been clearly related to reductions in cognitive functioning. Similarly, hormonal changes appear to be only modestly related to midlife distress or declining sexual activity. Unfortunately, health does tend to decline with increasing age for a variety of reasons. Engaging in regular exercise and eating a healthful diet can help maintain health.

• Intelligence seems to remain fairly stable during most of adulthood. Memory processes probably deteriorate less than believed. Attentional capacity, speed of learning, and success in problem solving all tend to decline slightly during old age. However, most people remain capable of sound intellectual functioning in their later years. The adult personality seems to be characterized by both stability and change.

Death and Dying
• Attitudes about death vary from one culture to another. Attitudes in Western culture are characterized by negativism, avoidance, and fear. Early research on the process of dying by Kübler-Ross indicated that individuals progress through a sequence of five stages. Later research has called into question the idea that people's reactions to dying follow such a straightforward path.

• There is wide variation between and within cultures regarding how death is acknowledged. John Bowlby theorized that grieving individuals go through a four-stage process. Later research has revealed several different patterns of grieving, calling into question traditional views of the process of mourning.

Application: Becoming an Effective Parent
• Attachment between infants and their primary caregivers develops very early in life. According to Mary Ainsworth, infants develop one of three different attachment styles with their caregivers: secure, anxious-ambivalent, and avoidant. Of Diana Baumrind's four parenting styles, authoritative parenting is associated with the most positive outcomes in children. Although rearing adolescents presents parents with some special challenges, parent-adolescent relations are not nearly as problematic as many suppose. Effective parenting involves the use of five key principles, as well as knowing how to use punishment effectively.

Key Terms

Bereavement
Death system
Egocentrism
Menarche
Menopause
Mourning
Neurons
Primary sex characteristics
Puberty
Pubescence
Secondary sex characteristics
Senile dementia
Social clock

Key People

Mary Ainsworth
Diana Baumrind
John Bowlby
David Elkind
Erik Erikson
Elisabeth Kübler-Ross

363

Work and Career Development

"The [telephone] dictates. This crummy little machine with buttons on it—you've just got to answer it. . . . Your job doesn't mean anything. Because you're just a little machine. A monkey could do what I do. . . .

"Until recently, I'd cry in the morning. I didn't want to get up. I'd dread Fridays because Monday was always looming over me. Another five days ahead of me. . . .

"I'll be at home and the telephone will ring and I get nervous. It reminds me of the telephone at work."

—A receptionist quoted in *Working* (Terkel, 1974)

"Piano tuning is not really business. It's a dedication. There's such a thing as piano tuning, piano rebuilding, and antique restoration. There's such a thing as scale designing and engineering, to produce the highest sound quality possible. I'm in all of this and I enjoy every second of it. . . . I don't see any possibility of separating my life from my work. . . . There seems something mystic about music, about piano tuning. There's so much beauty comes out of music. There's so much beauty comes out of piano tuning."

—A piano tuner quoted in *Working* (Terkel, 1974)

*T*hese quotations attest to the pivotal role of work in adult life. They speak poignantly of the tremendous impact, either positive or negative, that jobs can have on the quality of people's lives. Perhaps the significant role of work shouldn't be so surprising, given that many people's sense of identity is determined by the nature of their work. When adults meet for the first time, their initial "How do you do?" is often followed by the more crucial question, "What do you do for a living?" The answer may convey information not only about one's occupation but also about one's social status, lifestyle, personality, interests, and aptitudes.

Because work plays such an important role in life, psychologists take a great interest in it. Those who study human behavior in work settings are *industrial/organizational psychologists.* Among other things, they examine the workplace and its effects on worker productivity and psychological adjustment, and they study job stress and its effects. They are also becoming increasingly interested in how individuals balance work, family life, and leisure activities.

In this chapter, we'll survey some important background issues related to the world of work and review key factors in job satisfaction. Then we'll explore several models of career development and some important considerations in choosing a career. Next, we'll turn to the important issue of balancing work, relationships, and leisure. Finally we'll discuss some hazards in the workplace. In the Application, we'll offer some concrete suggestions for enhancing your chances of landing a desirable job.

Perspectives on Work

Before we plunge into to the world of work, let's take a look at several important background issues: contemporary trends in the workplace, the relationship between education and earnings, and diversity in the workforce.

Contemporary Trends

We'll define **work as an activity that produces something of value for others.** For some people, work is just a way to earn a living; for others, work is a way of life. For both types of workers, the nature of work is undergoing dramatic changes. Individuals need to be aware of trends in the workplace that can affect their later job prospects. We'll highlight five work-related trends you should know about.

1. *Temporary employment is increasing.* In 1988, temporary workers represented about 24% of the labor force; by the year 2000, some experts predict that the number of temporary workers will grow to 50% (Morrow, 1993). Corporations are

The growth of technology is significantly changing the nature of work, with both positive and negative effects.

downsizing and restructuring to cope with the changing economy and to be globally competitive. In doing so, they are eliminating large numbers of permanent jobs and doling out the work to temporary or contingent employees—clerical workers as well as professionals. By reducing the number of core (regular) workers, companies are able to cut dramatically their expenditures on payroll, health insurance, and pension plans, since temporary employees don't typically receive such benefits. A leaner workforce also enables organizations to respond quickly to fast-changing markets. Many professionals thrive on temporary work; they have freedom, flexibility, and high incomes. Those who want only part-time work like the increased opportunities for contingent employment. The majority of temporary workers, however are struggling to survive, with multiple jobs, low wages, erratic schedules, no benefits, and high anxiety (Morrow, 1993). If this trend continues, it will mean an almost unimaginable transformation of the relationship between Americans and their jobs (Kennedy & Laramore, 1993; Morrow, 1993).

2. *More and more jobs will be in the service sector.* The United States, like other industrialized nations, is shifting away from a manufacturing or "goods-producing" economy to a service-producing one (Kennedy & Laramore, 1993). Whereas the bulk of yesterday's jobs were in manufacturing, mining, construction, and agriculture, the jobs of today and tomorrow will be in service, government, finance, trade, and transportation. Figure 12.1 lists 26 specific occupations expected to grow the most between now and 2005.

3. *Dual-earner couples are becoming the norm.* Increasing numbers of women are entering the workforce, and these increases hold even for women with very young children. In 1975 only 31% of women with children under the age of 3 were employed outside the home. By 1994, this number had practically doubled to almost 60% (U.S. Bureau of the Census, 1995). These changes have implications not only for work and family life but also for men's and women's roles.

4. *Technological advances are changing the nature of work.* Computers have dramatically transformed the workplace. From the worker's point of view, these changes are having both positive and negative effects. On the negative side, computers have been used to automate many jobs, reducing the need for workers. On the positive side, computer technology enables workers to communicate with others in distant offices and while traveling. This same technology also makes it possible for employees to work at home as well as at the office. Because work-related technology changes rapidly, lifelong learning and training will become essential for employees. Workers who have "learned how to learn" will be able to keep pace with the rapidly changing workplace and will be highly valued. Those who cannot will be left behind.

**Figure 12.1
High growth occupations for the 21st century**
According to Kennedy and Laramore (1993), these 26 occupations are expected to grow the most in the *number of job openings* between now and the year 2005. Although some other occupations may grow at a more rapid rate, more opportunities will be available in the listed areas because they employ very large numbers of people.

Twenty-Six King-Size Occupations	
Retail salespeople	Registered nurses
Cashiers	General office clerks
Truck drivers	General managers
Janitors	Nursing aides
Food workers	High school teachers
Receptionists	Computer systems analysts
Child-care workers	Gardeners
Accountants	Computer programmers
Elementary teachers	Guards
Teacher aides	Licensed practical nurses
Clerical supervisors	Home health aides
Restaurant cooks	Maintenance repairers
Secretaries	Lawyers

5. *The boundaries between work and home are becoming blurred.* Computer technology is one force driving this change, because people can work at home and stay in touch with the office. At the same time, a traditional home function has moved to the office, with increasing numbers of companies providing on-site day care. This development is largely a response to increases in the number of dual-earner households and in the number of single-parent families. The availability of quality on-site daycare is obviously a big "draw" to these workers because it allows parents to interact with their children during the day.

Education and Earnings

Learning Objective

Explain the importance of education to work, and describe the relationship between education and salary.

Although a college education is certainly not a requirement for everyone, the ability to read, write, and do basic mathematical computations is essential to be competitive in the workplace. Ironically, as the number of years of education completed by the average American have increased, so have the problems of illiteracy and innumeracy. For example, in a national survey of 3600 young people aged 21–25 conducted by the Educational Testing Service, it was found that only 34% of whites, 20% of Hispanics, and 8% of African Americans could calculate the tip and change for a two-item restaurant meal (Hamilton, 1988). Hence, it is not surprising that companies are having difficulty recruiting qualified entry-level workers. Consider two chilling examples of what can happen when workers can't do basic math or read (Kennedy & Laramore, 1993): (1) an insurance clerk paid $2200.00 on a dental claim that should have been only $22.00 (she didn't understand decimals); (2) a plant worker nearly killed several co-workers by fitting the wrong heavy piece of machinery onto a machine (he couldn't read). To prevent these costly errors, many organizations are having to invest in expensive programs to educate new workers in the basic skills they should have learned in school (Hamilton, 1988).

As new jobs develop, they will require higher education and skill levels than those jobs that technology has rendered obsolete (K. Miller, 1989). Clearly, then, a good basic education will enhance a person's prospects for existing and future jobs. In addition, an essential complement to a good basic education is computer literacy (Broida, 1995). The more education a person has, the higher their income (see Figure 12.2). This relationship between level of education and salary holds for both males and females. However, this figure also shows that men are paid from approximately $6,000 to $22,000 more than women and that this gender gap increases as education increases.

Figure 12.2
Education and income
The median incomes of year-round, full-time workers ages 25 and over, by gender and educational attainment, are shown here for 1994. As you can see, the more education people have, the higher their income tends to be. However, women earn less than men with comparable education. (Data from U.S. Bureau of the Census, 1995)

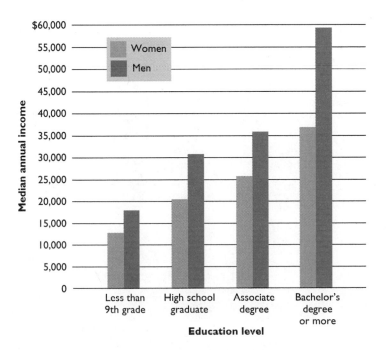

Diversity in the Workforce

Learning Objective

Summarize the important demographic changes that are transforming the workforce and some of the problems that women and minorities face in the workplace today.

The *labor force* consists of all those who are employed as well as those who are currently unemployed but looking for work. In this section, we'll examine some key characteristics of workers today and consider how women and other minorities fare in the workplace.

Demographic Changes

In 1994, the labor force included about 83% of males between the ages of 20 and 24 and about 92% of males between 24 and 54 (U.S. Bureau of the Census, 1995). Comparable rates for females were 71% (ages 20–24) and 75% (ages 24–54). Participation rates decline after age 55 for both genders and show an even sharper drop-off after age 65. In the last several decades, the labor force participation rates for males have remained largely stable, while the participation rates for females have risen steadily (see Figure 12.3).

Experts predict that a third of the new entrants to the workforce between now and the year 2000 will be minority group members (Johnston & Packer, 1987). More than half of these new workers will have been reared in families at or below the poverty level (Horowitz & O'Brien, 1989). Because personal income typically determines the quality of schools one attends, many of these new workers will not have had the benefit of an adequate education. Consequently, this group will be at a disadvantage when it comes to competing for the better jobs, as we'll see in the next section.

The increasingly diverse workforce presents challenges to both organizations and workers. There are important cultural differences in managing time and people, in identification with work, and in making decisions (Matsumoto, 1996). These differences can contribute to conflict. To minimize conflict and to maintain productivity and satisfaction, managers need to be knowledgeable about the values and needs of these new workers. Similarly, employees must be willing to learn to work comfortably with those who come from different backgrounds.

Today's Workplace for Women and Minorities

Economic and social changes in recent decades have resulted in a dramatic upsurge in the number of women and minorities in the workplace. Is today's workplace essentially the same for these groups as it is for white men? In many respects, the answer appears to be "no." Although job discrimination on the basis of race and gender has been illegal for more than 25 years, women and minority group mem-

Figure 12.3
Women in the workforce
The percentage of adult women (ages 20–64) who work outside the home has been increasing throughout the century. The rate of increase began to escalate in the 1950s. Experts estimate that 80% of adult women will be in the workforce by the year 2000. (From Matthews & Rodin, 1989)

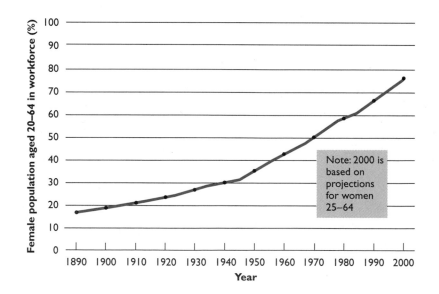

Today's workforce is becoming increasingly diverse.

bers continue to face subtle obstacles to occupational success. Foremost among these is *job segregation*. Jobs tend to be typed by gender and race (Amott & Matthaei, 1991; Green & Russo, 1993). Consider the position of railroad porter or skycap—most such jobs are held by African American males. Most white women and people of color have been concentrated in low-paying jobs with little opportunity for advancement or increase in salary. Still, both African American and Hispanic women are more likely to work in blue-collar jobs than white women are (National Committee on Pay Equity, 1987). Employees in female-dominated fields typically earn less than employees in male-dominated fields, even when the jobs require similar levels of training, skill, and responsibility (Betz, 1993).

Nonetheless, more women and minorities are entering higher-status occupations, even if at a low rate. Unfortunately, they still face discrimination because they are frequently *passed over for promotion* in favor of white men (Morrison & Von Glinow, 1990). This seems to be a problem especially at the higher levels of management. For example, less than 3% of the corporate officers of Fortune 500 companies are female (Gilbert, 1993). There appears to be a "glass ceiling" that prevents most women and ethnic minorities from advancing beyond middle-management positions (see Figure 12.4).

When there is only one woman or minority person in an office, that person becomes **a *token*—or a symbol of all the members of that group.** As we discussed in Chapter 6, tokens are more distinctive than members of the dominant majority. Because these individuals stand out, their actions are subject to intense scrutiny, stereotyping, and judgments. That is, if a white male makes a mistake, it is explained as an *individual* problem. When a token woman or minority person

Figure 12.4
The glass ceiling for women and minorities
According to a survey of Fortune 1000 corporations, women and minorities are underrepresented in management and executive positions. (Data from U.S. Department of Labor, 1992).

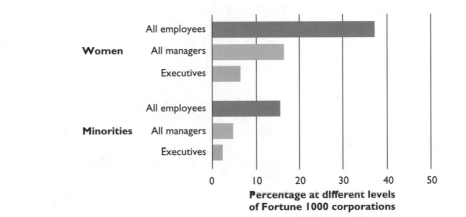

makes a mistake, it is seen as evidence that *all* members of that group are incompetent. Hence, tokens experience a lot of *performance pressure*. Interestingly, if tokens are perceived as being "too successful," they may be labeled "workaholics" or accused of trying to "show up" members of the dominant majority. These unfavorable perceptions may be reflected in performance appraisals. The performance of successful white men is less likely to be interpreted in these negative ways.

Another way the world of work is different for women and minorities is that they have *fewer opportunities to observe and emulate same-gender or same-group role models* who occupy professional positions (Betz, 1993; Fitzgerald & Crites, 1980). Also, women and members of minority groups have a *harder time finding a mentor* in the workplace than do men (Betz, 1993; Yoder et al., 1985). Finally, *sexual harassment*, a topic we'll take up later, is much more likely to be a problem for women in the workplace than it is for men.

In sum, women and minority individuals must contend with discrimination on the job in a number of forms. To escape these negative experiences in the workplace, many women are leaving organizations to start their own businesses (Morrison & Von Glinow, 1990).

Understanding Job Satisfaction

In making a career choice, in a sense people make a prediction about the future. They predict that the occupation they choose will lead to success and provide them with satisfaction. That is, they hope not only to do well in their chosen field but to *enjoy* it as well. **Job satisfaction refers to the favorability or unfavorability of people's attitudes toward their jobs.** Job satisfaction is related to employees' mental and physical health (Holt, 1982; Warr, 1987). Furthermore, job satisfaction is a significant issue for employers, because it can affect workers' performance, productivity, absenteeism, and tendency to look for another job (Carsten & Spector, 1987; Miller & Monge, 1986).

Measuring Job Satisfaction

Learning Objective

Explain why assessing job satisfaction is complicated.

Before describing the factors associated with job satisfaction, we want to stress the complexity of this issue. First, job satisfaction is a multidimensional concept that is not easily measured. A job has many aspects. A person might be satisfied with one aspect, such as promotion opportunities, and dissatisfied with another, such as job security.

Second, job satisfaction is a highly personal matter that depends on more than just the nature of one's work. Two people working at the same job may have very different levels of satisfaction. Your job satisfaction depends on your subjective *perception* of your working conditions. For example, imagine that your company institutes a new policy in which each worker will now perform a greater variety of tasks. If you view this change as an opportunity to broaden your skills and alleviate boredom, your job satisfaction will increase. But if you attribute this change to the company's desire to increase your duties without increasing your pay, your job satisfaction will probably decline.

To some extent, the tendency to feel satisfied with work may be a personality trait that transcends specific job characteristics. In one study, the job satisfaction of 5000 men was measured over a period of five years (Staw & Ross, 1985). Surprisingly, individuals' job satisfaction tended to remain very stable over this span of time, despite changes in their assignments, responsibilities, employers, and occupations.

As you can see, the assessment of job satisfaction is a complicated matter. Small wonder, then, that researchers have conducted well over 3000 studies on this issue (Locke, 1983). Although their findings are complex, they have isolated some factors that are related to job satisfaction for most people. We'll look at these factors next.

Ingredients of Job Satisfaction

Learning Objective

List the major ingredients of job satisfaction.

When you make career decisions, it's important to be aware of the key ingredients of job satisfaction. We'll highlight some of the more important factors in this section.

Meaningfulness

Meaningfulness as it relates to work is rather difficult to define. Generally, when people talk about their work being meaningful, they seem concerned with whether it gives them a sense of real accomplishment, which often translates into making a difference in the lives of others (London & Strumpf, 1986). The results of a Louis Harris Poll (1987) suggest that "meaningfulness" is a key component of work: 48% of the respondents rated "gives feeling of real accomplishment" as the "most important" aspect of work.

Challenge and Variety

Many people need challenge in their jobs. When asked to rate the importance of various aspects of their jobs, the respondents in a 1991 Gallup Poll ranked "interesting work" and "chance to learn new skills" second and fourth, respectively (see Figure 12.5). A closely related consideration is the variety of work that a job provides. People tend to find repetitive, assembly-line work boring and dissatisfying. One way companies can increase employee satisfaction is by restructuring jobs so that each worker is allowed to perform a variety of what would otherwise be routine tasks.

The issue of challenging work has taken on new significance since the early 1970s, when the sizable baby boom cohort began to enter the workforce. Since then, there has been an oversupply of professional talent. This has slowed the absorption of new workers into the labor force and increased the selectivity of employers. Many people have found that their college diplomas haven't won them the jobs they were trained for (Church, 1993), and many have found themselves underemployed. *Underemployment* **is settling for a job that does not fully utilize one's skills, abilities, and training.** This problem declined during the 1980s, because of economic expansion, but it has arisen again in the 1990s because of the dramatic changes in the economy. Between now and 2005, experts estimate that 30% of new college graduates will be underemployed (Church, 1993). Thus, lack of challenge may contribute to job dissatisfaction among these workers.

Figure 12.5
Workers' evaluation of job characteristics
A 1991 Gallup Poll asked workers to rate the importance of various aspects of their jobs and to rate their level of satisfaction with these aspects of their present jobs. Workers rated good health insurance and job security very high, no doubt reflecting concerns about corporate downsizing and layoffs. (Data from Hugick & Leonard, 1991a; based on Rathus & Nevid, 1995)

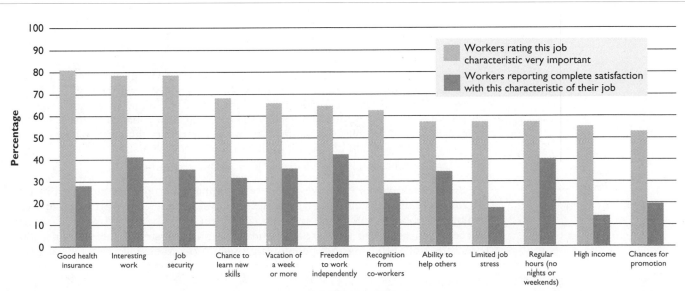

Legend: Workers rating this job characteristic very important / Workers reporting complete satisfaction with this characteristic of their job

Job characteristics

Autonomy

Most people prefer to have a sense of freedom while on the job (London & Strumpf, 1986). For example, respondents in the 1991 Gallup Poll ranked "freedom to work independently" as sixth in importance (see Figure 12.5). They also want to have some control over the decisions that will affect them on the job: how they perform their work, how to improve a product or the manufacture of it, and how to improve the work environment. One way organizations can increase employees' sense of autonomy is to involve them in decision making by developing Quality of Work Life programs (Offermann & Gowing, 1990). In these programs, workers at all levels are given maximum responsibility for how they do their jobs (Levering, 1988).

Friendship and Recognition

In Chapter 8, we discussed the prominent role that friendships play in people's lives. For many people, friendship circles emerge largely out of interactions at work. Consequently, it should come as no surprise that the social aspects of a job are a prime determinant of job satisfaction. When interpersonal relationships at work are pleasant, people are more likely to be content with their jobs.

Whether it is provided through pay raises, promotions, or praise, people crave recognition for their work. Most people need to have the value of their work validated by others, especially supervisors and co-workers. Many are quite willing to go beyond the minimum requirements of their jobs as long as their extra efforts are recognized and appreciated. In the absence of such feedback, they may feel undervalued and dissatisfied.

Good Pay

When workers are asked to rate the importance of various job features, they generally rank pay surprisingly low. For instance, in the 1991 Gallup Poll, "high income" was ranked only 11th in importance out of 12 items (see Figure 12.5). However, the relatively low ratings of the importance of pay may be misleading. Although workers often rank pay low in importance, it tends to be a major source of complaints. This paradoxical finding suggests that people may be more concerned about pay than they would like to believe.

Pay, by the way, is one of those things that is evaluated on a relative basis. People are very sensitive to what *others* earn. Workers tend to be satisfied with their pay to the extent that they perceive it as *fair*. For most people, a fair salary is one that (1) compares favorably with that of other employees with similar training and seniority who work in the same field and (2) is commensurate with the company's ability to pay (Levering, 1988). No matter how much workers make, they may feel undercompensated if others are earning more or if their employers are making large profits that do not filter down to employees.

Security

> "I used to joke at lunch. I'd say, 'If anybody hears that layoffs are comin', do me a favor. Send in my name.' Then a funny thing happened. I got laid off. I couldn't believe it. . . . I felt like a kid who wet his pants. I was afraid to go home and tell my wife. The rest of the day, nobody talked to me. They looked at me like I had cancer. I tried to smile, but I wanted to puke. The end of the day, I didn't want to leave. I even thought about just working through the next shift."
>
> —A man quoted in *Psychology of Work Behavior* (Landy, 1989)

Being unemployed can have a devastating impact on one's psychological health. Job loss is related to temporary increases in physical illnesses, depression, anxiety, drinking problems, and family conflict (Hamilton et al., 1993; Voydanoff, 1990). Indeed, unemployment rates are a significant predictor of suicide rates (Boor, 1980). Thus, it is not surprising that people value security in their jobs (see Figure 12.5). Rankings of this factor vary with the strength of the economy. When economic times are good, security is sometimes ranked low in importance because employees begin to take it for granted. But job security becomes very important as soon as it is undermined, as the quotation illustrates.

Models of Career Development

Psychologists have long been interested in understanding how individuals make decisions about career choices. Some theorists in this area approach the issue from a developmental (stage) perspective. Others take a nondevelopmental view. We'll examine a representative model from each orientation.

Trait Measurement and Matching Models

Learning Objective

Summarize Holland's hexagonal model of career development.

The nondevelopmental view asserts that career choice is related to an individual's personality traits. These traits, which are assumed to be relatively stable over time, are measured by psychological tests. In turn, the test results are used to match individuals to the jobs for which their personalities are best suited. The most influential model of this type has been developed by John Holland (1973, 1985). According to Holland, people have stereotypic views of the work environments associated with various occupations, and they search for a work environment that will fit their personality. Holland has identified six broad personality types, called *personal orientations*, and six matching *work environments*. For obvious reasons, Holland's approach is often called the *hexagonal model*. Here are the six orientations and their optimal work environments:

- *Realistic* people describe themselves as good at mechanical tasks and weak in social skills. They prefer jobs with tasks that are physical or mechanical and clearly defined, such as farming, auto mechanics, and engineering. They tend to avoid tasks that involve social skills, abstract thinking, subjectivity, or verbal skills.
- *Investigative* people enjoy abstract thinking and logical analysis, preferring understanding to action. They like working with ideas rather than with things or people. Investigative individuals can often be found working in research laboratories or libraries.
- *Artistic* people see themselves as imaginative and independent. They tend to be impulsive and creative and are socially aloof. These individuals dislike structured tasks, preferring instead to rely on their subjective impressions in dealing with the environment. They have a high need for emotional expression and often seek careers in art, music, or drama.
- *Social* people describe themselves as being understanding and wanting to help others. They prefer to interact with people, and they have the necessary social skills to do so comfortably. They typically have greater verbal ability than mathematical ability. Social types are often found in the helping professions, such as teaching, nursing, and social work.
- *Enterprising* people perceive themselves as happy, self-confident, sociable, and popular. They like to use their social skills to lead or persuade others. They prefer sales or supervisory positions, in which they can express these characteristics.
- *Conventional* people are conforming, systematic, and orderly. They typically have greater clerical and mathematical ability than verbal ability. They prefer working environments that are structured and predictable and may be well suited to occupations in the business world.

Holland has developed several tests to measure the six basic personal orientations. One of them, the Self-Directed Search (SDS), is actually a self-scoring test. Once individuals identify their personality type on the SDS, they can match it with various relevant occupations. Studies have shown that the SDS has helped students reduce career indecision and select occupations consistent with their personality traits (McGowan, 1977; Tay, Ward, & Hill, 1993). You can take a rough stab at cat-

Holland's Personal Orientations and Related Work Environments

Themes	Personal orientations	Work environments
Realistic	Values concrete and physical tasks. Perceives self as having mechanical skills and lacking social skills.	*Settings:* concrete, physical tasks requiring mechanical skills, persistence, and physical movement *Careers:* machine operator, truck driver, draftsperson, barber
Investigative	Wants to solve intellectual, scientific, and mathematical problems. Sees self as analytical, critical, curious, introspective, and methodical.	*Settings:* research laboratory, diagnostic medical case conference, work group of scientists *Careers:* marine biologist, computer programmer, clinical psychologist, architect, dentist
Artistic	Prefers unsystematic tasks or artistic projects: painting, writing, or drama. Perceives self as imaginative, expressive, and independent.	*Settings:* theater, concert hall, library, radio or TV studio *Careers:* sculptor, actor, designer, musician, author, editor
Social	Prefers educational, helping, and religious careers. Enjoys social involvement, church, music, reading, and dramatics. Is cooperative, friendly, helpful, insightful, persuasive, and responsible.	*Settings:* school and college classrooms, psychiatrist's office, religious meetings, mental institutions, recreational centers *Careers:* counselor, nurse, teacher, social worker, judge, minister, sociologist
Enterprising	Values political and economic achievements, supervision, and leadership. Enjoys leadership control, verbal expression, recognition, and power. Perceives self as extraverted, sociable, happy, assertive, popular, and self-confident.	*Settings:* courtroom, political rally, car sales room, real estate firm, advertising company *Careers:* realtor, politician, attorney, salesperson, manager
Conventional	Prefers orderly, systematic, concrete tasks with verbal and mathematical data. Sees self as conformist and having clerical and numerical skills.	*Settings:* bank, post office, file room, business office, Internal Revenue office *Careers:* banker, accountant, timekeeper, financial counselor, typist, receptionist

Figure 12.6
Overview of Holland's theory of vocational choice
According to John Holland, people can be divided into six personality types (personal orientations) that prefer different work environments. These connections between personality and vocational preferences are summarized here. (From Holland, 1985)

egorizing your own personal orientation by studying Figure 12.6. Look at the matching work environments to get some ideas for possible career options.

Holland's hexagonal model has prompted considerable research, and much of it supports his theory (Tracey & Rounds, 1993). Holland reports that people in occupations that are well matched to their personality are more satisfied with their jobs and are likely to remain in these jobs for a longer time than individuals who are not so well matched (Holland, 1985). Another study found that personal orientation was a much better predictor than other personal characteristics (age, gender, length of time on the job) of teachers' job satisfaction (Wiggins et al., 1983).

One of the assumptions of trait measurement and matching models is that occupational interests remain stable during adulthood. The research evidence is mixed on this question. On the positive side, one study found that the interests underlying career choices remain stable after about age 17 (Hansen & Campbell, 1985). It has also been found that when people change occupations, they frequently choose new jobs that correspond to the same personal orientation in Holland's model (Gottfredson, 1977). On the negative side, at least one study has found that accountants differed significantly in their needs and work attitudes at different life stages and also in the extent to which they fit Holland's conventional orientation (Adler & Aranya, 1984).

Developmental Models

Although the trait approach is useful, it fails to take into account the fact that people's interests, skills, motivations, aspirations, and situations change over time. In contrast, stage theories view occupational choice as a developmental process rather than a specific event (Crites, 1980; Osipow, 1987).

The most influential stage theory of career choice is one outlined by Donald Super (1957, 1985, 1988). He views occupational development as a process that unfolds gradually across most of the life span. This process begins in childhood and

Learning Objective

Summarize Super's five-stage model of career development.

ends with retirement. Super asserts that one's *self-concept* is the critical factor that governs this developmental process. According to him, decisions about work and career commitments reflect people's attempts to express their changing views of themselves. To map these changes, Super breaks the occupational life cycle into five major stages and a variety of substages (see Figure 12.7).

Growth Stage

The growth stage encompasses childhood, during which youngsters fantasize about exotic jobs they would enjoy. Generally, they imagine themselves as detectives, airplane pilots, and brain surgeons rather than plumbers, grocers, and bookkeepers. Until the very end of this period, youngsters are largely oblivious to realistic considerations such as the abilities or education required for specific jobs. Instead, they base their fantasies purely on their likes and dislikes.

Exploration Stage

Pressures from parents, teachers, and peers to develop a general career direction begin to intensify during high school. By the end of high school, individuals are expected to have narrowed a general career direction into a specific one. Whether through studying about it or through part-time work, a person tries to get a real taste of the projected occupation. During the later part of this stage, people typically attempt to enter the world of work on a full-time basis. Many individuals in this phase are still only tentatively committed to their chosen occupation. If their initial work experiences are gratifying, their commitment will be strengthened. However, if their first experiences are not rewarding, they may shift to another occupation, where they will continue the process of exploration.

Figure 12.7
Overview of Super's theory of vocational development
According to Donald Super, people go through five major stages (and a variety of substages) of vocational development over the life span. The approximate ages and key events for each stage are summarized here. (Adapted from Zaccaria, 1970)

Stages of Vocational Development

Stage	Approximate ages	Key events and transitions
Growth stage	**0–14**	**A period of general physical and mental growth**
Prevocational substage	0–3	No interest or concern with vocations
Fantasy substage	4–10	Fantasy is basis for vocational thinking
Interest substage	11–12	Vocational thought is based on individual's likes and dislikes
Capacity substage	13–14	Ability becomes the basis for vocational thought
Exploration stage	**15–24**	**General exploration of work**
Tentative substage	15–17	Needs, interests, capacities, values, and opportunities become bases for tentative occupational decisions
Transition substage	18–21	Reality increasingly becomes basis for vocational thought and action
Trial substage	22–24	First trial job is entered after the individual has made an initial vocational commitment
Establishment stage	**25–44**	**Individual seeks to enter a permanent occupation**
Trial substage	25–30	Period of some occupational change due to unsatisfactory choices
Stabilization substage	31–44	Period of stable work in a given occupational field
Maintenance stage	**45–65**	**Continuation in one's chosen occupation**
Decline stage	**65+**	**Adaptation to leaving workforce**
Deceleration substage	65–70	Period of declining vocational activity
Retirement substage	71+	A cessation of vocational activity

Establishment Stage

Vacillation continues to be moderately common during the first part of the establishment stage. For some people, doubts begin to surface for the first time as they reappraise the match between their personal attributes and their current position. Others simply carry earlier doubts into this stage. If a person's career choice turns out to be gratifying, however, he or she firmly commits to an occupation. With few exceptions, future job moves will take place *within* this occupational area. Having made a commitment, the person's task is now to demonstrate the ability to function effectively in the chosen occupation. To succeed, the individual must use previously acquired skills, learn new skills as necessary, and display flexibility in adapting to organizational changes.

Maintenance Stage

As the years go by, opportunities for further career advancement and occupational mobility decline. Around their mid-40s, many people cross into the maintenance stage, during which they worry more about *retaining* their achieved status than *improving* it. Rapidly changing technology may compel middle-aged employees to enhance and update their skills as they face competition from younger, more recently educated workers. The primary goal in this stage, however, is simply to protect the security, power, advantages, and perks that one has attained. With decreased emphasis on career advancement, many people shift energy and attention away from work concerns in favor of family concerns or leisure activities.

Decline Stage

Deceleration involves a decline in work activity during one's later years as retirement looms near. People redirect their energy and attention toward planning for this major transition. In his original formulation, which was based on research in the 1950s, Super projected that deceleration ought to begin around age 65. Since the 1970s, however, slowed economic growth and the entry of the large baby boom cohort into the workforce have combined to create an oversupply of skilled labor and professional talent. This social change has created pressures that promote early retirement. Because of these conditions, deceleration often begins earlier than Super initially indicated.

Retirement brings work activity to a halt. People approach this transition with highly varied attitudes. Many individuals look forward to it eagerly. Others approach it with apprehension, unsure about how they will occupy themselves and worried about their financial viability. Still others approach retirement with a combination of hopeful enthusiasm and anxious concern. Although concern about what lies ahead is understandable, many studies have shown that retirement has no adverse effect on overall health or life satisfaction (Smith, Patterson, & Grant, 1992). Although retirement may mean less income, it can also mean having more time to spend on hobbies, travel, and friends (George, Fillenbaum, & Palmore, 1984).

As a stage theorist, Super deserves credit for acknowledging that people follow different patterns in their career development. He identified several atypical patterns for both men and women that do not coincide with the conventional pattern we have described. In support of Super's model, it has been found that self-esteem and career maturity are positively correlated (Crook, Healy, & O'Shay, 1984). Also, recall the earlier-mentioned study reporting changes in accountants' personal orientations at different life stages (Adler & Aranya, 1984). On the other hand, a recent study of adolescents reported that identity status was a stronger predictor of career maturity than was self-esteem (Wallace-Broscious, Serafica, & Osipow, 1994).

Women's Career Development

Until fairly recently, most of the theories and research on career development have focused on *men's* careers. One reason for this is that relatively few women worked. Today, however, women can expect to spend about 30 years in the labor force (compared to 40 years for men) (U.S. Department of Labor, 1990). Once women began entering the workforce, it was simply taken for granted that the theories and concepts used to explain men's vocational development would apply equally well to women. However, Nancy Betz and other experts in this area say that men and women have different patterns of career development (Betz, 1993; Betz & Fitzgerald, 1987). Why might this be? For one thing, most women still subordinate their career goals to their husbands' goals (Unger & Crawford, 1992). If a married man wants or needs to move to another job, his wife typically follows him and takes the best job she can find in the new location. Hence, married women usually have less control over their careers than married men do.

Another reason women's career paths are different from men's is that women are more likely than men to interrupt their careers to concentrate on child-rearing or family crises. Historically, women's participation in the labor force has typically shown a sharp rise as women take their first jobs, then a sharp dip as they leave the labor force to concentrate on rearing children, and finally a second sharp rise when they return to work, usually after the children are grown. Interestingly, this pattern has been labeled the *M-curve*—both for its shape on the graph and for "mother" (Farley, 1980). However, as we've mentioned, more and more mothers are returning to work when their children are small. In fact, over 70% of working women return to the labor force within two years after their children are born (Hofferth & Phillips, 1987). As women's participation in the labor force increasingly resembles that of men, the M-curve is disappearing.

Still, many women do leave the labor force, even if for increasingly brief periods of time. This hiatus in employment is termed *labor force discontinuity*. Does labor force discontinuity pose any problems for women? Definitely. In fact, dropping out of the workforce is an important, but not the only, cause of the gender gap in salaries and employment status. Moreover, when women want to return to the workplace, they are unlikely to find the welcome mat out for any but entry-level positions (Treiman & Terrell, 1975). Studies show that women who do not have children remain in the labor force and have a typical pattern of career advancement, whereas women who have children usually drop out of the workforce and show downward mobility in their career paths (Betz, 1993; Betz & Fitzgerald, 1987). An implication of this finding is that economic hardship is likely if a married woman with children becomes a single parent. Changes in the family and the work setting are needed to accommodate the changing roles of women and men.

Important Considerations in Career Choice

One of your biggest decisions in life is choosing a career. The importance of this decision is enormous. It may determine whether you are employed or unemployed, financially secure or insecure, happy or unhappy. Given our rapidly advancing technology and the increased training and education required to break into most fields, it is more important than ever to choose thoughtfully. Along with being knowledgeable about the factors that promote job satisfaction, you need to have information about your personal characteristics and your job options. Let's review some important considerations to help you choose a career that's suitable for you.

General Principles

Learning Objective

List six general principles to keep in mind in choosing an occupation.

As you explore your personal characteristics and investigate career opportunities, keep the following points in mind:

1. *You have the potential for success in a variety of occupations.* Career counselors stress that people have multiple potentials (Carney & Wells, 1995). More than 20,000 occupations are listed in the U.S. Department of Labor's *Dictionary of Occupational Titles*. Considering the huge variety in occupational opportunities, it's foolish to believe that only one career would be right for you. If you expect to find one job that fits you perfectly, you may spend your entire lifetime searching for it.

2. *A career choice is an expression of your personality.* Various influential theories of occupational choice focus on how this process is related to personal orientation (Holland, 1985), self-concept (Super, 1988), ego functioning (Ginzberg, 1972), and psychological needs (Roe, 1977). Although these theories differ in their emphasis, they clearly agree that the choice of a career is an expression of one's personality.

3. *Chance may play a role in your career development.* Unplanned, accidental events can influence career development. For example, your career plans might be changed by a particular college course that you took only because the class you really wanted was full. This reality does not mean that you should leave career development to fate. Rather, your challenge is to minimize the role of chance in your work life through thoughtful planning.

4. *There are limits on your career options.* Entry into a particular occupation is not simply a matter of choosing what you want to do. It's a two-way street. You get to make choices, but you also have to persuade schools and employers to choose you. Your career options will be limited to some extent by factors beyond your control, including fluctuations in the economy and the job market (Lock, 1988).

5. *Some career decisions are not easily undone.* Although it's never too late to strike out in new career directions, it is important to recognize that many decisions are not readily reversed. One influential theory of occupational choice in the 1950s (Ginzberg, 1952) went so far as to propose that vocational decisions are characterized by *irreversibility.* That assertion has since been retracted as an overstatement (Ginzberg, 1972). Still, it's obvious that once you invest time, money, and effort in moving along a particular career path, it may not be easy to change paths. This potential problem highlights why it is important to devote systematic thought to your occupational choice.

6. *Career choice is a developmental process that extends throughout life.* Occupational choice involves not a single decision but a series of decisions. Although this process was once believed to extend only from prepuberty to one's early 20s, it is now recognized that the process often continues throughout life. In a 1993 Gallup Poll, 48% of American workers said that they were either "very likely" or "somewhat likely" to switch careers during their working life (Moore & McAneny, 1993). Nonetheless, many middle-aged people tend to underestimate the options available to them and therefore miss opportunities to make constructive changes. We want to emphasize that making occupational choices is not limited to one's youth.

Examining Your Personal Characteristics

Learning Objective

Discuss the personal characteristics that one should consider in making occupational decisions.

Our discussions of job satisfaction and career choice point to the importance of self-knowledge in making career decisions. To select an occupation that you will find rewarding, you need to have a clear picture of yourself. In piecing together this picture, you will want to consider your personality, your abilities, and your interests (Shertzer, 1985).

Personality

As we saw in our discussion of the career development models of Holland and Super, most vocational theorists agree that it is important to choose an occupation that is compatible with your personality. In assessing your personality, you should try to identify your dominant traits, needs, and values. Holland's Self-Directed Search can be useful in this regard. A particularly crucial characteristic to evaluate is how socially skilled you are. Some jobs require much more social dexterity than others.

Aptitudes and Abilities

Although intelligence does not necessarily predict occupational success, it does predict the likelihood of entering particular occupations. This is because intelligence is related to the academic success needed to enter many fields. Certain professions, such as law and medicine, are open only to people who can meet increasingly selective criteria as they move from high school to college to graduate education and professional training.

Other aptitudes and abilities are important as well. In many occupations, special talents are more important than general intelligence. Specific aptitudes that might make a person well suited for certain occupations include perceptual-motor coordination, creativity, artistic or musical talent, mechanical ability, clerical skill, mathematical ability, and persuasive talents.

Interests

As you meander through life, you acquire interests in different kinds of activities. Are you intrigued by the business world? the academic world? international affairs? agriculture? the outdoors? physical sciences? music? athletics? human services? The list of potential interests is virtually infinite. Although interests may change, they tend to be relatively stable, and they should definitely be considered as you develop your career plans.

Using Tests to Aid Career Planning

Numerous psychological tests are available that can be valuable in helping you arrive at a good picture of your personality, abilities, and interests. There are standardized tests of intellectual abilities, spatial and mechanical skills, perceptual accuracy, and motor abilities, as well as of personality and interests. If you are undecided about what kind of occupation might intrigue you, you might want to begin by taking a special kind of test. *Occupational interest inventories* **measure one's interests as they relate to various jobs or careers.** There are many tests in this category. The most widely used are the Strong Interest Inventory (SII) and the Kuder Occupational Interest Survey (KOIS), both of which can be taken at most college counseling centers.

Occupational interest inventories do not attempt to predict whether you would be successful in various occupations. They focus more on the likelihood of job *satisfaction* than of job *success*. When you take an occupational interest inventory, you receive many scores indicating how similar your interests are to the typical interests of people in various occupations. A high score on the accountant scale of a test means that your interests are similar to those of the average accountant. This correspondence in interests does not ensure that you would enjoy a career in accounting, but it is a moderately good predictor of job satisfaction (Swaney & Prediger, 1985).

The most recent revision of the Strong Interest Inventory groups occupations into six broad categories that correspond to the six types of work environments identified by John Holland (1985). Holland's six prototype work environments are called *general occupational themes*. Scores on these general themes indicate whether you have a realistic, investigative, artistic, social, enterprising, or conventional personality, as described by Holland. The SII divides each theme into a few basic interest scales and then breaks basic interests down into specific occupational scores—211 in all.

Interest inventories such as the SII can provide worthwhile food for thought about possible careers. The results may confirm your subjective guesses about your interests and strengthen already existing vocational preferences. Additionally, the test results may inspire you to investigate career possibilities that you had never thought of before. Unexpected results may stimulate you to rethink your career plans.

Although interest inventories can be helpful in working through career decisions, several cautions are worth noting. First, you may score high on some occupations that you're sure you would hate. Given the sheer number of occupational scales on the tests, this can easily happen by chance. However, you shouldn't dismiss the remainder of the test results just because you're sure that a few specific scores are "wrong." Second, don't let the test make career decisions for you. Some students naively believe that they should pursue whatever occupation yields their highest score. This is not how the tests are meant to be used. They merely provide information for you to consider. Ultimately, you will have to think things out for yourself.

Third, you should be aware that there is a lingering gender bias on most occupational interest inventories. Many of these scales were originally developed 30 to 40 years ago when outright discrimination or more subtle discouragement prevented women from entering many traditionally "male" occupations. Critics assert that interest inventories have helped channel women into gender-typed careers, such as nursing and secretarial work, while guiding them away from more prestigious "male" occupations, such as medicine and engineering (Betz, 1993; Betz & Fitzgerald, 1987). Undoubtedly, this was true in the past. Recently, progress has been made toward reducing gender bias in occupational tests, but it has not been eliminated yet. Thus, in interpreting interest inventory results, be wary of letting gender stereotypes limit your career options. A good career counselor should be able to help women—as well as men—sort through the effects of gender bias on their test results.

Researching Job Characteristics

Learning Objective

List some job characteristics that one should be concerned about in making occupational decisions.

To match yourself up with an occupation, you have to seek out information about jobs. As we have noted, there are over 20,000 occupations to choose from. Their sheer number is overwhelming. Obviously, you have to narrow down the scope of your search before you can start gathering information.

Once you have selected some jobs that might interest you, the next question is: Where do you get information on them? This is not a simple matter. The first step is usually to read some occupational literature. A good general reference is the *Occupational Outlook Handbook*, available in most libraries. This government document, published every two years by the U.S. Bureau of Labor Statistics, is a comprehensive guide to occupations. It includes job descriptions, education and training requirements, advancement possibilities, salaries, and employment outlooks for 250 occupations. In addition, it describes sources of career education, training, and financial aid, as well as resources for special groups such as youth, the handicapped, veterans, women, and minorities. Other helpful books are *Joyce Lain Kennedy's Career Book* by Joyce Lain Kennedy and Darryl Laramore (1993) and *The Where Am I Now? Where Am I Going? Career Manual* by William Lareau (1992). In addition to these general books, you can often get more detailed information on particular occupations from government agencies, trade unions, and professional organizations. For example, if you're interested in a career in psychology, you can obtain a number of pamphlets or books from the American Psychological Association.

After you read the available literature about an occupation, it's often a good idea to talk to some people working in that area. People in the field can provide you with more down-to-earth information than you can get by reading. Keep in mind, though, that the people you talk to may not be a representative sample of those who work in that occupation. Don't make the mistake of rejecting a potentially satisfying career just because one person hates it.

When you examine occupational literature and interview people, what kinds of information should you seek? To some extent, the answer depends on your unique values and needs. However, there are some general things that should be of concern to virtually anyone. The questions you can ask include the following:

- *The nature of the work.* What would your duties and responsibilities be on a day-to-day basis?
- *Working conditions.* Is the work environment pleasant or unpleasant, low-key or high-pressure?
- *Job entry requirements.* What education and training are required to break into this occupational area?
- *Potential earnings.* What are entry-level salaries, and how much can you hope to earn if you're exceptionally successful? What does the average person earn? What are the fringe benefits?
- *Potential status.* What is the social status associated with this occupation? Is it personally satisfactory for you?
- *Opportunities for advancement.* How do you "move up" in this field? Are there adequate opportunities for promotion and advancement?

- *Intrinsic job satisfaction.* Apart from money and formal fringe benefits, what can you derive in the way of personal satisfaction from this job? Will it allow you to have fun, help people, be creative, or shoulder responsibility?
- *Future outlook.* How is supply and demand projected to shape up in the future for this occupational area?

By the way, if you're wondering whether your college education will be worth the effort in terms of dollars and cents, the answer generally is yes. The jobs that you can obtain with a college degree *do* tend to yield higher pay than those available to people with less education (Murphy & Welch, 1989). Moreover, almost all the experts agree that the future belongs to those who are better educated (Church, 1993).

Balancing Work and Other Spheres of Life

A major challenge for workers today is balancing work, family, and leisure activities in ways that are personally satisfying. We noted that dual-earner families are becoming increasingly common and that the traditional boundaries between family and paid work life are breaking down. These two developments are related. Historically, traditional gender roles assigned women's work to the home and men's work outside the home. This division of labor created boundaries between family and work life. As more women enter the workforce, these boundaries are becoming blurred. The technology-based changes in the workplace are also eroding these distinctions between family and work life. Let's examine three issues related to balancing one's various roles.

Multiple Roles

Learning Objective

Explain the scarcity hypothesis and the enhancement hypothesis, and summarize the findings on the effects of multiple roles.

The biggest recent change in the labor force has been the emergence of the dual-earner family, which is now the dominant family form in the United States (Hayghe, 1990). Dual-earner couples are struggling to work out new ways of balancing family life and the demands of work. These changes in work and family life have sparked the interest of researchers in many disciplines, including psychology.

An important fact of life for dual-earner couples is that two workers juggle three jobs: two paid jobs and one unpaid job at home. (In truth, if a couple have children, it is probably more realistic to describe them as having *four* jobs: two paid jobs and two unpaid jobs—housework and child care.) It doesn't take too much thought to realize that what goes on at work can spill over to affect family life and vice versa. These *spillover effects* can be either positive or negative. For example, if you have a great day at the office, you will probably come home in a good mood. But if your children are ill, your worry about them might undermine your concentration at work.

Most of the burdens associated with dual-earner households are borne by wives (Crosby & Jaskar, 1993). A woman's unpaid work at home after her paid workday ends has been termed "the second shift" (Hochschild, 1989). Sometimes multiple

Reprinted with special permission of King Features Syndicate.

roles are incompatible and cause *role conflict*. Because the division of labor in many homes is still based on traditional gender roles, wives are more likely to experience role conflict than husbands are. Let's say that a woman is scheduled to make a major presentation at work on Tuesday morning and her 2-year-old son wakes up with a fever and can't go to day care. If her husband can stay home with the baby, all is well. If he can't, then she either has to find someone else to care for him or do so herself. Either way, she feels guilt, conflict, and stress. Because juggling multiple roles is still more of a problem for women than men, almost all the research on this topic has used women as subjects.

What are the effects on women of juggling multiple roles? There are two competing perspectives on this question (Baruch, Biener, & Barnett, 1987). The *scarcity hypothesis* assumes that everyone has a finite amount of energy. The more roles a person has, the more energy will be used. The more energy expended, the greater the stress and other negative consequences. In contrast, the *enhancement hypothesis* asserts that people's energy resources are not limited. Psychologists who espouse this view use the analogy of those who exercise (expend energy) yet say they actually feel less tired and more energetic. In this view, the more roles one has, the greater the opportunities for stimulation, social status, and self-esteem. Also, multiple roles should serve as a buffer against the assaults of painful experiences because negative events in one role can be balanced by the positive aspects of other roles.

Both hypotheses are supported by research. In support of the scarcity hypothesis, employed women report that the competing demands of work and family life are a major source of stress (Duxbury & Higgins, 1991). A study of 232 professional women (attorneys, physicians, and professors) reported that the majority of women often experienced career-family conflicts (Gray, 1983). For obvious reasons, the presence of young children reduces women's satisfaction with their professional work (Amaro, Russo, & Johnson, 1987). If working mothers can't find (or can't afford) high-quality care for their children, combining work and motherhood is stressful (Ross & Mirowsky, 1988). A high income can ease the strains and increase work satisfaction, but most women don't have high-paying jobs.

In support of the enhancement hypothesis, it has been found that working women are happier and healthier than full-time homemakers, except when their children are infants (Walker & Best, 1991). Other studies have reported similar findings (Amatea & Fong, 1991; Helson, Elliott, & Leigh, 1990). Still, because much of this research is correlational, we can't tell whether paid work, itself, makes women happier and healthier or whether they would be happier and healthier than homemakers even if they didn't work. Also, these studies haven't looked at whether the positive effects of working are due to some other factor, such as salary, rather than work per se. However, in one study that looked at a number of possible correlates of self-esteem (employment, income, education, marital status, and developmental status), the researchers reported that employment was the *only* significant predictor of self-esteem in midlife women (Coleman & Antonucci, 1983). Thus, although we have no definitive proof of the positive benefits of work for women, the evidence points strongly toward this conclusion. Again, the availability of high-quality child care and the involvement of the father in child care are key factors in the adjustment of working mothers (Ross & Mirowsky, 1988).

Most of the research on multiple roles has focused on women in high-paying jobs. Additional research is needed on women in lower-paying jobs and on the effects of multiple roles on men. It is possible, for example, that if men spent less time and energy on work and more time with their families, many of them would have more close and rewarding relationships with their children.

Leisure and Recreation

Learning Objective

List five types of leisure activities and summarize the benefits of leisure activities.

Computers and other machines are doing more of traditional human work these days, and this trend is likely to continue. Does this mean that the 40-hour work-week is on its way out? It seems not. The number of hours people work typically affects how much money they make. Hence, it isn't too surprising to learn that most American workers would rather work more hours and make more money (Kennedy & Laramore, 1993). Still, Americans' awareness of their need for leisure time seems to be increasing, according to a Gallup Poll (Moore & McAneny, 1993). In 1993, 67% of workers polled reported that they were satisfied with the amount of leisure and free time available, down from 76% in 1963.

We'll define *leisure* as **unpaid activities one chooses to engage in because they are personally meaningful.** How might we differentiate between activities that are meaningful and those that aren't? Although you may sometimes choose to veg out in front of the TV set for a few hours, most people would acknowledge that there is an important difference between using your time in this manner and spending that same few hours, say, taking photographs of dazzling spring flowers. What distinguishes these two uses of your time? While one activity merely provides respite from a boring or exhausting day (which you sometimes need), the other genuinely revitalizes you. Being a couch potato will probably contribute nothing to your state of mind and may even result in feelings of physical apathy and depression (Csikszentmihalyi & Kubey, 1981; Kubey & Csikszentmihalyi, 1990). On the other hand, participating in activities that are truly meaningful to you (photography, for example) can produce highly positive emotional states (Csikszentmihalyi & Kleiber, 1991).

Types of Leisure Activities

The types of leisure activities that people prefer are quite diverse (see Figure 12.8). Popular leisure pursuits include the following:

- *Hobbies.* Common hobbies include photography; acting; music (playing and listening); gardening; knitting; drawing; collecting stamps, autographs, and so forth; hiking; camping; fishing; and birdwatching.
- *Travel.* Many choose their destinations spontaneously, but others are more systematic in their travel plans. For example, some individuals want to travel to all the U.S. national parks or all the major Civil War battlefields. Those who can afford it may travel to other countries—to get a taste of real French cooking or a firsthand look at what remains of ancient Egyptian civilization.
- *Games.* Some individuals enjoy playing bridge for relaxation; others like to play board games such as Scrabble or chess. Computerized games attract others.
- *Sports.* Many people like to play team sports such as bowling and softball. This way, they get the benefits of both physical exercise and social interaction. Others

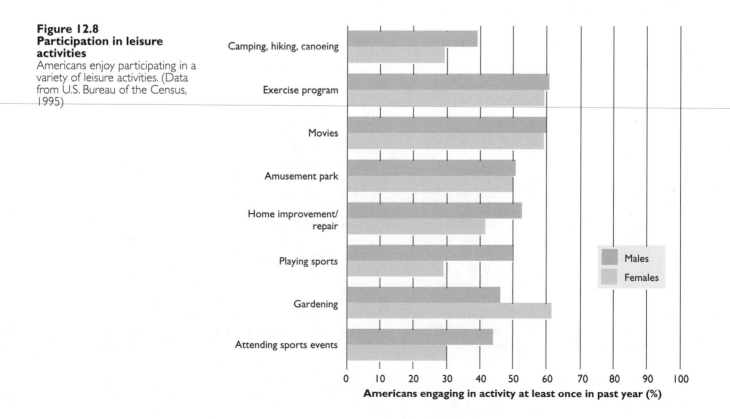

Figure 12.8
Participation in leisure activities
Americans enjoy participating in a variety of leisure activities. (Data from U.S. Bureau of the Census, 1995)

Americans engaging in activity at least once in past year (%)

enjoy individual sports such as jogging, swimming, surfing, ice skating, or skiing. And, of course, some people simply like to watch sporting events.

• *Volunteer activities.* Helping others appeals to individuals in almost all age groups. Moreover, volunteers can use their skills to help others in an incredibly diverse array of settings—homeless shelters, hospitals, schools, battered women's shelters, boys' and girls' clubs, and sports teams, to name only a few.

Being aware of the broad range of recreational activities heightens your chances of selecting those that are most meaningful to you.

Participation in leisure activities can help reduce stress.

Benefits of Leisure Activities

The idea that a satisfying balance of work, relationships, and leisure activities will lead to a more rewarding and healthy life has intuitive appeal. Is there any evidence to support this assumption? Amazingly, there isn't much research on this important question. Furthermore, the research that has been done has concentrated primarily on retirees rather than workers. One early, interview-based study found that higher "overall quality of life" was associated with satisfaction with one's job as well as with one's leisure activities (London, Crandall, & Seals, 1977). Some people include physical exercise in their leisure time. In a study of senior police officers in the United Kingdom, it was found that those who exercised showed higher levels of job satisfaction and better mental and physical health than officers who did not (Kirkcaldy et al., 1994). As you'll see in Chapter 14, regular exercise can also reduce the effects of stress and improve one's mood and self-concept.

Workaholism

Learning Objective

Summarize current perspectives on workaholism.

Most people cherish their leisure activities and their relationships with their families and friends. However, a small minority of people devote nearly all their time and energy to their jobs. These people tend to avoid nonwork activities. They put in considerable overtime, take few vacations, regularly bring work home from the office, and think about work most of the time. They are energetic, intense, and overly ambitious. In short, they are *workaholics.*

Psychologists are divided on the issue of whether workaholism is problematic. Should workaholics be praised for their dedication and encouraged in their single-minded pursuit of fulfillment through work? Or is workaholism a form of "addiction," a sign that an individual is driven by compulsions he or she cannot control? In support of the former view, Machlowitz (1980) found that workaholics tend to be highly satisfied with their jobs and with their lives. They work hard simply because work is the most meaningful activity they know. Yet other evidence suggests that workaholics may have a pathological need to exercise rigid control over themselves and their environments (Schwartz, 1982).

How can these conflicting findings be reconciled? Naughton (1987) has suggested that there may be two different types of workaholics. One type, the job-involved workaholic, works for the pure joy of it. Such people derive immense satisfaction from work and generally perform well in highly demanding jobs. The other type, the compulsive workaholic, is neither well adjusted nor an asset to an employer. Compulsive workaholics are addicted to work. Their devotion to work reflects a rigid, overcontrolling personality. They approach their jobs in a ritualized manner and cannot deviate from their set routines. They often alienate their supervisors and co-workers with their rigidity. Interestingly, compulsive workaholics are not necessarily satisfied with their jobs, and they may be prone to develop *burnout*, which we described in Chapter 3. Thus, it appears that workaholism may be either constructive or problematic, depending on the motivation underlying a person's dedication to work.

To summarize, meaningful work, rewarding family interactions and friendships, and revitalizing leisure pursuits are three components of a rewarding life. Maintaining a personally satisfying balance among these life components is a major challenge in contemporary times.

Occupational Hazards

Work can bring people deep satisfaction, but it can also be a source of frustration and conflict. Working in unsafe environments can cause injuries and disease—and, sometimes, death. In this last section, we'll explore three hazards in today's workplace: unsafe working conditions, job stress, and sexual harassment.

Unsafe Working Conditions

Many people work in unsafe conditions. Hazardous jobs that come easily to mind are fire fighting, police work, mining, and construction. Every year, about one in nine workers in private industry suffers an occupational injury (U.S. Bureau of the Census, 1995). Moreover, some 6000 workers lose their lives every year in work-related accidents, and thousands more are disabled (U.S. Bureau of the Census, 1995). Homicide has now moved to second place as a cause of workplace deaths (see Figure 12.9). The primary cause of on-the-job homicides is robbery, not assaults by co-workers or spillover from family conflicts (Rosato, 1995). Most robberies occur in convenience stores, fast-food restaurants, and gas stations. For men, the leading cause of death on the job is traffic incidents; for women, it is homicides (because they are more likely than men to work where robberies occur).

Unhealthful work environments can cause a variety of diseases in workers. Work-related injuries and diseases vary in type and severity. The five leading *work-related* diseases or injuries (based on the frequency of occurrence, severity to the individual, and amenability to prevention) are (1) lung diseases, (2) musculoskeletal injuries, (3) cancers, (4) severe traumatic injuries, and (5) cardiovascular diseases. Psychological disorders, including alcohol and drug dependency, rank tenth on this list (National Institute for Occupational Safety and Health, 1988).

Many unsafe conditions exist because equipment and work settings have typically been designed to maximize productivity and minimize expenses (Levi, 1990). Although the short-run benefits of these developments have been greater productivity, lower costs, and increased profits, the long-run disadvantages have been the ill health, dissatisfaction, and alienation of many workers (Levi, 1990). Some workers are going to court to change things. More than 2000 workers have filed lawsuits against several makers of computer equipment because they believe that the design of computer keyboards contributes to repetitive motion injuries (Elmer-Dewitt, 1994). **Repetitive strain injury (RSI) involves injuries to muscles and tendons caused by rapidly repeating the same motions for many hours over many days.** Artists, hair stylists, physical therapists, and other workers who repeatedly perform the same motions are also at risk for repetitive motion injuries. The tragedy of RSI is that it is difficult to cure, but relatively easy to prevent. Maintaining good posture, taking frequent rest breaks, and stretching occasionally can stave off these debilitating injuries. In some cases, better-designed equipment is needed.

In 1970, recognizing the problem of unsafe work environments, Congress passed the Occupational Safety and Health Act, which requires employers to make their workplaces safe and free of health hazards "as far as possible." Among other things, this law established the Occupational Safety and Health Administration (OSHA) to

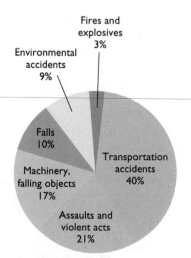

Figure 12.9
Fatal work injuries, 1993
Transportation accidents (auto, airplane, railroad, and boat) account for the largest number of on-the-job fatalities. The next two largest causes of death in the workplace are homicides and accidents involving machinery and falling objects. (Data from U.S. Bureau of the Census, 1995)

Repetitive strain injury is increasingly common in today's workplace.

set standards for workplace conditions and inspect places of employment to see whether those standards are being met. For instance, OSHA is currently reviewing steps companies should follow to reduce the number of repetitive strain injuries. OSHA can impose fines on employers who violate standards and order them to improve working conditions. Workers can file complaints with OSHA calling for inspections and evaluations of health hazards.

Many work-related injuries and diseases are preventable, either by the employer or the employee. Today more companies appear to be recognizing this fact, as well as the relationship between worker satisfaction and productivity. Consequently, organizations are taking a more active role in improving and maintaining the health and safety of their workers. For instance, many companies have instituted policies that relegate smoking to certain areas or ban it entirely, and some companies provide on-site health clubs for their employees.

Job Stress

We saw in Chapter 3 that stress can emerge from every corner of people's lives. However, many theorists suspect that the workplace is the primary source of stress in modern society. Let's examine stress on the job and what employers and workers can do about it.

Sources of Stress on the Job

Learning Objective

Describe some important sources of job stress and four conditions that seem to predict whether stress will develop.

Common job stressors include prolonged physical labor, tedious work, work overload, long hours, unusual hours (such as rotating shifts), and the pressure of deadlines (Marshall & Cooper, 1981; Shostak, 1980). High-pressure jobs such as air traffic controller and surgeon demand virtually perfect performance, as errors can have disastrous consequences. Coal miners and firefighters face frequent threats to their physical safety. Workers who must adapt to computers and automated offices experience "technostress" (Brod, 1988). Ultimately, many sources of occupational stress come from organizational factors, such as office politics, restrictions on communication, and the like (Blau, 1981). Another major cause of daily job stress is conflict with supervisors, subordinates, and co-workers (Bolger et al., 1989). The list of stressful job conditions is practically endless.

Women and minorities may experience certain stressors, such as sex discrimination and sexual harassment, at higher rates than men do (Ivancevich et al., 1990).

African Americans and ethnic minorities must cope with racism and other types of discrimination on the job (Keita & Jones, 1990). In addition, workers from lower socioeconomic groups work in more dangerous and more stressful jobs than do workers from higher socioeconomic statuses (Green, 1989).

According to Lennart Levi (1990), a well-known researcher in the area of job-related stress, four factors play a critical role in whether stress reactions develop:

1. *The degree of match between a worker and job.* A good match occurs when a person has the abilities needed to be successful at the job and when the job meets the worker's needs. When the employee and the job environment are compatible, stress is usually low. The greater the mismatch, the greater the worker's stress (French, Caplan, & Van Harrison, 1982).

2. *The degree of control over working conditions.* Robert Karasek has proposed an intriguing model of occupational stress that supports this idea (Karasek, 1979; Karasek & Theorell, 1990). He suggests that the *psychological demands* made on a worker and the *decision control* a worker has are the two key factors in occupational stress. Psychological demands are measured by asking employees such questions as "Is there excessive work?" and "Must you work fast (or hard)?" To measure decision control, employees are asked such questions as "Do you have a lot of say in your job?" and "Do you have freedom to make decisions?" According to Karasek, *stress is greatest in jobs characterized by high psychological demands and low decision control.* Based on survey data obtained from workers, he has tentatively mapped out where various jobs fall on these two key dimensions of job stress, as shown in Figure 12.10. The jobs thought to be most stressful are those in the lower right area of the diagram.

3. *A worker's coping skills.* Some of the personal qualities that may moderate the effects of job stress include physical stamina, tolerance for ambiguity, excellent job-related skills, and the ability to cope with change (French, Caplan, & Van Harrison, 1982; Matteson & Ivancevich, 1987). The impact of work stress may also be reduced by other factors that moderate the effects of stress in general, such as hardiness, optimism, sensation seeking, and autonomic reactivity (see Chapter 3).

Figure 12.10
Karasek's model of occupational stress as related to specific jobs
Robert Karasek theorizes that occupational stress is greatest in jobs characterized by high psychological demands and low decision control. Based on survey data, this chart shows where various familiar jobs fall on these two dimensions. According to Karasek's model, the most stressful jobs are those in the shaded area on the lower right. (Adapted from Landy, 1989)

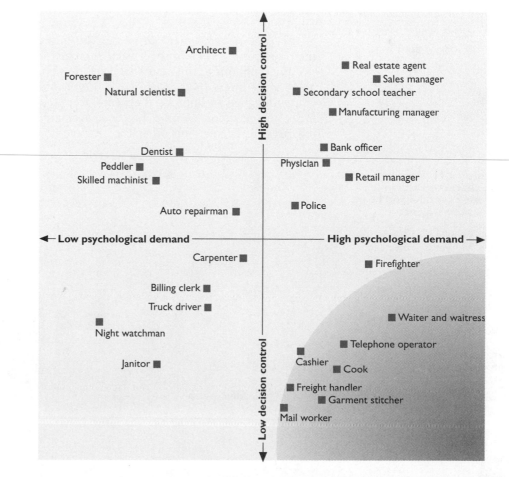

4. *Amount of social support.* As we noted in Chapter 3, supportive friends and family figure importantly in both physical and psychological health.

Those who develop work-related stress reactions respond in a variety of ways, as we'll see next.

Effects of Job Stress

Learning Objective

Summarize the effects of job stress on physical and mental health.

Like other forms of stress, occupational stress is associated with a host of negative effects. In the work arena itself, job stress has been linked to increases in industrial accidents (Levenson et al., 1983), poor job performance (Jackson & Schuler, 1985), higher turnover rates (Powell, 1973), and increased absenteeism (Rosch & Pelletier, 1987). Experts estimate that stress-related reductions in workers' productivity may cost American industry about $300 billion per year (Karasek & Theorell, 1990).

Of course, the negative effects of occupational stress extend beyond the workplace. Foremost among them are adverse effects on employees' physical health (Wolf, 1986). Work stress has been related to a variety of physical maladies, including heart disease, high blood pressure, stroke, ulcers, and arthritis (Holt, 1982). In a test of Karasek's model of work stress, more symptoms of heart disease were found among Swedish men whose jobs were high in psychological demands and low in decision control (Karasek et al., 1981) (see Figure 12.11). Job stress can also have a negative impact on workers' psychological health (Landy, Quick, & Kasl, 1994). Occupational stress has been related to decreased self-esteem, frequent anxiety, bouts of depression, and abuse of alcohol or drugs (Fleming, 1986; Matteson & Ivancevich, 1987). Experts estimate that the health care costs arising from occupational stress in the United States may run around $150 billion per year (Karasek & Theorell, 1990).

Dealing with Job Stress

Learning Objective

Describe what organizations are doing to reduce job stress.

There are essentially three avenues of attack for dealing with occupational stress (Ivancevich et al., 1990). The first is to intervene at the *individual* level by modifying workers' ways of coping with job stress. The second is to intervene at the *organizational* level by redesigning the work environment itself. The third is to intervene at the *individual-organizational interface* by improving the fit between workers and their companies. Let's consider each approach in turn.

Interventions at the *individual* level are the most widely used strategy for managing work stress (Ivancevich et al., 1990). Many companies have instituted programs designed to improve their employees' coping skills. These programs usually focus on relaxation training, time management, cognitive approaches to reappraising stressful events, and other constructive coping strategies that we discussed in

Figure 12.11
Job characteristics in Karasek's model and heart disease prevalence
Karasek et al. (1981) interviewed 1621 Swedish men about their work and assessed their cardiovascular health. The vertical bars in this figure show the percentage of the men with symptoms of heart disease as a function of the characteristics of their jobs. The highest incidence of heart disease was found among men who had jobs high in psychological demands and low in decision control, just as Karasek's model of occupational stress would predict.

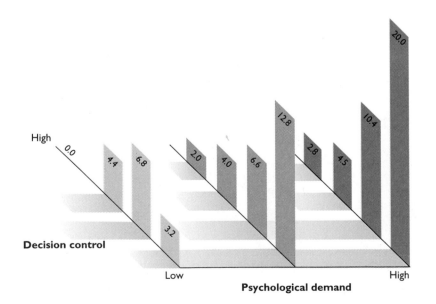

Figure 12.12
Worker-responsive innovations in the workplace
Increasingly, employers are recognizing that they have to address the needs of the changing labor force by providing new benefits that help employees meet family and leisure needs, as well as work demands. Among innovative benefits, flextime and flexible leave time were the most widely offered in 1987. (Data from Statistical Abstract of the United States, 1990)

Worker-Responsive Innovations in the Workplace

Benefit	Percentage of employers providing benefits	
	Private sector	Government
Flexible leave time	42.9	43.7
Flextime	43.6	37.5
Voluntary part-time work	35.3	26.7
Job sharing	15.0	23.5
Counseling services	4.2	18.2
Child-care information or referral services	4.3	15.8
Work at home	8.5	4.0
Employer-sponsored day care	1.6	9.4
Assistance with child-care expenses	3.1	2.9

Chapter 4. Also popular are workplace wellness programs that seek to improve employees' physical health (Gebhardt & Crump, 1990; Offermann & Gowing, 1990). These programs usually focus on exercise and fitness training, health screening, nutritional education, and the reduction of health-impairing habits, such as smoking and overeating.

Interventions at the *organizational* level are intended to make work environments less stressful. Some companies have attempted to reduce occupational stress by making the surroundings more comfortable and attractive and by giving workers different tools or responsibilities. The key is to give adequate decision control to people in jobs that have high psychological demands (Karasek & Theorell, 1990). Trends toward decentralizing management and giving workers greater participation in decision making may help reduce occupational stress (Offermann & Gowing, 1990).

Interventions at the *individual-organizational interface* can take many forms. In future years, the biggest challenge will probably be to accommodate the changing nature of the workforce. The workforce is now dominated by dual-earner couples rather than married men who are the sole wage earners in their families. Another 6% of workers are single parents (D. Friedman, 1987). What kinds of accommodations are companies making in response to the changing needs of their workers? Quite a few interesting innovations are under way (Zedeck & Mosier, 1990). The more common options include flextime, flexible leave time, voluntary part-time work, job sharing, and working at home (see Figure 12.12). Other, less frequently offered benefits include child care information or referral services, counseling services, assistance with child care expenses, and employer-sponsored day care (see Figure 12.12). The Family and Medical Leave Act requires larger organizations to provide workers with time off (unpaid) for the birth of a child or serious illness of a family member.

As we noted, workers from lower socioeconomic groups typically experience more work stress than those from higher groups. Ironically, these groups receive less attention through stress management and other programs (Ilgen, 1990). Researchers also pay limited attention to gender, race, and socioeconomic status in their research on job stressors and intervention programs (Keita & Jones, 1990).

Sexual Harassment

Learning Objective

Describe the prevalence and consequences of sexual harassment and how organizations are addressing this problem.

Sexual harassment burst into the American consciousness in the fall of 1991 during the televised confirmation hearings for the nomination of Clarence Thomas as a Justice of the U.S. Supreme Court. Although Justice Thomas survived the confirmation process, many would argue that his reputation was damaged by Anita Hill's public allegations of sexual harassment. Other public figures have suffered more serious consequences: Robert Packwood resigned his Senate seat in 1995 after multiple accusations of sexual harassment surfaced. Individuals and companies have now awakened to the fact that they could be sued for such behavior in the workplace (regulations were instituted in 1980). Moreover, as workers have recog-

Robert Packwood resigned from the U.S. Senate on the heels of numerous complaints about his sexually harassing behavior.

nized that they need to take the problem seriously, they also realize that they are relatively ignorant about what constitutes sexual harassment.

Sexual harassment occurs when employees are subjected to unwelcome sexually oriented behavior. According to law, there are two types of sexual harassment. The first is *quid pro quo* (from the Latin expression that translates as "something given or received in exchange for something else"). In the context of sexual harassment, quid pro quo involves subjecting an employee to unwanted sexual advances and making submission a condition of hiring or advancement, and firing the result of refusal. In other words, the worker's survival on the job depends on agreeing to have unwanted sex. The second type of harassment is *environmental.* This refers to any type of unwelcome sexual behavior that creates a hostile work environment.

Sexual harassment can take a variety of forms: unsolicited and unwelcome flirting, sexual advances, or propositions; insulting comments about an employee's appearance, dress, or anatomy; unappreciated dirty jokes and sexual gestures; intrusive or sexual questions about an employee's personal life; explicit descriptions of the harasser's own sexual experiences; abuse of familiarities such as "honey" or "dear"; catcalls; unnecessary and unwanted physical contact such as touching, hugging, pinching, or kissing; exposure of one's genitals; physical or sexual assault; and rape. As experts have pointed out, sexual harassment is an abuse of power by a person in authority. Figure 12.13 details the frequency of seven types of harassing behaviors of various severity reported by male and female federal workers in a 1987 survey (U.S. Merit Systems Protection Board, 1988).

Prevalence and Consequences

Sexual harassment in the workplace is more widespread than most people realize. A review of 18 studies suggested that approximately 42% of female workers in the United States report having been sexually harassed (Gruber, 1990). A liberal estimate for male workers is 15% (Gutek, 1993). The typical female victim is young and unmarried, has several years of technical training or college, and works in a male-dominated field (Tangri, Burt, & Johnson, 1982). Still, if we believe Anita Hill's testimony, even a Yale Law School graduate can experience the problem.

A review of research on the consequences of sexual harassment among women reported stress-related physical symptoms such as stomach disorders, inability to sleep, and weight loss (Gutek & Koss, 1993). Other problematic emotional reactions include lower self-esteem, depression, anxiety, and anger. In addition, victims have reported difficulties in their personal relationships and in sexual adjustment (loss of desire, for example). Sexual harassment can also produce negative fallout on the

Figure 12.13
Types of sexual harassment workers report
A stratified random sample of 8523 male and female federal workers were surveyed about seven types of harassing behaviors. The three behaviors at the top of the figure were classified as "less severe" and the next three, as "more severe." The behavior at the bottom of the figure, "actual or attempted rape," was categorized as "most severe." The less severe types of sexual harassment occurred more frequently than the more severe forms. (From U.S. Merit Systems Protection Board, 1988).

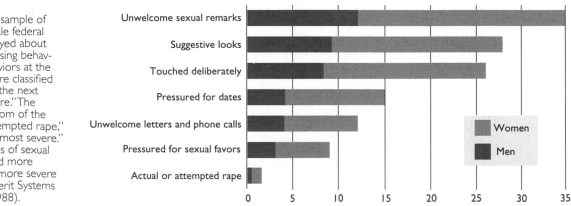

job: Women who are harassed may be less productive, less satisfied with their jobs, and less committed to their work and employer (Gutek, 1985).

Stopping Sexual Harassment

To predict the occurrence of sexual harassment, researchers have developed a two-factor model based on the person (prospective harasser) and the social situation (Pryor, Giedd, & Williams, 1995). According to this model, individuals vary in their proclivity for sexual harassment, as do organizational norms regarding the acceptability of sexual harassment. Research suggests that sexual harassment is most likely to occur when individual proclivity is high and organizational norms are accepting. Thus, it follows that organizations can reduce the incidence of sexual harassment by promoting norms that are intolerant of sexual harassment.

Acknowledging the prevalence and negative impact of sexual harassment, many organizations have taken steps to educate and protect their workers. Managers are speaking out publicly against sexual harassment, supporting programs designed to increase employees' awareness of the problem, issuing policies expressly forbidding harassment, and implementing formal grievance procedures for handling allegations of harassment. In the Recommended Reading box on this page, we describe a book that both employers and employees should find helpful in this regard.

In the Application, we'll describe how to conduct an effective job search.

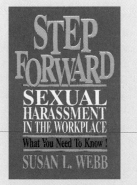
After the Clarence Thomas–Anita Hill sexual harassment controversy, both employers and workers were eager to learn what constitutes sexual harassment and what does not. Although Susan Webb wrote this book to address the questions of employers, workers will also find it quite informative. Chapters are devoted to the history of sexual harassment and to defining and clarifying the complexities of the issue. Webb also offers concrete steps for stopping sexual harassment, specific suggestions for handling sexual harassment complaints, and information about training and education. In addition, she lists and responds to the most-asked questions and details measures that all employees can adopt to stop and prevent sexual harassment. Some case studies and exercises are also included in the book.

How Can I Be Sure It's Sexual Harassment?

To recognize sexual harassment, first decide if the behavior in question is job-related. Does it go toward getting the work done? If the answer is "yes," the behavior is appropriate and will probably not cause a problem. If the answer is "no," and the behavior is social, then consider the following:

- Is the behavior directed toward employees of one gender only—only men or only women?
- Is it courting, flirting, or sexual behavior?
- Has the employee receiving the attention objected in any way, said or indicated "no," "stop," or "I don't like it"?
- Has the employee been asked if the attention is objected to or unwanted?
- Is the behavior or similar behavior repeated? Has it happened before?
- Does the offending employee behave this way deliberately, on purpose?
- Does the behavior interfere with the receiving employee's work performance?
- Does it create an environment that is hostile, intimidating, or offensive for an employee?
- Does the employee feel demeaned, degraded, or embarrassed by the behavior?

If the answer to several of the questions is "yes," the behavior may well be considered sexual harassment. [pp. 91–92]

Getting Ahead in the Job Game

Indicate whether each of the following is true or false.

1. The most common and effective job search method is answering classified ads.

2. Your technical qualifications are the most important factor in determining the success of your job search.

3. Employment agencies are a good source of leads to high-level professional jobs.

4. You should make sure that your résumé is very thorough and includes everything you have ever done.

5. It's a good idea to inject some humor into your job interviews. It will help both you and your interviewer relax.

Most career counselors would agree that all of these statements are generally false. Although there isn't a single "tried and true" method for obtaining desirable jobs, in this Application we'll summarize advice that can increase your chances of success.

Above all else, it is important to conduct a job search that is well organized, thorough, and systematic. Sending out a hastily written résumé to a few randomly selected companies is a waste of effort. An effective job search requires lots of time and careful planning. People who are desperate for a job tend to behave in ways that cause prospective employers to see them as bad risks. Thus, it is crucial that you begin your search well in advance of the time when you will need a job. The best time to look for a job is when you don't need one. Then you can select an employer, rather than seeking an employer who will select you.

Of course, no amount of planning and effort can guarantee favorable results in a job search. Luck is definitely a part of the picture. Success may hinge on being in the right place, or meeting the right person, at the right time. Moreover, becoming a top candidate for a position will depend on factors other than your technical competence. This is not to say that technical competence isn't necessary; it is. But given the realities of today's job market, employers are often inundated with applicants who possess all the required training and experience. The one who is ultimately selected often is *not* the one with the best technical qualifications. Rather, hiring decisions are made on the basis of subjective impressions gleaned from résumés, telephone conversations, and face-to-face interviews (Lareau, 1985). These impressions will be based on perceptions of your personality, your appearance, your social skills, and your body language. Knowing this, you can practice certain strategies that may increase the odds in your favor.

No matter what type of job you're looking for, successful searches have certain elements in common. First, you must prepare a résumé. Next, you need to target specific companies or organizations you would like to work for. Then, you must inform these companies of your interest in such a way as to get them interested in you.

Putting Together a Résumé

Learning Objective

Summarize the guidelines for putting together an effective résumé.

No matter what your job search strategy, an excellent résumé is a critical ingredient. The purpose of a résumé is not to get you a job. Rather, it is to get you an interview. To do so, it must communicate to the reader that you possess the minimum technical qualifications for the position, know the standard conventions of the work world, and are a person who is on the fast track to success. Furthermore, it must achieve these goals without being flashy or gimmicky.

Your résumé will project the desired positive, yet conservative, image if you follow these guidelines (Carney & Wells, 1995):

1. Use white, ivory, or beige (*never* any other color) paper high in rag content.
2. Make sure the résumé contains not a single typographical error.
3. Use the best professional printing service available.
4. Keep it short. The normal maximum is two sides of an 8.5" × 11" sheet of paper.
5. Don't write in full sentences, and avoid using the word "I." Instead, begin each statement with an "action" word that describes a specific achievement, as in "Supervised a staff of fifteen" or "Handled all customer complaints."
6. Avoid giving any personal information that is superfluous to the job. It is an unnecessary distraction and may give the reader cause to dislike you and therefore reject your application.

An effective résumé will generally contain the following information, laid out in an easy-to-read format (see Figure 12.14 for an attractively prepared résumé containing these elements):

Figure 12.14
Example of an attractively formatted résumé
The physical appearance of a résumé is very important. This example shows what a well-prepared résumé should look like. (Adapted from Lock, 1988)

TERESA M. MORGAN

Campus Address	**Permanent Address**
1252 River St., Apt. 808	1111 W. Franklin
East Lansing, MI 48823	Jackson, MI 49203
(517) 332-6086	(517) 782-0819

OBJECTIVE
To pursue a career in interior design, or a related field, in which I can utilize my design training. Willing to relocate after June 1996.

EDUCATION
Sept. 1994–
June 1996
Michigan State University, East Lansing, MI 48825. Bachelor of Arts–Interior Design, with emphasis in Design Communication and Human Shelter. Courses include Lighting, Computers, Public Relations and History of Art. (F.I.D.E.R. accredited) 3.0 GPA (4.0 = A).

July 1995–
Aug. 1995
Michigan State University overseas study, England and France, Decorative Arts and Architecture. 4.0 GPA (4.0 = A).

Sept. 1992–
June 1994
Jackson Community College, Jackson, MI 49201. Associate's Degree. 3.5 GPA (4.0 = A).

EMPLOYMENT
Sept. 1995–
June 1996
Food Service and Maintenance, Owen Graduate Center, Michigan State University.
• Prepared and served food.
• Managed upkeep of adjacent Van Hoosen Residence Hall.

Dec. 1994–
June 1995
Food Service and Maintenance, McDonel Residence Hall.
• Served food and cleaned facility.
• General building maintenance.

June 1993–
Dec. 1993
Waitress, Charlie Wong's Restaurant, Jackson, MI.
• Served food, dealt with a variety of people on a personal level.
• Additional responsibilities: cashier, hostess, bartender, and employee trainer.

HONORS AND ACTIVITIES
• Community College Transfer scholarship from MSU.
• American Society of Interior Design Publicity Chairman; Executive board, MSU Chapter.
• Sigma Chi Little Sisters.
• Independent European travel, summer 1995.
• Stage manager and performer in plays and musicals.

REFERENCES and **PORTFOLIO** available upon request.

- *Heading*. At the top of the page, give your name, address, and phone number. This is the only section of the résumé that is *not* given a label.
- *Objective*. State a precise career goal, remembering to use action words and to avoid the use of "I." An example might be "Challenging, creative position in the communication field requiring extensive background in newspaper, radio, and television."
- *Education*. List any degrees you possess, giving major field of study, date, and granting institution for each. (List the highest degree you received first. If you have a college degree, you don't need to mention your high school diploma.) If you received any academic honors or awards, mention them in this section.
- *Experience*. This section should be organized chronologically, beginning with your most recent job and working backward. For each position, describe your responsibilities and your achievements. Make them specific, and make sure your most recent position is the one with the greatest achievements. Never pad your résumé by listing trivial accomplishments. Readers find this annoying. Moreover, it just calls attention to the fact that you don't have more important items to list.

If you are currently a student or a recent graduate, your schooling will provide the basis for both your experience and your qualifications. You can give yourself a boost over the competition by taking part-time or summer jobs in the field in which you plan to work. If this option isn't feasible, do some volunteer work in this area and list it under "Honors and Activities" on your résumé.

Finding Companies You Want to Work For

Learning Objective

Discuss strategies for targeting companies you would like to work for.

Initially, you need to determine what general type of organization will best suit your needs. Do you want to work in a school? a hospital? a small business? a large corporation? a government agency? a human services agency? As you have seen, to select an appropriate work environment, you need an accurate picture of your personal qualities and knowledge of various occupations and their characteristics.

Once you've decided on a setting, you need to target specific companies. That's easy; you simply look for companies that have advertised openings in your field, right? Not necessarily. If you restrict yourself to this approach, you may miss many valuable opportunities. Experts estimate that up to 80% of all vacancies, especially those above entry level, are never advertised at all (Bolles, 1995).

How should you proceed? Certainly you should check the classified section in newspapers to identify the many positions that *are* advertised. If you are willing to relocate anywhere, a good source for business and professional jobs is the *National Business Employment Weekly*. You should also consult any trade or professional newspapers, magazines, or journals in your field.

There are two additional options to consider. You could go to an employment agency. However, keep in mind that these agencies generally handle only entry-level, hourly wage jobs. In addition, they can cost you thousands of dollars (Lareau, 1992). If you're interested in professional jobs, you might consider contacting executive recruiters, widely known as "headhunters." Executive recruiters work on commission for organizations that have vacancies to fill. They earn their livelihood by actively looking for people who have the qualifications being sought by the hiring organization. You can locate headhunters nationwide by consulting *The Directory of Executive Recruiters*.

What about the 80% of openings that are not advertised? Actually, this statistic is somewhat misleading. It includes a large number of vacancies that are filled by promotions within organizations (Lareau, 1985). Nonetheless, many organizations do have openings that are not accessible through traditional channels. If you have targeted companies that haven't advertised any vacancies, you may want to initiate the contact yourself. In support of this approach, a survey by the Bureau of the Census indicated that "direct application to an employer" was both the most commonly used and the most effective job search method (Bolles, 1995). Richard Bolles, author of *What Color Is Your Parachute?*, suggests the following strategy. First, identify a specific problem that the organization has and develop a strategy to solve it. Then, find out who has the power to hire and fire (either through library research or a network of personal contacts). Finally, approach this person directly to convince him or her of your unique capability to help.

Landing an Interview

Learning Objective

Describe several strategies for landing a job interview.

No one is going to hire you without first "checking out the goods." This inspection process typically involves one or more formal interviews. How do you go about getting yourself invited for an interview? If you are applying for an advertised vacancy, the traditional approach is to mail a résumé with a cover letter to the hiring organization. If your letter and résumé stand out from the crowd, you may be invited for an interview. One way to increase your chances is to persuade the prospective employer that you are interested enough in the company to have done some research on the organization. By taking the time to learn something about a company, you should be in a better position to make a convincing case about the ways in which your expertise will be particularly useful to the organization.

If you are approaching an organization in the absence of a known opening, your strategy might be somewhat different. You may still opt to send a résumé, along with a more detailed cover letter explaining why you have selected this particular company. Another option, suggested by Bolles (1995), is to introduce yourself (by

Recommended Reading

What Color Is Your Parachute? A Practical Manual for Job-Hunters and Career-Changers

by Richard Nelson Bolles (Ten Speed Press, 1990, 1995)

Richard Bolles is a clever, creative writer who has put together a landmark book on the process of hunting for a job. The book has been so successful that it's being updated yearly. Although Bolles devotes some attention to the matter of career choice, this book focuses mainly on the process of hunting for a job. Unlike many similar books, it does not assume that you're a recent college graduate seeking your first job. Instead, it devotes equal time to people shifting careers later in life.

Bolles's writing is humorous and opinionated. However, his opinions have merit because he has done his homework; the book is thoroughly researched and documented. He destroys many of the myths about what does and does not work in seeking jobs. Bolles discusses a variety of practical topics, including where the jobs are, what will get you hired, how to get in to see the boss, whom to go see, and whom to avoid.

> So dream, dream, dream. Never mind "being realistic." According to the experts, 80% of the workers in this country are "underemployed." That's what comes of "being realistic." You don't want to end up in the same fix. But you will, if while you dream you corrupt your dream by keeping one eye fixed on what you think you know about the job market. . . .
>
> Only one job offer is tendered for every 1,470 résumés that the average company receives.
>
> Well, okay, so maybe they don't always work. But what's the harm in trying out a résumé, just in case? Well, if you've got the money and the time, fine. But do keep in mind what we have discovered in the past: that job-hunters who invest a lot of time on sending out their résumé, often suffer tremendous damage to their self-esteem by having depended upon résumés. [1990, pp. 99, 152]

phone or in person) directly to the person in charge of hiring and request an interview. You can increase your chances of success by using your network of personal contacts to identify some acquaintance that you and the person in charge both know. Then, you can use this person's name to facilitate your approach. Once you do get in to see a potential employer, you should follow up with a thank-you note and a résumé that will jog the employer's memory about your training and talents.

Polishing Your Interview Technique

Learning Objective

List the do's and don'ts of interviewing for jobs.

The final, and most crucial, step in the process of securing a job is the face-to-face interview. If you've gotten this far, the employer already knows that you have the requisite training and experience to do the job. Now your challenge is to convince the employer that you're the kind of person who would fit in well in the organization. Your interviewer will attempt to verify that you have the intangible qualities that will make you a good team player. Even more important, the interviewer will attempt to identify any "red flag" behaviors, attitudes, or traits that mark you as an unacceptable risk.

To create the right impression, you must appear to be confident, enthusiastic, and ambitious. Your demeanor should be somewhat formal and reserved, and you should avoid any attempts at humor—you never know what might offend your interviewer (Lareau, 1985). Above all, never give more information than the interviewer requests, especially negative information. If asked directly what your weaknesses are—a common ploy—respond with a "flaw" that is really a positive, as in "I tend to work too hard at times" (Lareau, 1985). Don't interrupt or contradict your interviewer. And don't ever blame or criticize anyone, especially previous employers, even if you feel that the criticism is justified (Lipman, 1983).

Careful preparation helps applicants be more confident and put their best foot forward in a job interview.

Developing an effective interview technique requires practice. Many experts suggest that you never turn down an interview. Even if you know you don't want the job, you can always benefit from the practice. Advance preparation is also crucial. Never go into an interview cold. Find out all you can about the company before you go. Try to anticipate the questions that will be asked and have some answers ready. In general, you will not be asked simply to reiterate information from your résumé. Remember, it is your personal qualities that are being assessed now. A final word of advice: If possible, avoid any discussion of salary in an initial interview. The appropriate time for salary negotiation is *after* a firm offer of employment has been extended.

Key Ideas

Perspectives on Work

• Work is an activity that produces something of value for others. A number of contemporary trends are changing the world of work. Generally, the more education individuals obtain, the higher their salaries will be. Computer literacy is becoming increasingly important as a job skill.

• Between now and the year 2000, more women and minorities will join the labor force. Although women and minorities are participating in the workforce at all occupational levels, they tend to be concentrated in the lower-paying and lower-status positions. Furthermore, women and minorities also face discrimination in a number of areas.

Understanding Job Satisfaction

• Job satisfaction is a critical issue for both employees and employers. It is related to employees' physical and mental health, and it affects productivity, absenteeism, and the tendency to look for other employment. Important determinants of job satisfaction include meaningfulness, challenge and variety, autonomy, friendship and recognition, good pay, and security.

Models of Career Development

• Two major theories of career development are those of John Holland and Donald Super. John Holland's hexagonal model of career development asserts that we select careers based on our personality characteristics. Holland has identified six personality orientations and matching work environments. Super's stage theory holds that self-concept development is the basis for career choice. According to this model, there are five stages in the occupational life cycle: growth, exploration, establishment, maintenance, and decline.

• Models of women's career development are still being developed. Women's career paths are often less orderly and predictable than those of men because of the need to juggle multiple roles and because many women interrupt their careers to devote time to child rearing.

Important Considerations in Career Choice

• In making career decisions, individuals should consider how compatible their personality, abilities, and interests are with the demands of various jobs. Career-related interests can be assessed through interest inventories. To accurately evaluate their suitability for various jobs, people should seek information about the nature of the work, working conditions, entry requirements, potential earnings, potential status, opportunities for advancement, intrinsic satisfactions, and the future outlook for each occupational area they consider.

Balancing Work and Other Spheres of Life

• A major challenge for workers today is balancing work, family, and leisure activities in ways that are personally satisfying. As dual-earner families have become the family norm, juggling multiple roles has emerged as a challenge, especially for women. Leisure seems to play an important role in psychological and physical health. Workaholism may be constructive or problematic, depending on a person's underlying motives for work.

Occupational Hazards

• Major hazards in the workplace include unsafe working conditions, job stress, and sexual harassment. Many work-related injuries, diseases, and deaths are preventable, either by the employer or the employee. The negative effects of stress affect both employers and employees. Interventions for managing stress in the workplace can be made at the individual level, at the organizational level, and at the individual-organizational interface.

• Victims of sexual harassment often develop physical and psychological symptoms of stress that can lead to decreased work motivation and productivity. Many organizations are taking steps to educate their workers about this problem.

Application: Getting Ahead in the Job Game

• Career counselors are in agreement about the essential elements of a successful job search. The key factors include: (1) determining the type of organization that will best suit one's needs, (2) constructing an effective résumé, (3) winning a job interview, and (4) developing an effective interview technique.

Key Terms

Job satisfaction
Labor force
Leisure
Occupational interest inventories
Repetitive strain injury
Sexual harassment
Token
Underemployment
Work

Key People

Nancy Betz
John Holland
Robert Karasek
Donald Super

13 Development and Expression of Sexuality

Sex. To some people it's a sport, to others an oppressive duty. For some it's recreation, for others it's business. Some people find it a source of great intimacy and pleasure. Others find it a source of extraordinary anxiety and frustration. Whatever the case, sexuality plays a central role in people's lives. In our culture, it sometimes seems that everyone is obsessed with sex. People joke and gossip about it constantly. Magazines and novels are saturated with sex. The advertising industry uses sex to sell everything from automobiles to toothpaste. Americans have become voracious consumers of books purporting to tell them how to improve their sex lives. In spite of all this, many lovers find it excruciatingly difficult to talk to each other about sex, and misconceptions about sexual functioning abound.

In this chapter we'll consider how people express their sexuality and how this expression affects their adjustment. Specifically, we'll look at the development of sexuality, the interpersonal dynamics of sexual relationships, the psychology and physiology of sexual arousal, and patterns of sexual behavior. We'll also discuss contraception and sexually transmitted diseases. In the Application, we'll turn our attention to some things that people can do to enhance their sexual relationships.

Let's begin with a cautionary note. Several problems, though not unique to sex research, are especially troublesome in this area of inquiry. For one thing, it is particularly difficult to get representative samples of subjects in sex research. Many people are understandably reluctant to discuss their sex lives. The crucial problem is that people who *are* willing to volunteer information about their sexual behavior appear to be more liberal and more sexually experienced than the general population (Wolchik, Braver, & Jensen, 1985).

Furthermore, given the difficulties in doing direct observation, sex researchers have depended mostly on interviews and questionnaires. Unfortunately, when questioned about their sexual behavior, people may provide inaccurate information because of shame, embarrassment, boasting, or wishful thinking (Catania, McDermott, & Pollack, 1986). For these reasons, the results of sex research need to be evaluated with more than the usual caution.

Becoming a Sexual Person

There is immense variety in how people express their sexuality. Some people barely express it at all. Rather, they work to suppress their sexual feelings and desires. At the other extreme are individuals who express their sexual urges with abandon, engaging in casual sex with great ease. Some people need to turn the lights out before they can have sex, while others would like to be on camera with spotlights shining. Some cannot even bring themselves to use sexual words without embarrassment, while others are eager to reveal the intimate details of their sex lives. To understand this diversity, we need to examine developmental influences on human sexual behavior.

Key Aspects of Sexual Identity

Learning Objective

List four key aspects of sexual identity.

As we noted in Chapter 5, *identity* refers to a stable sense of who one is and what one stands for. We'll use the term *sexual identity* **to refer to the complex of personal qualities, self-perceptions, attitudes, values, and preferences that guide one's sexual behavior.** In other words, your sexual identity consists of your sense of yourself as a sexual person. This conception of sexual identity includes four key features: your sexual orientation, body image, sexual values and ethics, and erotic preferences.

1. *Sexual orientation.* We have noted that sexual orientation refers to an individual's preference for emotional and sexual relationships with individuals of one gender or the other. *Heterosexuals* **seek emotional-sexual relationships with members of the other gender.** *Bisexuals* **seek emotional-sexual relationships with members of both genders.** *Homosexuals* **seek emotional-sexual relationships with members of the same gender.** In recent years, the terms *gay* and

straight have become widely used to refer to homosexuals and heterosexuals, respectively. Generally, male homosexuals are more likely to be called gay, whereas female homosexuals are more likely to be called *lesbians*. As a social issue, sexual orientation has only recently come out of the closet. Because many people are ignorant about this topic, we'll discuss it in some detail a little later.

2. *Body image.* Your body image is how you see yourself physically. Accurate or not, your body image definitely affects how you feel about yourself in the sexual domain. A positive body image is correlated with greater sexual activity and higher sexual satisfaction (Berscheid, Walster, & Bohrnstedt, 1973; Hatfield & Rapson, 1996). The increasing use of plastic surgery for breast enhancements, face-lifts, and nose jobs testifies to the importance of body image (Hamburger, 1988).

3. *Sexual values and ethics.* All cultures impose morality-based constraints on how people are expected to behave sexually (Rubin, 1984). Thus, people are trained to believe that certain expressions of sexuality are "right" while others are "wrong." The nature of the sexual messages individuals receive from parents, peers, schools, religion, and the media vary depending on their gender, race, ethnicity, and socioeconomic status. For example, the double standard encourages sexual experimentation in males but not females. Individuals are faced with the daunting task of sorting through these varied messages to develop their own sexual values and ethics.

4. *Erotic preferences.* Within the limits imposed by sexual orientation and values, people still differ in what they find enjoyable (Blumstein & Schwartz, 1983). Your erotic preferences encompass your attitudes about self-stimulation, oral sex, styles of foreplay and intercourse, and other sexual activities.

The years of childhood and adolescence are especially important in the development of sexual identity (Miller & Simon, 1980). This shaping process involves a complex interplay between physiological and psychosocial influences.

Physiological Influences

Learning Objective

Discuss how hormones influence sexual differentiation and sexual behavior.

Of the various physiological factors involved in sexual behavior, hormones have been of particular interest to researchers.

Hormones and Sexual Differentiation

During prenatal development, a number of biological changes result in a fetus that is a male or a female. Hormones play an important role in this process, which is termed *sexual differentiation* (Money & Ehrhardt, 1972). Around the third month of prenatal development, different hormonal secretions begin to be produced by male and female **gonads—the sex glands.** In males, the testes produce **androgens, the principal class of male sex hormones.** *Testosterone* is the most important of the androgens. In females, the ovaries produce **estrogens, the principal class of female sex hormones.** Actually, both classes of hormones are present in both genders, but in different proportions. During prenatal development, the differentiation of the genitals depends primarily on the level of testosterone produced—high in males, low in females.

With the arrival of adolescence, hormones once again play a key role in sexual development (Brooks-Gunn & Reiter, 1990). As we saw in Chapter 11, adolescents attain reproductive capacity as hormonal changes stimulate the maturation of the *primary sex characteristics* (sex organs). Hormonal changes also regulate the development of *secondary sex characteristics* (physical features that distinguish the genders but are not directly involved in reproduction). In females, increased secretion of estrogens leads to breast development, widened hips, and more rounded body contours. In males, increased secretion of androgens leads to the development of facial hair, a deeper voice, and more angular body contours.

Hormones and Sexual Behavior

Hormonal fluctuations clearly regulate sex *drive* in many species of animals (Feder, 1984). Hormones also play a role in human sexuality, but their influence is much more modest. Androgen does seem related to sexual motivation in *both* men and women, although the effect is less strong in women (Everitt & Bancroft, 1991; Sherwin, 1991). Also, high levels of testosterone in female and male subjects correlate with higher rates of sexual activity (Knussmann, Christiansen, & Couwenbergs, 1986). Curiously, estrogen levels among women do *not* correlate well with sexual interest. There does appear to be an association between females' sex drive and their ovulation/menstruation cycles, but its hormonal basis is yet to be determined (Harvey, 1987; Stanislaw & Rice, 1988).

In summary, physiological factors have important effects on sexual development. Their influence on *anatomy,* however, is much greater than their influence on sexual *activity.*

Psychosocial Influences

Learning Objective

Discuss how families, peers, schools, and media shape individuals' sexual attitudes and behavior.

The principal psychosocial influences on sexual identity are essentially the same as the main sources of gender-role socialization discussed in Chapter 10. Sexual identity is shaped by families, schools and peers, and the media. We'll discuss each of these in turn.

Families

Parents and the home environment are significant influences on sexual identity in the early years. Children usually engage in some sex play and exploration before they reach school age (Reinisch, 1990). They also display curiosity about sexual matters, asking questions such as "Where do babies come from?" Parents frequently punish innocent, exploratory sex play and squirm miserably when kids ask sexual questions. These sorts of reactions tend to convey to children that sex is "dirty." They may begin to feel guilty about their sexual urges and curiosity. Thus, parents who are uncomfortable with their sexuality can pass that discomfort on to their children at very early ages (Reinisch, 1990).

When it comes time for more systematic sex instruction, many parents have difficulty talking with their children. One survey found that 31% of American teenagers have never talked to their parents about sex, and 42% were anxious about bringing up the topic with their parents (Harris & Associates, 1986). As you might expect, open communication about sexual topics in the home correlates with better sexual adjustment among college students (Lewis & Janda, 1988). Furthermore, adolescents' attitudes about sexual conduct are more similar to their parents' attitudes when they are reared in families that encourage open sexual communication (Fisher, 1988).

Ultimately, parents who make sex a taboo topic end up reducing their influence on their kids' evolving sexual identity. Their children turn elsewhere to seek information about sexuality. Thus, the conspiracy of silence about sex in the home often backfires by increasing the influence of peers, schools, and the media.

Peers and Schools

As you can see in Figure 13.1, friends are, by far, the principal source of sex information for both males and females (Reinisch, 1990). Of course, one's peer group can be a source of highly misleading information. Furthermore, peers are unlikely to instill the same kinds of sexual ethics that parents tend to champion. Adolescents who receive most of their sex education from a parent are less likely to be sexually active and more likely to use contraceptives if they are sexually active (Zellman & Goodchilds, 1983).

To allay parents' fears that sex education will encourage sexual behavior, many sex education programs are nothing more than "an organ recital—what is connected to what in the body with no discussion of how or why two bodies might connect with each other" (Zellman & Goodchilds, 1983, p. 53). Unfortunately, these programs ignore the important psychological and social aspects of sexuality (Fine, 1988). Research on the effectiveness of sex education programs suggests that they lead to neither the experimentation that parents worry about nor the restraint that the programs advocate (Eisen & Zellman, 1987).

Figure 13.1
Where children get sexual information
When questioned about where they got their information about sex during childhood, adult respondents cited friends as their most important source of information. (Adapted from Reinisch, 1990)

Main Sources of Sexual Information in Childhood

Sources of information	Percentage using source*
Friend	42
Mother	29
Books	22
Boyfriend or girlfriend	17
Sex education	14
Magazines	13
Father	12
Sister	8
Movies	6
Brother	6
Other relative	6
Television	5
Teacher	5

*Respondents could choose up to three sources.

Media

As Figure 13.1 indicates, books and magazines are another major source of information on sex. Unfortunately, many of these publications perpetuate myths about sex and miseducate their young readers. On television alone, American teenagers see nearly 14,000 sexual encounters a year (Cole, Emery, & Horowitz, 1993), and these TV portrayals of sexual relationships are likely to influence young people's emerging sexual values (Strouse & Fabes, 1985). The authors of one study concluded that soap operas portray sex "as a spur-of-the-moment activity pursued primarily by unmarried partners with little concern about either birth control or disease prevention" (Lowry & Towles, 1989, p. 82).

The lyrics of rock music also contain extensive references to sexual behavior and norms of sexual conduct (Ray, Soares, & Tolchinsky, 1988). Some rap music has come under fire because it portrays women as sex objects and advocates sexual violence against women (Cocks, 1991).

Exposure to erotic materials appears to elevate the likelihood of sexual activity for only a few hours (Cattell, Kawash, & DeYoung, 1972). Nonetheless, such materials may have long-term effects on attitudes that eventually influence sexual behavior. For instance, participants who were exposed to a large dose of (nonaggressive) pornography developed more liberal attitudes about acceptable sexual practices (Zillmann & Bryant, 1984). Men who view *aggressive* pornography may come to believe more strongly in the myth that women enjoy being raped (Malamuth, 1984) and may increase their aggressive behavior toward women (Malamuth & Donnerstein, 1982).

Sex-charged music videos, such as those starring Madonna, appear to affect viewers' attitudes about sexual behavior.

In summary, sexual identity is shaped by a host of intersecting influences. Given the multiplicity of factors at work, it is not surprising that people bring highly diverse expectations to their sexual relationships. This diversity can make sexual interactions exceedingly complicated.

Gender Differences in Sexual Socialization

Discuss gender differences in sexual socialization and how they affect individuals in heterosexual and homosexual relationships.

Sexuality typically has different meanings for males and females. Males are more genitally focused than females, for several reasons. For one thing, boys usually begin masturbating earlier and more often than girls (Hunt, 1974). Also, uncontrolled frequent erections at puberty (caused by the increase in male hormones) focus the boy's attention on his genitals.

At the same time, powerful societal expectations encourage boys to be aggressive and conquest-oriented regarding sex. Adolescent boys are encouraged to experiment sexually, to initiate sexual activities, and to enjoy sex without emotional involvement (Fracher & Kimmel, 1987; Gagnon & Simon, 1973). Also, sex becomes a vehicle by which adolescent males validate their social status with other males (Garnets & Kimmel, 1991; Miller & Simon, 1974). As a result, sex has multiple meanings for men: They may emphasize "sex for fun" in casual relationships and reserve "sex with love" for committed relationships (Oliver & Hyde, 1993).

Adolescent girls are usually taught to view sex in the context of a loving relationship (Peplau, Rubin, & Hill, 1977). They learn about romance and the importance of physical attractiveness and catching a mate (Gagnon & Simon, 1973). It isn't until women actually begin having sexual experiences that they start to see themselves as sexual persons.

Sexual socialization takes longer in females than in males. One reason for this is *sexual guilt* (Lott, 1987). Whereas social norms about sexual behavior encourage males to be sexually active, the norms typically discourage this behavior in females: Sexually active women may be looked on as "sluts" or "easy lays." Thus, women learn to feel guilty about having sexual feelings and wanting to act on them. A second reason is that women typically develop *negative associations about their genitals and sex* that males don't experience, because of the blood and pain associated with menstruation, fears of pregnancy, and fears of penetration. Also, girls hear negative messages about sex and about men from their mothers, siblings, and female peers ("Men

Because of gender differences in sexual socialization, females tend to begin seeing themselves as sexual persons at a later age than males.

only want one thing"). They are also aware of rape and incest. These negative associations about sex are combined with the positive rewards of dating and emotional intimacy. It isn't surprising, therefore, that the sexuality of adolescent and many adult females is characterized by ambivalence (Hyde, 1996). These feelings can tilt in the negative direction if early sexual partners are impatient, unskillful, or selfish.

With these different views of sexuality and relationships, males and females are likely to be out of sync with each other—particularly during adolescence and early adulthood (DeLamater, 1987; Whitley, 1988b). A meta-analysis of studies on gender differences in sexuality found men to be much more accepting of casual sex ("one-night stands") than women (Oliver & Hyde, 1993). Similarly, in one study of college students, 84% of the men reported having had sexual relationships without any emotional involvement, but only 42% of the women had done so (Carroll, Volk, & Hyde, 1985). It is not until adulthood that males become more comfortable with emotional intimacy and commitment and that women become more comfortable with themselves as sexual persons. Clearly, these gender differences in sexual socialization make communication a critical factor in developing and maintaining sexual relationships that are mutually satisfying.

What implications do these gender differences have for individuals in *homosexual* relationships? For one thing, homosexual couples are less likely to have "incompatibility problems" because both members of the couple are the same gender and therefore have been socialized similarly. Like heterosexual women, lesbians typically experience emotional attraction to their partners before experiencing sexual feelings (Blumstein & Schwartz, 1989; Garnets & Kimmel, 1991). In contrast, gay men (like heterosexual men) place much more importance on physical appearance and sexual compatibility in selecting partners (Blumstein & Schwartz, 1983) and develop emotional relationships out of sexual ones (Harry, 1983).

Sexual Orientation

Learning Objective

Describe Kinsey's seven-point scale of sexual orientation.

People usually view heterosexuality and homosexuality as two distinct categories: You're either one or the other. However, many people who define themselves as heterosexuals have had homosexual experiences, and vice versa (Kinsey et al., 1948, 1953; Laumann et al., 1994). Thus, experts believe that it is more accurate to view heterosexuality and homosexuality as end points on a continuum. Indeed, Alfred Kinsey devised a seven-point scale, shown in Figure 13.2, that can be used to characterize sexual orientation.

How are people distributed on this scale? No one knows for sure because it's difficult to get accurate data. Furthermore, there's some debate about where to draw the lines between heterosexuality, bisexuality, and homosexuality on the Kinsey scale. A frequently cited estimate of the number of people who are predominantly homosexual is 10%; however, several recent surveys conducted in France, Great Britain, and the United States have all reported lower estimates (ACSF Investigators, 1992; Johnson et al., 1992; Laumann et al., 1994). Each of these studies used relatively rigorous sampling techniques, and each reported that about 2% of males and around 1% of females are *exclusively* homosexual. Janet Hyde (1994), the author of a respected textbook on human sexuality, also uses these figures. Furthermore, she estimates that another 80% of men and 90% of women are exclusively heterosexual and that the rest have had varying amounts of sexual experience with members of both genders.

Origins

Learning Objective

Summarize the current thinking on the origins of sexual orientation.

Why do some people become straight and others, gay? A number of *environmental explanations* have been suggested as causes of homosexuality. Freud believed that the combination of a "binding" mother and distant father contributed to the development of male homosexuality. Sociologists propose that homosexuality develops because of poor relationships with same-gender peers or because being labeled a homosexual sets up a self-fulfilling prophecy. Learning theorists assert that homosexuality develops as a result of early negative heterosexual encounters or early positive homosexual experiences. Surprisingly, the most comprehensive study of the causes of sexual orientation found no compelling support for *any* of these leading environmental explanations (Bell, Weinberg, & Hammersmith, 1981). Regarding a

Figure 13.2
Heterosexuality and homosexuality as end points on a continuum
Kinsey and other sex researchers view heterosexuality and homosexuality as a continuum rather than an all-or-none distinction. Kinsey created this seven-point scale (from 0 to 6) for describing sexual orientation. He used the term *ambisexual* to describe those falling in the middle of the scale, but the term *bisexual* is more widely used today.

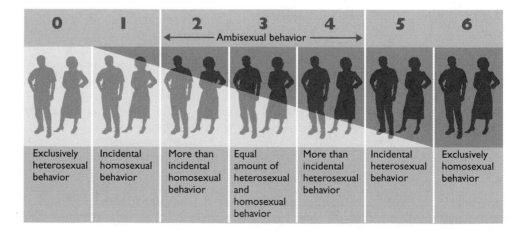

0	1	2	3	4	5	6
		← Ambisexual behavior →				
Exclusively heterosexual behavior	Incidental homosexual behavior	More than incidental homosexual behavior	Equal amount of heterosexual and homosexual behavior	More than incidental heterosexual behavior	Incidental heterosexual behavior	Exclusively homosexual behavior

Both biological and environmental factors appear to contribute to homosexuality, although its precise developmental roots remain obscure.

Figure 13.3
Genetics and sexual orientation
A concordance rate indicates the percentage of twin pairs or other pairs of relatives that exhibit the same characteristic. If relatives who share more genetic relatedness show higher concordance rates than relatives who share less genetic overlap, this evidence suggests a genetic predisposition to the characteristic. Recent studies of both gay men and lesbian women have found higher concordance rates among identical twins than fraternal twins, who, in turn, exhibit more concordance than adoptive siblings. These findings are consistent with the hypothesis that genetic factors influence sexual orientation. If only genetic factors were responsible for sexual orientation, the identical twin concordance rates would be 100%; because the rates are much lower, environmental factors must also play a role. (Data from Bailey & Pillard, 1991; Bailey et al., 1993)

related question, there is no evidence that parents' sexual orientation is linked to that of their children (Bozett, 1987; Falk, 1989). That is, heterosexual parents are as likely to produce homosexual (or heterosexual) offspring as homosexual parents.

Some theorists have speculated that *biological factors* may be involved in the development of homosexuality because many gay men and women can trace their homosexual leanings back to their childhood years (Bell, Weinberg, & Hammersmith, 1981; Garnets & Kimmel, 1991). One theory proposes that sexual orientation is determined during prenatal development by a complex process involving both hormonal and neurological factors (Ellis & Ames, 1987). To date, however, the research is inconclusive, so this theory must be viewed with caution (Bailey, Willerman, & Parks, 1991; Dorner et al., 1983). Other theorists have explored possible hormonal differences between heterosexuals and homosexuals. Again, however, there is no convincing evidence linking hormonal patterns to sexual orientation, although this possibility can't be ruled out. If hormones shape sexual orientation, their effects must be complex and subtle (Garnets & Kimmel, 1991; Gladue, 1987).

Researchers have also been looking at genetic factors as possible determinants of sexual orientation. In one study, researchers identified gay and bisexual men who had a twin brother (identical or fraternal) or an adopted brother (Bailey & Pillard, 1991). It was found that the concordance rates for identical twins were substantially higher than for fraternal twins or adopted siblings ("concordance" means that if one member of a pair has a characteristic, so does the other). These researchers found a similar pattern of results in a study of lesbian women with twin or adopted sisters (Bailey et al., 1993). The fact that the concordance rates for identical twins were substantially higher than for fraternal twins clearly points to a genetic contribution to sexual orientation (see Figure 13.3). However, if only genetic factors determined sexual orientation, we would see 100% concordance for the identical twin pairs. However, these concordance rates were 52% for gay men and 48% for lesbians, indicating that environmental factors also play a role in sexual orientation. Finally, there is evidence for a genetic marker for homosexuality in men (Hamer et al., 1993). Researchers speculate that a gene or genes on the X chromosome somehow contributes to male homosexuality. Researchers are currently looking at the chromosomes of female homosexuals. Obviously, this startling discovery must be replicated before we can place much confidence in it. Nonetheless, the study of possible genetic links to homosexuality appears to be a promising line of inquiry.

To conclude, we don't yet know what determines sexual orientation. This is an exceedingly complex issue and research is still in its infancy. The best we can say is that the explanation must lie in some complex interaction of biological and environmental factors (Byne & Parsons, 1993; Gladue, 1994).

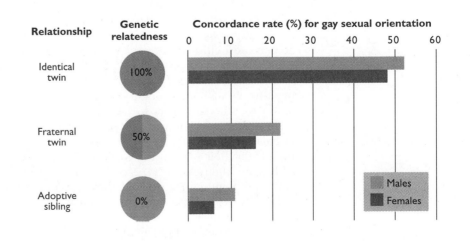

Adjustment

Homosexuality was initially classified as a psychological disorder by the mental health community. The pioneering research of Evelyn Hooker (1957) and others, however, demonstrated that view to be a myth: Gays and straights do not differ on overall measures of psychological adjustment (Bell & Weinberg, 1978; Rosen, 1974). The results of these studies, changes in public attitudes, and political lobbying eventually contributed to the deletion of homosexuality from the official list of psychological disorders in 1973 (Rothblum, Solomon, & Albee, 1986).

Researchers have also examined the adjustment of children from homosexual families. A study that compared children from lesbian and heterosexual families reported no differences in peer group relationships, popularity, or social adjustment (Green, 1982).

Lesbian and Gay Male Identity Development

Homosexuals seem to take longer to recognize their sexual orientation than heterosexuals do, for several reasons (Garnets & Kimmel, 1991; Vance & Green, 1984). For one thing, the widespread *assumption that heterosexuality is universal* means that some individuals never even consider the possibility that they might be homosexual until they have pretty strong evidence that they are. A second reason is tied to the *stigma* still associated with homosexuality—that is, even if individuals suspect they are homosexual, they may try to deny this fact for fear of social rejection. A third reason is that homosexuals report both same- and other-gender erotic arousal and sexual behavior during adolescence and early adulthood. Some experts speculate that *sexual experiences with the other gender* may cause gay men and lesbians to misclassify themselves as heterosexuals, thus delaying their awareness of their true sexual orientation (Hencken, 1984).

Clarity about sexual orientation seems to take longer for lesbians than for gay men. Possible reasons include the fact that lesbians are more likely than gay men to engage in heterosexual sex, less likely to be involved in same-gender erotic activity, more likely to continue other-gender sexual activities after questioning their sexual identity, and more likely to get married than gay men (Chapman & Brannock, 1987; Garnets & Kimmel, 1991).

Linda Garnets and Doug Kimmel (1991) have summarized the research on gay male and lesbian identity development. Developmental milestones in this process include the following:

1. *Initial awareness of same-gender erotic desires.* Individuals become aware of strong emotional and sexual attractions to members of the same gender. This recognition in turn triggers a "developmental transition in which individuals report feeling different and being off course" (Garnets & Kimmel, 1991, p. 154).

2. *Reconciling sexual orientation with negative societal attitudes.* Over time, individuals transform the category of "gay" or "lesbian" from a negative (societal stereotype) to a positive one and accept, by degrees, that the label applies to themselves. They use a number of cognitive strategies by which to reconcile negative societal attitudes with their own sexual orientation.

3. *Exploring gay and lesbian subcultures.* Contact with these subcultures is available in most cities, by newspaper subscription, and by toll-free information services. Such contact provides a range of role models and diminishes feelings of isolation.

4. *Disclosing sexual orientation to others.* Over time, homosexuals usually feel the need to disclose their identity to other people. Communicating one's sexual orientation to others appears to be a prerequisite for the emergence of a positive gay male or lesbian identity (Garnets & Kimmel, 1991). Nevertheless, individuals need to balance the psychological and social benefits of doing so against the costs (being fired from their jobs, losing custody of their children, falling victim to hate crimes). Although Americans are becoming more accepting of homosexuality, prejudice is still a problem, as Figure 13.4 shows. A pragmatic solution to this conflict is *rational outness*—being "as open as possible, because it feels healthy to be honest, and as closed as necessary to protect against discrimination" (Bradford & Ryan, 1987, p. 77). Homosexual individuals tend to disclose their sexual orientation to close heterosexual friends and siblings rather than to parents, co-workers, or employers.

Figure 13.4
Prejudice toward homosexuals
A 1993 Gallup Poll surveyed Americans on the acceptance of gays in American society. Responses to three selected questions show that attitudes are quite variable. (Data from Moore, 1993)

Attitudes Toward Homosexuals			
Poll Question	**Yes**	**No**	**No opinion**
1 Should homosexuals have equal rights in terms of job opportunities?	80%	14%	6%
2 Should homosexuals stay in the closet?	56%	37%	7%
3 Should civil rights laws include homosexuals?	46%	48%	6%

Interaction in Sexual Relationships

Because of their importance, sexual relationships stir up intense emotions. When things are going well, people feel "on top of the world"; when they're not, they feel in the grip of despair. In this section, we'll briefly discuss the interpersonal dynamics of sexual relationships.

Motives Underlying Sexual Interactions

Learning Objective

Summarize the findings on sexual motives.

What motivates individuals to engage in sexual encounters? As you might surmise, sexual motives are quite diverse (Nass, Libby, & Fisher, 1981). We'll mention only a few:

- *Affection.* Longing for love, closeness, and physical and emotional union.
- *Lust.* Having passion for intensifying and then gratifying sexual desires, with a focus on sensual arousal, fantasies, and delight in touching and being touched.
- *Duty.* Feeling that it's one's responsibility to have sex on schedule or to keep a partner from being uncomfortably frustrated. A woman often feels that she can't leave a man unsatisfied. The notion that he could masturbate or that she might feel equally uncomfortable if highly aroused but not satisfied is missing from the traditional script.
- *Boredom.* Using sex to enhance a dull environment or routine activities.
- *Self-affirmation.* Acting out one's perceived sexual identity so that the other will notice and approve of it.

Research suggests that the motives for sex vary by gender (Carroll et al., 1985; Whitley, 1988a). In one study, college students were asked, "What was your most important reason for having sexual intercourse on the most recent occasion?" (Whitley, 1988a). Lust and pleasure motives were cited by 51% of the men, but only 9% of the women. Love and emotional reasons were cited by 51% of the women, but only 24% of the men. Similar gender differences have been found in a community survey that looked at a broader sample of subjects than just college students (Leigh, 1989). Furthermore, these gender differences appear to transcend sexual orientation, as they were observed in homosexuals as well as heterosexuals. Some theorists speculate that these differences are attributable to gender-role socialization (Carroll et al., 1985); others believe that they are a product of biological influences (Knoth, Boyd, & Singer, 1988).

Sexual Scripts

Besides varying motives for sex, people may have different expectations about how romantic and sexual relationships should evolve (Gagnon & Simon, 1973; Simon & Gagnon, 1986). **Sexual scripts are culturally programmed sets of expectations about how individuals should behave sexually.** Individuals' sexual scripts are influenced by their social class, ethnic background, and religious upbringing. Although sexual scripts can be individualized, there are a handful of scripts that guide sexual conduct in most people. Nass et al. (1981) describe five common sexual scripts in modern Western culture:

- *Traditional religious script.* Sex is acceptable only within marriage. All other sexual activities are taboo, especially for women. Sex means reproduction, though it may also have something to do with affection.
- *Romantic script.* Sex means love. If one grows in love with someone, it's okay to "make love," either in or out of marriage. Without love, sex is a meaningless animal function. The romantic script is the predominant one in our society.
- *Sexual friendship script.* It's okay for people who are friends to have an intimate sexual relationship. Usually such arrangements are not sexually exclusive.
- *Casual/mutual horniness script.* Sex is defined as recreational fun. Here, people are casual acquaintances who are mutually sexually aroused. This script is increasingly publicized by the mass media.
- *Utilitarian-predatory script.* People have sex for some reason other than pleasure, reproduction, or love. The reasons for sex might include economic gain (as in prostitution), career advancement, or power achievement.

These sexual scripts focus broadly on the *formation* of sexual liaisons. However, sexual scripts also guide the day-to-day details of sexual interactions in *established relationships*. People have expectations about which partner should initiate sexual encounters, where and when sex should take place, and the sequencing of sexual activities (Gagnon & Simon, 1987). One person's sexual script might dictate that sex should occur only in the evening, progressing quickly from hugging and kissing to intercourse in a single position. Another individual's sexual script might dictate that sex should occur whenever the urge strikes, progressing slowly from mutual fondling to oral contact to intercourse in several different positions. Obviously, if these two people were an actual couple, their differing sexual scripts would be a source of considerable conflict.

Communicating About Sex

Couples bring differing motives, scripts, attitudes, and appetites to sexual liaisons. Hence, it is not surprising that disagreements about sex are commonplace (Blumstein & Schwartz, 1983; Levinger, 1970). These disparities are likely to be an ongoing source of frustration in a relationship if they cannot be resolved to the couple's mutual satisfaction. Intimate couples have to negotiate whether, when, and how often they will have sex. They also have to decide what kinds of erotic activities will take place and what it all means to their relationship. This negotiation process may not be explicit, but it's there. Unfortunately, many people find it difficult to talk to their partner about sex. Let's look at four common barriers to sexual communication.

1. *Fear of appearing ignorant.* According to a Kinsey Institute/Roper poll, most Americans are woefully ignorant about sex (Reinisch, 1990). Specifically, on an 18-item test of basic sexual knowledge, 55% of a statistically representative sample of American adults failed (could answer correctly only 50% or fewer of the questions). Another 27% received D's (could answer correctly only 56–66% of the questions). (You can test your own knowledge about some aspects of sex by responding to the questions in Figure 13.5.) Because most people feel that they should be experts about sex and know that they are not, they feel ashamed. To hide their ignorance, they avoid talking about sex.

2. *Concern about partner's response.* Sometimes the problem is that individuals worry that their partner might not continue to respect and love them if they express their authentic wishes about sex. So, they keep their preferences to themselves. As a result, one or both partners are often left feeling unsatisfied and frustrated.

3. *Conflicting attitudes about sex.* Many people, particularly women, carry into adulthood the negative sexual messages they learned as children. Also, most peo-

Figure 13.5
Sexual knowledge test
Check your basic sexual knowledge by answering 5 of the 18 questions on the Kinsey Institute's test. Information about each of the 5 questions is discussed in this chapter. (Based on Reinisch, 1990)

How Knowledgeable About Sex Are You?

1 Petroleum jelly, Vaseline Intensive Care, baby oil, and Nivea are *not* good lubricants to use with a condom or diaphragm.

_____True _____False _____Don't know

2 More than one out of four (25%) American men have had a sexual experience with another male during their teens or adult years.

_____True _____False _____Don't know

3 It is usually difficult to tell whether people are or are not homosexual just by their appearance or gestures.

_____True _____False _____Don't know

4 A woman or teenage girl can get pregnant during her menstrual flow (her "period").

_____True _____False _____Don't know

5 A woman or teenage girl can get pregnant even if the man withdraws his penis before he ejaculates (before he "comes").

_____True _____False _____Don't know

Scoring: 1. True. (Oil-based creams, lotions, and jellies can produce microscopic holes in rubber products within 60 seconds of their application.) 2. True. (A Kinsey Institute review of research estimated that at least 25% of American males have had at least one same-sex experience.) 3. True. (Gay males can be extremely masculine, average, or effeminate in their appearance and gestures. Lesbians can be extremely feminine, average, or masculine in their appearance and gestures.) 4. True. (While the chance of a woman's becoming pregnant during her menstrual period is lower than at other times, pregnancy *can* occur if she has unprotected sex during her period. Sperm can live for up to 8 days in a woman's reproductive tract, and if the menstrual cycle is irregular, as it is likely to be in adolescence, sperm may still be present in the reproductive tract a week later to fertilize a new egg.) 5. True. (The pre-ejaculatory fluid secreted from the tip of the penis during arousal may contain enough sperm to fertilize an egg.)

ple have contradictory beliefs about sex ("Sex is 'beautiful'" and "Sex is 'dirty'"), which produces psychological conflicts. These conflicting attitudes may also cause individuals to feel uncomfortable with themselves as sexual persons and to have difficulty talking about sex.

4. *Early negative sexual experiences.* Some people have had negative sexual experiences that inhibit their enjoyment of sex. If earlier negative experiences were the result of having ignorant or inconsiderate sexual partners, subsequent positive sexual interactions will usually resolve the problem over time. If earlier sexual experiences were traumatic, as in the case of rape or incest, counseling may be required to help the individual view sex positively and to enjoy it.

It's unfortunate that couples have difficulty talking about sex. Studies show that open communication is associated with greater relationship satisfaction and greater sexual satisfaction (Cupach & Comstock, 1990; Zimmer, 1983). Most of the advice in Chapter 7 on how to improve verbal and nonverbal communication can be applied to sexual relationships. Assertive communication and constructive conflict-resolution strategies can keep sexual negotiations healthy. Keeping in mind these thoughts about interpersonal aspects of sex, let's turn our attention to the physiological aspects of sexuality.

Unsatisfying sex can be a source of frustration in relationships if couples are not able to talk about their needs and preferences.

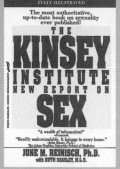
June Machover Reinisch, a psychologist and former director of the Kinsey Institute for Research on Sex, Gender, and Reproduction, provides the latest factual information about a wide variety of sexual topics. The book starts off with a test of basic sex information and provides readers with national norms by which to evaluate their expertise. The 19 chapters in the book range across a variety of topics: the anatomy and physical functioning of the male and female reproductive systems; sexual socialization; puberty; sex and the disabled; and sex and disease, surgery, and drugs, to name a few. Most of the book is written in a question-and-answer format (the questions are taken from those sent to the institute). Reinisch also includes the names and addresses of helpful organizations and support groups for many kinds of sex-related issues. The book's informal writing style makes for not only informative but enjoyable reading. Recommended readings are included at the end of each chapter, and there is an appendix on locating, selecting, and evaluating health care specialists.

> In the fall of 1989, The Kinsey Institute tested the basic sexual knowledge of a statistically representative group of 1,974 American adults. Unfortunately, Americans failed the test. . . . Of Americans taking our eighteen-question test, 55% failed. . . . Another 27% of respondents received D's. . . . 14% obtained C's. There were only five A students (less than .5%) and only sixty-eight people (4%) received B's.
>
> Who passed the test? These people tended to be 30–44 years old; with at least some college education; from higher income groups; with no religious affiliation; from the Midwest or West; politically liberal; single, married, divorced or separated but not widowed; and from more densely populated urban areas.
>
> Who failed? They were more likely to be 60 years or older; to have no high school diploma; to come from lower income groups; to have a religious affiliation; to live in the South or Northeast; to be politically conservative or moderate; widowed; and to come from less densely populated or more rural areas. [p. 1]

The Human Sexual Response

When people engage in sexual activity, exactly how does the body respond? Surprisingly, until William Masters and Virginia Johnson conducted their groundbreaking research in the 1960s, very little was known about the physiology of the human sexual response. Masters and Johnson used physiological recording devices to monitor the bodily changes of volunteers engaging in sex. Their observations and interviews with their subjects yielded a detailed description of the human sexual response that has won them widespread acclaim.

The Sexual Response Cycle

Learning Objective

Describe the four phases of the human sexual response cycle.

Masters and Johnson's (1966, 1970) description of the sexual response cycle is a generalized one, outlining typical rather than inevitable patterns. You should keep in mind that there is considerable variability among people. Figure 13.6 shows how the intensity of sexual arousal changes as women and men progress through the four phases of the sexual response cycle.

Excitement Phase

During the initial phase of excitement, the level of arousal usually escalates rapidly. In both sexes, muscle tension, respiration rate, heart rate, and blood pressure increase quickly. In males *vasocongestion*—**engorgement of blood vessels**—produces penile erection, swollen testes, and the movement of the scrotum (the sac

June Machover Reinisch

Figure 13.6
The human sexual response cycle
There are similarities and differences between men and women in patterns of sexual arousal. Pattern A, which culminates in orgasm and resolution, is the most typical sequence for both sexes. Pattern B, which involves sexual arousal without orgasm followed by a slow resolution, is also seen in both sexes, but it is more common among women. Pattern C, which involves multiple orgasms, is seen almost exclusively in women, as men go through a refractory period before they are capable of another orgasm. (Based on Masters & Johnson, 1966)

containing the testes) closer to the body. In females, vasocongestion leads to a swelling of the clitoris and vaginal lips, vaginal lubrication, and enlargement of the uterus. Most women also experience nipple erection and a swelling of the breasts.

Plateau Phase

The name given to the "plateau" stage is misleading, as physiological arousal does not level off. Instead, it continues to build, but at a much slower pace. In women, further vasocongestion produces a tightening of the lower third of the vagina and a "ballooning" open of the upper two-thirds. This lifts the uterus and cervix away from the end of the vagina. In men, the head of the penis may swell, and the testicles typically enlarge and move closer to the body. Many men secrete a bit of pre-ejaculatory fluid from the tip of the penis that may contain sperm.

Distractions during the plateau phase can delay or stop movement to the next stage. These include ill-timed interruptions such as a telephone call, the doorbell ringing, or a child's knocking—or not!—on the bedroom door. Equally distracting can be such things as physical discomfort, pain, guilt, frightening thoughts, feelings of insecurity or anger toward one's partner, and anxiety about being able to have an orgasm.

Orgasm Phase

Orgasm **occurs when sexual arousal reaches its peak intensity and is discharged in a series of muscular contractions that pulsate through the pelvic area.** Heart rate, respiration rate, and blood pressure increase sharply during this exceedingly pleasant spasmodic response. The male orgasm is usually accompanied by ejaculation of seminal fluid. Some women report that they ejaculate some kind of fluid at orgasm. The extent of this phenomenon as well as the source and nature of the fluid are matters still under debate (Reinisch, 1990). The subjective experience of orgasm appears to be similar for men and women. When investigators have asked subjects to provide written descriptions of what their orgasms feel like without using specific words for genitals, even psychologists and physicians have not

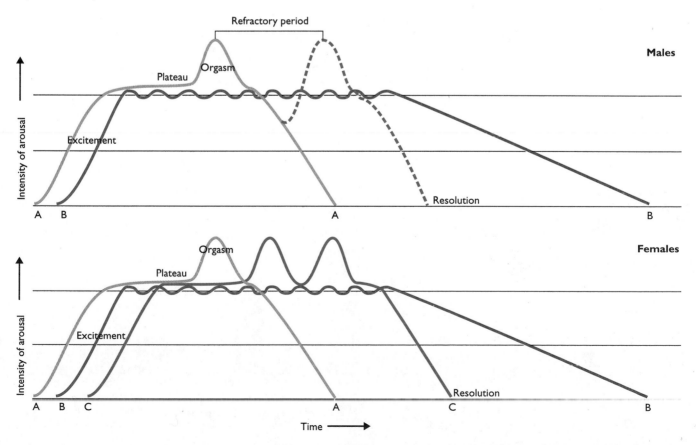

been able to tell which descriptions came from women and which came from men (Vance & Wagner, 1976; Wiest, 1977).

Resolution Phase

During the resolution phase, the physiological changes produced by sexual arousal subside. If one has not had an orgasm, the reduction in sexual tension may be relatively slow and sometimes unpleasant. After orgasm, men generally experience **a** *refractory period,* **a time following orgasm during which males are unable to experience another orgasm.** The refractory period varies from a few minutes to a few hours and increases with age.

Gender Differences in Patterns of Orgasm

Learning Objective

Discuss gender differences in patterns of orgasm and some reasons for them.

As a whole, the sexual responses of women and men parallel each other fairly closely. The similarities clearly outweigh the differences. Nonetheless, there are some interesting differences between the genders in their patterns of experiencing orgasm. During *intercourse*, women are somewhat less likely than men to reach orgasm (that is, they are more likely to follow pattern B in Figure 13.6). According to a recent survey of American sexual behavior (Laumann et al., 1994), about 30% of women reported that they "always" reached orgasm in their primary sexual relationships, compared to 75% of men (see Figure 13.7). The latest data from the Kinsey Institute indicate that about 10% of women have never had an orgasm by any means (Reinisch, 1990).

Masters and Johnson found that the men they studied took about 4 minutes to reach a climax with their partners in the laboratory. Women took about 10–20 minutes to reach orgasm with their partners, but they reached orgasm in about 4 minutes when they masturbated. Clearly, then, women are capable of reaching orgasm more quickly than they typically do. Our point here is not that men and women should race each other to the finish line but that physiological factors are not the likely cause of gender differences related to orgasm.

What, then, might account for these disparities? First, although most women report that they enjoy intercourse, it may not be the optimal mode of stimulation for them. Reinisch (1990) estimates that between 50% and 75% of women who have orgasms by other means of stimulation do not have orgasms when the *only* form of stimulation is penile thrusting during intercourse. This is because intercourse provides rather indirect stimulation to the clitoris, which appears to be the most sexually sensitive genital area in most women. Thus, more lengthy foreplay, including manual or oral stimulation, should enhance women's sexual pleasure. Unfortu-

Figure 13.7
Sexual satisfaction with primary partner
A recent major survey of American sexual behavior showed large gender differences in the consistency of orgasm, a physical measure of sexual satisfaction. Men's and women's subjective evaluations of physical and emotional sexual satisfaction are much more similar. These data indicate that not everyone who has an orgasm every time has a blissful sex life and that factors other than orgasm contribute to a satisfying sex life. (From Laumann et al., 1994)

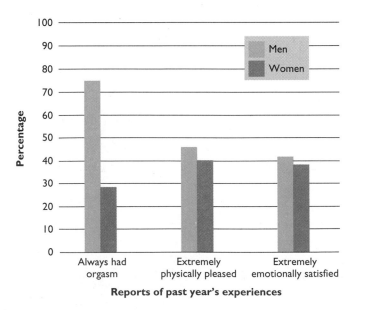

William Masters and Virginia Johnson

nately, many couples are locked into a sexual script that prescribes that orgasms should be achieved through intercourse. (Even the word "foreplay" suggests that any other form of sexual stimulation is merely preparation for the "main event.")

Orgasmic inconsistency in women can also be caused by intercourse that is too brief or too mechanical to be satisfying (Gebhard, 1966; Wolfe, 1981). Since women's sexual scripts usually call for affection, most women want to hear some tender words and expressions of love during a sexual encounter. If a man is ignorant about this fact, discounts its importance, or is uncomfortable expressing his affection verbally, his partner may be inhibited in her sexual response.

Data on the incidence of orgasm among lesbians also support a socialization-based explanation of gender differences in orgasmic consistency. Kinsey and his associates (1953) found that lesbians who had been sexually active for five years reached orgasm more consistently than heterosexual women who had been married for the same length of time. No doubt this is because female (lesbian) partners know more about women's sexuality and techniques for optimizing women's sexual satisfaction than male partners do. Also, female couples are more likely to emphasize the emotional aspects of lovemaking than heterosexual couples (Blumstein & Schwartz, 1983).

Because women reach orgasm through intercourse less consistently than men, they are more likely than men to fake an orgasm (Petersen et al., 1983). Surveys reveal that both sexes fake orgasms—women just do it more often. People appear to fake orgasms to make their partners feel better or to bring sexual activity to an end when they're fatigued. Generally, faking orgasms is not a good idea, as this practice undermines open communication about sex.

Sexual Arousal and Satisfaction

People engage in a wide variety of activities to elicit sexual arousal and satisfaction. *Erogenous zones* **are areas of the body that are sexually sensitive or responsive.** The genitals and breasts usually come to mind when people think of erogenous zones. These *are* particularly sensitive areas for most people. But it's worth noting that many individuals fail to appreciate the potential that lies in other areas of the body. Virtually any area of the body can function as an erogenous zone.

Indeed, the ultimate erogenous zone may be the mind. By this we mean that one's mental set is extremely important to sexual arousal. Skillful genital stimulation by a partner may have absolutely no impact if the person is not in the mood for sex. Yet fantasy in the absence of any other stimulation can produce great arousal. In this section, we'll discuss techniques for achieving sexual arousal and satisfaction.

Fantasy

Learning Objective

Discuss the role of fantasy and kissing and touching in sexual arousal.

Sexual fantasies are common and normal. Some of the more common themes in sexual fantasies are listed in Figure 13.8, based on research by Sue (1979). It should be emphasized that just because people fantasize about a particular encounter, such as forced sex, doesn't mean that they would really like to have such an experience. Only one-tenth of 1% of women say that they enjoy forced sex and only one-third of 1% of men say that they enjoy forcing a partner to have sex (Laumann et al., 1994). Thus, fantasizing about forced sexual encounters may actually be a way to absolve oneself of guilt that might come from enjoying sexual pleasure or from initiating sex (Reinisch, 1990).

Many people fantasize while masturbating (Hones & Barlow, 1990). Also, one study reported that 84% of males and 82% of females fantasized at least sometime during sexual activities with another person (Cado & Leitenberg, 1990). Research suggests that fantasies can help people of both sexes enhance their sexual excitement and achieve orgasm (Davidson, 1985).

Figure 13.8
Common sexual fantasies
The percentage of men and women reporting various sexual fantasies during intercourse is shown here. Sue (1979) concludes that people fantasize about experiences they wouldn't seek out in real life.

Fantasies During Intercourse

Theme	Subjects reporting fantasy (%)	
	Males	Females
A former lover	42.9	41.0
An imaginary lover	44.3	24.3
Oral-genital sex	61.2	51.4
Group sex	19.3	14.1
Being forced or overpowered into a sexual relationship	21.0	36.4
Others observing you engage in sexual intercourse	15.4	20.0
Others finding you sexually irresistible	55.2	52.8
Being rejected or sexually abused	10.5	13.2
Forcing others to have sexual relations with you	23.5	15.8
Others giving in to you after resisting you at first	36.8	24.3
Observing others engaging in sex	17.9	13.2
A member of the same sex	2.8	9.4
Animals	0.9	3.7

Note: For comparison, the responses of "frequently" and "sometimes" were combined for both males and females to obtain these percentages. The number of respondents answering for a specific fantasy ranged from 103 to 106 for males and from 105 to 107 for females.

Kissing and Touching

Most two-person sexual activities begin with kissing. Kissing usually starts with the lips but may be extended to almost any area of the partner's body. Mutual caressing is also an integral element of sexual stimulation for most couples. Like kissing, this tactile stimulation may be applied to any area of the body. Manual and oral stimulation of the other partner's genitals are related sexual practices. As with any type of sexual activity, specific techniques are not as important as good communication about one's preferences.

Men often underestimate the importance of kissing and touching (including clitoral stimulation). It is not surprising, therefore, that heterosexual women commonly complain that their partners are in too big of a hurry (Denny, Field, & Quadagno, 1984). Partners who seek to learn about each other's preferences and who try to accommodate each other are much more likely to have mutually satisfying sexual experiences than those who ignore these issues.

Self-Stimulation

Learning Objective

Discuss the prevalence of self-stimulation and attitudes about it.

Stimulation of one's own genitals is commonly called masturbation. This practice has traditionally been condemned as immoral because of its nonreproductive nature. In the 19th and early 20th centuries, disapproval and suppression of masturbation were truly intense because it was widely assumed that self-stimulation was harmful to one's physical and mental health. Children were often forced to sleep in manacles, and some were fitted with genital cages (Karlen, 1971). Because the term *masturbation* has negative connotations, many experts prefer such terms as *self-stimulation* and *autoeroticism*.

Kinsey discovered over four decades ago that most people masturbate with no ill effects. Sexologists now recognize that self-stimulation is a normal, healthy, and sometimes important component of sexual behavior (Gadpaille, 1975). Nonetheless, many people experience guilt about it.

DEVELOPMENTAL TRANSITIONS **PART III**

Self-stimulation is common in our society: By adulthood, nine out of ten males and eight out of ten females report having masturbated at least once (Atwood & Gagnon, 1987). Masturbation is less common among those with less education (Laumann et al., 1994). Also, women masturbate less than men, and African American males masturbate less than Asian, white, and Hispanic men.

Males almost always masturbate by stimulating the penis by hand (Kinsey et al., 1948). The most preferred technique in females is manipulating the clitoris and inner lips (Hite, 1976; Kinsey et al., 1953). Self-stimulation remains common among adults even after marriage. Among married couples, 57% of the husbands and 37% of the wives reported engaging in self-stimulation (Laumann et al., 1994). Marital partners usually don't talk to each other about their masturbation, no doubt for fear that their partner might view it as a sign of sexual discontent. However, the fact that self-stimulation is so widespread among married persons suggests that it probably is not a sign of dissatisfaction in most cases.

Oral and Anal Sex

Oral sex refers to oral stimulation of the genitals. ***Cunnilingus* is oral stimulation of the female genitals; *fellatio* is oral stimulation of the penis.** Partners may stimulate each other simultaneously, or one partner may stimulate the other without immediate reciprocation. Oral-genital sex may be one of several activities in a sexual encounter, or it may constitute the main event. Oral sex is a major source of orgasms for many heterosexual couples, and it plays a particularly central role in homosexual relationships. A positive aspect of oral sex is that it does not result in pregnancy. However, it is possible to contract AIDS through mouth-genital stimulation, especially if semen is swallowed (in fellatio).

There is a residue of negative attitudes about oral sex, particularly among African Americans, Hispanics, religious conservatives, and those who have less education (Laumann et al., 1994). However, the prevalence of oral sex appears to have increased dramatically since the Kinsey studies of the late 1940s and early 1950s (Gagnon & Simon, 1987). About 80% of men and about 70% of women (both gay

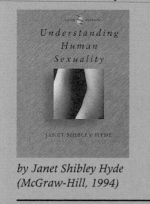

Recommended Reading

Understanding Human Sexuality

by Janet Shibley Hyde
(McGraw-Hill, 1994)

College courses on sexuality are gradually appearing all over the country, and a host of new books to serve these courses are now available. If you can't enroll in a course on sexuality, you may want to read one of the better textbooks. If so, *Understanding Human Sexuality* by Janet Shibley Hyde is an outstanding candidate. Hyde's text is accurate, thorough, up-to-date, well organized, and written in an engaging, highly readable manner. What sets it apart from other texts is its clarity and sensitivity to readers' personal needs. It discusses the interpersonal aspects of sex without getting bogged down in physiology. Other excellent sexuality texts of similar quality include *Our Sexuality* by Robert Crooks and Karla Baur (Brooks/Cole, 1996) and *Understanding Sexuality* by Adelaide Haas and Kurt Haas (Times Mirror/Mosby, 1993). Any of these three books can provide you with an excellent introduction to the realities of human sexual expression.

Throughout most of recorded history, at least until about 100 years ago, religion (and rumor) provided most of the information that people had about sexuality. . . . It was against this background of religious understandings of sexuality that the scientific study of sex began in the late nineteenth century, although, of course, religious notions continue to influence our ideas about sexuality to the present day. . . . The scientific study of sex has not emerged as a separate, unified academic discipline like biology or psychology or sociology. Rather, it tends to be interdisciplinary—a joint effort by biologists, psychologists, sociologists, anthropologists, and physicians. In a sense, this is a major virtue in our current approach to understanding sexuality, since it gives us a better view of humans in all their sexual complexity. [pp. 4, 5, 8] and straight) report that they have either given or received oral sex at least once (Laumann et al., 1994). It appears that oral sex is now a component in most couples' sexual relationships (Blumstein & Schwartz, 1983; Wyatt, Peters, & Guthrie, 1988).

Anal intercourse **is insertion of the penis into a partner's anus and rectum.** Legally, it is termed *sodomy* (and is still considered illegal in a few states). About 25% of men and women report that they have practiced anal sex at least once (Laumann et al., 1994). Anal intercourse is more popular among homosexual male couples than among heterosexual couples (Bell & Weinberg, 1978). However, even among gay men it ranks lower than oral sex and mutual masturbation in prevalence. AIDS is very easily transmitted by anal sex, so it's fortunate that the incidence of this practice is low.

Intercourse

Learning Objective

Discuss intercourse and the preferred sexual activities of gay males and lesbians.

Vaginal intercourse, known more technically as *coitus,* **involves insertion of the penis into the vagina and (typically) pelvic thrusting.** It is the most widely endorsed and widely practiced sexual act in our society. In the recent American sex survey, 95% of heterosexual respondents said that they had practiced vaginal sex the last time they had sex (Laumann et al., 1994). Insertion of the penis generally requires adequate vaginal lubrication, or it may be difficult and painful for the woman—as will intercourse itself. This is another good reason for couples to spend plenty of time on mutual kissing and touching. In the absence of adequate lubrication, partners may choose to use artificial lubricants such as K-Y jelly.

Partners may use any of a variety of positions in their intercourse. Many couples use more than one position in a single encounter. The man-above, or "missionary," position is the most common. When Kinsey's studies were done over 40 years ago, many couples limited themselves to this position exclusively. Studies indicate that there is more variation today, as you can see from the data in Figure 13.9.

Each position has its advantages and disadvantages, according to Masters and Johnson (1970). Although people are fascinated by the relative merits of various positions, specific positions may not be as important as the tempo, depth, and angle of movements in intercourse. As with other aspects of sexual relations, the crucial consideration is that partners talk to each other about their preferences.

What kinds of sexual activities do homosexuals prefer in the absence of coitus (which is, by definition, a heterosexual act)? Gay men tend to engage in mutual masturbation, fellatio, and, less frequently, anal intercourse. Lesbians engage in mutual masturbation, cunnilingus, and *tribadism,* in which one partner lies on top of the other and makes thrusting movements so that both receive genital stimulation at the same time. Contrary to stereotype, a dildo (an artificial penis) is rarely used by lesbian couples (Jay & Young, 1979).

Figure 13.9
Changes in the use of coital positions
About 20–25 years apart, Kinsey et al. (1948, 1953) and Hunt (1974) asked subjects about coital positions they used besides the man-above position. As you can see, Hunt's data indicate that by the 1970s couples were using a greater variety of positions for intercourse.

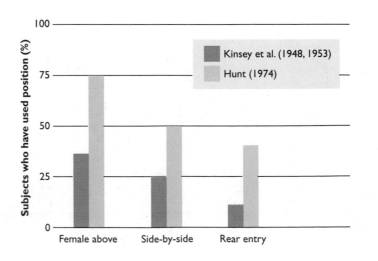

Public awareness of AIDS has had a significant effect on the sexual behavior of some groups, although the behavior of college-aged individuals is little changed.

Patterns of Sexual Behavior

In the previous section we focused on the sexual response itself. Our principal interests were physiology and techniques. In this section we'll discuss how variables such as age, gender, and type of relationship are related to patterns of sexual behavior. Let's begin by examining the so-called sexual revolution.

Sex in the Age of AIDS

Learning Objective

Describe how the fear of contracting AIDS has influenced sexual attitudes and practices.

During the 1960s and 1970s, American sexual attitudes and behaviors became more liberal than they had been previously. The unfortunate results of these changes in sexual practices were increases in teenage pregnancy and sexually transmitted diseases (Byrne, Kelley, & Fisher, 1993; Hatcher et al., 1994). In addition, the early 1980s saw the spread of the human immunodeficiency virus (HIV) that leads to acquired immune deficiency syndrome (AIDS). Has public awareness of this deadly sexually transmitted disease had any effects on sexual behavior?

In Figure 13.10, you can see that the incidence of premarital intercourse was just as high in 1985 as it had been in 1980, and higher than it had been in 1975.

Figure 13.10
Premarital sex among college students
The percentage of college students who report engaging in premarital intercourse did not decline between 1980 and 1985, indicating that concerns about AIDS did not affect this aspect of their sexual behavior. The graph also shows that premarital sex has increased among college students since 1965. Males are still more likely to engage in premarital sex than females, but the gap has been closing. (Data from Robinson et al., 1991)

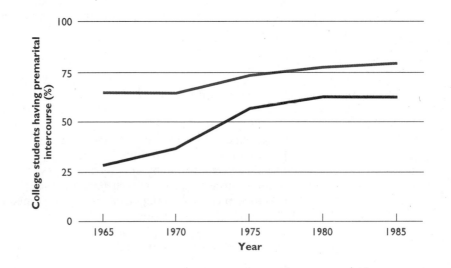

Thus, the results of this survey show no reduction in premarital intercourse since the early 1980s. On the other hand, the percentage of young couples using condoms the first time they had sex rose from 48% in the beginning of the 1980s to 65% by the end of the 1980s (Forrest & Singh, 1990). Also, there is some evidence that college students are becoming more disapproving of casual sex (Robinson et al., 1991). Older (non–college age) gay men are reducing the number of their sex partners and increasing their condom use, although younger gay men are not (Ehrhardt, Yingling, & Warne, 1991). Thus, there is evidence that concerns about contracting AIDS are affecting sexual practices; however, the behavior of college students seems to be less affected than the behavior of older individuals.

"Premarital" Sex

Learning Objective

Summarize attitudes toward and prevalence of "premarital" sex.

The term *premarital sex* conjures up images of furtive sex among teenagers. Of course, with more people delaying marriage, premarital sex increasingly involves relationships between mature adults. Obviously, the emotional implications of sex between a pair of 15-year-olds who still live with their parents and a pair of independent 30-year-olds are likely to be quite different. Another problem with the term *premarital* is that it doesn't apply to homosexuals, who aren't permitted to marry under the law. Although the term *premarital sex* is becoming dated, many contemporary researchers continue to use it to refer to early, youthful sexual encounters.

Attitudes

People hold a number of viewpoints regarding premarital sex. Ira Reiss (1967) has identified the following standards:

- *Traditional.* Both males and females should abstain from sexual intercourse prior to marriage.
- *Double standard.* Sex before marriage is acceptable for males but not for females.
- *Permissiveness with affection.* Sex before marriage is acceptable *if* it takes place in the context of a stable, loving relationship.
- *Permissiveness without affection.* Sex before marriage is acceptable whether or not two people care for each other.

Most parents and institutions (churches, schools, and so forth) in our society endorse abstinence, and many of them have voiced dismay at their perception that permissiveness without affection has become the norm. In fact, the evidence indicates that today's dominant standard is "permissiveness with affection" (Dreyer, 1982; Earle & Perricone, 1986). Although a meta-analysis of gender differences in sexuality found that males were more accepting than females of premarital sex under casual circumstances (Oliver & Hyde, 1993), a study of college students reported that only 33% of the men and 3% of the women endorsed premarital sex with a "casual acquaintance" (Earle & Perricone, 1986). Thus, the casual one-night stands that get so much attention in the media appear to be less frequent than commonly believed.

Prevalence

It is clear that the prevalence of premarital sex has increased since the 1960s (Robinson et al., 1991), as Figure 13.10 shows. Roughly 75% of Americans engage in premarital sex (Hyde, 1994). A survey of Los Angeles youth reported that the average age of first intercourse was between 15 and 16 (see Figure 3.11). Thus, most people no longer enter committed relationships as virgins. Some of the increase in premarital sex is attributable to later marriages, but premarital sex among teenagers *has* become more frequent as well (Dreyer, 1982). Teenagers who engage in premarital sex are typically less religious and less concerned about academic achievement; they also place a greater value on independence and report being more influenced by peers than by parents (Jessor et al., 1983). Interestingly, adult homosexuals report rates of *heterosexual* premarital intercourse that are nearly identical to those reported

Figure 13.11
Ethnicity and premarital intercourse
A survey of 16- to 25-year-olds from different ethnic groups in the Los Angeles area revealed that the average age for first having sex was relatively similar between males and females and among the groups. (Adapted from Moore & Erickson, 1985)

Subgroup	Mean age of first intercourse
Males (all ethnic groups combined)	14.9
Females (all ethnic groups combined)	15.9
Whites	16.2
Blacks	14.4
Hispanics	15.3
Asians	16.4

by heterosexuals (Saghir & Robins, 1973). Among other things, these findings support the view that adolescence is an important period for working out answers to questions about sexual orientation.

Males and females have different reactions to their first experience with sexual intercourse (Coles & Stokes, 1985). For instance, more than twice as many males as females report feeling glad (60% to 23%). Also, girls are more likely to feel sadness, disappointment, and ambivalence. Surprisingly, the girl's partner is not usually aware of her negative feelings. In a study that asked college women to rate their first coital experience on a scale ranging from 1 (no pleasure at all) to 7 (strongly experienced pleasure), the average pleasure rating was 3.9 (Weis, 1983). Thus, it seems that female sexuality involves more negative elements than male sexuality does.

Sex in Committed Relationships

Sex is an important element in most committed, romantic relationships. In this section, we'll examine patterns of sexual activity in dating couples, married couples, and gay couples.

Sex Between Dating Couples

Learning Objective

Summarize the findings on sex in dating couples and marital sex.

Sooner or later couples who are dating and in love confront the question of whether or when they should have sex. For some, the decision is easy, but for others, it isn't. Some worry that sex might adversely affect the relationship; others fear that *not* having sex will cause trouble. Is there evidence to support either view? Research suggests that dating couples who have sex are more likely to be dating the same person three months later than couples who don't have sex (Simpson, 1987). Of course, because this was a correlational study, it's possible that couples who were sexually active started out with closer relationships. If this were so, relationship satisfaction might be more significant than sexual activity. However, when the researchers took this factor into account, the relationships of the sexually active couples still lasted longer. It would be interesting to see if this same pattern of results was obtained six months or a year later.

Marital Sex

There is ample evidence that couples' overall marital satisfaction is highly related to their satisfaction with their sexual interaction (Henderson-King & Veroff, 1994; Kurdek, 1991). For example, Hunt (1974) found that spouses who characterized their marital relationship as "very close" were much more likely to rate their sex life as "very pleasurable" than those who characterized their marriage as "fairly close" or "not too close" (see Figure 13.12). Thus, good sex and a good marriage tend to go hand in hand. Of course, it is difficult to tell whether this is a matter of good sex promoting good marriages or good marriages promoting good sex. In all probability, it's a two-way street. It seems likely that marital closeness is conducive to sexual pleasure *and* that sexual satisfaction increases marital satisfaction.

Figure 13.12
Sexual satisfaction and marital satisfaction
Hunt (1974) found that the better the subjects' marital relationship, the more likely they were to rate their sex life as very pleasurable. Thus, there is a correlation between good marriages and good sex.

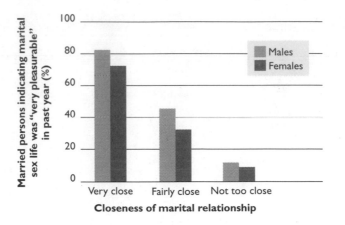

Married couples vary greatly in how often they have sex. *On the average*, couples in their 20s and 30s engage in sex about two or three times a week (Reinisch, 1990; Westoff, 1974). A recent, well-sampled survey of sexual behavior reported that Americans could be divided into three groups based on how frequently they have sex: One-third have sex twice a week or more; one-third have sex a few times a month; and another third have sex a few times a year or not at all (Laumann et al., 1994). Research indicates that the frequency of sex among married couples tends to decrease as the years wear on (Trussell & Westoff, 1980). Couples report that this decline is due to increasing fatigue from work and child-rearing and to growing familiarity with their sexual routine (Greenblat, 1983). As one man put it:

> "In the beginning it was five times a week, three times in one day. But it changed because the early adrenaline wore off. Karin took a trip for a month and when she came back we were both too busy because we were working sixteen-hour days. So we sort of settled down to your typical boring existence." [Quoted in Blumstein & Schwartz, 1983, p. 199]

A person's sexual response changes with age (Diamond & Karlen, 1981). Arousal tends to build more slowly in both sexes, and orgasms tend to diminish in frequency and intensity. Males' refractory periods lengthen, and females' vaginal lubrication and elasticity decrease. Nevertheless, people over 60 remain capable of rewarding sexual encounters. In a study of healthy 80- to 102-year-olds, 62% of the men and 30% of the women reported that they still engaged in sexual intercourse (Bretschneider & McCoy, 1988). About 80% of couples over the age of 60 continue to engage in intercourse every week or two (Brecher, 1984).

Sex in Homosexual Relationships

Learning Objective

Compare and contrast sexual behavior in married couples and committed homosexual couples.

On the average, homosexual couples have sex about as often as heterosexual couples of similar ages—two or three times a week (Blumstein & Schwartz, 1983). Similarly, homosexual individuals vary widely in their desire for sex. One well-known survey reported that about 45% of lesbian couples wished that they had sex more often than they actually did, whereas only 5% preferred a lower frequency. Among gay males, some 37% expressed a desire for sex more often and 21% preferred a lower frequency (Blumstein & Schwartz, 1983).

Gay and lesbian couples are more likely to have egalitarian relationships than heterosexual couples are (Blumstein & Schwartz, 1983; Kurdek & Schmitt, 1986b). This fact may account for some interesting differences between homosexual and heterosexual couples that Masters and Johnson (1979) discovered based on their observations and interviews.

First, both male and female homosexual couples seemed to have a *non-goal-oriented view* of their sexual activities. Gay and lesbian couples enjoyed a variety of mutually pleasurable sexual activities and didn't get focused on reaching orgasm. They took their time on preliminary sexual activities such as holding and kissing and communicated a lot with one another. In contrast, heterosexual couples were likely to spend just 30 seconds on preliminary activities of holding and kissing before they shifted to genital stimulation.

A second finding was that, compared to heterosexual couples, homosexual couples rated higher on the *subjective quality* of their sexual experiences—that is, total body contact, enjoyment of each aspect of the sexual experience, psychological involvement, and responsiveness to the needs and desires of the partner. Communication was a key factor responsible for this difference. Masters and Johnson believed that homosexual couples communicated their sexual feelings pretty well, but they criticized the "persistent neglect" of sexual communication they observed in heterosexual couples.

Infidelity in Committed Relationships

Learning Objective

Summarize the evidence on infidelity in committed relationships.

Sexual infidelity occurs when a person who is in a committed relationship engages in erotic activity with someone other than his or her partner. Among married couples, this behavior is also called *adultery* or *extramarital sex*. The vast majority of people (about 75%) in our society strongly disapprove of extramarital sex (Davis & Smith, 1991; Laumann et al., 1994). Generally, gay couples are more permissive about sexual activity with other individuals than lesbian and married couples are (Blumstein & Schwartz, 1989; Kurdek, 1991).

Prevalence

Despite the fact that a majority of people disapprove of infidelity, a substantial number of people get involved in extramarital activity. Because of the stigma and secrecy associated with this behavior, accurate estimates of infidelity are difficult to come by. One review of research on the topic suggests that about 40–50% of husbands and about 25–35% of wives engage in extramarital activity at least once (Thompson, 1983). Much more conservative estimates were reported in the recent American survey on sex: about 25% for men and about 10% for women (Laumann et al., 1994).

Motivations

Why do people pursue extramarital sexual encounters? Common reasons include anger toward a partner, dissatisfaction with a relationship (Thompson, 1983), and a desire for new and different sexual experiences (Buunk, 1980). Also, extramarital sexual activity sometimes occurs simply because two persons are attracted to each other. Erotic reactions to people other than one's spouse do not cease when one marries, but most people suppress these sexual desires because they disapprove of adultery.

The gender differences in motivations for infidelity parallel gender differences in sexual socialization: Men's motivations are tied to sex and women's, to emotions. When a man has an extramarital affair, it doesn't necessarily mean that he is unhappy with his marriage. On the other hand, when a woman has an affair, it may suggest that she is unhappy with her relationship (Glass & Wright, 1985; Thompson, 1984).

Impact

The impact of extramarital sexual activity on marriages has not been investigated extensively. Experts speculate that approximately 20% of all divorces are caused by infidelity (Reinisch, 1990). Occasionally, extramarital affairs may have a positive effect on a marriage. Some participants report experiencing a sense of self-discovery and self-recognition as a result of extramarital sexual experiences (Atwater, 1982). Regarding the impact of infidelity in gay relationships, the findings are contradictory. One investigator reported no differences in the perceived quality of "open" versus "closed" relationships in males (Kurdek, 1988). On the other hand, another study found that male couples in closed relationships reported greater feelings of closeness, more favorable attitudes toward their relationship, and lower tension than couples in open relationships (Kurdek & Schmitt, 1986a).

Practical Issues in Sexual Activity

Regardless of the context of sexual activity, two practical issues are often matters of concern: contraception and sexually transmitted diseases. These topics are more properly the concern of medicine than of psychology, but birth control and sex-related diseases certainly do have their behavioral aspects.

Contraception

Learning Objective

Describe common barriers to effective contraception and discuss the merits of condoms and the pill.

Most people want to control whether and when they will conceive a child, so they need reliable contraception. Despite the availability of effective contraceptive methods, however, many people fail to exercise much control.

Barriers to Effective Contraception

Effective contraception requires that intimate couples negotiate their way through a complex sequence of steps. First, they must define themselves as sexually active. Second, they must have accurate knowledge about fertility and conception. Third, their chosen method of contraception must be readily accessible. Finally, they must have the motivation and skill to use the method correctly and consistently. Failure to meet even one of these conditions can result in an unintended pregnancy.

Ineffective contraception is particularly prevalent among adolescents (Voydanoff & Donnelly, 1990). Teens are sexual novices and often have ambivalent feelings about their behavior. Hence, they are especially likely to deny their need for contraception. Many girls feel guilty about planned sex, so they may not use contraception; they try to rationalize their sexual behavior by telling themselves that "we got carried away." In addition, many teens are simply unable to grasp the idea that pregnancy is a possibility (Voydanoff & Donnelly, 1990). Finally, ready access to contraceptive devices is often a problem for adolescents.

Like their younger peers, college students engage in risky sexual practices for a variety of reasons. One contributing factor is alcohol, which doesn't increase sexual desire but does typically impair judgment. Many college students probably drink as a socially acceptable way to avoid potentially embarrassing discussions about sex.

Conflicting norms about gender and sexual behavior also contribute to ineffective contraceptive practices. Men are socialized to be the initiators of sexual activity, whereas women are socialized to take a passive role. However, when it comes to birth control, men frequently rely on women to take charge (Geis & Gerrard, 1984). It is difficult to maintain an image of sexual naiveté and also be responsible for contraception; telling her partner that she is "on the pill" or whipping out a condom at the appropriate time is likely to convey quite a different message. Studies have shown that when college women feel that their sexual partners are not supportive of contraception, couples are less likely to practice protected sex (Whitley & Hern, 1991). Also, women who engage in unprotected sex are higher in guilt and lower in self-esteem than those who practice contraception (Gerrard, 1987; Whitley & Schofield, 1986).

Selecting a Contraceptive Method

If couples are motivated to control their fertility, how should they go about selecting a technique? A rational choice requires accurate knowledge of the effectiveness, benefits, costs, and risks of the various methods. Figure 13.13 summarizes information on most of the methods currently available. The *ideal failure rate* estimates the probability of conception when the technique is used correctly and consistently. The *actual failure rate* is what occurs in the real world, when users' negligence is factored in.

Besides being informed about the various types of contraceptive methods, individuals must also put this information to use. Contraception is a joint responsibility. Hence, it's essential for couples to discuss their preferences for contraception with each other, to decide what method(s) they are going to use, and to *act* on their decision. Let's look in more detail at the two most widely used birth control methods in the Western world: oral contraceptives and condoms (Calderone & Johnson, 1989; Hatcher et al., 1994).

Oral contraceptives are pills taken daily by mouth. They contain synthetic forms of two hormones, estrogen and progesterone. "The pill" actually refers to over 50 different oral contraceptive products that inhibit ovulation in women. Oral contraception is preferred by many couples because it is the only widely available method that is separated in time from the sex act itself. No other method (except for the intrauterine device, which is rarely prescribed today) permits a similar degree of sexual spontaneity.

Despite much worrisome publicity, use of oral contraceptives does not appear to increase a woman's overall risk for cancer (Eichhorst, 1988). In fact, the likelihood of certain forms of cancer (such as uterine cancer) is reduced in women who use low-dosage oral contraceptives. The pill *does* slightly increase the risk of certain cardiovascular disorders, such as heart disease and stroke. Thus, alternative methods of contraception should be considered by smokers over age 35 and those with any suspicion of cardiovascular disease (Eichhorst, 1988).

Figure 13.13
A comparison of widely used contraceptive techniques
Couples can choose from a variety of contraceptive methods. This chart summarizes the advantages and disadvantages of each method. Note that the actual failure rate is much higher than the ideal failure rate for all methods, because couples do not use contraceptive techniques consistently and correctly. (Based on Hatcher et al., 1994; Masters, Johnson, & Kolodny, 1994)

Contraceptive Methods

Method	Ideal failure rate (%)	Actual failure rate (%)	Advantages	Disadvantages
Birth control pills (combination)	0.1	3	Highly reliable; coitus-independent; has some health benefits	Side effects; daily use; continual cost; health risks for some women; no protection against STDs*
Minipill (progestin only)	0.5	3	Thought to have low risk of side effects; coitus-independent; has some health benefits	Breakthrough bleeding; daily use; continual cost; health risks for some women; no protection against STDs*
IUD	1–2	1–2	No memory or motivation required for use; very reliable	Cramping, bleeding, expulsion; risk of pelvic inflammatory disease; no protection against STDs*
Diaphragm with cream or jelly	6	18	No major health risks; inexpensive	Aesthetic objections
Condom	3	12	Protects against STDs;* simple to use; male responsibility; no health risks; no prescriptions required	Unaesthetic to some; requires interruption of sexual activity; continual cost
Sponge	9	18	24-hour protection; simple to use; no taste or odor; inexpensive; effective with several acts of intercourse	Aesthetic objections; continual cost; no protection against STDs*
Cervical cap with cream or jelly	9	18	Can wear for weeks at a time; coitus-independent; no major health risks	May be difficult to insert; may irritate cervix
Spermicides	6	21	No major health risks; no prescription required; some protect against AIDS	Unaesthetic to some; must be properly inserted; continual cost
Rhythm	1–9	20	No cost; acceptable to Catholic church	Requires high motivation and periods of abstinence; unreliable; no protection against STDs*
Withdrawal	4	19	No cost or health risks	Reduces sexual pleasure; unreliable; requires high motivation
Implants	.09	.09	Highly reliable; continuous protection for up to 5 years; easily reversible; low risk of side effects; some health benefits	Slightly visible; costly; minor surgery required for insertion and removal; possible side effects; no protection against STDs*
No contraception	85	85	No immediate monetary cost	High risk of pregnancy and STDs*

*Sexually transmitted diseases

A *condom* is a sheath worn over the penis during intercourse to collect ejaculated semen. The condom is the only widely available contraceptive device for use by males. It can be purchased in any drugstore without a prescription. If used correctly, the condom is highly effective in preventing pregnancy (Hatcher et al., 1994). It must be placed over the penis after erection but before any contact with the vagina, and space must be left at the tip of the condom to collect the ejaculate. The man should withdraw before completely losing his erection and hold the rim of the condom during withdrawal to prevent any semen from spilling into the vagina.

Condoms are generally made of latex rubber but are occasionally made from animal membranes ("skin"). The polyurethane condom, introduced in 1994, claims to be thinner than latex and just as strong. The use of rubber and polyurethane condoms can reduce the chances of contracting or passing on various sexually transmitted diseases. However, couples should not use oil-based creams and lotions (petroleum jelly, hand creams, or baby oil, for example) as lubricants with *rubber* condoms (or diaphragms). Within 60 seconds, these products can make microscopic holes in the rubber membrane that are large enough to allow passage of the AIDS virus and organisms produced by other sexually transmitted diseases (Reinisch, 1990). Water-based lubricants such as K-Y jelly don't cause this problem. Polyurethane condoms are impervious to oils. Skin condoms do *not* offer protection against sexually transmitted diseases.

Sexually Transmitted Diseases

A *sexually transmitted disease* **(STD) is an illness that is transmitted primarily through sexual contact.** When people think of STDs they typically think of syphilis and gonorrhea, but these are only the tip of the iceberg. There are actually about 20 sexually transmitted diseases. Some of these diseases—for instance, pubic lice—are minor nuisances that can readily be treated. Some STDs, however, are severe afflictions that are difficult to treat. For instance, if it isn't detected early, syphilis can cause heart failure, blindness, and brain damage, and AIDS is eventually fatal. (We'll discuss AIDS in detail in Chapter 14.)

Prevalence and Transmission

Learning Objective

Describe the various types of STDs and discuss their prevalence and means of transmission.

No one is immune to sexually transmitted diseases. Even monogamous partners can develop some STDs (yeast infections, for instance). Sexually transmitted diseases occur more frequently than widely realized, and most STDs are increasing in prevalence. Health authorities estimate that there are about 13 million new cases in the United States each year (Hatcher et al., 1994). If you are between the ages of 15 and 55, you have about a one in four chance of developing a sexually transmitted disease—not including AIDS—during your lifetime (Gordon & Snyder, 1989). The highest incidence of STDs is seen in the under-25 age group (Hatcher et al., 1994).

The principal types of sexually transmitted diseases are listed in Figure 13.14, along with their symptoms and modes of transmission. Most of these diseases are spread from one person to another through intercourse, oral-genital contact, or anal-genital contact. Concerning the transmission of STDs, six points are worth emphasizing:

1. You should consider *any* activity that exposes you to blood, semen, vaginal secretions, menstrual blood, urine, feces, or saliva as high-risk behavior *unless* you and your partner are in a mutual, sexually exclusive relationship and neither of you is infected (Reinisch, 1990).

2. The more sexual partners you have, the higher your chances of exposure to a sexually transmitted disease.

3. Don't assume that the labels people attach to themselves (heterosexual or homosexual) accurately describe their actual sexual behavior. According to the director of the Kinsey Institute, "Studies of men from the general population show that more than 30% (1 out of 3) have had at least one sexual experience with another male since puberty" (Reinisch, 1990, pp. 465–466).

4. People can often be carriers of sexually transmitted diseases without being aware of it. For instance, in its early stages gonorrhea may cause no readily appar-

ent symptoms in women, who may unknowingly transmit the disease to their partners.

5. Even when people know they have a sexually transmitted disease, they may not remain sexually abstinent or inform their partners. Guilt and embarrassment cause many people to ignore symptoms of sexually transmitted diseases and continue their normal sexual activities (Kramer, Aral, & Curran, 1980). Close to half of the subjects in one study admitted that they had told dates that they had had fewer sexual partners than was actually the case (Reinisch, 1990). People are even more likely to lie about homosexual activity, sex with prostitutes, and drug use (Reinisch, 1990). So don't assume that sexual partners will warn you that they may be contagious.

6. Engaging in anal intercourse (especially being the receiving partner) puts one at very high risk for AIDS. Rectal tissues are very delicate and can be easily torn, thus letting the virus pass through the membrane. Oral-genital sex may also transmit AIDS, particularly if semen is swallowed.

Prevention

Abstinence is the best way to minimize the risk of acquiring sexually transmitted diseases. However, this is not an appealing or realistic option for most people. Short

Figure 13.14
Overview of common sexually transmitted diseases (STDs)
This chart summarizes the symptoms and modes of transmission of 10 STDs. Note that intercourse is not required to transmit all STDs—many STDs can be contracted through oral-genital contact or other forms of physical intimacy. (Adapted from Hatcher, et al., 1994; Hyde, 1994)

Sexually Transmitted Diseases (STDs)

STD	Transmission	Symptoms
Acquired immune deficiency syndrome (AIDS)	The AIDS virus is spread by coitus or anal intercourse. There is a chance the virus may also be spread by oral-genital sex, particularly if semen is swallowed. (AIDS can also be spread by non-sexual means: contaminated blood, contaminated hypodermic needles, and transmission from an infected woman to her baby during pregnancy or childbirth.)	Most people infected with the virus show no immediate symptoms; antibodies usually develop in the blood 2–8 weeks after infection. People with the virus may remain symptom-free for 5 years or more. No cure for the disease has yet been found, so once AIDS symptoms appear, death occurs within a few months to a few years.
Candidiasis (yeast infection)	The Candida albicans fungus may accelerate growth when the chemical balance of the vagina is disturbed; it may also be transmitted through sexual interaction.	White, "cheesy" discharge; irritation of vaginal and vulvar tissue.
Chlamydial infection	The Chlamydia trichomatis bacterium is transmitted primarily through sexual contact. It may also be spread by fingers from one body site to another.	In men, chlamydial infection of the urethra may cause a discharge and burning during urination. Chlamydia-caused epidydimitis may produce a sense of heaviness in the affected testicle(s), inflammation of the scrotal skin, and painful swelling at the bottom of the testicle. In women, pelvic inflammatory disease caused by chlamydia may disrupt menstrual periods, elevate temperature, and cause abdominal pain, nausea, vomiting, and headache.
Genital warts (venereal warts)	The virus is spread primarily through genital, anal, or oral-genital interaction.	Warts are hard and yellow-gray on dry skin areas, soft pinkish red and cauliflowerlike on moist areas.
Gonorrhea ("clap")	The Neisseria gonorrhoeae bacterium (gonococcus) is spread through genital, oral-genital, or genital-anal contact.	Most common symptoms in men are a cloudy discharge from the penis and burning sensations during urination. If the disease is untreated, complications may include inflammation of the scrotal skin and swelling at the base of the testicle. In women, some green or yellowish discharge is produced, but the disease commonly remains undetected. At a later stage, pelvic inflammatory disease may develop.
Herpes	The genital herpes virus (HSV-2) appears to be transmitted primarily by vaginal, oral-genital, or anal-sexual intercourse. The oral herpes virus (HSV-1) is transmitted primarily by kissing.	Small red, painful bumps (papules) appear in the region of the genitals (genital herpes) or mouth (oral herpes). The papules become painful blisters that eventually rupture to form wet, open sores.
Pubic lice ("crabs")	Phthirus pubis, the pubic louse, is spread easily through body contact or through shared clothing or bedding.	Persistent itching. Lice are visible and may often be located in pubic hair or other body hair.
Syphilis	The Treponema pallidum bacterium (spirochete) is transmitted from open lesions during genital, oral-genital, or genital-anal contact.	Primary stage: A painless chancre appears at the site where the spirochetes entered the body. Secondary stage: The chancre disappears and a generalized skin rash develops. Latent stage: There may be no observable symptoms. Tertiary stage: Heart failure, blindness, mental disturbance, and many other symptoms may occur. Death may result.
Trichomoniasis	The protozoan parasite Trichomonas vaginalis is passed through genital sexual contact or less frequently by towels, toilet seats, or bathtubs used by an infected person.	White or yellow vaginal discharge with an unpleasant odor; vulva is sore and irritated.
Viral hepatitis	The hepatitis B virus may be transmitted by blood, semen, vaginal secretions, and saliva. Manual, oral, or penile stimulation of the anus is strongly associated with the spread of this virus. Hepatitis A seems to be spread primarily via the fecal-oral route. Oral-anal sexual contact is a common mode of sexual transmission for hepatitis A.	Vary from nonexistent to mild, flulike symptoms to an incapacitating illness characterized by high fever, vomiting, and severe abdominal pain.

of abstinence, the best strategy is to engage in sexual activity only in the context of a long-term relationship, where you have an opportunity to know your partner reasonably well. Sexual interactions with casual acquaintances greatly increase your risk for STDs, including AIDS.

Along with being judicious about sexual relations, it's also essential that you talk openly about safer sexual practices with your partner. Still, if you don't carry the process one step further and practice what you preach, you remain at risk. Unfortunately, there is evidence that many people are still engaging in risky sexual behavior—a practice that no one can afford while we are in the grip of the deadly AIDS epidemic. A government-sponsored, nationwide survey of 10,630 heterosexuals between the ages of 18 and 75 found that condoms were always used by only 17% of those with multiple partners, by only 13% of those with risky sex partners (partners who were HIV-positive, injection drug users, nonmonogamous, transfusion recipients, or hemophiliacs), and by only 11% of untested transfusion recipients (Catania et al., 1992).

Safer sex practices have increased dramatically among older gay and bisexual males (Stall, Coates, & Hoff, 1988), but younger gay males may still be taking sexual risks (Griggs, 1990). Lesbians have the lowest rates of syphilis and gonorrhea among sexually active individuals, as well as extremely low rates of AIDS (Reinisch, 1990). Lesbian sexual behaviors don't typically involve penetration, so there is little risk of exposure to infectious organisms from breaks in oral, vaginal, or anal tissues. Lesbians also tend to have fewer sexual partners than other sexually active women or men. All the same, for reasons we have already mentioned, lesbians should still follow "safer sex" guidelines.

We offer the following suggestions for safer sex (Hyde, 1994; Reinisch, 1990):

- Because the AIDS virus is easily transmitted through anal intercourse, it's a good idea to avoid this type of sex.
- If you are not involved in a sexually exclusive relationship, always use rubber or polyurethane condoms. They have a good track record of preventing STDs and offer effective protection against the AIDS virus. (Never use oil-based lubricants with rubber condoms; use water-based lubricants instead.)
- The spermicide *nonoxynol 9* has been found to be relatively effective in killing the AIDS virus (Peterman & Curran, 1986; Reinisch, 1990). Use it with a condom to make sex safer. Read the labels on spermicides or ask a pharmacist to help you find those with nonoxynol. (LifeStyles condoms are lubricated on the inside and outside with nonoxynol.)
- Wash your genitals with soap and warm water before and after sexual contact.
- Urinate soon after intercourse.
- Don't have sex with someone who has had numerous previous partners. People won't always be honest about this, so it's important to know whether you can trust a prospective partner's word.
- Watch for sores, rashes, or discharge around the vulva or penis, or elsewhere on your body, especially the mouth. If you have cold sores, avoid kissing or oral sex.

If you have several sexual partners in a year, it is important to have regular STD checkups. You will have to ask for these checkups, as most doctors and health clinics won't perform STD tests unless they're asked to. Also, if you have any reason to suspect that you have an STD, find a good health clinic and get tested *as soon as possible*. It's normal to be embarrassed or afraid of getting bad news, but don't delay. Health professionals are in the business of helping people, not judging them.

Remember that the symptoms of some STDs disappear as the disease progresses. Don't make the mistake of thinking that you really don't have an STD when you might. To make really sure, have yourself tested twice. If both tests are negative, you can stop worrying. If your test results are positive, it's essential to get the proper treatment *right away*. Notify your sexual partners so they can be tested immediately, too. In addition, it's important to avoid sexual intercourse and oral sex until you and your partners are fully treated and a physician or clinic says you are no longer infectious.

In the Application, we'll focus on enhancing sexual satisfaction and discuss advances in the understanding and treatment of sexual problems.

Learning Objective

List seven suggestions for safer sexual practices.

Application

Enhancing Sexual Relationships

Answer the following statements "true" or "false."

1. *Sexual problems are very resistant to treatment.*

2. *Sexual problems belong to couples rather than individuals.*

3. *Most sexual problems have an organic basis.*

4. *Sex therapists sometimes recommend masturbation as a treatment for certain types of problems.*

The answers are (1) false, (2) true, (3) false, and (4) true. If you answered several of the questions incorrectly, you have misconceptions about sexual difficulties that may affect your sexual relations, but you are by no means unusual. As we saw in our earlier discussion of the results of the recent Kinsey Institute survey, misconceptions about sexuality are the norm rather than the exception. Fortunately, recent advances in our understanding of sexual functioning have yielded many useful ideas on how to improve sexual relationships.

In this Application, we take a practical look at sexual problems and their possible solutions. Obviously, many readers may not be involved in a sexual relationship at present. But if you're not, we'll assume that someday you will be. In the interest of simplicity, our advice is directed to heterosexual couples, but much of what we have to say is relevant to homosexual couples as well. For gay and lesbian students who want advice directed specifically to homosexual couples, we recommend *Permanent Partners* by Betty Berzon (1988) and Masters and Johnson's (1979) book *Homosexuality in Perspective*.

General Suggestions

Learning Objective

List six general suggestions for enhancing sexual relationships.

Let's begin with some general ideas about how to enhance sexual relationships, drawn from several excellent books on sexuality (Crooks & Baur, 1996; Hyde, 1994; Reinisch, 1990). Even if you are satisfied with your sexual relations, these ideas may be useful as preventive medicine.

1. *Pursue adequate sex education.* A surprising number of people are ignorant about the realities of sexual functioning. In a book titled *Sexual Myths and Fallacies*, James McCary (1971) discusses over 80 common misconceptions about sexuality. So, the first step in promoting sexual satisfaction is to acquire accurate information about sex. The shelves of most bookstores are bulging with popular books on sex, but many of them are loaded with inaccuracies. A good bet is to pick up a college textbook on human sexuality. The Recommended Readings in this chapter describe books on this topic that we think are excellent. Enrolling in a course on sexuality is also a good idea. More and more colleges are offering such courses today.

2. *Review your sexual values system.* Many sexual problems are derived from a negative sexual values system in which people associate sex with immorality. The guilt feelings caused by such an orientation can interfere with sexual functioning. Given this possibility, experts on sexuality often encourage adults to examine the sources and implications of their sexual values.

3. *Communicate about sex.* As children, people often learn that they shouldn't talk about sex. Many people carry this feeling into adulthood and have great difficulty discussing sex, even with their partner. Good communication is extremely impor-

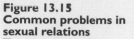

Figure 13.15
Common problems in sexual relations
The percentage of men and women reporting various types of problems in their sexual relationships is shown here, based on a sample of 100 couples. (Data from Frank, Anderson, & Rubinstein, 1978)

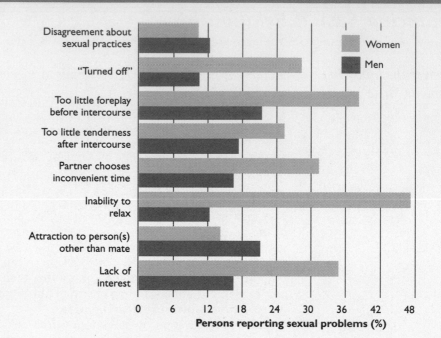

tant in a sexual relationship. Figure 13.15 lists common problems in sexual relations reported by a sample of 100 couples (Frank, Anderson, & Rubinstein, 1978). Many of the problems reported by the couples—such as choosing an inconvenient time, too little erotic activity before intercourse, and too little tenderness afterward—are traceable largely to poor communication. Your partner is not a mind reader. You have to share your thoughts and feelings to promote mutual satisfaction. Ask questions if you have doubts about your partner's preferences. Provide candid (but diplomatic) feedback when your partner asks about your reactions. Learn to make specific requests that effectively convey your erotic preferences.

4. *Avoid goal setting.* Sexual encounters are not tests or races. Sexual relations usually work out best when people relax and enjoy themselves. Some people get overly concerned about orgasms. A grim determination to climax typically makes it harder to do so. This mental set can lead to disruptive habits such as *spectatoring*, or stepping outside the sexual act to judge one's performance. It's better to adopt the philosophy that getting there is at least half the fun.

5. *Enjoy your sexual fantasies.* As we noted earlier, the mind is the ultimate erogenous zone. Fantasizing during a sexual encounter is normal, and both genders report that their sexual fantasies increase their excitement. Don't be afraid to use fantasy to enhance your sexual arousal. One woman's experience illustrates the potential value of both fantasy and open communication:

"I had this sexual fantasy that kept going through my mind. I would imagine coming home after a long, hard day of classes and being met by my partner, who would proceed to take me into the bedroom and remove all my clothes. He would then pick me up and carry me into the bathroom where a tub full of hot water and bubbles awaited. The fantasy would end with us making passionate love in the bathtub with bubbles popping off around us. Finally, I shared my fantasy with him. Guess what happened when I came home after the next long day? It was even better than I had imagined!" [Quoted in Crooks & Baur, 1996, p. 204]

6. *Be selective about sex.* Sexual encounters generally work out better when you have privacy and a relaxed atmosphere, when you are well rested, and when you are enthusiastic. If you consistently have sex in bad situations, your sexual relations may not be very rewarding. Realistically, you can't count on (or insist on) having

Figure 13.16
Sexual difficulties in normal couples
This graph shows the prevalence of various sexual problems during a year in a probability sample of American men and women. The most common problems among men are premature ejaculation and anxiety about performance; in women, they are lack of interest in sex and orgasmic difficulties. (From Laumann et al., 1994)

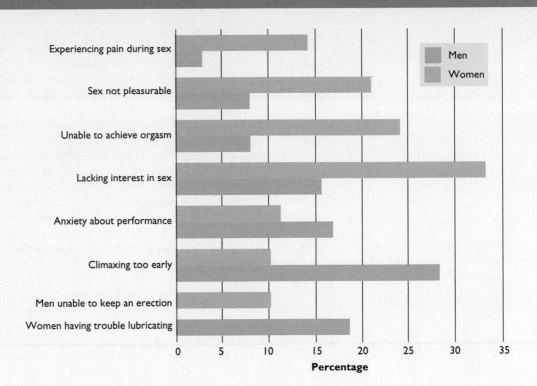

ideal situations all the time, but you should be aware of the value of being selective. If your heart isn't in it, it may be wise to wait. It also helps to remember that it is quite common for partners to disagree about when, where, and how often they should have sex. This sort of disagreement is normal and should not be a source of resentment. Couples simply need to work toward reasonable compromises—through open communication.

Understanding Sexual Dysfunction

Learning Objective

Discuss the nature, prevalence, and causes of common sexual dysfunctions.

Many people struggle with *sexual dysfunctions*—**impairments in sexual functioning that cause subjective distress.** One study of patients visiting a family practice center for medical treatment found that 75% had sexual problems of some kind (Schein et al., 1988). This estimate may be a little high for the population as a whole, since some of the sexual problems may have been spinoffs from the patients' medical problems. Nonetheless, it is clear that sexual difficulties are more common than widely appreciated. Figure 13.16 shows the percentage of subjects in the recent survey on American sexual behavior reporting some of the problems we will discuss (Laumann et al., 1994).

Traditionally, people have assumed that a sexual problem lies in one partner. Although it is convenient to refer to a man's erectile difficulties or a woman's orgasmic difficulties, research indicates that most sexual problems emerge out of partners' unique ways of relating to each other. In other words, sexual problems belong to couples rather than to individuals.

Masters and Johnson's research led them to conclude that a relatively small proportion of sexual dysfunctions have an organic basis. Most sexual problems are psychological in origin. In this section, we examine the symptoms and causes of three common sexual dysfunctions: erectile difficulties, premature ejaculation, and orgasmic difficulties (based on Levay, Weissberg, & Woods, 1981; Masters, Johnson, & Kolodny, 1994).

Erectile difficulties **occur when a man is persistently unable to achieve or maintain an erection adequate for intercourse.** Impotence is the traditional name for this problem, but sex therapists have discarded this term because of its demeaning connotation. A man who has never had an erection sufficient for intercourse is said to have *primary erectile difficulties*. A man who has had intercourse in the past but is currently having problems achieving erections is said to have *secondary erectile difficulties*. The latter problem is more common and easier to overcome.

The most common cause of erectile difficulties is anxiety about sexual performance, which can undermine sexual arousal. What leads to this troublesome anxiety? Its cause can range from a man's doubts about his virility to conflict about the morality of his sexual desires. Many temporary conditions, such as fatigue, worry about work, an argument with his partner, a depressed mood, or too much alcohol can cause such incidents. If either partner turns the incident into a major catastrophe, the man may begin to get unduly concerned about his sexual response, and the seeds of anxiety may be sown.

Recent research suggests that physiological factors may contribute to erectile difficulties more often than Masters and Johnson's data suggested (Buvat et al., 1990). A host of common diseases (such as diabetes) can produce erectile problems as a side effect (Melman & Leiter, 1983). So can many of the medications used to treat physical illnesses (Buffum et al., 1981). Experts now estimate that organic factors may contribute to as many as 50% of all cases of erectile dysfunction (Buvat et al., 1990).

Premature ejaculation **occurs when sexual relations are impaired because a man consistently reaches orgasm too quickly.** What is "too quickly"? Obviously, any time estimate is hopelessly arbitrary. The critical consideration is the subjective feelings of the partners. If either partner feels that the ejaculation is persistently too fast for sexual gratification, they have a problem.

What causes premature ejaculation? Some men simply don't exert much effort to prolong intercourse. Most of these men do not view their ejaculations as premature, even if their partners do. Among men who are concerned about their partners' satisfaction, problems may occur because their early sexual experiences emphasized the desirability of a rapid climax. Furtive sex in the backseat of a car, quick efforts at masturbation, and experiences with prostitutes are situations in which men typically attempt to achieve orgasm quickly. A pattern of rapid ejaculation established by these formative experiences may become entrenched.

Orgasmic difficulties **occur when people experience sexual arousal but have persistent problems in achieving orgasm.** When this problem occurs in men, it is often called retarded ejaculation. The traditional name for this problem in women, frigidity, is no longer used because of its derogatory implications. Since this problem is much more common among women, we'll limit our discussion to them. As with erectile difficulties, it is useful to distinguish between primary and secondary orgasmic difficulties. Women who have never experienced an orgasm through any kind of stimulation are said to have *primary orgasmic difficulties*. Women who formerly experienced orgasms but are currently unable to do so are said to have *secondary orgasmic difficulties*. Women who seek treatment because they experience orgasm only through noncoital techniques (oral, manual, and self-stimulation) fall into the latter category. Although primary orgasmic difficulties would seem to be the more severe problem, they are actually more responsive to treatment than secondary orgasmic difficulties.

A negative attitude toward sex is one of the leading causes of orgasmic difficulties among women. Those who have been taught that sex is dirty are likely to approach it with shame and guilt. These feelings can inhibit sexual expression, undermine arousal, and impair orgasmic responsiveness.

A lack of authentic affection for one's partner seems to undermine sexual arousal in women more than in men. Thus, women sometimes have orgasmic difficulties when the emotional closeness in their relationship deteriorates. Arousal may also be inhibited by fear of pregnancy or excessive concern about achieving orgasm. Some women have orgasmic difficulties because intercourse is too brief or because their partners are unconcerned about their needs and preferences. Another consideration is that intercourse provides less direct genital stimulation for women than it does for men. Thus, some women do not experience orgasms simply because they (and their partners) haven't explored sexual activities that they might find more rewarding than intercourse.

Coping with Specific Problems

Learning Objective

Describe the strategies for coping with erectile difficulties, premature ejaculation, and orgasmic difficulties.

With the advent of modern sex therapy, sexual problems no longer have to be chronic sources of frustration and shame. *Sex therapy* **involves the professional treatment of sexual dysfunctions.** Masters and Johnson have reported very high success rates for their treatments of specific problems, as Figure 13.17 shows. Some critics argue that the cure rates reported by Masters and Johnson are overly optimistic in comparison with those reported by other investigators (Zilbergeld & Evans, 1980). Nonetheless, there is a consensus that sexual dysfunctions can be overcome with encouraging regularity (McConaghy, 1993). If you're in the market for a sex therapist, be sure to get someone who is qualified to work in this specialized field. One professional credential to look for is that provided by the American Association of Sex Educators, Counselors, and Therapists (AASECT).

Of course, sex therapy isn't for everyone. It can be time-consuming and expensive. In some locations, it is difficult to find. However, many people can benefit from ideas drawn from the professional practice of sex therapy (Hartman & Fithian, 1994; Masters et al., 1994).

Erectile Difficulties

The key to overcoming psychologically based erectile difficulties is to decrease the man's performance anxiety. It is a good idea for a couple to discuss the problem openly. The woman should be reassured that the difficulty does not reflect lack of affection. Obviously, it is crucial for her to be emotionally supportive rather than hostile and demanding.

Masters and Johnson use a procedure called *sensate focus* in the treatment of erectile difficulties and other dysfunctions. *Sensate focus* **is an exercise in which**

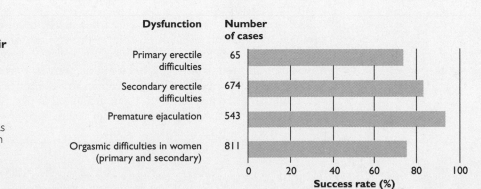

Figure 13.17
Success rates reported by Masters and Johnson in their treatment of sexual dysfunctions
This figure shows the success rates for cases treated between 1959 and 1985. Treatment was categorized as successful only if the change in sexual function was clear and enduring. The minimum follow-up period was two years, and in many cases it was five years. (Adapted from Masters, Johnson, & Kolodny, 1988)

partners take turns pleasuring each other while giving guided verbal feed-back and in which certain kinds of stimulation are temporarily forbidden. One partner stimulates the other, who simply lies back and enjoys it while giving instructions and feedback about what feels good. Initially, the partners are not allowed to touch each other's genitals or to attempt intercourse. This prohibition should free the man from feelings of pressure to perform. Over a number of sessions, the couple gradually include genital stimulation in their sensate focus, but intercourse is still banned. With the pressure to perform removed, many men spontaneously get erections. Repeated arousals should begin to restore the man's confidence in his sexual response. As his confidence returns, the couple gradually move on to attempts at intercourse.

Premature Ejaculation

Men troubled by premature ejaculation range from those who climax almost instantly to those who cannot last the time that their partner requires. In the latter case, simply slowing down the tempo of intercourse may help. Sometimes the problem can be solved indirectly by discarding the traditional assumption that orgasms should come through intercourse. If the female partner enjoys oral or manual stimulation, either can be used to provide her with an orgasm before or after intercourse. This strategy can reduce the performance pressure for the male partner, and couples may find that intercourse starts to last longer.

The problem of instant ejaculation is more challenging to remedy. Sex therapists rely primarily on certain sensate focus exercises in which the man is repeatedly brought to the verge of orgasm. These sensate focus exercises can gradually help a man to recognize preorgasmic sensations and improve his control over his ejaculation response.

Orgasmic Difficulties

Because orgasmic difficulties among women are often attributable to negative attitudes about sex, a restructuring of values is often the key to conquering the problem. Therapeutic discussions may be geared toward helping nonorgasmic women reduce their ambivalence about sexual expression. Sex therapists often suggest that women who have never had an orgasm try to have one through masturbation. Many women achieve orgasms in intercourse after an initial breakthrough with self-stimulation (LoPiccolo & Lobitz, 1972).

Treatment for orgasmic difficulties sometimes focuses on couples' relationship problems more than on sexual functioning as such. Efforts are often made to improve partners' communication skills. Thus, couples may discuss the complexities of initiating sexual overtures and the need to communicate openly about sexual turn-offs and turn-ons.

For reasons we have discussed earlier, it is not uncommon for women to be troubled by orgasmic difficulties only in the context of intercourse. This is particularly true for sexually inexperienced women. If partners don't assume that orgasms must come through coitus, this need not be seen as a problem. However, many couples feel that it is important for the woman to experience orgasm during intercourse. Sensate focus exercises can help them achieve this goal. The guided verbal feedback from the woman can greatly improve her partner's appreciation of her unique erotic preferences.

Key Ideas

Becoming a Sexual Person

• A person's sexual identity is made up of sexual orientation, body image, sexual values and ethics, and erotic preferences. Physiological factors such as hormones influence sexual differentiation, maturation, and anatomy more than they do sexual activity. Psychosocial factors appear to have more impact on sexual behavior. Sexual identity is shaped by families, peers and schools, and the media. Because of differences in sexual socialization, sexuality usually has different meanings for males and females.

• Many experts believe that sexual orientation is best viewed as a continuum, with end points of heterosexuality and homosexuality. The determinants of sexual orientation are not yet known but appear to be a complex interaction of biological and environmental factors. Although gay and straight people do not differ in adjustment, homosexuals take longer to recognize their sexual orientation than heterosexuals do.

Interaction in Sexual Relationships

• People frequently enter into sexual interactions with differing motivations. Men tend to be motivated more by physical gratification, whereas emotional motives tend to be more important for women. Sexual scripts regulate the formation and evolution of sexual relationships. Variations among people in erotic preferences are also shaped by their attitudes.

• Disparities between partners in sexual interest and erotic preferences understandably lead to conflicts that necessitate negotiation. Communication plays an important role in satisfaction with one's sex life and with the relationship in general.

The Human Sexual Response

• The physiology of the human sexual response was elucidated by Masters and Johnson. They analyzed the sexual response cycle into four phases: excitement, plateau, orgasm, and resolution. Women reach orgasm less consistently than men in intercourse, usually because foreplay and intercourse are too brief and because of gender differences in sexual socialization.

Sexual Arousal and Satisfaction

• Sexual fantasies are normal and can play an important part in sexual arousal. Kissing and touching are also important erotic activities, but their importance is often underestimated by heterosexual males. Self-stimulation, despite the negative attitudes about masturbation that are traditional in our society, is quite common, even among married people. Oral-genital sex has also become a common element in most couples' sexual repertoire.

• Coitus is the most widely practiced sexual act in our society. Four coital positions are commonly used, each with its advantages and disadvantages. Between gay males, sexual activities include mutual masturbation, fellatio, and, less often, anal intercourse. Lesbians engage in mutual masturbation, cunnilingus, and tribadism.

Patterns of Sexual Behavior

• The acceptability and prevalence of premarital sex have increased since the 1960s. Satisfaction with the sexual aspect of a relationship is correlated with the overall satisfaction with the relationship. Younger married couples tend to have sex about two or three times a week; this frequency declines with age. Homosexual couples appear to spend more time on mutual sexual activities before moving to orgasm, and they communicate more with each other, compared to heterosexual couples.

• Infidelity is uncommon among married couples and lesbians, and more common among gay male couples. Dissatisfaction, sexual discontent, curiosity, and chance attractions motivate people to get involved in sex outside of committed relationships.

Practical Issues in Sexual Activity

• Contraception and sexually transmitted diseases are two practical issues that concern many couples. Many people who do not want to conceive a child fail to use contraceptive procedures effectively, if at all. Contraceptive methods differ in effectiveness and have various advantages and disadvantages.

• STDs are increasing in prevalence, especially among teenagers. The danger of contracting STDs is higher among those who have had more sexual partners. The use of condoms with spermicides containing nonoxynol 9 decreases the risk of contracting STDs. Early treatment of STDs is important.

Application: Enhancing Sexual Relationships

• To enhance their sexual relationships, individuals need to have adequate sex education and positive values about sex. They also need to be able to communicate with their partners about sex and avoid goal setting in sexual encounters. Enjoying sexual fantasies and being selective about their sexual encounters are also important. Common sexual dysfunctions include erectile difficulties, premature ejaculation, and orgasmic difficulties. Treatments designed for specific sexual problems are extremely effective.

Key Terms

Anal intercourse
Androgens
Bisexuals
Coitus
Cunnilingus
Erectile difficulties
Erogenous zones
Estrogens
Fellatio
Gonads
Heterosexuals
Homosexuals
Orgasm
Orgasmic difficulties
Premature ejaculation
Refractory period
Sensate focus
Sex therapy
Sexual dysfunctions
Sexual identity
Sexual scripts
Sexually transmitted disease (STD)
Vasocongestion

Key People

Alfred Kinsey
William Masters and Virginia Johnson
June Machover Reinisch

14   *Psychology and Physical Health*

Learning Objective

Explain how patterns of disease and conceptions of illness have changed in modern society.

$\mathcal{T}$he patterns of illness found in a society tend to fluctuate over time. Before the 20th century, the principal threats to health were *contagious diseases* caused by an invasion of the body by a specific infectious agent. Because such diseases can be transmitted readily from one person to another, people used to live in fear of epidemics. The leading causes of death were diseases such as the plague, smallpox, typhoid fever, influenza, diphtheria, yellow fever, malaria, cholera, tuberculosis, polio, and scarlet fever. Today, the incidence of these diseases has declined to the point where none of them is among the leading killers in the United States (see Figure 14.1).

What neutralized these dreaded diseases? The general public tends to attribute the conquest of contagious diseases to advances in medical treatment. Although progress in medicine certainly played a role, Grob (1983) marshals evidence that the significance of such progress has been overrated. Of greater significance, he says, were trends such as (1) improvements in nutrition, (2) improvements in public hygiene and sanitation (water filtration, treatment of sewage, and so forth), and (3) evolutionary changes in the human immunal resistance to the diseases. Whatever the causes, infectious diseases are no longer the major threat to physical health in the industrialized nations of the world (many remain quite prevalent in Third World countries).

Unfortunately, the void left by contagious diseases has been filled all too quickly by various *chronic diseases*—illnesses that develop gradually over years (refer to Figure 14.1). Psychosocial factors, such as lifestyle and stress, play a much larger role in the development of chronic diseases than they do in contagious diseases. Today, the three leading chronic diseases (heart disease, cancer, and stroke) account for nearly two-thirds of the deaths in the United States! Moreover, these mortality statistics reveal only the tip of the iceberg. Many other less serious illnesses (such as headaches, backaches, skin disorders, asthma, and ulcers) are also influenced by psychosocial factors.

In light of these dramatic trends, it is not surprising that the way we think about illness is changing. Traditionally, illness has been thought of as a purely biological phenomenon produced by an infectious agent or some internal physical breakdown.

Figure 14.1
Changing patterns of illness
Trends in the death rates for various diseases during the 20th century reveal that contagious diseases (shown in green) have declined as a threat to human health. However, the death rates for stress-related chronic diseases (shown in red) have remained quite high. The pie chart (inset), which depicts the percentage of deaths caused by the leading killers today, shows the results of these trends. Three chronic diseases (heart disease, cancer, and stroke) account for over 60% of all deaths.

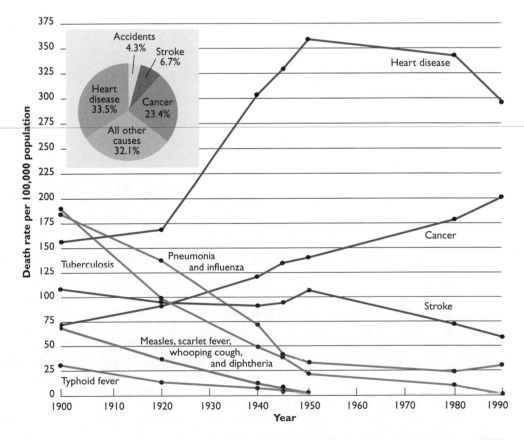

However, the shifting patterns of disease and new findings relating stress to physical illness have rocked the foundation of this biological model. In its place a new model is gradually emerging. **The *biopsychosocial model* holds that physical illness is caused by a complex interaction of biological, psychological, and sociocultural factors.** This new model does not suggest that biological factors are unimportant. Rather, it simply asserts that biological factors operate in a psychosocial context that can also be influential.

The growing recognition that psychological factors influence physical health led to the development of a new specialty within psychology. ***Health psychology* is concerned with the relation of psychosocial factors to the promotion and maintenance of health, and with the causation, prevention, and treatment of illness.** This specialty is relatively young, having emerged in the late 1970s. Our focus in this chapter will be on this exciting new area of psychology.

Psychological factors can influence physical health in three main ways:

Learning Objective

List three ways in which psychological factors can influence health.

1. *Direct effects of stress.* The most basic way in which psychological functioning can affect physical health is through the direct effects of stress on physiological processes. As we discussed in Chapter 3, stress tends to elicit wide-ranging physiological arousal, which can lead to bodily changes that may be damaging in the long run.
2. *Health-impairing habits.* Many habitual patterns of behavior can increase vulnerability to various kinds of illnesses. For instance, there is ample evidence that the likelihood of developing heart disease is influenced by cigarette smoking, physical inactivity, poor diet, and other aspects of lifestyle.
3. *Reactions to illness.* Behavioral responses to symptoms of illness can have a decided impact on health. Many people delay seeking needed medical consultation, thus increasing their risk of serious illness. Furthermore, a surprisingly great number of people ignore their doctors' advice or are unable to comply successfully with their doctors' instructions.

The three ways in which behavior can influence physical health will serve as our organizing scheme in this chapter. The first section analyzes the link between stress and illness. The second section examines common health-impairing habits, such as smoking and overeating. The third section discusses how people's reactions to illness can affect their health. In the Application we will expand on a particular type of health-impairing habit: the use of recreational drugs.

Stress, Personality, and Illness

As we noted in Chapter 3, during the 1970s researchers began to uncover new links between stress and a variety of diseases previously believed to be purely physiological in origin. In this section, we'll look at the evidence on the apparent link between stress and physical illness and discuss how personality factors contribute to this relationship. We'll begin with heart disease, which is far and away the leading cause of death in North America.

Type A Personality, Hostility, and Heart Disease

Learning Objective

Describe the Type A personality and its link to heart disease.

Heart disease accounts for nearly 40% of the deaths in the United States every year. ***Coronary heart disease* involves a reduction in blood flow from the coronary arteries, which supply the heart with blood.** This type of heart disease causes about 90% of heart-related deaths. Atherosclerosis is the principal cause of coronary disease. ***Atherosclerosis* is the gradual narrowing of the coronary arteries.** A buildup of fatty deposits and other debris on the inner walls of the arteries is the usual cause of this narrowing (see Figure 14.2). Atherosclerosis progresses slowly over periods of years. Narrowed coronary arteries may eventually lead to situations in which the heart is temporarily deprived of adequate blood flow, causing brief chest pain, a condition known as *angina pectoris*. If a coronary artery is blocked com-

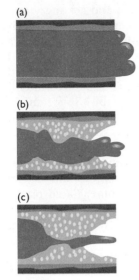

Figure 14.2
Atherosclerosis
Atherosclerosis, a narrowing of the coronary arteries, is the principal cause of coronary disease. (a) Blood flows through a normal artery. (b) Fatty deposits on the walls of the artery have narrowed the path for blood flow. (c) Advanced atherosclerosis. In this situation, a blood clot might suddenly block the flow of blood through the artery.

pletely (by a blood clot, for instance), the abrupt interruption of blood flow can produce a full-fledged heart attack, known as a *myocardial infarction.*

In the 1960s and 1970s a pair of cardiologists, Meyer Friedman and Ray Rosenman (1974), were investigating the causes of coronary disease. Originally, Friedman and Rosenman were interested in the usual factors thought to produce a high risk of heart attack: smoking, obesity, physical inactivity, and so forth. Although they found that these factors were important, they eventually recognized that a piece of the puzzle was missing. Many people would smoke constantly, get little exercise, and be severely overweight, yet avoid the ravages of heart disease. At the same time, other people who seemed to be in much better shape in regard to these risk factors experienced the misfortune of a heart attack. Gradually, Friedman and Rosenman unraveled the riddle. What was their explanation for these perplexing findings? Stress! Specifically, they found a connection between coronary risk and a pattern of behavior they called the *Type A personality*, which involves self-imposed stress and intense reactions to stress.

Elements of the Type A Personality

Friedman and Rosenman divided people into two basic types: Type A and Type B (Rosenman, 1993). **The *Type A personality* includes three elements: (1) a strong competitive orientation, (2) impatience and time urgency, and (3) anger and hostility.** Type A's are ambitious, hard-driving perfectionists who are exceedingly time conscious. They routinely try to do several things at once. Thus, a Type A person may watch TV, talk on the phone, work on a report, and eat dinner all at the same time. Type A's are so impatient that they frequently finish others' sentences for them! They fidget frantically over the briefest delays. Often they are highly competitive, achievement-oriented workaholics who drive themselves with many deadlines. They speak rapidly and emphatically. They are cynical about life and hostile

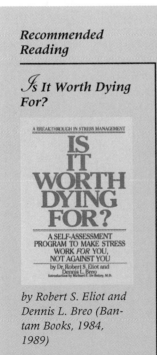
Robert S. Eliot is a cardiologist whose work on heart attack vulnerability has been attracting attention. Eliot believes that some people ("hot reactors") are particularly vulnerable to heart attacks because they have an overly reactive cardiovascular response to stress. These people may or may not exhibit Type A behavior. Hot reacting involves a *physiological* tendency that is probably affected by one's genetic inheritance. Type A behavior involves *behavioral* tendencies that are presumably acquired through learning over a lifetime. A person might be a hot reactor only, a Type A personality only, both, or neither. Those who are both a hot reactor and a Type A personality probably have a highly elevated risk of coronary problems.

Eliot and Breo explain all this and much more in their highly readable book, which focuses on the connections between stress and coronary risk. In addition to explaining how stress, hot reacting, and Type A behavior influence the risk of heart attack, they discuss the role of such health-impairing habits as physical inactivity, poor eating, and smoking. They construct a nice overview of how a diverse array of factors govern cardiac vulnerability and then offer a great deal of useful advice on how to minimize one's susceptibility to a heart attack.

Jeff was a living demonstration of the difference between Type A behavior and hot reacting. He was psychologically intense most of the time, but he was not physiologically intense. His blood pressure rose a little under mental stress, as everyone's does, but it did not rise very much.

Jeff was like a person driving without a muffler—the car may make plenty of noise, but that has nothing to do with how the engine is working. It could be in great shape or it could be burning up; you can't tell from the revved-up sound. At the same time, driving without a muffler isn't a good idea—the noise is a strain on everybody else, if not on the engine. Extreme Type A behavior is worth modifying for that reason alone. Jeff's psychological overreactions kept him in enough hot water to harm the overall quality of his life. [1984, p. 53]

Hard-driving, easy-to-anger, Type A personalities, such as Indiana basketball coach Bobby Knight, appear to be more vulnerable to heart attack than others.

toward others. They are easily aggravated and get angry quickly. In contrast, **the Type B personality is marked by relatively relaxed, patient, easygoing, amicable behavior.** Type B's are less hurried, less competitive, and less easily angered than Type A's. Are you a Type A or a Type B? The strength of one's Type A tendencies can be measured with either structured interviews or questionnaires. The checklist in Figure 14.3 lists some questions that are representative of those used in measurements of Type A behavior.

Which aspects of Type A behavior are most strongly related to increased coronary risk? Are competitiveness, time urgency, and hostility equally important? These are questions of current interest in research on the Type A syndrome. Based on recent studies, many researchers believe that hostility may be more important for coronary risk than other elements of the Type A personality (Houston et al., 1992; Smith, 1992; Williams & Barefoot, 1988). In particular, investigators have been impressed by the apparent relationship between *cynical hostility* and coronary disease, hypertension, and early mortality. People high in cynical hostility are moody, suspicious, resentful, and distrusting. They are quick to anger and to criticize others. When they get upset they tend to show relatively strong physiological reactions. In comparison to others, they exhibit elevated heart rate and blood pressure reactivity (Smith & Brown, 1991) and elevated secretions of stress hormones (Pope & Smith, 1991). More research is needed and the evidence is far from conclusive (Rosenman, 1991), but cynical hostility may prove to be the most toxic element of the Type A syndrome.

Evaluating the Risk

Learning Objective

Discuss the strength of the association between Type A behavior and heart disease and possible explanations for this relationship.

How strong is the link between Type A personality and coronary risk? Based on preliminary data, Friedman and his associates originally estimated that Type A's were *six* times more prone to heart attack than Type B's. At the other extreme, some studies have failed to find an association between Type A behavior and coronary risk (Ragland & Brand, 1988; Shekelle et al., 1985). What can we make of these inconsistent findings? Miller and his associates (1991) have demonstrated convincingly that most of the studies that have failed to find a link between Type A behavior and

Figure 14.3
The Type A personality
The ten questions shown here highlight some of the behavioral traits associated with the Type A personality.

Measuring the Type A Personality

You can use the checklist below to *estimate* the likelihood that you might be a Type A personality. However, the checklist should be regarded as providing only a rough estimate, because Friedman and Rosenman (1974) emphasize that *how* you answer certain questions in their interview is often more significant than the answers themselves. Nonetheless, if you answer "yes" to a majority of the items below, you may want to consider reading their book *Type A Behavior and Your Heart.*

_____ 1. Do you find it difficult to restrain yourself from hurrying others' speech (finishing their sentences for them)?

_____ 2. Do you often try to do more than one thing at a time (such as eat and read simultaneously)?

_____ 3. Do you often feel guilty if you use extra time to relax?

_____ 4. Do you tend to get involved in a great number of projects at once?

_____ 5. Do you find yourself racing through yellow lights when you drive?

_____ 6. Do you need to win in order to derive enjoyment from games and sports?

_____ 7. Do you generally move, walk, and eat rapidly?

_____ 8. Do you agree to take on too many responsibilities?

_____ 9. Do you detest waiting in lines?

_____ 10. Do you have an intense desire to better your position in life and impress others?

"While you've been learning to relax, Tom, I'm afraid a less enlightened 'Type A' personality got your job."

coronary disease have suffered from one or more methodological limitations (chief among them, poor sample selection). Nonetheless, the mixed findings suggest that the relationship between Type A behavior and coronary risk is more modest than originally believed. Taken as a whole, the data suggest that the increased coronary risk for Type A's is perhaps double that for Type B's (Lyness, 1993; Weaver & Rodnick, 1986). The modest nature of this relationship probably means that Type A behavior increases coronary risk for only a portion of the population.

Explaining the Connection

Why is Type A behavior associated with increased coronary risk? Research on the Type A syndrome has uncovered a number of possible explanations.

First, Type A individuals appear to exhibit greater physiological reactivity than Type B's (Lyness, 1993; Smith & Brown, 1991). The frequent ups and downs in heart rate and blood pressure may create wear and tear in their cardiovascular systems.

Second, Type A's probably create more stress for themselves than others do. For example, their competitiveness may lead them to put themselves under a lot of pressure, and their hostility may provoke many arguments and conflicts with others. Consistent with this line of thinking, Smith and colleagues (1988) found that subjects high in hostility reported more hassles, more negative life events, more marital conflict, and more work-related stress than subjects who were lower in hostility.

Third, thanks to their antagonistic ways of relating to others, Type A personalities tend to have less social support than others (Smith & Christensen, 1992). As we noted in Chapter 3, social support may be an important coping resource that promotes health and buffers the effects of stress (Leppin & Schwarzer, 1990; Spiegel, 1993).

Fourth, perhaps because of their cynicism and their tendency to push themselves to work hard, Type A's tend to exhibit health habits that may contribute to the development of cardiovascular disease. For example, in comparison to others, they drink more alcohol, get less exercise, and ignore symptoms of fatigue more often (Houston & Vavak, 1991; Leiker & Hailey, 1988).

In sum, there are a variety of plausible explanations for the connection between the Type A syndrome and heart disease. With all these mechanisms at work, it's not surprising that Type A behavior is associated with increased coronary risk. What's surprising is that the association isn't stronger.

Stress and Cancer

Learning Objective

Discuss whether stress is related to the causation or course of cancer.

If there is a single word that can strike terror in most people's hearts, it is probably *cancer*. We generally view cancer as the most sinister, tragic, loathsome, and unbearable of diseases. In reality, cancer is actually a *collection* of over 100 closely related diseases that vary in their characteristics and amenability to treatment. ***Cancer* refers to malignant cell growth, which may occur in many organ systems in the body.** The core problem in cancer is that cells begin to reproduce in a rapid, disorganized fashion. As this reproduction process lurches out of control, the teeming new cells clump together to form tumors. If this wild growth continues unabated, the spreading tumors create tissue damage and begin to interfere with normal functioning in the affected organ systems.

The research linking psychological factors to the *onset* of cancer is relatively weak. A few studies have found evidence that high stress precedes the development of cancer, but many others have failed to find any connection (Cooper, 1984). Investigators have also attempted to ascertain whether there is a *cancer-prone personality,* which might reflect unsuccessful patterns of coping with stress. These studies have yielded some intriguing threads of consistency, suggesting that lonely, depressed people who have difficulty expressing anger may have an elevated risk for cancer (Cox & Mackay, 1982; Eysenck, 1988; LeShan, 1966; Temoshok, 1987). However, this research must be viewed with caution, given the possibility that one's personality may change after the discovery that one has cancer (Scherg, 1987).

Although efforts to link psychological factors to the onset of cancer have largely failed, more convincing evidence indicates that stress and personality influence the *course* of the disease. The onset of cancer frequently sets off a chain reaction of stressful events. Patients typically have to grapple with fear of the unknown, difficult and aversive treatment regimens, nausea, fatigue, and other treatment side effects, dislocations in intimate relationships, career disruptions, job discrimination, and financial worries. Such stressors may often contribute to the progress of the disease, perhaps by impairing certain aspects of immune system functioning (Andersen, Kiecolt-Glaser, & Glaser, 1994). The impact of all this stress may depend in part on one's personality. Research suggests that mortality rates are higher among patients who respond to this stress with depression, repressed anger, and other negative emotions (Friedman, 1991). In contrast, prospects appear to be better for patients who can maintain their emotional stability and enthusiasm.

Stress and Other Diseases

Learning Objective

Summarize evidence linking stress to a variety of diseases and to immune functioning.

The development of questionnaires to measure life stress has allowed researchers to look for correlations between stress and a variety of diseases. These researchers have uncovered many connections between stress and illness. For example, Thomason et al. (1992) found an association between life stress and the course of rheumatoid arthritis. Working with a sample of female students, Williams and Deffenbacher (1983) found that life stress was correlated with the number of vaginal (yeast) infections the women reported in the past year. Other studies have connected stress to the development of genital herpes (VanderPlate, Aral, & Magder, 1988) and periodontal disease (Green et al., 1986). Researchers have also found an association between high stress and flare-ups of inflammatory bowel disease (Garrett et al., 1991).

These are just a handful of representative examples of studies relating stress to physical diseases. Figure 14.4 provides a longer list of health problems that have been linked to stress. Many of these stress-illness connections are based on tentative or inconsistent findings, but the sheer length and diversity of the list is remarkable. Why should stress increase the risk for so many kinds of illness? A partial answer may lie in immunal functioning.

Stress and Immune Functioning

The apparent link between stress and many types of illness raises the possibility that stress may undermine immunal functioning. **The *immune response* is the body's defensive reaction to invasion by bacteria, viral agents, or other foreign substances.** The immune response works to protect the body from many forms of disease. Immunal reactions are multifaceted, but they depend heavily on actions initiated by specialized white blood cells, called *lymphocytes.*

A wealth of studies indicate that experimentally induced stress can impair immunal functioning *in animals* (Ader & Cohen, 1984, 1993). Stressors such as crowding, shock, and restraint reduce various aspects of lymphocyte reactivity in laboratory animals.

Studies by Janice Kiecolt-Glaser and her colleagues have also related stress to suppressed immunal activity *in humans.* In one study, medical students provided researchers with blood samples so that their immunal response could be assessed (Kiecolt-Glaser et al., 1984). The students provided the baseline sample a month before final exams and contributed the "high stress" sample on the first day of their finals. The subjects also responded to the Social Readjustment Rating Scale (SRRS;

Janice Kiecolt-Glaser

see Chapter 3) as a measure of recent stress. Reduced levels of immune activity were found during the extremely stressful finals week. Reduced immunal activity was also correlated with higher scores on the SRRS.

In another study, investigators exposed quarantined volunteers to respiratory viruses that cause the common cold and found that those under high stress were more likely to be infected by the viruses (Cohen, Tyrrell, & Smith, 1993). Other studies have found evidence of reduced immunal activity among people who scored relatively high on a stress scale measuring daily hassles (Levy et al., 1989), among recently divorced or separated men (Kiecolt-Glaser et al., 1988), and among people struggling with the stress of loneliness (Glaser et al., 1985). Thus, scientists are beginning to assemble some impressive evidence that stress can temporarily suppress human immunal functioning, which may make people more vulnerable to infections.

Conclusions

Learning Objective

Discuss the strength of the relationship between stress and illness.

In summary, a wealth of evidence suggests that stress influences physical health. However, virtually all of the relevant research is correlational, so it cannot demonstrate conclusively that stress *causes* illness (Brett et al., 1990; Watson & Pennebaker, 1989). The association between stress and illness could be due to a third variable.

Health Problems That May Be Linked to Stress

Health problem	Representative evidence
Common cold	Stone et al. (1992)
Ulcers	Ellard et al. (1990)
Asthma	Mrazek (1993)
Headaches	Featherstone & Beitman (1984)
Menstrual discomfort	Siegel, Johnson, & Sarason (1979)
Vaginal infections	Williams & Deffenbacher (1983)
Genital herpes	VanderPlate, Aral, & Magder (1988)
Skin disorders	Fava et al. (1989)
Rheumatoid arthritis	Thomason et al. (1992)
Chronic back pain	Craufurd, Creed, & Jayson (1990)
Female reproductive problems	Seibel & McCarthy (1993)
Diabetes	Gonder-Frederick et al. (1990)
Complications of pregnancy	Pagel et al. (1990)
Hernias	Rahe & Holmes (1965)
Glaucoma	Cohen & Hajioff (1972)
Hyperthyroidism	H. Weiner (1978)
Hemophilia	Buxton et al. (1981)
Tuberculosis	Wolf & Goodell (1968)
Leukemia	Greene & Swisher (1969)
Stroke	Harmsen et al. (1990)
Appendicitis	Creed (1989)
Multiple sclerosis	Grant et al. (1989)
Periodontal disease	Green et al. (1986)
Hypertension	Egan et al. (1983)
Cancer	Holland & Lewis (1993)
Coronary heart disease	Rosengren, Tibblin, & Wilhelmsen (1991)
Inflammatory bowel disease	Garrett et al. (1991)

Figure 14.4
Stress and health problems
The onset or progress of the health problems listed here may be affected by stress. The evidence is fragmentary in many instances, but the number and diversity of problems on this list are alarming.

Based on the evidence as a whole, most health psychologists would probably accept the assertion that stress often contributes to the causation of illness. However, some critics argue that the stress-illness correlation could reflect other causal processes. One or more aspects of personality, physiology, or memory might contribute to the correlation between high stress and high incidence of illness (see Chapter 3 for additional discussion of this complex issue).

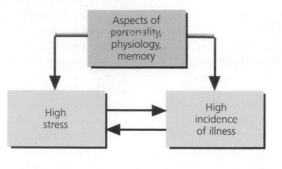

Perhaps some aspect of personality or some type of physiological predisposition makes people overly prone to interpret events as stressful *and* overly prone to interpret unpleasant physical sensations as symptoms of illness (see Figure 14.5). For instance, in the Chapter 3 Application we discussed how the personality trait of neuroticism might increase individuals' sensitivity to both stress and illness.

Moreover, critics of this research note that many of the studies used research designs that may have inflated the apparent link between stress and illness (Schroeder & Costa, 1984). For example, researchers often have subjects make after-the-fact reports of how much stress and illness they endured during the previous year or two. If some subjects have a tendency to recall more stress than others *and* to recall more illness than others, their better memories would artificially increase the correlation between stress and illness.

In spite of methodological problems favoring inflated correlations, the research in this area consistently indicates that the *strength* of the relationship between stress and health is modest. The correlations typically fall in the .20s and .30s. Clearly, stress is not an irresistible force that produces inevitable effects on health. Actually, this should come as no surprise. As we saw in Chapter 3, some people handle stress better than others. Furthermore, stress is only one actor on a crowded stage. A complex network of biopsychosocial factors influence health, including genetic endowment, exposure to infectious agents and environmental toxins, nutrition, exercise, alcohol and drug use, smoking, use of medical care, and cooperation with medical advice. In the next section we'll discuss some of these factors as we examine health-impairing habits and lifestyles.

Habits, Lifestyles, and Health

Learning Objective

Give some reasons why people develop health-impairing habits.

Some people seem determined to dig an early grave for themselves. They do precisely those things they have been warned are particularly bad for their health. For example, some people drink heavily even though they know they're corroding their liver. Others eat all the wrong foods even though they know they're increasing their risk for a heart attack. Such downright self-destructive behavior is much more common than most people realize. In fact, research reveals that *chronic self-destructiveness* is a measurable personality trait related to a variety of potentially harmful behaviors, from driving recklessly (as reflected by traffic tickets) to postponing important medical tests (Kelley et al., 1985).

It may seem puzzling that people behave in self-destructive ways. Why do they do it? Several considerations are involved. First, many health-impairing habits creep up on people slowly. For instance, drug use may grow imperceptibly over years, or exercise habits may decline ever so gradually. Second, many health-impairing habits involve activities that are quite pleasant at the time. Eating favorite foods, smoking cigarettes, and getting "high" are potent reinforcing events. Third, the risks associated with most health-impairing habits are chronic diseases, such as cancer, that usually lie 10, 20, or 30 years down the road. It is relatively easy to ignore risks that lie in the distant future. Fourth, it appears that *people have a tendency to underestimate the risks associated with their own health-impairing habits,* while viewing the risks associated with others' self-destructive behaviors much more accurately (van der Velde, van der Pligt, & Hooykaas, 1994; Weinstein, 1989). In other words, most people are aware of the dangers associated with certain habits. However, they often engage in *denial* when it is time to apply this information to themselves.

In this section we'll discuss how health is affected by smoking, drinking, overeating and obesity, poor nutrition, and lack of exercise. We'll also look at lifestyle factors that relate to AIDS. The health risks of alcohol and drug use are covered in the Application.

Smoking

The smoking of tobacco is widespread in our culture, with current consumption running around 2800 cigarettes a year per adult in the United States (Fiore, 1992). The percentage of people who smoke has declined noticeably since the mid-1960s. Nonetheless, about 28% of adult men and 24% of adult women in the United States continue to smoke regularly. Moreover, among those who continue to smoke, the proportion who smoke "heavily" has increased.

Health Effects

Learning Objective

Discuss the health effects of smoking.

Suspicions about the health risks associated with tobacco use were voiced in some quarters throughout the first half of the 20th century. However, the risks of smoking were not widely appreciated until the mid-1960s. Since then, accumulating evidence has clearly shown that smokers face a much greater risk of premature death than nonsmokers (Jarvik & Schneider, 1992; U.S. Department of Health and Human Services, 1989, 1990). For example, a 25-year-old male who smokes two packs a day has an estimated life expectancy that is *8.3 years shorter* than that of a similar nonsmoker (Schlaadt & Shannon, 1994). The overall risk is positively related to the number of cigarettes smoked and their tar and nicotine content. Cigar and pipe smoking is also associated with elevated health risks, although these habits are less hazardous than cigarette smoking. The health costs of smoking can be put in perspective by noting that smoking accounts for roughly 60 times as many deaths per year as cocaine and heroin use combined (Jarvik & Schneider, 1992).

Why are mortality rates higher for smokers? Smoking increases the likelihood of developing a surprisingly large range of diseases. Many of these diseases are highly lethal, including 7 of the 14 leading causes of death among people over age 65 (Rimer et al., 1990). Lung cancer and heart disease are the two types of illness that kill the largest number of smokers (Fielding, 1985). However, smokers also have an elevated risk for oral, bladder, and kidney cancer, as well as cancer of the larynx, esophagus, and pancreas (Newcomb & Carbone, 1992); for arteriosclerosis, hypertension, stroke, and other cardiovascular diseases (McBride, 1992); and for bronchitis, emphysema, and other pulmonary diseases (Sherman, 1992).

The increased prevalence of diseases among smokers may not be due to their smoking alone. Some studies suggest that smokers are more likely than nonsmokers to exhibit a *variety* of health-impairing habits (Castro et al., 1989). For example, they may tend to consume more alcohol, more coffee, and more unhealthful foods than nonsmokers, while exercising less as well.

The dangers of smoking are not limited to smokers themselves. Family members and co-workers who spend a lot of time around smokers are exposed to second-hand smoke, which can increase their risk for a variety of illnesses, especially lung cancer (Byrd, 1992). One report estimates that passive smoking is the third leading cause of preventable deaths in the United States (Glantz & Parmley, 1991). Young children with asthma are particularly vulnerable to the effects of passive smoking (Shephard, 1989).

Giving Up Smoking

Learning Objective

Discuss the dynamics of giving up smoking.

Studies show that if people can give up smoking, their health risks decline reasonably quickly (Samet, 1992). Five years after people stop smoking, their health risk is already noticeably lower than that of people who continue to smoke. The health risks of people who give up tobacco continue to decline until they reach a normal level after about 15 years (see Figure 14.6). Evidence suggests that most smokers would like to quit, but they are reluctant to give up a major source of pleasure, and they worry about craving cigarettes, gaining weight, and becoming tense and irritable (Grunberg, Bowen, & Winders, 1986; Orleans et al., 1991).

There are nearly 40 million ex-smokers in the United States. Collectively, they clearly demonstrate that it is possible to give up smoking successfully. But many didn't succeed until their third, fourth, or fifth attempt, and most would testify that quitting isn't easy. Research shows that long-term success rates for efforts to quit smoking are in the vicinity of only 25% (Cohen et al., 1989). However, light smokers (fewer than 20 cigarettes per day) are somewhat more successful at quitting than heavy smokers. The probability of a relapse after quitting is much greater among people who experience high levels of stress (Cohen & Lichtenstein, 1990). Discouragingly, people who enroll in formal smoking-cessation programs aren't any more successful than people who try to quit on their own (Cohen et al., 1989). In fact, it is estimated that 80–90% of the people who successfully give up smoking quit on their own, without professional help.

No single approach to quitting smoking is effective for everyone. However, if you attempt to give up smoking on your own (without entering a formal treatment program), you may want to consider the following advice.

1. *Educate yourself thoroughly about the dangers of smoking.* Giving up smoking requires strong motivation. You can increase your motivation by becoming familiar with the health problems caused by smoking. Programs that concentrate on education alone can be effective for some people (Windsor et al., 1985).
2. *Quit cold turkey.* Success rates for giving up smoking appear to be somewhat higher for people who quit cold turkey as opposed to reducing tobacco consumption gradually (Glasgow et al., 1985).
3. *Use self-modification techniques.* The self-modification techniques described in Chapter 4 can be invaluable in efforts to quit smoking. A good program should include careful monitoring of smoking habits, ample rewards for going without cigarettes, and control of antecedents to avoid situations that trigger smoking.
4. *If you don't succeed, try again.* People attempting to give up smoking often fail several times before eventually succeeding. Evidence suggests that the readiness to quit builds gradually as people cycle through periods of abstinence and relapse (Biener & Abrams, 1991; Prochaska et al., 1988). Hence, if your effort to quit smoking ends in failure, don't give up hope—try again in a few weeks or few months.

In recent years there has been considerable publicity about the potential value of *nicotine substitutes*—nicotine gum and the newer nicotine skin patch, which releases a steady dose of nicotine into the wearer. The rationale for nicotine substitutes is that insofar as nicotine is addictive, it might be helpful to employ a substitute during the transitional period as one tries to give up cigarettes. Thus, people trying to halt their smoking often wonder whether it would be helpful to use nicotine gum or the nicotine patch. Do nicotine substitutes work? The evidence is ambiguous. On the positive side of the ledger, controlled studies have demonstrated that nicotine substitutes increase long-term rates of quitting in comparison to placebos (Oster et al., 1986; Tonnesen et al., 1991). However, the increases are small and

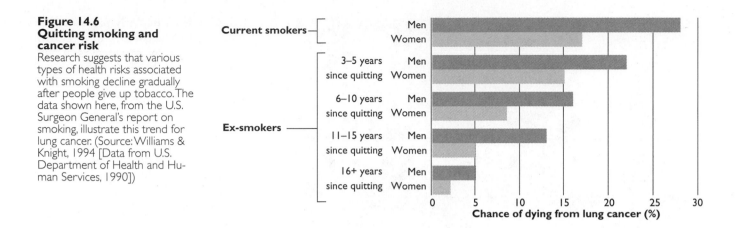

Figure 14.6
Quitting smoking and cancer risk
Research suggests that various types of health risks associated with smoking decline gradually after people give up tobacco. The data shown here, from the U.S. Surgeon General's report on smoking, illustrate this trend for lung cancer. (Source: Williams & Knight, 1994 [Data from U.S. Department of Health and Human Services, 1990])

the success rates are still discouragingly low. For instance, in one study (Tonneson et al., 1991), the "increased" abstinence rates for subjects using the nicotine patch were only 24% after 6 months and 17% after 12 months. Clearly, nicotine substitutes are not a panacea, and they are not a substitute for a firm determination to quit. Furthermore, some people experience side effects, such as nausea and headaches, from nicotine replacements. Finally, some experts question the wisdom of giving people nicotine in new forms, in light of the fact that one reason people attempt to quit smoking is that nicotine is bad for their health (Pomerleau & Pomerleau, 1988).

Drinking

Learning Objective

Summarize data on patterns of alcohol use and the short-term risks of drinking.

Alcohol rivals tobacco as one of the leading causes of health problems in American society. Alcohol encompasses a variety of beverages containing ethyl alcohol, such as beers, wines, and distilled spirits. The concentration of alcohol in these drinks varies from about 4% in most beers up to 40% in 80-proof liquor (occasionally more in higher-proof liquors). Survey data indicate that around 100 million people in the United States drink alcoholic beverages. About two-thirds of the adult population are drinkers, so they outnumber abstainers by about two to one. As Figure 14.7 shows, per capita consumption of alcohol in the United States declined in the 1980s, but this decrease followed decades of steady growth, and alcohol consumption remains relatively high, although certainly not the highest in the world (Williams et al., 1992).

Figure 14.7
Drinking in America
Drinking in the United States, as indexed by per capita consumption of ethanol in gallons, has risen steadily through most of the 20th century, although there was a modest decline during the 1980s. The inset shows the percentage of American adults who are abstainers or heavy, moderate, or light drinkers. Although only 9% of the population drinks heavily, drinkers outnumber abstainers by about two to one. (Data from Williams et al., 1992)

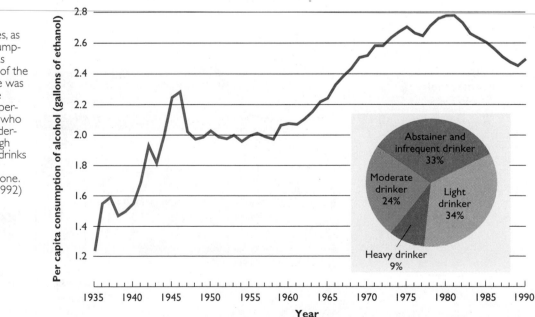

Overindulging in alcohol is particularly widespread among college students.

Drinking is particularly prevalent on college campuses, according to a recent, large-scale survey by researchers at the Harvard School of Public Health (Wechsler et al., 1994). This survey of over 17,000 undergraduates at 140 schools found that 85% of the students drank. Moreover, 50% of the men and 39% of the women reported that they engaged in binge drinking with the intention of getting drunk. Perhaps most telling, college students spend far more money on alcohol ($5.5 billion annually) than they do on their books.

Why Do People Drink?

The effects of alcohol are influenced by the user's experience, motivation, and mood, as well as by the presence of food in the stomach, the proof of the beverage, and the rate of drinking. Thus, there is great variability in how alcohol affects different people on different occasions. Nonetheless, the central effect is a "Who cares?" brand of euphoria that temporarily boosts self-esteem as one's problems melt away. Negative emotions such as tension, worry, anxiety, and depression are dulled, and inhibitions may be loosened. Thus, when first-year college students are asked why they drink, they mention such reasons as to relax, to feel less tense in social situations, to keep friends company, and to forget their problems (see Figure 14.8). Of course, other factors are also at work. Many people drink largely out of habit. Drinking is a widely endorsed and encouraged social ritual in our culture. Its central role in American culture is readily apparent if you think about all the alcohol consumed at weddings, sports events, holiday parties, and so forth. Moreover, the alcohol industry spends hundreds of millions of dollars on advertising to convince us that drinking is cool, sexy, sophisticated, and harmless.

Short-Term Risks and Problems

Alcohol has a variety of side effects, including some that can be very problematic. To begin with, there is that infamous source of regret, the "hangover," which may include headaches, dizziness, nausea, and vomiting. In the constellation of alcohol's risks, however, hangovers are downright trivial. For instance, life-threatening over-doses are more common than most people realize. Although it's possible to over-

Figure 14.8
Why students drink
Alcohol use among college students is higher than in the population as a whole. What motivates this drinking? A survey of 1669 first-year college students at 14 schools suggests that students drink primarily to relax and to ease tensions in social situations. (From Williams & Knight, 1994)

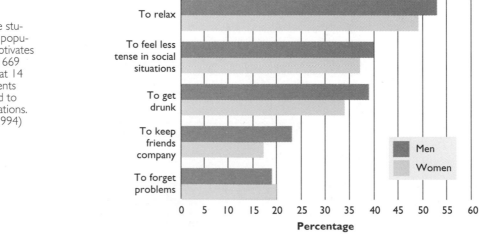

Figure 14.9
Drinking and impaired driving
This chart estimates how many drinks it takes to impair driving ability in people of various weights. As you can see, as few as three drinks in a two-hour period can elevate blood alcohol content (BAC) to a dangerous level.

	BAC to .05% Be careful driving		.05–.09% Driving will be impaired		.10% & up Do not drive							
Weight (lbs)												
100	1	2	3	4	5	6	7	8	9	10	11	12
120	1	2	3	4	5	6	7	8	9	10	11	12
140	1	2	3	4	5	6	7	8	9	10	11	12
160	1	2	3	4	5	6	7	8	9	10	11	12
180	1	2	3	4	5	6	7	8	9	10	11	12
200	1	2	3	4	5	6	7	8	9	10	11	12
220	1	2	3	4	5	6	7	8	9	10	11	12
240	1	2	3	4	5	6	7	8	9	10	11	12

Drinks (1½ oz liquor or 12 oz beer) in two-hour period

dose with alcohol alone, a much more frequent problem is overdosing on combinations of alcohol and sedative or narcotic drugs. These combinations result in about 140,000 emergency room visits annually in the United States.

In substantial amounts, alcohol has a decidedly negative effect on intellectual functioning and perceptual-motor coordination. The resulting combination of tainted judgment, slowed reaction time, and reduced coordination can be deadly when people attempt to drive automobiles after drinking. As Figure 14.9 shows, depending on one's weight, it may take only a few drinks before driving is impaired. It's estimated that alcohol contributes to 50% of all auto accidents. Drunk driving is a major social problem that costs about 20,000 lives every year and is the leading cause of death in young adults. Alcohol has also been implicated in about half of all home accidents and fire fatalities, and about 70% of drownings (Kinney & Leaton, 1987).

With their inhibitions released, some drinkers become argumentative and prone to aggression. In the Harvard survey of over 17,000 undergraduates, 34% of the students from "heavy drinking" schools reported that they had been insulted or humiliated by a drunken student, 20% had experienced serious arguments, and 13% had been pushed or assaulted (Wechsler et al., 1994). Worse yet, alcohol appears to contribute to about 90% of student rapes and 95% of violent crime on campus. In society at large, alcohol is associated with a host of violent crimes, including murder, assault, rape, child abuse, and spouse abuse (Maisto, Galizio, & Connors, 1995). Finally, alcohol can also contribute to reckless sexual behavior, which may have ramifications for one's health. In the Harvard survey, 41% of the binge drinkers reported that they had unplanned sex as a result of drinking, and 22% indicated that their drinking had led to unprotected sex.

Long-Term Health Effects and Social Costs

Learning Objective

Summarize the major long-term health risks and social costs of drinking.

Alcohol's long-term health risks are mostly (but not exclusively) associated with chronic, heavy consumption of alcohol. Estimates of the number of people at risk vary considerably. According to Winick (1992), there are approximately 19 million people in the United States with drinking problems, including about 8 million who should probably be characterized as *alcoholics*. **Alcoholism is a chronic, progressive disorder marked by a growing compulsion to drink and impaired control over drinking that eventually interfere with health and social behavior.** Whether alcoholism is best viewed as a disease or as a self-control problem is the source of considerable debate, but there is a reasonable consensus about the warning signs of alcoholism. These include preoccupation with alcohol, drinking to relieve uncomfortable feelings, gulping drinks, clandestine drinking, and the other indicators listed in Figure 14.10.

Alcoholism and problem drinking are associated with an elevated risk for a wide range of serious health problems (Goodwin, 1992). One of the most serious is cirrhosis of the liver, an irreversible scarring of the liver, which is the ninth leading cause of death in the United States. Although there is some thought-provoking (albeit controversial) evidence that moderate drinking may reduce one's risk for

Figure 14.10
Detecting a drinking problem
Experts estimate that as many as 19 million people in the United States may have a drinking problem (Winick, 1992). However, facing the reality that one has a problem with alcohol is always difficult. This list of the chief warning signs associated with problem drinking is intended to facilitate this process. (From Edlin & Golanty, 1992)

Warning Signs of Problem Drinking or Alcoholism

1. Gulping drinks.

2. Drinking to modify uncomfortable feelings.

3. Personality or behavioral changes after drinking.

4. Getting drunk frequently.

5. Experiencing "blackouts"—not being able to remember what happened while drinking.

6. Frequent accidents or illness as a result of drinking.

7. Priming—preparing yourself with alcohol before a social gathering at which alcohol is going to be served.

8. Not wanting to talk about the negative consequences of drinking (avoidance).

9. Preoccupation with alcohol.

10. Focusing social situations around alcohol.

11. Sneaking drinks or clandestine drinking.

coronary disease (Riman et al., 1991), it is clear that heavy drinking increases one's risk for heart disease, hypertension, and stroke. Excessive drinking is also correlated with an elevated risk for various types of cancer, including oral, stomach, pancreatic, colon, and rectal cancer. Among women, even moderate drinking may increase the likelihood of developing breast cancer (Willett et al., 1987). Moreover, serious drinking problems can lead to malnutrition, pregnancy complications, brain damage, and neurological disorders. Finally, alcoholism can produce severe psychotic states, characterized by delirium, disorientation, and hallucinations.

We have focused on the personal risks of alcohol abuse, but the enormous social costs of alcohol should also be emphasized. Drinking problems wreak havoc in millions of families. Children of alcoholics grow up in dysfunctional environments in which the risk of physical or sexual abuse is much higher than normal (Mathew et al., 1993). Homes of alcoholics tend to become tense battlegrounds as family members attempt to cope with the problem drinker's self-destructive behavior. Family members experience their own emotional crises as they struggle with feelings of frustration, anger, fear, pity, and resentment. Moreover, in the world of work, alcohol-related absenteeism and reduced efficiency on the job cost American industry billions of dollars annually. It is hard to put a dollar value on the diverse social costs of alcohol abuse, but experts estimate that alcohol costs the U.S. economy between $86 and $116 billion annually (NIAAA, 1991). Thus, the social costs of alcohol abuse are staggering.

Overeating

Learning Objective

Discuss the determinants and health risks of obesity.

Obesity, the condition of being overweight, is a common health problem. The criteria of obesity vary considerably. Typically, people are assumed to be obese if their weight exceeds their ideal body weight by 15–20%. Depending on where one draws the line between obesity and normality, 12–40% of American adults are overweight (Gray, 1989). Obesity is similar to smoking in that it exerts a relatively subtle impact on health that is easy for many people to ignore. Yet the long-range effects of obesity can be quite dangerous. Obese people have an increased risk of coronary disease, hypertension, stroke, respiratory problems, arthritis, diabetes, gall bladder disease, back problems, infertility, and at least four types of cancer (Kannel & Cupples, 1989; Kissebah, Freedman, & Peiris, 1989). Figure 14.11 shows estimates of just how much obesity elevates the risk for some of these diseases.

Determinants of Obesity

A few decades ago it was widely believed that obesity was a function of personality. Obesity was thought to occur mostly in depressed, anxious, compulsive people who overate to deal with their negative emotions. However, research eventually

Figure 14.11
Obesity and mortality
This graph shows the increased
mortality risks for men who are
either 20% or 40% above average
weight for their age and height.
Clearly, obesity is a significant
health risk. (Data from VanItallie,
1979)

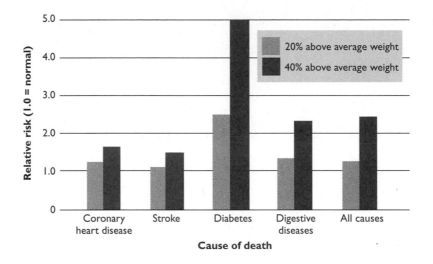

Obesity, which carries quite a
number of health risks, is a product of many factors, including
genetic predisposition.

showed that there is no such thing as an "obese personality" (Rodin, Schank, & Striegel-Moore, 1989). Instead, research revealed that a complex network of interacting factors determine whether people develop weight problems.

Chief among these factors is *genetic predisposition.* In one influential study, adults raised by foster parents were compared with their biological and foster parents in regard to *body mass index*—a measure of weight that controls for variations in height (Stunkard et al., 1986). The investigators found that the adoptees resembled their biological parents more than their adoptive parents. In a subsequent *twin study,* Stunkard and associates (1990) found that identical twins reared apart were far more similar in body mass index than fraternal twins reared together (see Chapter 2 for a discussion of the logic underlying twin studies). Based on their correlational data, Stunkard et al. (1990) estimate that genetic factors account for roughly 70% of the variation in weight among people. These genetic factors probably explain why some people can eat constantly without gaining weight, while other, less fortunate people grow chubby eating far less. Thus, it appears that some people inherit a genetic vulnerability to obesity.

People who lose weight on a diet have a rather strong (and depressing) tendency to gain back the weight they lose. The reverse is also true. People who have to work to put weight on often have trouble keeping it on. According to Richard Nisbett (1972), these observations suggest that each person's body may have a **set point, which represents its natural point of stability in body weight.** According to set point theory, the body monitors fat cell levels to keep them fairly stable (Keesey & Powley, 1975, 1986). When fat stores slip below a crucial set point, the body compensates for this change by increasing hunger and decreasing metabolism. The processes hypothesized by set point theory function to keep body weight within a limited range (not at one precise weight, as the theory's name suggests).

What determines one's set point? Advocates of set point theory note that gains or reductions in weight generally do *not* lead to increases or decreases in the *number* of fat cells. Instead, fat cells increase or decrease in average *size* (Hirsch et al., 1989). Although the number of fat cells in the body can be increased at any age (through persistent overeating), the count typically stabilizes in early childhood (Knittle et al., 1981). This curious stability suggests that the number of fat cells has something to do with one's set point. It also suggests that childhood eating habits may exert considerable influence over one's set point and one's vulnerability to obesity (Brownell, 1986).

Can one's set point be changed? The evidence on this issue is not very encouraging. Studies suggest that long-term excessive eating can gradually increase one's set point, but decreasing it seems to be very difficult (Keesey, 1986). This finding does *not* mean that all obese people are doomed to remain obese forever. However, it does suggest that most overweight people must be prepared to make *permanent* changes in their eating and exercise habits if they expect to keep their weight down (Keesey, 1988).

While a variety of physiological factors may influence vulnerability to obesity, chronic overeating undeniably plays a prominent role. Why is overeating such a routine habit for so many people? Stanley Schachter (1971) advanced the hypothesis that obese people are *overly sensitive to external cues* that affect their hunger and *relatively insensitive to internal physiological cues* that signal the true need for food. According to this notion, overweight people pay little attention to messages from their bodies but respond readily to external cues such as the availability of food, the attractiveness of the food, and the time of day. This formulation suggests that people overeat because they cannot ignore environmental cues that trigger hunger. For example, people who are not really hungry may be stimulated to pursue food simply by seeing a delectable commercial on TV.

Schachter's theory proved to be an incomplete explanation of obesity because it ignored the importance of the various physiological factors that we have discussed (Rodin, 1981). Furthermore, studies have raised doubts about whether obese people really eat all that much more than normal-weight people (Rodin et al., 1989). Nonetheless, Schachter deserves credit for showing how external food cues can contribute to overeating.

Losing Weight

Learning Objective

Discuss fad diets and the key elements in effective weight loss.

Whether out of concern about their health or just old-fashioned vanity, an ever-increasing number of people are trying to lose weight. One recent survey of over 4600 people found that 47% of the men and 75% of the women had dieted to lose weight at one time or another (Jeffery, Adlis, & Forster, 1991). Unfortunately, the obsession with weight loss can sometimes become dangerous. According to medical and nutritional experts, many of the popular fad diets promising large, rapid weight reductions can be perilous to one's health (Atkinson, 1989). For instance, an article in the *Journal of the American Medical Association* (Wadden et al., 1983) revealed that by the end of 1982 the U.S. Food and Drug Administration had received 138 complaints of illness (including six deaths) from people using the so-called Cambridge Diet. Wadden and colleagues also mentioned that liquid-protein diets were thought to be associated with some 58 deaths before they faded from view. Thus, it is important to understand that faddish, extreme nutritional programs are usually money-making ventures for their developers that have little genuine merit and may even be dangerous. What, by the way, do Wadden and colleagues (1983) recommend to achieve safe, durable weight loss? They advocate "behavior modification, nutrition counseling and exercise" (p. 2834).

While there may be a number of causes of obesity, there is only one way to lose weight. You must change your ratio of energy intake (from food consumption) to energy output (from physical activities). To be quite specific, to lose one pound you need to burn up 3500 more calories than you consume. You have three options in trying to change your ratio of energy input to energy output: (1) You can sharply reduce your food consumption. (2) You can sharply increase your exercise output. (3) You can simultaneously decrease your food intake and step up your exercise output in more moderate ways. Most experts recommend the third option, with an

emphasis on reducing food intake. Although exercise clearly can contribute to weight loss, its effects are limited (Segal & Pi-Sunyer, 1989). Even a vigorous, hour-long workout will burn off only an extra 200–300 calories—a drop in the bucket compared to what most people can achieve by eating less. (However, exercise does help, and it can yield many other benefits, which we will discuss momentarily.)

Although popular diet regimens promise rapid weight loss, experts agree that slow, gradual reductions in weight are more likely to have lasting effects (Brownell, 1989). Self-modification techniques (see Chapter 4) can be helpful in achieving gradual weight loss. It is important to avoid "yo-yo dieting," the syndrome in which one loses and regains the same weight over and over in a cyclical manner (Brownell, 1988). In fact, yo-yo dieting appears to alter metabolism in ways that gradually make it harder and harder to lose weight.

Recent evidence suggests that dieters should monitor the *kinds* of calories they consume as well as the *number* of calories. Foods with a high fat content are converted into body fat more readily than foods high in carbohydrates or protein (Gurin, 1989). Thus, people who want to "shape up" should consume low-fat diets. This point highlights the importance of nutritional patterns, which we consider in the next section.

Poor Nutrition

Nutrition **is a collection of processes (mainly food consumption) through which an organism utilizes the materials (nutrients) required for survival and growth.** The term also refers to the *study* of these processes. Unfortunately, most people don't study nutrition very much. Moreover, the cunning mass marketing of nutritionally worthless foods makes it more and more difficult to maintain sound nutritional habits.

Nutrition and Health

Evidence is accumulating that patterns of nutrition influence susceptibility to a variety of diseases and health problems. In addition to the problems associated with obesity, which we have already discussed, other possible connections between eating patterns and health include the following:

1. Heavy consumption of foods that elevate serum cholesterol level (eggs, cheeses, butter, shellfish, sausage, and the like) appears to increase the risk of heart disease (Muldoon, Manuck, & Matthews, 1990). Eating habits are only one of several factors that influence serum cholesterol level, but they do make an important contribution. Unfortunately, recent studies have turned up disturbing—and baffling—evidence that lower cholesterol levels are associated with increases in depression, suicide, and accidents (Kaplan, Manuck, & Shumaker, 1992).
2. High salt intake is thought to be a contributing factor to the development of hypertension (Kaplan, 1986), although there is still some debate about its exact role.
3. Some studies have suggested that high caffeine consumption may elevate one's risk for hypertension (France & Ditto, 1988) and for coronary disease (LaCroix et al., 1986). However, a recent large-scale study found no association between caffeine consumption and cardiovascular risk (Grobbee et al., 1990). Given these inconsistent findings, more research is needed to settle the issue.
4. High-fat diets have been implicated as possible contributors to some forms of cancer, especially cancers of the colon, prostate, and breast (Levy, 1985). Some studies also suggest that high-fiber diets may reduce one's risk for colon and rectal cancer (Rosen, Nystrom, & Wall, 1988), but the evidence is far from conclusive.
5. Vulnerability to osteoporosis, an abnormal loss of bone mass observed most commonly in postmenopausal women, appears to be elevated by a lifelong pattern of inadequate calcium intake (Fahey & Gallagher-Allred, 1990).
6. A recent study suggests that high intake of vitamin E may reduce one's risk for coronary disease (Rimm et al., 1993). The authors of the study emphasize that more research should be conducted before medical authorities recommend widespread use of vitamin E supplements, but their findings are very encouraging.

7. Nutritional patterns play a role in the course and management of a host of diseases. Prominent examples include gall stones, kidney stones, gout, peptic ulcers, and rheumatoid arthritis (Werbach, 1988). Eating habits may also contribute to the causation of some of these diseases, although the evidence is less compelling on this point.

Of course, nutritional habits interact with other factors—genetics, exercise, environment, and so on—to determine whether one develops a particular disease. Nonetheless, the examples just described indicate that our eating habits can influence our physical health.

The Basis for Poor Nutrition

Nutritional deficiencies are more widespread in the United States than most people realize. One recent study found that 70% of men and 80% of women consumed a diet that was deficient in at least 1 of 15 essential nutrients (Murphy et al., 1992). For the most part, these deficiencies are not attributable to low income or inability to afford appropriate foods. Instead, most malnutrition in America is attributable to lack of knowledge about nutrition and lack of effort to ensure good nutrition (Quillin, 1987).

In other words, most people's nutritional shortcomings are a result of ignorance and poor motivation. Collectively, Americans are remarkably naive about the basic principles of nutrition, and schools tend to provide very little education in this area. Most people are not highly motivated to make sure their food consumption is nutritionally sound. Instead, they approach eating casually, guided not by nutritional needs but by convenience, palatability, and clever advertising.

For most people, then, the first steps toward improved nutrition involve changing attitudes and acquiring information. First and foremost, people need to recognize the importance of good nutrition and commit themselves to making a real effort to regulate their eating patterns. Second, people should try to acquire a basic education about nutritional principles.

Nutritional Goals

Learning Objective

List three general goals intended to foster sound nutrition.

The evidence indicates that the most healthful approach to nutrition is to follow well-moderated patterns of food consumption that ensure nutritional adequacy while limiting the intake of certain substances that can be counterproductive. Some general guidelines for achieving these goals include the following:

1. *Consume a balanced variety of foods.* Food is made up of a variety of components, six of which are essential to your physical well-being. These six *essential nutrients* are proteins, fats, carbohydrates, vitamins, minerals, and fiber. Proteins, fats, and carbohydrates supply the body with its energy. Vitamins and minerals help release that energy and serve other important functions as well. Fiber provides roughage that facilitates digestion. It is probably a bit unrealistic to expect most people to keep track of which nutrients are found in which foods. However, it is fairly easy to promote adequate intake of all essential nutrients. All you have to do is to consume a balanced diet in terms of the *basic food groups,* which are described in the food guide pyramid shown in Figure 14.12.

2. *Avoid excessive consumption of fats, cholesterol, sugar, and salt.* These are all commodities that are overrepresented in the typical American diet. They are not inherently bad, but they can become problematic when consumed in excess. It is particularly prudent to limit the intake of saturated fats by consuming less beef, pork, ham, hot dogs, sausage, lunchmeats, whole milk, and fried foods. Consumption of many of the same foods should also be limited to help reduce cholesterol intake, which influences vulnerability to heart disease. In particular, beef, pork, lamb, sausage, cheese, butter, and eggs are high in cholesterol. Refined (processed) sugar is believed to be grossly overconsumed. Hence, people should limit their dependence on soft drinks, chocolate, candies, pies, cakes, and jams. Finally, many people should cut down on their salt intake. This may require more than ignoring your saltshaker, as many prepackaged foods are loaded with salt.

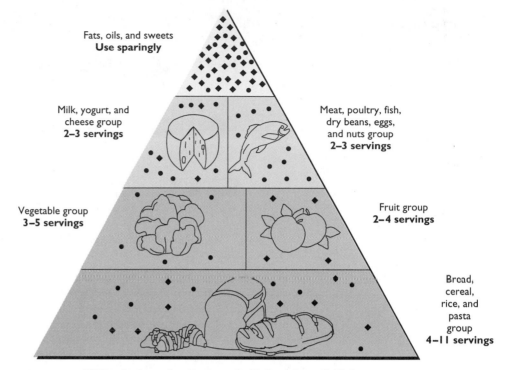

Figure 14.12
The food pyramid
The food pyramid, endorsed in 1991 by the U.S. Department of Agriculture, is intended to provide a simple and easy guide to nutritionally balanced eating. It identifies key categories of food and makes recommendations about how many daily servings one should have in each category. (From Williams & Knight, 1994)

Fats, oils, and sweets
Use sparingly

Milk, yogurt, and cheese group
2–3 servings

Meat, poultry, fish, dry beans, eggs, and nuts group
2–3 servings

Vegetable group
3–5 servings

Fruit group
2–4 servings

Bread, cereal, rice, and pasta group
4–11 servings

KEY • Fat (naturally occurring and added) ◆ Sugars (added)

3. *Increase consumption of complex carbohydrates, polyunsaturated fats, natural sugars, and foods with fiber.* If you're supposed to avoid all the foods mentioned in point 2, you may be wondering what's left to eat. Please note, however, that the experts suggest only that you reduce *excessive* consumption of those foods while increasing consumption in other areas. In particular, fruits, vegetables, and whole grains contain complex carbohydrates, natural sugars, and ample fiber. In order to substitute polyunsaturated fats for saturated ones, you can eat more fish, chicken, turkey, and veal. Additionally, you can trim meats of fat more thoroughly, use skim (nonfat) milk, and switch to vegetable oils high in polyunsaturated fats.

Lack of Exercise

In 1984 James Fixx, the noted author of several books touting the benefits of running, died from a heart attack while out jogging. All over the country, people who rarely exercise probably nodded their heads knowingly and made comments about exercise having little real value. Despite such rationalizations, there is considerable evidence of a link between exercise and health. Research indicates that regular exercise is associated with increased longevity (Paffenbarger, Hyde, & Wing, 1990). Moreover, one study showed that one need not be a dedicated athlete to benefit from exercise (Blair et al., 1989). In this study, even a moderate level of fitness—a level that could be achieved by taking a brisk half-hour walk each day—was associated with lower mortality rates (see Figure 14.13).

Benefits and Risks of Exercise

Learning Objective

Summarize evidence on the benefits and risks of exercise.

Why is exercise correlated with increased longevity? Because physical fitness promotes a diverse array of specific benefits. First, an appropriate exercise program can enhance cardiovascular fitness and thereby reduce one's susceptibility to deadly cardiovascular problems. Fitness is associated with reduced risk for both coronary disease and hypertension (Froelicher, 1990; Hagberg, 1990). Second, regular physical activity can help prevent obesity (Bray, 1990). Hence, fitness may indirectly reduce one's risk for a variety of obesity-related health problems, including diabetes, respiratory difficulties, arthritis, and back pain. Third, recent studies suggest that physi-

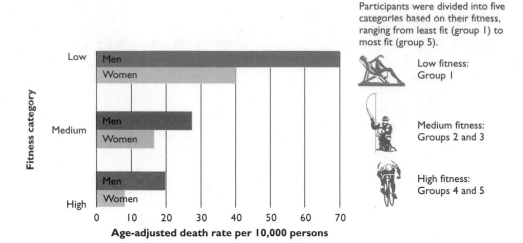

Figure 14.13
Physical fitness and mortality
Blair et al. (1989) studied death rates among men and women who exhibited low, medium, or high fitness. As you can see, even medium fitness was associated with lower mortality rates in both sexes. The investigators note that one could achieve this level of fitness by taking a brisk half-hour walk each day. (Data from Blair et al., 1989)

Participants were divided into five categories based on their fitness, ranging from least fit (group 1) to most fit (group 5).

Low fitness: Group 1

Medium fitness: Groups 2 and 3

High fitness: Groups 4 and 5

cal fitness is also associated with a decreased risk for colon cancer in men and for breast and reproductive cancer in women (Blair et al., 1992; Calabrese, 1990). The apparent link between exercise and reduced cancer risk has been a pleasant surprise for scientists, who are now scrambling to figure out the physiological mechanisms underlying this association. Fourth, exercise can serve as a buffer that reduces the potentially damaging physical effects of stress (Brown, 1991; Brown & Siegel, 1988). People high in fitness show less physiological reactivity to stress than those who are less fit. Fifth, successful participation in an exercise program can produce desirable personality changes that may promote physical wellness. Research suggests that fitness training can lead to improvements in one's mood, self-concept, and work efficiency, as well as reductions in tension, anxiety, and depression (D. R. Brown, 1990; Sacks, 1993).

It is important to note, however, that exercise programs have their own hazards. For example, jogging clearly elevates one's risk of muscular and skeletal injuries (it's especially hard on the knees) and can bring on heatstroke and possibly even a heart attack (Siscovick, 1990). The fact that exercise can both improve cardiovascular health and cause a heart attack may seem paradoxical. However, this contradiction was explained in a study by Siscovick and colleagues (1984). They found that men who participated in *regular* exercise activity lowered their cardiac risk. Vigorous exercise does temporarily (during the exercise) increase cardiac risk—but almost exclusively among those who do not exercise regularly. Although James Fixx's death appears inconsistent with the assertion that exercise decreases cardiac risk, Fixx took up jogging because he knew there was a history of heart problems in his family. In other words, he carried a hereditary vulnerability to heart attack that might have killed him 20 years earlier if he hadn't exercised regularly (his father had his first heart attack at age 35). In any case, an exercise program should be planned carefully to minimize the risks and maximize the benefits.

Devising an Exercise Program

List five guidelines for embarking on an effective exercise program.

Learning Objective

Putting together a good exercise program is difficult for many people. Exercise is time-consuming, and if you're out of shape, your initial attempts may be painful, aversive, and discouraging. To circumvent these problems, it is wise to heed the following advice (Greenberg, 1993):

1. *Look for an activity that you will find enjoyable.* You have a great many physical activities to choose from (see Figure 14.14). Shop around for one that you find intrinsically enjoyable. This will make it much easier for you to follow through and exercise regularly.

2. *Increase your participation gradually.* Don't try to do too much too quickly. An overzealous approach can lead to frustration, not to mention injury. An exercise regimen should be built up gradually. If you do experience injuries, avoid the common tendency to ignore them. Consult your physician to see whether continuing your exercise program is advisable.

How Beneficial Is Your Favorite Sport?

	Jogging	Bicycling	Swimming	Skating (ice or roller)	Handball/ Squash	Skiing— Nordic	Skiing— Alpine	Basketball	Tennis	Calisthenics	Walking	Golf	Softball	Bowling
Physical fitness														
Cardiorespiratory endurance (stamina)	21	19	21	18	19	19	16	19	16	10	13	8	6	5
Muscular endurance	20	18	20	17	18	19	18	17	16	13	14	8	8	5
Muscular strength	17	16	14	15	15	15	15	15	14	16	11	9	7	5
Flexibility	9	9	15	13	16	14	14	13	14	19	7	9	9	7
Balance	17	18	12	20	17	16	21	16	16	15	8	8	7	6
General well-being														
Weight control	21	20	15	17	19	17	15	19	16	12	13	6	7	5
Muscle definition	14	15	14	14	11	12	14	13	13	18	11	6	5	5
Digestion	13	12	13	11	13	12	9	10	12	11	11	7	8	7
Sleep	16	15	16	15	12	15	12	12	11	12	14	6	7	6
Total	148	142	140	140	140	139	134	134	128	126	102	67	64	51

Figure 14.14
A scorecard on the benefits of 14 sports and exercises
Here is a summary of how seven experts rated the value of 14 sporting activities (the highest rating possible on any one item was 21). The ratings were based on vigorous participation four times per week. (Adapted from Conrad, 1976)

3. *Exercise regularly without overdoing it.* Sporadic exercise will not improve your fitness. A widely cited rule of thumb is that you should plan on exercising vigorously for a minimum of 30 minutes three times a week, or you will gain little from your efforts. At the other extreme, don't try to become fit overnight by working out too vigorously and too frequently. Even highly trained athletes include days off in their schedules. These off days are necessary to allow muscles to recover from their hard work.

4. *Reinforce yourself for your participation.* To offset the inconvenience or pain that may be associated with exercise, it is a good idea to reinforce yourself for your participation. The behavior modification procedures discussed in the Application for Chapter 4 can be very helpful in shaping up a viable exercise program.

5. *Avoid the competition trap.* If you choose a competitive sport for your physical activity (for example, baseball, basketball, tennis), try to avoid becoming obsessed with victory. It is easy to get overly concerned with winning. When this happens, you put yourself under pressure. This is obviously self-defeating, in that it adds another source of stress to your life.

Behavior and AIDS

Learning Objective

Describe AIDS and summarize evidence on the transmission of the HIV virus.

At present, some of the most problematic links between behavior and health may be those related to AIDS. AIDS stands for *acquired immune deficiency syndrome,* **a disorder in which the immune system is gradually weakened and eventually disabled by the human immunodeficiency virus (HIV).** Being infected with the HIV virus is *not* equivalent to having AIDS. AIDS is the final stage of the HIV infection process, typically manifested about ten years after the original infection, during which a person is left virtually defenseless against a host of opportunistic infectious agents. AIDS inflicts its harm indirectly by opening the door to other diseases. The symptoms of AIDS vary widely depending on the specific constellation of diseases that one develops. Ultimately, AIDS is fatal, and there is no cure on the horizon. Unfortunately, the prevalence of this deadly disease continues to increase at an alarming rate, as Figure 14.15 shows.

Although the average length of survival for AIDS patients has increased slightly, the typical patient dies 18 to 24 months after the AIDS syndrome is manifested (Lib-

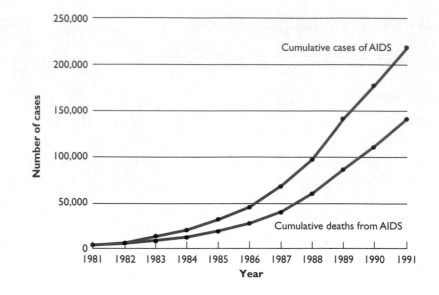

Figure 14.15
The grim statistics on AIDS
Cases of AIDS are increasing at a rapid rate, with no plateau yet in sight. After the discovery of AIDS in 1981, it took about eight years to accumulate the first 100,000 cases, but it took less than three years to accumulate the next 100,000 cases. The data shown here, from the Centers for Disease Control, refer only to diagnosed cases of AIDS. No one knows exactly how many people in the United States are infected with the HIV virus, but the number is surely much higher. Seage et al. (1990) estimated that there were 1.5 million HIV carriers in the United States in 1990.

man, 1992). Spurred by findings linking stress to immune function, researchers have begun to explore whether stress might speed up the progression of AIDS. Some studies have found a modest association between stress and the course of AIDS, but others have not (Kessler et al., 1991). One recent study suggests that depressed mood may be more important than stress per se, in accelerating the progress of the disease (Kemeny et al., 1994).

Transmission

The HIV virus is transmitted through person-to-person contact involving the exchange of bodily fluids, primarily semen and blood. The two principal modes of transmission in the United States have been sexual contact and the sharing of needles by intravenous (IV) drug users. In the United States, sexual transmission has occurred primarily among gay and bisexual men, but in the world as a whole, infection through heterosexual relations is more common, with male-to-female transmission particularly prevalent (Ickovics & Rodin, 1992). The HIV virus can be found in the tears and saliva of infected individuals, but the concentrations are low and there is no evidence that the infection can be spread through casual contact (Friedland et al., 1986). Even most forms of noncasual contact, including kissing, hugging, and sharing food with infected individuals, appear safe.

Misconceptions

Learning Objective

Identify common misconceptions about AIDS and discuss the prevention of AIDS.

After investigating attitudes about AIDS, Temoshok, Sweet, and Zich (1987) commented that "perhaps no medical phenomenon has been so feared or so misunderstood by the public." Misconceptions about AIDS are widespread. Ironically, the people who hold these misconceptions fall into two polarized camps. On the one hand, a great many people have unrealistic fears that AIDS can be readily transmitted through casual contact with infected individuals. These people worry unnecessarily about contracting AIDS from a handshake, a sneeze, or an eating utensil. They tend to be paranoid about interacting with homosexuals, thus fueling discrimination against gays in regard to housing, employment, and so forth. Some people also believe that it is dangerous to donate blood, when in fact blood donors are at no risk whatsoever.

On the other hand, many young heterosexuals who are sexually active with a variety of partners foolishly downplay their risk for HIV, naively assuming that they are safe as long as they avoid IV drug use and sexual relations with gay or bisexual men (Friedman & Goodman, 1992). They greatly underestimate the probability that their sexual partners may have previously used IV drugs or had unprotected sex with an infected individual. Also, because AIDS is usually accompanied by discernible symptoms, many young people believe that prospective sexual partners who carry the HIV virus will exhibit telltale signs of illness. However, as we have already

What Do You Know About HIV and AIDS?

Answer "true" or "false" to each of the following statements:

1 There is no known cure for AIDS.

2 AIDS is caused by inheriting faulty genes.

3 AIDS is caused by bacteria.

4 A person can "carry" and transmit the organism that causes AIDS without showing symptoms of the disease or appearing ill.

5 The organism that causes AIDS can be transmitted through semen.

6 Urinating after sexual intercourse makes infection with AIDS less likely.

7 Washing your genitals after sex makes infection with AIDS less likely.

8 Sharing drug needles increases the chance of transmitting the organism that causes AIDS.

9 The organism that causes AIDS can be transmitted through blood or blood products.

10 Donating blood makes it more likely you will be exposed to HIV.

11 You can catch AIDS like you catch a cold because whatever causes AIDS can be carried in the air.

12 You can get AIDS by being in the same classroom as someone who has AIDS.

13 You can get AIDS by shaking hands with someone who has AIDS.

14 A pregnant woman who has HIV can give AIDS to her baby.

15 Having a steady relationship with just one sex partner decreases the risk of getting AIDS.

16 Using condoms reduces the risk of getting AIDS.

17 A test to determine whether a person has been exposed to HIV is available.

18 A vaccine that protects people from getting AIDS is now available.

Correct Answers

1 True	**3** False	**5** True	**7** False	**9** True	**11** False	**13** False	**15** True	**17** True
2 False	**4** True	**6** False	**8** True	**10** False	**12** False	**14** True	**16** True	**18** False

Figure 14.16
A quiz on knowledge of AIDS
Misconceptions about AIDS abound, so it may be wise to take this brief quiz to test your knowledge of AIDS. (From Williams & Knight, 1994)

noted, having AIDS and being infected with HIV are not the same thing, and HIV carriers often remain healthy and symptom-free for years after they are infected. In sum, many myths about AIDS persist, in spite of extensive efforts to educate the public about this complex and controversial disease. Figure 14.16 contains a short quiz to test your knowledge of the facts about AIDS.

Prevention

The behavioral changes that minimize the risk of developing AIDS are fairly straightforward, although making the changes is often much easier said than done. In all groups, the more sexual partners a person has, the higher the risk that he or she will be exposed to the HIV virus. Thus, people can reduce their risk by having sexual contacts with fewer partners and by using condoms to control the exchange of semen. It is also important to curtail certain sexual practices (in particular, anal sex) that increase the probability of semen/blood mixing. Intravenous drug users could greatly reduce their risk by abandoning their drug use, but this is unlikely, since most are physically dependent on the drugs. Alternatively, they need to improve the sterilization of their needles and avoid sharing syringes with other users.

Efforts to alter high-risk behaviors that contribute to the spread of AIDS have met with considerable success in the gay male community, although there is still room for much more improvement (Fisher & Fisher, 1992). Unfortunately, there has been relatively little progress among IV drug users (Friedman, de Jong, & Des Jarlais, 1988). Experts are also disappointed because the evidence suggests that heterosexuals have not modified their sexual practices much in response to the threat of AIDS (Catania et al., 1992).

Reactions to Illness

So far we have emphasized the psychosocial aspects of maintaining health and minimizing the risk of illness. Health is also affected by how people *respond* to physical symptoms and illnesses. Some people engage in denial and ignore early warning signs of developing diseases. Others engage in active coping efforts to conquer their diseases. In this section, we discuss the decision to seek medical treatment, the sick role, and compliance with medical advice.

The Decision to Seek Treatment

Robin DiMatteo

Have you ever experienced nausea, diarrhea, stiffness, headaches, cramps, chest pains, or sinus problems? Of course you have; we all experience some of these problems periodically. However, whether we view these sensations as *symptoms* is a matter of individual interpretation. When two persons experience the same unpleasant sensations, one may shrug them off as a nuisance while the other may rush to a physician. Studies suggest that people who are relatively high in anxiety and low in self-esteem tend to report more symptoms of illness than others (Pennebaker, 1982). Those who are extremely attentive to bodily sensations and health concerns also report more symptoms than the average person (Barsky, 1988).

Variations in the perception of symptoms help to explain the differences among people in their readiness to seek treatment (Cameron, Leventhal, & Leventhal, 1993). Generally, people are more likely so seek medical care when symptoms are unfamiliar, frightening, or disruptive of their work or social activities (Bernard & Krupat, 1994). Another key consideration is how friends and family react to the symptoms. Medical consultation is much more likely when friends and family view symptoms as serious and encourage the person to seek medical care (Sanders, 1982).

The biggest problem in regard to seeking treatment is the tendency of many people to put off going to the doctor or clinic. It is common knowledge that quick intervention can facilitate more effective treatment of many health problems. Yet, procrastination is the norm even when people are faced with a medical emergency, such as a heart attack. Why do people dawdle in the midst of a crisis? Robin DiMatteo (1991) mentions a number of reasons, noting that people delay because they often (1) misinterpret and downplay the significance of their symptoms, (2) fret about looking silly if the problem turns out to be nothing, (3) worry about "bothering" their physician, (4) are reluctant to disrupt their plans (to go out to dinner, see a movie, and so forth), and (5) waste time on trivial matters (such as taking a shower or packing clothes) before going to a hospital emergency room.

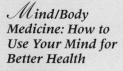
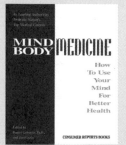
Edited by Daniel Goleman, a psychologist who writes for the *New York Times*, and Joel Gurin, editorial director of Consumers Union of U.S., Inc., publisher of *Consumer Reports* magazine, this book consists of 25 highly informative chapters on topics related to health psychology. Each chapter is written by a renowned expert on that topic. Recruiting experts to write for the general public is always a risky business, as their contributions are often too dry and technical to have any practical value for the typical reader. However, the editors of this volume have extensive experience in writing for the layperson, and they obviously provided effective guidance for their contributors, as the chapters are engaging, readable, and easy to understand, while still being scientifically accurate and up-to-date. Some of the topics covered include hostility and the heart, emotions and cancer, mind and immunity, stress and asthma, emotion and infertility, mindfulness meditation, hypnosis, the use of imagery to fight disease, biofeedback, social support, and stress management.

In short, one basic tenet of mind/body medicine is that it is best to treat the whole person. Treating emotional distress should be an essential complement to standard medical care. Another tenet is that people can be active participants in their own health care and may be able to prevent disease or shorten its course by taking steps to manage their own psychological states.

Of course, these principles must be tempered with a realistic view of the many other factors at work in health and illness. No one is promising that people can cure themselves of disease just by thinking happy thoughts. That simplistic idea ignores the complexities of biology and the wired-in destiny of our genes. Worse, it can leave people feeling guilty about being sick at all. This is not the message of mind/body medicine.

But the evidence is growing stronger that states of mind can affect physical health. And while that effect may not be as dramatic as, say, the power of penicillin to fight strep throat, it can be meaningful nonetheless. [p. 5]

The Sick Role

Although many people tend to delay medical consultations, others are positively eager to seek medical care. These people have learned that there are potential benefits to adopting the "sick role" (Lubkin, 1990; Parsons, 1979). For instance, fewer demands are placed on sick people, who can selectively decide which demands to ignore. Illness can provide a convenient, face-saving excuse for one's failures. Sick people may also find themselves to be the center of attention from friends and relatives. This increase in attention can be very rewarding, especially to those who received little attention previously. Moreover, much of this attention is favorable, in that the sick person is showered with affection, concern, and sympathy.

Thus, some people grow to *like* the sick role, although they may not be aware of it. Such people readily seek professional care, but they tend to behave in subtle ways that prolong their illness (Kinsman, Dirks, & Jones, 1982). For example, they may only pretend to go along with medical advice, a common problem that we discuss next.

Adherence to Medical Advice

Learning Objective

Discuss the prevalence of nonadherence to professional advice and its causes.

Many patients fail to adhere to the instructions they receive from physicians and other health care professionals. Such nonadherence is not limited to people who have come to like the sick role, and it's a major problem in our medical care system. The evidence suggests that noncompliance with medical advice may occur 30–60% of the time (Kaplan & Simon, 1990).

This point is not intended to suggest that you should passively accept all professional advice from medical personnel. However, when you have doubts about a prescribed treatment, you should speak up and ask questions. Passive resistance can backfire. For instance, if a physician sees no improvement in a patient who falsely insists that he has been taking his medicine, the physician may abandon an accurate diagnosis in favor of an inaccurate one. The inaccurate diagnosis could lead to inappropriate treatments that might be harmful to the patient.

Why don't people comply with the advice that they've sought out from highly regarded health care professionals? Physicians tend to attribute noncompliance to patients' personality traits, but research indicates that other factors are more important. Three considerations are especially prominent (DiMatteo & Friedman, 1982; Evans & Haynes, 1990):

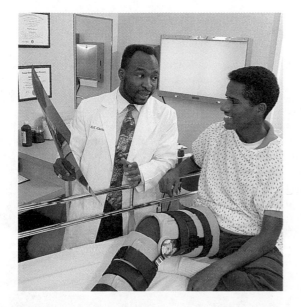

When physicians carefully explain their instructions, patients are more likely to comply with medical advice.

1. Frequently, noncompliance is due to a failure by the patient to understand the instructions as given. Highly trained professionals often forget that what seems obvious and simple to them may be obscure and complicated to many of their patients.

2. Another key factor is how aversive or difficult the instructions are. If the prescribed regimen is unpleasant, compliance will tend to decrease. And the more that following instructions interferes with routine behavior, the less probable it is that the patient will cooperate successfully.

3. If a patient has a negative attitude toward a physician, the probability of noncompliance will increase. When patients are unhappy with their interactions with the doctor, they're more likely to ignore the medical advice provided.

In response to the noncompliance problem, some health psychologists are exploring ways to increase patients' adherence to medical advice. They've found that the communication process between the practitioner and the patient is of critical importance. Courtesy, encouragement, reassurance, taking time to answer questions, and decreased reliance on medical jargon can improve compliance (DiNicola & DiMatteo, 1984; Hall, Roter, & Katz, 1988). Thus, the new emphasis is on enhancing health care professionals' communication skills.

Understanding the Effects of Drugs

Answer the following "true" or "false."

1. Smoking marijuana can make men impotent and sterile.

2. Overdoses caused by cocaine are relatively rare.

3. It is well documented that LSD causes chromosome damage.

4. Hallucinogens are addictive.

5. Snorting cocaine is safer than smoking crack.

As you will learn in this Application, all of the above statements are false. If you answered all of the above questions accurately, you may already be well informed about drugs. If not, you *should* be. Intelligent decisions about drugs require an understanding of their effects and risks.

This Application focuses on the use of drugs for their pleasurable effects, commonly referred to as *drug abuse* or *recreational drug use.* Drug abuse reaches into every corner of our society and is a problematic health-impairing habit. Although some small declines occurred in the abuse of certain drugs during the 1980s (Johnson & Muffler, 1992), it appears that recreational drug use is here to stay for the foreseeable future.

Like other controversial social problems, recreational drug use often inspires more rhetoric than reason. For instance, a former president of the American Medical Association made headlines when he declared that marijuana "makes a man of 35 sexually like a man of 70." In reality, the research findings do not support this assertion. This influential physician later retracted his statement, admitting that he had made it simply to campaign against marijuana use (Leavitt, 1982). Unfortunately, such scare tactics can backfire by undermining the credibility of drug education efforts.

Recreational drug use involves personal, moral, political, and legal issues that are not matters for science to resolve. However, the more knowledgeable you are about drugs, the more informed your decisions and opinions about them will be. Accordingly, this Application is intended to provide you with nonjudgmental, realistic coverage of issues related to recreational drug use. We'll begin by reviewing key drug-related concepts. Then we'll examine the effects and risks of five types of widely abused drugs: narcotics, sedatives, stimulants, hallucinogens, and cannabis.

Drug-Related Concepts

Learning Objective

Explain the concepts of tolerance, physical dependence, psychological dependence, and overdose.

The drugs that people use recreationally are *psychoactive*. **Psychoactive drugs are chemical substances that modify a person's mental, emotional, or behavioral functioning.** Not all psychoactive drugs produce effects that lead to drug abuse. Generally, people prefer drugs that elevate their mood or produce pleasant alterations in consciousness. The principal types of recreational drugs are described in Figure 14.17. This table lists representative drugs in each of five categories, how the drugs are taken, their principal medical uses, their desired effects, and their common side effects (based on Blum, 1984; Julien, 1995; Lowinson, Ruiz, & Millman, 1992).

Most drugs produce tolerance effects. **Tolerance is the progressive decrease in a person's responsiveness to a drug with continued use.** Tolerance effects usually lead people to consume larger and larger doses of a drug to attain the effects

Comparison of Major Abused Drugs

Drugs	Methods of administration	Principal medical uses	Desired effects	Short-term side effects
Narcotics (opiates) Morphine Heroin	Injected, smoked, oral	Pain relief	Euphoria, relaxation, anxiety reduction, pain relief	Lethargy, drowsiness, nausea, impaired coordination, impaired mental functioning, constipation
Sedatives Barbiturates (e.g., Seconal) Nonbarbiturates (e.g., Quaalude)	Oral, injected	Sleeping pill, anticonvulsant	Euphoria, relaxation, anxiety reduction, reduced inhibitions	Lethargy, drowsiness, severely impaired coordination, impaired mental functioning, emotional swings, dejection
Stimulants Amphetamines Cocaine	Oral, sniffed, injected, freebased, smoked	Treatment of hyperactivity and narcolepsy; local anesthetic (cocaine only)	Elation, excitement, increased alertness, increased energy, reduced fatigue	Increased blood pressure and heart rate, increased talkativeness, restlessness, irritability, insomnia, reduced appetite, increased sweating and urination, anxiety, paranoia, increased aggressiveness, panic
Hallucinogens LSD Mescaline Psilocybin	Oral		Increased sensory awareness, euphoria, altered perceptions, hallucinations, insightful experiences	Dilated pupils, nausea, emotional swings, paranoia, jumbled thought processes, impaired judgment, anxiety, panic reaction
Cannabis Marijuana Hashish THC	Smoked, oral	Treatment of glaucoma; other uses under study	Mild euphoria, relaxation, altered perceptions, enhanced awareness	Bloodshot eyes, dry mouth, reduced short-term memory, sluggish motor coordination, sluggish mental functioning, anxiety

Note: A major omission from this table is PCP (phencyclidine hydrochloride), which does not fit neatly into any of the listed categories. PCP has stimulant, hallucinogenic, and anesthetic effects. Its short-term side effects can be very dangerous. Common side effects include agitation, paranoia, confusion, and severe mental disorientation that has been linked to accidents and suicides.

Figure 14.17
Major categories of abused drugs
This chart summarizes the methods of ingestion, chief medical uses, and principal effects of five major types of recreational drugs. (Based on Blum, 1984; Julien, 1991; Lowinson, Ruiz, & Millman, 1992)

they desire. Tolerance builds more rapidly to some drugs than to others. The first column in Figure 14.18 indicates whether various groups of drugs tend to produce rapid or gradual tolerance.

In evaluating the potential problems associated with the use of various drugs, a key consideration is the likelihood of either physical or psychological dependence. Although evidence indicates that there is a physiological basis for both forms of drug dependence (Koob & Bloom, 1988; Ray & Ksir, 1990), there are important differences between the two syndromes. *Physical dependence* **exists when a person must continue to take a drug to avoid withdrawal illness (which occurs when drug use is terminated).** The symptoms of withdrawal illness vary depending on the drug. Withdrawal from heroin and barbiturates can produce fever, chills, tremors, convulsions, seizures, vomiting, cramps, diarrhea, and severe aches and pains. The agony of withdrawal from these drugs virtually compels addicts to continue using them. Withdrawal from stimulant use leads to a different and somewhat milder syndrome dominated by fatigue, apathy, irritability, depression, and disorientation.

Psychological dependence **exists when a person must continue to take a drug to satisfy intense mental and emotional craving for the drug.** Psychological dependence is more subtle than physical dependence, as it is not marked by a clear withdrawal reaction. However, psychological dependence can create a powerful, overwhelming need for a drug. Both types of dependence are established gradually with repeated use of a drug. Drugs vary greatly in their potential for creating

Figure 14.18
Specific risks for various categories of drugs
This chart shows estimates of the risk potential for tolerance, dependence, and overdose for the five major categories of drugs discussed in this Application.

Risks Associated with Abused Drugs

Drugs	Tolerance	Risk of physical dependence	Risk of psychological dependence	Fatal overdose potential
Narcotics (opiates)	Rapid	High	High	High
Sedatives	Rapid	High	High	High
Stimulants	Rapid	Moderate	High	Moderate to high
Hallucinogens	Gradual	None	Very low	Very low
Cannabis	Gradual	None	Low to moderate	Very low

either physical or psychological dependence. The second and third columns in Figure 14.18 provide estimates of the risk of each kind of dependence for the drugs covered in our discussion.

An *overdose* is an excessive dose of a drug that can seriously threaten one's life. Any drug can be fatal if a person takes enough of it, but some drugs have more potential for overdose than others. In Figure 14.18, column 4 estimates the risk of accidentally consuming a lethal overdose of various drugs. Drugs that are central nervous system (CNS) depressants—narcotics and sedatives—carry the greatest risk of overdose. It's important to understand that the effects of these drugs are additive. Many overdoses involve lethal *combinations* of CNS depressants (including alcohol). What happens when people overdose on these drugs? Their respiratory system usually grinds to a halt, producing coma, brain damage, and death within a brief period. In contrast, fatal overdoses with CNS stimulants (cocaine and amphetamines) usually involve a heart attack, stroke, or cortical seizure.

Now that our basic vocabulary is spelled out, we can begin to examine the effects and risks of major recreational drugs. Of course, we'll be describing the *typical* effects of each drug. Please bear in mind that the effects of any drug depend on the user's age, body weight, physiology, personality, mood, expectations, and previous experience with the drug. The dose and potency of the drug, the method of administration, and the setting in which the drug is taken also influence its effects. Our coverage is based largely on comprehensive books by Blum (1984), Julien (1995), and Lowinson et al. (1992), but we'll cite additional sources when discussing specific studies or controversial points.

Narcotics

Narcotics (or opiates) are drugs derived from opium that are capable of relieving pain. In legal regulations, the term *narcotic* is used in a haphazard way to refer to a variety of drugs besides opiates. Our discussion will focus on heroin and morphine, but many of the points would also apply to less potent opiates such as codeine, demerol, and methadone.

Effects

The most significant narcotics problem in modern, Western society is the use of heroin. Most users inject heroin intravenously with a hypodermic needle. The main effect of the drug is an overwhelming sense of euphoria. This euphoric effect has a "Who cares?" quality to it that makes the heroin high an attractive escape from reality. Common side effects include nausea, lethargy, drowsiness, constipation, and slowed respiration.

Risks

Narcotics carry a high risk for both *psychological dependence* and *physical dependence*. It is estimated that there are about a half-million heroin addicts in the United States (Jaffe, 1986). Although heroin withdrawal usually isn't life threatening, it can be terribly unpleasant, so that "junkies" have a desperate need to continue their drug use. Once dependence is entrenched, users tend to develop a *drug-centered lifestyle* that revolves around the need to procure more heroin. This happens because the drug is very expensive (up to $200 a day) and available only through highly undependable black market channels. Obviously it is difficult to lead a very productive life if one's existence is dominated by a desperate need to "score" heroin. The inordinate cost of heroin forces many junkies to resort to criminal activities to support their habit.

Overdose is also a very real danger with heroin (Jaffe, 1992). Part of the problem is that it is difficult to judge the purity of heroin obtained through black market sources. As noted earlier, opiates are additive with other CNS depressants, and most narcotic overdoses occur in combination with the use of sedatives or alcohol. Junkies also risk the *contraction of infectious disease* because they often share hypodermic needles and tend to be sloppy about sterilizing them. The most common of these diseases used to be hepatitis, but in recent years, AIDS has been transmitted at an alarming rate through the population of intravenous drug users (Des Jarlais et al., 1992).

Sedatives

Learning Objective

Summarize the main effects and risks of sedatives.

Sedatives are sleep-inducing drugs that tend to decrease central nervous system activation and behavioral activity. In street jargon they are often called "downers." Over the years, the most widely abused sedatives have been the barbiturates, which are compounds derived from barbituric acid. Although distinctions are made between barbiturate and nonbarbiturate sedatives, the functional differences are minimal.

Effects

People abusing sedatives generally consume larger doses than are prescribed for medical purposes. These overly large doses have a euphoric effect similar to that produced by drinking large amounts of alcohol (Wesson, Smith, & Seymour, 1992). Feelings of tension, anxiety, and depression are temporarily replaced by a relaxed, pleasant state of intoxication in which inhibitions may be loosened. Sedatives carry a truckload of dangerous side effects. Motor coordination suffers badly, producing slurred speech and a staggering walk, among other things. Intellectual functioning also becomes sluggish and judgment is impaired. The person's emotional tone may become unstable, with feelings of dejection often intruding on the intended euphoric mood.

Risks

Sedatives have the potential to produce both *psychological dependence* and *physical dependence*. They are also among the leading cause of *overdoses* in the United States (O'Brien & Woody, 1986) because of their additive interactions with other CNS depressants (especially alcohol) and because of the degree to which they impair one's judgment. In their drug-induced haze, sedative abusers may take doses that they would ordinarily recognize as dangerous. Also, with prolonged use, the dose of barbiturates needed to feel high increases more rapidly than the dose the body can handle. Thus, the margin of safety between an intoxicating dose and a lethal dose gradually narrows. Sedative users also elevate their risk for *accidental injuries* because of the drastic effects these drugs have on motor coordination. Many users trip down stairs, fall off bar stools, get into automobile accidents, and so forth.

Stimulants

Learning Objective

Summarize the main effects and risks of stimulant drugs.

Stimulants are drugs that tend to increase central nervous system activation and behavioral activity. They range from mild, widely available stimulants, such as caffeine and nicotine, to stronger, carefully regulated stimulants, such as cocaine and amphetamines ("speed"). We'll focus on the latter two drugs.

Cocaine is an organic substance extracted from the coca shrub, which grows most prominently in South America. It is usually consumed as a crystalline powder that is snorted through the nasal cavities. However, an increasing number of users are "freebasing" cocaine. Freebasing is a chemical treatment used to extract nearly pure cocaine concentrate from ordinary street cocaine. "Crack" is the most widely distributed by-product of this process, consisting of little chips of pure cocaine that are usually smoked. Smoking crack is far more dangerous than snorting cocaine powder because of its greater purity. Also, smoking leads to a more rapid absorption of the drug into the bloodstream (Cregler & Mark, 1986).

Synthesized in a pharmaceutical laboratory, amphetamines are usually consumed orally. However, speed is also sold as a crystalline powder (called "crank") that may be snorted or injected intravenously. Recently, a smokable form of methamphetamine (called "ice") has been developed.

Effects

Amphetamines and cocaine have almost indistinguishable effects, except that cocaine produces a very brief high (20–30 minutes unless more is taken), while a speed high can last many hours (Gold, Miller, & Jonas, 1992). Stimulants produce a euphoria very different from that created by narcotics or sedatives. They produce a bouyant, elated, enthusiastic, energetic, "I can conquer the world!" feeling accompanied by increased alertness. Common side effects include: increased blood pressure, muscle tension, sweating, and restlessness. Some users experience unpleasant feelings of irritability, anxiety, and paranoia.

Risks

Stimulants can cause *physical dependence,* but the physical distress caused by stimulant withdrawal is mild compared to that caused by narcotic or sedative withdrawal (Kleber & Gawin, 1986). *Psychological dependence* on stimulants is a more common problem. Cocaine can create an exceptionally powerful psychological dependence that compels the user to pursue the drug with a fervor normally seen only when physical dependence exists. Both cocaine and amphetamines can suppress appetite and disrupt sleep. Thus, heavy use of stimulants may lead to poor eating, poor sleeping, and ultimately, a *deterioration in physical health.* Stimulant use increases one's risk for stroke, heart attack, and other forms of cardiovascular disease, and crack smoking is associated with a host of respiratory problems (Gold, 1992). Heavy stimulant use occasionally leads to the onset of a severe psychological disorder called *amphetamine* or *cocaine psychosis* (depending on the drug involved), which is dominated by intense paranoia (King & Ellinwood, 1992). All of the risks associated with stimulant use increase *greatly* when more potent forms of the drugs (crack and ice) are used.

Overdoses on stimulants used to be relatively infrequent (Kalant & Kalant, 1979). However, in recent years cocaine overdoses have increased sharply as more people experiment with freebasing, smoking crack, and other more dangerous modes of ingestion (Gold, 1992). The dangers of cocaine were underscored in a study of rats that were given unlimited access to heroin or cocaine (Bozarth & Wise, 1985). The rats earned drug injections (delivered through implanted tubes) by pressing a lever in an experimental chamber. The health of the rats on heroin deteriorated rapidly, and 36% of them died by the end of the 30-day study. However, the health of the rats on cocaine deteriorated even more rapidly, and by the end of the study 90% of them had died! Many of the rats on cocaine experienced severe seizures, but they would resume their lever pressing as soon as their convulsions subsided. We must be cautious about generalizing from rats to humans, but this research suggests that the addictive potential and debilitating physical effects of cocaine have been underestimated.

Hallucinogens

Learning Objective

Summarize the main effects and risks of hallucinogens.

Hallucinogens **are a diverse group of drugs that have powerful effects on mental and emotional functioning, marked most prominently by distortions in sensory and perceptual experience.** The principal hallucinogens are LSD, mescaline, and psilocybin, which have similar effects, although they vary in potency. Mescaline comes from the peyote plant, psilocybin comes from a particular type of mushroom, and LSD is a synthetic drug.

Effects

Hallucinogens intensify and distort perception in ways that are difficult to describe, and they temporarily impair intellectual functioning as thought processes become meteoric and jumbled. They can produce awesome feelings of euphoria that sometimes include an almost mystical sense of "oneness" with the human race. This is why they have been used in religious ceremonies in various cultures. Unfortunately, at the other end of the emotional spectrum, they can also produce nightmarish feelings of anxiety, fear, and paranoia, commonly called a "bad trip."

Risks

Hallucinogens have no potential for physical dependence, and no deaths attributable to overdose are known to have occurred. Psychological dependence has been reported but appears to be very rare (Grinspoon & Bakalar, 1986). Research reports that LSD increases chromosome breakage were based on poor methodology (Dishotsky et al., 1971). However, as with most drugs, hallucinogens may be harmful to a fetus if taken by a pregnant woman.

Although the dangers of hallucinogens have probably been exaggerated in the popular press, there are some significant risks. Because emotion is highly volatile with these drugs, users can never be sure they won't experience *acute panic* from a terrifying bad trip. Generally, this disorientation subsides within a few hours, leaving no permanent emotional scars. However, in such a severe state of disorientation, *accidents and suicide* are possible. *Flashbacks* involve vividly reliving hallucinogenic experiences months after the original experience. Repetitious, frightening flashbacks can become troublesome. In a small minority of users, hallucinogens may contribute to the development of a variety of *psychological disorders* (psychoses, depressive reactions, paranoid states) that appear partially attributable to the drug (Ungerleider & Pechnick, 1992).

Learning Objective

Summarize the main effects and risks of marijuana.

***Cannabis* is the hemp plant from which marijuana, hashish, and THC are derived.** Marijuana is a mixture of dried leaves, flowers, stems, and seeds taken from the plant, while hashish comes from the plant's resin. THC is the active chemical ingredient in cannabis and can be synthesized for research purposes (for example, to give to animals).

Effects

When smoked, cannabis has an almost immediate impact that may last several hours. The effects of the drug vary greatly, depending on the user's expectations and experience with the drug, the potency of the drug, and the amount smoked. Marijuana has subtle effects on emotion, perception, and cognition. Emotionally, the drug tends to create a mild, relaxed state of euphoria. Perceptually, it enhances the impact of incoming stimulation, thus making music sound better, food taste better, and so on. Cannabis tends to produce a slight impairment in cognitive functioning (especially short-term memory) and perceptual-motor coordination while the user is high. However, there are huge variations among users.

Risks

Overdose and physical dependence are not problems, but like any other drug that produces pleasant feelings, marijuana has the potential to produce *psychological dependence* (Grinspoon & Bakalar, 1992). There is no solid evidence that cannabis causes psychological disorders. However, marijuana can cause *transient problems with anxiety and depression* in some people. Some studies also suggest that cannabis may have a more *negative effect on driving* than widely believed (Moskowitz, 1985). Like tobacco, marijuana smoke carries carcinogens and impurities into the lungs, thus increasing the user's chances for *respiratory and pulmonary diseases, as well as lung cancer* (Cohen, 1986; Gold, 1989). However, the evidence on other widely publicized risks remains controversial. Here is a brief overview of the evidence on some of these controversies:

• *Does marijuana cause brain damage?* The handful of studies linking marijuana to brain damage have been shown to be methodologically unsound (Kuehnle et al., 1977). Marijuana affects brain wave activity (Heath, 1976), but there is no clear evidence that these changes in brain activity are permanent or pathological (Jenike, 1987).

• *Does marijuana reduce one's immune response?* Cannabis may suppress the body's natural immune response slightly (Nahas, 1976). However, infectious diseases are no more common among marijuana smokers than nonsmokers. Hence, this effect apparently is too small to have any practical importance (Relman, 1982).

• *Does marijuana impair reproductive functioning?* Cannabis does appear to have endocrine and reproductive effects that merit further investigation. Marijuana appears to produce a small, reversible decline in sperm count among male smokers and may have temporary effects on hormone levels (Bloodworth, 1987). The popular media have frequently implied that marijuana therefore makes men sterile and impotent. In reality, there is no evidence that marijuana produces any lasting effects on male smokers' fertility or sexual functioning (Grinspoon & Bakalar, 1992). Of greater concern are reports that marijuana—like tobacco—may be hazardous to a developing embryo or fetus. Some studies suggest that marijuana use may be associated with an increased risk of premature birth and low birth weight (Day & Richardson, 1991; Fried, 1986).

Key Ideas

Stress, Personality, and Illness

• The biopsychosocial model holds that physical health is influenced by a complex network of biological, psychological, and sociocultural factors. Stress is one of the psychological factors that can affect physical health. In particular, Type A behavior has been implicated as a contributing cause of coronary heart disease. This competitive, impatient, hostile pattern of behavior may double one's coronary risk. However, the evidence is contradictory, and more research is needed.

• The connection between psychological factors and the onset of cancer is not well documented, but stress and personality may influence the course of the disease. Researchers have found associations between stress and the onset of a variety of other diseases. Stress may play a role in a host of diseases because it can temporarily suppress immune functioning. While there's little doubt that stress can contribute to the development of physical illness, the link between stress and illness is modest.

Habits, Lifestyles, and Health

• People commonly engage in health-impairing habits and lifestyles. These habits creep up slowly, and their risks are easy to ignore because the dangers often lie in the distant future. Smokers have much higher mortality rates than nonsmokers because they are more vulnerable to a variety of diseases. Giving up smoking is difficult in part because nicotine is addictive.

• Drinking rivals smoking as a source of health problems. In the short term, drinking can impair driving, cause various types of accidents, and increase the likelihood of aggressive interactions or reckless sexual behavior. In the long term, chronic, excessive alcohol consumption increases one's risk for a host of health problems, including cirrhosis of the liver, heart disease, hypertension, stroke, and cancer, among other things.

• Obesity elevates one's risk for many health problems. Body weight is influenced by genetic endowment, set point, and eating habits. Weight loss is best accomplished by decreasing caloric consumption while gradually increasing exercise. Poor nutritional habits have been linked to a host of health problems, although much of the evidence is tentative. One's health can best be served by following balanced food consumption patterns while limiting the intake of certain substances that can be counterproductive.

• Lack of exercise is associated with elevated mortality rates. Regular exercise can reduce one's risk for cardiovascular disease, cancer, and obesity-related diseases, buffer the effects of stress, and lead to desirable personality changes.

• Aspects of behavior are the key factors influencing one's risk of contracting AIDS. Although misconceptions abound, HIV is transmitted almost exclusively by sexual contact and the sharing of needles by IV drug abusers. One's risk for HIV infection can be reduced by avoiding IV drug use, having fewer sexual partners, using condoms, and curtailing certain sexual practices.

Reactions to Illness

• Everyone experiences physical symptoms, but people vary in how they respond to such symptoms. Variations in seeking treatment are influenced by the severity of the symptoms and the reactions of friends and family. The biggest problem is the tendency of many people to delay needed medical treatment. At the other extreme, a minority of people learn to like the sick role because it earns them attention and allows them to avoid stress.

• Noncompliance with medical advice is a major problem. The likelihood of noncompliance is greater when instructions are difficult to understand, when recommendations are difficult to follow, and when patients are unhappy with their doctor.

Application: Understanding the Effects of Drugs

• Recreational drugs vary in their potential for tolerance effects, psychological dependence, physical dependence, and overdose. The risks associated with narcotics use include both types of dependence, overdose, and the acquisition of infectious diseases. Sedatives can also produce both types of dependence, are subject to overdoses, and elevate one's risk for accidental injuries. Stimulant use can lead to psychological dependence, overdose, psychosis, and a deterioration in physical health.

• Hallucinogens can contribute to accidents, suicides, and psychological disorders, and can cause flashbacks. The risks of marijuana use include psychological dependence, transient problems with anxiety and depression, and respiratory and pulmonary diseases. Marijuana use can also impair driving.

Key Terms

Acquired immune deficiency syndrome (AIDS)
Alcoholism
Atherosclerosis
Biopsychosocial model
Cancer
Cannabis
Coronary heart disease
Hallucinogens
Health psychology
Immune response
Narcotics
Nutrition
Obesity
Overdose
Physical dependence
Psychoactive drugs
Psychological dependence
Sedatives
Set point
Stimulants
Tolerance
Type A personality
Type B personality

Key People

Robin DiMatteo
Meyer Friedman and Ray Rosenman
Janice Kiecolt-Glaser

15 *Psychological Disorders*

"The government of the United States was overthrown more than a year ago! I'm the president of the United States of America and Bob Dylan is vice president!" So said Ed, the author of a prominent book on journalism, who was speaking to a college journalism class as a guest lecturer. Ed also informed the class that he had killed both John and Robert Kennedy, as well as Charles de Gaulle, the former president of France. He went on to tell the class that all rock music songs were written about him, that he was the greatest karate expert in the universe, and that he had been fighting "space wars" for 2000 years. The students in the class were mystified by Ed's bizarre, disjointed "lecture," but they assumed that he was putting on a show that would eventually lead to a sensible conclusion. However, their perplexed but expectant calm was shattered when Ed pulled a hatchet from the props he had brought with him and hurled the hatchet at the class! Fortunately, he didn't hit anyone, as the hatchet sailed over the students' heads. At that point, the professor for the class realized that Ed's irrational behavior was not a pretense. The professor evacuated the class quickly while Ed continued to rant and rave about his presidential administration, space wars, vampires, his romances with female rock stars, and his personal harem of 38 "chicks." [Adapted from Pearce, 1974]

*C*learly, Ed's behavior was abnormal. Even *he* recognized that when he agreed later to be admitted to a mental hospital, signing himself in as the "President of the United States of America." What causes such abnormal behavior? Does Ed have a mental illness, or does he just behave strangely? What is the basis for judging behavior as normal versus abnormal? Are people who have psychological disorders dangerous? How common are such disorders? These are just a few of the questions that we will address in this chapter as we discuss psychological disorders and their complex causes.

Abnormal Behavior: Myths, Realities, and Controversies

Misconceptions about abnormal behavior are common. Hence, we need to clear up some preliminary issues before we describe the various types of disorders. In this section, we will discuss (1) the medical model of abnormal behavior, (2) the criteria of abnormal behavior, (3) the classification of psychological disorders, and (4) the prevalence of such disorders.

The Medical Model Applied to Abnormal Behavior

Learning Objective

Describe the medical model of abnormal behavior.

In Ed's case, there's no question that his behavior was abnormal. But does it make sense to view his unusual and irrational behavior as an illness? This is a controversial question. The *medical model* **proposes that it is useful to think of abnormal behavior as a disease.** This point of view is the basis for many of the terms used to refer to abnormal behavior, including mental *illness*, psychological *disorder*, and psycho*pathology* (*pathology* refers to manifestations of disease). The medical model gradually became the dominant way of thinking about abnormal behavior during the 18th and 19th centuries, and its influence remains strong today.

The medical model clearly represented progress over earlier models of abnormal behavior. Prior to the 18th century, most conceptions of abnormal behavior were based on superstition. People who behaved strangely were thought to be possessed by demons, to be witches in league with the devil, or to be victims of God's punishment. Their disorders were "treated" with chants, rituals, exorcisms, and such. If the people's behavior was seen as threatening, they were candidates for chains, dungeons, torture, and death (see Figure 15.1).

The rise of the medical model brought improvements in the treatment of those who exhibited abnormal behavior. As victims of an illness, they were viewed with more sympathy and less hatred and fear. Although living conditions in early asylums were often deplorable, gradual progress was made toward more humane care of the mentally ill. It took time, but ineffectual approaches to treatment eventually gave way to scientific investigation of the causes and cures of psychological disorders.

Figure 15.1
Historical conceptions of mental illness
Throughout most of history, psychological disorders were thought to be caused by demonic possession, and the mentally ill were candidates for chains and torture.

Problems with the Medical Model

Thomas Szasz

In recent decades, critics have suggested that the medical model may have outlived its usefulness. A particularly vocal critic has been Thomas Szasz (1974, 1993). Szasz asserts that "strictly speaking, disease or illness can affect only the body; hence there can be no mental illness. . . . Minds can be 'sick' only in the sense that jokes are 'sick' or economies are 'sick'" (1974, p. 267). He further argues that abnormal behavior usually involves a deviation from social norms rather than an illness. He contends that such deviations are "problems in living" rather than medical problems. According to Szasz, the medical model's disease analogy converts moral and social questions about what is acceptable behavior into medical questions. Under the guise of "healing the sick," this conversion allegedly allows modern society to lock up deviant people and to enforce its norms of conformity.

Other critics of the medical model are troubled because medical diagnoses of abnormal behavior pin potentially derogatory labels on people (Becker, 1973; Rothblum, Solomon, & Albee, 1986). Being labeled as psychotic, schizophrenic, or mentally ill carries a social stigma that can be difficult to shake. Even after a full recovery, someone who has been labeled mentally ill may have difficulty finding a place to live, getting a job, or making friends. Deep-seated prejudice against people who have been labeled mentally ill is commonplace.

The medical model has also been criticized because it suggests that people with behavioral problems should adopt the passive role of medical patient (Korchin, 1976). In this passive role, mental patients are implicitly encouraged to wait for their therapists to do the work to effect a cure. Such passiveness can be problematic even when an illness is purely physical. In psychological disorders, this passiveness can seriously undermine the likelihood of improvement in the person's condition. In general, people with psychological problems need to be actively involved in their recovery efforts.

Putting the Medical Model in Perspective

So, what position should we take on the medical model? In this chapter, we will assume an intermediate position, neither accepting nor discarding the model entirely. There certainly are significant problems with the medical model, and the issues raised by its critics deserve serious attention. However, in its defense, the medical model *has* stimulated scientific research on abnormal behavior. Moreover, some of the problems blamed on the disease analogy are not unique to this conception of abnormality. People who displayed strange, irrational behavior were labeled and stigmatized long before the medical model came along.

Hence, we'll take the position that the disease analogy can be useful, as long as we remember that it is *only* an analogy. Medical concepts such as *diagnosis, etiology,* and *prognosis* have proven useful in the treatment and study of abnormality. ***Diagnosis* involves distinguishing one illness from another. *Etiology* refers to the apparent causation and developmental history of an illness. A *prognosis* is a forecast about the probable course of an illness.** These medically based concepts have widely shared meanings that permit clinicians, researchers, and the public to communicate more effectively in their discussions of abnormal behavior. So, flawed though it may be, we will use the disease analogy and will use terms such as *abnormal behavior, mental illness, psychopathology,* and *psychological disorders* interchangeably. Do keep in mind, however, that the medical model *is* only an analogy.

Criteria of Abnormal Behavior

If your next-door neighbor scrubs his front porch twice every day and spends virtually all his time cleaning and recleaning his house, is he normal? If your sister-in-law goes to one physician after another seeking treatment for ailments that appear imaginary, is she psychologically healthy? How are we to judge what's normal and what's abnormal? More important, who's to do the judging?

These are complex questions. In a sense, *all* people make judgments about normality in that they express opinions about others' (and perhaps their own) mental health. Of course, formal diagnoses of psychological disorders are made by mental health professionals. In making these diagnoses, clinicians rely on an overlapping hodgepodge of criteria, which reflect the lack of scientific consensus on how to define the concept of mental disorder (Wakefield, 1992). Let's examine the three criteria that are most frequently used in judgments of abnormality. Although two or three criteria may apply in a particular case, people are often viewed as disordered when only one criterion is met.

1. *Deviance.* As Szasz has pointed out, people often are said to have a disorder because their behavior deviates from what their society considers acceptable. What constitutes normality varies somewhat from one culture to another, but all cultures have such norms. When people ignore these standards and expectations, they may be labeled mentally ill. Consider transvestites, for instance. ***Transvestism* is a sexual disorder in which a man achieves sexual arousal by dressing in women's clothing.** This behavior is regarded as disordered because a man who wears a dress, brassiere, and nylons is deviating from our culture's norms. The example of transvestism illustrates the arbitrary nature of cultural standards regarding normality, as in our society it is normal for women to dress in men's clothing, but not vice versa. Thus, the same overt behavior (cross-sex dressing) is acceptable for women and deviant for men.

2. *Maladaptive behavior.* In many cases, people are judged to have a psychological disorder because their everyday adaptive behavior is impaired. This is the key criterion in the diagnosis of substance use (drug) disorders. In and of itself, recreational drug use is not terribly unusual or deviant. However, when the use of cocaine, for instance, begins to interfere with a person's social or occupational functioning, a substance use disorder exists. In such cases, it is the maladaptive quality of the behavior that makes it disordered.

3. *Personal distress.* Frequently, the diagnosis of a psychological disorder is based on an individual's report of great personal distress. This is usually the criterion met by people who are troubled by depression or anxiety disorders. Depressed people, for instance, may or may not exhibit deviant or maladaptive behavior. Such people are usually labeled as having a disorder when they describe their subjective pain and suffering to friends, relatives, and mental health professionals.

The Cultural Bounds of Normality

Learning Objective

Discuss whether and how culture influences judgments of abnormality.

The major categories of psychological disorders transcend culture, and researchers have found considerable continuity across cultures in regard to what is considered normal or abnormal (Butcher, Narikiyo, & Vitousek, 1993). Nonetheless, judgments of abnormality are influenced to some extent by cultural norms and values (Lewis-Fernandez & Kleinman, 1994). Behavior that is considered deviant or maladaptive in one society may be quite acceptable in another. For example, in modern Western society people who "hear voices" are assumed to be irrational and are routinely placed in mental hospitals. However, in some cultures, hearing voices is commonplace and hardly merits a raised eyebrow.

Cultural norms regarding acceptable behavior can also change over time. For example, consider how views of homosexuality have changed in our society. Homosexuality used to be listed as a sexual disorder in the American Psychiatric Association's diagnostic system. However, in 1973 a committee appointed by the association voted to delete homosexuality from the official list of psychological disorders. This action occurred for several reasons (Rothblum, Solomon, & Albee, 1986). First, attitudes toward homosexuality in our society had become more accepting. Second, gay rights activists campaigned vigorously for the change. Third, research showed that gays and heterosexuals do not differ overall on measures of psychological health. As you might guess, this change stimulated a great deal of debate.

Gays are not the only group that has tried to influence the psychiatric diagnostic system. For example, in recent years women's groups have lobbied against adding a new diagnosis called *masochistic personality disorder* (since renamed *self-defeating personality disorder*) because they believe it will be applied in sexist ways to blame battered women for their partners' violence against them (Kass et al., 1989). Concerned groups have also campaigned against the inclusion of a new diagnosis called *premenstrual dysphoric disorder*, on the grounds that it has sexist overtones (Parlee, 1992).

The key point is that diagnoses of psychological disorders involve *value judgments* about what represents normal or abnormal behavior. The criteria of mental illness are not nearly as value-free as the criteria of physical illness. In evaluating physical diseases, people can usually agree that a weak heart or a bad kidney is pathological, regardless of their personal values. However, judgments about mental illness reflect prevailing cultural values, social trends, and political forces, as well as scientific knowledge (Kirk & Kutchins, 1992).

Normality and Abnormality as a Continuum

Learning Objective

Describe Rosenhan's pseudopatient study and explain what is meant by the continuum of normality and abnormality.

Antonyms such as *normal* versus *abnormal* and *mental health* versus *mental illness* imply that people can be divided neatly into two distinct groups: those who are normal and those who are not. In reality, it is often difficult to draw a line that clearly separates normality from abnormality. On occasion, everyone experiences personal distress. Everybody acts in deviant ways once in a while. And everyone displays some maladaptive behavior. People are judged to have psychological disorders only when their behavior becomes *extremely* deviant, maladaptive, or distressing. Thus, normality and abnormality exist on a continuum. It's a matter of degree, not an either-or proposition (see Figure 15.2).

For the most part, people with psychological disorders do *not* behave in bizarre ways that are very different from the behavior of normal people. At first glance, people with psychological disorders usually are indistinguishable from those without disorders. A study by David Rosenhan (1973) showed that even mental health professionals may have difficulty distinguishing normality from abnormality. To study diagnostic accuracy, Rosenhan arranged for a number of normal people to seek admission to mental hospitals. These "pseudopatients" arrived at the hospitals complaining of one false symptom—hearing voices. Except for this single symptom, they acted as they normally would and gave accurate information when interviewed about their personal histories. *All* the pseudopatients were admitted, and the average length of their hospitalization was 19 days! Why is it so hard to distinguish normality from abnormality? The pseudopatients' observations about life on the psychiatric wards offer a clue. They noted that the real patients acted normal most of

David Rosenhan

**Figure 15.2
Normality and abnormality as a continuum**
No sharp boundary exists between normal and abnormal behavior. Behavior is normal or abnormal in degree, depending on the extent to which it is deviant, personally distressing, or maladaptive.

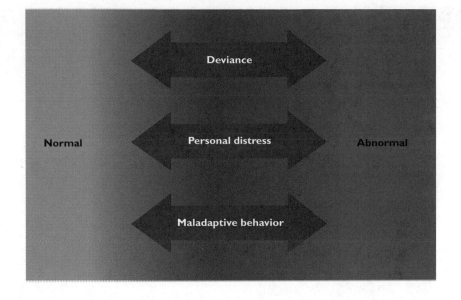

the time and only infrequently acted in a deviant manner. As you might imagine, Rosenhan's study evoked quite a controversy about our diagnostic system for mental illness. Let's take a look at how this diagnostic system has evolved.

Psychodiagnosis: The Classification of Disorders

Learning Objective

Discuss the history of the DSM system and describe the five axes of DSM-IV.

Obviously, we cannot lump all psychological disorders together without giving up all hope of understanding them better. A sound taxonomy of mental disorders can facilitate empirical research and enhance communication among scientists and clinicians (Adams & Cassidy, 1993). Hence, a great deal of effort has been invested in devising an elaborate system for classifying psychological disorders.

Guidelines for psychodiagnosis were vague and informal prior to 1952, when the American Psychiatric Association unveiled its *Diagnostic and Statistical Manual of Mental Disorders* (Grob, 1991). Known as DSM-I, this classification scheme described about 100 disorders. Revisions intended to improve the system were incorporated into the second edition (DSM-II), published in 1968, but the diagnostic guidelines were still pretty sketchy and there was widespread dissatisfaction with the lack of consistency in psychiatric diagnosis (Wilson, 1993). All too often, several clinicians evaluating the same patient would arrive at several different diagnoses. Thus, the revisions of the next two editions, DSM-III (1980) and DSM-III-R (1987), sought, first and foremost, to improve the consistency of psychodiagnosis. To achieve this end, diagnostic guidelines were made more explicit, concrete, and detailed. These revisions *did* lead to substantial increases in diagnostic consistency for many disorders, although there is still room for considerable improvement (Garfield, 1993). The current edition, DSM-IV, was introduced in 1994. More than ever before, the architects of the most recent DSM worked to base their revision on empirical research, as opposed to the consensus of experts (Widiger et al., 1991).

The Multiaxial System

The publication of DSM-III in 1980 introduced a new multiaxial system of classification, which asks for judgments about individuals on five separate dimensions or "axes." Figure 15.3 provides an overview of the entire system and the five axes. The diagnoses of disorders are made on Axes I and II. Clinicians record any major disorders that are apparent on Axis I (Clinical Syndromes). They use Axis II (Personality Disorders) to list milder, long-running personality disturbances, which often coexist with Axis I syndromes. People may receive diagnoses on both axes.

The remaining axes are used to record supplemental information. A patient's physical disorders are listed on Axis III (General Medical Conditions). On Axis IV (Psychosocial and Environmental Problems), the clinician makes notations regard-

Axis I
Clinical Syndromes

1   *Disorders usually first diagnosed in infancy, childhood, or adolescence*
    This category includes disorders that arise before adolescence, such as attention deficit disorders, autism, mental retardation, enuresis, and stuttering.

2   *Organic mental disorders*
    These disorders are temporary or permanent dysfunctions of brain tissue caused by diseases or chemicals. Examples are delirium, dementia, and amnesia.

3   *Substance-related disorders*
    This category refers to the maladaptive use of drugs and alcohol. Mere consumption and recreational use of such substances are not disorders. This category requires an abnormal pattern of use, as with alcohol abuse and cocaine dependence.

4   *Schizophrenia and other psychotic disorders*
    The schizophrenias are characterized by psychotic symptoms (for example, grossly disorganized behavior, delusions, and hallucinations) and by over 6 months of behavioral deterioration. This category also includes delusional disorder and schizoaffective disorder.

5   *Mood disorders*
    The cardinal feature is emotional disturbance. Patients may, or may not, have psychotic symptoms. These disorders include major depression, bipolar disorder, dysthymic disorder, and cyclothymic disorder.

6   *Anxiety disorders*
    These disorders are characterized by physiological signs of anxiety (for example, palpitations) and subjective feelings of tension, apprehension, or fear. Anxiety may be acute and focused (panic disorder) or continual and diffuse (generalized anxiety disorder).

7   *Somatoform disorders*
    These disorders are dominated by somatic symptoms that resemble physical illnesses. These symptoms cannot be accounted for by organic damage. There *must* also be strong evidence that these symptoms are produced by psychological factors or conflicts. This category includes somatization and conversion disorders and hypochondriasis.

8   *Dissociative disorders*
    These disorders all feature a sudden, temporary alteration or dysfunction of memory, consciousness, identity, and behavior, as in dissociative amnesia and multiple personality.

9   *Sexual and gender-identity disorders*
    There are three basic types of disorders in this category: gender identity disorders (discomfort with identity as male or female), paraphilias (preference for unusual acts to achieve sexual arousal), and sexual dysfunctions (impairments in sexual functioning).

Axis II
Personality Disorders

These disorders are patterns of personality traits that are longstanding, maladaptive and inflexible and involve impaired functioning or subjective distress. Examples include borderline, schizoid, and antisocial personality disorders.

Axis III
General Medical Conditions

Physical disorders or conditions are recorded on this axis. Examples include diabetes, arthritis, and hemophilia.

Axis IV
Psychosocial and Environmental Problems

Axis IV is for reporting psychosocial and environmental problems that may affect the diagnosis, treatment, and prognosis of mental disorders (Axes I and II). A psychosocial or environmental problem may be a negative life event, an environmental difficulty or deficiency, a familial or other interpersonal stress, an inadequacy of social support or personal resources, or another problem that describes the context in which a person's difficulties have developed.

Axis V
Global Assessment of Functioning (GAF) Scale

Code	Symptoms
100	Superior functioning in a wide range of activities
90	Absent or minimal symptoms, good functioning in all areas
80	Symptoms transient and expectable reactions to psychosocial stressors
70	Some mild symptoms or some difficulty in social, occupational, or school functioning, but generally functioning pretty well
60	Moderate symptoms or difficulty in social, occupational, or school functioning
50	Serious symptoms or impairment in social, occupational, or school functioning
40	Some impairment in reality testing or communication or major impairment in family relations, judgment, thinking, or mood
30	Behavior considerably influenced by delusions or hallucinations, serious impairment in communication or judgment, or inability to function in almost all areas
20	Some danger of hurting self or others, occasional failure to maintain minimal personal hygiene, or gross impairment in communication
10	Persistent danger of severely hurting self or others

**Figure 15.3 (opposite page)
Overview of the DSM
diagnostic system**
Published by the American Psychiatric Association, the *Diagnostic and Statistical Manual of Mental Disorders* is the formal classification system used in the diagnosis of psychological disorders. It is a *multiaxial* system, which means that information is recorded on the five axes described here. (Adapted from DSM-IV, 1994)

ing the types of stress experienced by the individual in the past year. On Axis V (Global Assessment of Functioning), estimates are made of the individual's current level of adaptive functioning (in social and occupational behavior, viewed as a whole), and of the individual's highest level of functioning in the past year.

Most theorists agree that the multiaxial system is a step in the right direction because it recognizes the importance of information besides a traditional diagnostic label. However, the distinction between Axis I disorders and Axis II disorders is plagued by conceptual inconsistencies (Frances et al., 1991), and it appears that clinicians make little use of Axis III (Maricle, Leung, & Bloom, 1987). Furthermore, Axes IV and V are poorly defined, and more evidence is needed regarding their validity (Goldman, Skodol, & Lave, 1992; Rey et al., 1988). It is hoped that research will lead to improvement of the supplementary axes in future editions of the DSM system.

Controversies Surrounding the DSM

Learning Objective

Discuss some controversial aspects of DSM-IV.

Since the publication of the third edition in 1980, the DSM system has become the dominant classification scheme for mental disorders around the world (Maser, Kaelber, & Weise, 1991; Williams, 1994). Nonetheless, the DSM system has garnered its share of criticism. First, some critics argue that the heavy focus on improving the consistency of psychodiagnosis has drawn attention away from an equally basic issue—the *validity* of the diagnostic categories (Carson, 1991). Precise, detailed descriptions of disorders are of little value unless the descriptions mesh well with the constellations of problems that people actually experience. Some theorists have even questioned the wisdom of the DSM's *categorical approach* to describing disorders, which assumes (incorrectly, they argue) that people can reliably be placed in discontinuous (nonoverlapping) diagnostic categories (Clark, Watson, & Reynolds, 1995). These critics argue that too many people qualify for two or more diagnoses and that patients in the same diagnostic category exhibit too much diversity in their symptoms.

Second, recent editions of the DSM sparked controversy by adding everyday problems that are not traditionally thought of as mental illnesses to the diagnostic system. For example, the DSM system includes a *developmental coordination disorder* (basically, extreme clumsiness in children), a *nicotine dependence disorder* (distress derived from quitting smoking), and a *pathological gambling disorder* (difficulty controlling one's gambling). Critics argue that this approach "medicalizes" everyday problems and casts the shadow of pathology on normal behavior (Kirk & Kutchins, 1992). In part, everyday problems were added to the diagnostic system so that more people could bill their insurance companies for professional treatment of the conditions (Garfield, 1986). Many health insurance policies permit reimbursement only for the treatment of disorders on the official (DSM) list. There's merit in making it easier for more people to seek needed professional help. Nonetheless, the pros and cons of including everyday problems in DSM are complicated.

Shifting definitions of normality and abnormality inevitably affect estimates regarding the number of people who suffer from psychological disorders. The changes made in DSM-III stimulated a flurry of research on the prevalence of specific mental disorders that has continued through the present. Let's examine some of this research.

The Prevalence of Psychological Disorders

Learning Objective

Summarize data on the prevalence of various psychological disorders.

How common are psychological disorders? What percentage of the population is afflicted with mental illness? Is it 10%? Perhaps 25%? Could the figure range as high as 40% or 50%?

Such estimates fall in the domain of **epidemiology—the study of the distribution of mental or physical disorders in a population.** In epidemiology, **prevalence refers to the percentage of a population that exhibits a disorder during a specified time period.** In the case of mental disorders, the most interesting data are the estimates of *lifetime prevalence*, the percentage of people who endure a specific disorder at any time in their lives.

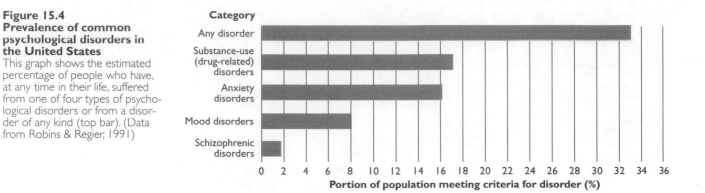

Estimates of lifetime prevalence suggest that psychological disorders are more common than most people realize. Prior to the advent of DSM-III, studies suggested that about *one-fifth* of the population exhibited clear signs of mental illness (Neugebauer, Dohrenwend, & Dohrenwend, 1980). However, the older studies did not assess drug-related disorders very effectively, because these disorders were vaguely described in DSM-I and DSM-II. More recent studies, using the explicit criteria for substance-use disorders in recent editions of the DSM system, have found psychological disorders in roughly *one-third* of the population! This increase in mental illness is more apparent than real, as it is mostly due to more effective tabulation of drug-related disorders. As Figure 15.4 shows, the most common disorders are (1) anxiety disorders, (2) substance-use (alcohol and drug) disorders, and (3) mood disorders (Robins, Locke, & Regier, 1991).

The raw numbers are even more dramatic than the prevalence rates in Figure 15.4. Estimates based on these prevalence rates suggest that the United States contains nearly 4 million people who will be troubled at some time in their lives by schizophrenic disorders. Roughly 20 million people will experience mood disorders (mostly depression). And over 40 million people will wrestle with substance-use disorders or anxiety disorders. Thus, it's clear that psychological disorders are widespread. When psychologists note that mental illness can strike anyone, they mean it quite literally.

We are now ready to start examining the specific types of psychological disorders. Obviously, we cannot cover all of the multitudinous disorders listed in DSM-IV. However, we will introduce most of the major categories of disorders to give you an overview of the many forms abnormal behavior takes. In discussing each set of disorders, we will begin with brief descriptions of the specific syndromes or subtypes that fall in the category. Then we'll focus on the *etiology* of the disorders in that category. Although many paths can lead to specific disorders, some are more common than others. We'll highlight some of the common paths to enhance your understanding of the roots of abnormal behavior.

Anxiety Disorders

Learning Objective

Describe four types of anxiety disorders.

Everyone experiences anxiety from time to time. It is a natural and common reaction to many of life's difficulties. For some people, however, anxiety becomes a chronic problem. These people experience high levels of anxiety with disturbing regularity. **Anxiety disorders are a class of disorders marked by feelings of excessive apprehension and anxiety.** There are four principal types of anxiety disorders: generalized anxiety disorders, phobic disorders, obsessive-compulsive disorders, and panic disorders. They are not mutually exclusive, as many people who develop one anxiety syndrome often suffer from another at some point in their lives (Massion, Warshaw, & Keller, 1993). People with anxiety disorders also exhibit elevated rates of depression (Clark, Beck, & Beck, 1994). Studies suggest that anxiety disorders are quite common, occurring in roughly 17% of the population (Robins & Regier, 1991). Most of these cases are generalized anxiety disorders or phobic disorders (Blazer et al., 1991; Eaton, Dryman, & Weissman, 1991).

Generalized Anxiety Disorder

The *generalized anxiety disorder* is marked by a chronic, high level of anxiety that is not tied to any specific threat. This anxiety is sometimes called "free-floating anxiety" because it is nonspecific. People with this disorder worry constantly about yesterday's mistakes and tomorrow's problems. In particular, they worry about minor matters related to family, finances, work, and personal illness (Sanderson & Barlow, 1990). They often dread decisions and brood over them endlessly. Their anxiety is frequently accompanied by physical symptoms, such as trembling, muscle tension, diarrhea, dizziness, faintness, sweating, and heart palpitations.

Phobic Disorder

In a phobic disorder, an individual's troublesome anxiety has a specific focus. **A *phobic disorder* is marked by a persistent and irrational fear of an object or situation that presents no realistic danger.** Although mild phobias are extremely common, people are said to have a phobic disorder only when their fears seriously interfere with their everyday behavior. The following case provides an example of a phobic disorder:

> Hilda is 32 years of age and has a rather unusual fear. She is terrified of snow. She cannot go outside in the snow. She cannot even stand to see snow or hear about it on the weather report. Her phobia severely constricts her day-to-day behavior. Probing in therapy revealed that her phobia was caused by a traumatic experience at age 11. Playing at a ski lodge, she was buried briefly by a small avalanche of snow. She had no recollection of this experience until it was recovered in therapy. [Adapted from Laughlin, 1967, p. 227]

As Hilda's unusual snow phobia illustrates, people can develop phobic responses to virtually anything. Nonetheless, certain types of phobias are relatively common, as the data in Figure 15.5 show. Particularly common are acrophobia (fear of heights), claustrophobia (fear of small, enclosed places), brontophobia (fear of storms), hydrophobia (fear of water), and various animal and insect phobias (Eaton et al., 1991). People troubled by phobias typically realize that their fears are irrational, but they still are unable to calm themselves when confronted by a phobic object.

Figure 15.5
Common phobias
Frequently reported phobias are listed here, along with their typical age of onset and information on gender differences. (From Marks, 1969)

Common Phobias		Percent of all phobias	Gender difference	Typical age of onset
Agoraphobia		10–50%	Large majority are women	Early adulthood
(fear of places of assembly, crowds, open spaces)				
Social phobia		10%	Majority are women	Adolescence
(fear of being observed doing something humiliating)				
Specific phobias				
Animals		5–15%	Vast majority are women	Childhood
Cats (ailurophobia)	Dogs (cynophobia)			
Insects (insectophobia)	Spiders (arachnophobia)			
Birds (avisophobia)	Horses (equinophobia)			
Snakes (ophidiophobia)	Rodents (rodentophobia)			
Inanimate objects		20%	None	Any age
Dirt (mysophobia)	Storms (brontophobia)			
Heights (acrophobia)	Darkness (nyctophobia)			
Closed spaces (claustrophobia)				
Illness-injury (nosophobia)		15–25%	None	Middle age
Death (thanatophobia)				
Cancer (cancerophobia)				
Venereal disease (venerophobia)				

AGORAPHOBIA SOCIETY

NICE TURNOUT

Panic Disorder and Agoraphobia

A *panic disorder* **is characterized by recurrent attacks of overwhelming anxiety that usually occur suddenly and unexpectedly.** These paralyzing attacks are accompanied by physical symptoms of anxiety. After a number of anxiety attacks, victims often become apprehensive, wondering when their next panic will occur. Their concern about exhibiting panic in public may escalate to the point where they are afraid to leave home. This creates a condition called agoraphobia, which is a common complication of panic disorders.

Agoraphobia **is a fear of going out to public places** (its literal meaning is "fear of the marketplace or open places"). Because of this fear, some people become prisoners confined to their homes, although many will venture out if accompanied by a trusted companion (Hollander, Simeon, & Gorman, 1994). As its name suggests, agoraphobia has traditionally been viewed as a phobic disorder. However, empirical research suggests that agoraphobia shares more kinship with panic disorders than phobic disorders (Turner et al., 1986). Nonetheless, agoraphobia can occur independently of panic disorder, and some theorists question the wisdom of lumping panic and agoraphobia together in the DSM classification system (Noyes, 1988). The vast majority of people who suffer from panic disorder or agoraphobia are female (Rapee & Barlow, 1993).

Obsessive-Compulsive Disorder

Obsessions are *thoughts* that repeatedly intrude on one's consciousness in a distressing way. Compulsions are *actions* that one feels forced to carry out. Thus, **an *obsessive-compulsive disorder* (OCD) is marked by persistent uncontrollable intrusions of unwanted thoughts (obsessions) and urges to engage in senseless rituals (compulsions).** To illustrate, let's examine the bizarre behavior of a man once reputed to be the wealthiest person in the world:

The famous industrialist Howard Hughes was obsessed with the possibility of being contaminated by germs. This led him to devise extraordinary rituals to minimize the possibility of such contamination. He would spend hours methodically cleaning a single telephone. He once wrote a three-page memo instructing assistants on exactly how to open cans of fruit for him. The following is just a small portion of the instructions that Hughes provided for a driver who delivered films to his bungalow. "Get out of the car on the traffic side. Do not at any time be on the side of the car between the car and the curb. . . . Carry only one can of film at a time. Step over the gutter opposite the place where the sidewalk dead-ends into the curb from a

Repeatedly cleaning things that are already clean is an example of compulsive behavior.

point as far out into the center of the road as possible. Do not ever walk on the grass at all, also do not step into the gutter at all. Walk to the bungalow keeping as near to the center of the sidewalk as possible." [Adapted from Barlett & Steele, 1979, pp. 227–237]

The typical age of onset for OCD is early adulthood (Sturgis, 1993). Obsessions often center on fear of contamination, inflicting harm on others, suicide, or sexual acts. Compulsions usually involve stereotyped rituals that temporarily relieve anxiety. Common examples include constant handwashing, repetitive cleaning of things that are already clean, and endless rechecking of locks, faucets, and such (Foa & Kozak, 1995). Unusual rituals intended to bring good luck are also a common form of compulsive behavior. Although many of us can be compulsive at times, full-fledged obsessive-compulsive disorders occur in roughly 2–4% of the population (Karno & Golding, 1991). The frequency of obsessive-compulsive disorder seems to be increasing, but this trend may simply reflect changes in clinicians' diagnostic tendencies. Recent years have seen increased research on OCD and advances in its treatment that may have made clinicians more sensitive to the syndrome (Stoll, Tohen, & Baldessarini, 1992).

Etiology of Anxiety Disorders

Like most psychological disorders, anxiety disorders develop out of complicated interactions among a variety of factors. Conditioning and learning appear especially important, but biological factors may also contribute to anxiety disorders.

Biological Factors

Learning Objective

Discuss the contribution of biological factors and conditioning to the etiology of anxiety disorders.

Recent studies suggest that there may be a weak genetic predisposition to anxiety disorders (Kendler et al., 1992; Pauls et al., 1995). These findings are consistent with the idea that inherited differences in temperament might make some people more vulnerable than others to anxiety disorders. Kagan and his colleagues (1992) have found that about 15–20% of infants display an *inhibited temperament,* characterized by shyness, timidity, and wariness, which appears to have a strong genetic basis. Recent research suggests that this temperament is a risk factor for the development of anxiety disorders (Rosenbaum, Lakin, & Roback, 1992). Thought-provoking connections have also been found between anxiety disorders and a common heart defect, *mitral valve prolapse.* This anatomical defect, which makes people prone to physiological sensations associated with anxiety (heart palpitations, faintness, and shortness of breath), *may* predispose some people to anxiety disorders (Agras, 1985; Dager et al., 1988). This finding fits well with a recent theory that *anxiety sensitivity* may make people vulnerable to anxiety disorders (Fowles, 1993; Reiss, 1991). According to this notion, some people are very sensitive to the internal physiological symptoms of anxiety and are prone to overreact with fear when they experience these symptoms. Anxiety sensitivity may fuel an inflationary spiral in which anxiety breeds more anxiety, which eventually spins out of control in the form of an anxiety disorder.

Recent evidence suggests that a link may exist between anxiety disorders and neurochemical activity in the brain. **Neurotransmitters are chemicals that carry signals from one neuron to another.** Therapeutic drugs (such as Valium) that reduce excessive anxiety appear to alter activity at synapses involving the neurotransmitter GABA. This finding and other lines of evidence suggest that disturbances in the neural circuits using GABA may play a role in some types of anxiety disorders (Paul, Crawley, & Skolnick, 1986). Abnormalities in other neural circuits (using the neurotransmitter serotonin) have recently been implicated in obsessive-compulsive disorders (Hollander et al., 1994). Thus, scientists are beginning to unravel the neurochemical bases for anxiety disorders.

Conditioning and Learning

Many anxiety responses may be *acquired through classical conditioning* and *maintained through operant conditioning* (see Chapter 6). According to Mowrer (1947), an originally neutral stimulus (the snow in Hilda's case, for instance) may be paired with a frightening event (the avalanche) so that it becomes a conditioned stimulus eliciting anxiety (see Figure 15.6). Once a fear is acquired through classical conditioning, the person may start avoiding the anxiety-producing stimulus. The avoidance response is negatively reinforced because it is followed by a reduction in anxiety. This process involves operant conditioning (see Figure 15.6). Thus, separate conditioning processes may create and then sustain specific anxiety responses (Levis, 1989).

The tendency to develop phobias of certain types of objects and situations may be explained by Martin Seligman's (1971) concept of *preparedness*. Like many theorists, Seligman believes that classical conditioning creates most phobic responses. *However, he suggests that people are biologically prepared by their evolutionary history to acquire some fears much more easily than others.* His theory would explain why people develop phobias of ancient sources of threat (such as snakes and spiders) much more readily than modern sources of threat (such as electrical outlets or hot irons). Some laboratory studies of conditioned fears have yielded evidence consistent with Seligman's theory. For example, Cook and Mineka (1989) found that monkeys acquired conditioned fears of stimuli that they should be prepared to fear, such as snakes, with relative ease in comparison to other stimuli, such as flowers. As a whole, however, research has provided only modest support for the role of preparedness in the acquisition of phobias (McNally, 1987; Ohman & Soares, 1993).

There are a number of problems with conditioning models of phobias (Rachman, 1990). For instance, many people with phobias cannot recall or identify a traumatic conditioning experience that led to their phobia. Conversely, many people endure extremely traumatic experiences that should create a phobia but do not. To provide better explanations for these complexities, conditioning models of anxiety disorders are currently being revised to include a larger role for cognitive factors.

Cognitive Factors

Cognitive theorists maintain that certain styles of thinking make some people particularly vulnerable to anxiety disorders. According to these theorists, some people are prone to suffer from problems with anxiety because they tend to (1) misinterpret harmless situations as threatening, (2) focus excessive attention on perceived threats, and (3) selectively recall information that seems threatening (Beck, 1988a;

Figure 15.6
Conditioning as an explanation for phobias
Many phobias appear to be acquired through classical conditioning when a neutral stimulus is paired with an anxiety-arousing stimulus. Once acquired, a phobia may be maintained through operant conditioning because avoidance of the phobic stimulus leads to a reduction in anxiety, resulting in negative reinforcement.

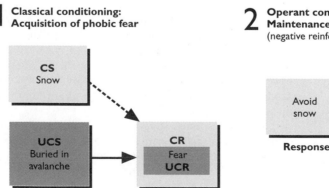
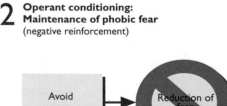

Figure 15.7
Cognitive factors in anxiety disorders
Eysenck and his colleagues (1991) compared how subjects with anxiety problems and nonanxious subjects tended to interpret sentences that could be viewed as threatening or nonthreatening. Consistent with cognitive models of anxiety disorders, anxious subjects were more likely to interpret the sentences in a threatening light. (From Eysenck et al., 1991)

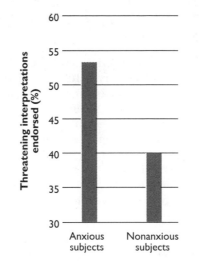

McNally, 1990). In one intriguing test of the cognitive view, anxious and nonanxious subjects were asked to read 32 sentences that could be interpreted in either a threatening or a nonthreatening manner (Eysenck et al., 1991). One such sentence was "The doctor examined little Emma's growth," which could mean that the doctor checked her height or the growth of a tumor. As Figure 15.7 shows, the anxious subjects interpreted the sentences in a threatening way more often than the nonanxious subjects. Thus, the cognitive view holds that some people are prone to anxiety disorders because they see threat in every corner of their lives.

Stress

Finally, recent studies have supported the long-held suspicion that anxiety disorders are stress related. For instance, Blazer, Hughes, and George (1987) found an association between stress and the development of generalized anxiety disorders. Men who experienced high stress were 8.5 times more likely to develop these disorders than men under low stress. In another study, Faravelli and Pallanti (1989) found that patients with panic disorder had experienced a dramatic increase in stress in the month prior to the onset of their disorder. Thus, there is reason to believe that high stress often helps to precipitate the onset of anxiety disorders.

Somatoform Disorders

Learning Objective

Distinguish somatoform disorders from psychosomatic disorders and describe three types of somatoform disorders.

Chances are, you have met people who always seem to be complaining about aches, pains, and physical maladies of doubtful authenticity. You may have thought to yourself, "It's all in his head," and concluded that the person exhibited a "psychosomatic" condition. However, as we discussed in Chapter 3, the term *psychosomatic* is widely misused. ***Psychosomatic diseases* are genuine physical ailments caused in part by psychological factors, especially emotional distress.** These diseases, which include maladies such as ulcers, asthma, and high blood pressure, have a genuine organic basis and are not imagined ailments. They are recorded on the DSM axis for physical problems (Axis III). When physical illness appears *entirely* psychological in origin, we are dealing with somatoform disorders, which are recorded on Axis I. ***Somatoform disorders* are physical ailments with no authentic organic basis that are due to psychological factors.** Although their symptoms are more imaginary than real, victims of somatoform disorders are *not* simply faking illness. Deliberate feigning of illness for personal gain is another matter altogether, called *malingering.*

People with somatoform disorders typically seek treatment from physicians practicing neurology, internal medicine, or family medicine, instead of from psychologists or psychiatrists. Making accurate diagnoses of somatoform disorders can be difficult, because the causes of physical ailments are sometimes hard to identify. In some cases, somatoform disorders are misdiagnosed when a genuine organic cause for a person's physical symptoms goes undetected in spite of extensive medical examinations and tests (Rubin, Zorumski, & Guze, 1986).

We will discuss three specific types of somatoform disorders: somatization disorder, conversion disorder, and hypochondriasis. Diagnostic difficulties make it hard to obtain sound data on the prevalence of somatoform disorders. Hypochondriasis seems to be fairly common, with somatization and conversion disorders less frequent (Barsky, 1989).

Somatization Disorder

Individuals with somatization disorders are often said to "cling to ill health." **A** *somatization disorder* **is marked by a history of diverse physical complaints that appear to be psychological in origin.** Somatization disorders occur mostly in women (Martin & Yutzy, 1994). Victims report an endless succession of minor physical ailments. They usually have a long and complicated history of medical treatment from many doctors. The distinguishing feature of this disorder is the diversity of victims' physical complaints. Over the years, they report a mixed bag of cardiovascular, gastrointestinal, pulmonary, neurological, and genitourinary symptoms. The unlikely nature of such a smorgasbord of symptoms occurring together often alerts a physician to the possible psychological basis for the patient's problems.

Conversion Disorder

Conversion disorder **is characterized by a significant loss of physical function (with no apparent organic basis), usually in a single organ system.** Common symptoms include partial or complete loss of vision, partial or complete loss of hearing, partial paralysis, severe laryngitis or mutism, and loss of feeling or function in limbs, such as that seen in the following case:

> Mildred was a rancher's daughter who lost the use of both of her legs during adolescence. Mildred was at home alone one afternoon when a male relative attempted to assault her. She screamed for help, and her legs gave way as she slipped to the floor. She was found on the floor a few minutes later when her mother returned home. She could not get up, so she was carried to her bed. Her legs buckled when she made subsequent attempts to walk on her own. Due to her illness, she was waited on hand and foot by her family and friends. Neighbors brought her homemade things to eat or to wear. She became the center of attention in the household. [Adapted from Cameron, 1963, pp. 312–313]

People with conversion disorders are usually troubled by more severe ailments than people with somatization disorders. In some cases of conversion disorder, there are telltale clues about the psychological origins of the illness because the patient's symptoms are not consistent with medical knowledge about their apparent disease. For instance, the loss of feeling in one hand that is seen in "glove anesthesia" is inconsistent with the known facts of neurological organization (see Figure 15.8).

Figure 15.8
Glove anesthesia
In conversion disorders, the physical complaints are sometimes inconsistent with the known facts of physiology. Such is the case in glove anesthesia, in which the patient complains of losing feeling in a hand. Given the patterns of nerve distribution in the arm (shown in a), a loss of feeling exclusively in the hand (as shown in b) is a physical impossibility, indicating that the patient's problem is psychological in origin.

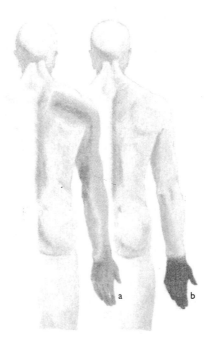

"THE WAY HE MOANS AND GROANS WHEN HE GETS A LITTLE COLD... I CAN'T DECIDE WHETHER HE SHOULD CALL A DOCTOR OR A DRAMA CRITIC."

Reprinted by permission of Edgar Argo.

Hypochondriasis

Hypochondriacs constantly monitor their physical condition, looking for signs of illness. Any tiny alteration from their physical norm leads them to conclude that they have contracted a disease. *Hypochondriasis* **(more widely known as hypochondria) is characterized by excessive preoccupation with health concerns and incessant worry about developing physical illnesses.** The following case illustrates the nature of hypochondria:

> Jeff is a middle-aged man who works as a clerk in a drugstore. He spends long hours describing his health problems to anyone who will listen. Jeff is an avid reader of popular magazine articles on medicine. He can tell you all about the latest medical discoveries. He takes all sorts of pills and vitamins to ward off possible illnesses. He's the first to try every new product on the market. Jeff is constantly afflicted by new symptoms of illness. His most recent problems were poor digestion and a heartbeat that he thought was irregular. He frequently goes to physicians who can find nothing wrong with him physically. They tell him that he is healthy. He thinks they use "backward techniques." He suspects that his illness is too rare to be diagnosed successfully. [Adapted from Suinn, 1984, p. 236]

When hypochondriacs are assured by their physician that they do not have any real illness, they often are skeptical and disbelieving. As in Jeff's case, they frequently assume that the physician must be incompetent, and they go shopping for another doctor. Hypochondriacs don't subjectively suffer from physical distress as much as they *overinterpret* every conceivable sign of illness. Hypochondria frequently appears alongside other psychological disorders, especially anxiety disorders and depression (Simon & VonKorff, 1991). For example, Howard Hughes's obsessive-compulsive disorder was coupled with profound hypochondria. Indeed, hypochondria coexists with other disorders so often that some theorists have raised doubts about whether it should be viewed as a separate diagnostic category (Iezzi & Adams, 1993).

Etiology of Somatoform Disorders

Learning Objective

Summarize what is known about the causes of somatoform disorders.

Inherited aspects of physiological functioning, such as a highly reactive autonomic nervous system, may predispose some people to somatoform disorders (Weiner, 1992). However, available evidence suggests that these disorders are largely a function of personality and learning. Let's look at personality factors first.

Personality Factors

People with certain types of personality traits seem to be particularly disposed to develop somatoform disorders. The prime candidates appear to be people with *histrionic* personality characteristics (Nemiah, 1985; Slavney, 1990). The histrionic personality tends to be self-centered, suggestible, excitable, highly emotional, and overly dramatic. Such people thrive on the attention that they get when they become ill. The personality trait of *neuroticism* also seems to elevate individuals' susceptibility to somatoform disorders (Kirmayer, Robbins, & Paris, 1994).

The Sick Role

As we discussed in Chapter 14, some people grow fond of the role associated with being sick (Lubkin, 1990; Pilowsky, 1978). Their complaints of physical symptoms may be reinforced by indirect benefits derived from their illness. What are the benefits commonly associated with physical illness? One payoff is that becoming ill is a superb way to avoid having to confront life's challenges. Many people with somatoform disorders are avoiding facing up to marital problems, career frustrations, family responsibilities, and the like. After all, when you're sick, others cannot place great demands on you. Another benefit is that physical problems can provide a convenient excuse when people fail, or worry about failing, in endeavors that are critical to their self-esteem (Organista & Miranda, 1991).

Attention from others is another payoff that may reinforce complaints of physical illness. When people become ill, they command the attention of family, friends, co-workers, neighbors, and doctors. The sympathy that illness often brings may strengthen the person's tendency to feel ill. This clearly occurred in Mildred's case of conversion disorder. Her illness paid handsome dividends in terms of attention, consolation, and kindhearted assistance from others.

Dissociative Disorders

Learning Objective

Describe three types of dissociative disorders.

Dissociative disorders are among the more unusual syndromes that we will discuss. *Dissociative disorders* **are a class of disorders in which people lose contact with portions of their consciousness or memory, resulting in disruptions in their sense of identity.** We'll describe three dissociative syndromes—dissociative amnesia, dissociative fugue, and multiple-personality disorder—all of which are relatively uncommon.

Dissociative Amnesia and Fugue

Dissociative amnesia and fugue are overlapping disorders characterized by serious memory deficits. *Dissociative amnesia* **is a sudden loss of memory for important personal information that is too extensive to be due to normal forgetting.** Memory losses may occur for a single traumatic event (such as an automobile accident or home fire) or for an extended period of time surrounding the event. **In** *dissociative fugue,* **people lose their memory for their entire lives along with their sense of personal identity.** These people forget their name, their family, where they live, and where they work! In spite of this wholesale forgetting, they remember matters unrelated to their identity, such as how to drive a car and how to do math.

Multiple-Personality Disorder

Multiple-personality disorder **(MPD) involves the coexistence in one person of two or more largely complete, and usually very different, personalities.** The formal name for this disorder was changed to *dissociative identity disorder* in the recent revision of the DSM system, but it remains more widely known by its traditional name. In multiple-personality disorders, the divergences in behavior go far beyond those that people normally display in adapting to different roles in life. People with multiple personalities feel that they have more than one identity. Each personality has his or her own name, memories, traits, and physical mannerisms. Although rare, this "Dr. Jekyl and Mr. Hyde" syndrome is frequently portrayed in novels, movies, and television shows. In popular media portrayals, the syndrome is often mistakenly called *schizophrenia*. As you will see later, schizophrenic disorders are entirely different.

In a multiple-personality disorder, the original personality often is unaware of the alternate personalities. In contrast, the alternate personalities usually are aware of the original one and have varying amounts of awareness of each other. The alternate personalities commonly display traits that are quite foreign to the original personality. For instance, a person who is shy and inhibited might develop a flamboyant, extraverted alternate personality. Transitions between personalities often occur suddenly.

During the 1980s, a dramatic increase occurred in the diagnosis of multiple-personality disorders (Ross et al., 1991). Some theorists believe that these disorders used to be underdiagnosed—that is, they often went undetected (Saxe et al., 1993). However, it appears more likely that a handful of clinicians have begun overdiagnosing the condition (Frankel, 1990; Thigpen & Cleckley, 1984). Consistent with this view, a survey of all the psychiatrists in Switzerland (Modestin, 1992) found that 90% of them had never seen a case of MPD, whereas three of the psychiatrists had each seen more than 20 MPD patients. The data from this study suggest that six psychiatrists (out of 655 surveyed) accounted for two-thirds of the MPD diagnoses in Switzerland.

Etiology of Dissociative Disorders

Learning Objective

Summarize what is known about the causes of dissociative disorders.

Dissociative amnesia and fugue are usually attributed to excessive stress. However, relatively little is known about why this extreme reaction to stress occurs in a tiny minority of people but not in the vast majority who are subjected to similar stress. There is speculation that certain personality traits—fantasy proneness and a tendency to become intensely absorbed in personal experiences—may make some people more susceptible to dissociative disorders, but adequate evidence on this line of thought is lacking (Kihlstrom, Glisky, & Angiulo, 1994).

The causes of multiple-personality disorders are particularly obscure. Some skeptical theorists believe that people with multiple personalities are engaging in intentional role playing to use mental illness as a face-saving excuse for their personal failings and to covertly manipulate people around them to gain attention, support, and other rewards (Spanos, 1994). Indeed, there is evidence that multiple-personality disorders are faked with some regularity, perhaps because of all the media attention garnered by the disorder. However, various lines of evidence suggest to most theorists that at least some cases are authentic (Kihlstrom, Tataryn, & Hoyt, 1993). Many of these cases seem to be rooted in severe emotional trauma that occurred during childhood. A substantial majority of people with multiple-personality disorder have a history of disturbed home life, beatings and rejection from parents, and sexual abuse (Ross et al., 1990; Spiegel, 1994). In the final analysis, however, very little is known about the causes of multiple-personality disorders.

Mood Disorders

Learning Objective

Describe the two major mood disorders and discuss their prevalence.

What did Abraham Lincoln, Marilyn Monroe, Ernest Hemingway, Winston Churchill, Janis Joplin, and Leo Tolstoy have in common? Yes, they all achieved great prominence, albeit in different ways at different times. But, more pertinent to our interest, they all suffered from severe mood disorders. Although mood disorders can be terribly debilitating, people with mood disorders may still achieve great-

Actress Patty Duke and statesman Winston Churchill suffered from depression, a common psychological disorder that causes its victims to feel worthless and hopeless.

ness, because such disorders tend to be episodic. In other words, emotional disorders often come and go. Thus, episodes of disturbance are interspersed among periods of normality. These episodes of disturbance can vary greatly in length, but they typically last several months (Coryell & Winokur, 1992).

Of course, we all have our ups and downs in terms of mood. Life would be dull indeed if our emotional tone was constant. Everyone experiences depression occasionally. Likewise, everyone has moments of euphoria. Such emotional fluctuations are natural, but some people experience extreme and prolonged distortions of mood. *Mood disorders* **are a class of disorders marked by emotional disturbances that may spill over to disrupt physical, perceptual, social, and thought processes.**

There are two basic types of mood disorders: unipolar and bipolar (see Figure 15.9). People with *unipolar disorders* experience emotional disturbances at just one end of the mood continuum—*depression*. People with *bipolar disorders* experience emotional extremes at both ends of the mood continuum, going through periods of both *depression and mania* (excitement and elation). The mood swings in bipolar disorders can be patterned in many different ways.

Figure 15.9
Episodic patterns in mood disorders
Episodes of emotional disturbance come and go unpredictably in mood disorders. People with unipolar disorders suffer from bouts of depression only, while people with bipolar disorders experience both manic and depressed episodes. The time between episodes of disturbance varies greatly.

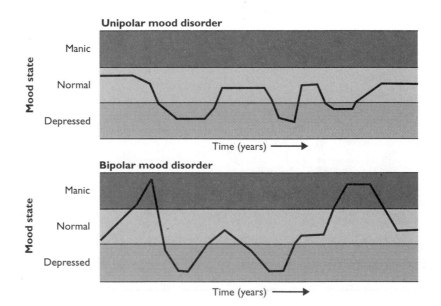

Depressive Disorder

The line between normal and abnormal depression can be difficult to draw (Grove & Andreasen, 1992). Ultimately, a subjective judgment is required. Crucial considerations in this judgment include the duration of the depression and its disruptive effects. When a depression significantly impairs everyday adaptive behavior for more than a few weeks, there is reason for concern.

In *depressive disorders* **people show persistent feelings of sadness and despair and a loss of interest in previous sources of pleasure.** The most common symptoms of depressive disorders are summarized in Figure 15.10. Negative emotions form the heart of the depressive syndrome, but many other symptoms may also appear. Depressed people often give up activities that they used to find enjoyable. For example, a depressed person might quit going bowling or give up a favorite hobby such as photography. Reduced appetite and insomnia are common. People with depression often lack energy. They tend to move sluggishly and talk slowly. Anxiety, irritability, and brooding are frequently observed. Self-esteem tends to sink as the depressed person begins to feel worthless. Depression plunges people into feelings of hopelessness, dejection, and boundless guilt. The severity of abnormal depression varies considerably. The onset of unipolar disorder can occur at any point in the life span and is *not* strongly related to age (Lewinsohn et al., 1986).

How common are depressive disorders? Very common. Studies in the 1980s suggested that about 7% of the U.S. population endures a depressive disorder at some time (Weissman et al., 1991). However, a recent, large-scale study using more probing interview techniques estimated that the lifetime prevalence of depression may be as high as 17% (Blazer et al., 1994). Moreover, evidence suggests that the prevalence of depression is increasing, as it is higher in more recent age cohorts (Lewinsohn et al., 1993). In particular, age cohorts born since World War II appear to have an elevated risk for depression (Smith & Weissman, 1992). The factors underlying this rise in depression are not readily apparent, and researchers are scrambling to collect data that might shed light on this unanticipated trend. Researchers are also hard at work trying to figure out why the prevalence of depression is about twice as high in women as it is in men (Nolen-Hoeksema & Girgus, 1994).

Bipolar Mood Disorder

Bipolar mood disorders **(formerly known as manic-depressive disorders) are marked by the experience of both depressed and manic periods.** The symptoms seen in manic periods generally are the opposite of those seen in depression (see Figure 15.10 for a comparison). In a manic episode, a person's mood becomes elevated to the point of euphoria. Self-esteem skyrockets as the person bubbles over

Figure 15.10
Common symptoms in manic and depressive episodes
The emotional, cognitive, and motor symptoms exhibited in manic and depressive illnesses are largely the opposite of each other. (From Sarason & Sarason, 1987)

Comparison of Manic and Depressive Symptoms

Characteristics	Manic episode	Depressive episode
Emotional	Elated, euphoric, very sociable, impatient at any hindrance	Gloomy, hopeless, socially withdrawn, irritable
Cognitive	Characterized by racing thoughts, flight of ideas, desire for action, and impulsive behavior; talkative, self-confident; experiencing delusions of grandeur	Characterized by slowness of thought processes, obsessive worrying, inability to make decisions, negative self-image, self-blame, and delusions of guilt and disease
Motor	Hyperactive, tireless, requiring less sleep than usual, showing increased sex drive and fluctuating appetite	Less active, tired, experiencing difficulty in sleeping, showing decreased sex drive and decreased appetite

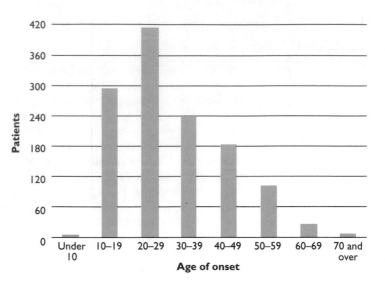

Figure 15.11
Age of onset for bipolar mood disorder
The onset of bipolar disorder typically occurs in adolescence or early adulthood. The data graphed here, which were combined from ten studies, show the distribution of age of onset for 1304 bipolar patients. As you can see, bipolar disorder emerges most frequently during the 20s decade. (From Goodwin & Jamison, 1990)

with optimism, energy, and extravagant plans. Manic individuals become hyperactive and may go for days without sleep. They talk rapidly and shift topics wildly as their minds race at breakneck speed. Judgment is often impaired. Some people in manic periods gamble impulsively, spend money frantically, or become sexually reckless. Like depressive disorders, bipolar disorders vary considerably in severity.

You may be thinking that the euphoria in manic episodes sounds appealing. If so, you are not entirely wrong. In their milder forms, manic states can seem attractive. The increases in energy, self-esteem, and optimism can be deceptively seductive. Because of the increase in energy, many bipolar patients report temporary surges of productivity and creativity (Goodwin & Jamison, 1990).

Although there may be some positive aspects to manic episodes, bipolar mood disorders ultimately prove to be troublesome for most victims. Manic periods often have a paradoxical negative undertow of uneasiness and irritability (Rehm & Tyndall, 1993). Moreover, mild manic episodes usually escalate to higher levels that become scary and disturbing. Impaired judgment leads many victims to do things that they greatly regret later, as you'll see in the following case:

> Robert, a dentist, awoke one morning with the idea that he was the most gifted dental surgeon in his tristate area. He decided that he should try to provide services to as many people as possible, so that more people could benefit from his talents. Thus, he decided to remodel his two-chair dental office, installing 20 booths so that he could simultaneously attend to 20 patients. That same day he drew up plans for this arrangement, telephoned a number of remodelers, and invited bids for the work. Later that day, impatient to get going on his remodeling, he rolled up his sleeves, got himself a sledgehammer, and began to knock down the walls in his office. Annoyed when that didn't go so well, he smashed his dental tools, washbasins, and X-ray equipment. Later, Robert's wife became concerned about his behavior and summoned two of her adult daughters for assistance. The daughters responded quickly, arriving at the family home with their husbands. In the ensuing discussion, Robert—after bragging about his sexual prowess—made advances toward his daughters. He had to be subdued by their husbands. [Adapted from Kleinmuntz, 1980, p. 309]

Although not rare, bipolar disorders are much less common than unipolar depression. Bipolar disorders affect a little under 1% of the population (Weissman et al., 1991). Unlike depressive disorders, bipolar disorders are seen equally often in men and women (Perris, 1992). As Figure 15.11 shows, onset of bipolar disorders is age-related, with the peak of vulnerability occurring between the ages of 20 and 29 (Goodwin & Jamison, 1990).

Etiology of Mood Disorders

We know quite a bit about the etiology of mood disorders, although the puzzle hasn't been assembled completely. There appear to be a number of routes into these disorders, involving intricate interactions between psychological and biological factors.

Genetic Vulnerability

The evidence strongly suggests that genetic factors influence the likelihood of developing major depression or a bipolar mood disorder. In studies that assess the impact of heredity on psychological disorders, investigators look at *concordance rates*. **A concordance rate indicates the percentage of twin pairs or other pairs of relatives that exhibit the same disorder.** If relatives who share more genetic similarity show higher concordance rates than relatives who share less genetic overlap, this finding supports the genetic hypothesis. Twin studies, which compare identical and fraternal twins (see Chapter 2), suggest that genetic factors are involved in mood disorders (Rieder, Kaufmann, & Knowles, 1994). Concordance rates average around 67% for identical twins but only 15% for fraternal twins, who share less genetic similarity. Thus, evidence suggests that heredity can create a *predisposition* to mood disorders. Environmental factors probably determine whether this predisposition is converted into an actual disorder. The influence of genetic factors appears to be stronger for bipolar disorders than for unipolar disorders (Nurnberger & Gershon, 1992).

Neurochemical Factors

Heredity may influence susceptibility to mood disorders by creating a predisposition toward certain types of neurochemical activity in the brain. Correlations have been found between mood disorders and the levels of three neurotransmitters in the brain: norepinephrine, serotonin, and acetylcholine, although the evidence on acetylcholine is modest (Delgado et al., 1992). The details remain elusive, but it seems clear that there is a neurochemical basis for at least some mood disorders. A variety of drug therapies are fairly effective in the treatment of severe mood disorders. Most of these drugs are known to affect the availability (in the brain) of the neurotransmitters that have been related to mood disorders (Davidson, 1992). Since this effect is unlikely to be a coincidence, it bolsters the plausibility of the idea that neurochemical changes produce mood disturbances.

If alterations in neurotransmitter activity are the basis for many mood disorders, what causes these alterations? Such neurochemical changes probably depend on one's reactions to environmental events. Thus, a number of psychological factors have been implicated in the etiology of mood disorders. We'll examine evidence on patterns of thinking, interpersonal style, and stress.

Cognitive Factors

A variety of theories emphasize how cognitive factors contribute to depressive disorders (Abramson, Metalsky, & Alloy, 1988; Beck, 1987; Ellis, 1984; Seligman, 1992). In recent years, theories that focus on people's patterns of *attribution* have generated a great deal of research on the cognitive roots of depression. As noted in Chapters 5 and 6, **attributions are inferences that people draw about the causes of events, others' behavior, and their own behavior.** People routinely make attributions because they want to *understand* their personal fates and the events that take place around them. For example, if your boss criticizes your work, you will probably ask yourself why. Was your work really that sloppy? Was your boss just in a grouchy mood? Was the criticism a manipulative effort to motivate you to work harder? Each of these potential explanations is an attribution.

Reprinted with special permission of King Features Syndicate.

Attributions can be analyzed along a number of dimensions. Three important dimensions are illustrated in Figure 15.12. The most prominent dimension is the degree to which people attribute events to *internal, personal factors versus external, situational factors*. For instance, if you performed poorly on a standardized mathematics test, you might attribute your poor showing to your lack of intelligence (an internal attribution) or to the horrible heat and humidity in the exam room (an external attribution).

Another key dimension is the degree to which people attribute events to factors that are *stable or unstable over time*. Thus, you might blame your poor test performance on exhaustion (an internal but unstable factor that could change next time) or on your low intelligence (an internal but stable factor). Some theories are also interested in the degree to which attributions have *global versus specific implications*. Thus, you might attribute your low test score to your lack of intelligence (which has very general, global implications) or to your poor math ability (the implications are specific to math). Figure 15.12 provides additional examples of attributions that might be made for poor test performance.

Theories that link attribution to depression are interested in the *attributional style* that people display, especially when they are trying to explain failures, setbacks, and other negative events. Studies show that *people who consistently tend to make internal, stable, and global attributions are more prone to depression* than people who exhibit the opposite attributional styles (Robins, 1988; Sweeney, Anderson, & Bailey, 1986). Why? Because in making internal, stable, and global attributions, people blame their setbacks on personal inadequacies (internal) they see as unchangeable (stable) and draw far-reaching (global) conclusions about their lack of worth as human beings. In other words, they draw depressing conclusions about themselves.

Thus, cognitive models of depression maintain that negative thinking is what makes many people feel helpless, hopeless, and dejected. The principal problem with cognitive theories is their difficulty in separating cause from effect (Barnett & Gotlib, 1988). Does negative thinking cause depression? Or does depression cause negative thinking? Could both be caused by a third variable, such as neurochemical changes (see Figure 15.13)? Evidence can be mustered to support all three of these possibilities, suggesting that negative thinking, depression, and neurochemical alterations may feed off of each other as a depression deepens.

Consistent with this line of thinking, Susan Nolen-Hoeksema has found that depressed people who *ruminate* about their depression remain depressed longer than those who try to distract themselves (Nolen-Hoeksema, 1991; Nolen-Hoeksema, Morrow, & Fredrickson, 1993). People who respond to depression with rumination repetitively focus their attention on their depressing feelings, thinking constantly about how sad, lethargic, and unmotivated they are. According to Nolen-Hoeksema, excessive rumination tends to extend and amplify individuals' episodes of depres-

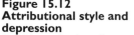
Susan Nolen-Hoeksema

**Figure 15.12
Attributional style and depression**
Possible attributions for poor performance on a standardized math exam are shown here. Note how these explanations vary in terms of whether causes are seen as internal-external, stable-unstable, and specific-global. People who consistently explain their failures with attributions that are internal, stable, and global are particularly vulnerable to depression.

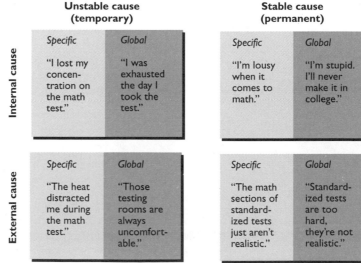

Figure 15.13
Interpreting the correlation between negative thinking and depression
Cognitive theories of depression assert that consistent patterns of negative thinking cause depression. Although these theories are highly plausible, depression could cause negative thoughts, or both could be caused by a third factor, such as neurochemical changes in the brain.

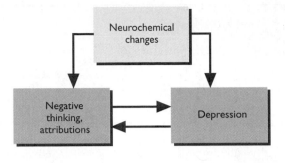

sion. She believes that women are more likely to ruminate than men and that this disparity may be the primary reason why depression is more common in women.

Ironically, depressed individuals' negative thinking may be more realistic than nondepressed individuals' more positive thinking, a phenomenon christened *depressive realism.* This unexpected possibility first surfaced in a study by Lauren Alloy and Lyn Abramson (1979). Depressed and nondepressed subjects worked on a laboratory task. The experimenters controlled how much the subjects' responses on the task (pressing or not pressing a button) influenced their outcomes (turning on a light, winning money). Afterward, subjects were asked to estimate how much their responses influenced their outcomes. As expected, the depressed subjects estimated that they had less control than the nondepressed subjects. However, this difference occurred because the nondepressed subjects *overestimated* their control. In comparison, the depressed subjects made fairly accurate estimates. Since then, numerous studies have shown that depressed subjects' self-evaluations, recall of feedback from others, and attributions for success and failure tend to be more realistic than those made by nondepressed subjects (Alloy & Abramson, 1988). This evidence suggests that depressed people may not be overly pessimistic as much as nondepressed people are overly optimistic.

Interpersonal Roots

Some theorists emphasize how inadequate social skills put people on the road to depressive disorders (Lewinsohn, 1974; Segrin & Abramson, 1994). According to this notion, depression-prone people lack the social finesse needed to acquire many important kinds of reinforcers, such as good friends, top jobs, and desirable spouses. This paucity of reinforcers could understandably lead to negative emotions and depression. Consistent with this theory, researchers have found correlations between poor social skills and depression (Dykman et al., 1991).

Another interpersonal consideration is that depressed people tend to be depressing (Joiner, 1994). Individuals suffering from depression often are irritable and pessimistic. They complain a lot, and they aren't very enjoyable companions. As a consequence, depressed people inadvertently court rejection from those around them (Coyne, Burchill, & Stiles, 1990). Depressed people thus have fewer sources of social support than nondepressed people (Billings, Cronkite, & Moos, 1983). In turn, social rejection and lack of support may aggravate and deepen a person's depression (Segrin & Dillard, 1992).

Precipitating Stress

Mood disorders sometimes appear mysteriously "out of nowhere" in people who are leading benign, nonstressful lives. For this reason, experts used to believe that mood disorders were not influenced much by stress. However, recent advances in the measurement of personal stress have altered this picture. The evidence available today suggests that a moderately strong link exists between stress and the onset of mood disorders (Paykel & Cooper, 1992). Some theorists believe that stress leads to disruptions of biological rhythms and sleep loss, which lead to neurochemical changes that cause mood disorders (Healy & Williams, 1988; Wehr, Sack, & Rosenthal, 1987).

Stress seems to act as a precipitating factor that triggers depression in some people. Of course, many people endure great stress without getting depressed. The impact of stress varies, in part because different people have different degrees of *vulnerability* to mood disorders (Monroe & Simons, 1991). Variations in vulnerability appear to depend primarily on biological makeup. Similar interactions between stress and vulnerability probably influence the development of many kinds of disorders, including those that are next on our agenda—the schizophrenic disorders.

Schizophrenic Disorders

Learning Objective

Describe the prevalence and general symptoms of schizophrenia.

Literally, *schizophrenia* means "split mind." However, when Eugen Bleuler coined the term in 1911, he was referring to the fragmenting of thought processes seen in the disorder—not to a "split personality." Unfortunately, writers in the popular media often assume that the split-mind notion refers to the rare syndrome in which a person manifests two or more personalities. As you have already learned, this syndrome is actually called *multiple-personality disorder.* Schizophrenia is a much more common, and altogether different, type of disorder.

Schizophrenic disorders are a class of disorders marked by disturbances in thought that spill over to affect perceptual, social, and emotional processes. How common is schizophrenia? Prevalence estimates suggest that about 1–1.5% of the population may suffer from schizophrenic disorders (Keith, Regier, & Rae, 1991). That may not sound like much, but it means that in the United States alone there may be 4 million people troubled by schizophrenic disturbances. Moreover, schizophrenia is a severe, debilitating disorder that places a heavy burden on our mental health system. Flynn (1994) estimates that schizophrenia accounts for about three-quarters of the total U.S. tax dollars spent on the treatment of mental illness.

General Symptoms

There are a number of distinct schizophrenic syndromes, but they share some general characteristics that we will examine before looking at the subtypes. Many of these characteristics are apparent in the following case history (adapted from Sheehan, 1982).

Recommended Reading

Surviving Schizophrenia: A Family Manual

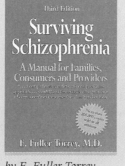

by E. Fuller Torrey
(HarperCollins, 1995)

E. Fuller Torrey is a prominent psychiatrist who has specialized in the treatment and study of schizophrenia. He has conducted basic research and written technical articles on schizophrenia, as well as this practical book intended for the lay public. Torrey points out that many myths surrounding schizophrenia have added to the anguish of families victimized by this illness. He explains that schizophrenia is *not* caused by childhood trauma, domineering mothers, or passive fathers. He discusses how genetic vulnerability, flawed brain chemistry, and other factors contribute to the development of schizophrenic disorders. Torrey discusses the treatment of schizophrenia at great length. He also explains the various ways in which the disease can evolve. Some of the best material is found in chapters on what the patient needs and what the family needs.

Throughout the book, Torrey writes with clarity, eloquence, and conviction. He's not reluctant to express strong opinions. For instance, in an appendix he lists the ten worst readings on schizophrenia (along with the ten best), and his evaluations are brutal. He characterizes one book as "absurd drivel" and dismisses another by saying, "If a prize were to be given to the book which has produced the most confusion about schizophrenia over the past 20 years, this book would win going away." Scientists and academicians are usually reluctant to express such strong opinions, and Torrey's candor is remarkably refreshing.

Psychoanalysis is to schizophrenia as Laetrile is to cancer. Both have enjoyed surprising popularity considering the fact that they lack scientific basis, are completely ineffective, may make the patient worse if administered in toxic doses, and still attract patients who are willing to pay vast sums of money in desperation for a cure. Freud himself recognized that schizophrenic patients "are inaccessible to the influence of psychoanalysis and cannot be cured by our endeavors," but that observation has not stopped his followers from trying. [p. 220]

Sylvia was first diagnosed as schizophrenic at age 15. She has been in and out of many different types of psychiatric facilities since then. She has never been able to hold a job for any length of time. During severe flare-ups of her disorder, her personal hygiene deteriorates. She rarely washes, wears clothes that neither fit nor match, smears makeup on heavily but randomly, and slops food all over herself. Sylvia occasionally hears voices talking to her. She tends to be argumentative, aggressive, and emotionally volatile. Over the years, she has been involved in innumerable fights with fellow patients, psychiatric staff members, and strangers. Her thoughts can be highly irrational, as is apparent from the following quotation:

> "Mick Jagger wants to marry me. If I have Mick Jagger, I don't have to covet Geraldo Rivera. Mick Jagger is St. Nicholas and the Maharishi is Santa Claus. I want to form a gospel rock group called the Thorn Oil, but Geraldo wants me to be the music critic on *Eyewitness News,* so what can I do? Got to listen to my boyfriend. Teddy Kennedy cured me of my ugliness. I'm pregnant with the son of God. I'm going to marry David Berkowitz and get it over with. Creedmoor is the headquarters of the American Nazi Party. They're eating the patients here. Archie Bunker wants me to play his niece on his TV show. I work for Epic Records. I'm Joan of Arc. I'm Florence Nightingale. The door between the ward and the porch is the dividing line between New York and California. Divorce isn't a piece of paper, it's a feeling. Forget about Zip Codes. I need shock treatment. The body is run by electricity. My wiring is all faulty. A fly is a teen-age wasp. I'm marrying an accountant. I'm in the Pentecostal Church, but I'm considering switching my loyalty to the Charismatic Church." [Sheehan, 1982, pp. 104–105]

Sylvia's case clearly shows that schizophrenic thinking can be bizarre and that schizophrenia is a brutally serious, psychologically disfiguring disorder. Although no single symptom is inevitably present, the following symptoms are commonly seen in schizophrenia (Black & Andreasen, 1994; Grebb & Cancro, 1989).

Irrational Thought

Disturbed, irrational thought processes are the central feature of schizophrenic disorders. Various kinds of delusions are common. *Delusions* **are false beliefs that are maintained even though they clearly are out of touch with reality.** For example, one patient's delusion that he is a tiger (with a deformed body) has persisted for 15 years (Kulick, Pope, & Keck, 1990). More typically, affected persons believe that their private thoughts are being broadcast to other people or that thoughts are being injected into their mind against their will (Maher & Spitzer, 1993). In *delusions of grandeur,* people maintain that they are extremely famous or important. Sylvia expressed an endless array of grandiose delusions, such as thinking that Mick Jagger wanted to marry her, that she dictated the hobbit stories to Tolkien, and that she was going to win the Nobel Prize for medicine.

In addition to delusions, the schizophrenic person's train of thought deteriorates. Thinking becomes chaotic rather than logical and linear. There is a "loosening of associations" as the schizophrenic shifts topics in disjointed ways. The quotation from Sylvia illustrates this symptom dramatically. The entire passage involves a wild flight of ideas, but at one point (beginning with the sentence "Creedmoor is the headquarters . . .") she rattles off ten consecutive sentences that have no apparent connection to one another.

Deterioration of Adaptive Behavior

Schizophrenia usually involves a noticeable deterioration in the quality of one's routine functioning in work, social relations, and personal care. Friends will often make remarks such as "Hal just isn't himself anymore." This deterioration is readily apparent in Sylvia's inability to get along with others or function in the work world. It's also apparent in her neglect of personal hygiene.

Distorted Perception

A variety of perceptual distortions may occur in schizophrenia, with the most common being auditory hallucinations. *Hallucinations* **are sensory perceptions that** occur in the absence of a real, external stimulus or that represent gross distortions of perceptual input. Schizophrenics frequently report that they hear voices of nonexistent or absent people talking to them. Sylvia, for instance, heard messages from former Beatle Paul McCartney. These voices often provide an insulting running commentary on the person's behavior ("You're an idiot for shaking his hand"). The voices may be argumentative ("You don't need a bath"), and they may issue commands ("Prepare your home for visitors from outer space").

Disturbed Emotion

Normal emotional tone can be disrupted in schizophrenia in a variety of ways. Some victims show a flattening of emotions. In other words, they show little emotional responsiveness. Others show inappropriate emotional responses that don't jell with the situation or with what they are saying. For instance, a schizophrenic patient might cry over a Smurfs cartoon and then laugh about a news story describing a child's tragic death. People with schizophrenia may also become emotionally volatile. This pattern was displayed by Sylvia, who often overreacted emotionally in erratic, unpredictable ways.

Subtypes

Learning Objective

Describe the four subtypes of schizophrenic disorders.

Four subtypes of schizophrenic disorders are recognized, including a category for people who don't fit neatly into any of the first three categories.

Paranoid Type

As its name implies, *paranoid schizophrenia* **is dominated by delusions of persecution, along with delusions of grandeur.** In this common form of schizophrenia, people come to believe that they have many enemies who want to harass and oppress them. They may become suspicious of friends and relatives, or they may attribute the persecution to mysterious, unknown persons. They are convinced that they are being watched and manipulated in malicious ways. To make sense of this persecution, they often develop delusions of grandeur. They believe that they must be enormously important, frequently seeing themselves as great inventors or as great religious or political leaders. For example, in the case described at the beginning of the chapter, Ed's belief that he was president of the United States was a delusion of grandeur.

Catatonic Type

Catatonic schizophrenia **is marked by striking motor disturbances, ranging from muscular rigidity to random motor activity.** Some catatonics go into an extreme form of withdrawal known as a catatonic stupor. They may remain virtually motionless and seem oblivious to the environment around them for long periods of time. Others go into a state of catatonic excitement. They become hyperactive and incoherent. Some alternate between these dramatic extremes. The catatonic subtype is not particularly common, and its prevalence seems to be declining.

Disorganized Type

In *disorganized schizophrenia*, **a particularly severe deterioration of adaptive behavior is seen.** Prominent symptoms include emotional indifference, frequent incoherence, and virtually complete social withdrawal. Aimless babbling and giggling are common. Delusions often center on bodily functions ("My brain is melting out my ears").

Undifferentiated Type

People who are clearly schizophrenic but who cannot be placed into any of the three previous categories are said to have *undifferentiated schizophrenia*, **which is**

Figure 15.14
Examples of positive and negative symptoms in schizophrenia

Some theorists believe that schizophrenic disorders should be classified into just two types, depending on whether patients exhibit mostly positive symptoms (behavioral excesses) or negative symptoms (behavioral deficits). Examples of negative symptoms seen in people with schizophrenic disorders are listed on the left, with examples of positive symptoms listed on the right. The percentages, based on a sample of 111 schizophrenic patients studied by Andreasen (1987), provide an indication of how common each specific symptom is.

Positive and Negative Symptoms in Schizophrenia

Negative symptoms	Percent of patients	Positive symptoms	Percent of patients
Few friendship relationships	96	Delusions of persecution	81
Few recreational interests	95	Auditory hallucinations	75
Lack of persistence at work or school	95	Delusions of being controlled	46
Impaired grooming or hygiene	87	Derailment of thought	45
Paucity of expressive gestures	81	Delusions of grandeur	39
Social inattentiveness	78	Bizarre social, sexual behavior	33
Emotional nonresponsiveness	64	Delusions of thought insertion	31
Inappropriate emotion	63	Aggressive, agitated behavior	27
Poverty of speech	53	Incoherent thought	23

Nancy Andreasen

marked by idiosyncratic mixtures of schizophrenic symptoms. The undifferentiated subtype is fairly common.

Some theorists are beginning to doubt the value of dividing schizophrenic disorders into these four subtypes (Nicholson & Neufeld, 1993). Critics note that the catatonic subtype is disappearing and that undifferentiated cases aren't a subtype as much as a hodgepodge of "leftovers." Critics also point out that the classic schizophrenic subtypes do not differ meaningfully in etiology, prognosis, or response to treatment. The absence of such differences casts doubt on the value of the current classification scheme.

Because of such problems, Nancy Andreasen (1990) and others (Carpenter, 1992; McGlashan & Fenton, 1992) have proposed an alternative approach to subtyping. This new scheme divides schizophrenic disorders into just two categories based on the predominance of negative versus positive symptoms (see Figure 15.14). *Negative symptoms* include behavioral deficits, such as flattened emotions, social withdrawal, apathy, impaired attention, and poverty of speech. *Positive symptoms* include behavioral excesses or peculiarities, such as hallucinations, delusions, bizarre behavior, and wild flights of ideas. Andreasen believes that researchers will find consistent differences between these two subtypes in etiology, prognosis, and response to treatment. Only time (and research) will tell whether the proposed subdivision based on positive versus negative symptoms will prove useful.

Course and Outcome

Learning Objective

Describe how the course of schizophrenia can unfold in three different patterns and identify factors related to the prognosis for schizophrenic patients.

Schizophrenic disorders usually emerge during adolescence or early adulthood and only rarely after age 45 (Murphy & Helzer, 1986). The emergence of schizophrenia may be either sudden or gradual. Once it clearly emerges, the course of schizophrenia is variable (Ciompi, 1980; Marengo et al., 1991), but patients tend to fall into three broad groups. Some patients, presumably those with milder disorders, are treated successfully and enjoy a full recovery. With other patients, treatment produces a partial recovery so that they can return to their normal life. However, they experience frequent relapses and are in and out of treatment facilities for much of the remainder of their lives. Finally, a third group of patients endure chronic illness that sometimes results in permanent hospitalization. Overall, less than half of schizophrenic patients enjoy a significant recovery (Hegarty et al., 1994).

A number of factors are related to the likelihood of recovery from schizophrenic disorders (Lehmann & Cancro, 1985). A patient has a relatively *favorable prognosis* when (1) the onset of the disorder has been sudden rather than gradual, (2) the onset has occurred at a later age, (3) the patient's social and work adjustment were relatively good prior to the onset of the disorder, and (4) the patient has a relatively healthy, supportive family situation to return to. All of these predictors are concerned with the etiology of schizophrenic illness, which is the matter we turn to next.

Etiology of Schizophrenia

Most of us can identify, at least to some extent, with people who suffer from mood disorders, somatoform disorders, and anxiety disorders. You probably can imagine events that might leave you struggling with depression, or grappling with anxiety, or worrying about your physical health. But what could possibly have led Ed to believe that he had been fighting space wars and vampires? What could account for Sylvia thinking that she was Joan of Arc? Or that she dictated the hobbit novels to Tolkien? As mystifying as these delusions may seem, you'll see that the etiology of schizophrenic disorders is not all that different from the etiology of other disorders. We'll begin our discussion by examining the matter of genetic vulnerability.

Genetic Vulnerability

Evidence is plentiful that hereditary factors play a role in the development of schizophrenic disorders (Rieder et al., 1994). For instance, in twin studies, concordance rates average around 48% for identical twins, in comparison to about 17% for fraternal twins (Gottesman, 1991). Studies also indicate that a child born to two schizophrenic parents has about a 46% probability of developing a schizophrenic disorder (as compared to the probability of about 1% for the population as a whole). These and other findings that demonstrate the genetic roots of schizophrenia are summarized in Figure 15.15. Overall, the picture is similar to that seen for mood disorders. Several converging lines of evidence indicate that people inherit a genetically transmitted *vulnerability* to schizophrenia (Fowles, 1992).

Neurochemical Factors

Like mood disorders, schizophrenic disorders appear to be accompanied by changes in neurotransmitter activity in the brain (Hollandsworth, 1990). Excess *dopamine* activity has been implicated as the probable cause of schizophrenia because most of the drugs that are useful in the treatment of schizophrenia are known to dampen dopamine activity in the brain (Black & Andreasen, 1994). However, the evidence linking schizophrenia to high dopamine levels has been riddled with inconsistencies, complexities, and interpretive problems (Carson & Sanislow, 1993). Many of these inconsistencies may be resolved by a new theory that links schizophrenia to abnormally high dopamine activity in subcortical areas of the brain, coupled with abnormally low dopamine activity in the prefrontal cortex (Davis et al., 1991). Thus,

Figure 15.15
Genetic vulnerability to schizophrenic disorders
Relatives of schizophrenic patients have an elevated risk for schizophrenia. This risk is greater among closer relatives. Although environment also plays a role in the etiology of schizophrenia, the concordance rates shown here suggest that there must be a genetic vulnerability to the disorder. These concordance estimates are based on pooled data from 40 studies conducted between 1920 and 1987. (Data from Gottesman, 1991)

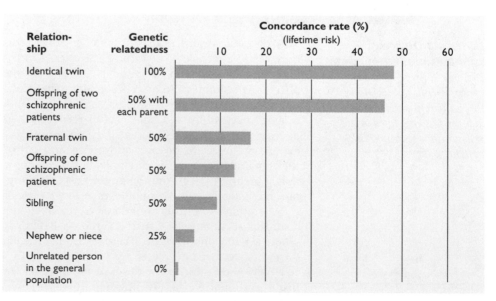

investigators are making progress in their search for the neurochemical bases of schizophrenia.

Structural Abnormalities in the Brain

Various studies have suggested that schizophrenic individuals have difficulty focusing their attention (Dawson et al., 1993). Some theorists believe that many bizarre aspects of schizophrenic behavior may be due mainly to an inability to filter out unimportant stimuli (Judd et al., 1992). This lack of selectivity supposedly leaves victims of the disorder flooded with overwhelming, confusing sensory input.

These problems with attention suggest that schizophrenic disorders may be caused by neurological defects (Perry & Braff, 1994). Until recently, this theory was based more on speculation than on actual research. However, new advances in brain-imaging technology are beginning to yield some intriguing data. The findings suggest an association between enlarged brain ventricles (the hollow, fluid-filled cavities in the brain shown in Figure 15.16) and chronic schizophrenic disturbance (Raz, 1993; Suddath et al., 1990).

The significance of enlarged ventricles in the brain is hotly debated, however. Enlarged ventricles are not unique to schizophrenia. They are a sign of many kinds of brain pathology. Furthermore, even if the association between enlarged ventricles and schizophrenia is replicated consistently, it will be difficult to sort out whether this brain abnormality is a cause or an effect of schizophrenia.

Communication Deviance

Over the years, hundreds of investigators have tried to relate patterns of family interaction to the development of schizophrenia. Popular theories have come and gone as empirical evidence has overturned once-plausible hypotheses (Goldstein, 1988). Vigorous research and debate in this area continue today. The current emphasis is on families' communication patterns and their expression of emotions.

Various theorists assert that vulnerability to schizophrenia is increased by exposure to defective interpersonal communication during childhood. Studies have found a relationship between schizophrenia and *communication deviance* (Goldstein, 1987;

Learning Objective
_____

Summarize how communication deviance, expressed emotion, and stress may contribute to schizophrenia.

Figure 15.16
Schizophrenia and the ventricles of the brain
Cerebrospinal fluid (CSF) circulates around the brain and spinal cord. The hollow cavities in the brain filled with CSF are called ventricles. The four ventricles in the human brain are depicted here. Recent studies with new brain-imaging techniques suggest that an association exists between enlarged ventricles in the brain and the occurrence of schizophrenic disturbance.

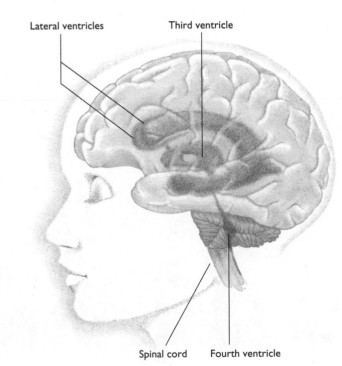

Lateral ventricles   Third ventricle

Spinal cord   Fourth ventricle

Singer, Wynne, & Toohey, 1978). Communication deviance includes unintelligible speech, stories with no endings, heavy use of unusual words, extensive contradictions, and poor attention to children's communication efforts. The evidence suggests that schizophrenia is more likely to develop when youngsters grow up in homes characterized by vague, muddled, fragmented communication. Researchers speculate that communication deviance gradually undermines a child's sense of reality and encourages youngsters to withdraw into their own private worlds, setting the stage for schizophrenic thinking later in life.

Expressed Emotion

Studies of expressed emotion have primarily focused on how this element of family dynamics influences the *course* of schizophrenic illness after the onset of the disorder (Leff & Vaughn, 1985). *Expressed emotion* reflects the degree to which a relative of a schizophrenic patient displays highly critical or emotionally overinvolved attitudes toward the patient. Audiotaped interviews are used to assess relatives' expressed emotion. The interviews are carefully evaluated for critical comments, resentment toward the patient, and excessive emotional involvement (overprotective, overconcerned attitudes).

Studies show that a family's expressed emotion is a good predictor of the course of a schizophrenic patient's illness (Parker & Hadzi-Pavlovic, 1990). After release from a hospital, schizophrenic patients who return to a family high in expressed emotion show relapse rates three or four times that of patients who return to a family low in expressed emotion. Part of the problem for patients returning to homes high in expressed emotion is that their families probably are sources of more stress than social support. And like virtually all mental disorders, schizophrenia is influenced to some extent by life stress.

Precipitating Stress

Most theories of schizophrenia assume that stress plays a key role in triggering schizophrenic disorders (Fowles, 1992; Zubin, 1986). According to this notion, various biological and psychological factors influence individuals' *vulnerability* to schizophrenia. High stress may then serve to precipitate a schizophrenic disorder in someone who is vulnerable. A recent study indicates that high stress can also trigger relapses in schizophrenic patients who have made progress toward recovery (Ventura et al., 1989).

Application

Understanding and Preventing Suicide

Answer the following "true" or "false."

1. *People who talk about suicide usually don't commit suicide.*

2. *Suicides usually take place with little or no warning.*

3. *People who attempt suicide are fully intent on dying.*

4. *People who are suicidal remain so forever.*

The four statements above are all false. They are myths about suicide that we will dispose of momentarily. First, however, let's discuss the magnitude of this tragic problem.

Prevalence of Suicide

It is estimated that there are about 250,000 suicide attempts in the United States each year. Roughly one in eight of these attempts is "successful." This makes suicide the ninth leading cause of death in the United States, accounting for about 30,000 deaths annually (Ghosh & Victor, 1994). Worse yet, official statistics may underestimate the scope of the problem. Many suicides are disguised as accidents, either by the suicidal person or by the survivors who try to cover up afterward. Thus, experts estimate that there may be far more suicides than officially reported (Hirschfeld & Davidson, 1988; K. Smith, 1991).

Who Commits Suicide?

Learning Objective

Outline how demographic factors are related to the prevalence of suicide.

Anyone can commit suicide. No segment of society is immune. Nonetheless, some groups are at higher risk than others (Buda & Tsuang, 1990; Cross & Hirschfeld, 1986). For instance, the prevalence of suicide varies according to *marital status*. Married people commit suicide less often than divorced, bereaved, or single people. In regard to race, suicide rates are higher among white Americans than African Americans.

Anyone can commit suicide—including successful individuals one might expect to be quite content with their lives. The roster of those who have committed suicide includes many well-known and widely admired people, such as the two pictured here: rock star Kurt Cobain and White House deputy counsel Vince Foster.

Figure 15.17
Suicide rates in the United States by age and gender
At all ages, more men than women commit suicide, but the age patterns for the two genders are noticeably different. The rate of male suicide peaks during the retirement years, whereas the rate of female suicide peaks in middle adulthood.

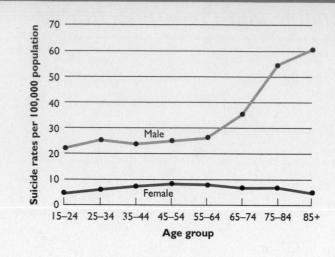

Gender and *age* have complex relations to suicide rates. On the one hand, women *attempt* suicide more often than men. On the other hand, men are more likely to actually kill themselves in an attempt, so they *complete* four times as many suicides as women. In regard to *age*, suicide attempts peak between ages 24 and 44, but completed suicides are most frequent after age 55. However, age trends are different for men and women, as you can see in Figure 15.17.

Unfortunately, suicide rates have tripled among adolescents and young adults in the last several decades (Brent & Kolko, 1990). Among *college students*, academic pressures and setbacks do *not* appear to be the principal cause of suicide. Interpersonal problems and loneliness seem to be more important (see Figure 15.18). Serious physical illness can increase the risk of suicide, as evidenced by elevated suicide rates among people with AIDS (Ghosh & Victor, 1994).

Suicide is *not* committed only by people with severe mental illness, although elevated suicide rates are found for most categories of psychological disorders (Black & Winokur, 1990). As you might predict, suicide rates are highest for people with mood disorders. Figure 15.19 shows how mood disorders and suicide attempts overlap. Experts estimate that about 15% of patients with mood disorders eventually commit suicide (Jefferson & Greist, 1994). Alcohol and drug disorders are also cor-

Figure 15.18
Personal problems reported by suicidal students
Westefeld and Furr (1987) gathered data on the problems mentioned by students who had attempted suicide or who reported suicidal thoughts. On the whole, interpersonal problems dominate this list.

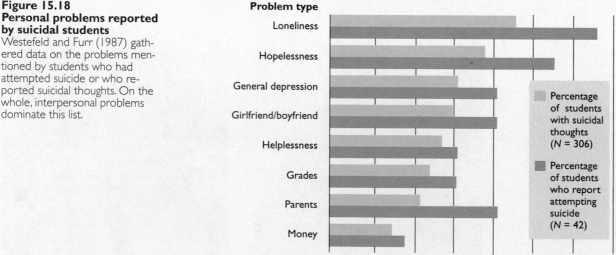

Figure 15.19
The relationship between suicide and mood disorders
Two groups with elevated risk of suicide are people with mood disorders and people who have made previous suicide attempts. Between them, these groups account for a high percentage of suicides. (Adapted from Avery & Winokur, 1978)

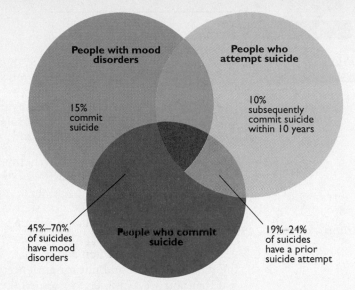

People with mood disorders

15% commit suicide

People who attempt suicide

10% subsequently commit suicide within 10 years

45%–70% of suicides have mood disorders

People who commit suicide

19%–21% of suicides have a prior suicide attempt

related with an elevated incidence of suicide (Lesage et al., 1994). Although the correlations between demographic factors and suicide rates are interesting, demographic factors have little practical value in predicting suicide at the individual level (Garland & Zigler, 1993).

Myths About Suicide

We began with four false statements about suicide. Let's examine these myths as they have been discussed by various suicide experts (Fremouw, de Perczel, & Ellis, 1990; Shneidman, 1985).

Myth 1: People who talk about suicide don't actually commit suicide. Undoubtedly, many people who threaten suicide never go through with it. Nonetheless, there is no group at higher risk for suicide than those who openly discuss the possibility. Many people who kill themselves have a history of earlier threats that they did not carry out.

Myth 2: Suicide usually takes place with little or no warning. It is estimated that eight out of ten suicide attempts are preceded by some kind of warning. These warnings may range from clear threats to vague statements. For example, at dinner with friends the night before he committed suicide, one prominent attorney cut up his American Express card, saying, "I'm not going to need this anymore." The probability of an actual suicide attempt is greatest when a threat is clear, when it includes a detailed plan, and when the plan involves a relatively deadly method.

Myth 3: People who attempt suicide are fully intent on dying. It appears that only about 3–5% of those who attempt suicide definitely want to die. About 30% of the people who make an attempt seem ambivalent. They arrange things so that their fate is largely a matter of chance. The remaining two-thirds of suicide attempts are made by people who appear to have no interest in dying. They only want to send out a very dramatic distress signal. Thus, they arrange their suicide so that a rescue is quite likely. These variations in intent probably explain why only about one-eighth of suicide attempts end in death.

Myth 4: People who are suicidal remain so forever. Many people who become suicidal do so for a limited period of time. If they manage to ride through their crisis period, thoughts of suicide may disappear entirely. Apparently, time heals many wounds—if it is given the opportunity.

Preventing Suicide

Learning Objective

Discuss advice on preventing suicide.

There is no simple and dependable way to prevent someone from going ahead with a threatened suicide. One expert on suicide (Wekstein, 1979) makes the point that "perhaps nobody really knows *exactly* what to do when dealing with an imminent suicide" (p. 129). However, we will review some general advice that may be useful if you ever have to help someone through a suicidal crisis (Fremouw et al., 1990; Rosenthal, 1988; Shneidman, Farberow, & Litman, 1970).

1. *Take suicidal talk seriously.* When people talk about suicide in vague generalities, it's easy to dismiss it as "idle talk" and let it go. However, people who talk about suicide are a high-risk group and their veiled threats should not be ignored. According to Rosenthal (1988), the first step in suicide prevention is to directly ask such people if they're contemplating suicide.

2. *Provide empathy and social support.* It is important to show the suicidal person that you care. People often contemplate suicide because they see the world around them as indifferent and uncaring. Hence, you must demonstrate to the suicidal person that you are genuinely concerned. Even if you are thrust into a situation where you barely know the suicidal person, you need to provide empathy. Suicide threats are often a last-ditch cry for help. It is therefore imperative that you offer to help.

3. *Identify and clarify the crucial problem.* The suicidal person is often terribly confused and feels lost in a sea of frustration and problems. It is a good idea to try to help sort through this confusion. Encourage the person to try to identify the crucial problem. Once it is isolated, the problem may not seem quite so overwhelming. It may also help to point out that the person's confusion is clouding his or her ability to rationally judge the seriousness of the problem.

4. *Suggest alternative courses of action.* People thinking about suicide often see it as the only solution to their problems. This is obviously an irrational view. Try to chip away at this premise by offering other possible solutions for the problem that has been identified as crucial. Suicidal people often are too distraught and disoriented to do this on their own. Therefore, it may help if you offer alternatives.

5. *Capitalize on any doubts.* For most people, life is not easy to give up. They are racked by doubts about the wisdom of their decision. Many people will voice their unique reasons for doubting whether they should take the suicidal path. Zero in on these doubts. They may be your best arguments for life over death. For instance, if a person expresses concern about how her or his suicide will affect family members, capitalize on this source of doubt.

6. *Encourage professional consultation.* Most mental health professionals have at least some experience in dealing with suicidal crises. Many cities have suicide prevention centers with 24-hour hotlines. These centers are staffed with people who have been specially trained to deal with suicidal problems. It is important to try to get a suicidal person to seek professional assistance. The mere fact that you have talked a person out of attempting a threatened suicide does not mean that the crisis is over. The contemplation of suicide indicates that a person is experiencing great distress. Given this reality, professional intervention is crucial.

Key Ideas

Abnormal Behavior: Myths, Realities, and Controversies
• The medical model assumes that it is useful to view abnormal behavior as a disease. There are serious problems with the medical model, but the disease analogy is useful if one remembers that it is only an analogy. Three criteria are used in deciding whether people suffer from psychological disorders: deviance, personal distress, and maladaptive behavior. Often, it is difficult to clearly draw a line between normality and abnormality.
• DSM-IV is the official psychodiagnostic classification system in the United States. This system describes over 200 disorders and asks for information about patients on five axes. Psychological disorders are more common than widely believed, affecting roughly one-third of the population.

Anxiety Disorders
• The anxiety disorders include generalized anxiety disorder, phobic disorder, panic disorder, and obsessive-compulsive disorder. These disorders have been linked to temperament, neurochemical abnormalities in the brain, and mitral valve prolapse. Many anxiety responses, especially phobias, may be caused by classical conditioning and maintained by operant conditioning. Certain patterns of thinking and stress may also contribute to the onset of these disorders.

Somatoform Disorders
• Somatoform disorders include somatization disorder, conversion disorder, and hypochondriasis. These disorders often emerge in people with highly suggestible, histrionic personalities. Somatoform disorders may be a learned avoidance strategy reinforced by attention and sympathy.

Dissociative Disorders
• Dissociative disorders include dissociative amnesia and fugue, and multiple personality. These disorders appear to be uncommon, although there is some controversy about the prevalence of multiple-personality disorder. Stress and childhood trauma may contribute to multiple-personality disorder, but overall, the causes of dissociative disorders are not well understood.

Mood Disorders
• The principal mood disorders are major (unipolar) depression and bipolar mood disorder. People vary in their genetic vulnerability to mood disorders, which are accompanied by changes in neurochemical activity in the brain. Cognitive models posit that an attributional style emphasizing internal, stable, and global attributions contributes to depression. Depression is often rooted in interpersonal inadequacies and sometimes is stress related.

Schizophrenic Disorders
• Schizophrenic disorders are characterized by deterioration of adaptive behavior, irrational thought, distorted perception, and disturbed mood. Schizophrenic disorders are classified as paranoid, catatonic, disorganized, or undifferentiated, although a new classification scheme is under study. Research has linked schizophrenia to genetic vulnerability, changes in neurotransmitter activity, and structural abnormalities in the brain. Precipitating stress and unhealthy family dynamics, especially communication deviance and expressed emotion, may also contribute.

Application: Understanding and Preventing Suicide
• Suicide attempts result in death about one-eighth of the time, and suicide is the ninth leading cause of death in the United States. People with psychological disorders, especially mood disorders, show elevated suicide rates. Suicidal people usually provide warnings, often are not intent on dying, and may not remain suicidal if they survive their crisis. Efforts at suicide prevention emphasize empathy, clarification of the person's problems, and professional assistance.

Key Terms

Agoraphobia
Anxiety disorders
Attributions
Bipolar mood disorder
Catatonic schizophrenia
Concordance rate
Conversion disorder
Delusions
Depressive disorder
Diagnosis
Disorganized schizophrenia
Dissociative amnesia
Dissociative disorders
Dissociative fugue
Dissociative identity disorder
Epidemiology
Etiology
Generalized anxiety disorder
Hallucinations
Hypochondriasis
Medical model
Mood disorders
Multiple-personality disorder
Neurotransmitters
Obsessive-compulsive disorder
Panic disorder
Paranoid schizophrenia
Phobic disorder
Prevalence
Prognosis
Psychosomatic diseases
Schizophrenic disorders
Somatization disorder
Somatoform disorders
Transvestism
Undifferentiated schizophrenia

Key People

Lauren Alloy and Lyn Abramson
Nancy Andreasen
Susan Nolen-Hoeksema
David Rosenhan
Martin Seligman
Thomas Szasz

16 *Psychotherapy*

$\mathcal{W}$hat comes to mind when you hear the term *psychotherapy*? If you're like most people, you probably picture a troubled patient lying on a couch in a therapist's office, with the therapist asking penetrating questions and providing sage advice. Typically, people believe that psychotherapy is only for those who are "sick" and that therapists have special powers that allow them to "see through" their clients. It is also widely believed that therapy requires years of deep probing into a client's innermost secrets. Many people further assume that therapists routinely tell their patients how to lead their lives. Like most stereotypes, this picture of psychotherapy is a mixture of fact and fiction, as you'll see in the upcoming pages.

In this chapter, we'll take a down-to-earth look at the complex process of psychotherapy. We'll start by discussing some general questions about the provision of therapy. Who seeks therapy? What kinds of professionals provide therapy? How many different types of therapy are there? After we've considered these general issues, we'll examine some of the more widely used approaches to psychotherapy, analyzing their goals, techniques, and effectiveness. In the Application at the end of the chapter, we focus on practical issues in case you ever have to advise someone about seeking psychotherapy.

The Elements of Psychotherapy: Treatments, Clients, and Therapists

It wasn't always so, but today people can choose from a bewildering array of approaches to psychotherapy. The immense diversity of therapeutic treatments makes it extremely difficult to define the concept of *psychotherapy*. After organizing an unprecedented conference that brought together many of the world's leading authorities on psychotherapy, Jeffrey Zeig (1987) commented, "I do not believe there is any capsule definition of psychotherapy on which the 26 presenters could agree" (p. xix). In lieu of a definition, we can identify a few basic elements that the various approaches to therapy have in common. All psychotherapies involve a helping relationship (the treatment) between a professional with special training (the therapist) and another person in need of help (the client). As we look at each of these elements—the treatment, the therapist, and the client—you'll see the diverse nature of modern psychotherapy.

This book is billed as a "consumer's guide to the ins and outs of therapy." The Ehrenbergs provide a frank and down-to-earth discussion of practical issues relating to psychotherapy. Most books on therapy are devoted to explaining the various theoretical approaches to therapy. The authors go far beyond this, tackling practical issues such as how to select a therapist, how to help make therapy work for you, and how to judge whether therapy is doing you any good. They also discuss mundane but important details such as fees, insurance, missed sessions, and emergency phone calls. The Ehrenbergs' goal is to make therapy less intimidating and mysterious. They succeed handsomely in this endeavor.

> Even without the cultural barriers, it's not easy to get started in psychotherapy. To begin with, there is the uncertainty about how to go about doing it: how do you pick a therapist, what do you say when you go to one, and what do you have to do once you're in therapy? If you are thinking of therapy for yourself, you probably feel anxious about starting off on a new experience in which a lot is at stake and the outcome is uncertain. You are not sure what is going to happen to you and how you are going to take to it. You might be worried about what other people are going to think of you. On top of all this, you have to overcome a certain amount of lethargy. Getting started means putting in time and effort, it means planning and committing yourself to a new routine, and it usually means having to make financial sacrifices. [p. 26]

Treatments: How Many Types Are There?

Learning Objective

Identify the three major categories of psychotherapy.

In their efforts to help people, psychotherapists use many different methods of treatment. Included among them are discussion, emotional support, persuasion, conditioning procedures, relaxation training, role playing, prescription of drugs, biofeedback, and group therapy. Some therapists also use a variety of less conventional procedures, such as rebirthing, poetry therapy, and primal therapy. No one knows exactly how many approaches to treatment are in use. One expert (Kazdin, 1994) estimates that there may be over 400 distinct types of psychotherapy! Fortunately, we can impose some order on this chaos. As varied as therapists' procedures are, approaches to treatment can be classified into three major categories:

1. *Insight therapies.* Insight therapy is "talk therapy" in the tradition of Freud's psychoanalysis. This is probably the approach to treatment that you envision when you think of psychotherapy. In insight therapies, clients engage in complex, often lengthy verbal interactions with their therapists. The goal in these discussions is to pursue increased insight regarding the nature of the client's difficulties and to sort through possible solutions. Insight therapy can be conducted with an individual or with a group.

2. *Behavior therapies.* Behavior therapies are based on the principles of learning and conditioning, which were introduced in Chapter 2. Instead of emphasizing personal insights, behavior therapists make direct efforts to alter problematic responses (phobic behaviors, for instance) and maladaptive habits (drug use, for instance). Behavior therapists work on changing clients' overt behaviors. They use different procedures for different kinds of problems. Most of their procedures involve either classical conditioning or operant conditioning.

3. *Biomedical therapies.* Biomedical approaches to therapy involve interventions into a person's biological functioning. The most widely used procedures are the prescription of drugs and electroconvulsive (shock) therapy. As the name bio*medical* therapies suggests, these treatments have traditionally been provided only by physicians with a medical degree (usually psychiatrists). However, this situation may change, as psychologists have recently begun to campaign for limited prescription privileges and the federal government has funded a pilot study to assess the feasibility of this proposal (VandenBos, Cummings, & DeLeon, 1992).

We will examine approaches to therapy that fall into each of these three categories. Although we'll find very different methods in each category, the three major classes of treatment are not entirely incompatible. For example, a client might be seen in insight therapy and be given medication at the same time.

Clients: Who Seeks Therapy?

Learning Objective

Discuss why people do or do not seek psychotherapy.

In the therapeutic triad (treatments, therapists, clients), the greatest diversity of all is seen among the clients. They bring to therapy the full range of human problems: anxiety, depression, unsatisfactory interpersonal relations, troublesome habits, poor self-control, low self-esteem, marital conflicts, self-doubt, a sense of emptiness, and feelings of personal stagnation. Therapy is sought by people who feel troubled, but the nature and severity of the trouble varies greatly from one person to another. The two most common presenting problems are excessive anxiety and depression (Lichtenstein, 1980).

A client in treatment does *not* necessarily have an identifiable psychological disorder. Some people seek professional help for everyday problems (career decisions, for instance) or vague feelings of discontent. Thus, therapy includes efforts to foster clients' personal growth as well as professional interventions for mental disorders.

People vary considerably in their willingness to seek psychotherapy. Women are more likely than men to enter therapy, and college-educated individuals use therapy more than those with less education (Olfson & Pincus, 1994). As one might expect, people who do not have medical insurance that covers psychotherapy are

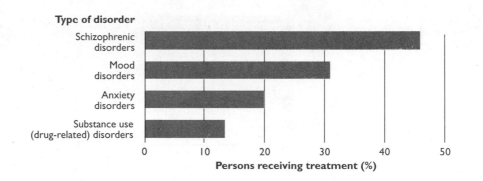

Figure 16.1
Patterns of seeking treatment
Not everyone who has a psychological disorder receives professional treatment. This graph shows the percentage of people with specific disorders who obtained mental health treatment during a six-month period. Research suggests that only a minority of people with disorders receive treatment. (Data based on Shapiro et al., 1984)

less likely to seek therapy than people who have insurance (Landerman et al., 1994). *Unfortunately, it appears that many people who need therapy don't receive it* (Pekarik, 1993). As Figure 16.1 shows, only a minority of people with actual disorders receive treatment (Robins, Locke, & Regier, 1991). People who could benefit from therapy do not seek it for a variety of reasons. Some are unaware of its availability, and some believe that it is always expensive. The biggest roadblock is that many people equate being in therapy with admitting personal weakness.

Therapists: Who Provides Professional Treatment?

Learning Objective

Describe the various types of mental health professionals involved in the provision of therapy.

Friends and relatives may provide excellent advice about personal problems, but their assistance does not qualify as therapy. Psychotherapy refers to *professional* treatment by someone with special training. However, a common source of confusion about psychotherapy is the variety of "helping professions" available to offer assistance. Psychology and psychiatry are the principal professions involved in the provision of psychotherapy, delivering the lion's share of mental health care (see Figure 16.2). However, therapy is also provided by psychiatric social workers, psychiatric nurses, and counselors, as outlined in Figure 16.3. Let's look at these mental health professions.

Psychologists

Two types of psychologists may provide therapy, although the distinction between them is more theoretical than real. **Clinical psychologists** and *counseling psychologists* **specialize in the diagnosis and treatment of psychological disorders and everyday behavioral problems.** In theory, the training of clinical psychologists emphasizes treatment of full-fledged disorders, whereas the training of counseling psychologists is slanted toward treatment of everyday adjustment problems in normal people. In practice, however, there is great overlap between clinical and counseling psychologists in training, in skills, and in the clientele they serve.

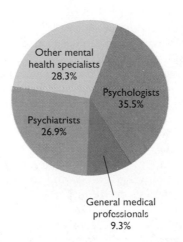

Figure 16.2
Who people see for therapy
Based on a national survey, Olfson and Pincus (1994) estimated that in 1987 Americans made 79.5 million outpatient psychotherapy visits. Information on the therapist's profession was missing for 11% of these visits. The pie chart shows how the remaining visits were distributed among psychologists, psychiatrists, other mental health professionals (social workers, counselors, and such), and general medical professionals (typically physicians specializing in family practice, internal medicine, or pediatrics). As you can see, psychologists and psychiatrists account for about 62% of outpatient treatment.

Both types of psychologists must earn a doctoral degree (Ph.D., Psy.D., or Ed.D.). A doctorate in psychology requires five to seven years of training beyond a bachelor's degree. The process of gaining admission to a Ph.D. program in clinical psychology is highly competitive (about as competitive as for medical school). Psychologists receive most of their training on university campuses, although they serve a one- to two-year internship in a clinical setting, such as a hospital.

In providing therapy, psychologists use either insight or behavioral approaches. In comparison to psychiatrists, they are more likely to use behavioral techniques and less likely to use psychoanalytic methods. Clinical and counseling psychologists do psychological testing as well as psychotherapy, and many also conduct research.

Figure 16.3
The principal mental health professions
Psychotherapists come from a variety of professional backgrounds. This chart provides an overview of various types of therapists' education and typical professional activities.

Types of Therapists

Title	Degree*	Years beyond bachelor's degree	Typical roles and activities
Clinical or counseling psychologist	Ph.D. Psy.D. Ed.D.	5–7	Diagnosis, psychological testing, insight and behavior therapy
Psychiatrist	M.D.	8	Diagnosis; insight, behavior, and biomedical therapy
Social worker	M.S.W.	2	Insight and behavior therapy, family therapy, helping patients return to the community
Psychiatric nurse	B.S., B.A., M.A.	0–2	Inpatient care, insight and behavior therapy
Counselor	M.A. M.S.	2	Insight and behavior therapy, working primarily with everyday adjustment problems and marital and career issues

*Ph.D. = Doctor of Philosophy; Psy.D. = Doctor of Psychology; Ed.D. = Doctor of Education; M.D. = Doctor of Medicine; M.S.W. = Master of Social Work; B.S. = Bachelor of Science; B.A. = Bachelor of Arts; M.A. = Master of Arts; M.S. = Master of Science

Psychiatrists

Psychiatrists **are physicians who specialize in the treatment of psychological disorders.** Many psychiatrists also treat everyday behavioral problems. However, in comparison to psychologists, psychiatrists devote more time to relatively severe disorders (schizophrenia, mood disorders) and less time to everyday marital, family, job, and school problems. Psychiatrists have an M.D. degree. Their graduate training requires four years of course work in medical school and a four-year apprenticeship in a residency at an approved hospital. Their psychotherapy training occurs during their residency, since the required course work in medical school is essentially the same for all students, whether they are going into surgery, pediatrics, or psychiatry.

In their provision of therapy, psychiatrists tend to emphasize biomedical treatments that have historically been their exclusive province (drug therapy, for instance). Psychiatrists use a variety of insight therapies, but psychoanalysis and its descendants remain dominant in psychiatry. In comparison to psychologists, psychiatrists are less likely to use group therapies or behavior therapies.

Other Mental Health Professionals

Several other mental health professions provide psychotherapy services. In hospitals and other institutions, *psychiatric social workers* and *psychiatric nurses* often work as part of a treatment team with a psychologist or psychiatrist. Psychiatric nurses, who may have a bachelor's or master's degree in their field, play a large role in hospital inpatient treatment. Psychiatric social workers generally have a master's degree and typically work with patients and their families to ease the patient's integration back into the community. Although social workers have traditionally worked in hospitals and social service agencies, in some states they are licensed as independent, private practitioners who provide a wide range of therapeutic services.

Many kinds of *counselors* also provide therapeutic services. Counselors are usually found working in schools, colleges, and human service agencies (youth centers, geriatric centers, family planning centers, and so forth). Counselors typically have a master's degree. They often specialize in particular types of problems, such as vocational counseling, marital counseling, rehabilitation counseling, and drug counseling.

Although there are clear differences among the helping professions in education and training, their roles in the treatment process overlap considerably. In this chapter, we will refer to psychologists or psychiatrists as needed, but otherwise we'll use the terms *clinician*, *therapist*, and *mental health professional* to refer to psychotherapists of all kinds, regardless of their professional degree.

Now that we have discussed the basic elements in psychotherapy, we can examine specific approaches to treatment in terms of their goals, procedures, and effectiveness. We'll begin with a few representative insight therapies.

Insight Therapies

Therapists with different theoretical orientations use different methods to pursue different kinds of insights. What these varied approaches have in common is that **insight therapies involve verbal interactions intended to enhance clients' self-knowledge and thus promote healthful changes in personality and behavior.** Although there may be hundreds of insight therapies, the leading eight or ten approaches appear to account for the lion's share of treatment. In this section, we'll delve into psychoanalysis, client-centered therapy, and cognitive therapy. We'll also discuss how insight therapy can be done with groups as well as individuals.

Psychoanalysis

Sigmund Freud

Sigmund Freud worked as a psychotherapist for almost 50 years in Vienna. Through a painstaking process of trial and error, he developed innovative techniques for the treatment of psychological disorders and distress. His system of *psychoanalysis* came to dominate psychiatry for many decades. Although the dominance of psychoanalysis has eroded in recent decades (Reiser, 1989), a diverse array of psychoanalytic approaches to therapy continue to evolve and to remain influential today (Eagle & Wolitzky, 1992).

Psychoanalysis **is an insight therapy that emphasizes the recovery of unconscious conflicts, motives, and defenses through techniques such as free association, dream analysis, and transference.** To appreciate the logic of psychoanalysis, we have to look at Freud's thinking about the roots of mental disorders. Freud treated mostly anxiety-dominated disturbances, such as phobic, panic, obsessive-compulsive, and conversion disorders, which were then called *neuroses*. He believed that neurotic problems are caused by unconscious conflicts left over from early childhood. As explained in Chapter 2, he thought that these inner conflicts involve battles among the id, ego, and superego, usually over sexual and aggressive impulses. Freud theorized that people depend on defense mechanisms to avoid confronting these conflicts, which remain hidden in the depths of the unconscious. However, he noted that defensive maneuvers often lead to self-defeating behavior. Furthermore, he asserted that defenses usually are only partially successful in alleviating anxiety, guilt, and other distressing emotions. With this model in mind, let's take a look at the therapeutic procedures used in psychoanalysis.

Probing the Unconscious

Given Freud's assumptions, we can see that the logic of psychoanalysis is very simple. The analyst attempts to probe the murky depths of the unconscious to discover the unresolved conflicts causing the client's neurotic behavior. In a sense, the analyst functions as a psychological detective. In this effort to explore the unconscious, the therapist relies on two techniques: free association and dream analysis.

In *free association*, **clients spontaneously express their thoughts and feelings exactly as they occur, with as little censorship as possible.** Clients lie on a couch so they will be better able to let their minds drift freely. In free associating, clients expound on anything that comes to mind, regardless of how trivial, silly, or embarrassing it might be. Gradually, most clients begin to let everything pour out without conscious censorship. The analyst studies these free associations for clues about what is going on in the unconscious.

In the psychoanalytic approach, the therapist encourages the client to reveal thoughts, feelings, and memories, which can then be interpreted in relation to the client's current problems.

In *dream analysis*, **the therapist interprets the symbolic meaning of the client's dreams.** For Freud, dreams were the "royal road to the unconscious," the most direct means of access to patients' innermost conflicts, wishes, and impulses. Clients are encouraged and trained to remember their dreams, which they describe in therapy. The therapist then analyzes the symbolism in these dreams to interpret their meaning.

To better illustrate these matters, let's look at an actual case treated through psychoanalysis (adapted from Greenson, 1967, pp. 40–41). Mr. N. was troubled by an unsatisfactory marriage. He claimed to love his wife, but he preferred sexual relations with prostitutes. Mr. N. reported that his parents also endured lifelong marital difficulties. His childhood conflicts about their relationship appeared to be related to his problems. Both dream analysis and free association can be seen in the following description of a session in Mr. N.'s treatment:

> Mr. N. reports a fragment of a dream. All that he can remember is that he is waiting for a red traffic light to change when he feels that someone has bumped into him from behind. . . . The associations led to Mr. N.'s love of cars, especially sports cars. He loved the sensation, in particular, of whizzing by those fat, old, expensive cars. . . . His father always hinted that he had been a great athlete, but he never substantiated it. . . . Mr. N. doubted whether his father could really perform. His father would flirt with a waitress in a cafe or make sexual remarks about women passing by, but he seemed to be showing off. If he were really sexual, he wouldn't resort to that.

As is characteristic of free association, Mr. N.'s train of thought meanders about with little direction. Nonetheless, clues about his unconscious conflicts are apparent. What did Mr. N.'s therapist extract from this session? The therapist saw sexual overtones in the dream fragment, where Mr. N. was bumped from behind. The therapist also inferred that Mr. N. had a competitive orientation toward his father, based on the free association about whizzing by fat, old, expensive cars. As you can see, analysts must *interpret* their clients' dreams and free associations. This is a critical process throughout psychoanalysis.

Interpretation

Learning Objective

Discuss interpretation, resistance, and transference in psychoanalysis.

Interpretation **is the therapist's attempt to explain the inner significance of the client's thoughts, feelings, memories, and behaviors.** Contrary to popular belief, analysts do not interpret everything, and they generally don't try to dazzle clients with startling revelations. Instead, analysts move forward inch by inch, offering interpretations that should be just out of the client's own reach. Mr. N.'s therapist eventually offered the following interpretations to his client:

> I said to Mr. N. near the end of the hour that I felt he was struggling with his feelings about his father's sexual life. He seemed to be saying that his father was sexually not a very potent man. . . . He also recalls that he once found a packet of con-

doms under his father's pillow when he was an adolescent and he thought, "My father must be going to prostitutes." I then intervened and pointed out that the condoms under his father's pillow seemed to indicate more obviously that his father used the condoms with his mother, who slept in the same bed. However, Mr. N. *wanted* to believe his wish-fulfilling fantasy: mother doesn't want sex with father and father is not very potent. The patient was silent and the hour ended.

As you may already have guessed, the therapist has concluded that Mr. N.'s difficulties are rooted in an oedipal complex (see Chapter 2). Mr. N. has unresolved sexual feelings toward his mother and hostile feelings about his father. These unconscious conflicts, which are rooted in his childhood, are distorting his intimate relations as an adult.

Resistance

How would you expect Mr. N. to respond to his therapist's suggestion that he was in competition with his father for the sexual attention of his mother? Obviously, most clients would have great difficulty accepting such an interpretation. Freud fully expected clients to display some resistance to therapeutic efforts. **Resistance involves largely unconscious defensive maneuvers intended to hinder the progress of therapy.** Why do clients try to resist the helping process? Because they don't want to face up to the painful, disturbing conflicts that they have buried in their unconscious. Although they have sought help, they are reluctant to confront their real problems.

Resistance may take many forms. Patients may show up late for their sessions, merely pretend to engage in free association, or express hostility toward the therapist. For instance, Mr. N.'s therapist noted that after the session just described, "The next day he began by telling me that he was furious with me." Analysts use a variety of strategies to deal with their clients' resistance. Often, a key consideration is the handling of *transference*, which we consider next.

Transference

Transference **occurs when clients start relating to their therapist in ways that mimic critical relationships in their lives.** Thus, a client might start relating to a therapist as if the therapist were an overprotective mother, rejecting brother, or passive spouse. In a sense, the client *transfers* conflicting feelings about important people onto the therapist. For instance, in his treatment, Mr. N. transferred some of the competitive hostility he felt toward his father onto his analyst.

Psychoanalysts often encourage transference so that clients begin to reenact relations with crucial people in the context of therapy. These reenactments can help bring repressed feelings and conflicts to the surface, allowing the client to work through them. The therapist's handling of transference is complicated and difficult because transference may arouse confusing, highly charged emotions in the client.

Undergoing psychoanalysis is not easy. It can be a slow, painful process of self-examination that routinely requires three to five years of hard work. Ultimately, if resistance and transference can be handled effectively, the therapist's interpretations should lead the client to profound insights. For instance, Mr. N. eventually admitted, "The old boy is probably right, it does tickle me to imagine that my mother preferred me and I could beat out my father. Later, I wondered whether this had something to do with my own screwed-up sex life with my wife." According to Freud, once clients recognize the unconscious sources of their conflicts, they can resolve these conflicts and discard their neurotic defenses.

Though still available, classical psychoanalysis as done by Freud is not widely practiced anymore. Freud's psychoanalytic method was geared to a particular kind of clientele that he was seeing in Vienna many years ago. As his followers fanned out across Europe and America, many found that it was necessary to adapt psychoanalysis to different cultures, changing times, and new kinds of patients. Thus, many variations on Freud's original approach to psychoanalysis have developed over the years. These descendants of psychoanalysis are collectively known as *psychodynamic approaches* to therapy.

Some of these adaptations, such as those by Carl Jung (1917) and Alfred Adler (1927), were sweeping revisions based on fundamental differences in theory. Other

Figure 16.4
**Comparing classical and
modern psychoanalysis**
Contemporary psychoanalytic
therapists continue to practice in
the tradition established by Freud,
but there are a number of differences, as pointed out by Baker
(1985). Baker divides contemporary psychodynamic therapies
into three subgroups. "Modern
psychoanalysis," profiled in the
right column, refers to the group
that has remained most loyal to
Freud's ideas while modifying his
clinical techniques. (Adapted from
Baker, 1985)

Some Differences Between Classical and Modern Psychoanalysis

Classical psychoanalysis	Modern psychoanalysis
Frequency of treatment is usually four to five times per week.	Frequency of treatment is typically one to two times per week.
Patient is treated "on the couch."	Patient is typically seen "face to face."
Treatment goals emphasize character reconstruction.	Treatment emphasizes problem resolution, enhanced adaptation, and support of ego functions with limited character change.
Treatment approach emphasizes the neutrality and nonintrusion of the analyst.	Therapist assumes an active and direct stance.
Technique emphasizes "free association," uncovering, interpretation, and analysis of transference and resistance.	A wide range of interventions are used, including interpretive, supportive, and educative techniques. Transference is typically kept less intense.

variations, such as those devised by Melanie Klein (1948) and Heinz Kohut (1971), involved more subtle changes in theory. Still other revisions (Alexander, 1954; Stekel, 1950) simply involved efforts to modernize and streamline psychoanalytic techniques (rather than theory), as outlined in Figure 16.4. Hence, today we have a rich diversity of psychodynamic approaches to therapy (Ursano & Silberman, 1994).

Client-Centered Therapy

You may have heard of people going into therapy to "find themselves" or to "get in touch with their real feelings." These now-popular phrases emerged out of the human potential movement, which was stimulated in part by Carl Rogers's work (Rogers, 1951, 1986). Taking a humanistic perspective, Rogers devised *client-centered therapy* (also known as *person-centered therapy*) in the 1940s and 1950s.

Client-centered therapy is an insight therapy that emphasizes providing a supportive emotional climate for clients, who play a major role in determining the pace and direction of their therapy. You may wonder why the troubled, untrained client is put in charge of the pace and direction of the therapy. Rogers (1961) provides a compelling justification:

> It is the client who knows what hurts, what directions to go, what problems are crucial, what experiences have been deeply buried. It began to occur to me that unless I had a need to demonstrate my own cleverness and learning, I would do better to rely upon the client for the direction of movement in the process. [pp. 11–12]

Rogers's theory about the principal causes of neurotic anxieties is quite different from the Freudian explanation. As discussed in Chapter 2, Rogers maintains that most personal distress is due to inconsistency, or "incongruence," between a person's self-concept and reality. According to his theory, incongruence makes people prone to feel threatened by realistic feedback about themselves from others. For example, if you inaccurately viewed yourself as a hardworking, dependable person, you would feel threatened by contradictory feedback from friends or co-workers. According to Rogers, anxiety about such feedback often leads to reliance on defense mechanisms, distortions of reality, and stifled personal growth. Excessive incongruence is thought to be rooted in clients' overdependence on others for approval and acceptance.

Given Rogers's theory, client-centered therapists stalk insights that are quite different from the repressed conflicts that psychoanalysts try to track down. Client-centered therapists help clients realize that they do not have to worry constantly about pleasing others and winning acceptance. They encourage clients to respect their own feelings and values. They help people to restructure their self-concept to correspond better to reality. Ultimately, they try to foster self-acceptance and personal growth.

Carl Rogers

Therapeutic Climate

In client-centered therapy, the *process* of therapy is not as important as the emotional *climate* in which the therapy takes place. According to Rogers, it is critical for the therapist to provide a warm, supportive, accepting climate in which clients can confront their shortcomings without feeling threatened. The lack of threat should reduce clients' defensive tendencies and thus help them open up. To create this atmosphere of emotional support, Rogers believes that client-centered therapists must provide three conditions:

1. *Genuineness*. The therapist must be genuine with the client, communicating in an honest and spontaneous manner. The therapist should not be phony or defensive.
2. *Unconditional positive regard*. The therapist must also show complete, nonjudgmental acceptance of the client as a person. The therapist should provide warmth and caring for the client with no strings attached. This does not mean that the therapist must approve of everything that the client says or does. A therapist can disapprove of a particular behavior while continuing to value the client as a human being.
3. *Empathy*. Finally, the therapist must provide accurate empathy for the client. This means that the therapist must understand the client's world from the client's point of view. Furthermore, the therapist must be articulate enough to communicate this understanding to the client.

Rogers firmly believed that a supportive emotional climate is the major force promoting healthful changes in therapy. However, in recent years some client-centered therapists have begun to place more emphasis on the therapeutic process (Rice & Greenberg, 1992).

Therapeutic Process

In client-centered therapy, the client and therapist work together as equals. The therapist provides relatively little guidance and keeps interpretation and advice to a minimum. So, just what does the client-centered therapist do, besides creating a supportive climate? Primarily, the therapist provides feedback to help clients sort out their feelings. The therapist's key task is *clarification*. Client-centered therapists try to function like a human mirror, reflecting statements back to their clients, but with enhanced clarity. They help clients become more aware of their true feelings by highlighting themes that may be obscure in the clients' rambling discourse. The reflective nature of client-centered therapy can be seen in the following exchange between a client and therapist:

Client: I really feel bad today . . . just terrible.

Therapist: You're feeling pretty bad.

Client: Yeah, I'm angry and that's made me feel bad, especially when I can't do anything about it. I just have to live with it and shut up.

Therapist: You're very angry and feel like there's nothing you can safely do with your feelings.

Client: Uh-huh. I mean . . . if I yell at my wife she gets hurt. If I don't say anything to her I feel tense.

Therapist: You're between a rock and a hard place—no matter what you do, you'll wind up feeling bad.

Client: I mean she chews ice all day and all night. I feel stupid saying this. It's petty, I know. But when I sit there and try to concentrate, I hear all these slurping and crunching noises. I can't stand it . . . and I yell. She feels hurt—I feel bad—like I shouldn't have said anything.

Therapist: So when you finally say something you feel bad afterward.

Client: Yeah, I can't say anything to her without getting mad and saying more than I should. And then I cause more trouble than it's worth. [Duke & Nowicki, 1979, p. 565]

By working with clients to clarify their feelings, client-centered therapists hope to gradually build toward more far-reaching insights. In particular, they try to help clients become more aware of and comfortable about their genuine selves. Obviously, these are ambitious goals. Client-centered therapy resembles psychoanalysis in that both seek to achieve a major reconstruction of a client's personality. We'll see more limited and specific goals in cognitive therapy, which we consider next.

Cognitive Therapy

Aaron Beck

In Chapter 3 we saw that cognitive interpretations of events make all the difference in the world as to how well people handle stress. In Chapter 15 we learned that cognitive factors play a key role in the development of depressive disorders. Citing the importance of findings such as these, two former psychoanalysts—Aaron Beck (1976, 1987) and Albert Ellis (1973, 1989)—independently devised cognitive-oriented therapies that became highly influential (Arnkoff & Glass, 1992). Because we covered the main ideas underlying Ellis's *rational-emotive therapy* in our discussion of coping strategies (see Chapter 4), we'll focus on Beck's system of *cognitive therapy* here. **Cognitive therapy is an insight therapy that emphasizes recognizing and changing negative thoughts and maladaptive beliefs.**

In recent years cognitive therapy has been applied fruitfully to a wide range of disorders (Beck, 1991; Hollon & Beck, 1994), but it was originally devised as a treatment for depression. According to Beck, depression is caused by "errors" in thinking (see Figure 16.5). He asserts that depression-prone people tend to (1) blame their setbacks on personal inadequacies without considering circumstantial explanations; (2) focus selectively on negative events while ignoring positive events; (3) make unduly pessimistic projections about the future; and (4) draw negative conclusions about their worth as persons based on insignificant events. For instance, imagine that you earned a low score on a minor quiz in a class. If you made the kinds of errors in thinking Beck identified, you might blame the score on your woeful stupidity, dismiss comments from a classmate that it was an unfair test, hysterically predict that you will surely flunk the course, and conclude that you are not genuine college material.

Goals and Techniques

The goal of cognitive therapy is to change the way clients think. To begin, clients are taught to detect their automatic negative thoughts. These are self-defeating statements that people are inclined to make when analyzing problems. Examples might include "I'm just not smart enough," "No one really likes me," and "It's all my fault." Clients are then trained to subject these automatic thoughts to reality testing. The therapist helps them see how unrealistically negative the thoughts are.

The therapist's goal is not to promote unwarranted optimism, but rather to help the client use more reasonable standards of evaluation. For example, a cognitive therapist might point out that a client's failure to get a desired promotion at work may be attributable to many factors and that this setback doesn't mean that the client is incompetent. Gradually, the therapist digs deeper, looking for the unrealistic assumptions that underlie clients' constant negative thinking. These, too, have to be changed.

Unlike client-centered therapists, cognitive therapists are actively involved in determining the pace and direction of treatment. They usually talk extensively in the therapy sessions. They may argue openly with clients as they try to persuade them to alter their patterns of thinking.

Kinship with Behavior Therapy

Cognitive therapy borrows heavily from behavioral approaches to treatment, which we will discuss shortly. Specifically, cognitive therapists often use "homework assignments" that focus on changing clients' overt behaviors (Wright & Beck, 1994). Clients may be instructed to engage in overt responses on their own, outside the clinician's office. For example, one shy, insecure young man was told to go to a sin-

Figure 16.5
Beck's cognitive theory of depression
According to Aaron Beck (1976, 1987), depression is caused by certain patterns of negative thinking. This chart lists some of the particularly damaging cognitive errors that can foster depression. (Adapted from Beck, 1976)

Cognitive Errors That Promote Depression

Cognitive error	Description
Overgeneralizing	If it is true in one case, it applies to any case that is even slightly similar.
Selective abstraction	The only events that matter are failures, deprivation, and so on. I should measure myself by errors, weaknesses, etc.
Excessive responsibility (assuming personal causality)	I am responsible for all bad things, failures, and so on.
Assuming temporal causality (predicting without sufficient evidence)	If it has been true in the past, then it is always going to be true.
Self-references	I am the center of everyone's attention, especially when it comes to bad performances or personal attributes.
"Catastrophizing"	Always think of the worst. It is most likely to happen to you.
Dichotomous thinking	Everything is either one extreme or another (black or white; good or bad).

gles bar and engage three different women in conversations for up to five minutes each (Rush, 1984). He was instructed to record his thoughts before and after each of the conversations. This assignment elicited various maladaptive patterns of thought that gave the young man and his therapist plenty to talk about in subsequent sessions. As this example illustrates, cognitive therapy is a creative blend of "talk therapy" and behavior therapy, although it is primarily an insight therapy.

Cognitive therapy was originally designed as a treatment for individuals. However, it has recently been adapted for use with groups (Covi & Primakoff, 1988). Most insight therapies can be conducted on either an individual or a group basis (Kaplan & Sadock, 1993), so let's take a look at the dynamics of group therapy.

Group Therapy

Although it dates back to the early part of the 20th century, group therapy came of age during World War II and its aftermath in the 1950s (Rosenbaum, Lakin, & Roback, 1992). During this period, the expanding demand for therapeutic services forced clinicians to use group techniques (Scheidlinger, 1993). **Group therapy involves the simultaneous treatment of several or more clients in a group.** Most major insight therapies have been adapted for use with groups. In fact, the ideas underlying Rogers's client-centered therapy spawned the much-publicized encounter group movement. Although group therapy can be conducted in a variety of ways, we can provide a general overview of the process as it usually unfolds (see Fuchs, 1984; Vinogradov & Yalom, 1994).

Participants' Roles

Learning Objective

Describe how group therapy is generally conducted.

A therapy group typically consists of about five to ten members. The therapist usually screens the participants. Most therapists exclude persons who seem likely to be disruptive. Some theorists maintain that judicious selection of participants is crucial to effective group treatment (Salvendy, 1993). There is some debate about whether or not it is best to have a homogeneous group (people who are similar in age, gender, and presenting problem). Practical necessities usually dictate that groups are at least somewhat diversified.

In group treatment, the therapist's responsibilities include selecting participants, setting goals for the group, initiating and maintaining the therapeutic process, and protecting clients from harm (Weiner, 1993). The therapist often plays a relatively subtle role in group therapy, staying in the background and focusing mainly on promoting group cohesiveness. The therapist always retains a special status, but the therapist and clients are on much more equal footing in group therapy than in individual therapy. The leader in group therapy expresses emotions, shares feelings, and copes with challenges from group members. In other words, group therapists participate in the group's exchanges and "bare their own souls" to some extent.

In group therapy, participants essentially function as therapists for one another. Group members describe their problems, trade viewpoints, share experiences, and discuss coping strategies. Most important, they provide acceptance and emotional support for each other. In this supportive atmosphere, group members work at peeling away the social masks that cover their insecurities. Once their problems are exposed, members work at correcting them. As members come to value one another's opinions, they work hard to display healthy changes to win the group's approval.

Advantages of the Group Experience

Learning Objective

Identify some advantages of group therapy.

Group therapies obviously save time and money, which can be critical in understaffed mental hospitals and other institutional settings. Therapists in private practice usually charge less for group than individual therapy, making therapy affordable for more people. However, group therapy is *not* just a less costly substitute for individual therapy. For many types of patients and problems, group therapy can be just as effective as individual treatment (Piper, 1993). Moreover, group therapy has unique strengths of its own. Irwin Yalom (1985), who has studied group therapy extensively, has described some of these advantages:

1. *In group therapy, participants often come to realize that their misery is not unique.* Clients often enter therapy feeling sorry for themselves. They think that they alone have a terribly burdensome cross to bear. In the group situation, they quickly see that they are not unique. They are reassured to learn that many other people have similar or even worse problems.
2. *Group therapy provides an opportunity for participants to work on their social skills in a safe environment.* Many personal problems essentially involve difficulties in effectively relating to people. Group therapy can provide a workshop for improving interpersonal skills that cannot be matched by individual therapy.
3. *Certain kinds of problems are especially well suited to group treatment.* Some specific types of problems and clients respond especially well to the social support that group therapy can provide. Peer self-help groups illustrate this advantage. In peer self-help groups, people who have a problem in common get together regularly to help one another out. The original peer self-help group was Alcoholics Anonymous. Today, there are similar groups made up of former psychiatric patients, single parents, drug addicts, and so forth.

Whether therapy is conducted on a group basis or an individual basis, clients usually invest considerable time, effort, and money in insight therapies. Are they worth the investment? Let's examine the evidence on the effectiveness of insight therapy.

Evaluating Insight Therapies

Learning Objective

Summarize evidence on the efficacy of insight therapies.

In 1952 Hans Eysenck shocked mental health professionals by reporting that there was no sound evidence that insight therapy actually helped people. What was the basis for this startling claim? Eysenck (1952) reviewed numerous studies of therapeutic outcome for clients suffering from neurotic problems. He found that about two-thirds of the clients recovered. A two-thirds recovery rate sounds reasonable, except that Eysenck found a similar recovery rate among *untreated* neurotics. As we noted in Chapter 15, psychological disorders sometimes clear up on their own. **A spontaneous remission is a recovery from a disorder that occurs without formal treatment.** Based on his estimate of the spontaneous remission rate for neurotic disorders, Eysenck concluded that the therapeutic effects of insight therapy are small or nonexistent.

Hans Eysenck

In the ensuing years, critics pounced on Eysenck's article looking for flaws. They found a variety of shortcomings in his data. For instance, Eysenck used different time frames in comparing the recovery rates of treated and untreated neurotics. The two-thirds recovery rate in the untreated groups was based on a *two-year* time period, whereas the two-thirds recovery rate for the treated groups occurred in a *two-month* time frame (Strupp & Howard, 1992). Moreover, the treated and untreated groups were not matched in terms of the severity of their disorders, their attitudes and expectations about therapy, or any other relevant variables that might influence therapeutic outcomes. Eysenck also made many arbitrary judgments about "recoveries" that were consistently favorable to the untreated groups. After taking a close look at Eysenck's data, Bergin (1971) argued that the data really suggested that the spontaneous remission rate for neurotic disorders was in the vicinity of 30–40%. Although Eysenck's conclusions were unduly pessimistic, he made an important contribution to the mental health field by sparking debate and research on the effectiveness of insight therapy.

Evaluating the effectiveness of any approach to psychotherapy is a complicated matter (Garfield, 1992; Persons, 1991). This is especially true for insight therapies. If you were to undergo insight therapy, how would you judge its effectiveness? By how you felt? By looking at your behavior? By asking your therapist? By consulting your friends and family? What would you be looking for? People enter therapy with different problems and needs. Different schools of thought seek to realize entirely different goals. Thus, measures of therapeutic outcome tend to be subjective, with little consensus about the best way to assess therapeutic progress (Lambert & Hill, 1994). Moreover, people enter therapy with diverse problems of varied severity, so the efficacy of treatment can be evaluated meaningfully only for specific clinical problems (Elliott, Stiles, & Shapiro, 1993).

Another problem is that both therapists and clients are biased strongly in the direction of evaluating therapy favorably (Rachman & Wilson, 1980). Why? Therapists want to see improvement because it reflects on their professional competence. Obviously, they hope to see clients getting better as a result of their work. Clients are slanted toward a favorable evaluation because they want to justify their effort, their heartache, their expense, and their time.

In spite of these difficulties, hundreds of therapy outcome studies have been conducted since Eysenck prodded researchers into action. These studies have examined a broad range of specific clinical problems and used diverse methods to assess therapeutic outcomes, including scores on psychological tests and ratings by family members, as well as therapists' and clients' ratings. Although Eysenck (1993) remains skeptical, these studies generally indicate that insight therapy *is* superior to no treatment or to placebo treatment and that the effects of therapy are reasonably durable (Lambert & Bergin, 1994; Lipsey & Wilson, 1993).

Admittedly, this outcome research does not indicate that insight therapy leads to miraculous results. The superiority of therapy over no treatment is usually characterized as modest. Moreover, when professional therapy is compared to paraprofessional interventions (mostly peer self-help groups), the differences in efficacy are often negligible (Christensen & Jacobson, 1994; Lambert & Bergin, 1994). In light of the cost of therapy, there is room for debate about its value. Overall, about 70–80% of clients appear to benefit from insight therapy, while 20–30% fail to show any clear improvement.

Therapy and the Recovered Memories Controversy

While debate about the efficacy of insight therapy has simmered for four decades, the 1990s brought an entirely new controversy that has rocked the psychotherapy profession like never before. The subject of this emotionally charged debate is the recent spate of prominent reports involving the recovery of repressed memories of sexual abuse and other childhood trauma through therapeutic techniques that some critics characterize as questionable. In recent years the media have been flooded with stories of people—including some celebrities—who have recovered long-lost recollections of sexual abuse, typically with the help of their therapists. For example, in 1991 TV star Roseanne Barr suddenly recalled years of abuse by her parents, and a former Miss America remembered being sexually assaulted by her father (Wielawski, 1991). Such recovered memories have led to a rash of lawsuits in which adult plaintiffs have sued their parents, teachers, neighbors, pastors, and so forth for alleged child abuse 20 or 30 years earlier (even the Archbishop of Chicago was sued, although the suit was soon dropped). For the most part, these parents, teachers, and neighbors have denied the allegations. Many of them have seemed genuinely befuddled by the accusations, which have torn some previously happy families apart. In an effort to make sense of the charges, many accused parents have argued that their children's recollections are false memories created inadvertently by well-intentioned therapists through the power of suggestion.

The crux of the debate is that child abuse usually takes place behind closed doors, and in the absence of corroborative evidence, there isn't any way to reliably distinguish genuine recovered memories from those that are false. Some recovered memories have been substantiated by independent witnesses or belated admissions of guilt from the accused (for example, see Horn, 1993). But in the vast majority of cases, the allegations of abuse have been vehemently denied and independent corroboration has not been available (Loftus, 1993). Astonishingly, recovered recollections of sexual abuse have become so common, a support group has been formed for people who feel that they have been victimized by "false memory syndrome." Thousands of families have sought help from the False Memory Syndrome Foundation (Ness & Salter, 1993).

Psychologists are sharply divided on the issue of recovered memories, leaving the public understandably confused. Many psychologists, especially therapists in clinical practice, accept most recovered memories at face value (Briere & Conte, 1993; Dawes, 1992; Terr, 1994). They assert that it is common for patients to bury traumatic incidents in their unconscious. Citing new evidence that sexual abuse in childhood is far more widespread than most people realize, they argue that most repressed memories of abuse are probably genuine. They attribute the recent upsurge in reports of recovered memories to therapists' and clients' increased sensitivity to an issue that people used to be reluctant to discuss.

In contrast, many other psychologists, especially memory researchers, have expressed skepticism about the recent flood of recovered memories (Frankel, 1993; Loftus, 1993; Lynn & Nash, 1994). These psychologists do not say that people are lying about their repressed memories. Rather, they maintain that some suggestible,

Reprinted by permission: Tribune Media Services.

confused people struggling to understand profound personal problems have been convinced by persuasive therapists that their emotional problems must be the result of abuse that occurred years ago. Critics blame a small minority of therapists who presumably have good intentions but who operate under the dubious assumption that virtually all psychological problems are attributable to childhood sexual abuse. Using hypnosis, dream interpretation, and leading questions, they supposedly prod and probe patients until they inadvertently create the memories of abuse that they are searching for. Consistent with this view, Yapko (1994) reviews evidence that some therapists are (1) prone to see signs of abuse where none has occurred, (2) unsophisticated about the extent to which memories can be distorted, and (3) naive about how much their expectations and beliefs can influence their patients' efforts to achieve self-understanding.

Psychologists who doubt the authenticity of repressed memories also point to published case histories that clearly involved suggestive questioning and to cases in which patients have recanted recovered memories of sexual abuse (see Figure 16.6) after realizing that these memories were implanted by their therapists (Goldstein & Farmer, 1993; Loftus, 1994). Those who question recovered memories also point to several lines of carefully controlled laboratory research demonstrating that it is not all that difficult to create "memories" of events that never happened (Belli & Loftus, 1994). For example, studies have shown that subtle suggestions made to hypnotized subjects can be converted into "memories" of things they never saw (Sheehan, Green, & Truesdale, 1992).

Of course, psychologists who believe in recovered memories have mounted rebuttals to these arguments. For example, Gleaves (1994) argues that a recantation of a recovered memory of abuse does not prove that the memory was false. He points out that individuals with a history of sexual abuse often vacillate between denying and accepting that the abuse occurred. Olio (1994) argues that laboratory demonstrations designed to show that it is easy to create false memories have involved trivial memory distortions that are a far cry from the vivid, emotionally wrenching recollections of sexual abuse that have generated the recovered memories controversy. She concludes that "the possibility of implanting entire multiple scenarios of horror that differ markedly from the individual's experience, such as memories of childhood abuse in an individual who does not have a trauma history, remains an unsubstantiated hypothesis" (p. 442).

Although both sides seem genuinely concerned about the welfare of the people involved, the debate about recovered memories of sexual abuse has grown increasingly bitter. Those who are skeptical about repressed memories argue that thousands of innocent families are being ripped to shreds by unquestioned acceptance of recovered memories of sexual abuse. The other camp raises an equally disturbing concern that the recent suspicions about repressed memories will turn the clock back to a time when women and children were reluctant to report abuse because they were often ignored, ridiculed, or made to feel guilty.

So, what can we conclude about the recovered memories controversy? It seems pretty clear that a significant portion of recovered memories of abuse are the product of suggestion, but we can't rule out the possibility that at least some cases are authentic. Thus, the matter needs to be addressed with great caution. On the one hand, peo-

Figure 16.6
False memory syndrome
Recovered memories of sexual abuse are viewed with skepticism in some quarters. One reason is that some people who have recovered previously repressed recollections of childhood abuse have subsequently realized that their "memories" were the product of suggestion. A number of case histories, such as the one summarized here (from Jaroff, 1993), have demonstrated that therapists who relentlessly search for memories of abuse in their patients sometimes create the memories they are seeking.

A Case History of False Memory Syndrome

Suffering from a prolonged bout of depression and desperate for help, Melody Gavigan, 39, a computer specialist from Long Beach, California, checked herself into a local psychiatric hospital. As Gavigan recalls the experience, her problems were just beginning. During five weeks of treatment there, a family and marriage counselor repeatedly suggested that her depression stemmed from incest during her childhood. While at first Gavigan had no recollection of any abuse, the therapist kept prodding. "I was so distressed and needed help so desperately, I latched on to what he was offering me," she says. "I accepted his answers."

When asked for details, she wrote page after page of what she believed were emerging repressed memories. She told about running into the yard after being raped in the bathroom. She incorporated into another lurid rape scene an actual girlhood incident, in which she had dislocated a shoulder. She went on to recall being molested by her father when she was only a year old—as her diapers were being changed—and sodomized by him at five. Following what she says was the therapist's advice, Gavigan confronted her father with her accusations, severed her relationship with him, moved away, and formed an incest survivors' group.

But she remained uneasy. Signing up for a college psychology course, she examined her newfound memories more carefully and concluded that they were false. Now Gavigan has begged her father's forgiveness and filed a lawsuit against the psychiatric hospital for the pain that she and her family suffered.

ple should be extremely careful about accepting recovered memories of abuse in the absence of convincing corroboration. On the other hand, recovered memories of abuse cannot be summarily dismissed, and it would be tragic if the repressed memories controversy made people overly skeptical about the all-too-real problem of childhood sexual abuse.

Behavior Therapies

Learning Objective

Outline the general approach and principles of behavior therapies.

Behavior therapy is different from insight therapy in that behavior therapists make no attempt to help clients achieve grand insights about themselves. Why not? Because behavior therapists believe that such insights aren't necessary to produce constructive change. For example, consider a client troubled by compulsive gambling. The behavior therapist doesn't care whether this behavior is rooted in unconscious conflicts or parental rejection. What the client needs is to get rid of the maladaptive behavior. Consequently, the therapist simply designs a program to eliminate the compulsive gambling. In some cases, behavior therapists may work with clients to attain limited insights into how environmental factors evoke troublesome behaviors (Franks & Barbrack, 1983), since such information can be helpful in designing a behavioral therapy program.

The crux of the difference between insight therapy and behavior therapy lies in how they view symptoms. Insight therapists treat pathological symptoms as signs of an underlying problem. In contrast, behavior therapists think that the symptoms *are* the problem. Thus, **behavior therapies involve the application of the principles of learning to direct efforts to change clients' maladaptive behaviors.**

Behaviorism has been an influential school of thought in psychology since the 1920s. But behaviorists devoted little attention to clinical issues until the 1950s, when behavior therapy emerged out of three independent lines of research fostered by B. F. Skinner and his colleagues (1953) in the United States, Hans Eysenck (1959) and his colleagues in Britain, and Joseph Wolpe (1958) and his colleagues in South Africa (Glass & Arnkoff, 1992). Since then, an explosion of interest has occurred in behavioral approaches to psychotherapy.

General Principles

Behavior therapies are based on certain assumptions (Agras & Berkowitz, 1994). *First, it is assumed that behavior is a product of learning.* No matter how self-defeating or pathological a client's behavior might be, the behaviorist believes that it is the result of past conditioning. *Second, it is assumed that what has been learned can be unlearned.* The same learning principles that explain how the maladaptive behavior was acquired can be used to get rid of it. Thus, behavior therapists attempt to change clients' behavior by applying the principles of classical conditioning, operant conditioning, and observational learning.

Behavior therapies are close cousins of the self-modification procedures described in the Chapter 4 Application. Both use the same principles of learning to alter behavior directly. In discussing *self-modification*, we examined some relatively simple procedures that people can apply to themselves to improve everyday self-control. In our discussion of *behavior therapy*, we will examine more complex procedures used by mental health professionals to treat more severe problems.

Like self-modification, behavior therapy requires that clients' vague complaints ("My life is filled with frustration") be translated into specific, concrete behavioral goals ("I need to increase my use of assertive responses in dealing with colleagues"). Once the troublesome behaviors have been targeted, the therapist designs a program to alter these behaviors. The nature of the therapeutic program depends on the types of problems identified. Specific procedures are designed for specific types of problems, as you'll see in our discussion of systematic desensitization.

Systematic Desensitization

Learning Objective

Describe the three steps in systematic desensitization and the logic underlying the treatment.

Joseph Wolpe

Devised by Joseph Wolpe (1958, 1987), systematic desensitization revolutionized psychotherapy by giving therapists their first useful alternative to traditional "talk therapy" (Fishman & Franks, 1992). *Systematic desensitization* **is a behavior therapy used to reduce clients' anxiety responses through counterconditioning.** The treatment assumes that most anxiety responses are acquired through classical conditioning. According to this model, a harmless stimulus (for instance, a bridge) may be paired with a frightening event (lightning strikes it), becoming a conditioned stimulus eliciting anxiety. The goal of systematic desensitization is to weaken the association between the conditioned stimulus (the bridge) and the conditioned response of anxiety. Systematic desensitization involves three steps.

First, the therapist helps the client to build an anxiety hierarchy. The hierarchy is a list of anxiety-arousing stimuli centering on the specific source of anxiety, such as flying, academic tests, or snakes. The client ranks the stimuli from the least anxiety arousing to the most anxiety arousing. This ordered list of related, anxiety-provoking stimuli is the anxiety hierarchy.

The second step involves training the client in deep muscle relaxation. This second phase may begin during early sessions while the therapist and client are still constructing the anxiety hierarchy. Different therapists use different relaxation training procedures. Whatever procedures are employed, the client must learn to engage in deep and thorough relaxation on command from the therapist.

In the third step, the client tries to work through the hierarchy, learning to remain relaxed while imagining each stimulus. Starting with the least anxiety-arousing stimulus, the client imagines the situation as vividly as possible while relaxing. If the client experiences strong anxiety, he or she drops the imaginary scene and concentrates on relaxation. The client keeps repeating this process until able to imagine a scene with little or no anxiety. Once a particular scene is conquered, the client moves on to the next stimulus situation in the anxiety hierarchy. Gradually, over a number of therapy sessions, the client progresses through the hierarchy, unlearning troublesome anxiety responses.

As clients conquer *imagined* phobic stimuli, they may be encouraged to confront the *real* stimuli. Although desensitization to imagined stimuli *can* be effective by itself, contemporary behavior therapists usually follow it up with direct exposures to the real anxiety-arousing stimuli (Emmelkamp & Scholing, 1990). Indeed, behavioral interventions emphasizing direct exposures to anxiety-arousing situations have become behavior therapists' treatment of choice for phobic and other anxiety disorders (Goldfried, Greenberg, & Marmar, 1990). Usually, these real-life confrontations prove harmless, and individuals' anxiety responses decline.

According to Wolpe (1958, 1990), the principle at work in systematic desensitization is simple. Anxiety and relaxation are incompatible responses. The trick is to recondition people so that the conditioned stimulus elicits relaxation instead of anxiety. This is *counterconditioning*—an attempt to reverse the process of classical conditioning by associating the crucial stimulus with a new conditioned response. Although Wolpe's explanation of how systematic desensitization works has been questioned, the technique's effectiveness in eliminating specific anxieties has been well documented (Spiegler & Guevremont, 1993; Wilson & O'Leary, 1980).

Aversion Therapy

Learning Objective

Describe the use of aversion therapy and social skills training.

Aversion therapy is far and away the most controversial of the behavior therapies. It's not something that you would sign up for unless you were pretty desperate. Psychologists usually suggest it only as a treatment of last resort, after other interventions have failed. What's so terrible about aversion therapy? The client has to endure decidedly unpleasant stimuli, such as shock or drug-induced nausea.

Aversion therapy **is a behavior therapy in which an aversive stimulus is paired with a stimulus that elicits an undesirable response.** For example,

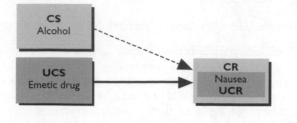

Figure 16.7
Aversion therapy
Aversion therapy uses classical conditioning to create an aversion to a stimulus that has elicited problematic behavior. For example, in the treatment of drinking problems, alcohol may be paired with a nausea-inducing drug to create a conditioned aversion to alcohol.

alcoholics have had drug-induced nausea paired with their favorite drinks during therapy sessions (Cannon, Baker, & Wehl, 1981). By pairing an *emetic drug* (one that causes vomiting) with alcohol, the therapist hopes to create a conditioned aversion to alcohol (see Figure 16.7).

Aversion therapy takes advantage of the automatic nature of responses produced through classical conditioning. Admittedly, alcoholics treated with aversion therapy know that they won't be given an emetic outside of their therapy sessions. However, their reflex response to the stimulus of alcohol may be changed to one of nausea and distaste. Obviously, this response should make it much easier to resist the urge to drink.

Troublesome behaviors treated successfully with aversion therapy include drug abuse, sexual deviance, gambling, shoplifting, stuttering, cigarette smoking, and overeating (Sandler, 1975; Wolpe, 1990). Typically, aversion therapy is only one element in a larger treatment program. Of course, this procedure should only be used with willing clients when other options have failed (Rimm & Cunningham, 1985).

Social Skills Training

Many psychological problems grow out of interpersonal difficulties. Behavior therapists point out that people are not born with social finesse. They acquire social skills through learning. Unfortunately, some people have not learned how to be friendly, how to make conversation, how to express anger appropriately, and so forth. Social ineptitude can contribute to anxiety, feelings of inferiority, and various kinds of disorders. In light of these findings, therapists are increasingly using social skills training in efforts to improve clients' social abilities (Liberman, Mueser, & DeRisi, 1989). This approach to therapy has yielded promising results in the treatment of depression, shyness, social anxiety, and even schizophrenia (Becker, 1990; Wixted, Bellack, & Hersen, 1990).

Social skills training **is a behavior therapy designed to improve interpersonal skills that emphasizes shaping, modeling, and behavioral rehearsal.** This type of behavior therapy can be conducted with individual clients or in groups. Social skills training depends on the principles of operant conditioning and observational learning. The therapist makes use of *modeling* by encouraging clients to watch socially skilled friends and colleagues, so that responses (eye contact, active listening, and so on) can be acquired through observation.

In *behavioral rehearsal*, the client tries to practice social techniques in structured role-playing exercises. The therapist provides corrective feedback and uses approval to reinforce progress. Eventually, clients try their newly acquired skills in real-world interactions. Usually, they are given specific homework assignments. *Shaping* is used in that clients are gradually asked to handle more complicated and delicate social situations. For example, a nonassertive client may begin by working on making requests of friends. Only much later will the client be asked to tackle standing up to his or her boss.

Evaluating Behavior Therapies

Learning Objective

Summarize evidence on the efficacy of behavior therapies.

Behavior therapists have historically placed more emphasis than insight therapists on the importance of measuring therapeutic outcomes. As a result, there is ample evidence regarding the effectiveness of behavior therapy (Liberman & Bedell, 1989; Rachman & Wilson, 1980). How does the effectiveness of behavior therapy compare to that of insight therapy? In direct comparisons, the differences between the therapies are usually small (Smith, Glass, & Miller, 1980). However, these modest differences tend to favor behavioral approaches for certain types of disorders (Lambert & Bergin, 1992). Of course, behavior therapies are not well suited to the treatment of some types of problems (vague feelings of discontent, for instance). Furthermore, it's misleading to make global statements about the effectiveness of behavior therapies because they include many different procedures designed for different purposes. For example, the value of systematic desensitization for phobias has no bearing on the value of aversion therapy for sexual deviance.

For our purposes, it is sufficient to note that there is favorable evidence on the efficacy of most of the widely used behavioral interventions (Wixted et al., 1990). Behavior therapies seem to be particularly effective in the treatment of anxiety problems, phobias, obsessive-compulsive disorders, sexual dysfunction, schizophrenia, drug-related problems, eating disorders, psychosomatic disorders, hyperactivity, autism, and mental retardation (Emmelkamp, 1994; Liberman & Bedell, 1989).

Many of these problems would not be amenable to treatment with the biomedical therapies, which we consider next. To some extent, the three major approaches to treatment have different strengths. Let's see where the strengths of the biomedical therapies lie.

Biomedical Therapies

In the 1950s, a French surgeon was looking for a drug that would reduce patients' autonomic response to surgical stress. The surgeon noticed that chlorpromazine produced a mild sedation. Based on this observation, Delay and Deniker (1952) decided to give chlorpromazine to hospitalized schizophrenic patients to see whether it would have calming effects. Their experiment was a dramatic success. Chlorpromazine became the first effective antipsychotic drug—and a revolution in psychiatry was begun. Hundreds of thousands of severely disturbed patients—patients who had appeared doomed to spend the remainder of their lives in mental hospitals—were gradually sent home, thanks to the therapeutic effects of antipsychotic drugs (see Figure 16.8). Today, biomedical therapies, such as drug treatment, lie at the core of psychiatric practice.

Biomedical therapies **are physiological interventions intended to reduce symptoms associated with psychological disorders.** These therapies assume that psychological disorders are caused, at least in part, by biological malfunctions. As we discussed in the previous chapter, this assumption clearly has merit for many disorders, especially the more severe ones. We will discuss two biomedical approaches to psychotherapy: drug therapy and electroconvulsive (shock) therapy.

**Figure 16.8
The declining inpatient population in mental hospitals**
The number of inpatients in public mental hospitals has declined dramatically since the late 1950s. In part, this has been due to "deinstitutionalization"—a philosophy that emphasizes outpatient care whenever possible. However, above all else, this decline was made possible by the development of effective antipsychotic medications.

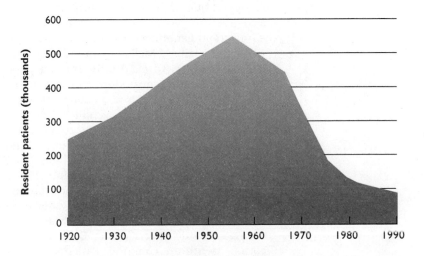

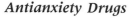

Treatment with Drugs

Learning Objective

Describe the principal drug therapies used in the treatment of psychological disorders.

Psychopharmacotherapy involves the treatment of mental disorders with medication. We will refer to this kind of treatment more simply as *drug therapy.* Therapeutic drugs for psychological problems fall into three major groups: (1) antianxiety drugs, (2) antipsychotic drugs, and (3) antidepressant drugs. Another important drug that does not fit neatly into any of these categories is lithium, which is used in the treatment of bipolar mood disorders. Of these drugs, the antianxiety agents are the most widely prescribed (see Figure 16.9). Surprisingly, only about 17% of the prescriptions for drugs used in the treatment of psychological problems are written by psychiatrists (Beardsley et al., 1988). The vast majority of these prescriptions are written by primary care physicians.

Antianxiety Drugs

Most of us know someone who pops pills to relieve anxiety. The drugs involved in this common coping strategy are *antianxiety drugs,* **which relieve tension, apprehension, and nervousness.** The most popular of these drugs are Valium and Xanax, the trade names (the proprietary names that pharmaceutical companies use in marketing drugs) for diazepam and alprazolam, respectively.

Valium, Xanax, and other drugs in the benzodiazepine family are often called *tranquilizers.* These drugs are routinely prescribed for people with anxiety disorders. They are also given to millions of people who simply suffer from chronic nervous tension. In the mid-1970s, pharmacists in the United States were filling nearly *100 million* prescriptions each year for Valium and similar antianxiety drugs. Many critics characterized this level of use as excessive (Lickey & Gordon, 1991).

Antianxiety drugs exert their effects almost immediately. They can be fairly effective in alleviating feelings of anxiety (Lader, 1984). However, their effects are measured in hours, so their impact is relatively short-lived. Common side effects of antianxiety drugs include drowsiness, depression, nausea, and confusion (Evans, 1981). There is some potential for abuse, dependency, and overdose problems with these drugs (Salzman, 1989). Another drawback is that patients who have been on antianxiety drugs for a while often experience withdrawal symptoms when their drug treatment is stopped (Lader, 1990). These problems led to a moderate decline in the prescription of Valium and similar drugs in the 1980s. Currently, clinicians and researchers are experimenting with a new antianxiety drug called BuSpar (buspirone). It appears to have little potential for abuse or dependence (Gorman & Davis, 1989). Unlike Valium, BuSpar is slow-acting, exerting its effects in one to three weeks, but with fewer sedative side effects (Norman & Burrows, 1990).

Antipsychotic Drugs

Antipsychotic drugs are used primarily in the treatment of schizophrenia. They are also given to people with severe mood disorders who become delusional. The trade names (and generic names) of some prominent drugs in this category are Thorazine (chlorpromazine), Mellaril (thioridazine), and Haldol (haloperidol). *Antipsychotic drugs* **are used to gradually reduce psychotic symptoms, including hyperactivity, mental confusion, hallucinations, and delusions.**

Studies suggest that about 90% of psychotic patients respond favorably (albeit in varied degrees) to antipsychotic medication (Davis, Barter, & Kane, 1989). When antipsychotic drugs are effective, they work their magic gradually, as shown in Figure 16.10. Patients usually begin to respond within two days to a week. Further improvement may occur for several months. Many schizophrenic patients are placed on antipsychotics indefinitely because these drugs can reduce the likelihood of a relapse into an active schizophrenic episode.

Antipsychotic drugs undeniably make a major contribution to the treatment of severe mental disorders, but they are not without problems. They have many unpleasant side effects (Lader & Herrington, 1990). Drowsiness, constipation, and cotton mouth are common. Patients may also experience tremors, muscular rigidity, and impaired coordination. After being released from a hospital, many schizo-

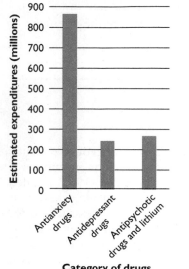

**Figure 16.9
Expenditures on drugs used in the treatment of psychological problems and disorders**
Hundreds of millions of dollars are spent on drug therapy in the United States each year. Of the three categories of therapeutic drugs, the antianxiety drugs are the most frequently prescibed, as these data on outpatient expenditures reflect. (Data based on Zorc et al., 1991)

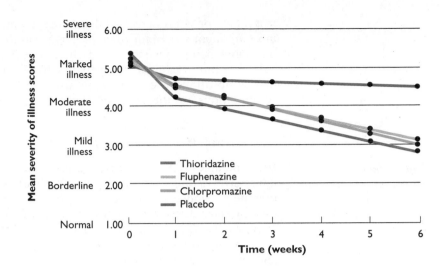

Figure 16.10
The time course of antipsychotic drug effects
Antipsychotic drugs reduce psychotic symptoms gradually, over a span of weeks, as graphed here. In contrast, patients given placebo pills show little improvement. (Data from Cole, Goldberg, & Davis, 1966; J. M. Davis, 1985)

phrenic patients, supposedly placed on antipsychotics indefinitely, discontinue their drug regimen because of the disagreeable side effects. Unfortunately, relapse into another schizophrenic episode often occurs within three to nine months after a patient stops taking antipsychotic medication (J. M. Davis, 1985). In addition to minor side effects, antipsychotics may cause a severe and lasting problem called *tardive dyskinesia*. **Tardive dyskinesia is a neurological disorder marked by chronic tremors and involuntary spastic movements.** This debilitating syndrome resembles Parkinson's disease, and there is no cure.

A new antipsychotic drug called Clozaril (clozapine) was introduced in 1990. Although it's not risk-free, this drug seems to produce fewer side effects than traditional antipsychotics (Davis, Barter, & Kane, 1989). Moreover, Clozaril appears to help a significant portion of the 10% of patients who do not respond to other antipsychotic medications (Perry et al., 1991). Unfortunately, Clozaril therapy is extremely expensive, running about $5000 per year for each patient (Jann, Jenike, & Lieberman, 1994).

Antidepressant Drugs

As their name suggests, *antidepressant drugs* **gradually elevate mood and help bring people out of a depression.** Until recently, there were two principal classes of antidepressants: *tricyclics* (such as Elavil) and *MAO inhibitors* (such as Nardil). These two classes of drugs affect neurochemical activity in different ways and tend to work with different patients. The tricyclics are effective for a larger percentage (60–80%) of depressed patients (Davis & Glassman, 1989). They also have fewer problematic side effects than the MAO inhibitors (Glenn & Taska, 1984). Like antipsychotic drugs, antidepressants exert their effects gradually over a period of weeks.

Psychiatrists are currently enthusiastic about a new class of antidepressants, called *selective serotonin reuptake inhibitors*, which slow the reuptake process at serotonin synapses. The drugs in this class, which include Prozac (fluoxetine), Paxil (paroxetine), and Zoloft (sertraline) seem to yield rapid therapeutic gains in the treatment of depression (Jann et al., 1994). Prozac also appears to have value in the treatment of obsessive-compulsive disorders (Jenike, Baer, & Greist, 1990). However, Prozac is not a "miracle drug" as suggested by some popular magazines. A minority of patients on Prozac have developed serious, unexpected side effects, such as intense suicidal preoccupations (Teicher, Glod, & Cole, 1990). Like all drugs for psychological disorders, Prozac has risks that must be carefully weighed against its benefits.

Lithium

Lithium is a chemical used to control mood swings in patients with bipolar mood disorders. Lithium has excellent value in preventing *future* episodes of both mania and depression in patients with bipolar illness (Jefferson & Greist, 1989). Lithium can also be used in efforts to bring patients with bipolar illness out of cur-

rent manic or depressive episodes. However, antipsychotics and antidepressants are more frequently used for these purposes. On the negative side of the ledger, lithium has some dangerous side effects if its use isn't managed skillfully (Abou-Saleh, 1992). Lithium levels in the patient's blood must be monitored carefully because high concentrations can be highly toxic and even fatal. Kidney and thyroid gland complications are the major problems associated with lithium therapy (Post, 1989).

Evaluating Drug Therapies

Learning Objective

Summarize evidence on the efficacy and problems of drug therapies.

Drug therapies can produce clear gains for many kinds of patients. What's especially impressive is that they can be effective with severe disorders that otherwise defy therapeutic endeavors. Nonetheless, drug therapies are controversial. Critics of drug therapy have raised a number of issues (Breggin, 1990, 1991; Cohen & McCubbin, 1990; Lickey & Gordon, 1991). First, some critics argue that drug therapies often produce superficial curative effects. For example, Valium does not really solve problems with anxiety. It merely provides temporary relief from an unpleasant symptom. Moreover, this temporary relief may lull patients into complacency about their problem and prevent them from working toward a more lasting solution. Second, critics charge that many drugs are overprescribed and many patients overmedicated. According to these critics, many physicians habitually hand out prescriptions without giving adequate consideration to more complicated and difficult interventions. This problem is compounded by the fact that drugs calm patients and make it easier for hospital staff to run their wards. Thus, critics argue that there is a tendency in some institutions to overmedicate patients to minimize disruptive behavior. Third, some critics charge that the side effects of therapeutic drugs are worse than the illnesses that the drugs are supposed to cure. Citing problems such as tardive dyskinesia, lithium toxicity, addiction to antianxiety agents, and so forth, these critics argue that the risks of therapeutic drugs aren't worth the benefits.

In their relatively even-handed evaluation of psychiatric drugs, Lickey and Gordon (1991) acknowledge that the issues raised by the critics of drug therapy are legitimate sources of concern, but after reviewing the evidence they defend the value of therapeutic drugs. They argue that drug therapies were never touted as *cures* and that "the relief of symptoms is a genuine benefit that must not be dismissed as trivial" (p. 358). They agree that some drugs are overprescribed and that most drugs have potentially serious side effects, but they conclude that overall, the benefits of drug therapy far exceed any harm done.

Obviously, drug therapies have stirred up some debate. However, this controversy pales in comparison to the furious debates inspired by electroconvulsive (shock) therapy (ECT). ECT is so controversial that the residents of Berkeley, California, voted to outlaw ECT in their city. However, in subsequent lawsuits, the courts ruled that scientific questions cannot be settled through a vote, and they overturned the law. What makes ECT so controversial? You'll see in the next section.

Electroconvulsive Therapy (ECT)

Learning Objective

Describe ECT and discuss its efficacy.

In the 1930s, a Hungarian psychiatrist named Ladislas Meduna speculated that epilepsy and schizophrenia could not coexist in the same body. On the basis of this observation (which turned out to be inaccurate), Meduna theorized that it might be useful to induce epileptic-like seizures in schizophrenic patients. Initially, a drug was used to trigger these seizures. However, by 1938 a pair of Italian psychiatrists (Cerletti & Bini, 1938) had demonstrated that it was safer to elicit the seizures with electric shock. Thus, modern electroconvulsive therapy was born.

Electroconvulsive therapy (ECT) is a biomedical treatment in which electric shock is used to produce a cortical seizure accompanied by convulsions. In ECT, electrodes are attached to the skull over the temporal lobes of the brain (see the photo on page 528). A light anesthesia is induced and the patient is given a variety of drugs to minimize the likelihood of complications, such as spinal fractures. An electric current is then applied for about a second. The current should trigger a brief (5–20 seconds) convulsive seizure, during which the patient usually loses consciousness. Patients normally awaken in an hour or two. People typically receive between 6 and 20 treatments as inpatients at a hospital (Fink, 1992).

The clinical use of ECT peaked in the 1940s and 1950s, before effective drug therapies were widely available. ECT has long been controversial, and its use declined in the 1960s and 1970s. Nonetheless, ECT is *not* a rare form of therapy. Estimates suggest that about 36,000 people receive ECT treatments yearly in the United States, mainly for mood disorders (Thompson, Weiner, & Myers, 1994).

Controversy about ECT is also fueled by patients' reports that the treatment is painful, dehumanizing, and terrifying. Additional concerns have been raised by allegations that staff members at some hospitals have used the threat of ECT to keep patients in line (Breggin, 1979). Using ECT for disciplinary purposes is unethical, but the essay in Figure 16.11 suggests that it has happened in some institutions. This essay, written by one of Wayne Weiten's former students who received ECT in the 1960s, also provides a moving description of how unpleasant and frightening ECT can be for some patients. Although improvements in the administration of ECT have made it less disagreeable than it once was, many patients continue to report that they find the treatment extremely aversive (Breggin, 1991).

Effectiveness of ECT

The evidence on the effectiveness of ECT is open to varied interpretations, and the therapeutic efficacy of the treatment is hotly debated. Ardent proponents maintain that it is a remarkably effective treatment (Abrams, 1992; Fink, 1992; Swartz, 1993). However, equally ardent opponents argue that it is no more effective than a placebo (Breggin, 1991; Friedberg, 1976). Reported improvement rates for ECT treatment range from negligible to very high (Small, Small, & Milstein, 1986). The findings on

Figure 16.11
One patient's experience with electroconvulsive therapy
Although some patients treated with electroconvulsive therapy (ECT) have much more favorable experiences, this moving memoir about ECT treatment paints a very unpleasant picture. (Quoted by permission from a former student)

A Personal Experience with ECT

I'm not saying this is what shock is all about, or that it happens this way everywhere. I am saying that this is what happened to me in this particular institution.

Slang for shock in that institution was known as "gettin' Kentucky fried," and being taken into shock was known as "a visit to the Colonel." I was going for a visit.

Along the way, I always started making deals with God: "If you get me out of this one . . ." They never worked out. When the deals fell through, I started making every promise I knew I could keep, and just to be safe, a few I knew I couldn't. Looking back, it all seems kind of funny. At the time, I was sure they were trying to kill me.

The room where it was done was in the very center of the ward. This was not surprising. Almost all of our shock was done as a disciplinary measure, our very lives revolved around staff's ability to enforce discipline and order upon us. So to me, it was not too surprising that the Colonel set up shop where he did.

When the door opened, the intense whiteness of the fluorescent lights blinded me. Staff took advantage of this by leading me to the gurney where I was to lie down. By the time my eyes adjusted, I was on my back with several pairs of hands holding me down.

A mouthpiece was crammed rather indelicately into place, and the conductant was smeared on my temples. There was some technical talk and someone said "Now" (I wanted desperately to say wait a moment). And then there it was—one of the most excruciating pains I have ever felt. My back ached in an attempt to jump off the gurney, all the air squeezed out of my lungs, my legs flexed until they felt as if they would break, my head felt as if it would pop off. I was out of control: it was not me anymore.

I don't know how long it took but finally I passed out. When I opened my eyes again, I had the headache of headaches. I was confused, I couldn't connect two thoughts.

The next two or three days were a nightmare of confusion and awkward movements, always feeling like a thought was there, on the tip of your tongue, but not able to grab it. The more you grabbed at it, the more elusive it became, and the more frustrated you became.

Eventually, I returned to normal, but before that happened, I would go through a deep dark depression. I could fight the system, I could fight Staff, I could fight the drugs, the aides, and the other patients.

I could not fight this. I was beaten. My thoughts were exactly that, mine. Before shock they were untouched, now they had been reached and, worse still, disorganized externally. The depression then seemed to come from a sense of defeat, of being violated, and of being mentally raped.

How can I make you feel that?

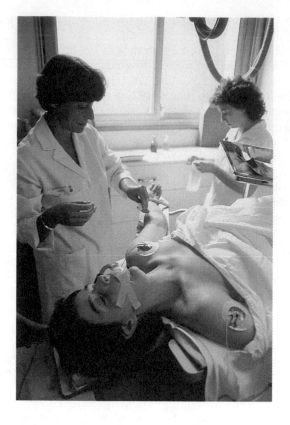

This patient is being prepared for electroconvulsive therapy. The mouthpiece keeps the patient from biting her tongue during the electrically induced seizures.

relapse rates after treatment are also inconsistent (Frank, 1990; Weiner, 1984).

In light of these problems, conclusions about the value of ECT must be tentative. Although ECT was once considered appropriate for a wide range of disorders, in recent decades it has primarily been recommended for the treatment of depression. Accumulating evidence suggests that it may also have value for manic patients (Mukherjee, Sackeim, & Schnur, 1994). Overall, there does seem to be enough favorable evidence to justify *conservative* use of ECT in treating severe mood disorders (Rudorfer & Goodwin, 1993; Weiner & Coffey, 1988). Curiously, to the extent that ECT may be effective, no one is sure why. The discarded theories about how ECT works could fill several books.

The debate about whether ECT works, and how it works, does *not* make ECT unique among approaches to psychotherapy. Controversies exist regarding the effectiveness of most psychotherapies. However, this controversy is especially problematic because ECT may carry substantial risks.

Risks Associated with ECT

Learning Objective

Identify some of the risks associated with ECT.

Even ECT proponents acknowledge that memory losses, impaired attention, and other cognitive deficits are common short-term side effects of electroconvulsive therapy. However, ECT proponents assert that these deficits are mild and usually disappear within six months (Calev et al., 1993). In contrast, ECT critics maintain that these cognitive losses are significant and often permanent (Breggin, 1991; Frank, 1990). Complicating the issue considerably, recent studies using objective measures of patients' memory performance show that former ECT patients tend to overestimate their memory deficits (Sachs & Gelenberg, 1988).

So, what can be concluded about ECT and cognitive deficits? The truth probably lies somewhere between the positions staked out by the proponents and opponents of ECT. In a relatively dispassionate review of the ECT controversy, Small and associates (1986) asserted that "there is little doubt that ECT produces both short- and long-term intellectual impairment." However, they concluded that this impairment isn't inevitable and that it isn't permanent in the vast majority of cases. Nonetheless, given the concerns about the risks of ECT and the doubts about its efficacy, it appears that the use of ECT will remain controversial for some time to come.

Blending Approaches to Psychotherapy

Learning Objective

Discuss the merits of blending approaches to therapy.

We have reviewed several approaches to therapy, which are summarized and compared in Figure 16.12. However, there is no law that a client must be treated with just one approach. Often, a clinician will use several different approaches in working with a client. For example, a depressed person might receive cognitive therapy

Major Approaches to Psychotherapy

Type of psychotherapy	Primary founders	Origin of disorder	Therapeutic goals	Therapeutic techniques
Psychoanalysis	Freud	Unconscious conflicts resulting from fixations in earlier development	Insights regarding unconscious conflicts and motives; personality reconstruction	Free association, dream analysis, interpretation, catharsis, transference
Client-centered therapy	Rogers	Incongruence between self-concept and actual experience; dependence on acceptance from others	Congruence between self-concept and experience; acceptance of genuine self; self-determination, personal growth	Genuineness, empathy, unconditional positive regard, clarification, reflecting back to client
Cognitive therapy	Beck Ellis	Irrational assumptions and negative, self-defeating thinking about events related to self	Detection of negative thinking; substitution of more realistic thinking	Thought stopping, recording automatic thoughts, refuting negative thinking, reattribution, homework assignments
Behavior therapies	Wolpe Skinner Eysenck	Maladaptive patterns of behavior acquired through learning	Elimination of symptomatic, maladaptive behaviors; acquisition of more adaptive responses	Classical and operant conditioning, reinforcement, punishment, extinction, shaping, aversive conditioning, systematic desensitization, social skills training
Biomedical therapies		Physiological malfunction, primarily abnormal neurotransmitter activity	Elimination of symptoms; prevention of relapse	Antipsychotic, antianxiety, and antidepressant drugs; lithium; electroconvulsive therapy (ECT)

**Figure 16.12
Comparison of psychotherapy approaches**
This chart compares behavior therapies, biomedical therapies, and three leading approaches to insight therapy.

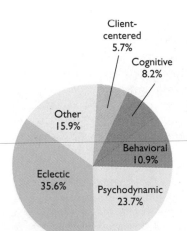

**Figure 16.13
The leading approaches to therapy among psychologists**
The pooled data from a survey of 415 clinical and counseling psychologists (Smith, 1982) and another survey of 479 clinical psychologists (Norcross & Prochaska, 1982) indicate that the most widely used approaches to therapy are (in order) the eclectic, psychodynamic, behavioral, cognitive, and client-centered approaches.

(an insight therapy), social skills training (a behavior therapy), and antidepressant medication (a biomedical therapy). Multiple approaches are particularly likely when a treatment *team* provides therapy.

Studies suggest that combining approaches to treatment has significant merit (Frank, 1991; Klerman et al., 1994). One representative study compared the value of insight therapy alone, drug therapy alone, and a combination of insight and drug therapies for unipolar depression (Weissman et al., 1979). The subjects were treated on an outpatient basis. The groups treated only with antidepressant medication or only with insight therapy both responded well. However, the greatest improvement was found in the group treated with both. Interestingly, the two treatments complemented each other nicely. The drug therapy was particularly effective in relieving certain symptoms, while the insight therapy was effective in relieving other symptoms. Thus, there is much to be said for combining approaches to treatment.

The value of multiple approaches may explain why a significant trend seems to have crept into the field of psychotherapy: a movement away from strong loyalty to individual schools of thought and a corresponding move toward integrating various approaches to therapy (Arkowitz, 1992; Norcross & Goldfried, 1992). Most clinicians used to depend exclusively on one system of therapy while rejecting the utility of all others. This era of fragmentation may be drawing to a close. In recent surveys of psychologists' theoretical orientations, researchers have been surprised to find that the greatest proportion of respondents describe themselves as *eclectic* in approach (Garfield & Bergin, 1994; see Figure 16.13).

Eclecticism in the practice of therapy involves drawing ideas from two or more systems of therapy, instead of committing to just one system. Therapists can be eclectic in a number of ways (Arkowitz, 1992). Two common approaches are theoretical integration and technical eclecticism. In *theoretical integration*, two or more systems of therapy are combined or blended to take advantage of the strengths of each. Paul Wachtel's (1977, 1991) efforts to blend psychodynamic and behavioral therapies is a prominent example. *Technical eclecticism* involves borrowing ideas, insights, and techniques from a variety of sources while tailoring the intervention strategy to the unique needs of each client. Advocates of technical eclecticism, such as Arnold Lazarus (1976, 1989), maintain that therapists should ask themselves, "What is the best approach for this specific client, problem, and situation?" and then adjust their strategy accordingly.

Looking for a Therapist

Answer the following "true" or "false."

1. Psychotherapy is an art as well as a science.

2. The type of professional degree that a therapist holds is relatively unimportant.

3. Psychotherapy can be harmful or damaging to a client.

4. Psychotherapy does not have to be expensive.

5. It is a good idea to shop around when choosing a therapist.

All of the statements above are true. Do any of them surprise you? If so, you're in good company. Many people know relatively little about the practicalities of selecting a therapist.

The task of finding an appropriate therapist is no less complex than shopping for any other major service. Should you see a psychologist or a psychiatrist? Should you opt for individual therapy or group therapy? Should you see a client-centered therapist or a behavior therapist? The unfortunate part of this complexity is that people seeking psychotherapy often feel overwhelmed by personal problems. The last thing they need is to be confronted by yet another complex problem.

Nonetheless, the importance of finding a good therapist cannot be overestimated. Therapy can sometimes have harmful rather than helpful effects. We have already discussed how drug therapies and ECT can sometimes be damaging, but problems are not limited to these interventions. Talking about your problems with a therapist may sound pretty harmless, but studies indicate that insight therapies can also backfire (Lambert & Bergin, 1994; McGlashan et al., 1990). Although a

Recommended Reading

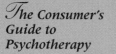

The Consumer's Guide to Psychotherapy

by Jack Engler & Daniel Goleman (Simon & Schuster, 1992)

This book, written by a clinical psychologist at the Harvard Medical School (Engler) and a psychologist who writes on the behavioral sciences for the *New York Times* (Goleman), follows in the highly practical tradition of the book by the Ehrenbergs recommended earlier in this chapter. However, the two books have different strengths, and both are worthwhile reading for anyone who is in therapy or is considering therapy. This remarkably thorough handbook provides advice on how to decide whether you need therapy, how to find the right therapist, what to realistically expect out of therapy, how to get the most out of therapy, and how to tell when therapy isn't working. Financial matters and ethical issues are discussed in detail. The book also includes extensive information about what types of treatment work best for various types of specific problems, such as bereavement, marital difficulties, anxiety disorders, eating disorders, hyperactivity, schizophrenia, and so forth. It also includes a chapter on psychiatric drugs and appendixes that list self-help groups, therapist referral sources, and other sources of information on mental health care.

Normally one of the most reliable sources of information about a professional service is satisfied consumers. However, just the opposite tends to be true in therapy. Recommendations from current or former clients are compromised by their emotional involvement. It is not that they don't know the therapist, but that their sense of the therapist is from their own perspective, which will not be yours. They are also too close to have an objective view. They rightfully need to believe that their therapy has worked for them. [p. 88] great many talented therapists are available, psychotherapy, like any other profession, has incompetent practitioners as well. Therefore, you should shop for a skilled therapist, just as you would for a good attorney or a good mechanic.

In this Application, we'll go over some information that should be helpful if you ever have to look for a therapist for yourself or for a friend or family member (based on Amada, 1985; Bruckner-Gordon, Gangi, & Wallman, 1988; Ehrenberg & Ehrenberg, 1986; Pittman, 1994).

When Should You Seek Professional Treatment?

There is no simple answer to the question of *when* (or whether) to seek professional treatment. Obviously, people *consider* the possibility of therapy when they are psychologically distressed. However, they have other options available to them. There is much to be said for seeking advice from family, friends, the clergy, and so forth. Insights about personal problems do not belong exclusively to people with professional degrees.

So, when should you turn to professionals for help? You should begin to think seriously about therapy when (1) you have no one to lean on, (2) the people you lean on indicate that they're getting tired of it, (3) you feel helpless and overwhelmed, or (4) your life is seriously disrupted by your problems. Of course, you do not have to be falling apart to justify therapy. You may want to seek professional advice simply because you want to get more out of life.

Where Do You Find Therapeutic Services?

Psychotherapy can be found in a variety of settings. Contrary to general belief, most therapists are not in private practice. Many work in institutional settings such as community mental health centers, hospitals, and human service agencies. The principal sources of therapeutic services are outlined in Figure 16.14. The exact configuration of therapeutic services available will vary from one community to another.

**Figure 16.14
Sources of therapeutic services**
Therapists work in a variety of organizational settings. Foremost among them are the five described here.

Principal Sources of Therapeutic Services

Source	Comments
Private practitioners	Self-employed therapists are listed in the Yellow Pages under their professional category, such as psychologists or psychiatrists. Private practitioners tend to be relatively expensive, but they also tend to be highly experienced therapists.
Community mental health centers	Community mental health centers have salaried psychologists, psychiatrists, and social workers on staff. The centers provide a variety of services and often have staff available on weekends and at night to deal with emergencies.
Hospitals	Several kinds of hospitals provide therapeutic services. There are both public and private mental hospitals that specialize in the care of people with psychological disorders. Many general hospitals have a psychiatric ward, and those that do not will usually have psychiatrists and psychologists on staff and on call. Although hospitals tend to concentrate on inpatient treatment, many provide outpatient therapy as well.
Human service agencies	Various social service agencies employ therapists to provide short-term counseling. Depending on your community, you may find agencies that deal with family problems, juvenile problems, drug problems, and so forth.
Schools and workplaces	Most high schools and colleges have counseling centers where students can get help with personal problems. Similarly, some large businesses offer in-house counseling to their employees.

To find out what your community has to offer, it is a good idea to consult your friends, your local phone book, or your local community mental health center.

Is the Therapist's Profession Important?

Learning Objective

Discuss the potential importance of a therapist's gender and professional background.

Psychotherapists may be trained in psychology, psychiatry, social work, counseling, psychiatric nursing, or marriage and family therapy. Researchers have *not* found any reliable associations between therapists' professional background and their therapeutic efficacy (Beutler, Machado, & Neufeldt, 1994), probably because many talented therapists can be found in all of these professions. Thus, the kind of degree that a therapist holds doesn't need to be a crucial consideration in your selection process. It *is* true that only a psychiatrist can prescribe drugs for disorders that merit drug therapy. However, some critics argue that many psychiatrists are too quick to use drugs to solve problems (Breggin, 1991). In any case, other types of therapists can refer you to a psychiatrist if they think that drug therapy would be helpful. If you have a health insurance policy that covers psychotherapy, you may want to check to see whether it carries any restrictions about the therapist's profession.

Is the Therapist's Gender Important?

The importance of the therapist's gender depends on your attitude. If *you* feel that the therapist's gender is important, then for you it is. The therapeutic relationship must be characterized by trust and rapport. Feeling uncomfortable with a therapist of one gender or the other could inhibit the therapeutic process. Hence, you should feel free to look for a male or female therapist if you prefer to do so. This point is probably most relevant to female clients whose troubles may be related to the extensive sexism in our society (A. G. Kaplan, 1985). It is entirely reasonable for women to seek a therapist with a feminist perspective if that would make them feel more comfortable.

On a related topic, you should be aware that sexual exploitation is an occasional problem in the context of therapy. Studies indicate that a small minority of therapists take advantage of their clients sexually (Pope, Keith-Spiegel, & Tabachnick, 1986). These incidents almost always involve a male therapist making advances to a female client. The available evidence indicates that these sexual liaisons are usually harmful to clients (Williams, 1992). There are absolutely no situations in which therapist-client sexual relations are an ethical therapeutic practice. If a therapist makes sexual advances, a client should terminate treatment.

Is Therapy Always Expensive?

Psychotherapy does not have to be prohibitively expensive. Private practitioners tend to be the most expensive, charging between $25 and $100 per (50-minute) hour. These fees may seem high, but they are in line with those of similar professionals, such as dentists and attorneys. Community mental health centers and social service agencies are usually supported by tax dollars. Hence, they can charge lower fees than most therapists in private practice. Many of these organizations use a sliding scale, so that clients are charged according to how much they can afford to pay. Thus, most communities have inexpensive opportunities for psychotherapy. Moreover, many health insurance plans provide at least partial reimbursement for the cost of psychotherapy.

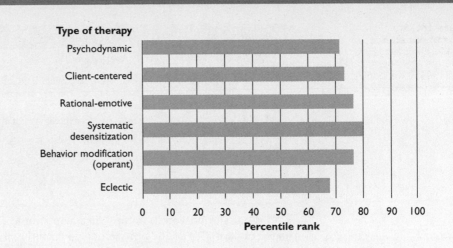

Figure 16.15
Efficacy of various approaches to therapy
Smith and Glass (1977) reviewed nearly 400 studies in which clients who were treated with a specific type of therapy were compared with a control group made up of people with similar problems who went untreated. The bars indicate the percentile rank (on outcome measures) attained by the average client treated with each type of therapy when compared to control subjects. The higher the percentile, the more effective the therapy was. As you can see, the various approaches were fairly close in their apparent effectiveness.

Is the Therapist's Theoretical Approach Important?

Learning Objective

Discuss whether therapists' theoretical approach influences their effectiveness.

Logically, you might expect that the diverse approaches to therapy vary in effectiveness. For the most part, this is *not* what researchers find, however. After reviewing the evidence, Jerome Frank (1961) and Lester Luborsky and his colleagues (1975) both quote the dodo bird who has just judged a race in *Alice in Wonderland:* "*Everybody* has won, and *all* must have prizes." Improvement rates for various theoretical orientations usually come out pretty close in most studies (Lambert & Bergin, 1994). In their landmark review of outcome studies, Smith and Glass (1977) estimated the effectiveness of many major approaches to therapy. As Figure 16.15 shows, the estimates cluster together closely.

These findings do not mean that all *therapists* are created equal. Some therapists unquestionably are more effective than others. However, these variations appear to depend more on therapists' personal skills rather than on their theoretical orientation (Beutler et al., 1994). Good, bad, and mediocre therapists are found within each school of thought.

The key point is that effective therapy requires skill and creativity. Arnold Lazarus (1989), who devised multimodal therapy, emphasizes that therapists straddle the fence between science and art. Therapy is scientific in that interventions are based on extensive theory and empirical research (Forsyth & Strong, 1986). Ultimately, though, each client is a unique human being, and the therapist has to creatively fashion a treatment program that will help that individual.

What Should You Look for in a Prospective Therapist?

Learning Objective

Summarize what one should look for in a prospective therapist and what one should expect out of therapy.

Some clients are timid about asking prospective therapists questions about their training, approach, fees, and so forth. However, these are reasonable questions, and the vast majority of therapists will be most accommodating in providing answers. Usually, you may ask your preliminary questions over the phone. If things seem promising, you may decide to make an appointment for an interview (you probably will have to pay for the interview). In this interview, the therapist will gather more information to determine the likelihood of helping you, given the therapist's training and approach to treatment. At the same time, you should be making a similar judgment about whether *you* believe the therapist can help you with your problems.

Figure 16.16
Signs of resistance
Resistance in therapy may be subtle, but Ehrenberg and Ehrenberg (1986) have identified some telltale signs to look for.

Signs of Resistance in Therapy

If you're dissatisfied with your progress in therapy, resistance may be the problem when:

1 You have nothing specific or concrete to complain about.

2 Your attitude about therapy changes suddenly just as you reach the truly sensitive issues.

3 You've had the same problem with other therapists in the past.

4 Your conflicts with the therapist resemble those that you have with other people.

5 You start hiding things from your therapist.

What should you look for? First, you should look for personal warmth and sincere concern. Try to judge whether you will be able to talk to this person in a candid, nondefensive way. Second, look for empathy and understanding. Is the person capable of appreciating your point of view? Third, look for self-confidence. Self-assured therapists will communicate a sense of competence without trying to intimidate you with jargon or boasting needlessly about what they can do for you. When all is said and done, you should *like* your therapist. Otherwise, it will be difficult to establish the needed rapport.

What If There Isn't Any Progress?

If you feel that your therapy isn't going anywhere, you should probably discuss these feelings with your therapist. Don't be surprised, however, if the therapist suggests that it may be your own fault. Freud's concept of resistance has some validity. Some clients *do* have difficulty facing up to their problems. Thus, if your therapy isn't progressing, you may need to *consider* whether your resistance may be slowing progress. This self-examination isn't easy, as you are not an unbiased observer. Some common signs of resistance identified by Ehrenberg and Ehrenberg (1986) are listed in Figure 16.16.

Given the very real possibility that poor progress may be due to resistance, you should not be too quick to leave therapy when dissatisfied. However, it *is* possible that your therapist isn't sufficiently skilled or that the two of you are incompatible. Thus, after careful and deliberate consideration, you should feel free to terminate your therapy.

What Is Therapy Like?

It is important to have realistic expectations about therapy, or you may be unnecessarily disappointed. Some people expect miracles. They expect to turn their life around quickly with little effort. Others expect their therapist to run their lives for them. These are unrealistic expectations.

Therapy usually is a slow process. Your problems are not likely to melt away quickly. Moreover, therapy is hard work, and your therapist is only a facilitator. Ultimately, *you* have to confront the challenge of changing your behavior, your feelings, or your personality. This process may not be pleasant. You may have to face up to some painful truths about yourself. As Ehrenberg and Ehrenberg (1986) point out, "Psychotherapy takes time, effort, and courage."

Key Ideas

The Elements of Psychotherapy: Treatments, Clients, and Therapists

• Psychotherapy involves three elements: treatments, clients, and therapists. Approaches to treatment are diverse, but they can be grouped into three categories: insight therapies, behavior therapies, and biomedical therapies.

Insight Therapies

• Insight therapies involve verbal interactions intended to enhance self-knowledge. In psychoanalysis, free association and dream analysis are used to explore the unconscious. When an analyst's probing hits sensitive areas, resistance can be expected. The transference relationship may be used to overcome this resistance. Classical psychoanalysis is not widely practiced anymore, but Freud's legacy lives on in a rich diversity of modern psychodynamic therapies.

• The client-centered therapist tries to provide a supportive climate in which clients can restructure their self-concepts. The process of therapy emphasizes clarification of the client's feelings and self-acceptance. Cognitive therapy concentrates on changing the way clients think about events in their lives. Most theoretical approaches to insight therapy have been adapted for use with groups. Group therapy has unique advantages in comparison to individual therapy.

• Eysenck's work in the 1950s raised doubts about the effectiveness of insight therapy and stimulated research on its efficacy. The weight of the evidence suggests that insight therapies can be effective. Repressed memories of childhood sexual abuse recovered through therapy are a new source of controversy in the mental health field. Although many recovered memories of abuse may be the product of suggestion, some may be authentic.

Behavior Therapies

• Behavior therapies use the principles of learning in direct efforts to change specific aspects of behavior. Systematic desensitization is a treatment for phobias. It involves the construction of an anxiety hierarchy, relaxation training, and step-by-step movement through the hierarchy.

• In aversion therapy, a stimulus associated with an unwanted response is paired with an unpleasant stimulus in an effort to eliminate the maladaptive response. Social skills training can improve clients' interpersonal skills through shaping, modeling, and behavioral rehearsal. There is ample evidence that behavior therapies are effective.

Biomedical Therapies

• Biomedical therapies involve physiological interventions for psychological problems. Two examples of biomedical treatments are drug therapy and electroconvulsive therapy. A great variety of disorders are treated with drugs. The principal types of therapeutic drugs include antianxiety drugs, antipsychotic drugs, antidepressant drugs, and lithium. Drug therapies can be very effective, but they have their pitfalls. Many drugs produce problematic side effects and some are overprescribed.

• Electroconvulsive therapy is used to trigger a cortical seizure that is believed to have therapeutic value for mood disorders, especially depression. There is contradictory evidence and heated debate about the effectiveness of ECT and about possible risks associated with its use.

Blending Approaches to Psychotherapy

• Combinations of insight, behavioral, and biomedical therapies are often used fruitfully in the treatment of psychological disorders. Many modern therapists are eclectic, using specific ideas, techniques, and strategies gleaned from a number of theoretical approaches.

Application: Looking for a Therapist

• Many practical considerations are relevant to the task of seeking professional treatment. Therapeutic services are available in many settings, and such services do not have to be expensive. Excellent therapists and mediocre therapists can be found in all of the mental health professions, using the full range of therapeutic approaches. Thus, therapists' personal skills are more important than their professional degree or their theoretical orientation.

• In selecting a therapist, warmth, empathy, confidence, and likability are desirable traits, and it is reasonable to insist on a therapist of one gender or the other. If progress is slow, your own resistance may be the problem. Therapy requires time, hard work, and the courage to confront your problems.

Key Terms

Antianxiety drugs
Antidepressant drugs
Antipsychotic drugs
Aversion therapy
Behavior therapies
Biomedical therapies
Client-centered therapy
Clinical psychologists
Cognitive therapy
Counseling psychologists
Dream analysis
Electroconvulsive therapy (ECT)
Free association
Group therapy
Insight therapies
Interpretation
Lithium
Psychiatrists
Psychoanalysis
Psychopharmacotherapy
Resistance
Social skills training
Spontaneous remission
Systematic desensitization
Tardive dyskinesia
Transference

Key People

Aaron Beck
Hans Eysenck
Sigmund Freud
Carl Rogers
Joseph Wolpe

acquaintance rape Forced and unwanted sexual intercourse with someone known to the victim.

acquired immune deficiency syndrome (AIDS) A disorder in which the immune system is gradually weakened and eventually disabled by the human immunodeficiency virus (HIV).

actor-observer effect The tendency to attribute one's own behavior to situation factors and others' behavior to personal factors.

adjustment The psychological processes through which people manage or cope with the demands and challenges of everyday life.

aggression Any behavior intended to hurt someone, either physically or verbally.

agoraphobia A fear of going out to public places.

alcoholism A chronic, progressive disorder marked by a growing compulsion to drink and impaired control over drinking that eventually interfere with health and social behavior.

ambient stress Chronic environmental conditions that, although not urgent, are negatively valued and place adaptive demands on people.

anal intercourse The insertion of the penis into a partner's anus and rectum.

androcentrism The belief that the male is the norm.

androgens The principal class of male sex hormones.

androgyny The coexistence of both masculine and feminine personality traits in an individual.

antecedents In behavior modification, events that typically precede a target response.

antianxiety drugs Drugs that relieve tension, apprehension, and nervousness.

antidepressant drugs Drugs that gradually elevate mood and help to bring people out of a depression.

antipsychotic drugs Drugs used to gradually reduce psychotic symptoms, including hyperactivity, mental confusion, hallucinations, and delusions.

anxiety disorders A class of psychological disorders marked by feelings of excessive apprehension and anxiety.

approach-approach conflict A conflict in which a choice must be made between two attractive goals.

approach-avoidance conflict A conflict in which a choice must be made about whether to pursue a single goal that has both attractive and unattractive aspects.

archetypes Emotionally charged images and thought forms that have universal meaning.

assertiveness Acting in one's own best interest by expressing one's feelings and thoughts honestly and directly.

atherosclerosis A disease characterized by gradual narrowing of the coronary arteries.

attitudes Beliefs and feelings about people, objects, and ideas.

attributional style The tendency to use similar causal explanations for a wide variety of events in one's life.

attributions Inferences that people draw about the causes of events, others' behavior, and their own behavior.

autonomic nervous system (ANS) That portion of the peripheral nervous system made up of the nerves that connect to the heart, blood vessels, smooth muscles, and glands.

aversion therapy A behavior therapy in which an aversive stimulus is paired with a stimulus that elicits an undesirable response.

avoidance-avoidance conflict A conflict in which a choice must be made between two unattractive goals.

basking in reflected glory The tendency to enhance one's image by publicly announcing one's association with those who are successful.

behavior Any overt (observable) response or activity by an organism.

behavior modification A systematic approach to changing behavior through the application of the principles of conditioning.

behavior therapies The application of the principles of learning to direct efforts to change clients' maladaptive behaviors.

behavioral contract A written agreement outlining a promise to adhere to the contingencies of a behavior modification program.

behaviorism A theoretical orientation based on the premise that scientific psychology should study observable behavior.

bereavement The painful loss of a loved one through death.

biomedical therapies Physiological interventions intended to reduce symptoms associated with psychological disorders.

biopsychosocial model The idea that physical illness is caused by a complex interaction of biological, psychological, and sociocultural factors.

bipolar mood disorders Psychological disorders marked by the experience of both depressed and manic periods.

bisexuals People who seek emotional-sexual relationships with members of both genders.

brainstorming Generating as many ideas as possible while withholding criticism and evaluation.

burnout Physical, mental, and emotional exhaustion that is attributable to work-related stress.

bystander effect The social phenomenon in which individuals are less likely to provide needed help when others are present than when they are alone.

cancer Malignant cell growth, which may occur in many organ systems in the body.

cannabis The hemp plant from which marijuana, hashish, and THC are derived.

case study An in-depth investigation of an individual subject.

catastrophic thinking Unrealistic appraisals of stress that exaggerate the magnitude of one's problems.

catatonic schizophrenia A type of schizophrenia marked by striking motor disturbances, ranging from muscular rigidity to random motor activity.

catharsis The release of emotional tension.

cerebral hemispheres The right and left halves of the cerebrum, which is the convoluted outer layer of the brain.

channel The medium through which a message reaches the receiver.

classical conditioning A type of learning in which a neutral stimulus acquires the capacity to evoke a response that was originally evoked by another stimulus.

client-centered therapy An insight therapy that emphasizes providing a supportive emotional climate for clients, who play a major role in determining the pace and direction of their therapy.

clinical psychologists Psychologists who specialize in the diagnosis and treatment of psychological disorders and everyday behavioral problems.

clinical psychology The branch of psychology concerned with the diagnosis and treatment of psychological problems and disorders.

close relationships Relatively long-lasting relationships in which frequent interactions occur in a variety of settings and in which the impact of the interactions is strong.

cognition The thought processes involved in acquiring knowledge.

cognitive dissonance The psychological discomfort that occurs when related cognitions are inconsistent—that is, when they contradict each other.

cognitive therapy An insight therapy that emphasizes recognizing and changing negative thoughts and maladaptive beliefs.

cohabitation Living together in a sexually intimate relationship without the legal bonds of marriage.

coitus The insertion of the penis into the vagina and (typically) pelvic thrusting.

collective unconscious According to Jung, a storehouse of latent memory traces inherited from people's ancestral past that is shared with the entire human race.

collectivism Putting group goals ahead of personal goals and defining one's identity in terms of the groups to which one belongs.

collusion The situation that occurs when two people have an unspoken agreement to deny some problematic aspect of reality in order to sustain their relationship.

commitment The decision and intent to maintain a relationship in spite of the difficulties and costs that may arise.

communication apprehension The anxiety caused by having to talk with others.

communication barrier Anything in the communication process that inhibits or blocks the accurate transmission and reception of messages.

comparison level One's standard of what constitutes an acceptable balance of rewards and costs in a relationship.

comparison level for alternatives One's estimation of the available outcomes from alternative relationships.

compensation A defense mechanism characterized by efforts to overcome imagined or real inferiorities by developing one's abilities.

compliance Yielding to social pressure in one's public behavior, even though one's private beliefs have not changed.

concordance rate A statistic indicating the percentage of twin pairs or other pairs of relatives that exhibit the same disorder.

conditioned response (CR) A learned reaction to a conditioned stimulus that occurs because of previous conditioning.

conditioned stimulus (CS) A previously neutral stimulus that has, through conditioning, acquired the capacity to evoke a conditioned response.

confirmatory hypothesis The tendency to behave toward others in ways that confirm one's hypotheses about them.

conflict The struggle that occurs when two or more incompatible motivations or behavioral impulses compete for expression.

conformity Yielding to real or imagined social pressure.

conscious According to Freud, whatever one is aware of at a particular point in time.

constructive coping Efforts to deal with stressful events that are judged to be relatively healthful.

control group Subjects in an experiment who do not receive the special treatment given to the experimental group.

conversion disorders Psychological disorders characterized by a significant loss of physical function (with no apparent organic basis), usually in a single organ system.

coping Active efforts to master, reduce, or tolerate the demands created by stress.

coronary heart disease A chronic disease characterized by a reduction in blood flow from the coronary arteries, which supply the heart with blood.

correlation The extent to which two variables are related to each other.

correlation coefficient A numerical index of the degree of relationship that exists between two variables.

counseling psychologists Psychologists who specialize in the treatment of everyday behavioral problems.

cunnilingus The oral stimulation of the female genitals.

date rape Forced and unwanted intercourse with someone in the context of dating.

death system The collection of rituals and procedures used by a culture to handle death.

defense mechanisms Largely unconscious reactions that protect a person from unpleasant emotions such as anxiety and guilt.

defensive attribution The tendency to blame victims for their misfortune, so that one feels less likely to be victimized in a similar way.

deindividuation The loss of self-awareness and evaluation apprehension that occur when individuals believe they are anonymous.

delusions False beliefs that are maintained even though they clearly are out of touch with reality.

dependent variable In an experiment, the variable that is thought to be affected by manipulations of the independent variable.

depressive disorders Psychological disorders characterized by persistent feelings of sadness and despair and a loss of interest in previous sources of pleasure.

designer drugs Illicitly manufactured variations of known recreational drugs.

diagnosis Distinguishing one illness from another.

diffusion of responsibility The expectation that others who are present will take responsibility for action.

discrimination Behaving differently, usually unfairly, toward members of a group.

disorganized schizophrenia A type of schizophrenia characterized by a particularly severe deterioration of adaptive behavior.

displacement Diverting emotional feelings (usually anger) from their original source to a substitute target.

display rules Norms that govern the appropriate display of emotions.

dissociative amnesia A sudden loss of memory for important personal information that is too extensive to be due to normal forgetting.

dissociative disorders A class of psychological disorders characterized by loss of contact with portions of one's consciousness or memory, resulting in disruptions in one's sense of identity.

dissociative identity disorder See multiple-personality disorder.

door-in-the-face technique Making a very large request that is likely to be turned down to increase the chance that people will agree to a smaller request later.

downward social comparison The defensive tendency to compare oneself with someone whose troubles are more serious than one's own.

dream analysis A psychotherapeutic technique in which the therapist interprets the symbolic meaning of the client's dreams.

ego According to Freud, the decision-making component of personality that operates according to the reality principle.

egocentrism The tendency to view reality in line with one's own idiosyncratic perceptions.

electroconvulsive therapy (ECT) A biomedical treatment in which electric shock is used to produce a cortical seizure accompanied by convulsions.

emotions Powerful, largely uncontrollable feelings, accompanied by physiological changes.

empathy Adopting another's frame of reference to understand his or her point of view.

empiricism The premise that knowledge should be acquired through observation.

endocrine system Glands that secrete chemicals called hormones into the bloodstream.

endogamy The tendency of people to marry within their own social group.

epidemiology The study of the distribution of mental or physical disorders in a population.

erectile difficulties The male sexual dysfunction characterized by the persistent inability to achieve or maintain an erection adequate for intercourse.

erogenous zones Areas of the body that are sexually sensitive or responsive.

estrogens The principal class of female sex hormones.

etiology The apparent causation and developmental history of an illness.

experiment A research method in which the investigator manipulates an (independent) variable under carefully controlled conditions and observes whether there are changes in a second (dependent) variable as a result.

experimental group The subjects in an experiment who receive some special treatment in regard to the independent variable.

expressive style A style of communication characterized by the ability to express tender emotions easily and to be sensitive to the feelings of others.

external attributions Ascribing the causes of behavior to situational demands and environmental constraints.

extinction The gradual weakening and disappearance of a conditioned response tendency.

extrovert A person who tends to be interested in the external world of things and people.

family life cycle An orderly sequence of developmental stages that families tend to progress through.

fellatio The oral stimulation of the penis.

fight-or-flight response A physiological reaction to threat that mobilizes an organism for attacking (fight) or fleeing (flight) an enemy.

fixation In Freud's theory, a failure to move forward from one stage to another as expected.

foot-in-the-door technique Getting people to agree to a small request to increase the chances that they will agree to a larger request later.

free association A psychotherapeutic technique in which clients spontaneously express their thoughts and feelings exactly as they occur, with as little censorship as possible.

frustration The feelings that occur in any situation in which the pursuit of some goal is thwarted.

fundamental attribution error The tendency to explain others' behavior as a result of personal rather than situational factors.

games Manipulative interactions progressing toward a predictable outcome, in which people conceal their real motivations.

gay See homosexuals.

gender The state of being male or female.

gender identity The ability to correctly classify oneself as male or female.

gender-role identity A person's identification with the traits regarded as masculine or feminine.

gender-role transcendence The idea that to be fully human, people need to move beyond gender roles as a way of organizing the world and of perceiving themselves and others.

gender roles Cultural expectations about what is appropriate behavior for each gender.

gender stereotypes Widely shared beliefs about males' and females' abilities, personality traits, and social behavior.

general adaptation syndrome A model of the body's stress response, consisting of three stages: alarm, resistance, and exhaustion.

generalized anxiety disorder A psychological disorder marked by a chronic high level of anxiety that is not tied to any specific threat.

gonads The sex glands.

group Two or more individuals who interact and are interdependent.

hallucinations Sensory perceptions that occur in the absence of a real, external stimulus or that represent gross distortions of perceptual input.

hallucinogens A diverse group of drugs that have powerful effects on mental and emotional functioning, marked most prominently by distortions in sensory and perceptual experience.

hardiness A personality syndrome marked by commitment, challenge, and control that is purportedly associated with strong stress resistance.

health psychology The subfield of psychology concerned with the relation of psychosocial factors to the promotion and maintenance of health, and with the causation, prevention, and treatment of illness.

heterosexism The assumption that all individuals and relationships are heterosexual.

heterosexuals People whose sexual desires and erotic behaviors are directed toward the other gender.

hierarchy of needs A systematic arrangement of needs, according to priority, in which basic needs must be met before less basic needs are aroused.

homogamy The tendency of people to marry others who have similar personal characteristics.

homophobia The intense fear and intolerance of homosexuality.

homosexuals People who seek emotional-sexual relationships with members of the same gender.

hormones Chemical substances released into the bloodstream by the endocrine glands.

humanism A theoretical orientation that emphasizes the unique qualities of humans, especially their free will and their potential for personal growth.

hypochondriasis (hypochondria) Excessive preoccupation with health concerns and incessant worry about developing physical illnesses.

id In Freud's theory, the primitive, instinctive component of personality that operates according to the pleasure principle.

identification Bolstering self-esteem by forming an imaginary or real alliance with some person or group.

identity A relatively clear and stable sense of who one is and what one stands for.

immune response The body's defensive reaction to invasion by bacteria, viral agents, or other foreign substances.

impression management Usually conscious efforts to influence the way others think of one.

incest Sexual activity between close relatives.

incongruence The disparity between one's self-concept and one's actual experience.

independent variable In an experiment, a condition or event that an experimenter varies in order to see its impact on another variable.

individualism Putting personal goals ahead of group goals and defining one's identity in terms of personal attributes rather than group memberships.

infant attachment The strong emotional bond that infants usually develop with their caregivers during the first year of their lives.

ingratiation Efforts to make oneself likable to others.

insight therapies A group of psychotherapies in which verbal interactions are intended to enhance clients' self-knowledge and thus promote healthful changes in personality and behavior.

instrumental style A style of communication that focuses on reaching practical goals and finding solutions to problems.

interference Forgetting information because of competition from other learned material.

internal attributions Ascribing the causes of behavior to personal dispositions, traits, abilities, and feelings rather than to external events.

interpersonal attraction Positive feelings toward another person.

interpersonal communication An interactional process whereby one person sends a message to another.

interpersonal conflict Disagreement among two or more people.

interpretation A therapist's attempts to explain the inner significance of the client's thoughts, feelings, memories, and behaviors.

intimacy Warmth, closeness, and sharing in a relationship.

intimate violence Aggression toward those who are in close relationships to the aggressor.

introvert A person who tends to be preoccupied with the internal world of his or her own thoughts, feelings, and experiences.

investments Things that people contribute to a relationship that they can't get back if the relationship ends.

job satisfaction The favorability or unfavorability of people's attitudes toward their jobs.

kinesics The study of communication through body movements.

labor force All people who are employed as well as those who are currently unemployed but are looking for work.

learned helplessness Passive behavior produced by exposure to unavoidable aversive events.

leisure Unpaid activities one chooses to engage in because they are personally meaningful.

life changes Any noticeable alterations in one's living circumstances that require readjustment.

lithium A chemical used to control mood swings in patients with bipolar mood disorders.

loneliness The emotional state that occurs when a person has fewer interpersonal relationships than desired or when these relationships are not as satisfying as desired.

lowball technique Getting people to commit themselves to an attractive proposition before its hidden costs are revealed.

marriage The legally and socially sanctioned union of sexually intimate adults.

matching hypothesis The idea that people of similar levels of physical attractiveness gravitate toward each other.

medical model The idea that it is useful to think of abnormal behavior as a disease.

meditation A family of mental exercises in which a conscious attempt is made to focus attention in a nonanalytical way.

menarche The first occurrence of menstruation.

menopause The cessation of menstruation.

message The information or meaning that is transmitted from one person to another.

meta-analysis A statistical technique that evaluates the results of many studies on the same question.

mnemonic devices Strategies for enhancing memory.

mood disorders A class of disorders marked by emotional disturbances that may spill over to disrupt physical, perceptual, social, and thought processes.

mourning Formal practices of an individual and a community in response to a death.

multiple-personality disorders Dissociative disorders involving the coexistence in one person of two or more largely complete, and usually very different, personalities. Also called dissociative identity disorder.

narcotics (opiates) Drugs derived from opium that are capable of relieving pain.

naturalistic observation An approach to research in which the researcher engages in careful observation of behavior without intervening directly with the subjects.

need for self-actualization The need to fulfill one's potential; the highest need in Maslow's motivational hierarchy.

negative reinforcement The strengthening of a response because it is followed by the removal of a (presumably) unpleasant stimulus.

neurons Individual cells that receive, integrate, and transmit information.

neuroticism A broad personality trait associated with chronic anxiety, insecurity, and self-consciousness.

neurotransmitters Chemicals that carry signals from one neuron to another.

nonverbal communication The transmission of meaning from one person to another through means or symbols other than words.

nutrition A collection of processes (mainly food consumption) through which an organism uses the materials (nutrients) required for survival and growth.

obedience A form of compliance that occurs when people follow direct commands, usually from someone in a position of authority.

obesity The condition of being overweight.

observational learning Learning that occurs when an organism's responding is influenced by observing others, who are called models.

obsessive-compulsive disorder A psychological disorder marked by persistent uncontrollable intrusions of unwanted thoughts (obsessions) and by urges to engage in senseless rituals (compulsions).

occupational interest inventories Tests that measure one's interests as they relate to various jobs or careers.

Oedipal complex According to Freud, a child's erotically tinged desires for the other-sex parent, accompanied by feelings of hostility toward the same-sex parent.

operant conditioning A form of learning in which voluntary responses come to be controlled by their consequences.

optimism A general tendency to expect good outcomes.

orgasm The release that occurs when sexual arousal reaches its peak intensity and is discharged in a series of muscular contractions that pulsate through the pelvic area.

orgasmic difficulties Sexual disorders characterized by an ability to experience sexual arousal but persistent problems in achieving orgasm.

overcompensation Making up for frustration in one area by seeking overgratification in another area.

overdose An excessive dose of a drug that can seriously threaten one's life.

overlearning The continued rehearsal of material after one first appears to have mastered it.

panic disorder Recurrent attacks of overwhelming anxiety that usually occur suddenly and unexpectedly.

paralanguage All vocal cues other than the content of the verbal message itself.

paranoid schizophrenia A type of schizophrenia dominated by delusions of persecution, along with delusions of grandeur.

passion The intense feelings (both positive and negative) experienced in love relationships, including sexual desire.

person perception The process of forming impressions of others.

personal space A zone of space surrounding a person that is felt to "belong" to that person.

personality An individual's unique constellation of consistent behavioral traits.

personality trait A durable disposition to behave in a particular way in a variety of situations.

perspective taking A component of empathy that involves the tendency to put oneself in another person's place.

persuasion The communication of arguments and information intended to change another person's attitudes.

phobic disorders Anxiety disorders marked by a persistent and irrational fear of an object or situation that presents no realistic danger.

physical dependence The need to continue to take a drug to avoid withdrawal illness.

placebo A substance that resembles a drug but has no actual pharmacological effect.

placebo effects Experiencing some change as the result of an empty, fake, or ineffectual treatment because of one's positive expectations about the treatment.

pleasure principle According to Freud, the principle according to which the id operates, demanding immediate gratification of its urges.

polygraph A device that records fluctuations in physiological arousal as a person answers questions.

positive reinforcement The strengthening of a response because it is followed by the arrival of a (presumably) pleasant stimulus.

possible selves One's conceptions about the kind of person one might become in the future.

posttraumatic stress disorder Disturbed behavior that emerges sometime after a major stressful event is over.

preconscious According to Freud, material just beneath the surface of awareness that can be easily retrieved.

prejudice A negative attitude toward members of a group.

premature ejaculation Impaired sexual relations because a man consistently reaches orgasm too quickly.

pressure Expectations or demands that one behave in a certain way.

prevalence The percentage of a population that exhibits a disorder during a specified time period.

primacy effect The fact that initial information tends to carry more weight than subsequent information.

primary appraisal An initial evaluation of whether an event is (1) irrelevant to one, (2) relevant, but not threatening, or (3) stressful.

primary sex characteristics The structures necessary for reproduction.

prognosis A forecast about the probable course of an illness.

projection Attributing one's own thoughts, feelings, or motives to another person.

projective tests Personality tests that ask subjects to respond to vague, ambiguous stimuli in ways that may reveal the subjects' needs, feelings, and personality traits.

proxemics The study of people's use of interpersonal space.

proximity Geographic, residential, and other forms of spatial closeness.

psychiatrists Physicians who specialize in the treatment of psychological disorders.

psychoactive drugs Chemical substances that modify a person's mental, emotional, or behavioral functioning.

psychoanalysis An insight therapy that emphasizes the recovery of unconscious conflicts, motives, and defenses through techniques such as free association, dream analysis, and transference.

psychodynamic theories All the diverse theories descended from the work of Sigmund Freud that focus on unconscious mental forces.

psychological dependence The need to continue to take a drug to satisfy intense mental and emotional craving for it.

psychological test A standardized measure of a sample of a person's behavior.

psychology The science that studies behavior and the physiological and mental processes that underlie it and the profession that applies the accumulated knowledge of this science to practical problems.

psychopharmacotherapy The treatment of mental disorders with medication.

psychosexual stages In Freud's theory, developmental periods with a characteristic sexual focus that leave their mark on adult personality.

psychosomatic diseases Genuine physical ailments caused in part by psychological factors, especially emotional distress.

puberty The stage during which sexual functions reach maturity and that marks the beginning of adolescence.

pubescence The two-year span preceding puberty during which the changes leading to physical and sexual maturity take place.

public self An image or facade presented to others in social interactions.

punishment The weakening (decrease in frequency) of a response because it is

followed by the arrival of a (presumably) unpleasant stimulus.

rational-emotive therapy An approach to therapy that focuses on altering clients' patterns of irrational thinking to reduce maladaptive emotions and behavior.

rationalization Creating false but plausible excuses to justify unacceptable behavior.

reactance The response that occurs when a person's freedom to behave in a certain way is impeded, thus leading to efforts to restore the threatened freedom.

reaction formation Behaving in a way that is exactly the opposite of one's true feelings.

reality principle According to Freud, the principle by which the ego seeks to delay gratification of the id's urges until appropriate outlets and situations can be found.

receiver The person to whom a message is targeted.

reciprocity Liking those who show they like you.

reciprocity norm The rule that one should pay back in kind what one receives from others.

reference group A set of people against whom one compares oneself.

refractory period A time after orgasm during which males are unable to experience another orgasm.

regression A reversion to immature patterns of behavior.

reliability The measurement consistency of a test.

repetitive strain injury (RSI) Injuries to muscles and tendons caused by rapidly repeating the same motions for many hours over many days.

repression Keeping distressing thoughts and feelings buried in the unconscious.

resistance Largely unconscious defensive maneuvers intended to hinder the progress of therapy.

schizophrenic disorders A class of disorders marked by disturbances in thought that spill over to affect perceptual, social, and emotional processes.

secondary appraisal An evaluation of one's coping resources and options for dealing with stress.

secondary sex characteristics The physical features that distinguish one gender from the other but are not essential for reproduction.

sedatives Sleep-inducing drugs that tend to decrease central nervous system activation and behavioral activity.

self-actualization See need for self-actualization.

self-attributions Inferences that people draw about the causes of their own behavior.

self-centered bias The tendency to take more than one's share of credit for a joint venture.

self-complexity How simple or elaborate one's self-concept is.

self-concept A collection of beliefs about one's basic nature, unique qualities, and typical behavior.

self-disclosure The voluntary act of verbally communicating private information about oneself to another person.

self-discrepancy The mismatching of self-perceptions.

self-efficacy One's belief about one's ability to perform behaviors that should lead to expected outcomes.

self-enhancement The tendency to maintain positive views of oneself.

self-esteem One's overall assessment of one's worth as a person; the evaluative component of the self-concept.

self-fulfilling prophecy The process whereby expectations about a person

cause the person to behave in ways that confirm the expectations.

self-handicapping The tendency to sabotage one's performance to provide an excuse for possible failure.

self-monitoring The degree to which people attend to and control the impressions they make on others.

self-regulation Directing and controlling one's behavior.

self-report inventories Personality scales that ask individuals to answer a series of questions about their characteristic behavior.

self-serving bias The tendency to attribute one's successes to personal factors and one's failures to situational factors.

self-verification theory The idea that people prefer to receive feedback from others that is consistent with their own self-views.

senile dementia The abnormal and progressive decline in general cognitive functioning observed in some people over age 65.

sensate focus A sex-therapy exercise in which partners take turns pleasuring each other with guided verbal feedback while certain kinds of stimulation are temporarily forbidden.

sensation seeking A generalized preference for high or low levels of sensory stimulation.

set point A natural point of stability in body weight, thought to involve the monitoring of fat cell levels.

sex therapy The professional treatment of sexual dysfunctions.

sexism Discrimination against people on the basis of their sex.

sexual dysfunctions Impairments in sexual functioning that cause subjective distress.

sexual harassment The subjection of individuals to unwelcome sexually oriented behavior.

sexual identity The complex of personal qualities, self-perceptions, attitudes, values, and preferences that guide one's sexual behavior.

sexual orientation A person's preference for emotional and sexual relationships with individuals of the same gender, the other gender, or either gender.

sexual scripts Culturally programmed sets of expectations about how individuals should behave sexually.

sexually transmitted disease (STD) An illness that is transmitted primarily through sexual contact.

shaping Modifying behavior by reinforcing closer and closer approximations of a desired response.

shyness Discomfort, inhibition, and excessive caution in interpersonal relations.

social clock A person's notion of a developmental schedule that specifies what the person should have accomplished by certain points in life.

social comparison theory The idea that people need to compare themselves with others in order to gain insight into their own behavior.

social constructionism The assertion that individuals construct their own reality based on societal expectations, conditioning, and self-socialization.

social exchange theory The idea that interpersonal relationships are governed by perceptions of the rewards and costs exchanged in interactions.

social penetration theory A theory that focuses on how relationships develop and sometimes dissolve.

social role theory The assertion that minor gender differences are exaggerated by the different social roles that males and females occupy.

social schemas Organized clusters of ideas about categories of people.

social skills training A behavior therapy designed to improve interpersonal skills that emphasizes shaping, modeling, and behavioral rehearsal.

social support Aid and succor provided by members of one's social networks.

socialization The process by which individuals acquire the norms and roles expected of people in a particular society.

sociobiology The study of the genetics and evolutionary basis of social behavior in all organisms, including humans.

sociology The scientific study of human society and its institutions.

somatization disorder A psychological disorder marked by a history of diverse physical complaints that appear to be psychological in origin.

somatoform disorders A class of psychological disorders involving physical ailments that have no authentic organic basis but are due solely to psychological factors.

source The person who initiates, or sends, a message.

spontaneous remission A recovery from a disorder that occurs without formal treatment.

SQ3R A study system designed to promote effective reading that includes five steps: survey, question, read, recite, and review.

standardization The uniform procedures used to administer and score a test.

stereotypes Widely held beliefs that people have certain characteristics simply because of their membership in a particular group.

stimulants Drugs that tend to increase central nervous system activation and behavioral activity.

stress Any circumstances that threaten or are perceived to threaten one's well-being and thereby tax one's coping abilities.

superego According to Freud, the moral component of personality that incorporates social standards about what represents right and wrong.

surveys Structured questionnaires designed to solicit information about specific aspects of subjects' behavior.

systematic desensitization A behavior therapy used to reduce clients' anxiety responses through counterconditioning.

tardive dyskinesia A neurological disorder marked by chronic tremors and involuntary spastic movements; a potential side effect of antipsychotic drugs.

test norms Statistics that provide information about where a score on a psychological test ranks in relation to other scores on that test.

token A symbol of all the members of a group.

token economy A system for doling out symbolic reinforcers that are exchanged later for a variety of genuine reinforcers.

tolerance A progressive decrease in responsiveness to a drug with continued use.

Transactional Analysis A broad theory of personality and interpersonal relations that emphasizes patterns of communication.

transference A phenomenon that occurs when clients start relating to their therapist in ways that mimic critical relationships in their lives.

transvestism A sexual disorder in which a man achieves sexual arousal by dressing in women's clothing.

twin studies Studies in which researchers assess hereditary influence by comparing the resemblance of identical twins and fraternal twins on a trait.

Type A personality A personality style marked by a competitive orientation, impatience and urgency, and anger and hostility.

Type B personality A personality style marked by relatively relaxed, patient, easygoing, amicable behavior.

unconditioned response (UCR) An unlearned reaction to an unconditioned stimulus that occurs without previous conditioning.

unconditioned stimulus (UCS) A stimulus that evokes an unconditioned response without previous conditioning.

unconscious According to Freud, thoughts, memories, and desires that are well below the surface of conscious awareness but that nonetheless exert great influence on our behavior.

underemployment Settling for a job that does not make full use of one's skills, abilities, and training.

undifferentiated schizophrenia A type of schizophrenia marked by idiosyncratic mixtures of schizophrenic symptoms.

validity The ability of a test to measure what it was designed to measure.

variables *See* dependent variable; independent variable.

vasocongestion Engorgement of blood vessels.

verbal communication The sending and receiving of messages through written or spoken words.

References

Abbey, A. (1991). Misperception as an antecedent of acquaintance rape: A consequence of ambiguity in communication between men and women. In A. Parrott & L. Bechhofer (Eds.), *Acquaintance rape: The hidden crime.* New York: Wiley.

Abou-Saleh, M. T. (1992). Lithium. In E. S. Paykel (Ed.), *Handbook of affective disorders.* (2nd ed.). New York: Guilford Press.

Abrams, R. (1992). *Electroconvulsive therapy.* New York: Oxford University Press.

Abramson, L. Y., Metalsky, G. I., & Alloy, L. B. (1988). The hopelessness theory of depression: Does the research test the theory? In L. Y. Abramson (Ed.), *Social cognition and clinical psychology: A synthesis.* New York: Guilford Press.

Abramson, L. Y., Seligman, M. E. P., & Teasdale, J. D. (1978). Learned helplessness in humans: Critique and reformulation. *Journal of Abnormal Psychology, 87,* 49–74.

Acock, A. C., & Demo, D. H. (1994). *Family diversity and well-being.* Thousand Oaks, CA: Sage Publications.

ACSF investigators (1992, December). AIDS and sexual behaviour in France. *Nature, 360,* 407–409.

Adams, G. R. (1992, Fall). Identity and intimacy: Some observations after a decade of investigations. *Society for Research on Adolescence Newsletter,* pp. 4–5.

Adams, H. E., & Cassidy, J. F. (1993). The classification of abnormal behavior: An overview. In P. B. Sutker & H. E. Adams (Eds.), *Comprehensive textbook of psychopathology* (2nd ed.). New York: Plenum.

Adams, K. A. (1980). Who has the final word? Sex, race, and dominance behavior. *Journal of Personality and Social Psychology, 38,* 1–8.

Adams, K. A. (1983). Aspects of social context as determinants of black women's resistance to challenges. *Journal of Social Issues, 39,* 69–78.

Ader, R., & Cohen, N. (1984). Behavior and the immune system. In W. D. Gentry (Ed.), *Handbook of behavioral medicine.* New York: Guilford Press.

Ader, R., & Cohen, N. (1993). Psychoneuroimmunology: Conditioning and stress. *Annual Review of Psychology, 44,* 53–85.

Adler, A. (1917). *Study of organ inferiority and its psychical compensation.* New York: Nervous and Mental Diseases Publishing.

Adler, A. (1927). *Practice and theory of individual psychology.* New York: Harcourt, Brace & World.

Adler, R., & Towne, N. (1987). *Looking out/looking in.* New York: Holt, Rinehart & Winston.

Adler, S., & Aranya, N. (1984). A comparison of the work needs, attitudes, and preferences of professional accountants at different career stages. *Journal of Vocational Behavior, 25,* 45–57.

Affleck, G., Tennen, H., Urrows, S., & Higgins, P. (1994). Person and contextual features of daily stress reactivity: Individual differences in relations of undesirable daily events with mood disturbance and chronic pain intensity. *Journal of Personality and Social Psychology, 66*(2), 329–340.

Agras, W. S. (1985). Stress, panic and the cardiovascular system. In A. H. Tuma & J. Maser (Eds.), *Anxiety and the anxiety disorders.* Hillsdale, NJ: Erlbaum.

Agras, W. S., & Berkowitz, R. (1994). Behavior therapy. In R. E. Hales, S. C. Yudofsky, & J. A. Talbott (Eds.), *The American Psychiatric Press textbook of psychiatry* (2nd ed.). Washington, DC: American Psychiatric Press.

Ainsworth, M. D. S., Blehar, M. C., Waters, E., & Wall, S. (1978). *Patterns of attachment: A psychological study of the strange situation.* Hillsdale, NJ: Erlbaum.

Alberti, R. E., & Emmons, M. L. (1990). *Your perfect right: A guide to assertive behavior* (6th ed.). San Luis Obispo, CA: Impact.

Albiston, C. R., Maccoby, E. E., & Mnookin, R. R. (1990, Spring). Does joint legal custody matter? *Stanford Law and Policy Review,* 167–179.

Albright, L., Kenny, D. A., & Malloy, T. E. (1988). Consensus in personality judgments at zero acquaintance. *Journal of Personality and Social Psychology, 55,* 387–395.

Alexander, C. N., Chandler, H. M., Langer, E. J., Newman, R. I., & Davies J. L. (1989). Transcendental meditation, mindfulness, and longevity: An experimental study with the elderly. *Journal of Personality and Social Psychology, 57,* 950–964.

Alexander, C. N., Davies, J. L., Dixon, C. A., Dillbeck, M. C., Druker, S. M., Oetzel, R. M., Muehlman, J. M., & Orme-Johnson, D. W. (1990). Growth of higher states of consciousness: The Vedic psychology of human development. In C. N. Alexander & E. J. Langer (Eds.), *Higher stages of human development: Perspectives on adult growth.* New York: Oxford University Press.

Alexander, C. N., & Knight, G. W. (1971). Situated identities and social psychological experimentation. *Sociometry, 34,* 65–82.

Alexander, C. N., Rainfourth, M. V., & Gelderloos, P. (1991). Transcendental Meditation, self-actualization, and psychological health: A conceptual overview and statistical meta-analysis. *Journal of Social Behavior and Personality, 6,* 189–247.

Alexander, F. (1954). Psychoanalysis and psychotherapy. *Journal of the American Psychoanalytic Association, 2,* 722–733.

Alicke, M. D., Smith, R. H., & Klotz, J. L. (1986). Judgments of personal attractiveness: The role of faces and bodies. *Personality and Social Psychology Bulletin, 12,* 381–389.

Allen, K. R., & Demo, D. H. (1995). The families of lesbians and gay men: A new frontier in family research. *Journal of Marriage and the Family, 79,* 111–127.

Allison, S. T., Messick, D. M., & Goethals, G. R. (1989). On being better but not smarter than others: The Muhammad Ali effect. *Social Cognition, 7,* 275–295.

Alloy, L. B., & Abramson, L. Y. (1979). Judgment of contingency in depressed and nondepressed students: Sadder but wiser. *Journal of Experimental Psychology: General, 108,* 441–485.

Alloy, L. B., & Abramson, L. Y. (1988). Depressive realism: Four theoretical perspectives. In L. B. Alloy (Ed.), *Cognitive processes in depression.* New York: Guilford Press.

Alloy, L. B., Clements, C., & Kolden, G. (1985). The cognitive diathesis-stress theories of depression: Therapeutic implications. In S. Reiss & R. R. Bootzin (Eds.), *Theoretical issues in behavior therapy.* Orlando, FL: Academic Press.

Allport, G. W. (1937). *Personality: A psychological interpretation.* New York: Holt.

Allport, G. W. (1961). *Pattern and growth in personality.* New York: Holt, Rinehart & Winston.

Almeida, D. M., Maggs, J. L., & Galambos, N. L. (1993). Wives' employment hours and spousal participation in family work. *Journal of Family Psychology, 7,* 233–244.

Altman, I., & Haythorn, W. W. (1965). Interpersonal exchange in socialization. *Sociometry, 23,* 411–426.

Altman, I., & Taylor, D. A. (1983). *Social penetration: The development of interpersonal relationships.* New York: Irvington.

Altman, I., Vinsel, A., & Brown, B. A. (1981). Dialectic conceptions in social psychology: An application to social penetration and privacy regulation. In L. Berkowitz (Ed.), *Advances in experimental social psychology* (Vol. 14). New York: Academic Press.

Amada, G. (1985). *A guide to psychotherapy.* Lanham, MD: Madison Books.

Amaro, H., Russo, N. F., & Johnson, J. (1987). Family and work predictors of psychological well-being among Hispanic women professionals. *Psychology of Women Quarterly, 11,* 523–532.

Amatea, E. S., & Fong, M. L. (1991). The impact of role stressors and personal resources on the stress experience of professional women. *Psychology of Women Quarterly, 15,* 419–430.

Amato, P. R. (1993). Children's adjustment to divorce: Theories, hypotheses, and empirical support. *Journal of Marriage and the Family, 55,* 23–28.

Amato, P. R., & Keith, B. (1991a). Parental divorce and adult well-being: A meta-analysis. *Journal of Marriage and the Family, 53,* 43–58.

Amato, P. R., & Keith, B. (1991b). Parental divorce and the well-being of children: A meta-analysis. *Psychological Bulletin, 110,* 26–46.

Ambady, N., & Rosenthal, R. (1992). Thin slices of expressive behavior as predictors of interpersonal consequences: A meta-analysis. *Psychological Bulletin, 111,* 256–274.

American Association of University Women. (1994). *Shortchanging girls, shortchanging America.* Washington, DC: Author.

American Psychiatric Association. (1994). *Diagnostic and statistical manual of mental disorders* (4th ed.). Washington, DC: Author.

Amott, T., & Matthaei, J. (1991). *Race, gender, and work: A multicultural economic history of women in the United States.* Boston, MA: South End Press.

Andersen, B. L., Kiecolt-Glaser, J. K., & Glaser, R. (1994). A biobehavioral model of cancer stress and disease course. *American Psychologist, 49,* 389–404.

Anderson, C. A., & Harvey, R. J. (1988). Discriminating between problems in living: An examination of depression, loneliness, shyness, and social anxiety. *Journal of Social and Clinical Psychology, 6,* 482–491.

Anderson, C. A., Horowitz, L. M., & French, R. D. (1983). Attributional style of lonely and depressed people. *Journal of Personality and Social Psychology, 45,* 127–136.

Anderson, C. A., Miller, R. S., Riger, A. L., Dill, J. C., & Sedikides, C. (1994). Behavioral and characterological attributional styles as predictors of depression and loneliness: Review, refinement, and test. *Journal of Personality and Social Psychology, 66,* 549–558.

Anderson, C. A., & Riger, A. L. (1991). A controllability attributional model of problems in living: Dimensional and situational interactions in the prediction of depression and loneliness. *Social Cognition, 9,* 149–181.

Anderson, D. M., & Christenson, G. M. (1991). Ethnic breakdown of AIDS-related knowledge and attitudes from the National Adolescent Student Health Survey. *Journal of Health Education, 2,* 30–34.

Anderson, J. R. (1980). *Cognitive psychology and its implications.* New York: Freeman.

Anderson, K. J. (1990). Arousal and the inverted-U hypothesis: A critique of Neiss's "reconceptualizing arousal." *Psychological Bulletin, 107,* 96–100.

Andersson, B. E. (1992). Effects of day-care on cognitive and socioemotional competence of thirteen-year-old Swedish schoolchildren. *Child Development, 63,* 20–36.

Andre, R. (1991). *Positive solitude: A practical program for mastering loneliness and achieving self-fulfillment.* New York: HarperCollins.

Andreasen, N. C. (1987). The diagnosis of schizophrenia. *Schizophrenia Bulletin, 13,* 9–22.

Andreasen, N. C. (1990). Positive and negative symptoms: Historical and conceptual aspects. In N. C. Andreasen (Ed.), *Modern problems of pharmacopsychiatry: Positive and negative symptoms and syndromes.* Basel: Karger.

Ankey, C. D. (1992). Sex differences in relative brain size: The mismeasure of woman, too? *Intelligence, 16,* 329–336.

Antill, J. K. (1983). Sex-role complementarity versus similarity in married couples. *Journal of Personality and Social Psychology, 45,* 145–155.

Antonucci, T. C. (1990). Social supports and social relationships. In R. H. Binstock & L. K. George (Eds.), *Handbook of aging and the social sciences* (3rd ed.). San Diego: Academic Press.

Antonucci, T. C., & Akiyama, H. (1987). Social networks in adult life and a preliminary examination of the convoy model. *Journal of Gerontology, 42,* 519–527.

Aquilino, W. S. (1990). The likelihood of parent-adult child coresidence: Effects of family structure and parental characteristics. *Journal of Marriage and the Family, 52,* 405–419.

Archer, S. L. (1982). The lower age boundaries of identity development. *Child Development, 53,* 1551–1556.

Argyle, M. (1987). *The psychology of happiness.* London: Metheun.

Argyle, M., & Henderson, M. (1984). The rules of friendship. *Journal of Social and Personal Relationships, 1,* 211–237.

Argyle, M., Henderson, M., Bond, M. H., Iizuka, Y., & Contarello, A. (1986). Cross-cultural variations in relationship rules. *International Journal of Psychology, 21,* 287–315.

Aries, E. (1987). Gender and communication. In P. Shaver & C. Hendrick (Eds.), *Sex and gender.* Newbury Park, CA: Sage Publications.

Arkin, R. M., & Baumgardner, A. H. (1985). Self-handicapping. In J. H. Harvey & G. Weary (Eds.), *Attribution: Basic issues and applications.* New York: Academic Press.

Arkowitz, H. (1992). Integrative theories of therapy. In D. K. Freedheim (Ed.), *History of psychotherapy: A century of change.* Washington, DC: American Psychological Association.

Arnkoff, D. B., & Glass, C. R. (1992). Cognitive therapy and psychotherapy. In D. K. Freedheim (Ed.), *History of psycho-therapy: A century of change.* Washington, DC: American Psychological Association.

Aron, A. (1988). The matching hypothesis reconsidered again: Comment on Kalick and Hamilton. *Journal of Personality and Social Psychology, 54,* 441–446.

Aronson, E., Willerman, B., & Floyd, J. (1966). The effect of a pratfall on increasing interpersonal attractiveness. *Psychonomic Science, 4,* 157–158.

Asch, S. E. (1946). Forming impressions of personality. *Journal of Abnormal and Social Psychology, 41,* 258–290.

Asch, S. E. (1951). Effects of group pressure on the modification and distortion of judgments. In H. Guetzkow (Ed.), *Groups, leadership and men.* Pittsburgh: Carnegie Press.

Asch, S. E. (1955). Opinions and social pressures. *Scientific American, 193*(5), 31–35.

Asch, S. E. (1956). Studies of independence and conformity: A minority of one against a unanimous majority. *Psychological Monographs, 70* (9, Whole No. 416).

Asendorpf, J. B. (1986). Shyness in middle and late childhood. In W. H. Jones, J. M. Cheek, & S. R. Briggs (Eds.), *Shyness: Perspectives on research and treatment.* New York: Plenum.

Asendorpf, J. B. (1989). Shyness as a final common pathway for two different kinds of inhibition. *Journal of Personality and Social Psychology, 57,* 481–492.

Aspinwall, L. G., & Taylor, S. E. (1992). Modeling cognitive adaptation: A longitudinal investigation of the impact of individual differences and coping on college adjustment and performance. *Journal of Personality and Social Psychology, 63,* 989–1003.

Asterita, M. F. (1985). *The physiology of stress.* New York: Human Sciences Press.

Astrachan, A. (1992). Men and the new economy. In M. S. Kimmel & M. A. Messner (Eds.), *Men's lives* (2nd ed.). New York: Macmillan.

Atchley, R. C. (1982). The process of retirement: Comparing women and men. In M. Szinovacz (Ed.), *Women's retirement.* Newbury Park, CA: Sage Publications.

Atchley, R. C. (1991). *Social forces and aging.* Belmont, CA: Wadsworth.

Atkins, A., Deaux, K., & Bieri, J. (1967). Latitude of acceptance and attitude change: Empirical evidence for a reformulation. *Journal of Personality and Social Psychology, 6,* 47–54.

Atkinson, R. L. (1989). Low and very low calorie diets. *Medical Clinics of North America, 73,* 203–215.

Atwater, L. (1982). *The extramarital connection: Sex, intimacy, and identity.* New York: Irvington.

Atwood, J. D., & Gagnon, J. H. (1987). Masturbatory behavior in college youth. *Journal of Sex Education and Therapy, 13*(2), 35–42.

Avery, D., & Winokur, G. (1978). Suicide, attempted suicide, and relapse rates in depression. *Archives of General Psychiatry, 35,* 749–753.

Baber, K. M., & Monaghan, P. (1988). College women's career and motherhood expectations: New options, old dilemmas. *Sex Roles, 19,* 189–203.

Baenninger, M., & Newcombe, N. (1989). The role of experience in spatial test performance: A meta-analysis. *Sex Roles, 20,* 327–344.

Bailey, J. M., & Pillard, R. C. (1991). A genetic study of male sexual orientation. *Archives of General Psychiatry, 48,* 1089–1096.

Bailey, J. M., Pillard, R. C., Neale, M. C., & Agyei, Y. (1993). Heritable factors influence sexual orientation in women. *Archives of General Psychiatry, 50,* 217–223.

Bailey, J. M., Willerman, L., & Parks, C. (1991). A test of maternal stress theory of human male homosexuality. *Archives of Sexual Behavior, 20,* 277–294.

Baker, E. L. (1985). Psychoanalysis and psychoanalytic therapy. In S. J. Lynn & J. P. Garske (Eds.), *Contemporary psychotherapies: Models and methods.* Columbus, OH: Merrill.

Baker, L. A., & Daniels, D. (1990). Nonshared environmental influences and personality differences in adult twins. *Journal of Personality and Social Psychology, 58,* 103–110.

Balswick, J., & Avertt, C. P. (1977). Differences in expressiveness: Gender, interpersonal orientation, and perceived expressiveness as contributing factors. *Journal of Marriage and the Family, 39,* 121–127.

Baltes, P. B., & Kleigl, R. (1992). Further testing of limits of cognitive plasticity: Negative age differences in a mnemonic skill are robust. *Developmental Psychology, 28,* 121–125.

Banaji, M. R., Hardin, C., & Rothman, A. J. (1993). Implicit stereotyping in person judgment. *Journal of Personality and Social Psychology, 65,* 272–281.

Bandura, A. (1973). *Aggression: A social learning analysis.* Englewood Cliffs, NJ: Prentice-Hall.

Bandura, A. (1977). *Social learning theory.* Englewood Cliffs, NJ: Prentice-Hall.

Bandura, A. (1986). *Social foundations of thought and action: A social-cognitive theory.* Englewood Cliffs, NJ: Prentice-Hall.

Bandura, A. (1989). Human agency in social cognitive theory. *American Psychologist, 44,* 1175–1184.

Bandura, A. (1990a). Perceived self-efficacy in the exercise of personal agency. *Journal of Applied Sport Psychology, 2,* 128–163.

Bandura, A. (1990b). Self-regulation of motivation through goal systems. In R. A. Dienstbier (Ed.), *Nebraska symposium on motivation* (Vol. 38). Lincoln: University of Nebraska Press.

Bandura, A. (1992). Self-efficacy mechanism in psychobiologic functioning. In R. Schwarzer (Ed.), *Self-efficacy: Thought control of action.* Washington, DC: Hemisphere.

Bandura, A. (1993). Perceived self-efficacy in cognitive development and functioning. *Educational Psychologist, 28,* 117–148.

Barber, B. K. (1994). Cultural, family, and personal contexts of parent-adolescent conflict. *Journal of Marriage and the Family, 56,* 375–386.

Barlett, D. L., & Steele, J. B. (1979). *Empire: The life, legend and madness of Howard Hughes.* New York: Norton.

Barnes, M. L., & Buss, D. M. (1985). Sex differences in the interpersonal behavior of married couples. *Journal of Personality and Social Psychology, 48,* 654–661.

Barnett, P. A., & Gotlib, I. H. (1988). Psychosocial functioning and depression: Distinguishing among antecedents, concomitants, and consequences. *Psychological Bulletin, 104,* 97–126.

Baron, R. S., Cutrona, C. E., Hicklin, D., Russell, D. W., & Lubaroff, D. M. (1990). Social support and immune function among spouses of cancer patients. *Journal of Personality and Social Psychology, 59,* 344–352.

Barret, R. L., & Robinson, B. E. (1994). Gay dads. In A. E. Gottfried & A. W. Gottfried (Eds.), *Redefining families: Implications for children's development.* New York: Plenum.

Barsky, A. J. (1988). The paradox of

health. *New England Journal of Medicine, 318,* 414–418.

Barsky, A. J. (1989). Somatoform disorders. In H. I. Kaplan & B. J. Sadock (Eds.), *Comprehensive textbook of psychiatry/V.* Baltimore: Williams & Wilkins.

Baruch, G. K., Biener, L., & Barnett, R. C. (1987). Women and gender in research on stress. *American Psychologist, 42,* 130–136.

Basow, S. A. (1992). *Gender: Stereotypes and roles* (3rd ed.). Pacific Grove, CA: Brooks/Cole.

Baugher, R. J., Burger, C., Smith, R., & Wallston, K. (1989–1990). A comparison of terminally ill persons at various time periods to death. *Omega, 20,* 103–115.

Baum, A. (1990). Stress, intrusive imagery, and chronic distress. *Health Psychology, 9,* 653–675.

Baumeister, R. F. (1984). Choking under pressure: Self-consciousness and paradoxical effects of incentives on skillful performance. *Journal of Personality and Social Psychology, 46,* 610–620.

Baumeister, R. F. (1989). The optimal margin of illusion. *Journal of Social and Clinical Psychology, 8,* 176–189.

Baumeister, R. F., & Steinhilber, A. (1984). Paradoxical effects of supportive audiences on performance under pressure: The home field disadvantage in sports championships. *Journal of Personality and Social Psychology, 47,* 85–93.

Baumeister, R. F., Tice, D. M., & Hutton, D. G. (1989). Self-presentational motivations and personality differences in self-esteem. *Journal of Personality, 57,* 547–579.

Baumgarder, A. H., & Brownlee, E. A. (1987). Strategic failure in social interaction: Evidence for expectancy disconfirmation process. *Journal of Personality and Social Psychology, 52,* 525–535.

Baumrind, D. (1964). Some thoughts on the ethics of reading Milgram's "Behavioral study of obedience." *American Psychologist, 19,* 421–423.

Baumrind, D. (1967). Child care practices anteceding three patterns of preschool behavior. *Genetic Psychology Monographs, 75,* 43–88.

Baumrind, D. (1971). Current patterns of parental authority. *Developmental Psychology Monographs, 4* (1, Part 2).

Baumrind, D. (1978). Parental disciplinary patterns and social competence in children. *Youth and Society, 9,* 239–276.

Baumrind, D. (1989). Rearing competent children. In W. Damon (Ed.), *Child development today and tomorrow.* San Francisco: Jossey-Bass.

Baumrind, D. (1991). Effective parenting during the early adolescent transition. In P. A. Cowan & M. Hetherington (Eds.), *Family transitions.* Hillsdale, NJ: Erlbaum.

Baxter, L. A. (1988). A dialectical perspective on communication strategies in relationship development. In S. Duck (Ed.), *Handbook of personal relationships.* New York: Wiley.

Baxter, L. A., & Wilmot, W. W. (1985). Taboo topics in close relationships. *Journal of Social and Personal Relationships, 2,* 253–269.

Beardsley, R. S., Gardocki, G. J., Larson, D. B., & Hidalgo, J. (1988). Prescribing of psychotropic medication by primary care physicians and psychiatrists. *Archives of General Psychiatry, 45,* 1117–1119.

Beattie, M. (1987). *Co-dependent no more.* New York: HarperCollins.

Beattie, M. (1989). *Beyond codependency: And getting better all the time.* New York: HarperCollins.

Beattie, M. (1993). *The language of letting go: Daily meditations for codependents.* San Francisco: Harper.

Beck, A. T. (1976). *Cognitive therapy and the emotional disorders.* New York: International Universities Press.

Beck, A. T. (1987). Cognitive therapy. In J. K. Zeig (Ed.), *The evolution of psychotherapy.* New York: Brunner/Mazel.

Beck, A. T. (1988a). Cognitive approaches to panic disorder: Theory and therapy. In S. Rachman & J. Maser (Eds.), *Panic: Psychological perspectives.* Hillsdale, NJ: Erlbaum.

Beck, A. T. (1988b). *Love is never enough.* New York: Harper & Row.

Beck, A. T. (1991). Cognitive therapy: A 30-year retrospective. *American Psychologist, 46,* 368–375.

Beck, J., & Morgan, P. A. (1986). Designer drug confusion: A focus on MDMA. *Journal of Drug Education, 16,* 287–302.

Becker, H. S. (1973). *Outsiders: Studies in the sociology of deviance.* New York: Free Press.

Becker, R. E. (1990). Social skills training. In A. S. Bellack & M. Hersen (Eds.), *Handbook of comparative treatments for adult disorders.* New York: Wiley.

Behar, R. (1991, May 6). The thriving cult of greed and power. *Time,* pp. 50–77.

Bell, A. P., & Weinberg, M. S. (1978). *Homosexualities: A study of diversity among men and women.* New York: Simon & Schuster.

Bell, A. P., Weinberg, M. S., & Hammersmith, K. S. (1981). *Sexual preference—Its development in men and women.* Bloomington: Indiana University Press.

Bell, I. P. (1989). The double standard: Age. In J. Freeman (Ed.), *Women: A feminist perspective* (4th ed.). Mountain View, CA: Mayfield.

Belli, R. F., & Loftus, E. F. (1994). Recovered memories of childhood abuse: A source monitoring perspective. In S. J. Lynn & J. W. Rhue (Eds.), *Dissociation: Clinical and theoretical perspectives.* New York: Guilford Press.

Belsky, J. (1985). Exploring differences in marital change across the transition to parenthood: The role of violated expectations. *Journal of Marriage and the Family, 47,* 1037–1044.

Belsky, J. (1988). The "effects" of infant day care reconsidered. *Early Childhood Research Quarterly, 3,* 235–272.

Belsky, J. (1990a). Children and marriage. In F. D. Fincham & T. N. Bradbury (Eds.), *The psychology of marriage: Basic issues and applications.* New York: Guilford Press.

Belsky, J. (1990b). Infant day care, child development, and family policy. *Society, 27,* 10–12.

Belsky, J. (1992). Consequences of child care for children's development: A deconstructionist view. In A. Booth (Ed.), *Child care in the 1990s.* Hillsdale, NJ: Erlbaum.

Belsky, J. (1993). Etiology of child maltreatment: A developmental-ecological analysis. *Psychological Bulletin, 114,* 413–434.

Bem, S. L. (1975, September). Androgyny vs. the tight little lives of fluffy women and chesty men. *Psychology Today,* pp. 58–62.

Bem, S. L. (1983). Gender schema theory and its implications for child development: Raising gender-aschematic children in a gender-schematic society. *Signs, 8,* 598–616.

Bem, S. L. (1985). Androgyny and gender schema theory: A conceptual and empirical integration. In T. B. Sonderegger (Ed.), *Nebraska symposium on motivation 1984: Psychology and gender* (Vol. 32). Lincoln: University of Nebraska Press.

Bem, S. L. (1993). *The lenses of gender: Transforming the debate on sexual inequality.* New Haven, CT: Yale University Press.

Benjamin, L. T., Jr., Cavell, T. A., & Shallenberger, W. R., III. (1984). Staying with initial answers on objective tests: Is it a myth? *Teaching of Psychology, 11,* 133–141.

Benson, H. (1975). *The relaxation response* (1st ed.). New York: Morrow.

Benson, H. (1984). *Beyond the relaxation response.* New York: Times Books.

Benson, H., & Klipper, M. Z. (1988). *The relaxation response* (2nd ed.). New York: Avon.

Berenbaum, S. A., & Hines, M. (1992). Early androgens are related to childhood sex-typed toy preferences. *Psychological Science, 3,* 203–206.

Berg, J. H., & Clark, M. S. (1986). Differences in social exchange between intimate and other relationships: Gradually evolving or quickly apparent? In V. J. Derlega & B. A. Winstead (Eds.), *Friendship and social interaction.* New York: Springer-Verlag.

Berg, J. H., & McQuinn, R. D. (1986). Attraction and exchange in continuing and noncontinuing dating relationships. *Journal of Personality and Social Psychology, 50,* 942–952.

Berg, S. (1987). Intelligence and terminal decline. In G. L. Maddox & E. W. Busse (Eds.), *Aging: The universal human experience.* New York: Springer.

Bergen, D. J., & Williams, J. E. (1991). Sex stereotypes in the United States revisited: 1972–1988. *Sex Roles, 24,* 413–423.

Bergin, A. E. (1971). The evaluation of therapeutic outcomes. In A. E. Bergin & S. L. Garfield (Eds.), *Handbook of psychotherapy and behavior change: An empirical analysis.* New York: Wiley.

Berglas, S., & Jones, E. E. (1978). Drug choice as a self-handicapping strategy in response to noncontingent success. *Journal of Personality and Social Psychology, 36,* 405–417.

Berkowitz, L. (1969). The frustration-aggression hypothesis revisited. In L. Berkowitz (Ed.), *Roots of aggression: A reexamination of the frustration-aggression hypothesis.* New York: Atherton.

Berkowitz, L. (1989). Frustration-aggression hypothesis: Examination and reformulation. *Psychological Bulletin, 106,* 59–73.

Berkowitz, L. (1993). *Aggression: Its causes, consequences, and control.* New York: McGraw-Hill.

Berlo, D. K. (1960). *The process of communication: An introduction to theory and practice.* New York: Holt, Rinehart & Winston.

Bernard, L. C., & Krupat, E. (1994). *Health psychology: Biopsychosocial factors in health and illness.* Fort Worth, TX: Harcourt Brace.

Berne, E. (1961). *Transactional analysis in psychotherapy.* New York: Ballantine.

Berne, E. (1964). *Games people play.* New York: Grove Press.

Berne, E. (1972). *What do you say after hello?* New York: Grove Press.

Berry, D. S., & McArthur, L. Z. (1985). Some components and consequences of a babyface. *Journal of Personality and Social Psychology, 48,* 312–323.

Berscheid, E. (1985). Interpersonal attraction. In G. Lindzey & E. Aronson (Eds.), *The handbook of social psychology: Vol. 2. Special fields and applications.* New York: Random House.

Berscheid, E. (1988). Some comments on love's anatomy: Or, whatever happened to old-fashioned lust? In R. J. Sternberg

& M. L. Barnes (Eds.), *The psychology of love.* New Haven, CT: Yale University Press.

Berscheid, E., Dion, K., Walster, E., & Walster, G. W. (1971). Physical attractiveness and dating choice: A test of the matching hypothesis. *Journal of Experimental Social Psychology, 7,* 173–189.

Berscheid, E., Snyder, M., & Omoto, A. M. (1989). The relationship closeness inventory: Assessing the closeness of interpersonal relationships. *Journal of Personality and Social Psychology, 57,* 792–807.

Berscheid, E., & Walster, E. (1978). *Interpersonal attraction.* Reading, MA: Addison-Wesley.

Berscheid, E., Walster, E., & Bohrnstedt, G. (1973, November). The happy American body, a survey report. *Psychology Today,* pp. 119–131.

Berzon, B. (1988) *Permanent partners: Building gay and lesbian relationships.* New York: E. P. Dutton.

Best, R. (1983). *We've all got scars: What boys and girls learn in elementary school.* Bloomington: Indiana University Press.

Bettelheim, B. (1943). Individual and mass behavior in extreme situations. *Journal of Abnormal and Social Psychology, 38,* 417–452.

Betz, N. E. (1993). Women's career development. In F. L. Denmark & M. A. Paludi (Eds.), *Psychology of women: A handbook of issues and theories.* Westport, CT: Greenwood Press.

Betz, N. E., & Fitzgerald, L. E. (1987). *The career psychology of women.* New York: Academic Press.

Betz, N. E., & Hackett, G. (1986). Applications of self-efficacy theory to understanding career choice behavior. *Journal of Social and Clinical Psychology, 4,* 279–289.

Beutler, L. E., Machado, P. P. P., & Neufeldt, S. A. (1994). Therapist variables. In A. E. Bergin & S. L. Garfield (Eds.), *Handbook of psychotherapy and behavior change* (4th ed.). New York: Wiley.

Biegel, D. E., Sales, E., & Schulz, R. (1991). *Family caregiving in chronic illness.* Newbury Park, CA: Sage Publications.

Biener, L., & Abrams, D. B. (1991). The contemplation ladder: Validation of a measure of readiness to consider smoking cessation. *Health Psychology, 10,* 360–365.

Billings, A. G., Cronkite, R. C., & Moos, R. H. (1983). Social-environment factors in unipolar depression. *Journal of Abnormal Psychology, 92,* 119–133.

Birchler, G. R. (1992). Marriage. In V. B. Van Hasselt & M. Hersen (Eds.), *Handbook of social development: A lifespan perspective.* New York: Plenum.

Birren, J. E., & Fisher, L. M. (1995). Aging and speed of behavior: Possible consequences for psychological functioning. *Annual Review of Psychology, 46,* 329–353.

Bitter, R. G. (1986). Late marriage and marital instability: The effects of heterogeneity and inflexibility. *Journal of Marriage and the Family, 48,* 631–640.

Black, D. W., & Andreasen, N. C. (1994). Schizophrenia, schizophreniform disorder, and delusional (paranoid) disorder. In R. E. Hales, S. C. Yudofsky, & J. A. Talbott (Eds.), *The American Psychiatric Press textbook of psychiatry* (2nd ed.). Washington, DC: American Psychiatric Press.

Black, D. W., & Winokur, G. (1990). Suicide and psychiatric diagnosis. In S. J. Blumenthal & D. J. Kupfer (Eds.), *Suicide over the life cycle: Risk factors, assessment, and treatment of suicidal patients.* Washington, DC: American Psychiatric Press.

Blair, S. L. (1993). Employment, family, and perceptions of marital quality among husbands and wives. *Journal of Family Issues, 14,* 189–212.

Blair, S. L., & Johnson, M. P. (1992). Wives' perceptions of the fairness of the division of household labor: The intersection of housework and ideology. *Journal of Marriage and the Family, 54,* 570–581.

Blair, S. N., Kohl, H. W., Gordon, N. F., & Paffenbarger, R. S. (1992). How much physical activity is good for health? In G. S. Omenn, J. E. Fielding, & L. B. Lave (Eds.), *Annual review of public health.* (Vol. 13). Palo Alto, CA: Annual Reviews.

Blair, S. N., Kohl, H. W., Paffenbarger, R. S., Clark, D. G., Cooper, K. H., & Gibbons, L. W. (1989). Physical fitness and all-cause mortality: A prospective study of healthy men and women. *Journal of the American Medical Association, 262,* 2395–2401.

Blake, R. R., & Mouton, J. S. (1964). *The managerial grid.* Houston: Gulf Publishing.

Blank, A. S., Jr. (1982). Stresses of war: The example of Viet Nam. In L. Goldberger & S. Breznitz (Eds.), *Handbook of stress: Theoretical and clinical aspects.* New York: Free Press.

Blasband, D., & Peplau, L. A. (1985). Sexual exclusivity versus openness in gay male couples. *Archives of Sexual Behavior, 14,* 395–412.

Blascovich, J., & Katkin, E. S. (1993). Cardiovascular reactivity to psychological stress and disease: Conclusions. In J. Blascovich & E. S. Katkin (Eds.), *Cardiovascular reactivity to psychological stress & disease.* Washington, DC: American Psychological Association.

Blau, G. (1981). An empirical investigation of job stress, social support, service length, and job strain. *Organizational Behavior and Human Performance, 27,* 279–302.

Blau, Z. S. *Old age in a changing society.* New York: Van Nostrand.

Blazer, D. G., Hughes, D., & George, L. K. (1987). Stressful life events and the onset of generalized anxiety syndrome. *American Journal of Psychiatry, 144,* 1178–1183.

Blazer, D. G., Hughes, D., George, L. K., Swartz, M., & Boyer, R. (1991). Generalized anxiety disorder. In L. N. Robins & D. A. Regier (Eds.), *Psychiatric disorders in America: The epidemiologic catchment area study.* New York: Free Press.

Blazer, D. G., Kessler, R. C., McGonagle, K. A., & Swartz, M. S. (1994). The prevalence and distribution of major depression in a national community sample: The national comorbidity survey. *American Journal of Psychiatry, 151,* 979–986.

Bleier, R. (1984). *Science and gender: A critique of biology and its theories on women.* New York: Pergamon Press.

Blieszner, R., & Adams, R. G. (1992). *Adult friendship.* Newbury Park, CA: Sage Publications.

Block, J. D. (1980). *Friendship: How to give it; how to get it.* New York: Macmillan.

Block, J. H. (1973). Conceptions of sex role: Some cross-cultural and longitudinal perspectives. *American Psychologist, 28,* 512–526.

Bloodworth, R. C. (1987). Major problems associated with marijuana abuse. *Psychiatric Medicine, 3,*173–184.

Bloomfield, H. H., & Kory, R. B. (1976). *Happiness: The TM program, psychiatry, and enlightenment.* New York: Simon & Schuster.

Blum, K. (1984). *Handbook of abusable drugs.* New York: Gardner Press.

Blumenthal, J. A., Emery, C. F., Madden, D. J., Schniebolk, S., Walsh-Riddle, M., George, L. K., McKee, D. C., Higginbotham, M. B., Cobb, F. R., & Coleman, R. E. (1991). Long-term effects of exercise on psychological functioning in older men and women. *Journal of Gerontology, 46,* 352–361.

Blumstein, P., & Schwartz, P. (1983). *American couples: Money, work, sex.* New York: Morrow.

Blumstein, P., & Schwartz, P. (1989). Intimate relationships and the creation of sexuality. In B. Risman & P. Schwartz (Eds.), *Gender in intimate relationships: A microstructural approach.* Belmont, CA: Wadsworth.

Blumstein, P., & Schwartz, P. (1990). Intimate relationships and the creation of sexuality. In D. P. McWhirter, S. A. Sanders, & J. M. Reinisch (Eds.), *Homosexuality/heterosexuality: Concepts of sexual orientation.* New York: Oxford University Press.

Bolger, N. (1990). Coping as a personality process: A prospective study. *Journal of Personality and Social Psychology, 59,* 525–537.

Bolger, N., DeLongis, A., Kessler, R. C., & Schilling, E. A. (1989). Effects of daily stress on negative mood. *Journal of Personality and Social Psychology, 57,* 808–818.

Bolles, R. N. (1987). *What color is your parachute? A practical manual for job-hunters and career-changers.* Berkeley, CA: Ten Speed Press.

Bolles, R. N. (1995). *What color is your parachute? A practical manual for job-hunters and career-changers.* Berkeley, CA: Ten Speed Press.

Boor, M. (1980). Relationships between unemployment rates and suicide rates in eight countries, 1962–1976. *Psychological Reports, 60,* 562–564.

Bores-Rangel, E., Church, A. T., Szendre, D., & Reeves, C. (1990). Self-efficacy in relation to occupational consideration and academic performance in high school equivalency students. *Journal of Counseling Psychology, 37,* 407–418.

Boskind-Lodahl, M. (1976). Cinderella's stepsisters: A feminist perspective on anorexia nervosa and bulimia. *Signs, 2,* 120–146.

Boster, F. J., & Mongeau, P. (1985). Fear-arousing persuasive messages. In R. N. Bostrom (Ed.), *Communication yearbook* (Vol. 8). Newbury Park, CA: Sage Publications.

Boston Women's Health Book Collective (1992). *The new our bodies ourselves: A book by and for women.* New York: Simon & Schuster.

Bower, G. H. (1970). Organizational factors in memory. *Cognitive Psychology, 1,* 18–46.

Bower, G. H., & Clark, M. C. (1969). Narrative stories as mediators of serial learning. *Psychonomic Science, 14,* 181–182.

Bower, S. A., & Bower, G. H. (1991). *Asserting yourself: A practical guide for positive change* (2nd ed.). Reading, MA: Addison-Wesley.

Bowers, J. W., Metts, S. M., & Duncanson, W. T. (1985). Emotion and interpersonal communication. In M. L. Knapp & G. R. Miller (Eds.), *Handbook of interpersonal communication.* Newbury Park, CA: Sage Publications.

Bowlby, J. (1980). *Attachment and loss: Vol. 3. Loss: Sadness and depression.* New York: Basic Books.

Bozarth, M. A., & Wise, R. A. (1985). Toxicity associated with long-term intravenous heroin and cocaine self-administration in the rat. *Journal of the American Medical Association, 254,* 81–83.

Bozett, F. W. (1987). Children of gay fathers. In F. W. Bozett (Ed.), *Gay and lesbian parents*. New York: Praeger.

Bradbury, T. N., & Fincham, F. D. (1988). Individual difference variables in close relationships: A contextual model of marriage as an integrative framework. *Journal of Personality and Social Psychology, 54,* 713–721.

Bradbury, T. N., & Fincham, F. D. (1990). Attributions in marriage: Review and critique. *Psychological Bulletin, 107,* 3–33.

Bradford, J., & Ryan, C. (1987). *National lesbian health care survey: Mental health implications.* Washington, DC: National Lesbian and Gay Health Foundation.

Bradley, P. H. (1981). The folk-linguistics of women's speech: An empirical examination. *Communications Monographs, 48,* 73–90.

Bradshaw, J. (1988). *Healing the shame that binds you.* Pompano Beach, FL: Health Communications.

Braiker, H. B., & Kelley, H. H. (1979). Conflict in the development of close relationships. In R. L. Burgess & T. L. Huston (Eds.), *Social exchange in developing relationships.* New York: Academic Press.

Bram, S. (1985). Childlessness revisited: A longitudinal study of voluntarily childless couples, delayed parents, and parents. *Lifestyles: A Journal of Changing Patterns, 8,* 46–66.

Brand, P. A., & Kidd, A. H. (1986). Frequency of physical aggression in heterosexual and female homosexual dyads. *Psychological Reports, 59,* 1307–1313.

Brannon, R. (1976). The male sex role: Our culture's blueprint of manhood, and what it's done for us lately. In D. David & R. Brannon (Eds.), *The forty-nine percent majority.* Reading, MA: Addison-Wesley.

Bray, G. A. (1990). Exercise and obesity. In C. Bouchard, R. J. Shephard, T. Stephens, J. R. Sutton, & B. D. McPherson (Eds.), *Exercise, fitness and health: A consensus of current knowledge.* Champaign, IL: Human Kinetics Books.

Bray, J. H., & Hetherington, E. M. (1993). Families in transition: Introduction and overview. *Journal of Family Psychology, 7,* 3–8.

Brecher, E. M. (1984). *Love, sex, and aging.* Boston: Little, Brown.

Breggin, P. R. (1979). *Electroshock: Its brain disabling effects.* New York: Springer.

Breggin, P. R. (1990). Brain damage, dementia and persistent cognitive dysfunction associated with neuroleptic drugs: Evidence, etiology, implications. *The Journal of Mind and Behavior, 11,* 425–464.

Breggin, P. R. (1991). *Toxic psychiatry.* New York: St. Martin's Press.

Brehm, J. W. (1966). *A theory of psychological reactance.* New York: Academic Press.

Brehm, S. S. (1992). *Intimate relationships* (2nd ed.). New York: McGraw-Hill.

Brehm, S. S., & Kassin, S. M. (1993). *Social psychology.* Boston: Houghton Mifflin.

Brent, D. A., & Kolko, D. J. (1990). The assessment and treatment of children and adolescents at risk for suicide. In S. J. Blumenthal & D. J. Kupfer (Eds.), *Suicide over the life cycle: Risk factors, assessment, and treatment of suicidal patients.* Washington, DC: American Psychiatric Press.

Bretl, D. J., & Cantor, J. (1988). The portrayal of men and women in U.S. television commercials: A recent content analysis and trends over 15 years. *Sex Roles, 18,* 595–609.

Bretschneider, J. G., & McCoy, N. L. (1988). Sexual interest and behavior in healthy 80- to 102-year-olds. *Archives of Sexual Behavior, 17,* 109–130.

Brett, J. F., Brief, A. P., Burke, M. J.,

George, J. M., & Webster, J. (1990). Negative affectivity and the reporting of stressful life events. *Health Psychology, 9,* 57–68.

Brett, J. M. (1980). The effect of job transfer on employees and their families. In C. L. Cooper & R. Payne (Eds.), *Current concerns in occupational stress.* New York: Wiley.

Brewer, M. (1975, August). Erhard Seminars Training: "We're gonna tear you down and put you back together." *Psychology Today,* pp. 35–40, 82, 88–89.

Brewer, M. B. (1988). A dual process model of impression formation. In T. K. Srull & R. S. Wyer, Jr. (Eds.), *Advances in social cognition* (Vol. 1). Hillsdale, NJ: Erlbaum.

Brewer, M. B., & Caporeal, L. R. (1990). Selfish genes vs. selfish people: Sociobiology as origin myth. *Motivation and Emotion, 14,* 237–243.

Briere, J., & Conte, J. R. (1993). Self-reported amnesia for abuse in adults molested as children. *Journal of Traumatic Stress, 6,* 21–31.

Briggs, S. R. (1989). The optimal level of measurement for personality constructs. In D.M. Buss & N. Cantor (Eds.), *Personality psychology: Recent trends and emerging directions.* New York: Springer.

Briton, N. J., & Hall, J. A. (1995). Beliefs about female and male nonverbal communication. *Sex Roles, 32,* 79–90.

Brockner, J. (1983). Low self-esteem and behavioral plasticity: Some implications. In L. Wheeler & P. Shaver (Eds.), *Review of personality and social psychology* (Vol. 4). Newbury Park, CA: Sage Publications.

Brockner, J., & Rubin, J. Z. (1985). *Entrapment in escalating conflicts: A social psychological analysis.* New York: Springer-Verlag.

Brod, C. (1988). *Technostress: Human cost of the computer revolution.* Reading, MA: Addison-Wesley.

Brody, J. E. (1992, December 9). Hip fracture: A potential killer that can be avoided. *The New York Times,* C16.

Broida, R. (1995, Winter). Tea and Tennyson. *Career Woman,* 34–36.

Bromage, B. K., & Mayer, R. E. (1986). Quantitative and qualitative effects of repetition on learning from technical text. *Journal of Educational Psychology, 78,* 271–278.

Brooks-Gunn, J. (1986). The relationship of maternal beliefs about sex typing to maternal and young children's behavior. *Sex Roles, 14,* 21–35.

Brooks-Gunn, J., & Reiter, E. O. (1990). The role of pubertal processes. In S. S. Feldman & G. R. Elliott (Eds.), *At the threshold: The developing adolescent.* Cambridge, MA: Harvard University Press.

Brown, D. R. (1990). Exercise, fitness, and mental health. In C. Bouchard, R. J. Shephard, T. Stephens, J. R. Sutton, & B. D. McPherson (Eds.), *Exercise, fitness, and health: A consensus of current knowledge.* Champaign, IL: Human Kinetics Books.

Brown, J., Childers, K. W., Bauman, K. E., & Koch, G. G. (1990). The influence of new media and family structure on young adolescents' television and radio use. *Communication Research, 17,* 65–82.

Brown, J. D. (1990). Evaluating one's abilities: Shortcuts and stumbling blocks on the road to self-knowledge. *Journal of Experimental Social Psychology, 26,* 149–167.

Brown, J. D. (1991). Staying fit and staying well: Physical fitness as a moderator of life stress. *Journal of Personality and Social Psychology, 60,* 555–561.

Brown, J. D., & McGill, K. L. (1989).

The cost of good fortune: When positive life events produce negative health consequences. *Journal of Personality and Social Psychology, 57,* 1103–1110.

Brown, J. D., & Siegel, J. M. (1988). Exercise as a buffer of life stress: A prospective study of adolescent health. *Health Psychology, 7,* 341–353.

Browne, A. (1993). Violence against women by male partners: Prevalence, outcomes, and policy implications. *American Psychologist, 48,* 1077–1087.

Browne, A., & Williams, K. R. (1993). Gender, intimacy, and lethal violence: Trends from 1976 through 1987. *Gender & Society, 7,* 78–98.

Brownell, K. D. (1986). Social and behavioral aspects of obesity in children. In N. A. Krasnegor, J. D. Arasteh, & M. F. Cataldo (Eds.), *Child health behavior: A behavioral pediatrics perspective.* New York: Wiley.

Brownell, K. D. (1988, January). Yo-yo dieting. *Psychology Today,* pp. 20–23.

Brownell, K. D. (1989, June). When and how to diet. *Psychology Today,* pp. 40–46.

Brubaker, T. (1990). Families in later life: A burgeoning research area. *Journal of Marriage and the Family, 52,* 959–982.

Bruckner-Gordon, F., Gangi, B. K., & Wallman, G. U. (1988). *Making therapy work: Your guide to choosing, using, and ending therapy.* New York: HarperCollins.

Bryan, J. H., & Test, M. A. (1967). Models and helping: Naturalistic studies in aiding behavior. *Journal of Personality and Social Psychology, 6,* 400–407.

Bryant, S., & Rokowski, W. (1992). Predictors of mortality among elderly African-Americans. *Research on Aging, 14,* 50–67.

Bryden, M. P. (1988). An overview of the dichotic listening procedure and its relation to cerebral organization. In K. Hugdahl (Ed.), *Handbook of dichotic listening.* Chichester, England: Wiley.

Bryer, K. B. (1979). The Amish way of death: A study of family support systems. *American Psychologist, 34,* 255–261.

Buck, E. B., Newton, B. J., & Muramatsu, Y. (1984). Independence and obedience in the U.S. and Japan. *International Journal of Intercultural Relations, 8,* 279–300.

Buckhout, R. (1980). Nearly 2,000 witnesses can be wrong. *Bulletin of the Psychonomic Society, 16,* 307–310.

Buda, M., & Tsuang, M. T. (1990). The epidemiology of suicide: Implications for clinical practice. In S. J. Blumenthal & D. J. Kupfer (Eds.), *Suicide over the life cycle: Risk factors, assessment, and treatment of suicidal patients.* Washington, DC: American Psychiatric Press.

Buehler, C., & Langenbrunner, M. (1987). Divorce-related stressors: Occurrence, disruptiveness, and area of life change. *Journal of Divorce, 11,* 25–50.

Buehlman, K. T., Gottman, J. M., & Katz, L. F. (1992). How a couple views their past predicts their future: Predicting divorce from an oral history interview. *Journal of Family Psychology, 5,* 295–318.

Buffum, J., Pharm, D., Smith, D. E., Moser, C., Apter, M., Buxton, M., & Davison, J. (1981). Drugs and sexual function. In H. I. Lief (Ed.), *Sexual problems in medical practice.* Chicago: American Medical Association.

Bull, R., & Rumsey, N. (1988). *The social psychology of facial appearance.* New York: Springer-Verlag.

Bullock, W. A., & Gilliland, K. (1993). Eysenck's arousal theory of introversion-extraversion: A converging measures investigation. *Journal of Personality and Social Psychology, 64,* 113–123.

Bumiller, E. (1989). First comes marriage—Then, maybe, love. In J. M. Henslin (Ed.), *Marriage and family in a changing society* (3rd ed.). New York: Free Press.

Bumpass, L. L., & Sweet, J. A. (1989). National estimates of cohabitation: Cohort levels and union stability. *Demography, 25,* 615–625.

Bumpass, L. L., Sweet, J. A., & Cherlin, A. (1991). The role of cohabitation in declining rates of marriage. *Journal of Marriage and the Family, 53,* 913–927.

Bumpass, L. L., Sweet, J. A., & Martin, T. C. (1990). Changing patterns of remarriage. *Journal of Marriage and the Family, 52,* 747–756.

Burg, B. (1974, November). Est: 60 hours to happiness. *Human Behavior,* pp. 16–23.

Burger, J. M. (1989). Negative reactions to increases in perceived personal control. *Journal of Personality and Social Psychology, 56,* 246–256.

Burger, J. M. (1993). *Personality.* Pacific Grove, CA: Brooks/Cole.

Burger, J. M., & Petty, R. E. (1981). The low-ball compliance technique: Task or person commitment? *Journal of Personality and Social Psychology, 40,* 492–500.

Burgoon, J. K. (1990). *Nonverbal Communication: The unspoken dialogue.* New York: HarperCollins.

Buri, J. R., Louiselle, P. A., Misukanis, T. M., & Mueller, R. A. (1988). Effects of parental authoritarianism and authoritativeness on self-esteem. *Personality and Social Psychology Bulletin, 14,* 271–282.

Burleson, B. R. (1982). The development of comforting communication skills in childhood and adolescence. *Child Development, 53,* 1578–1588.

Burns, D. (1980). *Feeling good: The new mood therapy.* New York: Signet.

Burns, D. (1989). *The feeling good handbook.* New York: Plume.

Burt, M. R. (1980). Cultural myths and supports for rape. *Journal of Personality and Social Psychology, 38,* 217–230.

Buscaglia, L. (1982). *Living, loving and learning.* Thorofare, NJ: Charles B. Slack.

Busch-Rossnagel, N. A., & Vance, A. K. (1982). The impact of the schools on social and emotional development. In B. B. Wolman (Ed.), *Handbook of developmental psychology.* Englewood Cliffs, NJ: Prentice-Hall.

Buss, D. M. (1985). Human mate selection. *American Scientist, 73,* 47–51.

Buss, D. M. (1988). The evolution of human intrasexual competition: Tactics of mate attraction. *Journal of Personality and Social Psychology, 54,* 616–628.

Buss, D. M. (1989). Sex differences in human mate preferences: Evolutionary hypotheses tested in 37 cultures. *Behavioral and Brain Sciences, 12,* 1–14.

Buss, D. M. (1994). Mate preferences in 37 cultures. In W. J. Lonner & R. S. Malpass (Eds.), *Psychology and culture.* Boston: Allyn & Bacon.

Buss, D. M., & Barnes, M. (1986). Preferences in human mate selection. *Journal of Personality and Social Psychology, 50,* 559–570.

Bussey, K., & Bandura, A. (1984). Influence of gender constancy and social power on sex-linked modeling. *Journal of Personality and Social Psychology, 47,* 1292–1302.

Butcher, J. N., Narikiyo, T., & Vitousek, K. B. (1993). Understanding abnormal behavior in cultural context. In P. B. Sutker & H. E. Adams (Eds.), *Comprehensive handbook of psychopathology.* New York: Plenum.

Butler, R., & Lewis, M. (1982). *Aging and mental health* (3rd ed.). St. Louis: Mosby.

Buunk, B. (1980). Extramarital sex in the Netherlands: Motivations in social and marital context. *Alternative Lifestyles, 3,* 11–39.

Buvat, J., Buvat-Herbaut, M., Lemaire, A., & Marcolin, G. (1990). Recent developments in the clinical assessment and diagnosis of erectile dysfunction. *Annual Review of Sex Research, 1,* 265–308.

Buxton, M. N., Arkel, Y., Lagos, J., Deposito, F., Lowenthal, H., & Simring, S. (1981). Stress and platelet aggregation in hemophiliac children and their family members. *Research Communications in Psychology, Psychiatry and Behavior, 6,* 21–48.

Byne, W., & Parsons, B. (1993). Human sexual orientation: The biologic theories reappraised. *Archives of General Psychiatry, 50,* 228–238.

Byrd, J. C. (1992). Environmental tobacco smoke: Medical and legal issues. *Medical Clinics of North America, 76,* 377–398.

Byrne, D. (1971). *The attraction paradigm.* New York: Academic Press.

Byrne, D., Clore, G. L., & Smeaton, G. (1986). The attraction hypothesis: Do similar attitudes affect anything? *Journal of Personality and Social Psychology, 51,* 1167–1170.

Byrne, D., Kelley, K., & Fisher, W. A. (1993). Unwanted teenage pregnancies: Incidence, interpretation, and intervention. *Applied and Preventive Psychology, 2,* 101–113.

Byrne, D., & Murnen, S. K. (1988). Maintaining loving relationships. In R. J. Sternberg & M. L. Barnes (Eds.), *The psychology of love.* New Haven, CT: Yale University Press.

Cado, S., & Leitenberg, H. (1990). Guilt reactions to sexual fantasies during intercourse. *Archives of Sexual Behavior, 19,* 49–64.

Calabrese, L. H. (1990). Exercise, immunity, cancer, and infection. In C. Bouchard, R. J. Shephard, T. Stephens, J. R. Sutton, & B. D. McPherson (Eds.), *Exercise, fitness, and health: A consensus of knowledge.* Champaign, IL: Human Kinetics Books.

Calderone, M. S., & Johnson, E. W. (1989). *The family book about sexuality.* New York: Harper & Row.

Caldwell, B. M. (1993). Impact of day care on the child. *Pediatrics, 91,* 225–228.

Caldwell, M. A., & Peplau, L. A. (1982). Sex differences in same-sex friendship. *Sex Roles, 8,* 721–732.

Calev, A., Phil, D., Pass, H. L., Shapira, B., Fink, M., Tubi, N., & Lerer, B. (1993). ECT and memory. In C. E. Coffey (Ed.), *The clinical science of electroconvulsive therapy.* Washington, DC: American Psychological Press.

Cameron, L., Leventhal, E. A., & Leventhal, H. (1993). Symptom representations and affect as determinants of care seeking in a community-dwelling, adult sample population. *Health Psychology, 12,* 171–179.

Cameron, N. (1963). *Personality development and psychopathology.* Boston: Houghton Mifflin.

Campbell, J. D. (1986). Similarity and uniqueness: The effects of attribute type, relevance, and individual differences in self-esteem and depression. *Journal of Personality and Social Psychology, 50,* 281–294.

Cannon, D. S., Baker, T. B., & Wehl, C. K. (1981). Emetic and electric shock alcohol aversion therapy: Six- and twelve-month follow-up. *Journal of Consulting and Clinical Psychology, 49,* 360–368.

Cannon, W. B. (1932). *The wisdom of the body.* New York: Norton.

Cantor, N. (1990). Social psychology and sociobiology: What can we leave to evolution? *Motivation and Emotion, 14,* 245–254.

Cappella, J. N., & Palmer, M. T. (1990). Attitude similarity, relational history, and attraction: The mediating effects of kinesic and vocal behaviors. *Communication Monographs, 57,* 161–183.

Cargan, L., & Melko, M. (1982). *Singles: Myths and realities.* Newbury Park, CA: Sage Publications.

Carli, L. J. (1990). Gender, language, and influence. *Journal of Personality and Social Psychology, 59,* 941–951.

Carlson, V., Cicchetti, D., Barnett, D., & Braunwald, K. (1989). Disorganized/disoriented attachment relationships in maltreated infants. *Developmental Psychology, 25,* 525–531.

Carney, C. G., & Wells, C. F. (1995). *Discover the career within you* (4th ed.). Pacific Grove, CA: Brooks/Cole.

Carpenter, W. T. (1992). The negative symptom challenge. *Archives of General Psychiatry, 49,* 236–237.

Carr, P. G., & Mednick, M. T. (1988). Sex role socialization and the development of achievement motivation in black preschool children. *Sex Roles, 18,* 169–180.

Carrington, P. (1987). Managing meditation in clinical practice. In M. A. West (Ed.), *The psychology of meditation.* Oxford: Clarendon Press.

Carrington, P. (1993). Modern forms of meditation. In P. M. Lehrer & R. L. Woolfolk (Eds.), *Principles and practice of stress management* (2nd ed.). New York: Guilford Press.

Carroll, J. L., Volk, K. D., & Hyde, J. S. (1985). Differences between males and females in motives for engaging in sexual intercourse. *Archives of Sexual Behavior, 14,* 131–139.

Carson, R. C. (1991). Dilemmas in the pathway of the DSM-IV. *Journal of Abnormal Psychology, 100,* 302–307.

Carson, R. C., & Sanislow, C. A., III. (1993). The schizophrenias. In P. B. Sutker & H. E. Adams (Eds.), *Comprehensive handbook of psychopathology* (2nd ed.). New York: Plenum.

Carsten, J. M., & Spector, P. E. (1987). Unemployment, job satisfaction, and employee turnover: A meta-analytic test of the Muchinsky model. *Journal of Applied Psychology, 72,* 75–80.

Carter, E. A., & McGoldrick, M. (1988). Overview: The changing family life cycle—A framework for family therapy. In E. A. Carter & M. McGoldrick (Eds.), *The changing family life cycle: A framework for family therapy* (2nd ed.). New York: Gardner Press.

Carter, R. J., & Myerowitz, B. E. (1984). Sex-role stereotypes: Self-reports of behavior. *Sex Roles, 10,* 293–306.

Carver, C. S., Pozo, C., Harris, S. D., Noriega, V., Scheier, M. F., Robinson, D. S., Ketcham, A. S., Moffat, F. L., Jr., & Clark, K. C. (1993). How coping mediates the effect of optimism on distress: A study of women with early stage breast cancer. *Journal of Personality and Social Psychology, 65,* 375–390.

Carver, C. S., & Scheier, M. F. (1994). Situational coping and coping dispositions in a stressful transaction. *Journal of Personality and Social Psychology, 66,* 184–195.

Carver, C. S., Scheier, M. F., & Weintraub, J. K. (1989). Assessing coping strategies: A theoretically based approach. *Journal of Personality and Social Psychology, 56,* 267–283.

Cashmore, J. A., & Goodnow, J. J. (1986). Influences on Australian parents' values: Ethnicity versus sociometric status. *Journal of Cross-Cultural Psychology, 17,* 441–454.

Caspi, A., Bolger, N., & Eckenrode, J.

(1987). Linking person and context in the daily stress process. *Journal of Personality and Social Psychology, 52,* 184–195.

Caspi, A., & Herbener, E. S. (1990). Continuity and change: Assortative marriage and the consistency of personality in adulthood. *Journal of Personality and Social Psychology, 58,* 250–258.

Castro, K. G., Newcomb, M. D., Mc-Creary, C., & Baezconde-Garbanati, L. (1989). Cigarette smokers do more than just smoke cigarettes. *Health Psychology, 8,* 107–129.

Catania, J. A., Coates, T. J., Stall, R., Turner, H., Peterson, J., Hearst, N., Dolcini, M. M., Hudes, E., Gagnon, J., Wiley, J., & Groves, R. (1992). Prevalence of AIDS-related risk factors and condom use in the United States. *Science, 258,* 1101–1106.

Catania, J. A., McDermott, L. J., & Pollack, L. M. (1986). Questionnaire response bias and face-to-face interview sample bias in sexuality research. *The Journal of Sex Research, 22,* 52–72.

Cate, R. M., & Lloyd, S. A. (1988). Courtship. In S. Duck (Ed.), *Handbook of personal relationships.* New York: Wiley.

Cate, R. M., & Lloyd, S. A. (1992). *Courtship.* Newbury Park, CA: Sage Publications.

Cate, R. M., Huston, T. L., & Nesselroade, J. R. (1986). Premarital relationships: Toward the identification of alternative pathways to marriage. *Journal of Social and Clinical Psychology, 4,* 3–22.

Cattell, R. B. (1950). *Personality: A systematic, theoretical and factual study.* New York: McGraw-Hill.

Cattell, R. B. (1966). *The scientific analysis of personality.* Chicago: Aldine.

Cattell, R. B. (1990). Advances in Cattellian personality theory. In L. A. Pervin (Ed.), *Handbook of personality: Theory and research.* New York: Guilford Press.

Cattell, R. B., Eber, H. W., & Tatsuoka, M. M. (1970). *Handbook of the Sixteen Personality Factor Questionnaire (16PF).* Champaign, IL: Institute for Personality and Ability Testing.

Cattell, R. B., Kawash, G. F., & DeYoung, G. E. (1972). Validation of objective measures of ergic tension: Response of the sex erg to visual stimulation. *Journal of Experimental Research in Personality, 6,* 76–83.

Cerletti, U., & Bini, L. (1938). Un nuevo metodo di shockterapie "L'elettroshock." *Boll. Acad. Med. Roma, 64,* 136–138.

Cermak, T. L. (1986). Diagnostic criteria for codependency. *Journal of Psychoactive Drugs, 18,* 15–20.

Cernovsky, Z. Z. (1989). Life stress measures and reported frequency of sleep disorders. In T. W. Miller (Ed.), *Stressful life events.* Madison, CT: International Universities Press.

Chaiken, S. (1979). Communicator's physical attractiveness and persuasion. *Journal of Personality and Social Psychology, 37,* 1387–1397.

Chapman, B. E., & Brannock, J. C. (1987). A proposed model of lesbian identity development: An empirical investigation. *Journal of Homosexuality, 14,* 69–80.

Charlesworth, W. R., & Dzur, C. (1987). Gender comparisons of preschoolers' behavior and resource utilization in group problem-solving. *Child Development, 58,* 191–200.

Charness, N. (1985). Aging and problem-solving performance. In N. Charness (Ed.), *Aging and human performance.* Chichester, England: Wiley.

Check, J. V. P., Perlman, D., & Malamuth, N. M. (1985). Loneliness and aggressive behavior. *Journal of Social and Personal Relationships, 2,* 243–252.

Cheek, J. M., & Busch, C. M. (1981). The influence of shyness on loneliness in a new situation. *Personality and Social Psychology Bulletin, 7,* 572–577.

Cheek, J. M., & Buss, A. H. (1981). Shyness and sociability. *Journal of Personality and Social Psychology, 41,* 330–337.

Chelune, G. J. (1987). A neuropsychological perpective of interpersonal communication. In V. J. Derlega & J. H. Berg (Eds.), *Self-disclosure: Theory, research, and therapy.* New York: Plenum.

Cherlin, A. J. (1981). *Marriage, divorce, remarriage.* Cambridge, MA: Harvard University Press.

Chiriboga, D. A. (1987). Personality in later life. In P. Silverman (Ed.), *The elderly as modern pioneers.* Bloomington: Indiana University Press.

Chiriboga, D. A. (1989). Mental health at the mid-point: Crisis, challenge, or relief? In S. Hunter & M. Sundel (Eds.), *Mid-life myths: Issues, findings, and practical implications.* Thousand Oaks, CA: Sage.

Chodorow, N. (1978). *The reproduction of mothering.* Berkeley, CA: University of California Press.

Chopra, D. (1993). *Ageless body, timeless mind.* New York: Crown.

Christensen, A., & Heavey, C. L. (1990). Gender and social structure in the demand/withdraw pattern of marital conflict. *Journal of Personality and Social Psychology, 59,* 73–81.

Christensen, A., & Jacobson, N. S. (1994). Who (or what) can do psychotherapy: The status and challenge of nonprofessional therapies. *Psychological Science, 5,* 8–14.

Chumlea, W. C. (1982). Physical growth in adolescence. In B. B. Wolman (Ed.), *Handbook of developmental psychology.* Englewood Cliffs, NJ: Prentice-Hall.

Church, A. T., & Burke, P. J. (1994). Exploratory and confirmatory tests of the Big Five and Tellegen's three- and four-dimensional models. *Journal of Personality and Social Psychology, 66,* 93–114.

Church, G. J. (1993, November 22). Jobs in an age of insecurity. *Time,* pp. 32–39.

Cialdini, R. B. (1993). *Influence: Science and practice* (3rd ed.). Glenview, IL: HarperCollins.

Cialdini, R. B., Borden, R. J., Thorne, A., Walker, M. R., Freeman, S., & Sloan, L. R. (1976). Basking in reflected glory: Three (football) field studies. *Journal of Personality and Social Psychology, 34,* 366–375.

Cicirelli, V. G. (1989). Feelings of attachment to siblings and well-being in later life. *Psychology and Aging, 4,* 211–216.

Ciompi, L. (1980). Catamnestic long-term study on the course of life and aging in schizophrenics. *Schizophrenia Bulletin, 6,* 607–618.

Clark, D. A., Beck, A. T., & Beck, J. S. (1994). Symptom differences in major depression, dysthymia, panic disorder, and generalized anxiety disorder. *American Journal of Psychiatry, 151,* 205–209.

Clark, H. H. (1985). Language use and language users. In G. Lindzey & E. Aronson (Eds.), *The handbook of social psychology: Vol. 2. Special fields and applications.* New York: Random House.

Clark, L. A., Watson, D., & Mineka, S. (1994). Temperament, personality, and the mood and anxiety disorders. *Journal of Abnormal Psychology, 103,* 103–116.

Clark, L. A., Watson, D., & Reynolds, S. (1995). Diagnosis and classification of psychopathology: Challenges to the current system and future directions. *Annual Reviews of Psychology, 46,* 121–153.

Clark, L. F. (1993). Stress and the cognitive-conversational benefits of social interaction. *Journal of Social and Clinical Psychology, 12,* 25–55.

Clark, M. S. (1984). Record-keeping in two types of relationships. *Journal of Personality and Social Psychology, 47,* 549–557.

Clark, M. S., & Bennett, M. E. (1992). Research on relationships: Implications for mental health. In D. N. Ruble, R. R. Costanzo, & M. E. Oliveri (Eds.), *The social psychology of mental health.* New York: Guilford Press.

Clark, M. S., Mills, J., & Powell, M. C. (1986). Keeping track of needs in communal and exchange relationships. *Journal of Personality and Social Psychology, 51,* 333–338.

Clark, R. L. (1988). The future of work and retirement. *Research on Aging, 10,* 169–193.

Clarke-Stewart, K. A., & Bailey, B. L. (1989). Adjusting to divorce: Why do men have it easier? *Journal of Divorce, 13,* 75–94.

Cleary, P. J. (1980). A checklist for life event research. *Journal of Psychosomatic Research, 24,* 199–207.

Cleek, M. G., & Pearson, T. A. (1985). Perceived causes of divorce: An analysis of interrelationships. *Journal of Marriage and the Family, 47,* 179–183.

Coates, D. L. (1987). Gender differences in the structure and support characteristics of black adolescents' social networks. *Sex Roles, 17,* 667–687.

Cocks, J. (1991, July 1). A nasty jolt for the top pops. *Time,* pp. 78–79.

Cocores, J. (1987). Co-addiction: A silent epidemic. *Psychiatry Letter, 5,* 5–8.

Cohen, C. E. (1981). Person categories and social perception: Testing some boundaries of the processing effects of prior knowledge. *Journal of Personality and Social Psychology, 40,* 441–452.

Cohen, D., & McCubbin, M. (1990). The political economy of tardive dyskinesia: Asymmetries in power and responsibility. *The Journal of Mind and Behavior, 11,* 465–488.

Cohen, F. (1979). Personality, stress and the development of physical illness. In G. C. Stone, F. Cohen, N. E. Adler, & associates (Eds.), *Health psychology—A handbook.* San Francisco: Jossey-Bass.

Cohen, S. (1986). Marijuana. In A. J. Frances & R. E. Hales (Eds.), *Psychiatry Update: Annual Review* (Vol. 5). Washington, DC: American Psychiatric Press.

Cohen, S. (1988). Psychosocial models of the role of social support in the etiology of physical disease. *Health Psychology, 7,* 269–297.

Cohen, S., Evans, G. W., Krantz, D. S., & Stokols, D. (1980). Physiological, motivational, and cognitive effects of aircraft noise on children: Moving from the laboratory to the field. *American Psychologist, 35,* 231–243.

Cohen, S., Glass, D. C., & Phillips, S. (1977). Environment and health. In H. E. Freeman, S. Levine, & L. G. Reeder (Eds.), *Handbook of medical sociology.* Englewood Cliffs, NJ: Prentice-Hall.

Cohen, S., Kamarck, T., & Mermelstein, R. (1983). A global measure of perceived stress. *Journal of Health and Social Behavior, 24,* 385–396.

Cohen, S., & Lichtenstein, E. (1990). Perceived stress, quitting smoking, and smoking relapse. *Health Psychology, 9,* 466–478.

Cohen, S., Lichtenstein, E., Prochaska, J. O., Rossi, J. S., Gritz, E. R., Carr, C. R., Orleans, C. T., Schoenbach, V. J., Biener, L., Abrams, D., DiClemente, C., Curry, S., Marlatt, G. A., Cummings, K. M., Emont, S. L., Giovino, A., & Ossip-Klein, D.

(1989). Debunking myths about self-quitting: Evidence from 10 prospective studies of persons who attempt to quit smoking by themselves. *American Psychologist, 44,* 1355–1365.

Cohen, S., Sherrod, D., & Clark, M. (1986). Social skills and the stress-protective role of social support. *Journal of Personality and Social Psychology, 50,* 963–973.

Cohen, S., & Syme, S. L. (Eds.). (1985). *Social support and health.* New York: Academic Press.

Cohen, S., Tyrrell, D. A., & Smith, A. P. (1993). Negative life events, perceived stress, negative affect, and susceptibility to the common cold. *Journal of Personality and Social Psychology, 64,* 131–140.

Cohen, S., & Wills, T. A. (1985). Stress, social support, and the buffering hypothesis. *Psychological Bulletin, 98,* 310–357.

Cohn, L. D., & Adler, N. E. (1992). Female and male perceptions of ideal body shapes: Distorted views among Caucasian college students. *Psychology of Women Quarterly, 16,* 69–79.

Cole, J. O., Goldberg, S. C., & Davis, J. M. (1966). Drugs in the treatment of psychosis. In P. Solomon (Ed.), *Psychiatric Drugs.* New York: Grune & Stratton.

Cole, W., Emery, M., & Horowitz, J. M. (1993, May 24). What should we teach our children about sex? *Time,* pp. 60–66.

Coleman, L. M., & Antonucci, T. C. (1983). Impact of work on women at midlife. *Developmental Psychology, 19,* 290–294.

Coles, R., & Stokes, G. (1985). *Sex and the American teenager.* New York: Harper.

Coley, S. M., & Beckett, J. O. (1988). Black battered women: A review of empirical literature. *Journal of Counseling and Development, 66,* 266–270.

Colgrove, M., Bloomfield, H., & McWilliams, P. (1991). *How to survive the loss of a love.* Los Angeles, CA: Prelude Press.

Collins, B. G. (1993). Reconstruing codependency using self-in-relation theory: A feminist perspective. *Social Work, 38,* 470–476.

Collins, N. L., & Miller, L. C. (1994). Self-disclosure and liking: A meta-analytic review. *Psychological Bulletin, 116,* 457–475.

Collins, N. L., & Read, S. J. (1990). Adult attachment, working models, and relationship quality in dating couples. *Journal of Personality and Social Psychology, 58,* 644–663.

Coltrane, S., & Ishii-Kuntz, M. (1992). Men's housework: A life course perspective. *Journal of Marriage and the Family, 54,* 43–57.

Comas-Diaz, L. (1987). Feminist therapy with mainland Puerto Rican women. *Psychology of Women Quarterly, 11,* 461–474.

Comas-Diaz, L. (1991). Feminism and diversity in psychology: The case of women of color. *Psychology of Women Quarterly, 15,* 597–609.

Conger, R., Elder, G., Lorenz, F., Conger, K., Simons, R., Whitbeck, L., Huck, S., & Melby, J. (1990). Linking economic hardship to marital quality and instability. *Journal of Marriage and the Family, 52,* 643–656.

Conley, J. J. (1985). Longitudinal stability of personality traits: A multitrait-multimethod-multioccasion analysis. *Journal of Personality and Social Psychology, 49,* 1266–1282.

Conrad, C. C. (1976, May). How different sports rate in promoting physical fitness. *Medical Times,* pp. 4–5.

Cook, M., & Mineka, S. (1989). Observational conditioning of fear to fear-relevant versus fear-irrelevant stimuli in Rhesus monkeys. *Journal of Abnormal Psychology, 98,* 448–459.

Cooney, T. M., Pedersen, F. A., Indelicato, S., & Palkovitz, R. (1993). Timing of fatherhood: Is "on-time" optimal? *Journal of Marriage and the Family, 55,* 205–215.

Coontz, S. (1992). *The way we never were: American families and the nostalgia trap.* New York: Basic Books.

Cooper, C. L. (1984). The social-psychological precursors to cancer. *Journal of Human Stress, 10,* 4–11.

Cooper, H., Okamura, L., & Gurka, V. (1992). Social activity and subjective well-being. *Personality and Individual Differences, 13,* 573–583.

Cooper, K. (1970). *The new aerobics.* New York: Bantam.

Coopersmith, S. (1967). *The antecedents of self-esteem.* San Francisco: Freeman.

Coopersmith, S. (1975). Studies in self-esteem. In R. C. Atkinson (Ed.), *Psychology in progress: Readings from Scientific American.* San Francisco: Freeman.

Coryell, W., & Winokur, G. (1992). Course and outcome. In E. S. Paykel (Ed.), *Handbook of affective disorders* (2nd ed.). New York: Guilford Press.

Costa, P. T., Jr., & McCrae, R. R. (1988). Personality in adulthood: A six-year longitudinal study of self-reports and spouse ratings on the NEO Personality Inventory. *Journal of Personality and Social Psychology, 54,* 853–863.

Costa, P. T., Jr., & McCrae, R. R. (1994). Set like plaster? Evidence for the stability of adult personality. In T. F. Heatherton & J. L. Weinberger (Eds.), *Can personality change?* Washington, DC: American Psychological Association.

Covi, L., & Primakoff, L. (1988). Cognitive group therapy. In A. J. Frances & R. E. Hales (Eds.), *Review of psychiatry* (Vol. 7). Washington, DC: American Psychiatric Association.

Cox, T., & Mackay, C. (1982). Psychosocial factors and psychophysiological mechanisms in the etiology and development of cancer. *Social Science and Medicine, 16,* 381–396.

Coyle, J. T., Price, D. L., & DeLong, M. R. (1983). Alzheimer's disease: A disorder of cortical cholinergic innervation. *Science, 219,* 1184–1190.

Coyne, J. C., Burchill, S. A. L., & Stiles, W. B. (1990). An interactional perspective on depression. In C. R. Snyder & D. R. Forsyth (Eds.), *Handbook of social and clinical psychology: The health perspective.* New York: Pergamon Press.

Crane, P. T. (1985). Voluntary childlessness: Some notes on the decision-making process. In D. B. Gutknecht & E. W. Butler (Eds.), *Family, self, and society: Emerging issues, alternatives, and interventions* (2nd ed.). New York: UPA.

Craufurd, D. I. O., Creed, F., & Jayson, M. D. (1990). Life events and psychological disturbance in patients with low-back pain. *Spine, 15,* 490–494.

Creed, F. (1989). Appendectomy. In G. W. Brown & T. O. Harris (Eds.), *Life events and illness.* New York: Guilford Press.

Creed, F. (1993). Stress and psychosomatic disorders. In L. Goldberger & S. Breznitz (Eds.), *Handbook of stress: Theoretical and clinical aspects* (2nd ed.). New York: Free Press.

Cregler, L. L., & Mark, H. (1986). Medical complications of cocaine abuse. *New England Journal of Medicine, 315,* 1495–1500.

Crimmins, E. M., & Ingegneri, D. G. (1990). Interaction and living arrangements of older parents and their children. *Research on Aging, 12,* 3–35.

Crites, J. O. (1980). Career development. In J. F. Adams (Ed.), *Understanding adolescence. Current developments in adolescent psychology* (4th ed.). Boston: Allyn & Bacon.

Crocker, J., & Major, B. (1989). Social stigma and self-esteem: The self-protective properties of stigma. *Psychological Review, 96,* 608–630.

Crocker, J., & McGraw, K. M. (1984). What's good for the goose is not good for the gander: Solo status as an obstacle to occupational achievement for males and females. *American Behavioral Scientist, 27,* 357–370.

Crook, R. H., Healy, C. C., & O'Shay, D. W. (1984). The linkage of work achievement to self-esteem, career maturity, and college achievement. *Journal of Vocational Behavior, 25,* 70–79.

Crooks, R., & Baur, K. (1983). *Our sexuality* (2nd ed.). Menlo Park, CA: Benjamin Cummings.

Crooks, R., & Baur, K. (1993). *Our sexuality* (5th ed.). Menlo Park, CA: Benjamin Cummings.

Crooks, R., & Baur K. (1996). *Our sexuality* (6th ed.). Pacific Grove, CA: Brooks/Cole.

Crosby, F., Bromley, S., & Saxe, L. (1980). Recent unobtrusive studies of black and white discrimination and prejudice: A literature review. *Psychological Bulletin, 87,* 546–563.

Crosby, F. J., & Jaskar, K. L. (1993). Women and men at home and at work: Realities and illusions. In S. OsKamp & M. Costanzo (Eds.), *Gender issues in contemporary society.* Newbury Park, CA: Sage Publications.

Cross, C. K., & Hirschfeld, R. M. A. (1986). Epidemiology of disorders in adulthood: Suicide. In G. L. Klerman, M. M. Weissman, P. S. Appelbaum, & L. H. Roth (Eds.), *Psychiatry: Vol. 5. Social, epidemiologic, and legal psychiatry.* New York: Basic Books.

Crovitz, H. F. (1971). The capacity of memory loci in artificial memory. *Psychonomic Science, 24,* 187–188.

Crozier, W. R. (1981). Shyness and self-esteem. *British Journal of Social Psychology, 20,* 220–222.

Csikszentmihalyi, M., & Kleiber, D. A. (1991). Leisure and self-actualization. In B. C. Drirer, P. J. Brown, & G. L. Peterson (Eds.), *Benefits of leisure.* State College, PA: Venture.

Csikszentmihalyi, M., & Kubey, R. (1981). Television and the rest of life. *Public Opinion Quarterly, 45,* 317–328.

Cunningham, J. A., Strassberg, D. S., & Haan, B. (1986). Effects of intimacy and sex-role congruency on self-disclosure. *Journal of Social and Clinical Psychology, 4,* 393–401.

Cupach, W. R., & Comstock, J. (1990). Satisfaction with sexual communication in marriage: Links to sexual satisfaction and dyadic adjustment. *Journal of Social and Personal Relationships, 7,* 179–186.

Curran, D. K. (1987). *Adolescent suicidal behavior.* Washington, DC: Hemisphere.

Curtis, R. C., & Miller, K. (1986). Believing another likes or dislikes you: Behaviors making the beliefs come true. *Journal of Personality and Social Psychology, 51,* 284–290.

Cutrona, C. E. (1982). Transition to college: Loneliness and the process of social adjustment. In L. A. Peplau & D. Perlman (Eds.), *Loneliness: A sourcebook of current theory, research, and therapy.* New York: Wiley.

Dager, S., Saai, A. K., Comess, K. A., & Dunner, D. L. (1988). Mitral valve prolapse and the anxiety disorders. *Hospital and Community Psychology, 39,* 517–527.

Dambrot, F. H., Papp, M. E., & Whitmore, C. (1984). The sex-role attitudes of three generations of women. *Personality and Social Psychology Bulletin, 10,* 469–473.

D'Andrade, R. G. (1966). Sex differences and cultural institutions. In E. Maccoby (Ed.), *The development of sex differences.* Stanford, CA: Stanford University Press.

Daniels, D., & Plomin, R. (1985). Origins of individual differences in infant shyness. *Developmental Psychology, 21,* 118–121.

Danziger, N. (1983). Sex-related differences in the aspirations of high school students. *Sex Roles, 9,* 683–695.

Darley, J. M., & Gilbert, D. T. (1985). Social psychological aspects of environmental psychology. In G. Lindzey & E. Aronson (Eds.), *Handbook of social psychology* (3rd ed., Vol. 2). New York: Random House.

Darley, J. M., & Latané, B. (1968). Bystander intervention in emergencies: Diffusion of responsibility. *Journal of Personality and Social Psychology, 8,* 377–383.

Davidson, J. (1985). The utilization of sexual fantasies by sexually experienced university students. *Journal of American College Health, 34,* 24–32.

Davidson, J. (1988). *The agony of it all.* Los Angeles: Tarcher.

Davidson, J. R. T. (1992). Monoamine oxidase inhibitors. In E. S. Paykel (Ed.), *Handbook of affective disorders* (2nd ed.). New York: Guilford Press.

Davidson, L. R., & Duberman, L. (1982). Friendship: Communication and interactional patterns in same-sex dyads. *Sex Roles, 8,* 809–822.

Davidson, N. (1988). The failure of feminism. Buffalo: Prometheus.

Davis, D. M. (1990). Portrayals of women in prime-time network television: Some demographic characteristics. *Sex Roles, 23,* 325–332.

Davis, J. A. (1966). The campus as a frog pond. *American Journal of Sociology, 72,* 17–31.

Davis, J. A., & Smith, T. (1991). *General social surveys, 1972–1991.* Storrs, CT: University of Connecticut, Roper Center for Public Opinion Research.

Davis, J. M. (1985). Antipsychotic drugs. In H. I. Kaplan & B. J. Sadock (Eds.), *Comprehensive textbook of psychiatry/IV.* Baltimore: Williams & Wilkins.

Davis, J. M., Barter, J. T., & Kane, J. M. (1989). Antipsychotic drugs. In H. I. Kaplan & B. J. Sadock (Eds.), *Comprehensive textbook of psychiatry/V.* Baltimore: Williams & Wilkins.

Davis, J. M., & Glassman, A. H. (1989). Antidepressant drugs. In H. I. Kaplan & B. J. Sadock (Eds.), *Comprehensive textbook of psychiatry/V.* Baltimore: Williams & Wilkins.

Davis, K. E. (1985, February). Near and dear: Friendship and love compared. *Psychology Today,* pp. 22–30.

Davis, K. L., Kahn, R. S., Ko, G., & Davidson, M. (1991). Dopamine in schizophrenia: A review and reconceptualization. *American Journal of Psychiatry, 148,* 1474–1486.

Davis, L. (1990). *The courage to heal workbook for women and men survivors of child sexual abuse.* New York: HarperCollins.

Davis, M. H., & Franzoi, S. L. (1986). Adolescent loneliness, self-disclosure, and private self-consciousness: A longitudinal investigation. *Journal of Personality and Social Psychology, 51,* 595–608.

Davis, S. F., Miller, K. M., Johnson, D., McAuley, H., & Dinges, D. (1992). The relationship between optimism-pessimism, loneliness, and death anxiety. *Bulletin of the Psychonomic Society, 30,* 135–136.

Dawes, R. M. (1992). Why believe that for which there is no good evidence? *Issues in Child Abuse Accusations, 4,* 214–218.

Dawson, M. E., Hazlett, E. A., Filion, D. L., Neuchterlein, K. H., & Schell, A. M. (1993). Attention and schizophrenia: Impaired modulation of the startle reflex. *Journal of Abnormal Psychology, 102,* 633–641.

Day, N. L., & Richardson, G. A. (1991). Prenatal marijuana use: Epidemiology, methodological issues, and infant outcome. *Chemical Dependency and Pregnancy, 18,* 77–91.

Deaux, K. (1972). To err is humanizing: But sex makes a difference. *Representative Research in Social Psychology, 3,* 20–28.

Deaux, K., & Hanna, R. (1984). Courtship in the personals column: The influence of gender and sexual orientation. *Sex Roles, 11,* 363–375.

Deaux, K., & Lewis, L. L. (1983). Components of gender stereotypes. *Psychological Documents, 13,* Ms. No. 2583.

Deaux, K., & Lewis, L. L. (1984). Structure of gender stereotypes: Interrelationships among components and gender label. *Journal of Personality and Social Psychology, 46,* 991–1004.

DeJong, W. (1979). An examination of self-perception mediation in the foot-in-the-door effect. *Journal of Personality and Social Psychology, 37,* 2221–2239.

DeLamater, J. (1987). A sociological perspective. In J. H. Geer & W. T. O'Donohue (Eds.), *Theories of human sexuality.* New York: Plenum.

Delay, J., & Deniker, P. (1952). *Trentehuit cas de psychoses traitees par la cure prolongee et continue de 4560 RP.* Paris: Masson et Cie.

Delgado, P. L., Price, L. H., Heninger, G. R., & Charney, D. S. (1992). Neurochemistry. In E. S. Paykel (Ed.), *Handbook of affective disorders* (2nd ed.). New York: Guilford Press.

DeLongis, A., Folkman, S., & Lazarus, R. S. (1988). The impact of daily stress on health and mood: Psychological and social resources as mediators. *Journal of Personality and Social Psychology, 54,* 486–495.

DeMaris, A., & MacDonald, W. (1993). Premarital cohabitation and marital instability: A test of the unconventionality hypothesis. *Journal of Marriage and the Family, 55,* 399–407.

DeMaris, A., & Rao, K. V. (1992). Premarital cohabitation and subsequent marital stability in the United States: A reassessment. *Journal of Marriage and the Family, 54,* 178–190.

Demo, D. H. (1992). Parent-child relations: Assessing recent changes. *Journal of Marriage and the Family, 54,* 104–117.

Demo, D. H., & Acock, A. C. (1988). The impact of divorce on children. *Journal of Marriage and the Family, 50,* 619–648.

Dennis, W. (1966). Creative productivity between the ages of 20 and 80 years. *Journal of Gerontology, 21,* 1–8.

Denny, N., Field, J., & Quadagno, D. (1984). Sex differences in sexual needs and desires. *Archives of Sexual Behavior, 13,* 233–245.

Densen-Gerber, J. (1984). Sexual abuse of children: Emerging issues. *New York Pediatrician, 2,* 3–6.

DePaulo, B. M. (1992). Nonverbal behavior and self-presentation. *Psychological Bulletin, 111,* 203–243.

DePaulo, B. M., Kenny, D. A., Hoover, C. W., Webb, W., & Oliver, P. (1987). Accuracy of person perception: Do people know what kinds of impressions they convey? *Journal of Personality and Social Psychology, 52,* 303–315.

DePaulo, B. M., Lanier, K., & Davis, T. (1983). Detecting the deceit of the motivated liar. *Journal of Personality and Social Psychology, 45,* 1096–1103.

DePaulo, B. M., LeMay, C. S., & Epstein, J. A. (1991). Effects of importance of success and expectations for success on effectiveness at deceiving. *Personality and Social Psychology Bulletin, 17,* 14–24.

DePaulo, B. M., Stone, J., & Lassiter, G. D. (1985). Deceiving and detecting deceit. In B. R. Schlenker (Ed.), *The self and social life.* New York: McGraw-Hill.

Derlega, V. J., Winstead, B. A., Wong, P. T. P., & Greenspan, M. (1987). Self-disclosure and relationship development: An attributional analysis. In M. E. Roloff & G. R. Miller (Eds.), *Interpersonal processes: New directions in communication research.* Newbury Park, CA: Sage Publications.

Derlega, V. J., Winstead, B. A., Wong, P. T. P., & Hunter, S. (1985). Gender effects in an initial encounter: A case where men exceed women in disclosure. *Journal of Social and Personal Relationships, 2,* 25–44.

Derogatis, L. R. (1982). Self-report measures of stress. In L. Goldberger & S. Breznitz (Eds.), *Handbook of stress: Theoretical and clinical aspects.* New York: Free Press.

Derogatis, L. R. (1987). The Derogatis Stress Profile (DSP): Quantification of psychological stress. *Advances in Psychosomatic Medicine, 17,* 30–54.

Derogatis, L. R., & Coons, H. L. (1993). Self-report measures of stress. In L. Goldberger & S. Breznitz (Eds.), *Handbook of stress: Theoretical and clinical aspects* (2nd ed.). New York: Free Press.

Des Jarlais, D. C., Friedman, S. R., Woods, J., & Milliken, J. (1992). HIV infection among intravenous drug users: Epidemiology and emerging public health perspectives. In J. H. Lowinson, P. Ruiz, & R. B. Millman (Eds.), *Substance abuse: A comprehensive textbook* (2nd ed.). Baltimore: Williams & Wilkins.

DeSpelder, L. A., & Strickland, A. L. (1983). *The last dance: Encountering death and dying.* Palo Alto, CA: Mayfield.

Deutsch, F. M., Sullivan, L., Sage, C., & Basile, N. (1991). The relations among talking, liking, and similarity between friends. *Personality and Social Psychology Bulletin, 17,* 406–411.

Deutsch, M., & Gerard, H. B. (1955). A study of normative and informational social influences upon individual judgment. *Journal of Abnormal and Social Psychology, 51,* 629–636.

Devine, P. G. (1989). Stereotypes and prejudice: Their automatic and controlled components. *Journal of Personality and Social Psychology, 56,* 5–18.

DeVito, J. A. (1992). *The interpersonal communication book.* New York: Harper-Collins.

de Wilde, E. J., Kienhorst, I. C. W. M., Diekstra, R. F. W., & Wolters, W. H. G. (1992). The relationship between adolescent suicidal behavior and life events in childhood and adolescence. *American Journal of Psychiatry, 149,* 45–51.

Diamond, M., & Karlen, A. (1981). The sexual response cycle. In H. I. Lief (Ed.), *Sexual problems in medical practice.* Chicago: American Medical Association.

Dickson, L. (1993). The future of marriage and the family in Black America. *Journal of Black Studies, 23,* 472–491.

DiClemente, C. C. (1986). Self-efficacy and the addictive behaviors. *Journal of Social and Clinical Psychology, 4,* 302–315.

Diener, E. (1984). Subjective well-being. *Psychological Bulletin, 93,* 542–575.

Diener, F. (1980). Deindividuation: The

absence of self-awareness and self-regulation in group members. In P. B. Paulus (Ed.), *Psychology of group influence.* Hillsdale, NJ: Erlbaum.

Dillard, J. P. (1991). The current status of research on sequential-request compliance techniques. *Personality and Social Psychology Bulletin, 17,* 283–288.

DiMatteo, M. R. (1991). *The psychology of health, illness, and medical care: An individual perspective.* Pacific Grove, CA: Brooks/Cole.

DiMatteo, M. R., & Friedman, H. S. (1982). *Social psychology and medicine.* Cambridge, MA: Oelgeschlager, Gunn & Hain.

Dimsdale, J. E. (1988). A perspective on Type A behavior and coronary disease. *New England Journal of Medicine, 318,* 110–112.

Dindia, K., & Allen, M. (1992). Sex differences in self-disclosure: A meta-analysis. *Psychological Bulletin, 112,* 106–124.

Dindia, K., & Fitzpatrick, M. A. (1985). Marital communication: Three approaches compared. In S. Duck & D. Perlman (Eds.), *Understanding personal relationships: An interdisciplinary approach.* London: Sage Publications.

DiNicola, D. D., & DiMatteo, M. R. (1984). Practitioners, patients, and compliance with medical regimens: A social psychological perspective. In A. Baum, S. E. Taylor, & J. E. Singer (Eds.), *Handbook of psychology and health: Vol. 4. Social psychological aspects of health.* Hillsdale, NJ: Erlbaum.

Dion, K. K. (1986). Stereotyping based on physical attractiveness: Issues and conceptual perspectives. In C. P. Herman, M. P. Zanna, & E. T. Higgins (Eds.), *Appearance, stigma and social behavior: The Ontario symposium on personality and social psychology* (Vol. 3). Hillsdale, NJ: Erlbaum.

Dion, K. K., Berscheid, E., & Walster, E. (1972). What is beautiful is good. *Journal of Personality and Social Psychology, 24,* 285–290.

Dion, K. K., & Dion, K. L. (1993). Individualistic and collectivistic perspectives on gender and the cultural context of love and intimacy. *Journal of Social Issues, 49,* 53–69.

Dion, K. L., & Dion, K. K. (1988). Romantic love: Individual and cultural perspectives. In R. J. Sternberg & M. L. Barnes (Eds.), *The psychology of love.* New Haven, CT: Yale University Press.

Dishotsky, N. I., Loughman, W. D., Mogar, R. E., & Lipscomb, W. R. (1971). LSD and genetic damage: Is LSD chromosome damaging, carcinogenic, mutagenic, or teratogenic? *Science, 172,* 431–440.

Dixon, N. F. (1980). Humor: A cognitive alternative to stress? In I. G. Sarason & C. D. Spielberger (Eds.), *Stress and anxiety* (Vol. 7). Washington, DC: Hemisphere.

Dobbins, G. H., Cardy, R. L., & Truxillo, D. M. (1986). Effects of ratee sex and purpose of appraisal on the accuracy of performance evaluations. *Basic and Applied Social Psychology, 7,* 225–241.

Dobbins, G. H., Cardy, R. L., & Truxillo, D. M. (1988). The effects of purpose of appraisal and individual differences in stereotypes of women on sex differences in performance ratings: A laboratory and field study. *Journal of Applied Psychology, 73,* 551–558.

Dohrenwend, B. P., Raphael, K. G., Schwartz, S., Stueve, A., & Skodol, A. (1993). The structured event probe and narrative rating method for measuring stressful life events. In L. Goldberger & S. Breznitz (Eds.), *Handbook of stress: Theoretical and*

clinical aspects (2nd ed.). New York: Free Press.

Dohrenwend, B. S., & Dohrenwend, B. P. (1981). Life stress and illness: Formulation of the issues. In B. S. Dohrenwend & B. P. Dohrenwend (Eds.), *Stressful life events and their contexts.* New York: Prodist.

Dohrenwend, B. S., Krasnoff, L., Askenasy, A. R., & Dohrenwend, B. P. (1978). Exemplification of a method for scaling life events: The PERI life events scale. *Journal of Health and Social Behavior, 19,* 205–229.

Dollard, J., Doob, L. W., Miller, N. E., Mowrer, O. H., & Sears, R. R. (1939). *Frustration and aggression.* New Haven, CT: Yale University Press.

Donnerstein, E., & Linz, D. (1984, January). Sexual violence in the media: A warning. *Psychology Today,* pp. 14–15.

Donovan, R. L., & Jackson, B. L. (1990). Deciding to divorce: A process guided by social exchange, attachment and cognitive dissonance theories. *Journal of Divorce, 13,* 23–35.

Dorner, G., Schenk, B., Schmiedel, B., & Ahrens, L. (1983). Stressful events in prenatal life of bi- and homosexual men. *Experimental and clinical endocrinology, 81,* 83–87.

Douvan, E., & Adelson, J. (1966). *The adolescent experience.* New York: Wiley.

Dovidio, J. F., Ellyson, S. L., Keating, C. F., Heltman, K., & Brown, C. E. (1988). The relationship of social power to visual display of dominance between men and women. *Journal of Personality and Social Psychology, 54,* 233–242.

Dovidio, J. F., & Gaertner, S. L. (Eds.). (1986). *Prejudice, discrimination, and racism.* New York: Academic Press.

Dovidio, J. F., & Gaertner, S. L. (1991). Changes in the expression of racial prejudice. In H. J. Knopke, R. J. Norrell, & R. W. Rogers (Eds.), *Opening doors: Perspectives in race relations in contemporary America.* Tuscaloosa: University of Alabama Press.

Doyle, J. A. (1989). *The male experience.* Dubuque, IA: William C. Brown.

Doyle, J. A., & Paludi, M. A. (1991). *Sex and gender.* Dubuque, IA: William C. Brown.

Drachman, D. A. (1986). Memory and cognitive function in normal aging. *Developmental Neuropsychology, 2,* 277–285.

Dreyer, P. H. (1982). Sexuality during adolescence. In B. B. Wolman (Ed.), *Handbook of developmental psychology.* Englewood Cliffs, NJ: Prentice-Hall.

Driskell, J. E., Willis, R. P., & Copper, C. (1992). Effect of overlearning on retention. *Journal of Applied Psychology, 77,* 615–622.

Duffy, S. M., & Rusbult, C. E. (1986). Satisfaction and commitment in homosexual and heterosexual relationships. *Journal of Homosexuality, 12,* 1–23.

Duke, M., & Nowicki, S., Jr. (1979). *Abnormal psychology: Perspectives on being different.* Pacific Grove, CA: Brooks/Cole.

Duncan, B. L. (1976). Differential social perception and attribution of intergroup violence: Testing the lower limits of stereotyping of blacks. *Journal of Personality and Social Psychology, 34,* 590–598.

Dutton, D. G., & Aron, A. P. (1974). Some evidence for heightened sexual attraction under conditions of high anxiety. *Journal of Personality and Social Psychology, 30,* 510–517.

Duxbury, L. E., & Higgins, C. A. (1991). Gender differences in work-family conflict. *Journal of Applied Psychology, 76,* 60–74.

Dyer, W. W. (1976). *Your erroneous zones.* New York: Crowell.

Dyk, P. H., & Adams, G. R. (1990). Identity and intimacy: An initial investigation of three theoretical models using cross-lag panel correlations. *Journal of Youth and Adolescence, 19,* 91–110.

Dykman, B. M., Horowitz, L. M., Abramson, L. Y., & Usher, M. (1991). Schematic and situational determinants of depressed and nondepressed students' interpretation feedback. *Journal of Abnormal Psychology, 100,* 45–55.

Dziech, B. W., & Weiner, L. (1990). *The lecherous professor: Sexual harassment on campus.* Urbana: University of Illinois Press.

D'Zurilla, T. J., & Sheedy, C. F. (1991). Relation between social problem-solving ability and subsequent level of psychological stress in college students. *Journal of Personality and Social Psychology, 61,* 841–846.

Eagle, M. N., & Wolitzky, D. L. (1992). Psychoanalytic theories of psychotherapy. In D. K. Freedheim (Ed.), *History of psychotherapy: A century of change.* Washington, DC: American Psychological Association.

Eagly, A. H. (1987). *Sex differences in social behavior: A social-role interpretation.* Hillsdale, NJ: Erlbaum.

Eagly, A. H., Ashmore, R. D., Makhijani, M. G., & Longo, L. C. (1991). What is beautiful is good, but . . . : A meta-analytic review of research on the physical attractiveness stereotype. *Psychology Bulletin, 110,* 107–128.

Eagly, A. H., & Carli, L. L. (1981). Sex of researchers and sex-typed communications as determinants of sex differences in influenceability: A meta-analysis of social influence studies. *Psychological Bulletin, 90,* 1–20.

Eagly, A. H., & Crowley, M. (1986). Gender and helping behavior: A meta-analytic review of the social psychological literature. *Psychological Bulletin, 100,* 283–308.

Earle, J. R., & Harris, C. T. (1985). Modern women and the dynamics of social psychological ambivalence. *Psychology of Women Quarterly, 9,* 65–80.

Earle, J. R., & Perricone, P. J. (1986). Premarital sexuality: A ten-year study of attitudes and behavior on a small university campus. *Journal of Sex Research, 22,* 304–310.

Easterbrooks, M. A., & Goldberg, W. A. (1985). Effects of early maternal employment on toddlers, mothers, and fathers. *Developmental Psychology, 21,* 774–783.

Eaton, W. W., Dryman, A., & Weissman, M. M. (1991). Panic and phobia. In L. N. Robins & D. A. Regier (Eds.), *Psychiatric disorders in America: The epidemiologic catchment area study.* New York: Free Press.

Ebbinghaus, H. (1885/1964). Memory: A contribution to experimental psychology. (H. A. Ruger & E. R. Bussemius, Trans.). New York: Dover. (Original work published 1885)

Eccles, J. S. (1989). Bringing young women to math and science. In M. Crawford & M. Gentry (Eds.), *Gender and thought.* New York: Springer-Verlag.

Eccles, J. S., Midgley, C., Wigfield, A., Buchanan, C. M., Reuman, D., Flanagan, C., & MacIver, D. (1993). Development during adolescence: The impact of stage-environment fit on young adolescents' experiences in schools and in families. *American Psychologist, 48,* 90–101.

Edlin, G., & Golanty, E. (1992). *Health and wellness: A holistic approach.* Boston: Jones and Bartlett.

Efran, J. S., Lukens, M. D., & Lukens, R. J. (1986). It's all done with mirrors. *Family Therapy Networker, 10,* 41–49.

Egan, G. (1990). *The skilled helper: A sys-*

tematic approach to effective helping. Pacific Grove, CA: Brooks/Cole.

Egan, K. J., Kogan, H. N., Garber, A., & Jarrett, M. (1983). The impact of psychological distress on the control of hypertension. *Journal of Human Stress, 9,* 4–10.

Ehrenberg, O., & Ehrenberg, M. (1986). *The psychotherapy maze.* Northvale, NJ: Aronson.

Ehrhardt, A. A., Yingling, S., & Warne, P. A. (1991). Sexual behavior in the era of AIDS: What has changed in the United States? *Annual Review of Sex Research, 2,* 25–48.

Eichhorst, B. C. (1988). Contraception. *Primary Care, 15,* 437–459.

Eisen, M., & Zellman, G. L. (1987). Changes in incidence of sexual intercourse of unmarried teenagers following a community-based sex education prgram. *Journal of Sex Research, 23,* 527–544.

Eisenberg, N., Roth, K., Bryniarski, K. A., & Murray, E. (1984). Sex differences in the relationship of height to children's actual and attributed social and cognitive competencies. *Sex Roles, 11,* 719–734.

Eisler, R. M., & Ragsdale, K. (1992). Masculine gender role and midlife transition in men. In V. B. Van Hasselt & M. Hersen (Eds.), *Handbook of social development: A lifespan perspective.* New York: Plenum.

Ekman, P. (1975, September). The universal smile: Face muscles talk every language. *Psychology Today,* pp. 35–39.

Ekman, P. (1992). Facial expressions of emotion: New findings, new questions. *Psychological Science, 3,* 34–38.

Ekman, P., & Friesen, W. V. (1984). *Unmasking the face.* Palo Alto, CA: Consulting Psychologists Press.

Ekman, P., & Friesen, W. V. (1986). A new pan-cultural facial expression of emotion. *Motivation and Emotion, 10,* 159–168.

Ekman, P. Friesen, W. V., & Ellsworth, P. (1982). What emotion categories or dimensions can observers judge from facial behavior? In P. Ekman (Ed.), *Emotion in the human face* (2nd ed.). Cambridge, MA: Cambridge University Press.

Ekman, P., Friesen, W. V., O'Sullivan, M., Chan, A., Diacoyanni-Tarlatzis, I., Heider, K., Krause, R., LeCompte, W. A., Pitcairn, T., Ricci-Bitti, P. E., Scherer, K. R., Tomita, M., & Tzavaras, A. (1987). Universals and cultural differences in the judgments of facial expressions of emotion. *Journal of Personality and Social Psychology, 53,* 712–717.

Elias, M. F., Elias, J. W., & Elias, P. K. (1990). Biological and health influences on behavior. In J. E. Birren & K. W. Schaie (Eds.), *Handbook of the psychology of aging.* San Diego: Academic Press.

Elicker, J., Englund, M., & Sroufe, L. A. (1992). Predicting peer competence and peer relationships in childhood from early parent-child relationships. In R. D. Parke & G. W. Ladd (Eds.), *Family-peer relationships.* Hillsdale, NJ: Erlbaum.

Eliot, R. S., & Breo, D. L. (1989). *Is it worth dying for?* New York: Bantam Books.

Elkind, D. (1988). *The hurried child: Growing up too fast, too soon.* Reading, MA: Addison-Wesley.

Ellard, K., Beaurepaire, J., Jones, M., Piper, D., & Tennant, C. (1990). Acute chronic stress in duodenal ulcer disease. *Gastroenterology, 99,* 1628–1632.

Elliott, E. (1989). Stress and illness. In S. Cheren (Ed.), *Psychosomatic medicine: Theory, physiology, and practice* (Vol. 1).

Madison, CT: International Universities Press.

Elliott, G. R., & Eisdorfer, C. (Eds.). (1982). *Stress and human health: Analysis and implications of research.* New York: Springer.

Elliott, R., Stiles, W. B., & Shapiro, D. A. (1993). Are some therapies more equivalent than others? In T. R. Giles (Ed.), *Handbook of effective psychotherapy.* New York: Plenum.

Ellis, A. (1973). *Humanistic psychotherapy: The rational-emotive approach.* New York: Julian Press.

Ellis, A. (1977). *Reason and emotion in psychotherapy.* Seacaucus, NJ: Lyle Stuart.

Ellis, A. (1984). *Reason and emotion in psychotherapy.* Seacaucus, NJ: Lyle Stuart.

Ellis, A. (1985). *How to live with and without anger.* New York: Citadel Press.

Ellis, A. (1987). The evolution of rational-emotive therapy (RET) and cognitive behavior therapy (CBT). In J. K. Zeig (Ed.), *The evolution of psychotherapy.* New York: Brunner/Mazel.

Ellis, A. (1989). Rational-emotive therapy. In R. J. Corsini & D. Wedding (Eds.), *Current Psychotherapies.* Itasca, IL: Peacock.

Ellis, A. (1993). The advantages and disadvantages of self-help therapy materials. *Professional Psychology: Research and Practice, 24,* 335–339.

Ellis, L., & Ames, M. A. (1987). Neurohormonal functioning and sexual orientation: A theory of homosexuality-heterosexuality. *Psychological Bulletin, 101,* 233–258.

Elmer-Dewitt, E. (1994, October 24). A royal pain in the wrist. *Time,* pp. 60–62.

Emanuel, H. M. (1987). Put time on your side. In A. D. Timpe (Ed.), *The management of time.* New York: Facts On File.

Emery, R. E. (1989). Family violence. *American Psychologist, 44,* 321–328.

Emmelkamp, P. M. G. (1994). Behavior therapy with adults. In A. E. Bergin & S. L. Garfield (Eds.), *Handbook of psychotherapy and behavior change* (4th ed.). New York: Wiley.

Emmelkamp, P. M. G., & Scholing, A. (1990). Behavioral treatment for simple and social phobias. In R. Noyes, Jr., M. Roth, & G. D. Burrows (Eds.), *Handbook of anxiety: The treatment of anxiety* (Vol. 4). Amsterdam: Elsevier.

Engel, J. W., & Saracino, M. (1986). Love preferences and ideals: A comparison of homosexual, bisexual, and heterosexual groups. *Contemporary Family Therapy, 8,* 241–250.

Engler, J., & Goleman, D. (1992). *The consumer's guide to psychotherapy.* New York: Simon & Schuster.

Enright, R. D., Shukla, D. G., & Lapsley, D. K. (1980). Adolescent egocentrism, sociocentrism and self-consciousness. *Journal of Youth and Adolescence, 9,* 101–116.

Eppley, K., Abrams, A., & Shear, J. (1989). The differential effects of relaxation techniques on trait anxiety: A meta-analysis. *Journal of Clinical Psychology, 45,* 957–974.

Epstein, S., & Brodsky, A. (1993). *You're smarter than you think.* New York: Simon & Schuster.

Epstein, S. P. (1990). Cognitive-experiential self-theory. In L. A. Pervin (Ed.), *Handbook of personality: Theory and research.* New York: Guilford Press.

Epstein, S. P., & Katz, L. (1992). Coping ability, stress, productive load, and symptoms. *Journal of Personality and Social Psychology, 62,* 813–825.

Epstein, S. P., & Meier, P. (1989). Constructive thinking: A broad coping variable with specific components. *Journal*

of Personality and Social Psychology, 57, 332–350.

Erikson, E. H. (1963). *Childhood and society.* New York: Norton.

Erikson, E. H. (1968). *Identity: Youth and crisis.* New York: Norton.

Esterling, B. A., Kiecolt-Glaser, J. K., Bodnar, J. D., & Glaser, R. (1994). Chronic stress, social support, and persistent alterations in the natural killer cell response to cytokines in older adults. *Health Psychology, 13,* 291–298.

Etaugh, C. (1993). Maternal employment: Effects on children. In J. Frankel (Ed.), *The employed mother and the family context.* New York: Springer.

Etaugh, C., & Liss, M. B. (1992). Home, school, and playroom: Training grounds for adult gender roles. *Sex Roles, 26,* 129–147.

Evans, C. E., & Haynes, R. B. (1990). Patient compliance. In R. E. Rakel (Ed.), *Textbook of family practice.* Philadelphia: Saunders.

Evans, R. G., & Dinning, W. D. (1982). MMPI correlates of the Bem Sex Role Inventory and Extended Personal Attributes Questionnaire in a male psychiatric sample. *Journal of Clinical Psychology, 38,* 811–815.

Evans, R. L. (1981). New drug evaluations: Alprazolam. *Drug Intelligence and Clinical Pharmacy, 15,* 633–637.

Everitt, B. J., & Bancroft, J. (1991). Of rats and men: The comparative approach to male sexuality. *Annual Review of Sex Research, 2,* 77–118.

Eysenck, H. J. (1952). The effects of psychotherapy: An evaluation. *Journal of Consulting Psychology, 16,* 319–324.

Eysenck, H. J. (1959). Learning theory and behaviour therapy. *Journal of Mental Science, 195,* 61–75.

Eysenck, H. J. (1967). *The biological basis of personality.* Springfield, IL: Charles C Thomas.

Eysenck, H. J. (1982). *Personality, genetics and behavior: Selected papers.* New York: Praeger.

Eysenck, H. J. (1988, December). Health's character. *Psychology Today,* pp. 28–35.

Eysenck, H. J. (1990). Biological dimensions of personality. In L. A. Pervin (Ed.), *Handbook of personality: Theory and research.* New York: Guilford Press.

Eysenck, H. J. (1991). Dimensions of personality: 16, 5, or 3?—Criteria for a taxonomic paradigm. *Personality and Individual Differences, 12,* 773–790.

Eysenck, H. J. (1992). Four ways five factors are not basic. *Personality and Individual Differences, 13,* 667–673.

Eysenck, H. J. (1993). Forty years on: The outcome problem in psychotherapy revisited. In T. R. Giles (Ed.), *Handbook of effective psychotherapy.* New York: Plenum.

Eysenck, H. J., & Eysenck, S. B. G. (1969). *Personality structure and measurement.* San Diego, CA: EDITS.

Eysenck, M. W., Mogg, K., May, J., Richards, A., & Mathews, A. (1991). Bias in interpretation of ambiguous sentences related to threat in anxiety. *Journal of Abnormal Psychology, 100,* 144–150.

Fagley, N. S. (1987). Positional response bias in multiple-choice tests of learning: Its relation to testwiseness and guessing strategy. *Journal of Educational Psychology, 79,* 95–97.

Fagot, B. I. (1985). Changes in thinking about early sex role development. *Developmental Review, 5,* 83–98.

Fagot, B. I., Hagan, R., Leinbach, M. D., & Kronsberg, S. (1985). Differential reactions to assertive and communicative acts of toddler boys and girls. *Child Development, 56,* 1499–1505.

Fagot, B. I., & Leinbach, M. D. (1987).

Socialization of sex roles within the family. In B. Carter (Ed.), *Current conceptions of sex roles and sex typing: Theory and research.* New York: Praeger.

Fagot, B. I., Leinbach, M. D., & O'Boyle, D. (1992). Gender labeling, gender stereotyping, and parenting behaviors. *Developmental Psychology, 28,* 225–230.

Fahey, P. J., & Gallagher-Allred, C. (1990). Nutrition. In R. E. Rakel (Ed.), *Textbook of family practice* (4th ed.). Philadelphia: Saunders.

Falk, P. (1989). Lesbian mothers: Psychosocial assumptions in family law. *American Psychologist, 44,* 941–947.

Falk, P. (1994). The gap between psychological assumptions and empirical research in lesbian-mother child custody cases. In A. E. Gottfried & A. W. Gottfried (Eds.), *Redefining families: Implications for children's development.* New York: Plenum.

Fancher, R. E. (1979). *Pioneers of psychology.* New York: Norton.

Faravelli, C., & Pallanti, S. (1989). Recent life events and panic disorders. *American Journal of Psychiatry, 146,* 622–626.

Farina, A., Burns, G. L., Austad, C., Bugglin, C., & Fischer, E. H. (1986). The role of physical attractiveness in the readjustment of discharged psychiatric patients. *Journal of Abnormal Psychology, 95,* 139–143.

Farley, J. (1980). Worklife problems for both women and men. In D. A. Neugarten & J. M. Shafritz (Eds.), *Sexuality in occupations: Romantic and coercive behavior at work.* Oak Park, IL: Moore.

Fausto-Sterling, A. (1992). *Myths of gender: Biological theories about women and men* (2nd ed.). New York: Basic Books.

Fava, G. A., Perini, G. I., Santonastaso, P., & Fornasa, C. V. (1989). Life events and psychological distress in dermatologic disorders: Psoriasis, chronic urticaria, and fungal infections. In T. W. Miller (Ed.), *Stressful life events.* Madison, CT: International Universities Press.

Featherstone, H. J., & Beitman, B. D. (1984). Marital migraine: A refractory daily headache. *Psychosomatics, 25,* 30–38.

Feder, H. H. (1984). Hormones and sexual behavior. *Annual Review of Psychology, 35,* 165–200.

Federal Bureau of Investigation (1995). *Uniform crime reports: Crime in the United States.* Washington, DC: U.S. Government Printing Office.

Feeney, J. A., & Noller, P. (1990). Attachment style as a predictor of adult romantic relationships. *Journal of Personality and Social Psychology, 58,* 281–291.

Fehr, B. J., & Exline, R. V. (1987). Social visual interaction: A conceptual and literature review. In A. W. Siegman & S. Feldstein (Eds.), *Nonverbal behavior and communication.* Hillsdale, NJ: Erlbaum.

Feingold, A. (1988). Matching for attractiveness in romantic partners and same-sex friends: A meta-analysis and theoretical critique. *Psychological Bulletin, 104,* 226–235.

Feingold, A. (1990). Gender differences in effects of physical attractiveness on romantic attraction: A comparison across five research paradigms. *Journal of Personality and Social Psychology, 59,* 981–993.

Feingold, A. (1992a). Gender differences in mate selection preferences: A test of the parental investment model. *Psychological Bulletin, 112,* 125–139.

Feingold, A. (1992b). Good-looking people are not what we think. *Psychological Bulletin, 111,* 304–341.

Feiring, C., & Lewis, M. (1987). The child's social network: Sex differences

from three to six years. *Sex Roles, 17,* 621–636.

Felmlee, D., Sprecher, S., & Bassin, E. (1990). The dissolution of intimate relationships: A hazard model. *Social Psychology Quarterly, 53,* 13–30.

Felson, R. B. (1989). Parents and the reflected appraisal process: A longitudinal analysis. *Journal of Personality and Social Psychology, 56,* 965–971.

Fenwick, P. (1987). Meditation and the EEG. In M. A. West (Ed.), *The psychology of meditation.* Oxford: Clarendon Press.

Fenz, W. D., & Epstein, S. (1967). Gradients of physiological arousal, skin conductance, heart rate, and respiration rate as a function of experience. *Psychosomatic Medicine, 29,* 33–51.

Ferree, M. M., & Hall, E. J. (1990). Visual images of American society: Gender and race in introductory sociology textbooks. *Gender and Society, 4,* 500–533.

Festinger, L. (1954). A theory of social comparison processes. *Human Relations, 7,* 117–140.

Festinger, L., Schachter, S., & Back, K. (1950). *Social pressures in informal groups: A study of human factors in housing.* Stanford, CA: Stanford University Press.

Field, D., Schaie, K. W., & Leino, E. V. (1988). Continuity in intellectual functioning: The role of self-reported health. *Psychology and Aging, 3,* 385–392.

Fielding, J. E. (1985). Smoking: Health effects and control. *New England Journal of Medicine, 313,* 491–498, 555–561.

Fincham, F. D., Beach, S. R., & Baucom, D. H. (1987). Attribution processes in distressed and nondistressed couples: 4. Self-partner attribution differences. *Journal of Personality and Social Psychology, 52,* 739–748.

Fincham, F. D., & Bradbury, T. N. (1992). Assessing attributions in marriage: The relationship attribution measure. *Journal of Personality and Social Psychology, 62,* 457–468.

Fine, M. A. (1992). Families in the United States: Their current status and future prospects. *Family Relations, 41,* 430–435.

Fine, R. (1990). *The history of psychoanalysis.* New York: Continuum.

Fink, M. (1992). Electroconvulsive therapy. In E. S. Paykel (Ed.), *Handbook of affective disorders* (2nd ed.). New York: Guilford Press.

Fiore, M. C. (1992). Trends in cigarette smoking in the United States: The epidemiology of tobacco use. *Medical Clinics of North America, 76,* 289–303.

Fischer, L. R. (1983). Mothers and mothers-in-law. *Journal of Marriage and the Family, 45,* 187–192.

Fisher, J. D., Bell, P. A., & Baum, A. S. (1984). *Environmental psychology.* New York: Holt, Rinehart & Winston.

Fisher, J. D., & Fisher, W. A. (1992). Changing AIDS-risk behavior. *Psychological Bulletin, 111,* 455–474.

Fisher, S., & Greenberg, R. P. (1985). *The scientific credibility of Freud's theories and therapy.* New York: Columbia University Press.

Fisher, T. D. (1988). The relationship between parent-child communication about sexuality and college students' sexual behavior and attitudes as a function of parental proximity. *Journal of Sex Research, 24,* 305–311.

Fishman, D. B., & Franks, C. M. (1992). Evolution and differentiation within behavior therapy: A theoretical epistemological review. In D. K. Freedheim (Ed.), *History of psychotherapy: A century of change.* Washington, DC: American Psychological Association.

Fiske, S. T. (1993). Social cognition and

social perception. *Annual Review of Psychology, 44,* 155–194.

Fiske, S. T., & Taylor, S. E. (1991). *Social cognition.* New York: McGraw-Hill.

Fitch, S. A., & Adams, G. R. (1983). Ego identity and intimacy status: Replication and extension. *Developmental Psychology, 19,* 839–845.

Fitzgerald, L. F., & Crites, J. O. (1980). Toward a career psychology of women: What do we know? What do we need to know? *Journal of Counseling Psychology, 27,* 44–62.

Fitzpatrick, M. A. (1987). Marriage and verbal intimacy. In V. J. Derlega & J. H. Berg (Eds.), *Self-disclosure: Theory, research, and therapy.* New York: Plenum.

Flanders, J. P. (1982). A general systems approach to loneliness. In L. A. Peplau & D. Perlman (Eds.), *Loneliness: A sourcebook of current theory, research and therapy.* New York: Wiley.

Fleming, T. C. (1986). Alcohol and other mood-changing drugs. In S. Wolf & A. J. Finestone (Eds.), *Occupational stress: Health and performance at work.* Littleton, MA: PSG Publishing.

Fletcher, G. J. O., Fincham, F. D., Cramer, L., & Heron, N. (1987). The role of attributions in the development of dating relationships. *Journal of Personality and Social Psychology, 53,* 481–489.

Fletcher, G. J. O., & Fitness, J. (1990). Occurrent social cognition in close relationship interaction: The role of proximal and distal variables. *Journal of Personality and Social Psychology, 59,* 464–474.

Flynn, L. M. (1994). Schizophrenia from a family point of view: A social economic perspective. In N. C. Andreasen (Ed.), *Schizophrenia: From mind to molecule.* Washington, DC: American Psychiatric Press.

Foa, E. B., & Kozak, M. J. (1995). DSM-IV field trial: Obsessive-compulsive disorder. *American Journal of Psychiatry, 152,* 90–96.

Folkes, V. S. (1982). Forming relationships and the matching hypothesis. *Personality and Social Psychology Bulletin, 8,* 631–636.

Folkman, S., Lazarus, R. S., Gruen, R. J., & DeLongis, A. (1986). Appraisal, coping, health status, and psychological symptoms. *Journal of Personality and Social Psychology, 50,* 571–579.

Forrest, J. D., & Singh, S. (1990). The sexual and reproductive behavior of American women, 1982–1988. *Family Planning Perspectives, 22,* 206–214.

Forsyth, D. R., & Strong, S. R. (1986). The scientific study of counseling and psychotherapy: A unificationist view. *American Psychologist, 41,* 113–119.

Foss, R. D., & Dempsey, C. B. (1979). Blood donation and the foot-in-the-door technique. *Journal of Personality and Social Psychology, 37,* 580–590.

Fowers, B. J., Applegate, B., Olson, D. H., & Pomerantz, B. (1994). Marital conventionalization as a measure of marital satisfaction: A confirmatory factor analysis. *Journal of Family Psychology, 8,* 98–103.

Fowers, B. J., & Olson, D. H. (1989). ENRICH Marital Inventory: A discriminant validity and cross-validation assessment. *Journal of Marital and Family Therapy, 15,* 65–79.

Fowles, D. C. (1992). Schizophrenia: Diathesis-stress revisited. *Annual Review of Psychology, 43,* 303–336.

Fowles, D. C. (1993). A motivational theory of psychopathology. In W. Spaulding (Ed.), *Nebraska Symposium on Motivation: Integrated views of motivation, cognition and emotion* (Vol. 41). Lincoln: University of Nebraska Press.

Fracher, J. C., & Kimmel, M. S. (1987). Hard issues and soft spots: Counseling men about sexuality. In M. Scher, M. Stevens, G. Good, & G. A. Eichenfield (Eds.), *Handbook of counseling and psychotherapy with men.* Newbury Park, CA: Sage Publications.

France, C., & Ditto, B. (1988). Caffeine effects on several indices of cardiovascular activity at rest and during stress. *Journal of Behavioral Medicine, 11,* 473–482.

Frances, A. J., First, M. B., Widiger, T. A., Miele, G. M., Tilly, S. M., Davis, W. W., & Pincus, H. A. (1991). An A to Z guide to DSM-IV conundrums. *Journal of Abnormal Psychology, 100,* 407–412.

Frank, E. (1991). Interpersonal psychotherapy as a maintenance treatment for patients with recurrent depression. *Psychotherapy, 28,* 259–266.

Frank, E., Anderson, C., & Rubinstein, D. (1978). Frequency of sexual dysfunction in "normal" couples. *New England Journal of Medicine, 299,* 111–115.

Frank, H. B. (1985). Gender differences in postmarital adjustment. In D. C. Goldberg (Ed.), *Contemporary marriage: Special issues in couples therapy.* Homewood, IL: Dorsey Press.

Frank, J. D. (1961). *Persuasion and healing.* Baltimore: John Hopkins University Press.

Frank, L. R. (1990). Electroshock: Death, brain damage, memory loss, and brainwashing. *The Journal of Mind and Behavior, 11,* 489–512.

Frankel, A., & Prentice-Dunn, S. (1990). Loneliness and the processing of self-relevant information. *Journal of Social and Clinical Psychology, 9,* 303–315.

Frankel, F. H. (1990). Hypnotizability and dissociation. *American Journal of Psychiatry, 147,* 823–829.

Frankel, F. H. (1993). Adult reconstruction of childhood events in the multiple personality disorder. *American Journal of Psychiatry, 150,* 954–958.

Franken, R. E., Gibson, K. J., & Rowland, G. L. (1992). Sensation seeking and the tendency to view the world as threatening. *Personality and Individual Differences, 13,* 31–38.

Frankl, V. (1984). *Man's search for meaning.* New York: Pocket Books.

Franks, C. M., & Barbrack, C. R. (1983). Behavior therapy with adults: An integrative perspective. In M. Hersen, A. E. Kazdin, & A. S. Bellack (Eds.), *The clinical psychology handbook.* New York: Pergamon.

Franzoi, S. L., & Herzog, M. E. (1987). Judging personal attractiveness: What body aspects do we use? *Personality and Social Psychology Bulletin, 13,* 19–33.

Frazier, P. A., & Esterly, E. (1990). Correlates of relationship beliefs: Gender, relationship experience, and relationship satisfaction. *Journal of Social and Personal Relationships, 7,* 331–352.

Freedman, J. (1978). *Happy people.* New York: Harcourt Brace Jovanovich.

Freedman, J. L., & Fraser, S. C. (1966). Compliance without pressure: The foot-in-the-door technique. *Journal of Personality and Social Psychology, 4,* 195–202.

Fremouw, W. J., de Perczel, M., & Ellis, T. E. (1990). *Suicide risk: Assessment and response guidelines.* New York: Pergamon.

French, J. R. P., Jr., Caplan, R. D., & Van Harrison, R. (1982). *The mechanisms of job stress and strain.* New York: Wiley.

Freud, S. (1901–1960). *The psychopathology of everyday life* (Standard ed., Vol. 6.) London: Hogarth. (Original work published 1901)

Freud, S. (1920/1924). *A general introduction to psychoanalysis.* New York: Boni and Liveright. (Original work published 1920)

Freud, S. (1923). *The ego and the id* (Standard ed., Vol. 19.) London: Hogarth.

Fried, P. A. (1986). Marijuana and human pregnancy. In I. J. Chasnoff (Ed.), *Drug use in pregnancy: Mother and child.* Lancaster, PA: MTP Press.

Friedan, B. (1964). *The feminine mystique.* New York: Dell.

Friedberg, J. (1976). *Shock treatment is not good for your brain.* San Francisco: Glide Publications.

Friedland, G. H., Saltzman, B. R., Rogers, M. F., Kahl, P. A., Lesser, M. L., Mayers, M. M., & Kelin, R. S. (1986). Lack of transmission of HTLV-III/LAV infection to household contacts of patients with AIDS or AIDS-related complex with oral candidiasis. *New England Journal of Medicine, 314,* 344–349.

Friedman, A. (1987). Getting powerful with age: Changes in women over the life cycle. *Israel Social Science Research, 5,* 76–86.

Friedman, D. E. (1987). Work vs. family: War of the worlds. *Personnel Administrator, 32,* 36–39.

Friedman, H. S. (1983). Social perception and face-to-face interaction. In D. Perlman & D. C. Cozby (Eds.), *Social psychology.* New York: Holt, Rinehart & Winston.

Friedman, H. S. (1991). *The self-healing personality: Why some people achieve health and others succumb to illness.* New York: Holt.

Friedman, H. S., & Miller-Herringer, T. (1991). Nonverbal display of emotion in public and private: Self-monitoring, personality, and expressive cues. *Journal of Personality and Social Psychology, 61,* 766–775.

Friedman, J. (1989). The impact of homophobia on male sexual development. *Siecus Report, 17,* 8–9.

Friedman, L. S., & Goodman, E. (1992). Adolescents at risk for HIV infection. *Primary Care, 19,* 171–190.

Friedman, M., & Rosenman, R. F. (1974). *Type A behavior and your heart.* New York: Knopf.

Friedman, S. R., de Jong, W. M., & Des Jarlais, D. C. (1988). Problems and dynamics of organizing intravenous drug users for AIDS prevention. *Health Education Research, 3,* 49–57.

Frieze, I. H., & Ramsey, S. J. (1976). Nonverbal maintenance of traditional sex roles. *Journal of Social Issues, 32,* 133–141.

Froelicher, V. F. (1990). Exercise, fitness, and coronary heart disease. In C. Bouchard, R. J. Shephard, T. Stephens, J. R. Sutton, & B. D. McPherson (Eds.), *Exercise, fitness, and health: A consensus of current knowledge.* Champaign, IL: Human Kinetics Books.

Fromm, E. (1963). *Escape from freedom.* New York: Holt.

Fromm, E. (1981). *Sane society.* New York: Fawcett.

Fuchs, R. M. (1984). Group therapy. In T. B. Karasu (Ed.), *The psychiatric therapies.* Washington, DC: American Psychiatric Association.

Fuller, R. G. C., & Sheehy-Skeffington, A. (1974). Effects of group laughter on responses to humorous materials: A replication and extension. *Psychological Reports, 35,* 531–534.

Funk, S. C. (1992). Hardiness: A review of theory and research. *Health Psychology, 11,* 335–345.

Furnham, A. F. (1984). Value systems and anomie in three cultures. *International Journal of Psychology, 19,* 565–579.

Furstenberg, F. F., Jr. (1990). Divorce and the American family. *Annual Review of Sociology, 16,* 379–403.

Furstenberg, F. F., Jr., & Cherlin, A. J. (1991). *Divided families: What happens to children when parents part.* Cambridge, MA: Harvard University Press.

Gadpaille, W. J. (1975). *The cycles of sex.* New York: Scribner's.

Gaertner, S. L., & Dovidio, J. F. (1986). The aversive form of racism. In J. F. Dovidio & S. L. Gaertner (Eds.), *Prejudice, discrimination, and racism: Theory and research.* Orlando, FL: Academic Press.

Gagnon, J. H., & Simon, W. (1973). *Sexual conduct: The social sources of human sexuality.* Chicago: Aldine.

Gagnon, J. H., & Simon, W. (1987). The sexual scripting of oral genital contacts. *Archives of Sexual Behavior, 16,* 1–25.

Galambos, N. L. (1992). Parent-adolescent relations. *Current Directions in Psychological Science, 1,* 146–149.

Galanter, H. (1989). *Cults: Faith, healing, and coercion.* New York: Oxford University Press.

Gale, A. (1983). Electroencephalographic studies of extraversion-introversion: A case study in the psychophysiology of individual differences. *Personality and Individual Differences, 4,* 371–380.

Gantt, W. H. (1975, April 25). Unpublished lecture, Ohio State University. Cited in D. Hothersall (1984), *History of psychology.* New York: Random House.

Garcia, M. E., Schmitz, J. M., & Doerfler, L. A. (1990). A fine-grained analysis of the role of self-efficacy in self-initiated attempts to quit smoking. *Journal of Consulting and Clinical Psychology, 58,* 317–322.

Gardner, R. A. (1971). *The boys and girls book about divorce.* New York: Bantam Books.

Garfield, S. L. (1986). Problems in diagnostic classification. In T. Millon & G. L. Klerman (Eds.), *Contemporary directions in psychopathology: Toward the DSM-IV.* New York: Guilford Press.

Garfield, S. L. (1992). Major issues in psychotherapy research. In D. K. Freedheim (Ed.), *History of psychotherapy: A century of change.* Washington, DC: American Psychological Association.

Garfield, S. L. (1993). Methodological problems in clinical diagnosis. In P. B. Sutker & H. E. Adams (Eds.), *Comprehensive handbook of psychopathology.* New York: Plenum.

Garfield, S. L., & Bergin, A. E. (1994). Introduction and historical overview. In A. E. Bergin & S. L. Garfield (Eds.), *Handbook of psychotherapy and behavior change* (4th ed.). New York: Wiley.

Garland, A. F., & Zigler, E. (1993). Adolescent suicide prevention: Current research and social policy implications. *American Psychologist, 48,* 169–182.

Garner, D., Garfinkel, P., Schwartz, D., & Thompson, M. (1980). Cultural expectations of thinness in women. *Psychological Reports, 47,* 483–491.

Garnets, L., & Kimmel, D. (1991). Lesbian and gay male dimensions in the psychological study of human diversity. In J. D. Goodchilds (Ed.), *Psychological perspectives on human diversity in America.* Washington, DC: American Psychological Association.

Garrett, V. D., Brantley, P. J., Jones, G. N., & McKnight, G. T. (1991). The relation between daily stress and Crohn's disease. *Journal of Behavioral Medicine, 14,* 87–96.

Gebhard, P. H. (1966). Factors in marital orgasm. *Journal of Social Issues, 22,* 88–95.

Gebhardt, D. L., & Crump, C. E. (1990). Employee fitness and wellness programs in the workplace. *American Psychologist, 45,* 262–272.

Gecas, V., & Schwalbe, M. L. (1986).

Parental behavior and adolescent self-esteem. *Journal of Marriage and the Family, 48,* 37–46.

Gecas, V., & Seff, M. A. (1990). Families and adolescents: A review of the 1980s. *Journal of Marriage and the Family, 52,* 941–958.

Geis, B. D., & Gerrard, M. (1984). Predicting male and female contraceptive behavior: A discriminant analysis of groups high, moderate, and low in contraceptive effectiveness. *Journal of Personality and Social Psychology, 46,* 669–680.

Geiser, R. L., Rarick, D. L., & Soldow, G. F. (1977). Deception and judgment accuracy: A study in person perception. *Personality and Social Psychology Bulletin, 3,* 446–449.

Gelderloos, P., Walton, K. G., Orme-Johnson, D. W., & Alexander, C. N. (1991). Effectiveness of the transcendental meditation program in preventing and treating substance misuse: A review. *The International Journal of Addictions, 26,* 293–325.

George, L. K., Fillenbaum, G. G., & Palmore, E. (1984). Sex differences in the antecedents and consequences of retirement. *Journal of Gerontology, 39,* 364–371.

Gergen, K. J., Gergen, M. M., & Barton, W. H. (1973, October). Deviance in the dark. *Psychology Today,* pp. 129–130.

Gerrard, M. (1987). Emotional and cognitive barriers to effective contraception: Are males and females really different? In K. Kelley (Ed.), *Females, males, and sexuality: Theories and research.* Albany: SUNY Press.

Gerstel, N. (1988). Divorce, gender, and social integration. *Gender and Society, 2,* 343–367.

Gesser, G., Wong, P. T. P., & Reker, G. T. (1987–88). Death attitudes across the life-span: The development and validation of the death attitude profile (DAP). *Omega, 18,* 113–128.

Ghosh, T. B., & Victor, B. S. (1994). Suicide. In R. E. Hales, S. C. Yudofsky, & J. A. Talbott (Eds.), *The American Psychiatric Press textbook of psychiatry* (2nd ed.). Washington, DC: American Psychiatric Press.

Gibbs, N. (1989, July 31). Sick and tired. *Time,* pp. 48–53.

Gibbs, N. (1993, May 3). Oh, my God, they're killing themselves. *Time,* pp. 27–43.

Gilbert, D. A. (1988). *Compendium of American public opinion.* New York: Facts On File.

Gilbert, L. A. (1993). *Two careers/one family.* Newbury Park, CA: Sage Publications.

Gilbert, L. A. (1994). Current perspectives on dual-career families. *Current Directions in Psychological Science, 3,* 101–104.

Gilder, G. F. (1986). *Men and marriage.* New York: Pelican.

Giles, H., & Street, R. L., Jr. (1985). Communicator characteristics and behavior. In M. L. Knapp & G. R. Miller (Eds.), *Handbook of interpersonal communication.* Newbury Park, CA: Sage Publications.

Giles-Sims, J. (1987). Social exchange in remarried families. In K. Pasley & M. Ihinger-Tallman (Eds.), *Remarriage and stepparenting: Current research and theory.* New York: Guilford Press.

Gilligan, C. (1982). *In a different voice.* Cambridge, MA: Harvard University Press.

Gillis, J. S. (1993). Effects of life stress and dysphoria on complex judgments. *Psychological Reports, 72,* 1355–1363.

Ginzberg, E. (1952). Toward a theory of occupational choice. *Occupations, 30,* 491–494.

Ginzberg, E. (1972). Toward a theory of occupational choice: A restatement. *Vocational Guidance Quarterly, 20,* 169–176.

Gladue, B. A. (1987). Psychobiological contributions. In L. Diamant (Ed.), *Male and female homosexuality: Psychological approaches.* Washington, DC: Hemisphere.

Gladue, B. A. (1994). The biopsychology of sexual orientation. *Current Directions in Psychological Science, 3,* 150–154.

Glantz, S. A., & Parmley, W. W. (1991). Passive smoking and heart disease: Epidemiology, physiology, and biochemistry. *Circulation, 83,* 1–12.

Glaser, R., Kiecolt-Glaser, J. K., Speicher, C. E., & Holliday, J. E. (1985). Stress, loneliness, and changes in herpesvirus latency. *Journal of Behavioral Medicine, 8,* 249–260.

Glasgow, R. E., Klesges, R. C., Mizes, J. S., & Pechacek, T. F. (1985). Quitting smoking: Strategies used and variables associated with success in a stop-smoking contest. *Journal of Consulting and Clinical Psychology, 53,* 905–912.

Glass, C. R., & Arnkoff, D. B. (1992). Behavior therapy. In D. K. Freedheim (Ed.), *History of psychotherapy: A century of change.* Washington, DC: American Psychological Association.

Glass, S. P., & Wright, T. L. (1985). Sex differences in type of extramarital involvement and marital dissatisfaction. *Sex Roles, 12,* 1101–1120.

Glazer, M. P., & Glazer, P. M. (1990). *The whistleblowers: Exposing corruption in government and industry.* New York: Basic Books.

Gleaves, D. H. (1994). On "The reality of repressed memories." *American Psychologist, 49,* 440–441.

Glenberg, A. M. (1992). Disturbed practice effects. In L. R. Squire (Ed.), *Encyclopedia of learning and memory.* New York: Macmillan.

Glenn, M., & Taska, R. J. (1984). Antidepressants and lithium. In T. B. Karasu (Ed.), *The psychiatric therapies.* Washington, DC: American Psychiatric Association.

Glenn, N. D. (1990). Quantitative research on marital quality in the 1980s: A critical review. *Journal of Marriage and the Family, 52,* 818–831.

Glenn, N. D., & McLanahan, S. (1982). Children and marital happiness: A further specification of the relationship. *Journal of Marriage and the Family, 44,* 63–72.

Glenn, N. D., & Weaver, C. N. (1988). The changing relationship of marital status to reported happiness. *Journal of Marriage and the Family, 50,* 317–324.

Glick, P. C. (1984). Marriage, divorce, and living arrangements: Prospective changes. *Journal of Family Issues, 5,* 7–26.

Glick, P. C., & Lin, S. (1986). More young adults are living with their parents: Who are they? *Journal of Marriage and the Family, 48,* 107–112.

Goethals, G. R. (1986). Social comparison theory: Psychology from the lost and found. *Personality and Social Psychology Bulletin, 12,* 261–278.

Goetting, A. (1986). Parental satisfaction: A review of research. *Journal of Family Issues, 7,* 83–109.

Goffman, E. (1959). *The presentation of self in everyday life.* Garden City, NY: Doubleday/Anchor.

Goffman, E. (1971). *Relations in public.* New York: Basic Books.

Gold, D. T. (1990). Late-life sibling relationships: Does race affect typological distribution? *The Gerontologist, 30,* 741–748.

Gold, M. S. (1989). *Marijuana.* New York: Plenum.

Gold, M. S. (1992). Cocaine (and crack): Clinical aspects. In J. H. Lowinson, P. Ruiz, & R. B. Millman (Eds.), *Substance abuse: A comprehensive textbook* (2nd ed.). Baltimore: Williams & Wilkins.

Gold, M. S., Miller, N. S., & Jonas, J. M. (1992). Cocaine (and crack): Neurobiology. In J. H. Lowinson, P. Ruiz, & R. B. Millman (Eds.), *Substance abuse: A comprehensive textbook* (2nd ed.). Baltimore: Williams & Wilkins.

Goldberg, L. R. (1993). The structure of phenotypic personality traits. *American Psychologist, 48,* 26–34.

Goldberg, M. (1985). Remarriage: Repetition versus new beginnings. In D. C. Goldberg (Ed.), *Contemporary marriage: Special issues in couples therapy.* Homewood, IL: Dorsey Press.

Goldberger, L. (1993). Sensory deprivation and overload. In L. Goldberger & S. Breznitz (Eds.), *Handbook of stress: Theoretical and clinical aspects* (2nd ed.). New York: Free Press.

Goldfried, M. R., Greenberg, L. S., & Marmar, C. (1990). Individual psychotherapy: Process and outcome. *Annual Review of Psychology, 41,* 659–688.

Goldman, H. H., Skodol, A. E., & Lave, T. R. (1992). Revising axis V for DSM-IV: A review of measures of social functioning. *American Journal of Psychiatry, 149,* 1148–1156.

Goldstein, E., & Farmer, K. (Eds.). (1993). *True stories of false memories.* Boca Raton, FL: Sirs Publishing.

Goldstein, M. J. (1987). Family interaction patterns that antedate the onset of schizophrenia and related disorders: A further analysis of data from a longitudinal prospective study. In K. Hahlweg & M. J. Goldstein (Eds.), *Understanding major mental disorder: The contribution of family interaction research.* New York: Family Process Press.

Goldstein, M. J. (1988). The family and psychopathology. *Annual Review of Psychology, 39,* 283–300.

Goleman, D. (1979, November). Interview with Richard S. Lazarus, Positive denial: The case for not facing reality. *Psychology Today,* pp. 44–60.

Gomberg, E. L. (1989). On terms used and abused: The concept of "codependency." *Drugs and Society, 3,* 113–122.

Gonder-Frederick, L. A., Carter, W. R., Cox, D. J., & Clarke, W. L. (1990). Environmental stress and blood glucose change in insulin-dependent diabetes mellitus. *Health Psychology, 9,* 503–515.

Gondolf, E. W. (1988). *Battered women as survivors.* Lexington, MA: Lexington Books.

Gonsiorek, J. C., & Weinrich, J. D. (1991). The definition and scope of sexual orientation. In J. C. Gonsiorek & J. D. Weinrich (Eds.), *Homosexuality: Research implications for public policy.* Newbury Park, CA: Sage Publications.

Gonzales, M. H., Davis, J. M., Loney, G. L., Lukens, C. K., & Junghans, C. H. (1983). Interactional approach to interpersonal attraction. *Journal of Personality and Social Psychology, 44,* 1192–1197.

Gonzales, M. H., & Meyers, S. A. (1993). "Your mother would like me": Self-presentation in the personals ads of heterosexual and homosexual men and women. *Personality and Social Psychology Bulletin, 19,* 131–142.

Goodall, K. (1972, November). Field report: Shapers at work. *Psychology Today,* pp. 53–63, 132–138.

Goodwin, D. W. (1992). Alcohol: Clinical aspects. In J. H. Lowinson, P. Ruiz, & R. B. Millman (Eds.), *Substance abuse: A comprehensive textbook* (2nd ed.). Baltimore: Williams & Wilkins.

Goodwin, F. K., & Jamison, K. R. (1990). *Manic-depressive illness.* New York: Oxford University Press.

Goodwin, R. (1990). Sex differences among partner preferences: Are the sexes really very similar? *Sex Roles, 23,* 501–513.

Gordon, S., & Snyder, C. W. (1989). *Personal issues in human sexuality: A guidebook for better sexual health.* Boston: Allyn & Bacon.

Gordon, T. (1970). *Parent effectiveness training.* New York: McKay.

Gorman, J. M., & Davis, J. M. (1989). Antianxiety drugs. In H. I. Kaplan & B. J. Sadock (Eds.), *Comprehensive textbook of psychiatry/V.* Baltimore: Williams & Wilkins.

Gotlib, I. H., & McCabe, S. B. (1990). Marriage and psychopathology. In F. D. Fincham & T. N. Bradbury (Eds.), *The psychology of marriage: Basic issues and applications.* New York: Guilford Press.

Gottesman, I. I. (1991). *Schizophrenia genesis: The origins of madness.* New York: Freeman

Gottfredson, G. D. (1977). Career stability and redirection in adulthood. *Journal of Applied Psychology, 62,* 436–445.

Gottman, J. M. (1979). *Marital interaction.* New York: Academic Press.

Gottman, J. M., & Levenson, R. S. (1988). The social psychophysiology of marriage. In P. Noller & M. A. Fitzpatrick (Eds.), *Perspectives on marital interaction.* Clevedon, England, and Philadelphia: Multilingual Matters.

Gould, R. L. (1972). The phases of adult life: A study in developmental psychology. *American Journal of Psychiatry, 129,* 521–531.

Gould, R. L. (1978). *Transformations: Growth and change in adult life.* New York: Simon & Schuster.

Graham, J. W. (1986). Principle organizational dissent: A theoretical essay. *Research in Organizational Behavior, 8,* 1–52.

Graig, E. (1993). Stress as a consequence of the urban physical environment. In L. Goldberger & S. Breznitz (Eds.), *Handbook of stress: Theoretical and clinical aspects* (2nd ed.). New York: Free Press.

Grant, I., McDonald, W. I., Patterson, T., & Trimble, M. R. (1989). Multiple sclerosis. In G. W. Brown & T. O. Harris (Eds.), *Life events and illness.* New York: Guilford Press.

Gray, D. S. (1989). Diagnosis and prevalence of obesity. *Medical Clinics of North America, 73,* 1–13.

Gray, J. D. (1983). The married professional woman: An examination of her role conflicts and coping strategies. *Psychology of Women Quarterly, 7,* 235–243.

Grebb, J. A., & Cancro, R. (1989). Schizophrenia: Clinical features. In H.I. Kaplan & B.J. Sadock (Eds.), *Comprehensive textbook of psychiatry/V.* Baltimore: Williams & Wilkins.

Green, B. L. (1991). Evaluating the effects of disasters. *Psychological Assessment, 3,* 538–546.

Green, B. L., & Russo, N. F. (1993). Work and family roles: Selected issues. In F. L. Denmark & M. A. Paludi (Eds.), *Psychology of women: A handbook of issues and theories.* Westport, CT: Greenwood Press.

Green, K. L. (1989). Healthy workers: Whose responsibility? *Advances, 6,* 12–14.

Green, L. W., Tryon, W. W., Marks, B., & Huryn, J. (1986). Periodontal disease as a function of life events stress. *Journal of Human Stress, 12,* 32–36.

Green, R. (1982). The best interests of the child with a lesbian mother. *American Academy of Psychiatry and the Law Bulletin, 10,* 7–15.

Green, S. K., Buchanan, D. R., & Heuer, S. K. (1984). Winners, losers, and choosers: A field investigation of dating initiation. *Personality and Social Psychology Bulletin, 10,* 502–511.

Greenberg, J., Pyszczynski, T., & Solomon, S. (1982). The self-serving attributional bias: Beyond self-presentation. *Journal of Experimental Social Psychology, 8,* 99–111.

Greenberg, J. S. (1993). *Comprehensive stress management.* Dubuque, IA: William C. Brown.

Greenberger, E., & Goldberg, W. A. (1989). Work, parenting, and the socialization of children. *Developmental Psychology, 25,* 22–35.

Greenberger, E., Goldberg, W. A., Crawford, T., & Granger, J. (1988). Beliefs about the consequences of maternal employment for children. *Psychology of Women Quarterly, 12,* 35–59.

Greenblat, C. S. (1983). The salience of sexuality in the early years of marriage. *Journal of Marriage and the Family, 45,* 289–299.

Greene, R. L. (1992). *Human memory: Paradigms and paradoxes.* Hillsdale, NJ: Erlbaum.

Greene, W. A., & Swisher, S. N. (1969). Psychological and somatic variables associated with the development and course of monozygotic twins discordant for leukemia. *Annals of the New York Academy of Sciences, 164,* 394–408.

Greenson, R. R. (1967). *The technique and practice of psychoanalysis* (Vol. 1). New York: International Universities Press.

Greenstein, T. N. (1993). Maternal employment and child behavioral outcomes. *Journal of Family Issues, 14,* 323–354.

Griggs, L. (1990, July 2). A losing battle with AIDS. *Time,* pp. 41–43.

Grinspoon, L., & Bakalar, J. B. (1986). Psychedelics and arylcyclohexylamines. In A. J. Frances & R. E. Hales (Eds.), *Psychiatric Update: Annual Review* (Vol. 5). Washington, DC: American Psychiatric Press.

Grinspoon, L., & Bakalar, J. B. (1992). Marihuana. In J. H. Lowinson, P. Ruiz, & R. B. Millman (Eds.), *Substance abuse: A comprehensive textbook* (2nd ed.). Baltimore: Williams & Wilkins.

Grob, G. N. (1983). Disease and environment in American history. In D. Mechanic (Ed.), *Handbook of health, health care, and the health professions.* New York: Free Press.

Grob, G. N. (1991). Origins of DSM-I: A study in appearance and reality. *American Journal of Psychiatry, 148,* 421–431.

Grobbee, D. E., Rimm, E. B., Giovannucci, E., Colditz, G., Stampfer, M., & Willett, W. (1990). Coffee, caffeine, and cardiovascular disease in men. *New England Journal of Medicine, 323,* 1026–1032.

Grolnick, W. S., & Ryan, R. M. (1989). Parent styles associated with children's self-regulation and competence in school. *Journal of Educational Psychology, 81,* 143–154.

Grove, W. M., & Andreasen, N. C. (1992). Concepts, diagnosis and classification. In E. S. Paykel (Ed.), *Handbook of affective disorders* (2nd ed.). New York: Guilford Press.

Grover, K. J., Russell, C. S., Schumm, W. R., & Paff-Bergen, L. A. (1985). Mate selection processes and marital satisfaction. *Family Relations, 34,* 383–386.

Gruber, J. E. (1990). Methodological problems and policy implication in sexual harassment research. *Population Research and Policy Review, 9,* 235–254.

Gruen, R. J. (1993). Stress and depression: Toward the development of integrative models. In L. Goldberger & S. Breznitz (Eds.), *Handbook of stress: Theoretical and clinical aspects.* New York: Free Press.

Grunberg, N. E., & Straub, R. O. (1992). The role of gender and taste class in the effects of stress on eating. *Health Psychology, 11,* 97–100.

Grunberg, N. E., Bowen, D. J., & Winders, S. E. (1986). Effects of nicotine on body weight and food consumption in female rats. *Psychopharmacology, 90,* 101–105.

Grynch, J. H., & Fincham, F. D. (1990). Marital conflict and children's adjustment: A cognitive-contextual framework. *Psychological Bulletin, 108,* 267–290.

Guidubaldi, J., Perry, J. D., & Nastasi, B. K. (1987). Growing up in a divorced family: Initial and long-term perspectives on children's adjustment. In S. Oskamp (Ed.), *Family processes and problems: Social psychological aspects* (Vol. 7, Applied Social Psychology Annual). Newbury Park, CA: Sage Publications.

Gupta, G. R. (1992). Love, arranged marriage, and the Indian social structure. In J. J. Macionis & N. V. Benokraitis (Eds.), *Seeing ourselves: Classic, contemporary and cross-cultural reading in sociology.* Englewood Cliffs, NJ: Prentice-Hall.

Gupta, U., & Singh, P. (1982). Exploratory study of love and liking type of marriages. *Indian Journal of Applied Psychology, 19,* 92–97.

Gurin, J. (1989, June). Leaner, not lighter. *Psychology Today,* pp. 32–36.

Gutek, B. A. (1985). *Sex and the workplace: Impact of sexual behavior and harassment on women, men and organizations.* San Francisco: Jossey-Bass.

Gutek, B. (1993). Responses to sexual harassment. In S. Oskamp & M. Costanzo (Eds.), *Gender issues in contemporary society.* Newbury Park, CA: Sage Publications.

Gutek, B., & Koss, M. P. (1993). Changed women and changed organizations: Consequences of and coping with sexual harassment. *Journal of Vocational Behavior, 42,* 28–48.

Haaken, J. (1990). A critical analysis of the co-dependence construct. *Psychiatry, 53,* 396–406.

Haaken, J. (1993). From Al-Anon to ACOA: Codependence and the reconstruction of caregiving. *Signs, 18,* 321–345.

Haas, A., & Haas, K. (1993). *Understanding sexuality.* St. Louis: Times Mirror/ Mosby.

Hagberg, J. M. (1990). Exercise, fitness, and hypertension. In C. Bouchard, R. J. Shephard, T. Stephens, J. R. Sutton, & B. D. McPherson (Eds.), *Exercise, fitness, and health: A consensus of current knowledge.* Champaign, IL: Human Kinetics Books.

Halford, W. K., & Sanders, M. R. (1990). The relationship of cognition and behavior during marital interaction. *Journal of Social and Clinical Psychology, 9,* 489–510.

Hall, E. T. (1990). *The hidden dimension.* Garden City, NY: Doubleday.

Hall, G. S. (1904). *Adolescence.* New York: Appleton.

Hall, J. A. (1978). Gender effects in decoding nonverbal cues. *Psychological Bulletin, 85,* 845–875.

Hall, J. A. (1984). *Nonverbal sex differences: Communication accuracy and expressive style.* Baltimore: Johns Hopkins University Press.

Hall, J. A. (1990). *Nonverbal sex differences: Communication accuracy and expressive style* (2nd ed.). Baltimore: Johns Hopkins University Press.

Hall, J. A., Roter, D. L., & Katz, N. R. (1988). Meta-analysis of correlates of provider behavior in medical encounters. *Medical Care, 26*, 1–19.

Hall, J. A., & Veccia, E. M. (1990). More "touching" observations: New insights on men, women, and interpersonal touch. *Journal of Personality and Social Psychology, 59*, 1155–1162.

Hall, J. A., & Veccia, E. M. (1991). Touch asymmetry between the sexes. In C. L. Ridgeway (Ed.), *Gender, interaction, and inequality*. New York: Springer-Verlag.

Hall, R. M., & Sandler, B. R. (1982). *The classroom climate: A chilly one for women?* Washington, DC: Association of American Colleges.

Hallie, P. P. (1971). Justification and rebellion. In N. Sanford & C. Comstock (Eds.), *Sanctions for evil*. San Francisco: Jossey-Bass.

Halpern, D. F. (1992). *Sex differences in cognitive abilities* (2nd ed.). Hillsdale, NJ: Erlbaum.

Hamachek, D. (1992). *Encounters with the self*. Fort Worth: Harcourt Brace Jovanovich.

Hamburger, A. C. (1988, May). Beauty quest. *Psychology Today*, pp. 28–32.

Hamer, D. H., Hu, S., Magnuson, V. L., Hu, N., & Pattatucci, A. M. L. (1993). A linkage between DNA markers on the X chromosome and male sexual orientation. *Science, 261*, 321–327.

Hamilton, M. H. (1988, July 10). Employing new tools to recruit workers. *Washington Post*, pp. H1, H3.

Hamilton, V. L., Hoffman, W. S., Broman, C. L., & Rauma, D. (1993). Unemployment, distress, and coping: A panel study of autoworkers. *Journal of Personality and Social Psychology, 65*, 234–247.

Hampton, R. L., Gelles, R. J., & Harrop, J. W. (1989). Is violence in black families increasing? A comparison of 1975 and 1985 national survey rates. *Journal of Marriage and the Family, 51*, 969–980.

Hansen, C. H., & Hansen, R. D. (1988). How rock music videos can change what is seen when boy meets girl: Priming stereotypic appraisal of social interations. *Sex Roles, 19*, 287–316.

Hansen, J. C., & Campbell, D. P. (1985). *Manual for the SVIB-SCII* (4th ed.). Stanford, CA: Stanford University Press.

Hansen, J. E., & Schuldt, W. J. (1984). Marital self-disclosure and marital satisfaction. *Journal of Marriage and the Family, 46*, 923–926.

Hanson, R. O., Jones, W. H., & Carpenter, B. N. (1984). Relational competence and social support. In P. Shaver (Ed.), *Review of personality and social psychology* (Vol. 5). Newbury Park, CA: Sage Publications.

Harmsen, P., Rosengren, A., Tsipogianni, A., & Wilhelmsen, L. (1990). Risk factors for stroke in middle-aged men in Goteborg, Sweden. *Stroke, 21*, 23–29.

Harper, J., & Capdevila, C. (1990). Codependency: A critique. *Journal of Psychoactive Drugs, 22*, 285–292.

Harrigan, J. A. (1985). Self-touching as an indicator of underlying affect and language processing. *Social Science and Medicine, 20*, 1161–1168.

Harriman, L. C. (1986). Marital adjustment as related to personal and marital changes accompanying parenthood. *Family Relations, 35*, 233–239.

Harris, L. (1987). *Inside America*. New York: Vintage Books.

Harris, L., & Associates (1986). *American teens speak: Sex, myths, TV and birth control*. New York: Planned Parenthood.

Harris, M. B., Harris, R. J., & Bochner, S. (1982). Fat, four-eyed, and female: Stereotypes of obesity, glasses, and gender. *Journal of Applied Social Psychology, 12*, 503–516.

Harris, T. (1967). *I'm OK—you're OK*. New York: HarperCollins.

Harrison, A. A., & Saeed, I. (1977). Let's make a deal: An analysis of revelations and stipulations in lonely heart advertisements. *Journal of Personality and Social Psychology, 35*, 257–264.

Harry, J. (1983). Gay male and lesbian relationships. In E. D. Macklin & R. H. Rubin (Eds.), *Contemporary families and alternative lifestyles: Handbook on research and theory*. Newbury Park, CA: Sage Publications.

Harter, S. (1990). Self and identity development. In S. S. Feldman & G. R. Elliott (Eds.), *The developing adolescent*. Cambridge, MA: Harvard University Press.

Hartley, R. (1959). Sex-role pressures and the socialization of the male child. *Psychological Reports, 5*, 457–468.

Hartman, W. E., & Fithian, M. A. (1994). *Treatment of sexual dysfunction: A bio-psycho-social approach*. New York: Aronson.

Hartmann, E. L. (1985). Sleep disorders. In H. I. Kaplan & B. J. Sadock (Eds.), *Comprehensive textbook of psychiatry* (4th ed.). Baltimore: Williams & Wilkins.

Harvey, J. H., Town, J. P., & Yarkin, K. L. (1981). How fundamental is "the fundamental attribution error"? *Journal of Personality and Social Psychology, 40*, 346–349.

Harvey, S. M. (1987). Female sexual behavior: Fluctuations during the menstrual cycle. *Journal of Psychosomatic Research, 31*, 101–110.

Hass, R. G. (1981). Effects of source characteristics on cognitive responses and persuasion. In R. E. Petty, T. M. Ostrom, & T. C. Brock (Eds.), *Cognitive responses in persuasion*. Hillsdale, NJ: Erlbaum.

Hatcher, R. A., Trussell, J., Stewart, F., Stewart, G. K., Kowal, D., Guest, F., Cates, W., Jr., & Policar, M. S. (1994). *Contraceptive technology* (16th ed.). New York: Irvington.

Hatfield, E. (1988). Passionate and companionate love. In R. J. Sternberg & M. L. Barnes (Eds.), *The psychology of love*. New Haven, CT: Yale University Press.

Hatfield, E., & Rapson, R. L. (1993). *Love, sex, and intimacy: Their psychology, biology, and history*. New York: HarperCollins.

Hatfield, E., & Rapson, R. L. (1996). *Love and sex: Cross-cultural perspectives*. Boston: Allyn & Bacon.

Haugaard, J. J., & Reppucci, N. D. (1988). *The sexual abuse of children*. San Francisco: Jossey-Bass.

Hauser, S. T., & Bowlds, M. K. (1990). Stress, coping, and adaptation. In S. S. Feldman & G. R. Elliott (Eds.), *At the threshold: The developing adolescent*. Cambridge, MA: Harvard University Press.

Hayghe, H. V. (1990, March). Family members in the work force. *Monthly Labor Review*, pp. 14–19.

Hays, R. B. (1984). The development and maintenance of friendship. *Journal of Social and Personal Relationships, 1*, 75–98.

Hays, R. B. (1985). A longitudinal study of friendship development. *Journal of Personality and Social Psychology, 48*, 909–924.

Hazan, C., & Shaver, P. (1986). *Parental caregiving style questionnaire*. Unpublished questionnaire.

Hazan, C., & Shaver, P. (1987). Romantic love conceptualized as an attachment process. *Journal of Personality and Social Psychology, 52*, 511–524.

Heady, B., & Wearing, A. (1989). Personality, life events, and subjective well-being: Toward a dynamic equilibrium model. *Journal of Personality and Social Psychology, 57*, 731–739.

Healy, D., & Williams, J. M. G. (1988). Dysrhythmia, dysphoria, and depression: The interaction of learned helplessness and circadian dysrhythmia in the pathogenesis of depression. *Psychological Bulletin, 103*, 163–178.

Heath, R. G. (1976). Cannabis sativa derivatives: Effects on brain function of monkeys. In G.G. Nahas (Ed.), *Marijuana: Chemistry, biochemistry and cellular effects*. New York: Springer.

Heatherington, L., Daubman, K. A., Bates, C., Ahn, A., Brown, H., & Preston, C. (1993). Two investigations of "female modesty" in achievement situations. *Sex Roles, 29*, 739–754.

Hegarty, J. D., Baldessarini, R. J., Tohen, M., Waternaux, C., & Oepen, G. (1994). One hundred years of schizophrenia: A meta-analysis of the outcome literature. *American Journal of Psychiatry, 151*, 1409–1416.

Heider, F. (1958). *The psychology of interpersonal relations*. New York: Wiley.

Helgeson, V. S. (1994). Relation of agency and communion to well-being: Evidence and potential explanations. *Psychological Bulletin, 116*, 412–428.

Helson, H., Blake, R. R., & Mouton, J. S. (1958). Petition-signing as adjustment to situational and personal factors. *Journal of Social Psychology, 48*, 3–10.

Helson, R., Elliott, T., & Leigh, J. (1990). Number and quality of roles. *Psychology of Women Quarterly, 14*, 83–101.

Helson, R., Mitchell, V., & Moane, G. (1984). Personality and patterns of adherence and nonadherence to the social clock. *Journal of Personality and Social Psychology, 46*, 1079–1096.

Helson, R., & Moane, G. (1987). Personality change in women from college to midlife. *Journal of Personality and Social Psychology, 53*, 176–186.

Helson, R., & Stewart, A. (1994). Personality change in adulthood. In T. F. Heatherton & J. L. Weinberger (Eds.), *Can personality change?* Washington, DC: American Psychological Association.

Helzer, J. E., Robins, L. N., & McEvoy, L. (1987). Post-traumatic stress disorder in the general population: Findings of the epidemiologic catchment area survey. *The New England Journal of Medicine, 317*, 1630–1634.

Hembre, R. (1988). Correlates, causes, effects, and treatment of test anxiety. *Review of Educational Research, 58*, 47–77.

Hencken, J. (1984). Conceptualizations of homosexual behavior which preclude homosexual self-labeling. *Journal of Homosexuality, 9*, 53–63.

Henderson, C. W. (1975). *Awakening: Ways to psychospiritual growth*. Englewood Cliffs, NJ: Prentice-Hall.

Henderson-King, D. H., & Veroff, J. (1994). Sexual satisfaction and marital well-being in the first years of marriage. *Journal of Social and Personal Relationships, 11*, 509–534.

Hendrick, C., & Hendrick, S. S. (1989). Research on love: Does it measure up? *Journal of Personality and Social Psychology, 56*, 784–794.

Hendrick, S. S., & Hendrick, C. (1992). *Liking, loving, and relating* (2nd ed.). Pacific Grove, CA: Brooks/Cole.

Hendrick, S. S., Hendrick, C., & Adler, N. L. (1988). Romantic relationships: Love, satisfaction, and staying together. *Journal of Personality and Social Psychology, 54*, 980–988.

Henley, N. M. (1977). *Body politics: Power,*

sex and nonverbal communication. Englewood Cliffs, NJ: Prentice-Hall.

Henley, N. M. (1986). Body politics: Power, sex, and nonverbal communication (2nd ed.). New York: Simon & Schuster.

Henley, N. M., & Freeman, J. (1981). The sexual politics of interpersonal behavior. In S. Cox (Ed.), Female psychology: The emerging self. New York: St. Martin's Press.

Herek, G. M. (1986). On heterosexual masculinity: Some psychical consequences of the social construction of gender and sexuality. American Behavioral Scientist, 29, 563–577.

Herek, G. M. (1988). Heterosexuals' attitudes toward lesbians and gay men: Correlates and gender differences. Journal of Sex Research, 25, 451–477.

Herek, G. M. (1991). Stigma, prejudice, and violence against lesbians and gay men. In J. C. Gonsiorek & J. D. Weinrich (Eds.), Homosexuality: Research implications for public policy. Newbury Park, CA: Sage Publications.

Hertzog, C., & Schaie, K. W. (1988). Stability and changes in adult intelligence: 2. Simultaneous analysis of longitudinal means and covariance structures. Psychology and Aging, 3, 122–130.

Herzog, A. R., House, J. S., & Morgan, J. N. (1991). Relation of work and retirement to health and well-being in older age. Psychology and Aging, 6, 202–211.

Hetherington, E. M. (1991). The role of individual differences and family relationships in children's coping with divorce and remarriage. In P. A. Cowan & M. Hetherington (Eds.), Family transitions. Hillsdale, NJ: Erlbaum.

Hetherington, E. M., & Clingempeel, W. G. (1992). Coping with marital transitions: A family systems perspective. Monographs of the Society for Research in Child Development, 227 (whole No. 57, Nos. 2–3).

Hettich, P. I. (1992). Learning skills for college and career. Pacific Grove, CA: Brooks/Cole.

Heun, L. R., & Heun, R. E. (1978). Developing skills for human interactions. Columbus, OH: Charles E. Merrill.

Higgins, E. T. (1989). Self-discrepancy theory: What patterns of self-beliefs cause people to suffer? In L. Berkowitz (Ed.), Advances in experimental social psychology (Vol. 22). New York: Academic Press.

Higgins, E. T., Bond, R. N., Klein, R., & Strauman, T. (1986). Self-discrepancies and emotional vulnerability: How magnitude, accessibility, and type of discrepancy influence affect. Journal of Personality and Social Psychology, 51, 5–15.

Hilgard, E. R. (1987). Psychology in America: A historical survey. San Diego: Harcourt Brace Jovanovich.

Hill, C. T., Rubin, Z., & Peplau, L. A. (1976). Breakups before marriage: The end of 103 affairs. Journal of Social Issues, 32, 147–168.

Hill, C. T., & Stull, D. E. (1987). Gender and self-disclosure: Strategies for exploring the issues. In V. J. Derlega & J. H. Berg (Eds.), Self-disclosure: Theory, research, and therapy. New York: Plenum.

Hill, R. D., Storandt, M., & Malley, M. (1993). The impact of exercise training on psychological function in older adults. Journal of Gerontology, 48, 12–17.

Hilton, J. L., & Darley, J. M. (1985). Constructing other persons: A limit on the effect. Journal of Experimental Social Psychology, 21, 1–18.

Hilton, J. L., Fein, S., & Miller, D. T. (1993). Suspicion and dispositional in-

ference. Personality and Social Psychology Bulletin, 19, 501–512.

Hines, M. (1982). Prenatal gonadal hormones and sex differences in human behavior. Psychological Bulletin, 92, 56–80.

Hines, M. (1990). Gonadal hormones and human cognitive development. In J. Balthazart (Ed.), Hormones, brain and behavior in vertebrates: 1. Sexual differentiation, neuroanatomical aspects, neurotransmitters and neuropeptides. Basel: Karger.

Hines, M., & Kaufman, F. R. (1994). Androgen and the development of human sex typical behavior: Rough-and-tumble play and sex of preferred playmates in children with congenital adrenal hyperplasia (CAH). Child Development, 65, 1042–1053.

Hiroto, D. S., & Seligman, M. E. P. (1975). Generality of learned helplessness in man. Journal of Personality and Social Psychology, 31, 311–327.

Hirsch, J., Fried, S. K., Edens, N. K., & Leibel, R. L. (1989). The fat cell. Medical Clinics of North America, 73, 83–96.

Hirschfeld, R. M. A., & Davidson, L. (1988). Risk factors for suicide. In A. J. Frances & R. E. Hales (Eds.), Review of psychiatry (Vol. 7). Washington, DC: American Psychiatric Press.

Hirt, E. R., Deppe, R. K., & Gordon, L. J. (1991). Self-reported versus behavioral self-handicapping: Empirical evidence for a theoretical distinction. Journal of Personality and Social Psychology, 61, 981–991.

Hite, S. (1976). The Hite report. New York: Macmillan.

Hobfoll, S. E. (1989). Conservation of resources: A new attempt at conceptualizing stress. American Psychologist, 44, 513–524.

Hobfoll, S. E., & Vaux, A. (1993). Social support: Resources and context. In L. Goldberger & S. Breznitz (Eds.), Handbook of stress: Theoretical and clinical aspects (2nd ed.). New York: Free Press.

Hochschild, A. (1989). The second shift: Working parents and the revolution at home. New York: Viking Penguin.

Hochswender, W. (1990, June 17). For today's fathers, their holiday seems a bit set in its ways. New York Times, pp. 1, 22.

Hock, E., Schirtzinger, M. B., Lutz, W. J., & Widaman, K. (1995). Maternal depressive symptomatology over the transition to parenthood: Assessing the influence of marital satisfaction and marital sex role traditionalism. Journal of Family Psychology, 9, 79–88.

Hodges, B. H. (1974). Effects of valence on relative weighting in impression formation. Journal of Personality and Social Psychology, 30, 378–381.

Hofferth, S. L., & Phillips, D. A. (1987). Child care in the United States: 1970–1995. Journal of Marriage and the Family, 49, 559–571.

Hoffman, L. (1987). The effects on children of maternal and paternal employment. In N. Gerstel & H. Gross (Eds.), Families and work. Philadelphia: Temple University Press.

Hoffman, L. W. (1991). The influence of the family environment on personality: Accounting for sibling differences. Psychological Bulletin, 110, 187–203.

Hofstede, G. (1980). Culture's consequences: International differences in work-related values. Newbury Park, CA: Sage Publications.

Hofstede, G. (1983). Dimensions of national cultures in fifty countries and three regions. In J. Deregowski, S. Dziurawiec, & R. Annis (Eds.), Explications in cross-cultural psychology. Lisse: Swets and Zeitlinger.

Hokanson, J. E., & Burgess, M. (1962).

The effects of three types of aggression on vascular processes. Journal of Abnormal and Social Psychology, 65, 446–449.

Holahan, C. J. (1986). Environmental psychology. Annual Review of Psychology, 37, 381–407.

Holahan, C. J., & Moos, R. H. (1985). Life stress and health: Personality, coping, and family support in stress resistance. Journal of Personality and Social Psychology, 49, 739–747.

Holahan, C. J., & Moos, R. H. (1990). Life stressors, resistance factors, and improved psychological functioning: An extension of the stress resistance paradigm. Journal of Personality and Social Psychology, 58, 909–917.

Holahan, C. J., & Moos, R. H. (1994). Life stressors and mental health: Advances in conceptualizing stress resistance. In W. R. Avison & I. H. Gotlib (Eds.), Stress and mental health: Contemporary issues and prospects for the future. New York: Plenum.

Holland, D. C., & Eisenhart, M. A. (1990). Educated in romance: Women, achievement, and college culture. Chicago: University of Chicago Press.

Holland, J. C., & Lewis, S. (1993). Emotions and cancer: What do we really know? In D. Goleman & J. Gurin (Eds.), Mind/body medicine: How to use your mind for better health. Yonkers, NY: Consumer Reports Books.

Holland, J. L. (1973). Making vocational choices: A theory of careers. Englewood Cliffs, NJ: Prentice-Hall.

Holland, J. L. (1985). Making vocational choices: A theory of vocational personalities and work environments. Englewood Cliffs, NJ: Prentice-Hall.

Hollander, E., Simeon, D., & Gorman, J. M. (1994). Anxiety disorders. In R. E. Hales, S. C. Yudofsky, & J. A. Talbott (Eds.), The American Psychiatric Press textbook of psychiatry (2nd ed.). Washington, DC: American Psychiatric Press.

Hollandsworth, J. G., Jr. (1990). The physiology of psychological disorders: Schizophrenia, depression, anxiety, and substance abuse. New York: Plenum.

Hollon, S. D., & Beck, A. T. (1994). Cognitive and cognitive-behavioral therapies. In A. E. Bergin & S. L. Garfield (Eds.), Handbook of psychotherapy and behavior change (4th ed.). New York: Wiley.

Holman, T. B., & Jacquart, M. (1988). Leisure-activity patterns and marital satisfaction: A further test. Journal of Marriage and the Family, 50, 69–77.

Holmes, D. S. (1984). Meditation and somatic arousal reduction: A review of the experimental evidence. American Psychologist, 39, 1–10.

Holmes, D. S. (1987). The influence of meditation versus rest on physiological arousal: A second examination. In M.A. West (Ed.), The psychology of meditation. Oxford: Clarendon Press.

Holmes, T. H., & Rahe, R. H. (1967). The Social Readjustment Rating Scale. Journal of Psychosomatic Research, 11, 213–218.

Holt, R. R. (1982). Occupational stress. In L. Goldberger & S. Breznitz (Eds.), Handbook of stress: Theoretical and clinical aspects. New York: Free Press.

Hones, J. C., & Barlow, D. H. (1990). Self-reported frequency of sexual urges, fantasies, and masturbatory fantasies in heterosexual males and females. Archives of Sexual Behavior, 19, 269–280.

Honeycutt, J. M. (1986). A model of marital functioning based on an attraction paradigm and social-penetration dimensions. Journal of Marriage and the Family, 48, 651–667.

Hood, K. E., Draper, P., Crockett, L. J., & Petersen, A. C. (1987). The ontogeny and phylogeny of sexual differences in development: A biopsychosocial synthesis. In B. Carter (Ed.), *Current conceptions of sex roles and sex typing: Theory and research*. New York: Praeger.

Hooker, E. (1957). The adjustment of the male overt homosexual. *Journal of Projective Techniques, 21,* 18–31.

Horn, M. (1993, November 29). Memories lost and found. *U.S. News & World Report,* pp. 52–63.

Horowitz, F. D., & O'Brien, M. (1989). In the interest of the nation: A reflective essay on the state of our knowledge and the challenges before us. *American Psychologist, 44,* 441–445.

Hotaling, G. T., & Sugarman, D. B. (1986). An analysis of risk markers in husband to wife violence: The current state of knowledge. *Violence and Crimes, 1,* 101–124.

House, J. S., Landis, K. R., & Umberson, D. (1988). Social relationships and health. *Science, 241,* 540–545.

Houston, B. K., Chesney, M. A., Black, G. W., Cates, D. S., & Hecker, M. H. L. (1992). Behavioral clusters and coronary heart disease. *Psychosomatic Medicine, 54,* 447–461.

Houston, B. K., & Vavak, C. R. (1991). Hostility: Developmental factors, psychosocial correlates, and health behaviors. *Health Psychology, 10,* 9–17.

Howes, C., Phillips, D. A., & Whitebrook, M. (1992). Thresholds of quality: Implications for the social development of children in center-based child care. *Child Development, 63,* 449–460.

Hubbard, L. R. (1989). *Scientology: The fundamentals of thought.* Los Angeles: Bridge.

Huesmann, L. R., & Morikawa, S. (1985). Learned helplessness and depression: Cognitive factors in treatment and inoculation. In S. Reiss & R. R. Bootzin (Eds.), *Theoretical issues in behavior therapy.* Orlando, FL: Academic Press.

Hugick, L., & Leonard, J. (1991a, September). Job dissatisfaction grows. *Gallup Poll Monthly,* pp. 2–15.

Hugick, L., & Leonard, J. (1991b, October). Sex in America. *The Gallup Poll Monthly,* pp. 60–73.

Hull, J. G., & Young, R. D. (1983). Self-consciousness, self-esteem, and success-failure as determinants of alcohol consumption in male social drinkers. *Journal of Personality and Social Psychology, 44,* 1097–1109.

Hultsch, D. F., & Dixon, R. A. (1990). Learning and memory in aging. In J. E. Birren & K. W. Schaie (Eds.), *Handbook of the psychology of aging* (3rd ed.). San Diego: Academic Press.

Hunt, J. M., Smith, M. F., & Kernan, J. B. (1985). The effects of expectancy disconfirmation and argument strength on message processing level: An application to personal selling. In E. C. Hirschman & M. B. Holbrook (Eds.), *Advances in consumer research* (Vol. 12). Provo, UT: Association for Consumer Research.

Hunt, M. (1974). *Sexual behavior in the 1970s.* Chicago: Playboy Press.

Huseman, R. C., Lahiff, J. M., & Hatfield, J. D. (1976). *Interpersonal communication in organizations.* Boston: Holbrook Press.

Huston, A. C., Wright, J. C., Rice, M. L., Kerkman, D., & St. Peters, M. (1990). Development of television viewing patterns in early childhood: A longitudinal investigation. *Developmental Psychology, 26,* 409–420.

Huyck, M. H., & Hoyer, W. J. (1982). *Adult development and aging.* Belmont, CA: Wadsworth.

Hyde, J. S. (1981). How large are cognitive gender differences? *American Psychologist, 36,* 892–901.

Hyde, J. S. (1984). How large are gender differences in aggression? A developmental meta-analysis. *Developmental Psychology, 20,* 722–736.

Hyde, J. S. (1994). *Understanding human sexuality* (5th ed.). New York: McGraw-Hill.

Hyde, J. S. (1996). *Half the human experience: The psychology of women* (5th ed.). Lexington, MA: Heath.

Hyde, J. S., Fennema, E., & Lamon, S. J. (1990). Gender differences in mathematics performance: A meta-analysis. *Psychological Bulletin, 107,* 139–155.

Hyde, J. S., & Frost, L. A. (1993). Meta-analysis in the psychology of women. In F. L. Denmark & M. A. Paludi (Eds.), *Psychology of women: A handbook of issues and theories.* Westport, CT: Greenwood Press.

Hyde, J. S., & Linn, M. C. (1988). Gender differences in verbal ability: A meta-analysis. *Psychological Bulletin, 104,* 53–69.

Hyman, B. T., Van Hoesen, G. W., Damasio, A. R., & Barnes, C. L. (1984). Alzheimer's disease: Cell-specific pathology isolates the hippocampal formation. *Science, 225,* 1168–1170.

Ickes, W. (1993). Traditional gender roles: Do they make and then break our relationships? *Journal of Social Issues, 3,* 71–85.

Ickovics, J. R., & Rodin, J. (1992). Women and AIDS in the United States: Epidemiology, natural history, and mediating mechanisms. *Health Psychology, 11,* 1–16.

Iezzi, A., & Adams, H. E. (1993). Somatoform and factitious disorders. In P. B. Sutker & H. E. Adams (Eds.), *Comprehensive handbook of psychopathology* (2nd ed.). New York: Plenum.

Ilgen, D. R. (1990). Health issues at work: Opportunities for industrial/organization psychology. *American Psychologist, 45,* 252–261.

Ineichen, B. (1979). The social geography of marriage. In M. Cook & G. Wilson (Eds.), *Love and attraction.* New York: Pergamon.

Inkeles, A., & Usui, C. (1989). Retirement patterns in cross-national perspective. In D. I. Kertzer & K. W. Schaie (Eds.), *Age structuring in comparative perspective.* Hillsdale, NJ: Erlbaum.

Inoff-Germain, G., Arnold, G. S., Nottelmann, E. D., Susman, E. J., Cutler, G. B., Jr., & Chrousos, G. P. (1988). Relations between hormone levels and observational measures of aggressive behavior of young adolescents in family interactions. *Developmental Psychology, 24,* 129–139.

Isabella, R. A., & Belsky, J. (1991). Interactional synchrony and the origins of infant-mother attachment: A replication study. *Child Development, 62,* 373–384.

Ivancevich, J. M., Matteson, M. T., Freedman, S. M., & Phillips, J. S. (1990). Worksite stress management interventions. *American Psychologist, 45,* 252–261.

Iwao, S. (1993). *The Japanese woman: Traditional image and changing reality.* New York: Free Press.

Jackson, L. A., Ialongo, N., & Stollak, G. A. (1986). Parental correlates of gender role: The relations between parents' masculinity, femininity, and child-rearing behaviors and their children's gender roles. *Journal of Social and Clinical Psychology, 4,* 204–224.

Jackson, S., & Schuler, R. (1985). A meta-analysis and conceptual critique of research on role ambiguity and role conflict in work settings. *Organizational Behavior and Human Decision Processes, 36,* 16–78.

Jacobs, J. (1971). *Adolescent suicide.* New York: Wiley-Interscience.

Jacobson, E. (1938). *Progressive relaxation.* Chicago: University of Chicago Press.

Jaffe, J. H. (1986). Opioids. In A. J. Frances & R. E. Hales (Eds.), *Psychiatric Update: Annual Review* (Vol. 5). Washington, DC: American Psychiatric Press.

Jaffe, J. H. (1992). Opiates: Clinical aspects. In J. H. Lowinson, P. Ruiz, & R. B. Millman (Eds.), *Substance abuse: A comprehensive textbook* (2nd ed.). Baltimore: Williams & Wilkins.

Jahoda, M. (1958). *Current concepts of positive mental health.* New York: Basic Books.

Janis, I. L. (1958). *Psychological stress.* New York: Wiley.

Janis, I. L. (1993). Decision making under stress. In L. Goldberger & S. Breznitz (Eds.), *Handbook of stress: Theoretical and clinical aspects* (2nd ed.). New York: Free Press.

Jann, M. W., Jenike, M. A., & Lieberman, J. A. (1994). The new psychopharmaceuticals. *Patient Care, 28,* 47–61.

Janus, S. S., & Janus, C. L. (1993). *The Janus report on sexual behavior.* New York: Wiley.

Jaroff, L. (1993, November 29). Lies of the mind. *Time,* pp. 52–59.

Jarvik, M. E., & Schneider, N. G. (1992). Nicotine. In J. H. Lowinson, P. Ruiz, & R. B. Millman (Eds.), *Substance abuse: A comprehensive textbook* (2nd ed.). Baltimore: Williams & Wilkins.

Jay, K., & Young, A. (1979). *The gay report.* New York: Summit Books.

Jefferson, J. W., & Greist, J. H. (1989). Lithium therapy. In H. I. Kaplan & B. J. Sadock (Eds.), *Comprehensive textbook of psychiatry/V.* Baltimore: Williams & Wilkins.

Jefferson, J. W., & Greist, J. H. (1994). Mood disorders. In R. E. Hales, S. C. Yudofsky, & J. A. Talbott (Eds.), *The American Psychiatric Press textbook of psychiatry* (2nd ed.). Washington, DC: American Psychiatric Press.

Jeffery, R. W., Adlis, S. A., & Forster, J. L. (1991). Prevalence of dieting among working men and women: The healthy worker project. *Health Psychology, 10,* 274–281.

Jemmott, J. B., III, & Magloire, K. (1988). Academic stress, social support, and secretory Immunoglobin A. *Journal of Personality and Social Psychology, 55,* 803–810.

Jenike, M. A. (1987). Drug abuse. In E. Rubenstein & D. D. Federman (Eds.), *Scientific American medicine.* New York: Scientific American Press.

Jenike, M. A., Baer, L., & Greist, J. H. (1990). Clomipramine versus fluoxetine in obsessive-compulsive disorder: A retrospective comparison of side effects and efficacy. *Journal of Clinical Psychopharmacology, 10,* 122–124.

Jennison, K. M. (1992). The impact of stressful life events and social support on drinking among older adults: A general population survey. *International Journal of Aging and Human Development, 35,* 99–123.

Jepson, C., & Chaiken, S. (1986). *The effect of anxiety on the systematic processing of persuasive communications.* Washington, DC: Paper presented at the annual meeting of the American Psychological Association.

Jessor, R., Costa, F., Jessor, L., & Donovan, J. E. (1983). Time of first intercourse: A prospective study. *Journal of Personality and Social Psychology, 44*, 608–626.

John, O. P. (1990). The "big five" factor taxonomy: Dimensions of personality in the natural language and in questionnaires. In L. A. Pervin (Ed.), *Handbook of personality: Theory and research*. New York: Guilford Press.

Johnson, A. M., Wadsworth, J., Wellings, K., Bradshaw, S., & Field, J. (1992). Sexual lifestyles and HIV risk. *Nature, 360*, 410–412.

Johnson, B. D., & Muffler, J. (1992). Sociocultural aspects of drug use and abuse in the 1990s. In J. H. Lowinson, P. Ruiz, & R. B. Millman (Eds.), *Substance abuse: A comprehensive textbook* (2nd ed.). Baltimore: Williams & Wilkins.

Johnson, B. T. (1991). Insights about attitudes: Meta-analytic perspectives. *Personality and Social Psychology Bulletin, 17*, 289–299.

Johnson, C. L. (1982). Sibling solidarity: Its origin and functioning in Italian-American families. *Journal of Marriage and the Family, 44*, 155–167.

Johnson, D. R., White, L. K., Edwards, J. N., & Booth, A. (1986). Dimensions of marital quality: Toward methodological and conceptual refinement. *Journal of Family Issues, 7*, 31–49.

Johnson, D. W. (1981). *Reaching out: Interpersonal effectiveness and self-actualization*. Englewood Cliffs, NJ: Prentice-Hall.

Johnson, D. W., & Johnson, F. (1994). *Joining together* (5th ed.). Englewood Cliffs, NJ: Prentice-Hall.

Johnson, J. G., & Bornstein, R. F. (1991). Does daily stress independently predict psychopathology? *Journal of Social and Clinical Psychology, 10*, 58–74.

Johnson, R. D., & Downing, L. L. (1979). Deindividuation and valence of cues: Effects on prosocial and antisocial behavior. *Journal of Personality and Social Psychology, 37*, 1532–1538.

Johnston, W. B., & Packer, A. H. (1987). *Workforce 2000: Work and workers for the twenty-first century*. Indianapolis, IN: Hudson Institute.

Joiner, T. E. (1994). Contagious depression: Existence, specificity to depressed symptoms, and the role of reassurance seeking. *Journal of Personality and Social Psychology, 67*, 287–296.

Jones, E. E. (1964). *Ingratiation*. New York: Appleton-Century-Crofts.

Jones, E. E. (1990). *Interpersonal perception*. New York: Freeman.

Jones, E. E., & Davis, K. (1965). From acts to dispositions: The attribution process in person perception. In L. Berkowitz (Ed.), *Advances in experimental social psychology* (Vol. 2). New York: Academic Press.

Jones, E. E., & Pittman, T. S. (1982). Toward a general theory of strategic self-presentation. In J. Suls (Ed.), *Psychological perspectives on the self*. Hillsdale, NJ: Erlbaum.

Jones, E. E., Rhodewalt, F., Berglas, S., & Skelton, J. A. (1981). Effects of strategic self-presentation on subsequent self-esteem. *Journal of Personality and Social Psychology, 41*, 407–421.

Jones, M. (1993, July 5). Getting away from the "R" word. *Publishers Weekly*, pp. 42–45.

Jones, R. A., & Brehm, J. W. (1970). Persuasiveness of one- and two-sided communications as a function of awareness there are two sides. *Journal of Experimental Social Psychology, 6*, 47–56.

Jones, S. C. (1973). Self- and interpersonal evaluations: Esteem theories versus consistency theories. *Psychological Bulletin, 79*, 185–199.

Jones, W. H., Briggs, S. R., & Smith, T. G. (1986). Shyness: Conceptualization and measurement. *Journal of Personality and Social Psychology, 51*, 629–639.

Jones, W. H., & Carpenter, B. N. (1986). Shyness, social behavior, and relationships. In W. H. Jones, J. M. Cheek, & S. R. Briggs (Eds.), *Shyness: Perspectives on research and treatment*. New York: Plenum.

Jones, W. H., Freeman, J. A., & Goswick, R. A. (1981). The persistence of loneliness: Self and other determinants. *Journal of Personality, 49*, 27–48.

Jones, W. H., Hobbs, S. A., & Hockenbury, D. (1982). Loneliness and social skill deficits. *Journal of Personality and Social Psychology, 42*, 682–689.

Jones, W. H., Sansome, C., & Helm, B. (1983). Loneliness and interpersonal judgments. *Personality and Social Psychology Bulletin, 9*, 437–442.

Josselson, R. (1987). *Finding herself: Pathways to identity development in women*. San Francisco: Jossey-Bass.

Jourard, S. M. (1971). *The transparent self*. New York: Van Nostrand Reinhold.

Jourard, S. M., & Landsman, T. (1980). *Healthy personality: An approach from the viewpoint of humanistic psychology*. New York: Macmillan.

Judd, L. L., McAdams, L. A., Budnick, B., & Braff, D. L. (1992). Sensory gating effects in schizophrenia: New results. *American Journal of Psychiatry, 149*, 488–493.

Julien, R. M. (1995). *A primer of drug action* (7th ed.). New York: W. H. Freeman.

Jung, C. G. (1917). *On the psychology of the unconscious*. In Collected Works (Vol. 7). Princeton, NJ: Princeton University Press.

Jung, C. G. (1921). *Psychological types*. In Collected Works (Vol. 6). Princeton, NJ: Princeton University Press.

Jung, C. G. (1933). *Modern man in search of a soul*. New York: Harcourt, Brace & World.

Kacerguis, M. A., & Adams, G. R. (1980). Erikson stage resolution: The relationship between identity and intimacy. *Journal of Youth and Adolescence, 9*, 117–126.

Kagan, J., Snidman, N., & Arcus, D. M. (1992). Initial reactions to unfamiliarity. *Current Directions in Psychological Science, 1*, 171–174.

Kahle, L. R., & Homer, P. M. (1985). Physical attractiveness of the celebrity endorser: A social adaptation perspective. *Journal of Consumer Research, 11*, 954–961.

Kahn, S., Zimmerman, G., Csikszentmihalyi, M., & Getzels, J. W. (1985). Relations between identity in young adulthood and intimacy at midlife. *Journal of Personality and Social Psychology, 49*, 1316–1322.

Kalant, H., & Kalant, O. J. (1979). Death in amphetamine users: Causes and rates. In D. E. Smith (Ed.), *Amphetamine use, misuse and abuse*. Boston: G. K. Hall.

Kalick, S. M., & Hamilton, T. E., III. (1986). The matching hypothesis reexamined. *Journal of Personality and Social Psychology, 51*, 673–682.

Kalish, R. A. (1985). The social context of death and dying. In R. H. Binstock & E. Shanas (Eds.), *Handbook of aging and the social sciences* (2nd ed.) (pp. 149–170). New York: Van Nostrand Reinhold.

Kalish, R. A. (1986). Cemetery visits. *Death Studies, 10*, 55–58.

Kalmuss, D., Davidson, A., & Cushman, L. (1992). Parenting expectations, experiences, and adjustment to parenthood: A test of the violated expectations framework. *Journal of Marriage and the Family, 52*, 516–526.

Kamen-Siegel, L., Rodin, J., Seligman, M. E. P., & Dwyer, J. (1991). Explanatory style and cell-mediated immunity in elderly men and women. *Health Psychology, 10*, 229–235.

Kaminer, W. (1992). *I'm dysfunctional, you're dysfunctional*. Reading, MA: Addison-Wesley.

Kandel, D. B. (1978). Similarity in real-life adolescent friendship pairs. *Journal of Personality and Social Psychology, 36*, 306–312.

Kane, J. (1991). *Be sick well: A healthy approach to chronic illness*. Oakland, CA: New Harbinger.

Kannel, W. B., & Cupples, L. A. (1989). Cardiovascular and noncardiovascular consequences of obesity. In A. J. Stunkard & A. Baum (Eds.), *Perspectives in behavioral medicine: Eating, sleeping, and sex*. Hillsdale, NJ: Erlbaum.

Kanner, A. D., Coyne, J. C., Schaefer, C., & Lazarus, R. S. (1981). Comparison of two modes of stress measurement: Daily hassles and uplifts versus major life events. *Journal of Behavioral Medicine, 4*, 1–39.

Kanter, R. M. (1977). *Men and women of the corporation*. New York: Basic Books.

Kaplan, A. G. (1985). Female or male therapists for women patients: New formulations. *Psychiatry, 48*, 111–121.

Kaplan, H. I. (1985). History of psychosomatic medicine. In H. I. Kaplan & B. J. Sadock (Eds.), *Comprehensive textbook of psychiatry/IV* (4th ed.). Baltimore: Williams & Wilkins.

Kaplan, H. I. (1989). History of psychosomatic medicine. In H. I. Kaplan & B. J. Sadock (Eds.), *Comprehensive textbook of psychiatry/V* (Vol. 2) (5th ed.). Baltimore: Williams & Wilkins.

Kaplan, H. I., & Sadock, B. J. (Eds.). (1993). *Comprehensive group psychotherapy*. Baltimore: Williams & Wilkins.

Kaplan, H. S. (1979). *Disorders of sexual desire and other new concepts and techniques in sex therapy*. New York: Simon & Schuster.

Kaplan, H. S. (1983). *The evaluation of sexual disorders: Psychological and medical aspects*. New York: Brunner/Mazel.

Kaplan, N. M. (1986). Dietary aspects of the treatment of hypertension. In L. Breslow, J. E. Fielding, & L. B. Lave (Eds.), *Annual review of public health* (Vol. 7). Palo Alto, CA: Annual Reviews.

Kaplan, R. M., & Simon, H. J. (1990). Compliance in medical care: Reconsideration of self-predictions. *Annals of Behavioral Medicine, 12*, 66–71.

Kaplan, R. M., Manuck, S. B., & Shumaker, S. (1992). Does lowering cholesterol cause increases in depression, suicide, and accidents? In H. S. Freidman (Ed.), *Hostility coping and health*. Washington, DC: American Psychological Association.

Karasek, R. A., Jr. (1979). Job demands, job decision latitude, and mental strain: Implications for job redesign. *Administrative Science Quarterly, 24*, 285–308.

Karasek, R. A., Jr., Baker, D., Marxer, F., Ahlbom, A., & Theorell, T. (1981). Job decision latitude, job demands, and cardiovascular disease: A prospective study of Swedish men. *American Journal of Public Health, 71*, 694–705.

Karasek, R. A., Jr., & Theorell, T. (1990). *Healthy work: Stress, productivity, and the reconstruction of working life*. New York: Basic Books.

Karlen, A. (1971). *Sexuality and homosexuality*. New York: Norton.

Karney, B. R., Bradbury, T. N., Fincham, F. D., & Sullivan, K. T. (1994). The role of negative affectivity in the association between attributions and marital satisfaction. *Journal of Personality and Social Psychology, 66,* 413–424.

Karno, M., & Golding, J. M. (1991). Obsessive compulsive disorder. In L. N. Robins & D. A. Regier (Eds.), *Psychiatric disorders in America: The epidemiologic catchment area study.* New York: Free Press.

Kass, F., Spitzer, R. L., Williams, J. B. W., & Widiger, T. (1989). Self-defeating personality disorder and DSM-III-R: Development of the diagnostic criteria. *American Journal of Psychiatry, 146,* 1022–1026.

Kassler, J. (1994). *Bitter medicine.* New York: Birch Lane Press.

Kastenbaum, R. (1986). *Death, dying, and human experience.* Columbus, OH: Charles E. Merrill.

Katz, B. L. (1991). The psychological impact of stranger versus nonstranger rape on victims' recovery. In A. Parrot & L. Bechhofer (Eds.), *Acquaintance rape: The hidden crime.* New York: Wiley.

Katz, I., Wackenhut, J., & Hass, G. (1986). Racial ambivalence, value duality, and behavior. In J. F. Dovidio & S. L. Gaertner (Eds.), *Prejudice, discrimination, and racism: Theory and research.* Orlando, FL: Academic Press.

Katz, L., & Epstein, S. (1991). Constructive thinking and coping with laboratory-induced stress. *Journal of Personality and Social Psychology, 61,* 789–800.

Katz, P. A., Boggiano, A., & Silvern, L. (1993). Theories of female personality. In F. L. Denmark & M. A. Paludi (Eds.), *Psychology of women: A handbook of issues and theories.* Westport, CT: Greenwood Press.

Kauffman, D. R., & Steiner, I. D. (1968). Conformity as an ingratiation technique. *Journal of Experimental Social Psychology, 4,* 404–414.

Kausler, D. H. (1985). Episodic memory: Memorizing performance. In N. Charness (Ed.), *Aging and human performance.* Chichester, England: Wiley.

Kavesh, L., & Lavin, C. (1988). *Tales from the front.* New York: Doubleday.

Kazdin, A. E. (1982). History of behavior modification. In A.S. Bellack, M. Hersen, & A.E. Kazdin (Eds.), *International handbook of behavior modification and behavior therapy.* New York: Plenum.

Kazdin, A. E. (1994). Methodology, design, and evaluation in psychotherapy research. In A. E. Bergin & S. L. Garfield (Eds.), *Handbook of psychotherapy and behavior change* (4th ed.). New York: Wiley.

Keating, D. P. (1990). Adolescent thinking. In S. S. Feldman & G. R. Elliott (Eds.), *At the threshold: The developing adolescent.* Cambridge, MA: Harvard University Press.

Keefe, S. E. (1984). Real and ideal extended familism among Mexican Americans and Anglo Americans: On the meaning of "close" family ties. *Human Organization, 43,* 65–70.

Keen, S. (1991). *Fire in the belly: On being a man.* New York: Bantam Books.

Keesey, R. E. (1986). A set-point theory of obesity. In K. D. Brownell & J. P. Foreyt (Eds.), *Handbook of eating disorders: Physiology, psychology, and treatment of obesity, anorexia, and bulimia.* New York: Basic Books.

Keesey, R. E. (1988). The body-weight set point. *Postgraduate Medicine, 83,* 114–127.

Keesey, R. E., & Powley, T. L. (1975). Hypothalamic regulation of body weight. *American Scientist, 63,* 558–565.

Keesey, R. E., & Powley, T. L. (1986). The regulation of body weight. *Annual Review of Psychology, 37,* 109–133.

Kegan, R. (1994). *In over our heads: The mental demands of modern life.* Cambridge, MA: Harvard University Press.

Keinan, G. (1987). Decision making under stress: Scanning of alternatives under controllable and uncontrollable threats. *Journal of Personality and Social Psychology, 52,* 639–644.

Keita, G. P., & Jones, J. M. (1990). Reducing adverse reaction to stress in the workplace. *American Psychologist, 45,* 1137–1141.

Keith, P. M. (1986). The social context and resources of the unmarried in old age. *International Journal of Aging and Human Development, 23,* 81–96.

Keith, S. J., Regier, D. A., & Rae, D. S. (1991). Schizophrenic disorders. In L. N. Robins & D. A. Regier (Eds.), *Psychiatric disorders in America: The epidemiologic catchment area study.* New York: Free Press.

Kelley, H. H. (1950). The warm-cold dimension in first impressions of persons. *Journal of Personality, 18,* 431–439.

Kelley, H. H. (1967). Attribution theory in social psychology. In D. Levine (Ed.), *Nebraska Symposium on Motivation* (Vol. 15). Lincoln: University of Nebraska Press.

Kelley, H. H., & Thibaut, J. W. (1978). *Interpersonal relations: A theory of interdependence.* New York: Wiley-Interscience.

Kelley, K., Byrne, D., Przybyla, D. P. J., Eberly, C., Eberly, B., Greendlinger, V., Wan, C. K., & Gorsky, J. (1985). Chronic self-destructiveness: Conceptualization, measurement and initial validation of the construct. *Motivation and Emotion, 9,* 135–151.

Kelsey, R. M. (1993). Habituation of cardiovascular reactivity to psychological stress: Evidence and implications. In J. Blascovich & E. S. Katkin (Eds.), *Cardiovascular reactivity to psychological stress and disease.* Washington, DC: American Psychological Association.

Kemeny, M. E., Weiner, H., Taylor, S. E., Schneider, S., Visscher, B., & Fahey, J. L. (1994). Repeated bereavement, depressed mood, and immune parameters in HIV seropositive and seronegative gay men. *Health Psychology, 13,* 14–24.

Kendler, K. S., Neale, M. C., Kessler, R. C., Heath, A. C., & Eaves, L. J. (1992). Generalized anxiety disorder in women: A population-based twin study. *Archives of General Psychiatry, 49,* 267–272.

Kennedy, J. L., & Laramore, D. (1993). *Joyce Lain Kennedy's career book* (2nd ed.). Lincolnwood, IL: VGM Career Horizons.

Kenny, D. A., & DePaulo, B. M. (1993). Do people know how others view them? An empirical and theoretical account. *Psychological Bulletin, 114,* 145–161.

Kenny, D. A., & La Voie, L. (1982). Reciprocity of interpersonal attraction: A confirmed hypothesis. *Social Psychology Quarterly, 45,* 54–58.

Kenny, D. A., & Nasby, W. (1981). Splitting the reciprocity correlation. *Journal of Personality and Social Psychology, 38,* 249–256.

Kenrick, D. T. (1987). Gender, genes, and the social environment. In P. C. Shaver & C. Hendrick (Eds.), *Review of Personality and Social Psychology* (Vol. 8). Newbury Park, CA: Sage Publications.

Kenrick, D. T., Groth, G. E., Trost, M. R., & Sadalla, E. K. (1993). Integrating evolutionary and social exchange perspectives on relationships: Effects of gender, self-appraisal, and involvement level on mate selection criteria. *Journal of Personality and Social Psychology, 64,* 951–969.

Kenrick, D. T., & Keefe, R. C. (1992). Age preferences in mates reflect sex differences in human reproductive strate-

gies. *Behavioral and Brain Sciences, 15,* 75–133.

Kessler, R. C., Foster, C., Joseph, J., Ostrow, D., Wortman, C., Phair, J., & Chmiel, J. (1991). Stressful life events and symptom onset in HIV infection. *American Journal of Psychiatry, 148,* 733–738.

Keyes, R. (1980). We, the lonely people. In J. Hartog, J. R. Audy, & Y. A. Cohen (Eds.), *The anatomy of loneliness.* New York: International Universities Press.

Keyes, R. (1991). *Timelock: How life got so hectic and what you can do about it.* New York: HarperCollins.

Kiecolt-Glaser, J. K., Garner, W., Speicher, C., Penn, G. M., Holliday, J., & Glaser, R. (1984). Psychosocial modifiers of immunocompetence in medical students. *Psychosomatic Medicine, 46,* 7–14.

Kiecolt-Glaser, J. K., Glaser, R., Williger, D., Stout, J., Messick, G., Sheppard, S., Ricker, D., Romisher, S. C., Briner, W., Bonnell, G., & Donnerberg, R. (1985). Psychosocial enhancement of immunocompetence in a geriatric population. *Health Psychology, 4,* 25–42.

Kiecolt-Glaser, J. K., Kennedy, S., Malkoff, S., Fisher, L., Speicher, C. E., & Glaser, R. (1988). Marital discord and immunity in males. *Psychosomatic Medicine, 50,* 213–229.

Kiesler, S. B., & Baral, R. L. (1970). The search for a romantic partner: The effects of self-esteem and physical attractiveness on romantic behavior. In K. J. Gergen & D. Marlowe (Eds.), *Personality and social behavior.* Reading, MA: Addison-Wesley.

Kihlstrom, J. F. (1990). The psychological unconscious. In L. A. Pervin (Ed.), *Handbook of personality: Theory and research.* New York: Guilford Press.

Kihlstrom, J. F., Glisky, M. L., & Angiulo, M. J. (1994). Dissociative tendencies and dissociative disorders. *Journal of Abnormal Psychology, 103,* 117–124.

Kihlstrom, J. F., Tataryn, D. J., & Hoyt, I. P. (1993). Dissociative disorders. In P. B. Sutker & H. E. Adams (Eds.), *Comprehensive handbook of psychopathology* (2nd ed.). New York: Plenum.

Kilmartin, C. T. (1994). *The masculine self.* New York: Macmillan.

Kimball, M. M. (1986). Television and sex-role attitudes. In T. M. Williams (Ed.), *The impact of television: A natural experiment in three communities.* Orlando, FL: Academic Press.

Kimball, M. M. (1989). A new perspective on women's math achievement. *Psychological Bulletin, 105,* 198–214.

Kimura, D. (1987). Are men's and women's brains really different? *Canadian Psychology, 28,* 133–147.

Kinard, E. M. (1982). Experiencing child abuse: Effects on emotional adjustment. *American Journal of Orthopsychiatry, 52,* 82–91.

King, G. R., & Ellinwood, E. H. (1992). Amphetamines and other stimulants. In J. H. Lowinson, P. Ruiz, & R. B. Millman (Eds.), *Substance abuse: A comprehensive textbook* (2nd ed.). Baltimore: Williams & Wilkins.

King, L. A., & Emmons, R. A. (1990). Conflict over emotional expression: Psychological and physical correlates. *Journal of Personality and Social Psychology, 58,* 864–877.

Kinney, J., & Leaton, G. (1987). *Loosening the grip: A handbook of alcohol information* (3rd ed.). St. Louis: Times Mirror/Mosby.

Kinsey, A. C., Pomeroy, W. B., & Martin, C. E. (1948). *Sexual behavior in the human male.* Philadelphia: Saunders.

Kinsey, A. C., Pomeroy, W. B., Martin, C. E., & Gebhard, P. H. (1953). *Sexual behavior in the human female.* Philadelphia: Saunders.

Kinsman, R. A., Dirks, J. F., & Jones, N. F. (1982). Psychomaintenance of chronic physical illness: Clinical assessment of personal styles affecting medical management. In T. Millon, C. Green, & R. Meagher (Eds.), *Handbook of clinical health psychology.* New York: Plenum.

Kirk, S. A., & Kutchins, H. (1992). *The selling of DSM: The rhetoric of science in psychiatry.* New York: Aldine de Gruyter.

Kirkcaldy, B. D., Cooper, C. L., Shephard, R. J., & Brown, J. S. (1994). Exercise, job satisfaction, and well-being among superintendent police officers. *European Review of Applied Psychology, 44,* 117–123.

Kirmayer, L. J., Robbins, J. M., & Paris, J. (1994). Somatoform disorders: Personality and the social matrix of somatic distress. *Journal of Abnormal Psychology, 103,* 125–136.

Kissebah, A. H., Freedman, D. S., & Peiris, A. N. (1989). Health risks of obesity. *Medical Clinics of North America, 73,* 111–138.

Kite, M. E. (1984). Sex differences in attitudes towards homosexuals: A meta-analytic review. *Journal of Homosexuality, 10,* 69–81.

Kitson, G. C. (1992). *Portrait of divorce: Adjustment to marital breakdown.* New York: Guilford Press.

Kitson, G. C., & Morgan, L. A. (1990). The multiple consequences of divorce: A decade review. *Journal of Marriage and the Family, 52,* 913–924.

Klassen, M. (1987). How to get the most out of your time. In A. D. Timpe (Ed.), *The management of time.* New York: Facts On File.

Klebanov, P. K., Brooks-Gunn, J., & Duncan, G. J. (1994). Does neighborhood and family poverty affect mothers' parenting, mental health, and social support? *Journal of Marriage and the Family, 56,* 441–455.

Kleber, H. D., & Gawin, F. H. (1986). Cocaine. In A. J. Frances & R. E. Hales (Eds.), *Psychiatric Update: Annual Review* (Vol. 5). Washington, DC: American Psychiatric Press.

Klein, D. N., & Rubovits, D. R. (1987). The reliability of subjects' reports of life events inventories: A longitudinal study. *Journal of Behavioral Medicine, 10,* 501–512.

Klein, M. (1948). *Contributions to psychoanalysis.* London: Hogarth.

Kleinginna, P. R., & Kleinginna, A. M. (1988). Current trends toward convergence of the behavioristic, functional, and cognitive perspectives in experimental psychology. *The Psychological Record, 38,* 369–392.

Kleinke, C. L. (1986). Gaze and eye contact: A research review. *Psychological Bulletin, 100,* 78–100.

Kleinke, C. L. (1991). *Coping with life challenges.* Pacific Grove, CA: Brooks/Cole.

Kleinke, C. L., & Staneski, R. A. (1980). First impressions of female bust size. *Journal of Social Psychology, 110,* 123–134.

Kleinmuntz, B. (1980). *Essentials of abnormal psychology.* San Francisco: Harper & Row.

Kleinmuntz, B., & Szucko, J. J. (1984). Lie detection in ancient and modern times: A call for contemporary scientific study. *American Psychologist, 39,* 766–776.

Klerman, G. L., Weissman, M. M., Markowitz, J. C., Glick, I., Wilner,

P. J., Mason, B., & Shear, M. K. (1994). Medication and psychotherapy. In A. E. Bergin & S. L. Garfield (Eds.), *Handbook of psychotherapy and behavior change* (4th ed.). New York: Wiley.

Knight, R. A., Rosenberg, R., & Schneider, B. (1985). Classification of sexual offenders: Perspectives, methods, and validation. In A. W. Burgess (Ed.), *Rape and sexual assault.* New York: Garland.

Knittle, J. L., Merritt, R. J., Dixon-Shanies, D., Ginsberg-Fellner, F., Timmers, K. I., & Katz, D. P. (1981). Childhood obesity. In R. M. Suskind (Ed.), *Textbook of pediatric nutrition.* New York: Raven Press.

Knoth, R., Boyd, K., & Singer, B. (1988). Empirical tests of sexual selection theory: Predictions of sex differences in onset, intensity, and time course of sexual arousal. *Journal of Sex Research, 24,* 73–89.

Knox, D., & Wilson, K. (1981). Dating behaviors of university students. *Family Relations, 30,* 255–258.

Knussman, R., Christiansen, K., & Couwenbergs, C. (1986). Relations between sex hormone levels and sexual behavior in men. *Archives of Sexual Behavior, 15,* 429–445.

Kobak, R. R., & Sceery, A. (1988). Attachment in late adolescence: Working models, affect regulation, and representations of self and others. *Child Development, 59,* 135–146.

Kobasa, S. C. (1979). Stressful life events, personality, and health: An inquiry into hardiness. *Journal of Personality and Social Psychology, 37,* 1–11.

Kobasa, S. C. (1984, September). How much stress can you survive? *American Health,* pp. 64–77.

Kogan, N. (1990). Personality and aging. In J. E. Birren & K. W. Schaie (Eds.), *Handbook of the psychology of aging.* San Diego: Academic Press.

Kohn, P. M., Lafreniere, K., & Gurevich, M. (1991). Hassles, health, and personality. *Journal of Personality and Social Psychology, 61,* 478–482.

Kohut, H. (1971). *Analysis of the self.* New York: International Universities Press.

Kollock, P., Blumstein, P., & Schwartz, P. (1985). Sex and power in interaction: Conversational privileges and duties. *American Sociological Review, 50,* 34–46.

Koob, G. F., & Bloom, F. E. (1988). Cellular and molecular mechanisms of drug dependence. *Science, 242,* 715–723.

Koopman, C., Classen, C., & Spiegel, D. (1994). Predictors of posttraumatic stress symptoms among survivors of the Oakland/Berkeley, Calif., firestorm. *American Journal of Psychiatry, 151,* 888–894.

Koranyi, E. K. (1989). Physiology of stress reviewed. In S. Cheren (Ed.), *Psychosomatic medicine: Theory, physiology, and practice* (Vol. 1). Madison, CT: International Universities Press.

Korchin, S. J. (1976). *Modern clinical psychology: Principles of intervention in the clinic and community.* New York: Basic Books.

Koren, P., Carlton, K., & Shaw, D. (1980). Marital conflict: Relations among behaviors, outcomes, and distress. *Journal of Consulting and Clinical Psychology, 48,* 460–468.

Koss, M. P. (1985). The hidden rape victim: Personality, attitudinal, and situational characteristics. *Psychology of Women Quarterly, 9,* 193–212.

Koss, M. P. (1993). Rape: Scope, impact, interventions, and public policy. *American Psychologist, 48,* 1062–1069.

Koss, M. P., Gidycz, C. A., & Wisniewski, N. (1987). The scope of rape: Inci-

dence and prevalence of sexual aggression and victimization in a national sample of higher education students. *Journal of Consulting and Clinical Psychology, 55,* 162–170.

Koss, M. P., Goodman, L. A., Browne, A., Fitzgerald, L. F., Keita, G. P., & Russo, N. F. (1994). *No safe haven: Male violence against women at home, at work, and in the community.* Washington, DC: American Psychological Association.

Koss, M. P., Leonard, K. E., Beezley, D. A., & Oros, C. (1985). Nonstranger sexual aggression: A discriminant analysis of the psychological characteristics of undetected offenders. *Sex Roles, 12,* 981–992.

Kotkin, M. (1985). To marry or live together? *Lifestyles: A Journal of Changing Patterns, 7,* 156–170.

Kowalski, R. M. (1993). Inferring sexual interest from behavioral cues: Effects of gender and sexually relevant attitudes. *Sex Roles, 29,* 13–36.

Kraemer, D. L., & Hastrup, J. L. (1988). Crying in adults: Self-control and autonomic correlates. *Journal of Social and Clinical Psychology, 6,* 53–68.

Kramer, H. (1994). *Liberating the adult within.* New York: Simon & Schuster.

Kramer, M. A., Aral, S. O., & Curran, J. W. (1980). Self-reported behavior pattern of patients attending a sexually transmitted disease clinic. *American Journal of Public Health, 70,* 997–1000.

Krilov, L. R. (1988, March). Sexually transmitted diseases in adolescents. *Medical Aspects of Human Sexuality,* pp. 67–77.

Kristiansen, C. M., & Giulietti, R. (1990). Perceptions of wife abuse: Effects of gender, attitudes toward women, and just-world beliefs among college students. *Psychology of Women Quarterly, 14,* 177–189.

Krueger, W. C. F. (1929). The effect of overlearning on retention. *Journal of Experimental Psychology, 12,* 71–78.

Kubey, R., & Csikszentmihalyi, M. (1990). *Leisure and the benefits of television.* Hillsdale, NJ: Erlbaum.

Kübler-Ross, E. (1969). *On death and dying.* New York: Macmillan.

Kübler-Ross, E. (1970). The dying patient's point of view. In O. G. Brim, Jr., H. E. Freeman, S. Levine, & N. A. Scotch (Eds.), *The dying patient.* New York: Russell Sage Foundation.

Kuehnle, J., Mendelson, J. H., Davis, K. R., & New, P. F. J. (1977). Computerized tomographic examination of heavy marijuana smokers. *Journal of the American Medical Association, 237,* 1231–1232.

Kulick, A. R., Pope, H. G., & Keck, P. E. (1990). Lycanthropy and self-identification. *Journal of Nervous and Mental Disease, 178,* 134–137.

Kunkel, S. R., & Applebaum, R. A. (1992). Estimating the prevalence of long-term disability for an aging society. *Journal of Gerontology, 47,* S253–260.

Kurdek, L. A. (1988). Perceived social support in gays and lesbians in cohabitating relationships. *Journal of Personality and Social Psychology, 54,* 504–509.

Kurdek, L. A. (1991). Sexuality in homosexual and heterosexual couples. In K. McKinney & S. Sprecher (Eds.), *Sexuality in close relationships.* Hillside, NJ: Erlbaum.

Kurdek, L. A. (1993). Nature and prediction of changes in marital quality for first-time parent and nonparent husbands and wives. *Journal of Family Psychology, 6,* 255–265.

Kurdek, L. A. (1994a). Areas of conflict for gay, lesbian, and heterosexual couples: What couples argue about influences relationship satisfaction. *Journal of Marriage and the Family, 56,* 923–934.

Kurdek, L. A. (1994b). Conflict resolution styles in gay, lesbian, heterosexual nonparent, and heterosexual parent couples. *Journal of Marriage and the Family, 56,* 705–722.

Kurdek, L. A. (1995). Predicting change in marital satisfaction from husbands' and wives' conflict resolution styles. *Journal of Marriage and the Family, 57,* 153–164.

Kurdek, L. A., & Schmitt, J. P. (1986a). Early development of relationship quality in heterosexual married, heterosexual cohabiting, gay, and lesbian couples. *Developmental Psychology, 22,* 305–309.

Kurdek, L. A., & Schmitt, J. P. (1986b). Interaction of sex role self-concept with relationship quality and relationship beliefs in married, heterosexual cohabiting, gay, and lesbian couples. *Journal of Personality and Social Psychology, 51,* 365–370.

Kurdek, L. A., & Schmitt, J. P. (1988). Relationship quality of gay men in closed or open relationships. In J. P. De Cecco (Ed.), *Gay relationships.* New York: Harrington Park Press.

LaCroix, A. Z., Mead, L. A., Liang, K. Y., Thomas, C. B., & Pearson, T. A. (1986). Coffee consumption and the incidence of coronary heart disease. *New England Journal of Medicine, 315,* 977–982.

Lader, M. H. (1984). Antianxiety drugs. In T. B. Karasu (Ed.), *The psychiatric therapies.* Washington, DC: American Psychiatric Association.

Lader, M. H. (1990). Benzodiazepine withdrawal. In R. Noyes, Jr., M. Roth, & G. D. Burrows (Eds.), *Handbook of anxiety: The treatment of anxiety* (Vol. 4). Amsterdam: Elsevier.

Lader, M. H., & Herrington, R. (1990). *Biological treatments in psychiatry.* New York: Oxford University Press.

LaFrance, M., & Mayo, C. (1976). Racial differences in gaze behavior during conversations: Two systemic observational studies. *Journal of Personality and Social Psychology, 33,* 547–552.

Lakein, A. (1973). *How to get control of your time and your life.* New York: Wyden.

Lakoff, R. (1973). Language and woman's place. *Language and Society, 2,* 45–79.

Lamb, M. E., Sternberg, K. J., & Prodromidis, M. (1992). Nonmaternal care and the security of infant-mother attachment: A reanalysis of the data. *Infant Behavior and Development, 15,* 71–83.

Lambert, M. J., & Bergin, A. E. (1992). Achievements and limitations of psychotherapy research. In D. K. Freedheim (Ed.), *History of psychotherapy: A century of change.* Washington, DC: American Psychological Association.

Lambert, M. J., & Bergin, A. E. (1994). The effectiveness of psychotherapy. In A. E. Bergin & S. L. Garfield (Eds.), *Handbook of psychotherapy and behavior change* (4th ed.). New York: Wiley.

Lambert, M. J., & Hill, C. E. (1994). Assessing psychotherapy outcomes and processes. In A. E. Bergin & S. L. Garfield (Eds.), *Handbook of psychotherapy and behavior change* (4th ed.). New York: Wiley.

Landau, E. (1988). *Teenagers talk about school.* Englewood Cliffs, NJ: Julian Messner.

Landerman, L. R., Burns, B. J., Swartz, M. S., Wagner, H. R., & George, L. K. (1994). The relationship between insurance coverage and psychiatric disorder in predicting use of mental health services. *American Journal of Psychiatry, 151,* 1785–1790.

Landrine, H. (1985). Race × class stereotypes of women. *Sex Roles, 13,* 65–75.

Landy, F. J. (1989). *Psychology of work behavior.* Pacific Grove, CA: Brooks/Cole.

Landy, F. J., Quick, J. C., & Kasl, S. (1994). Work, stress, and well being. *International Journal of Stress Management, 1,* 33–73.

Laner, M. R. (1988). Permanent partner priorities: Gay and straight. In J. P. De Cecco (Ed.), *Gay relationships.* New York: Harrington Park Press.

Langone, J. (1988). *AIDS: The facts.* Boston: Little, Brown.

Lareau, W. (1985). *Inside track: A successful job search strategy.* Piscataway, NJ: New Century.

Lareau, W. (1992). *The where am I now? Where am I going? career manual.* Clinton, NJ: New Win.

Larson, R., & Asmussen, L. (1991). Anger, worry, and hurt in early adolescence: An enlarging world of negative emotions. In M. E. Colten & S. Gore (Eds.), *Adolescent stress: Causes and consequences.* New York: Aldine de Gruyter.

Larson, R., & Ham, M. (1993). Stress and "storm and stress" in early adolescence: The relationship of negative events with dysphoric affect. *Developmental Psychology, 29,* 130–140.

Lassner, J. B., Matthews, K. A., & Stoney, C. M. (1994). Are cardiovascular reactors to asocial stress also reactors to social stress? *Journal of Personality and Social Psychology, 66,* 69–77.

Latané, B., & Darley, J. M. (1970). *The unresponsive bystander: Why doesn't he help?* New York: Appleton-Century-Crofts.

Latané, B., & Nida, S. A. (1981). Ten years of research on group size and helping. *Psychological Bulletin, 89,* 308–324.

Lau, S., & Gruen, G. E. (1992). The social stigma of loneliness: Effect of target person's and perceiver's sex. *Personality and Social Psychology Bulletin, 18,* 182–189.

Lauer, J., & Lauer, R. (1985, June). Marriages made to last. *Psychology Today,* pp. 22–26.

Laughlin, H. (1967). *The neuroses.* Washington, DC: Butterworth.

Laughlin, H. (1979). *The ego and its defenses.* New York: Aronson.

Laumann, E. O., Gagnon, J. H., Michael, R. T., & Michaels, S. (1994). *The social organization of sexuality: Sexual practices in the United States.* Chicago: University of Chicago Press.

Lavine, L. O., & Lombardo, J. P. (1984). Self-disclosure: Intimate and non-intimate disclosures to parents and best friends as a function of Bem sex-role category. *Sex Roles, 11,* 735–744.

Lavrakas, P. J. (1975). Female preferences for male physiques. *Journal of Research in Personality, 9,* 324–334.

Lazarus, A. A. (1976). *Multimodal behavior therapy.* New York: Springer.

Lazarus, A. A. (1987). The need for technical eclecticism: Science, breadth, depth, and specificity. In J. K. Zeig (Ed.), *The evolution of psychotherapy.* New York: Brunner/Mazel.

Lazarus, A. A. (1989). Multimodal therapy. In R. J. Corsini & D. Wedding (Eds.), *Current Psychotherapies.* Itasca, IL: Peacock.

Lazarus, R. S. (1991). *Emotion and adaptation.* New York: Oxford.

Lazarus, R. S. (1993). Why we should think of stress as a subset of emotion. In L. Goldberger & S. Breznitz (Eds.), *Handbook of stress: Theoretical and clinical aspects* (2nd ed.). New York: Free Press.

Lazarus, R. S., & Folkman, S. (1984). *Stress, appraisal and coping.* New York: Springer.

Leavitt, F. (1982). *Drugs and behavior.* New York: Wiley.

Leavy, R. L. (1983). Social support and psychological disorder: A review. *Journal of Community Psychology, 11,* 3–21.

LeBoeuf, M. (1980, February). Managing time means managing yourself. *Business Horizons,* pp. 41–46.

Lebov, M. (1980). *Practical tools and techniques for managing time.* Englewood Cliffs, NJ: Prentice-Hall.

Ledray, L. E. (1994). *Recovering from rape* (2nd ed.). New York: Henry Holt.

Lee, G. R. (1988). Marital satisfaction in later life: The effects of nonmarital roles. *Journal of Marriage and the Family, 50,* 775–783.

Lee, G. R., Seccombe, K., & Shehan, C. L. (1991). Marital status and personal happiness: An analysis of trend data. *Journal of Marriage and the Family, 53,* 839–844.

Lee, G. R., & Shehan, C. L. (1989). Retirement and marital satisfaction. *Journal of Gerontology, 44,* S226–230.

Leff, J., & Vaughn, C. (1985). *Expressed emotion in families.* New York: Guilford Press.

Lehmann, H. E., & Cancro, R. (1985). Schizophrenia: Clinical features. In H. I. Kaplan & B. J. Sadock (Eds.), *Comprehensive textbook of psychiatry/IV.* Baltimore: Williams & Wilkins.

Lehrer, P. M., & Woolfolk, R. L. (1984). Are stress reduction techniques interchangeable, or do they have specific effects? A review of the comparative empirical literature. In R. L. Woolfolk & P. M. Lehrer (Eds.), *Principles and practice of stress management.* New York: Guilford Press.

Lehrer, P. M., & Woolfolk, R. L. (1993). Specific effects of stress management techniques. In P. M. Lehrer & R. L. Woolfolk (Eds.), *Principles and practice of stress management* (2nd ed.). New York: Guilford Press.

Leigh, B. C. (1989). Reasons for having and avoiding sex: Gender, sexual orientation, and relationship to sexual behavior. *Journal of Sex Research, 26,* 199–209.

Leigh, G. K., Holman, T. B., & Burr, W. R. (1984). An empirical test of sequence in Murstein's SVR Theory of mate selection. *Family Relations, 33,* 225–231.

Leigh, G. K., Holman, T. B., & Burr, W. R. (1987). Some confusions and exclusions of the SVR theory of dyadic pairing: A response to Murstein. *Journal of Marriage and the Family, 49,* 933–937.

Leiker, M., & Hailey, B. J. (1988). A link between hostility and disease: Poor health habits. *Behavioral Medicine, 14,* 129–133.

Leo, J. (1987, January 12). Exploring the traits of twins. *Time,* p. 63.

Lepore, S. J. (1992). Social conflict, social support, and psychological distress: Evidence of cross-domain buffering effects. *Journal of Personality and Social Psychology, 63,* 857–867.

Leppin, A., & Schwarzer, R. (1990). Social support and physical health: An updated meta-analysis. In L. R. Schmidt, P. Schwenkmezger, J. Weinman, & S. Maes (Eds.), *Theoretical and applied aspects of health psychology.* London: Harwood.

Lerner, H. (1985). *The dance of anger: A woman's guide to changing the patterns of intimate relationships.* New York: Harper Perennial.

Lerner, H. (1989). *The dance of intimacy: A woman's guide to courageous acts of change in key relationships.* New York: Harper Perennial.

Lerner, M. J., & Miller, D. T. (1978). Just world research and the attribution process: Looking back and ahead. *Psychological Bulletin, 85,* 1030–1051.

Lesage, A. D., Boyer, R., Grunberg, F., Vanier, C., Morissette, R., Menard-Buteau, C., & Loyer, M. (1994). Suicide and mental disorders: A case-control study of young men. *American Journal of Psychiatry, 151,* 1063–1068.

LeShan, L. (1966). An emotional life-history pattern associated with neoplastic disease. *Annals of the New York Academy of Sciences, 125,* 780–793.

Lester, N., Nebel, L. E., & Baum, A. (1994). Psychophysiological and behavioral measurement of stress: Applications to mental health. In W. R. Avison & I. H. Gotlib (Eds.), *Stress and mental health: Contemporary issues and prospects for the future.* New York: Plenum.

Levay, A. N., Weissberg, J. H., & Woods, S. M. (1981). Intrapsychic factors in sexual dysfunctions. In H. I. Lief (Ed.), *Sexual problems in medical practice.* Chicago: American Medical Association.

LeVay, S. (1991). A difference in hypothalamic structure and homosexual men. *Science, 253,* 1034–1037.

Levenkron, S. (1982). *Treating and overcoming anorexia nervosa.* New York: Scribner's.

Levenson, H., Hirschfeld, M. L., Hirschfeld, A., & Dzubay, B. (1983). Recent life events and accidents: The role of sex differences. *Journal of Human Stress, 9,* 4–11.

Levering, R. (1988). *A great place to work.* New York: Random House.

Levi, L. (1990). Occupational stress: Spice of life or kiss of death? *American Psychologist, 45,* 1142–1145.

Levinger, G. (1970). Husbands' and wives' estimates of coital frequency. *Medical Aspects of Human Sexuality, 4,* 42–57.

Levinson, D. J., Darrow, C. M., Klein, E. G., Levinson, M. H., & McKee, B. (1978). *The seasons of a man's life.* New York: Knopf.

Levis, D. J. (1989). The case for a return to a two-factor theory of avoidance: The failure of non-fear interpretations. In S. B. Klein & R. R. Bowrer (Eds.), *Contemporary learning theories: Pavlovian conditioning and the status of traditional learning theory.* Hillsdale, NJ: Erlbaum.

Levy, M. B., & Davis, K. E. (1988). Love-styles and attachment styles compared: Their relations to each other and to various relationship characteristics. *Journal of Social and Personal Relationships, 5,* 439–471.

Levy, S. M. (1985). *Behavior and cancer.* San Francisco: Jossey-Bass.

Levy, S. M., Herberman, R. B., Simons, A., Whiteside, T., Lee, J., McDonald, R., & Beadle, M. (1989). Persistently low natural killer cell activity in normal adults: Immunological, hormonal and mood correlates. *Natural Immune Cell Growth Regulation, 8,* 173–186.

Lewin, K. (1935). *A dynamic theory of personality.* New York: McGraw-Hill.

Lewinsohn, P. M. (1974). A behavioral approach to depression. In R. J. Friedman & M. M. Katz (Eds.), *The psychology of depression: Contemporary theory and research.* New York: Halsted.

Lewinsohn, P. M., & Arconad, M. (1981). Behavioral treatment of depression: A social learning approach. In J. F. Clarkin & H. I. Glazer (Eds.), *Depression: Behavioral and directive intervention strategies.* New York: Garland STPM.

Lewinsohn, P. M., Duncan, E. M., Stanton, A. K., & Hautzinger, M. (1986). Age at first onset for nonbipolar depression. *Journal of Abnormal Psychology, 95,* 378–383.

Lewinsohn, P. M., Rohde, P., Seeley, J. R., & Fischer, S. A. (1993). Age-cohort changes in the lifetime occurrence of depression and other mental disorders. *Journal of Abnormal Psychology, 102,* 110–120.

Lewis, J. M. (1988). The transition to parenthood: II. Stability and change in marital structure. *Family Process, 27,* 273–283.

Lewis, R. J., & Janda, L. H. (1988). The relationship between adult sexual adjustment and childhood experiences regarding exposure to nudity, sleeping in the parental bed, and parental attitudes toward sexuality. *Archives of Sexual Behavior, 17,* 349–362.

Lewis-Fernandez, R., & Kleinman, A. (1994). Culture, personality, and psychology. *Journal of Abnormal Psychology, 103,* 67–71.

Lewontin, R. C., Rose, S., & Kamin, L. (1984). *Not in our genes: Biology, ideology and human nature.* New York: Pantheon.

Liberman, R. P., & Bedell, J.R. (1989). Behavior therapy. In H.I. Kaplan & B.J. Sadock (Eds.), *Comprehensive textbook of psychiatry/V.* Baltimore: Williams & Wilkins.

Liberman, R. P., Mueser, K. T., & DeRisi, W. J. (1989). *Social skills training for psychiatric patients.* New York: Pergamon.

Libman, H. (1992). Pathogenesis, natural history, and classification of HIV infection. *Primary Care, 19,* 1–17.

Lichtenstein, E. (1980). *Psychotherapy: Approaches and applications.* Pacific Grove, CA: Brooks/Cole.

Lichter, S. R., Lichter, L. S., Rothman, S., & Amundson, D. (1987, July-August). Prime-time prejudice: TV's images of blacks and Hispanics. *Public Opinion,* pp. 13–16.

Lickey, M. E., & Gordon, B. (1991). *Medicine and mental illness: The use of drugs in psychiatry.* New York: Freeman.

Liebert, R. M., & Spiegler, M. D. (1990). *Personality: Strategies and issues.* Pacific Grove, CA: Brooks/Cole.

Liebert, R. M., & Sprafkin, J. N. (1988). *The early window: Effects of television on children and youth.* New York: Pergamon.

Lightsey, O. R. (1994). "Thinking positive" as a stress buffer: The role of positive automatic cognitions in depression and happiness. *Journal of Counseling Psychology, 41,* 325–334.

Linden, W. (1993). The autogenic training method of J. H. Schultz. In P. M. Lehrer & R. L. Woolfolk (Eds.), *Principles and practice of stress management* (2nd ed.). New York: Guilford Press.

Lindgren, H. C. (1969). *The psychology of college success: A dynamic approach.* New York: Wiley.

Linn, M. C., & Petersen, A. C. (1986). A meta-analysis of gender differences in spatial ability: Implications for mathematics and science achievement. In J. S. Hyde & M. C. Linn (Eds.), *The psychology of gender: Advances through meta-analysis.* Baltimore: Johns Hopkins University Press.

Linville, P. W. (1985). Self-complexity and affective extremity: Don't put all of your eggs in one cognitive basket. *Social Cognition, 3,* 94–120.

Linville, P. W. (1987). Self-complexity as a cognitive buffer against stress-related illness and depression. *Journal of Personality and Social Psychology, 52,* 663–676.

Linville, P. W., & Fischer, G. W. (1991). Preferences for separating or combining events. *Journal of Personality and Social Psychology, 60,* 5–23.

Lipman, B. E. (1983). *The personal job search program: How to market yourself.* New York: Wiley.

Lippa, R. A. (1994). *Introduction to social psychology.* Pacific Grove, CA: Brooks/Cole.

Lipsey, M. W., & Wilson, D. B. (1993). The efficacy of psychological, educational, and behavioral treatment: Confirmation from meta-analysis. *American Psychologist, 48,* 1181–1209.

Litt, I. F., & Vaughan, V. C., III. (1992). Adolescence. In R. E. Behrman (Ed.), *Nelson textbook of pediatrics.* Philadelphia: Saunders.

Litwack, M., & Resnick, M. R. (1984). *The art of self-fulfillment.* New York: Simon & Schuster.

Lloyd, C., Alexander, A. A., Rice, D. G., & Greenfield, N. S. (1980). Life events as predictors of academic performance. *Journal of Human Stress, 6,* 15–26.

Lloyd, M. A. (1985). *Adolescence.* New York: HarperCollins.

Lobel, K. (1986). *Naming the violence.* Seattle: Seal Press.

Lock, R. D. (1988). *Taking charge of your career direction: Career planning guide, Book I.* Pacific Grove, CA: Brooks/Cole.

Locke, E. A. (1983). The nature and causes of job satisfaction. In M. D. Dunnette (Ed.), *Handbook of industrial and organizational psychology.* New York: Wiley.

Loftus, E. F. (1993). The reality of repressed memories. *American Psychologist, 48,* 518–537.

Loftus, E. F. (1994). The repressed memory controversy. *American Psychologist, 49,* 443–445.

London, K. A., & Wilson, B. F. (1988). Divorce. *American Demographics, 10,* 22–26.

London, M., Crandall, R., & Seals, G. W. (1977). The contribution of job and leisure satisfaction to the quality of life. *Journal of Applied Psychology, 62,* 328–334.

London, M., & Strumpf, S. A. (1986). Individual and organizational career development in changing times. In D. T. Hall & associates (Eds.), *Career development in organizations.* San Francisco: Jossey-Bass.

Long, E. C. J., & Andrews, D. W. (1990). Perspective taking as a predictor of marital adjustment. *Journal of Personality and Social Psychology, 59,* 126–131.

Longman, D. G., & Atkinson, R. H. (1991). *College learning and study skills.* St. Paul, MN: West.

Loomis, L. S., & Booth, A. (1995). Multigenerational caregiving and well-being: The myth of the beleaguered sandwich generation. *Journal of Family Issues, 16,* 131–148.

LoPiccolo, J., & Lobitz, C. (1972). The role of masturbation in the treatment of sexual dysfunction. *Archives of Sex Research, 2,* 163–171.

Lott, B. (1981). A feminist critique of androgyny: Toward the elimination of gender attributions for learned behavior. In C. Mayo & N. M. Henley (Eds.), *Gender and nonverbal behavior.* New York: Springer-Verlag.

Lott, B. (1987). *Women's lives: Themes and variations in gender learning.* Pacific Grove, CA: Brooks/Cole.

Loughead, T. A. (1991). Addictions as a process: Commonalities or codependence. *Contemporary Family Therapy: An International Journal, 13,* 455–470.

Lovdal, L. T. (1989). Sex role messages in television commercials: An update. *Sex Roles, 21,* 715–724.

Lowe, C. A., & Goldstein, J. W. (1970). Reciprocal liking and attributions of ability: Mediating effects of perceived intent and personal involvement. *Journal of Personality and Social Psychology, 16,* 291–297.

Lowinson, J. H., Ruiz, P., & Millman, R. B. (1992). *Substance abuse: A comprehensive textbook* (2nd ed.). Baltimore: Williams & Wilkins.

Lowry, D. T., & Towles, D. E. (1989). Soap opera portrayals of sex, contraception, and sexually transmitted diseases. *Journal of Communication, 39,* 76–83.

Lubkin, I. M. (1990). Illness roles. In I. M. Lubkin (Ed.), *Chronic Illness: Impact and interventions* (2nd ed.). Boston: Jones and Bartlett.

Luborsky, L., Singer, B., & Luborsky, L. (1975). Comparative studies of psychotherapies: Is it true that everyone has won and all must have prizes? *Archives of General Psychiatry, 32,* 995–1008.

Lumsdaine, A., & Janis, I. (1953). Resistance to counterpropaganda presentation. *Public Opinion Quarterly, 17,* 311–318.

Lye, D. N., & Biblarz, T. J. (1993). The effects of attitudes toward family life and gender roles on marital satisfaction. *Journal of Family Issues, 14,* 157–188.

Lykes, M. B. (1985). Gender and individualistic vs. collectivist bases for notions about the self. *Journal of Personality, 53,* 356–383.

Lykken, D. T. (1981). *A tremor in the blood: Uses and abuses of the lie detector.* New York: McGraw-Hill.

Lyman, B., Hatlelid, D., & Macurdy, C. (1981). Stimulus-person cues in first-impression attraction. *Perceptual and Motor Skills, 52,* 59–66.

Lyness, S. A. (1993). Predictors of differences between Type A and Type B individuals in heart rate and blood pressure reactivity. *Psychological Bulletin, 114,* 266–295.

Lynn, M., & Shurgot, B. A. (1984). Responses to lonely hearts advertisements: Effects of reported physical attractiveness, physique, and coloration. *Personality and Social Psychology Bulletin, 10,* 349–357.

Lynn, S. J., & Nash, M. (1994). Truth in memory: Ramifications for psychotherapy and hypnotherapy. *American Journal of Clinical Hypnosis, 36,* 194–208.

Lyon, D., & Greenberg, J. (1991). Evidence of codependency in women with an alcoholic parent: Helping out Mr. Wrong. *Journal of Personality and Social Psychology, 61,* 435–439.

Lytton, H., & Romney, D. M. (1991). Parents' differential socialization of boys and girls: A meta-analysis. *Psychological Bulletin, 109,* 267–296.

Maccoby, E. E. (1988). Gender as a social category. *Developmental Psychology, 24,* 755–765.

Maccoby, E. E. (1990). Gender and relationships: A developmental account. *American Psychologist, 45,* 513–520.

Maccoby, E. E., & Jacklin, C. N. (1974). *The psychology of sex differences.* Stanford, CA: Stanford University Press.

Maccoby, E. E., & Jacklin, C. N. (1987). Gender segregation in childhood. In E. H. Reese (Ed.), *Advances in child development.* New York: Academic Press.

Maccoby, E. E., & Martin, J. A. (1983). Socialization in the context of the family: Parent-child interaction. In P. H. Mussen (Series Ed.) & E. M. Hetherington (Vol. Ed.), *Handbook of child psychology: Vol. 4. Socialization, personality, and social development.* New York: Wiley.

MacEwen, K. E., & Barling, J. (1991). Effects of maternal employment experiences on children's behavior via mood, cognitive difficulties, and parenting behavior. *Journal of Marriage and the Family, 53,* 635–644.

Machlowitz, M. M. (1980). *Workaholics: Living with them, working with them.* Reading, MA: Addison-Wesley.

Machung, A. (1989). Talking career, thinking job: Gender differences in career and family expectations of Berkeley seniors. *Family Studies, 15,* 35–58.

Macke, A. S., Richardson, L. W., &

Cook, J. (1980). *Sex-typed teaching styles of university professors and student reactions.* Columbus, OH: Ohio State University Research Foundation.

Mackenzie, R. A. (1972). *The time trap.* New York: Amacom.

Mackie, D. M., Worth, L. T., & Asuncion, A. G. (1990). Processing of persuasive in-group messages. *Journal of Personality and Social Psychology, 58,* 812–822.

Macklin, E. D. (1983). Nonmarital heterosexual cohabitation: An overview. In E. D. Macklin & R. H. Rubin (Eds.), *Contemporary families and alternative lifestyles: Handbook on research and theory.* Newbury Park, CA: Sage Publications.

Macklin, E. D. (1987). Nontraditional family forms. In M. B. Sussman & S. K. Steinmetz (Eds.), *Handbook of marriage and the family.* New York: Plenum.

Maddi, S. R. (1989). *Personality theories: A comparative analysis.* Chicago, IL: Dorsey Press.

Maher, B. A., & Spitzer, M. (1993). Delusions. In P. B. Sutker & H. E. Adams (Eds.), *Comprehensive handbook of psychopathology* (2nd ed.). New York: Plenum.

Mahoney, M. J. (1979). *Self-change: Strategies for solving personal problems.* New York: Norton.

Main, M., & Solomon, J. (1990). Procedures for identifying infants as disorganized/disoriented during the Ainsworth Strange Situation. In M. T. Greenberg, D. Cicchetti, & E. M. Cummings (Eds.), *Attachment in the preschool years: Theory, research, and intervention.* Chicago: University of Chicago Press.

Maisto, S. A., Galizio, M., & Connors, G. J. (1995). *Drug use and abuse* (2nd ed.). Fort Worth, TX: Harcourt Press.

Major, B. (1981). Gender patterns in touching behavior. In C. Mayo & N. M. Henley (Eds.), *Gender and nonverbal behavior.* New York: Springer-Verlag.

Major, B., Schmidlin, A. M., & Williams, L. (1990). Gender patterns in social touch: The impact of setting and age. *Journal of Personality and Social Psychology, 58,* 634–643.

Malamuth, N. M. (1984). Violence against women: Cultural and individual cases. In N. M. Malamuth & E. Donnerstein, *Pornography and sexual aggression.* New York: Academic Press.

Malamuth, N. M., & Check, J. V. P. (1981). The effects of mass media exposure on acceptance of violence against women: A field experiment. *Journal of Research in Personality, 15,* 436–446.

Malamuth, N. M., & Donnerstein, E. (1982). The effects of aggressive-pornographic mass media stimuli. In L. Berkowitz (Ed.), *Advances in Experimental Social Psychology* (Vol. 15). New York: Academic Press.

Malatesta, V. J., & Adams, H. E. (1984). The sexual dysfunctions. In H. E. Adams & P. B. Sutker (Eds.), *Comprehensive handbook of psychopathology.* New York: Plenum.

Malina, R. M. (1990). Physical growth and performance during the transitional years (9–16). In G. R. Adams & T. P. Gullota (Eds.), *From childhood to adolescence: A transitional period?* Newbury Park, CA: Sage Publications.

Malinosky-Rummell, R., & Hansen, D. J. (1993). Long-term consequences of childhood physical abuse. *Psychological Bulletin, 114,* 68–79.

Maltz, D. N., & Borker, R. A. (1983). A cultural approach to male-female miscommunication. In J. A. Gumperz (Ed.), *Language and social identity.* New York: Cambridge University Press.

Mandler, G. (1993). Thought, memory, and learning: Effects of emotional stress.

In L. Goldberger & S. Breznitz (Eds.), *Handbook of stress: Theoretical and clinical aspects* (2nd ed.). New York: Free Press.

Mangelsdorf, S., Gunnar, M., Kestenbaum, R., Lang, S., & Andreas, D. (1990). Infant proneness-to-distress temperament, maternal personality, and mother-infant attachment: Associations and goodness of fit. *Child Development, 61,* 830–831.

Manuck, S. B., Kamarck, T. W., Kasprowicz, A. S., & Waldstein, S. R. (1993). Stability and patterning of behaviorally evoked cardiovascular reactivity. In J. Blascovich & E. S. Katkin (Eds.), *Cardiovascular reactivity to psychological stress and disease.* Washington, DC: American Psychological Association.

Marcia, J. E. (1976). Identity six years after: A follow-up study. *Journal of Youth and Adolescence, 5,* 145–160.

Marcia, J. E. (1980). Identity in adolescence. In J. Adelson (Ed.), *Handbook of adolescent psychology.* New York: Wiley.

Marcia, J. E. (1991). Identity and self-development. In R. M. Lerner, A. C. Petersen, & J. Brooks-Gunn (Eds.), *Encyclopedia of adolescence* (Vol. 1). New York: Garland.

Marecek, J., Finn, S. E., & Cardell, M. (1988). Gender roles in the relationships of lesbians and gay men. In J. P. De Cecco (Ed.), *Gay relationships.* New York: Harrington Park Press.

Marengo, J., Harrow, M., Sands, J., & Galloway, C. (1991). European versus U.S. data on the course of schizophrenia. *American Journal of Psychiatry, 148,* 606–611.

Margolin, G., & Wampold, B. E. (1981). A sequential analysis of conflict and accord in distressed and nondistressed marital partners. *Journal of Consulting and Clinical Psychology, 49,* 554–567.

Maricle, R., Leung, P., & Bloom, J. D. (1987). The use of DSM-III axis III in recording physical illness in psychiatric patients. *American Journal of Psychiatry, 144,* 1484–1486.

Marini, M. M. (1978). Sex differences in the determination of adolescent aspirations: A review of research. *Sex Roles, 4,* 723–753.

Markides, K. S., Coreil, J., & Rogers, L. P. (1989). Aging and health among southwestern Hispanics. In K. S. Markides (Ed.), *Aging and health.* Newbury Park, CA: Sage Publications.

Markides, K. S., & Krause, N. (1985). Intergenerational solidarity and psychological well-being among older Mexican Americans: A three generations study. *Journal of Gerontology, 40,* 390–392.

Marks, I. M. (1987). *Fears, phobias, and rituals: Panic, anxiety, and their disorders.* New York: Oxford University Press.

Markus, H., & Cross, S. (1990). The interpersonal self. In L. A. Pervin (Ed.), *Handbook of personality: Theory and research.* New York: Guilford Press.

Markus, H., & Kitayama, S. (1991). Culture and the self: Implications for cognition, emotion, and motivation. *Psychological Review, 98,* 224–253.

Markus, H., & Nurius, P. (1986). Possible selves. *American Psychologist, 41,* 954–969.

Markus, H., & Ruvolo, A. (1989). Possible selves: Personalized representations of goals. In L. A. Pervin (Ed.), *Goal concepts in personality and social psychology.* Hillsdale, NJ: Erlbaum.

Markus, H., & Wurf, E. (1987). The dynamic self-concept: A social psychological perspective. *Annual Review of Psychology, 38,* 299–337.

Marotz-Baden, R., & Cowan, D. (1987). Mothers-in-law and daughters-in-law:

The effects of proximity on conflict and stress. *Family Relations, 36,* 385–390.

Marsh, H. W., & Parker, J. W. (1984). Determinants of student self-concept: Is it better to be a relatively large fish in a small pond even if you don't learn to swim well? *Journal of Personality and Social Psychology, 47,* 213–231.

Marsh, P. (Ed). (1988). *Eye to eye: How people interact.* Topsfield, MA: Salem House.

Marshall, J., & Cooper, C. L. (1981). The causes of managerial stress: A research note on methods and initial findings. In E. N. Corlett & J. Richardson (Eds.), *Stress, work, design, and productivity.* Chichester, England: Wiley.

Marshall, V. W., & Levy, J. A. (1990). Aging and dying. In R. H. Binstock & L. K. George (Eds.), *Handbook of aging and the social sciences.* San Diego, CA: Academic Press.

Martin, C. L. (1987). A ratio measure of sex stereotyping. *Journal of Personality and Social Psychology, 52,* 489–499.

Martin, C. L., & Halverson, C. F., Jr. (1987). The role of cognition in sex role acquisition. In D. B. Carter (Ed.), *Current conceptions of sex roles and sex typing: Theory and research.* New York: Praeger.

Martin, R. A., & Lefcourt, H. M. (1983). Sense of humor as a moderator of the relation between stressors and moods. *Journal of Personality and Social Psychology, 45,* 1313–1324.

Martin, R. L., & Yutzy, S. H. (1994). Somatoform disorders. In R. E. Hales, S. C. Yudofsky, & J. A. Talbott (Eds.), *The American Psychiatric Press textbook of psychiatry* (2nd ed.). Washington, DC: American Psychiatric Press.

Martin, T. C., & Bumpass, L. L. (1989). Recent trends in marital disruption. *Demography, 26,* 37–51.

Maser, J. D., Kaelber, C., & Weise, R. E. (1991). International use and attitudes toward DSM-III and DSM-III-R: Growing consensus in psychiatric classification. *Journal of Abnormal Psychology, 100,* 271–279.

Maslach, C. (1982). Understanding burnout: Definitional issues in analyzing a complex phenomenon. In W. S. Paine (Ed.), *Job stress and burnout: Research, theory and intervention perspectives.* Newbury Park, CA: Sage Publications.

Maslow, A. (1968). *Toward a psychology of being.* New York: Van Nostrand.

Maslow, A. (1970). *Motivation and personality.* New York: Harper & Row.

Massion, A. O., Warshaw, M. G., & Keller, M. B. (1993). Quality of life and psychiatric morbidity in panic disorder and generalized anxiety disorder. *American Journal of Psychiatry, 150,* 600–607.

Mastekaasa, A. (1994). Psychological well-being and marital dissolution. *Journal of Family Issues, 15,* 208–228.

Masters, W. H., & Johnson, V. E. (1966). *Human sexual response.* Boston: Little, Brown.

Masters, W. H., & Johnson, V. E. (1970). *Human sexual inadequacy.* Boston: Little, Brown.

Masters, W. H., & Johnson, V. E. (1979). *Homosexuality in perspective.* Boston: Little, Brown.

Masters, W. H., & Johnson, V. E. (1980). *Human sexual inadequacy* (2nd ed.). New York: Bantam Books.

Masters, W. H., Johnson, V. E., & Kolodny, R. C. (1994). *Heterosexuality.* New York: HarperCollins.

Mathes, E. W., Brennan, S. M., Haugen, P. M., & Rice, H. B. (1985). Ratings of physical attractiveness as a function of age. *Journal of Social Psychology, 125,* 157–168.

Mathew, R., Wilson, W., Blazer, D., &

George, L. (1993). Psychiatric disorders in adult children of alcoholics: Data from the epidemiologic catchment area project. *American Journal of Psychiatry, 150,* 793–796.

Matsumoto, D. (1994). *People: Psychology from a cultural perspective.* Pacific Grove, CA: Brooks/Cole.

Matsumoto, D. (1996). *Culture and psychology.* Pacific Grove, CA: Brooks/Cole.

Matteson, M. T., & Ivancevich, J. M. (1987). *Controlling work stress: Effective human resource and management strategies.* San Francisco: Jossey-Bass.

Mattessich, P., & Hill, R. (1987). Life cycle and family development. In M. B. Sussman & S. K. Steinmetz (Eds.), *Handbook of marriage and the family.* New York: Plenum.

Matthews, K. A. (1992). Myths and realities of menopause. *Psychosomatic Medicine, 54,* 1–9.

Matthews, K. A., & Rodin, J. (1989). Women's changing work roles: Impact on health, family, and public policy. *American Psychologist, 44,* 1389–1393.

Matthews, K. A., Scheier, M. F., Brunson, B. I., & Carducci, B. (1989). Why do unpredictable events lead to reports of physical symptoms? In T. W. Miller (Ed.), *Stressful life events.* Madison, CT: International Universities Press.

Matthews, K. A., Woodall, K. L., & Stoney, C. M. (1990). Changes in and stability of cardiovascular responses to behavioral stress. *Child Development, 61,* 1134–1144.

Mattley, C., & Schwartz, M. D. (1990). Emerging from tyranny: Using the battered woman scale to compare the gender identities of battered and non-battered women. *Symbolic Interaction, 13,* 281–289.

Mayo, C., & Henley, N. (1981). *Gender and nonverbal behavior.* New York: Springer-Verlag.

McAdams, D. P. (1982). Intimacy motivation. In A. J. Stewart (Ed.), *Motivation and society.* San Francisco: Jossey-Bass.

McAdams, D. P., & Bryant, F. B. (1987). Intimacy motivation and subjective mental health in a nationwide sample. *Journal of Personality, 55,* 395–414.

McAdams, D. P., Healy, S., & Krause, S. (1984). Social motives and friendship patterns. *Journal of Personality and Social Psychology, 47,* 828–838.

McArthur, L. Z., & Berry, D. S. (1987). Cross-cultural agreement in perceptions of babyfaced adults. *Journal of Cross Cultural Psychology, 18,* 165–192.

McBride, P. E. (1992). The health consequences of smoking: Cardiovascular diseases. *Medical Clinics of North America, 76,* 333–353.

McCann, C. D., & Hancock, R. D. (1983). Self-monitoring in communicative interactions: Social cognitive consequences of goal-directed message modification. *Journal of Experimental Social Psychology, 19,* 109–121.

McCary, J. L. (1971). *Sexual myths and fallacies.* New York: Schocken Books.

McConaghy, N. (1993). *Sexual behavior: Problems and management.* New York: Plenum.

McConahay, J. B. (1986). Modern racism, ambivalence, and the modern racism scale. In J. F. Dovidio & S. L. Gaertner (Eds.), *Prejudice, discrimination, and racism: Theory and research.* Orlando FL: Academic Press.

McCrae, R. R. (1984). Situational determinants of coping responses: Loss, threat and challenge. *Journal of Personality and Social Psychology, 46,* 919–928.

McCrae, R. R., & Costa, P. T., Jr. (1984).

Emerging lives, enduring dispositions: Personality in adulthood. Boston: Little, Brown.

McCrae, R. R., & Costa, P. T., Jr. (1985). Updating Norman's "adequate taxonomy": Intelligence and personality dimensions in natural language and in questionnaires. *Journal of Personality and Social Psychology, 49,* 710–721.

McCrae, R. R., & Costa, P. T., Jr. (1987). Validation of the five-factor model of personality across instruments and observers. *Journal of Personality and Social Psychology, 52,* 81–90.

McCrae, R. R., & Costa, P. T., Jr. (1990). *Personality in adulthood.* New York: Guilford Press.

McCreary, D. R. (1994). The male role and avoiding femininity. *Sex Roles, 31,* 517–531.

McCroskey, J. C., & Beatty, M. J. (1986). Oral communication apprehension. In W. H. Jones, J. M. Cheek, & S. R. Briggs (Eds.), *Shyness: Perspectives on research and treatment.* New York: Plenum.

McDaniel, M. A., & Einstein, G. O. (1986). Bizarre imagery as an effective memory aid: The importance of distinctiveness. *Journal of Experimental Psychology: Learning, Memory & Cognition, 12,* 54–65.

McDougle, L. G. (1987). Time management: Making every minute count. In A. D. Timpe (Ed.), *The management of time.* New York: Facts On File.

McGinnies, E., & Ward, C. D. (1980). Better liked than right: Trustworthiness and expertise as factors in credibility. *Personality and Social Psychology Bulletin, 6,* 467–472.

McGlashan, T. H., & Fenton, W. S. (1992). The positive-negative distinction in schizophrenia: Review of natural history validators. *Archives of General Psychiatry, 49,* 63–72.

McGlashan, T. H., Mohr, D. C., Beutler, L. E., Engle, D., Shoham-Salomon, V., Bergan, J., Kaszniak, A. W., & Yost, E. B. (1990). Identification of patients at risk for nonresponse and negative outcome in psychotherapy. *Journal of Consulting and Clinical Psychology, 58,* 622–628.

McGoldrick, M., & Carter, E. A. (1989). The family life cycle—its stages and dislocations. In J. M. Henslin (Ed.), *Marriage and family in a changing society.* New York: Free Press.

McGowan, A. S. (1977). Vocational maturity and anxiety among vocationally undecided and indecisive students. *Journal of Vocational Behavior, 10,* 196–204.

McGrath, J. E. (1977). Settings, measures and themes: An integrative review of some research on social-psychological factors in stress. In A. Monat & R. S. Lazarus (Eds.), *Stress and coping: An anthology.* New York: Columbia University Press.

McGuigan, F. J. (1993). Progressive relaxation: Origins, principles, and clinical applications. In P. M. Lehrer & R. L. Woolfolk (Eds.), *Principles and practice of stress management* (2nd ed.). New York: Guilford Press.

McGuire, W. J. (1964). Inducing resistance to persuasion. In L. Berkowitz (Ed.), *Advances in Experimental Psychology* (Vol. 1). New York: Academic Press.

McHale, S. M., & Crouter, A. C. (1992). You can't always get what you want: Incongruence between sex-role attitudes and family work roles and its implications for marriage. *Journal of Marriage and the Family, 54,* 537–547.

McHale, S. M., Bartko, W. T., Crouter, A. C., & Perry-Jenkins, M. (1990). Children's housework and psychosocial functioning: The mediating effects of parents' sex-role behaviors and attitudes. *Child Development, 61,* 1413–1426.

McHugh, M. C., Frieze, I. H., & Browne, A. (1993). Research on battered women and their assailants. In F. L. Denmark & M. A. Paludi (Eds.), *Psychology of women: A handbook of issues and theories.* Westport, CT: Greenwood Press.

McKay, M., Davis, M., & Fanning, P. (1995). *Messages: The communication skills book.* Oakland, CA: New Harbinger.

McKay, M., & Fanning, P. (1992). *Self-esteem.* Oakland, CA: New Harbinger.

McKeon, J., Roa, B., & Mann, A. (1989). Life events and personality traits in obsessive-compulsive neurosis. In T. W. Miller (Ed.), *Stressful life events.* Madison, CT: International Universities Press.

McKillip, J., & Riedel, S. L. (1983). External validity of matching on physical attractiveness for same and opposite sex couples. *Journal of Applied Social Psychology, 13,* 328–337.

McKinlay, J. B., McKinlay, S. M., & Brambilla, D. (1987). The relative contributions of endocrine changes and social circumstances to depression in mid-aged women. *Journal of Health and Social Behavior, 28,* 345–363.

McLeod, J. D. (1995). Social and psychological bases of homogamy for common psychiatric disorders. *Journal of Marriage and the Family, 57,* 201–214.

McMillan, J. R., Clifton, A. K., McGrath, D., & Gale, W. S. (1977). Women's language: Uncertainty or interpersonal sensitivity and emotionality? *Sex Roles, 3,* 545–560.

McNally, R. J. (1987). Preparedness and phobias: A review. *Psychological Bulletin, 101,* 283–303.

McNally, R. J. (1990). Psychological approaches to panic disorder: A review. *Psychological Bulletin, 108,* 403–419.

Mead, M. (1950). *Sex and temperament in three primitive societies.* New York: Mentor Books.

Mednick, M. T., & Thomas, V. G. (1993). Women and the psychology of achievement: A view from the eighties. In F. L. Denmark & M. A. Paludi (Eds.), *Psychology of women: A handbook of issues and theories.* Westport, CT: Greenwood Press.

Meehan, P. J., Lamb, J. A., Saltzman, L. E., & O'Carroll, P. W. (1992). Attempted suicide among young adults: Progress toward a meaningful estimate of prevalence. *American Journal of Psychiatry, 149,* 41–44.

Mehrabian, A. (1971). *Silent messages.* Belmont, CA: Wadsworth.

Mehrabian, A. (1972). *Nonverbal communication.* Chicago: Aldine-Atherton.

Meichenbaum, D. (1993). Stress inoculation training: A 20-year update. In P. M. Lehrer & R. L. Woolfolk (Eds.), *Principles and practice of stress management* (2nd ed.). New York: Guilford Press.

Meilman, P. W. (1979). Cross-sectional age changes in ego identity status during adolescence. *Developmental Psychology, 15,* 230–232.

Melman, A., & Leiter, E. (1983). The urologic evaluation of impotence (male excitement phase disorder). In H. S. Kaplan (Ed.), *The evaluation of sexual disorders: Psychological and medical aspects.* New York: Brunner/Mazel.

Menaghan, E. G., & Parcel, T. L. (1990). Parental employment and family life: Research in the 1980s. *Journal of Marriage and the Family, 52,* 1079–1098.

Mendenhall, W. (1989). Co-dependency definitions and dynamics. *Alcoholism Treatment Quarterly, 6,* 3–17.

Mentzer, R. L. (1982). Response biases in multiple-choice test item files. *Educational and Psychological Measurement, 42,* 437–448.

Merckelbach, H., De Ruiter, C., Van Den Hout, M. A., & Hoekstra, R. (1989). Conditioning experiences and phobias. *Behavior Research and Therapy, 27,* 657–662.

Merton, R. (1948). The self-fulfilling prophecy. *Antioch Review, 8,* 193–210.

Meyerhoff, J. L., Oleshansky, M. A., & Mougey, M. S. (1988). Psychologic stress increases plasma levels of prolactin, cortisol, and POMC-derived peptides in man. *Psychosomatic Medicine, 50,* 295–303.

Michela, J. L., Peplau, L. A., & Weeks, D. G. (1982). Perceived dimensions of attributions for loneliness. *Journal of Personality and Social Psychology, 43,* 929–936.

Mikulincer, M., & Nachshon, O. (1991). Attachment styles and patterns of self-disclosure. *Journal of Personality and Social Psychology, 61,* 321–331.

Milgram, S. (1963). Behavioral study of obedience. *Journal of Abnormal and Social Psychology, 67,* 371–378.

Milgram, S. (1968). Reply to the critics. *International Journal of Psychiatry, 6,* 294–295.

Milgram, S. (1974). *Obedience to authority.* New York: Harper & Row.

Miller, A. G. (1986). *The obedience experiments: A case study of controversy in social science.* New York: Praeger.

Miller, B. C., & Sollie, D. L. (1986). Normal stresses during the transition to parenthood. In R. H. Moos (Ed.), *Coping with life crises: An integrated approach.* New York: Plenum.

Miller, D. T., & Ross, M. (1975). Self-serving biases in the attribution of causality: Fact or fiction? *Psychological Bulletin, 82,* 213–225.

Miller, G. P. (1978). *Life choices: How to make the critical decisions—about your education, career, marriage, family, life style.* New York: Thomas Y. Crowell.

Miller, J. G. (1984). Culture and the development of everyday social explanation. *Journal of Personality and Social Psychology, 46,* 961–978.

Miller, K. (1989). *Retraining the American workforce.* Reading, MA: Addison-Wesley.

Miller, K. I., & Monge, P. R. (1986). Participation, satisfaction, and productivity: A meta-analytic review. *Academy of Management Journal, 29,* 727–753.

Miller, L. C., Berg, J. H., & Archer, R. L. (1983). Openers: Individuals who elicit intimate self-disclosure. *Journal of Personality and Social Psychology, 44,* 1234–1244.

Miller, N. E. (1944). Experimental studies of conflict. In J. McV. Hunt (Ed.), *Personality and the behavior disorders* (Vol. 1). New York: Ronald.

Miller, N. E. (1959). Liberalization of basic S-R concepts: Extension to conflict behavior, motivation, and social learning. In S. Koch (Ed.), *Psychology: A study of a science.* (Vol. 2). New York: McGraw-Hill.

Miller, N. E. (1983). Behavioral medicine: Symbiosis between laboratory and clinic. *Annual Review of Psychology, 34,* 1–31.

Miller, P. Y., & Simon, W. (1974). Adolescent sexual behavior: Context and change. *Social Problems, 22,* 58–76.

Miller, P. Y., & Simon, W. (1980). The development of sexuality in adolescence. In J. Adelson (Ed.), *Handbook of adolescent psychology.* New York: Wiley.

Miller, R. S. (1991). On decorum in close relationships: Why aren't we polite to those we love? *Contemporary Social Psychology, 15,* 63–65.

Miller, T. Q., Turner, C. W., Tindale, R. S., Posavac, E. J., & Dugoni, B. L. (1991). Reasons for the trend toward null findings in research on Type A behavior. *Psychological Bulletin, 110,* 469–485.

Miller, T. W. (Ed.). (1989). *Stressful life events.* Madison, CT: International Universities Press.

Millett, K. (1970). *Sexual politics.* Garden City, NY: Doubleday.

Millstein, S. G., & Litt, I. F. (1990). At the threshold: The developing adolescent. In S. S. Feldman & G. R. Elliott (Eds.), *At the threshold: The developing adolescent.* Cambridge, MA: Harvard University Press.

Mischel, W. (1970). Sex-typing and socialization. In P. H. Mussen (Ed.), *Carmichael's manual of child psychology* (Vol. 2). New York: Wiley.

Mischel, W. (1973). Toward a cognitive social learning conceptualization of personality. *Psychological Review, 80,* 252–283.

Mischel, W. (1990). Personality dispositions revisited and revised: A view after three decades. In L. A. Pervin (Ed.), *Handbook of personality: Theory and research.* New York: Guilford Press.

Mischel, W., & Mischel, H. N. (1976). A cognitive social learning approach to morality and self-regulation. In T. Lickona (Ed.), *Moral development and behavior: Theory, research and social issues.* New York: Holt, Rinehart & Winston.

Mitchell, V. F. (1987). Rx for improving staff effectiveness. In A. D. Timpe (Ed.), *The management of time.* New York: Facts On File.

Modestin, J. (1992). Multiple personality disorder in Switzerland. *American Journal of Psychiatry, 149,* 88–92.

Moghaddam, F. M., Taylor, D. M., & Wright, S. C. (1993). *Social psychology in cross-cultural perspective.* New York: Freeman.

Money, J., & Ehrhardt, A. A. (1972). *Man and woman, boy and girl: Differentiation and dimorphism of gender identity.* Baltimore: Johns Hopkins University Press.

Monroe, S. M., & McQuaid, J. R. (1994). Measuring life stress and assessing its impact on mental health. In W. R. Avison & I. H. Gotlib (Eds.), *Stress and mental health: Contemporary issues and prospects for the future.* New York: Plenum.

Monroe, S. M., & Simons, A. D. (1991). Diathesis-stress theories in the context of life stress research: Implications for the depressive disorders. *Psychological Bulletin, 110,* 406–425.

Monteith, M. J. (1993). Self-regulation of prejudiced responses: Implications for progress in prejudice-reduction efforts. *Journal of Personality and Social Psychology, 65,* 469–485.

Montepare, J. M., & Zebrowitz-McArthur, L. (1987). Perceptions of adults with childlike voices in two cultures. *Journal of Experimental Social Psychology, 23,* 331–349.

Moore, D. S., & Erickson, P. I. (1985). Age, gender, and ethnic differences in sexual and contraceptive knowledge, attitudes, and behaviors. *Family and Community Health, 8*(3), 38–51.

Moore, D. W. (1993, April). Public polarized on gay issue. *The Gallup Poll Monthly,* pp. 30–34.

Moore, D. W. (1994, May). One in seven Americans victim of child abuse. *The Gallup Poll Monthly,* pp. 18–22.

Moore, D. W., & McAneny, L. (1993, May). Workers concerned they can't afford to retire. *The Gallup Poll Monthly,* pp. 16–25.

Moos, R. H., & Billings, A. G. (1982). Conceptualizing and measuring coping resources and processes. In L. Goldberger & S. Breznitz (Eds.), *Handbook of stress: Theoretical and clinical aspects.* New York: Free Press.

Moos, R. H., & Schaefer, J. A. (1993). Coping resources and processes: Current concepts and measures. In L. Goldberger & S. Breznitz (Eds.), *Handbook of stress: Theoretical and clinical aspects* (2nd ed.). New York: Free Press.

Morell, M. A., Twillman, R. K., & Sullaway, M. E. (1989). Would a Type A date another Type A? Influence of behavior type and personal attributes in the selection of dating partners. *Journal of Applied Social Psychology, 19*, 918–931.

Moretti, M. M., & Higgins, E. T. (1990). Relating self-discrepancy to self-esteem: The contribution of discrepancy beyond actual-self ratings. *Journal of Experimental Social Psychology, 26*, 108–123.

Morgan, E., & Farber, B. A. (1982). Toward a reformulation of the Eriksonian model of identity development. *Adolescence, 17*, 199–211.

Morgan, J. P. (1992). Controlled substance analogues: Current clinical and social issues. In J. H. Lowinson, P. Ruiz, & R. B. Millman (Eds.), *Substance abuse: A comprehensive textbook* (2nd ed.). Baltimore: Williams & Wilkins.

Morgan, M. (1982). Television and adolescents' sex role stereotypes: A longitudinal study. *Journal of Personality and Social Psychology, 43*, 947–955.

Morris, M. W., & Peng, K. (1994). Culture and cause: American and Chinese attributions for social and physical events. *Journal of Personality and Social Psychology, 67*, 949–971.

Morrison, A. M., & Von Glinow, M. A. (1990). Women and minorities in management. *American Psychologist, 45*, 200–208.

Morrow, L. (1993, March 29). The temping of America. *Time*, pp. 40–44, 46–47.

Morse, S., & Gergen, K. J. (1970). Social comparison, self-consistency, and the concept of self. *Journal of Personality and Social Psychology, 16*, 148–156.

Mosher, D. L. (1991). Macho men, machismo, and sexuality. *Annual Review of Sex Research, 2*, 199–248.

Moskowitz, H. (1985). Marijuana and driving. *Accident Analysis & Prevention, 17*, 323–345.

Mowrer, O. H. (1947). On the dual nature of learning: A reinterpretaton of "conditioning" and "problem-solving." *Harvard Educational Review, 17*, 102–150.

Mrazek, D. A. (1993). Asthma: Stress, allergies, and the genes. In D. Goleman & J. Gurin (Eds.), *Mind/body medicine: How to use your mind for better health*. Yonkers, NY: Consumer Reports Books.

Mrazek, P. B., & Mrazek, D. A. (1978). The effects of child sexual abuse. In R. S. Kempe & C. H. Kempe (Eds.), *Child abuse*. Cambridge, MA: Harvard University Press.

Muehlenhard, C. L. (1988). Misinterpreted dating behaviors and the risk of date rape. *Journal of Social and Clinical Psychology, 6*, 20–37.

Muehlenhard, C. L., & Hollabaugh, L. C. (1988). Do women sometimes say no when they mean yes? The prevalence and correlates of women's token resistance to sex. *Journal of Personality and Social Psychology, 54*, 872–879.

Muehlenhard, C. L., & Linton, M. A. (1987). Date rape and sexual aggression in dating situations: Incidence and risk factors. *Journal of Counseling Psychology, 34*, 186–196.

Muehlenhard, C. L., & McCoy, M. L. (1991). Double standard/double bind: The sexual double standard and women's communication about sex. *Psychology of Women Quarterly, 15*, 447–461.

Mukherjee, S., Sackeim, H. A., & Schnur, D. B. (1994). Electroconvulsive therapy of acute manic episodes: A review of 50 years' experience. *American Journal of Psychiatry, 151*, 169–176.

Muldoon, M. F., Manuck, S. B., & Matthews, K. A. (1990). Effects of cholesterol lowering on mortality: A quantitative review of primary prevention trials. *British Medical Journal, 301*, 309–314.

Mullen, B., & Baumeister, R. F. (1987). Group effects on self-attention and performance: Social loafing, social facilitation, and social impairment. In C. Hendrick (Ed.), *Group processes and intergroup relations* (Vol. 9). Newbury Park, CA: Sage Publications.

Mullen, B., & Felleman, B. (1990). Tripling in the dorms: A meta-analytic integration. *Basic and Applied Social Psychology, 11*, 33–44.

Mullis, R. L., Youngs, G. A., Mullis, A. K., & Rathge, R. (1993). Adolescent stress: Issues of measurement. *Adolescence, 28*, 267–279.

Multon, K. D., Brown, S. D., & Lent, R. W. (1991). Relation of self-efficacy beliefs to academic outcomes: A meta-analytic investigation. *Journal of Counseling Psychology, 38*, 30–38.

Munroe, R. L., & Munroe, R. H. (1975). *Cross-cultural human development*. Pacific Grove, CA: Brooks/Cole.

Murphy, J. M., & Helzer, J. E. (1986). Epidemiology of schizophrenia in adulthood. In G. L. Klerman, M. M. Weissman, P. S. Appelbaum, & L. H. Roth (Eds.), *Psychiatry: Vol. 5. Social, epidemiologic, and legal psychiatry*. New York: Basic Books.

Murphy, K., & Welch, F. (1989). Wage premiums for college graduates: Recent growth and possible explanations. *Educational Researcher, 18*, 17–26.

Murphy, S. P., Rose, D., Hudes, M., & Viteri, F. E. (1992). Demographic and economic factors associated with dietary quality for adults in the 1987–88 nationwide food consumption theory. *Journal of the American Diet Association, 92*, 1352–1357.

Murstein, B. I. (1976). *Who will marry whom? Theories and research in marital choice*. New York: Springer.

Murstein, B. I. (1986). *Paths to marriage*. Newbury Park, CA: Sage Publications.

Myers, D. G. (1980). *Inflated self: Human illusions and the biblical call to hope*. New York: Seabury Press.

Myers, D. G. (1992). *The pursuit of happiness: Who is happy—and why*. New York: Morrow.

Nahas, G. G. (1976). *Marijuana: Chemistry, biochemistry and cellular effects*. New York: Springer.

Nass, G. D., Libby, R. W., & Fisher, M. P. (1981). *Sexual choices: An introduction to human sexuality*. Monterey, CA: Brooks/Cole.

Natale, M., Entin, E., & Jaffe, J. (1979). Vocal interruptions in dyadic communication as a function of speech and social anxiety. *Journal of Personality and Social Psychology, 37*, 865–878.

National Center on Child Abuse and Neglect. (1988). *Study findings: Study of national incidence and prevalence of child abuse and neglect*. Washington, DC: U.S. Department of Health and Human Services.

National Committee on Pay Equity. (1987). *Pay equity: An issue of race, ethnicity, and sex*. Washington, DC: U.S. Government Printing Office.

National Institute for Occupational Safety and Health. (1988). *A proposed national strategy for the prevention of work-related psychological disorders*. Cincinnati, OH: Author.

Naughton, T. J. (1987). A conceptual view of workaholism and implications for career counseling and research. *The Career Development Quarterly, 35*, 180–187.

Naylor, T. H., Willimon, W. H., & Naylor, M. R. (1994). *The search for meaning*. Nashville: Abingdon Press.

Neimeyer, R. A., & Chapman, K. M. (1980–81). Self/ideal discrepancy and fear of death: The test of an existential hypothesis. *Omega, 11*, 233–239.

Neiss, R. (1988). Reconceptualizing arousal: Psychobiological states in motor performance. *Psychological Bulletin, 103*, 345–366.

Neiss, R. (1990). Ending arousal's reign of error: A reply to Anderson. *Psychological Bulletin, 107*, 101–105.

Nemiah, J. C. (1985). Somatoform disorders. In H. I. Kaplan & B. J. Sadock (Eds.), *Comprehensive textbook of psychiatry/IV*. Baltimore: Williams & Wilkins.

Ness, C., & Salter, S. (1993, December 26). Bitter debate over recovered memories. *San Francisco Examiner*, pp. A1, A12.

Neugebauer, R., Dohrenwend, B. P., & Dohrenwend, B. S. (1980). Formulation about hypotheses about the true prevalence of functional psychiatric disorders among adults in the United States. In B. P. Dohrenwend, B. S. Dohrenwend, M. S. Gould, B. Link, R. Neugebauer, & R. Wunsch-Hitzig (Eds.), *Mental illness in the United States: Epidemiological estimates*. New York: Praeger.

Nevid, J. S. (1984). Sex differences in factors of romantic attraction. *Sex Roles, 11*, 401–411.

Newcomb, M. D. (1983). Relationship qualities of those who live together. *Alternative Lifestyles, 6*, 78–102.

Newcomb, M. D. (1990). Social support and personal characteristics: A developmental and interactional perspective. *Journal of Social and Clinical Psychology, 9*, 54–68.

Newcomb, P. A., & Carbone, P. P. (1992). The health consequences of smoking: Cancer. *Medical Clinics of North America, 76*, 305–331.

Newcomb, T. M. (1961). *The acquaintance process*. New York: Holt, Rinehart & Winston.

Newman, M., & Berkowitz, B. (1976). *How to be awake and alive*. Westminster, MD: Ballantine.

Newsom, C., Favell, J. E., & Rincover, A. (1983). Side effects of punishment. In S. Axelrod & J. Apsche (Eds.), *The effects of punishment on human behavior*. New York: Academic Press.

Newtson, D. (1974). Dispositional inference from effects of actions: Effects chosen and effects forgone. *Journal of Experimental Social Psychology, 10*, 487–496.

Nezu, A. M. (1986). Efficacy of a social-problem therapy approach for unipolar depression. *Journal of Consulting and Clinical Psychology, 54*, 196–202.

Nezu, A. M., Nezu, C. M., Blissett, S. E. (1988). Sense of humor as a moderator of the relation between stressful events and psychological distress: A prospective analysis. *Journal of Personality and Social Psychology, 54*, 520–525.

NIAAA. (1991). *Alcohol alert 11: Estimating the economic cost of alcohol abuse*. Rockville, MD: Author.

Nichols, M. (1990). Lesbian relationships: Implications for the study of sexuality and gender. In D. P. McWhirter, S. A. Sanders, & J. M. Reinisch (Eds.), *Homosexuality/heterosexuality: Concepts of sexual orientation*. New York: Oxford University Press.

Nicholson, I. R., & Neufeld, R. W. J. (1993). Classification of the schizophrenias according to symptomatology: A two-factor model. *Journal of Abnormal Psychology, 102,* 259–270.

Nicol, S. E., & Gottesman, I. I. (1983). Clues to the genetics and neurobiology of schizophrenia. *American Scientist, 71,* 398–404.

Nielsen, J. M. (1990). *Sex and gender in society: Perspective on stratification* (2nd ed.). Prospect Heights, IL: Waveland.

Niemann, Y. F., Jennings, L., Rozelle, R. M., Baxter, J. C., & Sullivan, E. (1994). Use of free responses and cluster analysis to determine stereotypes of eight groups. *Personality and Social Psychology Bulletin, 20,* 379–390.

Nisbett, R. E. (1972). Hunger, obesity, and the ventromedial hypothalamus. *Psychological Review, 79,* 433–453.

Noddings, N. (1992). Gender and the curriculum. In P. W. Jackson (Ed.), *Handbook of research on curriculum.* New York: Macmillan.

Noel, J. G., Wann, D. L., & Branscombe, N. R. (1995). Peripheral ingroup membership status and public negativity toward outgroups. *Journal of Personality and Social Psychology, 68,* 127–137.

Nolen-Hoeksema, S. (1991). Responses to depression and their effects on the duration of depressive episodes. *Journal of Abnormal Psychology, 100,* 569–582.

Nolen-Hoeksema, S., & Girgus, J. S. (1994). The emergence of gender differences in depression during adolescence. *Psychological Bulletin, 115,* 424–443.

Nolen-Hoeksema, S., & Morrow, J. (1991). A prospective study of depression and posttraumatic stress symptoms after a natural disaster: The 1989 Loma Prieta earthquake. *Journal of Personality and Social Psychology, 61,* 115–121.

Nolen-Hoeksema, S., Morrow, J., & Fredrickson, B. L. (1993). Response styles and the duration of episodes of depressed mood. *Journal of Abnormal Psychology, 102,* 20–28.

Noller, P. (1982). Channel consistency and inconsistency in the communications of married couples. *Journal of Personality and Social Psychology, 43,* 732–741.

Noller, P. (1985). Negative communications in marriage. *Journal of Social and Personal Relationships, 2,* 289–301.

Noller, P. (1987). Nonverbal communication in marriage. In D. Perlman & S. Duck (Eds.), *Intimate relationships: Development, dynamics, and deterioration.* Newbury Park, CA: Sage Publications.

Noller, P., & Fitzpatrick, M. A. (1990). Marital communication in the eighties. *Journal of Marriage and the Family, 52,* 832–843.

Noller, P., & Gallois, C. (1988). Understanding and misunderstanding in marriage: Sex and marital adjustment differences in structured and free interaction. In P. Noller & M. A. Fitzpatrick (Eds.), *Perspectives on marital interaction.* Clevedon, England: Multilingual Matters.

Norcross, J. C., & Goldfried, M. R. (Eds.). (1992). *Handbook of psychotherapy integration.* New York: Basic Books.

Norcross, J. C., & Prochaska, J. O. (1982). National survey of clinical psychologists: Affiliations and orientations. *Clinical Psychologist, 35,* 1, 4–6.

Norman, T. R., & Burrows, G. D. (1990). Buspirone for the treatment of generalized anxiety disorder. In R. Noyes, Jr., M. Roth, & G. D. Burrows (Eds.), *Handbook of anxiety: The treatment of anxiety* (Vol. 4). Amsterdam: Elsevier.

Novello, A., Rosenberg, M., Saltzman, L., & Shosky, J. (1992). From the Surgeon General, U.S. Public Health Service. *The Journal of the American Medical Association, 267,* 3132.

Noyes, R. Jr. (1988). Revision of the DSM-III classification of anxiety disorders. In R. Noyes, Jr., M. Roth, & G. D. Burrows (Eds.), *Handbook of anxiety: Classification, etiological factors and associated disturbances* (Vol. 2). Amsterdam: Elsevier.

Nurnberger, J. I., & Gershon, E. S. (1982). Genetics. In E. S. Paykel (Ed.), *Handbook of affective disorders.* New York: Guilford Press.

Nurnberger, J. I., & Gershon, E. S. (1992). Genetics. In E. S. Paykel (Ed.), *Handbook of affective disorders* (2nd ed.). New York: Guilford Press.

Nurnberger, J. I., & Zimmerman, J. (1970). Applied analysis of human behavior: An alternative to conventional motivational inferences and unconscious determination in therapeutic programming. *Behavior Therapy, 1,* 59–69.

Nye, R. D. (1992). *Three psychologies: Perspectives from Freud, Skinner, and Rogers.* Pacific Grove, CA: Brooks/Cole.

O'Brien, C. P., & Woody, G. E. (1986). Sedative-hypnotics and antianxiety agents. In A. J. Frances & R. E. Hales (Eds.), *Psychiatric Update: Annual Review* (Vol. 5). Washington, DC: American Psychiatric Press.

O'Brien, P. E., & Gaborit, M. (1992). Codependency: A disorder separate from chemical dependency. *Journal of Clinical Psychology, 48,* 129–136.

Offer, D., Ostrov, E., Howard, K. I., & Atkinson, R. (1988). *The teenage world: Adolescents' self-image in ten countries.* New York: Plenum.

Offermann, L. R., & Gowing, M. K. (1990). Organizations of the future: Changes and challenges. *American Psychologist, 45,* 95–108.

Ohman, A., & Soares, J. J. F. (1993). On the automatic nature of phobic fear: Conditioned electrodermal responses to masked fear-relevant stimuli. *Journal of Abnormal Psychology, 102,* 121–132.

O'Keefe, D. J. (1990). *Persuasion: Theory and research.* Newbury Park, CA: Sage Publications.

Okun, L. (1985). *Woman abuse.* Albany, NY: SUNY Press.

O'Leary, V. E. (1977). *Toward understanding women.* Pacific Grove, CA: Brooks/Cole.

Olfson, M., & Pincus, H. A. (1994). Outpatient psychotherapy in the United States, I: Volume, costs, and user characteristics. *American Journal of Psychiatry, 151,* 1281–1288.

Olio, K. (1994). Truth in memory. *American Psychologist, 49,* 442–443.

Oliver, M. B., & Hyde, J. S. (1993). Gender differences in sexuality: A meta-analysis. *Psychological Bulletin, 114,* 29–51.

Olmstead, R. E., Guy, S. M., O'Malley, P. M., & Bentley, P. M. (1991). Longitudinal assessment of the relationship between self-esteem, fatalism, loneliness and substance use. *Journal of Social Behavior and Personality, 6,* 749–770.

O'Neil, R., & Greenberger, E. (1994). Patterns of commitment to work and parenting: Implications for role strain. *Journal of Marriage and the Family, 56,* 101–118.

Oppenheimer, V. K. (1988). A theory of marriage timing. *American Journal of Sociology, 94,* 563–591.

Orenstein, P. (1994). *School girls: Young women, self-esteem, and the confidence gap.* New York: Doubleday.

Organista, P. B., & Miranda, J. (1991). Psychosomatic symptoms in medical outpatients: An investigation of self-handicapping theory. *Health Psychology, 10,* 427–431.

Orleans, C. T., Rimer, B. K., Cristinzio, S., Keintz, M. K., & Fleisher, L. (1991). A national survey of older smokers: Treatment needs of a growing population. *Health Psychology, 10,* 343–351.

Orlofsky, J. L., Marcia, J. E., & Lesser, I. M. (1973). Ego identity status and the intimacy versus isolation crisis of young adulthood. *Journal of Personality and Social Psychology, 27,* 211–219.

Orme-Johnson, D. W. (1987). Transcendental Meditation and reduced health care utilization. *Psychosomatic Medicine, 49,* 493–507.

Orne, M. T., & Holland, C. C. (1968). On the ecological validity of laboratory deceptions. *International Journal of Psychiatry, 6,* 282–293.

Osipow, S. H. (1987). Counseling psychology: Theory, research, and practice in career counseling. *Annual Review of Psychology, 38,* 257–278.

Oster, G., Huse, D. M., Delea, T. E., & Colditz, G. A. (1986). Cost-effectiveness of nicotine gum as an adjunct to physician's advice against cigarette smoking. *Journal of the American Medical Association, 256,* 1315–1318.

Otto, L. B. (1988). America's youth: A changing profile. *Family Relations, 37,* 385–391.

Ouellette, S. C. (1993). Inquiries into hardiness. In L. Goldberger & S. Breznitz (Eds.), *Handbook of stress: Theoretical and clinical aspects* (2nd ed.). New York: Free Press.

Ozer, D. J., & Reise, S. P. (1994). Personality assessment. *Annual Review of Psychology, 45,* 357–388.

Ozer, E. M., & Bandura, A. (1990). Mechanisms governing empowerment effects: A self-efficacy analysis. *Journal of Personality and Social Psychology, 58,* 472–486.

Packard, V. (1972). *A nation of strangers.* New York: David McKay.

Paffenbarger, R. S., Hyde, R. T., & Wing, A. L. (1990). Physical activity and physical fitness as determinants of health and longevity. In C. Bouchard, R. J. Shephard, T. Stephens, J. R. Sutton, & B. D. McPherson (Eds.), *Exercise, fitness, and health: A consensus of current knowledge.* Champaign, IL: Human Kinetics Books.

Pagel, M. D., Erdly, W. W., & Becker, J. (1987). Social networks: We get by with (and in spite of) a little help from our friends. *Journal of Personality and Social Psychology, 53,* 793–804.

Pagel, M. D., Smilkstein, G., Regen, H., & Montano, D. (1990). Psychosocial influences on new-born outcomes: A controlled prospective study. *Social Science Medicine, 30,* 597–604.

Paivio, A. (1986). *Mental representations: A dual coding approach.* New York: Oxford University Press.

Palkovitz, R. J., & Lore, R. K. (1980). Note taking and note review: Why students fail questions based on lecture material. *Teaching of Psychology, 7,* 159–161.

Pallak, S. R. (1983). Salience of a communicator's physical attractiveness and persuasion: A heuristic versus systematic processing interpretation. *Social Cognition, 2,* 158–170.

Papalia, D. E., & Olds, C. W. (1994). *Human Development* (6th ed.). New York: McGraw-Hill.

Pardeck, J. T. (1991). Using books in clinical practice. *Psychotherapy in Private Practice, 9,* 105–119.

Park, C. C., & Shapiro, L. N. (1979). *You are not alone: Understanding and dealing with mental illness.* Boston: Little, Brown.

Park, C. L., Cohen, L. H., & Murch, R. L. (1994). *Assessment and prediction of stress-related growth.* Paper presented at the meeting of the American Psychological Association, Los Angeles, CA.

Park, C. W., & Young, S. M. (1986). Consumer response to television commercials: The impact of involvement and background music on brand attitude formation. *Journal of Marketing Research, 23,* 11–24.

Parker, G., & Hadzi-Pavlovic, D. (1990). Expressed emotion as a predictor of schizophrenic relapse: An analysis of aggregated data. *Psychological Medicine, 20,* 961–965.

Parlee, M. B. (1992). On PMS and psychiatric abnormality. *Feminism and Psychology, 2,* 105–108.

Parlee, M. B., & the editors of *Psychology Today.* (1979, September). The friendship bond: PT's survey report on friendship in America. *Psychology Today,* pp. 43–54, 113.

Parrott, W. G., & Smith, R. H. (1993). Distinguishing the experiences of envy and jealousy. *Journal of Personality and Social Psychology, 64,* 906–920.

Parsons, T. (1979). Definitions of health and illness in light of the American values and social structure. In E. G. Jaco (Ed.), *Patients, physicians and illness: A sourcebook in behavioral science and health.* New York: Free Press.

Pasley, K., Ihinger-Tallman, M., & Lofquist, A. (1994). Remarriage and stepfamilies: Making progress in understanding. In K. Pasley & M. Ihinger-Tallman (Eds.), *Stepparenting: Issues in theory, research, and practice.* Westport, CT: Greenwood Press.

Patai, D. (1991, October 30). Minority status and the stigma of "surplus visibility." *The Chronicle of Higher Education,* p. A52.

Patterson, M. L. (1988). Functions of nonverbal behavior in close relationships. In S. Duck (Ed.), *Handbook of personal relationships: Theory, research, and interventions.* New York: Wiley.

Paul, S. M., Crawley, J. N., & Skolnick, P. (1986). The neurobiology of anxiety: The role of the GABA/benzodiazepine receptor complex. In P. A. Berger & H. K. H. Brodie (Eds.), *American hand-book of psychiatry: Biological psychiatry* (Vol. 8) (2nd ed.). New York: Basic Books.

Paulhus, D. L. (1989). Socially desirable responding: Some new solutions to old problems. In D. M. Buss & N. Cantor (Eds.), *Personality psychology: Recent trends and emerging directions.* New York: Springer-Verlag.

Paulhus, D. L. (1991). Measurement and control of response bias. In J. P. Robinson, P. Shaver, & L. S. Wrightsman (Eds.), *Measures of personality and social psychological attitudes.* San Diego: Academic Press.

Pauls, D. L., Alsobrook, J. P., II, Goodman, W., Rasmussen, S., & Leckman, J. F. (1995). A family study of obsessive-compulsive disorder. *American Journal of Psychiatry, 152,* 76–84.

Pavlov, I. P. (1906). The scientific investigation of psychical faculties or processes in the higher animals. *Science, 24,* 613–619.

Paykel, E. S. (1974). Life stress and psychiatric disorder. In B. S. Dohrenwend & B. P. Dohrenwend (Eds.), *Stressful life events: Their nature and effects.* New York: Wiley.

Paykel, E. S., & Cooper, Z. (1992). Life events and social stress. In E. S. Paykel (Ed.), *Handbook of affective disorders* (2nd ed.). New York: Guilford Press.

Pearce, L. (1974). Duck! It's the new journalism. *New Times, 2,* 40–41.

Pekarik, G. (1993). Beyond effectiveness: Uses of consumer-oriented criteria in defining treatment success. In T. R. Giles (Ed.), *Handbook of effective psychotherapy.* New York: Plenum.

Pennebaker, J. W. (1982). *The psychology of physical symptoms.* New York: Springer-Verlag.

Pennebaker, J. W. (1990). *Opening up: The healing power of confiding in others.* New York: Morrow.

Pennebaker, J. W., Colder, M., & Sharp, L. K. (1990). Accelerating the coping process. *Journal of Personality and Social Psychology, 58,* 528–537.

Pennebaker, J. W., Kiecolt-Glaser, J. K., & Glaser, R. (1988). Disclosure of traumas and immune function: Health implications for psychotherapy. *Journal of Consulting and Clinical Psychology, 56,* 239–245.

Pennebaker, J. W., & O'Heeron, R. C. (1984). Confiding in others and illness rate among spouses of suicide and accidental death victims. *Journal of Abnormal Psychology, 93,* 473–476.

Pennebaker, J. W., & Susman, J. R. (1988). Disclosure of traumas and psychosomatic processes. *Social Science and Medicine, 26,* 327–332.

Peplau, L. A. (1981, March). What homosexuals want. *Psychology Today,* pp. 28–38.

Peplau, L. A. (1988). Research on homosexual couples: An overview. In J. P. De Cecco (Ed.), *Gay relationships.* New York: Harrington Park Press.

Peplau, L. A. (1991). Lesbian and gay relationships. In J. C. Gonsiorek & J. D. Weinrich (Eds.), *Homosexuality: Research implications for public policy.* Newbury Park, CA: Sage Publications.

Peplau, L. A., Bikson, T. K., Rook, K. S., & Goodchilds, J. D. (1982). Being old and living alone. In L. A. Peplau & D. Perlman (Eds.), *Loneliness: A sourcebook of current theory, research, and therapy.* New York: Wiley-Interscience.

Peplau, L. A., & Cochran, S. D. (1990). A relational perspective on homosexuality. In D. P. McWhirter, S. A. Sanders, & J. M. Reinisch (Eds.), *Homosexuality/heterosexuality: Concepts of sexual orientation.* New York: Oxford University Press.

Peplau, L. A., & Gordon, S. L. (1983). The intimate relationships of lesbians and gay men. In E. R. Allgeier & N. B. McCormick (Eds.), *The changing boundaries: Gender roles and sexual behavior.* Palo Alto, CA: Mayfield.

Peplau, L. A., Hill, C. T., & Rubin, Z. (1993). Sex role attitudes in dating and marriage: A 15-year follow-up of the Boston couples study. *Journal of Social Issues, 49,* 31–52.

Peplau, L. A., Rubin, Z., & Hill, C. T. (1977). Sexual intimacy in dating relationships. *Journal of Social Issues, 33,* 86–109.

Perloff, R. M. (1993). *The dynamics of persuasion.* Hillsdale, NJ: Erlbaum.

Perls, F. S. (1969). *Gestalt therapy verbatim.* Lafayette, CA: Real People Press.

Perris, C. (1992). Bipolar-unipolar distinction. In E. S. Paykel (Ed.), *Handbook of affective disorders.* New York: Guilford Press.

Perry, D. G., & Bussey, K. (1979). The social learning theory of sex differences: Imitation is alive and well. *Journal of Personality and Social Psychology, 37,* 1699–1712.

Perry, P. J., Miller, D. D., Arndt, S. V., & Cadoret, R. J. (1991). Clozapine and norclozapine plasma concentrations and clinical response of treatment-refractory schizophrenic patients. *American Journal of Psychiatry, 148,* 231–235.

Perry, W., & Braff, D. L. (1994). Information-processing deficits and thought disorder in schizophrenia. *American Journal of Psychiatry, 151,* 363–367.

Persons, J. B. (1991). Psychotherapy outcome studies do not accurately represent current models of psychotherapy: A proposed remedy. *American Psychologist, 46,* 99–106.

Pervin, L. A. (1994). Personality stability, personality change, and the question of process. In T. F. Heatherton & J. L. Weinberger (Eds.), *Can personality change?* Washington, DC: American Psychological Association.

Peterman, T. A., & Curran, J. W. (1986). Sexual transmission of human immunodeficiency virus. *Journal of the American Medical Association, 256,* 2222–2226.

Petersen, A. C. (1987, September). Those gangly years. *Psychology Today,* pp. 28–34.

Petersen, A. C. (1988). Adolescent development. *Annual Review of Psychology, 39,* 583–607.

Petersen, A. C., Compas, B. E., Brooks-Gunn, J., Stemmler, M., Ey, S., & Grant, K. E. (1993). Depression in adolescence. *American Psychologist, 48,* 155–168.

Petersen, A. C., Crockett, L., & Tobin-Richards, M. H. (1982). Sex differences. In H. E. Mitzel (Ed.), *Encyclopedia of education research* (5th ed.). New York: Free Press.

Peterson, C., & Seligman, M. E. P. (1984). Causal explanations as a risk factor for depression: Theory and evidence. *Psychological Review, 91,* 347–374.

Peterson, C., & Seligman, M. E. P. (1987). Explanatory style and illness. *Journal of Personality, 55,* 237–265.

Peterson, C., Seligman, M. E. P., & Vaillant, G. E. (1988). Pessimistic explanatory style is a risk factor for physical illness: A thirty-five-year longitudinal study. *Journal of Personality and Social Psychology, 55,* 23–27.

Pettigrew, T. F. (1979). The ultimate attribution error: Extending Allport's cognitive analysis of prejudice. *Personality and Social Psychology Bulletin, 5,* 461–476.

Pettigrew, T. F., & Martin, J. (1987). Shaping the organizational context for black American inclusion. *Journal of Social Issues, 43,* 41–78.

Petty, R. E., & Cacioppo, J. T. (1979). Effects of forewarning of persuasive intent and involvement on cognitive responses and persuasion. *Personality and Social Psychology Bulletin, 5,* 173–176.

Peyser, H. S. (1993). Stress, ethyl alcohol, and alcoholism. In L. Goldberger & S. Breznitz (Eds.), *Handbook of stress: Theoretical and clinical aspects* (2nd ed.). New York: Free Press.

Pfau, M., Kenski, H. C., Nitz, M., & Sorenson, J. (1990). Efficacy of inoculation strategies in promoting resistance to political attack messages: Application to direct mail. *Communication Monographs, 57,* 25–43.

Phelps, S., & Austin, N. (1987). *The assertive woman.* San Luis Obispo, CA: Impact.

Philpott, J. S. (1983). *The relative contribution to meaning of verbal and nonverbal channels of communication: A meta-analysis.* Unpublished master's thesis, University of Nebraska, Omaha.

Pillow, D. R., West, S. G., & Reich, J. W. (1991). Attributional style in relation to self-esteem and depression: Mediational and interactive models. *Journal of Research in Personality, 25,* 57–69.

Pilowsky, I. (1978). A general classification of abnormal illness behaviors. *British Journal of Psychology, 51,* 131–137.

Pines, A. M. (1993). Burnout. In L. Goldberger & S. Breznitz (Eds.), *Handbook of stress: Theoretical and clinical aspects* (2nd ed.). New York: Free Press.

Pines, A. M., & Aronson, E. (1983). Antecedents, correlates, and consequences of sexual jealousy. *Journal of Personality, 51,* 108–136.

Pines, A. M., & Aronson, E. (1988). *Career burnout: Causes and cures.* New York: Free Press.

Pines, A. M., Aronson, E., & Kafry, D. (1981). *Burnout: From tedium to personal growth.* New York: Free Press.

Piotrkowski, C. S., Rapoport, R. N., & Rapoport, R. (1987). Families and work. In M. B. Sussman & S. K. Steinmetz (Eds.), *Handbook of marriage and the family.* New York: Plenum.

Piper, W. E. (1993). Group psychotherapy research. In H. I. Kaplan & B. J. Sadock (Eds.), *Comprehensive group psychotherapy.* Baltimore: Williams & Wilkins.

Pittman, F., III. (1994, January/February). A buyer's guide to psychotherapy. *Psychology Today*, pp. 50–53, 74–81.

Pittman, J. F., & Lloyd, S. A. (1988). Quality of family life, social support, and stress. *Journal of Marriage and the Family, 50,* 53–67.

Pleck, J. H. (1976). The male sex role: Definitions, problems, and sources of change. *Journal of Social Issues, 32,* 155–164.

Pleck, J. H. (1981a). *The myth of masculinity.* Cambridge, MA: MIT Press.

Pleck, J. H. (1981b). The work-family problem: Overloading the system. In B. Forisha & B. Goldman (Eds.), *Outsiders on the inside: Women in organizations.* Englewood Cliffs, NJ: Prentice-Hall.

Pleck, J. H., Sonenstein, F. L., & Ku, L. C. (1993). Masculinity ideology: Its impact on adolescent males' heterosexual relationships. *Journal of Social Issues, 49,* 11–29.

Plomin, R. (1990). *Nature and nurture: An introduction to human behavioral genetics.* Pacific Grove, CA: Brooks/Cole.

Plomin, R., Chipuer, H. M., & Loehlin, J. C. (1990). Behavioral genetics and personality. In L. A. Pervin (Ed.), *Handbook of personality: Theory and research.* New York: Guilford Press.

Plomin, R., & Daniels, D. (1987). Why are children in the same family so different from each other? *Behavioral and Brain Sciences, 10,* 1–16.

Plude, D. J., & Hoyer, W. J. (1985). Attention and performance: Identifying and localizing age deficits. In N. Charness (Ed.), *Aging and human performance.* Chichester, England: Wiley.

Polivy, J., & Thomsen, L. (1988). Dieting and other eating disorders. In E. A. Blechman & K. D. Brownell (Eds.), *Handbook of behavioral medicine for women.* New York: Pergamon.

Pomerleau, O. F., & Pomerleau, C. S. (Eds.). (1988). *Nicotine replacement: A critical evaluation.* New York: Liss.

Ponterotto, J. G., & Pedersen, P. B. (1993). *Preventing prejudice: A guide for counselors and educators.* Newbury Park, CA: Sage Publications.

Pope, H. G., & Hudson, J. I. (1992). Is childhood sexual abuse a risk factor for bulimia nervosa? *American Journal of Psychiatry, 4,* 455–463.

Pope, K. S., Keith-Spiegel, P., & Tabachnick, B. G. (1986). Sexual attraction to clients. *American Psychologist, 41,* 147–158.

Pope, M. K., & Smith, T. W. (1991). Cortisol excretion in high and low cynically hostile men. *Psychosomatic Medicine, 53,* 386–392.

Popenoe, D. (1993). American family decline, 1960–1990: A review and appraisal. *Journal of Marriage and the Family, 55,* 527–555.

Post, R. M. (1989). Mood disorders: Somatic treatment. In H. I. Kaplan & B. J. Sadock (Eds.), *Comprehensive textbook of psychiatry/V* (Vol. 2). Baltimore: Williams & Wilkins.

Powell, L. H., Friedman, M., Thoresen, C. E., Gill, J. J., & Ulmer, D. K. (1984). Can the Type A behavior pattern be altered after myocardial infarction? A second year report from the recurrent coronary prevention unit. *Psychosomatic Medicine, 46,* 293–313.

Powell, M. (1973). Age and occupational change among coal-miners. *Occupational Psychology, 47,* 37–49.

Pratkanis, A. R., & Aronson, E. (1992). *Age of propaganda: The everyday use and abuse of persuasion.* New York: Freeman.

Prentice-Dunn, S., & Rogers, R. W. (1989). Deindividuation and the self-regulation of behavior. In P. B. Paulis (Ed.), *Psychology of group influence* (2nd ed.). Hillsdale, NJ: Erlbaum.

Pressman, S. (1993). *Outrageous betrayal: The real story of Werner Erhard, Est and the Forum.* New York: St. Martin's Press.

Prest, L. A., & Protinsky, H. (1993). Family systems theory: A unifying framework for codependence. *American Journal of Family Therapy, 21,* 352–360.

Price, S. J., & McKenry, P. C. (1988). *Divorce.* Newbury Park, CA: Sage Publications.

Prochaska, J. O., Velicer, W. F., DiClemente, C. C., & Fava, J. (1988). Measuring processes of change: Applications to the cessation of smoking. *Journal of Consulting and Clinical Psychology, 56,* 520–528.

Pryor, J. B., Giedd, J. L., & Williams, K. B. (1995). A social psychological model for predicting sexual harassment. *Journal of Social Issues, 51,* 69–84.

Punetha, D., Giles, H., & Young, L. (1987). Ethnicity and immigrant values: Religion and language choice. *Journal of Language and Social Psychology, 6,* 229–241.

Purcell, P., & Stewart, L. (1990). Dick and Jane in 1989. *Sex Roles, 22,* 177–185.

Pursell, S. A., & Banikiotes, P. G. (1978). Androgyny and initial interpersonal attraction. *Personality and Social Psychology Bulletin, 4,* 235–243.

Quillin, P. (1987). *Healing nutrients.* New York: Random House.

Quina, K., & Carlson, N. L. (1989). *Rape, incest, and sexual harassment: A guide for helping survivors.* New York: Praeger.

Rabbitt, P., & McGinnis, L. (1988). Do clever old people have earlier and richer first memories? *Psychology and Aging, 3,* 338–341.

Rabinowitz, F. E., & Cochran, S. V. (1994). *Man alive: A primer of men's issues.* Pacific Grove, CA: Brooks/Cole.

Rabkin, J. G., & Streuning E. L. (1976). Life events, stress and illness. *Science, 194,* 1013–1020.

Rachman, S. J. (1990). *Fear and courage.* New York: Freeman.

Rachman, S. J. (1992). Behavior therapy. In L. R. Squire (Ed.), *Encyclopedia of learning and memory.* New York: Macmillan.

Rachman, S. J., & Wilson, G. T. (1980). *The effects of psychological therapy.* New York: Pergamon.

Ragland, D. R., & Brand, R. J. (1988). Type A behavior and mortality from coronary heart disease. *The New England Journal of Medicine, 318,* 65–69.

Rahe, R. H., & Arthur, R. H. (1978). Life change and illness studies. *Journal of Human Stress, 4,* 3–15.

Rahe, R. H., & Holmes, T. H. (1965). Social, psychologic and psychophysiologic aspects of inguinal hernia. *Journal of Psychosomatic Research, 8,* 487–491.

Rakowski, W., & Mor, V. (1992). The association of physical activity with mortality among older adults in the longitudinal study of aging (1984–1988). *Journals of Gerontology, 47*(4), 122–129.

Rapaport, K., & Burkhart, B. R. (1984). Personality and attitudinal characteristics of sexually coercive college males. *Journal of Abnormal Psychology, 93,* 216–221.

Rapee, R. M., & Barlow, D. H. (1993). Generalized anxiety disorder, panic disorder, and the phobias. In P. B. Sutker & H. E. Adams (Eds.), *Comprehensive handbook of psychopathology* (2nd ed.). New York: Plenum.

Raphael, K. G., Cloitre, M., & Dohrenwend, B. P. (1991). Problems of recall and misclassification with checklist methods of measuring stressful life events. *Health Psychology, 10,* 62–74.

Raschke, H. J. (1987). Divorce. In M. B. Sussman & S. K. Steinmetz (Eds.), *Handbook of marriage and the family.* New York: Plenum.

Rashid, H. M. (1989). Divergent paths in the development of African-American males: A qualitative perspective. *Urban Research Review, 12,* 1–2, 12–13.

Raskin, P. M. (1986). The relationship between identity and intimacy in early adulthood. *Journal of Genetic Psychology, 147,* 167–181.

Raugh, M. R., & Atkinson, R. C. (1975). A mnemonic method for learning a second-language vocabulary. *Journal of Educational Psychology, 67,* 1–16.

Raush, H. L., Barry, W. A., Hertel, R. K., & Swain, M. A. (1974). *Communication, conflict and marriage.* San Francisco: Jossey-Bass.

Ray, L., Soares, E. J., & Tolchinsky, B. (1988). Explicit lyrics: A content analysis of top 100 songs from the 50's to the 80's. *The Speech Communication Annual, 2,* 43–56.

Ray, O., & Ksir, C. (1990). *Drugs, society & human behavior.* St. Louis: Times Mirror/Mosby.

Raz, S. (1993). Structural cerebral pathology in schizophrenia: Regional or diffuse? *Journal of Abnormal Psychology, 102,* 445–452.

Read, C. R. (1991). Achievement and career choices: Comparisons of males and females. *Roeper Review, 13,* 188–193.

Reese, H. W., & Rodeheaver, D. (1985). Problem solving and complex decision making. In J. E. Birren & K. W. Schaie (Eds.), *Handbook of the psychology of aging* (2nd ed.). New York: Van Nostrand Reinhold.

Regier, D. A., Boyd, J. H., Burke, J. D., Rea, D. S., Myers, J. K., Kramer, M., Robins, L. N., George, L. K., Karno, M., & Locke, B. Z. (1988). One-month prevalance of mental disorders in the United States. *Archives of General Psychiatry, 45,* 977–986.

Rehm, L. P., & Tyndall, C. I. (1993). Mood disorders: Unipolar and bipolar. In P. B. Sutker & H. E. Adams (Eds.), *Comprehensive handbook of psychopathology* (2nd ed.). New York: Plenum.

Reid, P. T., & Paludi, M. A. (1993). Developmental psychology of women: Conception to adolescence. In F. L. Denmark & M. A. Paludi (Eds.), *Psychology of women: A handbook of issues and theories.* Westport, CT: Greenwood Press.

Reinisch, J. M. (1990). *The Kinsey Institute new report on sex: What you must know to be sexually literate.* New York: St. Martin's.

Reinke, B. J., Ellicott, A. M., Harris, R. L., & Hancock, E. (1985). Timing of psychosocial changes in women's lives. *Human Development, 28,* 259–280.

Reis, H. T., Senchak, M., & Solomon, B. (1985). Sex differences in the intimacy of social interaction: Further examination of potential explanation. *Journal of*

Personality and Social Psychology, 48, 1204–1217.

Reis, T. J., Gerrard, M., & Gibbons, F. X. (1993). Social comparison and the pill: Reactions to upward and downward comparison of contraceptive behavior. *Personality and Social Psychology Bulletin, 19,* 13–21.

Reiser, M. F. (1989). The future of psychoanalysis in academic psychiatry: Plain talk. *Psychoanalytic Quarterly, 58,* 185–209.

Reiss, I. L. (1967). *The social context of premarital sexual permissiveness.* New York: Holt, Rinehart & Winston.

Reiss, M., Rosenfeld, P., Melburg, V., & Tedeschi, J. T. (1981). Self-serving attributions: Biased private perceptions and distorted public descriptions. *Journal of Personality and Social Psychology, 41,* 224–231.

Reiss, S. (1991). Expectancy model of fear, anxiety and panic. *Clinical Psychology Review, 11,* 141–154.

Relman, A. (1982). Marijuana and health. *New England Journal of Medicine, 306,* 603–604.

Repetti, R. L. (1992). Social withdrawal as a short-term coping response to daily stressors. In H. S. Friedman (Ed.), *Hostility coping and health.* Washington, DC: American Psychological Association.

Repetti, R. L. (1993). Short-term effects of occupational stressors on daily mood and health complaints. *Health Psychology, 12,* 125–131.

Revenson, T. A., & Felton, B. J. (1989). Disability and coping as predictors of psychological adjustment to rheumatoid arthritis. *Journal of Consulting and Clinical Psychology, 57,* 344–348.

Rey, J. M., Stewart, G. W., Plapp, J. M., Bashir, M. R., & Richards, I. N. (1988). DSM-III axis IV revisited. *American Journal of Psychiatry, 145,* 286–292.

Rhodewalt, F., & Agustsdottir, S. (1986). Effects of self-presentation on the phenomenal self. *Journal of Personality and Social Psychology, 50,* 47–55.

Rhodewalt, F., Morf, C., Hazlett, S., & Fairfield, M. (1991). Self-handicapping: The role of discounting and augmentation in the preservation of self-esteem. *Journal of Personality and Social Psychology, 61,* 122–131.

Rhodewalt, F., & Zone, J. B. (1989). Appraisal of life change, depression, and illness in hardy and nonhardy women. *Journal of Personality and Social Psychology, 56,* 81–88.

Rice, L. N., & Greenberg, L. S. (1992). Humanistic approaches to psychotherapy. In D. K. Freedheim (Ed.), *History of psychotherapy: A century of change.* Washington, DC: American Psychological Association.

Richardson, J. G., & Simpson, C. H. (1982). Children, gender and social structure: An analysis of the contents of letters to Santa Claus. *Child Development, 53,* 429–436.

Rieder, R. O., Kaufmann, C. A., & Knowles, J. A. (1994). Genetics. In R. E. Hales, S. C. Yudofsky, & J. A. Talbott (Eds.), *The American Psychiatric Press textbook of psychiatry* (2nd ed.). Washington, DC: American Psychiatric Press.

Rierdan, J., & Koff, E. (1991). Depressive symptomatology among very early maturing girls. *Journal of Youth and Adolescence, 20,* 415–425.

Rifkin, J. (1987). *Time wars: The primary conflict in human history.* New York: Simon & Schuster.

Rimer, B. K., Orleans, C. T., Keintz, M. K., Cristinzio, S., & Fleisher, L. (1990). The older smoker: Status, chal-

lenges and opportunities for intervention. *Chest, 97,* 547–553.

Rimm, D. C., & Cunningham, H. M. (1985). Behavior therapies. In S. J. Lynn & J. P. Garske (Eds.), *Contemporary psychotherapies: Models and methods.* Columbus, OH: Merrill.

Rimm, E. B., Giovannucci, E. L., Willet, W. C., Coditz, G. A., Ascherio, A., Rosner, B., & Stampfer, M. J. (1991). Prospective study of alcohol consumption and risk of coronary disease in men. *The Lancet, 338,* 464–468.

Rimm, E. B., Stampfer, M. J., Ascherio, A., Giovannucci, E., Colditz, G. A., & Willett, W. C. (1993). Vitamin E consumption and the risk of coronary heart disease in men. *New England Journal of Medicine, 328,* 1450–1456.

Rindfuss, R. R. (1991). The young adult years: Diversity, structural change, and fertility. *Demography, 28,* 493–512.

Rindfuss, R. R., Morgan, S. P., & Swicegood, G. (1988). *First births in America.* Berkeley: University of California Press.

Ringer, R. J. (1978). *Winning through intimidation.* New York: Fawcett.

Rivera, R. R. (1991). Sexual orientation and the law. In J. C. Gonsiorek & J. D. Weinrich (Eds.), *Homosexuality: Research implications for public policy.* Newbury Park, CA: Sage Publications.

Robbins, A. (1991). *Awaken the giant within: How to take immediate control of your mental, emotional, physical, and financial destiny.* New York: Simon & Schuster (Summit Books).

Roberts, J. V., & Herman, C. P. (1986). The psychology of height: An empirical review. In C. P. Herman, M. P. Zanna, & E. T. Higgins (Eds.), *Physical appearance, stigma, and social behavior: The Ontario symposium* (Vol. 3). Hillsdale, NJ: Erlbaum.

Roberts, P., & Newton, P. M. (1987). Levinsonian studies of women's adult development. *Psychology and Aging, 2,* 154–163.

Robins, C. J. (1988). Attributions and depression: Why is the literature so inconsistent? *Journal of Personality and Social Psychology, 54,* 880–889.

Robins, E. (1990). The study of interdependence in marriage. In F. D. Fincham & T. N. Bradbury (Eds.), *The psychology of marriage: Basic issues and applications.* New York: Guilford Press.

Robins, L. N., Helzer, J. E., Weissman, M. M., Orvaschel, H., Gruenberg, E., Burke, J. D., & Regier, D. A. (1984). Lifetime prevalence of specific psychiatric disorders in three sites. *Archives of General Psychiatry, 41,* 949–958.

Robins, L. N., Locke, B. Z., & Regier, D. A. (1991). An overview of psychiatric disorders in America. In L. N. Robins & D. A. Regier (Eds.), *Psychiatric disorders in America: The epidemiologic catchment area study.* New York: Free Press.

Robins, L. N., & Regier, D. A. (Eds.). (1991). *Psychiatric disorders in America: The epidemiologic catchment area study.* New York: Free Press.

Robinson, F. P. (1970). *Effective study* (4th ed.). New York: HarperCollins.

Robinson, I., Ziss, K., Ganza, B., & Katz, S. (1991). Twenty years of the sexual revolution, 1965–1985: An update. *Journal of Marriage and the Family, 53,* 216–220.

Rodin, J. (1981). Current status of the internal-external hypothesis for obesity: What went wrong? *American Psychologist, 36,* 361–372.

Rodin, J., Schank, D., & Striegel-Moore, R. H. (1989). Psychological features of obesity. *Medical Clinics of North America, 73,* 47–66.

Rodman, H., & Sidden, J. (1992). A critique of pessimistic views about U.S. families. *Family Relations, 41,* 436–439.

Roe, A. (1977). *The psychology of occupations.* New York: Wiley.

Rogers, C. R. (1951). *Client-centered therapy: Its current practice, implications, and theory.* Boston: Houghton Mifflin.

Rogers, C. R. (1959). A theory of therapy, personality, and interpersonal relationships, as developed in the client-centered framework. In S. Koch (Ed.), *Psychology: A study of a science* (Vol. 3). New York: McGraw-Hill.

Rogers, C. R. (1961). *On becoming a person: A therapist's view of psychotherapy.* Boston: Houghton Mifflin.

Rogers, C. R. (1977). *Carl Rogers on personal power.* New York: Delacorte.

Rogers, C. R. (1980). *A way of being.* Boston: Houghton Mifflin.

Rogers, C. R. (1986). Client-centered therapy. In I. L. Kutash & A. Wolf (Eds.), *Psychotherapist's casebook.* San Francisco: Jossey-Bass.

Rokowski, W., & Mor, V. (1992). The association of physical activity with mortality among older adults in The Longitudinal Study of Aging. *Journal of Gerontology, 47,* M122–129.

Rollins, B., & Feldman, H. (1970). Marital satisfaction over the family life cycle. *Journal of Marriage and the Family, 32,* 20–28.

Romer, N., & Cherry, D. (1980). Ethnic and social class differences in children's sex-role concepts. *Sex Roles, 6,* 245–263.

Romzek, B. S., & Dubnick, M. J. (1987). Accountability in the public sector: Lessons from the Challenger tragedy. *Public Administration Review, 47,* 227–238.

Rook, K. S. (1984). Research on social support, loneliness, and social isolation: Toward an integration. In P. Shaver (Ed.), *Review of personality and social psychology* (Vol. 5). Newbury Park, CA: Sage Publications.

Rook, K. S. (1990). Parallels in the study of social support and social strain. *Journal of Social and Clinical Psychology, 9,* 118–132.

Rook, K. S., Dooley, D., & Catalano, R. (1991). Stress transmission: The effects of husbands' job stressors on the emotional health of their wives. *Journal of Marriage and the Family, 53,* 165–177.

Roosa, M. W. (1988). The effect of age in the transition to parenthood: Are delayed childbearers a unique group? *Family Relations, 37,* 322–327.

Rosato, D. (1995, August 4–6). On-the-job deaths: Homicide no. 2 cause. *USA Today,* p. 1.

Rosch, P. J., & Pelletier, K. R. (1987). Designing worksite stress management programs. In L. R. Murphy & T. F. Schoenborn (Eds.), *Stress management in work settings.* Washington, DC: National Institute for Occupational Safety and Health.

Rose, R. M., Gordon, T. P., & Bernstein, I. (1972). Plasma testosterone levels in the male rhesus: Influence of sexual and social stimuli. *Science, 178,* 643–645.

Rosen, D. H. (1974). *Lesbianism: A study of female homosexuality.* Springfield, IL: Charles C Thomas.

Rosen, G. M. (1987). Self-help treatment books and the commercialization of psychotherapy. *American Psychologist, 42,* 46–51.

Rosen, M., Nystrom, L., & Wall, S. (1988). Diet and cancer mortality in the counties of Sweden. *American Journal of Epidemiology, 127,* 42–49.

Rosen, R. D. (1977). *Psychobabble.* New York: Atheneum.

Rosenbaum, J. F., Biederman, J., Bolduc, E. A., Hirschfeld, D. R.,

Faraone, S. V., & Kagan, J. (1992). Comorbidity of parental anxiety disorders as risk for childhood-onset anxiety in inhibited children. *American Journal of Psychiatry, 149,* 475–481.

Rosenbaum, M., Lakin, M., & Roback, H. B. (1992). Psychotherapy in groups. In D. K. Freedheim (Ed.), *History of psychotherapy: A century of change.* Washington, DC: American Psychological Association.

Rosenbaum, M. E. (1986). The repulsion hypothesis: On the nondevelopment of relationships. *Journal of Personality and Social Psychology, 51,* 1156–1166.

Rosenberg, M. (1979). *Conceiving the self.* New York: Basic Books.

Rosenberg, M. (1985). Self-concept and psychological well-being in adolescence. In R. L. Leahy (Ed.), *The development of the self.* Orlando, FL: Academic Press.

Rosenfeld, L. B., Civikly, J. M., & Herron, J. R. (1979). Anatomical and psychological sex differences. In G. J. Chelune & associates (Eds.), *Self-disclosure: Origins, patterns, and implications of openness in interpersonal relationships.* San Francisco: Jossey-Bass.

Rosengren, A., Tibblin, G., & Wilhelmsen, L. (1991). Self-perceived psychological stress and incidence of coronary artery disease in middle-aged men. *American Journal of Cardiology, 68,* 1171–1175.

Rosenhan, D. L. (1973). On being sane in insane places. *Science, 179,* 250–258.

Rosenheim, E., & Muchnik, B. (1984–1985). Death concerns in differential levels of consciousness as functions of defense strategy and religious beliefs. *Omega, 155,* 15–24.

Rosenman, R. H. (1991). Type A behavior pattern and coronary heart disease: The hostility factor? *Stress Medicine, 7,* 245–253.

Rosenman, R. H. (1993). Relationships of the Type A behavior pattern with coronary heart disease. In L. Goldberger & S. Breznitz (Eds.), *Handbook of stress: Theoretical and clinical aspects* (2nd ed.). New York: Free Press.

Rosenthal, H. (1988). *Not with my life I don't: Preventing your suicide and that of others.* Muncie, IN: Accelerated Development.

Rosenthal, R. (1985). From unconscious experimenter bias to teacher expectancy effects. In J. B. Dusek, V. C. Hall, & W. J. Meyer (Eds.), *Teacher expectancies.* Hillsdale, NJ: Erlbaum.

Rosenthal, R., Hall, J. A., DiMatteo, M. R., Rodgers, P. L., & Archer, D. (1979). *Sensitivity to non-verbal cues: The P Test.* Baltimore: Johns Hopkins University Press.

Roskos-Ewoldsen, D. R., & Fazio, R. H. (1992). The accessibility of source likability as a determinant of persuasion. *Personality and Social Psychology, 18,* 19–25.

Ross, C. A., Anderson, G., Fleisher, W. P., & Norton, G. R. (1991). The frequency of multiple personality disorder among psychiatric inpatients. *American Journal of Psychiatry, 148,* 1717–1720.

Ross, C. A., Miller, S. D., Reagor, P., Bjornson, L., Fraser, G. A., & Anderson, G. (1990). Structured interview data on 102 cases of multiple personality disorder from four centers. *American Journal of Psychiatry, 147,* 596–601.

Ross, C. W., & Mirowsky, J. (1988). Child care and emotional adjustment to wives' employment. *Journal of Health and Social Behavior, 29,* 127–138.

Ross, L. D. (1977). The intuitive psychologist and his shortcomings: Distortions in the attribution process. In L. Berkowitz (Ed.), *Advances in experimental social psychology* (Vol. 10). New York: Academic Press.

Ross, L. D. (1988). The obedience experiments: A case study of controversy. *Contemporary Psychology, 33,* 101–104.

Ross, M., & Conway, M. (1986). Remembering one's own past: The construction of personal histories. In R. M. Sorrentino & E. T. Higgins (Eds.), *Handbook of motivation and cognition: Foundations of social behavior.* New York: Guilford Press.

Ross, M., McFarland, C., & Fletcher, G. J. O. (1981). The effect of attitude on the recall of personal histories. *Journal of Personality and Social Psychology, 10,* 627–634.

Ross, M., & Sicoly, F. (1979). Egocentric biases in availability and attribution. *Journal of Personality and Social Psychology, 37,* 322–337.

Rotenberg, K. J., & Kmill, J. (1992). Perception of lonely and non-lonely persons as a function of individual differences in loneliness. *Journal of Social and Personal Relationships, 9,* 325–330.

Rothbart, M., & Park, B. (1986). On the confirmability and disconfirmability of trait concepts. *Journal of Personality and Social Psychology, 50,* 131–142.

Rothblum, E. D., Solomon, L. J., & Albee, G. W. (1986). A sociopolitical perspective of DSM-III. In T. Millon & G. L. Klerman (Eds.), *Contemporary directions in psychopathology: Toward the DSM-IV.* New York: Guilford Press.

Rotter, J. B. (1982). *The development and application of social learning theory.* New York: Praeger.

Rotton, J., & Frey, J. (1984). Psychological costs of air pollution: Atmospheric conditions, seasonal trends, and psychiatric emergencies. *Population and Environmental Behavior and Social Issues, 7,* 3–16.

Rowlison, R. T., & Felner, R. D. (1988). Major life events, hassles, and adaptation in adolescence: Confounding in the conceptualization and measurement of life stress and adjustment revisited. *Journal of Personality and Social Psychology, 55,* 432–444.

Rozee, P. D., Bateman, P., & Gilmore, T. (1991). The personal perspective of acquaintance rape prevention: A three-tier approach. In A. Parrot & L. Bechhofer (Eds.), *Acquaintance rape: The hidden crime.* New York: Wiley.

Rubenstein, C. M., & Shaver, P. (1980). Loneliness in two northeastern cities. In J. Hartog, J. R. Audy, & Y. A. Cohen (Eds.), *The anatomy of loneliness.* New York: International Universities Press.

Rubenstein, C. M., & Shaver, P. (1982). The experience of loneliness. In L. A. Peplau & D. Perlman (Eds.), *Loneliness: A sourcebook of current theory, research and therapy.* New York: Wiley.

Rubin, E. H., Zorumski, C. F., & Guze, S. B. (1986). Somatoform disorders. In T. Millon & G. L. Klerman (Eds.), *Contemporary directions in psychopathology: Toward the DSM-IV.* New York: Guilford Press.

Rubin, G. (1984). Thinking sex: Notes for a radical theory of the politics of sexuality. In C. S. Vance (Ed.), *Pleasure and anger: Exploring female sexuality.* Boston: Routledge & Kegan Paul.

Rubin, L. (1985). *Just friends: The role of friendship in our lives.* New York: HarperCollins.

Rubin, Z. (1973). *Liking and loving: An introduction to social psychology.* New York: Holt, Rinehart & Winston.

Rubin, Z. (1974). Lovers and other strangers: The development of intimacy in encounters and relationships. *American Scientist, 62,* 182–190.

Rubin, Z., Hill, C. T., Peplau, L. A., & Dunkel-Schetter, C. (1980). Self-disclosure in dating couples: Sex roles and the ethic of openness. *Journal of Marriage and the Family, 42,* 305–317.

Rubin, Z., Peplau, L. A., & Hill, C. T. (1981). Loving and leaving: Sex differences in romantic attachments. *Sex Roles, 7,* 821–835.

Ruble, D. N., Fleming, A. S., Hackel, L. S., & Stangor, C. (1988). Changes in the marital relationship during the transition to first time motherhood: Effects of violated expectations concerning division of household labor. *Journal of Personality and Social Psychology, 55,* 78–87.

Ruble, T. L. (1983). Sex stereotypes: Issues of change in the 1970s. *Sex Roles, 9,* 397–402.

Rubonis, A. V., & Bickman, L. (1991). Psychological impairment in the wake of disaster: The disaster-psychopathology relationship. *Psychological Bulletin, 109,* 384–399.

Rudorfer, M. V., & Goodwin, F. K. (1993). Introduction. In C. E. Coffey (Ed.), *The clinical science of electroconvulsive therapy.* Washington, DC: American Psychiatric Press.

Ruse, M. (1987). Sociobiology and knowledge: Is evolutionary epistemology a viable option? In C. Crawford, M. Smith, & D. Krebs (Eds.), *Sociobiology and psychology: Ideas, issues and applications.* Hillsdale, NJ: Erlbaum.

Rush, A. J. (1984). Cognitive therapy. In T. B. Karasu (Ed.), *The psychiatric therapies.* Washington, DC: American Psychiatric Association.

Rushton, J. P. (1992). Cranial capacity related to sex, rank, and race in a stratified random sample of 6,325 U.S. Military personnel. *Intelligence, 16,* 401–413.

Rushton, J. P., Fulker, D. W., Neale, M. C., Nias, D. K. B., & Eysenck, H. J. (1986). Altruism and aggression: The heritability of individual differences. *Journal of Personality and Social Psychology, 50,* 1192–1198.

Russell, D. E. H. (1984). *Sexual exploitation.* Newbury Park, CA: Sage Publications.

Russo, N. F. (1979). Overview: Sex roles, fertility, and the motherhood mandate. *Psychology of Women Quarterly, 4,* 7–15.

Russo, N. F., & Green, B. L. (1993). Women and mental health. In F. L. Denmark & M. A. Paludi (Eds.), *Psychology of women: A handbook of issues and theories.* Westport, CT: Greenwood Press.

Sabatelli, R. M. (1988). Exploring relationship satisfaction: A social exchange perspective on the interdependence between theory, research, and practice. *Family Relations, 37,* 217–222.

Sabini, J. (1992). *Social psychology.* New York: Norton.

Sachs, G. S., & Gelenberg, A. J. (1988). Adverse effects of electroconvulsive therapy. In A. J. Frances & R. E. Hales (Eds.), *Review of psychiatry* (Vol. 7). Washington, DC: American Psychiatric Press.

Sacks, M. H. (1993). Exercise for stress control. In D. Goleman & J. Gurin (Eds.), *Mind/body medicine: How to use your mind for better health.* Yonkers, NY: Consumer Reports Books.

Sadker, M., & Sadker, D. (1985, March). Sexism in the schoolroom of the '80s. *Psychology Today,* pp. 54–57.

Saghir, M. T., & Robins, E. R. (1973). *Male and female homosexuality: A comprehensive investigation.* Baltimore: Williams & Wilkins.

Salminen, S. (1992). Defensive attribution hypothesis and serious occupational accidents. *Psychological Reports, 70,* 1195–1199.

Salthouse, T. A. (1991). Mediation of

adult age differences in cognition by reductions in working memory and speed of processing. *Psychological Science, 2,* 179–183.

Salvendy, J. T. (1993). Selection and preparation of patients and organization of the group. In H. I. Kaplan & B. J. Sadock (Eds.), *Comprehensive group psychotherapy.* Baltimore: Williams & Wilkins.

Salzman, C. (1989). Treatment with antianxiety agents. In *Treatment of psychiatric disorders* (Vol. 3). Washington, DC: American Psychiatric Association.

Samet, J. M. (1992). The health benefits of smoking cessation. *Medical Clinics of North America, 76,* 399–414.

Sanders, G. S. (1982). Social comparison and perceptions of health and illness. In G. S. Sanders & J. Suls (Eds.), *Social psychology of health and illness.* Hillsdale, NJ: Erlbaum.

Sanderson, W. C., & Barlow, D. H. (1990). A description of patients diagnosed with DSM-III-R generalized anxiety disorder. *Journal of Nervous and Mental Disease, 178,* 588–591.

Sandler, J. (1975). Aversion methods. In F. H. Kanfer & A. P. Goldstein (Eds.), *Helping people change: A textbook of methods.* New York: Pergamon.

Santrock, J. W., Minnett, A. M., & Campbell, B. D. (1994). *The authoritative guide to self-help books.* New York: Guilford Press.

Sarason, I. G. (1984). Stress, anxiety and cognitive interference: Reactions to stress. *Journal of Personality and Social Psychology, 46,* 929–938.

Sarason, I. G., Johnson, J. H., & Siegel, J. M. (1978). Assessing the impact of life changes: Development of the Life Experiences Survey. *Journal of Consulting and Clinical Psychology, 46,* 932–946.

Sarason, I. G., Pierce, G. R., & Sarason, B. R. (1994). General and specific perceptions of social support. In W. R. Avison & I. H. Gotlib (Eds.), *Stress and mental health: Contemporary issues and prospects for the future.* New York: Plenum.

Sarrel, P., & Masters, W. (1982). Sexual molestation of men by women. *Archives of Human Sexuality, 11,* 117–131.

Saxe, G. N., van der Kolk, B. A., Berkowitz, R., Chinman, G., Hall, K., Lieberg, G., & Schwartz, J. (1993). Dissociative disorders in psychiatric inpatients. *American Journal of Psychiatry, 150,* 1037–1042.

Scarr, S., Phillips, D., McCartney, K., & Abbott-Shim, M. (1993). Quality of child care as an aspect of family and child care policy in the United States. *Pediatrics, 91,* 182–188.

Schachter, S. (1959). *The psychology of affiliation.* Stanford, CA: Stanford University Press.

Schachter, S. (1964). The interaction of cognitive and physiological determinants of emotional state. In L. Berkowitz (Ed.), *Advances in experimental social psychology* (Vol. 1). New York: Academic Press.

Schachter, S. (1971). *Emotion, obesity and crime.* New York: Academic Press.

Schaef, A. W. (1986). *Codependence misdiagnosed-mistreated.* Minneapolis: Winston Press.

Schaef, A. W. (1992). *Meditations for women who do too much.* San Francisco: Harper San Francisco.

Schaefer, E. S., & Burnett, C. K. (1987). Stability and predictability of quality of women's marital relationships and demoralization. *Journal of Personality and Social Psychology, 53,* 1129–1136.

Schaefer, J., & Moos, R. (1992). Life crises and personal growth. In B. Carpenter (Ed.), *Personal coping: Theory, research, and application.* Westport, CT: Praeger.

Schaeffer, M., Street, S., Singer, J., & Baum, A. (1988). Effects of control on the stress reactions of commuters. *Journal of Applied Social Psychology, 18,* 944–957.

Schaffer, D. R. (1989). *Developmental psychology: Childhood and adolescence.* Pacific Grove, CA: Brooks/Cole.

Schaie, K. W. (1990). Intellectual development in adulthood. In J. E. Birren & K. W. Schaie (Eds.), *Handbook of the psychology of aging* (3rd ed.). San Diego: Academic Press.

Schaninger, C. M., & Buss, W. C. (1986). A longitudinal comparison of consumption and finance handling between happily married and divorced couples. *Journal of Marriage and the Family, 48,* 129–136.

Schau, C. G., & Scott, K. P. (1984). Impact of gender characteristics of instructional materials: An integration of the research literature. *Journal of Educational Psychology, 76,* 183–193.

Scheidlinger, S. (1993). History of group psychotherapy. In H. I. Kaplan & B. J. Sadock (Eds.), *Comprehensive group psychotherapy.* Baltimore: Williams & Wilkins.

Scheier, M. F., & Carver, C. S. (1985). Optimism, coping and health: Assessment and implications of generalized expectancies. *Health Psychology, 4,* 219–247.

Scheier, M. F., & Carver, C. S. (1992). Effects of optimism on psychological and physical well-being: Theoretical overview and empirical update. *Cognitive Theory and Research, 16,* 201–228.

Scheier, M. F., Matthews, K. A., Owens, J. F., Magovern, G. J., Sr., Lefebvre, R. C., Abbott, R. A., & Carver, C. S. (1989). Dispositional optimism and recovery from coronary artery bypass surgery: The beneficial effects on physical and psychological well-being. *Journal of Personality and Social Psychology, 57,* 1024–1040.

Schein, M., Zyzanski, S. J., Levine, S., & Medalie, J. H. (1988). The frequency of sexual problems among family practice patients. *Family Practice Research Journal, 7,* 122–134.

Scherg, H. (1987). Psychosocial factors and disease bias in breast cancer patients. *Psychosomatic Medicine, 49,* 302–312.

Schilit, W. K. (1987). Thinking about managing your time. In A. D. Timpe (Ed.), *The management of time.* New York: Facts On File.

Schlaadt, R. G., & Shannon, P. T. (1994). *Drugs: Use, misuse, and abuse* (4th ed.). Englewood Cliffs, NJ: Prentice-Hall.

Schlegel, A., & Barry, H., III. (1991). *Adolescence: An anthropological inquiry.* New York: Free Press.

Schlenger, W. E., Kulka, R. A., Fairbank, J. A., Hough, R. L., et al. (1992). The prevalence of post-traumatic stress disorder in the Vietnam generation: A multimethod, multisource assessment of psychiatric disorder. *Journal of Traumatic Stress, 5,* 333–363.

Schlenker, B. R., Weigold, M. F., & Hallam, J. R. (1990). Self-serving attributions in social context: Effects of self-esteem and social pressure. *Journal of Personality and Social Psychology, 58,* 855–863.

Schmidt, N., & Sermat, V. (1983). Measuring loneliness in different relationships. *Journal of Personality and Social Psychology, 44,* 1038–1047.

Schoen, R. (1992). First unions and the stability of first marriages. *Journal of Marriage and the Family, 54,* 281–284.

Schoen, R., & Wooldredge, J. (1989). Marriage choices in North Carolina and Virginia, 1969–71 and 1979–81. *Journal of Marriage and the Family, 51,* 465–481.

Schroeder, D. H., & Costa, P. T., Jr. (1984). Influence of life events stress on physical illness: Substantive effects or methodological flaws? *Journal of Personality and Social Psychology, 46,* 853–863.

Schuller, R. A., & Vidmar, N. (1992). Battered woman syndrome evidence in the courtroom: A review of the literature. *Law and Human Behavior, 16,* 273–291.

Schultz, J. H., & Luthe, W. (1969). *Autogenic therapy: Vol. 1. Autogenic methods.* New York: Grune & Stratton.

Schwartz, H. S. (1982). Job involvement as obsession. *Academy of Management Review, 7,* 429–432.

Seage, G. R., Landers, S., Lamb, G. A., & Epstein, A. M. (1990). Effect of changing patterns of care and duration of survival on the cost of treating the acquired immunodeficiency syndrome (AIDS). *American Journal of Public Health, 80,* 835–839.

Sears, D. O. (1987). Symbolic racism. In P. Katz & D. Taylor (Eds.), *Towards the elimination of racism: Profile in controversy.* New York: Plenum.

Seashore, S. E., & Barnowe, J. T. (1972, August). Collar color doesn't count. *Psychology Today,* pp. 53–54, 80–82.

Sebald, H. (1981). Adolescents' concept of popularity and unpopularity, comparing 1960 with 1976. *Adolescence, 16,* 187–193.

Seccombe, K. (1987). Children: Their impact on the elderly in declining health. *Research on Aging, 9,* 312–326.

Seccombe, K. (1991). Assessing the costs and benefits of children: Gender comparisons among childfree husbands and wives. *Journal of Marriage and the Family, 53,* 191–202.

Segal, K. R., & Pi-Sunyer, F. X. (1989). Exercise and obesity. *Medical Clinics of North America, 73,* 217–236.

Segal, M. W. (1974). Alphabet and attraction: An unobtrusive measure of the effect of propinquity in a field setting. *Journal of Personality and Social Psychology, 30,* 654–657.

Segrin, C., & Abramson, L. Y. (1994). Negative reactions to depressive behaviors: A communication theories analysis. *Journal of Abnormal Psychology, 103,* 655–668.

Segrin, C., & Dillard, J. P. (1992). The interactional theory of depression: A meta-analysis of the research literature. *Journal of Social and Clinical Psychology, 11,* 43–70.

Seibel, M. M., & McCarthy, J. A. (1993). Infertility, pregnancy, and the emotions. In D. Goleman & J. Gurin (Eds.), *Mind/body medicine: How to use your mind for better health.* Yonkers, NY: Consumer Reports Books.

Seidlitz, L., & Diener, E. (1993). Memory for positive versus negative life events: Theories for the differences between happy and unhappy persons. *Journal of Personality and Social Psychology, 64,* 654–664.

Seligman, M. E. P. (1971). Phobias and preparedness. *Behavior Therapy, 2,* 307–321.

Seligman, M. E. P. (1974). Depression and learned helplessness. In R. J. Friedman & M. M. Katz (Eds.), *The psychology of depression: Contemporary theory and research.* New York: Wiley.

Seligman, M. E. P. (1990). *Learned optimism: How to change your mind and your life.* New York: Pocket Books.

Seligman, M. E. P. (1992). *Helplessness: On depression, development, and death.* New York: Freeman.

Seligman, M. E. P. (1994). *What you can change and what you can't.* New York: Knopf.

Seltzer, J. A. (1991). Relationships between fathers and children who live apart: The father's role after separation. *Journal of Marriage and the Family, 53,* 79–101.

Selye, H. (1936). A syndrome produced by diverse nocuous agents. *Nature, 138,* 32.

Selye, H. (1956). *The stress of life.* New York: McGraw-Hill.

Selye, H. (1974). *Stress without distress.* New York: Lippincott.

Selye, H. (1982). History and present status of the stress concept. In L. Goldberger & S. Breznitz (Eds.), *Handbook of stress: Theoretical and clinical aspects.* New York: Free Press.

Seta, J. J., Seta, C. E., & Wang, M. A. (1991). Feelings of negativity and stress: An averaging-summation analysis of impressions of negative life experiences. *Personality and Social Psychology Bulletin, 17,* 376–384.

Shaffer, D. R. (1989). *Developmental psychology: Childhood and adolescence.* Pacific Grove, CA: Brooks/Cole.

Shapiro, D. H., Jr. (1984). Overview: Clinical and physiological comparison of meditation with other self-control strategies. In D. H. Shapiro, Jr. & R. N. Walsh (Eds.), *Meditation: Classic and contemporary perspectives.* New York: Aldine.

Shapiro, D. H., Jr. (1987). Implications of psychotherapy research for the study of meditation. In M. A. West (Ed.), *The psychology of meditation.* Oxford: Clarendon Press.

Shapiro, S., Skinner, E. A., Kessler, L. G., Von Korff, M., German, P. S., Tischler, G. L., Leaf, P. J., Benham, L., Cottler, L., & Regier, D. A. (1984). Utilization of health and mental health services. *Archives of General Psychiatry, 41,* 971–978.

Shavelson, R. J., Hubner, J. J., & Stanton, G. C. (1976). Self-concept: Validation of construct interpretations. *Review of Educational Research, 46,* 407–411.

Shaver, P. R., & Brennan, K. A. (1992). Attachment styles and the "Big Five" personality traits: Their connections with each other and with romantic relationship outcomes. *Personality and Social Psychology Bulletin, 18,* 536–545.

Shaver, P. R., & Hazan, C. (1992). Adult romantic attachment: Theory and evidence. In D. Perlman & W. Jones (Eds.), *Advances in personal relationships* (Vol. 4). Bristol, PA: Taylor & Francis.

Shaver, P. R., & Hazan, C. (1993). Adult attachment: Theory and research. In W. Jones & D. Perlman (Eds.), *Advances in personal relationships* (Vol. 4). London: Jessica Kingsley.

Shaver, P. R., & Hazan, C. (1994). Attachment. In A. L. Weber & J. H. Harvey (Eds.), *Perspectives on close relationships.* Boston: Allyn & Bacon.

Shaver, P. R., & Rubenstein, C. (1980). Childhood attachment experience and adult loneliness. In L. Wheeler (Ed.), *Review of personality and social psychology* (Vol. 1). Newbury Park, CA: Sage Publications.

Shaver, P. R., Wu, S., & Schwartz, J. C. (1991). Cross-cultural similarities and differences in emotion and its representation: A prototype approach. In M. S. Clark (Ed.), *Review of personality and social psychology* (Vol. 13). Newbury Park, CA: Sage Publications.

Sheehan, P. W., Green, V., & Truesdale, P. (1992). Influence of rapport on hypnotically induced pseudomemory. *Journal of Abnormal Psychology, 101,* 690–700.

Sheehan, S. (1982). *Is there no place on earth for me?* Boston: Houghton Mifflin.

Sheehy, G. (1976). *Passages.* Toronto: Bantam Books.

Sheehy, G. (1982). *Pathfinders.* New York: Morrow.

Sheehy, G. (1984). *Passages.* Toronto: Bantam Books.

Shekelle, R. B., Hulley, S. B., Neaton, J. D., Billings, J. H., Borhani, N. O., Gerace, T. A., Jacobs, D. R., Lasser, N. L., Mittlemark, M. B., & Stamler, J. (1985). The MRFIT behavior pattern study: II. Type A behavior and incidence of coronary heart disease. *American Journal of Epidemiology, 122,* 559–570.

Shephard, R. J. (1986). Passive smoking: Attitudes, health, and performance. In T. Ney & A. Gale (Eds.), *Smoking and human behavior.* Chichester: Wiley.

Shepperd, J. A., & Arkin, R. M. (1989). Self-handicapping: The moderating roles of public self-consciousness and task importance. *Personality and Social Psychology Bulletin, 15,* 252–265.

Sher, T. G., & Baucom, D. H. (1993). Marital communication: Differences among maritally distressed, depressed, and nondistressed-nondepressed couples. *Journal of Family Psychology, 7,* 148–153.

Sherer, M., Maddox, J. E., Mercandante, B., Prentice-Dunn, S., Jacobs, B., & Rogers, R. W. (1982). The self-efficacy scale: Construction and validation. *Psychological Reports, 51,* 663–671.

Sherif, M., & Hovland, C. I. (1961). *Social judgment: Assimilation and contrast effects in communication and attitude change.* New Haven, CT: Yale University Press.

Sherman, C. B. (1992). The health consequences of cigarette smoking: Pulmonary diseases. *Medical Clinics of North America, 76,* 355–375.

Sherrod, D. (1989). The influence of gender on same-sex friendships. In C. Hendrick (Ed.), *Review of personality and social psychology: Vol. 10. Close relationships.* Newbury Park, CA: Sage Publications.

Shertzer, B. (1985). *Career planning: Freedom to choose.* Boston: Houghton Mifflin.

Sherwin, B. B. (1991). The psychoendocrinology of aging and female sexuality. *Annual Review of Sex Research, 2,* 181–198.

Sherwood, A. (1993). Use of impedance cardiography in cardiovascular reactivity research. In J. Blascovich & E. S. Katkin (Eds.), *Cardiovascular reactivity to psychological stress and disease.* Washington, DC: American Psychological Association.

Shneidman, E. S. (1985). *At the point of no return.* New York: Wiley.

Shneidman, E. S., Farberow, N. L., & Litman, R. E. (Eds.). (1970). *The psychology of suicide.* New York: Science House.

Shore, T. H. (1992). Subtle gender bias in the assessment of managerial potential. *Sex Roles, 27,* 499–515.

Shostak, A. (1987). Singlehood. In M. B. Sussman & S. K. Steinmetz (Eds.), *Handbook of marriage and the family.* New York: Plenum.

Shostak, A. B. (1980). *Blue-collar stress.* Reading, MA: Addison-Wesley.

Shotland, R. L. (1989). A model of the causes of date rape in developing and close relationships. In C. Hendrick (Ed.), *Review of personality and social psychology: Vol. 10. Close relationships.* Newbury Park, CA: Sage Publications.

Shotland, R. L., & Hunter, B. A. (1995). Women's "token resistant" and compliant sexual behaviors are related to uncertain sexual intentions and rape. *Personality and Social Psychology Bulletin, 21,* 226–236.

Showers, C. (1992). Compartmentalization of positive and negative self-knowledge: Keeping bad apples out of the bunch. *Journal of Personality and Social Psychology, 62,* 1036–1049.

Shuval, J. T. (1993). Migration and stress. In L. Goldberger & S. Breznitz (Eds.), *Handbook of stress: Theoretical and clinical aspects* (2nd ed.). New York: Free Press.

Siegel, J. M. (1990). Stressful life events and use of physician services among the elderly. *Journal of Personality and Social Psychology, 58,* 1081–1086.

Siegel, J. M., Johnson, J. H., & Sarason, I. G. (1979). Life changes and menstrual discomfort. *Journal of Human Stress, 5,* 41–46.

Siegel, O. (1982). Personality development in adolescence. In B. B. Wolman (Ed.), *Handbook of developmental psychology.* Englewood Cliffs, NJ: Prentice-Hall.

Siegler, I. C., Nowlin, J. B., & Blumenthal, J. A. (1980). Health and behavior: Methodological considerations for adult development and aging. In L. W. Poon (Ed.), *Aging in the 1980s: Psychological issues.* Washington, DC: American Psychological Association.

Sifneos, P. E. (1972). *Short-term psychotherapy and emotional crisis.* Cambridge, MA: Harvard University Press.

Signorielli, N., & Lears, M. (1992). Children, television, and conceptions about chores: Attitudes and behaviors. *Sex Roles, 27,* 157–170.

Silberstein, L. R. (1992). *Dual-career marriage, a system in transition.* Hillsdale, NJ: Erlbaum.

Silva, J., & Miele, P. (1977). *The Silva mind control method.* New York: Simon & Schuster.

Silverberg, S. B., Tennenbaum, D. L., & Jacob, T. (1992). Adolescence and family interaction. In V. B. Van Hasselt & M. Hersen (Eds.), *Handbook of social development: A lifespan perspective.* New York: Plenum.

Simmons, C. H., von Kolke, A., & Shimizu, H. (1986). Attitudes toward romantic love among American, German, and Japanese students. *Journal of Social Psychology, 126,* 327–336.

Simmons, R. G., & Blyth, D. A. (1987). *Moving into adolescence: The impact of pubertal change and school context.* New York: Aldine de Gruyter.

Simon, G. E., & VonKorff, M. (1991). Somatization and psychiatric disorder in the NIMH epidemiologic catchment area study. *American Journal of Psychiatry, 148,* 1494–1500.

Simon, W., & Gagnon, J. (1977). Psychosexual development. In D. Byrne & L. A. Byrne (Eds.), *Exploring human sexuality.* New York: Crowell.

Simon, W., & Gagnon, J. (1986). Sexual scripts: Permanance and change. *Archives of Sexual Behavior, 15,* 97–120.

Simonton, D. K. (1990). Creativity and wisdom in aging. In J. E. Birren & K. W. Schaie (Eds.), *Handbook of psychology of aging.* San Diego: Academic Press.

Simpson, J. A. (1987). The dissolution of romantic relationships: Factors involved in relationship stability and emotional distress. *Journal of Personality and Social Psychology, 53,* 683–692.

Simpson, J. A. (1990). Influence of attachment styles on romantic relationships. *Journal of Personality and Social Psychology, 59,* 971–980.

Singer, M. T., Wynne, L. C., & Toohey, M. L. (1978). Communication disorders and the families of schizophrenics. In L. C. Wynne, R. L. Cromwell, & S. Matthysse (Eds.), *The nature of schizophrenia: New approaches to research and treatment.* New York: Wiley Medical.

Singh, R., & Tan, L. S. C. (1992). Attitudes and attraction: A test of the similarity-repulsion hypotheses. *British Journal of Social Psychology, 31,* 227–238.

Siscovick, D. S. (1990). Risks of exercising: Sudden cardiac death and injuries. In C. Bouchard, R. J. Shephard, T. Stephens, J. R. Sutton, & B. D. McPherson (Eds.), *Exercise, fitness, and health: A consensus of current knowledge.* Champaign, IL: Human Kinetics Books.

Siscovick, D. S., Weiss, N. S., Fletcher, R. H., & Lasky, T. (1984). The incidence of primary cardiac arrest during vigorous exercise. *New England Journal of Medicine, 311,* 874–877.

Skinner, B. F. (1953). *Science and human behavior.* New York: Macmillan.

Skinner, B. F. (1974). *About behaviorism.* New York: Knopf.

Skinner, B. F. (1987). Whatever happened to psychology as the science of behavior? *American Psychologist, 42,* 780–786.

Skinner, B. F. (1990). Can psychology be a science of mind? *American Psychologist, 45,* 1206–1210.

Skinner, B. F., Solomon, H. C., & Lindsley, O. R. (1953). *Studies in behavior therapy: Status report I.* Waltham, MA: Unpublished report, Metropolitan State Hospital.

Slavney, P. R. (1990). *Perspectives on hysteria.* Baltimore: John Hopkins University Press.

Sloan, W. W., Jr., & Solano, C. H. (1984). The conversational style of lonely males with strangers and roommates. *Personality and Social Psychology Bulletin, 10,* 293–301.

Small, I. F., Small, J. G., & Milstein, V. (1986). Electroconvulsive therapy. In P. A. Berger & H. K. H. Brodie (Eds.), *American handbook of psychiatry: Biological psychiatry* (Vol. 8) (2nd ed.). New York: Basic Books.

Small, S. A., & Riley, D. (1990). Toward a multidimensional assessment of work spillover into family life. *Journal of Marriage and the Family, 52,* 51–61.

Smeaton, G., Byrne, D., & Murnen, S. K. (1989). The repulsion hypothesis revisited: Similarity irrelevance or dissimilarity bias. *Journal of Personality and Social Psychology, 56,* 54–59.

Smith, A. L., & Weissman, M. M. (1992). Epidemiology. In E. S. Paykel (Ed.), *Handbook of affective disorders* (2nd ed.). New York: Guilford Press.

Smith, C. A., & Lazarus, R. S. (1993). Appraisal components, core relational themes, and the emotions. *Cognition and Emotion, 7,* 233–269.

Smith, E. R., & Mackie, D. M. (1995). *Social psychology.* New York: Worth.

Smith, J. C. (1993). *Understanding stress and coping.* New York: Macmillan.

Smith, K. (1991). Comments on "Teen suicide and changing cause-of-death certification, 1953–1987." *Suicidal Life-Threatening Behavior, 21,* 260–262.

Smith, L. W., Patterson, T. L., & Grant, I. (1992). Work, retirement, and activity: Coping challenges for the elderly. In V. B. Van Hasselt & M. Hersen (Eds.), *Handbook of social development: A lifespan perspective.* New York: Plenum.

Smith, M. (1985). *When I say no I feel guilty.* New York: Bantam Books.

Smith, M. L., & Glass, G. V. (1977). Meta-analysis of psychotherapy outcome studies. *American Psychologist, 32,* 752–760.

Smith, M. L., Glass, G. V., & Miller, R. L. (1980). *The benefits of psychotherapy.* Baltimore: Johns Hopkins University Press.

Smith, P. A., & Midlarsky, E. (1985). Empirically derived conceptions of femaleness and maleness: A current view. *Sex Roles, 12,* 313–328.

Smith, R. E. (1989). Effects of coping skills training on generalized self-efficacy and locus of control. *Journal of Personality and Social Psychology, 56,* 228–233.

Smith, T. (1991). *Ethnic images. GSS Topical Report No. 19.* Chicago: National Opinion Research Center.

Smith, T. W. (1992). Hostility and health: Current status of a psychosomatic hypothesis. *Health Psychology, 11,* 139–150.

Smith, T. W., & Brown, P. C. (1991). Cynical hostility, attempts to exert social control, and cardiovascular reactivity in married couples. *Journal of Behavioral Medicine, 14,* 581–592.

Smith, T. W., & Christensen, A. J. (1992). Hostility, health, and social contexts. In H. S. Friedman (Ed.), *Hostility coping and health.* Washington, DC: American Psychological Association.

Smith, T. W., Pope, M. K., Sanders, J. D., Allred, K. D., & O'Keefe, J. L. (1988). Cynical hostility at home and work: Psychosocial vulnerability across domains. *Journal of Research in Personality, 22,* 525–548.

Smith, T. W., Turner, C. W., Ford, M. H., Hunt, S. C., Barlow, G. K., Stults, B. M., & Williams, R. R. (1987). Blood pressure reactivity in adult male twins. *Health Psychology, 6,* 209–220.

Smoll, F. L., & Schutz, R. W. (1990). Quantifying gender differences in physical performance: A developmental perspective. *Developmental Psychology, 26,* 360–369.

Smollar, J., & Youniss, J. (1985). Adolescent self-concept development. In R. L. Leahy (Ed.), *The development of the self.* Orlando, FL: Academic Press.

Smyth, M. M., & Fuller, R. G. C. (1972). Effects of group laughter on responses to humorous materials. *Psychological Reports, 30,* 132–134.

Snelling, R. O., & Snelling, A. M. (1985). *Jobs! What they are . . . Where they are . . . What they pay!* New York: Simon & Schuster.

Snyder, C. R., Lassegard, M., & Ford, C. E. (1986). Distancing after group success and failure: Basking in reflected glory and cutting off reflected failure. *Journal of Personality and Social Psychology, 51,* 382–388.

Snyder, M. (1979). Self-monitoring processes. In L. Berkowitz (Ed.), *Advances in experimental social psychology* (Vol. 12). New York: Academic Press.

Snyder, M. (1986). *Public appearances/ Private realities: The psychology of self-monitoring.* New York: Freeman.

Snyder, M., & Campbell, B. (1982). Self-monitoring: The self in action. In J. Suls (Ed.), *Psychological perspectives on the self.* Hillsdale, NJ: Erlbaum.

Snyder, M., Tanke, E. D., & Berscheid, E. (1977). Social perception and interpersonal behavior: On the self-fulfilling nature of social stereotypes. *Journal of Personality and Social Psychology, 35,* 655–666.

Soares, L. M., & Soares, A. T. (1971). Comparative differences in the self-perceptions of disadvantaged and advantaged students. *Journal of School Psychology, 9,* 424–429.

Solano, C. H., Batten, P. G., & Parish, E. A. (1982). Loneliness and patterns of self-disclosure. *Journal of Personality and Social Psychology, 43,* 524–531.

Solano, C. H., & Koester, N. H. (1989). Loneliness and communication problems: Subjective anxiety or objective skills? *Personality and Social Psychology Bulletin, 15,* 126–133.

Solomon, Z., Weisenberg, M., Schwarzwald, J., & Mikulincer, M. (1988). Combat stress reaction and post-traumatic stress disorder as determinants of perceived self-efficacy in battle. *Journal of Social and Clinical Psychology, 6,* 356–370.

Somers, M. D. (1993). A comparison of voluntarily childfree adults and parents. *Journal of Marriage and the Family, 55,* 653–650.

Sontag, S. (1972, October). The double standard of aging. *Saturday Review,* pp. 29–38.

Sotiriou, P. E. (1984). *Integrating college study skills: Reasoning in reading, listening and writing.* Belmont, CA: Wadsworth.

Sotiriou, P. E. (1993). *Integrating college study skills: Reasoning in reading, listening and writing.* Belmont, CA: Wadsworth.

South, S. J. (1991). Sociodemographic differentials in mate selection preferences. *Journal of Marriage and the Family, 53,* 928–940.

Spanos, N. P. (1994). Multiple identity enactments and multiple personality disorder: A sociocognitive perspective. *Psychological Bulletin, 116,* 143–165.

Spence, J. T. (1983). Comment on Lubinski, Tellegen, and Butcher's "Masculinity, femininity, and androgyny viewed and assessed as distinct concepts." *Journal of Personality and Social Psychology, 44,* 440–446.

Spiegel, D. (1993). Social support: How friends, family, and groups can help. In D. Goleman & J. Gurin (Eds.), *Mind/body medicine: How to use your mind for better health.* Yonkers, NY: Consumer Reports Books.

Spiegel, D. (1994). Dissociative disorders. In R. E. Hales, S. C. Yudofsky, & J. A. Talbott (Eds.), *The American Psychiatric Press textbook of psychiatry* (2nd ed.). Washington, DC: American Psychiatric Press.

Spiegler, M. D., & Guevremont, D. C. (1993). *Contemporary behavior therapy.* Pacific Grove, CA: Brooks/Cole.

Spielberger, C. D., Johnson, E. H., Russell, S. F., Crane, R. J., Jacobs, G. A., & Worden, T. J. (1985). The experience and expression of anger. In M. A. Chesney, S. E. Goldston & R. H. Rosenman (Eds.), *Anger and hostility in behavioral medicine.* New York: McGraw-Hill.

Spitze, G. (1988). Women's employment and family relations: A review. *Journal of Marriage and the Family, 50,* 595–618.

Spivey, C. B., & Prentice-Dunn, S. (1990). Assessing the directionality of deindividuated behavior: Effects of deindividuation, modeling, and private self-consciousness on aggressive and prosocial responses. *Basic and Applied Social Psychology, 11,* 387–403.

Sporakowski, M. J. (1988). A therapist's views on the consequences of change for the contemporary family. *Family Relations, 37,* 373–378.

Sprecher, S. (1989). The importance to males and females of physical attractiveness, earning potential and expressiveness in initial attraction. *Sex Roles, 21,* 591–607.

Sprecher, S., & Metts, S. (1989). Development of the "Romantic Beliefs Scale" and examination of the effects of gender and gender-role orientation. *Journal of Personal and Social Relationships, 6,* 387–411.

Sprecher, S., Sullivan, Q., & Hatfield, E. (1994). Mate selection preferences: Gender differences examined in a national sample. *Journal of Personality and Social Psychology, 66,* 1074–1080.

Spring, B. (1989). Stress and schizophrenia: Some definitional issues. In T. W. Miller (Ed.), *Stressful life events.* Madison, CT: International Universities Press.

Springer, S. P., & Deutsch, G. (1993). *Left brain, right brain* (4th ed.). New York: Freeman.

Sroufe, L. A., Egeland, B., Kreutzer, T. (1990). The fate of early experience following developmental change: Longitudinal approaches to individual adaptation in childhood. *Child Development, 61,* 1363–1373.

Stacy, A. W., Newcomb, M. D., & Bentler, P. M. (1993). Cognitive motivations and sensation seeking as long-term predictors of drinking problems. *Journal of Social and Clinical Psychology, 12,* 1–24.

Stall, R. D., Coates, T. J., & Hoff, C. (1988). Behavioral risk reduction for HIV infection among gay and bisexual men: A review of results from the United States. *American Psychologist, 43,* 878–885.

Stanford, M. W. (1987). Designer drugs: Medical aspects and clinical management. *Alcoholism Treatment Quarterly, 4,* 97–125.

Stanislaw, H., & Rice, F. J. (1988). Correlation between sexual desire and menstrual cycle characteristics. *Archives of Sexual Behavior, 17,* 499–508.

Stankov, L. (1988). Aging, attention, and intelligence. *Psychology and Aging, 3,* 59–74.

Stark, E. (1984, May). The unspeakable family secret. *Psychology Today,* pp. 41–46.

Starker, S. (1990). Self-help books: Ubiquitous agents of health care. *Medical Psychotherapy: An International Journal, 3,* 187–194.

Starker, S. (1992). Characteristics of self-help book readers among VA medical outpatients. *Medical Psychotherapy: An International Journal, 5,* 89–93.

Stattin, H., & Magnusson, D. (1990). *Pubertal maturation in female development.* Hillsdale, NJ: Erlbaum.

Staw, B. M., & Ross, J. (1985). Stability in the midst of change: A dispositional approach to job attitudes. *Journal of Applied Psychology, 70,* 469–480.

Steele, B. (1980). Psychodynamic factors in child abuse. In C. H. Kempe & F. E. Helfer (Eds.), *The battered child.* Chicago: University of Chicago Press.

Stein, M., & Miller, A. H. (1993). Stress, the immune system, and health and illness. In L. Goldberger & S. Breznitz (Eds.), *Handbook of stress: Theoretical and clinical aspects* (2nd ed.). New York: Free Press.

Stein, N., Marshall, N. L., & Tropp, L. R. (1993). *Secrets in public: Sexual harassment in our schools.* Wellesley, MA: Center for Research on Women at Wellesley College and the NOW Legal Defense and Education Fund.

Stein, P. J. (1975). Singlehood: An alternative to marriage. *Family Coordinator, 24,* 489–503.

Stein, P. J. (1976). *Single.* Englewood Cliffs, NJ: Prentice-Hall.

Stein, P. J. (1989). The diverse world of single adults. In J. M. Henslin (Ed.), *Marriage and family in a changing society* (3rd ed.). New York: Free Press.

Steinberg, L., & Silverberg, S. B. (1987). Influences on marital satisfaction during the middle stages of the family life cycle. *Journal of Marriage and the Family, 49,* 751–760.

Stekel, W. (1950). *Techniques of analytical psychotherapy.* New York: Liveright.

Stephan, W. G. (1989). A cognitive approach to stereotyping. In D. Bartal, C. F. Graumann, A. W. Kruglanski, & W. Stroebe (Eds.), *Stereotyping and prejudice: Changing conceptions.* New York: Springer-Verlag.

Stephen, T. D. (1985). Fixed-sequence and circular-causal models of relationship development: Divergent views on the role of communication in intimacy. *Journal of Marriage and the Family, 47,* 955–963.

Stern, G. S., McCants, T. R., & Pettine, P. W. (1982). Stress and illness: Controllable and uncontrollable events' relative

contributions. *Personality and Social Psychology Bulletin, 8,* 140–145.

Sternberg, R. J. (1986). A triangular theory of love. *Psychological Review, 93,* 119–135.

Sternberg, R. J. (1988). Triangulating love. In R. J. Sternberg & M. L. Barnes (Eds.), *The psychology of love.* New Haven, CT: Yale University Press.

Sternberg, R. J., & Grajek, S. (1984). The nature of love. *Journal of Personality and Social Psychology, 47,* 312–329.

Sternberg, R. J., & Soriano, L. J. (1984). Styles of conflict resolution. *Journal of Personality and Social Psychology, 47,* 115–126.

Sterns, H. L., Barrett, G. V., & Alexander, R. A. (1985). Accidents and the aging individual. In J. E. Birren & K. W. Schaie (Eds.), *Handbook of the psychology of aging.* New York: Van Nostrand Reinhold.

Stevens, G., Owens, D., & Schaefer, E. C. (1990). Education and attractiveness in marriage choices. *Social Psychology Quarterly, 53,* 62–70.

Stoffer, G. R., Davis, K. E., & Brown, J. B., Jr. (1977). The consequences of changing initial answers on objective tests: A stable effect and a stable misconception. *Journal of Educational Research, 70,* 272–277.

Stoll, A. L., Tohen, M., & Baldessarini, R. J. (1992). Increasing frequency of the diagnosis of obsessive-compulsive disorder. *American Journal of Psychiatry, 149,* 638–640.

Stone, A. A., Bovbjerg, D. H., Neale, J. M., Napoli, A., Valdimarsdottir, H., Cox, D., Hayden, F. G., & Gwaltney, J. M. (1992). Development of the common cold symptoms following experimental rhinovirus infection is related to prior stressful events. *Behavioral Medicine, 18,* 115–120.

Stone, A. A., & Neale, J. M. (1984). New measure of daily coping: Development and preliminary results. *Journal of Personality and Social Psychology, 46,* 892–906.

Stone, A. A., Neale, J. M., Cox, D. S., Napoli, A., Valdimarsdottir, H., & Kennedy-Moore, E. (1994). Daily events are associated with a secretory immune response to an oral antigen in men. *Health Psychology, 13,* 440–446.

Stone, L. (1977). *The family, sex and marriage in England 1500–1800.* New York: Harper & Row.

Strauman, T. J., Vookles, J., Berenstein, V., Chaiken, S., & Higgins, E. T. (1991). Self-discrepancies and vulnerability to body dissatisfaction and disordered eating. *Journal of Personality and Social Psychology, 61,* 946–956.

Straus, M. A., & Gelles, R. J. (1986). Societal change and change in family violence from 1975 to 1985 as revealed by two national surveys. *Journal of Marriage and the Family, 48,* 465–479.

Strickland, B. R. (1988). Sex-related differences in health and illness. *Psychology of Women Quarterly, 12,* 381–399.

Strober, M. (1989). Stressful life events associated with bulimia in anorexia nervosa: Empirical findings and theoretical speculations. In T. W. Miller (Ed.), *Stressful life events.* Madison, CT: International Universities Press.

Stroebe, M., Gergen, M. M., Gergen, K. J., & Stroebe, W. (1992). Broken hearts or broken bonds: Love and death in historical perspective. *American Psychologist, 47,* 1205–1212.

Strouse, J., & Fabes, R. A. (1985). Formal vs. informal sources of sex education: Competing forces in the sexual socialization of adolescents. *Adolescence, 78,* 251–263.

Strupp, H. H., & Howard, K. I. (1992).

A brief history of psychotherapy research. In D. K. Freedheim (Ed.), *History of psychotherapy: A century of change.* Washington, DC: American Psychological Association.

Stull, D. E., & Hatch, L. R. (1984). Unraveling the effects of multiple life changes. *Research on Aging, 6,* 560–571.

Stunkard, A. J., Harris, J. R., Pederson, N. L., & McClearn, G. E. (1990). The body-mass index of twins who have been reared apart. *New England Journal of Medicine, 322,* 1483–1487.

Stunkard, A. J., Sorensen, T., Hanis, C., Teasdale, T. W., Chakraborty, R., Schull, W. J., & Schulsinger, F. (1986). An adoption study of human obesity. *New England Journal of Medicine, 314,* 193–198.

Sturgis, E. T. (1984). Obsessional and compulsive disorders. In H. E. Adams & P. B. Sutker (Eds.), *Comprehensive handbook of psychopathology.* New York: Plenum.

Sturgis, E. T. (1993). Obsessive-compulsive disorders. In P. B. Sutker & H. E. Adams (Eds.), *Comprehensive handbook of psychopathology* (2nd ed.). New York: Plenum.

Suddath, R. L., Christison, G. W., Torrey, E. F., Casanova, M. F., & Weinberger, D. L. (1990). Anatomical abnormalities in the brains of monozygotic twins discordant for schizophrenia. *The New England Journal of Medicine, 322,* 789–794.

Sue, D. (1979). Erotic fantasies of college students during coitus. *Journal of Sex Research, 15,* 299–305.

Suedfeld, P. (1979). Stressful levels of environmental stimulation. In I. G. Sarason & C. D. Spielberger (Eds.), *Stress and anxiety* (Vol. 6). Washington, DC: Hemisphere.

Suinn, R. M. (1984). *Fundamentals of abnormal psychology.* Chicago: Nelson-Hall.

Sulloway, F. J. (1991). Reassessing Freud's case histories: The social construction of psychoanalysis. *ISIS, 82,* 245–275.

Sundstrom, E. (1978). Crowding as a sequential process: Review of research on the effects of population density on humans. In A. Baum & Y. M. Epstein (Eds.), *Human response to crowding.* Hillsdale, NJ: Erlbaum.

Super, D. E. (1957). *The psychology of careers.* New York: HarperCollins.

Super, D. E. (1985). Career and life development. In D. Brown & L. Brooks (Eds.), *Career choice and development.* San Francisco: Jossey-Bass.

Super, D. E. (1988). Vocational adjustment: Implementing a self-concept. *The Career Development Quarterly, 36,* 351–357.

Surra, C. A. (1990). Research and theory on mate selection and premarital relationships in the 1980s. *Journal of Marriage and the Family, 52,* 844–865.

Sussman, N. M., & Rosenfeld, H. M. (1982). Influence of culture, language, and sex on conversational distance. *Journal of Personality and Social Psychology, 42,* 66–74.

Swacker, M. (1975). The sex of the speaker as a sociolinguistic variable. In B. Thorne & N. Henley (Eds.), *Language and sex: Difference and dominance.* Rowley, MA: Newbury House.

Swaney, K., & Prediger, D. (1985). The relationship between interest-occupation congruence and job satisfaction. *Journal of Vocational Behavior, 26,* 13–24.

Swann, W. B., Jr., & Ely, R. J. (1984). A battle of wills: Self-verification versus behavioral confirmation. *Journal of Personality and Social Psychology, 46,* 1287–1302.

Swann, W. B., Jr., Hixon, J. G., Stein-Seroussi, A., & Gilbert, D. T. (1990).

The fleeting gleam of praise: Behavioral reactions to self-relevant feedback. *Journal of Personality and Social Psychology, 43*, 59–66.

Swann, W. B., Jr., Pelham, B. W., & Krull, D. S. (1989). Agreeable fancy or disagreeable truth? How people reconcile their self-enhancement and self-verification needs. *Journal of Personality and Social Psychology, 57*, 782–791.

Swann, W. B., Jr., & Read, S. J. (1981). Acquiring self-knowledge: The search for feedback that fits. *Journal of Personality and Social Psychology, 41*, 1119–1128.

Swann, W. B., Jr., Stein-Seroussi, A., & Giesler, R. B. (1992). Why people self-verify. *Journal of Personality and Social Psychology, 62*, 392–401.

Swann, W. B., Jr., Stein-Seroussi, A., & McNulty, S. E. (1992). Outcasts in a white-lie society: The enigmatic worlds of people with negative self-conceptions. *Journal of Personality and Social Psychology, 62*, 618–624.

Swartz, C. M. (1993). Clinical and laboratory predictors of ECT response. In C. E. Coffey (Ed.), *The clinical science of electroconvulsive therapy*. Washington, DC: American Psychiatric Press.

Sweeney, P. D., Anderson, K., & Bailey, S. (1986). Attributional style in depression: A meta-analytic review. *Journal of Personality and Social Psychology, 50*, 974–991.

Swenson, C. H., Jr. (1973). *Introduction to interpersonal relations*. Glenview, IL: Scott, Foresman.

Swim, J. K., Aikin K. J., Wayne, S. H., & Hunter, B. A. (1995). Sexism and racism: Old-fashioned and modern prejudices. *Journal of Personality and Social Psychology, 68*, 199–214.

Szasz, T. S. (1974). *The myth of mental illness*. New York: HarperCollins.

Szasz, T. S. (1993). *A lexicon of lunacy: Metaphoric malady, moral responsibility, and psychiatry*. New Brunswick, NJ: Transaction.

Tajfel, H., Billig, M., Bundy, R. P., & Flament, C. (1971). Social categorization and intergroup behavior. *European Journal of Social Psychology, 1*, 149–177.

Takanishi, R. (1993). The opportunities of adolescence—Research, interventions, and policy. *American Psychologist, 48*, 85–87.

Tanfer, K. (1987). Patterns of premarital cohabitation among never-married women in the United States. *Journal of Marriage and the Family, 49*, 483–497.

Tangri, S. S., Burt, M. R., & Johnson, L. B. (1982). Sexual harassment at work: Three explanatory models. *Journal of Social Issues, 38*, 33–54.

Tannen, D. (1990). *You just don't understand: Women and men in conversation*. New York: Ballantine.

Tanner, J. M. (1978). *Fetus into man: Physical growth from conception to maturity*. Cambridge, MA: Harvard University Press.

Tavris, C. (1977, January). Men and women report their views on masculinity. *Psychology Today*, pp. 34–42, 82.

Tavris, C. (1982). *Anger: The misunderstood emotion*. New York: Simon & Schuster.

Tavris, C. (1989). *Anger: The misunderstood emotion* (2nd ed.). New York: Simon & Schuster.

Tavris, C. (1991). The mismeasure of woman: Paradoxes and perspectives in the study of gender. In J. D. Goodchilds (Ed.), *Psychological perspectives on human diversity in America*. Washington, DC: American Psychological Association.

Tavris, C. (1992). *The mismeasure of woman*. New York: Simon & Schuster.

Tavris, C., & Sadd, S. (1977). *The Redbook report on female sexuality*. New York: Delacorte.

Tay, K. H., Ward, C. M., & Hill, J. A. (1993, August). *Holland's congruence and certainty of career aspirations in Asian graduate students*. Paper presented at the meeting of the American Psychological Association, Toronto, Canada.

Taylor, D. A., & Altman, I. (1987). Communication in interpersonal relationships: Social penetration processes. In M. E. Roloff & G. R. Miller (Eds.), *Interpersonal processes: New directions in communication research*. Newbury Park, CA: Sage Publications.

Taylor, M. C., & Hall, J. A. (1982). Psychological androgyny: Theories, methods, and conclusions. *Psychological Bulletin, 92*, 347–366.

Taylor, R. J., Chatters, L. M., Tucker, M. B., & Lewis, E. (1990). Developments in research on black families: A decade review. *Journal of Marriage and the Family, 52*, 993–1014.

Taylor, S. E. (1989). *Positive illusions: Creative self-deception and the healthy mind*. New York: Basic Books.

Taylor, S. E., & Brown, J. D. (1988). Illusion and well-being: A social psychological perspective on mental health. *Psychological Bulletin, 103*, 193–210.

Taylor, S. E., & Brown, J. D. (1994). Positive illusions and well-being revisited: Separating fact from fiction. *Psychological Bulletin, 116*, 21–27.

Teachman, J. D., Polonko, K. A., & Scanzoni, J. (1987). Demography of the family. In M. B. Sussman & S. K. Steinmetz (Eds.), *Handbook of marriage and the family*. New York: Plenum.

Teicher, M. H., Glod, C., & Cole, J. O. (1990). Emergence of intense suicidal preoccupation during fluoxetine treatment. *American Journal of Psychiatry, 147*, 207–210.

Tellegen, A., Lykken, D. T., Bouchard, T. J., Jr., Wilcox, K. J., Segal, N. L., & Rich, S. (1988). Personality similarity in twins reared apart and together. *Journal of Personality and Social Psychology, 54*, 1031–1039.

Temoshok, L. (1987). Personality, coping style, emotion and cancer: Towards an integrative model. *Cancer Surveys, 6*, 545–567.

Temoshok, L., Sweet, D. M., & Zich, J. (1987). A three city comparison of the public's knowledge and attitudes about AIDS. *Psychology & Health, 1*, 43–60.

Terkel, S. (1974). *Working: People talk about what they do all day and how they feel about what they do*. New York: Pantheon.

Terpstra, D. E., & Baker, D. D. (1989). The identification and classification of reactions to sexual harassment. *Journal of Organizational Behavior, 10*, 1–14.

Terr, L. (1994). *Unchained memories: True stories of traumatic memories, lost and found*. New York: Basic Books.

Terry, D. J. (1994). Determinants of coping: The role of stable and situation factors. *Journal of Personality and Social Psychology, 66*, 895–910.

Terry, R. L., & Kroger, D. L. (1976). Effects of eye correctives on ratings of attractiveness. *Perceptual and Motor Skills, 42*, 562.

Tesch, S. A., & Whitbourne, S. K. (1982). Intimacy and identity status in young adults. *Journal of Personality and Social Psychology, 43*, 1041–1051.

Tesser, A., & Rosen, S. (1975). The reluctance to transmit bad news. In L. Berkowitz (Ed.), *Advances in experimental social psychology* (Vol. 8). San Diego, CA: Academic Press.

Thibaut, J. W., & Kelley, H. H. (1959). *The social psychology of groups*. New York: Wiley.

Thigpen, C. H., & Cleckley, H. M. (1984). On the incidence of multiple personality disorder: A brief communication. *International Journal of Clinical and Experimental Hypnosis, 32*, 63–66.

Thomas, K. (1976). Conflict and conflict management. In M. D. Dunnette (Ed.), *Handbook of industrial and organizational psychology*. Chicago: Rand McNally.

Thomason, B. T., Brantkey, P. J., Jones, G. N., Dyer, H. R., & Morris, J. L. (1992). The relation between stress and disease activity in rheumatoid arthritis. *Journal of Behavioral Medicine, 15*, 215–220.

Thompson, A. P. (1983). Extramarital sex: A review of the research literature. *Journal of Sex Research, 19*, 1–22.

Thompson, A. P. (1984). Emotional and sexual components of extramarital relations. *Journal of Marriage and the Family, 46*, 35–42.

Thompson, J. W., Weiner, R. D., & Myers, C. P. (1994). Use of ECT in the United States in 1975, 1980, and 1986. *American Journal of Psychiatry, 151*, 1657–1661.

Thompson, S. C., & Kelley, J. J. (1981). Judgments of responsibility for activities in close relationships. *Journal of Personality and Social Psychology, 41*, 469–477.

Thompson, S. C., & Spacapan, S. (1991). Perceptions of control in vulnerable populations. *Journal of Social Issues, 47*, 1–21.

Thomson, E., & Colella, U. (1992). Cohabitation and marital stability: Quality or commitment? *Journal of Marriage and the Family, 54*, 259–267.

Thorndyke, P. W., & Hayes-Roth, B. (1979). The use of schemata in the acquisition and transfer of knowledge. *Cognitive Psychology, 11*, 83–106.

Thornton, A. (1989). Changing attitudes toward family issues in the United States. *Journal of Marriage and the Family, 51*, 873–893.

Thornton, B. (1984). Defensive attribution of responsibility: Evidence for an arousal-based motivational bias. *Journal of Personality and Social Psychology, 46*, 721–734.

Thornton, B. (1992). Repression and its mediating influence on the defensive attribution of responsibility. *Journal of Research in Personality, 26*, 44–57.

Tice, D. M. (1991). Esteem protection or enhancement? Self-handicapping motives and attributions differ by trait self-esteem. *Journal of Personality and Social Psychology, 5*, 711–725.

Ting-Toomey, S. (1991). Intimacy expressions in three cultures: France, Japan and the United States. *International Journal of Intercultural Relations, 15*, 29–46.

Tobin-Richards, M. H., Boxer, A. M., & Petersen, A. C. (1983). The psychological significance of pubertal change: Sex differences in perceptions of self during early adolescence. In J. Brooks-Gunn & A. C. Petersen (Eds.), *Girls at puberty: Biological and psychosocial perspectives*. New York: Plenum.

Toffler, A. (1970). *Future shock*. New York: Random House.

Toffler, A. (1980). *The third wave*. New York: Bantam Books.

Tolstedt, B. E., & Stokes, J. P. (1984). Self-disclosure, intimacy, and the depenetration process. *Journal of Personality and Social Psychology, 46*, 84–90.

Tonnesen, P., Norregaard, J., Simonsen, K., & Sawe, U. (1991). A double-blind trial of a 16-hour transdermal nicotine patch in smoking cessation. *New England Journal of Medicine, 325*, 311–315.

Torrey, E. F. (1992). *Freudian fraud: The*

malignant effect of Freud's theory on American thought and culture. New York: Harper Perennial.

Tougas, F., Brown, R., Beaton, A. M., & Joy, S. (1995). Neosexism: Plus ça change, plus ç'est pareil. *Personality and Social Psychology Bulletin, 21,* 842–849.

Tracey, T. J., & Rounds, J. (1993). Evaluating Holland's and Gati's vocational-interest models: A structural meta-analysis. *Psychological Bulletin, 113,* 229–246.

Travis, C. B. (1988). *Women and health psychology: Mental health issues.* Hillsdale, NJ: Erlbaum.

Treas, J. (1983). Aging and the family. In D. S. Woodruff & J. E. Birren (Eds.), *Aging: Scientific perspectives and social issues.* Pacific Grove, CA: Brooks/Cole.

Treiman, D. J., & Terrell, K. (1975). Sex and the process of status attainment: A comparison of working women and men. *American Sociological Review, 40(2),* 174–200.

Triandis, H. C. (1989). Self and social behavior in differing cultural contexts. *Psychological Review, 96,* 269–289.

Triandis, H. C. (1994). *Culture and social behavior.* New York: McGraw-Hill.

Trickett, P. K., & Putnam, F. M. (1993). Impact of child sexual abuse on females: Toward a developmental, psychobiological interpretation. *Psychological Science, 4,* 81–87.

Tripp, C. A. (1987). *The homosexual matrix.* New York: Meridian.

Trivers, R. L. (1972). Parental investment and sexual selection. In B. Campbell (Ed.), *Sexual selection and the descent of man.* Chicago: Aldine.

Trovato, F., & Lauris, G. (1989). Marital status and mortality in Canada: 1951–1981. *Journal of Marriage and the Family, 51,* 907–922.

Trussell, J., & Westoff, C. F. (1980). Contraceptive practice and trends in coital frequency. *Family Planning Perspectives, 12,* 246–249.

Tsai, M., & Uemura, A. (1988). Asian Americans: The struggles, the conflicts, and the successes. In P. Bronstein & K. Quina (Eds.), *Teaching a psychology of people.* Washington, DC: American Psychological Association.

Tschann, J. M., Johnston, J. R., Kline, M., & Wallerstein, J. S. (1989). Family process and children's functioning during divorce. *Journal of Marriage and the Family, 51,* 431–444.

Tschann, J. M., Johnston, J. R., Kline, M., & Wallerstein, J. S. (1990). Conflict, loss, change and parent-child relationships: Predicting children's adjustment during divorce. *Journal of Divorce, 13,* 1–22.

Turner, B. F., & Adams, C. G. (1988). Reported change in preferred sexual activity over the adult years. *Journal of Sex Research, 25,* 289–303.

Turner, J. R., & Wheaton, B. (1995). Checklist measurement of stressful life events. In S. Cohen, R. C. Kessler, & L. U. Gordon (Eds.), *Measuring stress: A guide for health and social scientists.* New York: Oxford University Press.

Turner, S. M., McCann, B. S., Beidel, D. C., & Mezzich, J. E. (1986). DSM-III classification of the anxiety disorders: A psychometric study. *Journal of Abnormal Psychology, 95,* 168–172.

Uhle, S. M. (1994). Codependence: Contextual variables in the language of social pathology. *Issues in Mental Health Nursing, 15,* 307–317.

Unger, R. (1981). Sex as a social reality: Field and laboratory research. *Psychology of Women Quarterly, 5,* 645–653.

Unger, R., & Crawford, M. (1992). *Women*

and gender: A feminist psychology. New York: McGraw-Hill.

Ungerleider, J. T., & Pechnick, R. (1992). Hallucinogens. In J. H. Lowinson, P. Ruiz, & R. B. Millman (Eds.), *Substance abuse: A comprehensive textbook* (2nd ed.). Baltimore: Williams & Wilkins.

Upshaw, H. S. (1969). The personal reference scale: An approach to social judgment. In L. Berkowitz (Ed.), *Advances in experimental social psychology* (Vol. 4). New York: Academic Press.

Ursano, R. J., & Silberman, E. K. (1994). Psychoanalysis, psychoanalytic psychotherapy, and supportive psychotherapy. In R. E. Hales, S. C. Yudofsky, & J. A. Talbott (Eds.), *The American Psychiatric Press textbook of psychiatry* (2nd ed.). Washington, DC: American Psychiatric Press.

U.S. Bureau of the Census. (1992). *Sixty-five plus in America* (Current Population Reports, Special Studies, Series P23–178). Washington, DC: U.S. Government Printing Office.

U.S. Bureau of the Census. (1994). *Statistical abstract of the United States: 1994* (114th ed.). Washington, DC: U.S. Government Printing Office.

U.S. Bureau of the Census. (1995). *Statistical abstract of the United States: 1995* (115th ed.). Washington, DC: U.S. Government Printing Office.

U.S. Department of Health and Human Services. (1989). *Reducing the health consequences of smoking: 25 years of progress.* Rockville, MD: U.S. Government Printing Office.

U.S. Department of Health and Human Services. (1990). *The health benefits of smoking cessation: A report of the surgeon general.* Washington, DC: U.S. Government Printing Office.

U.S. Department of Justice. (1988). *Report to the nation on crime and justice: The data.* Washington, DC: U.S. Government Printing Office.

U.S. Department of Labor. (1990, September). *Twenty facts on women workers.* Washington, DC: U.S. Government Printing Office.

U.S. Department of Labor. (1992). *Pipelines of progress: An update on the glass ceiling initiative.* Washington, DC: U.S. Government Printing Office.

U.S. Merit Systems Protection Board. (1988). *Sexual harassment of federal workers: An update.* Washington, DC: U.S. Government Printing Office.

Vaillant, G. E. (1977). *Adaptation to life.* Boston: Little, Brown.

Vaillant, G. E. (1994). Ego mechanisms of defense and personality psychopathology. *Journal of Abnormal Psychology, 103,* 44–50.

Vance, B. K., & Green, V. (1984). Lesbian identities: An examination of sexual behavior and sex role acquisition as related to age of initial same-sex encounter. *Psychology of Women Quarterly, 8,* 293–307.

Vance, E. B., & Wagner, N. N. (1976). Written descriptions of orgasm: A study of sex differences. *Archives of Sexual Behavior, 5,* 87–98.

VandenBos, G. R., Cummings, N. A., & DeLeon, P. H. (1992). A century of psychotherapy: Economic and environmental influences. In D. K. Freedheim (Ed.), *History of psychotherapy: A century of change.* Washington, DC: American Psychological Association.

VanderPlate, C., Aral, S. O., & Magder, L. (1988). The relationship among genital herpes simplex virus, stress, and social support. *Health Psychology, 7,* 159–168.

van der Velde, F. W., van der Pligt, J., & Hooykaas, C. (1994). Perceiving AIDS-related risk: Accuracy as a func-

tion of differences in actual risk. *Health Psychology, 13,* 25–33.

Van Houten, R. (1983). Punishment: From the animal laboratory to the applied setting. In S. Axelrod & J. Apsche (Eds.), *The effects of punishment on human behavior.* New York: Academic Press.

VanItallie, T. B. (1979). Obesity: Adverse effects on health and longevity. *American Journal of Clinical Nutrition, 32,* 2727.

Van Wormer, K. (1989). Co-dependency: Implications for women and therapy. *Women and Therapy, 8,* 51–63.

Vaux, A. (1988). Social and personal factors in loneliness. *Journal of Social and Clinical Psychology, 6,* 462–471.

Vemer, E., Coleman, M., Ganong, L. H., & Cooper, H. (1989). Marital satisfaction in remarriage: A meta-analysis. *Journal of Marriage and the Family, 51,* 713–725.

Ventura, J., Nuechterlein, K. H., Lukoff, D., & Hardesty, J. P. (1989). A prospective study of stressful life events and schizophrenic relapse. *Journal of Abnormal Psychology, 98,* 407–411.

Verderber, R. F., & Verderber, K. S. (1995). *Inter-act: Using interpersonal communication skills.* Belmont, CA: Wadsworth.

Vinogradov, S., & Yalom, I. D. (1994). Group therapy. In R. E. Hales, S. C. Yudofsky, & J. A. Talbott (Eds.), *The American Psychiatric Press textbook of psychiatry* (2nd ed.). Washington, DC: American Psychiatric Press.

Vinokur, A. D., & van Ryn, M. (1993). Social support and undermining in close relationships: Their independent effects on the mental health of unemployed persons. *Journal of Personality and Social Psychology, 65,* 350–359.

Vitaliano, P. P., Katon, W., Maiuro, R. D., & Russo, J. (1989). Coping in chest pain patients with and without psychiatric disorders. *Journal of Consulting and Clinical Psychology, 57,* 338–343.

Vogt, T., Mullooly, J., Ernst, D., Pope, C., & Hollis, J. (1992). Social networks as predictors of ischemic heart disease, cancer, stroke and hypertension: Incidence, survival and mortality. *Journal of Clinical Epidemiology, 45,* 659–666.

Von Baeyer, C. L., Sherk, D. L., & Zanna, M. P. (1981). Impression management in the job interview: When the female applicant meets the male (chauvinist) interviewer. *Personality and Social Psychology Bulletin, 7,* 45–51.

Voydanoff, P. (1990). Economic distress and family relations: A review of the eighties. *Journal of Marriage and the Family, 52,* 1099–1115.

Voydanoff, P., & Donnelly, B. W. (1990). *Adolescent sexuality and pregnancy.* Newbury Park, CA: Sage Publications.

Wachtel, P. L. (1977). *Psychoanalysis and behavior therapy: Toward an integration.* New York: Basic Books.

Wachtel, P. L. (1989). *The poverty of affluence: A psychological portrait of the American way of life.* Philadelphia: New Society.

Wachtel, P. L. (1991). From eclecticism to synthesis: Toward a more seamless psychotherapeutic integration. *Journal of Psychotherapy Integration, 1,* 43–54.

Wadden, T. A., Stunkard, A. J., Brownell, K. D., & VanItallie, T. B. (1983). The Cambridge diet. *Journal of the American Medical Association, 250,* 2833–2834.

Wade, C., & Tavris, C. (1990). *Learning to think critically: A handbook to accompany psychology.* New York: HarperCollins.

Wakefield, J. C. (1992). The concept of mental disorder: On the boundary between biological facts and social values. *American Psychologist, 47,* 373–388.

Walker, L. E. (1989). Psychology and violence against women. *American Psychologist, 44,* 695–702.

Walker, L. O., & Best, M. A. (1991). Well-being of mothers with infant children: A preliminary comparison of employed women and homemakers. *Women and Health, 17,* 71–89.

Wallace, R. K., & Benson, H. (1972). The physiology of meditation. *Scientific American, 226,* 84–90.

Wallace-Broscious, A., Serafica, F. C., & Osipow, S. H. (1994). Adolescent career development: Relationships to self-concept and identity status. *Journal of Research on Adolescence, 4,* 127–149.

Walster, E., Aronson, E., Abrahams, D., & Rottman, L. (1966). Importance of physical attractiveness in dating behavior. *Journal of Personality and Social Psychology, 4,* 508–516.

Walster, E., & Berscheid, E. (1974). A little bit about love: A minor essay on a major topic. In T. L. Huston (Ed.), *Foundations of interpersonal attraction.* New York: Academic Press.

Walster, E., Walster, G. W., Piliavin, J., & Schmidt, L. (1973). Playing hard-to-get: Understanding an elusive phenomenon. *Journal of Personality and Social Psychology, 26,* 113–121.

Walter, T., & Siebert, A. (1990). *Student success: How to succeed in college and still have time for your friends.* Fort Worth: Holt, Rinehart & Winston.

Ward, S. E., Leventhal, H., & Love, R. (1988). Repression revisited: Tactics used in coping with a severe health threat. *Personality and Social Psychology Bulletin, 14,* 735–746.

Warner, R. E. (1991). Bibliotherapy: A comparison of the prescription practices of Canadian and American psychologists. *Canadian Psychology, 32,* 529–530.

Warr, P. B. (1987). *Work, unemployment, and mental health.* Oxford: Clarendon.

Warshaw, M. G., Fierman, E., Pratt, L., Hunt, M., Yonkers, K. A., Massion, A. O., & Keller, M. B. (1993). Quality of life and dissociation in anxiety disorder patients with histories of trauma or PTSD. *American Journal of Psychiatry, 150,* 1512–1516.

Watson, A., & Boundy, D. (1989). *Willpower's not enough.* New York: Harper & Row.

Watson, D., & Pennebaker, J. W. (1989). Health complaints, stress, and distress: Exploring the central role of negative affectivity. *Psychological Review, 96,* 234–254.

Watson, D. L., & Tharp, R. G. (1989). *Self-directed behavior: Self-modification for personal adjustment* (5th ed.). Pacific Grove, CA: Brooks/Cole.

Watson, D. L., & Tharp, R. G. (1993). *Self-directed behavior: Self-modification for personal adjustment* (6th ed.). Pacific Grove, CA: Brooks/Cole.

Watson, J. B. (1913). Psychology as the behaviorist views it. *Psychological Review, 20,* 158–177.

Weaver, R. C., & Rodnick, J. E. (1986). Type-A behavior: Clinical significance, evaluation, and management. *Journal of Family Practice, 23,* 255–261.

Webb, S. L. (1991). *Step forward: Sexual harassment in the workplace — What you need to know!* New York: Mastermedia.

Wechsler, H., Davenport, A., Dowdall, G., Moeykens, B., & Castillo, S. (1994). Health and behavioral consequences of binge drinking in college: A national survey of students at 140 campuses. *Journal of the American Medical Association, 272,* 1672–1677.

Weeks, M. O., & Gage, B. A. (1984). A comparison of the marriage-role expectations of college women enrolled in a functional marriage course in 1961, 1972, and 1978. *Sex Roles, 11,* 377–388.

Wehr, T. A., Sack, D. A., & Rosenthal, N. E. (1987). Sleep reduction as a final common pathway in the genesis of mania. *American Journal of Psychiatry, 144,* 201–204.

Weinberg, C. (1979). *Self creation.* New York: Avon.

Weinberger, D. A. (1990). The construct validity of the repressive coping style. In J. L. Singer (Ed.), *Repression and dissociation.* Chicago: University of Chicago Press.

Weiner, B. (Ed.). (1974). *Achievement motivation and attribution theory.* Morristown, NJ: General Learning Press.

Weiner, B. (1985). "Spontaneous" causal thinking. *Psychological Bulletin, 97,* 74–84.

Weiner, B. (1986). *An attribution theory of emotion and motivation.* New York: Springer-Verlag.

Weiner, B., Frieze, I., Kukla, A., Reed, L., Rest, S., & Rosenbaum, R. M. (1972). Perceiving the causes of success and failure. In E. E. Jones, D. E. Kanouse, H. H. Kelley, R. E. Nisbett, S. Valins, & B. Weiner (Eds.), *Perceiving the causes of behavior.* Morristown, NJ: General Learning Press.

Weiner, H. (1978). Emotional factors. In S. C. Werner & S. H. Ingbar (Eds.), *The thyroid.* New York: HarperCollins.

Weiner, H. (1992). *Perturbing the organism: The biology of stressful experience.* Chicago: University of Chicago Press.

Weiner, H., & Fawzy, F. I. (1989). An integrative model of health, disease, and illness. In S. Cheren (Ed.), *Psychosomatic medicine: Theory, physiology, and practice* (Vol. 1). Madison, CT: International Universities Press.

Weiner, M. F. (1993). Role of the leader in group psychotherapy. In H. I. Kaplan & B. J. Sadock (Eds.), *Comprehensive group psychotherapy.* Baltimore: Williams & Wilkins.

Weiner, R. D. (1984). Does electroconvulsive therapy cause brain damage? *Behavioral and Brain Sciences, 7,* 1–22.

Weiner, R. D., & Coffey, C. E. (1988). Indications for use of electroconvulsive therapy. In A. J. Frances & R. E. Hales (Eds.), *Review of psychiatry* (Vol. 7). Washington, DC: American Psychiatric Press.

Weinstein, N. D. (1980). Unrealistic optimism about future life events. *Journal of Personality and Social Psychology, 39,* 806–820.

Weinstein, N. D. (1989). Perceptions of personal susceptibility to harm. In V. M. Mays, G. W. Albee, & S. F. Schneider (Eds.), *Primary prevention of AIDS: Psychological approaches.* Newbury Park, CA: Sage Publications.

Weis, D. L. (1983). Affective reactions of women to their initial experience of coitus. *Journal of Sex Research, 19,* 209–237.

Weisaeth, L. (1993). Disasters: Psychological and psychiatric aspects. In L. Goldberger & S. Breznitz (Eds.), *Handbook of stress: Theoretical and clinical aspects* (2nd ed.). New York: Free Press.

Weisner, T. S., & Wilson-Mitchell, J. E. (1990). Nonconventional family lifestyles and sex typing in six-year-olds. *Child Development, 61,* 1915–1933.

Weiss, B., Dodge, K. A., Bates, J. E., & Petit, G. S. (1992). Some consequences of early harsh discipline: Child aggression and a maladaptive social information processing style. *Child Development, 63,* 1321–1335.

Weiss, R. S. (1975). *Marital separation.* New York: Basic Books.

Weissman, M. M., Bruce, M. L., Leaf, P. J., Florio, L. P., & Holzer, C., III. (1991). Affective disorders. In L. N. Robins & D. A. Regier (Eds.), *Psychiatric disorders in America: The epidemiologic catchment area study.* New York: Free Press.

Weissman, M. M., Prusoff, B. A., DiMascio, A., Neu, C., Goklaney, M., & Klerman, G. L. (1979). The efficacy of drugs and psychotherapy in the treatment of acute depressive episodes. *American Journal of Psychiatry, 136,* 555–558.

Weisz, J. R., Rothbaum, F. M., & Blackburn, T. C. (1984). Standing out and standing in: The psychology of control in America and Japan. *American Psychologist, 39,* 955–969.

Weiten, W. (1988). Pressure as a form of stress and its relationship to psychological symptomatology. *Journal of Social and Clinical Psychology, 6,* 127–139.

Weitzman, L. J. (1985). *The divorce revolution: The unexpected social and economic consequences for women and children in America.* New York: Free Press.

Weitzman, L. J. (1989). The divorce revolution and the feminization of poverty. In J. M. Henslin (Ed.), *Marriage and the family in a changing society.* (3rd ed.). New York: Free Press.

Wekstein, L. (1979). *Handbook of suicidology.* New York: Brunner/Mazel.

Wells, L. E., & Marwell, G. (1976). *Self-esteem: Its conceptualization and measurement.* Newbury Park, CA: Sage Publications.

Werbach, M. R. (1988). *Nutritional influences on illness: A sourcebook of clinical research.* Tarzana, CA: Third Line Press.

Weschler, H., Davenport, A., Dowdall, G., Moeykens, B., & Castillo, S. (1994). Health and behavioral consequences of binge drinking in college: A national survey of students at 140 campuses. *Journal of the American Medical Association, 272,* 1672–1677.

Wesson, D. R., Smith, D. E., & Seymour, R. B. (1992). Sedative-hypnotics and tricyclics. In J. H. Lowinson, P. Ruiz, & R. B. Millman (Eds.), *Substance abuse: A comprehensive textbook* (2nd ed.). Baltimore: Williams & Wilkins.

West, C., & Zimmerman, D. H. (1983). Small insults: A study of interruptions in cross-sex conversations between unacquainted persons. In B. Thorne, C. Kramarae, & N. Henley (Eds.), *Language, gender, and society.* Rowley, MA: Newbury House.

Westefeld, J. S., & Furr, S. R. (1987). Suicide and depression among college students. *Professional Psychology: Research and Practice, 18,* 119–123.

Westen, D. (1990). Psychoanalytic approaches to personality. In L. A. Pervin (Ed.), *Handbook of personality: Theory and research.* New York: Guilford Press.

Westoff, C. (1974). Coital frequency and contraception. *Family Planning Perspectives, 6,* 136–141.

Whitbourne, S. K. (1985). *The aging body: Physiological changes and psychological consequences.* New York: Springer-Verlag.

Whitbourne, S. K., Zuschlag, M. K., Elliot, L. B., & Waterman, A. S. (1992). Psychosocial development in adulthood: A 22–year sequential study. *Journal of Personality and Social Psychology, 63,* 260–271.

White, J. M. (1987). Premarital cohabitation and marital stability in Canada. *Journal of Marriage and the Family, 49,* 641–647.

White, J. W., & Koss, M. P. (1991). Courtship violence: Incidence in a national sample of higher education students. *Violence and Victims, 6,* 247–256.

White, L. K. (1990). Determinants of divorce: A review of research in the eighties. *Journal of Marriage and the Family, 32,* 904–912.

White, L. K. (1991). Determinants of

divorce: A review of research in the eighties. In A. Booth (Ed.), *Contemporary families: Looking forward, looking back.* Minneapolis: National Council on Family Relations.

White, L. K., & Booth, A. (1985). Stepchildren in remarriages. *American Sociological Review, 50,* 689–698.

Whitehead, W. E. (1994). Assessing the effects of stress on physical symptoms. *Health Psychology, 13,* 99–102.

Whitfield, C. L. (1987). *Healing the child within: Discovery and recovery for adult children of dysfunctional families.* Deerfield Beach, FL: Health Communications.

Whitfield, C. L. (1991). *Co-dependence: Healing the human condition.* Deerfield Beach, FL: Health Communications.

Whitfield, C. L. (1993). *Boundaries and relationships: Knowing, protecting and enjoying the self.* Deerfield Beach, FL: Health Communications.

Whiting, J. W. M., Burbank, V. K., & Ratner, M. S. (1986). The duration of maidenhood. In J. B. Lancaster & B. A. Hamburg (Eds.), *School age pregnancy and parenthood.* Hawthorne, NY: Aldine de Gruyter.

Whitley, B. E., Jr. (1983). Sex-role orientation and self-esteem: A critical meta-analytic review. *Journal of Personaltiy and Social Psychology, 44,* 765–778.

Whitley, B. E., Jr. (1984). Sex-role orientation and psychological well-being: Two meta-analyses. *Sex Roles, 12,* 207–225.

Whitley, B. E., Jr. (1988a). *College students' reasons for sexual intercourse: A sex role perspective.* Paper presented at the 96th Annual Meeting of the American Psychological Association, Atlanta, GA.

Whitley, B. E., Jr. (1988b). Masculinity, femininity, and self-esteem: A multitrait-multimethod analysis. *Sex Roles, 18,* 419–432.

Whitley, B. E., Jr., & Hern, A. L. (1991). Perceptions of vulnerability to pregnancy and the use of effective contraception. *Personality and Social Psychology Bulletin, 17,* 104–110.

Whitley, B. E., Jr., & Schofield, J. W. (1986). A meta-analysis of research on adolescent contraceptive use. *Population and Environment, 8,* 173–203.

Widiger, T. A., Frances, A. J., Pincus, H. A., Davis, W. W., & First, M. B. (1991). Toward an empirical classification for the DSM-IV. *Journal of Abnormal Psychology, 100,* 280–288.

Wiebe, D. J. (1991). Hardiness and stress moderation: A test of proposed mechanisms. *Journal of Personality and Social Psychology, 60,* 89–99.

Wielawski, I. (1991, October 3). Unlocking the secrets of memory. *Los Angeles Times,* p. 1.

Wiest, W. (1977). Semantic differential profiles of orgasm and other experiences among men and women. *Sex Roles, 3,* 399–403.

Wiggins, J. D., Lederer, D. A., Salkowe, A., & Rys, G. S. (1983). Job satisfaction related to tested congruence and differentiation. *Journal of Vocational Behavior, 23,* 112–121.

Wiggins, J. S. (1992). Have model, will travel. *Journal of Personality, 60,* 527–532.

Willett, W. C., Stampfer, M. F., Colditz, G. A., Rosner, B. A., Hennekens, C. H., & Speizer, F. E. (1987). Moderate alcohol consumption and the risk of breast cancer. *New England Journal of Medicine, 316,* 1174–1180.

Williams, B. K., & Knight, S. M. (1994). *Healthy for life: Wellness and the art of living.* Pacific Grove, CA: Brooks/Cole.

Williams, G. D., Stinson, F. S., Clem, D., & Noble, J. (1992). *Surveillance report 23, Apparent per capita alcohol consumption:*

National, state, and regional trends, 1977–1990. Rockville, MD: National Institute on Alcohol Abuse and Alcoholism.

Williams, J. B. W. (1994). Psychiatric classification. In R. E. Hales, S. C. Yudofsky, & J. A. Talbott (Eds.), *The American Psychiatric Press textbook of psychiatry* (2nd ed.). Washington, DC: American Psychiatric Press.

Williams, J. C., & Solano, C. H. (1983). The social reality of feeling lonely: Friendship and reciprocation. *Personality and Social Psychology Bulletin, 9,* 237–242.

Williams, J. E., & Best, D. L. (1982). *Measuring sex stereotypes: A thirty-nation study.* Newbury Park, CA: Sage Publications.

Williams, J. E., & Best, D. L. (1990). *Measuring sex stereotypes: A multination study* (Rev. ed.). Newbury Park, CA: Sage Publications.

Williams, M. H. (1992). Exploitation and inference: Mapping the damage from therapist-patient sexual involvement. *American Psychologist, 47,* 412–421.

Williams, N. A., & Deffenbacher, J. L. (1983). Life stress and chronic yeast infections. *Journal of Human Stress, 9,* 26–31.

Williams, R. B., & Barefoot, J. C. (1988). Coronary-prone behavior: The emerging role of the hostility complex. In B. K. Houston & C. R. Snyder (Eds.), *Type A behavior pattern: Research, theory, and intervention.* New York: Wiley.

Wills, T. A. (1981). Downward comparison principles in social psychology. *Psychological Bulletin, 90,* 245–271.

Wilson, E. O. (1980). *Sociobiology.* Cambridge, MA: Harvard University Press.

Wilson, G. (1990). Personality, time of day and arousal. *Personality and Individual Differences, 11,* 153–168.

Wilson, G. T., & O'Leary, K. D. (1980). *Principles of behavior therapy.* Englewood Cliffs, NJ: Prentice-Hall.

Wilson, M. (1993). DSM-III and the transformation of American psychiatry: A history. *American Journal of Psychiatry, 150,* 399–410.

Windsor, R. A., Cutter, G., Morris, J., Reese, Y., Manzella, B., Bartlett, E. E., Samuelson, C., & Spanos, D. (1985). The effectiveness of smoking cessation methods for smokers in public health maternity clinics: A randomized trial. *American Journal of Public Health, 75,* 1389–1392.

Winick, C. (1992). Epidemiology of alcohol and drug abuse. In J. H. Lowinson, P. Ruiz, & R. B. Millman (Eds.), *Substance abuse: A comprehensive textbook* (2nd ed.). Baltimore, MD: Williams & Wilkins.

Winn, K. I., Crawford, D. W., & Fischer, J. (1991). Equity and commitment in romance versus friendship. *Journal of Social Behavior and Personality, 6,* 301–314.

Wisensale, S. K. (1992). Toward the 21st century: Family change and public policy. *Family Relations, 41,* 417–422.

Wittenberg, M. T., & Reis, H. T. (1986). Loneliness, social skills, and social perception. *Personality and Social Psychology Bulletin, 12,* 121–130.

Wixted, J. T., Bellack, A. S., & Hersen, M. (1990). Behavior therapy. In A. S. Bellack & M. Hersen (Eds.), *Handbook of comparative treatments for adult disorders.* New York: Wiley.

Wolchik, S. A., Braver, S. L., & Jensen, K. (1985). Volunteer bias in erotica research: Effects of intrusiveness of measure and sexual background. *Archives of Sexual Behavior, 14,* 93–107.

Wolf, S. (1986). Common and grave disorders identified with occupational stress. In S. Wolf & A. J. Finestone (Eds.), *Occupational stress: Health and performance at work.* Littleton, MA: PSG Publishing.

Wolf, S., & Goodell, H. (1968). *Stress and disease.* Springfield, IL: Charles C. Thomas.

Wolfe, L. (1981). *The Cosmo report.* New York: Arbor House.

Woll, S. (1986). So many to choose from: Decision strategies in videodating. *Journal of Social and Personal Relationships, 3,* 43–52.

Wolpe, J. (1958). *Psychotherapy by reciprocal inhibition.* Stanford, CA: Stanford University Press.

Wolpe, J. (1987). The promotion of scientific therapy: A long voyage. In J. K. Zeig (Ed.), *The evolution of psychotherapy.* New York: Brunner/Mazel.

Wolpe, J. (1990). *The practice of behavior therapy.* Elmsford, NY: Pergamon.

Wood, J. T. (1994). *Gendered lives: Communication, gender, and culture.* Belmont, CA: Wadsworth.

Wood, J. V. (1989). Theory and research concerning social comparisons of personal attributes. *Psychological Bulletin, 106,* 231–248.

Wood, W., & Kallgren, C. A. (1988). Communicator attributes and persuasion: Recipients' access to attitude-relevant information in memory. *Personality and Social Psychology Bulletin, 14,* 172–182.

Woolfolk, R. L., & Richardson, F. C. (1978). *Stress, sanity and survival.* New York: Sovereign/Monarch.

Wortman, C. B., & Silver, R. C. (1990). Successful mastery of bereavement and widowhood: A life-course perspective. In P. B. Baltes & M. M. Baltes (Eds.), *Successful aging.* Cambridge, MA: Cambridge University Press.

Wright, J. C., & Dawson, V. L. (1985). Distortion in control attributions for real life events. *Journal of Research in Psychology, 19,* 54–71.

Wright, J. H., & Beck, A. T. (1994). Cognitive therapy. In R. E. Hales, S. C. Yudofsky, & J. A. Talbott (Eds.), *The American Psychiatric Press textbook of psychiatry* (2nd ed.). Washington, DC: American Psychiatric Press.

Wright, M. H., Zautra, A. J., & Braver, S. L. (1985). Distortion in control attributions for real life events. *Journal of Research in Personality, 19*(1), 54–71.

Wright, P. H. (1982). Men's friendships, women's friendships, and the alleged inferiority of the latter. *Sex Roles, 8,* 1–20.

Wright, P. H. (1989). Gender differences in adults' same- and cross-gender friendships. In R. G. Adams & R. Blieszner (Eds.), *Older adult friendship.* Newbury Park, CA: Sage Publications.

Wright, P. H., & Wright, K. D. (1991). Codependency: Addictive love, adjustive relating, or both? *Contemporary Family Therapy: An International Journal, 13,* 435–454.

Wurman, R. S. (1989). *Information anxiety.* New York: Doubleday.

Wyatt, G. E., Peters, S. D., & Guthrie, D. (1988). Kinsey revisited, Part I: Comparison of the sexual socialization and sexual behavior of white women over 33 years. *Archives of Sexual Behavior, 17,* 201–239.

Wyler, A. R., Masuda, M., & Holmes, T. H. (1971). Magnitude of life events and seriousness of illness. *Psychosomatic Medicine, 33,* 115–122.

Wylie, R. C. (1979). *The self-concept: Theory and research on selected topics.* Lincoln: University of Nebraska Press.

Xiaohe, X., & Whyte, M. K. (1990). Love matches and arranged marriages: A Chinese replication. *Journal of Marriage and the Family, 52,* 709–722.

Yalom, I. D. (1985). *The theory and practice*

of group psychotherapy. New York: Basic Books.

Yapko, M. D. (1994). *Suggestions of abuse: True and false memories of childhood sexual trauma.* New York: Simon & Schuster.

Yoder, J. D., Adams, J., Grove, S., & Priest, R. F. (1985). To teach is to learn: Overcoming tokenism with mentors. *Psychology of Women Quarterly, 9,* 119–132.

Young, J. E. (1982). Loneliness, depression and cognitive therapy: Theory and application. In L. A. Peplau & D. Perlman (Eds.), *Loneliness: A sourcebook of current theory, research and therapy.* New York: Wiley.

Young, T. J. (1990, June). Sensation seeking and self-reported criminality among student-athletes. *Perceptual and Motor Skills, 70,* 959–962.

Zacks, E., Green, R. J., & Marrow, J. (1988). Comparing lesbian and heterosexual couples on the Circumplex Model: An initial investigation. *Family Process, 27,* 471–484.

Zammichieli, M. E., Gilroy, F. D., & Sherman, M. F. (1988). Relation between sex-role orientation and marital satisfaction. *Personality and Social Psychology Bulletin, 14,* 747–754.

Zanna, M. P., & Olson, J. M. (1982). Individual differences in attitudinal relations. In M. P. Zanna, E. T. Higgins, & C. P. Herman (Eds.), *Consistency in social behavior: The Ontario symposium, Vol. 2.* Hillsdale, NJ: Erlbaum.

Zechmeister, E. B., & Nyberg, S. E. (1982). *Human memory: An introduction to research and theory.* Pacific Grove, CA: Brooks/Cole.

Zedeck, S., & Mosier, K. L. (1990). Work in the family and employing organization. *American Psychologist, 45,* 240–251.

Zeig, J. K. (1987). Introduction: The evolution of psychotherapy—Fundamental issues. In J. K. Zeig (Ed.), *The evolution of psychotherapy.* New York: Brunner/Mazel.

Zellman, G. L., & Goodchilds, J. D. (1983). Becoming sexual in adolescence. In E. R. Allgeier & N. B. McCormick (Eds.), *Changing boundaries.* Palo Alto, CA: Mayfield.

Zilbergeld, B., & Evans, M. (1980, August). The inadequacy of Masters and Johnson. *Psychology Today,* pp. 28–34, 37–43.

Zillmann, D., & Bryant, J. (1984). Effects of massive exposure to pornography. In N. M. Malamuth & E. Donnerstein (Eds.), *Pornography and sexual aggression.* New York: Academic Press.

Zimbardo, P. G. (1970). The human choice: Individuation, reason, and order versus deindividuation, impulse, and chaos. In W. J. Arnold & D. Levine (Eds.), *Nebraska symposium on motivation: 1969* (Vol. 17). Lincoln: University of Nebraska Press.

Zimbardo, P. G. (1977). *Shyness: What it is, what to do about it.* Reading, MA: Addison-Wesley.

Zimbardo, P. G. (1990). *Shyness.* Reading, MA: Addison-Wesley.

Zimbardo, P. G., & Leippe, M. R. (1991). *The psychology of attitude change and social influence.* New York: McGraw-Hill.

Zimmer, D. (1983). Interaction patterns and communication skills in sexually

distressed and normal couples: Two experimental studies. *Journal of Sex and Marital Therapy, 9,* 251–265.

Zorc, J. J., Larson, D. B., Lyons, J. S., & Beardsley, R. S. (1991). Expenditures for psychotropic medications in the United States in 1985. *American Journal of Psychiatry, 148,* 644–647.

Zubin, J. (1986). Implications of the vulnerability model for DSM-IV with special reference to schizophrenia. In T. Millon & G. L. Klerman (Eds.), *Contemporary directions in psychopathology: Toward the DSM-IV.* New York: Guilford Press.

Zuckerman, M. (1971). Dimensions of sensation seeking. *Journal of Consulting and Clinical Psychology, 36,* 45–52.

Zuckerman, M. (1979). *Sensation seeking: Beyond the optimal level of arousal.* Hillsdale, NJ: Erlbaum.

Zuckerman, M. (1990). The psychophysiology of sensation seeking. *Journal of Personality, 58,* 313–345.

Zuckerman, M. (1991). *Psychobiology of personality.* New York: Cambridge University Press.

Zuckerman, M., Lazzaro, M. M., & Waldgeir, D. (1979). Undermining effects of the foot-in-the-door technique with extrinsic rewards. *Journal of Applied Social Psychology, 9,* 292–296.

Zuo, J. (1992). The reciprocal relationship between marital interaction and marital happiness: A three-wave study. *Journal of Marriage and the Family, 54,* 870–878.

Chapter 1 **6:** Cover image from *I'm Dysfunctional, You're Dysfunctional,* by Wendy Kraminer. Cover design by Julie Metz. Copyright © 1992 Addison-Wesley Publishing Company. Reprinted by permission of J. Metz. **10:** Cover image from *What You Can Change & What You Can't,* by Martin E. P. Seligman. Copyright © 1994 Alfred A. Knopf, Inc. Reprinted by permission. **13:** Figure 1.2 from *Learning to Think Critically: A Handbook to Accompany Psychology,* by Carole Wade and Carol Tavris. Copyright © 1990 by Harper & Row Publishers, Inc. Reprinted by permission of HarperCollins, Publishers, Inc. **22:** Cover image from *The Pursuit of Happiness: Who is Happy—and Why?* by David G. Myers. Copyright © 1992 William Morrow & Co., Inc. Reprinted by permission. **28:** Figure 1.10 adapted from *The Psychology of College Success: A Dynamic Approach,* by permission of H. C. Lindgren, 1969. **29:** Cover image from *Learning Skills for College and Career,* by Paul I. Hettich. Copyright © 1992 Brooks/Cole Publishing Company. **31:** Figure 1.11 adapted from *"Narrative Stories as Mediators of Serial Learning,"* by G. H. Bower and M. C. Clark, 1969, *Psychonomic Science, 14,* 181–182. Copyright © 1969 by the Psychonomic Society. Adapted by permission of the Psychonomic Society. **32:** Figure 1.12 adapted from *"Analysis of a Mnemonic Device,"* by G. H. Bower, 1970, *American Scientist* (September–October), *58,* 496–499. Copyright © 1970 by American Scientist. Reprinted by permission.

Chapter 2 **43:** Figure 2.5 adapted from *Psychology,* Second Edition, by C. R. Lefrancois. Copyright © 1983 by Wadsworth, Inc. Reprinted by permission of Brooks/Cole Publishing Company. **52:** Figure 2.12 reproduced with permission of authors and publisher from Sherer, M., Maddox, J. E., Mercandante, B., Prentice-Dunn, S., Jacobs, B., and Rogers, R. W., "The Self-Efficacy Scale: Construction and Validation." *Psychological Reports,* 1982, *51,* 663–671. © Psychological Reports 1982. **53:** Cover image from *Three Psychologies,* by Robert D. Nye. Copyright © 1992 Brooks/Cole Publishing Company. **56:** Figure 2.15 adapted from *Personality: Theory, Research and Application,* by C. R. Potkay and B. P. Allen, p. 246. Copyright © 1986 by Wadsworth, Inc. **59:** Figure 2.16 from H. J. Eysenck, *The Biological Basis of Personality* (1st Edition), p. 36, 1967. Courtesy of Charles C. Thomas, Publisher, Springfield, IL. **64:** Figure 2.20 adapted from *Personality Structure and Measurement,* by H. J. Eysenck and S. B. G. Eysenck. Copyright © 1969 by EdITS publishers. Reprinted by permission. **65:** Figure 2.21 from R. B. Cattell in *Psychology Today,* July 1973, 40–46. Reprinted with permission from Psychology Today Magazine. Copyright © 1973 (Sussex Publishers, Inc.).

Chapter 3 **76:** Figure 3.3 from "The Social Readjustment Rating Scale," by T. H. Homes and R. H. Rahe, 1967, *Journal of Psychosomatic Research, 11,* 213–218. Copyright © 1967 by Pergamon Press, Inc. Adapted by permission. **78:** Figure 3.5 from W. D. Fenz and S. Epstein, "Gradients of Physiological Arousal, Skin Conductance, Heart Rate, and Respiration Rate as Function of Experience," *Psychosomatic Medicine, 29,* 33–51, © American Psychosomatic Society, 1967. Reprinted by permission. **85:** Cover image from *Comprehensive Stress Management,* 4th Edition, by Jerrold S. Greenberg, 1993, Wm. C. Brown. Cover photo © David Gilo. Reprinted by permission of D. Gilo. **86:** Figure 3.12 based on "Paradoxical Effects of Supportive Audiences on Performance Under Pressure: The Home Field Disadvantages in Sports Championships," by R. F. Baumeister and A. Steinhilber, 1984, *Journal of Personality and Social Psychology,* 47(1), 85–93. Copyright © 1984 by the American Psychological Association. Adapted by permission. **93:** Figure 3.14 reprinted by permission from page 101 of *Adjustment and Competence: Concepts and Applications,* by A. F. Grasha & D. S. Kirschenbaum. Copyright © 1986 by West Publishing Company. All rights reserved. **94:** Cover image from *Learned Optimism: How to Change Your Mind and Your Health,* by Martin E. P. Seligman. Copyright © 1990 Pocket Books. Reprinted by permission of Bob Silverman. **97:** Figure 3.16 from "Assessing the Impact of Life Changes," by I. G. Sarason, J. H. Johnson, and J. M. Siegel, 1978, *Journal of Consulting and Clinical Psychology, 46,* 932–946. Copyright © 1978 by the American Psychological Association. Reprinted by permission of the author. **100:** Figure 3.17 from "Assessing the Impact of Life Changes," by I. G. Sarason, J. H. Johnson, and J. M. Siegel, 1978, *Journal of Consulting and Clinical Psychology, 46,* 932–946. Copyright © 1978 by the American Psychological Association. Reprinted by permission of the author.

Chapter 4 **104:** Figure 4.1 from "Assessing Coping Strategies: A Theoretically Based Approach," by C. S. Carver, M. F. Scheier, and J. K. Weintraub, 1989, *Journal of Personality and Social Psychology, 56*(2), 267–283. Copyright 1989 by the American Psychological Association. Reprinted by permission. **106:** Cover image reprinted with the permission of Simon & Schuster from *Anger: The Misunderstood Emotion,* by Carol Tavris. Copyright © 1989 by Jackie Seow-Pracher. **106:** Figure 4.2 adapted from "The Effects of Three Types of Aggression on Vascular Processes," by J. E. Hokanson and M. Burgess, 1962, *Journal of Abnormal and Social Psychology, 65,* 446–449. Copyright 1962 by the American Psychological Association. Adapted by permission. **109:** Figure 4.3 adapted from *Abnormal Psychology and Modern Life,* Eighth Edition, by R. C. Carson, J. N. Butcher, and J. C. Coleman, pp. 64–65, 1988. Copyright © 1988 by Scott, Foresman and Company. Adapted by permission. **111:** Cover image from *You're Smarter Than You Think,* by Seymour Epstein, with Archie Brodsky. Copyright © 1993 Simon & Schuster, Inc. **112:** Figure 4.4 adapted from *Adaptation to Life,* by George E. Vaillant. Copyright © 1977 by George E. Vaillant. By permission of Little, Brown and Company. **116:** Cover image from *How to Stubbornly Refuse to Make Yourself Miserable About Anything—Yes, Anything!* by Albert Ellis. Copyright © 1988 Carol Publishing Group. Reprinted by permission. **117:** Figure 4.7 adapted from "Sense of Humor as a Moderator of the Relation Between Stressors and Moods," by R. A. Martin and H. M. Lefcourt, 1983, *Journal of Personality and Social Psychology, 45*(6), 1313–1324. Copyright 1983 by the American Psychological Association. Adapted by permission. **120:** Figure 4.8 from Le Boeuf, "Managing Time Means Managing Yourself," Questionnaire, p. 45. Reprinted from *Business Horizons Magazine,* February 1980. Copyright by the Foundation for the School of Business at Indiana University. Used with permission. **123:** Cover image from *Timelock: How Life Got So Hectic and What You Can Do About It,* by Ralph Keyes. Copyright © 1991 HarperCollins Publishers, Inc. Reprinted by permission. **126:** Figure 4.11 (based on illustration on p. 86 by Lorelle A. Raboni of *Scientific American, 226,* 85–90, February 1972) adapted from "The Psychology of Meditation," by R. K. Wallace and H. Bensen. Copyright © 1972 by Scientific American, Inc. All rights reserved. Adapted by permission. **127:** Figure 4.12 adapted from figure on pp. 114–115 from *The Relaxation Response* by Herbert Benson with Miriam Z. Klipper. Copyright © 1975 by William Morrow and Company. By permission of William Morrow and Company, Inc. **131:** Figure 4.15 from *Self-Directed Behavior: Self-Modification for Personal Adjustment,* Fourth Edition, by D. L. Watson and R. L. Tharp, pp. 213–214. Copyright © 1972, 1977, 1981, 1985, 1993 by Brooks/Cole Publishing Company.

Chapter 5 **138:** Cover image from *Encounters with the Self,* by Don Hamachek. Copyright © 1992 Harcourt, Brace, Jovanovich. **141:** Figure 5.4 from "Self-Consciousness, Self-Esteem, and Success-Failure as Determinants of Alcohol Consumption in Male Social Drinkers," by J. G. Hull and R. D. Young, 1983, *Journal of Personality and Social Psychology, 44*(6), 1097–1109. Copyright © 1983 American Psychological Association. Reprinted by permission of the author. **145:** Figure 5.6 adapted from "Culture and the Self: Implications for Cognition, Emotion, and Motivation," by H. R. Markus and Shinobu Kitayama, 1991, *Psychological Review, 98*(2), pp. 224–253. Copyright 1991 American Psychological Association. Reprinted by permission of the author. **147:** Figure 5.8 from *Social Psychology,* Second Edition, by S. S. Brehm and S. M. Kassin. Copyright © 1993 Houghton-Mifflin Company. Reprinted by permission. **152:** Figure 5.11 from "Perceiving the Causes of Success and Failure," by B. Weiner, I. Frieze, A. Kukla, L. Reed, and R. M. Rosenbaum. In E. E. Jones, D. E. Kanuouse, H. H. Kelly, R. E. Nisbett, S. Valins, and B. Weiner (Eds.), *Perceiving Causes of Behavior,* 1972, General Learning Press. Reprinted by permission of the author. **163:** Cover image from *Self-Esteem,* by Matthew McKay and Patrick Fanning. Copyright © 1993 New Harbinger Publications. Reprinted by permission.

Chapter 6 **169:** Figure 6.2 adapted from *Social Psychology,* Second Edition, by S. S. Brehm and S. M. Kassin, p. 137. Copyright © 1993 Houghton Mifflin Company. Reprinted by permission. **171:** Figure 6.3 adapted from *Social Psychology* by E. R. Smith and D. M. Mackie, p. 103. Copyright © 1995 Worth Publishing. Reprinted by permission. **183:** Figure 6.8 (adapted from illustrations by Sarah Love on p. 35, *Scientific American,* November 1955) from "Opinion and Social Pressure," by Solomon Asch. Copyright © 1955 by Scientific American, Inc. All rights reserved. Adapted by permission. **183:** Figure 6.9 (adapted from illustrations by Sarah Love on p. 32, *Scientific American,* November 1955) from "Opinion and Social Pressure," by Solomon Asch. Copyright © 1955 by Scientific American, Inc. All rights reserved. Adapted by permission. **185:** Figure 6.10 copyright 1965 by Stanley Milgram, from the film *Obedience,* distributed by the New York University Film Division and The Pennsylvania State University, PCR. By permission of the Estate of Stanley Milgram. **193:** Cover image from *Influence: Science and Practice,* Third Edition, by Robert B. Cialdini, 1993, HarperCollins Publishers, Inc. Cover photo by James H. Karales/Peter Arnold, Inc. Reprinted by permission of Peter Arnold, Inc.

Chapter 7 **205:** Figure 7.5 adapted from *Eye to Eye: How People Interact,* by Peter Marsh. Copyright © 1988 by Andromeda Oxford Ltd. Reprinted by permission of HarperCollins, Publishers, Inc. **210:** Cover image from *Messages: The Communication Skills Book,* by Matthew McKay, Martha Davis, and Patrick

Fanning. Copyright © 1983 New Harbinger Publications. Reprinted by permission. **218:** Cover image from *Recovering from Rape,* by Linda Ledray. Copyright © 1994 by Henry Holt & Co. Inc. Reprinted by permission of Henry Holt and Co., Inc. **220:** Figure 7.11 adapted from "Cultural Myths and Supports for Rape," by M. R. Burt, 1980, *Journal of Personality and Social Psychology, 38,* 217–230. Copyright © 1980 by the American Psychological Association. Adapted by permission of the author. **223:** Figure 7.13 adapted from David W. Johnson, *Reaching Out: Interpersonal Effectiveness and Self-Actualization,* Second Edition, © 1981, p. 204. Reprinted by permission of Prentice-Hall, Englewood Cliffs, NJ. **227:** Cover image from *Asserting Yourself: A Practical Guide for Positive Change,* by Sharon Anthony Bower and Gordon H. Bower. Cover design by Richard Rossiter. Copyright © 1991 Addison-Wesley Publishing Co. Reprinted by permission of R. Rossiter.

Chapter 8 **233:** Figure 8.1 adapted from Sharon S. Brehm and Saul M. Kassin, *Social Psychology,* Second Edition. Copyright © 1993 by Houghton Mifflin Company. Adapted with permission. **235:** Cover image from *Love and Sex: Cross-Cultural Perspectives,* by Elaine Hatfield and Richard L. Rapson. Copyright © 1996 by Allyn and Bacon. Reprinted by permission. **237:** Figure 8.2 from "Sex Differences in Human Mate Preferences: Evolutionary Hypotheses Tested in 37 Cultures," by D. M. Buss, 1989, *Behavioral and Brain Sciences, 12,* 1–14. Copyright © 1989 by Cambridge University Press. Reprinted with the permission of Cambridge University Press. **239:** Figure 8.4 adapted from "The Evolution of Human Intrasexual Competition: Tactics of Mate Attraction," by D. M. Buss, 1988, *Journal of Personality and Social Psychology, 54*(4), 616–628. Copyright © 1988 by the American Psychological Association. Adapted by permission of the author. **243:** Figure 8.5 adapted from "Interactional Approach to Interpersonal Attraction," by M. H. Gonzales, J. M. Davis, G. L. Loeny, C. K. Lukens, and C. H. Junghans, 1983, *Journal of Personality and Social Psychology, 44,* 1191–1197. Copyright 1983 by the American Psychological Association. Adapted by permission. **245:** Figure 8.7 from "The Friendship Bond," by Mary Brown Parlee and the Editors of *Psychology Today, 13*(4), 49. Reprinted with permission from Psychology Today Magazine. Copyright © 1979 (Sussex Publishers, Inc.). **246:** Cover image from *Just Friends: The Role of Friendship in Our Lives,* by Lillian Rubin. Copyright © 1986 Harper & Row. Reprinted by permission. **246:** Figure 8.8 adapted from "The Rules of Friendship," by M. Argyle and M. Henderson, 1984, *Journal of Social and Personal Relationships, 1,* 211–237. **250:** Figure 8.9 from "A Triangular Theory of Love," by R. J. Sternberg, 1986, *Psychological Review, 93,* 119–135. Copyright 1986 by the American Psychological Association. Reprinted by permission. **253:** Figure 8.12 adapted from "Breakups Before Marriage: The End of 103 Affairs," by C. T. Hill, Z. Rubin, and L. A. Peplau, 1976, *Journal of Social Issues, 32,* 147–168. Basic Books Publishing Co., Inc. Adapted by permission of the author. All rights reserved. **258:** Figure 8.13 from a paper presented at the annual convention of the American Psychological Association, September 2, 1979. An expanded version of this paper appears in *New Directions in Cognitive Therapy,* edited by Emery, Hollon, and Bedrosian, Guilford Press, 1981, and in *Loneliness: A Sourcebook of Current Theory, Research and Therapy,* by L. A. Peplau and D. Perlman (Eds.). Copyright 1982 by John Wiley & Sons, Inc. Reprinted by permission of John Wiley & Sons, Inc., and Jeffrey Young. **259:** Cover image from P. Zimbardo, *Shyness,* © 1977 Phillip Zimbardo Inc. Cover illustration © 1989 by Bart Goldman. Reprinted by permission of Addison-Wesley Publishing Company, Inc. and Bart Goldman. **261:** Figure 8.14 from P. Zimbardo, *Shyness,* © 1977 by Philip Zimbardo. Reprinted by permission of Addison-Wesley Publishing Company, Inc.

Chapter 9 **265:** Figure 9.1 data from U.S. Bureau of the Census, *Current Population Reports,* Series P-20, No. 412, "Households, Families, Marital Status and Living Arrangements," March 1986 (Advance Report), Washington, DC: U.S. Government Printing Office, p. 4. **267:** Figure 9.3 data from the National Center for Health Statistics, U.S. Bureau of the Census, 1991. **268:** Figure 9.4 adapted from Peter J. Stein, "Singlehood: An Alternative to Marriage," *The Family Coordinator, 24*(4), 500. Copyright 1975 by the National Council on Family Relations, 3989 Central Ave. N. E., Suite 550, Minneapolis, MN 55421. Reprinted by permission. **273:** Figure 9.7 adapted from "Marital Satisfaction over the Family Life Cycle," by Boyd C. Rollins and Harold Feldman, *Journal of Marriage and the Family, 32* (February 1970), 25. Copyright 1975 by the National Council on Family Relations, 3989 Central Ave., N.E., Suite 550, Minneapolis, MN 55421. Reprinted by permission. **280:** Cover image from *Love Is Never Enough,* by Aaron T. Beck. Copyright © 1988 Harper & Row. Reprinted by permission. **288:** Figure 9.13 data from Glick & Norton, 1979. Population Reference Bureau, Washington, DC: U.S. Bureau of the Census. **291:** Figure 9.15 from "What Homosexuals Want," by L. A. Peplau, March 1981, *Psychology Today, 3,* 28–38. Reprinted with permission from Psychology Today Magazine. Copyright © 1981 (Sussex Publishers, Inc.).

Chapter 10 **300:** Figure 10.2 adapted from "Sex Stereotypes: Issues of Change in the 70s," by T. L. Ruble, 1983, *Sex Roles, 9,* 397–402. Copyright © 1983 Plenum Publishing Company. Adapted by permission. **303:** Figure 10.4 data from the U. S. Bureau of the Census, *Statistical Abstract of the United States: 1994* (114th edition), Washington, D.C., 1994. **306:** Figure 10.7 adapted from *Social Psychology,* by John Brigham. Copyright © 1986 by John Brigham. Reprinted by permission of HarperCollins Publishers. **307:** Cover image from *The New Our Bodies, Ourselves: A Book By and For Women,* by The Boston Women's Health Book Collective. Copyright © 1992 Simon & Schuster, Inc. Reprinted by permission. **312:** Figure 10.8 adapted from "Children, Gender and Social Structure: An Analysis of the Contents of Letters to Santa Claus," by J. G. Richardson and C. H. Simpson, 1982, *Child Development, 53,* 429–436. Copyright © 1982 by the Society for Research in Child Development, Inc. Adapted by permission. **314:** Figure 10.9 from Graph B on page 7 of the Executive Summary of the American Association of University Women's Report, *Shortchanging Girls, Shortchanging America,* Revised Edition, August 1994. Washington, D.C.: AAUW. Reprinted by permission. **314:** Figure 10.10 data from Robert M. Liebert and Joyce Sprafkin, *The Early Window: Effects of Television on Children and Youth,* Third Edition. Copyright © 1988. Reprinted by permission of Allyn and Bacon. **319:** Figure 10.11 data from U. S. Bureau of the Census, *Statistical Abstract of the United States: 1994* (114th edition). Washington D.C., 1994. **320:** Figure 10.12 data from U. S. Bureau of Labor Statistics, *Employment and Earnings, 42*(1), January, 1995, Table 39, pp. 209–213. **320:** Figure 10.13 adapted from *Secrets in Public: Sexual Harassment in Our Schools,* by N. Stein, N. L. Marshall, and L. R. Tropp, p. 4. Copyright © 1993 Center for Research on Women at Wellesley College and the NOW Legal Defense and Education Fund. **321:** Cover image reprinted with permission of Simon & Schuster from *The Mismeasure of Woman, by Carol Tavris.* Copyright © 1992 by Jackie Seow. **326:** Cover image from *You Just Don't Understand: Women and Men in Conversation,* by D. Tannen. Copyright © 1990 Ballantine Books. Reprinted by permission of William Morrow & Co., Inc. **330:** Figure 10.15 based on *You Just Don't Understand: Women and Men in Conversation,* by D. Tannen. Copyright © 1990 by William Morrow & Company, Inc. Reprinted by permission of William Morrow & Company, Inc. **330:** Figure 10.16 based on *You Just Don't Understand: Women and Men in Conversation,* by D. Tannen. Copyright © 1990 by William Morrow & Company, Inc. Reprinted by permission of William Morrow & Company, Inc.

Chapter 11 **335:** Cover image from *The Hurried Child: Growing Up Too Fast, Too Soon,* by D. Elkind. Copyright © 1988 David Elkind. Reprinted by permission of Addison-Wesley Publishing Company, Inc. **337:** Figure 11.2 adapted from "The Psychological Significance of Pubertal Change: Sex Differences in Perceptions of Self During Early Adolescence," by M. H. Tobin-Richards, A. M. Boxer, and A. C. Petersen. In J. Brooks-Gunn and A. C. Petersen (Eds.), *Girls at Puberty: Biological and Psychosocial Perspectives,* p. 137. Copyright 1983 Plenum Publishing Inc. Reprinted by permission. **338:** Figure 11.3 adapted from *Childhood and Society,* Second Edition, by Erik H. Erikson. Copyright 1950, © 1963 by W. W. Norton & Co., Inc. Copyright renewed 1978, 1991 by Erik H. Erikson. **341:** Figure 11.4 data from U.S. Bureau of the Census, *Statistical Abstract of the United States: 1994* (114th edition), Washington, D.C., 1994. **343:** Cover image from *Necessary Losses,* by Judith Viorst. Copyright © 1986 Ballantine Books (A Fawcett Gold Medal Book). **351:** Figure 11.5 data from U. S. Bureau of the Census, *Statistical Abstract of the United States: 1994* (114th edition), Table 208, p. 140, Washington D.C., 1994. **353:** Figure 11.6 based on data from "Creative Productivity between the Ages of 20 and 80 Years," by W. Dennis, 1966. *Journal of Gerontology, 2*(1), 1–8. Copyright © 1966 the Gerontological Society of America. Adapted by permission. **359:** Figure 11.8 table constructed from Diana Baumrind (1971). Current patterns of parental authority (Monograph). *Developmental Psychology, 4*(1, Part 2), 1–103. Copyright © 1971 by the American Psychological Association. Adapted by permission of the author. **360:** Figure 11.9 based on data from "Socialization Determinants of Personal Agency," a paper presented at the biennial meeting of the Society for Research in Child Development, New Orleans, 1977.

Chapter 12 **366:** Figure 12.1 from *Joyce L. Kennedy's Career Book,* by J. L. Kennedy and Laramore, p. 62. Copyright © 1993 by VGM Career Horizons. Reprinted by permission. **368:** Figure 12.3 adapted from K. A. Matthews and J. Rodin, 1989, *American Psychologist, 44*(11), 1391. Copyright 1989 by the American Psychological Association. Adapted by permission. **369:** Figure 12.4 data from U. S. Department of Labor, *Pipelines of Progress: A Status Report on the Glass Ceiling,* 1992, Washington, D.C., U. S. Government Printing Office. **374:** Figure 12.6 from John L. Holland, *Making Vocational Choices: A Theory of Vocational Personalities and Work Environments* (2nd ed.). © 1985, pp. 19–23, 36–40. Adapted by permission of Prentice-Hall, Inc., Englewood Cliffs, NJ. **375:** Figure 12.7 adapted from *Theories of Occupational Choice and Vocational Development,* by J. Zaccaria, pp. 51–52. Copyright © 1970 by Time Share Corporation, New Hampshire. **387:** Figure 12.10 adapted from *Psychology of Work Behavior* (4th ed.), by F. J. Landy, p. 638. Copyright © 1989 by Wadsworth, Inc. Reprinted by permission of Brooks/Cole Publishing Company. **388:** Figure 12.11 redrawn from "Job Decision Latitude, Job Demands, and Cardiovascular Disease: A Prospective Study of Swedish Men," by R. A. Karasek, D. Baker, F. Marxer, A. Ahlbom, and T. Theorell, 1981, *American Journal of Public Health, 71,* 694–705. Reprinted by permission. **390:** Figure 12.13 from U.S. Merit Systems Protection Boards, 1981. *Sexual Harassment of Federal Workers: Is It a Problem?* Washington, DC: U.S. Government Printing Office. **391:** Cover image from *Step Forward: Sexual Harrassment in the Workplace—What You Need to Know,* by S. L. Webb. Copyright © 1991 MasterMedia Ltd. Reprinted by permission. **393:** Figure 12.14 adapted from *Job Search: Career Planning Guidebook, Book II,* by R. D. Lock, Brooks/Cole Publishing Company, 1988. **395:** Cover image from *What Color Is*

Your Parachute—1995? A Practical Manual for Job-Hunters and Career-Changers, by R. N. Bolles. Copyright © 1995 Ten Speed Press. Reprinted by permission.

Chapter 13 **402:** Figure 13.1 adapted from *The Kinsey Institute New Report on Sex* by J. M. Reinisch, 1990, p. 21. Copyright © 1990 by The Kinsey Institute for Research in Sex, Gender, and Reproduction. Reprinted with permission by St. Martin's Press, Incorporated. **409:** Figure 13.5 based on *The Kinsey Institute New Report on Sex,* by J. M. Reinisch, 1990, p. 4. Copyright © 1990 by The Kinsey Institute for Research in Sex, Gender, and Reproduction. Reprinted with permission from St. Martin's Press, Incorporated. **410:** Cover image from *The Kinsey Institute New Report on Sex: What You Must Know to Be Sexually Literate,* by J. M. Reinisch with R. Beasley. Copyright © 1990 by The Kinsey Institute for Research in Sex, Gender, and Reproduction. Reprinted with permission by St. Martin's Press, Incorporated. **412:** Figure 13.7 from *The Social Organization of Sexuality: Sexual Practices in the United States,* by E. O. Laumann, J. H. Gagnon, R. T. Michael, and S. Michaels. Copyright © 1994 University of Chicago Press. Reprinted by permission. **414:** Figure 13.8 from "The Erotic Fantasies of College Students During Coitus," by David Sue, 1979, *Journal of Sex Research, 15,* 303. Reprinted by permission. **415:** Cover image from *Understanding Human Sexuality,* by Janet Shibley Hyde. Copyright © 1994 McGraw-Hill, Inc. Reprinted by permission. **419:** Figure 13.11 from "Age, Gender, and Ethnic Differences in Sexual and Contraceptive Knowledge, Attitudes, and Behavior," by D. S. Moore, and P. I. Erickson, *Family and Community Health, 8*(3), November 1985, pp. 38–51. Copyright © 1985, Aspen Publishers, Inc. **420:** Figure 13.12 reprinted with permission of PEI Books, Inc. from *Sexual Behavior in the 1970s,* by Morton Hunt. Copyright 1974 by Morton Hunt. **428:** Figure 13.15 adapted from "Frequency of Sexual Dysfunction in 'Normal' Couples," by E. Frank, C. Anderson, and D. Rubenstein, 1978, *New England Journal of Medicine, 299,* 1111–1115. Copyright 1978 by the New England Journal of Medicine. Reprinted by permission. **429:** Figure 13.16 from *The Social Organization of Sexuality: Sexual Practices in the United States,* by E. O. Laumann, J. H. Gagnon, R. T. Michael, and S. Michaels, p. 369. Copyright © 1994 University of Chicago Press. Reprinted by permission. **431:** Figure 13.17 adapted from Human Sexuality, 3rd Edition by William H. Masters, Virginia E. Johnson, and Robert C. Kolodny, p. 527. Copyright © 1988 by William H. Masters, Virginia E. Johnson, and Robert C. Kolodny. Reprinted by permission of HarperCollins Publishers.

Chapter 14 **437:** Cover image from *Is It Worth Dying For?* by Robert S. Eliot and Dennis L. Breo. Copyright © 1984, 1989 Bantam Books. Reprinted by permission. **445:** Figure 14.6 data from *Smoking and Health* (1990). Rockville, MD: Health and Human Services; Graph from *Healthy for Life: Wellness and the Art of Living* by B. K. Williams and S. M. Knight, p. 4.12, Brooks/Cole Publishing Company, 1994. **446:** Figure 14.8 from *Healthy for Life: Wellness and the Art of Living,* by B. K. Williams and S. M. Knight, p. 11.28, Brooks/Cole Publishing Company, 1994. Based on Wechsler and McFadden for AAA Foundation for Traffic Safety, survey of 1669 college freshmen at 14 Massachusetts institutions. **448:** Figure 14.10 from *Health and Wellness,* Third Edition, by Edlin and Golanty, p. 294. Copyright © 1992, Boston: Jones & Bartlett Publishers, Inc. Reprinted with permission. **453:** Figure 14.12 from *Healthy for Life: Wellness and the Art of Living,* by B. K. Williams and S. M. Knight, p. 6.40, Brooks/Cole Publishing Company, 1994. **455:** Figure 14.14 adapted from "How Different Sports Rate in Promoting Physical Fitness," by C. C. Conrad, *Medical Times,* May 1976, 4–5. Copyright 1976 by Romaine Pierson Publishers. Reprinted by permission. **457:** Figure 14.16 from *Healthy for Life: Wellness and the Art of Living,* by B. K.

Williams and S. M. Knight, p. 11.28, Brooks/Cole Publishing Company, 1994. Based on Anderson & Christenson, 1991; Temosok et al., 1987. **458:** Cover image from *Mind Body Medicine: How to Use Your Mind for Better Health,* edited by Daniel Goleman and Joel Gurin. Copyright 1993 Consumers Union of U.S., Inc., Yonkers, NY 10703-1057. Reprinted by permission from Consumer Reports Books, January 1993. To order, call 1-800-500-9760.

Chapter 15 **474:** Figure 15.3 adapted with permission from the *Diagnostic and Statistical Manual of Mental Disorders,* 4th ed. (1994). Copyright © 1994 American Psychiatric Association. **477:** Figure 15.5 from *Fears and Phobias,* by I. M. Marks, 1969, Academic Press. Copyright 1969 by Isaac Marks. Reprinted by permission. **481:** Figure 15.7 from "Bias in Interpretation of Ambiguous Sentences Related to Threat in Anxiety," by M. W. Eysenck, K. Mogg, J. May, A. Richards, and A. Mathews, 1991, *Journal of Abnormal Psychology, 100,* pp. 144–150. Copyright © 1991 by the American Psychological Association. Reprinted by permission of the author. **487:** Figure 15.10 from Sarason/Sarason, *Abnormal Psychology: The Problem of Maladaptive Behavior* (5th Ed.), © 1987, p. 283. Reprinted by permission of Prentice-Hall, Inc., Englewood Cliffs, NJ. **488:** Figure 15.11 from *Manic-Depressive Illness,* by Frederick K. Goodwin and Kay R. Jamison (p. 132). Copyright © 1990 by Oxford University Press, Inc. Reprinted by permission. **492:** Cover image from *Surviving Schizophrenia: A Family Manual,* by E. Fuller Torrey. Copyright © 1988 Harper & Row. Reprinted by permission of HarperCollins Publishers, Inc. **500:** Figure 15.18 adapted from "Suicide and Depression Among College Students," by J. S. Westefeld and S. R. Furr, 1987, *Professional Psychology: Research and Practice, 18,* 119–123. Copyright 1987 by the American Psychological Association. Adapted by permission. **501:** Figure 15.19 adapted from "Suicide, Attempted Suicide and Relapse Rates in Depression," by D. Avery and G. Winokur, 1978, *Archives of General Psychiatry* (June), *35,* 749–753. Copyright 1978 by the American Medical Association. Adapted by permission.

Chapter 16 **505:** Cover image from *The Psychotherapy Maze,* by O. Ehrenberg and M. Ehrenberg. Copyright © 1986 Aronson. Reprinted by permission. **512:** Figure 16.4 adapted from "Psychoanalysis and Psychoanalytic Therapy," by E. L. Baker. In S. J. Lynn and J. P. Garske (Eds.), *Contemporary Psychotherapies: Models and Methods,* p. 52, 1982. Reprinted by permission of the authors. **515:** Figure 16.5 adapted from *Cognitive Therapy and the Emotional Disorders,* by A. T. Beck, 1976, International Universities Press. Copyright © 1976 by International Universities Press, Inc. Adapted by permission of the publisher. **519:** Figure 16.6 from "Lies of the Mind," by Leon Jaroff, 1993, *Time Magazine,* November 29, 1993, p. 52. Copyright © 1993 Time Inc. Reprinted by permission. **525:** Figure 16.10 from data in NIMH-PSC Collaborative Study I and reported in "Drugs in the Treatment of Psychosis," by J. O. Cole, S. C. Goldberg and J. M. Davis, 1966. In P. Solomon (Ed.), *Psychiatric Drugs,* Grune & Stratton. By permission of the author. **530:** Cover image from *The Consumer's Guide to Psychotherapy,* by J. Engler and D. Goleman. Copyright © 1992 Simon & Schuster. Reprinted by permission. **533:** Figure 16.15 adapted from "Meta Analysis of Psychotherapy Outcome Series," by M. L. Smith and G. V. Glass, 1977, *American Psychologist, 32* (September), 752–760. Copyright © 1977 by the American Psychological Association. Adapted by permission.

Photo Credits

Contents **xii:** (top left) Pete McArthur, (bottom right) William McCoy/Rainbow; **xiii:** (top left) Geoffrey Gove/The Image Bank, (top right) John Curtis/Offshoot Stock; **xiv:** Steven Hunt/The Image Bank; **xv:** (top left) Jeremy Gardiner/The Image Bank,

(below) Tom McCarthy/Rainbow; **xvi:** (top left) Pierre-Yves Goavec/The Image Bank, (middle) Bruce Ayres/Tony Stone Images, (bottom left) Alfred Gescheidt/The Image Bank; **xvii:** (bottom left) Michel Tcherevkoff/The Image Bank, (bottom right) Billy E. Barnes/Stock Boston; **xviii:** (top left) Bruce Ayres/Tony Stone Images, (center left) David Murir/Masterfile, (far right) Penny Tweedie/Tony Stone Images, (bottom left) Ken Fisher/Tony Stone Images; **xix:** (top left) Steve Krongard/The Image Bank, (center right) Myrleen Ferguson/PhotoEdit; **xx:** (top left) Michel Tcherevkoff/The Image Bank, (top right) Brylak/Gamma Liaison, (center) Tony Freeman/PhotoEdit, (bottom left) Geoffrey Gove/The Image Bank, (bottom right) David Young-Wolff/PhotoEdit; **xxi:** (top left) Elena Rooraid/PhotoEdit, (top right) Tony Arruza/Tony Stone Images, (bottom left) Will Crocker/The Image Bank; **xxii:** (top right) Ben Davidson/Photo 20-20, (center left) David Gaz/The Image Bank, (bottom right) J. R. Holland/Stock Boston; **xxiii:** (left) Ellen Schuster/The Image Bank, (far right) Bob Daemmrich/Stock Boston, (bottom left) Christopher Brown/Stock Boston; **xxiv:** Pete McArthur; **xxv** (left) Pete McArthur, (right) Michael Newman/PhotoEdit.

Chapter 1 **2:** (left) Coco McCoy/Rainbow, (right) Rob Crandall/Rainbow; **9:** William McCoy/Rainbow; **21:** Christopher Brown/Stock Boston; **26:** Bill Stanton/Rainbow.

Chapter 2 **34:** Geoffrey Gove/The Image Bank; **37:** (top) The Granger Collection; (bottom) Reuters/Bettmann; **41:** David Young-Wolff/Tony Stone Images; **46:** National Library of Medicin; **48:** Harvard University News Office; **49:** Courtesy B. F. Skinner Foundation; **54:** Carl Rogers Memorial Library; **57:** 1982 Michael Nichols/Magnum Photos Inc.; **58:** Mark Gerson /Courtesy, Dr. H. J. Eysenck; **65:** John Curtis/Offshoot Stock; **66:** Harvard University.

Chapter 3 **68:** Steven Hunt/The Image Bank; **70:** Courtesy, Richard Lazarus; **71:** (left) David Grossman, (right) Lionel Delevingne/Stock Boston; **73:** Courtesy, Dr. Neal E. Miller; **75:** Michael Newman/PhotoEdit; **83:** The Bettmann Archives; **86:** AP/Wide World Photos; **88:** Rick Browne/Stock Boston; **91:** Courtesy, Suzanne C. Ouelette; **92:** Robert Aschenbrenner/Stock Boston; **95:** Courtesy, Eleanor Holmes Williams.

Chapter 4 **102:** Jeremy Gardiner/The Image Bank; **105:** Courtesy, Dr. Martin Seligman; **107:** (left) Perlsteir/Jerrican/Photo Researchers, (right) Offshoot Stock; **110:** Courtesy, Shelley Taylor; **113:** Courtesy, Albert Ellis; **125:** Tom McCarthy/Rainbow; **127:** Courtesy, Herbert Benson, M.D./Michael Lutch Photo; **128:** Dan McCoy/Rainbow.

Chapter 5 **136:** Pierre-Yves Goavec/The Image Bank; **142:** (above) Frank Siteman/Stock Boston, (center) 1982 Karen Zebulon; **143:** Brooks/Cole photo; **144:** Bruce Ayres/Tony Stone Images; **148:** Bill Stanton/Rainbow; **157:** (below) L. A. Cicero, Stanford News Service, David Young-Wolff/PhotoEdit; **159:** Courtesy, Robert Cialdini.

Chapter 6 **166:** Alfred Gescheidt/The Image Bank; **170:** Courtesy, Susan Fiske; **173:** (right) The Bettmann Archive, (left) The Bettmann Archive; **175:** Craig McClain Photography; **176:** (above) Stanford University News Service, (below) Michael Newman/PhotoEdit; **184:** Eric Kroll; **185:** 1965 by Dr. Stanley Milgram from the film *Obedience;* **187:** Reuters/Corbis-Bettmann; **188:** 1987 Shelly Katz.

Chapter 7 **196:** Michel Tcherevkoff/The Image Bank; **201:** From *Unmasking the Face,* by P. Ekman & W. V. Friesens, Consulting Psychologists Press. Copyright © 1984.

TO THE OWNER OF THIS BOOK:

We hope that you have found *Psychology Applied to Modern Life: Adjustment in the 90s*, Fifth Edition, useful. So that this book can be improved in a future edition, would you take the time to complete this sheet and return it? Thank you.

School and address: _____

Department: _____

Instructor's name: _____

1. What I like most about this book is: _____

   _____

   _____

2. What I like least about this book is: _____

   _____

   _____

3. My general reaction to this book is: _____

   _____

4. The name of the course in which I used this book is: _____

   _____

5. Were all of the chapters of the book assigned for you to read? _____

   If not, which ones weren't? _____

6. In the space below, or on a separate sheet of paper, please write specific suggestions for improving this book and anything else you'd care to share about your experience in using the book.

   _____

   _____

   _____

   _____

   _____

   _____

   _____

   _____

Optional:

Your name: _____ Date: _____

May Brooks/Cole quote you, either in promotion for *Psychology Applied to Modern Life: Adjustment in the 90s,* Fifth Edition, or in future publishing ventures?

Yes: _____ No: _____

Sincerely,

Wayne Weiten
Margaret A. Lloyd

FOLD HERE

FOLD HERE